5th EDITION

Psychology

James S. Nairne
Purdue University

THOMSON

WADSWORTH

Australia • Brazil • Canada • Mexico • Singapore • Spain • United Kingdom • United States

Psychology, **Fifth Edition**
James S. Nairne

Publisher: Michele Sordi
Associate Development Editor: Dan Moneypenny
Assistant Editor: Magnolia Molcan
Editorial Assistant: Erin Miskelly
Managing Technology Project Manager: Amy Cohen
Marketing Manager: Sara Swangard
Marketing Assistant: Melanie Cregger
Marketing Communications Manager: Linda Yip
Project Manager, Editorial Production: Mary Noel
Creative Director: Rob Hugel

Art Director: Vernon T. Boes
Print Buyer: Karen Hunt
Permissions Editors: John Hill, Tim Sisler
Production Service: Margaret Pinette, Heckman & Pinette/Newgen
Text Designer: Lisa Buckley
Photo Researcher: Sarah Evertson, Image Quest
Copy Editor: Margaret Pinette
Cover Designer: Larry Didona
Cover Image: Robert Llewellyn/zefa/Corbis
Compositor: Newgen Book Services

Library of Congress Control Number: 2007937380

Student Edition:
ISBN-13: 978-0-495-50455-9
ISBN-10: 0-495-50455-6

Paper Edition:
ISBN-13: 978-0-495-50611-9
ISBN-10: 0-495-50611-7

Loose-leaf Edition:
ISBN-13: 978-0-495-50612-6
ISBN-10: 0-495-50612-5

Thomson Higher Education
10 Davis Drive
Belmont, CA 94002-3098
USA

For more information about our products, contact us at:
Thomson Learning Academic Resource Center
1-800-423-0563

For permission to use material from this text or product, submit a request online at **http://www.thomsonrights.com.**
Any additional questions about permissions can be submitted by e-mail to **thomsonrights@thomson.com.**

To Virginia and Stephanie

About the Author

James S. Nairne is the Reece McGee Distinguished Professor of Psychological Sciences at Purdue University, where he specializes in human memory. Recognized internationally as both a scholar and a teacher, he has received numerous teaching honors at Purdue, including the Liberal Arts Excellence in Education Award in 2000 and the Outstanding Undergraduate Teaching Award in 2001. Also in 2001, he was named a Fellow of the Purdue Teaching Academy, and in 2004 he was given a permanent position in Purdue's Book of Great Teachers. He is director of the Honors Program for the College of Liberal Arts. Professor Nairne received his Ph.D. in Human Memory and Cognition from Yale University.

Brief Contents

Contents

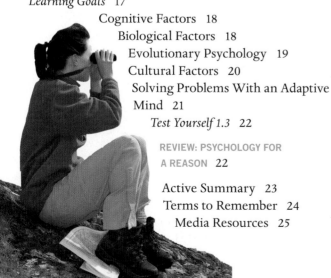

8 | Memory 244

9 | Language and Thought 278

10 | Intelligence 310

11 | Motivation and Emotion 342

12 | Personality 378

13 | Social Psychology 408

14 | Psychological Disorders 448

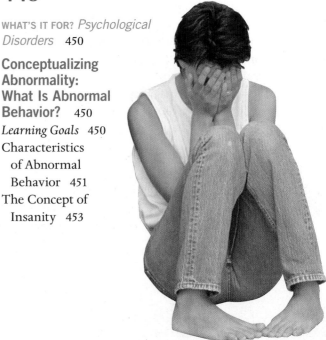

15 | Therapy 484

16 | Stress and Health 516

Preface

TO THE STUDENT

Psychology is the scientific study of behavior and mind. It can be a tough subject, but I'm confident that you'll find it fun and even surprising at the same time. You'll find scores of research studies and hundreds of isolated facts scattered throughout this book, but my main goal is to help you understand the value and usefulness of psychology in your life—to tell you what psychology is for! Toward that end, I'll show you how your behaviors, thoughts, and emotions help you solve important problems every day.

Everything we do is influenced, in part, by our need to solve specific problems in our environment. By "problems" I simply mean the challenges we face or the demands we confront as we move through everyday life. We're constantly dipping into our psychological "tool kit" to solve one problem or another. For example, before you can react, your brain needs to communicate with the environment and with the rest of your body. To communicate internally, your body uses the nervous system, the endocrine system, and to some extent, even the genetic code. We also need to translate the messages from the environment, which come in a variety of forms, into the internal language of the nervous system (which is electrochemical). We solve this problem through our various sensory systems, such as vision and audition. Our survival also depends on our ability to communicate through language and other, nonverbal forms of communication.

You'll soon see that many of our behaviors and thoughts can be viewed as solutions to such problems or demands. Each chapter begins with a brief preview section entitled "What's It For?" that describes the function and purpose of the psychological processes that we'll be studying. Throughout the chapter I'll then show you how these particular processes help us solve the problems and challenges that we face. Again, I don't think you should be expected to understand a topic unless you first know what it's for! I invite you to browse through the rest of the preface for a preview of how this book is organized. And I hope you will soon begin applying what you learn to situations in your daily life. The study of psychology may be challenging, but above all else it is relevant to everything we do. Have fun!

TO THE INSTRUCTOR

One of the first hurdles we face as instructors of introductory psychology is convincing students that psychology is more than just the study of abnormal behavior. Introduce yourself as a psychologist, and you're likely to get a response like "Don't analyze me!" or "I'd better watch what I say around you!" It takes time for students to realize that psychology is a vast interdisciplinary field that includes all aspects of both normal and abnormal behavior. Even after exposure to its breadth, the topics of psychology can remain mysterious and forbidding. Take a look at a typical chapter on learning, for example, and its contents seem to bear little resemblance to our everyday understanding of what it means to "learn." There are extended discussions of drooling dogs and key-pecking pigeons, but little about the connection between conditioning procedures and the learning problems we face on a daily basis.

In *Psychology,* Fifth Edition, I focus extensively on the function and purpose of psychological processes. Instead of leading with the facts and methods specific to a topic, I introduce each topic as a kind of "solution" to a pressing environmental or conceptual challenge. For example, if you want to understand how we learn about the signaling properties of events (problem), we can look to classical conditioning (solution). Notice the shift in emphasis: Instead of topic followed by function, it's function followed by topic. I believe this kind of "functional approach" offers a number of advantages:

1. The student has a reason to follow the discussion.
2. Because the discussion is about an adaptive or conceptual problem, it naturally promotes critical thinking. The student sees the connection between the problem and the solution.
3. The adaptive problem-solving theme extends across chapters.
4. The organization provides an effective learning framework.

Each chapter is organized around a set of topics that (a) focus the discussion on the functional relevance of the material and (b) demonstrate that we think and act for adaptive reasons. When we view behavior as the product of adaptive systems, psychology begins to make more sense. Students learn that behaviors (including the methods of psychologists!) are reactions to particular problems. When we emphasize adaptiveness, we relax our egocentric view of the world and increase our sensitivity to why behavior is so diverse, both within and across species. Our appreciation of individuality and diversity is enhanced by understanding that differences are natural consequences of adaptations to the environment.

CONTENT CHANGES FOR THE FIFTH EDITION

Some of the major content changes in the fifth edition are highlighted below. In addition, there are numerous editorial changes throughout these chapters—I've tried to make the writing simpler and clearer. I've added new references throughout, although I've tried to keep the primary and classic references in place where appropriate.

- Updated discussion of prescription drug privileges for psychologists
- New "Practical Solutions" entitled "How Should a Teacher Grade?"
- Improvement of the clarity of the section on split brains
- Expanded coverage of gender effects and the endocrine section
- New coverage of brain development during adolescence
- New coverage of cross-cultural differences in attachment
- New coverage of peer group influences on development
- Updated and reworked section on the long-term effects of day care, reflecting the latest results from the NICHD Early Child Care Research Network (2007)
- Expanded coverage of auditory perception
- Expanded coverage of neuroimaging in higher-order vision and audition
- New work on effectiveness of subliminal messages
- New work on sleep's role in memory consolidation
- Expanded section on cell phones and driving
- Improved explanations of reinforcement, punishment, shaping, and biological constraints
- Expanded section on observational learning in animals
- New section on evolutionary determinants of memory
- Improved focus in the sections on short-term forgetting and memory illusions
- Expanded coverage of the linguistic relativity hypothesis
- New work on functional fixedness
- Expanded discussion of the confirmation bias and belief persistence
- Reworked definitions of analytic, practical, and creative intelligence
- Expanded section on human instincts
- Revised and updated sections on internal controls of hunger
- Updated assessment of the validity of projective tests
- Reworked coverage of Freud

- Expanded discussion of how stereotypes are activated
- Additional discussion of deindividuation
- New reference to the ICD-10
- New section on social anxiety disorder
- Added coverage of borderline personality disorder
- Expanded section on schizophrenia, including subtypes and cognitive symptoms
- Expanded coverage of biomedical treatments
- New coverage of exposure therapy
- Expanded coverage of external stressors
- New data on obesity in the United States

LEARNING SUPPLEMENTS FOR STUDENTS

Psychology, Fifth Edition, is supported by a state-of-the-art teaching and learning package.

Study Guide

(0495508438)
By Janet Proctor of Purdue University
The Study Guide contains a variety of study and review tools for students. Each chapter provides learning goals for every major chapter section; a "mastering the vocabulary" section; a "mastering the concepts" fill-in exercise; a multiple-choice "evaluating your progress" quiz for every major chapter section; a language development guide for each chapter; a final review section with short-answer, matching, and multiple-choice questions; and a phonetic pronunciation guide for appropriate glossary words. The answer key contains main text page references and rejoinders for all items.

Lecture Outlines Booklet

(049550940X)
By Matthew Isaak, University of Louisiana, Lafayette
This booklet is a handy tool that allows students to take notes while following the lecture.

ThomsonNOW™ for *Psychology*, Fifth Edition

A web-based intelligent study system, ThomsonNow provides a complete package of assignable diagnostic quizzes tied directly to the text's learning goals, written by Steven Elias of Auburn University–Montgomery; personalized study plans; integrated learning modules; and an instructor gradebook. More information is available at www.thomsonedu.com/thomsonnow.

Companion Website

www.thomsonedu.com/psychology/nairne
This site features a variety of teaching and learning resources, including chapter-by-chapter learning goals, online tutorial quizzing, chapter-related weblinks, flash cards, critical thinking lessons, and internet activities.

PsykTrek™: A Multimedia Introduction to Psychology

CD ROM: 0495090352
Online: 0495186708
By Wayne Weiten, University of Nevada–Las Vegas
PsykTrek 3.0 is a student tutorial available on CD-ROM or online, organized in 65 individual learning modules that parallel the core content of any introductory psychology course. The intuitive landscape and easy navigation of PsykTrek encourage students to explore psychological topics, interact with numerous simulations, and participate in classical and contemporary experiments. PsykTrek is rich with impressive illustrations, animations, and video clips that help students to commit psychological concepts to memory; it contains over 150 concept checks with quizzing to help students attain set learning goals. Version 3.0 includes new multiple-choice tests, unit-level exams, critical thinking exercises, and learning objectives.

WebTutor™

on Blackboard: 049559699X
on WebCT: 0495596981
Ready to use as soon as you log in, WebTutor is a complete course management and communication tool preloaded with text-specific content organized by chapter for convenient access.

SUPPLEMENTS FOR TEACHING

Instructor's Resource Manual

(0495555460)
By Gregory Robinson-Riegler of the University of St. Thomas
The manual is provided in a three-ring binder for ease of use and contains a preface that includes a section mapping the main text to American Psychological Association Goals and Objectives and a Resource Integration Guide. Each chapter contains content organized by major chapter section: chapter outlines, learning goals, lecture elaborations, demonstrations/activities/student projects, student critical thinking journal, making connections, incorporating diversity, focus on research, extending the practical solutions, questions for study and review, answers to the in-text critical thinking questions, film and video suggestions (ABC videos, Psychology Digital Video 3.0), recommended reading, "What's on the Web," Web activities, and InfoTrac activities.

Test Bank

(0495555479)
By Sheila Kennison of Oklahoma State University
Including more than 300 questions per chapter, this comprehensive *Test Bank* offers a great variety of items for test creation. Question types include multiple-choice, fill-in-the-blank, essay, and true-false (with selected questions marked for the web and for the PsykTrek 3.0 CD-ROM). Each question is also marked with its associated *Learning Goal* (correlated with the *Learning Goals* feaure in this textbook), as well as page number, type of question, difficulty level, and correct answer.

- Approximately 250 multiple-choice questions per chapter
  - 20 marked with www, available on the web
  - 5 based on material from the PsykTrek 3.0 CD

- Approximately 40 sentence fill-in-the-blanks
  - 10 marked with www, available on the web
- Approximately 20 essay questions per chapter
  - 5 marked with www, available on the web
- Approximately 20 true/false questions per chapter
  - 5 marked with www, available on the web
  - Each test item is marked with the *Learning Goal*, page number, type of question, difficulty level, and correct answer
  - Each chapter contains a grid that indicates which multiple-choice, sentence completion, essay, and t/f questions correspond to each other and the main learning goal (from main text) for the chapter

PowerLecture With JoinIn™ and ExamView®

(0495555533)
By Matthew Isaak, University of Louisiana, Lafayette
This one-stop resource provides you with tools to help you enhance your PowerPoint lectures, create exams, and create interactive PowerPoint lectures.
The CD includes

- Chapter-by-chapter lecture outline slides with integrated art, a video library, and other integrated media.
- ExamView® Computerized testing software. You can quickly create customized tests in print or online. The software contains all Test Bank questions in electronic format. It helps you create and customize tests in minutes. You can easily edit and import your own questions and graphics and edit and maneuver existing questions. ExamView® offers flexible delivery and the ability to test and grade online.
- JoinIn™ student response software enables you to engage students and assess their progress with instant in-class quizzes and polls. You can pose book-specific questions with the Microsoft® PowerPoint® slides of your own lecture, in conjunction with the "clicker" hardware of your choice.
- Full text files of the Instructor's Resource Manual and print Test Bank.

ABC Video: Introductory Psychology

DVD: 0495503061
VHS: 0495031739
These ABC videos feature short, high-interest clips about current studies and research in psychology. These videos are perfect to start discussions or to enrich lectures. Topics include mental illness and suicide, prescription drug abuse in teenagers, stem cell research, gay teens, rules of attraction, foster care, and suicide bomber profile.

Wadsworth Psychology: Research in Action Videos, Volumes I and II

Demo ISBN: 0495510203
By Roger D. Klein
Roger Klein received his B.S. in Psychology from the City College of New York and his Ph.D. in Educational Psychology from the State University of New York at Buffalo. His dissertation research, in the area of classroom behavior management, was conducted at the University of Pittsburgh's Learning Research and Development Center (LRDC) under the supervision of Dr. Lauren Resnick. Dr. Klein's most recent award, received in 2007, recognized his video production work for Wadsworth Publishing and his radio series. He has also received the Chancellor's Distinguished Public Ser-

vice Award from the University of Pittsburgh, in recognition of his long-standing efforts to use the media to further the public's knowledge about the field of psychology.

The Wadsworth *Psychology: Research in Action* videos provide an opportunity for students to learn about cutting-edge research—who's doing it, how it's done, and how and where the results are being used. By taking students into the laboratories of both established and up-and-coming researchers and by showing research results being applied outside the laboratory, these videos offer insight into both the research process and the many real ways in which people's lives are affected by psychology. The videos' subjects span the full range of subfields in the study of psychology. Titles include: *Trust and the Brain, Stress and Health, Internet Relationships,* and *Issues in Multiracial Development.*

Critical Thinking in Psychology: Separating Sense from Nonsense, 2nd Edition

(0534634591)
By John Ruscio, Elizabethtown College
Can your students distinguish between the true science of human thought and behavior and pop psychology? *Critical Thinking in Psychology: Separating Sense From Nonsense* provides a tangible and compelling framework for making that distinction by using concrete examples of people's mistaken analysis of real-world problems. Stressing the importance of assessing the plausibility of claims, John Ruscio uses empirical research (such as the Milgram experiment) to strengthen evidence for his claims and to illustrate deception, self-deception, and psychological tricks throughout the text.

ACKNOWLEDGMENTS

My publisher deserves enormous credit for organizing the team and for helping me carry out my original plan for this book. I've had the opportunity to work with a number of very talented individuals during the past decade, especially my editors Jim Brace-Thompson, Stacey Purviance, Marianne Taflinger, and Michele Sordi. Each has been a supporter, friend, and source of countless ideas. The current edition also benefited greatly from the work of a fine developmental editor, Dan Moneypenny.

On the production side, the captain of the fifth edition team is Mary Noel, Content Project Manager, who held together the tight production schedule and coordinated the efforts of numerous people. Extra-special thanks also go to Margaret Pinette of Newgen-Austin Publishing and Sarah Evertson of ImageQuest—great job!

Of course, I could never have written this book without the help and guidance I received from the reviewers listed below. I hope they can see their mark on the book, because it's substantial.

Reviewers of the Fifth Edition
Ellen Carpenter, Old Dominion University; Verne C. Cox, University of Texas at Arlington; Darlene Earley-Hereford, Southern Union State Community College; Jessica Dennis, California State University at Los Angeles; Bert Hayslip, Jr., University of North Texas; Stacy Harkins, University of Texas at Arlington; Kim Kinzig, Purdue University; Christopher E. Overtree, University of Massachusetts at Amherst; and Kathleen Torsney, William Paterson University.

I'd like to express continued thanks to reviewers of previous editions, as well.

Reviewers of the Fourth Edition
Michael Allen, University of Northern Colorado; Deborah Bryant, Rutgers–The State University of New Jersey; Wendy Chambers, University of Georgia; Julia Chester, Purdue University; Gloria Cowan, California State University–San Bernardino; Leslie Cramblet, Northern Arizona University; David Denton, Austin Peay State University;

Emily Elliott, Louisiana State University; August Hoffman, California State University–Northridge; Linda Jones, Blinn College; Linda Juang, San Francisco State University; Laura Madson, New Mexico State University; Glenn Meyer, Trinity University; Todd Nelson, California State University–Stanislaus; David Perkins, Ball State University; Peter Pfordresher, University of Texas at San Antonio; Robert Smith, Marian College; Michael Strube, Washington University; Noreen Stuckless, York University; Cheryl Terrance, University of North Dakota; Sheree Watson, University of Southern Mississippi.

Reviewers of the Third Edition

Cody Brooks, Denison University; Brad Caskey, University of Wisconsin, River Falls; Lynn Coffey, Minneapolis Community College; Donna Dahlgren, Indiana University Southeast; George Diekhoff, Midwestern State University; Diana Finley, Prince George's Community College; Jill Folk, Kent State University; Nancy Franklin, State University of New York–Stony Brook; Adam Goodie, University of Georgia; Linda Jackson, Michigan State University; Joseph Karafa, Ferris State University; David Kreiner, Central Missouri State University; Daniel Leger, University of Nebraska; David Mitchell, Loyola University of Chicago; Sanford Pederson, University of Indianapolis; Faye Plascak-Craig, Marian College; Bridget Robinson-Riegler, Augsburg College; Kraig Schell, Angelo State University; Valerie Scott, Indiana University Southeast; Annette Taylor, University of San Diego; Orville Weiszhaar, Minneapolis Community College; Jennifer Wenner, Macalester College; and Leonard Williams, Rowan University. Survey Respondents: Tim Curran, University of Colorado; Ellen Cotter, Georgia Southwestern State University; Jeffery Scott Mio, California State Polytechnic University, Pomona; Andrew R. Getzfeld, New Jersey City University; Wendy James-Aldridge, University of Texas–Pan American; Sam Gosling, University of Texas– Austin; Jeff Sandoz, The University of Louisiana at Lafayette; Kim Mac-Lin, University of Texas, El Paso; Charles R. Geist, University of Alaska, Fairbanks; Dawn Blasko, Pennsylvania State University–Erie; Shirley-Anne Hensch, University of Wisconsin Center–Marshfield/Wood County; David P. J. Przybyla, Dension University; Anthony Hendrix, Waycross College; Mary Beth Ahlum, Nebraska Wesleyan University; David Carscaddon, Gardner-Webb University; Michael Vitevitch, Indiana University; John Harrington, University of Maine at Presque Isle; Romona Franklin, LBW College; Glen Adams, Harding University; John Salamone, University of Connecticut; C. James Goodwin, Wheeling Jesuit University; Bradley J. Caskey, University of Wisconsin–River Falls; Daniel Linwick, University of Wisconsin–River Falls; Everett Bartholf, Missouri Baptist College; Haig Kouyoumdjian, University of Nebraska–Lincoln; Lynn L. Coffey, Minneapolis Community and Technical College; Randy Sprung, Dakota Wesleyan University; Patrick Conley, University of Illinois at Chicago; Sheryl Hartman, Miami-Dade Community College; Lisa M. Huff, Washington University; Jim Rafferty, Bemidji State University; Barbara Blatchely, Agnes Scott College; Carolyn Becker, Trinity University; Frank Hager, Allegany College of Maryland; Maria Lynn Kessler, The Citadel; Charles Jeffreys, Seattle Central Community College; Valerie B. Scott, Indiana University Southeast; Pat Crowe, NIACC; Edward Rossini, Roosevelt University; Richard S. Cimbalo, Daemen College; Donna Dahlgren, Indiana University Southeast; Thomas Frangicetto, Northampton Community College; Brenda Karns, Austin Peay State University; Buddy Grah, Austin Peay State University; Milton A. Norville, Florida Memorial College; S. F. A. Gates, Ohio University–Lancaster; Neil Sass, Heidelberg College; Christine Panyard, University of Detroit Mercy; Hoda Badr, University of Houston; Jon Springer, Kean University; Morton Heller, Eastern Illinois University; Robert B. Castleberry, University of South Carolina–Sumter; Petri Paavilainen, University of Helsinki; Victoria Bedford, University of Indianapolis; Marilyn Schroer, Newberry College; Terri Bonebright, DePauw University; Mark Smith, Davidson College; and Bruce J. Diamond, William Paterson University.

Dr. Valerie Scott of Indiana University Southeast generously agreed to solicit diary reviews from the following students. Their responses were helpful and encouraging: Angela Lashley, Theresa Raymer, Brent Saylor, Mindy Goodale, Scott Hall, D. Jones, Heather Wenning, Rebecca Thompson, Holly Martin, Dan Abel, Edith Groves, Kim Krueger, J. Kittle, and Jennifer Hall.

Reviewers of the Second Edition

Glen M. Adams, Harding University; Jeffrey Adams, St. Michael's College; Marlene Adelman, Norwalk Community College; Robert Arkin, Ohio State University; Cheryl Arnold, Marietta College; Nolan Ashman, Dixie College; Elaine Baker, Marshall University; Charles Blaich, Wabash College; Dawn Blasko, Pennsylvania State University–Erie; Susan Bovair, College of Charleston; Stephen E. Buggie, University of New Mexico; Brian Burke, University of Arizona; James Butler, James Madison University; James F. Calhoun, University of Georgia; Kenneth Carter, Emory University; Jill Cermele, Drew University; Catherine Cowan, Southwest State University; Patricia Crowe, North Iowa Community College; Tim Curran, Case Western Reserve University; Robert M. Davis, Indiana University–Purdue University, Indianapolis; Crystal Dehle, Idaho State University; Gina Dow, Denison University; Susann Doyle, Gainesville College; Patrick Drumm, Ohio University; Maryann Dubree, Madison Area Tech College; Peter Dufall, Smith College; Joseph Ferrari, DePaul University; Paul Foos, University of North Carolina–Charlotte; Kathleen Flannery, Saint Anselm College; Susan Frantz, New Mexico State University; William R. Fry, Youngstown State University; Grace Galliano, Kennesaw State University; Stella Garcia, University of Texas–San Antonio; Robert Gehring, University of Southern Indiana; Judy Gentry, Columbus State Community College; Sandra Goss, University of Illinois at Urbana–Champaign; Lynn Haller, Morehead State University; Suzy Horton, Mesa Community College; Wendy James-Aldridge, University of Texas–Pan American; Cynthia Jenkins, Creighton University; Scott Johnson, John Wood Community College; Robert Kaleta, University of Wisconsin–Milwaukee; Deric Kenne, Mississippi State University; Stephen Kiefer, Kansas State University; Kris Klassen, North Idaho College; Stan Klein, University of California–Santa Barbara; Richard Leavy, Ohio Wesleyan University; Judith Levine, State University of New York–Farmingdale; Arlene Lundquist, Mount Union College; Molly Lynch, University of Texas–San Antonio; Salvador Macias III, University of South Carolina–Sumter; Douglas W. Matheson, University of the Pacific; Yancy McDougal, University of South Carolina–Spartanburg; Susan H. McFadden, University of Wisconsin; Glenn E. Meyer, Trinity University; David B. Mitchell, Loyola University, Chicago; William Nast, Bishop State Community College; Donald Polzella, University of Dayton; Pamela Regan, California State University–Los Angeles; Linda Reinhardt, University of Wisconsin–Rock County; Catherine Sanderson, Amherst College; Stephen Saunders, Marquette University; Susan Shapiro, Indiana University East; John E. Sparrow, University of New Hampshire–Manchester; Jon Springer, Kean University; Tracie Stewart, Bard College; Bethany Stillion, Clayton College and State University; Thomas Swan, Siena College; Dennis Sweeney, California University–Pennsylvania; Thomas Timmerman, Austin Peay State University; Peter Urcuioli, Purdue University; Lori R. Van Wallendael, University of North Carolina–Charlotte; David Wasieleski, Valdosta State University; Diane Wentworth, Fairleigh Dickinson University; Lisa Weyandt, Central Washington University; Fred Whitford, Montana State University; and Steve Withrow, Guilford Tech Community College.

Reviewers of the First Edition

Karin Ahlm, DePauw University; Mary Ann Baenninger, Trenton State College; Daniel R. Bellack, Trident Technical College; Ira Bernstein, University of Texas at Arlington; Kenneth Bordens, Indiana University–Purdue University Fort Wayne; Nancy S. Breland, Trenton State College; James Calhoun, University of Georgia; D. Bruce Carter, Syracuse University; John L. Caruso, University of Massachusetts–Dartmouth; Regina Conti, Colgate University; Eric Cooley, Western Oregon State College; Randall Engle, University of South Carolina, Columbia; Roy Fontaine, Pennsylvania College of Technology; Nelson L. Freedman, Queen's University, Ontario, Canada; Richard Froman, John Brown University; Grace Galliano, Kennesaw State College; Eugene R. Gilden, Linfield College; Perilou Goddard, Northern Kentucky University; Tim Goldsmith, University of New Mexico; Joel Grace, Mansfield University; Charles R. Grah, Austin Peay State University; Terry R. Greene, Franklin & Marshall College; George Hampton, University of Houston–Downtown; Linda Heath, Loyola University of Chicago; Phyllis Heath, Central Michigan University; Shirley-Anne Hensch, University of Wisconsin Center–Marshfield/Wood County; Michael Hillard, University of New Mexico; Vivian Jenkins, University of Southern Indiana; James J. Johnson, Illinois State University; Timothy Johnston, University of North Carolina at Greensboro; John Jung, California State University–Long Beach; Salvador Macias III, University of South Carolina at Sumter; Carolyn Mangelsdorf, University of Washington; Edmund Martin, Georgia Tech Michael McCall, Ithaca College; Laurence Miller, Western Washington University; Carol Pandey, Pierce College; Blaine F. Peden, University of Wisconsin–Eau Claire; William J. Pizzi, Northeastern Illinois University; Anne D. Simons, University of Oregon; Stephen M. Smith, Texas A & M University; John E. Sparrow, University of New Hampshire–Manchester; Irene Staik, University of Montevallo; Robert Thompson, Shoreline Community College; Diane Tucker, University of Alabama–Birmingham; John Uhlarik, Kansas State University; Lori Van Wallendael, University of North Carolina at Charlotte; Fred Whitford, Montana State University; Carsh Wilturner, Green River Community College; and Deborah Winters, New Mexico State University.

We offer special thanks to the following professors and their students for conducting student reviews of the manuscript: F. Samuel Bauer, Christopher Newport University; Gabriel P. Frommer, Indiana University; R. Martin Lobdell, Pierce College; Robert M. Stern, Pennsylvania State University; and the students of Dominican College.

Many colleagues and students at Purdue also played very important roles in creating the final product, often suffering through questions about one research area or another, especially Peter Urcuioli, Susie Swithers, and Julia Chester. One of my graduate students, Fabian Novello, helped me a great deal on the first edition, as did Alicia Knoedler, Georgia Panayiotou, and Esther Strahan. Undergraduates Jennifer Bataille, Lauren Baker, Julie Flynn, and Kate Gapinski—now all graduated—read portions of the manuscript and also provided valuable feedback. Julie Smith, as always, helped me in innumerable ways, especially with the references and glossary.

Finally, and perhaps most important, I want to thank my entire family. Everyone, including my parents, experienced the writing of this book in one way or another. My wife and daughter, Virginia and Stephanie, lived the book as I did, and I dedicate it to them with love.

An Introduction to Psychology

Let's talk about psychology—the scientific study of behavior and mind. If this is your first psychology course, you might be surprised by what you find covered in this book. Most people think psychology deals mainly with the study of mental illness—that is, depression, schizophrenia, or the things you commonly see on *Dr. Phil*. It's true that psychologists often treat psychological problems, but the image of psychology presented on the afternoon talk shows can be misleading. Did you know, for example, that psychologists tend to focus just as much on the study of normal behavior as they do on abnormal behavior?

In fact, most of the material in this book comes from the study of normal people. Why? Well, there are two reasons. First, when you develop a psychological problem, such as depression, it usually means there's been a breakdown in normal psychological functioning. Something in your brain might no longer be working properly, perhaps you've developed a set of faulty internal beliefs, or maybe you've just learned to cope in a weird and unproductive way. To understand the abnormal, we need to understand normal functioning first, in the same way that medical doctors need to understand healthy bodies before they can understand sickness and disease.

Second, psychologists want to understand how and why people think and act. Lots of time has been spent studying normal human and animal behavior, and psychologists are using the accumulated knowledge to build a science of behavior and mind. The goal is to understand the causes of behavior so that we can ultimately gain better control over our environment and live more productive lives. As you'll soon see, modern psychology has something to say about everything from the treatment of irrational fears (such as the fear of spiders) to the development of effective study skills—even to the design of the kitchen stove.

Is a science of psychology even possible? Human behavior is notoriously difficult to predict. You're probably skeptical about the chances of a psychologist ever predicting your behavior. After all, don't we have free will? Can't we control our own behavior? Look, I just raised my arm up and down—you find me any psychologist who could have predicted that! However, importantly, just because behavior varies, or seems unpredictable, doesn't mean that general principles aren't at work. Physicists can't predict exactly how a ball will travel down an inclined ramp or how a piece of paper will flutter in the wind, but all would agree that motion in the physical world is controlled by understandable principles.

Psychologists believe human actions are governed by general principles, just like a ball rolling down a ramp, but any given example of behavior—such as how you'll act at dinner tomorrow night—is determined by multiple causes. The motion of a ball is hard to predict because it's influenced by friction, atmospheric pressure, the texture of the ramp, and other factors. Similarly, your actions are hard to predict because they're shaped by your current environment, the culture in which you were raised, the genetic material you received from your biological parents, and your moment-to-moment experiences.

Recognizing that your actions are determined by multiple factors is important and has many implications that we'll discuss throughout this book. It's one reason psychologists are often concerned with the study of individual differences among people. To understand behavior, it's necessary to understand the context in which the behavior occurs. You can't expect to understand the actions of a person living in the barrio if you only take the perspective of someone living in a White suburban neighborhood (and vice versa). Different cultural and environmental forces are at work, and different strategies may be needed to solve the problems at hand.

What's It For?   *The Function of Psychology*

Inside this book you'll find the topics of psychology presented from a "functional" perspective—this means that I'll explain what a psychological process is *for* before attempting to explain how it works. Our brains are filled with psychological "tools," controlling everything from emotion to memory to how we choose a potential mate, and each one helps us adapt and solve important everyday problems. I'll describe these tools in detail and show you how they're used, and we'll focus on the specific situations in which they are applied. Each chapter begins with a preview section just like this, called "What's It For?," that explains how and why each psychological process is important—both in life and in your efforts to succeed as a student. To understand any psychological process completely, I'm convinced, you first must have some idea of what the process is *for*.

Let's consider a few examples: Suppose you're walking along a mountain

trail and hear a sudden rattle. You stop quickly because that sound may signal the presence of a rattlesnake. One important thing you learn about in your environment is that certain events, such as a rattling sound, predict or signal other events, such as dangerous snakes. Our brains are designed, in part, to help us learn associations between significant events so that we can adapt to our environment more efficiently. In Chapter 7, we'll discuss a procedure called *classical conditioning* that shows us how this important learning process works. Likewise, in Chapter 13 you'll learn how we use psychological processes to interpret the behavior of others. If a shadowy figure emerges suddenly from an alleyway, it's imperative that you size up the situation quickly and decide on an appropriate response. Is this person a threat, potentially hurt, or just having a little fun? For a broad overview of the types of situations that we'll be considering, take a look at ▌Table 1.1.

In some chapters, our focus will be on the methods psychologists use to understand behavior and mind. For instance, what are the best strategies for understanding the cause of a behavior (Chapter 2)? What are the best ways to conceptualize and then measure intelligence (Chapter 10)? How can abnormal behavior be classified and, once identified, how can it be treated (Chapter 14)? These are practical problems that psychologists face; and, again, the key to understanding the methods psychologists employ is to understand the specific problems that these methods are designed to solve.

This first chapter is designed simply to acquaint you with the scientific study of behavior and mind. Toward that end, I'll try to answer three questions: (1) What is the proper way to define and describe psychology? (2) How did current psychological perspectives evolve? (3) What trends and directions are shaping modern psychology?

Defining and Describing Psychology

LEARNING GOALS
• Understand the modern definition of psychology.
• Distinguish among clinical, applied, and research psychologists.

PSYCHOLOGY IS THE SCIENTIFIC STUDY of behavior and mind. The word comes from the Greek *psyche,* which translates as "soul" or "breath," and *logos,* which means the study or investigation of something (as in biology or physiology). The word **psychology** was not in common use before the 19th century, and the field of

psychology The scientific study of behavior and mind.

psychology didn't become an independent science until the middle of the 19th century (Boring, 1950). Prior to that point, "the study of the mind," as psychology was widely known, was conducted mainly by philosophers and physiologists. Neither Sigmund Freud nor Ivan Pavlov was trained in psychology, despite their reputations as famous psychologists—the field simply didn't exist as we know it now.

Notice that today's definition of psychology is quite precise—it is not simply the study of the mind; rather, it is the scientific study of behavior and mind. The emphasis on science, and particularly the scientific method, distinguishes psychology from the closely related field of philosophy. The essential characteristic of the scientific method, as you'll see in Chapter 2, is observation: Scientific knowledge is always based on some kind of direct or indirect observation. Psychologists collect observations, look for regularities, and then generate predictions based on what they've observed.

By **mind**, psychologists mean the contents and processes of subjective experience: sensations, thoughts, and emotions. Behavior and mind are kept separate in the definition because only behavior can be directly measured. You should understand, though, that psychologists use the term **behavior** in a quite general way. Besides obvious actions such as moving about, talking, gesturing, and so on, the activities of cells within the brain and even internal thoughts and feelings can be considered types of "behavior"— as long as they can be observed and measured in a systematic way.

Psychologists often seek to understand how and why people act, think, and feel.

mind The contents and processes of subjective experience: sensations, thoughts, and emotions.

behavior Observable actions such as moving about, talking, gesturing, and so on; behaviors can also refer to the activities of cells and to thoughts and feelings.

What Psychologists Do

Psychologists are engaged in the scientific study of behavior and mind, but if you're a psychologist, where do you work, and what kinds of specific problems are you tackling? How do you actually earn a living? As you can see in the Concept Review on page 7, we can divide the job description into three main types: *clinical psychologists, applied psychologists,* and *research psychologists.* These are somewhat artificial categories—for example, clinical psychologists often work in applied settings and conduct research—but they provide a useful way of defining the profession.

Chapter	Functional Problem	Example	Solution Tools
2	Determining the causes of behavior	Sally watches a TV program and becomes aggressive.	Experimental research
3	Communicating internally	A bicyclist weaves suddenly into the path of your car.	Electrochemical transmission in the nervous system
7	Learning what events signal	You hear a rattling tail on a mountain path.	Associations acquired through classical conditioning
8	Remembering over the short term	You try to remember a telephone number as you cross the room.	Rehearsal in short-term memory
10	Conceptualizing intelligence	Andy is excellent at fixing mechanical devices but is terrible at reading and math.	Psychometric tests designed to measure the mind
13	Interpreting the behavior of others	A shadowy figure emerges suddenly from an alleyway.	Knowledge-based social schemas used to predict outcomes
14	Defining abnormality	Lucinda hears voices and thinks she's immortal.	*Diagnostic and Statistical Manual of Mental Disorders*
15	Treating the mind	Ralph is mired in the depths of depression.	Psychoactive drug therapy or "insight" therapy

TABLE 1.1 Examples of Functional Problems Considered in the Book

CRITICAL THINKING

Do you think it's possible to study behavior independently of the mind? Or does all behavior result from the actions of a willful mind? Cockroaches, snails, and starfish all behave, but do they have minds?

clinical psychologists Psychologists who specialize in the diagnosis and treatment of psychological problems.

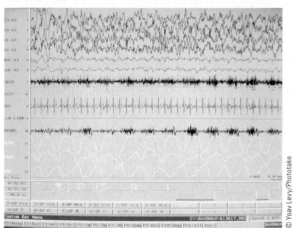

The term *behavior* can mean many things to a psychologist—observable actions, thoughts and feelings (as revealed through written reports), and even electrical activity in the brain.

Clinical Psychologists   A **clinical psychologist** diagnoses and treats psychological problems—such as depression, anxiety, phobias, or schizophrenia—or gives advice on things such as how to raise your children or get along with your boss. Clinical psychologists typically work in clinics or in private practice, delivering human services such as psychotherapy or counseling. To become a clinical psychologist, it is necessary to obtain a postgraduate degree such as a Ph.D. (Doctor of Philosophy) or a Psy.D. (Doctor of Psychology).

Counseling psychologists also deliver human services, but they tend to work on different kinds of problems. Counseling psychologists are more likely to deal with adjustment problems (marriage and family problems), whereas clinical psychologists tend to work with psychological disorders. Counseling psychology also requires a postgraduate degree, perhaps a Ph.D. from a graduate program specializing in counseling psychology or an Ed.D. (Doctor of Education). Together, clinical and counseling psychologists make up the majority of the profession. Currently, over half of the professionals working in psychology are actively involved in the treatment of mental health (American Psychological Association, 2002b).

Psychiatrists also specialize in the treatment of psychological problems, but psychiatrists are medical doctors. To become a psychiatrist you must graduate from medical school and complete further specialized training in psychiatry. Like clinical psychologists, psychiatrists treat mental disorders, but, unlike psychologists, they are licensed to prescribe medication.

As you'll see in Chapter 15, certain medications are useful in treating problems of the mind. Currently, there is an ongoing debate among mental health professionals about whether psychologists should be allowed to prescribe medication or whether it is practical for the profession to move in that direction (Fagan et al., 2007). Some states are considering legislation that will extend prescription privileges to licensed clinical psychologists; New Mexico and Louisiana, as well as the U.S. territory of Guam, recently passed legislation giving properly trained psychologists the right to prescribe drugs. At present, though, psychologists and medical doctors typically work together. A clinical psychologist is likely to refer a client to a psychiatrist or a general practitioner if he or she suspects that a physical problem might be involved.

Applied Psychologists   The goal of **applied psychologists** is to extend the principles of scientific psychology to practical, everyday problems in the real world. Applied psychologists work in many settings. For example, a *school psychologist* might work with students in primary and secondary schools to help them perform well academically and socially; an *industrial/organizational psychologist* might be employed in industry to help improve morale, train new recruits, or help managers establish effective lines of communication with their employees. *Human factors psychologists* play a key role in the design and engineering of new products: For example, why do you think telephone numbers are seven digits long, grouped in three, then four (e.g., 555-9378)? How about traffic lights—why red and green?

Human factors psychologists even work on the design of the kitchen stove. Does your stove look like the one shown in the left panel of ∎ Figure 1.1? Mine does. There are four burners, arranged in a rectangle, and four control knobs that line up horizontally along the front (or sometimes the back). To use the stove properly, you need to learn the relationship, or what psychologists call the *mapping*, between the control knobs and the burners. In this case you need to learn that the far left knob controls the back burner on the left. Or is it the front burner on the left? If you have a stove like this, which is psychologi-

  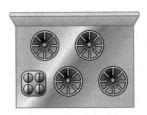

FIGURE 1.1 The Human Factors of Stove Design
The stove on the left does not provide a natural mapping between the control knobs and the burners and is therefore difficult to use. The stoves in the middle and on the right provide psychologically correct designs that reduce user errors.

cally incorrect, you probably have trouble remembering which knob controls which burner. Many a time I've placed a pot of water on one of the burners and turned a control knob, only to find moments later that I've turned on the wrong burner. The reason is simple: The stove has been designed with an unnatural mapping between its controls and the burners. (By the way, the stove came with the house.)

Mapping is easier to understand when you look at a psychologically correct design, as shown in the middle panel of Figure 1.1. Notice that the arrangement of the burners naturally aligns with the controls. The left-to-right display of the control knobs matches the left-to-right arrangement of the burners. There is no need to learn the mapping in this case—it's obvious which knob you need to turn to activate the appropriate burner. Alternatively, if you want to keep the rectangular arrangement of the stove top, then simply arrange the control knobs in a rectangular manner that matches the burners, as shown in the far right panel. The point is that there are natural and unnatural ways to express the relationship between product control and product function. Taking advantage of the natural mapping requires that you consider the human factor—in this case, the fact that humans tend to rely on spatial similarity (left knob to left burner; right knob to right burner).

We'll be considering the work of applied psychologists throughout this book. Applied psychologists usually have a postgraduate degree, often a Ph.D., although a master's in psychology can be sufficient for a successful career in an industrial setting.

Research Psychologists Some psychologists primarily conduct experiments or collect observations in an attempt to discover the basic principles of behavior and mind; they are called **research psychologists**, and, like applied psychologists, they usually specialize. *Biopsychologists*, for instance, seek to understand how biological or genetic

psychiatrists Medical doctors who specialize in the diagnosis and treatment of psychological problems.

applied psychologists Psychologists who extend the principles of scientific psychology to practical problems in the world.

research psychologists Psychologists who try to discover the basic principles of behavior and mind.

Concept Review Types of Psychologists

TYPE OF PSYCHOLOGIST	GUIDING FOCUS	PRIMARY WORKPLACE	EXAMPLES OF WHAT THEY DO
Clinical psychologists	The diagnosis and treatment of psychological problems	Clinics Private practice Academic settings	Counsel clients suffering from adjustment problems or more severe psychological problems; evaluate diagnostic techniques and therapy effectiveness
Applied psychologists	Extending psychological principles to practical problems in the world	Private industry Schools Academic settings	Help performance of students in school; improve employee morale and performance at work; design computers so that humans can use them efficiently
Research psychologists	Conduct research to discover the basic principles of behavior and mind	Academic settings Private industry	Conduct experiments on the best study method for improving memory; assess the impact of day care on children's attachment to their parents; observe the effects of others on a person's helping behavior

factors influence and determine behavior. *Personality psychologists* are concerned with the internal factors that lead people to act consistently across situations and also with how people differ. *Cognitive psychologists* focus on higher mental processes such as memory, learning, and reasoning. *Developmental psychologists* study how behavior and internal mental processes change over the course of the life span. *Social psychologists* are interested in how people think about, influence, and relate to each other. You'll be reading about the efforts of research psychologists in every chapter of this book. (Sometimes research psychologists work on problems of special interest to society—for an example, read the Practical Solutions feature.)

Practical Solutions

Can Racial Diversity Improve the Way We Think?

As part of the scientific analysis of behavior and mind, psychologists often confront "hot" topics, issues of relevance to society. Consider affirmative action, for example. Is it appropriate to give extra "points" on college entrance scales because of racial, ethnic, or cultural concerns? From the perspective of a psychologist, ignoring the political issue, you might wonder about the effect of group diversity on subsequent behavior and thought. Do we think better or learn more when surrounded by people of differing color or cultural backgrounds? Do diverse educational environments improve outcomes in college relative to homogeneous ones? Psychologists have developed tools, particularly the experimental method, that allow questions like these to be attacked empirically—that is, from a scientific perspective (see Crosby et al., 2006). One study by Anthony Antonio and colleagues (2004) looked at the effects of racial diversity on complex thinking in college students. White college students were assigned to small-group discussions in which

one of the research collaborators acted as a participant. The collaborator was either Black or White and was instructed to either agree or disagree with other members of the group on an assigned discussion topic (e.g., the merits of the death penalty). None of the real participants was aware that the collaborator was secretly part of the experiment.

After discussing the issue in the presence of the collaborator, the participants were asked to make a judgment on a different issue and to write a short essay expressing and justifying their opinion. They were also asked to rate how each of the other members of their group influenced their thinking during the group discussion. Perhaps not surprisingly, when the collaborator was Black (remember, the "real" participants were always White), his or her contribution was deemed more influential than when the collaborator was White. Moreover, because all the collaborators were instructed to say exactly the same things during the group discussion (they followed a script), it was presumably race rather

than message content that made the contribution influential.

Of main interest, though, was the effect of the collaborator on the essay written following the discussion. Again, this essay was written on a new topic, and there was no group discussion, yet those who had a Black collaborator in the earlier discussion tended to show less rigidity, were more willing to consider alternative perspectives, and revealed overall more complexity in their written essay than those with a same-race (White) collaborator. (Note: All the essays were rated by independent judges who were unaware of the earlier group assignments.) The differences were not large and depended to a certain extent on the particular discussion topic, but they indicate that racial diversity can, in some circumstances, positively affect the flexibility and complexity of one's thoughts and opinions. Positive effects of racial diversity have also been detected on jury deliberations in simulated courtroom trials (Sommers, 2006).

Test Yourself 1.1

Test your knowledge about how best to define and describe psychology by deciding whether each of the following statements is True or False. *(You will find the answers in the Appendix.)*

1. Psychologists use the term *behavior* to refer only to observable responses, such as moving about, talking, and gesturing. Internal events, such as thoughts and feelings, fall outside the domain of scientific psychology. *True or False?*

2. Psychology did not exist as a separate field of science 150 years ago. To explore questions about behavior and mind, it was necessary to study philosophy and physiology. *True or False?*

3. Clinical psychologists are generally interested in diagnosing and treating psychological problems such as depression or schizophrenia. *True or False?*

4. Psychiatrists differ from psychologists primarily in their focus of interest. Psychiatrists tend to work on severe and chronic problems, such as schizophrenia, whereas psychologists treat milder problems, such as phobias and anxiety disorders. *True or False?*

The Science of Psychology: A Brief History

LEARNING GOALS
- Understand what is meant by the mind–body problem.
- Contrast the different viewpoints on the origins of knowledge.
- Trace the development of the first scientific schools of psychology.
- Note the early clinical contributions of Freud and the humanists.
- Highlight the contributions of women to the development of psychology as a field.

THE FIELD OF PSYCHOLOGY has a relatively short past, but it has a long and distinguished intellectual history. Thousands of years ago the Greek philosopher Aristotle (384–322 B.C.) wrote extensively on topics that are central to modern psychology—topics like memory, sleep, and sensation. It was Aristotle who first argued that the mind is a kind of *tabula rasa*—a blank tablet—on which experiences are written. As you'll see shortly, the idea that knowledge arises directly from experience, a philosophical position known as **empiricism**, continues to be an important theme in modern psychological thought.

empiricism The idea that knowledge comes directly from experience.

Modern psychology actually developed out of the disciplines of philosophy and physiology. In a sense, psychology has always occupied a kind of middle ground between the two. Aristotle, Plato, and other philosophers helped frame many of the basic questions that occupy the attention of psychologists today: Where does knowledge come from? What are the laws, if any, that govern sensation? What are the necessary conditions for learning and remembering? Physiologists, on the other hand, focused their attention on the workings of the human body. Before psychology was formally established, physiologists collected volumes of data on the mechanics of physical movement and the anatomy of sensory systems, which proved essential in the development of a scientific understanding of behavior and mind.

CRITICAL THINKING

Psychology is the scientific study of behavior and mind. Is it really surprising then that its intellectual roots lie in physiology and philosophy?

Mind and Body: Are They the Same?

What exactly is the relationship between the physical body, as studied by physiologists, and the mind, as studied by philosophers? Are the mind and body separate and distinct, or are they one and the same? In the 17th century, the French philosopher René Descartes (1596–1650) argued that the mind and body are separate: The physical body, he claimed, cannot think, nor is it possible to explain thinking by appealing to physical matter. He did allow for the possibility that one could have an important influence on the other. He believed the mind controlled the actions of a mechanical body through the *pineal gland*, a small structure at the base of the brain (see ∎ Figure 1.2). He was never clear about the details.

Descartes offered some ingenious descriptions of the human body, and his writings influenced generations of physiologists. His specific ideas about the body turned out to be largely incorrect—the pineal gland, for example, plays a role in producing hormones, not muscle movements—but a few of his ideas remain influential today. It was Descartes, for instance, who first introduced the concept of a *reflex*. Reflexes are automatic, involuntary reactions of the body to events in the environment (such as pulling your hand away from the hot burner on a stove). As you'll see in Chapter 3, reflexes play a very important role in our survival. But Descartes did little to advance the scientific study of the mind. To separate the mind from the physical world essentially places psychology outside the boundaries of science. The scientific method is based on observation, and it's impossible to study something scientifically that cannot be observed in some way.

Today, most psychologists approach the mind–body problem quite differently. They reject the separation of mind and body and assume they're one and the same. What we call the "mind" today is really nothing more than brain activity; put

∎ **FIGURE 1.2** Descartes and the Reflex
René Descartes introduced the concept of the reflex, which he described as an automatic, involuntary reaction of a physical body to an event in the outside world. He thought the mediating structure was the pineal gland, shown here as a tear-shaped area at the back of the head.

simply, the mind is what the brain does (Pinker, 1997). As you'll see throughout this text, there is an extremely close link between the operation of the brain and behavior. Many psychological problems appear to come directly from problems in the brain, and many of the symptoms can be treated effectively through biological means (usually medication). Exactly how we infer mental "states" and processes from the study of brain action remains a tricky problem (Schall, 2004), but it's a problem that most psychologists believe will ultimately be solved.

Nature and Nurture: Where Does Knowledge Come From?

nativism The idea that some knowledge is innate, or present at birth.

Philosophers and psychologists have long been interested in determining where our knowledge comes from. As noted earlier, Aristotle adopted an empiricist position: He believed that knowledge comes directly from our day-to-day experiences. Empiricism can be contrasted with a philosophical position called **nativism**, which holds that certain kinds of knowledge and ideas are inborn, or innate.

The Nativist Argument Nativists believe that we arrive in the world knowing certain things. The German philosopher Immanuel Kant (1724–1804) proposed that humans are born with a certain mental "structure" that determines how they perceive the world. People, he argued, are born with a natural tendency to see things in terms of cause and effect and to interpret the world in terms of space and time (Bolles, 1993; Wertheimer, 1987). Of course, nativists don't believe that *all* knowledge is present at birth—we certainly learn a variety of things—but some kinds of knowledge, they argue, do not depend on experience.

As you can probably guess, the question of whether humans are born knowing fundamental things about their world is difficult to answer. For one thing, no one is really sure at what point experience begins. We could draw a line at birth and say that any knowledge or abilities that exist at that very moment are innate, but, as you'll see in Chapter 4, the environment exerts tremendous influences on embryos as they develop in the womb. We can never eliminate the influence of experience completely; so we're always faced with the tricky problem of disentangling which portions of the knowledge we observe are inborn and which are produced by experience.

It is possible to demonstrate that people use certain organizing principles of perception that cannot be altered by experience. Take a look at ▌Figure 1.3. If I showed you (a) and then (b), do you think you could easily recognize that (a) is in fact embedded in (b)? It's not easy to see, is it? More important, it doesn't really matter how many times I show you (a). Even if I force you to look at (a) one hundred times, it's always going to be difficult to find when you look at (b). The reason for this, according to a movement called **Gestalt psychology**, is that humans are born with a certain fixed way of viewing the world. The visual system, in this case, naturally organizes the sensory input in (b) in such a way that (a) is hard to see. These organizing principles are innate, and experience cannot change them (Ellis, 1938).

I'll have more to say about organizing principles of perception, and about Gestalt psychology, when we take up the topics of sensation and perception in Chapter 5. At that time, we'll return to this issue of experience and its effects on perception, and you'll see that experience is

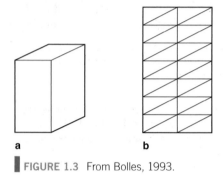

a   b

▌ **FIGURE 1.3** From Bolles, 1993.

Separated at birth, the Mallifert twins meet accidentally.

not always irrelevant to perception. In fact, very often the knowledge we gain from experience fundamentally affects the way we perceive the world.

Darwin's Theory of Evolution   By the end of the 19th century, the ideas of Charles Darwin (1809–1882) had taken hold in the debate about the origins of knowledge. Darwin proposed that all living things are the end products of an extended period of evolution, guided by the principles of natural selection. Cats have fur, seals have thick skin, and babies cry because these traits have been passed along—selected for—during the evolutionary history of the species. By *natural selection* Darwin meant that some individuals are better than others at overcoming obstacles and solving the problems present in their environment.

Because animals compete for survival and for opportunities to reproduce, those inherited characteristics that further survival and reproduction will be the traits most likely to persist from generation to generation. If an inborn tendency to cry helps us communicate feelings about hunger effectively, then it's more likely that we'll live long enough to pass this tendency on to our offspring. Such tendencies are selected for naturally because they are adaptive—they improve the chances for meeting the needs demanded by the environment (Darwin, 1859, 1871).

Notice that the emphasis is on inherited tendencies. Darwin believed that the principles of natural selection apply to characteristics that pass from parents to their offspring—not only physical traits, but behavioral and psychological ones as well. We now know that the principal vehicle for the transmission of inherited traits is genetic material inside the cells of the body. During development, the activity of the genes, together with other environmental influences, gives rise to the physical structure of the brain and the rest of the body.

By emphasizing the adaptive value of inherited characteristics, including psychological characteristics, Darwin was destined to have an enormous influence on the thinking of psychologists (Dennett, 1995). If natural selection plays a role in the evolution of mental abilities, then it's easier to accept the idea that people may inherit certain ways of thinking or of viewing the world (the nativist position). Researchers now commonly argue, for example, that humans may have an inherited predisposition to acquire language, much as birds have an inherited predisposition to fly (Pinker, 1994).

Nature via Nurture   Today, virtually all psychologists accept that psychological characteristics, such as intelligence, emotion, and personality, are influenced by genetic factors. We're not born with a blank slate but rather with a brain that is predisposed to act and think in particular ways (Pinker, 2002; Ridley, 2003). At the same time, genes never act alone; they always act in concert with experience. Experience determines how genetic material is expressed, which, in turn, means that physical and psychological traits will always depend on both. Nature works via nurture (experience) and vice versa—one can't happen without the other.

You'll be reading more about nature and nurture in upcoming chapters. From an adaptive perspective, it makes sense that both factors are involved. The newborn, for example, arrives in the world with a set of basic reflexes that helps the infant to survive. At the same time, it would make no sense to "hardwire" the brain with fixed responses to all environmental events. We live in a constantly changing world, and it is to our advantage that we can shape our responses to best meet the needs of individual situations. One of the unique features of humans is that they do a lot of developing outside the womb, thereby allowing the environment to exert a powerful effect on our neural and psychological development.

The First Schools: Psychology as Science

The first psychology laboratory was established in 1879 at the University of Leipzig by a German professor named Wilhelm Wundt (1832–1920). Wundt was a medical doctor by training, and early in his career he worked with some of the great physiologists

© Bettmann/CORBIS

Charles Darwin believed that both physical and psychological characteristics were naturally selected for their adaptive value.

Gestalt psychology A movement proposing that certain organizing principles of perception are innate and cannot be altered by experience.

Certain physical characteristics, including the ability to self-camouflage, are selected for in nature because they are adaptive—they improve the chances of an organism surviving.

©Steve Kaufman/Corbis

Wilhelm Wundt, shown here in about 1912, established the first psychological laboratory in 1879, at the University of Leipzig.

Archives, History of American Psychology, University of Akron, OH

structuralism An early school of psychology; structuralists tried to understand the mind by breaking it down into basic parts, much as a chemist might try to understand a chemical compound.

systematic introspection An early technique used to study the mind; systematic introspection required people to look inward and describe their own experiences.

of the 19th century. Fittingly, his laboratory was established during the time he spent as a professor of philosophy. (Remember, the intellectual roots of psychology lie at the union of philosophy and physiology.) Wundt is traditionally recognized as the founder, or father, of modern psychology, and 1879 is seen as the year that psychology finally started as a unique field. Prior to Wundt, it was not possible to major in psychology because there were no official psychologists or psychology departments (Bolles, 1993).

It is noteworthy that the birth of psychology coincides with the establishment of an experimental laboratory. Wundt's background in physiological research convinced him that the proper approach to the study of mental events was to conduct experiments. He believed that controlled observations should be collected about the mind in the same way that one might observe twitching frog legs in an effort to understand the principles of nerve conduction. Wundt didn't think all mental processes could be studied in this way, but he committed himself wholeheartedly to the use of scientific techniques (see Fuchs & Milar, 2003).

Structuralism   Wundt (1896) was convinced that the focus of psychology should be the study of immediate conscious experience, by which he meant the things that people sense and perceive when they reflect inward on their own minds. This view was strongly shared by one of Wundt's students, Edward Titchener (1867–1927), who proposed that immediate experience could be broken down into *elements*—primarily sensations and feelings. Titchener believed it was the job of the psychologist to (1) identify these elements and then (2) discover how they combine to produce meaningful wholes. He later named this approach **structuralism**: Essentially, psychologists should seek the *structure* of the mind by breaking it down into elementary parts, much as a chemist might try to understand a chemical compound (Titchener, 1899).

One problem with structuralism, however, is that while you can directly observe and measure a chemical compound, it's not easy to observe the internal workings of the human mind. Mental events are subjective, personal, and difficult to record. To solve this problem, the structuralists relied on a technique called **systematic introspection**, which required people to provide rigorous self-reports of their own internal experiences. Introspectionists were trained to describe the elements that they perceived in simple colors, sounds, and tastes. As a result, volumes of data about elementary sensory experiences were collected. Titchener's laboratory, for example, was one of the first to document that complex tastes could be broken down into combinations of four elementary tastes: salty, bitter, sour, and sweet (Webb, 1981).

Once psychology was established as a laboratory science by Wundt and his contemporaries, psychology departments began to spring up rapidly throughout the world. This was particularly true in North America, where dozens of laboratories were established in the last two decades of the 19th century (Hilgard, 1987). Titchener immigrated to the United States and established his own psychological laboratory at Cornell University. By 1890 a number of professional journals had been established, and highly influential textbooks of psychology started to appear (e.g., James, 1890). In 1892 the American Psychological Association (APA) was founded, and G. Stanley Hall (1846–1924), an American who had trained under Wundt in Germany, was installed as its first president.

Functionalism   The nature of North American psychology quickly shifted, however, away from the strict structuralist approach advocated by European psychologists. Whereas structuralists tended to focus exclusively on the content of immediate experience, dissecting the mind into parts, North American psychologists worried more about the *function* of immediate experience. What is the purpose of immediate conscious experience? How do internal psychological processes help us solve problems related to survival? Because of the emphasis on function rather than content, this school of thought became generally known as **functionalism** (Angell, 1903; Dewey, 1896; James, 1890).

functionalism An early school of psychology; functionalists believed that the proper way to understand mind and behavior is to first analyze their function and purpose.

Functionalists such as William James (1842–1910) and James Rowland Angell (1869–1949) were convinced that the mind couldn't be understood by looking simply at its parts—that's like trying to understand a house by analyzing the underlying bricks and mortar (James, 1884). You need to determine the goal of the mental operation first, and then, perhaps, you can discover how the individual parts work together to achieve that goal. To understand how memory works, for example, a functionalist would argue that you first need to consider its purpose—what specific kinds of problems do our memory systems help us solve (Nairne, 2005)?

Darwin's ideas about evolution through natural selection were extremely influential in the development of functionalism. To analyze the color markings on a butterfly's wings, a Darwinian would argue, you must ask how those markings help the butterfly survive, or at least reproduce. Similarly, when analyzing the operations and processes of mind, a functionalist would argue, you need to understand the adaptive value of those operations—how do they help people solve the problems they face?

William James, shown here in 1868, was convinced that to understand a mental process its function must be considered: How does it help the individual solve problems in the environment?

Functionalism had a liberalizing effect on the development of psychology in North America. It greatly expanded the acceptable range of topics. For example, it became fashionable to study how an organism interacts with its environment, which led to an early emphasis on how experience affects behavior (Thorndike, 1898) and to the study of individual differences. Later, some functionalists turned their attention to applied issues, such as how people solve practical problems in industry and in educational settings (Taylor, 1911). To a functionalist, almost any aspect of behavior was considered fair game for study, and psychology boomed in North America.

Behaviorism   Despite the differences between structuralism and functionalism, both still considered the fundamental problem in psychology to be understanding immediate conscious experience. The great functionalist William James is well known for his superb analysis of consciousness, which he compared to a flowing and ever-changing stream (see Chapter 6). Around 1900, the technique of introspection—systematic self-reflection—remained the dominant method of analysis in the tool kit of the experimental psychologist.

Yet, not all psychologists were convinced that self-observation could produce valid scientific results. In fact, throughout the early days of psychology controversies raged over the proper role for introspection. By definition, self-observations are

Archives, History of American Psychology, University of Akron, OH

John Watson, shown here at age 30, rejected the study of the mind in favor of the study of observable behavior.

behaviorism A school of psychology proposing that the only proper subject matter of psychology is observable behavior rather than immediate conscious experience.

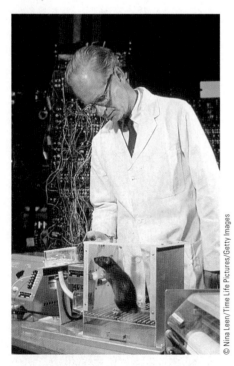

B. F. Skinner, shown here with one of his famous "Skinner boxes," championed the behaviorist approach and was one of the most influential psychologists of the 20th century.

© Nina Leen/Time Life Pictures/Getty Images

psychoanalysis A term used by Freud to describe his theory of mind and system of therapy.

personal, so, one might argue, how can we ever know whether the reports are truly accurate or representative of all people? It was also recognized that introspection can change the mental operations being observed. If you're concentrating intently on the "elements" of a banana, you experience "banana" in an atypical way—not as something to eat but rather as a complex collection of sensations. Introspection also limited the range of populations and topics that could be covered—it's difficult to ask someone with a severe mental disorder, for example, to introspect systematically on his or her condition (Marx & Cronan-Hillix, 1987).

By 1910 psychologists were seriously questioning the usefulness of studying immediate conscious experience. Increasingly, the focus shifted toward the study of observable *behavior*. The intellectual leader of this new movement was a young professor at Johns Hopkins University named John B. Watson (1878–1958). Watson was convinced that psychology should discard all references to consciousness because mental events cannot be publicly observed and therefore fall outside the proper domain of science. Observable behavior should be the proper subject matter of psychology; consequently, the task for the scientific researcher should be to discover how changes in the environment can lead to changes in measurable behavior. Because its entire emphasis was on behavior, Watson called this new approach **behaviorism** (Watson, 1913, 1919).

Behaviorism had an enormous impact on the development of psychology, particularly in North America. Remember: The psychology of Wundt and James was the psychology of mind and immediate experience. Yet by the second and third decades of the 20th century, references to consciousness had largely vanished from the psychological vocabulary, as had the technique of systematic introspection. Researchers now concerned themselves with measuring behavior, especially in animals, and noting how carefully controlled laboratory experiences could change behavior (Hull, 1943; Skinner, 1938). Influential psychologists such as B. F. Skinner (1904–1990) repeatedly demonstrated the practical value of the behaviorist approach. Skinner discovered the principles of behavior modification—how actions are changed by reinforcement and nonreinforcement—that are now widely used in mental hospitals, schools, and the workplace (Skinner, 1969). We'll discuss these principles in some detail in Chapter 7.

The behaviorist approach dominated psychology for decades. However, as you'll see later in this chapter, many psychologists have returned to the study of mental events (but with a healthy insistence on defining those events in observational terms). Behaviorism continues to be influential in modern psychology, but it no longer commands the dominant position it once held. To help you put everything in perspective, the top half of the Concept Review describes the three main schools of psychology in its early days.

Freud and the Humanists: The Influence of the Clinic

At roughly the same time American psychology was drifting toward behaviorism, a medical doctor in Vienna was mounting his own psychological revolution. Sigmund Freud (1856–1939) was trained as a neurologist (someone who studies the nervous system). He regularly treated patients whose physical problems, he felt, were actually psychological in origin. His experiences led him to develop an all-encompassing theory of mind that was to have a huge impact on future psychologists and psychiatrists (Freud, 1900, 1910, 1940).

Psychoanalysis Freud called his theory and system of therapy **psychoanalysis**, because he believed that the mind and its contents—the psyche—must be analyzed extensively before effective treatments can begin. Freud believed that psychological problems are best solved through insight: The patient, or client, must understand

Concept Review | Approaches to the Study of Psychology

GENERAL FOCUS	SPECIFIC APPROACH	IMPORTANT FIGURE(S)	FOCUSES OF APPROACH
Research	Structuralism	Wundt, Titchener	Determining the structure of immediate conscious experience through the use of *systematic introspection,* in which one attempts to describe the fundamental elements associated with simple thoughts and sensations.
	Functionalism	James, Angell	Determining the *functions* of conscious experience through the use of introspection, naturalistic observation, and the measurement of individual differences. Influenced by Darwin, it greatly expanded the range of topics studied in psychology.
	Behaviorism	Watson, Skinner	Establishing laws of observable *behavior.* The approach rejects the study of immediate conscious experience and mental events, unless they are defined in terms of observable behavior. It was the dominant approach to scientific psychology until the "cognitive revolution" of the 1950s.
Clinical	Psychoanalytic	Freud	Analyzing personality and treating psychological disorders by focusing on *unconscious* determinants of behavior. Also contends that childhood experiences play an important role in shaping adult behavior.
	Humanistic	Rogers, Maslow	Each person's unique self, and capacity for growth. A reaction against Freud, it emphasized that humans are basically good and have a unique capacity for self-awareness, choice, responsibility, and growth.

exactly how memories and other mental processes lead to problem behaviors. For this reason, psychoanalysis is often referred to as a form of "insight" therapy.

One of Freud's unique contributions was his emphasis on unconscious determinants of behavior. Freud believed each person houses a hidden reservoir in the mind, filled with memories, urges, and conflicts that guide and control actions. By "unconscious" he meant that these conflicts and memories cannot be accessed directly through conscious introspection—you might try, but your mind prevents you from consciously experiencing certain feelings and memories on your own. As a result, Freud largely dismissed the study of immediate conscious experience. He relied instead on the analysis of dreams, which he believed were largely symbolic, and on the occasional slip of the tongue for his primary investigative data. He spent hours listening to his patients relate their latest dreams or fantasies in the hope of discovering a symbolic key that would unlock their unconscious minds. Freud's complex analyses of the mind and its symbols led to a theory of how the unconscious mind defends itself from those seeking to discover its secrets. We'll consider this theory, as well as its applications for the treatment of psychological disorders, in more detail in Chapters 12 and 15.

Sigmund Freud developed the therapeutic technique of psychoanalysis.

Hulton Archive/Getty Images

The Humanistic Response Freud's influence was substantial, especially among clinicians seeking to provide effective therapy for psychologically disturbed patients. The familiar image of the client lying on a couch talking about his or her childhood, while the therapist silently jots down notes, is a fairly accurate depiction of early psychoanalysis. However, not all psychologists were comfortable with this approach. Freudian psychology paints a rather dark view of human nature, a view in which human actions are the product of unconscious urges related to sex and aggression. Moreover, it dismisses as symbolic and misleading any awareness that people might

humanistic psychology A movement in psychology that focuses on people's unique capacities for choice, responsibility, and growth.

Carl Rogers helped develop the humanistic perspective, which focuses on our unique capacity for self-awareness, personal responsibility, and psychological growth.

© Bettmann/CORBIS

Mary Whiton Calkins was the first female president of the American Psychological Association.

Wellesley College Archives/© Notman

have about why they act the way they do; instead, people's actions are really motivated by deeply hidden conflicts of which they are unaware.

In the 1950s negative reactions to Freud's view of therapy and mind led to the development of a new movement, **humanistic psychology**. Humanistic psychologists such as Carl Rogers (1905–1987) and Abraham Maslow (1908–1970) rejected Freud's pessimism and focused instead on what they considered to be humans' unique capacity for self-awareness, choice, responsibility, and growth. Humanists argued that people are not helpless unknowing animals controlled by unconscious forces—they are ultimately in control of their own destinies and can rise above whatever innate sexual or animalistic urges they possess. Humans are built for personal growth, to seek their fullest potential, to become all they are capable of being (Maslow, 1954; Rogers, 1951).

The optimistic message of the humanists played a significant role in theories of personality development, as well as in the treatment of psychological disorders. Carl Rogers, for example, promoted the idea of client-centered therapy, in which the therapist is seen not as an analyst or judge but rather as a supporter and friend. Humanistic psychologists believe that all individuals have a considerable amount of untapped potential that should be nurtured by an empathetic therapist. This idea remains influential among modern psychological approaches to therapy (see Chapters 12 and 15).

The First Women in Psychology

Mary Whiton Calkins (1863–1930) was elected president of the American Psychological Association in 1905. It's worth pausing and drawing special attention to this accomplishment because women have often been overlooked in historical treatments of psychology (Maracek et al., 2003; Scarborough & Furumoto, 1987). Significant discrimination existed against women in the early days of psychology. Women were denied admittance to Harvard University, and Mary Calkins was allowed to take classes with William James only as a special "guest" graduate student. She passed the final examinations for the Ph.D. but was never officially awarded the degree. Calkins went on to make a number of contributions to the science of psychology, including the development of the paired-associate learning technique (a method for studying memory that is still in use today), and she was a major contributor to philosophy as well.

The first woman to receive a Ph.D. in psychology (in 1894) was Margaret Floy Washburn (1871–1939), who in 1921 became the second female president of the American Psychological Association. Washburn's early contributions were in the structuralist tradition—she published her dissertation in one of Wundt's journals—and she became quite well known for her book *The Animal Mind* (1908) and for her behavioral views on consciousness. Helen Thompson Wooley (1874–1947) helped pioneer the study of sex differences, abolishing a number of myths about women that were widely accepted at the time. Never one to mince words, Wooley had this to say about the treatment of women in psychology circa 1910: "There is perhaps no field aspiring to be scientific where flagrant personal bias, logic martyred in the cause of supporting a prejudice, unfounded assertions, and even sentimental rot and drivel have run riot to such an extent as here" (Wooley, 1910, p. 340).

Calkins, Washburn, and Wooley are notable examples of female pioneers in psychology, but they were hardly alone. Many others overcame significant hardships to become active contributors to the developing science. For example, Christine Ladd-Franklin (1847–1930) was famous for her early work on color vision, and Lillien Martin (1851–1943), who made significant contributions in perception as well, rose to head the psychology department at Stanford University in 1915. Ruth Howard (1900–1997) was the first African American woman to receive a Ph.D. in psychology, and she is known for her significant contributions in clinical and developmental psychology. Martha Bernal (1931–2001), the first Latina to receive a doctorate in psychology, contributed significantly to the study of ethnic issues. Today women work in all aspects of psychological research, and they continue to be among the most important

Test Yourself 1.2

Test your knowledge about the development of psychology by answering the following questions. (You will find the answers in the Appendix.)

1. Most modern psychologists believe that the mind and the body are:
   a. controlled by different sections of the pineal gland.
   b. best considered as one and the same.
   c. separate, but both can be studied with the scientific method.
   d. best studied by philosophers and physiologists, respectively.

2. Fill in the blanks in the following paragraph. Choose your answers from the following set of terms: behavior, behaviorism, emotions, empiricists, functionalists, introspection, structuralists, thoughts.
   Functionalists and structuralists used the technique of _____ to understand immediate conscious experience. The _____ believed that it was best to break the mind down into basic parts, much as a chemist would seek to understand a chemical compound. The _____ were influenced by Darwin's views on natural selection and focused primarily on the purpose and adaptive value of mental events. _____, founded by John Watson, steered psychology away from the study of immediate conscious experience to an emphasis on _____.

3. Freud's psychoanalysis differs from Rogers' humanistic approach in which of the following ways?
   a. Psychoanalysis is "client centered" rather than "therapist centered."
   b. Psychoanalysis is designed to promote self-awareness and personal growth.
   c. Psychoanalysis minimizes the influence of early childhood experiences.
   d. Psychoanalysis is designed to reveal hidden urges and memories related to sex and aggression.

---

contributors to psychological thought. As you'll see in upcoming chapters, there is also a healthy interest in the psychology of women and in the study of gender differences (Kimura, 1999; Stewart & McDermott, 2004).

The Focus of Modern Psychology

LEARNING GOALS

- Understand what it means to adopt an eclectic approach.
- Understand the factors that started the cognitive revolution.
- Trace recent developments in biology and evolutionary psychology and note how they influence modern psychology.
- Explain why psychologists think cultural factors are important determinants of behavior and mind.

AS YOU'VE SEEN, psychology has undergone many changes since Wundt established the first psychological laboratory in 1879. Psychologists have argued—often for decades—about the proper focus for psychology (mind or behavior?) and about how to conceive of human nature (e.g., is there free will?). Debates still rage about the proper form that theories should take and about the right kinds of methods to employ (Proctor & Capaldi, 2001). You shouldn't be too surprised by the presence of controversy, however. Remember, the discipline is only a little over a century old; psychology is still getting its theoretical feet wet.

In the 21st century, most psychologists refuse to accept just one school of thought, such as behaviorism or psychoanalysis, and instead adopt a more **eclectic approach**. The word *eclectic* means that one selects or adopts information from many different sources rather than relying on one perspective. Eclecticism is common among clinicians working in the field and among research psychologists working in the laboratory.

In the case of the clinical psychologist, the best technique often depends on the preferences of the client and on the particular problem. Some kinds of phobias—for example, irrational fears of heights or spiders—can be treated effectively by focusing on the fearful behavior itself and ignoring its ultimate origin. (We don't need to know why you're afraid of snakes; we can just try to deal with the fear itself.) Other kinds of

Margaret Floy Washburn was the first woman to receive a Ph.D. in psychology.

eclectic approach The idea that it's useful to select information from several sources rather than to rely entirely on a single perspective or school of thought.

Archives, History of American Psychology, University of Akron, OH

problems may require the therapist to determine how factors in childhood contribute to troublesome adult behavior. Modern clinical psychologists tend to pick and choose among perspectives in an effort to find the approach that works best for their clients.

Research psychologists also take an eclectic approach. For example, depending on the circumstance, a researcher might try to determine the biological origins of a behavior or seek simply to describe the conditions under which it occurs. Once the conditions are cataloged, the behavior can be modified in a number of positive ways. Researchers recognize that it's possible to understand behavior and mind from many different perspectives, at many different levels of detail.

At the same time, several trends or perspectives have become influential in recent years. Modern psychologists remain eclectic, but they increasingly find themselves appealing to cognitive, biological, evolutionary, and cultural factors to explain behavior. Because of the special emphasis these factors currently receive, I highlight them briefly in the following sections.

Cognitive Factors

By the 1950s researchers showed renewed interest in the fundamental problems of consciousness and mental processes (Miller, Galanter, & Pribram, 1960; Neisser, 1967). A shift away from behaviorism began with an influential movement that is sometimes called the **cognitive revolution**. The word *cognitive* refers to the process of knowing or perceiving; as you may remember from our earlier discussion, cognitive psychologists are research psychologists who study processes such as memory, learning, and reasoning.

Psychologists returned to the study of internal mental phenomena for several reasons. One factor was the development of research techniques that allowed them to infer the characteristics of mental processes directly from observable behavior. Regularities in behavior, as measured by reaction times or forgetting rates, can provide detailed information about internal mental processes—as long as the experiments are conducted properly. You'll learn about some of these specific techniques later in the book.

Another important factor was the development of the computer, which became a model of sorts for the human mind. As you know, computers function through hardware—the fixed structural features of the machine such as the processor and hard drive—and software, the programs that tell the hardware what to do. Although the human mind cannot be compared directly to a computer, behavior is often influenced by "hardwired" biological (or genetic) factors and by the strategies (the "software") that we learn from the environment. Cognitive psychologists often explain behavior by appealing to information processing systems—internal structures in the brain that process information from the environment in ways that help us solve problems (see Chapters 8 and 9).

Much of our behavior is determined by how we think. Everything from perceptions and memories, to decisions about what foods to eat, to our choice of friends is critically influenced by our prior knowledge and beliefs. Many psychologists are convinced that the key to understanding psychological disorders, such as depression, lies in the analysis of a person's thought patterns. Depressed individuals tend to think in rigid and inflexible ways, and some forms of therapy are directed specifically at challenging existing thoughts and beliefs. You'll see many references to thoughts and cognitions as we investigate psychological phenomena.

Biological Factors

Modern psychologists have also benefited significantly from recent discoveries in biology. Over the years, researchers have uncovered fascinating links between structures in the brain and the phenomena of behavior and mind (see ▌Figure 1.4). It is

cognitive revolution The shift away from strict behaviorism, begun in the 1950s, characterized by renewed interest in fundamental problems of consciousness and internal mental processes.

now possible to record the activity of brain cells directly, and we know that individual brain cells often respond to particular kinds of events in the environment. For example, there are cells in the "visual" part of the brain that respond actively only when particular colors, or patterns of light and dark, are viewed. Cells in other parts of the body and brain respond to inadequate supplies of nutrients by "motivating" us to seek food.

Moreover, technology is now allowing psychologists to take "snapshots" of mental life in action. It is now possible to create images of how mental activities change as the mind processes its environment. These pictures of the brain in action can help researchers understand normal as well as abnormal brain activity. For example, it's possible to record brain activity during depression, extreme anxiety, or even during auditory and visual hallucinations. This information helps pinpoint where problems in the brain occur and acts as a road map for treatment.

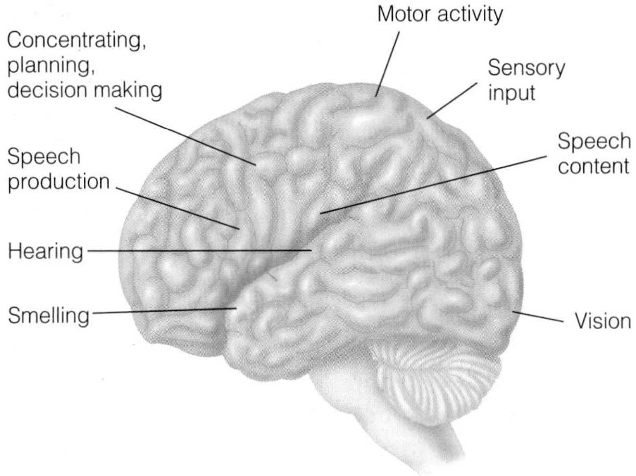

Great strides have also been made in the understanding of brain chemistry—that is, how natural drugs inside the brain control a range of behaviors. It turns out that certain psychological problems, such as depression and schizophrenia, may be related to imbalances among the chemical messengers in the brain. These developments, which we'll discuss in detail in Chapters 3, 14, and 15, are shaping the way psychological theories are constructed and how psychological problems are treated.

FIGURE 1.4 Specificity in the Brain
Scientists have discovered that certain functions in the body appear to be controlled by specific areas of the brain. Biological research has an enormous impact on the thinking of psychologists.

Evolutionary Psychology

From our earlier discussion about the origins of knowledge, you know that psychologists have been influenced by Darwin's theory of natural selection. Although it was widely accepted in the 19th century that the principles of natural selection apply to psychological characteristics, few psychologists advanced these ideas after the rise of behaviorism. Instead, psychologists focused their attention on the environment (nurture) and on learning in particular, and they essentially ignored evolutionary and inborn contributions (nature) to behavior. John Watson is known for claiming that any human infant might, under the right environmental conditions, be turned into a "doctor, lawyer, artist, merchant-chief and yes, even beggar-man and thief, regardless of his talents, penchants, tendencies, abilities, vocations and race of ancestors" (Watson, 1930, p. 104).

The rise of behaviorism was helped along by persistent attacks on Darwin's theory. Critics wondered, for example, why people and animals often engage in actions that don't seem very adaptive. Across the animal kingdom, it's easy to find examples of social behavior that seems to occur largely for the benefit of another—often putting the actor in great personal danger. Parents might deny themselves food and water to help their children survive. In the face of a predator, some animals call attention to themselves by emitting warning cries that help save others in their group. How do these nonadaptive behaviors help promote an individual's "fitness" for survival?

It wasn't until the second half of the 20th century that evolutionary theorists began to address these problems successfully. Some have argued that "altruistic" helping behavior can be handled by the mechanism of natural selection as long as one considers the unit of selection to be the gene rather than the individual (Dawkins, 1976; Hamilton, 1964). Sometimes actions that appear harmful to the individual can increase the chances that an adaptive gene will pass from one generation to the next. Moreover, it is now widely recognized that at least some of our actions are designed specifically to secure a mating partner and not necessarily to promote long-term survival (Buss, 2007). You'll read more about possible inherited mechanisms for mate selection when we discuss sexual behavior in Chapter 11.

evolutionary psychology A movement proposing that we're born with mental processes and "software" that guide our thinking and behavior. These innate mechanisms were acquired through natural selection in our ancestral past and help us to solve specific adaptive problems.

Evolutionary psychology is a recent movement that seeks to identify exactly how our behaviors and thought processes have been molded by evolutionary pressures. Evolutionary psychologists believe that we're born with mental software that guides our thinking and behavior. These natural tendencies, which were acquired through natural selection in our ancestral past, help us solve adaptive problems such as learning language, finding a mate, and acting socially in groups. For instance, it's been suggested that we're born with an ability to detect cheaters in social groups—those who violate social contracts or agreements (Cosmides & Tooby, 1992). We may also have been born with the natural distaste for incest, or sexual intercourse with relatives, because of its negative genetic consequences (Crawford, 2007). Not surprisingly, many of the claims of the evolutionary psychologists are controversial. Critics often argue that satisfactory environmental explanations can be given for behaviors that seem hardwired and universal (Buller, 2005; Eagly & Wood, 1999; Gould & Lewontin, 1979).

Cultural Factors

culture The shared values, customs, and beliefs of a group or community.

Finally, it's not possible to understand modern psychology without also discussing culture and the role it plays in determining how we act and think. By **culture**, psychologists generally mean the shared values, customs, and beliefs of a group or community (Lehman, Chiu, & Schaller, 2004). Cultural groups can be based on obvious characteristics such as ethnicity, race, or socioeconomic class but also on political, religious, or other factors (e.g., those who share the same sexual orientation might be considered a cultural group). Culture is a broad construct, and its influences can be found in virtually all aspects of behavior and mind.

Recognizing that culture has a strong influence may seem obvious, but it was largely ignored in mainstream psychology for many years. In the introductory textbook that I used as a college student, group influences were not discussed except for a mere three paragraphs covering why individuals might differ in intelligence. Psychologists have always recognized that behavior is influenced by the environment, which can mean one's culture, but it was the behavior of individuals in isolation rather than the behavior of individuals in groups that received the most attention. Researchers spent their time looking for universal principles of behavior, those that cut across all people in all groups, rather than exploring how the shared values of a community might affect how people think and act. The search for universal principles is still actively pursued today, as noted in our discussion of evolutionary psychology,

Cultural groups can reflect such obvious characteristics as shared ethnicity, race, or socioeconomic class but may also be based on political, religious, professional, or other factors.

© Brian A. Vikander/Corbis

but cross-cultural influences are now considered to be an integral part of the story of psychology.

Early on a few notable psychologists acknowledged the influence of culture on cognitive and social development. Over half a century ago, the Russian psychologist Lev Vygotsky proposed that children's thoughts and actions originate from their social interactions, particularly with parents. Vygotsky didn't think it was possible to understand the mind of a child without carefully considering the child's social and cultural world. In an important sense, the properties of a child's mind are actually created by his or her social and cultural interactions. At first these ideas were not very influential in psychology, partly because Vygotsky died young in the 1930s, but they've recently been rediscovered by psychologists and are now being actively pursued. (You'll read a bit more about Vygotsky in Chapter 4.)

Why have cultural factors finally become so important to psychologists? There are a number of reasons, but perhaps the most important is that research continues to show that culture matters, even when studying basic psychological principles such as memory (Nilsson & Ohta, 2006), perception (Jameson, 2005), and reasoning (Tarlowski, 2006). For example, as you'll see in upcoming chapters, members of Eastern societies (e.g., China and Japan), on average, think more in terms of the "group" than do Westerners (e.g., Americans), who tend to focus more on the individual. Members of these two culture types also categorize and remember different things about encounters and even simple visual scenes. Japanese responders, for example, are more likely to remember and report about the background elements of a visual scene ("there was a pond or lake"); Americans tend to focus on active elements ("there was a trout swimming to the right") and ignore the background (Nisbett et al., 2001).

The important lesson learned by psychologists, perhaps reluctantly at first but now actively embraced, is that a full understanding of psychology cannot be achieved without considering the individual in his or her social and cultural context. Cultural factors play a role in how we think and interact with each other and even in how we see the world.

Solving Problems With an Adaptive Mind

Psychologists are in the business of explaining behavior—discovering general principles—but the thoughts and actions of most people seem to change all the time. Pick any two people (or animals for that matter) and put them in the same situation. You may well see two different reactions. Haven't your actions ever made you wonder: "Why did I do that? I didn't mean to react like that."

As discussed at the beginning of the chapter, it's difficult to predict behavior because our view of the world is highly personal and subjective. No two people have exactly the same experiences; no two people are born with the same physical or genetic attributes (even identical twins have some differences). Given that behavior is almost always determined by multiple causes, it's hard to gather the information needed to generate a reasonable prediction. At the same time, psychologists are convinced that we don't act in haphazard ways; we act the way we do for a reason, and one job of the psychologist is to discover what those reasons are. The cause of a particular behavior may lie completely in the environment: It might be that you've been rewarded or punished for acting a certain way in the past. Alternatively, your actions might be caused by internal biological systems that lie outside of your direct conscious control.

We're constantly using our vast array of psychological processes to help us solve problems, everything from learning about the consequences of our behavior to choosing the right kitchen stove. It's useful to think about psychology in this functional way—not only will it help you understand your own actions, but it'll also help you think critically about the material presented in this book. When you read about a topic, don't just memorize—stop and think about how it helps you solve a problem. For example, how does a procedure such as classical conditioning (discussed in Chapter 7) tell us how people learn associations between significant events? How

CRITICAL THINKING

Behavior can be difficult to predict but still be governed by understandable principles. Think about how hard it is to predict the weather or even the movement of a ball rolling down an inclined plane. Would you claim that these activities are not controlled by principled "laws of nature"?

does the nervous system actually solve the problem of internal communication? Exactly how do existing diagnostic procedures help psychologists understand and treat psychological problems?

Most behaviors are tailored to solve particular problems. Once you understand those problems, it's a lot easier to see why specific behaviors or psychological processes developed. It's also easier to understand why behavior can be so diverse, both within and across species. People often differ because they face different problems—they're reacting to unique situations or using strategies that are culturally bound. To understand behavior, you first need to understand what it's for.

Test Yourself 1.3

Test your knowledge about the focus of modern psychology by answering the following questions. (You will find the answers in the Appendix.)

1. According to the eclectic approach, in choosing the best technique to use in therapy, you should consider:
   a. the specific unconscious urges that are driving behavior.
   b. the training and biases of the therapist/researcher.
   c. the preferences of the client and the particular problem under investigation.
   d. the availability of relevant monitoring equipment.
2. Fill in the blanks in the following paragraph. Choose your answers from the following set of terms: biology, cognitive, computer, cultural, philosophy.
   Over the past several decades, psychologists have returned to the study of internal mental phenomena such as consciousness. This shift away from strict behaviorism has been labeled the _____ revolution. An important factor that helped fuel this revolution was the development of the _____, which became a model of sorts for the human mind. Developments in _____ are also playing an important role in shaping modern psychology and in creating effective treatments for psychological problems.

3. Evolutionary psychologists believe that we're born with certain mental mechanisms, acquired through natural selection in our ancestral past, that help us solve specific adaptive problems such as learning language, finding a mate, and acting socially in groups. *True or False?*
4. Increasingly, psychologists are appealing to cultural factors to help explain human behavior. Which of the following statements about culture and psychology is false?
   a. Cultural influences were largely ignored by psychologists for many years.
   b. Culture influences social processes but not basic psychological processes such as memory or reasoning.
   c. A few notable psychologists, such as Lev Vygotsky, studied cultural influences many decades ago.
   d. By "culture," psychologists mean the shared values, customs, and beliefs of a group or community.

Review   *Psychology for a Reason*

At the end of every chapter, you'll find a section like this, which summarizes the main points of the chapter. This is a good point to stop and think about what you've read and to relate the topics to the functional "problem-solving" perspective introduced at the beginning of the chapter. Remember, the psychological processes that we'll be discussing exist for a reason—they help us solve problems every minute of every day. In this chapter, though, my goal was simply to introduce you to the science of psychology. I framed our discussion around three main issues.

Defining and Describing Psychology
Psychology is the scientific study of behavior and mind. Notice this definition makes no specific reference to psychological problems or to any kind of abnormal behavior. Although many psychologists (especially clinical psychologists) do indeed work to promote mental health, applied psychologists and research psychologists work primarily to understand "normal" people. The goal of the scientific study of behavior and mind is to discover general principles that can be applied widely to help people adapt more successfully—in

the workplace, in school, or at home—and to unravel the great scientific mystery of how and why people do the things they do.

The Science of Psychology: A Brief History Psychology has existed as a separate scientific subject for little more than a century, but people have pondered the mysteries of behavior and mind for thousands of years. Psychology has its primary roots in the areas of philosophy and physiology. Thinkers in these fields addressed several fundamental psychological issues, including the relationship between mind and body and the origins of knowledge. Most modern psychologists solve the mind–body problem by assuming that the two are essentially one and the same—thoughts, ideas, and emotions arise out of the biological processes of the brain. It is a common belief among psychologists that many basic behaviors originate from innate tendencies (nature) as well as from lifetime experiences (nurture).

Once the discipline of psychology was established by Wundt in 1879, psychologists struggled with the proper way to characterize and study the mind. Structuralists, such as Wundt and Titchener, believed the world of immediate experience could be broken down into elements, much as a chemist seeks to understand a chemical compound. The functionalists argued that the proper focus should be on the function and purpose of behavior. The behaviorists rejected the world of immediate experience in favor of the exclusive study of behavior. Added to the mix were the insights of Sigmund Freud, with his emphasis on the unconscious mind, and the arguments of the humanists, who strongly advocated free will and the power of personal choice.

The Focus of Modern Psychology

Each of the early psychological perspectives remains influential to a certain extent today, but most modern psychologists adopt an eclectic approach—they pick and choose from the perspectives. The study of behavior remains of primary importance, but the world of inner experience is also considered fair game for study, as evidenced by the cognitive revolution and by recent developments in the biological sciences. The possibility that some of our thoughts and actions are controlled by innate mental mechanisms, acquired through natural selection, is also being actively pursued by evolutionary psychologists. Finally, psychologists increasingly point to cultural factors in their attempts to explain behavior and mind.

Active Summary (You will find the answers in the Appendix.)

Defining and Describing Psychology

• Psychology is the scientific study of (1) _____ and (2) _____. Scientific knowledge is based on (3) _____. Psychologists infer how the mind works from directly measuring (4) _____.

• (5) _____ psychologists diagnose and treat psychological problems. (6) _____ psychologists extend the principles of scientific psychology to practical, everyday problems in the real world. (7) _____ psychologists conduct experiments and collect data to discover the basic principles of behavior and mind.

• Modern psychology developed out of the disciplines of (8) _____ and (9) _____.

The Science of Psychology: A Brief History

• (10) _____ believed that the mind is separate from the body, which the mind controls through the pineal gland. Modern psychologists believe that the mind and body are the same, because the (11) _____ is what the brain does.

• (12) _____ holds that we learn everything through experience. (13) _____ holds that certain kinds of knowledge and ideas are innate (inborn). (14) _____ proposed that natural selection guides evolution and that certain tendencies are inherited. Today, virtually all psychologists accept that psychological characteristics are influenced by both (15) _____ and (16) _____.

• (17) _____ was founded by Wundt, who established an experimental lab to study the elementary components of immediate experience and how they add up to a meaningful whole. (18) _____ was developed by North American psychologists who studied the adaptive purpose (function) of immediate experience. (19) _____, led by Watson, was based on the premise that because immediate conscious experience cannot be observed, measurable behavior is the proper subject of psychology.

• Freud was a neurologist and clinician who developed (20) _____, which used dreams and free association to analyze both the mind and (21) _____ determinants of behavior. Rogers and Maslow rejected Freud's pessimism and focused instead on positive traits. (22) _____ psychology holds that we control our destinies and can attain our full potential as human beings.

• (23) _____, who developed a paired-association technique, was the first female president of the American Psychological Association. (24) _____ was the first woman to receive a doctorate in psychology and is well known for her behavioral views on consciousness. (25) _____ helped pioneer the study of sex differences. (26) _____ and (27) _____ did significant work on color vision and perception. (28) _____ made important contributions to the study of clinical and developmental psychology. (29) _____ contributed significantly to the study of ethnic issues.

The Focus of Modern Psychology

• (30) _____ means that information is selected from many different sources rather than just one. Cognition is the process of knowing that involves learning,

(31) _____, and reasoning and that importantly influences behavior. Biology influences thought and behavior. Certain psychological problems may be caused by imbalances among the (32) _____ messengers in the brain. (33) _____ factors may be the basis for the thoughts and actions that are controlled by innate mental mechanisms. Culture is influenced by the thoughts and actions of group members along with their shared (34) _____, customs, and beliefs.

Terms to Remember

applied psychologists, 7
behavior, 5
behaviorism, 14
clinical psychologists, 6
cognitive revolution, 18
culture, 20
eclectic approach, 17

empiricism, 9
evolutionary psychology, 20
functionalism, 13
Gestalt psychology, 11
humanistic psychology, 16
mind, 5
nativism, 10

psychiatrists, 7
psychoanalysis, 14
psychology, 4
research psychologists, 7
structuralism, 12
systematic introspection, 12

Media Resources

 ThomsonNOW

www.thomsonedu.com/ThomsonNOW
Go to this site for the link to ThomsonNOW, your one-stop study shop. Take a Pre-Test for this chapter, and ThomsonNOW will generate a Personalized Study Plan based on your results. The Study Plan will identify the topics you need to review and direct you to online resources to help you master those topics. You can then take a Post-Test to help you determine the concepts you have mastered and what you still need to work on.

 Companion Website

www.thomsonedu.com/psychology/nairne
Go to this site to find online resources directly linked to your book, including a glossary, flashcards, quizzing, weblinks, and more.

 Psyk.trek 3.0

Check out the Psyk.trek CD-ROM for further study of the concepts in this chapter. Psyk.trek's interactive learning modules, simulations, and quizzes offer additional opportunities for you to interact with, reflect on, and retain the material:

History & Methods: Psychology's Timeline.

The Tools of Psychological Research

Todd leaned back on his bed, headphones firmly in place, and cranked up the volume. He couldn't hear the hidden message, the one announcing the arrival of Satan, just the steady "thump-thump-thump" of the bass.

He noticed nothing at all in particular, in fact, but he didn't feel much like going to church on Sunday either. . . .

Are there secret messages lurking about in advertisements or flowing backward on the tracks of your favorite CD? Maybe these messages are everywhere, hidden from the naked eye and ear by greedy advertisers and dark-natured rock stars. Some have assumed that subliminal ("below the threshold") stimuli are responsible for much of society's ills, such as sudden buying urges or especially abnormal thoughts (Key, 1973). Do you have an opinion?

Research psychologists have studied subliminal influence, and fortunately they've found little need for concern (Greenwald et al., 1991; Merikle & Skanes, 1992). Although subliminal stimuli may have an influence in some circumstances (Karremans et al., 2006), there's very little evidence that subliminal messages are used by advertisers, and even if they are, their power to influence is weak at best. So if Todd decides against church on Sunday, it's almost certainly not due to a subliminal message playing backward on his CD. It's an interesting topic for us, however, because this chapter deals with the techniques of psychological research. How do psychologists determine whether an event in the environment, such as a subliminal message, can affect our behavior?

In Chapter 1 you learned that the methods of psychology rely primarily on observation, on information gathered by the senses. Because psychologists depend on observation, they typically use the **scientific method** as the main tool for investigating behavior and mind. To understand the effect of subliminal messages, then, we must first employ the scientific method. Reduced to its barest essentials, the scientific method contains four important steps (see ▌Figure 2.1 on page 29):

1. *Observe.* The scientific method always begins, appropriately, with observation. In psychology, we choose the behavior of interest and begin recording its characteristics as well as the conditions under which the behavior occurs.
2. *Detect regularities.* Next the researcher looks for regularities in the observations—are there certain consistent features or conditions under which the behaviors commonly appear?

> **scientific method** A multistep technique that generates empirical knowledge—that is, knowledge derived from systematic observations of the world.

operational definitions Definitions that specify how concepts can be observed and measured.

3. *Generate a hypothesis*. In step three, the researcher forms a hypothesis, which is essentially a prediction about the characteristics of the behavior under study. Hypotheses are normally expressed in the form of testable if-then statements: If some set of conditions is present and observed, then a certain kind of behavior will occur.

4. *Observe*. Finally, the predictions of the hypothesis are checked for accuracy—once again through observation. If new data are consistent with the prediction of the hypothesis, the hypothesis is supported.

Notice that the scientific method is anchored on both ends by observation: Observation always begins and ends the scientific process. This means that psychological terms must be defined in a way that allows for observation. To make certain that terms and concepts meet this criterion, psychologists often use **operational definitions**, which define concepts specifically in terms of how those concepts can be measured (Levine & Parkinson, 1994; Stevens, 1939). For example, *intelligence* might be defined operationally as performance on a psychological test, and *memory* might be defined as the number of words correctly recalled on a retention test. If your goal is to investigate the topic of *subliminal influence*, you'll need an operational definition for subliminal influence. Can you think of one? I'll return to the topic of subliminal messages later in the chapter.

What's It For? *Unlocking the Secrets of Behavior and Mind*

In this chapter we'll focus on the methods researchers use to help describe and understand behavior and mind. Like psychological processes, research techniques are designed to solve specific kinds of problem for the psychologist, such as determining cause and effect or predicting and selecting. So, to understand the method you must first understand its goals—what kind of information about behavior and mind is the psychologist attempting to obtain?

Observing and Describing Behavior
Because the scientific process hinges on observation, one of the most important steps in any psychological research project is to choose a behavior and begin recording its characteristics. However, observation in research is more than casual looking or listening—the methods of observation must be systematic. To solve problems associated with observation and description, psychologists have developed a set of procedures known collectively as descriptive research.

Predicting Behavior
Once behavioral data have been collected and described, the researcher typically begins to think about the possibility of prediction. Descriptive research yields facts about behavior, but we need a different set of techniques to decide when and how the behavior will reoccur. Prediction is valuable because it allows for more effective control of future environments. To solve the problem of prediction, psychologists often employ correlational research.

Explaining Behavior
To determine cause and effect, as you'll soon see, it's necessary to conduct experimental research. The researcher must systematically manipulate the environment to determine its effect on behavior. If conducted properly, experiments allow the researcher to understand why behavior occurs or changes in a particular situation.

Treating Participants Ethically
Is it proper for the psychologist to hide in the shadows, carefully recording someone's every move in an attempt to advance scientific knowledge? Is it proper to experiment on animals—depriving them of food or water or destroying portions of their brain—simply to learn about the mechanisms underlying behavior? These are not easy questions to answer, but researchers have developed a set of ethical principles to help ensure that all research subjects are treated with dignity and respect.

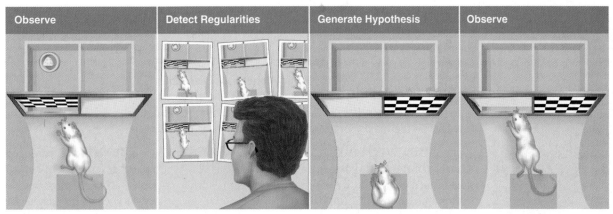

Observe	Detect Regularities	Generate Hypothesis	Observe
The rat receives food for jumping through the checkerboard panel on the left.	Over trials, the rat consistently chooses to jump toward the checkerboard panel on the left.	The rat has learned to associate the checkerboard with food, so if the checkerboard is moved to the right, the rat will jump to the right.	The rat jumps to the left, suggesting it has learned that jumping left produces food.

▌**FIGURE 2.1** The Scientific Method: Four Major Steps

1. Observe. The rat jumps toward the checkerboard panel on the left. 2. Detect regularities in behavior. The researcher notes that the rat, over repeated trials, consistently jumps to the checkerboard on the left. 3. Generate a hypothesis: If I move the checkerboard to the right, the rat will jump to the right. 4. Observe to test the hypothesis. Here the hypothesis turns out to be wrong. The rat jumps left again instead of following the checkerboard.

© Jim Richardson/Corbis

In attempting to understand why people act the way they do, psychologists study both ordinary and unusual behaviors.

Observing Behavior: Descriptive Research

LEARNING GOALS

- Describe the techniques and goals of descriptive research.
- Explain how psychologists conduct naturalistic research.
- Discuss the gains and costs of case studies and surveys.
- Explain how statistics can summarize and help interpret data.
- Describe the major purpose of psychological tests.

Psychologists must keep in mind the problem of reactivity: Are the behaviors they're observing simply a reaction to being observed? If these children behave differently because of the observer's presence, the observations may not generalize well to other situations.

descriptive research Methods designed to observe and describe behavior.

reactivity When behavior changes as a result of the observation process.

external validity The extent to which results generalize to other situations or are representative of real life.

WE BEGIN WITH A DISCUSSION of descriptive research. **Descriptive research** consists of the methods that underlie the direct observation and description of behavior. At face value, the act of observation seems simple enough—after all, most people can watch and record the behavior of themselves or others. However, it's easy to be misled, even when the goal is simply to record behavior passively (Rosenthal & Rosnow, 1969; Rosnow & Rosenthal, 1996).

Let's suppose you want to observe the behavior of preschoolers in the local day-care center. You arrive with cameras and recording devices to observe the children at play. After a few moments, you notice that the children distract easily—many seem uneasy and hesitant to engage in the activities suggested by the teacher. Several children show outward signs of fear and eventually withdraw, crying, to a corner of the room. Later, in describing your results, you conclude that children in day-care centers adjust badly, and some even show early signs of poor psychological health.

Is this a valid conclusion? Probably not. Whenever you observe the actions of another, the very act of observing can affect the behavior you're recording. In the case of the day-care center, it's likely that your unexpected presence (with cameras and the like) made the children feel uncomfortable and led them to act in ways that were not representative of their normal behavior. Psychologists call this a problem of reactivity. **Reactivity** occurs when an individual's behavior is changed by the process of being observed. It's called reactivity because the behavior is essentially a reaction to the observation process (Orne, 1969; Webb et al., 1981). The children are probably not naturally hesitant and distracted—they were simply startled by your presence. One consequence of reactivity is the loss of external validity. **External validity** tells us how well the results of an observation generalize to other situations or are representative of real life (Campbell & Stanley, 1966; Cook & Campbell, 1979). If a child's behavior is largely a reaction to your presence, it is clearly not representative of real life. More generally, even if these children are naturally fearful, your one set of observations cannot guarantee that your conclusions are representative of how children at other day-care centers will act. To improve external validity, you must record the behavior of children at another day-care center, or preferably many day-care centers, to see whether similar patterns emerge.

Naturalistic Observation: Focusing on Real Life

naturalistic observation A descriptive research technique that records naturally occurring behavior as opposed to behavior produced in the laboratory.

One way to reduce the problem of reactivity and improve external validity is to observe behavior in natural settings (Martin & Bateson, 1993; Timberlake & Silva, 1994). In **naturalistic observation**, the researcher records only naturally occurring behavior, as opposed to behavior produced in the laboratory, and tries hard not to interfere in any way. Because the recorded behavior is natural and has not been manufactured by the researcher, the observations are generally considered to be representative of real life (of course, it is also necessary to repeat the observations in different settings to be certain the results generalize). Also, if the subjects are unaware of being observed, their behavior cannot simply be a reaction to the observation process. Naturalistic observation has been used with great success by psychologists as well as by ethologists, biologists who study the behavior of animals in the wild (Goodall, 1990; Lorenz, 1958).

Researchers sometimes use a naturalistic technique called participant observation. In participant observation, the observer attempts to become a part of the ac-

© Galen Rowell/Corbis

In naturalistic observation the researcher records only behavior that occurs naturally (in contrast to behavior produced in the laboratory) and makes an effort not to interfere in any way.

tivities being studied, to blend into the group. In the 1950s a group of psychologists joined a doomsday cult group by passing themselves off as believers. People in the cult were convinced that the world was going to end, on a particular date, from a natural disaster. Once they were on the inside, the psychologists recorded and studied the reactions of the cultists when the prophesized "day of doom" failed to materialize (Festinger et al., 1956). In another classic project that you'll read more about in Chapter 14, a group of researchers committed themselves to local mental hospitals—they complained of hearing voices—in an effort to obtain an honest record of patient life inside an institution (Rosenhan, 1973). Participant observation could easily be used in our day-care center example: You could introduce yourself as a new teacher, rather than as a researcher, and hide your cameras or other recording equipment.

Another way to reduce reactivity is to measure behavior indirectly, by looking at the results of the behavior rather than the behavior itself. For example, you might be able to learn something about the shopping habits of teenagers at the local mall by analyzing the litter they leave behind. Administrators at museums have determined the popularity of various exhibits by noting how quickly floor tiles in front of each display wear out and need to be replaced (Webb et al., 1981; see ▮ Figure 2.2 on page 32). Neither of these examples requires direct observation; it is the aftereffects of the behavior that provide the insightful clues.

Naturalistic observation can also be used to verify the results of laboratory experiments (Miller, 1977; Timberlake & Silva, 1994). To gain control over a behavior, and to understand its causes, researchers usually manipulate the behavior directly through an experiment. Because it is difficult to conduct an experiment in natural settings, laboratory studies usually generate concerns about external validity. Most studies of human memory, for example, have been conducted by having subjects learn lists of words in the laboratory (Bruce, 1985; Neisser, 1978). Do the psychological principles established from such studies apply to learning and remembering in natural settings? To answer this question, psychologists also record natural instances of remembering and forgetting, such as eyewitness accounts of naturally occurring events, to determine whether the patterns resemble those collected in the lab (Conway et al., 1994; Neisser & Hyman, 1999). For reasons that will become clear later in this chapter, naturalistic observation, by itself, is a poor vehicle for determining causality. However, it can be used effectively to gather basic information about a phenomenon and, in conjunction with laboratory research, to establish the generality of psychological principles.

CRITICAL THINKING

Do you see any ethical problems with the technique of participant observation? After all, isn't the researcher misleading people by assuming a false identity?

FIGURE 2.2 Naturalistic Observation of Behavioral Results
At the Chicago Museum of Science and Industry, researchers gauged the popularity of exhibits by noting how quickly the vinyl tiles in front of each display wore out. The chick-hatching exhibit proved to be extremely popular.

Case Studies: Focusing on the Individual

case study A descriptive research technique in which the effort is focused on a single case, usually an individual.

Another widely used descriptive research technique is the case study. In a **case study** the researcher focuses on a single case, usually one individual (Bromley, 1986; Elmes, Kantowitz, & Roediger, 2006; Heiman, 1995). Because lots of information can be collected about the background and behavior of a single person, case studies give researchers an important historical perspective; this, in turn, helps the researcher form hypotheses about the possible causes of a behavior or psychological problem.

It's easy to find examples of case studies. Just browse around at your local bookstore, and you're find lots of books written about interesting cases; often the main characters in these books suffer from psychological problems or bizarre neurological disorders. Sybil, depicted in a television miniseries of the same name, is a well-known case study of multiple personality disorder (now known as dissociative identity disorder). The neurologist Oliver Sacks has written a number of delightful books about clinical cases, such as *The Man Who Mistook His Wife for a Hat* (Sacks, 1985). One of the most influential psychological theories of the 20th century, the psychoanalytic theory of Sigmund Freud, was based primarily on descriptive data gathered from case studies.

Like naturalistic observation, case studies suffer from limitations (Yin, 1998). By focusing on a single case, researchers essentially place all of their theoretical eggs in one basket. This raises concerns about external validity: Are the experiences of the research subject truly representative of others (Elmes et al., 2006)? Sybil's frightening descent into madness may not be representative of how psychological disorders normally develop (see Rieber, 1999, for a very interesting critique of the Sybil case). Another problem is verification: It can be difficult to verify the claims of the studied person. If the observations of the subject are somehow tainted—the subject is lying, for example—the entire study must be viewed with suspicion. In fact, sophisticated techniques are available to help researchers "catch" people with bogus symptoms (Slick et al., 1996). Case studies are excellent vehicles for generating hypotheses but are generally ineffective for determining cause-and-effect relationships.

Surveys: Focusing on the Group

Whereas a case study focuses on a single individual, psychologists use a **survey** to sample behavior broadly, usually by gathering responses from many people. Most surveys use questionnaires—individuals or groups are asked to answer questions about some personal behavior or psychological characteristic. You're familiar, of course, with opinion surveys conducted by political campaigns. Surveys can also be used purely for research purposes to gain valuable descriptive information about behavior and mind. For example, researchers have recently used surveys to determine whether there are gender differences in online (Internet) buying behavior (Dittmar, Long, & Meek, 2004), and to see whether television viewing habits in the days immediately following the September 11 terrorist attacks affected the likelihood of developing posttraumatic stress disorder (Ahern et al., 2004).

■ Figure 2.3 shows the results of a survey conducted by Michael Yapko (1994) in which 869 psychotherapists with differing degrees of academic training responded to questions about the use of hypnosis for recovering forgotten or repressed memories. As you may know, hypnosis is sometimes used by therapists as a memory aid to help people recover forgotten instances of trauma. Ninety-seven percent of Yapko's survey respondents agreed that hypnosis is a worthwhile tool in psychotherapy, and nearly 54% were convinced that hypnosis could be used to recover memories of actual events as far back as birth. More than 1 in 4 of the respondents believed that hypnosis could be used to recover accurate memories of past lives. (Huh?) If conducted properly, surveys are useful because they provide researchers with valuable insight into what people believe. In this case, Yapko's results are alarming because they reveal how widespread misinformed views can be, even among professional psychotherapists (don't worry, the Yapko data do not represent the majority opinion among psychologists—for reasons that will be described later). As you'll discover in Chapters 6, 8, and 12, memories recovered through hypnosis may not be especially accurate; plus, there is no scientific evidence to support the existence of past lives (remembered or otherwise)! These survey findings indicate a need for improved education and training, at least for this group of respondents. However before survey results can be accepted as truly representative of a group, such as practicing psychotherapists, the researchers must make certain that the participants in the survey have been sampled randomly (see Lindsay & Poole, 1998).

survey A descriptive research technique designed to gather limited amounts of information from many people, usually by administering some kind of questionnaire.

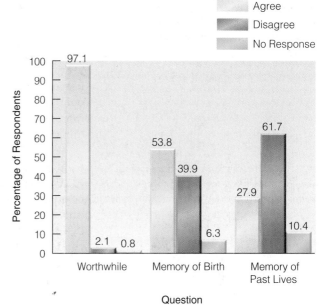

FIGURE 2.3 Opinions About Hypnosis A survey of psychotherapists shows the percentage of respondents who agreed, disagreed, or gave no response to the following statements: "Hypnosis is a worthwhile psychotherapy tool," "Hypnosis can be used to recover memories of actual events as far back as birth," and "Hypnosis can be used to recover accurate memories of past lives." (Yapko, 1994)

Sampling From a Population The purpose of a survey is to gather lots of observations to help determine the characteristics of a larger group or population. If the population of interest is extremely large, such as everyone between ages 18 and 25 in the United States, researchers must decide how to select a representative subset of individuals to measure. A subset of individuals from a target population is referred to as a sample.

Researchers must consider a number of technical details when sampling from a population. For example, it's easy to end up with an unrepresentative, or biased, sample unless the proper precautions are taken (Tourangeau, 2004). Let's imagine that a researcher named Rosa wants to know how often college-aged adults practice safe sex. She puts an ad containing a toll-free telephone number in selected college newspapers. Her hope is that students will call the number and answer questions about their sexual practices. However, not every college-aged student in the country will choose to participate, so Rosa will end up with only a subset, or sample, of the

random sampling A procedure guaranteeing that everyone in the population has an equal likelihood of being selected for the sample.

population of interest. Do you think the data collected from her subset will be truly representative of college students?

In this case the answer is clearly "No," because the method of sampling depends on people choosing to participate. Volunteers tend to produce biased samples, because people who volunteer usually have strong feelings or opinions about the study (Rosenthal & Rosnow, 1975). Think about it—would you tell a researcher that you regularly fail to practice safe sex? Representative samples are produced through **random sampling**, which means that everyone in the target population has an equal likelihood of being selected for the survey. Because everyone has an equal chance of participating, random sampling helps to ensure that all possible biases, viewpoints, and backgrounds will be represented. In principle, for Rosa to achieve a truly unbiased sample she would need to sample randomly from the entire population of college students—everyone in the group must have an equal chance of being selected. Because this is difficult to achieve in practice, Rosa will probably limit herself to sampling randomly from the population of students going to her particular college.

Now let's return to Yapko's (1994) survey, in which 869 practicing psychotherapists gave their views on the use of hypnosis as an effective memory aid. The results showed that some psychotherapists erroneously believe that memories recovered through hypnosis are accurate. Unfortunately, Yapko did not use a random sample of psychotherapists in his study—he simply asked therapists who attended certain conventions and workshops for their opinions. His data may therefore suffer from a volunteer problem that limits their generalizability. Only psychotherapists with strong opinions about hypnosis may have chosen to participate. To claim his results are truly representative of psychotherapists as a whole, he would need to use random sampling (for a similar study that does use random sampling, see Gore-Felton et al., 2000).

Even if a proper sample of the population has been selected, surveys can suffer from additional problems (Taylor, 1997; Tourangeau, 2004). Because large numbers of people are tested, it is usually not possible to gain detailed information about the behavior or opinion of interest. For example, researchers who use surveys are typically unable to obtain the in-depth historical information that can be collected in a case study. Surveys also consist mainly of self-reports, and people cannot always be counted on to provide accurate observations. Some people lie or engage in wishful thinking; others answer questions in ways they think might please the researcher.

Fortunately, psychologists have developed methods of checking for these types of strategies, but there is no perfect way to assure honest and accurate responses from a participant. The results of a survey can also depend on the particular wording of the questions or even on the order in which the questions are asked. Surveys can be written in ways that minimize the risk of inconsistent responses—for example, particular questions can be asked several times with slightly different wording—but inaccurate responding remains a concern and is difficult to eliminate.

Psychological Tests: Assessing Individual Differences

One of the most useful descriptive research techniques is psychological testing. Psychological tests come in a variety of forms, and they're designed primarily to measure differences among people. For example, *achievement tests* measure a person's current level of knowledge or competence in a particular subject (such as mathematics or psychology); *aptitude tests* are designed to measure the potential for success in a given profession or area of study. Researchers also use intelligence and personality tests to classify ability, or to characterize a person's tendencies to act in consistent ways.

Psychological tests have enormous practical value, and they help to advance basic research (Kaplin & Saccuzzo, 2005). Intelligence tests can be used to identify children who might need extra help in school or who are gifted and can benefit from an enriched curriculum; for adults, intelligence test scores are sometimes used to predict

Psychologists use tests to predict and select the fundamental components of mind, as well as to help decipher them.

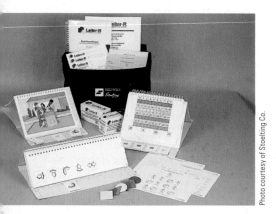

Photo courtesy of Stoelting Co.

Observational Research Methods

SPECIFIC METHOD	DESCRIPTION	ADVANTAGES AND DISADVANTAGES
Naturalistic observation	Record naturally occurring behavior	A: Behavior is natural; results are generalizable D: Research lacks control; can't determine cause
Case studies	Gather a great deal of information on a single case	A: Gives historical perspective D: Difficulties in generalization based on one case
Surveys	Gather responses from many participants	A: Can easily gather large amounts of information D: Sample bias; people misrepresenting selves
Psychological tests	Measure individual differences among people	A: Potential practical uses; assess basics of mind D: Difficulties in test construction and validation

future performance on the job (Kuncel, Hezlett, & Ones, 2004; Ree & Earles, 1992). Of course, a number of tests also help diagnose psychological problems and verify the effectiveness of treatment.

Psychologists also use the analysis of test performance to answer fundamental questions about psychology. For example, do people have a fixed amount of intelligence, present at birth, or do they have multiple kinds of intelligence that rise and fall with experience? Do people have consistent personality traits, such as honesty or pleasantness, or do their behaviors change haphazardly across situations? You'll hear more about these specific topics when we treat psychological tests in detail in Chapters 10 and 12.

Statistics: Summarizing and Interpreting the Data

At the end of any research project, the observations must be organized and summarized. Researchers look for patterns in the data so that hypotheses can be formulated and tested. It would be inappropriate simply to pick and choose from the results based on what looks interesting, because selective analyses of data can introduce systematic biases into the interpretation; you might draw conclusions that are not representative of the group as a whole (Barber, 1976; Rosenthal, 1994).

Central Tendencies If the observations can be expressed in the form of numbers, it is possible to calculate statistics, or values derived from mathematical manipulations of the data, to summarize and interpret the results. For any set of numerical observations, it's often useful to begin with a measure of central tendency, or the value around which scores tend to cluster. You're probably familiar with the **mean**, which is the arithmetic average of a set of scores. To calculate a mean, you simply add up the numbers for each of the observations and divide the total by the number of observations. Suppose you're a server at a local restaurant. You work a 5-day week, and your tips for the week are $30, $20, $20, $60, and $70. The mean of these scores would be 40 (30 + 20 + 20 + 60 + 70 = 200; 200 / 5 = 40). The mean summarizes the data into a single representative number: On average, you made $40 in tips. Notice, though, you never actually made $40 on any given day. The mean provides only an estimate of central tendency; it does not indicate anything about particular scores.

Other measures of central tendency include the **mode**, which is the most frequently occurring score (in the tip example the mode is $20), and the **median**, which is the middle point in the set of scores. Because the mode has the advantage of representing a real score—you did actually receive $20 on some days—and it's easy to calculate, it's sometimes a more meaningful measure of central tendency than the

mean The arithmetic average of a set of scores.

mode The most frequently occurring score in a set of scores.

median The middle point in an ordered set of scores; half of the scores fall at or below the median score, and half fall at or above the median score.

CRITICAL THINKING

Grade point average is typically calculated using the mean. Suppose the mean was replaced with a grade point mode or a grade point median. What would be the advantages and disadvantages of calculating grade point in these ways?

mean. Calculating the median takes a bit more work. First, order the scores from smallest to largest (20, 20, 30, 60, 70), then look for the middle score. For tips, half the scores fall below 30, and half fall above, so 30 is the median. If the number of scores is even, with no single middle score (e.g., 20, 20, 30, 40, 60, 70), the median is typically calculated by taking the midpoint of the two middle scores (the midpoint between 30 and 40 is 35).

Researchers usually like to compute several measures of central tendency. The mean is an excellent summary of the average score, but it can be misleading. Suppose, for example, that instead of $70 on your last workday you actually pull in $150! If we replace the old number with the new one, we now have the following set of scores: 20, 20, 30, 60, 150. The arithmetic average, or mean, will shift rather dramatically because of the extreme score, from 40 to 56, but neither the mode nor the median will change at all (see ▌Figure 2.4). Because of the way they are calculated, means are very sensitive to extreme scores—the value shifts in the direction of the extreme score. On the other hand, the mode and the median are unaffected. In our example, the median or the mode is probably a better summary of your daily income than the mean.

Variability In addition to calculating measures of central tendency, researchers are also interested in **variability**, or how much the scores in a set differ from one another. The mean indicates the average, but it provides no information about how far apart the individual scores are from each other. Why is this important? Well, think about your last exam score. Let's assume that you received a 79 and the average score was 75. How did you do? Your best guess is probably that you did about average because your score was relatively close to the mean—but perhaps not. If the scores were all bunched toward the middle, your performance might have been spectacular—in fact, a 79 could have been the highest grade in the class. As a result, researchers need to

variability A measure of how much the scores in a distribution of scores differ from one another.

▌FIGURE 2.4 Comparing the Mean, the Median, and the Mode
The top row shows the differences between the mean (arithmetic average), the median (middle point in a set of scores), and the mode (most frequently occurring score) for tips earned per day in a restaurant. The bottom row shows how the mean can be affected by an extreme score, in this case for the day you received $150 in tips. Notice that the extreme score has no effect on the median or mode.

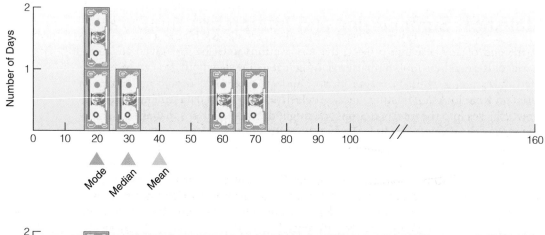

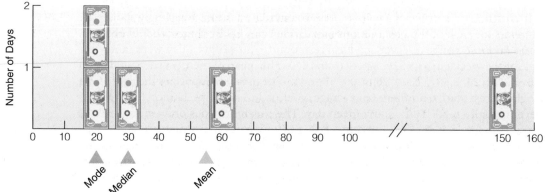

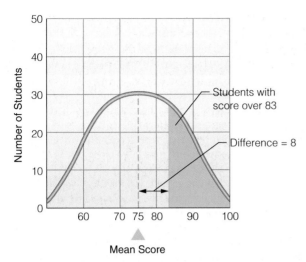
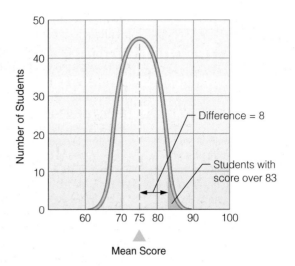

FIGURE 2.5 Variability

Researchers are often interested in variability, the extent to which scores in a set differ from one another. Each of these two distributions has the same average, or mean, but the distribution on the left has more variability. Notice that the difference between the mean and a particular score, such as 83, is the same in the two cases. But scoring 8 points above the mean is highly unusual in the distribution on the right, and more common in the distribution on the left. If you received a score of 83, which class would you rather be in?

know more than the average of a set of scores; they also need to know something about variability (see ▮ Figure 2.5).

Several measures of variability are available to researchers. A simple one is the **range**, which measures the difference between the largest and smallest scores in the distribution. If the highest score in the class was 90 and the lowest score was 50, the range would be $90 - 50 = 40$. A more widely used index is the **standard deviation**, which provides an indication of how much individual scores vary from the mean. It's calculated by (1) finding the difference (or deviation) of each score from the mean; (2) squaring those deviations; (3) finding the average, or mean, of the squared deviations; and (4) calculating the square root of this average. We'll return to the concept of standard deviation later in the text, particularly in Chapter 10, because psychologists often define psychological characteristics, such as intelligence, in terms of how far away a measured score "sits" from the mean in a distribution of scores. (To apply what you have learned about variability, see the Practical Solutions feature on page 38.)

range The difference between the largest and smallest scores in a distribution.

standard deviation An indication of how much individual scores differ or vary from the mean.

Inferential Statistics   Statistics such as the mean and the standard deviation form a part of what is called **descriptive statistics**—they help researchers describe their data. But it's also possible to use statistics to draw inferences from data—to help interpret the results. Researchers use **inferential statistics** to decide (1) whether the behaviors recorded in a sample are representative of some larger population, or (2) whether the differences among observations can be attributed to chance or to some other factor.

Inferential statistics are based on the laws of probability. Researchers always assume that the results of an observation, or group of observations, might be due to chance. For example, suppose you find that the male servers in your restaurant average $38 a day in tips for the week whereas the female servers average $42 (a difference of $4). Is there really a gender difference in tip income? It could be that your recorded gender difference is accidental and unrepresentative of a true difference. Had you recorded tip income in a different week, you might have found that men produced more income. It is in your interest, then, to determine how representative your data are of true tipping behavior.

descriptive statistics Mathematical techniques that help researchers describe their data.

inferential statistics Mathematical techniques that help researchers decide whether data are representative of a population or whether differences among observations can be attributed to chance.

How Should a Teacher Grade?

Now let's apply what you just learned about statistical "variability" to an important topic: GRADING! Every teacher needs a method for discriminating among people. If you work really hard and perform well on tests, you should be rewarded with a higher grade than someone who skips class and never bothers to learn the material, right? Students are often skeptical about grading techniques, whatever method is employed, but most teachers adopt one of two strategies, absolute grading or relative grading (sometimes called grading "by the curve"). One depends on variability, and the other does not. Let's consider each in turn.

Absolute grading is simple and easy to understand. Your grade is determined by the number, or percentage, of items that you answer correctly on a test. So, if there are 100 questions on your final exam, you might need to answer 90 or more correctly to receive an A, if you correctly answer between 80 and 90 questions you get a B, and so on. With this method, you immediately know where you stand once you know your test score, and your grade does not depend on how the rest of the

students in the class performed. Variability, or how much the scores in the class differ from one another, is not involved in the calculation.

Relative grading, or grading "by the curve," means that your grade is determined by your relative performance in the class. If there are 100 students in the class, an A might be given to the top 10 students (or 10%), a B to the next 10, and so on. In this case your absolute score means nothing by itself—you need to know something about how the test scores were distributed among the students in your class. Variability is critical in determining your grade, as in the example shown in Figure 2.5.

Which is the best technique? Both are easy to justify, but they both have problems. For example, suppose your teacher doesn't have a very good "sense" of what the class understands and writes an extremely difficult test—in fact, the best student in the class answers only 50% of the questions correctly. Does this mean that everyone in the class should get an F? That's what would probably happen if the grades were determined by an absolute scale. Relative grading takes the

teacher's test out of the equation. It doesn't matter whether the test is easy or hard. What matters is where your test score "sits" in the distribution of class scores—how well you performed relative to everyone else in the class. So even if you only get half of the test questions correct, you might still get an A. But here's the trouble with relative grading: Suppose you happen to be in a class of brilliant students. You might learn the material quite well, perhaps you answer 90% of the test questions correctly, but you could still be at the bottom of the class distribution. Do you deserve to flunk just because you are in a "smart" class?

Lots of factors are involved in picking the best way to grade, such as the size of the class, the experience of the teacher, whether the material is introductory or advanced, and many more. Talk to your teacher about his or her chosen method. Try to determine the role that "variability" is playing in your teacher's method—it should help you understand why variability is important to the psychologist as well!

Through inferential statistics, researchers try to determine the likelihood, or probability, that results could have occurred by chance. The details of the procedures are beyond the scope of this text, but if you find that the chance probability is extremely low, then your findings can be treated as statistically significant. In most psychological studies, the probability that an outcome is due to chance must be lower than 0.05 (5%) for the outcome to be accepted as statistically significant. This means you can treat a female tipping advantage of $4 as significant only if that difference occurs less than 5 times out of 100 by chance factors alone.

Test Yourself 2.1

To test your knowledge of descriptive research methods, fill in the blanks with one of the following words or terms: reactivity, external validity, case study, random sampling, survey, mean, median, mode, standard deviation. *(You will find the answers in the Appendix.)*

1. The middle point in an ordered set of scores is the _____.

2. The _____ technique, which focuses on the study of a single instance of a behavior or condition, is open to criticism because its results may lack _____; that is, the results may not generalize or be representative of the population as a whole.

3. When behavior changes as a result of the observation process, the recorded data are said to suffer from a problem of _____.

4. The descriptive research technique used to gather limited amounts of information from many people is called a _____.

Predicting Behavior: Correlational Research

LEARNING GOALS
- Define correlation and explain how correlations can be used to predict behavior.
- Explain why correlations cannot normally be used to determine the cause of behavior.

PSYCHOLOGISTS ARE RARELY SATISFIED with just describing behavior. They're also interested in making predictions about future behavior. As we discussed earlier, prediction allows one to determine how individuals are likely to perform in the future. Thus the manager of a company can select the best potential employee based on present performance; the school administrator can manage a student's curriculum to maximize future performance.

Correlational Research

One way to predict future performance is to determine whether a relationship exists between two measures of behavior, the one recorded and the one expected. Psychologists often use a statistical measure called a **correlation** to help make this determination. A correlation tells you whether two variables, or measures that can take on more than one value (such as a test score), vary together systematically. Correlations are computed by gathering observations on both measures of interest from a single set of individuals and then computing a mathematical index called a correlation coefficient. A correlation coefficient gives the researcher a feel for how well the value of one variable, such as job success, can be predicted if the value of a second variable, such as an achievement test score, is known.

When there is a correlation between two measures of behavior, those behaviors will tend to vary together in some way. For example, there is probably a strong correlation between the number of hours worked and the number of tips a waiter or waitress will receive. The two measures vary together—the more hours you spend working, the more tips you get. In this particular case, we have a positive correlation, which means that the two measures move in the same direction—the more of one, the more of the other. A negative correlation exists when the two measures still vary together but in opposite directions. For example, there is a negative, or inverse, relationship between the number of hours that Beverly practices on the piano and the number of errors she makes during her recital performance. The more she practices, the fewer errors she is likely to make. A relationship still exists—we can predict one when we know the other—but the correlation is negative.

Calculating a correlation coefficient requires that you collect observations from a relatively large number of individuals. Moreover—and this is important—data must be recorded initially on both measures. The details of the calculation are beyond the scope of this text, but if calculated properly correlation coefficients always range between +1.00 and −1.00. The absolute value of the coefficient (the range between 0 and 1 without the sign) indicates the strength of the correlation. The closer the value is to 1.00 (either positive or negative), the stronger the relationship between the two measures and the more likely you'll make an accurate prediction. The sign of the coefficient indicates whether the correlation is positive or negative. Positive correlations fall within the range from 0 to +1.00; negative correlations fall within the range from 0 to −1.00.

∎ Figure 2.6 on page 40 shows how positive and negative correlations can be represented graphically, in the form of a scatterplot. Each point in a scatterplot represents a person's scores on the two measures. In Figure 2.6b you can find how many hours an individual spent practicing and the number of errors made during the recital. Once the correlation has been computed, it can then be applied to new individuals who have a score on only one of the measures. So, if a correlation is present, you

correlation A statistic that indicates whether two variables vary together in a systematic way; correlation coefficients vary from +1.00 to −1.00.

The building skills of the young girl on the top may or may not predict a professional career in architecture.

FIGURE 2.6 Positive and Negative Correlations
Each point in the scatterplot shows an individual's scores on each of the two variables.
(a) In a strong positive correlation, the values for both variables move in the same direction; that is, as more hours are worked, more tips are received. **(b)** In a negative correlation, the values for the two variables move in opposite directions; that is, as more time is spent practicing, fewer errors are made during the recital.

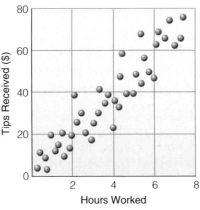

a Strong Positive Correlation

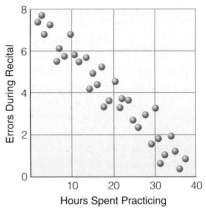

b Strong Negative Correlation

can predict how many errors Natasha will make during her recital by simply knowing how many hours she practiced. The closer the correlation is to 1.00 (positive or negative), the more accurate your prediction is likely to be. This is the logic used by most college admissions committees—they know there is a correlation between SAT and college performance, so they try to predict how well people will do in college by looking at their SAT scores.

Zero Correlations When a correlation coefficient is not statistically different from zero, the two measures are said to be uncorrelated. Technically, this means that knowing that the value of one measure does not allow you to predict the value of the second measure with an accuracy greater than chance. Imagine, for example, trying to predict college grade point average by measuring how many times people wash their hands during the day. In this case, the correlation is almost certainly zero—you can't use hand-washing behavior to predict GPA. Note: It's important not to confuse the concept of a zero correlation with negative correlation. If the correlation between two variables is zero, no statistical relationship is present—a value on one measure reveals nothing about the other measure. In a negative correlation, a clear relationship exists; it's just that the values move in opposite directions.

Interestingly, the fact that two measures are uncorrelated (they have a zero correlation) doesn't mean that similar values can't occur on each. Look at the scatterplot in ▌Figure 2.7. It shows a zero correlation between hand washing and GPA. Each point shows how many times a particular person washed his or her hands in a day (x-axis) along with his or her GPA (y-axis). If there's no correlation between the two, as the figure depicts, then we can't predict GPA simply by knowing hand-washing behavior. Yet notice that some instances in the figure (marked in orange) show that a high value on the hand-washing variable can be associated with a high value on the GPA variable. Suppose you only looked at these instances—"Boy, people who wash their hands a lot sure have high GPAs"—you might mistakenly conclude that the key to obtaining a high GPA is make sure your hands are clean!

Once again, the point to remember is that when two variables are unrelated we can't predict what will happen. Sometimes a high value on one measure will be associated with a high value on the other measure; sometimes it will be associated with a low value. A mistake people often make is to look only at the cases where the two variables appear to be related. Consider the ability of "psychics" to predict the future. Many people believe in precognition, the ability to predict the future, based on a few anecdotal examples (e.g., "I dreamed my dog was hit by a car, and the next day it happened"). In all likelihood, however, the correlation between predictions and outcomes is zero. We ignore those instances in which our feelings ("I have a feeling something bad is going to happen to the dog tomorrow") don't come true ("My

FIGURE 2.7 Zero Correlation
This scatterplot shows a zero correlation between numbers of times hands are washed and grade point average. Overall, it is not possible to predict the value on one of the variables by knowing a value on the other, although high values on each variable (orange) sometimes occur together.

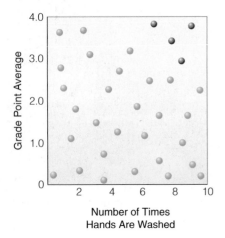

Number of Times
Hands Are Washed

dog turned out to be fine"); instead, we focus only on those few instances where, by chance, predictions and events occur together.

Behavioral measures rarely correlate perfectly—most correlations are only moderate. When researchers make predictions about behavior based on correlations, the accuracy of their predictions is usually limited. For example, the correlation between scores on the SAT and the grade point average of college freshmen is only around +0.40, not 1.0 (Morgan, 1990). Researchers can use SAT scores to predict college performance to an extent greater than chance, but the test's predictive abilities are far from perfect (Stricker, Rock, & Burton, 1996). Similarly, the correlation between height and weight is only about +0.60; on average, taller people do tend to weigh more, but there are obvious exceptions to this general rule. Correlation coefficients give researchers some important predictive ability, but they do not completely capture the variability present in the world.

CRITICAL THINKING

Imagine a scenario in which every time you dreamed about your dog getting hurt, your dog was certain to be okay. Wouldn't you be truly predicting the future? What kind of correlation would this scenario represent?

Correlations and Causality

Determining that a relationship exists between two measures of behavior is important because it helps people make educated guesses about their environment. It is useful to know that if a person acts in a certain way at time 1, he or she is likely to act in a predictable way at time 2. Suppose, for example, that we could demonstrate a meaningful correlation between the amount of violence that a child watches on television and how aggressively that child will act later in life. Knowing about such a relationship would probably influence the behavior of parents and might even lead to a social outcry to monitor televised violence (Bushman & Anderson, 2001).

Correlations are useful devices for helping psychologists describe how behaviors co-occur in our world, but they are of only limited value when it comes to understanding why. The presence of a correlation between two behaviors may help psychologists predict, but correlations do not allow them to determine causality. A correlation between watching violence on television and later aggression does not mean that television violence causes aggression, even if the correlation is perfect.

Third Variables   The main reason it's not possible to determine causality from a correlation is the presence of other potentially uncontrolled factors. Two variables can appear to be connected—that is, they might rise or fall together in a regular way—but the connection could be due to a common link with some third variable. Let's consider an example close to home. It's commonly argued, correctly, that annual income will be higher if a person graduates from college. Put in terms of a correlation, annual income is positively correlated with years of schooling. Does that mean that a good education causes better jobs and higher income? Perhaps, but not necessarily. A third factor could explain the relationship.

Think for a moment about the kinds of people who go to college. Do they represent a random sample of the population as a whole? Of course not. College students tend to be brighter, they tend to come from better secondary schools, and they tend to be people who have worked hard and succeeded in high school. None of these other factors is controlled for in the calculation of a correlation. You can predict with a correlation, but you can't isolate the particular factor that is responsible for the relationship. College students might end up with higher incomes because they're smarter, work harder, or because they're better educated. Any or all of these factors could be contributing to the relationship that the correlation describes (Cook & Campbell, 1979).

Now let's return to the example we considered earlier—the relationship between TV violence and aggression. Can you think of any third variable that might explain the correlation? One possibility is that some children have personalities that make violent programs on television enjoyable. It is not the violence on TV that is causing the aggression; it is the child's personality that is influencing both program choice and aggression. Still other factors could be involved—perhaps children who are

Concept Review | Correlational Patterns

QUESTION TO BE ADDRESSED	PATTERN OF CORRELATION	INTERPRETATION
How does the number of hours worked relate to the tips received?	Positive	The more hours worked, the more tips received; the fewer hours worked, the fewer tips received (more/more; fewer/fewer).
How does performance on the SAT relate to college GPA?	Positive	The greater the score on the SAT, the higher the GPA; the lower the score on the SAT, the lower the GPA.
How does the amount of piano practice relate to the number of errors during a recital?	Negative	The more practice, the fewer errors are made; the less practice, the more errors are made.
How does the amount of time spent partying relate to college GPA?	Negative	The more time spend partying, the lower the GPA; the less time spent partying, the higher the GPA.
How does a person's shoe size relate to his or her score on an intelligence test?	No correlation	Knowing one's shoe size tells you nothing about his or her IQ test score and vice versa.

allowed to watch violence on television tend to be raised in households where aggression is the norm. Once again, correlations describe relationships, but they typically provide no insight into cause and effect. To determine causality, as you'll see shortly, researchers cannot simply describe and predict behavior; they must manipulate it.

Test Yourself | 2.2

Test your understanding of correlations by identifying whether the following statements represent positive, negative, or zero correlations. (You will find the answers in the Appendix.)

1. The more Larry studies his psychology, the fewer errors he makes on the chapter test: _____
2. As Sadaf reduces her rate of exercising, her heart rate begins to slow: _____
3. The longer that Yolanda waits for her date to arrive, the higher her blood pressure rises: _____

4. Eddie finds no relationship between his dreams about plane crashes and the number of planes that actually crash: _____

Explaining Behavior: Experimental Research

LEARNING GOALS
- Explain how and why experiments are conducted.
- Discuss the differences between independent and dependent variables.
- Explain what is meant by experimental control and how it allows for the determination of causality.
- Describe the problems created by expectancies and biases and how these problems are solved.
- Discuss the problems associated with generalizing experimental conclusions.

WE NOW TURN OUR ATTENTION to techniques that help us understand why behavior occurs. Suppose you wanted to determine whether, in fact, watching violent programs really does cause later aggression. If Blake becomes aggressive after watching a violent television program, is it really the program that's responsible for the change? Alternative possibilities need to be eliminated, or at least accounted for, before you can confidently conclude that things are causally related. As you've just seen, the mere description of a relationship is not enough—correlation does not imply causation. Establishing causality requires control, one of the most important functions of an experiment.

In **experimental research**, the investigator actively manipulates the environment to observe its effect on behavior. By "environment," psychologists can mean just about anything. For instance, they might manipulate the external setting (room temperature, lighting, time of day), a person's internal state (hunger, mood, motivation to perform), or social factors (presence or absence of an authority figure or popular peer group). The particular manipulation is determined by the researcher's hypothesis. As mentioned earlier, hypotheses in psychology are usually expressed as if-then statements: If some set of conditions is present and observed, then a certain kind of behavior will occur. The purpose of the experiment is to set up the proposed conditions and see what happens.

To examine the role of television violence on aggressive behavior, an experimenter would directly manipulate the amount of violence the person watches. Perhaps one group of children would be picked to watch a violent superhero cartoon while a second group watches the playful antics of a lovable purple dinosaur. The experimenter would then carefully measure the effect of the manipulation on the behavior of interest: aggression. This strategy of directly manipulating the viewing habits, rather than simply observing them, is the essential feature of the experimental approach. Notice the difference from correlational research, where the investigator simply records the viewing habits of children and then measures later aggressive acts. It is only through a direct manipulation by the experimenter, as you'll see shortly, that control over the environment can be exercised and causality determined. Figure 2.8 compares experimental research to the other two approaches previously discussed: descriptive and correlational research.

experimental research A technique in which the investigator actively manipulates the environment to observe its effect on behavior.

Descriptive Method	**Correlational Method**	**Experimental Method**
Purpose Observing and describing behavior	Predicting and selecting behavior	Determining why behavior occurs: Establishing cause and effect
Research Tactics Naturalistic observation Case studies Survey research Psychological tests	Statistical correlations based on two or more variables	Experiments manipulating the independent variable to note effects on the dependent variable

FIGURE 2.8 Major Research Methods

Independent and Dependent Variables

independent variable The aspect of the environment that is manipulated in an experiment. It must consist of at least two conditions.

The aspect of the environment that is manipulated in an experiment is called the **independent variable**. Because it is a variable (that is, something that can take on more than one value), any experimental manipulation must consist of at least two different conditions. In our example, the independent variable is the amount of television violence, and the two conditions are (1) watching a violent program and (2) watching a nonviolent program. The aspect that is manipulated is called an independent variable because the experimenter produces the change—independently of the subject's wishes, desires, or behavior.

dependent variable The behavior that is measured or observed in an experiment.

The behavior that is measured in an experiment is called the **dependent variable**. In our example, the dependent variable is the amount of aggressive behavior that is seen after watching the programs. The experimenter manipulates the independent variable, the level of TV violence, and observes whether the behavior measured by the dependent variable, aggression, changes. Notice that the experimenter is interested in whether the dependent variable depends on the experimental manipulation (hence the name *dependent variable*).

Now let's return to the topic that opened this chapter: subliminal perception. Can evil advertisers improve product sales by hiding messages such as "BUY NOW" in their advertising material? Remember, a subliminal message is presented below a person's normal threshold for perception. You won't be able to see the message consciously, but it influences you nonetheless. Let's begin by forming a hypothesis: If people are exposed to advertising material containing a hidden message then product sales will increase (see ▌Figure 2.9). To test this prediction, let's give two groups of people an advertisement to study. One group receives an ad containing a hidden message and the other group receives the same advertisement without the message. Later, we can check to see how likely the people in each group are to purchase the product described in the ad.

What is the independent variable in this experiment? To answer this question, look for the aspect of the environment that is being manipulated: The independent variable is the presence or absence of the hidden message (half of the participants receive the message in the ad, and half do not). What is the dependent variable? In this case, the researcher wants to know whether sales of the advertised product will change due to the presence of the subliminal message. The dependent variable is the number of times the people in each group buy the advertised product.

Experimental Control

To conclude that changes in the dependent variable are really caused by the independent variable, you need to be certain that the independent variable is the only thing changing systematically in the experiment. This is the main reason at least two conditions are needed in an experiment. Researchers compare subjects who get the change, often called the experimental group, with those who do not, called the control group. In the subliminal perception experiment, the experimental group consisted of the subjects who received the hidden message, and the control group consisted of those who did not. If product sales subsequently differ between these two groups, and we know that the only difference between them was the presence of the hidden message in the ad, then it's possible to conclude that hidden messages can indeed cause changes in sales.

Confounding Variables The determination of cause and effect requires that the experimental and control groups be identical in all respects, except for the critical independent variable manipulation. But how can we ever be certain that this is the case? If some factor other than the independent variable differs across the groups, it will be exceedingly difficult, if not impossible, to interpret the results (Elmes et al., 2006; Rosnow & Rosenthal, 1996). Uncontrolled variables that change systematically with

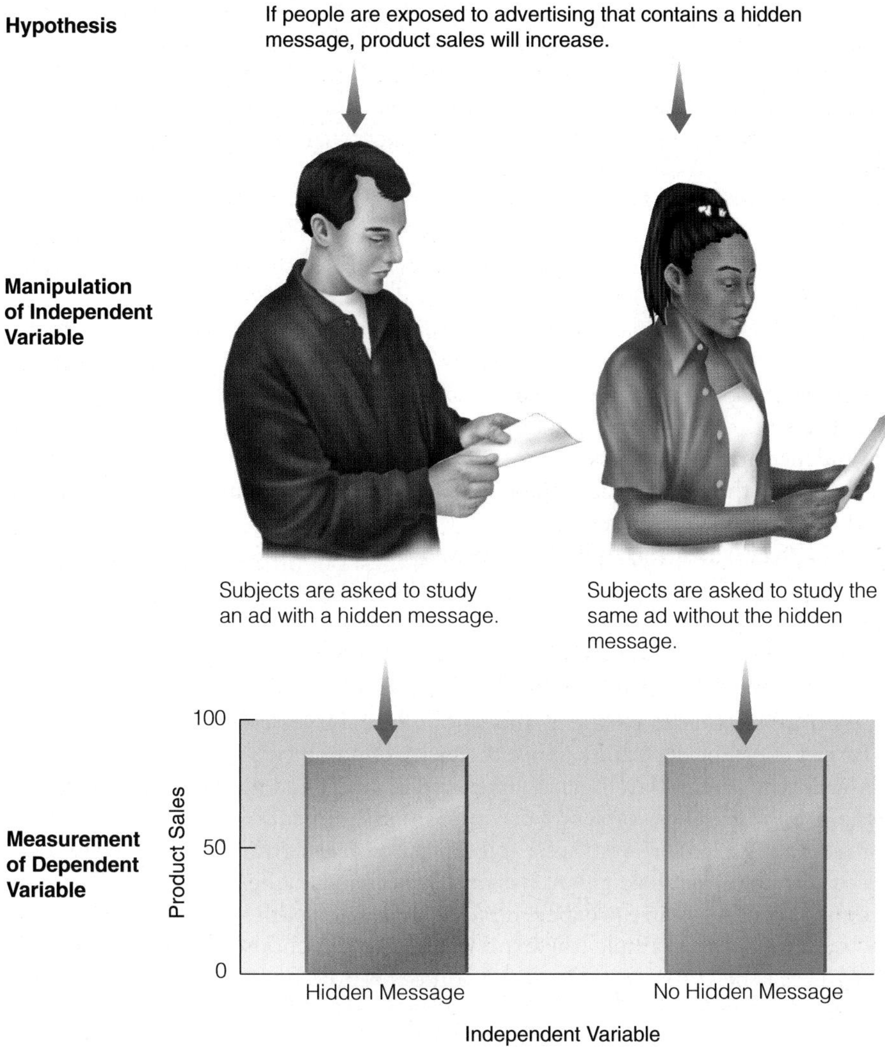

Hypothesis If people are exposed to advertising that contains a hidden message, product sales will increase.

Manipulation of Independent Variable

Subjects are asked to study an ad with a hidden message.

Subjects are asked to study the same ad without the hidden message.

Measurement of Dependent Variable

FIGURE 2.9 Major Components of an Experiment
The hypothesis is tested by manipulating the independent variable and then assessing its effects on the dependent variable. If the only systematic changes are in the independent variable, the experimenter can assume that they are causing the changes measured by the dependent variable.

the independent variable are called **confounding variables** (the word *confound* means to throw into confusion or dismay). Suppose we decide to use one kind of advertisement in the experimental group and a different advertisement in the control group. Any differences in sales could then be attributed to the effectiveness of the individual ad, or the product advertised, rather than to the presence or absence of the subliminal message. Changes in the dependent variable could not be attributed uniquely to the hidden message because there is a confounding variable.

To solve the problem of confounding variables, you need to hold constant all of the factors that can vary along with the experimental manipulation. You should definitely give everyone exactly the same advertisement, and you should probably conduct the experimental session at the same time of day for both groups. You should also make certain that people in both groups are given the same amount of time to study the ad and the same length of time to buy, or indicate that they'll buy, the advertised product. Any factor that might affect the likelihood of purchase, other than the independent variable manipulation, should be controlled—that is, held constant—across the different groups. When potential confounding variables are effectively controlled, allowing for the determination of cause and effect, the experiment is said to have **internal validity**.

Knowing what factors to worry about comes, in part, from experience. The more you know about the phenomenon under study, the more likely you are to identify and control confounding variables. Consumer researchers recognize, for example,

confounding variable An uncontrolled variable that changes along with the independent variable.

internal validity The extent to which an experiment has effectively controlled for confounding variables; internally valid experiments allow for the determination of causality.

Concept Review | The Experimental Method

RESEARCH QUESTION (VARIABLES IN BOLD)	INDEPENDENT VARIABLE (EXPERIMENTER *MANIPULATES*)	DEPENDENT VARIABLE (EXPERIMENTER *MEASURES*)
Does **watching television violence** affect **aggression**?	Experimenter *manipulates* the amount of exposure to TV violence.	Experimenter *measures* the amount of aggression displayed.
Does **exposure to subliminal messages** have an effect on **product sales?**	Experimenter *manipulates* whether or not subjects receive a hidden message.	Experimenter *measures* product sales.
Does **forming images of words** to be remembered enhance **memory for those words?**	Experimenter *manipulates* whether or not subjects form images of words as they're being presented.	Experimenter *measures* memory for the words.

that it's essential to give everyone the same advertisement and product in the experimental and control conditions; obviously, some ads will be liked better than others regardless of whether they contain hidden messages. But other variables, such as the length of the participants' hair or their eye color, probably have no effect on buying behavior and require no control.

random assignment A technique ensuring that each participant in an experiment has an equal chance of being assigned to any of the conditions in the experiment.

Random Assignment People differ in many ways: intelligence, personal preferences, their motivation to perform, and so on. Researchers can't possibly hold all of these factors constant. Just think about the task of finding two groups of people with exactly the same level of intelligence, likes and dislikes, and motivation. It would be impossible. So researchers typically use random assignment, which is similar to the random sampling used for survey research. In **random assignment**, the experimenter makes certain that each participant has an equal chance of being assigned to any of the groups or conditions in the experiment. At the outset, each subject is assigned randomly to a group. For example, the experimenter might choose a number randomly and assign the subject to one group if the number is even and a different group if the number is odd.

Random assignment does not eliminate differences among people—some subjects will still be more intelligent than others, and some will be more naturally inclined to buy the advertised product. It simply increases the chances that these differences will be equally represented in each of the groups (see ▐ Figure 2.10). As a result, the researcher knows that the results of the experiment cannot easily be caused by some special characteristic of the individual subjects.

Expectancies and Biases in Experimental Research

Anyone who participates in a psychology experiment is likely to have expectations about the process. People are rarely passive participants in research—they might, for example, attempt to guess the true purpose of the project. Expectations like these can affect a subject's behavior, clouding interpretation of the results (Barber, 1976; Rosenthal & Rosnow, 1969). Let's suppose that on the first day of class your teacher randomly selects half of the students, including you, to participate in a special enrichment program. You receive instruction in a special room, with carefully controlled lighting and temperature, to see whether your learning will improve. The rest of the students, forming the control group, are left in the original classroom. The end of the semester arrives and, sure enough, the enrichment group consistently outperforms the control group. What can you conclude from these results?

At first glance, this seems to be a well-designed experiment. It includes both an experimental and a control group, the subjects were randomly assigned to groups, and let's assume that all other known potentially confounding variables were care-

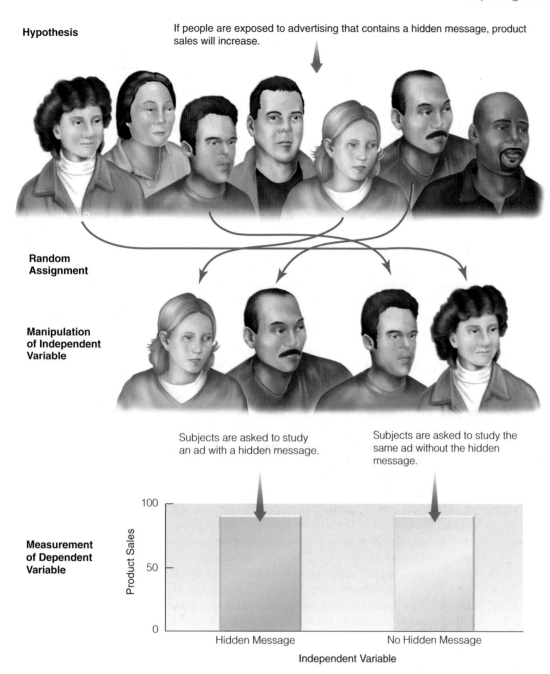

Hypothesis If people are exposed to advertising that contains a hidden message, product sales will increase.

Random Assignment

Manipulation of Independent Variable

Subjects are asked to study an ad with a hidden message.

Subjects are asked to study the same ad without the hidden message.

Measurement of Dependent Variable

Product Sales

100

50

0

Hidden Message   No Hidden Message

Independent Variable

FIGURE 2.10 Random Assignment
Volunteers are randomly assigned to two levels of the independent variable. Each participant has an equal likelihood of being assigned to any of the groups or conditions in the experiment. Random assignment increases the chances that unique subject characteristics will be represented equally in each condition.

fully controlled. However, there is still a problem. The subjects in the enrichment group expected to perform better, based on their knowledge about the experiment. After all, they were selected to be in an enrichment group. Consequently, these students may have simply tried harder, or studied more, in an effort to live up to the expectations of the researcher. At the same time, subjects in the control group knew they were failing to get special instruction; this knowledge might have lowered their motivation to perform, leading to poorer performance. The fact that the groups differed in what they learned is not necessarily due to the enrichment program itself.

Researchers can control for these kinds of expectancy effects in two ways. First, the investigator can be somewhat misleading in initially describing the study—subjects can be deceived to disguise the true purpose of the experiment. This approach raises obvious ethical questions, although it is possible, under some conditions, to omit telling the subjects some critical feature of the study without severely violating ethical standards. (I'll return to the issue of ethics in research later in the chapter.)

placebo An inactive, or inert, substance that resembles an experimental substance.

single-blind study Experimental participants do not know to which condition they have been assigned (e.g., experimental versus control); it's used to control for subject expectancies.

double-blind study Neither participants nor research observers are aware of who has been assigned to the experimental and control groups; it's used to control for both subject and experimenter expectancies.

Second, the investigator can try to match expectations for both the experimental and control groups. For example, the researchers can lead the people in the control group to believe that they, too, are receiving an experimental treatment. This technique is often used in drug studies. Participants in both groups receive a pill or an injection, but the drug is actually present only in the medication given to the experimental group. The control subjects are given a **placebo**—an inactive, or inert, substance (a "sugar pill") that looks just like the true drug (Shapiro, 1960; White, Tursky, & Schwartz, 1985).

Blind Controls   The kind of experimental procedure just described for drug studies is called a **single-blind study**. That is, the participants are kept "blind" about the particular group in which they've been placed (experimental or control). Single-blind studies control for expectancies because people have no idea which group they are in. This helps to ensure that any overall expectations are equally represented in both groups. It is even possible to inform the participants that some of them will be given a placebo—the inactive pill or injection—as long as no one knows who is in which group. Notice that the single-blind technique does not eliminate subject expectancies; it simply reduces the chances that expectancies will contribute more to the experimental group than to the control group (or vice versa).

The people participating in the experiment aren't the only ones who expect certain things to happen—the experimenter does too (Rosenthal, 1966). Remember, it is the experimenter who formulated the hypothesis. Experimenters are often convinced that behavior will change in a certain way, and these expectations can also influence the results. Imagine that a researcher has developed a drug designed to cure all forms of influenza. The researcher has worked hard on its development but still needs convincing scientific evidence to show that it's effective. So the researcher designs a single-blind experiment composed of two groups of flu-sufferers. One group receives the drug and the other a placebo. Later, after analyzing the results, the researcher is satisfied to report that indeed people in the experimental group recovered more quickly than those in the control group.

There are two ways that the experimenter's expectations might influence these results. First, there is the unlikely possibility that the investigator has deliberately "cooked" the results to be consistent with his or her hypothesis. Intentional errors on the part of researchers are rare, but they have been documented on occasion in most branches of scientific research (for a discussion, see Barber, 1976; Broad & Wade, 1982). A second and more likely possibility is that the experimenter unknowingly influenced the results in some subtle way. Perhaps, for example, the researcher gave slightly more attention to the flu-stricken people in the experimental group; the researcher expected these people to get well and so was more responsive to changes in their medical condition. Alternatively, the researcher might simply have been more encouraging to the people who actually received the drug, leading them to adopt a more positive outlook on their chances for a quick recovery. Such biases are not necessarily deliberate on the part of researchers. Nevertheless, these unintentional effects can cloud a meaningful interpretation of the results. The solution to experimenter expectancy effects is to keep the researcher blind about the assignment of people to groups. If those administering the study do not know which individuals are receiving the experimental treatment, they are unlikely to treat members of each group differently. Obviously, someone needs to know the group assignments, but the information can be coded in such a way that the person doing the actual observations remains blind about the condition. After the data have been collected, based on the code, the experimenter can determine the particular manipulation that the subject received. To control for both experimenter and subject expectancies in the same context, a **double-blind study** is conducted, in which neither the subject nor the observer is aware of who is in the experimental and control conditions. Double-blind studies, often used in drug research, are considered to be an effective way for reducing bias effects.

Generalizing Experimental Conclusions

Properly designed experiments help an investigator determine the causes of behavior. The determination of causality is possible whenever the experimenter has sufficient control over the situation to eliminate confounding factors. But experimental control is occasionally gained at a cost. Sometimes, in the search for appropriate controls, the researcher creates an environment that is sterile or artificial and not representative of situations in which a person normally behaves. The results of the experimental research then cannot easily be generalized to real-world situations; as you learned previously, such results are said to have little external validity.

Consider again the issue of television violence and aggression: Does one really cause the other? A number of experimental studies have been conducted to explore this question (Anderson et al., 2003; Bushman & Anderson, 2001), but most have been conducted in the laboratory under controlled conditions. People are randomly assigned to groups who watch violent programs or neutral programs, and their behavior is then observed for aggressive tendencies, again under controlled conditions. In one study, preschool children were exposed to neutral or aggressive cartoons and then were given the opportunity to play with aggressive toys (such as toy guns); more aggressive acts were recorded for the children who watched the violent cartoon (Sanson & Di Muccio, 1993). These results clearly demonstrate that watching violence can increase the likelihood of aggressiveness. But this does not necessarily mean that these children would act similarly in their homes or that the effects of the brief exposure to violence will be long lasting. In short, the experiment may lack external validity. Concerns about generalizability should not, however, be taken as a devastating critique of the experimental method—results demonstrated in the laboratory often do generalize to real-world environments. Moreover, the true purpose of an experiment is to gain control, not external validity. Still, it's legitimate to raise questions about how widely the results apply. As you might expect, we'll return to the problem of external validity in later chapters.

CRITICAL THINKING

Experiments are sometimes criticized because they are considered artificial. Many psychology experiments use college students in introductory psychology courses as participants. Do you feel there is a problem in generalizing the findings from these studies to the whole population?

Test Yourself 2.3

Answer the following questions to test your knowledge about experimental research. (You will find the answers in the Appendix.)

1. Fill in the blanks with the terms *independent* or *dependent*. In experimental research, the researcher actively manipulates the environment to observe its effect on behavior. The aspect of the environment that is manipulated is called the _____ variable; the behavior of interest is measured by the _____ variable. To draw conclusions about cause and effect, the experimenter must make certain that the _____ variable is the only thing changing systematically in the environment.

2. Javier wants to determine whether the presence of Tom Cruise in a movie increases the box office take. He randomly forms two groups of subjects. One group sees *Mission Impossible III*, starring Cruise, and the other group sees *Barney's Big Adventure*, without Cruise. Sure enough, the Tom Cruise movie is later rated as more enjoyable than the movie starring the purple dinosaur. Javier concludes that Tom Cruise movies are sure winners. What's wrong with this experiment?
   a. The dependent variable—Tom Cruise versus Barney—is confounded with the content of the movie.
   b. The independent variable—Tom Cruise versus Barney—is not the only factor changing across the groups.
   c. Nothing has been manipulated—it's really a correlational study.
   d. Experiments of this type require independent variables with at least three conditions.

3. Random assignment is an important research tool because it helps the researcher control for potential confounding variables. Which of the following statements about random assignment is true? Random assignment
   a. eliminates individual differences among people.
   b. ensures that some participants will get the experimental treatment and others will not.
   c. increases the likelihood that subject differences will be equally represented in each group.
   d. controls for bias by ensuring that biased subjects will be placed in the control group.

The Ethics of Research: Human and Animal Guidelines

LEARNING GOALS
- Explain the principle of informed consent.
- Discuss the roles of debriefing and confidentiality in research.
- Discuss the ethical issues involved in animal research.

DO YOU REMEMBER the problem of reactivity? The act of observation can importantly change the way people behave. Although psychologists have developed techniques for reducing reactivity—designing noninterfering measures, keeping participants blind to their true role in the study, fooling individuals into thinking the observer is really part of the environment—each method raises significant ethical questions. Is it appropriate to deceive people into thinking they're not really being recorded? Is it appropriate to withhold treatment from some participants, through the use of placebos, in the interest of achieving proper experimental control (Kirsch, 2003)? To deal with such issues, formal organizations such as the American Psychological Association (APA) develop and publish ethical guidelines and codes of conduct for their members (American Psychological Association, 2002a; Smith, 2003).

Psychologists have a responsibility to respect the rights and dignity of all people. This responsibility is recognized around the world (Leach & Harbin, 1997), and it goes beyond simple research activities. The code of conduct applies to everything that psychologists do, from administering therapy, to working in the field, to giving testimony in the courtroom. First and foremost, respecting the rights of others means showing concern for their health, safety, and welfare; no diabolical mind-altering treatments are allowed, even "in the name and pursuit of science." Psychologists are expected to act responsibly in advertising their services, representing themselves in the media, pricing their services, and collecting their fees.

Informed Consent

informed consent The principle that before consenting to participate in research, people should be fully informed about any significant factors that could affect their willingness to participate.

The cornerstone of the ethics code is the principle of **informed consent**. Participants in any form of research or therapy must be informed, in easy-to-understand language, of any significant factors that could affect their willingness to participate (Smith, 2003). Physical and emotional risks should be explained, as should the general nature of the project and any therapeutic procedures to be used. Once informed, participants must then willingly give their written consent to participate in the research. They should understand as well that if for any reason they choose not to participate, they will suffer no negative consequences. Unfortunately, informed consent can raise significant problems for the researcher.

People cannot give truly informed consent unless they understand the details of the project, yet full disclosure could critically affect their behavior in the study. You've seen that it's often necessary to keep people blind about group assignments so that their expectations won't affect the outcome of the study. Imagine that you're interested in how readily bystanders at an accident will come to the aid of a victim. To gain experimental control, you might stage a mock accident in the laboratory, in front of waiting research subjects, to see how they react. Conducting the study in the laboratory would enable you to investigate the likelihood of intervention under a variety of conditions (such as whether the person is alone or with others in the room when the accident occurs). But people in this situation would need to be misled—you certainly couldn't fully inform them about the procedure by telling them the accident isn't real.

The psychological research community recognizes that it's sometimes necessary to use deception as part of a research procedure. Not all psychologists agree with this conclusion (Baumrind, 1985; Ortmann & Hertwig, 1997), but it represents the major-

ity opinion. According to the APA code of ethics, deception in research is justified only if the scientific, educational, or applied value of the study is clear and if there is no way to answer the research questions adequately without deceiving the participants (American Psychological Association, 2002a). It is agreed also that whatever deception might be involved, it should not cause physical or emotional harm or affect someone's willingness to participate in the study. Experimenters have a responsibility to respect the rights and dignity of research participants at all times. Most universities and colleges make certain that subjects' rights are protected by requiring investigators to submit detailed descriptions of their studies to oversight review committees before any human or animal subjects can be tested. If a study fails to protect the subjects adequately, permission to conduct the study is denied.

Debriefing and Confidentiality

Two other key ingredients of the psychologist's code of ethics are debriefing and confidentiality. Psychologists are expected to debrief people fully at the end of the experimental session, meaning that everyone involved is to be informed about the general purpose of the study. **Debriefing** is intended to clear up any misunderstandings that the person might have about the research and to explain in detail why certain procedures were used (Gurman, 1994; Holmes, 1976). Certainly if deception was a part of the study, the full nature of the deception should be disclosed during the debriefing process. Debriefing gives the researcher an opportunity to counteract any anxieties that a person might have developed as a result of the research. If a participant failed to help the victim of a staged accident, for example, the experimenter could explain that bystander passivity is a characteristic of most people (Darley & Latané, 1968).

    Finally, once the participation is completed, a person's right to privacy continues. Psychologists are obligated to respect the privacy of the individual by maintaining **confidentiality**—the researcher or therapist is not to discuss or report personal information obtained in research or in therapy without the permission of the individual (American Psychological Association, 2002a). Confidentiality makes sense for more than just ethical reasons. Research participants, as well as people seeking help for psychological problems, are likely to feel more comfortable with the process, and to act more naturally, if they are convinced that their right to privacy will be respected.

debriefing At the conclusion of an experimental session, informing the participants about the general purpose of the experiment, including any deception that was involved.

confidentiality The principle that personal information obtained from a participant in research or therapy should not be revealed without the individual's permission.

The Ethics of Animal Research

In laboratories all over the world, animals actively participate in basic research. They're pressing metal bars for food, receiving small doses of electrical stimulation in the brain, and being raised in enriched environments designed to improve their ability to learn. Although animals are probably used in less than 10% of all current psychological research studies, the famous "laboratory rat" has been an important source of basic data for decades (Coile & Miller, 1984). As you'll see in later chapters, many significant psychological principles were originally discovered through the study of animal behavior (Domjan & Purdy, 1995).

    Why use animal subjects? The reason most often cited is experimental control. It is possible to raise and house nonhuman subjects in relatively ideal environments. Researchers can control diet, experience, and genetic background, thereby eliminating many of the potential confounding variables that plague human research studies. Researchers can also study phenomena such as life-span development in ways that cannot be accomplished with human subjects. Studies that would take 70 or 80 years with humans take only a few years with rats. Others use nonhuman subjects because they're thought to contain simple, rather than complex, internal systems. The basic biological machinery that underlies learning, for example, has been studied extensively with sea slugs; the number of neural connections in a sea slug is tiny compared with the billions of connections residing in a human brain. Research with nonhuman

Many important psychological insights have come from studying animals, but using animals as laboratory subjects also raises serious ethical questions.

© Paul Conklin/PhotoEdit

subjects often serves as a vehicle for developing hypotheses that can later be tested, when feasible, with humans (Saucier & Cain, 2006).

But is research with animal subjects ethical? There can be no informed consent in animal research, as animal rights activists point out. Can we justify the invasive procedures sometimes used in animal research—for example, is it okay to destroy a part of a cat's brain to learn how localized brain structures control behavior? Obviously, the use of animals in research is a highly controversial subject. Many millions of dollars are spent every year by animal rights groups; many of these groups oppose any sort of animal research (see Hubbel, 1990). Other critics question the basic value of animal studies, arguing that an understanding of animals reveals little about human beings and may even mislead researchers into drawing inappropriate conclusions (see Ulrich, 1991). In one survey of animal rights activists, 85% advocated the complete elimination of all animal research (Plous, 1991).

Despite the claims of these critics, most psychologists believe that animal research has value. Animal studies have repeatedly led to significant breakthroughs (see Miller, 1991). To cite one instance, animal research has led to significant advances in our understanding of depression, as well as to the development of drugs that lessen the symptoms of this disorder (see Chapters 14 and 15). Similarly, through the study of monkeys' natural fear of snakes in the wild, psychologists have discovered that phobias (such as the fear of heights or of being locked in small places) can be learned by imitating the behavior of others rather than through a traumatic life experience (see Chapter 7).

The American Psychological Association enforces strict guidelines with regard to the ethical treatment of nonhuman subjects (American Psychological Association, 2002a). Psychologists who conduct research that uses animals are expected to treat their subjects humanely. They are responsible for ensuring the animals' proper care, and any treatments that cause discomfort, pain, or illness must be avoided unless absolutely necessary. When surgical procedures are performed, the animals must be given the appropriate anesthesia, and proper medical procedures must be followed to eliminate infection and minimize pain. Failure to stick to these standards can result in censure or termination of membership by the governing body of the association.

The issue of animal research is controversial, in part, because of misinformation. Experiments that inflict pain and suffering on animals are extremely rare and do not fairly characterize the majority of animal studies (see Coile & Miller, 1984). Psychologists also haven't done a very good job of promoting the true value of animal research (Johnson & Morris, 1987). At the same time, all researchers need to recognize that the nature of the research subject can importantly determine the results (Gluck & Bell, 2003). Findings established from research with nonhuman subjects may, in fact, not always apply to humans—because animals have evolved to solve different problems than humans. Despite these legitimate concerns, animal research continues to be a valuable tool in the search for an understanding of behavior and mind (see Miller, 1991).

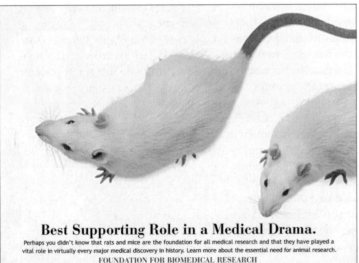

Best Supporting Role in a Medical Drama.

Perhaps you didn't know that rats and mice are the foundation for all medical research and that they have played a vital role in virtually every major medical discovery in history. Learn more about the essential need for animal research.
FOUNDATION FOR BIOMEDICAL RESEARCH
www.fbresearch.org

© 2005. Foundation for Biomedical Research

Test Yourself 2.4

You can test what you've learned about ethics and research by answering the following questions. (You will find the answers in the Appendix.)

1. Fill in the banks. Psychologists have a responsibility to respect the rights and dignity of all people. To ensure that research participants are treated ethically, psychologists use (a) informed _____, which means that everyone is fully informed about the potential risks of the project, (b) _____, which assures that the subject's right to privacy will be maintained, and (c) _____, which is designed to provide more information about the purpose and procedures of the research.

2. Sometimes it is necessary to deceive research participants in some way, such as keeping them blind about group assignments, so that expectations won't determine the outcome. Most psychologists believe that deception

   a. is always justified as long as it furthers scientific knowledge.
   b. is never justified unless the research involves clinical treatment.
   c. is justified, but only under some circumstances.
   d. is not necessary if you design the project correctly.

3. The majority of psychologists believe that animal research has enormous value. But some question the ethics of using animals primarily because

   a. no real scientific advancements have come from animal research.
   b. animals are often treated cruelly.
   c. animals can give no informed consent.
   d. animal research is too expensive.

Review *Psychology for a Reason*

Psychologists rely on a set of established research methods. Understanding research methodology is important because the conclusions reached in research studies are importantly influenced by the methods used. Whether the behavior of children in a day-care center will accurately represent real life, for example, depends on what methods of observation have been employed. In addition, whether an experiment can determine if television violence truly causes aggression depends on the use of proper controls and the appropriate selection of participants. In this chapter we considered various tools and guidelines that psychologists use to uncover the basic principles of behavior and mind.

Observing Behavior: Descriptive Research To observe and describe behavior properly, psychologists use the techniques of descriptive research. In naturalistic observation the researcher observes behavior in natural settings rather than in a laboratory environment. Naturalistic observation is a useful technique for generating ideas and for verifying whether conclusions reached in the lab generalize to more realistic settings. In case studies the focus is on a single instance of a behavior. This technique allows the researcher to get lots of background information, but the results may not always generalize to wider populations. In survey research behavior is sampled broadly, usually by gathering responses from many people in the form of a questionnaire. Surveys typically provide information that is representative of the group being examined, but the amount of information that can be gathered is limited. Finally, through psychological tests differences among individuals can be measured.

Once the observational data have been collected, they are summarized through the application of statistics. Statistical applications include measures of central tendency—the mean, median, and mode—and measures of variability, or how far apart individual scores are from each other in a set of scores. Researchers use inferential statistics, based on the laws of probability, to test hypotheses. Inferential statistics can help the researcher decide whether a difference between an experimental and a control group, for example, is likely to have occurred by chance.

Predicting Behavior: Correlational Research In correlational research the researcher determines whether a relationship exists between two measures of behavior. For instance, does high school grade point average predict college performance? Correlation coefficients, which provide an index of how well one measure predicts another, are statistics that vary between +1.00 and −1.00. Correlations are useful primarily because they enable the researcher to predict and select. If employers know there is a correlation between achievement test scores and job performance, they can use someone's score on an achievement test to predict that person's success on the job. Correlations are useful tools for predicting and selecting, but they do not allow us to draw conclusions about causality.

Explaining Behavior: Experimental Research If you want to know whether an activity, such as watching violence on television, causes a change in behavior, you must conduct an experiment. In doing so, the researcher manipulates the environment in a systematic way and then observes the effect of that manipulation on behavior. The aspect of the environment that is manipulated is called the independent variable; the measured behavior is called the dependent variable. To determine that the independent variable is really responsible for the changes in behavior, the researcher must exert experimental control—the only thing that can change systematically is the manipulation of the independent variable. Researchers conducting experiments encounter a variety of potential pitfalls that need to be controlled, including subject and experimenter expectancies. Control strategies include the use of random assignment and blind research designs.

The Ethics of Research: Human and Animal Guidelines It is important to maintain a strict code of ethical conduct throughout the research process. An important safeguard is informed consent, which is designed to guarantee that participants will be informed of any significant factors that could influence their willingness to participate. Other ethical standards govern proper debriefing and maintaining confidentiality. All researchers, regardless of the nature of the research, have a professional responsibility to respect the rights and dignity of their research participants. This applies not only to human participants but also to animal subjects.

Active Summary *(You will find the answers in the Appendix.)*

Observing Behavior: Descriptive Research

• The goal of psychologists is to study behavior by using the scientific method: (1) observe; (2) detect regularities; (3) generate a hypothesis; (4) observe again to test the hypothesis.

• (1) _____ research is used primarily to (2) _____ and describe behavior.

• (3) _____ is observed in natural settings with (4) _____ measures.

• (5) _____ studies focus on a single case, usually a single individual. A case study can yield historical information that is useful for generating (6) _____, but the results may not always generalize to the population as a whole.

• Surveys gather limited (7) _____ from many people. The data are likely to be (8) _____ of the population as a whole but often lack historical perspective.

• Psychological tests are primarily designed to measure (9) _____ differences.

• Data analyses reveal (10) _____ in psychological observations that are used to test (11) _____.
(12) _____ statistics summarize and describe data.
(13) _____ statistics help researchers determine whether behaviors are representative of the larger population, or whether differences among observations can be attributed to chance.

Predicting Behavior: Correlational Research

• A (14) _____ helps determine whether there is a relationship between two (15) _____, or measures of behavior. When there is a correlation between two measures of behavior, it is possible to (16) _____ the value of one variable on the basis of knowledge about the other.

• A correlation between two measures of behavior allows for prediction but does not determine (17) _____.
Causality requires (18) _____ _____.

Explaining Behavior: Experimental Research

• In (19) _____ research, the investigator actively manipulates the (20) _____ to observe its effect on behavior. The particular manipulation is determined by the researcher's (21) _____.

• A(n) (22) _____ variable is the aspect of the environment that is (23) _____ in an experiment.
A(n) (24) _____ variable is the behavior that is (25) _____ or measured in an experiment.

• Experimental (26) _____ is achieved by making certain that the only thing changing systematically in an experiment is the (27) _____ variable. The independent variable must include at least (28) _____ conditions: Often there is a (29) _____ _____, which doesn't get the experimental treatment, and an (30) _____ group that does get the treatment.

• Expectations and biases, held by both subjects and researchers, can influence the results of experiments. Expectancy effects on the part of the subject are controlled for with the use of (31) _____ _____ experiments, and (32) _____ _____ experiments control for expectancies on the part of both the subject and the (33) _____.

• Necessary experimental (34) _____ can limit the relevance of one set of research results to other subjects and situations.

The Ethics of Research: Human and Animal Guidelines

• Research subjects must be informed of any factors that could affect their willingness to (35) _____.

• (36) _____ is the process of explaining to research participants why the study is being conducted. (37) _____ protects the participant's privacy.

• A primary reason for using animals in psychological research is that it allows for greater experimental (38) _____. The APA enforces strict guidelines for the (39) _____ treatment of laboratory animals. However, some controversy remains over their use in psychological research.

Terms to Remember

case study, 32
confidentiality, 51
confounding variable, 45
correlation, 39
debriefing, 51
dependent variable, 44
descriptive research, 30
descriptive statistics, 37
double-blind study, 48
experimental research, 43

external validity, 30
independent variable, 44
inferential statistics, 37
informed consent, 50
internal validity, 45
mean, 35
median, 35
mode, 35
naturalistic observation, 30
operational definitions, 28

placebo, 48
random assignment, 46
random sampling, 34
range, 37
reactivity, 30
scientific method, 27
single-blind study, 48
standard deviation, 37
survey, 33
variability, 36

Media Resources

 ThomsonNOW

www.thomsonedu.com/ThomsonNOW
Go to this site for the link to ThomsonNOW, your one-stop study shop. Take a Pre-Test for this chapter, and ThomsonNOW will generate a Personalized Study Plan based on your results. The Study Plan will identify the topics you need to review and direct you to online resources to help you master those topics. You can then take a Post-Test to help you determine the concepts you have mastered and what you still need to work on.

 Companion Website

www.thomsonedu.com/psychology/nairne
Go to this site to find online resources directly linked to your book, including a glossary, flashcards, quizzing, weblinks, and more.

 Psyk.trek 3.0

Check out the Psyk.trek CD-ROM for further study of the concepts in this chapter. Psyk.trek's interactive learning modules, simulations, and quizzes offer additional opportunities for you to interact with, reflect on, and retain the material:

History and Methods: Correlation
History and Methods: The Experimental Method

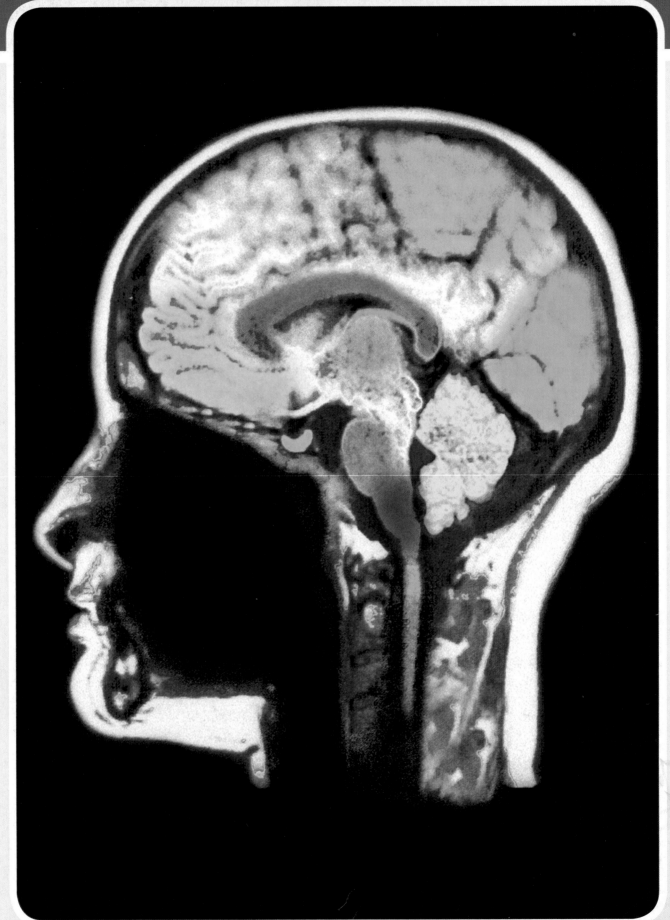

Biological Processes

Located within the confines of a protective layer of bone floats a 3- to 4-pound mass of tissue called the brain. Fueled by simple blood sugar and amino acids, the brain's billions of cells are engaged in a continuous, frenetic dance of activity. At the moment, the rhythms and movements of this dance are not well understood, but a "whole" is somehow created that is collectively greater than the sum of the individual parts. From what seem to be chaotic patterns of cellular activity arise the complexities of human behavior, thought, emotion, and creativity.

Throughout this book, and this chapter in particular, we'll assume that all of our actions arise from the activities of this brain—not just mundane things like breathing, maintaining a beating heart, and walking, but our intimate thoughts and deepest feelings as well. Every time you think, act, or feel, biological activity in your brain plays a critical, if not primary, role. Disorders of the mind, such as schizophrenia or clinical depression, are products of the brain as well. This chapter introduces you to the field of **neuroscience**, which studies the connection between the brain and behavior. Although I'll focus primarily on the brain, behavior is actually controlled by a broader system that includes the spinal cord as well as the connections between the brain and muscles, sensory organs, and other internal structures. More specifically, the brain and spinal cord comprise what is called the **central nervous system**. An additional network of nerves, the **peripheral nervous system**, acts as the communication link between the central nervous system and the rest of the body. It's the job of the peripheral nervous system to relay messages from the central nervous system to the muscles that produce actual responses. Later in this chapter I'll expand on these basic divisions and outline their functions in greater detail.

A vast communication network in the body helps us monitor the environment and produce quick adaptive responses when they're needed.

© PhotoDisc/Getty Images

neuroscience An interdisciplinary field of study directed at understanding the brain and its relation to behavior.

central nervous system The brain and the spinal cord.

peripheral nervous system The network of nerves that links the central nervous system with the rest of the body.

Our discussion of biological processes revolves around four central problems of adaptation: How do we communicate internally, how do we initiate and control behavior, how do we regulate growth and other internal functions, and how do we adapt and transmit the genetic code? Each of these problems must be solved by the systems in our bodies and, not surprisingly, we've evolved a set of sophisticated tools to meet these needs.

Communicating Internally: Connecting World and Brain

Our actions are often adaptive because we're able to monitor the environment continuously and produce quick and appropriate responses. If a dog suddenly runs in front of your car, you quickly jam on the brake, saving the animal. These nearly instantaneous world-to-behavior links are possible because of a sophisticated communication network linking the outside world to the brain. Informa-tion from the environment is translated into the language of the nervous system and relayed to appropriate processing sites throughout the body.

Initiating Behavior: A Division of Labor

The nervous system may handle the complicated task of receiving and communicating information, but information by itself does not translate into hand movements, quick reactions, or artistic creativity. Somehow the body must assign meaning to the information it receives and coordinate the appropriate responses. As you'll see, there are specific structures in the brain that initiate and coordinate our thoughts, actions, and emotions.

Regulating Growth and Internal Functions: Extended Communication

Besides relying on the rapid transmission of information from one point to the next, the systems in the body also have widespread and long-term internal communication needs. To resolve these needs, structures in the body control the release of chemicals into the bloodstream that serve important regulatory functions, influencing growth and development, sexual behavior, the desire to eat or drink, and even emotional expression.

Adapting and Transmitting the Genetic Code

The genetic code you inherited from your parents has been shaped by the forces of natural selection. It determines much of who you are and what you have the potential to become. Molecules carrying the genetic code influence more than eye color, height, or hair color. Intelligence, personality, and even susceptibility to mental disorders can be influenced significantly by genetic information. We'll review the basic principles of genetics and discuss how nature and nurture interact to guide and constrain behavior.

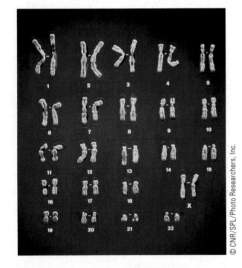

The genetic record we inherit from our parents shapes our physical and psychological characteristics in significant ways.

Communicating Internally: Connecting World and Brain

LEARNING GOALS
- Describe the structure, type, and function of neurons.
- Explain how neurons transmit information.
- Discuss how neurons work together to communicate.

STRIKE A MATCH AND HOLD IT an inch or so away from the tip of your index finger. Now move it a bit closer. Closer. Closer still. Let the flame approach and momentarily touch the flesh of your finger. On second thought, skip this experiment. You already know the outcome. Flame approaches flesh, and you withdraw your finger quickly, automatically, and efficiently. Let's consider the nervous system mechanisms that produce this kind of reaction, because it represents one of the simplest kinds of world-to-brain communications. The main components of the nervous system are individual cells, called **neurons**, that receive, transmit, and integrate information. The language used by the neurons to communicate is *electrochemical*—that is, it's part electrical and part chemical. There are three major types of neurons:

1. **Sensory neurons** make the initial contact with the environment and are responsible for carrying the message inward toward the spinal cord and brain.

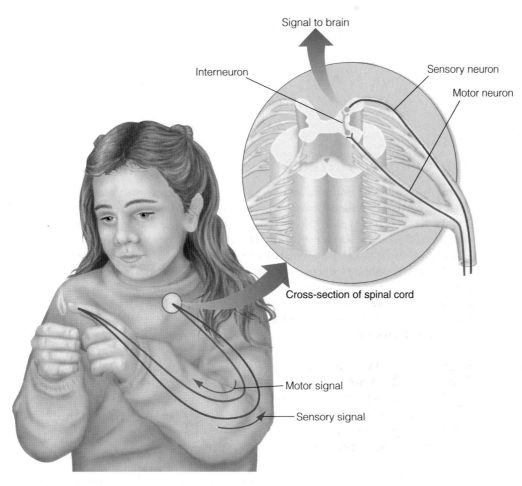

Signal to brain

Interneuron

Sensory neuron

Motor neuron

Cross-section of spinal cord

Motor signal

Sensory signal

FIGURE 3.1 A Simple Reflex Pathway
The information that flame has touched flesh travels through a sensory neuron to the spinal cord, which directs it to an interneuron, which sends it on to a motor neuron. The motor neuron then alerts the finger muscles, which quickly withdraw from the heat. The original information is also passed upward to the brain, which registers pain.

The heat of the flame excites receptor regions in the sensory neurons in your fingertip, which then pass the message along to the spinal cord.

2. **Interneurons**, the most plentiful type of neurons, make no direct contact with the world, but they convey information from one internal processing site to another. Interneurons in the spinal cord receive the message from the sensory neurons, then pass it on to the motor neurons.

3. **Motor neurons** carry the messages and commands away from the central nervous system to the muscles and glands that produce responses. In the match example in ▌Figure 3.1, the motor neurons contact the muscles of the finger, which leads to a quick and efficient finger withdrawal.

The nervous system also contains **glial cells**, which greatly outnumber neurons (by a factor of about 10 to 1), but these cells don't directly communicate messages on their own. Glial cells perform a variety of functions in the nervous system, such as removing waste, filling in empty space, and helping neurons to communicate efficiently. Some types of glial cells wrap around portions of neurons, acting as a kind of insulation. This insulation, called the **myelin sheath**, protects the neuron and helps speed up neural transmission. Unfortunately, glial cells also play an important role in some kinds of brain dysfunction, including brain cancer and Alzheimer disease.

You may have noticed that so far the brain hasn't figured into our discussion of fingers and flames. Actually, the message is passed upward to the brain, through the activity of more interneurons, and it is in the brain that you consciously experience the heat of the flame. But in situations requiring a quick response, as in the case of a flame touching your finger, the nervous system is capable of producing a collection of largely automatic reactions. These reactions, called **reflexes**, are controlled

neurons The cells in the nervous system that receive and transmit information.

sensory neurons Cells that carry environmental messages toward the spinal cord and brain.

interneurons Cells that transfer information from one neuron to another; interneurons make no direct contact with the outside world.

motor neurons Cells that carry information away from the central nervous system to the muscles and glands that directly produce behavior.

glial cells Cells that fill in space between neurons, remove waste, or help neurons to communicate efficiently.

myelin sheath An insulating material that protects the axon and helps to speed up neural transmission.

reflexes Largely automatic body reactions—such as the knee jerk—that are controlled primarily by spinal cord pathways.

CRITICAL THINKING

A reflex is a type of adaptive behavior that does not arise directly from activity of the brain. If you were building a body from scratch, what types of reflexes would you include and why?

FIGURE 3.2 The Components of a Neuron
The dendrites are the primary information receivers, the soma is the cell body, and the axon transmits the cell's messages. The myelin sheath that surrounds the axon helps speed up neural transmission. Terminal buttons at the end of the axon contain the chemicals that carry messages to the next neuron.

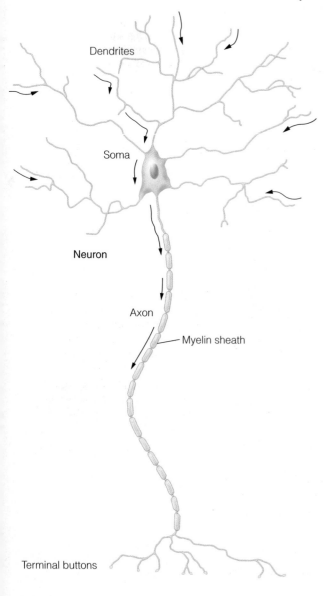

primarily by spinal cord pathways. A reflex requires no input from the brain. If your spinal cord were to be cut, blocking communication between most of the body and brain, you wouldn't feel the pain or react with a facial grimace, but your finger would still twitch. Reflex pathways allow the body to respond quickly to environmental events in a relatively simple and direct way. People don't think or feel with their spinal cords, but reflex pathways are an important part of our ability to adapt successfully to the world.

The Anatomy of Neurons

Before it's possible to understand how information passes from one neuron to another, we need to consider the basic anatomical hardware of these cells. As shown in Figure 3.2, neurons typically have four major structural features: *dendrites*, a *soma*, an *axon*, and *terminal buttons*. For any communication system to work properly, it must have a way to receive information, a way to process any received messages, and a means for sending an appropriate response. The four components of the neuron play these distinct roles in the communication chain.

The **dendrites**, which look like tree branches extending outward from the main body of the cell, are the primary information receivers. A sensory neuron passes information about a burning flame along to an interneuron by interacting with the interneuron's dendrites. A particular neuron may have thousands of these dendritic branches, enabling the cell to receive input from many different sources. Once received, the message is processed in the **soma**, the main body of the cell. The soma is also the cell's metabolic center, and it is where genetic material is stored. The **axon** is the cell's transmitter. When a neuron transmits a message, it sends an electrical signal called the *action potential* down its axon toward other neurons. Axons are like biological transmission cables, although the action potential in a neuron is considerably slower than a household electrical current. Axons can vary dramatically in size and shape; in some cases, such as in your legs, they can be several feet in length. Near its end the axon branches out to make contact with other cells. At the tip of each branch are tiny swellings called **terminal buttons**. Chemicals released by these buttons pass the message on to the next neuron.

Neurons don't actually touch. The **synapse** is a small gap between cells, typically between the terminal buttons of one neuron and the dendrite or cell body of another. The chemicals released by the terminal buttons flow into this gap. The synapse and the chemicals released into it are critical factors in the body's communication network, as you'll see next.

Neural Transmission: The Electrochemical Message

Neurons may differ in size and shape, but the direction of information flow is predictable and consistent:

DENDRITES → SOMA → AXON → TERMINAL BUTTONS

Information usually arrives at the dendrites from multiple sources—many thousands of contacts might be made—and is passed along to the soma. Here all the received messages sum together; if a sufficient electrical signal is present, an action potential will be generated. The action potential travels down the axon toward the terminal buttons, where it causes the release of chemicals into the synapse. These chemicals move the message from the end of the axon to the dendrites of the next neuron, starting the process all over again. That's the general sequence of information flow: Messages travel electrically from one point to another within a neuron, but the message is transmitted chemically between neurons. Now let's consider each of these processes in more detail.

The Resting Potential Neurons possess electrical properties even when they aren't receiving or transmitting messages. Specifically, a tiny electrical charge, called the **resting potential**, exists between the inside and the outside of the cell. This resting potential is created by the presence of electrically charged atoms and molecules, called *ions*, which are distributed unevenly between the inside and the outside of the cell. The main ions in neural transmission are positively charged *sodium* and *potassium* ions and negatively charged *chloride* ions. Normally, ions will distribute themselves evenly in an environment through a process called *diffusion*. However, they are unable to do so around a resting neuron because free movement is blocked by the neuron's cell wall, or *membrane*. The membrane of a neuron is selectively permeable, which means that it only allows certain ions to pass in and out through special ion "channels." As shown in ▌Figure 3.3, when the neuron is resting, the sodium and chloride ions are concentrated outside of the cell and the potassium ions are largely contained inside. These unequal concentrations are maintained, in part, by a sodium-potassium pump that actively moves the ions into and out of the cell. If you measured the electrical potential of the neuron with an electrode, you would find that the fluid inside the cell is *negative* with respect to the outside (between −60 and − 70 millivolts). This negative charge defines the resting potential for the cell. Most of the negative charge comes from large protein molecules inside the cell, which are too big to pass through ion channels.

Why is it adaptive for neurons to have a resting potential? It's likely that the resting potential helps the cell respond quickly when it's contacted by other neurons. When one neuron communicates with another, it releases chemicals that change the contacted neuron's membrane. Ions that are normally outside the cell can rush in quickly through newly opened channels. This changes the electrical potential inside the cell, which, as you'll see shortly, can lead to the production of an action potential.

dendrites The fibers that extend outward from a neuron and receive information from other neurons.

soma The cell body of a neuron.

axon The long tail-like part of a neuron that serves as the cell's transmitter.

terminal buttons The tiny swellings at the end of the axon that contain chemicals important to neural transmission.

synapse The small gap between the terminal buttons of a neuron and the dendrite or cell body of another neuron.

resting potential The tiny electrical charge in place between the inside and the outside of the resting neuron.

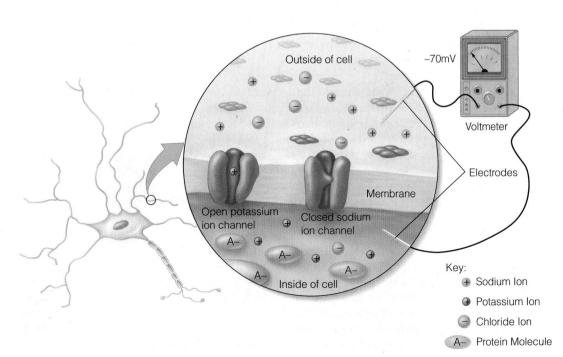

▌**FIGURE 3.3 The Resting Potential**
Neurons possess electrical properties even when they are neither receiving nor transmitting messages. The resting potential, a tiny negative electrical charge across the inside and outside of a resting cell, is created by an uneven distribution of ions across the cell membrane.

Outside of cell

−70mV

Voltmeter

Electrodes

Membrane

Open potassium ion channel

Closed sodium ion channel

Inside of cell

Key:
⊕ Sodium Ion
⊕ Potassium Ion
⊖ Chloride Ion
Ⓐ⁻ Protein Molecule

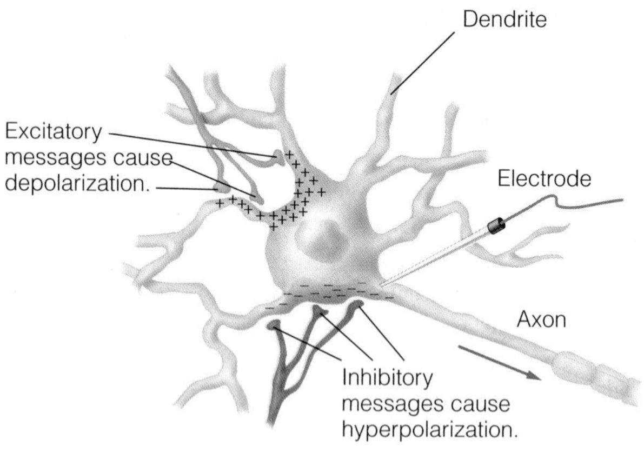

FIGURE 3.4 Summing Excitatory and Inhibitory Messages

Each neuron is in contact with many other neurons. Some contacts initiate excitatory messages, or depolarization, and others initiate inhibitory messages, or hyperpolarization. A neuron generates its own action potential only if the summed messages produce sufficient depolarization (the negative potential moves close enough to zero).

action potential The all-or-none electrical signal that travels down a neuron's axon.

neurotransmitters Chemical messengers that relay information from one neuron to the next.

Generating an Action Potential   For a neuron to stop resting and generate an **action potential**, the electrical signal that travels down the axon, the electrical potential inside the cell must become less negative. This necessary change occurs primarily as a result of contact from other neurons. Two types of messages can be passed from one neuron to the next, excitatory messages and inhibitory messages. If the message is excitatory, the membrane of the contacted neuron changes, and sodium ions begin to flow into the cell. This process, called *depolarization*, moves the electrical potential of the cell from negative toward zero and increases the chances of an action potential. When the message is inhibitory, the opposite happens: The cell membrane either pushes more positive ions out of the cell or allows negative ions to move in. The result is *hyperpolarization*: The electrical potential of the cell becomes more negative, and the chances of an action potential decrease.

It's important to remember that each neuron in the nervous system is in contact with many other neurons. As a result, small changes in potential regularly occur in many input regions of the neuron as messages are received (see Figure 3.4). Near the point where the axon leaves the cell body, in a special trigger zone called the *axon hillock*, all of the excitatory and inhibitory potentials combine. If enough excitatory messages have been received—that is, if the electrical potential inside the cell has become sufficiently less negative—an action potential will be initiated. If not, the resting potential of the axon will be maintained.

Action potentials are generated in an *all-or-none* fashion; that is, they will not begin until sufficient excitatory input has been received. But once the firing threshold is reached, action potentials begin and always travel completely down the length of the axon to its end. The process is somewhat like firing a gun (or flushing a toilet). Once sufficient pressure is delivered to the trigger (handle), a bullet fires and moves down the barrel in a characteristic way (the water flushes). Action potentials, like bullets, travel independent of the intensity of the messages. Bullets don't travel farther or faster if you pull the trigger harder. (Ditto for the toilet—the water doesn't flush harder if you yank on the handle.)

Action potentials also travel down the axon in a fixed and characteristic way. It really doesn't matter whether the neuron is carrying a message about pain or pleasure; the characteristics of the signal won't vary from one neuron to the next or from one point on the axon to the next. The overall speed of transmission, however, depends on the size and shape of the axon; in general, the thicker the axon, the faster the message will travel. Impulse speed varies among neuron types in a range from about 2 to 200 miles per hour (which is still significantly slower than the speed of electricity through a wire or printed circuit).

One feature that increases the speed of transmission in many neurons is the myelin sheath. Myelin provides insulation for the axon, similar to the plastic around copper wiring. At regular points there are gaps in the insulation, called *nodes of Ranvier*, that permit the action potential to jump down the axon rather than traveling from point to point. This method of transmission from node to node is called *saltatory conduction*; it comes from the Latin *saltare*, which means "to jump." The myelin sheath speeds transmission, and it also protects the message from interference from other neural signals.

Neurotransmitters: The Chemical Messengers   When the action potential reaches the end of the axon, it triggers the release of chemical messengers from small sacs, or vesicles, in the terminal buttons (see Figure 3.5). These chemical molecules, called **neurotransmitters**, spill out into the synapse and interact chemically with the cell membrane of the next neuron (called the *postsynaptic membrane*). Depending on the particular characteristics of this membrane, the neurotransmitter will transfer either an excitatory or an inhibitory message.

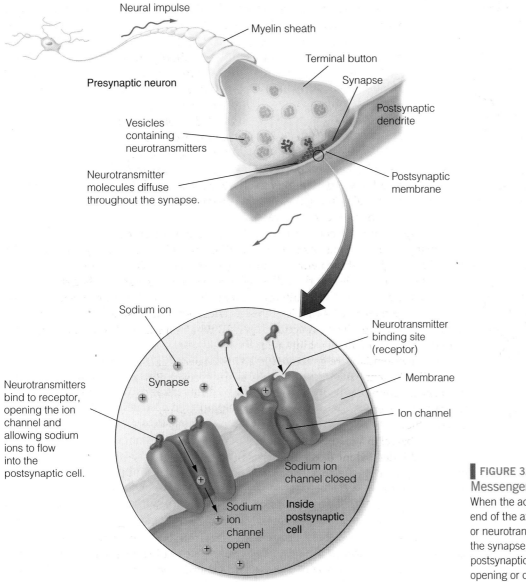

Neural impulse

Myelin sheath

Terminal button

Synapse

Presynaptic neuron

Postsynaptic dendrite

Vesicles containing neurotransmitters

Neurotransmitter molecules diffuse throughout the synapse.

Postsynaptic membrane

Sodium ion

Neurotransmitter binding site (receptor)

Synapse

Membrane

Neurotransmitters bind to receptor, opening the ion channel and allowing sodium ions to flow into the postsynaptic cell.

Ion channel

Sodium ion channel closed

Sodium ion channel open

Inside postsynaptic cell

FIGURE 3.5 Releasing the Chemical Messengers
When the action potential reaches the end of the axon, chemical messengers, or neurotransmitters, are released into the synapse, where they interact with the postsynaptic membrane of the next neuron, opening or closing its ion channels.

The released neurotransmitter molecule acts as a kind of key in search of the appropriate lock. The substance moves quickly across the synapse—it takes only about 1/10,000 of a second—and activates receptor molecules contained in the postsynaptic membrane. Depending on the particular type of receptor molecule, the neurotransmitter then either increases or decreases the electrical potential of the receiving cell. When the message is excitatory, the neurotransmitter causes channels in the postsynaptic membrane to open, allowing positive sodium ions to flow into the receiving cell. When the message is inhibitory, negative chloride ions are allowed to enter the cell, and positive potassium ions are allowed to leave. It's worth pointing out that neurotransmitters, by themselves, are neither excitatory nor inhibitory. It is really the nature of the receptor molecule that determines whether a particular neurotransmitter will produce an excitatory or inhibitory effect; the same neurotransmitter can produce quite different effects at different sites in the nervous system.

Dozens of neurotransmitters have been identified in the brain. The neurotransmitter **acetylcholine** is a major messenger in both the central and peripheral

acetylcholine A neurotransmitter that plays multiple roles in the central and peripheral nervous systems, including the excitation of muscle contractions.

For much of recorded history, psychological disorders were attributed to possession by evil spirits. Today psychologists recognize that some disorders are the result of brain malfunctioning.

dopamine A neurotransmitter that often leads to inhibitory effects; decreased levels have been linked to Parkinson disease, and increased levels have been linked to schizophrenia.

serotonin A neurotransmitter that has been linked to sleep, dreaming, and general arousal and may also be involved in some psychological disorders such as depression and schizophrenia.

gamma-amino-butyric acid (GABA) A neurotransmitter that may play a role in the regulation of anxiety; it generally produces inhibitory effects.

nervous systems; it acts as the primary transmitter between motor neurons and muscles in the body. When released into the synapse between motor neurons and muscle cells, acetylcholine tends to create excitatory messages that lead to muscle contraction. The neurotransmitter **dopamine** often produces inhibitory effects that help dampen and stabilize communications in the brain and elsewhere. Inhibitory effects help to keep the brain on an even keel and allow us to produce smooth voluntary muscle movements, sleep without physically acting out our dreams, and maintain posture. If neurotransmitters had only excitatory effects, there would be an endless chain of communication, producing a blooming, buzzing ball of confusion in the brain.

Dopamine is of particular interest to psychologists because it's thought to play a role in schizophrenia, a serious psychological disorder that disrupts thought processes and produces delusions and hallucinations. When patients with schizophrenia take drugs that inhibit the action of dopamine, their hallucinations and delusions are sometimes reduced or even eliminated. It's been speculated that perhaps an excess supply of dopamine is partly responsible for the disorder (Sigmundson, 1994; Snyder, 1976). Further support linking dopamine and schizophrenia comes from the study of Parkinson disease, a movement disorder that results from the underproduction of dopamine. Parkinson patients are often given the drug L-dopa, which increases the levels of dopamine in the brain, to reduce the tremors and other movement problems caused by the disease. For some patients, however, one of the side effects of L-dopa is a mimicking of the thought disorders characteristic of schizophrenia (Jaskiw & Popli, 2004).

Neurotransmitters in the brain drive our thoughts and actions, but the particular mechanisms involved are not well understood. We know, for example, that people with Alzheimer disease have suffered destruction of cells that play a role in producing acetylcholine. Because memory loss is a common problem for Alzheimer patients, a close connection may exist between acetylcholine and certain kinds of memory functioning (Pepeu & Giovannini, 2004). We also know that **serotonin**, another neurotransmitter that often acts in an inhibitory fashion, affects sleep, dreaming, and general arousal and may also be involved in such psychological disorders as depression, schizophrenia, and obsessive–compulsive disorder (Barlow & Durand, 2005). As you'll learn in Chapter 15, some medications used to treat depression, such as Prozac (fluoxetine), act by modulating the effectiveness of serotonin (Jacobs, 2004). Similarly, researchers have suspected for some time that a neurotransmitter called **gamma-amino-butyric acid (GABA)** plays an important role in the regulation of anxiety. Many medications for anxiety (e.g., tranquilizers such as Valium) regulate GABA in the brain.

Researchers haven't pinned down all the neural pathways involved in these effects and disorders. Unfortunately, much of our knowledge remains correlational at this point—we know that as the levels of particular neurotransmitters vary in the body, so too do the symptoms of disorders. This is useful information for treatment, but it doesn't establish a true cause-and-effect link between neurotransmitters and psychological characteristics.

Drugs and the Brain   Because the transmission of messages between neurons is chemical, chemicals that are ingested into the body can significantly affect the communication networks in the brain. Some drugs, called *agonists*, mimic the action of neurotransmitters. For example, the nicotine in cigarette smoke can act like the neurotransmitter acetylcholine. Nicotine has a general stimulatory effect in the body, such as increasing heart rate, because it produces excitatory messages in much the same way as acetylcholine.

Other drugs act as *antagonists*, which means that they oppose or block the action of neurotransmitters. The lethal drug curare, which is sometimes used on the tips of hunting arrows and blow darts in South America, is antagonistic to acetylcholine. Curare blocks the receptor systems involved in muscle movements, including those

Concept Review | Neurotransmitters and Their Effects

NEUROTRANSMITTER	NATURE OF EFFECT	INVOLVED IN . . .
Dopamine	Generally inhibitory*	Dampening and stabilizing communication in the brain and elsewhere; helps ensure smooth motor function. Plays a role in both schizophrenia and Parkinson disease.
Acetylcholine	Generally excitatory*	Communication between motor neurons and muscles in the body, leading to muscle contraction. May also play a role in Alzheimer disease.
Serotonin	Generally inhibitory*	Regulating sleep, dreaming, and general arousal. Also may play a role in some psychological disorders, including depression.
GABA	Generally inhibitory*	The regulation of anxiety; tranquilizing drugs act on GABA to decrease anxiety.

*Note: No neurotransmitter, on its own, is excitatory or inhibitory; the nature of its action depends on specific characteristics of the receiving cell's membrane.

muscles that move the diaphragm during breathing. The result is paralysis and likely death from suffocation.

In the early 1970s membrane receptor systems were discovered in the brain that react directly to morphine, a painkilling and highly addictive drug derived from the opium plant (Pert & Snyder, 1973). It turns out that we have receptor systems that are sensitive to morphine because the brain produces its own morphinelike substances called **endorphins**. Endorphins serve as natural painkillers in the body. They're thought to act as *neuromodulators*, or chemicals that modulate (increase or decrease) the effectiveness of neurotransmitters. Apparently, the brain has evolved systems for releasing endorphins under conditions of stress or exertion to reduce pain and possibly to provide pleasurable reinforcement (Pert, 2002). We'll return to the study of drugs, particularly their effects on conscious awareness, in Chapter 6.

The Communication Network

Up to this point we've tapped briefly into the electrochemical language of the nervous system. You've seen how information is transmitted electrically within a neuron, through the flow of charged ions, and how one neuron signals another through the release of chemical messengers. But understanding the dynamics of neuron-to-neuron communication is only part of the story.

To unravel the complex relationship between the brain and mental processes, we must understand how neurons work together. A vast communication network exists within the brain, involving the operation of thousands of neurons, and the way in which these cells interact is of critical importance. Behaviors, thoughts, feelings, ideas—they don't arise from the activation of single neurons; instead, it is the *pattern of activation* produced by groups of neurons operating at the same time that underlies both conscious experiences and complex behaviors. As a result, we need to be mindful of the specific ways in which neurons are connected and the means through which those connections can be modified by experience.

Information is also communicated in the nervous system by the *firing rate* of a neuron, defined as the number of action potentials it generates per unit of time. The stronger the incoming message, the more rapidly a message-sensitive neuron tends to fire. These firing rates, however, are subject to some natural limitations. For instance, a **refractory period** usually follows the generation of an action potential; during this period, additional action potentials cannot be generated. Even with the refractory period, though, neurons are still able to fire off a relatively steady stream of messages in response to environmental input. Many neurons even appear to have spontaneous firing rates, which means that they generate a steady stream of action potentials with

© Steve McDonough/CORBIS

Coffee and many other natural substances contain chemicals that affect the action of neurotransmitters in the brain and body.

endorphins Morphinelike chemicals that act as the brain's natural painkillers.

refractory period The period of time following an action potential when more action potentials cannot be generated.

Better Thinking Through Chemistry?

Neuroscientists believe that our thoughts, memories, and emotions are linked to specific activities in the brain. Your memory for where you went on vacation last year, or for where you left your keys last night, ultimately comes from interactions among large numbers of neurons firing together in organized patterns. This raises an intriguing possibility: If we can understand these interactions, then why can't we intervene biologically to improve our ability to think and remember? Shouldn't it be possible, in principle, to develop a drug that can improve the way we think?

We've all been exposed to messages from the media promising better thinking through chemistry. Commercials and infomercials offer pills to enhance concentration, solve problems, and improve memory. Usually these pills are sold with a disclaimer or two (often in small print), and "evidence" for the pill's effectiveness comes merely from testimonials and anecdotes. As a further hook, we're often told that the product is completely "natural" and has been used for centuries, outside of mainstream medicine, as a natural cure or remedy. To take a case in point, an extract from leaves of the deciduous tree ginkgo biloba has been touted as a natural and effective way to improve memory. Does it really work?

Actually, in the case of ginkgo, there is some evidence that it can produce small improvements in memory, at least for certain populations of people (Burns, Bryan, & Nettelbeck, 2006). To test the effectiveness of a drug properly, as we discussed in Chapter 2, it's best to conduct a double-blind study. In such a study, neither the subject/patient nor the person administering the drug knows who actually receives it; half of the participants receive the medication and the other

half receive a placebo, or inactive substance (e.g., a sugar pill). Double-blind studies help control for expectancies, and the placebo provides a necessary comparison control. There haven't been large numbers of double-blind studies conducted on ginkgo, but promising results have been reported. In one study, for example, more than 250 healthy people were tested in a double-blind study of the effects of ginkgo (combined with the root panax ginseng) on a variety of cognitive and memory tests (Wesnes et al., 2000). On average, the experimental group (those receiving the ginkgo compound) showed a 7 to 8% improvement on the memory tasks relative to the control group, and the advantage actually persisted for some time after participants stopped taking the medication. Unfortunately, the improvement seemed to depend on what time of the day the people were tested (McDaniel, Maier, & Einstein, 2002), and follow-up work has found that prolonged use of ginkgo produces little, if any, benefit on a variety of memory tests (Persson et al., 2004). Ginkgo may eventually turn out to be an effective treatment for individuals suffering from dementia (biologically based thought problems), such as the memory loss that accompanies Alzheimer disease, but it's too early to draw any firm conclusions (Gold, Cahill, & Wenk, 2002).

Overall, claims about better thinking through chemistry are best viewed with caution—perhaps in the same way that you think about ads promising weight loss. Is there really a pill that "melts away fat" as you sit in front of the TV? Perhaps, but in virtually every case these weight-loss pills either don't work or are sold as part of an overall program recommending exercise and changes in diet. The same is true for so-called cognitive en-

Tests indicate that ginkgo biloba may live up to its popular reputation as a plant that enhances memory.

hancers. These supplements are often sold with established strategies for improving memory and problem solving (such as using mental imagery—see Chapter 8), making it difficult to tell whether it's the drug or the strategies that are responsible for any success. It's also a wise idea to consult a physician before starting medications of any kind. Many supplements, even ginkgo, can have dangerous side effects.

In principle, though, most neuroscientists are optimistic about the future—most believe that drugs will be developed to improve a variety of mental functions, such as helping us to learn. At the same time, these developments are bound to raise a host of ethical questions. Do we really want our children taking drugs to improve their learning potential or to make them more competitive intellectually? Perhaps, but the widespread implications of such actions are not yet understood (see Schacter, 2001, for some discussion of these ethical issues).

little or no apparent input from the environment. A continuously active cell is adaptive because more information can be coded by increasing or decreasing a firing rate than by simply turning a neuron on or off.

Because the brain contains roughly 100 billion neurons, which is comparable to the number of stars in the Milky Way Galaxy, it's impractical to try to map out individual neural connections. So how can we ever hope to discover how everything works together to produce behavior? One solution is to study lower organisms, whose circuits of neurons are less complex and more easily mapped. Another option is to try to simulate activities of the mind—such as simple learning and memory processes—by creating artificial networks of neurons on computers.

At this point, no one has come close to achieving anything resembling an artificial brain, but simple computerized networks have been developed that show brain-like properties. For example, computerized neural networks can recognize objects when given incomplete information and can perform reasonably well if artificially damaged. If a subset of input units is turned off, perhaps mimicking damage to the brain, activation of the remaining units can still be sufficient to reproduce the correct output response. This is an adaptive characteristic of both neural circuits in the brain and neural networks. Each is able to sustain damage, or lesion, and still produce the correct responses (see Kolb, 1999).

Test Yourself | 3.1

Test your knowledge about neurons and how they communicate. Select your answers from the following list of terms: dendrites, soma, axon, terminal buttons, action potential, neurotransmitters, refractory period. *(You will find the answers in the Appendix.)*

1. The main body of the cell, where excitatory and inhibitory messages combine: _____
2. The long tail-like part of a neuron that serves as the cell's main transmitter device: _____
3. The all-or-none electrical signal that travels to the end of the axon, causing the release of chemical messengers: _____

4. The branchlike fibers that extend outward from a neuron and receive information from other neurons: _____
5. Acetylcholine, serotonin, GABA, and dopamine are all examples of _____.

Initiating Behavior: A Division of Labor

LEARNING GOALS
- Describe the basic organization of the nervous system.
- Explain the techniques researchers use to study the brain.
- Describe the major structures of the brain and their functions.
- Discuss how the two hemispheres coordinate brain functions.

AS A WHOLE, THE NERVOUS SYSTEM has a lot of tough problems to solve. Besides generating behavior and mental processes such as thinking and feeling, the brain must maintain a beating heart, control breathing, and signal the body that it's time to eat. If your body is deprived of food or water or if its constant internal temperature gets out of whack, you must be motivated to find food, water, or the appropriate shelter. Even the simplest of everyday activities—producing spoken language, walking, perceiving a complex visual scene—requires a great deal of coordination among the muscles and sensory organs of the body. To accomplish these different functions, the nervous system divides its labor.

The Central and Peripheral Nervous Systems

As noted earlier, the nervous system is divided into two major parts, the central nervous system and the peripheral nervous system. The central nervous system consists of the brain and spinal cord and acts as the central executive of the body. Decisions are made here, and messages are then communicated to the rest of the body via bundles of axons called **nerves**. The nerves outside the brain and spinal cord form the peripheral nervous system.

It is through the peripheral nervous system that muscles are moved, internal organs are regulated, and sensory input is directed toward the brain. As you can see in ▌Figure 3.6, the peripheral nervous system can be divided further into the somatic and autonomic systems. Information travels to the brain and spinal cord through

nerves Bundles of axons that make up neural "transmission cables."

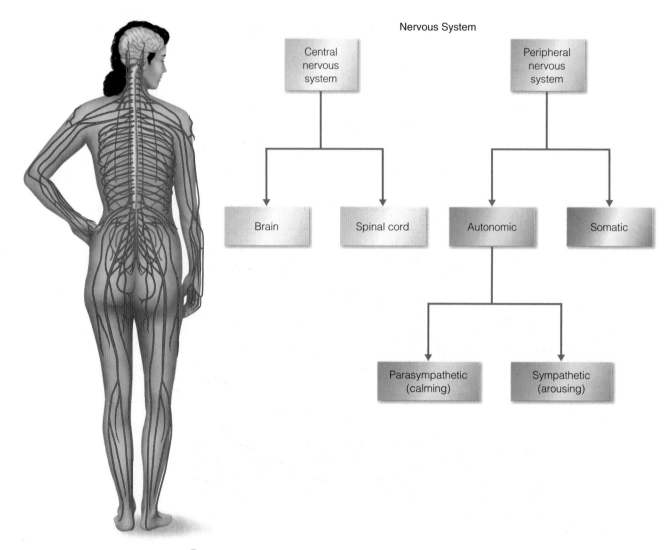

Nervous System

Central nervous system		Peripheral nervous system	
Brain	Spinal cord	Autonomic	Somatic

Autonomic:
- Parasympathetic (calming)
- Sympathetic (arousing)

▌FIGURE 3.6 The Nervous System
The central nervous system contains the brain and the spinal cord, and the peripheral nervous system has various subsystems. (Based on Kalat, 1996)

somatic system The collection of nerves that transmits information toward the brain and connects to the skeletal muscles to initiate movement; part of the peripheral nervous system.

autonomic system The collection of nerves that controls the more automatic needs of the body (such as heart rate, digestion, blood pressure); part of the peripheral nervous system.

afferent (sensory) nerve pathways; *efferent* (motor) nerve pathways carry central nervous system messages outward to the muscles and glands. The **somatic system** consists of the nerves that transmit sensory information toward the brain, as well as the nerves that connect to the skeletal muscles to initiate movement. Without the somatic system, information about the environment could not reach the brain, nor could we begin a movement of any kind. The **autonomic system** controls the more automatic needs of the body, such as heart rate, digestion, blood pressure, and the activities of internal glands. These two systems work together to make certain that information about the world is communicated to the brain for interpretation, that movements are carried out, and that the life-sustaining activities of the body are continued.

One critical function of the autonomic system, besides performing the automatic "housekeeping" activities that keep the body alive, is to help us handle and recover from emergency situations. When we're faced with an emergency, such as a sudden attack, our bodies typically produce a fight-or-flight response. The *sympathetic division* of the autonomic system triggers the release of chemicals, creating a state of readiness (e.g., by increasing heart rate, blood pressure, and breathing rate). After the emergency has passed, the *parasympathetic division* calms the body down by slowing heart rate and lowering blood pressure. Parasympathetic activity also helps increase the body's supply of stored energy, which may be diminished in response to the emergency situation.

How We Determine Brain Function

Before we embark on a detailed examination of the structure of the brain, let's consider the techniques that researchers use to determine how various parts of the brain actually work. The anatomical features of the nervous system as a whole—the various nerve tracts and so on—can be studied through dissection of the body. But the dissection of brain tissue, which contains billions of neurons, tells only a limited story. To determine the architecture of the brain, researchers need a broader set of tools. We'll briefly consider three popular techniques: (1) the study of brain damage, (2) activating the brain, and (3) monitoring the brain in action.

Brain Damage   The study of brain damage is one of the oldest methods for determining brain function. A patient arrives with an injury—such as a blow to the right side of the head—and complains of a particular problem, such as trouble moving the left side of the body. In this way, a link is established between a brain area and its function. As early as the 19th century, it was known that damage to the left side of the brain can create very specific speech difficulties. Destruction of *Wernicke's area* results in a patient who cannot easily understand spoken language (Wernicke, 1874); damage to *Broca's area* produces a patient who can understand but not easily produce spoken language (Broca, 1861). Cases such as these suggest that different psychological functions are controlled by specific areas of the brain.

Neuroscientists continue to make significant advances by studying brain injury. For example, brain damaged patients have recently taught us a great deal about how knowledge is represented in the brain (Martin, 2007) and about how we interact with objects and tools (Daprati & Sirigu, 2006). But case studies of brain damage have limitations. For one thing, researchers have no control over when and where the injury occurs. In addition, most instances of brain damage, either from an accident or from a tumor or a stroke, produce widespread damage. So it's difficult to know exactly which portion of the damaged brain is responsible for the behavioral or psychological problem. As we saw in Chapter 2, case studies can be rich sources of information, but the researcher typically lacks important controls.

To learn whether this man may be suffering from some kind of brain damage, assessment tests are performed at a memory disorders clinic.

© Dan McCoy/Rainbow

Electrical stimulator

Connection
to stimulator

Rotating drum

Pen

Connection
to recorder

Cumulative
response recorder

FIGURE 3.7 Electrical Stimulation
When the rat presses a bar, a small pulse of electric current is delivered to its brain. Stimulation of certain brain areas appears to be quite rewarding to the rat because it presses the bar very rapidly.

Researchers can observe the electrical activity of a person's brain with the EEG device, which records gross electrical activity in different regions.

© Richard T. Nowitz/CORBIS

To establish the true function of a particular brain structure, it helps to observe the effect of damage or lesion in a controlled way. Researchers have taken advantage of the fact that brain tissue contains no pain receptors to explore brain function in lower animals. It's possible to destroy, or *lesion*, particular regions of an animal's brain by administering an electric current, injecting chemicals, or cutting tissue. Even here it is difficult to pinpoint the damage exactly (because everything in the brain is interconnected), but lesioning techniques have become increasingly accurate in recent years (Bergvall, Fahlke, & Hansen, 1996; Jarrad, 1993). Animal lesioning studies have frequently led to significant advances in our understanding of the brain (Pinel, 1999).

Activating the Brain It's also possible to activate the brain directly by capitalizing on the electrochemical nature of the communication network. Essentially, messages can be created where none would have normally occurred. Chemicals can be injected that excite, rather than destroy, the neurons in a particular area of the brain. Researchers can also insert small wire electrodes into brain tissue, allowing an area's cells to be stimulated electrically. The researcher initiates a message externally, then observes behavior.

Electrical stimulation techniques have been used primarily with animals. It's possible to implant an electrode in such a way as to allow an animal to move freely about in its environment (see ▌Figure 3.7). A small pulse of current can then be delivered to various brain regions whenever the researcher desires. Studies have shown that electrical brain stimulation can cause animals to suddenly start eating, drinking, engaging in sexual behavior, or preparing for an attack. Using electrical stimulation, researchers have discovered what might be "reward" or "pleasure" centers in the brains of rats, leading the animals to engage repeatedly in whatever behavior led to the stimulation (Leon & Gallistel, 1998; Olds, 1958). For example, if rats are taught that pressing a metal bar leads to electrical stimulation of a reward area, they will press the bar thousands of times an hour. (The natural inference, of course, is that the stimulation is pleasurable, although we really have no way to tell what a concept like "pleasure" means to a rat.)

The electrical stimulation technique is used to link behavior to activity in specific areas in the brain. For example, a behavior that is produced by stimulation of brain region X but not by stimulation of brain region Y suggests that region X plays at least some role in the overall behavior. However, the precise mapping of behaviors to brain locations remains difficult. It's always possible to argue, for example, that a stimulated area is required to produce a particular behavior but that it does not act alone—it might serve only as a communication link, or relay connection, to some other brain region that actually starts the behavior.

Under some circumstances, it's possible to stimulate cells in the human brain and note the effects. During certain kinds of brain surgery (such as surgery to reduce the seizures produced by epilepsy), the patient is kept awake while the brain is stimulated from time to time with an electrode. Because there are no pain receptors in the brain, the patient typically receives only a local anesthetic prior to the surgery (along with some drugs for relaxation). Keeping the patient awake is necessary because the surgeon can stimulate an abnormal area, prior to removal, to make sure that vital capabilities such as speech or movement will not be affected. Electrical stimulation under these conditions has caused patients to produce involuntary movement, hear buzzing noises, and in some rare instances even experience what they report to be memories (Penfield & Perot, 1963).

Monitoring the Brain   Brain lesioning and electrical stimulation are effective research tools, but they're really not practical (or always ethical) for use with humans. Fortunately, other techniques can be applied more readily to the study of people. The **electroencephalograph** (**EEG**) is a device that simply monitors the gross electrical activity of the brain. Recording electrodes attached to the scalp measure global changes in the electrical potentials of thousands of brain cells in the form of line tracings, or brain waves. The EEG is useful not only as a research tool but also for diagnostic purposes. Brain disorders, including psychological disorders, can sometimes be detected through abnormalities in brain waves (Clementz, Keil, & Kissler, 2004).

A three-dimensional picture of the brain, including abnormalities in brain tissue, can be obtained through a **computerized tomography scan** (or **CT scan**). CT scanners use computers to detect how highly focused beams of X-rays change as they pass through the body at various angles and orientations. CT scans are most often used by physicians to detect tumors or injuries to the brain, but they can also be used to determine whether there is a physical basis for some chronic behavioral or psychological disorder.

Other imaging devices are designed to obtain a snapshot of the brain *at work*. These techniques help the researcher determine how various tasks, such as reading a book, affect individual parts of the brain. In **positron emission tomography** (**PET**), the patient ingests a harmless radioactive substance, which is then absorbed into the cells of active brain regions. When the person is performing a specific task, such as speaking or reading, the working areas of the brain absorb more of the ingested radioactive material. The PET scanner then develops a picture that reveals how the radioactive substance has distributed itself over time. It is assumed that those parts of the brain with the most concentrated traces of radioactive material probably play a significant role in the task being performed.

Another technique that can be used to isolate both structure and function in the brain is **magnetic resonance imaging** (**MRI**). MRI has two main advantages over PET scanning: It doesn't require the participant to ingest any chemicals, and it's capable of producing extremely detailed, three-dimensional images of the brain. MRI technology capitalizes on the fact that atoms behave in systematic ways in the presence of magnetic fields and radio-wave pulses. Although expensive to build and use, MRIs have proven to be excellent diagnostic tools for spotting brain damage, tumor growth, and other abnormalities.

More recent applications of what is called "functional MRI" use the MRI technology to map changes in blood flow or oxygen use as the patient thinks or behaves. Functional MRI, like PET scanning, is helping researchers determine where task-specific

electroencephalograph (EEG) A device used to monitor the gross electrical activity of the brain.

computerized tomography scan (CT scan) The use of highly focused beams of X-rays to construct detailed anatomical maps of the living brain.

positron emission tomography (PET) A method for measuring how radioactive substances are absorbed in the brain; it can be used to detect how specific tasks activate different areas of the living brain.

magnetic resonance imaging (MRI) A device that uses magnetic fields and radio-wave pulses to construct detailed, three-dimensional images of the brain; "functional" MRIs can be used to map changes in blood oxygen use as a function of task activity.

PET scans can demonstrate how a harmless radioactive substance is absorbed into the cells of brain regions active during various degrees of visual stimulation.

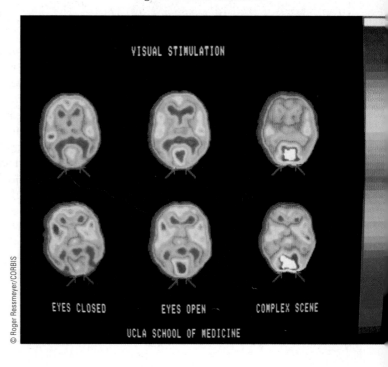

VISUAL STIMULATION

EYES CLOSED   EYES OPEN   COMPLEX SCENE

UCLA SCHOOL OF MEDICINE

© Roger Ressmeyer/CORBIS

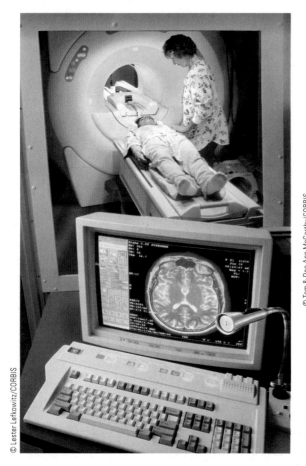

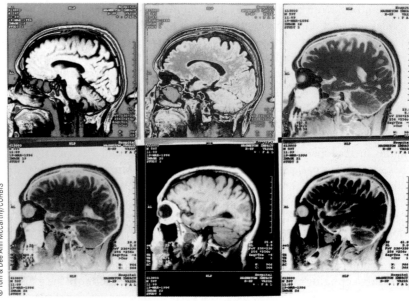

The magnetic resonance imaging device (MRI) can clarify structure and pinpoint some functions in the brain. Because MRIs produce extremely detailed images of the brain, they are excellent tools for diagnosing damage, tumor growth, and other physical abnormalities.

processing occurs in the brain. So far, this popular new technique has helped to isolate the brain regions associated with visual processing, language, attention, and memory (Gabrieli, 1998; Poldrack & Wagner, 2004). There is some evidence to suggest that functional MRIs may even help psychologists distinguish between true and false memories: When we falsely remember something that didn't occur, the blood flow patterns in the brain are somewhat different from those seen when we remember an actual event (Schacter, Gallo, & Kensinger, 2007). Exactly what these results mean is still a matter of debate, but functional MRI is clearly a very powerful investigative tool.

Brain Structures and Their Functions

Let's now turn our attention to the brain itself. Remember, it's here that mental processes are represented through the simultaneous activities of billions of individual neurons. Particular regions in the brain contribute unique features to an experience, helping to create a psychological whole. Your perception of a cat is not controlled by a single cell, or even by a single group of cells, but rather by different brain areas that detect the color of the fur or recognize a characteristic meow.

I'll divide our discussion of the brain into sections that correspond to the brain's three major anatomical regions: the *hindbrain*, the *midbrain*, and the *forebrain*.

The Hindbrain: Basic Life Support The **hindbrain** is the most primitive part of the brain, and it sits at the juncture point where the spinal cord and brain merge (see ▌Figure 3.8). *Primitive* is an appropriate term for two reasons. First, structures in the hindbrain act as the basic life-support system for the body—no creative thoughts or complex emotions originate here. Second, from the standpoint of evolution, the hindbrain is the oldest part of the brain. Similar structures, with similar functions, can be found throughout the animal kingdom. You can think of the hindbrain as a kind of base camp, with higher structures that are situated farther up into the brain controlling increasingly more complex mental processes. Not surprisingly, damage to these lower regions of the brain seriously affects the ability of the organism to survive.

hindbrain A primitive part of the brain that sits at the juncture point where the brain and spinal cord merge. Structures in the hindbrain, including the medulla, pons, and reticular formation, act as the basic life-support system for the body.

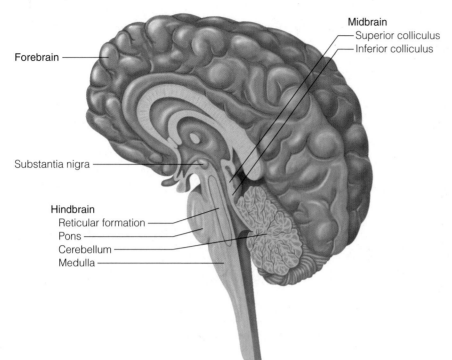

FIGURE 3.8 The Hindbrain and Midbrain
The hindbrain (blue) acts as the basic life-support system for the body, controlling such things as heart rate, blood pressure, and respiration. The midbrain (orange) contains structures that help coordinate and relay information to higher centers.

As Figure 3.8 shows, the hindbrain contains several important anatomical substructures. The *medulla* and the *pons* are associated with the control of heart rate, breathing, blood pressure, and reflexes such as vomiting, sneezing, and coughing. Both areas serve as pathways for neural impulses traveling to and from the spinal cord (the word *pons* means "bridge"). These areas are particularly sensitive to the lethal effects of drugs such as alcohol, barbiturates, and cocaine. The hindbrain also contains the *reticular formation*, a network of neurons and nerves linked to the control of general arousal, sleep, and consciousness (Parvizi & Damasio, 2001).

Finally, at the base of the brain sits a structure that resembles a smaller version of the brain—a kind of "brainlet." This is the **cerebellum** (which means "little brain"), a structure involved in the preparation, selection, and coordination of complex motor movements such as hitting a golf ball, playing the piano, or learning how to use and manipulate tools (Lewis, 2006). No one is certain about the exact role the cerebellum plays in movement—for instance, it may be a critical component of how we learn to time motor movements (Mauk et al., 2000). Brain-imaging studies have shown that the cerebellum is actually involved in a whole host of tasks, including language, memory, reasoning, and perhaps even the perception of pain (Saab & Willis, 2003).

cerebellum A hindbrain structure at the base of the brain that is involved in the coordination of complex motor skills.

The Midbrain: Neural Relay Stations
The **midbrain** lies deep within the brain atop the hindbrain. Perhaps because of its central position, the midbrain and its accompanying structures receive input from multiple sources, including the sense organs. The *tectum* and its component structures, the *superior colliculus* and *inferior colliculus*, serve as important relay stations for visual and auditory information and help coordinate reactions to sensory events in the environment (such as moving the head in response to a sudden sound).

The midbrain also contains a group of neurons, collectively called the *substantia nigra*, that release the neurotransmitter dopamine from their terminal buttons. As you saw earlier in the chapter, dopamine tends to produce inhibitory effects in the body, and it seems to be involved in a number of physical and psychological disorders. For example, the rigidity of movement that characterizes Parkinson disease apparently results from decreased levels of dopamine in the brain. Indeed, the death

midbrain The middle portion of the brain, containing such structures as the tectum, superior colliculus, and inferior colliculus; midbrain structures serve as neural relay stations and may help coordinate reactions to sensory events.

Concept Review | Brain Investigation Techniques

TECHNIQUE	OVERVIEW	WHAT CAN IT SHOW?
Brain damage and lesion	Associate areas of brain damage with changes in behavioral function	The areas of the brain that may be responsible for different functions
Electrical brain stimulation	Uses electrical or chemical stimulation to excite brain areas	How activation of certain brain regions affects behavior
EEG (Electroencephalograph)	Uses electrodes to record gross electrical activity of the brain	How overall activity in the brain changes during certain activities, such as sleeping, and may allow for detection of disorders
Computerized tomography (CT) scan	Passes X-rays through the body at various angles and orientations	Tumors or injuries to the brain, as well as the structural bases for chronic behavioral or psychological disorders
Positron emission tomography (PET)	A radioactive substance is ingested; active brain areas absorb the substance; PET scanner reveals distribution of the substance	How various tasks (such as reading a book) affect different parts of the brain
Magnetic resonance imaging (MRI)	Monitors systematic activity of atoms in the presence of magnetic fields and radio-wave pulses.	A three-dimensional view of the brain, serving as a diagnostic tool for brain abnormalities, such as tumors. Functional MRI allows for observation of brain function.

of neurons in the substantia nigra is believed to be the cause of the disorder. Exactly why this portion of the midbrain degenerates is not known, although both genetic and environmental factors are thought to be involved (Przedborski, 2005).

The Forebrain: Higher Mental Functioning Moving up past the midbrain we encounter the **forebrain** (see ▌Figure 3.9). The most recognizable feature of the forebrain is the **cerebral cortex**, which is the grayish matter full of fissures, folds, and crevices that covers the outside of the brain (*cortex* is Latin for "bark"). The cortex is quite large in humans, accounting for approximately 80% of the total volume of the human brain (Kolb & Whishaw, 2003). We'll look at the cerebral cortex in depth after a review of the other structures of the forebrain. Beneath the cerebral cortex are subcortical structures, including the thalamus, the hypothalamus, and the limbic system. The **thalamus** is positioned close to the midbrain and is an important gathering point for input from the various senses. Indeed, the thalamus is the main processing center for sensory input prior to its being sent to the upper regions of the cortex. Besides acting as an efficient relay center, information from the various senses is probably combined in some way here.

The **hypothalamus**, which lies just below the thalamus, is important in motivation, particularly the regulation of eating, drinking, body temperature, and sexual behavior. In experiments on lower animals, stimulating different regions of the hypothalamus kick-starts a variety of behaviors. For example, male and female rats will show characteristic sexual responses when one portion of the hypothalamus is stimulated (Marson & McKenna, 1994), whereas damage to another region of the hypothalamus can seriously affect regular eating behavior (Sclafani, 1994). Neuroimaging studies have shown that the hypothalamus becomes active when monkeys are exposed to sexually arousing odors from receptive females (Ferris et al., 2001). The hypothalamus also plays a key role in the release of hormones by the pituitary gland; you'll read about the actions of hormones shortly when we discuss the endocrine system.

The **limbic system** is made up of several interrelated brain structures, including the amygdala and the hippocampus. The *amygdala* is a small, almond-shaped piece of brain (from the Greek word meaning "almond") that's linked to a number of moti-

forebrain The outer portion of the brain, including the cerebral cortex and the structures of the limbic system.

cerebral cortex The outer layer of the brain, considered to be the seat of higher mental processes.

thalamus A relay station in the forebrain thought to be an important gathering point for input from the senses.

hypothalamus A forebrain structure thought to play a role in the regulation of various motivational activities, including eating, drinking, and sexual behavior.

limbic system A system of structures thought to be involved in motivational and emotional behaviors (the amygdala) and memory (the hippocampus).

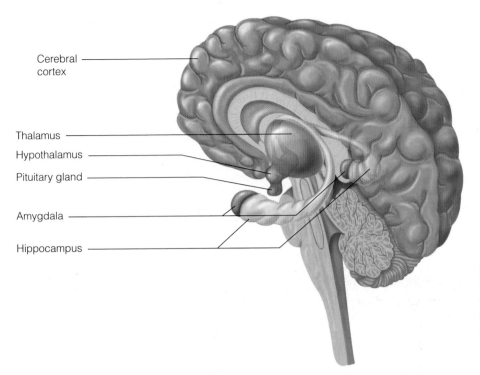

Cerebral cortex

Thalamus

Hypothalamus

Pituitary gland

Amygdala

Hippocampus

▌ FIGURE 3.9 The Forebrain
The forebrain includes structures such as the limbic system and the cerebral cortex. Structures in the limbic system are thought to be involved in motivation, emotion, and memory. The cerebral cortex controls higher mental processes.

vational and emotional behaviors, including fear, aggression, and defensive actions. Destruction of portions of the amygdala in lower animals, through brain lesioning, can produce an extremely passive animal—one that will do nothing in response to provocation. Neuroimaging studies in humans have found that activation in the amygdala increases when people look at faces showing fear, anger, sadness, or even happiness (Yang et al., 2002); moreover, people with damage to the amygdala sometimes have difficulty recognizing emotions like sadness in facial expressions (Adolphs & Tranel, 2004). The *hippocampus* (Greek for "seahorse," which it resembles anatomically) is important for the formation of memories, particularly our memory for specific personal events (Eichenbaum, 2003). People with severe damage to the hippocampus sometimes live in a kind of perpetual present—they are aware of the world around them, and they recognize people and things known to them prior to the damage, but they remember almost nothing new. These patients act as if they are continually awakening from a dream; experiences slip away, and they recall nothing from only moments before. We'll consider the hippocampus and the role it plays in memory in more detail in Chapter 8.

The Cerebral Cortex   On reaching the cerebral cortex, we finally find the seat of higher mental processes. Thoughts, the sense of self, the ability to reason and solve problems—each arises from neurons firing in patterns somewhere in specialized regions of the cerebral cortex. The cortex is divided into two *hemispheres*, left and right. The left hemisphere controls the sensory and motor functions for the right side of the body, and the right hemisphere controls these functions for the left side of the body. A structure called the corpus callosum, which I'll discuss later, serves as a communication bridge between the two hemispheres.

Each hemisphere can be further divided into four parts, or lobes: the *frontal, temporal, parietal,* and *occipital lobes* (see ▌ Figure 3.10). These lobes appear to control particular body functions, such as visual processing by the occipital lobe and language processing by the frontal and temporal lobes. A slight warning is in order here, however: Although researchers have discovered that particular areas in the brain seem to control highly specialized functions, there is almost certainly considerable overlap of function in the brain. Most brain regions are designed to play multiple roles.

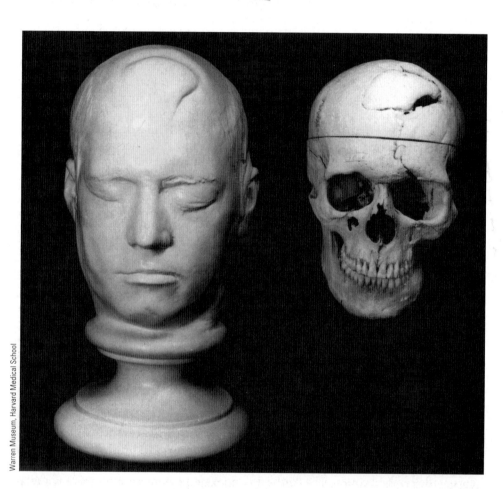

Left hemisphere

Right hemisphere

Frontal lobe

Motor cortex

Somatosensory cortex

Broca's area

Parietal lobe

Temporal lobe

Occipital lobe

Wernicke's area

FIGURE 3.10 The Cerebral Cortex
The cerebral cortex is divided into two hemispheres—left and right—each consisting of four lobes. The lobes are specialized to control particular functions, such as visual processing in the occipital lobe and language processing in the frontal and temporal lobes.

Warren Museum, Harvard Medical School

After Phineas Gage suffered a blasting accident that substantially damaged his frontal lobe, he was "no longer Gage," according to friends and acquaintances.

How can we possibly assign something like a "sense of self" to a specific area of the cerebral cortex? The evidence is primarily correlational—some portion of the cortex is damaged, or stimulated electrically, and behavioral changes are observed. We know, for example, that damage to the frontal lobe of the cortex can produce dramatic changes in personality. In 1848 a railroad foreman named Phineas Gage was packing black powder into a blasting hole when, accidentally, the powder discharged, driving a thick iron rod through the left side of his head (entering just below his left eye and exiting the left-top portion of his skull). The result was a 3-inch hole in his skull and a complete shredding of a large portion of the left frontal lobe of his brain. Remarkably, Gage recovered, and with the exception of the loss of vision in his left eye and some slight facial paralysis, he was able to move about freely and perform a variety of tasks. But he was "no longer Gage" in the minds of his friends and acquaintances—his personality changed completely. Whereas prior to his injury he was known to all as someone with "a well-balanced mind" and as "a shrewd businessman," after the meeting of brain and iron rod he became "fitful, irreverent, indulging at times in the grossest profanity (which was not previously his custom)" (Bigelow, 1850).

The **frontal lobes** are the largest lobes in the cortex and play a role in many functions, including planning and decision making, certain kinds of memory, and personality (as our description of Phineas Gage indicated). The frontal lobes were once the site of a famous surgical operation, the prefrontal lobotomy, which was performed on people suffering from severe and untreatable psychological disorders. The operation was performed to calm the patient and reduce symptoms, which it sometimes did, but the side effects were often severe. Patients lost their ability to take initiative or make plans, and they often appeared to lose their social inhibitions (like Gage). For these reasons, the operation fell out of favor as an acceptable treatment for psychological disorders.

The frontal lobes also contain the *motor cortex,* which controls voluntary muscle movements, as well as areas involved in language production and, possibly, higher-level thought processes (Baldo & Shimamura, 1998). Broca's area, which is involved in speech production, is located in a portion of the left frontal lobe in most people. The motor cortex sits at the rear of the frontal lobe in both hemispheres; axons from the motor cortex project down to motor neurons in the spinal cord and elsewhere. If neurons in this area of the brain are stimulated electrically, muscle contractions—the twitch of a finger or the jerking of a foot—can occur. Researchers have also discovered an intriguing relation between body parts and regions of the motor cortex. It turns out that there is a mapping, or *topographic* organization, in which adjacent areas of the body, such as the hand and the wrist, are activated by adjacent neurons in the motor cortex.

Among the most startling discoveries in recent years are so-called mirror neurons in these regions of the brain. Neuroimaging studies have revealed, not surprisingly, that regions in the motor cortex become active when we engage in simple motor movements, such as biting an apple or clapping our hands. However, neurons in these same regions become active when we simply *observe* someone else performing the same actions. This suggests that we may be able to recognize actions performed by others through matching activation in our own motor systems (Buccino, Binkofski, & Riggio, 2003). Even more amazing, these neurons become active even when we observe members of other species, such as dogs and monkeys, engaging in simple motor activities (Buccino et al., 2004). Some neuroscientists are convinced that mirror neurons play a role in our ability to learn from others, empathize with their actions, and in some developmental disorders such as autism (Iacoboni & Dapretto, 2006).

Topographic organization is found in many regions of the cerebral cortex. For example, the **parietal lobe** contains the *somatosensory cortex,* through which we experience the sensations of touch, temperature, and pain. The brush of a lover's kiss on the cheek excites neurons that lie close to those that would be excited by the same kiss to the lips. In addition, as ▌Figure 3.11 on page 78 demonstrates, there is a relationship between sensitivity to touch (or the ability to control a movement) and size of the representation in the cortex. Those areas of the body that show particular sensitivity to touch, or are associated with fine motor control (such as the face, lips, and fingers), have relatively large areas of neural representation in the cortex. It's not surprising, as a consequence, that we display affection by kissing on the lips rather than, say, rubbing our backs together!

The **temporal lobes,** which lie on either side of the cortex, are involved in processing auditory information received from the left and right ears. As you'll see in Chapter 5, there is a close relationship between the activities of particular neurons in the temporal lobe and the perception of certain frequencies of sound. As noted earlier, one region of the temporal lobe, Wernicke's area, is involved in language

---

frontal lobe One of four anatomical regions of each hemisphere of the cerebral cortex, located on the top front of the brain; it contains the motor cortex and may be involved in higher-level thought processes.

CRITICAL THINKING

Do you think it's possible that personality is completely localized in one portion of the brain? If so, how could you explain the fact that someone's personality can seem to change depending on the situation?

parietal lobe One of four anatomical regions of each hemisphere of the cerebral cortex, located roughly on the top middle portion of the brain; it contains the somatosensory cortex, which controls the sense of touch.

temporal lobe One of four anatomical regions of each hemisphere of the cerebral cortex, located roughly on the sides of the brain; it's involved in certain aspects of speech and language perception.

Concept Review | Brain Areas, Structures, and Functions

BRAIN AREA	GENERAL FUNCTION	STRUCTURES AND SPECIFIC FUNCTION
Hindbrain	Basic life support	**medulla** and **pons**: associated with the control of heart rate, breathing, and certain reflexes **reticular formation**: control of general arousal, sleep, and some movement of the head **cerebellum**: involved in preparation, selection, and coordination of complex motor movement
Midbrain	Houses neural relay stations	**tectum** (components are superior colliculus and inferior colliculus): relay stations for visual and auditory information **substantia nigra**: group of neurons that release the neurotransmitter dopamine
Forebrain	Higher mental functions	**thalamus**: initial gathering point for sensory input; information combined and relayed here **hypothalamus**: helps regulate eating, drinking, body temperature, and sexual behavior **hippocampus**: important to the formation of memories **amygdala**: linked to fear, aggression, and defensive behaviors **cerebral cortex**: the seat of higher mental processes, including sense of self and the ability to reason and solve problems

comprehension (the ability to understand what someone is saying). A person with damage to Wernicke's area might be able to repeat a spoken sentence aloud with perfect diction and control yet not understand a word of it; brain-imaging studies also reveal that Wernicke's area becomes active when people are asked to perform tasks that require meaningful verbal processing (Abdullaev & Posner, 1997). For most people, speech is localized in the temporal lobe of the left hemisphere.

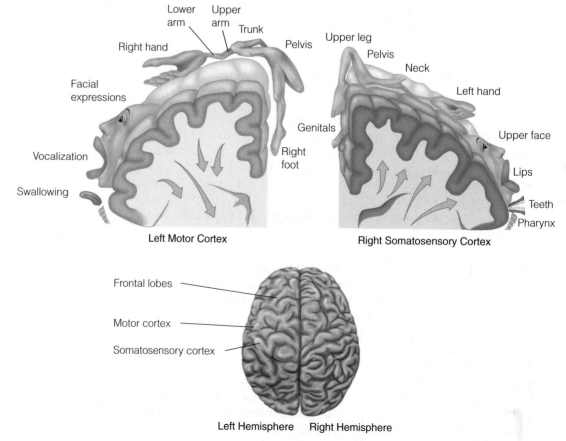

FIGURE 3.11 Cortex Specialization
The motor cortex is at the back of the frontal lobe in each cerebral hemisphere. In a systematic body-to-brain relationship, adjacent parts of the body are activated by neurons in adjacent areas of the cortex. The somatosensory cortex, in the parietal lobe of each hemisphere, controls the sense of touch; again, there is a systematic mapping arrangement. Notice that in each type of cortex, the size of the cortical representation is related to the sensitivity of the body part.

Finally, at the far back of the brain sit the **occipital lobes**, where most visual processing occurs. I'll consider the organization of this part of the brain in more detail in Chapter 5; for now, recognize that it is here that the information received from receptor cells in the eyes is analyzed and turned into visual images. The brain paints an image of the external world through a remarkable division of labor—there appear to be processing stations in the occipital lobe designed to integrate separate signals about color, motion, and form (Sincich & Horton, 2005). Not surprisingly, damage to the occipital lobe tends to produce highly specific visual problems—you might lose the ability to recognize a face, a contour moving in a particular direction, or a color (Bouvier & Engel, 2006; Zeki, 1992).

The Divided Brain

The division of labor in the brain is particularly striking in the study of the two separate halves, or hemispheres, of the cerebral cortex. Although the brain is designed to operate as a whole, the hemispheres are *lateralized*, which means that each side is responsible for performing unique and independent functions (Hellige, 1990). As you've seen, the right hemisphere of the brain controls the movements of the left side of the body; the left hemisphere governs the right side. This means that stimulating a region of the motor cortex in the left cerebral hemisphere would cause a muscle on the right side of the body to twitch. Similarly, if cells in the occipital lobe of the right cerebral hemisphere are damaged, a blind spot develops in the left portion of the visual world. Lateralization undoubtedly serves some adaptive functions. For example, it may allow the brain to divide its labor in ways that produce more efficient processing.

Figure 3.12 shows how information received through the eyes travels to one side of the brain or the other. If you're looking straight ahead, an image coming from the left side of your body (the left visual field) falls on the inside half of the left eye and the outside half of the right eye; receptor cells in these locations transmit their images to the back of the right cerebral hemisphere. Both eyes project information directly to each hemisphere, as the figure shows, but information from the left visual field goes to the right hemisphere and vice versa.

Under normal circumstances, if an object approaches you from your left side, the information eventually arrives on both sides of your brain. There are two reasons for this. First, if you turn your head or eyes to look at the object—from left to right—its image is likely to fall on both the inside and the outside halves of each eye over time. It might start off on the inside half of the left eye, but as your eyes turn, the outside half will soon receive the message. Second, as noted earlier, a major communication bridge—the corpus callosum—connects the two brain halves. Information arriving at the right hemisphere, for example, is transported to the left hemisphere via the **corpus callosum** in just a few thousandths of a second (Saron & Davidson, 1989). This transfer process occurs automatically and requires no head or eye turning.

Splitting the Brain It's important for both sides of the brain to receive information about objects in the environment. To understand why, imagine what visual perception would be like for someone without a corpus callosum—someone with a "split brain." Suppose an object appears suddenly, with great velocity, in the person's left visual field. There's no time to move the head or eyes, only enough for a reflexive response. Our patient would be incapable of a coordinated response because the image would be registered only in the right hemisphere, which contains the machinery to control only the left side of the body. The split-brain patient would also be unable to name the menacing object, because the language comprehension and production centers are located, typically, on the left side of the brain.

occipital lobe One of four anatomical regions of each hemisphere of the cerebral cortex, located at the back of the brain; visual processing is controlled here.

corpus callosum The collection of nerve fibers that connects the two cerebral hemispheres and allows information to pass from one side to the other.

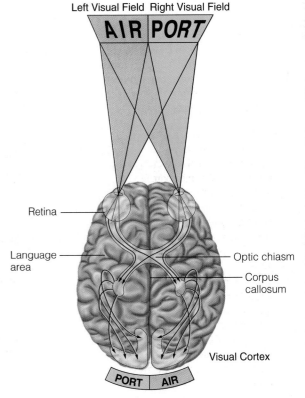

▌ **FIGURE 3.12 Visual Processing in the Two Hemispheres**
Images originating in the left visual field are projected to the right hemisphere, and information appearing in the right visual field is projected to the left hemisphere. Most language processing occurs in the left hemisphere, so split-brain patients can vocally report only stimuli that are shown in the right visual field. Here the subject can say only "port," the word available for processing in the left hemisphere.

Actually, hypothetical patients like the one just described really do exist; a number of people have split brains. Some were born without a corpus callosum (Sanders, 1989); others had their communication gateway cut on purpose by surgeons seeking to reduce the spread of epileptic seizures (Springer & Deutsch, 1989). The two hemispheres of split-brain patients are not broken or damaged by the operation. Information simply cannot easily pass from one side of the brain to the other. In fact, the behavior of most split-brain patients is essentially normal because most input from the environment still reaches both sides of their brain. These patients can turn their heads and eyes freely as they interact with the environment, allowing information to fall on receptor regions that transmit to both hemispheres. The abnormal nature of their brain becomes apparent only under manufactured conditions. For example, in a classic study by Gazzaniga, Bogen, and Sperry (1965), a variety of images (pictures, words, or symbols) were presented quickly to either the left or right visual fields of split-brain patients. Just like our hypothetical patient, when an image was shown to the right visual field, it was easily named because it could be processed by the language centers of the left hemisphere. For left visual field presentations, the patients remained perplexed and silent. It was later learned, however, that their silence did not mean that the brain failed to process the image. If the split-brain patients were asked to point to a picture of the object just shown, they could do so, but only with the left hand (Gazzaniga & LeDoux, 1978). The brain had received the input but could not respond verbally.

Hemispheric Specialization The two hemispheres of the cerebral cortex are clearly specialized to perform certain kinds of tasks. The right hemisphere, for example, appears to play a more important role in spatial tasks, such as fitting together the pieces of a puzzle or orienting oneself spatially in an environment. Patients with damage to the right hemisphere characteristically have trouble with spatial tasks, as do split-brain patients who must assemble a puzzle with their right hand. The right hemisphere also contributes uniquely to some aspects of emotional processing—for example, patients with damage to the right hemisphere have more trouble recognizing vocal emotional expressions. The left hemisphere—perhaps in part because of the lateralized language centers—contributes more to verbal tasks such as reading and

It's adaptive for both sides of the brain to process information from the environment; otherwise this woman would probably have difficulty developing a coordinated response to the rapidly arriving ball.

© John Livzey

writing.Still, a great deal of cooperation and collaboration goes on between the hemispheres. They interact continuously, and most mental processes, even language to a certain extent, depend on activity in both sides of the brain (Schirmer & Kotz, 2006). You think and behave with a whole brain, not a fragmented one. Moreover, if one side of the brain is damaged, regions in the other hemisphere can sometimes take over the lost functions (Gazzaniga et al., 1996). Specialization in the brain exists because it's sometimes adaptive for the two hemispheres to work independently—much in the same way that it's beneficial for members of a group to divide components of a difficult task rather than trying to cooperate on every small activity (Hellige, 1993).

Test Yourself 3.2

Test what you've learned about research into brain structures and their functions. Fill in each blank with one of the following terms: EEG, PET scan, hindbrain, midbrain, forebrain, cerebellum, hypothalamus, cortex, frontal lobes, limbic system, corpus callosum. (You will find the answers in the Appendix.)

1. A primitive part of the brain that controls basic life support functions such as heart rate and respiration: _____
2. A structure thought to be involved in a variety of motivational activities, including eating, drinking, and sexual behavior: _____
3. The portion of the cortex believed to be involved in higher-order thought processes (such as planning) as well as the initiation of voluntary motor movements: _____

4. A structure near the base of the brain that is involved in coordination of complex activities such as walking and playing the piano: _____
5. A device that is used to monitor the gross electrical activity of the brain: _____

Regulating Growth and Internal Functions: Extended Communication

LEARNING GOALS
- Explain how the endocrine system controls long-term and widespread communication needs.
- Discuss the role hormones play in gender-specific behaviors.

THE HUMAN BODY actually has two communication systems. The first, the nervous system, starts and controls most behaviors—thoughts, voluntary movements, and sensations and perceptions of the external world. But the body also has long-term communication needs. For example, the body must initiate and control growth and provide long-term regulation of numerous internal biological systems. Consequently, a second communication system has developed: a network of glands called the **endocrine system**, which uses the bloodstream, rather than neurons, as its main information courier. Chemicals called **hormones** are released into the blood by the various endocrine glands and control a variety of internal functions.

The word *hormone* comes from the Greek *hormon*, which means "to set into motion." Hormones play a role in many basic, life-sustaining activities in the body. Hunger, thirst, sexual behavior, and the fight-or-flight response are all regulated in part by an interplay between the nervous system and hormones released by the endocrine glands. The fact that the body has two communication systems rather than one makes sense from an adaptive standpoint. One system, communication among neurons, governs transmissions that are quick and detailed; the other, the endocrine system, initiates the slower but more widespread and longer-lasting effects. In the

endocrine system A network of glands that uses the bloodstream, rather than neurons, to send chemical messages that regulate growth and other internal functions.

hormones Chemicals released into the blood by the various endocrine glands to help control a variety of internal regulatory functions.

following section, I'll consider the endocrine system in more detail and then consider how hormones influence some fundamental differences between men and women.

The Endocrine System

The chemical communication system of the endocrine glands differs in some important ways from the rapid-fire electrochemical activities of the nervous system. Communication in the nervous system tends to be localized, which means that a given neurotransmitter usually affects only cells in a small area. Hormones have widespread effects. Because hormones are carried by the blood, they travel throughout the body and interact with numerous target sites. Also in contrast to neurotransmitters, hormones have long-lasting effects. Whereas neural communication operates in time scales bordering on the blink of an eye, the endocrine system can produce effects lasting minutes, hours, or even days. In some animals, for example, it is circulating hormones that prepare them for seasonal migration or hibernation. Thus the endocrine system provides the body with a mechanism for both widespread and long-term communication that cannot be produced by interactions among neurons.

Although the endocrine and nervous systems communicate in different ways, their activities are closely coordinated. Structures in the brain (especially the hypothalamus) stimulate or inhibit the release of hormones by the glands; once released, these chemicals then feed back and affect the firing rates of neural impulses. The feedback loop balances and controls the regulatory activities of the body. The hypothalamus is of particular importance because it controls the pituitary gland. The **pituitary gland**, a kind of master gland, controls the secretion of hormones in response to signals from the hypothalamus; these hormones, in turn, regulate the activity of many of the other vital glands in the endocrine system. It is the pituitary gland, for example, that signals the testes in males to produce *testosterone* and the ovaries in females to produce *estrogen*—both of critical importance in sexual behavior and reproduction.

Let's consider one example of the endocrine system at work. You leave a party late, convinced you can walk home without incident. The streets, quiet without the noise of traffic, exert a calming influence as you pass the flashing traffic lights and the parked cars. But suddenly, across the street, two shadowy figures emerge from an alleyway and move in your direction. You draw in your breath, your stomach tightens, and your rapidly beating heart seems ready to explode from your chest. These whole-body reactions, critical in preparing you to fight or flee, are created by signals from the brain that lead to increased activity of the endocrine glands. The hypothalamus signals the *adrenal glands* (located above the kidneys) to begin secreting such hormones as *norepinephrine* and *epinephrine* into the blood. These hormones, in turn, produce energizing effects on the body, increasing heart rate and directing blood and oxygen flow to energy-demanding cells throughout the body. The body is now prepared for action, enhancing the likelihood of survival (see ▌Figure 3.13).

Are There Gender Effects?

Prior to birth, hormones released by the pituitary gland determine whether a child ends up with male or female sex organs. At puberty, an increase in sex hormones (testosterone and estrogen) leads males to develop facial hair and deep speaking voices and females to develop breasts and to begin menstruation. It is now suspected that hormones released during development affect the basic wiring patterns of men's and women's brains as well. Evidence suggests that men and women may think differently as the result of gender-specific activities of the endocrine system.

Psychologists Doreen Kimura and Elizabeth Hampson (1994) report, for example, that the performance of women and men on certain tasks changes significantly as the levels of sex hormones increase or decrease in the body. Women traditionally perform

pituitary gland A kind of master gland in the body that controls the release of hormones in response to signals from the hypothalamus.

CRITICAL THINKING

Initiation of the fight-or-flight response clearly has adaptive value. Can you think of any circumstances in which this response might actually lower the chances of an adaptive response?

Hypothalamus
Stimulates adrenal glands.

Adrenal Glands
Secrete norepinephrine and epinephrine into bloodstream.

Norepinephrine and Epinephrine
Cause energy surge and heart rate increase; blood is shunted away from the stomach and intestine to areas that require it; glucose is made available to the muscles.

❚ FIGURE 3.13 The Fight-or-Flight Response
In potentially dangerous situations, the endocrine system releases hormones that produce energizing effects in the body, increasing our chances of survival through fighting back or running away.

better than men on some tests of verbal ability, and their performance improves with high levels of estrogen in their body. Similarly, men show slightly better performance on some spatial tasks (such as imagining that three-dimensional objects are rotating), and their performance seems to be related to their testosterone levels. The evidence is correlational, which means we can't be sure it's the hormones that are causing the performance changes, but the data are suggestive of endocrine-based gender differences in thought (Janowsky, 2006; Kimura, 1999). Testosterone levels typically decline with age, and there is evidence that testosterone replacement therapy in elderly men can improve cognitive ability, particularly on memory and spatial tasks (Cherrier et al., 2005).

It's also the case that girls who have been exposed to an excess of male hormones during the initial stages of prenatal development, either because of a genetic disorder or from chemicals ingested by the mother during pregnancy, tend to be particularly tomboyish during development (Resnick et al., 1986), preferring to engage in play activities that are more traditionally associated with boys. In one study reported by Kimura (1992), researchers at UCLA compared the choice of toys by girls who either had or had not been exposed to excess male hormones during early development. The girls who had been exposed tended to prefer the typical masculine activities— smashing trucks and cars together, for example—more than the control girls did (also see Ogilvie et al., 2006).

Male and female brains also show anatomical differences, although such differences have often been exaggerated historically (Shields, 1975). Animal studies have confirmed that male and female rat brains are different; moreover, the differences are clearly attributable, in part, to the early influence of hormones (see Hines, 1982, for a review). For humans, the data are less clear and more controversial. Imaging studies have revealed gender differences in the thickness of cortical tissue, sometimes favoring female brains, but whether these anatomical differences account for behavioral differences in performing certain tasks is unclear (Luders et al., 2006). Interesting differences have also been found in response to brain damage. For example, damage can sometimes lead to specific deficits in knowledge categories, such as loss in knowledge about plants; women rarely, if ever, show selective deficits in plant knowledge, which may stem from how evolution has selectively shaped the development of male and female brains (Laiacona, Barbarotto, & Capitani, 2006).

The evidence supporting gender-based differences in brain anatomy and mental functioning is provocative and needs to be investigated further. Hormones released by the endocrine system are known to produce permanent changes early in human development, and it's certainly possible that actions later in life are influenced by these changes. But no direct causal link has yet been established between anatomical differences and the variations in intellectual functioning that are sometimes found between men and women. In fact, some researchers have argued that sex-based differences in brain organization may actually cause men and women to act more similarly than they would otherwise (De Vries & Boyle, 1998).

In addition, the performance differences of women and men on certain laboratory tasks aren't very large and don't reflect general ability. Many of the studies report that gender-based differences are extremely small (Halpern, 2000). To repeat a theme discussed in Chapter 1, it is very difficult to separate the effects of biology (nature) from the ongoing influences of the environment (nurture). Men and women are faced with different environmental demands and cultural expectations during their lifetimes. Without question, these demands help determine the actions they take and produce many of the behavioral differences that we see between the sexes. We will return to gender issues often in later chapters of this text.

There may indeed be sex differences in brain anatomy and functioning, but the decision of girls and boys to engage in stereotypical activities is strongly influenced by the environment as well.

© Justin Pumfrey/Getty Images/Taxi

© Angela Wyant/Getty Images/The Image Bank

Test Yourself 3.3

Test your knowledge about the differences between the endocrine system and the nervous system. For each statement, decide whether the endocrine *or* nervous system *is the most appropriate term to apply. (You will find the answers in the Appendix.)*

1. Communication effects tend to be localized, affecting only a small area: _____
2. Responsible for whole-body reactions, such as the fight-or-flight response: _____
3. The major determinant of sexual identity: _____
4. Communicates through the release of epinephrine and norepinephrine: _____
5. Operates quickly, with time scales bordering on the blink of an eye: _____

Adapting and Transmitting the Genetic Code

LEARNING GOALS
- Review natural selection and adaptation.
- Describe the basic principles of genetic transmission.
- Explain how psychologists study genetic influences on behavior.

BRAINS TEND TO ACT in regular and predictable ways. When you read a book or perform any visual task, a neuroimaging "scan" is certain to reveal activity in the occipital lobe of your cortex. If a stroke occurs in the left cerebral hemisphere, there's a good chance you'll find paralysis occurring on the right side of the body. But behavior, the main interest of psychology, remains remarkably difficult to predict. People react differently to exactly the same event—even if they're siblings raised in the same household. How do we explain this remarkable diversity of behavior, given that everyone carries around a similar 3- to 4-pound mass of brain tissue?

One answer is that no two brains are exactly alike. The patterns of neural activity that determine how we think and act are uniquely determined by our individual experiences and by the genetic material we've inherited from our parents. Most of us have no trouble accepting that experience is critical, but genetic influences are a little tougher to accept. Sure, hair color, eye color, and blood type may be expressions of fixed genetic influences, but how could genetics govern intelligence, personality, or emotionality?

Recognizing that heredity has a role is a given to the psychologist. As you'll see, I'll appeal to genetic principles repeatedly throughout our discussions—on a whole host of topics. But it's also important to remember that the genetic code serves two adaptive functions. First, genes provide us with a flexible plan, a recipe of sorts, for our physical and psychological development. Second, genes provide a means through which we're able to pass on physical and psychological characteristics to our offspring, thereby helping to maintain qualities that have adaptive significance.

Natural Selection and Adaptations

Let's return briefly to the topic of natural selection, first addressed in Chapter 1. Darwin proposed the mechanism of natural selection to explain how species change, or evolve, over time. He recognized that certain traits, physical or psychological, can help an organism's reproductive "fitness" and that these features, in turn, are likely to be passed forward from one generation to the next. For example, if a bird is born with a special capacity to store, remember, and relocate seeds, then its chances of living long enough to mate and produce offspring increase. If the bird's offspring share the same capacity for obtaining food, then over many generations the seed-storing trait is likely to become a stable characteristic of the species. It becomes an **adaptation**, or a feature that has been selected for by nature because it increases the chances of the organism to survive and multiply.

adaptation A trait that has been selected for by nature because it increases the reproductive "fitness" of the organism.

Virtually all scientists accept that natural selection is the main mechanism for producing lasting change within and across species. However, not all features of the body and mind are necessarily adaptations. Consider your ability to read and write. These are highly adaptive psychological abilities, yet neither could have evolved through natural selection. Both developed relatively recently in human history—too short a time period for evolutionary change—and emerged long after the human brain had achieved its current size and form (Gould, 2000). On the other hand, the human eye and the psychological experience of perception are almost certainly specific adaptations that have been molded through generations of evolutionary change (Cosmides & Tooby, 1992; Dawkins, 1976).

How do we identify which features of our body and mind are adaptations? This is a controversial topic among evolutionary biologists and psychologists, particularly with respect to mental processes. As noted in Chapter 1, evolutionary psychologists are convinced that we're born with a number of psychological adaptations (Buss, 2004; Cosmides & Tooby, 1992); others believe that our thought processes are shaped largely by the environment—that is, by how we're taught and by the cultural messages we receive (see Rose & Rose, 2000). To qualify as an adaptation, the physical or psychological trait should be (a) *universal*, which means that it develops regularly in all members of the species; (b) *economical*, which means that its presence isn't costly to survival; and (3) *adaptive*, which means that the trait solves specific adaptive problems faced by the organism (Symons, 1992; Williams, 1966). Learned behaviors can sometimes satisfy these criteria as well, so building the case for an adaptation requires that you develop strong arguments against alternative accounts (Andrews, Gangestad, & Matthews, 2002).

For natural selection to produce an adaptation, there needs to be a mechanism for producing variation, or differences, within a species. If all the members of a species are exactly the same, then obviously there can be no special features for nature to select. In addition, there needs to be some way to guarantee that an adaptive feature can pass from one generation to the next. During Darwin's time, the mechanism for ensuring variability and inheritance was unknown; Darwin made his case by documenting the abundance of variability and inherited characteristics that exist in nature. It was later learned that the mechanism that enables natural selection is the genetic code.

Genetic Principles

Let's briefly review some of the important principles of genetics. How is the genetic code stored, and what are the factors that produce genetic variability? The genetic message resides within *chromosomes*, which are thin, threadlike strips of DNA. Human cells, with the exception of sperm cells and the unfertilized egg cell, contain a total of 46 chromosomes, arranged in 23 pairs. Half of each chromosome pair is contributed originally by the mother through the egg, and the other half arrives in the father's sperm. **Genes** are segments of a chromosome that contain instructions for influencing and creating particular hereditary characteristics. For example, each person has a gene that helps determine height or hair color and another that may determine susceptibility to disorders such as muscular dystrophy or even Alzheimer disease.

Because humans have *23 pairs* of chromosomes, they have two genes for most developmental characteristics, or traits. People have two genes, for example, for hair color, blood type, and the possible development of facial dimples. If both genes are designed to produce the same trait (such as nearsightedness), there's little question the characteristic will develop (you'll definitely need glasses). But if the two genes differ—for example, the father passes along the gene for nearsightedness, but the mother's gene is for normal distance vision—the trait is determined by the *dominant gene*; in the case of vision, the "normal" gene will dominate the *recessive gene* for nearsightedness.

The fact that a dominant gene will mask the effects of a recessive gene means that everybody has genetic material that's not actually expressed in physical or psychological characteristics. A person may see perfectly but still carry around the recessive gene for faulty distance vision. This is the reason parents with normal vision can produce a nearsighted child or two brown-haired parents can produce a child with blond hair—it is the particular combination of genes that determines the inherited characteristics.

Another important distinction is between the **genotype**, which is the actual genetic message, and the **phenotype**, which is the trait's observable characteristics. The phenotype, such as good vision or brown

CRITICAL THINKING
Do you think a trait could be universal, economical, and adaptive but still be due primarily to the environment? How can we ever be certain that a trait is an adaptation?

genes Segments of chromosomes that contain instructions for influencing and creating particular hereditary characteristics.

genotype The actual genetic information inherited from one's parents.

phenotype A person's observable characteristics, such as red hair. The phenotype is controlled mainly by the genotype, but it can also be influenced by the environment.

Genetic background is important in determining physical appearance, and many researchers believe that it also helps shape certain psychological characteristics.

© Dan McCoy/Rainbow

hair, is controlled mainly by the genotype, but it can be strongly influenced by the environment. A person's height and weight, for example, are shaped largely by the genotype, but environmental factors such as diet and physical health contribute significantly to the final phenotype. This is an important point to remember: Genes provide the materials from which characteristics develop, but the environment shapes the final product. As I stressed in Chapter 1, it's nature via nurture. The environment provides the means through which nature can express itself (Ridley, 2003).

Across individuals, variations in the genetic message arise because there are trillions of different ways that the genetic information from each parent can be combined at fertilization. Each egg or sperm cell contains a random half of each parent's 23 chromosome pairs. According to the laws of probability, this means that some 8 million (2^{23}) different combinations can reside in either an egg cell or a sperm cell. The particular meeting of egg and sperm is also a matter of chance, which means that the genetic material from both parents can be combined in some 64 trillion ways—and this is from a single set of parents!

Clearly, there are many ways by which a trait, or combination of traits, can emerge and produce a survival "advantage" for one person over another. But variation in the genetic code can also occur by chance in the form of a **mutation**. A mutation is a spontaneous change in the genetic material that occurs during the gene replication process. Most genetic mutations are harmful to the organism, but occasionally they lead to traits that confer a survival advantage to the organism. Mutations, along with the variations produced by unique combinations of genetic material, are key ingredients for natural selection—together, they introduce novelty, or new traits, into nature.

mutation A spontaneous change in the genetic material that occurs during the gene replication process.

Genes and Behavior

Now let's return to the link between genetics and psychology—what is the connection between genotypes, phenotypes, and behavior? In some sense, all behavior is influenced by genetic factors because genes help to determine the structure and function of the brain. At the same time, no physical or mental trait will ever be determined entirely by genetic factors—the environment always plays some role. At issue is the extent to which we can predict, at least on average, the psychological traits of an individual by knowing something about his or her genetic record. Susceptibility to the psychological disorder schizophrenia is a case in point. Natural children of parents who have schizophrenia (where either one or both have the disorder) have a greater chance of developing the disorder themselves, when compared to the children of normal parents. This is the case even if the children have been adopted at birth and never raised in an abnormal environment (Gottesman, 1991; Moldin & Gottesman, 1997), so genetic similarity probably plays some role in the increased tendency to develop schizophrenia. (I'll return to this issue in more detail in Chapter 14.)

One way that psychologists study the link between genes and behavior is to investigate family histories in detail. In **family studies**, researchers look for similarities and differences among biological (blood) relatives to determine the influence of heredity. As you've just seen, the chances of schizophrenia increase with a family history, and there are many other traits that seem to run in families as well (e.g., intelligence and personality). The trouble with family studies, however, is that members of a family share more than just common genes. They are also exposed to similar environmental experiences, so it's difficult to separate the relative roles of nature and nurture in behavior. Family studies can be useful sources of information—it helps to know, for instance, if someone is at a greater than average risk of developing schizophrenia—but they can't be used to establish true links between genes and behavior.

family studies The similarities and differences among biological (blood) relatives are studied to help discover the role heredity plays in physical or psychological traits.

In **twin studies**, researchers compare traits between *identical* twins, who share essentially the same genetic material, and *fraternal* twins, who were born at the same time but whose genetic overlap is only roughly 50% (fraternal twins can even be of different sexes). In studies of intelligence, for example, identical twins tend to have much more similar intelligence scores than fraternal twins, even when environmental

twin studies Identical twins, who share genetic material, are compared to fraternal twins in an effort to determine the roles heredity and environment play in psychological traits.

factors are taken into account (Bouchard, 1997; Bouchard et al., 1990). Identical twins make ideal research subjects because researchers can control for genetic factors. Because these twins have virtually the same genetic makeup, emerging from a single fertilized egg, any physical or psychological differences that arise during development must be attributable to environmental factors. Similarly, if identical twins are raised in different environments but still show similar traits, it's a strong indication that genetic factors are involved in expression of the trait.

You've been given only a brief introduction to "behavioral genetics" in this section because we'll be returning to the interplay between heredity and environment throughout the book. For now, recognize that how you think and act is indeed influenced by the code that is stored in the your body's chromosomes. Through the random processes that occur at fertilization, nature guarantees diversity within the species—everyone receives a unique genetic message that, in combination with environmental factors, helps determine brain structure as well as human psychology. From an evolutionary standpoint, diversity is of great importance because it increases the chances that at least some members of a species will have the necessary tools to deal successfully with the problems of survival.

Test Yourself | 3.4

To check on your understanding of genetics, choose the best answer to each of the following statements. (You will find the answers in the Appendix.)

1. Reading and writing are examples of adaptations, and therefore result from the mechanism of natural selection: *True or False*? _____
2. The actual genetic information inherited from one's parents: *genotype or phenotype*? _____
3. If the two inherited genes for a specific trait differ, which plays a stronger role: *dominant or recessive*? _____
4. Psychologists can study genetic effects on a variety of characteristics, such as intelligence or susceptibility to schizophrenia, by studying which kind of twins raised in different environments: *identical or fraternal*? _____

Review *Psychology for a Reason*

The human brain, along with the rest of the nervous system, is a biological solution to problems produced by constantly changing and sometimes hostile outside environments. Fortunately, out of these biological solutions arise those attributes that make up the human mind, including intellect, emotion, and artistic creativity. In this chapter we've considered four central problems of adaptation.

Communicating Internally: Connecting World and Brain

Networks of individual cells, called neurons, establish a marketplace of information called the nervous system. To communicate internally, the nervous system uses an electrochemical language. Messages travel electrically within a neuron, usually from dendrite to soma to axon to terminal button, and then chemically from one neuron to the next. Combining electrical and chemical components creates a quick, efficient, and extremely versatile communication system. Neurotransmitters regulate the rate at which neurons fire by producing excitatory or inhibitory messages, and the resulting patterns of activation shape how we think and act.

Initiating Behavior: A Division of Labor

To accomplish the remarkable variety of functions it controls, the nervous system divides its labor. Through the use of sophisticated techniques, including brain-imaging devices, researchers have begun to map out the regions of the brain that support particular psychological and life-sustaining functions. At the base of the brain, in the hindbrain region, structures control such basic processes as respiration, heart rate, and the coordination of muscle movements. Higher up are regions that control motivational processes such as eating, drinking, and sexual behavior. Finally, in the cerebral cortex more complex mental processes—such as thought, sensations, and language—are represented. Some functions in the brain appear to be lateralized, which means that they're controlled primarily by one cerebral hemisphere or the other. Through the development of specialized regions of cells, the human brain has become capable of extremely adaptive reactions to its changing environment.

Regulating Growth and Internal Functions: Extended Communication

To solve its widespread and long-term communication needs, the body uses the endocrine system to release chemicals called hormones into the bloodstream. These chemical messengers serve a variety of regulatory functions, influencing growth and development, hunger, thirst, and sexual behavior, in addition to helping the body prepare for action. Hormones released early in development and into adulthood may partly explain some of the behavioral differences between men and women.

Adapting and Transmitting the Genetic Code

Adaptations are traits that arise through the mechanism of natural selection. Although it's difficult to establish which psychological traits are truly adaptations, psychologists acknowledge that our thoughts and behaviors are influenced by genetic factors. The particular combinations of genes that are inherited from the parents, along with influences from the environment, determine individual characteristics. Psychologists often try to disentangle the relative contributions of genes and the environment by conducting twin studies, comparing the behaviors and abilities of identical and fraternal twins who have been raised in similar or dissimilar environments. When identical twins show similar characteristics, even though they have been raised in quite different backgrounds, psychologists assume that the underlying genetic code may be playing an influential role.

Active Summary *(You will find the answers in the Appendix.)*

• The field of (1) _____ studies the connection between the brain and behavior.

Communicating Internally: Connecting World and Brain

• Neurons receive, (2) _____, and transmit information (3) _____.

• A neuron consists of (4) _____, soma, (5) _____, and terminal buttons. Sensory neurons carry information through the spinal cord to the brain. (6) _____ convey information between internal processing sites. (7) _____ neurons carry messages from the central nervous system to the muscles and glands that produce a (8) _____ response.

• Within a neuron, messages travel electrically from one point to another. From one neuron to another, messages travel (9) _____, through neurotransmitters.

• Groups of neurons operating simultaneously create an (10) _____ pattern that underlies both conscious experiences and complex behaviors.

Initiating Behavior: A Division of Labor

• We think, feel, and function physically because of a biological division of labor.

• The central nervous system consists of the brain and (11) _____, which communicate to the rest of the body through bundles of (12) _____ or nerves. The peripheral nervous system, which includes the (13) _____ and (14) _____ systems, sends sensory information to the brain, moves muscles, and regulates (15) _____ function.

• Studying brain damage and (16) _____ can reveal brain function. Chemical injection and (17) _____ let scientists stimulate the brain. They can also observe the brain through noninvasive techniques, including monitoring electrical brain activity using an (18) _____ and using X-rays (CT scan) and neuroimaging devices such as (19) _____ and magnetic resonance imaging (MRI) to create three-dimensional pictures or live snapshots of the brain.

• The (20) _____ provides basic life support, through the medulla, (21) _____, reticular formation, and cerebellum. The (22) _____ relays sensory messages. Higher mental functioning takes place in the (23) _____ using the cerebral cortex, thalamus, hypothalamus, and (24) _____ system.

• The two hemispheres (halves) of the cerebral cortex are (25) _____; that is, each side is responsible for somewhat different functions.

Regulating Growth and Internal Functions: Extended Communication

• Endocrine glands release (26) _____ into the blood that interact with the nervous system to regulate such basic activities as the fight-or-flight response.

• The (27) _____ gland releases hormones that determine sexual identity before birth and direct sexual maturity at puberty. Activities in the (28) _____ system may account for basic differences in the ways females and males think and behave.

Adapting and Transmitting the Genetic Code

• Gene-based physical and psychological traits that increase the chances for (29) _____, or of finding a mate, can be selected for by nature and become adaptations. (30) _____, especially psychological ones, can be difficult to identify.

• Inside the cell are 23 pairs of (31) _____, threadlike strips of DNA. (32) _____ are segments of chromosomes that contain instructions for creating or influencing a particular hereditary characteristic. Genes can be dominant or (33) _____.

• (34) _____ studies identify similarities and differences that may reveal the influence of heredity. In (35) _____ studies, researchers compare the behavioral traits of identical twins, who have the same genetic material, and (36) _____ twins, who have only about half their genes in common. Traits that aren't accounted for by genetics are attributed to (37) _____ influences.

Terms to Remember

acetylcholine, 63
action potential, 62
adaptation, 85
autonomic system, 68
axon, 61
central nervous system, 57
cerebellum, 73
cerebral cortex, 74
computerized tomography scan (CT scan), 71
corpus callosum, 79
dendrites, 61
dopamine, 64
electroencephalograph (EEG), 71
endocrine system, 81
endorphins, 65
family studies, 87
forebrain, 74
frontal lobe, 77
gamma-amino-butyric acid (GABA), 64

genes, 86
genotype, 86
glial cells, 59
hindbrain, 72
hormones, 81
hypothalamus, 74
interneurons, 59
limbic system, 74
magnetic resonance imaging (MRI), 71
midbrain, 73
motor neurons, 59
mutation, 87
myelin sheath, 59
nerves, 67
neurons, 59
neuroscience, 57
neurotransmitters, 62
occipital lobe, 79
parietal lobe, 77
peripheral nervous system, 57

phenotype, 86
pituitary gland, 82
positron emission tomography (PET), 71
reflexes, 59
refractory period, 65
resting potential, 61
sensory neurons, 59
serotonin, 64
soma, 61
somatic system, 68
synapse, 61
temporal lobe, 77
terminal buttons, 61
thalamus, 74
twin studies, 87

Media Resources

ThomsonNOW

www.thomsonedu.com/ThomsonNOW
Go to this site for the link to ThomsonNOW, your one-stop study shop. Take a Pre-Test for this chapter, and Thomson-NOW will generate a Personalized Study Plan based on your results. The Study Plan will identify the topics you need to review and direct you to online resources to help you master those topics. You can then take a Post-Test to help you determine the concepts you have mastered and what you still need to work on.

Companion Website

www.thomsonedu.com/psychology/nairne
Go to this site to find online resources directly linked to your book, including a glossary, flashcards, quizzing, weblinks, and more.

Psyk.trek 3.0

Check out the Psyk.trek CD-ROM for further study of the concepts in this chapter. Psyk.trek's interactive learning modules, simulations, and quizzes offer additional opportunities for you to interact with, reflect on, and retain the material:

Biological Bases of Behavior: The Neuron and the Neural Impulse

CHAPTER 4

Human Development

Do you ever wish you could hop into a time machine and start over? Maybe you could return to that point in the third grade where you tripped in front of the whole school or to middle school, where the answer you blurted out became the focus of jokes for months. In fact, while you're at it, why not return to early childhood? Maybe if your parents had been more sympathetic when you just couldn't get the hang of toilet training, things would be different now . . . right? Psychologists believe that you are, in many ways, a product of your environment. But as you saw in Chapter 1, debate continues about the true origins of knowledge and behavior. If you could rerun your life, controlling your environment, would you really end up as a different person? Maybe, but remember that your personality—your likes and dislikes—also comes from the genetic recipe you inherited from your parents. The origins of thought and action don't lie exclusively in either the environment or in nature (genes), but always in both. So rerun your life a hundred times, and you might well end up with the same likes, dislikes, anxieties, and fears. Food for thought.

The topic of this chapter is human **development**, the age-related physical, intellectual, and social changes that occur throughout life. Why do humans develop? There's one very straightforward reason: Extending the process of development over time enables us to fine-tune our physical, intellectual, and social capabilities to better meet the needs of varied environments

> **development** The age-related physical, intellectual, social, and personal changes that occur throughout an individual's lifetime.

(continued next page)

Nature has built a considerable amount of flexibility, or plasticity, into the developmental process. This flexibility has given us an exceptional degree of adaptability to environmental influences—in fact, as you'll soon see, the environment can change the course of development in profound ways. Keep the adaptive significance of development in mind as you consider how we effectively solve the problems associated with developing physically, intellectually, and socially.

Developing Physically The environment helps shape the physical process of growth and can determine its ultimate outcome, but most physical changes are surprisingly consistent and predictable.

We lift our heads before we crawl; we crawl before we can walk. In general, the timing of development is a product of evolutionary history and partly reflects the survival problems that our species has been required to solve.

Developing Intellectually The developmental changes that occur in how people think—what is called cognitive development—are of major importance to psychologists. Intellectually, the newborn is hardly an "adultlet" (or miniature adult). You'll discover there are good reasons to believe that infants see and think about the world somewhat differently from adults. Infants are faced with infant problems, and these problems don't always overlap with those faced by adults.

Developing Socially and Personally Humans are social animals. We're continually interacting with each other, and these relationships help us adapt successfully to our environment. In this section we'll consider the milestones of social development, beginning with the formation of attachments to parents and caregivers and ending with a discussion of how relationships change in middle and late adulthood.

Developing physically

Developing intellectually

Developing socially and personally

Developing Physically

LEARNING GOALS
- Describe the physical changes that occur prenatally.
- Discuss how we grow from infancy through adolescence.
- Discuss adulthood and the aging body and brain.

TO A CHILD, IT SEEMS to take forever to grow up. In fact, we do take a relatively long time to reach full physical maturity compared to other species. At birth a human newborn's brain has about 25% of its ultimate weight; the chimpanzee newborn's brain has about 60% (Corballis, 1991; Lenneberg, 1967). We do a lot of developing outside of the womb. Still, the main components of the body—the nervous system, the networks of glands, and so on—develop at an astonishingly rapid rate from the point of conception.

Guided by the genetic code and influenced by hormones released by the endocrine system, in the early years we change physically at rates that will never again be matched in our lifetimes. To place the growth rate in some perspective, if we continued to develop at the rate we show in the first two years of life, we'd end up over 12 feet tall and weighing several tons! Fortunately, things slow down considerably after the first few years of life; but they never completely stop—we continue to change both physically and mentally until the very moment of death.

The Stages of Prenatal Development

Let's start at the beginning. The human developmental process begins with the union of egg and sperm at conception. Within the fertilized egg, or **zygote**, the 23 chromosomes from the father and the 23 chromosomes from the mother pair up to form the genetic recipe. Over the next 266 days or so (approximately 9 months), the newly formed organism undergoes a steady and quite remarkable transformation. It begins as a single cell and ends as an approximately 7-pound newborn composed of literally billions of cells. The period of development that occurs before birth is called *prenatal development*, and it's divided into three main stages: *germinal*, *embryonic*, and *fetal*.

It takes about two weeks after conception for the zygote to migrate down from the mother's fallopian tubes (where the sperm and egg meet) and implant itself in the wall of the uterus (often called the womb). The period from conception to implantation is called the **germinal period**, and it's a make-or-break time for the fertilized egg. In fact, most fertilized eggs do not complete the process; well over half fail to achieve successful implantation, either because of abnormalities or because the implantation site is nutritionally inadequate for proper growth (Roberts & Lowe, 1975; Sigelman & Rider, 2006).

Once successful implantation occurs, the **embryonic period** begins. During the next six weeks, the human develops from an unrecognizable mass of cells to a somewhat familiar creature with arms, legs, fingers, toes, and a distinctly beating heart. Near the end of the embryonic period—in the seventh and eighth weeks after fertilization—sexual differentiation begins. Depending on whether the father has contributed an X or a Y chromosome (the mother always contributes an X), the embryo starts to develop either male or female sexual characteristics (see ▌ Figure 4.1). If the developing embryo has inherited a Y chromosome, it begins to secrete the sex hormone *testosterone*, which leads to the establishment of a male sexual reproductive system. In the absence of testosterone, the natural course of development in humans is to become female. At the ninth week of prenatal development, the **fetal period** begins and continues until birth. Early in this period, the bones and muscles of what is now called the

zygote The fertilized human egg, containing 23 chromosomes from the father and 23 chromosomes from the mother.

germinal period The period in prenatal development from conception to implantation of the fertilized egg in the wall of the uterus.

embryonic period The period of prenatal development lasting from implantation to the end of the eighth week.

fetal period The period of prenatal development lasting from the ninth week until birth.

Prenatal human development

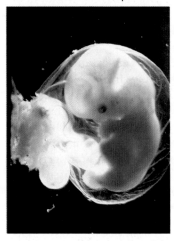

5–6 weeks postconception

4 months

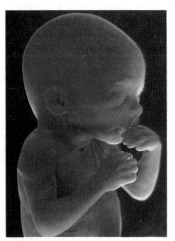

6 months

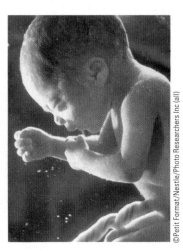

8 months

©Petit Format/Nestle/Photo Researchers Inc (all)

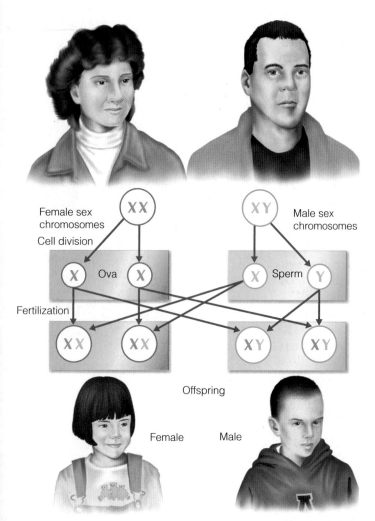

FIGURE 4.1 Genetic Determinants of Gender

If the father contributes an X chromosome, the child will be a girl; a Y chromosome from the father leads to the development of a boy.

teratogens Environmental agents—such as disease organisms or drugs—that can potentially damage the developing embryo or fetus.

fetus start to develop. By the end of the third month, the skeletal and muscular systems allow for extensive movement—even somersaults—although the fetus at this point is still only about 3 inches long (Apgar & Beck, 1974). By the end of the sixth month, the fetus has grown to over a foot long, weighs in at about 2 pounds, and may be capable of survival if delivered prematurely. The last three months of prenatal development are marked by extremely rapid growth, both in body size and in the size and complexity of brain tissue. The fetus also develops a layer of fat under the skin during this period, which acts as protective insulation, and the lungs mature in preparation for the baby's first gasping breath of air.

Environmental Hazards Although the developing child is snugly tucked away within the confines of its mother's womb, it is by no means completely isolated from the effects of the environment. The mother's physical health and diet, as well as exposure to toxins in the environment, can seriously affect the developing child. Mother and child are linked physically, so if the mother gets sick, smokes, drinks, or uses drugs, the effects can transfer to the fetus or embryo. Some psychologists even believe that the mother's psychological state, such as her level of anxiety or stress during pregnancy, can exert an effect and may actually influence the personality of the child (Dawson, Ashman, & Carver, 2000; but see DiPietro, 2004).

Environmental agents that potentially damage the developing child are called **teratogens**. As a rule, the structures and systems of the fetus or embryo are most susceptible to teratogens during formation. For example, if the mother contracts German measles (rubella) during the first six weeks of pregnancy, the child is at risk for heart defects because it's during this period that the structures of the heart are formed. In general the embryonic period is the point of greatest susceptibility, although the critical structures of the central nervous system can be affected throughout prenatal development.

Interestingly, some researchers have suggested that morning sickness, which usually affects the mother during the first three months of pregnancy, may be a natural defense against the influence of teratogens (Profet, 1992). Pregnant women sometimes show increased sensitivity to foods and odors and even develop aversions to certain tastes, which could help prevent potentially dangerous foods from being ingested. Remember, a food that's perfectly harmless to the adult mother might be damaging to the developing child. Morning sickness occurs across the world, in every culture, which suggests that it may be an evolutionary adaptation. Women who experience morning sickness are somewhat less likely to suffer miscarriages than women who do not (Flaxman & Sherman, 2000).

It's very important to recognize the powerful influence the environment can have on the developing child. If you're pregnant and drink heavily—five or more drinks a day—you're at least 30% more likely to give birth to a child suffering from *fetal alcohol syndrome*, a condition marked by physical deformities, a reduction in the size of certain brain structures, and an increased risk of mental retardation (Manning & Hoyme, 2007). Negative long-term effects can also result from drug consumption—including over-the-counter and prescription drugs—as well as from improper nutrition, smoking, and possibly excessive caffeine (Day & Richardson, 1994; Sussman & Levitt, 1989).

We can't predict with any certainty how an environmental agent will affect development because susceptibility is largely a matter of timing and genetics. Some mothers can abuse themselves terribly and still give birth to normal children; others who drink only moderately, perhaps as few as seven drinks a week, may produce a child with significant disabilities (Abel, 1981; Jacobson & Jacobson, 1994). Because the effects of maternal activities are impossible to predict in any particular case, most doctors recommend against playing Russian roulette with the developing fetus or embryo; it's best to stay sober, well fed, and under a doctor's care throughout pregnancy.

Growth During Infancy

Don't let all this bad news about the environment get you down too much—in the vast majority of cases the environment has a nurturing effect on the developing child. The internal conditions of the mother's uterus are perfectly "tuned" for physical development. The temperature is right, the fetus floats cushioned in a protective fluid, and regular nourishment is provided through the umbilical cord and placenta. More often than not, the result is a healthy baby who is ready to take on the world.

The average newborn weighs about 7 pounds and is roughly 20 inches in length. Over the next two years, as the child grows from baby to toddler, this weight will quadruple and the child will reach about half of his or her adult height. Along with the rest of the body, the brain continues its dramatic growth spurt during this period. As mentioned earlier, a newborn enters the world with a brain that is only 25% of its final weight; but by the second birthday, the percentage has increased to 75%. Remarkably, this increase in brain size is not due primarily to the formation of new neurons, as most of the cells that make up the cerebral cortex are in place well before birth (Nowakowski, 1987; Rakic, 1991). Instead, the cells grow in size and complexity, and a number of supporting glial cells are added. There is some evidence that new neurons may be added in the developing human brain through a process called *neurogenesis*, but this evidence remains controversial (see Gould et al., 1999; Bhardwaj et al., 2006).

This child is one of thousands born each year with fetal alcohol syndrome.

Experience Matters   The fact that substantial numbers of neurons are intact at birth does not mean that the brain of the newborn infant is mature—far from it. The brain still needs to build its vast internal communication network, and it requires experience to accomplish this task. During the final stages of prenatal development, and especially during the first year or two after birth, lots of changes occur in the neural circuitry. More branches (dendrites) sprout off from the existing cells, and the number of connections, or synapses, greatly increases. There is even a kind of neural pruning process in which neurons that are not used simply die (Dawson & Fischer, 1994).

Again, the key principle at work is plasticity. The genetic code does not rigidly fix the internal circuitry of the brain; instead, a kind of rough wiring pattern is established during prenatal development, which is filled in during the important first few years of life (Kolb, Gibb, & Robinson, 2003). Studies with animals have shown that the quality of early experience may be extremely important during this period. For example, rats raised in enriched environments (with lots of social contact and external stimulation) show significantly more complex and better functioning brain tissue than rats raised in sterile, barren environments (Greenough, Black, & Wall, 1987; Rosenzweig, 1984). Rats also show better recovery of function after brain injury if their recovery time is spent in an enriched environment (Nithianantharaja & Hannan, 2006).

From Crawling to Walking

Of course, parents don't see their baby's burgeoning neural circuitry—what they notice are the observable things, such as when the baby begins to sit up, crawl, stand alone, and walk. Before a baby can do these things, however, both the brain and the neuron-to-muscle links that radiate throughout the body need to develop adequately.

For example, the insulated coating of the axons (myelin sheath), which helps speed up neural transmission, must develop properly. Generally, the nervous system matures in a "down-and-out" fashion—that is, from the head down and from the center out (Shirley, 1933). Infants can lift their heads before they can roll over because the neuron-to-muscle connections in the upper part of the body mature before those in the lower part of the body. Babies crawl before they walk because they're able to control their arms efficiently before they're able to control their legs.

CRITICAL THINKING

Given that the environment plays such an important role in shaping brain development, what advice would you give new parents to maximize enriched development of their baby's intellectual capabilities?

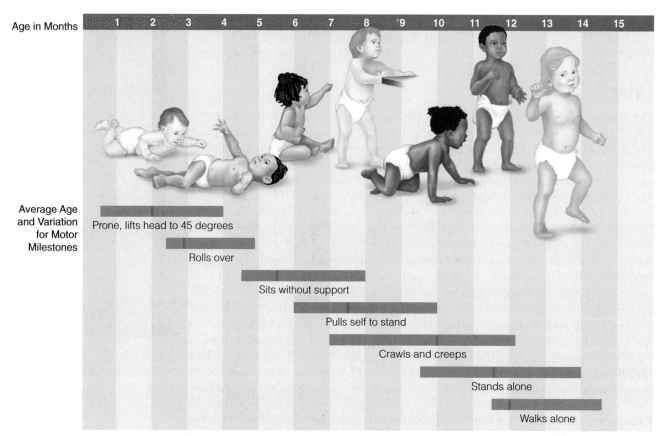

FIGURE 4.2 Major States of Motor Development
Although psychologists are reluctant to tie developmental milestones closely to age, most children learn to crawl, stand alone, and walk at about the same age.

Child-rearing practices reflect cultural differences. Hopi babies are traditionally swaddled and bound to cradle boards for much of the first year of life but show no developmental delays in walking.

Psychologists don't like to tie developmental milestones directly to age—because not all children develop at the same rate—but most children learn to crawl, then stand alone, and walk at about the same time. ▌Figure 4.2 shows the major stages of infant motor development. The sequence of development is generally stable, orderly, and predictable. Also, notice that each stage is associated with a range of ages, although the range is not large. Roughly 90% of all babies can roll over at 5 months of age, sit without support at 8 months, and then walk alone by 15 months. One baby might stand alone consistently at 9 months, whereas another might not accomplish the same feat until nearly 14 months of age; both fall within the normal range of development.

Why Is My Baby Different? What accounts for the individual differences? It's hard to tell for any particular case, but both nature and nurture contribute. Each person has a genetic recipe that determines when he or she will develop physically, although environmental experiences can speed up or slow down the process (Schmuckler, 1996). Some cultures place great value on early motor development and nurture such skills in children. If a baby is routinely exercised and handled during the early months of life, there is some evidence that he or she will progress through the landmark stages of motor development more quickly (Hopkins, 1991; Zelazo, Zelazo, & Kolb, 1972).

But these differences are usually small, and they play little, if any, role in determining final motor development. Hopi babies are traditionally swaddled and bound to cradle boards for much of the first year of life, yet these babies begin walking at roughly the same time as unbound babies (Dennis & Dennis, 1940). To learn to walk at a reasonable age, the baby simply needs to be given the opportunity to move around at some point—to "test the waters" and explore things on his or her own (Bertenthal, Campos, & Kermoian, 1994). Hopi babies are bound to cradle boards for only their first nine or ten months; then they're given several months to explore their motor capabilities before they begin to walk (Shaffer, 2007).

From Toddlerhood to Adolescence

From the onset of toddlerhood through puberty, the growth rate continues but at a less rapid pace. The average child grows several inches and puts on roughly 6 to 7 pounds annually. These are significant changes, but they're often hard for parents to detect because they represent only a small fraction of the child's current size (2 inches added to a 20-inch baby are far easier to spot than 2 inches added to someone who is 40 inches tall). More noticeable are the changes that occur in hand-to-eye coordination as the child matures. Three-year-olds lack the grace and coordination that are so obvious in 6-year-olds. The brain continues to mature, although again at a pace far slower than during prenatal development or during the first two years of life. General processing speed—how quickly we think and react to sudden changes in our environment—increases consistently throughout childhood (Kail, 1991; Kail & Salthouse, 1994).

Between the end of childhood and the beginning of young adulthood lies an important physical and psychological transition period called *adolescence*. Physically, the two most dramatic changes that occur during this time are the adolescent growth spurt and the onset of **puberty**, or sexual maturity (the word *puberty* is from the Latin for "to grow hairy"). Just like with crawling and walking, it's not possible to pinpoint the timing of these changes exactly, particularly for a specific individual, but changes usually start occurring for girls at around age 11 and for boys at about 13. Hormones released by the endocrine system rock us out of childhood by triggering a rapid increase in height and weight accompanied by the enlargement and maturation of internal and external sexual organs.

puberty The period during which a person reaches sexual maturity and is potentially capable of producing offspring.

Maturing Sexually Puberty is the developmental period when we mature sexually and acquire the ability to reproduce. For the adolescent girl, high levels of *estrogen* in the body lead to external changes, such as breast development and broadening hips, and eventually to the beginning of *menarche* (the first menstrual flow) at around age 12 or 13. For boys, hormones called *androgens* lead to the appearance of facial hair, a lower voice, and the ability to ejaculate (release semen) at around age 13 or 14. Neither menarche nor the first ejaculation necessarily means that the adolescent is ready to reproduce—ovulation and sperm production may not occur until months later—but psychologically these "firsts" tend to be highly memorable and emotional events (Golub, 1992).

The onset of puberty shows, yet again, the importance of both nature and nurture in development. Did you know that the average onset age for menarche has dropped from about 16 in the 1880s to the current 12 to 13? Physically, we're maturing earlier than in past generations, and it's not due to systematic changes in the genetic recipe. Instead, better nutrition, better living conditions, and improved medical care are responsible for the trend (Tanner, 1990). Even today, in parts of the world where living conditions are difficult, the average age of menarche is later than in industrialized countries such as the United States (Chumlea, 1982). Other factors, such as ethnicity and even family conflict, seem to matter as well (Romans, Martin, & Herbison, 2003). The environment does not cause sexual maturation—that's controlled by the genetic code—but the environment is clearly capable of accelerating or delaying the point when changes start to occur (Susman, Dorn, & Schliefelbein, 2003).

Becoming an Adult

The adolescent years are marked by dramatic changes in appearance and strength. Motor skills, including hand-to-eye coordination, improve to adult levels during the teenage years. As you know, there are world-class swimmers and tennis players who

©Ellen Senisi /The Image Works

Children reach the adolescent growth spurt at varying ages. Boys typically lag behind girls by as much as two years.

©PhotoDisc./Getty Images

A strenuous daily exercise program may delay the onset of puberty.

menopause The period during which a woman's menstrual cycle slows down and finally stops.

dementia Physically based losses in mental functioning.

| **FIGURE 4.3** Age and Reaction Time
Average reaction time changes between ages 20 and 80, as demonstrated in a cognitive task requiring subjects to match numbers with symbols on a computer screen. Although reaction time gradually quickens from childhood through adolescence, it gradually slows after age 20. (Based on Salthouse, 1994)

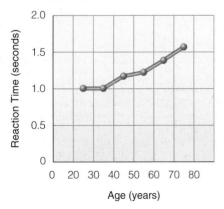

are barely into their teens. The brain reaches adult weight by about age 16, although the myelination of the neurons—so critical in early motor development—continues throughout the adolescent years (Benes, 1989; Benes et al., 1994). The continued development of the brain can also be seen in the gradual quickening of reaction times that occurs throughout adolescence (Kail, 1991).

Interestingly, researchers using neuroimaging technology (fMRI) have recently discovered that significant changes in both myelination and neural "pruning" occur just before and after puberty. These changes, in turn, are believed to alter the internal communication networks, particularly in the regions of the brain that control higher-level cognitive abilities. These same areas are thought to control aspects of social processing, such as the ability to understand what other people are thinking and the ability to take the perspective of another person. Although their results are speculative, some researchers have suggested that these brain changes may be responsible for the well-documented and even turbulent changes in social functioning that are associated with adolescence (Blakemore & Choudhury, 2006).

When do we actually cross the threshold to adulthood? That's a tough question to answer because becoming an adult is, in some sense, a state of mind. There are differences in how the transition from adolescent to adult is defined across the world. Some cultures have specific rites of passage, and others do not. Moreover, as you know, some adolescents are willing to accept the responsibilities of adulthood quite early, and others are not (Eccles, Wigfield, & Byrnes, 2003). Regardless, by the time we reach our 20s we're physically mature and at the height of our physical prowess.

The Aging Body   Now for the downside. It's barely noticeable at first, but most of us begin slowly and steadily to decline physically, at least with respect to our peak levels of strength and agility, at some point during our 20s. The loss tends to be across the board, which means it applies to virtually all physical functions, from strength, to respiration rate, to the heart's pumping capacity (Whitbourne, 1985). Individual differences occur in the rate of decline, of course, depending on such factors as exercise, illness, and heredity. (I'm sure you can think of a 40-year-old who is in better physical shape than a 25-year-old.) But wrinkles, age spots, sagging flesh, and loss of muscle tone are all reliable and expected parts of the aging process.

By about age 50, the average woman begins **menopause**, the period when the menstrual cycle slows down and finally stops. Ovulation also stops, so women lose the ability to conceive children. These events are caused by hormonal changes, in particular by a decline in the level of female hormones in the body. Despite what you might have heard, menopause is not disruptive for all women, either physically or psychologically (McKinlay, Brambilla, & Posner, 1992). The main physical symptoms, such as hot flashes, are not experienced by everyone, and the idea that women typically undergo a sustained period of depression or crankiness is simply a myth (Matthews, 1992). In fact, some women view menopause as a liberating experience, accompanied by an increased sense of sexual freedom (Lachman, 2004).

The Aging Brain   As we age, significant physical changes begin to occur in the brain as well. Some people suffer serious brain degeneration—the loss of brain cells—which leads to senility and, in some cases, to a disabling condition called Alzheimer disease. The good news is that the majority of older people never experience these problems; fewer than 1% of people at age 65 are afflicted with **dementia**, the technical name for physically based loss in mental functioning. Although that percentage may rise to as

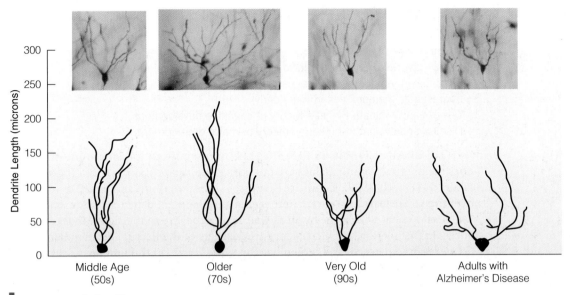

FIGURE 4.4 Aging Neurons

Notice that the dendrites of adult hippocampal neurons actually increase in length and complexity between 50 and 70, declining only in late old age or with Alzheimer disease.

(Photos courtesy Dr. Dorothy G. Flood/University of Rochester Medical Center)

much as 20% for individuals over age 80 (Cavanaugh & Blanchard-Fields, 2006), significant losses in mental functioning are still the exception rather than the rule. Everyone loses brain cells with age, and as you'll see later, declines also occur in certain kinds of memory, sensory ability, and reaction time (see ▌Figure 4.3; Salthouse, 1994).

But the physical changes that occur in the aging brain are not all bad. Neurons are lost, and the loss may be permanent, but the remaining neurons sometimes increase in complexity. In a famous autopsy study by Buell and Coleman (1979), dendrites were significantly longer and more complex in samples of normal brain tissue taken from elderly adults when compared to those of middle-aged adults (see ▌Figure 4.4). It appears that the brain may compensate for the losses it experiences by making better use of the structures that remain intact. Some researchers believe that sustained mental activity in later years helps promote neural growth, thereby counteracting some of the normal decline in mental skills and even reducing the risk of Alzheimer disease (Wilson et al., 2002).

CRITICAL THINKING

How might you test the idea that mental activity or exercise helps to counteract the decline in mental skills that occurs with age? Can you make predictions based on choice of profession? Should people who choose intellectually challenging professions show less mental decline with age?

Test Yourself 4.1

Check your knowledge about the physical changes that occur during development by deciding whether the following statements are True or False. (You will find the answers in the Appendix.)

1. The period in prenatal development lasting from implantation of the fertilized egg to the end of the eighth week is called the germinal period. *True or False?*
2. The initial development of arms, legs, fingers, and toes occurs during the embryonic period of prenatal development. *True or False?*
3. The large increases in brain size that occur in the first two years of life are due primarily to increases in the number of neurons in the brain. *True or False?*
4. The timing of motor development—when a baby begins to crawl, walk, and so on—is affected to a small extent by nature (biology) and to a large extent by nurture (the environment). *True or False?*
5. Everyone loses brain cells with age, and roughly half of all people over age 70 can expect to develop dementia. *True or False?*

Developing Intellectually

LEARNING GOALS

- Explain the research tools used to study infant perception and memory.
- Describe an infant's perceptual capabilities.
- Characterize memory loss in the elderly.
- Discuss and evaluate Piaget's theory of cognitive development.
- Discuss and evaluate Kolhberg's theory of moral development.

AS THE BRAIN CHANGES PHYSICALLY in response to the environment, so too does mental functioning. Babies are not born seeing and thinking about the world as adults do (Flavell, 1999). Cognitive processes—how we think and perceive—develop over time. Like learning to walk, intellectual development depends on adequate physical development within the brain as well as on exposure to the right kinds of experiences. In this section, we'll consider three aspects of intellectual development: How do we learn to perceive and remember the world? How do thought processes change with age? How do we develop a sense of right and wrong?

The Tools of Investigation

What does the world look like to a newborn child? Is it a complex three-dimensional world, full of depth, color, and texture? Or is it a "blooming, buzzing confusion," as claimed by the early psychologist William James? Let's stop for a moment and think about how a psychologist might answer these questions. Detecting the perceptual capabilities of an infant is not a simple matter. Babies can't tell us what they see or hear.

longitudinal design A research design in which the same people are studied or tested repeatedly over time.

Researchers who study development typically use two kinds of research design, *longitudinal* or *cross-sectional*. In a **longitudinal design**, you test the same person (or group of people) repeatedly over time, at various points in childhood or even through adulthood. If you wanted to study perceptual development, for instance, you would track the perceptual capabilities of baby Howard at various points in Howard's life. In a **cross-sectional design**, which is conducted over a more limited span of time, you assess the abilities of *different* people of different ages at the same time. So, rather than just testing Howard when he turns 2, 5, or 10, you would test groups of 2-, 5-, or 10-year-old children simultaneously. There are advantages and disadvantages associated with each research strategy.

cross-sectional design A research design in which people of different ages are compared at the same time.

If you're interested in studying infants or small children, though, you face additional problems. Because infants don't communicate as adults do, the analysis of perceptual development (or any other intellectual capacity) requires some creative research methods. It's necessary to devise a way to infer perceptual capabilities from what are essentially immobile, largely uncommunicative infants. Fortunately, babies possess several characteristics that make the job a little easier: (1) They show *preferences*, which means they prefer some stimuli over others; (2) they notice *novelty*, which means they notice new or different things in their environment; and (3) they

Concept Review | Research Designs for Studying Development

TYPE OF DESIGN	OVERVIEW	ADVANTAGES AND DISADVANTAGES
Cross-sectional	Researchers compare performance of different people of different ages.	A: Faster, more practical than longitudinal. D: Other variables may be confounded with age.
Longitudinal	Researchers test the same individuals repeatedly over time.	A: Can examine changes in individuals. D: Cost-intensive; subject loss over time.

FIGURE 4.5 The Preference
Technique
Babies prefer some visual stimuli over
others. In this case, the infant demonstrates
a preference for a female face by tracking its
location across trials. (The preference can
be determined by simply recording how long
the baby looks at each face.)

can *learn* to repeat activities that produce some kind of reward. As you'll see shortly,
researchers have developed techniques that capitalize on each of these tendencies.

The Preference Technique   In the "preference technique" developed by Robert Fantz (1961), an infant is presented with two visual displays simultaneously, and
the investigator simply records how long the infant looks at each (see ▌Figure 4.5).
Suppose one of the displays shows a male face and the other a female face, and the
baby looks at the female face for a significantly longer period of time. By "choosing"
to look longer at the female face, the infant has shown a preference. By itself, this
preference indicates very little. To infer things about what the baby can really see, it's
necessary to present the same two displays a number of times, switching their relative positions from trial to trial. If the baby continues to look longer at the female face
even though it appears on the left on some trials and on the right on others, we can
infer that the baby has the visual capability to differentiate between the two displays.
The infant "tells" us that he or she can detect differences by exclusively tracking the
female face. Notice that we didn't need to ask the baby anything—we simply inferred
things about his or her visual system by measuring overt behavior.

Habituation Techniques   One of the preferences babies consistently show is for
novelty—they like to look at new things. But they tend to ignore events that occur
repeatedly without consequence. For instance, if you show newborns a blue-colored
card and track how their eyes move (or how their heart rate changes), you'll find that
they spend a lot of time looking at the card when it first appears—it's something new.
But if you present the same card over and over again, their interest wanes, and they'll
begin to look at something else. This decline in responsiveness to repeated stimulation, called **habituation**, provides an effective tool for mapping out the infant's perceptual world (Bornstein, 1992; Colombo, Frick, & Gorman, 1997; Flavell, Miller, &
Miller, 1993). By acting bored, which is defined operationally by how long they look
at the card, babies reveal that they remember the stimulus from its previous presentation and recognize that it hasn't changed. It's as if the baby is saying, "Oh, it's that
blue card again."

habituation The decline in responsiveness to
a stimulus that is repeatedly presented.

Habituation can be used to discover specific information about how babies perceive and remember their world (DeSaint et al., 1997; Granrud, 1993). For example,
suppose we wanted to discover whether newborns have the capacity to see color.
We could show the blue card for a while, then suddenly switch to a green card that
matches on all other visual dimensions (such as size and brightness). If the infant
shows renewed interest in the card—treating the stimulus as if it were novel—we can
infer that the baby can discriminate, or tell the difference, between blue and green.

If, on the other hand, the baby continues to ignore the new green card, it suggests
that perhaps the baby lacks color vision at this stage in development (although there
may be other interpretations). We can also study memory by varying the time that
elapses between presentations of the card. If the baby continues to act bored by the
blue card even though we insert long pauses between successive presentations, we
know that he or she is remembering the card over those particular time intervals.

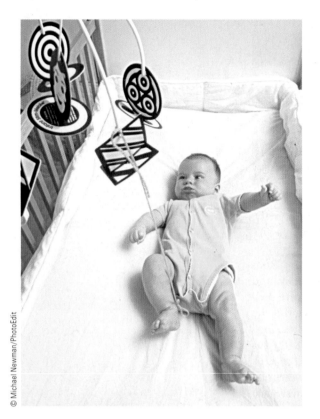

Researcher Carolyn Rovee-Collier showed that infants can learn to kick their legs to get an overhead mobile moving.

Using Rewards It's also possible to gain insight into what a baby sees, knows, and remembers by *rewarding* a simple motor movement, such as kicking a leg or sucking on an artificial nipple, in the presence of particular kinds of events (Siqueland & DeLucia, 1969). For example, in research by Carolyn Rovee-Collier (1993), 2- and 3-month-old infants were taught that kicking their legs could produce movement of a mobile hanging overhead. A moving mobile is quite rewarding to babies at this age, and they'll double or triple their rate of leg kicking in a matter of minutes if it leads to movement. We can then study cognitive abilities— such as memory—by taking the mobile away, waiting for some period of time, and then replacing the mobile. If the baby begins leg kicking again at rates comparable to those produced at the end of training, we can infer that the baby has remembered what he or she has learned. We can also change the characteristics of the mobile after training and learn things about a baby's perceptual abilities. For example, if we train an infant with a blue mobile and then switch to a green one, any differences in leg kicking should help to tell us whether the baby can discriminate between green and blue.

The Growing Perceptual World

Using such techniques, researchers have discovered that babies greet the world with reasonably well-functioning sensory systems. Although none is operating at peak efficiency, because the biological equipment is still maturing, babies still see a world of color and shape (Banks & Shannon, 1993). They even arrive with built-in preferences. One-day-old babies, for example, respond more to patterned stimuli than to unpatterned ones. As shown in ∎ Figure 4.6, they also prefer to look at correctly drawn faces rather than scrambled facial features (Johnson et al., 1991; see also Walton & Bower, 1993). It's likely that learning plays a role in some of these preferences (Turati, 2004), but reasonably sophisticated perceptual processing occurs soon after birth.

∎ **FIGURE 4.6** Infant Preferences
In this experiment, babies were shown either a blank stimulus, a stimulus with scrambled facial features, or a face. Each stimulus was first positioned over the baby's head and then moved from side to side. The dependent variable measured the extent to which the baby tracked each stimulus by head turning. As the results show, the babies tracked the face stimulus more than the others. (Graph adapted from Johnson et al., 1991)

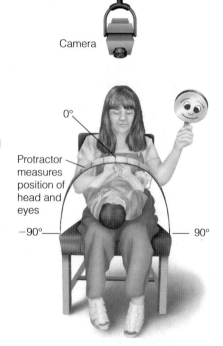

Experimental Setup

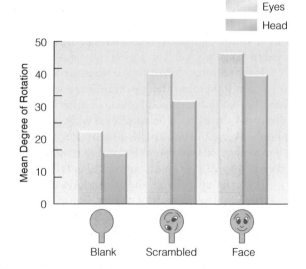

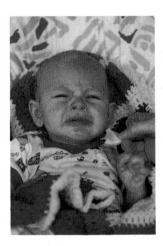

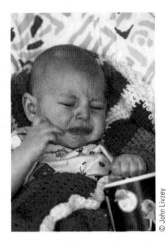

© John Livzey

This baby is a few months old, but even newborn infants show distinctive reactions to a variety of tastes (lemon, sugar, and salt are shown here).

Newborns also hear reasonably well, and they seem to recognize their mother's voice within a day or two (DeCasper & Fifer, 1980). Remarkably, there is even evidence to suggest that newborns can hear and remember things that happen *prior* to birth. By the 28th week, fetuses will close their eyes in response to loud noises presented near the mother's abdomen (Parmelee & Sigman, 1983). Infants will also choose to suck on an artificial nipple that produces a recording of a story that was read aloud to them repeatedly before birth. It's unlikely that the baby is actually remembering the story—but it does indicate that babies are sensitive to particular experiences that happen in the womb (DeCasper & Spence, 1986). If you think about it, you'll realize this is an adaptive quality for the newborn. Remember, babies need nourishment and are dependent on others for survival. Consequently, those born into the world with a visual system that can detect shapes and forms and an auditory system tuned to the human voice have a better chance of survival.

In addition to sights and sounds, babies are quite sensitive to touch, smell, pain, and taste. Place a drop of lemon juice in the mouth of a newborn, and you'll see a distinctive grimace. Place a small amount of sugar in the baby's mouth, and the baby will smack his or her lips. These distinctive reactions are present at birth and are found even before the infant has had a single taste of food (Steiner, 1977). A baby's sense of smell is developed well enough that the newborn quickly learns to recognize the odor of its mother's breast (Porter et al., 1992). As for pain and touch, babies will reject a milk bottle that is too hot, and, as every parent knows, the right kind of pat on the baby's back is pleasurable enough to soothe the newborn into sleep.

Babies even seem to perceive a three-dimensional world. When placed on a visual cliff, such as the one shown in the photo, 6-month-old babies are reluctant to cross over the apparent drop-off, or cliff, to reach a parent (Gibson & Walk, 1960). Babies as young as 2 months show heart rate changes when they're placed on the glass portion covering the deep side of the visual cliff (Campos, Langer, & Krowitz, 1970).

Still, these are infant perceptions, and the infant's world is not the same as that of an adult. Newborn babies cannot see as well as adults. They're not very good at discriminating fine detail in visual patterns: Compared with the ideal acuity level of 20/20, babies see a blurry world that is more on the order of 20/400, meaning that what newborns see at 20 feet is what adults with ideal vision see at 400 feet. In addition, newborns probably can't perceive shapes and forms in the same way adults do (Bornstein, 1992; Johnson, 1997), nor can they hear as well as adults. For example, infants seem to have some trouble listening selectively for certain kinds of sounds, and they require sounds to be louder than adults do before those sounds can be detected (Bargones & Werner, 1994).

Infants' perceptual systems improve markedly during the first few months, partly because of continued physical development but also because experience fine-tunes their sensory abilities. In the visual cliff experiments mentioned above, infants with extensive locomotor experience (e.g., crawling) are more reluctant to cross over the

© Mark Richards/PhotoEdit

In the visual cliff apparatus, a plate of glass covers an abrupt drop-off. From the age of approximately 6 months, babies are reluctant to cross the cliff to reach a beckoning parent.

"cliff" and show more fear (e.g., an elevated heart rate) when lowered over the cliff's deep side (Witherington et al., 2005). Moreover, research with nonhuman subjects, such as cats or chimpanzees, has shown that if animals are deprived of visual stimulation during the early weeks or months of life, permanent visual impairments can result (Gandelman, 1992). Thus perceptual development relies on experience as well as on physically mature sensory equipment.

By the time we leave infancy, our perceptual systems are reasonably intact. Most of the changes that occur during childhood and adolescence affect our ability to use the equipment we have. For example, as children grow older, their attention span improves, and they're better able to attend selectively to pertinent information. Memory improves throughout childhood, partly because kids learn strategies for organizing and maintaining information in memory (Courage & Howe, 2004). Moreover, as you'll see in Chapters 5 and 8, how we perceive and remember the world depends on what we know about it. We use our general knowledge about people and events to help us interpret ambiguous stimuli and to remember things that happen in our lives. Perception and memory are influenced by the knowledge gained from experience, which is one of the reasons perceptual development is really a lifelong process.

Do We Lose Memory With Age?

By the time people hit their 40s or 50s, the odds are pretty good they'll start complaining about memory problems—maybe they'll have trouble coming up with the right word or the name of someone they've recently met. These are normal trends, nothing to worry about, but overall, there isn't any simple or straightforward relationship between aging and memory. Some kinds of memory falter badly with age, but others do not.

For example, psychologists are now reasonably convinced that the ability to *recall* recent events, such as items from a grocery list, declines regularly with age. However, in other tests, such as *recognition*, where information is re-presented and the task is to tell whether it's been seen or heard before, little or no age differences might be found. So your 50-year-old Dad might fail to recall your best friend's name (it's on the tip of his tongue), but he'll easily recognize the name when he hears it.

Age-related deficits are also restricted primarily to tasks that require conscious memory. If memory is tested in ways that don't require conscious awareness (such as testing whether your ability to solve a puzzle increases if you've seen it before), age-related differences largely disappear (see Balota, Dolan, & Duchek, 2000).

Let's consider a specific example to illustrate how research in this area is typically done. Craik and McDowd (1987) used a cross-sectional design to compare recall and recognition performance for two age groups: a "young" group of college students, with an average age of 20.7 years; and an "old" group, volunteers from a senior citizen center, with an average age of 72.8 years. All of the participants were asked to learn memory lists that consisted of short phrases ("a body of water") presented together with associated target words ("pond"). The lists were followed by either (1) an immediate recall test in which the short phrase was given and the subject was to recall the target word or (2) a delayed recognition test that required the subjects to decide whether a word had or had not been presented in one of the earlier lists.

In such experiments, attempts are made to match the participants on as many variables as possible—such as educational level and verbal ability—so that the only difference between the groups is age. Any performance differences can then be attributed uniquely to the independent variable (age) and not to some other confounding factor (see Chapter 2). The results of the Craik and McDowd (1987) study are shown in ▌ Figure 4.7. As you can see, the younger group outperformed the older group on the test of recall, but the advantage vanished on the recognition test. So memory losses in the elderly depend importantly on how memory is actually tested. Other studies have shown that performance also depends on the types of materials tested. When older individuals are asked to remember materials that fit naturally into their personal ar-

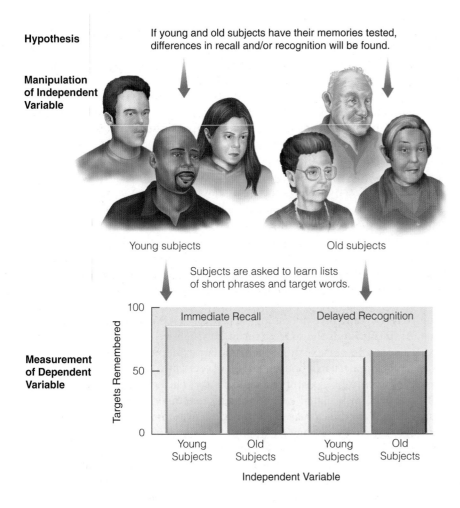

Hypothesis

If young and old subjects have their memories tested, differences in recall and/or recognition will be found.

Manipulation of Independent Variable

Young subjects   Old subjects

Subjects are asked to learn lists of short phrases and target words.

Measurement of Dependent Variable

Targets Remembered

Immediate Recall   Delayed Recognition

Young Subjects   Old Subjects   Young Subjects   Old Subjects

Independent Variable

FIGURE 4.7 Memory and Aging
A group with an average age of 20.7 years and a group with an average age of 72.8 years were asked to learn and then recall or recognize target words. Although the younger subjects recalled more targets than the older subjects, the advantage disappeared for recognition. (Craik & McDowd, 1987)

eas of expertise, they often perform better than their younger counterparts (Zacks & Hasher, 1994). Age-related memory problems can also be reduced, to a certain extent, if the elderly are given more time to study material and supportive cues are given at the time memory is required.

Researchers are actively trying to determine why age-related memory deficits occur (see Anderson & Craik, 2000). One possibility is that older adults lose the ability to suppress irrelevant thoughts or ignore irrelevant stimuli (Hasher et al., 1991). Because they're unable to focus selectively on the task at hand, they fail to process the to-be-remembered information in ways that help later recall (Craik, 1994). As you'll see in Chapter 8, memory depends greatly on the kinds of mental processing that occur during study. There's also some evidence that prior beliefs, or stereotypes, such as the belief that memory should decline with age, may influence memory performance in the aged. For example, there are generally fewer negative stereotypes about aging in mainland China, and Chinese residents tend to show smaller age-related memory differences than do residents of the United States (see Levy & Langer, 1994).

Piaget and the Development of Thought

Much of what we know about how thought develops during childhood comes from the collective works of a Swiss scholar named Jean Piaget (1896–1980). It was Piaget who first convinced psychologists that children think quite differently from adults. Children are not little adults, he argued, who simply lack knowledge and experience; instead, they view the world in a unique way. Piaget believed that everyone is born with a natural tendency to organize the world meaningfully. People construct mental models of the world—called **schemata**—and use these schemata to guide and

Jean Piaget

schemata Mental models of the world that we use to guide and interpret our experiences.

interpret their experiences. But these schemata are not very adultlike early in development—in fact, they tend not to reflect the world accurately—so much of early intellectual development is spent changing and fine-tuning our worldviews. One of Piaget's primary contributions was to demonstrate that children's reasoning errors can provide a window into how the schema construction process is proceeding.

For example, consider the two tilted cups shown in the margin. If young children are asked to draw a line indicating how the water level in a tilted cup might look, they tend to draw a line that's parallel to the top and bottom of the cup, as shown in the cup on the left, rather than parallel to the ground, as shown in the cup on the right. This kind of error is important, Piaget argued, because children can't have learned such a thing directly from experience (water never tilts that way in real life). Instead, the error reflects a fundamental misconception of how the world is structured. Young children have an inaccurate internal view, or model, of the world.

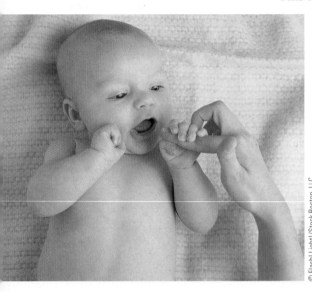

The rooting reflex is adaptive because it helps the newborn receive needed sustenance.

© Flash! Light/Stock Boston, LLC

assimilation The process through which we fit—or assimilate—new experiences into existing schemata.

accommodation The process through which we change or modify existing schemata to accommodate new experiences.

sensorimotor period Piaget's first stage of cognitive development, lasting from birth to about 2 years of age; schemata revolve around sensory and motor abilities.

Assimilation and Accommodation   As their brains and bodies mature, children are able to use experience to build more sophisticated and correct mental models of the world. Piaget suggested that cognitive development is guided by two adaptive psychological processes, *assimilation* and *accommodation*. **Assimilation** is the process through which we fit—or assimilate—new experiences into our existing schemata. For example, suppose a small child who has been raised in a household full of cats mistakenly concludes that the neighbor's new rabbit is simply a kind of kitty. The new experience—the rabbit—has been assimilated into the child's existing view of the world: Small furry things are cats. The second function, **accommodation**, is the process through which we change or modify existing schemata to accommodate new experiences. When the child learns that the new "kitty" hops rather than walks and seems reluctant to purr, he or she will need to modify and revise the existing concept of small furry things; the child is forced to change the existing schemata to accommodate the new information. Notice that the child plays an active role in constructing schemata by interacting directly with the world (Piaget, 1929).

Piaget believed that children develop an adult worldview by moving systematically through a series of four stages or developmental periods: *sensorimotor, preoperational, concrete operational,* and *formal operational.* Each of these periods is tied roughly to a particular age range—for example, the preoperational period usually lasts from age 2 to about age 7—but individual differences can occur in how quickly the child moves from one stage to the next. Although the timing may vary from child to child, Piaget believed that the order in which individuals progress through the stages is invariant—it remains the same for everyone. Let's consider these cognitive developmental periods in more detail.

The Sensorimotor Period: Birth to Two Years

From birth to about age 2, schemata about the world revolve primarily around the infant's sensory and motor abilities (hence the name **sensorimotor period**). Babies initially interact with the world through a collection of survival reflexes. For example, they'll start sucking when an object is placed in their mouth (called the *sucking reflex*), and they'll automatically turn their head in the direction of a touch or brush on the cheek (called the *rooting reflex*). This behavior is different from an adult's, but it's adaptive for a newborn. These reflexes increase the likelihood that adequate nourishment will follow, and attaining adequate nourishment is a significant problem the newborn needs to solve.

As infants develop intellectually over the first year, they use their maturing motor skills to understand how they can interact with the world voluntarily. Babies start to vocalize to gain attention; they learn they can kick their legs to make sounds; they acquire the ability to reach with their arms to touch or grasp objects. In essence, they

According to Piaget, babies who haven't yet mastered the concept of object permanence don't understand that objects still exist when they're no longer in view. Notice how this boy loses interest when he can no longer see his favorite toy.

begin acting like "little scientists," exploring their world, learning to repeat actions, and testing rudimentary hypotheses about cause and effect (although not in the same conscious way that we might). The initial stirrings of symbolic thought begin during this period. The infant gradually develops the ability to construct internal mental images or symbols.

Early in the first year babies lack **object permanence**, which means they fail to recognize that objects exist when they're no longer in sight. The accompanying photos illustrate how psychologists have measured object permanence. Notice that the baby loses interest when the toy is covered, suggesting that the baby is only capable of thinking about objects that are directly in view. Babies at this point are unable to represent objects symbolically—out of sight equals out of mind. But by the end of the first year, Piaget argued, the child has a different reaction to the disappearance of a favored toy; as object permanence develops, the child will begin to search actively for the lost toy.

object permanence The ability to recognize that objects still exist when they're no longer in sight.

The Preoperational Period: Two to Seven Years

From about ages 2 through 7, the child's schemata continue to grow in sophistication. Children in the **preoperational period** no longer have difficulty thinking about absent objects, and they can use one object to stand for another. A 4-year-old, for example, can effortlessly use a stick to represent a soaring airplane or a cardboard box for a stove. The child realizes these are not the real objects, but he or she can imagine them to be real for the purposes of play. At the same time, as Piaget demonstrated in a number of clever ways, the child still thinks about the world quite differently from an adult. As you'll see momentarily, the child lacks the ability to perform certain basic mental operations—hence Piaget's use of the term *preoperational* to describe a child's mental abilities during this period.

preoperational period Piaget's second stage of cognitive development, lasting from ages 2 to about 7; children begin to think symbolically but often lack the ability to perform mental operations such as conservation.

Conservation　Something that children at the preoperational stage often fail to understand is the **principle of conservation**. To understand conservation, one needs to be able to recognize that certain physical properties of an object remain the same despite superficial changes in its appearance (see ▌ Figure 4.8 on page 110). If 4- or 5-year-old children are shown two play dough balls of exactly the same size and are asked which object contains more play dough, most of the children will say that the two balls contain the same amount. But if one of the balls is then rolled into a long sausage-like shape, the children are likely to think that the two quantities of play dough are no longer the same, saying that either the sausage or the ball has more play dough.

Children at this age are unable to understand that a basic property of an object, in this case its mass, doesn't change as the object changes shape. Typically, preoperational children will fail to conserve a basic quantity even if they directly observe the change in appearance taking place. Suppose we ask 5-year-old Sam to pour a cup of water into each of two identical glasses. Sam performs the task and accepts that the two glasses now contain the same amount. We then instruct him to pour the water

principle of conservation The ability to recognize that the physical properties of an object remain the same despite superficial changes in the object's appearance.

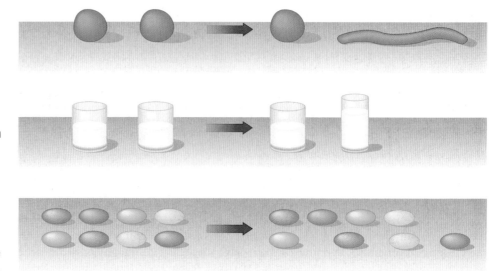

FIGURE 4.8 Examples of Conservation Problems
Understanding conservation means recognizing that the physical properties of objects remain the same, even though the objects may superficially change in appearance. Preoperational children often fail conservation problems—they fail to detect, for example, that the objects to the right of the arrows still retain the same volume or number.

from one of the glasses into another glass that is tall and thin. Do the glasses now contain the same amount of water? "No," Sam explains, "now the tall one has more water." Sam is not showing any evidence of conservation; he does not yet recognize that how the water looks in the glass has no effect on its volume.

The reason children in the preoperational period make these kinds of errors, Piaget argued, is that they lack the capacity to think in truly adultlike ways. For example, preoperational children suffer from *centration*—they tend to focus their attention on one particular aspect of a situation and to ignore others. Sam is convinced that the tall glass has more water because he cannot simultaneously consider both the height and width of the glass; he focuses only on the height and therefore is convinced that the taller glass must contain more water. In addition, children at this age have difficulty understanding the concept of *reversibility*—that one kind of operation can produce change and that another kind of operation can undo that change. For example, Sam is unlikely to consider what will happen if the water from the tall glass is poured back into the original glass. The capacity to understand that operations are reversible doesn't develop until the next stage.

Piaget also discovered that children in the preoperational period tend to see the world, and the objects in it, from primarily one perspective: their own. Children at this stage have a tough time imagining themselves in another person's position. If you ask a child in the preoperational period to describe what another person will see or think, you're likely to find the child simply describing what he or she personally sees or thinks. Piaget called this characteristic **egocentrism**—the tendency to view the world from your own unique perspective only.

The Concrete Operational Period: Seven to Eleven Years

Between the ages of 7 and about 11, children enter the **concrete operational period** and acquire true mental operations. By mental *operations*, Piaget meant the ability to perform mental actions on objects—to verbalize, visualize, and mentally manipulate objects. A child of 8 can consider the consequences of rolling a long strip of play dough into a ball before the action is actually performed. Children in the concrete operational period have fewer difficulties with conservation problems because they are capable of reversing operations on objects—they can mentally consider the effects of both doing and undoing an action.

Children at the concrete operational stage also show the initial stirrings of logical thought, which means they can now mentally order and compare objects and per-

egocentrism The tendency to see the world from one's own unique perspective only; a characteristic of thinking in the preoperational period of development.

concrete operational period Piaget's third stage of cognitive development, lasting from ages 7 to 11. Children acquire the capacity to perform a number of mental operations but still lack the ability for abstract reasoning.

Concept Review | Piaget's Stages of Cognitive Development

STAGE	BASIC CHARACTERISTICS	ACCOMPLISHMENTS	LIMITATIONS
Sensorimotor period (birth–2 years)	Schemata about the world revolve primarily around sensory and motor abilities.	Child develops **object permanence**; learns how to control body; learns how to vocalize, and learns first words.	Schemata are limited primarily to simple sensory and motor function; problems in thinking about absent objects (early).
Preoperational period (2–7 years)	Schemata grow in sophistication. Children can think about absent objects, and can use one object to stand for another.	Children readily symbolize objects, and imaginary play is common; great strides in language development.	Children are prelogical; they fail to understand **conservation**, due to **centration** and a failure to understand **reversibility**; children show **egocentricity** in thinking.
Concrete operational period (7–11 years)	Children gain the capacity for true mental operations, i.e., verbalizing, visualizing, mental manipulation.	Child understands reversibility and other simple logical operations like categorizing and ordering.	Mental operations remain concrete, tied to actual objects in the real world. Difficulty with problems that do not flow from everyday experience.
Formal operational period (11 years–adulthood)	Mastery is gained over abstract thinking.	Adolescents can think and answer questions in general and abstract ways.	No limitations; development of reasoning is complete. However, not all reach this stage.

form more sophisticated classifications. These children can do simple math and solve problems that require elementary reasoning. Consider the following example: Martin is faster than Jose; Jose is faster than Conrad. Is Martin faster or slower than Conrad? Children of 9 or 10 have little trouble with this problem because they can keep track of ordered relations in their heads. Younger preoperational children will probably insist on actually seeing Martin and Conrad race—they can't easily solve the problem in their heads.

Although concrete operational children possess a growing array of mental operations, Piaget believed they are still limited intellectually in an important way. The mental operations they can perform remain *concrete*, or tied directly to actual objects in the real world. Children at this age have great difficulty with problems that do not flow directly from everyday experience. Ask an 8-year-old to solve a problem involving four-armed people and barking cats and you're likely to see a blank look on his or her face. Basically, if something can't be seen, heard, touched, tasted, or smelled, it's going to be tough for these children to think about (although they can imagine non-real-world objects they have encountered, for example, in cartoons or fairy tales). The ability to think truly abstractly doesn't develop until the final stage of cognitive development.

© David Young-Wolff/PhotoEdit

Most children reach the formal operational period by their teenage years, when they master abstract thinking.

The Formal Operational Period: Eleven to Adulthood

By the time children reach their teenage years, most will be in the formal operational period, during which thought processes become increasingly more like those of an adult. Neither teenagers nor adults have problems thinking about imaginary or artificial concepts; they can consider hypothetical outcomes or make logical deductions about places they've never visited or that might not even exist. Teenagers can develop systematic strategies for solving problems—such as using trial and error—that are beyond the capability of most preteens.

formal operational period Piaget's last stage of cognitive development; thought processes become adultlike, and people gain mastery over abstract thinking.

The **formal operational period** is the stage at which we start to gain mastery over *abstract* thinking. Ask a concrete operational child about the meaning of education, and you'll be likely to hear about teachers and grades. The formal operational adolescent is able to answer the question in a general and abstract way, perhaps describing education as a system organized by parents and the government to foster the acquisition of useful knowledge. Piaget believed that the transition from concrete operational thinking to formal operational thinking probably occurs gradually, over several years, and may not be achieved by everyone (Piaget, 1970). Once this stage is reached, the adolescent is no longer tied to concrete, real-world constructs and can invent and experiment with the possible rather than just with the here and now.

Challenges to Piaget's Theory

Piaget's contributions to our understanding of cognitive development were substantial. He successfully convinced the psychological community that children have unique internal schemata, and he provided convincing demonstrations that those schemata, once formed, tend to change systematically over time. However, not all of Piaget's ideas have withstood the rigors of experimental scrutiny. Researchers now commonly challenge the specifics of his theory, primarily his assumptions about what children really know and when they know it (Feldman, 2003).

It turns out that children and young infants are considerably more sophisticated in their models of the world than Piaget believed. For example, Piaget was convinced that object permanence doesn't develop until late in the child's first year. Although it's true that children will not search for a hidden toy in the first few months of life, more sensitive tests have revealed that even 1- to 4-month-old infants are capable of recognizing that vanished objects still exist (Baillargeon, 2004).

In research by child psychologist T. G. R. Bower (1982), very young infants watched as a screen was moved in front of a toy, blocking it from view (see ▐ Figure 4.9). Moments later, when the screen was removed, the infants acted surprised

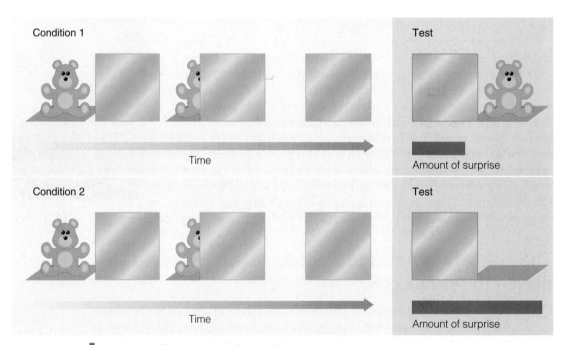

▐ **FIGURE 4.9** Reevaluating Object Permanence
In this experiment a screen was moved in front of a toy, blocking it from the infant's view. Moments later, when the screen was removed, the baby's level of surprise (defined as a change in heart rate) was measured. In one condition the toy appeared behind the screen; in a second condition it had vanished. Babies showed more surprise when the toy was absent, suggesting that object permanence may develop earlier than Piaget suspected. (Bower, 1982)

if the toy was absent (it could be secretly removed by the experimenter). If objects no longer exist when removed from view, then infants shouldn't be surprised by a sudden absence (see also Baillargeon, 1994; Hofstadter & Reznick, 1996). Other researchers have demonstrated that small infants can show symbolic thought—they understand, for instance, that objects move along continuous paths and do not jump around—and they gain this understanding at points in development far earlier than Piaget imagined (see Mandler, 1992; Spelke et al., 1992).

Piaget has also been criticized for sticking to the notion of distinct stages, or periods of development (Flavell et al., 1993). Piaget recognized that not all children develop at the same rate, but he remained convinced that a child's thought processes undergo sharp transitions from one stage to the next. Most developmental psychologists now believe that cognitive development is better viewed as a process of continual change and adaptation (Siegler, 1996). According to the stage view, once a child undergoes a stage transition—say, from the preoperational to the concrete operational—he or she should be able to perform a variety of new tasks relatively quickly. But this is not usually the case.

Children in nomadic societies, who move from one place to another often, may be able to orient themselves in an environment faster and more efficiently than children raised in fixed locales.

Children's thought processes do not seem to undergo rapid transitions; in fact, they often change slowly over long periods of time (Flavell, 1971). For example, it's not uncommon to find a 5-year-old who understands conservation of number but has no idea about conservation of mass or volume. A given child might show mental schemata that are characteristic of more than one stage. Children are learning to adapt to their world, to tasks and problems that might occur only in particular situations, so it's not surprising that they don't always fit into a specific cognitive stage, or that the transitions from one developmental point to the next are not rapid and well defined (Munakata et al., 1997).

The Role of Culture   Piaget was rather fuzzy about the mechanisms that produce cognitive change. He recognized that infants, toddlers, and school-age children think in fundamentally different ways, but he never clearly accounted for the psychological processes that produce those changes (Siegler, 1994, 1996). He also largely ignored the importance of social context in explaining individual differences in cognitive ability. Cross-cultural research has shown that children across the world develop cognitively in similar ways, but significant cultural differences occur in the rate of development (Matsumoto, 1994). For example, children raised in nomadic societies, which move frequently from place to place, seem to acquire spatial skills (the ability to orient themselves in their environment) earlier than children raised in single, fixed locales. Schooling may also be a factor: Ample cross-cultural evidence indicates that people who never attend school may have a difficult time reaching the formal operational stage of thinking, at least as measured through traditional Piagetian tasks (Cole, 1992; Segall et al., 1990).

The importance of social and cultural influences was promoted by a Russian psychologist, Lev Vygotsky, around the same time that Piaget was developing his theoretical ideas. Vygotsky died in 1934, after only a decade of work in psychology, but his ideas remain very influential (Daniels, Cole, & Wertsch, 2007). Vygotsky argued that cognitive abilities emerge *directly* out of our social interactions with others. He proposed, for example, that inner speech, which we use to think and plan activities, is a natural extension of the outer speech that we use to communicate. He was convinced that intellectual development is tied to social interaction—it grows out of each person's attempts to master social situations. Development can't be understood by considering the individual alone—you must always consider the individual in his or her social context (Vygotsky, 1978).

For example, imagine asking a 3-year-old child to describe how meals are prepared in the household. It's unlikely that you'll get much of a response—beyond, perhaps, a shrugging of the shoulders or shake of the head. Yet, if we engage the child

According to Vygotsky, cognitive abilities arise directly out of children's social and verbal interactions with other people.

in some form of social interaction—we provide clues or ask leading questions (e.g., Where is food stored? Where is it cooked?)—we're likely to find that the child actually has quite a bit of knowledge about how food is prepared. Every child has what Vygotsky called a "zone of proximal development," which is the difference between what the child can accomplish on his or her own and what he or she can do in the context of a social interaction (such as interacting with Mom or Dad). It is our social interactions, Vygotsky argued, that energize development and help to shape how we think.

Moral Development: Learning Right From Wrong

morality The ability to distinguish between appropriate and inappropriate actions.

Developing intellectually means more than learning to think logically and form correct internal models of the world. As children mature intellectually, they also need to develop *character*. They need to acquire a sense of **morality**, which provides them with a way to distinguish between appropriate and inappropriate actions. Piaget had strong opinions on this topic, arguing that the sense of morality is closely tied to one's stage of cognitive development and to one's social experiences with peers. For example, from Piaget's perspective children in the concrete operational stage shouldn't show sophisticated moral reasoning skills because morality is basically an abstract concept—something that cannot be handled until the formal operational stage of development. Partly for this reason, most of the work on moral development has been conducted with adolescents and adults.

Kohlberg's Stage Theory   The most influential theory of moral development is the stage theory proposed by Lawrence Kohlberg. Kohlberg was strongly influenced by Piaget, and like Piaget, he believed that people move through stages of moral development (Kohlberg, 1963, 1986). He would give people a moral dilemma, ask them to solve it, and use their reasoning to help identify their state of moral development. Let's consider an example, based on Kohlberg (1969):

> A woman is stricken with a rare and deadly form of cancer. There is a drug that can save her, a form of radium recently discovered by a druggist in town. But the druggist is charging $2,000 for the medicine, 10 times what the drug cost him to make. The sick woman's husband, Heinz, tries desperately to raise the money but can raise only half of the needed amount. He pleads with the druggist to sell him the drug at a reduced cost, or at least to allow him to pay for the drug over time, but the druggist refuses. "No," the druggist says, "I discovered the drug, and I'm going to make money from it." Frantic to save his wife, Heinz considers breaking into the druggist's office to steal the drug.

What do you think? Should the husband steal the drug? Why or why not? It is the reasoning behind your answer, the kind of intellectual justification you give, that was important to Kohlberg. He believed that people can be classified into stages of moral development based on how they answer such moral problems. Although Kohlberg's theory actually proposes as many as six stages of moral development, I'll focus on his three main levels only: *preconventional, conventional,* and *postconventional.*

preconventional level In Kohlberg's theory, the lowest level of moral development, in which decisions about right and wrong are made primarily in terms of external consequences.

At the lowest level of moral development—the **preconventional level**—decisions about right and wrong are based primarily on external consequences. Young children will typically interpret the morality of a behavior in terms of its immediate individual consequences—that is, whether the act will lead directly to a reward or to a punishment: "Heinz shouldn't steal the drug because he might get caught and punished" or "Heinz should steal the drug because people will get mad at him if his wife dies." Notice the rationale is based on the immediate external consequences of the action rather than on some abstract moral principle.

conventional level In Kohlberg's theory of moral development, the stage in which actions are judged to be right or wrong based on whether they maintain or disrupt the social order.

At the **conventional level** of moral reasoning, people justify their actions based on internalized rules. Now an action is right or wrong because it maintains or disrupts the *social order*. Someone at this level might argue that "Heinz shouldn't steal the drug because stealing is against the law" or that "Heinz should steal the drug be-

Concept Review | Kohlberg's Stage Theory of Moral Development

STAGE	BASIS FOR MORAL JUDGMENT	POSSIBLE RESPONSE TO "WAS HEINZ RIGHT?"
Preconventional	External consequences	Yes: "He can't be happy without his wife." No: "If he gets caught, he'll be put in jail."
Conventional	Social order	Yes: "Spouses are responsible for protecting one another." No: "Stealing is against the law."
Postconventional	Abstract ethical principles	Yes: "Individual lives are more important than society's law against stealing." No: "Laws are necessary in a civilized society; they need to be followed by all to prevent chaos."

cause husbands have an obligation to protect their wives." Notice here that the moral reasoning has moved away from immediate individual consequences to societal consequences. Moral behavior is that which conforms to the rules and conventions of society. In general, people at the conventional level of moral reasoning tend to consider the appropriateness of their actions from the perspective of the resident authority figures in the culture.

At the final level of moral development, the **postconventional level**, morality is based on abstract principles that may even conflict with accepted standards. The person adopts a moral standard not to seek approval from others or an authority figure but to follow some universal ethical principle. "An individual human life is more important than society's dictum against stealing," someone at this level might argue. In this case, moral actions are driven by general and abstract personal codes of ethics that may not agree with societal norms.

postconventional level Kohlberg's highest level of moral development, in which moral actions are judged on the basis of a personal code of ethics that is general and abstract and that may not agree with societal norms.

Evaluating Kohlberg's Theory Developmental psychologists continue to believe that we progress through periods of moral development, from an early focus on immediate individual consequences toward a final principled code of ethics. A number of observational studies have confirmed aspects of Kohlberg's views. For example, people do seem to move through the various types of moral reasoning in the sequence suggested by Kohlberg (Walker, 1989). Furthermore, the link that both Piaget and Kohlberg made between moral reasoning and level of cognitive development has clear merit. But Kohlberg's critics argue that he ties the concept of morality too closely to an abstract code of justice—that is, to the idea that moral acts are those that ensure fairness to the individual (Damon & Hart, 1992).

For example, suppose your sense of morality is not based on fairness but rather on concern for the welfare of others. You might believe that the appropriate action is always one that doesn't hurt anyone and takes into account the happiness of the affected individual. Under these conditions, as analyzed by Kohlberg, your behavior will appear to be driven more by an individual situation than by a consistent code of justice. Psychologist Carol Gilligan (1982) has argued that women in our culture often adopt such a view (a moral code based on caring), whereas men tend to make moral decisions on the basis of an abstract sense of justice. According to Kohlberg's theory, however, this means that women will tend to be classified at a lower level of moral development than men. Gilligan sees this as an unfair and unjustified gender bias.

The Role of Culture Gilligan may have overstated the case for sex differences in moral reasoning. Men and women often think in much the same way about the moral dilemmas studied by Kohlberg (Walker, 1989). At the same time, cross-cultural differences do occur in moral thinking that are not captured well by Kohlberg's classification system. For example, studies of moral decision making in India reveal striking differences from those typically found in Western cultures. Richard Shweder and his colleagues (1990) found that both Hindu children and adults are likely to find it

CRITICAL THINKING

Based on what you've learned about moral development, what advice would you give parents who are trying to teach their children about right and wrong?

morally acceptable for a husband to beat a disobedient wife—in fact, keeping disobedient family members in line is considered to be the moral obligation of the head of the family. In the United States, such actions would be widely condemned.

Western cultures also tend to place more value on individualism and stress individual goals more than other cultures, where the emphasis may be on collective goals. These kinds of cultural values must be factored into any complete theory of moral development (Miller, 1994). Moreover, the importance a culture places on teaching moral values can affect the speed with which moral development proceeds (Snarey, 1995). The bottom line: Morality seems to develop in a consistent manner across the world—that is, people tend to interpret morality first in terms of external consequences and only later in terms of abstract principles—but, not surprisingly, culture exerts its influence in powerful ways (Saltzstein, 1997).

Developmental psychologists also question whether the concept of morality can be easily captured by a simple analysis of reasoning. For example, Hart and Fegley (1995) interviewed inner-city adolescents who had been singled out by community leaders for exceptional volunteer work and commitment to social services. These kids expressed high degrees of moral commitment and often described themselves in terms of moral values, yet they didn't show a higher than average level of moral development when tested using Kohlberg's theory. Many developmental psychologists believe that we need to broaden our conception of morality to make it more representative of the diversity of social experiences (Arnold, 2000).

Test Yourself 4.2

Check your knowledge of intellectual development by answering these questions. (You will find the answers in the Appendix.)

1. Pick the appropriate research technique from among the following terms: *cross-sectional, habituation, longitudinal, preference,* and *reward*.
   a. Baby learns to kick her leg because it moves the mobile: _____

   b. Baby grows bored and stops looking at repeated presentations of the same event: _____
   c. Comparisons are made among three groups of children; each group contains children of a different age: _____

   d. The development of memory is studied by testing the same individual repeatedly throughout his or her lifetime: _____

2. According to Piaget, children develop mental models of the world, called schemata, that change as the child grows. During the preoperational period of development, children often fail to recognize that the physical properties of an object can stay the same despite superficial changes in its appearance (e.g., rolling a ball of dough into a sausage shape doesn't change its mass). Piaget referred to this ability as
   a. conservation.
   b. object permanence.
   c. accommodation.
   d. relativistic thinking.

3. Pick the appropriate level of moral development, as described by Kohlberg. Possible answers include *conventional, preconventional,* and *postconventional*.
   a. Actions are justified on the basis of whether they disrupt the social order: _____
   b. Actions are justified on the basis of abstract moral principles: _____
   c. Actions are justified on the basis of their immediate consequences: _____

Developing Socially and Personally

LEARNING GOALS
- Discuss the short- and long-term characteristics of early attachments.
- Explain Erik Erikson's stage theory of personal identity development.
- Describe the issues that affect gender-role development.
- Discuss the psychological issues associated with death and dying.

PEOPLE DO NOT DEVELOP IN ISOLATION. We're social animals, and the relationships we form with others affect how we act and view ourselves. For infants, relationships with caregivers—usually their parents—guarantee them adequate nourishment and a safe and secure environment. Children work hard to become part of a social group, learning how to get along with peers and to follow the rules and norms of society. For adults, whose social bonds become increasingly intimate, the task is to learn to accept responsibility for the care and support of others. As with most aspects of development, social and personal growth is shaped partly by biology and partly by what we learn from experience.

Forming Bonds With Others

Think again about the problems faced by the newborn infant: limited motor skills, somewhat fuzzy vision, yet a powerful sustained need for food, water, and warmth. To gain the nourishment needed to live, as well as protection from danger, the newborn relies on interactions with others—usually the mother. The newborn forms **attachments**, strong emotional ties to one or more intimate companions. The need for early attachments is so critical that researchers commonly argue that bonding behavior is built directly into our nature (Bowlby, 1969; Sable, 2004).

attachments Strong emotional ties formed to one or more intimate companions.

According to child psychiatrist John Bowlby, both caregiver and infant are pre-programmed from birth to respond to certain signals with attachment behavior. The newborn typically cries, coos, and smiles, and these behaviors lead naturally to attention and support from the caregiver. It's no accident that adults like to hear babies coo or watch them smile—these preferences may be built directly into the genetic code (Bowlby, 1969). At the same time, the baby arrives into the world with a bias to respond to care and particularly to comfort from the caregiver. Newborns imitate the facial expressions of their parents (Maratos, 1998), for example, which presumably enhances their social interactions with Mom and Dad (Bjorklund, 1997; Heimann, 1989).

Notice that both the infant and the caregiver are active participants—the attachment is formed because both parties are prepared to respond with bonding to the right kind of events. The bond usually is formed initially between baby and mother because it is the mother who provides most of the early care.

The Origins of Attachment

The idea that humans are built to form strong emotional attachments makes sense from an adaptive standpoint—it helps to guarantee survival. But what determines the strength or quality of the attachment? The quality of the bond that forms between infant and caregiver can vary enormously—some infants are securely attached to their caregivers, others are not. Research with animal subjects suggests that one very important factor is the amount of actual *contact comfort*—the degree of warm physical contact—provided by the caregiver.

Contact Comfort   In classic research on early attachment, psychologist Harry Harlow noticed that newborn rhesus monkeys, when separated from their mothers at birth, tended to become attached to soft cuddly objects left in their cages, such as baby blankets. If one of these blankets was removed for cleaning, the monkeys became extremely upset and would cling to it frantically when the blanket was returned. Intrigued, Harlow began a series of experiments in which he isolated newborn monkeys and raised them in cages with a variety of surrogate, or artificial, "mothers" (Harlow & Zimmerman, 1959). In one condition, baby monkeys were raised with a mother made simply of wire mesh and fitted with an artificial nipple that delivered food; in another condition, the babies were exposed to a nippleless cloth mother made of wire mesh that had been padded with foam rubber and wrapped in soft terrycloth.

Which of the two surrogate mothers did the monkeys prefer? If early attachments are formed primarily to caregivers who provide nourishment—that is, infants

When a mother nurses her newborn child, she provides more than sustenance for survival. The "contact comfort" helps secure the bond of mutual attachment.

When forced to choose between surrogate mothers, baby monkeys prefer the soft and cuddly one, even when the wire "mother" provides the food.

© Martin Rogers/Stock Boston, LLC

© Joseph Polleross/The Image Works

Children orphaned by the 1989 war in Romania were sometimes housed in hospitals with very poor infant-to-caretaker ratios; not surprisingly, these children subsequently showed significant social and intellectual deficits compared to children reared at home.

temperament A child's general level of emotional reactivity.

love the one who feeds them—we would expect the monkeys to prefer and cling to the wire mother because it provides the food. But in the vast majority of cases the monkeys preferred the cloth mother. If startled in some way, perhaps by the introduction of a foreign object into the cage, the monkeys ran immediately to the cloth mother, hung on tight, and showed no interest in the wire mother that provided the food. Harlow and his colleagues concluded that *contact comfort*—the warmth and softness provided by the terrycloth—was the primary motivator of attachment (Harlow, Harlow, & Meyer, 1971).

For obvious reasons, similar experiments have never been conducted with human babies. However, we have every reason to believe that human infants are like rhesus infants in their desire and need for contact comfort. Many studies have looked at how children progress in institutional settings that provide relatively low levels of contact comfort (Hodges & Tizard, 1989; Provence & Lipton, 1962; Spitz, 1945). Children reared in orphanages with poor infant-to-caregiver ratios (e.g., one caregiver for every 10 to 20 infants) often show more developmental problems than children reared in less deprived environments (Shaffer, 2007).

Temperament Given that physical contact is such a necessary part of a secure attachment, what determines whether infants will receive the contact they need? One contributing factor may be a baby's **temperament**, the general level of his or her emotional reactivity. Difficult or fussy babies tend to get fewer comforting and responsive reactions, and the quality of the attachment between parent and child suffers as a result (Thomas & Chess, 1977). Links also exist between early temperament and various cognitive abilities, particularly language development (e.g., Dixon & Smith, 2000).

Psychologists who study temperament find that infants can be categorized into types. As you might guess, some babies are easy; they're basically happy, readily establish daily routines, and tend not to get upset very easily. Other babies are difficult; they have trouble accepting new experiences, establishing routines, and maintaining a pleasant mood. Fortunately, only about 10% of babies fall into this difficult group, and about 40% of sampled babies are readily classified as easy (Thomas & Chess,

1977). The remaining 50% are more difficult to categorize. Some babies are "slow to warm up," which means they roughly fall between easy and difficult and show a mixture of different temperaments.

Psychologists are convinced that these differences in moodiness, or temperament, can't be explained completely by the environment. Babies are probably born easy or difficult, although experience certainly plays some kind of role (Cummings, Baumgart-Ricker, & Du Rocher-Schudlich, 2003). It's possible that biological factors, tied to specific structures in the brain, control a baby's degree of emotional reactivity. Jerome Kagan discovered that infants tend to be either *inhibited*—they're generally shy and fearful of unfamiliar people or new events—or *uninhibited*, which means they show little negative reaction to the unfamiliar or novel. Kagan has argued that natural differences in the activity levels of certain brain structures contribute to these inhibited and uninhibited temperaments (Kagan, 1997).

If temperament is based in biology, then you might expect it to remain stable across the life span. In other words, if you're a moody baby, then you should be a moody adolescent and a moody adult. In general, research has supported this conclusion (Caspi & Silva, 1995; Cummings et al., 2003). Infants who seem very shy or inhibited tend to remain so as they age. Identical twins, who share the same genes, also show more similarities in temperament than do fraternal twins or siblings raised in the same home (Braungart et al., 1992). As you'll see when you read the discussion of personality in Chapter 12, genetic factors probably influence many aspects of personality, not just temperament.

Types of Attachment

Not all attachments are created equal: There are systematic differences in the bonds that children form with their caregivers. To investigate these differences, psychologists often use a technique called the **strange situation test**. This test classifies 10- to 24-month-old children into four different attachment groups based on the children's reactions to stressful situations (Ainsworth & Wittig, 1969; Ainsworth et al., 1978). After arrival in the lab, the parent and child are ushered into a waiting room filled with toys; the child is encouraged to play with the toys. Various levels of infant stress are then introduced. A stranger might enter the room, or the parent might be asked to step out for a few moments leaving the child alone. Of main interest to the psychologist are the child's reactions: Initially, how willing is the child to move away from the parent and play with the toys? How much crying or distress does the child show when the parent leaves the room? How does the child react when the parent comes back into the room—does the child greet and cling to the parent, or does he or she move away?

Most infants—approximately 60 to 70%—react to the strange situation test with what psychologist Mary Ainsworth calls *secure attachment*. With the parent present, even if the situation is new and strange, these children play happily and are likely to explore the room looking for interesting toys or magazines to shred. But as the level of stress increases, they become increasingly uneasy and clingy. If the mother leaves the room, the child will probably start to cry but will calm down rapidly if the mother returns.

About 10% of children show a pattern called *resistant attachment*; these children react to stress in an ambiguous way, which may indicate a lack of trust for the parent. Resistant children will act wary in a strange situation, refusing to leave their mother's side and explore the room, and they do not deal well with the sudden appearance of strangers. They cry if the mother leaves the room, yet they're unlikely to greet her with affection on her return. Instead, these children act ambivalent: They remain by her side but resist her affections.

A third group of children—about 20 to 25%—show a pattern of *avoidant attachment*. These children show no strong attachment to the mother in any aspect of the

strange situation test Gradually subjecting a child to a stressful situation and observing his or her behavior toward the parent or caregiver. This test is used to classify children according to type of attachment—secure, resistant, avoidant, or disorganized/disoriented.

strange situation test. They're not particularly bothered by the appearance of strangers in the room, nor do they show much concern when the mother leaves the room or much interest when she returns. Ainsworth discovered that the parents of these children tend to be unresponsive and impatient when it comes to the child's needs and may even actively reject the child on a regular basis (Ainsworth, 1979).

The final attachment group—about 5 to 8%—is made up of children who show a pattern of *disorganized/disoriented* attachment. This fourth group was not part of Ainsworth's original classification scheme but was added to capture children with a history of possible abuse (Main & Soloman, 1990). These children react to the strange situation test with inconsistent responses. Sometimes they mimic securely attached children; sometimes they react with fear or anxiety to the returning mother. These children appear to have no consistent strategy for interacting with their caregivers.

What determines the kind of attachment a child will form? Unfortunately, there's no easy way to tell. The parent–child relationship depends on several factors: the particular personality characteristics of the parent, the temperament of the child, even the child-rearing practices of the culture. In Japan caregivers are less likely to encourage independence and exploration because the Japanese culture tends to value group-oriented accomplishments. This, in turn, can affect how attachments develop and are measured. When babies in the United States are raised according to Japanese practices, they are less likely to be labeled as "securely attached" using the criteria listed above, presumably because less of an emphasis has been placed on acting independently (see Rothbaum et al., 2000). Psychologists are convinced that attachment behavior is universal, because forming early attachments is critical to survival, but exactly how the attachment is expressed and how it should be appropriately measured may well depend importantly on cultural factors (Rothbaum & Morelli, 2005).

As a final note to parents, the strange situation test is a laboratory procedure and observations are made under carefully controlled conditions. You need to take care when drawing conclusions based on your own personal experiences. You shouldn't conclude that your child has an avoidant attachment, for example, just because he or she might not cry when left at day care. The strange situation test is not based on haphazard observations but on a careful examination of specific behaviors in a controlled setting.

CRITICAL THINKING

Do you think the findings of the strange situation test would change if the test was conducted in the child's home? Why or why not?

Do Early Attachments Matter Later in Life?

Given that infants can be easily divided into these attachment groups by around age 1, it's reasonable to wonder about the long-term consequences. For instance, are the avoidant children doomed to a life of insecurity and failed relationships? There's some evidence to suggest that children with an early secure attachment do indeed have some social and intellectual advantages, at least throughout middle and later childhood. For example, teachers rate these children as more curious and self-directed in school (Waters, Wippman, & Sroufe, 1979). By age 10 or 11, securely attached children also tend to have closer and more mature relationships with their peers than children who were classified as insecurely attached (Elicker, Englund, & Sroufe, 1992).

However, early patterns of attachment are not perfect predictors of later behavior. One problem is stability: Sometimes a child who appears to be insecurely attached at 12 months can act quite differently in the strange situation test a few months later (Lamb, Ketterling, & Fracasso, 1992). In addition, a child who has a particular kind of attachment to one parent may show quite a different pattern to the other. It's also important to remember that when psychologists talk about predicting later behavior based on early attachment patterns they are referring mainly to correlational studies. As you learned in Chapter 2, it's not possible to draw firm conclusions about causality from simple correlational analyses. The fact that later behavior can be predicted from early attachment patterns does not mean that early bonding necessarily causes the later behavior patterns—other factors might be responsible. For instance, children who form secure attachments in infancy typically have caregivers who remain warm and responsive throughout childhood, adolescence, and adulthood. So it could be that securely attached infants tend to have successful relationships later in life because they live most of their lives in supportive environments.

Friends and Peers   Early attachments are important. But the relationships formed after infancy, especially during later childhood and adolescence, matter as well. Under the right circumstances, people can counteract negative experiences of infancy or childhood (Lamb et al., 1992). The significance of friendship is a case in point. Psychologists now recognize that a child's social network—the number and quality of his or her friends—can have a meaningful impact on social development and well-being (Berndt, 2004; Hartup & Stevens, 1997).

Children with friends interact more confidently in social situations, they are more cooperative, and they report higher levels of self-esteem (Newcomb & Bagwell, 1995). Children with friends are also less likely to seek help for psychological problems, and they're more likely to be seen as well adjusted by teachers and adult caretakers. These trends are true for young children and adolescents, and they continue on into adulthood (Berndt & Keefe, 1995). When you read Chapter 16, which deals with stress and health, you'll find that social support—particularly our network of friends—predicts how well we're able to cope and deal with stressful situations and how well we're able to recover from injury or disease. This is just as true for children as it is for adults (Hartup & Stevens, 1997).

Obviously, general conclusions like these need to be qualified a bit. For example, the quality (or closeness) of the friendship matters, but so does the identity of the friends. If you have very close friends who recommend drug use or a life of crime, the developmental consequences obviously will be less than ideal. We also don't know what aspects of friendship matter most. For instance, people often share similarities with their friends (such as common attitudes and values). Does this mean that friends merely play the role of reinforcing our values and making us more secure in our attitudes? In-depth research on friendships is ongoing, in part because psychologists recognize the value of friendship across the life span. When asked to rank what is most important in their lives, children, adolescents, and adults often pick "friends" as the answer (Klinger, 1977).

Another very important influence—perhaps even more important than friends—is the child's peer group. Some psychologists believe that acceptance or rejection by the peer group is a more significant influence on later development than the actual rearing practices of the parent (e.g., Harris, 1998). When you examine language, for instance, children tend to speak like their peers, not like their parents. If a child grows up in a Spanish-speaking home but his or her peers speak English, then that child not only acquires the new language but prefers it. The same is true for behavior—children tend to adapt their behavior to the local norms, at least when they are outside of the home (Harris, 2000). Exactly what role the parents play in determining social and personality development, outside of the obvious genetic influence, remains controversial among developmental psychologists (Vandell, 2000).

Child Care: What Are the Long-Term Effects?

What about child care and its long-term impact on development? Most parents of preschool children face a dilemma: Do I stay at home and provide full-time care for my child, or do I work outside the home and place my child in child care? In contemporary American society, day care often turns out to be the answer, although it's not always a choice made voluntarily. For many parents, day care has simply become an economic necessity. Over the last several decades there has been a steady rise in the number of mothers employed outside the home. In 1960, for example, 16.5% of mothers with children under 3 years of age worked outside the home; by the middle 1980s the

Placing a child in day care is an economic necessity for many parents.

personal identity A sense of who one is as an individual and how well one measures up against peers.

Erik Erikson

figure had risen to more than 50%; by 1995 it was more than 60% (Hofferth, 1996; Lamb & Sternberg, 1990).

What are the long-term consequences of day care? Will leaving our children in the hands of nonparental caretakers, often for many hours a day, have positive or negative long-term effects on their social and mental development? Well, the answer is "it depends." The data are somewhat mixed, and the results (not surprisingly) depend on the quality, quantity, and type of care involved. For example, there is a relationship between the quality of day care and later academic performance. Children who experience high-quality care tend to have slightly higher vocabulary scores in school, at least through the fifth grade, and there is some evidence that day-care quality is a predictor of reading skills as well (Belsky et al., 2007). At the same time, children who go to day care "centers," as opposed to in-home care, can show more problem behaviors as measured through the sixth grade (Belsky et al., 2007). It is important to understand, though, that these findings do not apply to all children; instead, these are statistical relationships based on the study of large numbers of children who have been tested in well-controlled longitudinal studies.

Psychologists recognize that "day care" is a multifaceted concept—the term can mean anything from occasional babysitting by a neighbor for a few hours a week, to care by nonparental relatives, to extended care by licensed professionals in for-profit day-care centers. Consequently, it's difficult to draw general conclusions. As with most environmental effects, the role that day care plays in the life of a child will depend on many factors interacting together, including the individual characteristics of the child, the parents, the home environment, as well as the quality, type, and quantity of the service provided. There is no firm evidence that regular day care produces widespread negative effects on development—so don't worry too much. And, as noted above, it can have significant positive effects. Moreover, importantly, the quality of parenting turns out to be a much stronger and more consistent predictor of development than early child-care experiences (Belsky et al., 2007). For some guidelines on choosing a day-care facility, see the Practical Solutions feature.

Forming a Personal Identity: Erikson's Crises of Development

Another important aspect of social development is the formation of **personal identity**—a sense of self, of who you are as an individual and how well you measure up against peers. We recognize that we're unique people, different from others, quite early in our development. Children as young as 6 months will reach out and touch an image of themselves in a mirror; by a year and a half, if they look into a mirror and notice a smudge mark on their nose, they'll reach up and touch their own face (Butterworth, 1992; Lewis & Brooks-Gunn, 1979).

As noted earlier in the chapter, most psychologists are convinced that we use social interactions—primarily those with parents during childhood and with peers later in life—to help us come to grips with who we are as individuals. One of the most influential theories of how this process of identity formation proceeds is the stage theory of Erik Erikson. Erikson (1963, 1968, 1982) believed that our sense of self is shaped by a series of psychosocial *crises* that we confront at characteristic stages in development.

Choosing a Day-Care Center

If you decide to place your child in day care, it's important to choose a high-quality center. As noted in our discussion, you'll find considerable variation in the quality of existing day-care facilities. And, importantly, quality does matter: Factors such as the child-to-staff ratio, the size of the child's care group, and the education of the staff have been shown to correlate with measures of cognitive development. Several professional organizations provide recommendations for assessing the quality of child care (e.g., Child Care Action Campaign, 1996). I've summarized some of the main recommendations here:

1. *Check the physical environment.* It's a must to visit the center and make sure the physical structure and play environments are safe. For example, are there fences around the grounds? Is the facility clean? Do you see the staff washing their hands regularly? Hands should be washed before and after diapering, after washing surfaces, and before any kind of food preparation. Is the play equipment well constructed? Look to see if the electrical outlets are covered, and make certain there are no dangerous or toxic substances within reach of the children. Note: If you're restricted in any way from fully examining the environment, go someplace else for care.

2. *Listen and watch.* Spend some time watching the children who are currently enrolled. Do they look happy? Do they interact easily with each other and with the staff? Do the staff speak to the children in a positive and cheerful tone? Is the setting noisy? High noise levels can signal a lack of control on the part of the staff. If possible, also check with other parents and get their perspectives on the quality of the care.

3. *Count group and staff sizes.* As a general rule, the younger the child, the smaller should be the size of his or her care group. For infants or toddlers, no more than three to four children should be cared for by a single adult. For 2-year-olds, the size can increase to four to six; for 3-year-olds seven to eight; for 4-year-olds eight to nine; for 5-year-olds eight to ten children. If the child-to-staff ratios exceed these guidelines, the quality of your child's care may suffer.

4. *Ask about staff training.* Although legal requirements vary from state to state, it's a good idea to ask whether the center has been accredited by a professional organization. You should also inquire about the staff turnover rate. Qualified staff should have some specific training in early childhood education or child development. A number of studies have shown that caregiver background—specifically college training—influences the quality of the care provided. The better educated the staff, the more likely your child will be given activities that are appropriate for his or her developmental stage.

In a perfect world, all parents would be able to pick and choose the best from a wide array of child-care facilities. Unfortunately, high-quality centers are not always available or are too costly for the average parent or guardian. You can, however, be an active participant in choosing the best possible option. Take your time, use the guidelines listed here, and do your best to maximize a quality environment for your child.

Infancy and Childhood As you know, for the first few years of life babies are largely at the mercy of others for their survival. According to Erikson, this overwhelming dependency leads infants to their first true psychosocial crisis, usually in the first year of life: *trust versus mistrust*. Psychologically and practically, babies face an important problem: Are there people out there in the world who will meet my survival needs? Resolution of this crisis leads to the formation of an initial sense of either trust or mistrust, and the infant begins to understand that people differ. Some people can be trusted, and some can't. It's through social interactions, learning who to trust and who not to trust, that the newborn ultimately resolves the crisis and learns how to deal more effectively with the environment.

As the child progresses through toddlerhood and on into childhood, other fundamental conflicts appear. During the "terrible twos," the child struggles with breaking his or her dependence on parents. The crisis at this point, according to Erikson, is *autonomy versus shame or doubt*: Am I capable of independent self-control of my actions, or am I generally inadequate? Between the ages of 3 and 6, the crisis becomes one of *initiative versus guilt*: Can I plan things on my own, with my own initiative, or should I feel guilty for trying to carry out my own bold plans for action? In late childhood, beginning around age 6 and ending at around age 12, the struggle is for a basic sense of *industry versus inferiority*: Can I learn and master new skills, can I be industrious and complete required tasks, or do I lack fundamental competence?

© Dan McCoy/Rainbow

Developing a personal identity is part of the process of maturing socially and individually. Ellen demonstrates self-awareness as she discovers her nose in the mirror.

Again, what's important in determining how these crises are resolved is the quality of the child's interactions with parents, peers, and other significant role models. If 5-year-old Roberta's parents repeatedly scold her for taking the initiative to get her own drink of milk, she may develop strong feelings of guilt for trying to become independent. According to Erikson, children with highly critical parents or teachers can acquire a self-defeating attitude that carries over later in life. Children who resolve these crises positively learn to trust themselves and their abilities and acquire a strong positive sense of personal identity.

Adolescence and Young Adulthood By the time adolescence rolls around, our intellectual development has proceeded to the point where we begin to consider personal qualities that are pretty general and abstract. For example, Erikson argued, adolescents have to deal with the crisis of *identity versus role confusion*. They become concerned with testing roles and with finding their true identity: Who am I? What kind of person do I really represent? In a very real sense, the teenager acts as a kind of personality theorist, attempting to integrate various self-perceptions about abilities and limitations into a single unified concept of self. Erikson (1968) coined the term *identity crisis* to describe this transition period, which he believed can be filled with turmoil.

Observational studies of how adolescents come to grips with the identity crisis reveal many individual differences (Offer & Schonert-Reichl, 1992; Peterson, 1988). Not all teenagers become paralyzed with identity angst and anxiety—most, in fact, show no more anxiety during this transition period than at other points in their lives. Young people also vary widely in how they commit to a particular view of themselves (Marcia, 1966). Some adolescents choose an identity by modeling others: "I'm honest, open, and cooperative because that's the way I was brought up by my parents." Others develop a personal identity through a soul-searching evaluation of their feelings and abilities. Some adolescents even reject the crisis altogether, choosing instead not to commit to any particular view of themselves. The specific path an individual takes depends on many things, including his or her level of cognitive development, the quality of the parent–child relationship, and outside experiences (Compas, Hinden, & Gerhardt, 1995).

Entrance into young adulthood is marked by the crisis of *intimacy versus isolation*. Resolution of the identity crisis causes us to question the meaning of our relationships with others: Am I willing or able to form an intimate, committed relationship with another person? Or will my insecurities and fears about losing independence lead to a lifetime of isolation and loneliness? People who lack an integrated conception of themselves, Erikson argued, cannot commit themselves to a shared identity with someone else. Some have argued that this particular conclusion may be more applicable to men than women (Gilligan, 1982). Historically, women have been forced to deal with intimate commitments—raising a family and running a home—either at the same time as, or before, the process of searching for a stable personal identity. Things are a bit different now, of course, because many women are establishing professional careers prior to marriage.

Adulthood, Middle Age, and Beyond With the establishment of career and family arrives the crisis of *generativity versus stagnation*. The focus at this point shifts from resolving intimacy to concern about children and future generations: Am I contributing successfully to the community at large? Am I doing enough to assure the survival and productivity of future generations? Failure to resolve this crisis can induce a sense of meaninglessness in middle life and beyond—a condition Erikson calls stagnation.

For some people, especially men in their 40s, this point in psychosocial development is marked by soul-searching questions about personal identity reminiscent of those faced in adolescence (Gould, 1978; Levinson et al., 1978). A "midlife crisis" arises

Concept Review | Erikson's Stages of Personal Identity Development

LIFE PERIOD	STAGE	CONFLICTS REVOLVE AROUND . . .
Infancy and childhood	Trust vs. mistrust (first year of life)	Developing a sense of trust in others: Will the people around me fulfill my needs?
	Autonomy vs. shame or doubt ("terrible twos")	Developing a sense of self-control: Am I in charge of my own actions?
	Initiative vs. guilt (ages 3–6)	Developing a sense of one's own drive and initiative: Can I carry out plans? Should I feel guilty for trying to carry out my own plans?
	Industry vs. inferiority (ages 6–12)	Developing a sense of personal ability and competence: Can I learn and develop new skills?
Adolescence and young adulthood	Identity vs. role confusion (adolescence)	Developing a single, unified concept of self, a sense of personal identity: Who am I?
	Intimacy vs. isolation (young adulthood)	Questioning the meaning of our relationships with others: Can I form a committed relationship with another person, or will my personal insecurities lead to isolation?
Adulthood and older adulthood	Generativity vs. stagnation	Concern over whether one has contributed to the success of children and future generations: Have I contributed to the community at large?
	Integrity vs. despair	Acceptance of one's life—successes and failures: Am I content, looking back on my life?

as people begin to confront their own mortality—the inevitability of death—and as they come to grips with the fact that they may never achieve their lifelong dreams and goals. Although this can be an emotionally turbulent period for some, most of the evidence suggests that the midlife crisis is a relatively rare phenomenon. It gets a lot of attention in the media, and it's certainly consuming for those affected, but probably fewer than 5% of people in middle age undergo anything resembling a turbulent midlife crisis (McCrae & Costa, 2003).

The final stage in the process of psychosocial development, which occurs from late adulthood to the point of death, is the crisis of *integrity versus despair*. It's at this point in people's lives, Erikson believed, that they strive to accept themselves and their pasts—both failures and successes. Older people undergo a kind of life review in an effort to resolve conflicts in the past and to find ultimate meaning in their accomplishments. If successful in this objective search for meaning, they acquire wisdom; if unsuccessful, they wallow in despair and bitterness. An important part of the process is the preparation for death and dying, which I'll discuss in more detail near the end of the chapter.

Evaluating Erikson's Theory   Erikson's stage theory of psychosocial crises has been quite influential in shaping how psychologists view personal identity development (see Steinberg & Morris, 2001). Among its most important contributions is the recognition that personal development is a lifelong process. Individuals don't simply establish a rigid identity around the time they reach Piaget's formal operational stage; the way people view themselves and their relationships changes regularly throughout their lives. Erikson's theory is also noteworthy for its emphasis on the role of social and cultural interactions in shaping human psychology. Human beings don't grow up in a psychological vacuum; the way we think and act is critically influenced by our interactions with others, as Erikson's theory fully acknowledges (Douvan, 1997; Eagle, 1997).

Nevertheless, Erikson's theory suffers from the same kinds of problems as any stage theory. Although there may be an orderly sequence of psychosocial crises, overlap occurs across the stages (Whitbourne et al., 1992). As noted earlier, the search for identity is not confined to one turbulent period in adolescence—it is likely to continue

CRITICAL THINKING

How well do Erikson's ideas describe your own personal identity development? Are you going through any fundamental crisis at the moment, or are you aware of having solved one in the past?

throughout a lifetime. Furthermore, like Piaget, Erikson never clearly articulated how a person actually moves from one crisis stage to the next: What are the psychological mechanisms that allow for conflict resolution, and what determines when and how they will operate (Achenbach, 1992)? Finally, Erikson's theory of identity development, although useful as a general organizing framework, lacks sufficient scientific rigor. His concepts are vague enough to make scientific testing difficult.

Gender-Role Development

In our discussion of Erikson's theory, I touched briefly on the role of gender in establishing personal identity. Women are sometimes forced to struggle with questions about intimacy and relationships before addressing the identity crisis, as the task of establishing a home and rearing children typically falls on their shoulders. But gender is itself a kind of identity; children gain a sense of themselves as male or female quite early in life, and this gender identity has a long-lasting effect on how people behave and on how others behave toward them.

The rudimentary foundations of *gender identity* are already in place by the age of 2 or 3. Children at this age recognize that they're either a boy or a girl (Thompson, 1975), and they sometimes even give stereotypical responses about gender when asked. For example, when shown a picture of an infant labeled as either a boy or a girl, 3-year-olds are more likely to identify the infant "boy" as the one who is strong, big, or hard and the infant "girl" as the one who is weak, small, and soft (Cowan & Hoffman, 1986). Even so, children at this age have not developed sufficiently to recognize gender as a general and abstract characteristic of individuals. They might believe, for instance, that a boy can become a girl by changing hairstyle or clothing (Marcus & Overton, 1978). To understand that gender is a stable and unchanging condition requires some ability to conserve—to recognize that the qualities of objects remain the same despite superficial changes in appearance.

By the time children are firmly entrenched in elementary school, gender is seen as a permanent condition—"I'm a boy (or a girl) and I always will be." At this point, children tend to follow reasonably well-established **gender roles**—specific patterns of behavior consistent with society's dictums. As Martin and Ruble (2004) recently noted, children at this age become "gender detectives who search for cues about gender—who should and should not engage in a particular activity, who can play with whom, and why girls and boys are different" (p. 67). Can you imagine the reaction a 7-year-old boy might receive if he walked into his second-grade class wearing a dress or with his fingernails polished a bright shade of pink?

Nature or Nurture? How do these firm ideas about gender roles develop? Are they due to biological differences between male and female brains, or do they grow out of experience? We encountered this issue in Chapter 3, where we considered the evidence supporting gender-based differences in brain anatomy and functioning. Although hormones released by the endocrine system early in development may account for some gender differences in behavior and thought (Kimura, 1999), psychologists are just as likely to appeal to the environment to explain gender-role development.

According to *social learning* accounts of gender-role development, children learn to act in a masculine or feminine manner because they grow up in environments that reward them for doing so. Parents across the world look for and reward specific kinds of behavior from their male and female children. The socialization process begins the moment the new parents learn the answer to their question, "Is it a boy or a girl?" Parents become preoccupied with dressing Adorable Ginnie in pink bows and Active Glenn in blue. Television and movies continue the process: Children are exposed to hour after hour of stereotypical children acting in gender-appropriate ways (Hansen, 1989; Lovdal, 1989). Studies have indicated, for example, that children who watch a

gender roles Specific patterns of behavior that are consistent with how society dictates males and females should act.

Children are often rewarded for behaving in ways that are gender-role appropriate.

© Peter Cade/Getty Images/Stone

lot of television are more likely to prefer toys that are "gender appropriate" than children who watch little television (McGhee & Frueh, 1980).

Growing up in societies with well-defined gender roles helps establish *gender schemas* (Bem, 1981). A gender schema is an organized set of beliefs and perceptions held about men and women. Gender schemas guide and direct how we view others, as well as our own behavior. For example, as a male, my gender schema leads me to interpret my own behavior, as well as the behavior of other males, in terms of concepts such as "strength," "aggression," and "masculinity." We encountered the concept of schemas (or schemata) earlier in the chapter when we talked about Piaget, and I'll have more to say in later chapters about schemas and the role they play in guiding behavior. For the moment, you can think of schemas as little knowledge packages that people carry around inside their heads. Gender schemas are acquired through learning. They set guidelines for behavior, and they help us decide whether actions are appropriate. As you can probably guess, gender schemas are generally adaptive—they help us interpret the behavior of others—but they can lead to inaccurate perceptions of specific individuals and even to discrimination.

CRITICAL THINKING

Do you think that we as a society should work hard to eliminate specific gender roles? Do you believe that men and women can ever be taught to think and act similarly?

Growing Old in Society

As Bette Davis once famously said, "Growing old ain't for sissies." True enough—the physical declines that accompany the aging process are certain to present new challenges for the developing individual. Yet not all of the changes that greet us in our older years are negative—far from it. In fact, some kinds of intelligence seem to increase with age (see Chapter 10). Marital satisfaction often grows (Carstensen, 1995), and many elderly people remain actively involved in the community and report high levels of contentment (Lawton et al., 1992). One survey found that people in their 70s report more confidence in their ability to perform tasks than do people in their 50s (Wallhagen, Strawbridge, & Shema, 1997)!

At the same time, there are definite hurdles in the pathways of the elderly, many related to health care. The elderly need more physical care, require more doctor visits, and can be at an economic disadvantage due to retirement. Although most elderly adults do not live in nursing homes, many are in need of continuing care. Whatever form it takes, it's likely to be expensive; the costs of nursing homes continue to rise (Stewart, 2004). To make matters worse, the bulk of the costs often must be borne by family members because Medicare (health care for the elderly funded by the federal government) doesn't cover custodial, or chronic, care. The scope of the problem is troubling, especially as the "graying of America" continues. Over the next 50 years, there's expected to be a huge increase (perhaps as much as sixfold) in the number of people over age 85.

Ageism   The elderly face another problem as well: the potential for **ageism**, or prejudice against someone based on his or her age. We'll discuss the basis for prejudice, and particularly the formation of stereotypes, in detail in Chapter 13. For the moment, it is sufficient for you to understand that we all have beliefs about the traits and behaviors of individuals belonging to groups. The elderly comprise such a group, and our attitudes and beliefs toward the elderly can affect their ability to cope with the problems of everyday life.

Stereotypes about the elderly are complex and depend on cultural factors and the age of the individual holding the stereotype, but surveys often reveal beliefs that are inaccurate. Palmore (1990) has listed some of the more common myths, including the belief that most elderly people are sick, in mental decline, disabled and therefore unable to work, isolated and lonely, and depressed. In each of these cases, the negative stereotype is misleading or simply not true. Most elderly people are not sick or disabled and, as mentioned earlier, the elderly may often be more contented and less

ageism Discrimination or prejudice against an individual based on physical age.

Negative stereotypes about the elderly are very often false. Most elderly people are not sick or disabled but live active and productive lives.

prone to depression than younger people (Lawton et al., 1992; Palmore, 1990). Not surprisingly, negative stereotypes can lead to negative consequences, including the fact that older people are generally evaluated less positively (Kite & Johnson, 1988) and may be subject to job discrimination (Kite, 1996).

Some psychologists believe that prejudice toward the elderly arises partly from our anxiety about death (Martens, Goldenberg, & Greenberg, 2005). Terror management theory proposes that each of us is threatened by the idea of dying, and we defend ourselves against the threat by attempting to suppress thoughts about death and by avoiding things that remind us of our mortality. The elderly serve as symbols of our mortality and also of our impending physical decline, which helps feed the negative stereotypes. If college students are asked open-ended questions about death, they subsequently view themselves as less similar to the elderly, and they rate the attitudes of the elderly in a more negative light (Martens et al., 2004).

However, as you'll learn in Chapter 13, stereotypes can be quite adaptive. Like schemas, stereotypes help us organize and make predictions about the world, and not all of the beliefs that accompany stereotypes are negative. For example, people tend to believe that the elderly are kinder, wiser, more dependable, and have more personal freedom than younger people (Palmore, 1990). Stereotypic beliefs such as these, although not necessarily accurate, can lead to a kind of favorable discrimination that helps to counteract the negative stereotypes mentioned previously. One of the lessons of social psychology is that how we view others is often tied to our expectations; age can be a powerful determinant of what those expectations will be.

Death and Dying

As we close our discussion of the developmental process, it's fitting that we turn our attention to the final stage of life: death and dying. As just noted, research suggests that people are threatened by death and thoughts about death. It's the process of death that troubles us the most—the unpredictability, the uncertainty, the inability to understand what the end will be like. There are many psychological aspects to death and the dying process, including how people come to grips with their own mortality and how they grieve and accept the loss of others. Historically, one of the most influential approaches to the dying process itself has been the stage theory of Elisabeth Kübler-Ross (1969, 1974).

Kübler-Ross proposed that people progress through five distinct psychological stages as they face death. Based on extensive interviews with hundreds of terminally ill patients, she found that people react to their own impending death via a characteristic sequence: (1) *denial*—"There must be some terrible mistake"; (2) *anger*—"Why is this happening to me?"; (3) *bargaining*—"What can I do to stop this terrible thing?"; (4) *depression*—"Blot out the sun because all is lost"; and (5) *acceptance*—"I am ready to die." As a stage theorist, Kübler-Ross believed that people move through each of these five stages, from denial to acceptance, as a normal part of their emotional acceptance of death.

Kübler-Ross' views on the dying process have been highly influential, in both psychological and medical circles, and rightly so. She was one of the first people to treat the topic of dying thoroughly and systematically. She sensitized legions of physicians to the idea that denial, anger, and depression are normal reactions to dying that should be treated with respect rather than dismissed out of hand. However, many psychologists question whether people progress through a fixed set of orderly stages in exactly the way Kübler-Ross described. There are simply too many individual differences to support the theory. Not all dying people move through distinct emotional stages, and, even if they do, the stages don't seem to follow any particular set order. Stages might be skipped, be experienced out of order, or alternate, with the person being angry one day and accepting the next.

Many psychologists find it more appropriate to talk about *dying trajectories*. A dying trajectory is the psychological path people travel as they face their impending death. Different people show different trajectories, and the shape and form of the path depends on the particular illness as well as on the personality of the patient (Bortz, 1990; Glaser & Strauss, 1968). Trajectories are preferred to stages because stages imply that all people react to impending death in fixed and characteristic ways. But there is no right or wrong way to deal with dying—some people may react with anger and denial, others with calm acceptance. Witnesses to the dying process can best serve the dying by offering support and allowing the individual to follow his or her own unique path.

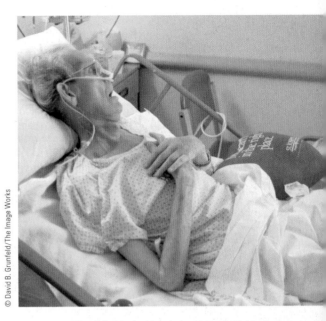

The dying trajectory depends on individual personality, the effects of age or illness, and what sort of care is received.

End-of-Life Decisions   We end the chapter with a little controversy: the decision-making processes that surround the end of life. Should people have the right to control how and when they die, especially if they're faced with a poor quality of life (e.g., constant pain, immobility, or dependency)? Is suicide, assisted suicide, or the termination of medical intervention justified under any circumstance? In some sense, these are legal and ethical questions rather than psychological ones, but questions about controlling the end of life occupy the attention of many people, especially the elderly.

Very little research has been conducted on the psychological factors that influence end-of-life decisions. It seems likely that religious convictions, value systems, life satisfaction, and even fear of death play a role in how people feel about end-of-life options. A study by Cicirelli (1997) confirms these expectations. Older adults, ranging in age from 60 to 100, were asked their views of various end-of-life options. Each person was given sample decision situations such as the following: Mrs. Lee is an elderly widow who has terminal bone cancer. She has had chemotherapy to try to cure the cancer, but it has not helped her, and the side effects from the chemotherapy itself have been difficult to deal with. She is slowly getting worse, and the pain is unbearable. Drugs for pain help some, but leave her in a stupor.

The participants were then asked to make judgments about various end-of-life options, such as strive to maintain life, refuse medical treatment or request that it be removed, commit suicide, or allow someone else to the make the decision about terminating life. Cicirelli (1997) found that people were often willing to endorse more than one option, but the majority opinion was to strive to continue life (51% of the participants endorsed this view). Psychosocial factors, such as religious convictions and fear of death, played a significant role in the decision-making process.

Death can mean many different things to the elderly (Cicirelli, 2002). For some older adults, death is associated with the beginning of the afterlife; for others it means complete extinction or annihilation. Not surprisingly, how one interprets death influences everyday living, reactions to death, and preparations for death. For those who believe that death provides the opportunity to be reunited with deceased friends and family in an afterlife, stressful end-of-life decisions are often easier to make. The fact that the elderly hold so many different personal meanings of death suggests that it will be difficult for society to reach consensus about the difficulties that surround end-of-life decisions.

Test Yourself 4.3

Test your knowledge about social and personal development by answering the following questions. (You will find the answers in the Appendix.)

1. The strange situation test is often used to study attachment. Identify the type of attachment that best characterizes the following reactions. Choose from *avoidant, resistant, secure,* or *disorganized/disoriented.*
   a. When Mom leaves the room, the child begins to cry but calms down rapidly when she returns: _____
   b. When Mom leaves the room, the child couldn't care less. There is little reaction or interest when she returns: _____
   c. When Mom leaves the room, the child cries; when Mom returns the child remains close by but pushes her away when she tries to show affection: _____
   d. When Mom is in the room, the child refuses to leave her side and does not react well to the sudden appearance of strangers: _____

2. According to Erik Erikson, adolescents face a psychosocial crisis called *identity versus role confusion.* Current research suggests that
   a. this is a time of rebellion for all adolescents.
   b. Erikson made a mistake—no such crisis occurs.
   c. the identity crisis has mostly a genetic basis.
   d. not all teenagers suffer anxiety during this period.

3. Gender identity doesn't develop until a child enters elementary school—it's only at that point that gender roles begin to exert an effect. *True or False?*

4. Which of the following statements about the elderly and growing old in society are True, and which are False?
   a. Most elderly people are sick and disabled. *True or False?*
   b. Stereotypes about the elderly are always harmful. *True or False?*
   c. Most elderly people have little, if any, confidence in their abilities. *True or False?*
   d. The elderly, on average, would rather die than suffer the consequences of a painful and terminal disease. *True or False?*

Review *Psychology for a Reason*

As we grow from infancy through childhood to adulthood, fundamental changes occur in physical, intellectual, and social functioning. Most of these changes serve adaptive functions. We're not biological machines, predestined to develop in fixed and inflexible ways from birth. Instead, we're born with a genetic recipe that mixes innate potential with the rigors and demands of the environment. It's nature via nurture, and the final product is a better-functioning person, someone who is fine-tuned to his or her environment.

In many ways this chapter acts as a concise summary of the topics you'll encounter throughout the book. Understanding human development requires that we take into account all aspects of the psychology of the individual: how people change physically; learn to perceive, think, and remember; and develop socially.

Developing Physically We begin life as a fertilized egg, or zygote, which contains genetic material packed into chromosomes received from the mother and father. During the prenatal period, we develop rapidly and are especially susceptible to environmental influences. Infancy and childhood are marked by rapid growth in height and weight and by a further maturing of the nervous system. One of the by-products of nerve cell maturation is motor development, the major milestones of which—crawling, standing alone, walking—tend to occur at similar times for most people, in part because the nervous system develops systematically.

As we move through adolescence and into early adulthood, our physical systems continue to change. During puberty people mature sexually and experience hormone-driven changes in physical appearance. Once people reach their 20s, their bodies become mature, and most begin a gradual decline in physical ability. Some declines occur in mental ability over time, especially in old age, although significant losses in mental functioning are the exception, not the rule.

Developing Intellectually Psychologists use the term *cognitive development* to refer to changes in intellectual functioning that accompany physical aging. Newborns have remarkably well-developed tools for investigating the world around them: They can see, hear, smell, feel, and taste, although not at the same level as they will in later childhood. We leave infancy with well-developed perceptual systems and use the experiences of childhood to help fine-tune our sensory equipment.

Much of what we know about thought processes during infancy and childhood comes from the work of Jean Piaget. Piaget's theory of cognitive development proposes that children use mental models of the world—called schemata—to guide and interpret ongoing experience. Central to the theory is the idea that as children grow and acquire new experiences their mental models of the world change. Piaget believed that children pass through a series of cognitive stages (sensorimotor, preoperational, concrete operational, and formal operational), each characterized by unique ways of thinking. Lawrence Kohlberg also proposed a stage theory, suggesting that individuals pass through levels of moral development that differ in the extent to which moral actions are seen as being driven by immediate external consequences or by general abstract principles. Not all psychologists agree that cognitive development progresses through fixed stages, but it's clear that qualitative differences in cognitive ability do occur over the course of development.

Developing Socially and Personally
Our relationships with others help us solve problems that arise throughout development. Infants form attachments to gain the nourishment they need for survival. Both infant and caregiver are active participants in the attachment process and are prepared to respond, given the right kinds of environmental events, with mutual bonding. Ainsworth identified several categories of attachment based on the strange situation test. In general, the responsiveness of the parent early in life influences, but does not absolutely determine, the relationships formed by the child later in life.

Another aspect of social development is the formation of personal identity. Erik Erikson argued that personal identity is shaped by a series of psycho-social crises over the life span. During infancy and childhood, we address questions about our basic abilities and independence and learn to trust or mistrust others. During adolescence and adulthood, we deal with the identity crisis and come to grips with our roles as participants in intimate relationships. In later years we struggle with questions of accomplishment, concern for future generations, and meaning. Other important components of social development include learning gender roles, growing old in society, and confronting the important stages and decisions of dying.

Active Summary (You will find the answers in the Appendix.)

Developing Physically

• Life begins with the fertilized egg, or (1) _____.
The (2) _____ period is from conception to (3) _____ of the zygote in the uterine wall. The next six weeks are the (4) _____ period. The (5) _____ period includes development of the skeletal and muscular systems, and lasts from the ninth week of gestation until birth.

• The average newborn weighs about (6) _____ pounds and is about 20 inches long. A newborn's brain shows (7) _____; that is, changes are constantly occurring in the neural circuitry. The sequence of development from lifting the head to walking alone is stable and (8) _____ across cultures. As the infant progresses from crawling to walking, the nervous system develops from the head down and from the center out.

• Past toddlerhood, general processing speed and coordination improve greatly. (9) _____ is an important physical and (10) _____ transition period that features growth spurts and the onset of (11) _____.

• By our 20s we are (12) _____ mature and at the height of our physical prowess. Reaching adulthood, however, is in some sense a mental rather than a physical state. Small physical declines begin to occur in the 20s. Some people eventually suffer brain degeneration with age, but fewer than 1% of people aged 65 are afflicted with (13) _____, or physically based loss in mental functioning.

Developing Intellectually

• In the (14) _____ technique, an infant is presented with two visual displays simultaneously, and the researcher notes how long the baby looks at each one. Researchers also use (15) _____, the decline in responsiveness to repeated stimulation, to investigate infants' preferences and abilities. Insight into infants' abilities can also be gained by (16) _____ simple motor movements.

• Newborns' (17) _____ systems function reasonably well. They prefer some colors and (18) _____; they recognize their mothers' voices a day or two after birth; they are sensitive to smell, taste, and touch; and they seem to perceive the world in three dimensions.

• The elderly commonly report memory problems, and evidence suggests that some kinds of memory do falter with age, but most do not. Age-related memory deficits appear to depend on the particular type of (19) _____ task being used.

• Piaget believed that everyone has a natural tendency to organize the world meaningfully, and that to do so we use (20) _____, or mental models of the world. Cognitive development is guided by (21) _____ (fitting new experiences into existing schemata), and (22) _____ (modifying existing schemata to accommodate new experiences). Piaget proposed four basic stages of cognitive development: (23) _____, (24) _____, (25) _____, and (26) _____ operational.

• At the (27) _____ level, decisions about right and wrong are based primarily on external consequences. At the (28) _____ level, children justify their actions on the basis of internalized rules and on whether an action will maintain or disrupt the social order. At the (29) _____ level, morality is based on abstract principles—such as right and wrong—that may at times conflict with accepted standards.

Developing Socially and Personally

• Some researchers believe that a newborn is preprogrammed to respond to environmental signals with (30) _____ behavior. Early attachments are formed primarily on the basis of (31) _____ comfort rather than nourishment. (32) _____, an individual type of emotional reactivity, is also an important factor. Attachment bonds have been investigated with the (33) _____ situation test, in which the child is observed reacting to a gradually developed stressful situation.

Most children show (34) _____ attachment, though some show resistant, (35) _____, or disorganized/disoriented attachments.

• Erikson believed that personal identity is shaped by a series of (36) _____ crises. During infancy and childhood these involve trust versus mistrust, (37) _____ versus shame or doubt, initiative versus guilt, and industry versus (38) _____. During adolescence and young adulthood, we experience identity versus (39) _____ confusion.

• Gender identity is usually in place by the time a child is 2 or 3. By the time children are in grade school, they tend to act in accordance with (40) _____ _____. Our sexual perceptions and behaviors are directed by gender (41) _____.

• (42) _____ is prejudice based on a person's age. That the elderly are sick, depressed, or in mental decline are common (43) _____, although the elderly do face the challenges of physical decline.

• Elisabeth Kübler-Ross proposed that the terminally ill pass through five (44) _____ as they approach death: denial, anger, (45) _____, depression, and acceptance. Many psychologists prefer to speak of dying trajectories, the individual paths that are traveled on the way to death.

Terms to Remember

accommodation, 108
ageism, 127
assimilation, 108
attachments, 117
concrete operational period, 110
conventional level, 114
cross-sectional design, 102
dementia, 100
development, 93
egocentrism, 110
embryonic period, 95

fetal period, 95
formal operational period, 112
gender roles, 126
germinal period, 95
habituation, 103
longitudinal design, 102
menopause, 100
morality, 114
object permanence, 109
personal identity, 122
postconventional level, 115

preconventional level, 114
preoperational period, 109
principle of conservation, 109
puberty, 99
schemata, 107
sensorimotor period, 108
strange situation test, 119
temperament, 118
teratogens, 96
zygote, 95

Media Resources

 ThomsonNOW

www.thomsonedu.com/ThomsonNOW

Go to this site for the link to ThomsonNOW, your one-stop study shop. Take a Pre-Test for this chapter, and Thomson-NOW will generate a Personalized Study Plan based on your results. The Study Plan will identify the topics you need to review and direct you to online resources to help you master those topics. You can then take a Post-Test to help you determine the concepts you have mastered and what you still need to work on.

Companion Website

www.thomsonedu.com/psychology/nairne

Go to this site to find online resources directly linked to your book, including a glossary, flashcards, quizzing, weblinks, and more.

 Psyk.trek 3.0

Check out the Psyk.trek CD-ROM for further study of the concepts in this chapter. Psyk.trek's interactive learning modules, simulations, and quizzes offer additional opportunities for you to interact with, reflect on, and retain the material:

Human Development: Prenatal Development
Human Development: Piaget's Theory of Cognitive Development

© Pete Atkinson/Getty Images/Stone

Sensation and Perception

Have you ever stared at the Necker cube? Take a look at ▌Figure 5.1 for a minute or so. Notice the lines, the angles, the colors. Each remains fixed on the page—how could it be otherwise?—but the cube itself shifts its shape from moment to moment to moment. For a time, the shaded surface of the image forms the front of the cube; in the blink of an eye, magically, it shifts and forms the rear. First you see it from one perspective, and then from another. How is this possible, given that the picture remains fixed, and what does it tell us about the world of inner experience?

We're constantly bombarded by messages from the environment. Some arrive as light energy, such as the words you see printed on this page; others, like the spoken sounds of language, arrive as regular changes in air pressure over time. Ultimately, these messages are translated into an electrochemical language for delivery deep within the brain. The products of this translation process, and their subsequent interpretation, serve as the focus of this chapter. It is through sensation and perception that we construct the world of immediate experience.

To understand the difference between the psychological terms *sensation* and *perception*, return momentarily to the Necker cube. It's a geometric figure, a cube, but it's describable in other ways as well. For example, it's made up of lines, angles, patterns of light and dark, colors, and so on. These elementary features—the building blocks of the meaningful image—are processed by the visual system through reasonably well-understood physiological systems, and the products are visual sensations. Psychologists have historically thought of **sensations**—such as a pattern of light and dark, a bitter taste, a change in temperature—as the fundamental, elementary components of an experience. **Perception**, on the other hand, is the collection of processes used to arrive at a meaningful interpretation of those sensations. The simple components are organized into a recognizable form—here, obviously, you perceive a cube.

In the case of the Necker cube, though, the message delivered to the brain is ambiguous. There's more than

▌**FIGURE 5.1** The Necker Cube

sensations The elementary components, or building blocks, of an experience (such as a pattern of light and dark, a bitter taste, or a change in temperature).

perception The collection of processes used to arrive at a meaningful interpretation of sensations.

It's not hard to understand why psychologists care about the topics of sensation and perception. But to appreciate how the brain actually builds its representation of the world, we must consider how the brain solves three fundamental problems that cut across all the sensory systems. Regardless of whether we're dealing with vision, hearing, touch, smell, or taste, the brain needs to figure out a way to translate the incoming message, identify the key components of the message, and produce a stable interpretation (see ▮ Figure 5.2). Keep these three problems in mind as you discover why our sensory systems work the way they do.

Translating the Message

As you learned in Chapter 3, communication in the nervous system is electrochemical. When the world "talks" to the brain, however, the messages arrive in forms that are not electrochemical. For example, you see with light, which arrives in the form of electromagnetic energy; you hear by interpreting sound vibrations or repetitive changes in air pressure. In a sense, it's like trying to listen to someone who speaks a language you don't understand. The brain needs an interpreter—a process through which the incoming message can be changed into an understandable form.

Identifying the Message Components

Once the message has been successfully translated—appearing now in the form of neural impulses—the message components must be extracted or pulled out of the complex sensory pattern. To solve this problem, the newly formed sensory code is delivered to processing stations deep within the brain. Along each pathway, which differs for each of the sensory systems, are specialized regions that perform specific sensory functions.

Producing a Stable Interpretation

How do these message components, represented as the activities of many thousands of neurons, combine to produce perceptual experiences? You see objects, not patterns of colored light and dark; you hear melodies, not sequences of irregularly timed sounds. The biological bases of perception—the processes that produce the interpretation—are still poorly understood, but the brain uses certain principles of organization, along with existing knowledge, to help construct the world of experience.

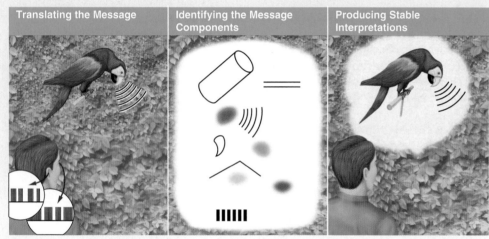

FIGURE 5.2 Adaptive Problems of Sensation and Perception

To build an internal representation of the outside world, the brain solves three fundamental adaptive problems for each of its sensory systems. (1) It translates messages from the environment into the language of the nervous system; (2) it identifies the elementary components of the messages, such as colors, sounds, simple forms, and patterns of light and dark; and (3) it builds a stable interpretation of those components once they've been identified.

From the Physical to the Psychological

Learning Goals
Stimulus Detection
Difference Thresholds
Sensory Adaptation
Test Yourself 5.5

REVIEW
Psychology for a Reason

one interpretation of the physical image, so the brain engages in a perceptual dance, shifting from one interpretation to the other and then back again. What you see, therefore, is not necessarily a faithful reflection of what the world presents; instead, you see an interpretation, or perception, of the message delivered by the physical world. As I'll discuss shortly, sometimes the brain gets it wrong altogether—in those cases, perceptual illusions are produced.

Vision: The World of Color and Form

LEARNING GOALS
- Explain how light is translated into the electrochemical language of the brain.
- Discuss how the basic features of the visual message, such as color, are identified by the brain.
- Explain how a stable interpretation of visual information is created and why the interpretation process sometimes produces visual illusions.

OUR DISCUSSION OF SENSATION and perception begins with vision: the sense of sight. To understand vision, it's first necessary to understand how the physical message—*light*—is translated into the electrochemical language of the brain. Next, we'll trace the brain pathways that are used to identify the basic components of the visual message once it's been translated (e.g., lines and colors). Finally, we'll tackle the topic of visual perception: How does the brain create its stable interpretation of the light information it receives?

Translating the Message

Light is a form of electromagnetic energy. What we think of as visible light is actually a small part of an electromagnetic spectrum that includes other energy forms, such as X-rays, ultraviolet rays, and even radio and television waves (see ▐ Figure 5.3). Visible light is typically classified by three main physical properties. The first is *wavelength*, which corresponds to the physical distance from one energy cycle to the next. Changes in the wavelength of light are generally experienced as changes in color, or

light The small part of the electromagnetic spectrum that is processed by the visual system.

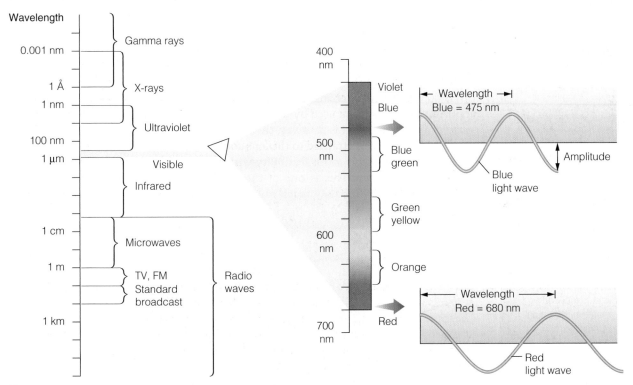

▐ **FIGURE 5.3** Light and the Electromagnetic Spectrum
Visible light is actually only a small part of the electromagnetic spectrum, which includes such other energy forms as X-rays and radio and TV waves. Changes in the wavelength of light from about 400 nanometers to 700 nanometers are experienced as changes in color; short wavelengths are seen as violets and blues; medium wavelengths as yellows and greens; and long wavelengths as reds.

hue The dimension of light that produces color; hue is typically determined by the wavelength of light reflecting from an object.

brightness The aspect of the visual experience that changes with light intensity; in general, as the intensity of light increases, so does its perceived brightness.

transduction The process by which external messages are translated into the internal language of the brain.

cornea The transparent and protective outer covering of the eye.

lens The flexible piece of tissue that helps focus light toward the back of the eye.

pupil The hole in the center of the eye that allows light to enter.

iris The ring of colored tissue surrounding the pupil.

accommodation In vision, the process through which the lens changes its shape temporarily to help focus light on the retina.

CRITICAL THINKING

It's been reported that pupil size increases with interest or level of emotional involvement. What do you think the adaptive value might be?

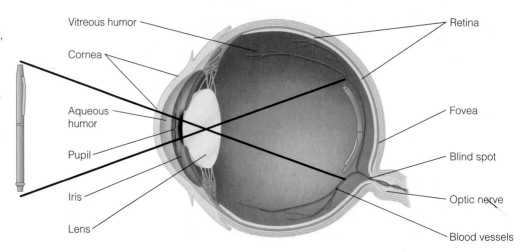

FIGURE 5.4 The Human Eye
Light enters the eye through the cornea, pupil, and lens. As the lens changes shape in relation to the distance of the object, the reflected light is focused at the back of the eye where, in the retina, the visual message is translated.

---

hue. As shown in Figure 5.3, our visual system is sensitive to wavelengths ranging from about 400 to 700 nanometers (billionths of a meter). Psychologically, these wavelengths are experienced as colors ranging roughly from violet to red. The second physical property is *intensity*, or amplitude, which is determined by the amount of light falling on an object. Changes in intensity are generally experienced as increases or decreases in **brightness**. Finally, the *purity* of the light, which is determined by the mix of wavelengths present, can influence the saturation, or richness, of perceived colors.

Light comes from a source, such as the sun or a lightbulb, and usually enters the eye after bouncing off objects in its path. Most of the time light is a mixture of many different wavelengths. After hitting an object, some of these wavelengths are absorbed—which ones depends on the physical properties of the object—and the remaining wavelengths reflect outward, where they eventually enter the eyes. It is here that the important translation process, called **transduction**, actually occurs.

Entering the Eye The first step in the translation process is to direct the light toward the light-sensitive receptor cells at the back of each eye. When light bounces off an object, the reflected wavelengths are scattered about. They need to be brought back together—or focused—for a clear image to be processed. In the human eye, the focusing process is accomplished by the **cornea**, the protective outer layer of the eye, and by the **lens**, a clear, flexible piece of tissue that sits behind the pupil.

As shown in ▌Figure 5.4, light first passes through the cornea and the pupil before traveling through the lens. The **pupil**, which looks like a black spot, is actually a hole in a ring of colored tissue called the **iris**. The iris gives the eye its distinctive color (a person with green eyes has green irises), but the color of the iris plays no real role in vision. Relaxing or tightening the muscles around the iris changes the size of the pupil, thereby regulating the amount of light that enters the eye. In dim light, the pupil gets larger, which allows more light to get in; in bright light, the pupil gets smaller, allowing less light to enter.

The lens focuses the light on the sensory receptors, which are at the back of the eye, much as the lens in a camera focuses light on film. But when you focus light in a camera, you change the distance between the lens and the film. Focusing the human eye is accomplished by changing the shape of the lens itself. This process, known as accommodation, is influenced by the distance between the lens and the object being viewed. When an object is far away, the lens is relatively long and thin; as the object moves closer, muscles attached to the lens contract, and the lens becomes thicker and rounder. You lose some of this flexibility with age, which makes the **accommodation** process much harder. This is one of the reasons people typically require reading glasses or bifocals when they reach middle age. The corrective lenses in the glasses help the accommodation process, which the eyes can no longer successfully perform on their own.

By the way, you may have noticed in Figure 5.4 that the image on the retina is actually inverted, or upside down. This may seem strange, given that we don't see an upside-down world. The inverted image is created by the optical properties of the lens—it tells us, yet again, that our perceptual world is built mainly in our brains. The main function of the eyes is to solve the translation problem and to pass the information to the brain. The brain later corrects the inversion problem, and we see a stable, orderly, and right-side-up world.

Rods and Cones Light completes its journey when it reaches a thin layer of tissue, called the **retina**, that covers the back of the eye. It is here that the electromagnetic energy gets translated into the inner language of the brain. Embedded in the retina of each eye are about 126 million light-sensitive receptor cells that *transduce*, or change, the light energy into electrochemical impulses. The translation process is chemically based. Each of the receptor cells contains a substance, known as a *photopigment*, that reacts to light. The light causes a chemical reaction that ultimately leads to a neural impulse. Thus what begins as a pattern of electromagnetic information ends as a pattern of electrochemical signals: the language of the brain.

There are two types of receptor cells contained in the retina, **rods** and **cones**. Of the roughly 126 million receptor cells within each eye, about 120 million are rods and 6 million are cones. Each receptor type is named for its visual appearance—rods are generally long and thin, whereas cones are short, thick, and tapered to a point. Rods are more sensitive to light than cones; they can generate visual signals when very small amounts of light strike their surface. This makes rods useful at night and in any situation in which the overall level of illumination is low. Rods also tend to be concentrated along the periphery, or sides, of the retina. This is one reason dim images can sometimes be seen better out of the corners of your eyes. (Did you ever notice this?) Cones tend to be concentrated in the very center of the retina, bunched in a small central pit called the **fovea** (which means "central pit"). Unlike rods, cones need relatively high levels of light to operate efficiently, but cones perform a number of critical visual functions. For example, cones are used for processing fine detail, an ability called **visual acuity**. Unlike rods, cones also play an extremely important role in the early processing of color, as you'll see later in the chapter.

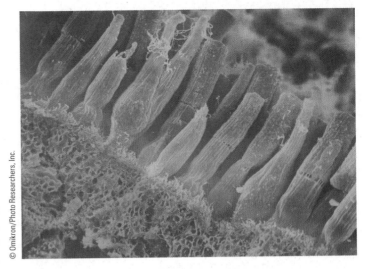

© Omikron/Photo Researchers, Inc.

Each human retina contains two types of photoreceptor cells: rods and cones. As shown in this color-enhanced photo, the rods are rod shaped in appearance and the cones are cone shaped.

retina The thin layer of tissue that covers the back of the eye and contains the light-sensitive receptor cells for vision.

rods Receptor cells in the retina, located mainly around the sides, that transduce light energy into neural messages; these visual receptors are highly sensitive and are active in dim light.

cones Receptor cells in the central portion of the retina that transduce light energy into neural messages; they operate best when light levels are high, and they are primarily responsible for the ability to sense color.

fovea The "central pit" area in the retina where the cone receptors are located.

visual acuity The ability to process fine detail in vision.

Concept Review | Comparing Rods and Cones

CHARACTERISTIC	RODS	CONES
Number	Approximately 120 million per retina	Approximately 6 million per retina
Shape	Generally long and thin	Short, thick, tapered to a point
Location	Concentrated in the periphery of the retina	Concentrated in the center of the retina, the *fovea*
Sensitivity		
—Light	Sensitive at low levels of illumination	Not very sensitive at low levels of illumination
—Detail	Not sensitive to visual detail	High level of sensitivity to detail; high *visual acuity*
—Color	Indistinguishable among different wavelengths	Three types, each maximally sensitive to a different wavelength

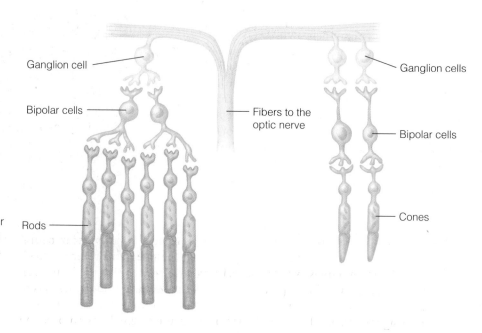

FIGURE 5.5 Rods, Cones, and Receptive Fields
Rods and cones send signals to other cells in the retina. Ganglion cells in the fovea, which receive input from cones, tend to have smaller receptive fields than cells located in the sides of the retina, which receive input from rods. This helps to explain why we see fine detail better in the fovea and why we see better out of the sides of our eyes when light levels are low.

receptive field In vision, the portion of the retina that, when stimulated, causes the activity of higher order neurons to change.

Processing in the Retina   Once the neural impulse is generated by a rod or a cone, it's passed along to other cells in the retina, particularly *bipolar* cells, which feed information from the receptors to *ganglion cells* where further processing occurs (see Figure 5.5). Even at this early stage in visual processing, cells in the retina are beginning to "interpret" the incoming visual message. For example, each ganglion cell has a **receptive field**, which means it receives input from a group of receptor cells and responds only when a particular pattern of light shines across the retina.

This concept of a receptive field is very important. The fact that a cell, such as a ganglion cell, receives input from a number of receptor cells means it can pass on more complex information to the brain. For example, many cells in the retina have *center–surround* receptive fields, as shown in Figure 5.6. In this case, if light falls into

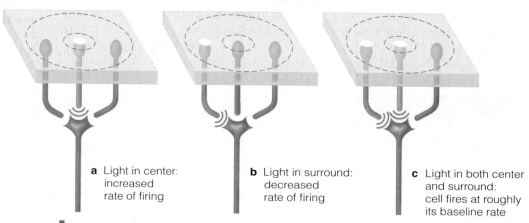

a Light in center: increased rate of firing

b Light in surround: decreased rate of firing

c Light in both center and surround: cell fires at roughly its baseline rate

FIGURE 5.6 Center-Surround Receptive Fields
Receptive fields in the retina often have a center-surround arrangement. Light falling in the center of the field has an opposite effect from light falling in the surround. **(a)** Light in the center of the field produces an excitatory response (green). **(b)** Light falling in the surround produces an inhibitory response (purple). **(c)** When light falls equally in both regions, there is no net increase in the cell's activity compared to its no-light baseline activity level. This kind of receptive field helps the brain detect edges.

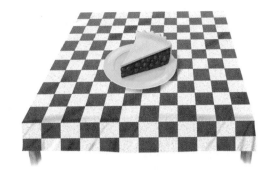

FIGURE 5.7 The Blind Spot
To experience your blind spot, simply close your left eye and focus with your right eye on the boy's face. Then hold this book only a few inches from your eyes and slowly move it away until the pie mysteriously disappears. Notice that your brain fills in the spot—complete with the checkerboard pattern.

the "center" of the cell's receptive field, it reacts by increasing the number of neural signals it sends to the brain. In contrast, if light falls on the sides of its receptive field, the cell will stop sending signals or decrease its firing rate. By detecting the firing rate, the brain determines how light is spread out across the retina and identifies where light stops and starts. This allows us, among other things, to easily detect *edges*.

The visual signals eventually leave the retina, en route to the deeper processing stations of the brain, through a collection of nerve fibers (actually the axons of ganglion cells) called the *optic nerve*. The optic nerve consists of roughly 1 million axons that wrap together to form a kind of visual transmission cable. Because of its size, at the point where the optic nerve leaves each retina there is no room for visual receptor cells. This creates a biological **blind spot** because there are no receptor cells in this location to transduce the visual message. Interestingly, people normally experience no holes in their visual field; as part of its interpretation process, the visual system fills in the gaps to create a continuous visual scene (Grossberg, 2003; Zur & Ullman, 2003). You can locate your blind spot by following the exercise described in ▌Figure 5.7.

blind spot The point where the optic nerve leaves the back of the eye.

dark adaptation The process through which the eyes adjust to dim light.

FIGURE 5.8 The Dark Adaptation Curve
Your eyes gradually adjust to the dark and become more sensitive; that is, you can detect light at increasingly low levels of intensity. The rods and cones adapt at different rates and reach different final levels of sensitivity. The dark adaptation curve represents the combined adaptation of the two receptor types. At about the 8-minute mark there is a point of discontinuity; this is where further increases in sensitivity are due to the functioning of the rods.

Dark Adaptation Another phenomenon that's linked to processing in the retina is dark adaptation. When we first enter a darkened room, we can't see much of anything (anyone who has ever gone out for popcorn during a movie knows this phenomenon). Gradually, over a span of about 20 to 25 minutes, our eyes adjust. This process is called **dark adaptation**, and it's caused by a regeneration process in the rods and cones. Remember, visual transduction occurs when light reacts chemically with photopigments in the receptor cells. In bright light, many of these photopigments break down, or become "bleached," and are no longer useful for generating a neural impulse. When you enter a dark movie theater from a bright environment, your receptor cells simply don't have enough of the depleted photopigments to detect the low levels of light. The photopigments must be regenerated by the cells, a process that takes time.

The timing of the adaptation process is shown in ▌Figure 5.8. The dark adaptation curve is produced by measuring the smallest amount of light that can reliably be seen, plotted as a function of time spent in the dark. Over 20 to 25 minutes, smaller and smaller amounts of light are needed to achieve accurate detection. Sensitivity increases over time because the visual receptor cells are recovering from their earlier interactions with bright light. Notice there's a break, or point of discontinuity, at about the 8-minute mark. This occurs because rods and cones adapt at different rates. Early in dark adaptation, cones show the most sensitivity, but they achieve their maximum sensitivity rather quickly. After about 7 or 8 minutes in the dark, the rods begin to take over. This

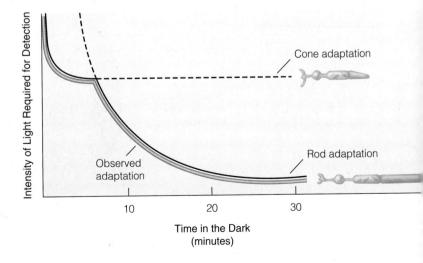

is one of the reasons you can't see color very well at night; in low illumination levels, you're relying almost entirely on your rods—which don't do much, if any, color processing.

Identifying the Message Components

After leaving the retina, the neural impulses flow along each optic nerve until they reach the *optic chiasm* (from the Greek word meaning "cross"), where the information travels to the separate hemispheres of the brain (see ▌ Figure 5.9). Information that has been detected on the right half of each retina (from the left visual field) is sent to the right hemisphere, and information falling on the left half of each retina (from the right visual field) projects to the left hemisphere. The majority of the visual signals move directly toward a major relay station in the thalamus called the *lateral geniculate nucleus*; other signals, perhaps 10% of the total, detour into a midbrain structure called the *superior colliculus*.

The Visual Cortex   From the lateral geniculate nucleus, the visual message moves to the back of the brain, primarily to portions of the occipital lobe. Here, in the visual cortex, more components of the message are picked out and identified. For example, **feature detectors** have been discovered in the visual cortex of cats and monkeys (Hubel & Weisel, 1962, 1979). Feature detectors are cells that respond best to very specific visual events, such as patterns of light and dark. One type of feature detector, called a *simple cell*, responds actively only when a small bar of light is shown into the eye. Cells of this type also turn out to be orientation specific, which means that the visual bar needs to be presented at a particular angle for the cell to respond. The properties of these cells were discovered by measuring neural impulses in individual cells using implanted recording electrodes. An example of this type of experiment, and

feature detectors Cells in the visual cortex that respond to very specific visual events, such as bars of light at particular orientations.

▌ **FIGURE 5.9** Visual Pathways
Input from the left visual field falls on the inside half of the left eye and the outside half of the right eye and projects to the right hemisphere of the brain; input from the right visual field projects to the left hemisphere. Visual processing occurs at several places along the pathway, ending in the visual cortex, where highly specialized processing takes place.

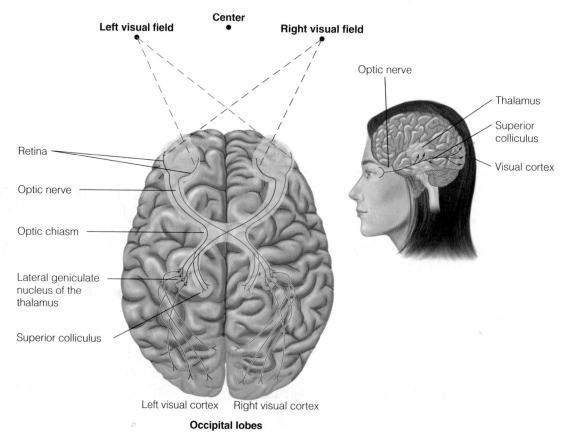

Center
Left visual field
Right visual field

Optic nerve
Thalamus
Superior colliculus
Visual cortex

Retina
Optic nerve
Optic chiasm
Lateral geniculate nucleus of the thalamus
Superior colliculus

Left visual cortex   Right visual cortex
Occipital lobes

the equipment used, is shown in ▌Figure 5.10. Remember, there are no pain receptors in the brain, which makes it possible to explore the reactions of brain cells without causing an animal severe discomfort. The recorded cells were found to increase, decrease, or show no changes in their firing rates in response to specific visual stimuli. In Figure 5.10 experimenters are recording the reaction to the presentation of a small bar of light presented at a particular angle. Again, it was discovered that certain feature detectors in the cat's brain would react to this stimulus, and not to others, and only when the bar was shown at this particular angle.

Feature detectors are not randomly organized in the visual cortex; rather, there is a kind of master plan to the organization in the brain. Cells that respond to stimuli shown at one orientation, say 20 degrees, tend to sit together in the same "columns" of brain tissue. If a recording electrode is moved across neighboring columns, cells show regular shifts in their orientation specificity. So, if cells in a particular column A respond to bars at an angle of 20 degrees, then cells in a physically adjacent column B might respond actively only to bars presented at a 30-degree angle. This is generally thought to mean that cells in the visual cortex break down the visual message in a systematic and highly organized way.

Obviously, the brain is sensitive to more than just bars or orientation-specific patterns of light and dark. Some cells respond selectively to more complex patterns—for example, corners, edges, bars that move through the visual field, and bars of a certain characteristic length. Researchers have also found cells—once again in monkey brains—that respond most actively to faces. Moreover, to get the most active response from these cells, the face needed to look realistically like a monkey—if the face was distorted or cartoonish, the cells did not respond as actively (Perrett & Mistlin, 1987). There's even evidence suggesting that some cells are "tuned" to respond selectively to certain kinds of facial expressions (Hasselmo, Rolls, & Baylis, 1989).

In humans, researchers have studied how the brain analyzes the visual message by examining brain-damaged patients and through the use of neuroimaging techniques. When certain parts of the human brain are damaged because of stroke or injury, very selective, even bizarre, visual problems can start to appear. For example,

CRITICAL THINKING

Can you think of any reason it might be adaptive for the brain to first break the visual pattern down into basic features—such as a bar or a pattern of light and dark—before recombining those features together into a unified whole?

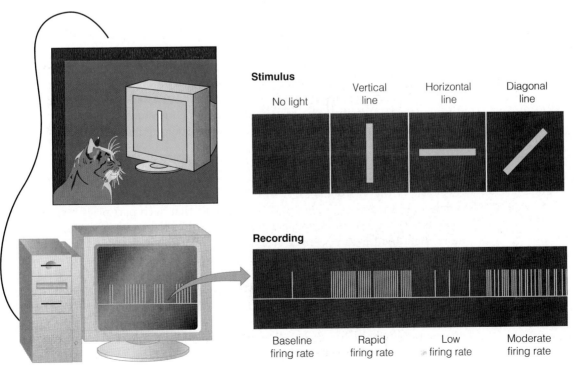

▌FIGURE 5.10
Feature Detectors in the Visual Cortex
Hubel and Wiesel discovered feature detectors in the brains of cats and monkeys. Feature detectors increase their firing rates to specific bars of light presented at particular orientations.

Stimulus

No light | Vertical line | Horizontal line | Diagonal line

Recording

Baseline firing rate | Rapid firing rate | Low firing rate | Moderate firing rate

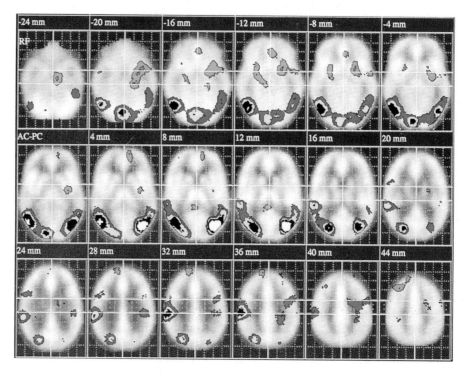

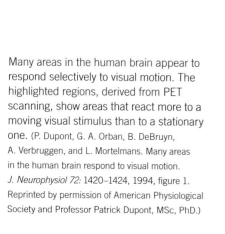

Many areas in the human brain appear to respond selectively to visual motion. The highlighted regions, derived from PET scanning, show areas that react more to a moving visual stimulus than to a stationary one. (P. Dupont, G. A. Orban, B. DeBruyn, A. Verbruggen, and L. Mortelmans. Many areas in the human brain respond to visual motion. *J. Neurophysiol 72:* 1420–1424, 1994, figure 1. Reprinted by permission of American Physiological Society and Professor Patrick Dupont, MSc, PhD.)

in the condition called *prosopagnosia*, the ability to recognize faces is lost (Sala & Young, 2003). People with prosopagnosia can fail to recognize acquaintances, family members, and even their own reflection in a mirror! In another condition, called *akinetopsia*, patients possess normal vision only for objects at rest; if an object is placed in motion, it seems to vanish, only to reappear if it becomes stationary once more (Nawrot, 2003).

Additional evidence for brain specialization comes from the fMRI neuroimaging technique. For example, consistent with the single-cell recording findings discussed previously, researchers have found regions in the cortex that become highly active when people view faces (Pelphrey et al., 2003). Moreover, these regions fail to show the same levels of activation when patients suffering from prosopagnosia are tested (Hadjikhani & de Gelder, 2002). The fMRI technique is also proving to be an effective tool for mapping visual pathways in the brain (Rao et al., 2003) and for detecting whether specific areas of the brain might be involved in the processing of visual images, such as when we imagine an object rotating in space (Zacks, Vettel, & Michelon, 2003).

Studies such as these strongly suggest that the human brain, like the monkey brain, divides its labor. Certain regions of the cortex are specifically designed to process parts of the visual message. In other words, there is specificity in the organization and function of the brain. The exact role that each part plays remains to be worked out, and it's quite possible that particular cells or regions of the brain perform more than one function (Pessig & Tarr, 2007), but the mysteries of how the brain solves the basic problems of vision are beginning to unravel.

Color Vision: Trichromatic Theory We turn our attention now to color, which is processed along virtually the entire visual pathway. In the retina, as you'll see shortly, early color information is detected by comparing the activity levels of different types of cone receptors; higher up in the brain, messages encounter cells that are "tuned" to respond only to particular colors.

trichromatic theory A theory of color vision proposing that color information is extracted by comparing the relative activations of three different types of cone receptors.

Earlier you learned that color is determined primarily by the wavelength of light reflected back into the eye. In general, short wavelengths (around 450 nanometers) produce blues, medium wavelengths (around 530 nanometers) produce greens, and long wavelengths (around 670 nanometers) produce reds. White light, which most people classify as colorless, is actually a combination of all of the wavelengths of the visible spectrum. The reason your neighbor's shirt looks red is because chemical pigments in the fabric of the shirt absorb all but the long wavelengths of light; the long wavelengths are reflected back into the eyes, and you see the shirt as red.

When reflected wavelengths reach the retina, they activate cones in the fovea. The human eye has three types of cone receptors: One type generates neural impulses primarily to short wavelengths (420 nanometers); another type responds most energetically to medium wavelengths (530 nanometers); and a final type responds most to long wavelengths (560 nanometers) of light. The activity levels of each of the cone types are determined by the photopigment contained in the receptor. ▌Figure 5.11 shows the sensitivities for each of the cones, as well as for the rods.

The **trichromatic theory** of color vision proposes that color information is identified by comparing the activations of these three types of cones (trichromatic means "three-color"). An early version of the theory was proposed in the 19th century by Thomas Young and Hermann von Helmholtz—long before modern techniques had verified the existence of the different cone types. Young and Helmholtz noted that most colors can be matched by mixing three basic, or *primary*, colors. They suggested that the brain must determine the color of an object by comparing the activity levels of three primary receptors. When just one receptor type is strongly activated, you see one of the primary colors. For example, when a short-wavelength cone is strongly activated, you might see something in the violet to blue region of the spectrum; when a medium cone is active, you would see something resembling green. For long wavelengths, which activate the third type of cone, you see the color red. All other colors, such as pumpkin orange, require the activation of more than one of the receptor types. Most colors correspond to a mixture of wavelengths and are sensed by comparing the activations of the three receptors.

The trichromatic theory explains a number of interesting aspects of color vision. For example, it explains certain kinds of color blindness. At times, nature makes a mistake and fills someone's red cones with green photopigment or the green cones with red photopigment (Boynton, 1979). Under these rare conditions, which affect more males than females, people are left with two rather than three cone receptors. The trichromatic theory predicts that these *dichromats* (only two rather than three cone types) should lose their ability to discriminate successfully among certain colors. These people can compare the activity levels of only two cone receptors, so, for example, the colors red, yellow, and orange might be perceived as the same shade of yellow. The particular type of color deficiency depends on the type of lost receptor.

Color Vision: Opponent Processes

The trichromatic theory is well supported, but it fails to account completely for color vision. For one thing, the theory has a problem with yellow. Human observers seem convinced that *yellow* is every bit as "pure" a color as red, green, and blue; even 4-month-old infants prefer dividing the color

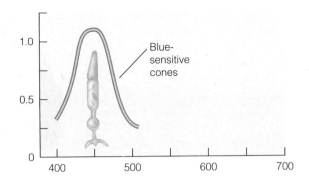

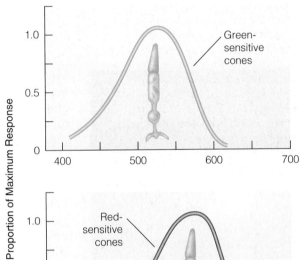

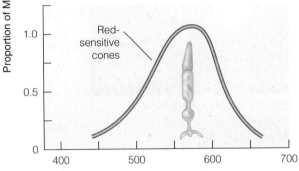

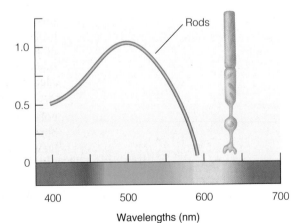

Proportion of Maximum Response

Wavelengths (nm)

▌**FIGURE 5.11** Receptor Sensitivity Curves
Blue-sensitive cones are most likely to respond to short wavelengths of light; green-sensitive cones respond best to medium wavelengths; red-sensitive cones respond best to long wavelengths. Notice that rods are not sensitive to long wavelengths of light. (Based on Jones & Childers, 1993)

● **FIGURE 5.12** Color Afterimage
Stare closely at the middle of this face for about a minute. Then focus on the black dot on the right. What do you see now? The demo works better in a brightly lit environment.

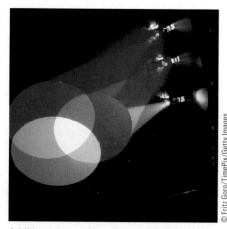

Additive mixing of lights with different wavelengths creates a variety of perceived colors—even white.

spectrum into four color categories rather than three (Bornstein, Kessen, & Weiskopf, 1976). In addition, most people have no problem reporting a yellowish red or a bluish green but almost never report seeing anything resembling a yellowish blue or, for that matter, a greenish red. Why?

It turns out that certain colors are specially linked, such as blue and yellow, and red and green. You can see this for yourself by taking a look at ▌Figure 5.12. You'll find that if you stare at a vivid color like blue for a while and then switch over to a blank white space, you will see an afterimage of its complementary color. Exposure to blue results in an afterimage of yellow; exposure to red produces an afterimage of green. Also, when you mix complementary colored lights, you get white, or at least various shades of gray (Hurvich & Jameson, 1951). The special status of yellow, along with the linking of complementary colors, is quite difficult for the trichromatic theory to explain.

The difficulties with the trichromatic view were recognized in the 19th century by the German physiologist Ewald Hering, who proposed an alternative view of color vision: **opponent-process theory**. He suggested that there are receptors in the visual system that respond positively to one color type (such as red) and negatively to another (such as green). Instead of three primary colors, Hering proposed six: *blue*, which is linked to *yellow* (therefore solving the problem with yellow); *green*, which is linked to *red*; and finally, *white*, which is linked to *black*. According to the opponent-process theory, people have difficulty perceiving a yellowish blue because activation of, say, the blue mechanism is accompanied by inhibition, or decreased activation, of the yellow mechanism. A yellowish red does not present a problem in this scheme because yellow and red are not linked in an opponent fashion.

Like Young and Helmholtz, Hering had no solid physiological evidence to support his notion of specially linked opponent-process cells. However, a century later, opponent-process cells were discovered in various parts of the visual pathway (see DeValois & DeValois, 1980). The rate at which these cells generate neural impulses increases to one type of color (for example, red) and decreases to another (green).

This means that the visual system must be pulling color information out of the visual message by relying on multiple processing stations. Color information is processed first in the retina through the cones (the trichromatic theory); further up in the brain, opponent-process cells fine-tune and further process the message. Finally, at the level of cortex, groups of neurons again appear to be selectively "tuned" to process color, although they may be involved in the processing of other information as well. The specific pathways and combination rules have yet to be fully worked out, but elements of both the trichromatic and opponent-process views appear to play a role in color vision (Gegenfurtner & Kiper, 2003).

opponent-process theory A theory of color vision proposing that cells in the visual pathway increase their activation levels to one color and decrease their activation levels to another color—for example, increasing to red and decreasing to green.

| Concept Review | Comparing Trichromatic and Opponent-Process Theory |

THEORY	STAGE OF PROCESSING	PROCESSING MECHANISM	BASIC DESCRIPTION
Trichromatic	Early in the retina	Three different cone types, maximally sensitive to short, medium, or long wavelengths of light	Brain compares the relative activity levels among the three cone types to determine the color of a stimulus; helps to explain certain types of color blindness (e.g., dichromats)
Opponent-process	Later in the visual pathway	Three types of mechanisms (e.g., cells) that respond positively and negatively to certain color pairs (red-green; blue-yellow; black-white)	Mechanism responds positively to one member of a particular color pair (e.g., blue) and negatively to the other (e.g., yellow); helps to explain complementary-color afterimages and prominence of yellow as a primary color

Producing Stable Interpretations: Visual Perception

Let's return, for a moment, to the cube in ▌Figure 5.1. You've seen how light bouncing off the page gets translated into an electrochemical signal and how specialized regions of the visual pathway break the message down—the brain pulls lines, edges, colors, even angles of orientation from the visual scene. But your fundamental perception is still of a cube—an object with form—not some complex combination of elementary particles.

To understand how the human brain can see "wholes" with visual machinery that seems designed to analyze parts, it helps to remember that perception is only partly determined by what comes in through the eyes. We also rely a great deal on our knowledge and expectations to construct what we see. Let's consider a simple example: Take a look at the two images depicted in ▌Figure 5.13. If you were raised in North America, you probably have no trouble seeing the image in panel (a): It's the word SKY, written in white, against a solid black background. Panel (b), on the other hand, might look like a meaningless collection of black shapes. Actually, panel (b) also shows the word SKY, but it's written in Chinese calligraphy. People who can read English, but not Chinese, see panel (a) as a meaningful image; if Chinese is your native language, and you can't read English, panel (b) presents the meaningful image (Coren, Porac, & Theodor, 1987). Prior knowledge plays a critical role in helping us interpret and organize what we see.

> **CRITICAL THINKING**
>
> Based on what you've learned about color vision, why do you think traffic lights change between red and green?

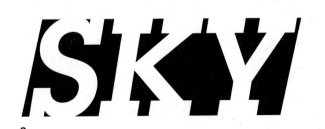

a

b

▌FIGURE 5.13 Prior Knowledge and Perception
Whether you detect meaningful images in **(a)** and **(b)** depends on how much prior knowledge you bring to perceptual interpretation. (From Coren, Ward, & Enns, 1994)

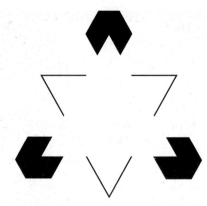

FIGURE 5.14 Illusory Contours
Can you see the white triangle embedded in this figure? No physical stimulus corresponds to the triangular form. Nonetheless, people interpret the pattern as a triangle.

bottom-up processing Processing that is controlled by the physical message delivered to the senses.

top-down processing Processing that is controlled by one's beliefs and expectations about how the world is organized.

Gestalt principles of organization The organizing principles of perception proposed by the Gestalt psychologists. These principles include the laws of proximity, similarity, closure, continuation, and common fate.

We also typically use one part of a visual display to help us interpret other parts. Exactly the same "object" is shown in positions 2 and 4 of the following two lines:

$$A \ B \ C \ D \ E \ F \ G$$
$$10 \ 11 \ 12 \ 13 \ 14 \ 15 \ 16$$

but you see the letter B or the number 13 depending on which line you read. The surrounding letters and digits act as *context* and lead us to expect a particular "whole" in positions 2 and 4. In some cases, the elements can be arranged to make us see things that aren't really there. Is there a white triangle embedded in the middle of ▌Figure 5.14? It sure looks like there is, but the perception is really an illusion—there is no physical stimulus, no reflected pattern of electromagnetic energy on the retina, that corresponds to the triangular form. Yet you interpret the pattern as a triangle.

Psychologists have recognized for some time that there's more to perception than what meets the eye. Our perceptual world is built by combining two important mental activities. First, the visual system performs an analysis of the actual sensory message, the pattern of electromagnetic information on the retina. Psychologists refer to this as **bottom-up processing**—the processing that starts with the actual physical message. Second, we use our knowledge, beliefs, and expectations about the world to interpret and organize what we see, something psychologists call **top-down processing**. Perception results from these two processes working together. What you see is determined by what's out there in the world but also by what you expect to be out there (Snowden & Schyns, 2006).

Principles of Organization   We're also born with strong tendencies to group, or organize, incoming visual information in sensible ways. We considered this process briefly in Chapter 1 when we discussed the work of *Gestalt psychologists* (*Gestalt* translates from German as "configuration" or "pattern"). The Gestalt psychologists believed that we're born with certain organizing principles of perception. For example, we have a natural, automatic tendency to divide any visual scene into a figure and a ground—we see the wine glass as separate from the table, the printed word as separate from the page. The rules governing the separation of *figure* and *ground* are complex, but as you can see from ▌Figure 5.15, the task is easy or hard depending on whether strong or weak cues are available to guide the interpretation.

The Gestalt psychologists outlined a number of compelling and systematic rules, known generally as the **Gestalt principles of organization**, that govern how people organize what they see:

1. *The law of proximity.* If the elements of a display are close to each other—that is, they lie in close spatial proximity—they tend to be grouped together as part of the same object. Here, for example, you see three groups of dots rather than a single collection.

Proximity

2. *The law of similarity.* Items that share physical properties—that physically resemble each other—are placed into the same set. Thus, here you see rows of X's and rows of O's rather than mixed-object columns.

Similarity

FIGURE 5.15 Separating Figure from Ground

We have a natural tendency to divide any visual scene into a discernible "figure" and "(back)ground." This task can be difficult, as with the "hidden faces" painting **(a)**; or it can be easy but ambiguous **(b)**: Which do you see—a vase or a pair of profiles?

3. *The law of closure.* Even if a figure has a gap, or a small amount of its border is missing, people still tend to perceive the object as a whole (e.g., a circle).

Closure

4. *The law of good continuation.* If lines cross or are interrupted, people tend to still see continuously flowing lines. In the following figure you have no trouble perceiving the snake as a whole object, even though part of it is blocked from view.

Continuation

5 *The law of common fate.* If things appear to be moving in the same direction, people tend to group them together. Here the moving dots are classified together as a group, with some fate in common.

Common fate

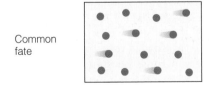

Object Recognition   By imposing organization on the visual scene, these natural grouping rules simplify the problem of object recognition. Psychologist Irving Biederman (1987, 1990) has suggested that the Gestalt principles of organization may help

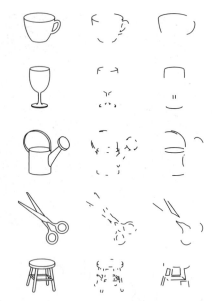

FIGURE 5.16 Recognition by Components
Biederman proposed that we recognize visual forms in part by extracting simple geometric forms (geons) from the visual message. Degraded versions of the objects on the left are in the other columns. We have no trouble recognizing the objects in the middle column, but most of us cannot identify those in the right column because the geons are degraded in the right column but not in the middle column. (From "Higher-Level Vision," by I. Biederman. In D. H. Osherson, S. M. Kosslyn, and J. M. Hollerback (eds.), *An Invitation to Cognitive Science: Visual Cognition and Action*, Vol. 2, p. 135. Copyright © 1990 MIT Press. Reprinted by permission.)

recognition by components The idea proposed by Biederman that people recognize objects perceptually via smaller components called geons.

the visual system break down complex visual messages into components called geons (short for "geometric icons"). *Geons* are simple geometrical forms, such as blocks, cylinders, wedges, and cones. From a collection of no more than 36 geons, Biederman argues, more than 150 million possible complex and meaningful objects can be created—far more than people need to capture the richness of their perceptual world. Once the brain is familiar with the geons, it can recognize the basic components of just about any perceptual experience. Just as the 26 letters of the alphabet form the basis for an incredible variety of words, geons form the "alphabet" for visualizing any object.

Biederman's theory, which he calls **recognition by components**, helps to explain how people can successfully identify fuzzy or incomplete images. Nature rarely provides all the identifying characteristics of a physical object: Cars are usually partially hidden behind other cars; a hurried glimpse of a child's face in a crowd might be all the information that reaches the eye. Yet the viewer has no trouble recognizing the car or the child. According to Biederman (1987), only two or three geons can be sufficient for the rapid identification of most objects. To illustrate, Biederman asked people to identify objects such as the ones shown in the left column of ▌Figure 5.16. In some cases, the items were presented intact; in other conditions, the images were made more difficult to see by removing bits of information that either maintained (the middle column) or disrupted (the right column) the component geons. Not surprisingly, people had no problem recognizing the objects in the middle column but had considerably more trouble when the geons were obscured. In fact, Biederman found that identification of the right-column objects was almost impossible—most people in this condition failed to identify any of the objects correctly.

It remains to be seen whether Biederman's theory will provide a complete account of object recognition. Not all researchers are convinced that a relatively small set of basic shapes is sufficient to allow us to identify and discriminate among all objects (Liu, 1996). Many objects share basic parts, yet we're able to quickly and efficiently tell them apart. Moreover, there may be certain kinds of objects, such as faces, that are perceived and remembered immediately as wholes, without any breaking down or building up from parts. As you learned earlier, some cells in the brain respond selectively to faces; also, certain kinds of brain damage make recognizing faces, but not other objects, difficult or impossible. We're capable of recognizing an enormous range of objects in our world without hesitation, and it may well be that our brains solve the problems of object recognition in a number of different ways (Pessig & Tarr, 2007).

Perceiving Depth Depth perception is another amazing capability of the visual system. Think about it: The visual message that arrives for processing at the retina is essentially two-dimensional. Yet, somehow, we're able to extract a rich three-dimensional world from the "flat" image plastered on the retina. How is this possible? As we discussed in Chapter 4, the ability to perceive depth develops relatively early in life. Infants as young as a few months can clearly tell the differences between the shallow and deep sides of a visual cliff (Campos et al., 1970; Gibson & Walk, 1960).

Depth perception results from a combination of bottom-up and top-down processing. People use their knowledge about objects, in combination with bottom-up processing of the actual visual message, to create a three-dimensional world. For example, the brain knows and adjusts for the fact that distant objects produce smaller reflections on the retina. If you see two people whom you know to be roughly the same height, but the retinal images they produce are of different sizes, your brain figures out that one person must be standing closer than the other. Experience also makes it clear that closer objects tend to block the images of objects that are farther away.

Another cue for distance, one that artists often use to depict depth in paintings, is *linear perspective*. As shown in the photos on the next page, parallel lines that recede into the distance tend to converge toward a single point. Generally, the farther away

© Lester Lefkowitz

© Maggie Leonard/Rainbox

© John Eik III/Stock Boston, LLC

Can you identify the types of cues present in these "flat" pictures that allow us to perceive depth?

two lines are, the closer together those lines will appear to be. The relative shading of objects in a scene can provide important clues as well: If one object casts a shadow on another, you can often tell which of the two is farther away. Objects that are far away also tend to look blurry and slightly bluish. If you look at a realistic painting of a mountain scene, you'll see that the distant hills lack fine detail and are painted with a tinge of blue.

The depth cues that we've been considering are called **monocular depth cues**, which means they require input from only one eye. A person can close one eye and still see a world full of depth based on the use of monocular cues such as those just discussed; you don't need two eyes to perceive depth. But the brain also uses **binocular depth cues**; these are cues produced by two eyes, each with a slightly different view of the world. Hold your index finger up about an inch or so in front of your eyes. Now quickly close and open each eye alternately. You should see your finger jumping back and forth as you switch from one open eye to the other. The finger appears to move because each eye has a slightly different angle of view on the world, producing different images in each retina.

The differences between the locations of the images in the two eyes is called **retinal disparity**. It's a useful cue for depth because the amount of disparity changes with distance from a point of fixation. The farther away an object is from the fixation point, the greater will be the differences in the locations of the images in each eye. The brain derives depth information, in part, by calculating the amount of disparity between the image in the left eye and the image in the right eye. The brain can also use the degree that the two eyes turn inward, called **convergence**, to derive information about depth. The closer an object is to the face, the more the two eyes must turn inward, or converge, to see the object properly. Not surprisingly, our brain is also able to monitor how these various cues change with motion, such as shifting our head or walking about, to compile an increasingly accurate view of the world in three dimensions (Wexler & van Boxtel, 2005).

monocular depth cues Cues for depth that require input from only one eye.

binocular depth cues Cues for depth that depend on comparisons between the two eyes.

retinal disparity A binocular cue for depth that is based on location differences between the images in each eye.

convergence A binocular cue for depth that is based on the extent to which the two eyes move inward, or converge, when looking at an object.

Concept Review | Depth Cues

TYPE OF CUE	CUE	DESCRIPTION
Monocular	Relative size	Comparably sized stimuli that produce different-sized retinal images are perceived as varying in distance from the observer.
	Overlap	Closer objects tend to block the images of objects farther away.
	Linear perspective	Parallel lines that recede into the distance appear to converge on a single point.
	Shading	Shadows cast by objects on other objects assist in depth perception.
	Haze	Distant objects tend to look blurry and slightly bluish.
Binocular	Retinal disparity	The differences between the locations of the images in the two eyes; the amount of disparity changes with distance from a point of fixation.
	Convergence	The closer the stimulus, the more the eyes turn inward toward one another.

Motion Perception We see a three-dimensional world, full of depth, but we experience a world rich in movement as well. Cars speed by us as we walk, birds soar and dive through the sky, and leaves scatter in the wind. Our ability to perceive motion effortlessly is extremely adaptive. Movement helps us determine the positions of objects over time, and it helps us to identify objects as well. For example, movement gives us information about shape, because we're able to see the object from more than one viewpoint, and it also helps us solve figure–ground problems—once an object begins to move, we can easily separate its image from a still background.

How do we perceive movement? You might think the brain could solve this problem by simply tracking the movement of images across the retina. Although this is true to a certain extent, motion perception is actually more complex. Images are constantly moving across our retinas as we turn our eyes or walk about, yet we don't necessarily see objects as moving. Moreover, sometimes we perceive motion when there is none. Think about those flashing arrows you see in front of stores or motels—they beckon us in, but they're actually made up of fixed lights that are blinking on and off at regular intervals. We experience an illusion of motion, called the **phi phenomenon**, even though nothing in the environment is actually moving. We experience a similar *illusion of motion* every time we watch a movie. Movies are really nothing more than still pictures presented rapidly in succession, but we certainly experience smooth and flowing images.

Neuroscientists believe there are designated pathways in the brain that helps us process movement, and a variety of cells that respond specifically to movement have been discovered in the cortex (Battelli, Alvaro, & Cavanagh, 2007). Changes in the retinal image, changes in the motion of the eyes, as well as changes in the relative positions of objects in the environment all contribute to our general perception of movement. For example, our brain infers movement when the retinal image of one object changes over time but the images of other objects in the background do not. As with depth, there are many cues in the environment that can help in the interpretation process.

Perceptual Constancies Another remarkable feature of the human visual system is its capacity to recognize that an object remains the same even when the image in the retina changes. As you watch a car pull away, the size of its retinal image becomes smaller and smaller—so small, in fact, that it eventually resembles the image that might be reflected from a toy car held at arm's distance. But you never think the car has been mysteriously transformed into a toy. Your visual system maintains a stable

phi phenomenon An illusion of movement that occurs when stationary lights are flashed in succession.

interpretation of the image despite the changes in its retinal size.

When you perceive an object, or its properties, to remain the same even though the physical message delivered to the eyes is changing, you are showing what's called a **perceptual constancy**. In the case of the car, it is *size constancy*—the perceived size of the car remains constant even though the actual size of the reflected image is changing with distance. ▮ Figure 5.17 provides an example of *shape constancy*. Consider how many changes occur in the reflected image of a door as it slowly moves from closed to open. Yet you still recognize it as a door, not as some bizarre shape that evolves unpredictably over time (Pizlo & Stevenson, 1999). Size and shape constancies turn out to be related; both result, at least in part, from the visual system's use of cues to determine distance.

To see what kind of cues produce constancy, look at ▮ Figure 5.18. Take particular note of the rectangular shapes on the ground marked as A, B, and C. You see these planters as the same size and shape in part because of the texture patterns covering the ground. Each of the open boxes covers three texture tiles in length and an additional three in width. The actual retinal image, however, differs markedly for each of the shapes (take a ruler and measure the physical size of each shape). You interpret and see them as the same because your experiences in the world have taught you that size and distance are related in systematic ways.

We experience perceptual constancies for a variety of object dimensions. In addition to size and shape constancy, the brightness and color of an object can appear to remain constant even though the intensity and wavelength of the light changes. Once again, these characteristics help us maintain a stable and orderly interpretation of a constantly changing world. Think about how chaotic the world would appear if you saw a new and different object every time the physical properties of its reflected image changed. For example, instead of seeing the same dancer gliding across the

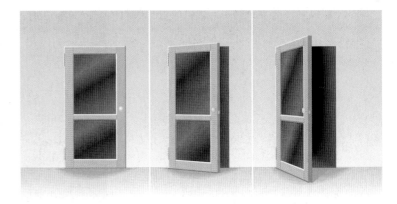

▮ **FIGURE 5.17** Shape Constancy
Notice all the changes in the image of a door as it moves from closed to open. Yet we perceive it as a constant rectangular shape.

perceptual constancy Perceiving the properties of an object to remain the same even though the physical properties of the sensory message are changing.

▮ **FIGURE 5.18** Constancy Cues
We see these three planters as matching in size and shape partly because of depth cues in the environment: Each covers three tiles in length and three in width.

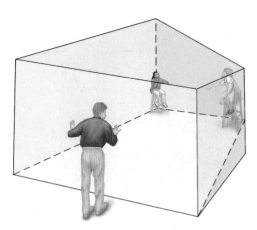

FIGURE 5.19 The Ames Room
The girl on the right appears to be much larger than the girl on the left, but this is an illusion induced by the belief that the room is rectangular. In fact, the sloping ceiling and floors provide misleading depth cues. To the viewer looking through the peephole, the room appears perfectly normal. This famous illusion was designed by Adelbert Ames.

perceptual illusions Inappropriate interpretations of physical reality. Perceptual illusions often occur as a result of the brain's using otherwise adaptive organizing principles.

© Richard Nowitz/Phototake

floor, you might be forced to see a string of dancers each engaged in a unique and unusual pose.

Perceptual Illusions   The perception of constancy is not gained without a cost. In its effort to maintain a stable image, the visual system can be tricked—**perceptual illusions**, or inappropriate interpretations of physical reality, can be created. Take a look at the two people sitting in the room depicted in ▌ Figure 5.19. The girl sitting on the right appears much larger than the girl sitting on the left. In reality, the two girls are approximately the same size. You're tricked because your brain uses cues in the environment—combined with the belief that rooms are vertically and horizontally rectangular—to interpret the size of the inhabitants. Actually, as the rest of the figure shows, it's the room, not the difference in size of the girls, that is unusual.

Based partly on your expectations about the shape of rooms and partly on the unique construction of the room, as you look through the peephole you think you see two people who are the same distance away from your eyes. But the person on the left is actually farther away, so a smaller image is projected onto the retina. Because the brain assumes the two are the same distance away, it compensates for the differences in retinal size by making the person on the right appear larger (Dorward & Day, 1997).

The Ponzo illusion, shown in ▌ Figure 5.20(a), operates in a similar way. You see two lines that are exactly the same length as slightly different because the linear perspective cue—the converging parallel lines—tricks the brain into thinking that the horizontal line near the top of the display is farther away. Because it has the same size retinal image as the bottom line (remember, the two are physically the same size) the brain compensates for the distance by making the top line appear larger. ▌ Figure 5.20(b) shows a similar illusion: The monsters are really the same size, but the one on the top certainly appears larger!

Similar principles create the Müller-Lyer illusion, which is shown in ▌ Figure 5.21. The vertical line with the wings turned out (a) appears longer than the line with the wings turned in (b), even though each line is identical in length. As (c) shows, this particular illusion may have a real-life model—the interior and exterior corners of a room or building. Notice that for the outside corner of this building the wings are really perspective cues signaling that the front edge is thrusting forward and the walls are sloping away. For the inside corner, the perspective cues signal the opposite—the inside edge is farther away. In the Müller-Lyer illusion the two lines produce the same retinal image, but your visual system assumes that (a), which is just like the interior corner, is likely to be farther away, and consequently must be larger in size.

Cultural Influences If the Müller-Lyer illusion is based partly on our experiences with rooms and buildings, then suppose we tested people raised in environments with few rectangular corners—would they be less susceptible to the illusion? When a group of Navajos who had been raised in traditional circular homes (called hogans) were tested, they were more likely to consider the lines as equal in length, although the illusion was still present to some degree (Leibowitz, 1971; Pedersen & Wheeler, 1983). Similar effects have been reported for other "circular" cultures, such as rural, isolated Zulus living in South Africa.

It's unlikely that experience alone can account for the perceptual illusions we've demonstrated, even the Müller-Lyer illusion, but it's reasonable to assume that experience can exert an influence. After all, perception is driven partly by our interpretation of the sensory message, and prior knowledge plays a big role in the interpretation process. An anecdote from the anthropologist Colin Turnbull (1961) provides another case in point: Turnbull was observing the behavior of Bambuti Pygmies, who live in a dense rain forest in the Congo. Because of the terrain, members of this culture rarely, if ever, are exposed to vast open spaces; their visual experiences are limited to short distances. One particular day, Turnbull took his Bambuti guide, Kenge, to a broad, flat plain—the guide's first venture out of the rain forest—and they observed a herd of buffalo some distance away. Here's Turnbull's description of Kenge's reaction:

> Kenge looked over the plains and down to where a herd of about a hundred buffalo were grazing some miles away. He asked me what kind of insects they were, and I told him they were buffalo, twice as big as the forest buffalo known to him. He laughed loudly and told me not to tell such stupid stories. (p. 252)

Although it's speculation, the grazing buffalo might have looked like insects to Kenge because he lacked experience with the depth cues that produce size constancy. We know that small retinal images don't necessarily mean small objects because we

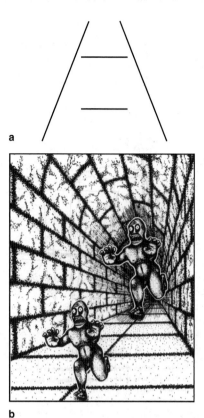

a

b

■ FIGURE 5.20 Illusion of Depth
These two figures, based on the Ponzo illusion, show that depth cues can lead to perceptual errors. In **(a)** the horizontal lines are actually the same length, and the monsters in **(b)** are the same size.
("A Monster of an Illusion, Explaining Ponzo Illusion," p. 47 from *Mind Sights* by Roger N. Shepard, © 1990 by Roger N. Shepard. Reprinted by permission of Henry Holt and Company.)

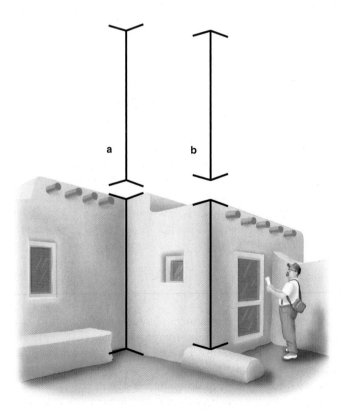

c

■ FIGURE 5.21 The Müller-Lyer Illusion
The vertical line with the wings turned up **(a)** appears longer than the line with the wings turned down **(b)**. This particular illusion may be influenced by experiences with the interior and exterior corners of buildings **(c)**.

Creating Illusions of Depth

Have you ever seen a movie presented in 3-D? Have you ever used a stereoscope—perhaps in its modern form, the View-Master? How about a stereogram? The image shown in ▌Figure 5.22 may look like a bunch of random color waves, but if you look at it just right, you'll see an image presented in astonishing depth.

Each of these examples represents an instance in which we can see depth from what is essentially a two-dimensional visual message. In the case of the stereogram, the 3-D image emerges out of a flat, and meaningless, two-dimensional picture—no special equipment is needed. How is this possible?

Not surprisingly, these visual tricks rely on the same perceptual principle—retinal disparity—that we discussed in the section on depth perception. We see with two eyes, and each of our eyes sees the world from a slightly different viewpoint. Through a process that is not completely understood, our brain is able to perceive an object in depth by noting, in part, the differences that exist between the left- and right-eye images. As you know from reading the text, this is not the only cue we use to perceive depth (our top-down knowledge of the world is also important), but it's a sufficiently strong cue to trick the brain into seeing depth when it's not really there.

In the case of a 3-D movie, the film actually contains two slightly offset images. By wearing special glasses, with one green lens and one red lens, the two images can be selectively filtered to your left and right eyes. This creates the image disparity that is needed to create depth. (The 3-D effect is achieved in the film production process, not by the glasses, which is why your 3-D glasses won't work on just any movie.) A stereoscope is based on a similar principle; when you look through the View-Master, you're actually seeing two different images of the same scene, drawn or photographed from two slightly different perspectives. The View-Master delivers one of the images to each eye, producing the illusion of depth.

A stereogram, such as the one shown in Figure 5.22, is slightly more difficult to see. There is a repeating pattern that is slightly offset. If you focus beyond the image in a certain way, your brain picks up on the disparity, and a 3-D image "mysteriously" appears. Here are some simple steps to view the image: First, make sure you're sitting in a brightly lit environment. Hold the book up in front of your face, relatively close to your nose, and imagine you're focusing on a distant object beyond the page. This will make the stereogram seem blurry, but that doesn't matter. (You're not really looking at anything in particular, and especially not the stereogram; instead, you're staring blankly forward.) Now start to move the book slowly away from you, trying to keep your eyes focused on the imaginary distant object. Eventually, if you're lucky, the 3-D image will appear. Don't get discouraged—it may take a long time for the effect to work.

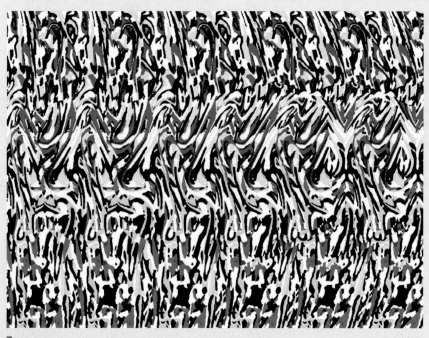

▌**FIGURE 5.22** A Single-Picture Random-Dot Stereogram

have experience viewing large objects at great distances. To Kenge, who had little, if any, experience with long distances, the small retinal image produced by the distant animals was interpreted as a small object—an insect (remember the toy car example mentioned earlier?). Importantly, this is just an anecdote and not systematic science. At the same time, given what we know about top-down processing in perception, it's reasonable to assume that our experiences teach us about cues in our world and, as a consequence, help to shape the world that we see.

Test Yourself 5.1

Check your knowledge about vision by answering the following questions. (You will find the answers in the Appendix.)

1. To test your understanding of how the visual message is translated into the language of the brain, choose the best answers from among the following terms: *accommodation, cones, cornea, fovea, lens, opponent-process, pupil, receptive field, retina, rods, trichromatic*.
   a. The "central pit" area where the cone receptors tend to be located: _____
   b. Receptors that are responsible for visual acuity, or our ability to see fine detail: _____
   c. The process through which the lens changes its shape temporarily to help focus light: _____
   d. The "film" at the back of the eye that contains the light-sensitive receptor cells: _____
   e. The protective outer layer of the eye: _____

2. Decide whether each of the following statements about how the brain extracts message components is True or False.
   a. Visual messages tend to be analyzed primarily by structures in the superior colliculus, although structures in the lateral geniculate are important too. *True or False?*
   b. It's currently believed that information about color and movement are probably processed in separate pathways in the brain. *True or False?*

   c. The opponent-process theory of color vision makes it easier to understand why most people think there are four, rather than three, primary colors (red, green, blue, yellow). *True or False.*
   d. Some feature detectors in the brain are "tuned" to respond only when certain patterns of light enter the eye at specific angles of orientation. *True or False?*

3. Test your knowledge about visual perception by filling in the blanks. Choose your answers from the following terms: *binocular depth cues, bottom-up processing, convergence, monocular depth cues, perceptual constancy, perceptual illusion, phi phenomenon, retinal disparity, recognition by components, top-down processing*.
   a. The part of perception that is controlled by our beliefs and expectations about how the world is organized: _____
   b. Perceiving an object, or its properties, to remain the same even though the physical message delivered to the eyes is changing: _____
   c. An illusion of motion: _____
   d. The depth cue that is based on calculating the degree to which the two eyes have turned inward: _____
   e. The view that object perception is based on the analysis of simple building blocks, called geons: _____

Hearing: Identifying and Localizing Sounds

LEARNING GOALS
- Explain how sound, the physical message, is translated into the electrochemical language of the brain.
- Discuss how pitch information is pulled out of the auditory message.
- Explain how the auditory message is interpreted and how sound is localized.

IMAGINE A WORLD WITHOUT SOUND. There wouldn't be music, or speech, or laughter. Sounds help us identify and locate objects; through sound, we're able to produce and comprehend the spoken word. Even our most private sense of self—the world inside our heads—often appears in the form of an inner voice, or an ongoing speech-based monologue (see Chapter 8)

A stereogram shows how the intensity and frequencies of sounds change over time.

David R. Frazier Photolibrary, Inc.

Translating the Message

The physical message delivered to the auditory system, **sound**, is a form of energy, like light, that travels as a wave. However, sound is mechanical energy and requires a *medium* (such as air or water) to move. Sound begins with a vibrating stimulus, such as the movement of vocal cords or the plucking of a tight string. The vibration pushes air molecules out into space, where they collide with other air molecules, and a kind of traveling chain reaction begins. Want to feel a pressure wave? Simply put your hand in front of the pounding diaphragm of a stereo speaker.

sound The physical message delivered to the auditory system; a mechanical energy that requires a medium such as air or water in order to move.

pitch The psychological experience that results from the auditory processing of a particular frequency of sound.

The rate of the vibrating stimulus determines the *frequency* of the sound, defined as the number of times the pressure wave moves from peak to peak per second (measured in units called *hertz*, where 1 Hz = 1 cycle [repetition]/second). Psychologically, when the frequency of a sound varies, we hear a change in **pitch**, which corresponds roughly to how high or low a tone sounds. For example, middle C on a piano has a frequency of 262 Hz, and the highest note corresponds to about 4000 Hz. Humans are sensitive to frequencies from roughly 20 to 20,000 Hz, but we're most sensitive to frequencies in the 1000 to 5000 Hz range. Many important sounds fall into this range, including most of the sounds that make up speech.

The other major dimension of sound is intensity, or *pressure amplitude*. Psychologically, changes in intensity are experienced as changes in *loudness*. As the intensity level increases, it generally seems louder to the ear. The amplitude of a wave is measured in units called *decibels* (dB). To give you some perspective, a normal conversation measures around 60 dB, whereas an incredibly loud rock band can produce sounds over 100 dB. (Just for your information, prolonged exposure to sounds at around 90 dB can produce permanent hearing loss.)

pinna The external flap of tissue normally referred to as the "ear"; it helps capture sounds.

tympanic membrane The eardrum, which responds to incoming sound waves by vibrating.

middle ear The portion between the eardrum and the cochlea containing three small bones (the malleus, incus, and stapes) that help to intensify and prepare the sound vibrations for passage into the inner ear.

Entering the Ear Let's follow a sound as it enters the auditory pathway (see ❚ Figure 5.23). The first stop, of course, is the ears. The external flap of tissue usually referred to as the "ear" is known technically as the **pinna**; it helps capture the sound, which then funnels down the auditory canal toward the *eardrum*, or **tympanic membrane**.

The tympanic membrane responds to the incoming sound wave by vibrating. The particular vibration pattern, which changes for different sound frequencies, is then transmitted through three small bones in the **middle ear**: the *malleus* (or hammer), the *incus* (or anvil), and the *stapes* (or stirrup). These bones help intensify the vibration pattern and prepare it for passage into the inner ear. Inside the inner ear

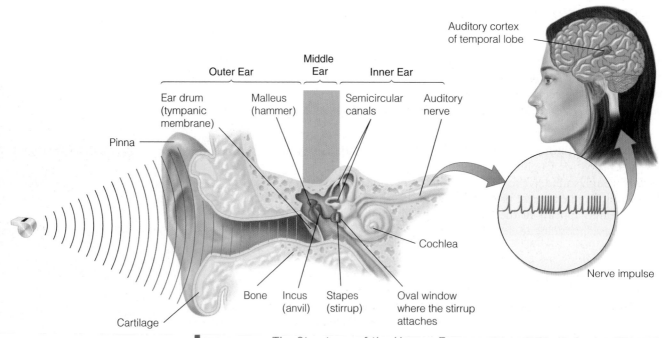

❚ **FIGURE 5.23** The Structures of the Human Ear
Sound enters the auditory canal and causes the tympanic membrane to vibrate in a pattern that is then transmitted through three small bones in the middle ear to the oval window. The oval window vibrates, causing fluid inside the cochlea to be displaced, which moves the basilar membrane. The semicircular canals contribute to our sense of balance.

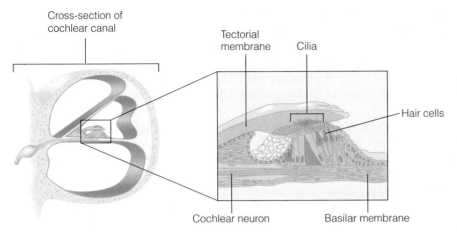

FIGURE 5.24 The Basilar Membrane
This figure shows an open slice of the cochlea. Sound vibrations cause fluid inside the cochlea to displace the basilar membrane that runs throughout the cochlear shell. Different frequencies trigger different patterns along the membrane. Transduction takes place through bending hair cells. The hair cells nearest the point of maximum displacement will be stimulated the most, helping the brain extract information about pitch.

is a bony, snail-shaped sound processor called the **cochlea**; here the sound energy is translated into neural impulses.

The third bone in the middle ear, the stapes, is connected to an opening in the cochlea called the *oval window*. As the stapes vibrates, it causes fluid inside the cochlea to move a flexible membrane, called the **basilar membrane**, that runs throughout the cochlear shell. Transduction takes place through the activation of tiny auditory receptor cells, called *hair cells*, that lie along the basilar membrane. As the membrane starts to ripple—like a cat moving under a bedsheet—tiny hairs, called cilia, that extend outward from the hair cells are bent (because they knock into something called the tectorial membrane). The bending of these hairs causes the auditory receptor cells to fire, creating a neural impulse that travels up the auditory pathways to the brain (see ▌Figure 5.24).

Different sound frequencies trigger different movement patterns along the basilar membrane. Higher frequencies of sound cause the membrane to be displaced the most near the oval window; low frequencies produce a traveling wave that reaches its peak deep inside the spiraling cochlea. As you'll learn shortly, the brain determines pitch by recognizing which of the receptor cells are activated by a particular sound pattern. If hair cells near the oval window are responding the most, the incoming sound is perceived as high in pitch. If many cells along the membrane are active, and the most active ones are far away from the oval window, the incoming sound is perceived as low in pitch.

Identifying the Message Components

The neural impulses generated by the hair cells leave the cochlea in each ear along the *auditory nerve*. Messages that have been received in the right ear travel mainly along pathways leading to the left hemisphere of the brain; left-ear messages go primarily to the right hemisphere. Just as in the visual system, auditory nerve fibers are "tuned" to transmit a specific kind of message. In the visual system, the ganglion cells transmit information about light and dark. In the auditory system, fibers in the auditory nerve pass on rough *frequency* information. Electrophysiological measurements of individual auditory nerve fibers show tuning curves—for example, a fiber might respond best to an input stimulus of around 2000 Hz and less well to others (Ribaupierre, 1997).

Detecting Pitch   Complex sounds, such as speech patterns, are built from combinations of simple sound frequencies. The auditory system pulls out information about the simple frequencies, which correspond

cochlea The bony, snail-shaped sound processor in the inner ear where sound is translated into nerve impulses.

basilar membrane A flexible membrane running through the cochlea that, through its movement, displaces the auditory receptor cells, or hair cells.

Prolonged exposure to intense noise can create hearing loss.

place theory The idea that the location of auditory receptor cells activated by movement of the basilar membrane underlies the perception of pitch.

frequency theory The idea that pitch perception is determined partly by the frequency of neural impulses traveling up the auditory pathway.

to different pitches, in several ways. Pitch is determined, in part, by the particular place on the basilar membrane that is active. For example, as we discussed earlier, activation of hair cells near the oval window leads to the perception of a high-pitched sound. This is called the **place theory** of pitch perception (Békésy, 1960). We hear a particular pitch because certain hair cells are responding actively. "Place" in this instance refers to the location of the activated hair cell along the basilar membrane.

Place theory helps to explain certain kinds of hearing loss. As people grow older, they typically have trouble hearing the higher frequencies of sound (such as those in whispered speech). Why? Because most sounds activate the hair cells that lie nearest the oval window. Cells in the interior portions of the cochlea respond actively only when low-frequency sounds are present. If receptor cells wear out from years of prolonged activity, then those nearest the oval window should be among the first to do so. Place theory partly explains, as a result, why older people have difficulty hearing high-pitched sounds.

At the same time, place theory does not offer a complete account of pitch perception. One problem with place theory is that hair cells do not act independently—often many are activated at the same time. As a result, it's thought that the brain must also rely on the *rate* at which cells fire their neural impulses. According to **frequency theory**, pitch is determined partly by the frequency of neural impulses traveling up the auditory pathway: The higher the rate of firing, the higher the perceived pitch. Like place theory, frequency theory does a reasonable job of explaining many aspects of pitch perception, but it runs into difficulties with high-frequency sounds. Because of their *refractory periods*, individual neurons cannot fire fast enough to deliver high-frequency information. To solve this problem, the brain tracks the patterns of firing among large groups of neurons. When groups of cells generate neural impulses rapidly in succession, they create *volleys* of impulses that provide additional clues about the pitch of the incoming message (Wever, 1949).

To sum up, the brain uses several kinds of information to extract pitch. The brain uses information about where on the basilar membrane activation is occurring (place theory) as well as the rate at which signals are generated (frequency theory). Neither place nor frequency information, by itself, is sufficient to explain our perception of pitch—both kinds of information are needed.

The Auditory Cortex The auditory message eventually reaches the auditory cortex, which is located mainly in the temporal lobes of the brain. Cells in the auditory cortex are frequency sensitive, which means they respond best to particular frequencies of sound. There is also a well-developed organizational scheme, just like in the visual system. Cells that sit in nearby areas of the auditory cortex tend to be tuned to similar frequencies of sound. For example, cells that respond to low-frequency sounds are clustered together in one area of the auditory cortex, whereas cells responsive to high-frequency sounds sit in another area (Scheich & Zuschratter, 1995).

Some cells in the auditory cortex respond best to complex combinations of sounds. For example, a cell might respond only to a sequence of tones that moves from one frequency to another, or to a burst of noise (Pickles, 1988). In animals, cortical cells have been discovered that respond only to sounds that exist in the animal's natural vocabulary, such as a particular shriek, cackle, or trill (Wollberg & Newman, 1972). In people, neuroimaging studies have found specific areas of the brain that "light up" when complex auditory sequences are played; different regions seem to be involved in detecting the identity of a sound and its location in space (Clarke & Thiran, 2004). Much remains to be learned about how complex sounds—such as patterns of speech—are represented in the cortex, but recent advances in imaging technology are opening many new doors for the researcher. For example, recent imaging studies have made it clear that multiple pathways are involved in speech comprehension, just as there are multiple processing pathways in vision (Hickok & Poeppel, 2007).

Producing Stable Interpretations: Auditory Perception

Say the phrase "kiss the sky," then repeat it aloud in rapid succession. Now do the same thing with the word "stress" or "life." You'll notice that your perception of what you're saying undergoes some interesting changes. "Kiss the sky" begins to sound like "kiss this guy"; "stress" will probably turn into "dress" and "life" into "fly." This is a kind of auditory analog to the Necker cube, which was discussed at the beginning of the chapter.

Organizing the Auditory Message   As with the ever-changing cube, the brain is often faced with ambiguous auditory messages—it seeks meaning where it can, usually by relying on established organizational rules (Bregman, 1990; Hirsh & Watson, 1996). The brain separates the incoming auditory stream into figure and ground; it groups auditory events that are similar and that occur close together in time. Sound frequency can be used as a grouping cue to distinguish among voices. Females generally speak at higher frequencies than males. As a result, it is easier to tell the difference between a male and a female talking than it is to tell the difference between two speakers of the same sex. At the same time, the auditory system shows a remarkable ability to maintain perceptual constancy: We can easily recognize the same melody played by different instruments, even though the physical characteristics of the sounds reaching the ears are very different (Zatorre, 2005).

The fact that the brain organizes the incoming sound message should not come as much of a surprise. Think about how easily you can listen to a band or orchestra, filled with many different instruments, and pick out the trumpet, violin, or piano. Think about how easily you can focus on the voice of a friend, to the exclusion of other voices, when you're in the middle of a noisy party. Moreover, your ability to identify and organize sounds increases with experience. We use our knowledge and expectations, through top-down processing, to help us interpret the incoming auditory sequence. Car mechanics, after years of experience, can identify an engine problem simply by listening to the particular "knocking" that the engine makes; cardiologists can use the sounds of the heartbeat to diagnose the health of a cardiovascular system. In one recent neuroimaging study, people were asked to listen to familiar or unfamiliar songs while being "scanned" in an fMRI machine. At certain points in the song the music was turned off unexpectedly. During these silent "gaps," activity continued in auditory regions of the brain but to a much greater extent if the participants were familiar with the song. Everyone reported still "hearing" the song during the gaps—a kind of auditory imagery—but only if he or she was familiar with the song (Kraemer et al., 2005).

Prior knowledge not only influences how we perceive sounds, it also influences how we produce sequences of sounds. Try saying the following aloud, and listen closely to the sounds: *Mairzi doats n doze edoats n lidul lamzey divey.* Recognize anything familiar? Well, actually this is a lesson in the dietary habits of familiar barnyard animals; it's taken from a popular 1940s song (Sekular & Blake, 1990). (Here's a hint: Mares eat oats and . . .) With a little knowledge, and some expectations about the content of the message, you should eventually arrive at an agreeable interpretation of the lyric. Notice how once you've arrived at that interpretation, the same groupings of letters produce quite a different reading aloud.

Sound Localization   Another adaptive characteristic of the auditory sense is the ability to determine location. For example, if you're driving down the street fiddling with your car radio and hear a sudden screech of brakes, you're able to identify the source of the sound rapidly and efficiently. How do you accomplish this feat? Just as comparisons between the retinal locations of images in the two eyes provide

CRITICAL THINKING

Can you think of any songs that you like now but didn't like when you first heard them? One possibility is that you've learned to organize the music in a way that makes it more appealing.

information about visual depth, message comparisons between the ears help people *localize* objects in space.

Let's assume that the braking car is approaching yours from the left side. Because your left ear is closer to the source of the sound, it will receive the relevant sound vibrations slightly sooner than your right ear. If an object is directly in front of you, the message will arrive at both ears simultaneously. By comparing the arrival times between the left and right ears, the brain is able to localize the sound fairly accurately. What's amazing is that these arrival time differences are extremely small. For example, the maximum arrival time difference, which occurs when an object is directly opposite one ear, is less than one-tenth of a second.

Another important cue for sound localization is *intensity*—more precisely, intensity differences between the ears. The sound that arrives first—to either the left or right ear—will be somewhat louder, or more intense, than the sound arriving second. These intensity differences are not large, and they depend partly on the frequency of the arriving sound, but they are useful cues for sound localization. Your brain can calculate the differences in arrival times, plus any differences in loudness, and use this information to localize the source. Plus, as noted earlier, imaging studies have found specific regions in the auditory cortex that are dedicated to the localization of sound (Clarke & Thiran, 2004).

Test Yourself 5.2

Check your knowledge about the auditory system by determining whether each of the following statements is True or False. (You will find the answers in the Appendix.)

1. Sound is a form of mechanical energy that requires a medium, such as air or water, in order to move. *True or False?*
2. According to the frequency theory of pitch perception, the location of activity on the basilar membrane is the primary cue for determining pitch. *True or False?*
3. Sound pressure causes tiny hair cells, located in the pinna, to bend, thereby generating a neural impulse. *True or False?*
4. The separation of a sensory message into figure and ground occurs for vision but not for hearing. *True or False?*
5. We use multiple cues to help us localize a sound, including comparisons of arrival times and intensity differences between the two ears. *True or False?*

The Skin and Body Senses: From Touch to Movement

LEARNING GOALS
- Explain how sensory messages delivered to the skin (touch and temperature) are translated and interpreted by the brain.
- Describe how we perceive and interpret pain.
- Discuss the operation and function of the body senses: movement and balance.

IN THIS SECTION we turn to the three skin senses—touch, temperature, and pain—as well as to the body senses related to movement and balance. Not surprisingly, the skin and body senses have tremendous adaptive value. You need to detect that spider crawling up your leg; if a blowing ember from the fireplace happens to land on your forearm, it is certainly adaptive for you to respond quickly. It's also important for us to detect and control the movement and position of our own bodies. We need to know, for example, whether we're hanging upside down and the current positions of our arms and legs. Human sensory systems have developed not only to detect the presence of objects in the environment but also to provide accurate information about the body itself. As in our earlier discussions, in each case the environmental message must be translated, transmitted to the brain, and interpreted in a meaningful way.

Touch

For touch or pressure, the physical message delivered to the skin is mechanical. An object makes contact with the body—perhaps your fingers actively reach out and initiate the contact—and receptor cells embedded in the skin are disturbed. The mechanical pressure on the cell (it is literally deformed) produces a neural impulse, and the message is then transmitted to the spinal cord and up into the brain.

There are several different types of pressure-sensitive receptor cells in the skin. Some respond to constant pressure; others respond best to intermittent pressure, such as tapping on the skin or a stimulus that vibrates at a particular frequency (Bolanowski, Gescheider, & Verillo, 1994). As with vision and hearing, touch information is transmitted up the neural pathway through distinct channels to processing stations in the brain, where the inputs received from various points on the body are combined (Bolanowski, 1989). One kind of nerve fiber might carry information about touch location; other fibers might transmit information about whether the touch has been brief or sustained.

At the level of the *somatosensory cortex*, located in the parietal lobe of the brain, a close connection is found among regions of the skin and representation in the cortex (Prud'homme. Cohen, & Kalaska, 1994). As you learned in Chapter 3, the cortex contains multiple "body maps," where adjacent cortical cells have areas of sensitivity that correspond to adjacent areas on the skin. Moreover, as in the visual cortex, some areas are represented more elaborately than others. For example, a relatively large amount of cortical tissue is devoted to the hands and lips, whereas the middle portion of the back, despite its size, receives little representation in the cortex. Maybe that's the reason we kiss to display intense affection rather than simply pat someone on the back. There's a lot more cortex devoted to the lips than to the back.

Everyone has the ability to recognize complex objects exclusively through touch. When blindfolded, people show near-perfect identification of common objects (such as toothbrushes and paperclips) after examining them by active touch (Klatzky, Lederman, & Metzger, 1985). Active skin contact with an object produces not only shape information but information about firmness, texture, and weight. Moreover, as with seeing and hearing, a person's final interpretation of an object depends on what the person feels as well as on what he or she expects to feel. For instance, if you expect to be touched by an object on a particular finger, you are more likely to identify

CRITICAL THINKING

Can you tell the difference between the touch of a loved one and the touch of a stranger? Do you think you could learn to interpret a touch differently with experience?

Humans use touch to acquire information about shape, firmness, texture, and weight.

Gary S. and Vivian Chapman/Getty Images/The Image Bank

The popularity of winter swimming among Russians demonstrates how the perception of temperature can be influenced by psychological factors.

the object correctly (Craig, 1985). There are also measurable changes in blood flow in the somatosensory cortex when a person simply expects to be touched (Drevets et al., 1995).

Temperature

At present researchers have only a limited idea of how the body records and processes temperature. Electrophysiological research has detected the presence of **cold fibers** that respond to a cooling of the skin by increasing the production of neural impulses, as well as **warm fibers** that respond vigorously when the temperature of the skin increases. But the behavior of these temperature-sensitive receptor systems is not particularly well understood (Zotterman, 1959). We do know, however, that the perception of warm and cold is only indirectly related to the actual temperature of the real-world object. To demonstrate, try plunging one hand into a bowl of cold water and the other hand into a bowl of hot water. Now place both hands into a third bowl containing water sitting at room temperature. The hand that was in the cold water will sense the water as warm; the other hand will experience it as cold. Same water, same temperature, but two different perceptual experiences. It's the temperature *change* that determines your perception. When your cold hand touches warmer water, your skin begins to warm; it is the increase in skin temperature that you actually perceive.

At times these perceptual processes can lead to temperature "illusions." For instance, metal seems cooler than wood even when both are at the same physical temperature. Why? Metal is a better conductor of heat than wood, so it absorbs more warmth from the skin. Consequently, the brain perceives the loss of heat as a cooler physical temperature.

Experiencing Pain

Pain is a unique kind of sensory experience. It's not a characteristic of the world that the brain tries to interpret, such as an object or an energy source. Instead **pain** is an adaptive reaction that the body generates in response to a stimulus that is intense enough to cause tissue damage. The stimulus can be just about anything. It can come from outside or inside the body; it doesn't even need to be particularly intense (consider the effect of salt on an open wound).

Little is known about pain receptors in the skin, although cells have been discovered in animals that react to painful stimuli (such as intense heat) by sending signals to the cortex (Dong et al., 1994). Pain is a complex psychological experience, however, and it often relies on much more than just a physical stimulus. There are well-documented examples of soldiers who report little or no pain after receiving serious injuries in battle; the same is true of many individuals entering an emergency room. In addition, certain non-Western cultures use rituals that should, from a Western perspective, inflict great pain but apparently do not (Melzack, 1973).

Gate-Control Theory   The interplay between the physical and the psychological in pain perception forms the basis for the **gate-control theory** (Melzack & Wall, 1965, 1982). The basic idea is that the neural impulses generated by pain receptors can be blocked, or gated, in the spinal cord by signals produced in the brain. If you've just sliced your finger cutting carrots on the kitchen counter, you would normally feel pain. But if a pan on the stove suddenly starts to smoke, the pain seems to evaporate while you try to prevent your house from burning down. According to gate-control

cold fibers Neurons that respond to a cooling of the skin by increasing the production of neural impulses.

warm fibers Neurons that respond vigorously when the temperature of the skin increases.

pain An adaptive response by the body to any stimulus that is intense enough to cause tissue damage.

gate-control theory The idea that neural impulses generated by pain receptors can be blocked, or gated, in the spinal cord by signals produced in the brain.

theory, the brain can block the critical pain signals from reaching higher neural centers when it is appropriate to do so.

How is the gating action actually carried out? The details of the mechanisms are unclear, but two types of nerve fibers appear to be responsible for opening and closing the gate. So-called large fibers, when stimulated, produce nervous system activity that closes the gate; other "small" fibers, when stimulated, inhibit those neural processes and effectively open the gate. External activities—such as rubbing or placing ice on a wound—also apparently stimulate the large fibers, which close the gate, preventing further passage of the pain message toward the brain. Again, the details of the neural circuitry remain to be worked out, and it's worth noting that the neural connections proposed in the original gate-control theory were wrong, but the idea of a *pain gate* that opens and closes remains popular among researchers (Sufta & Price, 2002).

In addition to gating the pain signals, as we discussed in Chapter 3, the brain can also control the experience of pain through the release of chemicals called *endorphins*, which produce painkilling effects like those obtained through morphine. The release of endorphins may help explain those instances in which pain should be experienced but is not. For example, swallowing a sugar pill can sometimes reduce pain even though there's no medical reason it should work (a placebo effect). The locus of such effects, and other analgesic procedures such as acupuncture, might lie in the brain's internal production of its own antipain medication.

The Kinesthetic Sense

The word **kinesthesia** literally means "movement"; when used in connection with sensation, the term refers to the ability to sense the position and movement of one's body parts. For example, as you reach toward a blossoming flower, feedback from your skin, tendons, muscles, and especially joints helps you maintain the correct line toward the target. The kinesthetic sense shares many properties with the sense of touch—a variety of receptors in the muscles that surround the joints react to the physical forces produced by moving the limbs (Gandevia, McCloskey, & Burke, 1992; Verschueven, Cordo, & Swinnen, 1998).

kinesthesia In perception, the ability to sense the position and movement of one's body parts.

The nerve impulses generated by the kinesthetic receptors travel to the somatosensory cortex, where, it is presumed, increasingly complex cells respond only when body parts (such as the arms) are placed in certain positions (Gardner & Costanzo, 1981). But the psychological experience of movement is most likely influenced by multiple factors, as with other kinds of perception. The visual system, for example, provides additional feedback about current position, as does the sense of touch.

The Vestibular Sense

We have another complex receptor system, attached to the cochlea of the inner ear, that responds not only to movement but also to acceleration and to changes in upright posture. Each ear contains three small fluid-filled **semicircular canals** that are lined with hair cells similar to those found in the cochlea. If you quickly turn your head toward some object, these hair cells are displaced, and nerve impulses signaling acceleration are transmitted throughout the brain. Some of the nerve fibers project to the cortex; others direct messages to the eye muscles, allowing you to adjust your eyes as your head is turning.

semicircular canals A receptor system attached to the inner ear that responds to movement and acceleration and to changes in upright posture.

The vestibular system is also responsible for the sense of balance. If you tilt your head, or encounter a 360-degree loop on a roller coaster, receptor cells located in other inner ear organs, called **vestibular sacs**, quickly transmit the appropriate orientation information to the brain. Continual disturbance of the semicircular canals or the vestibular sacs can produce dizziness, nausea, and motion sickness (Lackner & DiZio, 1991).

vestibular sacs Organs of the inner ear that contain receptors thought to be primarily responsible for balance.

The vestibular sense helps people maintain balance by monitoring the position of the body in space.

©Duomo/Corbis

Test Yourself 5.3

Check your knowledge about the skin and body senses by answering the following multiple-choice questions. (You will find the answers in the Appendix.)

1. Alicia holds her left hand in a bowl of cold water and her right hand in a bowl of hot water. She then transfers both hands to a bowl containing water at room temperature. She finds that her left hand now feels warm and her right hand cool. Why?
   a. Cold and hot fibers rebound after continued activity.
   b. It's temperature change that determines perception.
   c. She expects a change; therefore, a change is experienced.
   d. Opponent-process cells in the cortex are reacting.
2. According to gate-control theory, psychological factors can influence the perception of pain by
   a. channeling pain signals to the occipital lobe.

   b. reducing the supply of endorphins in the body.
   c. blocking pain signals from reaching higher neural centers.
   d. blocking pain receptors from relaying messages to the spinal cord.
3. The vestibular sacs contain receptor cells that help us maintain our sense of balance. Where are they located?
   a. In the lateral geniculate nucleus
   b. In the superior colliculus
   c. In the joints and limbs of the body
   d. In the inner ear

The Chemical Senses: Smell and Taste

LEARNING GOAL
• Describe how chemical stimuli lead to neural activities that are interpreted as different odors and tastes.

WE END OUR REVIEW of the individual sensory systems with the chemical senses, *smell* and *taste*. We receive lots of messages from the environment, but few carry as much emotional impact as chemically based input. You can appreciate the touch of a loved one, or the visual beauty of a sunset, but consider your reaction to the smell of decaying meat or to the distinctive taste of milk left a bit too long in the sun! Smells and tastes are enormously adaptive because they possess powerful signaling properties: Like other animals, humans learn to avoid off odors and bitter tastes.

The perception of both smell and taste begins with the activity of receptor cells, called **chemoreceptors**, that react to invisible molecules scattered about in the air or dissolved in liquids. These receptors solve the translation problem and project the

chemoreceptors Receptor cells that react to invisible molecules scattered about in the air or dissolved in liquids, leading to the senses of smell and taste.

newly formed neural impulses toward the brain. Psychologically, the two senses are related: Anyone who has ever had a cold knows that things "just don't taste right" with a plugged nose. You can demonstrate this for yourself by holding your nose and trying to taste the difference between an apple and a piece of raw potato. In fact people can identify a taste far more efficiently if they are also allowed a brief sniff (Mozell et al., 1969). Let's consider each of these chemical senses in more detail.

Smell

The technical name for the sense of smell is **olfaction**, which comes from the Latin word *olfacere*, meaning "to smell." Airborne molecules enter through the nose or the back of the throat and interact with receptor cells embedded in the upper region of the nasal cavity (Lancet et al., 1993). As with the receptor systems used to hear and detect motion, the olfactory receptor cells contain tiny hairs, or *cilia*. The airborne molecules are thought to bind with the cilia, causing the generation of a neural impulse. Receptor fibers then move the message forward to the *olfactory bulb*, located at the bottom front region of the brain. From here the information is sent to several areas in the brain.

olfaction The sense of smell.

©Joe Cornish/Getty Images/Stone

Studies have shown that people probably have a thousand or more different kinds of olfactory receptor cells (Buck & Axel, 1991). It's not yet known whether each receptor type is tied to the perception of a particular odor, but there's almost certainly no simple one-to-one connection. For one thing, olfactory receptor cells are often activated by more than one kind of chemical stimulus. In addition, most odors are complex psychological experiences. People have no problem recognizing the smell of frying bacon or the aroma of fresh coffee, but a chemical analysis of these events fails to reveal the presence of any single defining molecule. Clearly, the ability to apply the label "frying bacon" to a set of airborne chemicals arises from complex perceptual processes. It's even possible to produce smell *illusions*—if you're led to expect that a particular odor is present, even though it's not, you're likely to report detecting its presence (O'Mahony, 1978). Similar to other sensory systems, odor perception is likely signaled by a pattern of activation across the olfactory bulb and by changes in the firing rates of neurons (Shepard, 2006).

The neural pathway for smell is somewhat unusual, compared with other sensory systems, because connections are made with forebrain structures such as the amygdala, hippocampus, and the hypothalamus (Buck, 1996). As you learned in Chapter 3, these areas have been linked with the regulation of feeding, drinking, sexual behavior, and even memory. It's speculation, but part of the emotional power of olfactory cues might be related to the involvement of this motivational pathway. Certainly in lower animals, whose behavior is often dominated by odor cues, brain structures such as the hypothalamus and the amygdala seem likely to play a major role in the animal's reaction to odors in its environment.

A taster's ability to identify the smell, or "bouquet," of wine depends on the constellation of airborne chemicals produced by the wine and on the experience of the taster.

Many animals release chemicals, called *pheromones*, that cause highly specific reactions when detected by other members of the species (Brennan & Zufall, 2006). Pheromones often induce sexual behavior or characteristic patterns of aggression, but other reactions can be produced. Ants, for example, react to the smell of a dead member of the colony by carrying the decaying corpse outside the nest (Wilson, 1963). So far, much to the disappointment of the perfume industry, little support has been found for human pheromones; at least no scents have been discovered that reliably induce sexual interest (Hays, 2003). There is some tantalizing evidence suggesting that women prefer the scents of men who show physical traits suggestive of "good genes," such as facial symmetry; moreover, these preferences are strongest when the women are most fertile (Thornhill et al., 2003).

gustation The sense of taste.

flavor A psychological term used to describe the gustatory experience. Flavor is influenced by taste, smell, and the visual appearance of food, as well as by expectations about the food's quality.

taste buds The receptor cells on the tongue.

Taste

Smell's companion sense, taste, is known by the technical term **gustation**, which comes from the Latin *gustare*, meaning "to taste." Unlike odors, which are difficult to classify, there appear to be four basic tastes: sweet, bitter, salty, and sour. Growing evidence suggests there is a fifth basic taste as well, called umami (which translates from the Japanese as "meaty" or "savory"). When psychologists use the term *taste*, they are referring to the sensations produced by contact with the taste receptors; they are not referring to the overall richness of the psychological experience that accompanies eating. Typically, the term flavor is used to describe the meal experience. **Flavor** is influenced by taste, smell, and the visual appearance of the food, as well as by expectations about the quality of the meal (Shepard, 2006).

Taste receptors are distributed throughout the mouth but mainly occur across the tongue. If you coat your tongue with a mouthful of milk and glance in a mirror, you'll see that your tongue is covered with tiny bumps called *papillae*. The **taste buds**, which contain the actual receptor cells, are embedded within the folds of the papillae. Currently, lots of questions remain about how the transduction process for taste actually occurs. One possibility is that taste stimuli directly penetrate the membrane of the receptor cell, causing the cell to fire; another idea is that taste stimuli simply alter the chemical structure of the cell membrane (Shirley & Persaud, 1990; Teeter & Brand, 1987). In any case, the neural impulse is generated and passed to the brain.

The neural pathway for taste takes a more traditional route than the one for smell: Information is passed to the thalamus and then up to the somatosensory area of the cortex (Rolls, 1995). Little work has been done on how cortical taste cells react, although taste-sensitive cells have been discovered (Scott, Plata-Salamn, & Smith-Swintosky, 1994; Yamamoto et al., 1981). Stronger evidence for taste "tuning" has been found in analysis of the receptor fibers, but, as with many of the other senses, a given receptor cell seems to react to a broad range of gustatory stimuli. The neural code for taste is probably determined, to some extent, by the particular fiber that happens to react and by the relative patterns of activity across large groups of fibers (Chandrashekar et al., 2006). For example, there is evidence that similar tasting foods tend to produce similar patterns of activity across groups of taste neurons (Smith & Margolskee, 2001). One possibility is that our brains compare activity levels across

Taste buds, which contain the receptor cells for taste, are embedded within the folds of the large circular papillae.

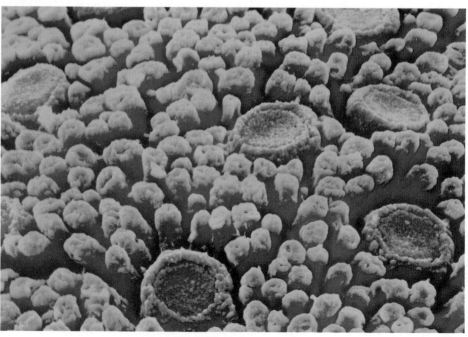

taste neurons, perhaps similar to the way the visual system compares output from the three cone receptors to help determine color.

The brain can produce stable interpretations of taste stimuli, but the identification process is complex. For one thing, prior exposure to one kind of taste often changes the perception of another. Anyone who has ever tried to drink orange juice after brushing his or her teeth understands how tastes interact. To some extent, the interaction process depends on the similarity of successive tastes. For example, a taste of a sour pickle, but not a salty cracker, will reduce the "sourness" of lemon juice. There are even natural substances that can completely change the normal perception of taste. One substance extracted from berries, called "miracle fruit," turns extremely sour tastes (such as from raw lemons) sweet. Another substance, taken from the leaves of a plant found in India and Africa, temporarily eliminates the sweet taste of sugar.

Test Yourself   **5.4**

Check your knowledge about smell and taste by filling in the blanks. Choose the best answer from among the following terms: chemoreceptors, flavor, gustation, hypothalamus, olfaction, olfactory bulb, pheromones, taste, taste buds. *(You will find the answers in the Appendix.)*

1. The general term for receptor cells that are activated by invisible molecules scattered about in the air or dissolved in liquids: _____
2. One of the main brain destinations for odor messages: _____

3. A psychological term used to describe the entire gustatory experience: _____
4. The technical name for the sense of smell: _____
5. The technical name for the sense of taste: _____

From the Physical to the Psychological

LEARNING GOALS
- Explain stimulus detection, including techniques designed to measure it.
- Define difference thresholds and explain Weber's law.
- Discuss stimulus adaptation and its adaptive value.

THROUGHOUT THIS CHAPTER, you've learned that there's a kind of transition from the physical to the psychological. Messages originate in the physical world, but our conscious experience of those messages is influenced by our expectations and beliefs about how the world is organized. We *interpret* the physical message, and this means our conscious experience of the sensory message can be different from the one that is actually delivered by the environment. In the field of **psychophysics**, researchers search for ways to describe the transition from the physical to the psychological in the form of mathematical laws. By quantifying the relationship between the physical properties of a stimulus and its subjective experience, psychophysicists hope to develop *general laws* that apply across all kinds of sensory input. Let's consider some examples of how such laws are established.

psychophysics A field of psychology in which researchers search for ways to describe the transition from the physical stimulus to the psychological experience of that stimulus.

Stimulus Detection

Psychophysics is one of the oldest research areas in psychology; it dates back to the work of Wilhelm Wundt, Gustav Fechner, and others in the 19th century. One of the first questions these early researchers asked was this: What is the minimum amount of stimulus energy needed to produce a sensation? Suppose I present you with a very faint pure tone—one that you cannot hear—and gradually make it louder. At some point you will hear the tone and respond accordingly. This point is known as the **absolute threshold** for the stimulus; it represents the level of intensity that lifts the

absolute threshold The level of intensity that lifts a stimulus over the threshold of conscious awareness; it's usually defined as the intensity level at which people can detect the presence of the stimulus 50% of the time.

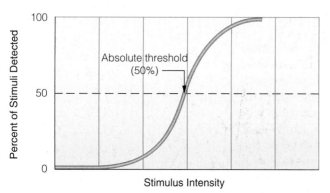

FIGURE 5.25 Absolute Threshold
The more intense the stimulus, the greater the likelihood that it will be detected. The absolute threshold is the intensity level at which we can detect the presence of the stimulus 50% of the time.

CRITICAL THINKING

Can you think of any occupations requiring detection—such as air traffic controller—in which it might be advantageous to be biased toward saying "Yes" that a stimulus has occurred?

FIGURE 5.26 Signal Detection Outcomes
There are four possible outcomes in a signal detection experiment: (1) If the stimulus is present and correctly detected, it's called a hit. (2) If the stimulus is absent but the observer claims it's present, it's a false alarm. (3) A miss is when the stimulus is present but not detected. (4) A correct rejection is when the observer correctly recognizes that the stimulus was not presented.

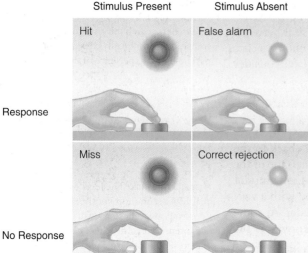

stimulus over the threshold of conscious awareness. One of the early insights of psychophysicists such as Fechner was the realization that absolute thresholds are really not absolute. It turns out that there is no single point in an intensity curve at which detection reliably begins. For a given intensity level, sometimes people will hear the tone, other times not (the same situation applies to detection in all the sensory modalities, not just auditory). For this reason, absolute thresholds were redefined as the intensity level at which people can detect the presence of a stimulus 50% of the time (see ▌Figure 5.25).

It might seem strange that detection abilities change from moment to moment. Part of the reason is that trial-to-trial observations turn out to be "noisy." It's virtually impossible for a researcher to control all the things that can potentially affect someone's performance. For example, a person might have a momentary lapse in attention that causes him or her to miss a presented stimulus on a given trial. Some random activity in the nervous system might even create brief changes in the sensitivity of the receptor systems. Experimenters try to take these factors into account by presenting many detection opportunities and averaging performance over trials.

Psychologists have also tried to develop reasonably sophisticated statistical techniques to pull the truth out of noisy data. Human participants often have built-in biases that influence their responses. For example, people will sometimes report the presence of a stimulus even though none has actually been presented. Why? Sometimes the observer is simply worried about missing a presented stimulus, so he or she says "Yes" on every trial. To control for these tendencies, researchers use a technique called **signal detection** that mathematically compares *hits*—in which a stimulus is correctly detected—to *false alarms*—in which the observer claims a stimulus was presented when it actually was not.

Four types of outcomes can occur in a detection situation. Besides hits and false alarms, you can also fail to detect a stimulus when it was actually presented—called a *miss*—or correctly recognize that a stimulus was, in fact, not presented on that trial—called a *correct rejection*. These four outcomes are shown in ▌Figure 5.26. Researchers compare these outcomes over trials in an attempt to infer true detection ability.

To see why it's important to compare different outcomes, imagine Lois is participating in a simple detection experiment and that her strategy is to say, "Yes, a stimulus occurred," on every trial (even when no stimulus was actually presented). If the researcher pays attention only to hits, it will appear as if Lois has perfect detection ability—she always correctly identifies a stimulus when it occurs. But saying "Yes" on every trial will also lead to false alarms—she will say "Yes" on trials when no stimulus was actually presented. By comparing hits and false alarms, the researcher is able to determine whether her high number of "hits" is really due to detection ability or whether it's due to some other strategic bias on her part. If Lois can truly detect the stimulus when it occurs, she should show lots of hits and very few false alarms.

Difference Thresholds

Researchers in psychophysics have also been concerned with the measurement of **difference thresholds**: the smallest detectable difference in the magnitude of two stimuli. Suppose I present you with two tones, each equally loud. I then gradually increase the intensity of one of the tones until you notice it as being louder than the other (called the *standard*). How much of a change do I need to make for you to detect the difference? As with absolute thresholds, the required amount changes from one moment to the next, but an important general principle emerges.

(a)   **(b)**

The addition of a few candles to a brightly lit room has little effect on perceived brightness **(a)**; but when candles are added to a dimly lit room **(b)**, the increase in brightness is quite noticeable.

It turns out that detection of a *just noticeable difference* (or jnd) depends on how intense the standard was in the first place. If you have your stereo cranked up, small changes in the volume will not be noticed; but if the volume starts out low, the same changes are likely to produce a very noticeable difference. If you're at a rock concert and your friend Gillian wants to tell you something, she needs to yell; if you're in a library, a whisper will do. We can state this relationship more formally as follows: The jnd for stimulus magnitude is a constant proportion of the size of the standard stimulus. In other words, the louder the standard stimulus (the stereo), the more volume will be needed before a difference in loudness will be detected. This general relationship, called **Weber's law**, doesn't work just for loudness—it applies across all the sensory systems. If the lights in your house go off, two candles will make the room a lot brighter than one; if the lights are on, the addition of one or two candles will lead to little, if any, noticeable increase in brightness (see the accompanying photos). Weber's law demonstrates once again that the relationship between the physical and the psychological is not always direct; increases in the magnitude of a physical stimulus will not always lead to increases in the psychological experience.

signal detection A technique used to determine the ability of someone to detect the presence of a stimulus.

difference threshold The smallest detectable difference in the magnitude of two stimuli.

Weber's law The principle stating that the ability to notice a difference in the magnitude of two stimuli is a constant proportion of the size of the standard stimulus. Psychologically, the more intense a stimulus is to begin with, the more intense it will need to become for one to notice a change.

Sensory Adaptation

One other feature of all sensory systems is important to remember: Sensory systems are more sensitive to a message when it first arrives than to its continued presence. Through **sensory adaptation**, the body quickly adapts, by reducing sensitivity, to a message that remains constant—such as the feel of a shirtsleeve on your forearm, your hand resting on your knee, or the hum of computers in the background. Think about what the world would be like without sensory adaptation. The water in the pool would never warm up; the smell of garlic from last night's dinner would remain a pervasive force; you would constantly be reminded of the texture of your sock pressing against your foot.

sensory adaptation The tendency of sensory systems to reduce sensitivity to a stimulus source that remains constant.

Adaptation is a feature of each of the sensory systems we've discussed. Images that remain stable on the retina will vanish; this doesn't normally occur because the eyes are constantly moving and refreshing the retinal image. If you are presented with a continuous tone, your perception of its loudness decreases over time (Evans,

1982). If auditory adaptation didn't occur, no one would ever be able to work in a noisy environment. Human sensory systems are designed to detect *changes* in the incoming message; sensitivity is reduced to those aspects of the message that remain the same.

Test Yourself | 5.5

Check your understanding of psychophysics by deciding whether each of the following statements is True or False. *(You will find the answers in the Appendix.)*

1. The intensity level that is required to perceive a stimulus varies across individuals but remains constant for any given individual. *True or False?*
2. A "false alarm" occurs in signal detection when an observer claims a signal was present when, in fact, it was not. *True or False?*
3. According to Weber's law, the detection of a just noticeable difference in magnitude is constant across all intensity levels. *True or False?*
4. Sensory adaptation is a characteristic of all sensory systems. *True or False?*

Review | *Psychology for a Reason*

To navigate successfully in the world, we rely on multiple sensory systems. As you've seen, the outside world itself is not very user friendly—it bombards the body with energy-based messages, but none arrives in a form appropriate for the language of the brain. Moreover, the messages that our sensory systems receive are complex and ever changing. To build an accurate view of the world, our sensory systems need to solve three problems: (1) the external message must be translated into the internal language of the nervous system; (2) the elementary components must be identified and pulled from the message; (3) a stable and lasting interpretation of the message components must be built.

Translating the Message To solve the translation problem, the body relies on specialized receptor cells that generate neural impulses in the presence of particular energy sources.

In the visual system, receptor cells—rods and cones—react to light; in the auditory system, sound leads to movement of the basilar membrane, which in turn causes tiny hair cells to generate a neural impulse. The body also has specialized receptors that react to pressure on the skin, free-floating chemicals in the air, and the relative position or movement of muscles. Each of these receptor systems acts as a kind of "translator," changing the messages delivered by the world into the electrochemical language of the nervous system.

Identifying the Message Components Once translated, systems in the brain work to pull components out of the sensory message. A variety of neural pathways are specialized to look for particular kinds of sensory information. For example, opponent-process cells in the lateral geniculate are specialized to process color; they signal the presence of one kind of color by increasing the rate at which they generate neural impulses, and they signal another kind of color by decreasing their firing rate. Similarly, highly specialized cells in

the visual cortex respond only to particular patterns of light and dark. One kind of cell might respond only to a bar of light presented at a particular orientation; another cell might respond only to a pattern of light that moves in a particular direction across the retina.

In the auditory cortex, the brain detects information about the frequencies of sound in an auditory message. Psychologically, changes in frequency correspond to changes in perceived pitch. The brain extracts frequency information by noting the particular place on the basilar membrane where hair cells are stimulated and by noting the rate at which neural impulses are generated over time. It's not unusual for the brain to rely on multiple kinds of processing to extract a particular message component. The perception of color, for instance, relies not only on opponent-process cells but also on the relative activations of three different cone types in the retina.

Producing a Stable Interpretation To build a stable interpretation of the sensory message, we use a combination of bottom-up and top-down processing—beliefs and expectations work with the actual sensory input to build perceptions of the external world. In many respects our perceptual abilities are truly amazing. The pattern of light reflected from a moving object changes continuously with time, yet we have no trouble recognizing a dancer moving effortlessly across the stage. We also have no trouble identifying the voice of a friend in a crowded room, even though the actual auditory message reaching our ears may be filled with frequency information from many different voices.

The brain solves these problems of perception, in part, by relying on organizational "rules." For example, we're born with built-in tendencies to group message components in particular ways. Figures are separated from ground, items that share physical properties are perceived together, and so on. But we also rely on prior knowledge for help in the interpretation process.

We use what we know about how cues are related in the environment to arrive at sensible interpretations of ambiguous objects. For instance, if two parallel lines converge in the visual field, the brain assumes that the lines are moving away—like railroad tracks moving off in the distance. Such top-down processing is usually extremely adaptive—it helps us maintain a stable interpretation—although in some cases perceptual illusions may be produced.

Active Summary (You will find the answers in the Appendix.)

Vision: The World of Color and Form

• Light reflected from an object enters the (1) _____ through the cornea, (2) _____, and (3) _____. Light reaches the back of the eye, or (4) _____, where light-sensitive receptor cells called (5) _____ and (6) _____ translate the message into the language of the brain.

• After leaving the retina, neural activation flows first to the (7) _____ _____ and then primarily through the lateral geniculate nucleus in the (8) _____. (9) _____ _____ in the visual cortex respond to particular aspects of a stimulus, such as orientation and patterns of light and dark. The trichromatic theory proposes that color information is extracted from (10) _____ different kinds of cones; (11) _____ - _____ proposes that cells respond positively to one color type and negatively to others. Each theory accounts for certain aspects of color vision.

• Bottom-up processing starts with a physical message, and (12) _____ - _____ processing applies knowledge and expectation. We group incoming visual messages according to Gestalt principles of organization, which include the laws of (13) _____, similarity, (14) _____, good continuation, and common fate. Monocular and (15) _____ cues help us perceive (16) _____. We use top-down processing to help us identify objects and achieve perceptual (17) _____, although sometimes inappropriate interpretations of physical reality can occur.

Hearing: Identifying and Localizing Sounds

• Sound varies in (18) _____ and (19) _____. Sound wave vibrations enter the ear through the pinna and travel to the tympanic membrane, or (20) _____, and then to the middle ear, inner ear, and cochlea. Vibrating fluid in the (21) _____ displaces the (22) _____ _____, which activates auditory receptors called hair cells.

• The (23) _____ uses several types of information to identify pitch. The (24) _____ _____ of pitch perception holds that we hear a particular pitch because (25) _____ _____ at a certain location on the basilar membrane are responding actively. According to frequency theory, pitch is partly determined by the (26) _____ of neural impulses traveling up the auditory pathway. Final processing of the auditory message takes place in the auditory cortex. Cells in certain areas of the (27) _____ _____ are sensitive to different sound information.

• The brain uses existing knowledge and (28) _____ to impose structure on and (29) _____ incoming auditory messages. Sound (30) _____ depends on comparing how the arrival (31) _____ and (32) _____ of a sound differs from one ear to another.

The Skin and Body Senses: From Touch to Movement

• Touch information is transmitted from different types of (33) _____ - _____ skin cells through distinct neural pathways to the brain, where it is processed by the (34) _____ cortex in the (35) _____ lobe. Cold fibers respond to skin cooling and warm fibers respond to skin warming by (36) _____ neural firing. Temperature perception depends on (37) _____ in temperature.

• According to (38) _____-_____ theory, pain receptors generate impulses that are gated, or blocked, in the (39) _____ _____ by brain signals. This can prevent critical pain signals from reaching higher neural centers when appropriate. The (40) _____ also controls our experience of pain by releasing (41) _____, chemicals that produce pain-relieving effects.

• (42) _____ is the ability to sense the (43) _____ and movement of the various parts of the body. Kinesthetic receptors generate nerve impulses that travel to the (44) _____ cortex. The (45) _____ sense responds to movement, (46) _____, and changes in upright posture. (47) _____ canals and vestibular sacs in the ear help us detect the position of the head and influence our sense of balance.

The Chemical Senses: Smell and Taste

• The sense of smell, or (48) _____, and taste, or gustation, depends on the activity of (49) _____ that react to molecules in the air or dissolved fluids. Olfaction relies on airborne molecules that enter the nose or back of the throat and interact with chemoreceptors in the (50) _____ cavity to produce a message that travels to the olfactory (51) _____ in the brain. Gustation relies on taste buds that contain chemoreceptors embedded in the tiny bumps on the tongue called papillae. Taste appears to have four categories: sweet, salty, bitter, and sour. Taste messages travel first to the (52) _____ and then to the somatosensory cortex.

From the Physical to the Psychological

• The (53) _____ _____ of a stimulus is the level of intensity at which we can detect the presence of the stimulus (54) _____ percent of the time. To account for varying responses, researchers developed (55) _____ _____, a technique that mathematically compares hits to (56) _____ alarms.

• A (57) _____ _____ is the smallest difference in the (58) _____ of two stimuli that can be (59) _____. According to Weber's law, detecting a (60) _____ _____ _____ (jnd) depends on the intensity or size of the standard stimulus.

• Sensory (61) _____ is an important function that allows the body to adapt quickly to a (62) _____ by reducing (63) _____ to sensory messages that remain (64) _____, such as the feel of a sleeve on your arm.

Terms to Remember

Media Resources

 **ThomsonNOW**

www.thomsonedu.com/ThomsonNOW

Go to this site for the link to ThomsonNow, your one-stop study shop. Take a Pre-Test for this chapter and Thomson-Now will generate a personalized Study Plan based on your test results! The Study Plan will identify the topics you need to review and direct you to online resources to help you master those topics. You can then take a Post-Test to help you determine the concepts you have mastered and what you still need to work on.

 Companion Website

www.thomsonedu.com/psychology/nairne

Go to this site to find online resources directly linked to your book, including a glossary, flashcards, quizzing, weblinks, and more.

 Psyk.trek 3.0

Check out the Psyk.trek CD-ROM for further study of the concepts in this chapter. Psyk.trek's interactive learning modules, simulations, and quizzes offer additional opportunities for you to interact with, reflect on, and retain the material:

Sensation and Perception: The Retina
Sensation and Perception: The Sense of Hearing

CHAPTER 6

Consciousness

Stop for a moment and take a look inside your own head. Try to grab hold of conscious thought and take it for a ride. Forget about its contents—ideas, images, sounds—concentrate only on the movements from thought-to-thought-to-thought-to-thought. Notice the transitions, the ways ideas and feelings spring forth, only to disappear a moment later. Would you call the movements bumpy? Smooth? The American psychologist William James (1890) was convinced that consciousness *flows*. Consciousness isn't something that can be chopped up in bits, he argued, "words such as 'chain' or 'train' do not describe it fitly . . . a 'river' or 'stream' are the metaphors by which it is most naturally described" (p. 233).

Psychologists define **consciousness** as the subjective *awareness* of internal and external events. The key term here, of course, is *awareness*, but what does it mean to be aware? Intuitively, the concept is clear: To be aware is to experience the here and now, to experience the past in the form of memories, to think internally and develop a guiding view of the world (Klatzky, 1984). Awareness has the additional property of focus: You can choose to attend to that bug walking up the page of your text or to the voice of your roommate telling you to turn out the light. You can also use conscious thought to develop strategies for behavior; you can think about what you want to say or do, and you can imagine the outcomes of those actions without actually performing the behaviors. You can also use conscious thought to imagine the content of other minds—to predict the behavior of other people and to understand their motivation (Weiskrantz, 1992).

At the same time, our actions are also controlled by processes that operate *below* levels of awareness. To take an extreme case, you're not aware of the processes controlling your heartbeat or breathing rate, yet these functions carry on like clockwork. Your awareness also takes on different properties when you sleep, when you're hypnotized, or when you take certain types of drugs. These are some of the topics that we'll be considering in this chapter, and you'll see how altering awareness plays an important and adaptive role in our lives.

consciousness The subjective awareness of internal and external events.

To appreciate the value of consciousness, as well as to understand how psychologists study it, we'll consider four situations in which the processes of consciousness importantly apply.

Setting Priorities for Mental Functioning

There are limits to the number of things we can think about at the same time or to the number of tasks we can perform. Have you ever tried to solve a difficult thought problem while someone talks nearby? What about driving and talking on a cell phone—having trouble? Obviously, it's critical to be selective about what we choose to focus on. In this section we'll discuss how the psychological processes of *attention* help focus our resources on the important tasks at hand.

Sleeping and Dreaming

Sleep clearly serves an adaptive function, and it represents a change in level or state of awareness. But what are the functions of sleep and dreaming? Some researchers believe that we sleep in order to give the brain a chance to rest and restore itself from the day's activities. Others believe that sleep protects us during periods when our sensory equipment is unlikely to function well (such as at night). Dreaming may help us work out hidden conflicts or simply help us exercise the neural circuitry of the brain.

Altering Awareness: Psychoactive Drugs

You know that psychoactive drugs, such as those contained in alcohol and marijuana, can produce mind-bending alterations of consciousness. But did you know that the biological processes that produce these changes are actually natural and important ingredients of the adaptive mind? Make no mistake—consuming psychoactive drugs can have harmful and long-lasting consequences, but it's important to understand that artificial drugs operate, in part, by tapping natural adaptive systems.

Altering Awareness: Induced States

We'll end the chapter by discussing hypnosis, a procedure that induces a heightened state of suggestibility. Does hypnosis tell us anything about awareness and its function? Through hypnosis, it's possible to break bad habits (such as smoking), drastically reduce the experience of pain, and eliminate the nausea caused by chemotherapy. The techniques of meditation have proven effective in the treatment of stress and psychological disorders. You'll discover that both hypnosis and meditation can have adaptive benefits.

Setting priorities for mental functioning

Sleeping and dreaming

Altering awareness: Psychoactive drugs

Altering awareness: Induced states

Setting Priorities for Mental Functioning: Attention

LEARNING GOALS
- Define attention and discuss its adaptive value.
- Explain how experiments on dichotic listening can be used to study attention.
- Describe automaticity and its effects on awareness.
- Describe such disorders as visual neglect and attention deficit/hyperactivity disorder.

AS YOU SAW IN CHAPTER 5, the world is a teeming smorgasbord of sensory information. We don't experience every sight and sound, of course; we sample selectively from the table based on current needs. If you're searching for a friend adrift in the neighborhood saloon, you focus on the familiar sound of his voice or the color of her shirt. If you're trying to determine what's for dinner tonight, you sniff the air for the odor of cooking pot roast or simmering spaghetti sauce. You notice those things that are important to the task at hand—you sift through, block out, and focus on those messages that solve the particular problem you face. Psychologists use the term **attention** to refer to the internal processes that set priorities for mental functioning. For adaptive reasons, the brain uses attention to focus selectively on certain parts of the environment while ignoring others. Obviously, the concepts of attention and consciousness are closely linked—you're consciously aware only of those things that receive some measure of attention (although see Koch & Tsuchiya, 2007). But why is awareness selective? One reason is that the resources of the brain and nervous system are limited. The brain has only so many neurons, and there are limits to how fast and efficiently those neurons can communicate. These limitations require us to make choices about which parts of the environment to process (Broadbent, 1958; Kahneman, 1973).

Even if we had unlimited resources, it would be in our interest to make choices. In a mystery novel, certain events are important for solving a murder and others are "red herrings"—irrelevant points that lead the reader in the wrong direction and delay solving the crime. The trick is to be selective about which clues to pursue. A first-rate detective knows not only what to look for but also what information to avoid. The same is true for even the simplest kind of action, such as walking across the room or reaching for a cup. The visual and motor systems must focus on objects in your path, not every single object in the room. If you looked at and thought about everything, you would suffer interference from irrelevant input. Prioritizing mental functioning is an important part of how we coordinate and control our actions (Allport, 1989).

attention The internal processes used to set priorities for mental functioning.

CRITICAL THINKING

Can you think of any circumstances in which your brain attends to things of which you are not aware?

Experiments on Attention: Dichotic Listening

Research on the phenomenon of attention really began in the 1950s with the development of the **dichotic listening** technique (Broadbent, 1952; Cherry, 1953). As shown in ▌Figure 6.1, in a typical experiment people are asked to listen to spoken messages presented individually to each ear through headphones. To promote selective attention, the task is to *shadow*, or repeat aloud, one of the two messages while ignoring the other. This kind of listening is called *dichotic*, meaning "divided into two," because two messages are involved, delivered separately into each of the two ears.

A dichotic listening experiment requires you to listen to two voices at the same time. Have you ever tried to watch television while someone next to you is blathering on endlessly? Not an easy task. In fact, in all likelihood you had to either ignore one of the two or switch back and forth from one message to the other. This is essentially what happens in a dichotic listening experiment. Forcing a person to repeat just one of the messages aloud usually results in poor processing of the other message. For example, if people are given a surprise test for the unattended message at the end of

dichotic listening Different auditory messages are presented separately and simultaneously to each ear. The subject's task is to repeat aloud one message while ignoring the other.

Attended Channel
"Four-score and seven years ago our fathers ..."

Unattended Channel
"When asked the question, 'what is consciousness?' we become conscious of consciousness ..."

"Four-score and seven years ago our fathers ..."

FIGURE 6.1 The Dichotic Listening Technique

In dichotic listening, a subject listens to different spoken messages presented simultaneously to each ear and shadows—or repeats aloud—one of the messages while ignoring the other. The task taps the ability to attend selectively.

cocktail party effect The ability to focus on one auditory message and ignore others; also refers to the tendency to notice when your name suddenly appears in a message that you've been actively ignoring.

the experiment, they can usually remember very little, if anything, about its content. They might pick up on the fact that one speaker was male and the other female, but they remember virtually nothing else about the unattended message (Cherry, 1953; Moray, 1959).

At the same time, we don't just shut off the part of the world that isn't bathed in the spotlight of attention. If we did, our actions wouldn't be adaptive because the world is constantly changing—something new, and possibly important, can happen at any time. Instead, the brain monitors many things simultaneously, although the monitoring may be minimal and beyond our current awareness. A case in point is the **cocktail party effect**. Imagine you're at a large party, filled with noisy conversation, and you're trying really hard to hear what your companion is saying. In all likelihood you won't be consciously aware of all the conversations around you. It's doubtful, for example, that you could repeat what the couple standing next to you is saying. But suppose someone across the room suddenly speaks your name. There's a

The processes of attention let us filter out competing conversations in a noisy environment. But if someone across the room suddenly speaks your name, you'll probably notice it. This is the "cocktail party effect."

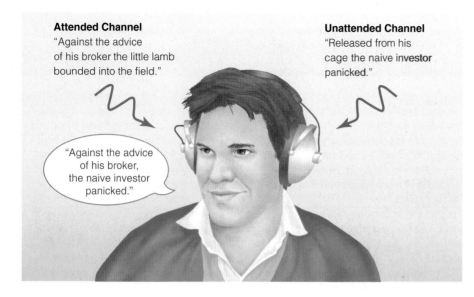

Attended Channel

"Against the advice of his broker the little lamb bounded into the field."

Unattended Channel

"Released from his cage the naive **investor** panicked."

"Against the advice of his broker, the naive investor panicked."

FIGURE 6.2 Treisman's "Ear-Switching" Experiment

At one point in a dichotic listening experiment by Treisman, unknown to the participant, the to-be-shadowed message was suddenly and without warning switched to the unattended channel. Interestingly, subjects often continued to repeat the meaningful sentence even though it was now presented in the unattended ear.

reasonable chance that you'll turn your head immediately. People in dichotic listening experiments have shown the same effect: They appear to ignore the contents of the unattended message, but if their name appears in it, they notice and remember it later. This is the cocktail party effect, and it suggests that our brains are aware of more than we think.

Another compelling example of how we can monitor multiple messages at the same time comes from an experiment by Treisman (1960), again using the dichotic listening technique. People were presented with compound sentences such as "Against the advice of his broker, the naive investor panicked" in one ear and "Released from his cage, the little lamb bounded into the field" in the other (see ▌ Figure 6.2). Subjects were asked to attend to the message in just one of the ears by repeating it aloud, but in the middle of some of the sentences Treisman switched things around—the second half of each sentence moved to the opposite ear. So in the attended ear the subject heard something like "Against the advice of his broker, the little lamb bounded into the field," whereas in the unattended ear the message became "Released from his cage, the naive investor panicked." The interesting finding was that about 30% of the time people continued to repeat the meaningful sentence ("Against the advice of his broker, the naive investor panicked") even though the message had switched midway from the attended to the unattended ear. Moreover, many reported being unaware that the message had switched.

These findings suggest that the brain doesn't simply filter out what goes on in the unattended message. It focuses the spotlight of attention on the task at hand, but it carries on at least some unconscious monitoring of the rest of the environment as well. If something important happens, the brain shifts its attention and allows the new event to enter conscious awareness. In Treisman's experiment, the brain must have been following the meaning of the messages in both ears, even though the people who participated were only aware of monitoring one thing. Exactly how all this works has been the subject of considerable debate over the last several decades (see Johnson & Proctor, 2004), but the process itself is clearly adaptive. Humans wouldn't live for long in a world where they processed only those things in the realm of immediate awareness.

Processing Without Attention: Automaticity

The idea that the brain and body are active beyond current awareness may seem strange at first, but not if you think about it. After all, when's the last time you thought about breathing or keeping your heart beating? You can drive a car and carry on a

Cell Phones and Driving

You've seen how the resources of the brain are limited. We use the processes of attention to help us attend selectively to current priorities because we simply cannot attend to multiple messages at the same time—at least, not very well. There are some exceptions. Automatic tasks can be performed without the need for sustained attention. Yet tasks that sometimes seem automatic, such as driving, often are not. Certain components of driving are well-practiced and require little conscious thought, yet driving demands vigilance at all times. It's been estimated that perhaps 50% of all traffic accidents on U.S. highways are influenced by driver inattention (U.S. Department of Transportation, 1998). The culprits? We're conversing with a friend, listening to a cranked-up radio, or talking on a cell phone.

Quite a bit of research has been done recently on cell phone use during driving. Cellular phones have become extremely popular worldwide—there are well over 100 million subscribers in the United States alone—and surveys indicate that as many as 85% of cell phone users talk on the phone at least occasionally while driving (Goodman et al., 1999).

Studies have established solid connections between cell phone use and traffic accidents. In fact, talking on a cell phone increases the risk of accident to levels comparable to those of driving with a blood alcohol level above the legal limit (Redelmeier & Tibshirani, 1997). The presence of a correlation between phone use and accidents, however, is not sufficient to infer that cell phone use causes accidents. It could be that people who use cell phones while driving are just bad drivers. As you know, correlations do not imply causality.

To determine a causal link, we must have experimental control. A number of experiments have examined the link between cell phone use and driving. Typically, these studies manipulate the type and extent of cell phone use during simulated driving—either in a driving simulator or by requiring people to perform a tracking task on a computer. In a study by Strayer and Johnston (2001), people were asked to use a joystick to move a cursor on a computer screen; the task was to keep the cursor aligned as closely as possible to a moving target (meant to correspond roughly to maintaining location on a road). At random

points, either a red or a green light flashed on the computer screen. The participants were instructed to react to the red light by pressing a "brake" button on the joystick. Strayer and Johnston found that when people were engaged in a cell phone conversation while performing the simulated driving task, they missed twice as many red lights. Even when the red light was detected, and the brake applied, people were considerably slower to respond. Moreover, the impairments were found regardless of whether the cell phone was handheld while "driving" or a hands-free model.

More recent research suggests that cell phone conversations induce a kind of inattention blindness—you literally fail to remember seeing objects in the road because your attention is directed toward the cell phone conversation. Although any kind of in-vehicle conversation can lead to some impairment in driving ability, the effects of cell phone conversations appear to be particularly disruptive (Strayer & Drews, 2007). The implications of this and other recent studies are clear: Turn off the cell phone when you drive.

---

automaticity Fast and effortless processing that requires little or no focused attention.

conversation at the same time—you don't need to focus attention on every turn of the wheel or on pressing the brake. These things occur automatically. In the case of driving, people have developed a skill that demands less and less attention with practice.

Psychologists use the term **automaticity** to refer to fast and effortless processing that requires little or no focused attention (Logan, 1991). When you practice a task, such as playing Mozart on the piano, overall speed steadily improves. You may even reach a point where performing the task seems automatic—Mozart rolls off your fingertips with such ease that you're not even consciously aware of finger movement. Automatic processes, once they develop, no longer seem to require conscious control. The mind is free to consider other things while the task itself is performed without a hitch. Many of the activities we take for granted—such as reading, talking, and walking—are essentially automatic processes. (For another viewpoint on driving, see the Practical Solutions feature on the hazards of driving while using a cell phone.)

It's possible to measure automaticity through a *divided attention* task (Logan, 1988). In a typical experiment, people are asked to perform two tasks at the same time, such as playing a piece by Mozart on the piano while simultaneously trying to remember a short list of unrelated words. Automaticity is demonstrated when one task, the automatic one, fails to interfere with performance on the other task (Hasher & Zacks, 1979; Shiffrin & Schneider, 1977). Clearly, if you've just learned to play the Mozart piece, your mind will need to focus on every note, and you'll have enough trouble just getting through it without error, let alone recalling a list of words. But if you're an accomplished pianist—if your Mozart performance has become automatic—you can let your fingers do the playing and your mind can concentrate on remembering the word list.

Notice the relationship between automaticity and awareness, because it tells us something important about the function of consciousness. The better you are at performing a task—the more automatic the task has become—the less likely you are to attend consciously to the details. In fact, some studies have found that highly trained athletes actually improve their skilled performance when they are slightly distracted by other attention-demanding tasks (see Koch & Tsuchiya, 2007). This is a very important characteristic of mental functioning. If we assume that the resources of the brain and nervous system are limited, then automaticity can help free up needed resources for conscious thought. Environmental conditions can change at any moment, so we often need to use conscious awareness as a kind of work space for developing new and creative reactions. We use consciousness for handling the new and demanding while relying on the steady and effortless processes of automaticity to keep moving and acting normally (Johnson, 2003).

Subliminal Influences

The cocktail party effect tells us that we sometimes process messages that sit outside the focus of awareness, but what about true subliminal messages—that is, messages presented at levels so hard to detect that they essentially bypass conscious awareness? We briefly considered this topic in Chapter 2, but it's worthwhile to consider it again. You've seen how the brain uses attention to prioritize mental functioning; automatic processes allow for fast and effortless actions that require little or no conscious thought. From an adaptive perspective, it's certainly reasonable to assume that we might be influenced by things that bypass conscious awareness. But do these messages work?

We don't know whether advertisers really try to influence people subliminally (the advertisers are not talking) or, in fact, whether subliminal tapes for weight loss or increased confidence really do contain the promised embedded messages (some evidence suggests that the messages might not even be present). It is possible, however, to conduct controlled experiments where such messages are purposely embedded in advertisements or on tapes. Dozens of such studies have been conducted (Druckman & Bjork, 1991; Merikle, 1988; Rosen & Singh, 1992); the general consensus seems to be that the effects of subliminal influence are mild or nonexistent. For example, it is sometimes claimed that subliminal messages lead to enhanced memory. In a study by Vokey and Read (1985), three or four instances of the word *SEX* were inserted into vacation slides; the words were placed in the pictures in such a way that they were not directly noticeable but could be detected easily if pointed out by the experimenters. Immediately after viewing the slides, or after a delay, people were given a memory test for the slides. Did the provocative "embed" *SEX* lead to better memory of the overall slide? Even though we know in this instance that the message was actually there and could be detected, participants showed no improvement in the recognition of the slides relative to the proper control groups.

In a study by Rosen and Singh (1992), the embedded messages were of three types: (1) the word *SEX*, (2) a picture of a naked woman and several phallic symbols, or (3) the word *DEATH* combined with pictures of skulls. The embeds were placed in black-and-white print ads for liquor or cologne, and people were asked to view each ad as part of an experiment on advertising effectiveness. No direct mention was made of the embeds, which were present in some of the ads but not in others. This study of subliminal messages is noteworthy because it used a variety of measures of advertising effectiveness. None turned out to be affected in any significant way by the hidden information.

With regard to self-help tapes, again the data are clear. Greenwald and his colleagues (1991) recruited people to help evaluate the effectiveness of tapes designed to improve either memory or self-esteem. Unknown to the participants, the labels on some of the tapes had been switched, and those who thought they were listening to a self-esteem tape were actually given a memory tape, and vice versa. After regular

If you practice a task for extended periods, your performance may become automatic. Once acquired, automatic processes no longer require much conscious control.

With a little imagination, people can "find" subliminal messages almost anywhere. However, research indicates that subliminal messages have only limited effects on behavior.

listening, people seemed to improve on posttests of self-esteem or memory, but it didn't matter which tape they had actually been given. A weight-loss study by Merikle and Skanes (1992) produced similar results. People improved as a result of participating in the study (in this case, they lost weight), but it didn't matter whether the tape actually contained the subliminal message, or even if the people had listened to a tape at all! Why the improvement? Certainly, one would think, people would stop buying these tapes if they were completely ineffective. From a psychological perspective, though, it's important to remember that those who buy such tapes are motivated to improve. Thus the people who volunteer for a weight-loss study may simply be more conscious of their weight during the course of the experiment (Merikle & Skanes, 1992). Alternatively, a tape may act as a kind of placebo, leading to improvement because the listener believes in its powers. If subliminal self-help is placebo-related, we would expect the person to improve regardless of whether the message was actually embedded in the background. All that's necessary is that people *think* they're receiving something that will work.

So what can we conclude about subliminal messages? Is it possible to alter behavior without awareness? Perhaps. Not all experiments on subliminal messages have produced negative results: Cooper and Cooper (2002) had people watch an episode of *The Simpsons* containing "thirsty" images flashed throughout at subliminal levels; afterward the participants reported increased levels of thirst compared to control subjects who viewed the same film without the hidden images. Similar results were obtained recently by Karremans and colleagues (2006): Subliminal presentations of a tasty drink increased the likelihood that people would select the drink in a choice situation, but the effect occurred only for participants who were thirsty. So it's conceivable that subliminal messages might work under some circumstances. But it's a bad idea to waste a lot of time worrying about subliminal conspiracies. There's not much evidence that these messages exist, and even if they do, their influence is certainly weak at best.

Disorders of Attention

We've stressed the link between attention and consciousness because, in many respects, attention is the gateway to consciousness. It follows that if the brain systems that control attention are damaged, there should be a corresponding loss in conscious awareness. Brain researchers have used clinical cases of brain damage to examine this possibility, and they're using neuroimaging techniques to map out attention-related areas of the brain (Posner & Rothbart, 2007; Roser & Gazzaniga, 2004). Let's briefly consider two attention disorders that may be related to brain dysfunction, *visual neglect* and the inattention associated with *attention deficit/hyperactivity disorder.*

Visual Neglect Damage to the right parietal lobe of the cerebral cortex can produce an odd and complex disorder of attention called **visual neglect**. People with visual neglect show a tendency to ignore things that appear toward the left side of the body (remember from earlier chapters that the right side of the brain generally controls the left side of the body). Visual neglect can cause people to read only from the right side of pages and copy only the right side of pictures. They may even dress, shave, or apply makeup only to the right side of the body (Bisiach & Rusconi, 1990). It's as if an entire side of their visual field has vanished from awareness. Fortunately, the condition sometimes recovers with time, although it's often associated with other kinds of processing deficits in the brain. It can also arise from damage to the left side of the brain, which then creates problems in the right visual field, but it occurs more frequently with right brain damage (Posner, 1993). There are also patients who show auditory neglect; after damage to the right hemisphere, they seem somewhat unresponsive to voices and noises that come from their left side (Clarke & Thiran, 2004).

Is the brain really shutting off all the information it receives from one side of the body? Probably not. In one study, a patient suffering from visual neglect was shown

visual neglect A complex disorder of attention characterized by a tendency to ignore things that appear on one side of the body (usually the left side).

FIGURE 6.3 Visual Neglect
Patients suffering from visual neglect might consciously detect no differences between these two houses. But they would probably choose to live in the house without the flames.

drawings of two houses (see ▌Figure 6.3). One house was normal in appearance; the other was normal on the right side but had bright red flames and smoke billowing out from a window on its left side. The patient was asked to choose which of the two houses she would prefer to live in. "The houses look the same to me," she reported, presumably because she was attending only to the right side of each picture. Nevertheless, she consistently chose to live in the house without the flames (Marshall & Halligan, 1988). She showed no conscious awareness of the full image, but her brain was still able to use all the available information to help determine the appropriate behavior (Bisiach, 1992).

CRITICAL THINKING

In what ways are the symptoms of visual neglect similar to the symptoms of the split-brain patients who were discussed in Chapter 3?

Attention Deficit/Hyperactivity Disorder A much more common disorder of attention, **attention deficit/hyperactivity disorder (ADHD)**, is associated with general difficulties in concentrating. People with ADHD have trouble paying attention for long periods—they're easily distracted and can't finish the tasks they begin. It's one of the most common psychological problems in school-aged children, although it probably affects only about 3 to 5% of all children (Cantwell, 1996). In addition to attention problems, which affect the quality of their schoolwork, ADHD children are often hyperactive and impulsive—they squirm and fidget and regularly blurt out answers to questions before the questions are completely asked. Attention problems are not always associated with hyperactivity, although the diagnosis is known generally as attention deficit/hyperactivity disorder (Barlow & Durand, 2005).

attention deficit/hyperactivity disorder (ADHD) A psychological disorder marked by difficulties in concentrating or in sustaining attention for extended periods; can be associated with hyperactivity.

Psychologists are actively searching for the brain mechanisms involved in ADHD. Neuroimaging studies, for instance, have indicated that various regions of the brain, including the frontal and parietal lobes, may be selectively involved (Tamm, Menon, & Reiss, 2006). There's some evidence that the problem may be associated with an imbalance in neurotransmitter action, particularly serotonin, or even mild brain damage, but no firm conclusions have been reached (Sagvolden & Sergeant, 1998). It's unlikely that any single brain location is responsible because the disorder is complex and expresses itself in a variety of ways. There are even ongoing debates about the disorder's proper definition (Barkley, 1997; Shaywitz, Fletcher, & Shaywitz, 1994). It may take some time before researchers arrive at a complete neurological understanding of the problem. Not surprisingly, it's almost certainly the case that experience plays a role in the onset and maintenance of the disorder as well (DeGrandpre, 2000).

Attention deficit/hyperactivity disorder is sometimes, but not always, associated with hyperactivity.

What about treatment? The news is promising. It turns out that a majority of children who have attention problems can be helped with either medication, directed training, or some combination of both (Arnold et al., 2004). Children with attention problems need to learn coping strategies to help them perform well in school and in social settings. A training program typically includes teaching study skills, such as learning to write down important information (rather than relying on memory), and offering rewards for sitting still and not being disruptive in social situations. Medications, such as Ritalin, seem to help concentration, and they often reduce hyperactivity and disruptive behavior. It's interesting to note that Ritalin, as well as many other drugs used to treat the disorder, actually comes from a class of drugs—called stimulants—that generally increase nervous system activity (you'll read more about stimulants later in this chapter). In low doses Ritalin improves a person's ability to concentrate and focus attention selectively (Mattay et al., 1996).

Finally, there is some concern among psychologists that attention deficit/hyperactivity disorder may be overdiagnosed; in fact, there has been rapid growth recently in the use of medications to treat both children and adults (Castle et al., 2007). It's important to be cautious about applying the label "attention disorder" to a child simply because he or she has trouble sitting still in school or paying attention. All children are restless from time to time, and certainly most ignore their parents in some situations, but that doesn't mean that medication or a directed training program is in order. Many psychologists feel, in particular, that medications such as Ritalin are being overprescribed as a kind of quick fix to what may be essentially normal behavior. Children with true attention deficit/hyperactivity disorder are usually identified quite early in childhood, by around age 3 or 4. They have trouble in social settings and don't make friends easily; their behavior, either because of the hyperactivity or the difficulties in concentrating, is simply too much for their peer group to bear.

Test Yourself 6.1

To test your knowledge about how we set priorities for mental functioning, decide whether each of the following statements about attention and its disorders is True or False. *(You will find the answers in the Appendix.)*

1. The cocktail party effect suggests that we cannot attend to more than one message at a time; we focus our attention on one thing, and the rest of the environment is effectively filtered out. *True or False?*
2. In dichotic listening tasks, people are presented with two auditory messages, one in each ear, and the task is to repeat one of the messages aloud while essentially ignoring the other. *True or False?*
3. If a task—such as playing Mozart on the piano—has become automatic, then you can perform a second task—

remembering a list of letters—without interfering with performance on the first task. *True or False?*
4. When visual neglect is caused by damage to the right side of the brain, people seem not to notice things that appear on the right side of the body. *True or False?*
5. Attention deficit/hyperactivity disorder is primarily learned and easily treated by special skills training. *True or False?*

Sleeping and Dreaming

LEARNING GOALS

- Define biological rhythms and discuss how they are controlled.
- Describe the various stages and characteristics of sleep.
- Discuss the function and adaptive significance of sleep.
- Discuss the function of REM sleep and theories of dreaming.
- Describe the various sleep disorders.

TO SET PRIORITIES FOR MENTAL FUNCTIONING, we focus our attention selectively. If you're trying to read a book, you focus on the page and try to block out distracting sounds. If you're listening to music, you might close your eyes to focus on the rhythms and harmonies of the sound patterns. Notice, however, when you redirect your attention in these cases, that you're not really changing anything fundamental about the processes of consciousness; instead, you're simply altering the *content* of conscious awareness. In the case of sleep, the change is more fundamental—you're no longer consciously aware of the external world, yet your mind is still quite active. For this reason, sleep is sometimes referred to as a different "state" of consciousness.

Biological Rhythms

The regular daily transition from waking to sleep is an example of what is known generally as a *biological rhythm*. Actually, many body functions work in cycles, which is something we share with all other members of the animal kingdom. Sleep and waking vary daily, along with body temperature, hormone secretions, blood pressure, and other processes (for a review, see Aschoff & Wever, 1981). Activities that rise and fall along a 24-hour cycle are called **circadian rhythms** (*circa* means "about," and *dies* means "day"). Other biological activities may follow cycles that are either shorter or longer. The female menstrual cycle operates on an approximately 28-day cycle, whereas changes in appetite and the ability to perform certain tasks may change several times throughout the day.

> **circadian rhythms** Biological activities that rise and fall in accordance with a 24-hour cycle.

These rhythmic activities are controlled automatically by structures in the brain called **biological clocks**. These clocks trigger the needed activities at just the right time and schedule the internal functions of the body to make sure everything is performing as it should. Animal research has determined that a particular area of the hypothalamus, called the *suprachiasmatic nucleus*, may play a key role in regulating the clock that controls circadian rhythms (Latta & Van Cauter, 2003). It's thought that the human brain probably has several clocks, each controlling functions such as body temperature or activity level.

> **biological clocks** Brain structures that schedule rhythmic variations in bodily functions by triggering them at the appropriate times.

Setting Our Biological Clocks The environment helps our brains synchronize—or set—our internal clocks. Light is a particularly important controller, or *Zeitgeber* (meaning "time giver"). If you were suddenly forced to spend all your time in the

The activity levels of many animals are controlled by internal clocks that are "set," in part, by the environment. Bears are active during the warm summer months and hibernate during the winter.

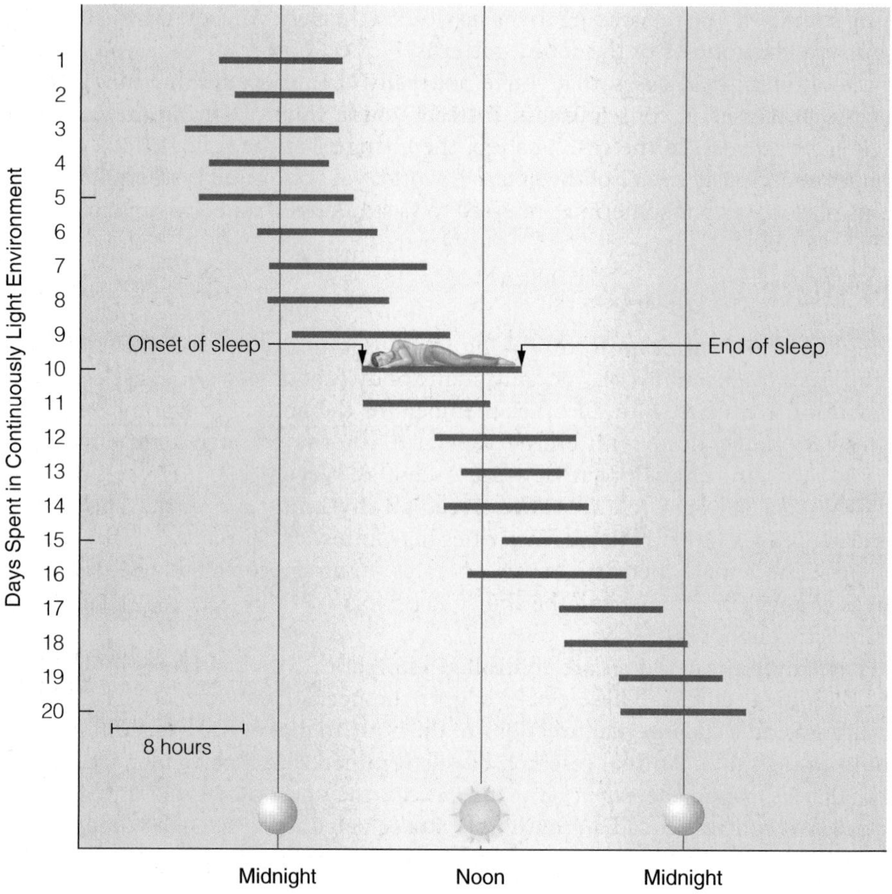

FIGURE 6.4 Pacing the Internal Clock
Light strongly influences our internal biological clocks. If you were suddenly forced to live without darkness, you would still sleep a normal 8 hours (shown by the length of the bar). But sleep onset times would probably drift. For example, if you usually fall asleep at 11:00 P.M. and wake at 7:00 A.M., after a while you might find yourself becoming sleepy at 2:00 A.M. and rising at 10:00 A.M.

CRITICAL THINKING

Can you think of any workplace environments that might lead to symptoms similar to jet lag?

dark or in a continuously lit environment, you would still sleep regularly, but your sleeping and waking cycles would begin to drift (see Figure 6.4). Rather than falling asleep at your usual 11:00 P.M. and waking at 7:00 A.M., after a while you might find yourself becoming sleepy at 2:00 A.M. and rising at 10:00 A.M. People use light during the day, as well as the absence of light at night, as a way of setting their internal sleep clock (Lavie, 2001).

The fact that the environment is so important in maintaining internal body rhythms makes considerable adaptive sense. Remember, the environment also shows regular cycles. The sun rises and sets approximately every 24 hours. There are daily changes in air pressure and temperature caused, in part, by the continuous rotation of the Earth about its axis. It's perfectly reasonable to assume that animals, including humans, have adapted to remain in harmony with these cycles. As the cold of winter approaches, birds fly south for a warmer climate and more abundant food supplies; other animals stay put and prepare for hibernation. These changes in behavior are sensible adaptations to fixed changes in the environment that are not under the animal's control.

Jet lag is a good example of how the environment can play havoc with our internal clocks. When you travel to a new time zone, especially if you move east (which shortens your day), your usual signals for sleeping and waking become disrupted—it gets light and dark at unusual times for you. The net result is that you have trouble going to sleep, you get up at the "wrong" time, and you generally feel lousy. Your body needs to reset its clocks in line with your new environment, and this process takes time. This is one reason diplomats and business travelers often arrive at their destinations a few days before an important event or meeting; it gives them time to adjust their internal clocks and shrug off the jet lag.

The Characteristics of Sleep

As mentioned earlier, the transition from waking to sleep can be described as a change in one's state or level of consciousness. Rather than "death's counterfeit" (as Shakespeare called it), sleep does involve awareness, although the focus of that awareness no longer connects directly to events in the world. The sticky problem facing researchers, of course, is that they can't directly measure the internal experience (because the subject is unresponsive). What researchers can do is eavesdrop on the electrical activity of the brain through EEG recordings and draw conclusions about how consciousness is changing based on changes in the patterns of brain activity.

As you may recall from Chapter 3, the *electroencephalograph*, or EEG, is a device that monitors the electrical activity of the brain. Electrodes are attached to the scalp, and changes in the electrical potentials of large numbers of brain cells are recorded in the form of line tracings, or brain waves. It's possible to record EEG-based brain waves at any time, including when someone is asleep. The EEG was first applied to the sleeping brain in the 1930s, and by the 1950s researchers had discovered some very intriguing and unexpected things about the sleep process. For example, EEG tracings revealed that during sleep there are regular, or cyclic, changes in brain activity. The EEG also revealed that at certain points the electrical activity of the sleeping brain bears a striking similarity to the brain activity of a person who is wide awake (Aserinsky & Kleitman, 1955).

❚ Figure 6.5 on page 190 presents typical EEG recordings made during waking and sleep states. The main things to notice are (1) the *height*, or amplitude, of the brain waves; (2) the *frequency*, or number of cycles per second (usually described in hertz); and (3) the *regularity*, or smoothness, of the pattern. Regular high-amplitude waves of low frequency reflect neural synchrony, meaning that large numbers of neurons are working together. In the first row of tracings, measured when a subject was awake, you'll see no evidence of neural synchrony—the EEG pattern is fast and irregular, and the waves are of low amplitude. Presumably, when we're awake, the brain is busy dividing its labor; lots of cells are working on specialized individual tasks, so the combined brain activity tends to look irregular. In contrast, when the brain is in a relaxed state, it produces **alpha waves**, which have a higher amplitude and cycle in a slower, more regular manner.

The Four Stages of Sleep   As you settle down for the night and prepare for sleep, the fast and irregular wave patterns of the waking state are soon replaced by slower, more regular alpha waves. You're not really asleep at this point—just relaxed and perhaps a little drowsy. The first official sign of sleep—what is called *stage 1* sleep—is marked by a return to waves that are bit lower in amplitude and slightly more irregular. The dominant wave patterns of stage 1 sleep are called **theta waves**; as you can see in Figure 6.5, they're different from the patterns found in the waking state. Even here, however, people often report that they're not really asleep; instead they might claim that their thoughts are simply drifting.

The next stage of sleep, *stage 2* sleep, is marked by another change in the EEG pattern. Specifically, the theta activity that defines stage 1 sleep begins to be interrupted occasionally by short bursts of activity called *sleep spindles*. There are also sudden, sharp, intermittent waveforms called *K complexes*. You're definitely asleep at this point, although your brain still shows some sensitivity to events in the external world. Loud noises, for example, tend to be reflected immediately in the EEG pattern by triggering a K complex (Bastien & Campbell, 1992). Your brain reacts, as revealed

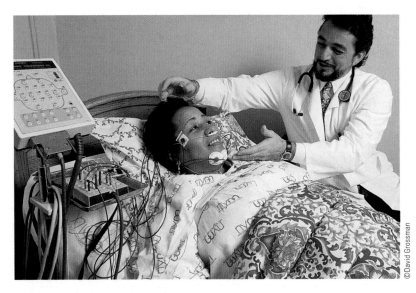

In sleep disorder clinics, changes in the gross electrical activity of the brain are monitored throughout the night.

alpha waves The pattern of brain activity observed in someone who is in a relaxed state.

theta waves The pattern of brain activity observed in stage 1 sleep.

CRITICAL THINKING

Can you think of any adaptive reasons sleep occurs in stages? What might be the advantage to starting off in a light sleep and moving to a deeper sleep?

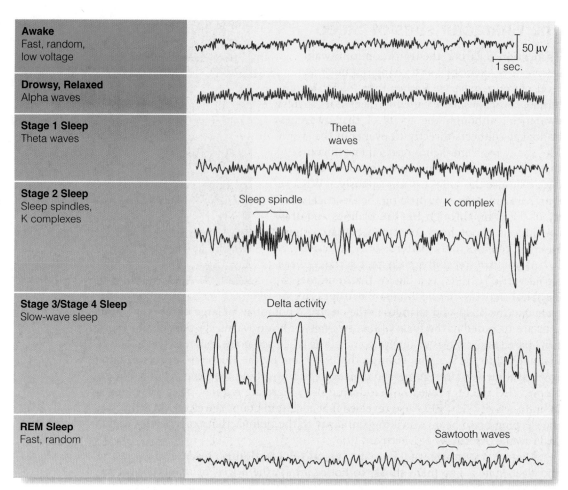

FIGURE 6.5 EEG Patterns Associated with Sleeping and Wakefulness
As we move from a waking state into sleep, characteristic changes occur in the electrical activity of the brain. Generally, as we become drowsy and move through the four stages of sleep, our brain waves become slower and more regular and show more amplitude. But during REM sleep, when we are presumed to be dreaming, the EEG shows a pattern more closely resembling the waking state. (From *Current Concepts: The Sleep Disorders*, by P. Hauri, 1982, The Upjohn Company, Kalamazoo, Michigan. Reprinted by permission of the author.)

delta activity The pattern of brain activity observed in stage 3 and stage 4 sleep; it's characterized by synchronized slow waves. Also called slow-wave sleep.

by the K complex, but you're not really consciously aware of the environment. For instance, you won't do a very good job of responding to signals delivered by an experimenter (say, by raising your finger or hand).

The final two stages of sleep, *stage 3* and *stage 4*, are progressively deeper states and show more synchronized slow-wave brain patterns called **delta activity**; these stages are sometimes called *delta* or *slow-wave sleep*. Notice that the wave patterns in Figure 6.5 appear large (high in amplitude) and cycle slower than the patterns of the earlier sleep stages. You're really asleep now and tough to arouse (Kelly, 1991). If I shake you awake during slow-wave sleep, you won't be very responsive. You'll act confused and disoriented, and it'll take quite some time for you to reach a normal state of conscious awareness.

REM Sleep   As you move from stage 1 to stage 4 sleep, you're progressing from light to deep sleep. Not surprisingly, other internal measures of arousal, such as breathing

FIGURE 6.6 Sleep Cycles
During an average night, most adults pass through the various stages of sleep four or five times. A complete cycle usually takes about 90 minutes. As morning approaches, we tend to spend more time in REM sleep, presumably dreaming. (Based on Kalat, 1996.)

rate, heart rate, and blood pressure, decline as you pass through each of the stages. But about 70 to 90 minutes into the sleep cycle, something very unexpected happens—abrupt changes appear in the entire physiological pattern. Heart rate increases rapidly and becomes more irregular; twitching movements might begin in the hands, feet, and face; in males, the penis becomes erect, and in females vaginal lubrication begins; the eyes begin to move rapidly and irregularly, darting back and forth or up and down behind the eyelids. The EEG pattern loses its synchrony and takes on low-amplitude irregular patterns that resemble those of the waking state. But you're not awake—you've entered *paradoxical*, or **REM** (rapid eye movement), sleep.

REM sleep is called "paradoxical" for an obvious reason: The electrical activity of the brain during REM sleep resembles the "awake" pattern, yet you remain deeply asleep. Muscle tone is extremely relaxed, and you're somewhat difficult to arouse. But as the EEG indicates, the brain is extremely active during this period—if jostled awake from REM sleep, you'll seem instantly alert. Again, this contrasts sharply with the confused reaction that people typically have when they're awakened from the early stages of sleep. Perhaps most interesting, people who awaken from REM sleep are likely to report an emotional and storylike dream. In fact REM-based dreaming is reported well over 80% of the time, even in people who have previously denied that they dream (Goodenough, 1991; Snyder, 1967).

There is still debate among sleep researchers about the exact relationship between the REM state and dreaming. It's true that people often report dreaming if they're awakened during REM, but dreaming also seems to occur during the earlier stages of sleep. Have you ever experienced a dream moments after going to sleep? Most people have, but it's unlikely that your brain was in an official REM state. Systematic studies of dreaming and the sleep stages have revealed conflicting results. Some studies report low levels of dreaming during non-REM stages (Dement, 1978); other studies have found the percentages to be relatively high (over 50%; see Foulkes, 1985). It remains an open question whether dreaming is an exclusive result of REM, which seems unlikely, or whether dreaming is simply highly correlated with REM activity. I'll have more to say about the REM state momentarily when we consider the function of dreaming.

The Sleep Cycle During an average night, we cycle through the various stages of sleep, including REM sleep, about four or five times. Each sleep cycle takes about 90 minutes: You progress from stage 1 through stage 4, then back from stage 4 toward stage 1, ending in REM (see ▮ Figure 6.6). This sequence remains intact throughout much of the night, but the time spent in each stage changes as morning approaches. During the first cycle of sleep, the majority of time is spent in stages 3 and 4 (slow-wave sleep), but REM sleep tends to dominate the later cycles. The amount of time spent in REM sleep, presumably dreaming, increases, and the interval between successive REM states becomes shorter (Ellman et al., 1991). In fact, by the end of the night you end up spending almost all of your time in REM sleep (Webb, 1992). As you're aware, many dreams seem to occur toward the end of the sleep period, and these are the dreams you're most likely to remember.

The Function of Sleep

If you sleep eight hours a night and reach the ripe old age of 75, you'll have spent a quarter century with your eyes closed, your limbs lying useless at your sides, and your outstretched body seemingly open to attack. Doesn't this seem a bit strange?

REM A stage of sleep characterized by rapid eye movements and low-amplitude, irregular EEG patterns resembling those found in the waking brain. REM is typically associated with dreaming.

Think about it. What could be the adaptive value, beyond the exercising of neurons during REM sleep, of redirecting the focus of awareness inward, away from potential threats in the environment?

Repairing and Restoring   Researchers aren't exactly sure why people sleep. One possibility is that sleep functions to *restore* or *repair* the body and brain. Our daily activities produce wear and tear on the body, and some mind–brain "down time" may be needed to put things back in order. There are definitely periods during sleep, especially slow-wave sleep, when the metabolic activity of the brain is dramatically lowered (Sakai et al., 1979). Moreover, if people are deprived of sleep for any extended period of time, their ability to perform complex tasks, especially those requiring problem solving, deteriorates (Linde & Bergstrom, 1992).

Is the brain really working overtime during sleep—repairing disorganized circuits or restoring depleted resources? In general, there isn't strong empirical support for this idea (Horne, 1988). Many restorative activities do go on during sleep, but these activities also occur regularly throughout the day, so sleep doesn't appear to be special in this regard. There also doesn't appear to be a strong relationship between the amount of activity in a day and the depth and length of the sleep period that follows. Sleep researchers have tried to tire people during the day by having them engage in vigorous exercise or spend a long day at a shopping center or amusement park, but no great changes in their subsequent sleep patterns have been observed (Horne & Minard, 1985). On the other hand, there is growing evidence that sleep helps us consolidate memories, making them less susceptible to later interference (Drosopoulos et al., 2007). Rest and restoration may be one of the important consequences of a good night's sleep, but that's clearly not the whole story.

Survival Value   Another possibility is that sleep is simply an adaptive response to changing environmental conditions, a form of behavior that's useful because it increases the likelihood that we'll survive. Humans rely significantly on their visual systems; as a result, we aren't very efficient outside at night when light levels are low. Our ancestors could have moved about at night looking for food, trying to avoid being eaten or killed by some lurking predator, but it was probably a better idea for them to stay sheltered until dawn. Sleep thus became adaptive—particularly sleeping at night—because it stopped people from venturing forth into a hostile environment (Kavanau, 2002).

We can find evidence supporting this view in the sleeping patterns of animal species in the wild. If sleep is an adaptive reaction to light–dark cycles and susceptibility to predators, then we might expect animals that rely on senses other than vision to be active primarily at night, when vision-based predators would be at a hunting disadvantage. This is indeed the case for mice, rats, and other rodents. Second, large animals that must eat continuously and can't easily find places to hide should sleep very little. And, indeed, grazing animals such as sheep, goats, horses, and cattle, which are vulnerable to surprise attack by predators, sleep only a few hours a day (see ▌ Figure 6.7). In one study, researchers found that body weight and susceptibility to attack could explain the majority of the sleeping patterns among different species (Allison & Chichetti, 1976).

Sleep Deprivation   Earlier I mentioned that our ability to perform complex tasks is disrupted if we haven't received much sleep. Surprised? Well, you've probably performed an all-nighter at some point, only to find yourself irritable and out of sorts the next day. But how serious is prolonged sleep deprivation? From time to time people have tried to remain awake for very long periods—approaching two weeks—and the results have been generally quite disruptive: Symptoms include slurred speech, sharp declines in mental ability, and even the development of paranoia and hallucinations. Although severely sleep-deprived in-

FIGURE 6.7 Sleep Times for Various Species
Large grazing animals, such as cows and horses, eat frequently and are quite vulnerable to surprise attacks from predators. Such animals tend to sleep very little. Small, quick animals, such as cats and rodents, are less vulnerable to attack and sleep a great deal.

dividuals can appear normal for brief periods, extensive loss of sleep generally hurts virtually all aspects of normal functioning (Coren, 1996).

Even more dramatic are the consequences in animal studies. When rats and dogs are deprived of sleep for extended periods, the results can be fatal. Sleep deprivation disrupts the ability of the animal to regulate internal functions, such as temperature, and leads to considerable loss of weight (despite an increased intake of food). The immune system also starts to fail, along with various organs in the body. After roughly three weeks of no sleep, the survival rate among these animals is virtually zero (Coren, 1996; Rechtschaffen & Bergmann, 1995). Fortunately, people don't ever reach these levels of sleep deprivation because we simply can't stay awake. Indirectly, however, sleep loss contributes to thousands of deaths each year, mostly through traffic accidents and job-related mishaps.

The Function of REM and Dreaming

It's easy to see how sleep might have developed as an adaptive response, whether to repair, restore, or protect the organism struggling to survive. But why are there stages of sleep? Why, if people want to protect or rest the body, do they spend a significant amount of time in an internally active state like REM sleep? REM sleep is strongly correlated with the recall of dreams: Does dreaming serve some unique biological or psychological function? Unfortunately, at this point we have no definitive answers to these questions.

It's not clear whether REM sleep is even a necessary component of normal functioning. It's possible to deprive people selectively of REM sleep by carefully monitoring the EEG and then waking the person whenever characteristic REM patterns appear in the recordings. Unlike the findings for sleep loss in general, losing significant amounts of REM sleep usually does not lead to drastic impairment. People may be a bit more irritable (compared to controls who are shaken awake during non-REM periods), and their performance on tasks requiring logical reasoning and problem solving

Why do people sleep? It could be to restore or repair depleted resources, but research suggests that vigorous activity during the day does not necessarily change one's sleep patterns.

is impaired, but not much (Ellman et al., 1991). Interestingly, some forms of severe depression appear to be helped by REM sleep deprivation, and some effective antidepressant drugs suppress REM sleep as a side effect (Vogel et al., 1990).

On the other hand, intriguing changes do occur in sleep patterns after periods of REM deprivation. Sleep researchers have noticed that on the second or third night of REM deprivation it's necessary to awaken the subject with much greater frequency. When people lose sleep, particularly REM sleep, their bodies attempt to make up for the loss during the next sleep period by increasing the total amount of time spent in the REM stage. The more REM sleep lost, the more the body tries to make it up the next night. This tendency, known as **REM rebound**, is one reason many researchers remain convinced that REM sleep serves some unspecified but extremely important purpose. One possibility, although it remains controversial, is that REM sleep plays a role in strengthening or consolidating certain kinds of memories (Karni et al., 1994; Vertes & Eastman, 2000).

Wish Fulfillment   Why do we dream? Historically, psychologists have considered dreaming to be extremely significant. Sigmund Freud believed that dreams, once interpreted, could serve as a "royal road to the unconscious." Freud believed that dreaming was a psychological mechanism for *wish fulfillment*, a way to satisfy forbidden wishes and desires—especially sexual ones. Dreams often look bizarre, he argued, because the objects within our dreams tend to be symbolic. We hide our true wishes and desires because they're often too unsettling for direct conscious awareness. So the appearance of a cigar or a gun in a dream (in fact, any elongated object) might represent a penis, whereas a tunnel (or any entryway) could stand for a vagina. To establish the true meaning of the dream, Freud believed it was necessary to distinguish between the dream's **manifest content**—the actual symbols of the dream—and its **latent content**, the hidden desires that are too disturbing to be expressed consciously.

Modern psychologists are reluctant to search for hidden meaning in dreams. Although certain kinds of dream events cut across people and cultures (people often dream of flying or falling, for example), and most people have the unsettling experience of recurring dreams, there is no consensus among psychologists about how to interpret dreams. Whether a cigar represents a penis, or just a cigar, isn't immediately obvious—even to the most thoughtful or well-trained psychologist. Moreover, just because you repeatedly dream about being chased by a poodle that looks like your brother Ed doesn't mean the dream is significant psychologically. A troubling dream, for example, might simply cause you to wake up suddenly and think about what has just occurred. As a result, the dream becomes firmly ingrained in memory and likely to occur again.

Activation-Synthesis   An alternative view, the **activation-synthesis hypothesis** of Hobson and McCarley (1977; Hobson et al., 2000) proposes that dreaming is a consequence of random activity in the brain. During REM sleep, for reasons that are not particularly clear, cells in the hindbrain tend to spontaneously activate the higher centers of the brain. This activity might arise simply to exercise the brain circuitry (Edelman, 1987), or it could be a consequence of random events in the room (e.g., the cat snoring or a mosquito buzzing around your face). Whatever the reason, the higher brain centers have evolved to interpret lower brain signals in meaningful ways. Thus the brain creates a story in an effort to make some sense out of the signals it receives. But in the activation-synthesis view, there's little of psychological significance here: Dreams typically represent only random activity in the brain (Weinstein et al., 1991).

The activation-synthesis hypothesis has received a lot of attention because it takes into account how biological activity in the brain changes during sleep. It also provides another explanation for why dream content can be bizarre: Because the activated signals that produce dreams are random in nature, the brain has a tough time creating a story line that is meaningful and consistent. Consequently, there may be some psychological significance to reported dreams after all, but not for the reasons

---

REM rebound The tendency to increase time spent in REM sleep after REM deprivation.

manifest content According to Freud, the actual symbols and events experienced in a dream.

latent content According to Freud, the true psychological meaning of dream symbols.

activation-synthesis hypothesis The idea that dreams represent the brain's attempt to make sense of the random patterns of neural activity generated during sleep.

suggested by Freud. The biological mechanisms that generate the REM state are not psychologically driven, but the brain's interpretations of those purely physiological activities may have psychological meaning. The story your brain creates probably tells us something about how you think when you're awake (Domhoff, 2003).

The activation-synthesis hypothesis is an intriguing alternative to the traditional Freudian view, but much remains to be worked out. The theory remains vague and difficult to test, and some have argued as well that the theory is inconsistent with current neurological evidence (Domhoff, 2005). Moreover, as noted earlier, we also dream during non-REM states, but the theory focuses primarily on brain activity that occurs during REM sleep. It is also of interest to note that REM activity is commonplace in numerous nonhuman organisms (Durie, 1981). Virtually all mammals experience REM, as do birds and some reptiles, such as turtles. Moreover, human infants spend a remarkable amount of time in REM sleep; even human fetuses show REM patterns in the womb. Perhaps a fetus dreams, but it's unlikely that the fetus is creating an internal "story" to make sense of random activity.

We've discussed two prominent views of dreaming—Freud and activation-synthesis—but there are others. Some psychologists have suggested that dreams help us solve pressing problems in our lives. We may dream to focus our attention on current problems in order to work toward possible solutions (Cartwright, 1991; Fiss, 1991). Unfortunately, the evidence for the problem-solving view is not very strong, relying primarily on anecdotes that seem to support the position (Blagrove, 1996; Domhoff, 1996). Cartwright (1996) found that depressed individuals who dreamed about the source of their negative emotions (e.g., their spouse during a painful separation) were better adjusted a year later, but something other than dreaming may have been responsible for the improvement. Our dreams usually don't deal with current events, and we often have trouble remembering what we dream, so it's unlikely that dreaming evolved simply to help us solve pressing problems (Domhoff, 2003). Another recent view comes from evolutionary psychology: Dreaming may allow us to simulate threats from the environment and mentally practice the skills needed to avoid those threats (Revonsuo, 2000). We do sometimes dream about aggressive events and threatening situations and take appropriate defense actions (Zadra, Desjardines, & Marcotte, 2006), but whether dreaming really evolved to help us handle real-world threats remains highly speculative (Flanagan, 2000). It's safe to assume that REM sleep and dreaming reflect some important property of the brain, but at the moment the major questions remain unanswered.

Disorders of Sleep

We end our treatment of sleep and dreaming with a brief discussion of sleep disorders. Psychologists and other mental health professionals divide sleep disorders into two main categories: (1) *dyssomnias*, which are problems connected with the amount, timing, and quality of sleep; and (2) *parasomnias*, which are abnormal disturbances that occur during sleep. Let's consider some prominent examples of each type.

Dyssomnias The most common type of dyssomnia is **insomnia**, where you have difficulty starting or maintaining sleep. Everyone has trouble getting to sleep from time to time, and everyone has awakened in the middle of the night and been unable to get back to sleep. For the clinical diagnosis of insomnia, these difficulties must be chronic—lasting for at least a month. It's been estimated that perhaps 30% of the population suffers from some degree of insomnia, although the number of truly severe sufferers is thought to be closer to 15% (Bootzin et al., 1993; Gillin, 1993). There are many causes for the condition, including stress, emotional problems, and alcohol and other drug use, as well as medical conditions. Some kinds of insomnia may even be learned—for example, children who regularly fall asleep in the presence of their parents often have trouble getting back to sleep if they wake up later alone in their room (Adair et al., 1991). Presumably, these children have learned to associate sleeping

insomnia A chronic condition marked by difficulties in initiating or maintaining sleep, lasting for a period of at least one month.

hypersomnia A chronic condition marked by excessive sleepiness.

narcolepsy A rare sleep disorder characterized by sudden extreme sleepiness.

nightmares Frightening and anxiety-arousing dreams that occur primarily during the REM stage of sleep.

with the presence of a parent and consequently can't return to sleep without the parent present.

Whereas insomnia is characterized by an inability to sleep, in **hypersomnia** the problem is too much sleep. People diagnosed with hypersomnia show excessive sleepiness—they're often caught catnapping during the day, and they complain about being tired all the time. The cause of this condition is unknown; it's been suggested that genetic factors might be involved (Parkes & Block, 1989). Excessive sleepiness can also be caused by infectious diseases, such as mononucleosis or chronic fatigue syndrome, and by a sleep disorder called *sleep apnea*. Sleep apnea is a relatively rare condition in which the sleeper repeatedly stops breathing throughout the night, usually for short periods lasting up to a minute or so. The episodes typically end with the person waking up gasping for breath. Because these episodes occur frequently throughout the night, the affected person feels tired during the day. Significant sleep apnea problems are found in less than 5% of the population, although a higher percentage of people may experience occasional episodes (Latta & Van Cauter, 2003).

There is yet another even rarer sleep disorder, called **narcolepsy**, that is characterized by sudden extreme sleepiness. Sleep attacks can occur at any time during the day and can last from a few seconds to several minutes. What makes this disorder unusual is that the person seems to directly enter a kind of REM sleep state. The person loses all muscle tone and can even fall to the ground in a sound sleep! Fortunately, not all instances of narcolepsy are this extreme, although it can be a disabling condition. There is some evidence to suggest that the disorder may also have a genetic link (Barlow & Durand, 2005). Again, it's very rare and probably affects only a few people in a thousand.

Parasomnias The second category of sleep disorders, parasomnias, includes such abnormal sleep disturbances as nightmares, night terrors, and sleepwalking. **Nightmares** are frightening and anxiety-arousing dreams that occur primarily during the REM stage of sleep. They inevitably cause the sleeper to awaken; if they recur frequently, they can lead to the symptoms of insomnia. What causes nightmares? No

Concept Review | Functions of Sleep and Dreaming

WHY DO WE SLEEP?

Theory	Description	Evaluation
Repair and restoration	Sleep restores and/or repairs the body and brain.	Not strongly supported by data; restorative activities of the body are not limited to sleep. Changes in physical activity do not lead to consistent changes in subsequent sleep patterns.
Survival value	Sleep increases chances of survival.	Receives some support from observation of sleep patterns in different species of animals.

WHY DO WE DREAM?

Theory	Description	Evaluation
Wish fulfillment (Freud)	Dreaming is a psychological mechanism for fulfillment of wishes, often sexual in nature.	Difficult to assess; psychologists are reluctant to ascribe hidden meaning to dreams.
Activation synthesis	Dreaming is a consequence of random activity that occurs in the brain during REM sleep. The brain creates a story to make sense of these random signals.	Theory is vague and difficult to test. Dreaming is not limited to REM sleep.
Problem solving	Dreaming helps us focus on our current problems to find solutions.	Evidence is weak and anecdotal.
Threat simulation	Dreaming evolved to help us practice the skills needed to avoid threats.	Still speculation at this point.

one is certain at this point, although frequent nightmares may indicate the presence of a psychological disorder.

Night terrors, which occur mainly in children, are terrifying experiences in which the sleeper awakens suddenly in an extreme state of panic—the child may sit in bed screaming and will show little responsiveness to others who are present. Fortunately, night terrors are not considered to be indicators of serious psychological or medical problems, and they tend to go away with age.

Finally, **sleepwalking** occurs when the sleeper rises during sleep and wanders about. Sleepwalking happens mainly in childhood, tends to vanish as the child reaches adolescence, and, again, it's not thought to result from a serious psychological or medical problem. There's some evidence that sleepwalking runs in families, so you may be born with a genetic susceptibility for the condition (Lecendreux et al., 2003). It's interesting to note that both night terrors and sleepwalking occur during periods of non-REM sleep, which suggests that neither may be related entirely to dreaming.

night terrors Terrifying experiences, which occur mainly in children, in which the sleeper awakens suddenly in an extreme state of panic.

sleepwalking The sleeper arises during sleep and wanders about.

Test Yourself 6.2

To check your understanding of sleep and dreaming, answer the following questions. (You will find the answers in the Appendix.)

1. Choose the EEG pattern that best fits the following descriptions. Choose from the following: *alpha waves, delta activity, K complex, sleep spindles, theta waves, REM*.
   a. The characteristic pattern found in stage 1 sleep: _____
   b. Often triggered by loud noises during stage 2 sleep: _____
   c. Another name for the slow-wave patterns that are found during stage 3 and stage 4 sleep: _____
   d. The characteristic pattern of paradoxical sleep: _____

2. Which of the following statements is most consistent with the view that we sleep because it keeps us away from hostile environments during times when we can't see well?
   a. Sleep deprivation leads to a breakdown in normal functioning.
   b. Fearful dreams make us wary of venturing outside.
   c. Cats sleep more than cows.
   d. People sleep less as they age.

3. Diagnose the following sleep disorders based on the information provided. Choose from the following: *hypersomnia, insomnia, nightmare, night terror, sleep apnea, sleepwalking*.
   a. Difficulty initiating and maintaining sleep: _____
   b. Sleeper awakens suddenly, screaming, but the EEG pattern indicates a period of non-REM sleep: _____
   c. Sleeper repeatedly stops breathing during the night, usually for short periods lasting less than 1 minute: _____
   d. An anxiety-arousing dream that usually occurs during the REM stage of sleep: _____

Altering Awareness: Psychoactive Drugs

LEARNING GOALS
- Compare neurotransmitters with psychoactive drugs.
- Discuss the different categories of psychoactive drugs, with examples of each.
- Discuss the psychological factors that influence the effects of psychoactive drugs.

THE RHYTHMIC CYCLES OF SLEEP reveal how conscious awareness shifts as the electrical activity of the brain changes. We haven't talked much about the factors that control these brain changes, but the brain's chemical messengers, the neurotransmitters, are primarily responsible. The brain is a biochemical factory, altering moods and shifting awareness by enhancing or inhibiting the actions of its various neurotransmitters. As we've discussed previously, the brain sometimes reacts to stress or injury by releasing brain chemicals called endorphins, which reduce pain and serve to elevate mood. Altering awareness can be highly adaptive, because the delay of pain can allow an organism to escape from a life-threatening situation.

If you allow an external agent, such as a drug, to enter your body, it too can radically alter the delicate chemical balance that controls awareness and other mental

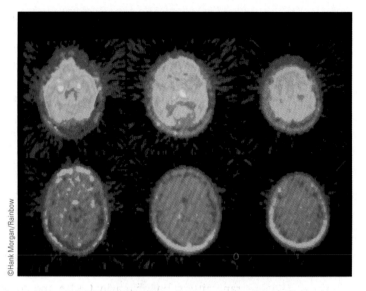

©M. Antman/The Image Works

©Hank Morgan/Rainbow

This series of PET scans shows how administration of a drug affects general activity in the brain over time. The first PET scan in the top row shows a normal active brain; the last PET scan in the bottom row shows diminished activity after the drug has taken full effect.

processes. Obviously, drugs can have tremendously beneficial effects, especially in the treatment of psychological and medical disorders (see Chapter 15). But drugs can have negative effects as well, even though they might seem to change awareness in a highly pleasurable way. As you probably know, *drug abuse*, particularly of alcohol and tobacco, is directly or indirectly responsible for hundreds of thousands of deaths annually in the United States (Coleman, 1993). In this section, we'll consider the actions of drugs labeled **psychoactive**—those that affect behavior and mental processes through alterations of conscious awareness.

Drug Actions and Effects

Psychologists are interested in psychoactive drugs for two main reasons. First, they produce powerful effects on behavior and mental processes. Second, they help us understand more about the neural mechanisms that cause behavior. Psychoactive drugs, like most natural drugs produced by the brain, exert their effects primarily by changing the normal communication channels of neurons. Some drugs, such as *nicotine*, duplicate the action of neurotransmitters by actually attaching themselves to the receptor sites of membranes; this allows the drug to produce the same effect as the brain's natural chemical messenger. Other drugs depress or block the action of neurotransmitters; some sleeping pills, for instance, decrease norepinephrine or dopamine stimulation. The psychoactive drug *fluoxetine* (known commercially as Prozac) has been used successfully to treat depression; it acts by slowing the process through which the neurotransmitter serotonin is broken down and taken back up into the transmitting cell (Kramer, 1993).

Long-term drug use often changes the way the body reacts. For example, you can develop a drug **tolerance**, which means that increasing amounts of the drug will be needed to produce the same physical and behavioral effects. Tolerance is a kind of adaptation that compensates for the effects of the drug. **Drug dependency** is often linked to the development of tolerance—dependency is manifested as either a physical or a psychological *need* for continued use (Woody & Cacciola, 1997). With physical dependency, the person typically experiences **withdrawal** symptoms when he or she stops taking the drug. These are clear, measurable physical reactions such as sweating, vomiting, changes in heart rate, or tremors. Drug dependency is the primary

psychoactive drugs Drugs that affect behavior and mental processes through alterations of conscious awareness.

tolerance An adaptation made by the body to compensate for the continued use of a drug, such that increasing amounts of the drug are needed to produce the same physical and behavioral effects.

drug dependency A condition in which one experiences a physical or a psychological need for continued use of a drug.

withdrawal Physical reactions, such as sweating, vomiting, changes in heart rate, or tremors, that occur when a person stops taking certain drugs after continued use.

cause of substance abuse, although the mechanisms that lead to dependency are still a matter of some debate. At this point, it's not certain whether dependency develops as a consequence of "urgings" produced by biological withdrawal or whether people essentially learn to become dependent on the drug with repeated use (Berridge & Robinson, 2003).

Categories of Psychoactive Drugs

It's useful to classify psychoactive drugs into one of four categories—depressants, stimulants, opiates, and hallucinogens—based on their specific mind-altering characteristics. We'll briefly examine each type and then conclude with a discussion of some psychological factors involved in drug use.

Depressants   In general, drugs classified as **depressants** slow, or depress, the ongoing activity of the central nervous system. *Ethyl alcohol*, which is present in beer, wine, and distilled drinks, is a well-known example of a depressant. Alcohol affects a number of neurotransmitters, but primarily GABA and dopamine. The GABA system is involved in the regulation of anxiety and generally reduces, or inhibits, neural activity. (Drugs that block the action of GABA can reduce alcohol's effects.) Alcohol stimulates the release of dopamine as well, which acts as a natural reinforcer and, at low doses, produces a general stimulatory effect. Animals, by the way, find the effects of alcohol quite reinforcing—they will perform tasks that yield small amounts of alcohol as a reward (Wise & Bozarth, 1987).

> **depressants** A class of drugs that slow or depress the ongoing activity of the central nervous system.

As the consumption of alcohol increases, more complex psychological effects emerge as the brain centers that control judgment become sluggish from inhibition. As you're undoubtedly aware, after a few drinks people can start acting in ways that are contrary to their usual behavioral tendencies. The normally demure become loud and aggressive; the sexually inhibited become flirtatious and provocative. These behavioral changes are produced, in part, because alcohol reduces self-awareness. Drinkers are less likely to monitor their behaviors and actions closely, and they tend to forget about current problems (Hull & Bond, 1986). These carefree moments are stolen at a cost, of course, because the body eventually reacts to the drug in a more negative way. Fatigue, nausea, and depression are likely consequences of overconsumption. If too much alcohol is consumed, the results can even be fatal. Alcohol poisoning, which comes from drinking large quantities of alcohol in a short period of time, often leads to death. The indirect costs are great as well: As activity in the sympathetic nervous system slows, so too does reaction time, which increases the chances of an accident while driving or in the workplace. Many people die every year as a result of alcohol-related incidents.

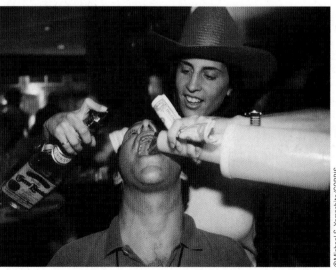

Despite the pleasurable properties of alcohol, too much alcohol consumption can have severe negative consequences on your health and well-being.

Barbiturates and *tranquilizers* are also classified as depressant drugs. Both are widely prescribed for the treatment of anxiety and insomnia, and they produce effects in the brain similar to those induced by alcohol (the neurotransmitter GABA is again involved; Gardner, 1997). Like alcohol, at low doses tranquilizing agents tend to produce pleasurable feelings of relaxation. But at higher doses your ability to concentrate easily is lost, memory is impaired, and speech becomes slurred. Barbiturate use also commonly leads to tolerance and dependency. With continued use, your metabolism changes so that larger and larger doses of the drug are required to obtain the same effect, and you become physically and psychologically dependent on the drug. Tranquilizers (such as the widely prescribed Valium and Xanax) are less habit forming than barbiturates and for this reason are more likely to be prescribed.

stimulants A class of drugs that increase central nervous system activity, enhancing neural transmission.

Stimulants   A **stimulant** is a drug that increases central nervous system activity, enhancing neural transmission. Examples of stimulants include *caffeine, nicotine, amphetamines,* and *cocaine*. These agents generally increase alertness and can affect mood by inducing feelings of pleasure. The morning cup of coffee is an excellent example of how a stimulant in low doses—caffeine—can improve your mood significantly and even increase concentration and attention. Other side effects of stimulants include dilated pupils, increased heart and respiration rate, and decreased appetite. In large doses, stimulants can produce extreme anxiety and even convulsions and death.

Both amphetamines and cocaine produce their stimulating effects by increasing the effectiveness of the neurotransmitters norepinephrine and dopamine. Dopamine seems to be primarily responsible for the positive, reinforcing qualities of these drugs (Dackis & Miller, 2003). Research has shown that animals work hard to self-administer drugs that increase the activity of dopamine-based synapses. In the case of cocaine, which is derived from the leaves of the coca plant, the drug blocks the reabsorption of both norepinephrine and dopamine. When reabsorption is blocked, these transmitter substances are able to exert their effects for a longer period of time. Cocaine produces intense feelings of euphoria, although the effects of the drug generally wear off quickly. A half hour or so after the drug enters the body the user crashes, in part because the drug has temporarily depleted the user's internal supply of norepinephrine and dopamine. Regular use of cocaine produces a number of harmful side effects, including intense episodes of paranoia and even hallucinations and delusions (Adeyemo, 2002).

Cocaine and amphetamines are also available in crystallized forms that can be smoked, snorted, or injected. *Crack*, the crystallized form of cocaine, tends to be purer than street cocaine, and its effects are generally faster acting and more intense. The effects also last for a shorter amount of time, which leads to heightened cravings and a desire for more of the drug—fast. The low that follows crack is also more intense; again, this increases the desire for more of the drug. These factors produce a lethal combination—a substantial increase in the likelihood of overdose and death, even in occasional and first-time users.

Another stimulant that's shown an alarming increase in popularity recently is a self-labeled designer drug called *Ecstasy*. The active ingredient in Ecstasy is methylenedioxymethamphetamine, or MDMA. Like other stimulants, it produces feelings of well-being, or even euphoria, and increased energy levels. The dangerous side effects of Ecstasy are similar to those produced by the other stimulants. Research with animals has found that it can lead to brain damage (the destruction of serotonin-producing neurons), and it's been shown to interfere with memory and even sleep in people (Montoya et al., 2002). Ecstasy, which comes in pill or liquid form, has the added disadvantage that it's street-made; as a result, the user never knows exactly what substances he or she has ingested.

opiates A class of drugs that reduce anxiety, lower sensitivity to pain, and elevate mood; opiates often act to depress nervous system activity.

Opiates   Drugs classified as **opiates** (also sometimes called *narcotics*) depress nervous system activity, thereby reducing anxiety, elevating mood, and lowering sensitivity to pain. Well-known examples of opiates include opium, heroin, and morphine. As you learned previously, morphine—which is derived from the flowering opium plant—acts on existing membrane receptor sites in the nervous system. Its painkilling effects and pleasurable mood shifts (it's named after Morpheus, the Greek god of dreams) apparently arise from mimicking the brain's own chemicals, specifically *endorphins*, that are involved in reducing pain. Opiates can produce strong physical and psychological dependence. Once usage is stopped, the body rebels with intense and prolonged withdrawal symptoms.

People who are regular users of opiates, such as heroin or morphine, suffer in many ways despite any fleeting pleasures that might immediately follow drug use. Kicking an opiate habit is extremely tough because the withdrawal symptoms—which can in-

The left photo shows the bud of an opium poppy, cut to release the narcotic sap. The middle photo shows psilocybin, a type of mushroom that produces hallucinogenic effects; the right photo shows a marijuana plant.

clude everything from excessive yawning, to nausea, to severe chills—last for days. Users who opt for the normal method of administration—intravenous injection—run additional risks from disease, especially HIV. Longitudinal studies of heroin addicts paint a grim picture: Addicts tend to die young (at an average age of about 40) from a variety of causes including suicide, homicide, and overdose (Hser et al., 1993).

Hallucinogens   For the final category of psychoactive drug, **hallucinogens** (sometimes called *psychedelics*), the term *psychoactive* is particularly apt. Hallucinogens play havoc with the normal internal construction of reality. Perception itself is fractured, and the world becomes awash in fantastic colors, sounds, and tactile sensations. Two of the best-known examples of these drugs, *mescaline* and *psilocybin*, occur naturally in the environment. Mescaline comes from a certain kind of cactus; psilocybin is a type of mushroom. Both have been used for centuries, primarily in the context of religious rituals and ceremonies. Since the 1960s they have served as potentially dangerous recreational drugs for those seeking alternative realities.

    Lysergic acid diethylamide (LSD) is a synthetic version of a psychedelic drug. LSD is thought to mimic the action of the neurotransmitter serotonin (Strassman, 1992); the drug acts on specific serotonin-based receptor sites in the brain, producing stimulation. For reasons that are not particularly clear, variations in sensation and perception are produced. A typical LSD experience, which can last for up to 16 hours, consists of profound changes in perception. Some users report a phenomenon called *synesthesia*, which is a blending of sensory experiences—colors may actually feel warm or cold, and rough textures may begin to sing. Also for unknown reasons, a user's experience can turn sharply wrong. Panic or depression can develop, increasing the likelihood of accidents and personal harm. Users also sometimes report the occurrence of "flashbacks," in which the sensations of the drug are reexperienced long after the drug has presumably left the body.

    Marijuana, which comes from the naturally occurring plant *Cannabis*, can also be classified as a hallucinogenic drug. It is unusual to see profound distortions of perceptual reality with this drug unless large amounts are ingested. Marijuana is usually smoked or swallowed, and its effects last around four hours. Users typically report a melting away of anxiety, a general sense of well-being, and increased awareness of normal sensations. Changes in the perception of time and its passage are sometimes reported, along with increased appetite. The pleasant effects of the drug are usually followed by fatigue and sometimes sleep.

hallucinogens A class of drugs that tends to disrupt normal mental and emotional functioning, including distorting perception and altering reality.

Marijuana does not always produce a pleasant experience. Some users report anxiety, extreme fearfulness, and panic. A number of studies have shown that marijuana use impairs concentration, motor coordination, and the ability to track things visually (Bolla et al., 2002); these side effects probably contribute to the likelihood of traffic accidents when driving under the influence. Less is known about the long-term effects of regular use, but there's some evidence that marijuana may impair the formation of memories (Sim-Selley, 2003). On the positive side, marijuana helps reduce some of the negative symptoms of chemotherapy (e.g., nausea), and in some cases it's proved helpful in treating eye disorders such as glaucoma. But the medical evidence in this area remains somewhat controversial.

Psychological Factors

Psychoactive drugs often produce individual differences. Two people can take the same drug, in exactly the same quantity, but experience completely different effects. A small amount of LSD consumed by Teo produces a euphoric "religious experience"; the same amount for Jane produces a frightening descent into a whirlpool of terror and fear. Why? Shouldn't the pharmacological effects on the neurotransmitters in the brain produce similar or at least consistent psychological effects?

Many factors influence the psychological experience: biological, genetic, and environmental. Smoking marijuana for the first time in a car speeding 75 miles per hour seriously limits the anxiety-reducing effects of the drug. Many users report that familiarity is also critical—users claim you need to learn to smoke marijuana or take LSD before the innermost secrets of the drug are revealed. In fact, experienced users of marijuana have reported experiencing a "high" after smoking a cigarette they only *thought* was marijuana; similar effects did not occur for novice users (Jones, 1971). Both familiarity and environment affect the user's *mental set*—his or her expectations about the drug's harmful and beneficial consequences. Finally, the user's physical state is critical. Some people develop resistance or tolerance to a drug faster than others do. The experience of a drug may even depend on such things as whether the person has eaten or is well rested.

The setting in which the drug is experienced can also mask or hide effects. In a study by Johnson and colleagues (2000), male college students were asked to judge the

Concept Review | Psychoactive Drugs

CATEGORY	EXAMPLES	GENERAL EFFECTS
Depressants	Ethyl alcohol Barbiturates Tranquilizers	Believed to enhance the effectiveness of GABA and dopamine, which often act as inhibitory messengers in the brain. Produce pleasurable feelings of relaxation, but at high doses concentration and memory are impaired.
Stimulants	Caffeine Nicotine Amphetamines Cocaine Ecstasy	Amphetamines and cocaine may work primarily by increasing the effectiveness of dopamine and norepinephrine. Stimulants tend to increase alertness, elevate mood, and produce physical changes such as increased heart and respiration rate.
Opiates	Opium Morphine Heroin	Depressing nervous system activity, resulting in reduced anxiety, mood elevation, and lower sensitivity to pain. Can produce strong physical and psychological dependence.
Hallucinogens	LSD Mescaline Psilocybin Marijuana	Produce variations in sensation and perception. LSD is believed to mimic the action of serotonin. Some users report synesthesia, a blending of sensory experiences. Marijuana leads to a general sense of well-being and heightened awareness of normal sensations. Negative side effects can include anxiety, fearfulness, and panic.

acceptability of forced sexual aggression toward a blind date. Everyone saw a video of a couple interacting: For one group, the female in the video acted friendly and cheerful toward the male date (e.g., touching his arm from time to time and sitting close); in a second condition, the woman acted unresponsive and distant. Afterward everyone was asked to judge how acceptable it would be for the male to force himself sexually on the woman.

Overall the men found such behavior to be unacceptable, but their rating depended, in part, on whether they had just consumed a moderate amount of alcohol. Interestingly, when the woman in the video acted unfriendly and unresponsive, alcohol had essentially no effect—all the men thought sexual aggression toward the woman was unacceptable. However, when the woman in the video acted friendly and responsive, drinking began to matter: Men who had consumed a moderate amount of alcohol were significantly more likely to view sexual aggression as an acceptable response. In this case, alcohol's effect depended importantly on the behavior of others present in the situation.

Test Yourself | 6.3

Test your knowledge about psychoactive drugs by picking the category of drug that best fits each of the following statements. Choose from among these terms: depressant, hallucinogen, opiate, stimulant. *(You will find the answers in the Appendix.)*

1. Increases central nervous system activity: _____
2. Reduces pain by mimicking the brain's own natural pain-reducing chemicals: _____
3. Tends to produce inhibitory effects by increasing the effectiveness of the neurotransmitter GABA: _____

4. Distorts perception and may lead to flashbacks: _____
5. The type of active ingredient found in your morning cup of coffee: _____

Altering Awareness: Induced States

LEARNING GOALS
- Describe the physiological and behavioral effects of hypnosis.
- Discuss whether hypnosis can be used effectively to enhance memory.
- Describe the dissociation and role-playing accounts of hypnosis.
- Describe the physical, behavioral, and psychological effects of meditation.

THE SETTING IS PARIS, late in the year 1783. Dressed in a silk robe, German-born physician Franz Anton Mesmer seeks to restore his patients' balance of "universal fluids." He rhythmically passes an iron rod over their outstretched bodies affecting, he thinks, their innate animal magnetism. Some quickly fall into a trancelike state; others become agitated and fitful. All enter what looks to be an alternative form of consciousness accompanied by a loss of voluntary control. On later awakening, many feel better, apparently cured of their various physical and psychological problems.

Although Mesmer himself eventually fell into disrepute, rejected by the scientific community of his time, the phenomenon of "mesmerizing" did not. We recognize today, of course, that the artificial state of awareness he induced in his patients had nothing to do with magnets or the balancing of universal fluids. Instead, the bizarre behavior of his patients is better explained as an example of hypnosis. **Hypnosis** can be defined generally as any form of social interaction that produces a *heightened state of suggestibility* in a willing participant. It is of interest to psychologists, like the related topic of meditation, because it's a technique specifically designed to alter conscious awareness. As you'll see shortly, hypnosis has many useful and adaptive properties (Santarcangelo & Sabastiani, 2004).

hypnosis A form of social interaction that produces a heightened state of suggestibility in a willing participant.

The Phenomenon of Hypnosis

Much remains to be learned about hypnosis and its effects. For example, researchers are still not sure whether it's truly an altered state of awareness or simply a kind of social playacting—more on that later. But we do know a few things about what *hypnosis* is not. For one thing, people who are hypnotized never really enter into anything resembling a deep sleep. The word *hypnosis* comes from the Greek *hypnos*, meaning "to sleep," but hypnosis bears little physiological relation to sleep. The EEG patterns of a hypnotized subject, along with other physiological indices, more closely resemble those of someone who is relaxed rather than deeply asleep (Graffen et al., 1995). Moreover, certain reflexes that are commonly absent during sleep, such as the knee jerk, are still present under hypnosis (Pratt et al., 1988). Not surprisingly, there are a host of ongoing studies using the techniques of modern cognitive neuroscience, such as neuroimaging, so we are likely to learn a lot more about the biological basis of hypnosis in the near future (see Burgess, 2007).

Another myth is that only weak-willed people are susceptible to hypnotic induction. We're all susceptible to a degree, in the sense that we show heightened suggestibility under some circumstances. Hypnotic "suggestibility" scales, which measure susceptibility to induction, indicate that only about 20% of the population is highly hypnotizable (Hilgard, 1965). But it's not clear exactly what factors account for these differences. Personality studies have shown that people who are easy to hypnotize are not weak willed or conforming, although they may have more active imaginations than people who resist hypnosis (Nadon et al., 1991).

There are many ways to induce the hypnotic state. In the most popular technique, the hypnotist acts as an authority figure, suggesting to the client that he or she is growing increasingly more relaxed and sleepy with time: "Your eyes are getting heavier and heavier, you can barely keep your lids open," and so on. The client is often asked to fixate on something, perhaps a spot on the wall or a swinging pendulum. The logic here is that eye fixation leads to muscle fatigue, which helps convince clients that they are indeed becoming increasingly relaxed. Other approaches to induction rely more on subtle suggestions (Erickson, 1964), but in general no one method

In the late 18th century, Anton Mesmer helped promote the belief that physical and psychological problems could be cured by passing magnets over the body. In this engraving, Mesmer and a subject are portrayed at far left.

LE MAGNÉTISME ANIMAL
Importante Découverte par Mr. Mesmer, Docteur en Médecine, de la Faculté de Vienne en Autriche.

is necessarily better than another. In the words of one researcher, "The art of hypnosis relies on not providing the client with grounds for resisting" (Araoz, 1982, p. 106).

Once hypnotized, people become highly suggestible, responding to commands from the hypnotist in ways that seem automatic and involuntary. The hypnotist can use the power of suggestion to achieve adaptive ends, such as helping people kick unwanted habits like smoking or overeating. Anesthetic effects are also possible at certain deep stages of hypnosis. Hypnotized patients report less pain during childbirth (Harmon et al., 1990) and typically suffer less during dental work (Houle et al., 1988). It's even been possible to perform major surgeries (such as appendectomies) using hypnosis as the primary anesthesia (Kihlstrom, 1985). Research is ongoing to determine the biological basis for these striking analgesic effects. It was once thought, for example, that the release of endorphins by the brain might be responsible, although this possibility now seems less likely (Moret et al., 1991).

Memory Enhancement   Another frequent claim is that hypnosis can dramatically improve memory, a phenomenon called **hypnotic hypermnesia**. There have been criminal cases in which hypnotized witnesses have suddenly and miraculously recalled minute details of a crime. In one famous kidnapping case from the 1970s, a bus driver was buried 6 feet underground along with 26 children inside a tractor trailer. Later, under hypnosis, the driver was able to reconstruct details of the kidnapper's license plate—digit by digit. There is a long-standing belief among some psychotherapists that hypnosis is an excellent tool for uncovering hidden memories of abuse or other forms of psychological trauma (Pratt et al., 1988; Yapko, 1994). There have even been well-publicized examples of *age regression* under hypnosis, in which a person mentally traveled backward to some earlier place (such as his or her second-grade classroom) and was able to recall numerous details.

Unfortunately, there's little hard evidence to support these phenomena scientifically. Memory does sometimes improve after a hypnotic session, but this doesn't allow us to conclude that the hypnotic state was responsible (Spiegel, 1995). One possibility is that hypnotic induction procedures (the relaxation techniques) simply create effective and supportive environments in which to remember (Geiselman et al., 1985). It's also difficult to judge whether memories recovered during hypnosis are, in fact, accurate representations of what actually occurred. You may "remember" a particularly unfortunate experience from the second-grade classroom, but can you be sure that this traumatic episode indeed occurred as you remember it?

As you'll see in a moment, hypnotized people often adopt roles designed to please the hypnotist. What appear to be memories are sometimes *fabrications*—stories that the person unintentionally makes up to please the hypnotist. For this reason, many states have banned the use of hypnotic testimony in criminal court cases. It's simply too difficult to tell whether the memory recovered after hypnosis is accurate or a product of suggestion. Controlled experiments in the laboratory have been unable to find good evidence for true memory enhancement—at least, memory enhancement that can be tied directly to the properties of hypnosis (Dinges et al., 1992; Steblay & Bothwell, 1994).

Explaining Hypnosis

What exactly is hypnosis? As noted earlier, the EEG patterns of someone in a hypnotic deep sleep resemble those of a relaxed waking state; in fact, there don't appear to be any reliable physiological measures that can be used to define the hypnotized condition. So how do we explain the heightened suggestibility? Currently, there are two prominent interpretations: (1) Hypnosis is a kind of dissociation, or true splitting

hypnotic hypermnesia The supposed enhancement in memory that occurs under hypnosis; there is little if any evidence to support the existence of this effect.

Although hypnosis is often used for entertainment, it can have considerable clinical value.

of conscious awareness; and (2) hypnosis represents a kind of social role playing. Let's consider each of these ideas in more detail.

hypnotic dissociation A hypnotically induced splitting of consciousness during which multiple forms of awareness exist.

Hypnotic Dissociations Some researchers believe that hypnosis produces **hypnotic dissociations**. "Dissociation" means that the individual experiences a kind of splitting of consciousness where multiple forms of awareness exist simultaneously (Hilgard, 1986, 1992). Hilgard (1986) has argued that conscious awareness in a hypnotized subject is actually divided into two components. One stream of consciousness follows the commands of the hypnotist—for example, feeling no pain in response to a painful stimulation. The second kind of awareness, called the "hidden observer," experiences the pain but reveals nothing to the observer.

Support for these ideas comes from experiments in which people are hypnotized and asked to submerge one arm into a bucket of extremely cold ice water (a common procedure to test for the analgesic effects of hypnosis). "You'll be aware of no pain," the participant is told, "but that other part of you, the hidden part that is aware of everything going on, can signal any true pain by pressing this key." A button is made available that the person is allowed to press, at will, with the nonsubmerged hand. It turns out that people press this key repeatedly—reporting the pain—and the key presses become much more frequent the longer the arm is kept submerged. During hypnosis, as well as afterward, people claim to have no knowledge of what the nonsubmerged hand is doing. There is a hidden part of consciousness, Hilgard argues, that maintains realistic contact with what's going on; it is the other hypnotized stream of awareness that feels no pain (also see Spiegel, 1998).

This idea that conscious awareness is divided or split during hypnosis may seem mystical, strange, and worthy of skepticism. But as you know, the brain often divides its labor to arrive at adaptive solutions. You walk and talk at the same time, and you certainly don't consciously think about picking up each leg and putting it down while making a point in the conversation. The idea that consciousness is regularly dissociated, or divided, is not really an issue to most psychologists; it's accepted as a given, as a normal part of psychological functioning. But whether it's correct to characterize hypnosis as a true splitting of consciousness is still undecided.

Social Role Playing Many psychologists remain skeptical about hypnosis because hypnotized subjects often seem to be playing a kind of role. The behavior of a hypnotized person is easily modified by expectations and by small changes in the suggestions of the hypnotist. For example, if people are told before being hypnotized that a rigid right arm is a prominent feature of the hypnotized state, then rigid right arms are likely to be reported after hypnosis even when no such specific suggestion is made during the induction process (Orne, 1959). It often appears as if people are trying desperately to do whatever they can to act in the suggested way (Kihlstrom & McConkey, 1990).

A number of researchers have suggested that hypnotic behavior may, in fact, be a kind of social role playing. Everyone has some idea of what hypnotized behavior looks like—when hypnotized, you fall into a trance state and obey the commands of the all-powerful hypnotist. So when people agree to be hypnotized, they implicitly agree to act out this role (Barber, Spanos, & Chaves, 1974; Sarbin & Coe, 1972; Spanos, 1982). You don't actually lose voluntary control over your behavior; instead, you follow the lead of the hypnotist and obey his or her every command because you think, perhaps unconsciously, that involuntary compliance is an important part of what it means to be hypnotized (Lynn, Rhue, & Weekes, 1990).

Quite a bit of evidence supports this role-playing interpretation of hypnosis. One compelling finding is that essentially all hypnotic phenomena can be reproduced with *simulated subjects*—people who are never actually hypnotized but who are told to act as if they're hypnotized (Spanos, 1986, 1996). Moreover, many of the classic phenomena—such as posthypnotic suggestions—turn out to be controlled mainly by expectations rather than by the hypnotist. For instance, if subjects are told to respond to a cue, such as tugging on their ear every time they hear a particular word, they will often do so after hypnosis. However, such posthypnotic suggestions work only if the subjects believe they're still participating in the experiment; if the hypnotist leaves the room, or if the subjects believe the experiment is over, they stop responding to the cue (see Lynn et al., 1990, for a review).

Meditation

There are similarities between hypnosis and meditation—both are claimed to produce an altered state of consciousness, and both tend to rely on relaxation. In **meditation**, of course, it's the participant alone who seeks to manipulate awareness. Most meditation techniques require you to perform some time-honored mental exercise, such as concentrating on repeating a particular string of words or sounds called a *mantra*.

meditation A technique for self-induced manipulation of awareness, often used for the purpose of relaxation and self-reflection.

The variations in awareness achieved through meditation, as with hypnosis, are often described in mystical or spiritual ways. Meditators report, for example, that they're able to obtain an expanded state of awareness, one that is characterized by a pure form of thought unburdened by self-awareness. There are many forms of meditation and numerous induction procedures; most trace their roots back thousands of years to the practices of Eastern religions.

Daily sessions of meditation have been prescribed for many physical and psychological problems. As with hypnosis, the induction procedure usually begins with relaxation, but the mind is kept alert through focused concentration on breathing, internal repetition of the mantra, or efforts to clear the mind. The general idea is to step back from the ongoing stream of mental activity and set the mind adrift in the oneness of the universe. Great insights, improved physical health, and release from desire are some of the reported benefits.

Scientifically, it's clear that meditation can produce significant changes in physiological functions. Arousal is lowered, so heart rate, respiration rate, and blood pressure tend to decrease. EEG recordings of brain activity during meditation reveal a relaxed mind—specifically, there is a significant increase in alpha-wave activity (Benson, 1975). Such changes are, of course, to be expected during any kind of relaxed state and do not necessarily signify anything special about a state of consciousness. Indeed, there appear to be no significant differences between the physiological patterns of accomplished meditators and those of nonmeditators who are simply relaxing (Holmes, 1987; Travis & Wallace, 1999). At this point, researchers have little to say about the subjective aspects of the meditative experience—whether, in fact, the meditator has indeed merged with the oneness of the universe—but most researchers agree that inducing a relaxed state once or twice a day has beneficial effects. Daily meditation sessions have helped people deal effectively with chronic anxiety as well as lower blood pressure and cholesterol levels (Seeman, Dublin, & Seeman, 2003).

Daily meditation can produce significant reductions in anxiety and improve physical and psychological well-being.

Test Yourself 6.4

Check what you've learned about hypnosis and meditation by deciding whether each of the following statements is True or False. *(You will find the answers in the Appendix.)*

1. The EEG patterns of a hypnotized person resemble those of non-REM sleep. *True or False?*
2. Hypnosis improves memory under some circumstances because it reduces the tendency to fabricate, or make things up, to please the questioner. *True or False?*
3. Hypnotic dissociations represent a kind of splitting of consciousness, in which more than one kind of awareness is present at the same time. *True or False?*
4. Hilgard's "hidden observer" experiments provide support for the social role-playing explanation of hypnosis. *True or False?*
5. Meditation leads primarily to alpha wave rather than theta wave EEG activity. *True or False?*

Review *Psychology for a Reason*

It's difficult to study consciousness because consciousness is a subjective, personal experience. It's tough to define consciousness objectively, and appealing to the scribblings of an EEG pattern or to a pretty picture from a neuroimaging device may, in the minds of many, fail to capture the complexities of the topic adequately. Is consciousness some classifiable thing that can change its state, like water as it freezes, boils, or evaporates? For the moment, psychologists are working with a set of rather loose ideas about the topic, although conscious awareness is agreed to have many adaptive properties. We considered four adaptive characteristics of consciousness in this chapter.

Setting Priorities for Mental Functioning
The processes of attention allow the mind to prioritize its functioning. Faced with limited resources, the brain must be selective about the enormous amount of information it receives. Through attention, we can focus on certain aspects of the environment while ignoring others; through attention, we can adapt our thinking in ways that allow for more selective and deliberate movement toward a problem solution. Attentional processes enable the brain to divide its processing. People don't always need to be consciously aware of the tasks they perform; automatic processes allow one to perform multiple tasks—such as walking and talking—simultaneously. Certain disorders of attention, including visual neglect and attention deficit/hyperactivity disorder, provide insights into attention processes. In both of these cases, which may be caused by malfunctioning in the brain, the person's ability to adapt to the environment is compromised.

Sleeping and Dreaming
Sleep is one part of a daily (circadian) rhythm that includes wakefulness, but sleep itself turns out to be composed of regularly changing cycles of brain activity. Studies using the EEG reveal that we move through several distinct stages during sleep, some of which are characterized by intense mental activity. Sleeping may allow the brain a chance to rest and restore itself from its daily workout, or it may simply be adaptive as a period of time out. Remaining hidden and motionless may have protected our ancestors at night when their sensory equipment was unlikely to function well. Dreaming, which occurs mainly during the REM period of sleep, remains a mystery to psychologists. Some believe that dreaming may reveal conflicts that are normally hidden to conscious awareness, or that dreaming may be one way to work out troubling problems. A third possibility is that dreaming is simply a manifestation of the brain's attempt to make sense of spontaneous neural activity. Dreaming may even help us practice, or rehearse, our responses to threatening situations.

Altering Awareness: Psychoactive Drugs
Psychoactive drugs alter behavior and awareness by tapping into natural brain systems that have evolved for adaptive reasons. The brain, as a biochemical factory, is capable of reacting to stress or injury by releasing chemicals that help reduce pain or improve mood. Many of the drugs that are abused regularly in our society activate these natural systems. As a result, the study of psychoactive drugs has enabled researchers to learn more about communication systems in the brain. There are four main categories of psychoactive drugs. Depressants, such as alcohol and barbiturates, lower the ongoing activity of the central nervous system. Stimulants, such as caffeine, nicotine, and cocaine, stimulate central nervous system activity by increasing the likelihood that neural transmissions will occur. Opiates, such as opium, morphine, and heroin, depress nervous system activity by mimicking the chemicals involved in the brain's own pain control system. Finally, hallucinogens, such as LSD, play havoc with the user's normal internal construction of reality. Although the mechanisms involved are not known, it's believed that LSD mimics the actions of the neurotransmitter serotonin.

Altering Awareness: Induced States
Two techniques have been designed specifically to alter conscious awareness, hypnosis and meditation. Hypnosis is a form of social interaction that induces a heightened state of suggestibility in people. Hypnotic techniques usually promote relaxation, although once achieved, brain activity under hypnosis more closely resembles the waking rather than the sleeping state. In meditation, it is the participant alone who manipulates awareness, often by mentally repeating a particular word or string of words. The biological mechanisms of both hypnosis and meditation are poorly understood at present, but each has some positive consequences. Pain and discomfort can be significantly reduced through hypnotic suggestion, and the continued use of meditation has been linked to the reduction of stress and anxiety. Psychologists study hypnosis and meditation, in part, because they believe these techniques may provide important insight into how we respond to the suggestions of others, particularly authority figures.

Active Summary *(You will find the answers in the Appendix.)*

Setting Priorities for Mental Functioning: Attention

• (1) _____ refers to the internal process of setting (2) _____ for mental functioning. The brain uses attention to focus selectively on certain aspects of the environment and not others. Why? In part because there are (3) _____ to how fast and efficiently (4) _____ communicate.

• Different messages are received simultaneously by each ear. In (5) _____ _____, the participant tries to repeat one message aloud while ignoring the other. Although the brain appears to (6) _____ many things at the same time, some of the monitoring may be minimal or beyond current (7) _____. One example of this monitoring is the (8) _____ _____ _____.

• (9) _____ refers to mental processing that is (10) _____ and easy, requiring little or no focused (11) _____. Once developed, automatic processing does not seem to require (12) _____ control or awareness. Automaticity can be measured in a (13) _____ attention task.

• Visual (14) _____ is caused most often by damage to the right (15) _____ lobe and results in the tendency to ignore everything on the (16) _____ side of the body. Attention deficit/hyperactivity disorder (ADHD) is a psychological condition that occurs in 3 to 5% of children and is characterized by (17) _____, which is often combined with impulsivity or hyperactivity.

Sleeping and Dreaming

• Structures in the brain called biological (18) _____ trigger biological, or circadian, (19) _____. Sleeping and (20) _____, body temperature, (21) _____ secretions and other biological processes follow a 24-hour (22) _____ cycle.

• Repeated cycles of brain activity, each about (23) _____ minutes long, occur during sleep. EEG recordings show cyclic changes in brain wave patterns that vary in (24) _____, frequency, and regularity. The sleep cycle contains (25) _____ stages of sleep and REM (rapid eye movement). Stage 1: Theta waves are dominant. Stage 2: Theta waves are interrupted by K complexes. Stages 3 and 4: Delta or (26) _____-wave sleep waves are dominant. REM sleep occurs 70 to (27) _____ minutes into the sleep cycle, and the EEG pattern is similar to the awake state. During REM sleep, abrupt physiological changes occur, and we dream the most.

• Sleep may help (28) _____ and restore the body and brain. Sleep may also help us respond adaptively to changing environmental conditions (for example, by causing us to remain hidden and motionless at night) and increase our likelihood for (29) _____. Sleep deprivation results in a decline in both (30) _____ and physical function.

• REM sleep may strengthen certain kinds of (31) _____. Freud believed that dreams are a form of (32) _____ _____. The activation-(33) _____ hypothesis holds that dreams are a product of (34) _____ activity in the brain. The problem-solving view suggests that dreaming may be a way for us to find solutions to our problems. Dreaming may help us mentally practice our survival skills by allowing us to simulate (35) _____ from the environment.

• Insomnia, (36) _____, and (37) _____ are (38) _____ that involve problems with the amount, quality, and timing of sleep. Nightmares, night (39) _____, and sleepwalking are (40) _____ that involve abnormal sleep disturbances.

Altering Awareness: Psychoactive Drugs

• Drugs influence the action of (41) _____. Like neurotransmitters, certain drugs alter behavior and (42) _____ processes. A person's physical response to a drug may change with repeated use. With (43) _____, increasing amounts of the substance are required to produce the desired effects. A physical or (44)_____ need for continued drug use indicates (45) _____. Withdrawal involves measurable physical reactions when drug use stops.

• (46) _____, which include (47) _____, barbiturates, and tranquilizers, reduce the activity of the central nervous system. Stimulants, including caffeine, nicotine, amphetamines, and cocaine, (48) _____ central nervous system activity. Opiates (or narcotics), such as opium, heroin, and morphine, depress central nervous system activity and reduce both anxiety and sensitivity to (49) _____. (50) _____ (or psychedelics), including mescaline, psilocybin, and LSD, drastically alter normal (51) _____.

• Psychoactive drugs produce different effects in different people due to biological, genetic, and (52) _____ factors. Reactions to psychoactive drugs can be influenced by the environment, (53) _____ with the effects of the substance, physical state, and mental (54) _____ or expectations.

Altering Awareness: Induced States

• Hypnosis produces a heightened state of (55) _____ and physiological indices resemble a (56) _____ state. Hypnosis can produce profound (57) _____ relieving effects and has been used to eliminate unwanted habits.

• A controversial claim is that hypnosis can (58) _____ memory, a phenomenon called hypnotic hypermnesia, but it's not certain that any kind of hypnotic state is responsible. It may be that the (59) _____ techniques create an effective and supportive environment that facilitates remembering.

• Hypnosis may produce hypnotic (60) _____, where (61) _____ is split into multiple forms of awareness. Some researchers suggest that hypnotic behavior may be a form of (62) _____ role playing, in which the subject responds in a way designed to please the hypnotist.

• Meditation, characterized by self-induced altered (63) _____, can cause significant physiological changes, promote relaxation, and reduce (64) _____.

Terms to Remember

Media Resources

 **ThomsonNOW**

www.thomsonedu.com/ThomsonNOW

Go to this site for the link to ThomsonNow, your one-stop study shop. Take a Pre-Test for this chapter and Thomson-Now will generate a personalized Study Plan based on your test results! The Study Plan will identify the topics you need to review and direct you to online resources to help you master those topics. You can then take a Post-Test to help you determine the concepts you have mastered and what you still need to work on.

 Companion Website

www.thomsonedu.com/psychology/nairne

Go to this site to find online resources directly linked to your book, including a glossary, flashcards, quizzing, weblinks, and more.

 Psyk.trek 3.0

Check out the Psyk.trek CD-ROM for further study of the concepts in this chapter. Psyk.trek's interactive learning modules, simulations, and quizzes offer additional opportunities for you to interact with, reflect on, and retain the material:

Consciousness: Biological Rhythms
Consciousness: Sleep
Consciousness: Drugs and Synaptic Transmission

Learning From Experience

We turn our attention now to learning, one of the most basic of all psychological processes. What exactly is learning? Well, obviously, it's the process of acquiring knowledge. You go to school, you take classes, you learn how the world works. In essence, that's the same way psychologists think about learning. But, as you know from Chapter 2, psychologists like to define concepts by how those concepts can be measured. "Knowledge" can't be measured directly; instead, **learning** is defined by behavior—more precisely, as a change in behavior, or potential behavior, that results from experience. Notice the emphasis is on behavior, which, unlike acquired knowledge, can be directly observed. We make inferences about learning by observing behavior and noting how it changes over time.

Like most definitions, this one needs a little tweaking. Sometimes behavior changes as a result of experience in ways that we wouldn't classify as learning. For example, your behavior changes as you age. Experience plays a role in development, as you know, but some changes occur purely as a result of physical development. Your behavior also changes when you get injured or sick. Suppose you're stuck in bed for two days with a high fever; your behavior is going to change—you sleep a lot more than normal—but these changes have nothing to do with learning. The concept of learning is reserved for those cases when behavior changes in a way that reflects the experience—we change our behavior, either as a reaction to the experience or as a result of practice, so we can act more sensibly in the future.

> learning A relatively permanent change in behavior, or potential behavior, that results from experience.

(continued on page 215)

213

It's easy to see why psychologists are interested in learning. The ability to alter behavior over time in response to changing environments is highly adaptive. Historically, as you'll see in this chapter, psychologists have tended to focus on very simple kinds of learning processes, often using animals as subjects. We'll discuss more complex forms of learning, particularly as they relate to memory, in Chapter 8. Here our discussion revolves around four simple problems that are resolved, in part, by our ability to learn.

Learning About Events: Noticing and Ignoring

We need to recognize new events but also learn to ignore events that occur repeatedly without consequence. A baby crying, the screech of automobile brakes—these sounds demand our attention and cause us to react. Humans and animals notice sudden changes in their environment; they notice those things that are new and potentially of interest. However, our reactions to these novel events change with repeated experience, and these changes are controlled by some of the most basic and important of all learning processes.

Learning What Events Signal: Classical Conditioning

When does one event predict that a second event is likely to follow? Many things that happen in our world signal the occurrence of other events. For instance, you know that lightning precedes thunder and that a rattling sound can signal the presence of a venomous snake. Often you can't do anything about the co-occurrence of such events, but if you recognize the relationship, you can respond accordingly (you can take cover or move to avoid the snake).

Learning About the Consequences of Our Behavior: Operant Conditioning

All species, sea snails as well as people, need to learn that some behaviors have consequences. The child who flicks the tail of a cat once too often receives an unwelcome surprise. The family dog learns that if he hangs around the dinner table, an occasional scrap of food might come his way. Behaviors are instrumental in producing rewards and punishments, and it's clearly adaptive for us to learn when and how to act.

Learning from Others: Observational Learning

Often our most important teachers are not our own actions and their consequences but the actions of others. We can learn by example, through observational learning. Obviously, observational learning has considerable adaptive significance: A teenager learns about the consequences of drunk driving, one hopes, not from direct experience but from observing others whose fate has already been sealed. A young monkey in the wild learns to be afraid of snakes not from a deadly personal encounter but from observing its mother's fear.

The bright colors and screeching sirens of a fire engine are designed to draw our attention and signal us to get out of the way.

It's clearly adaptive to learn about the signaling properties of events. A distinctive rattle on a wilderness trail signals the potential strike of the western diamondback rattlesnake.

This family dog knows about the consequences of hanging around the dinner table. She's learned that her begging behavior is instrumental in producing a tasty reward.

Learning About Events:
Noticing and Ignoring

LEARNING GOAL

• Describe and compare habituation and sensitization.

How do we learn to notice and ignore events that occur and repeat in our world? We're constantly surrounded by sights, sounds, and sensations—from the traffic outside the window, to the color of the paint on the wall, to the feel of denim jeans against our legs. As you discovered in Chapter 6, we can't attend to all of these stimuli. Instead, because the human nervous system has limited resources, we must prioritize our mental functioning. And this is not only a human problem: Animals, too, have limited resources, and they constantly need to decide whether events in their environment are important or unimportant.

It's adaptive for all living things to notice sudden changes in the environment. In this case, the unexpected appearance of a red-tailed hawk elicits distinctive orienting reactions from an opossum family.

Allen Roberts

Habituation and Sensitization

People and animals are programmed from birth to notice novelty; when something new or different happens, we pay close attention. Suppose you hear a funny ticking noise in your car engine when you press the gas pedal. When you first notice the sound, it occupies your attention. You produce an **orienting response**, which means you orient toward the new sound, maybe by leaning forward and listening. After driving with the problem for a while, however, your behavior changes—the ticking becomes less bothersome, and you may even stop reacting to it altogether. Your behavior in the presence of the event changes with repeated experience, which is the hallmark of learning.

Habituation occurs when you slow or stop responding to an event that has become familiar through repeated presentation; you may remember that we talked about this process in Chapter 4. Most birds will startle and become agitated when the shadow of a hawk passes overhead, but their level of alarm will rapidly decline if the object is presented repeatedly and there's no subsequent attack (Tinbergen, 1951). It makes sense for animals to produce a strong initial orienting response to a sudden change in their environment. If a bird fails to attend quickly to the shape of a predator, it's not likely to survive. Through the process of habituation, organisms learn to be selective about what they orient toward. They attend initially to the new and unusual but subsequently ignore events that occur repeatedly without consequence.

A related phenomenon, called **sensitization**, occurs when our response to an event increases rather than decreases with repeated exposure. For example, if you're exposed repeatedly to a loud noise, you're likely to become sensitized to the noise—your reactions become more intense and prolonged with repeated exposure. (This happens to me when our cat constantly yells for food.) Both habituation and sensitization are natural responses to repeated events. They help us respond appropriately to the environment. Whether repetition of a stimulus will lead to habituation or sensitization depends on several factors (Groves & Thompson, 1970). Generally, sensitization is more likely when the repeated stimulus is intense or punishing. If the stimulus is mild or modest in intensity, repeated exposure usually leads to habituation. Habituation and sensitization also depend importantly on the timing of presentations—for example, habituation typically occurs faster when the repetitions occur close together in time (Miller & Grace, 2003).

Both habituation and sensitization are examples of learning because they produce changes in behavior as a function of experience. In some cases, particularly with

orienting response An inborn tendency to notice and respond to novel or surprising events.

habituation The decline in the tendency to respond to an event that has become familiar through repeated exposure.

sensitization Increased responsiveness, or sensitivity, to an event that has been repeated.

Day 1   Day 2   Day 3   Day 4   Day 5

FIGURE 7.1 Long-Term Habituation

Organisms notice sudden changes in the environment but learn to ignore those that occur repeatedly. A novel sound initially makes an eating cat panic, but if the sound is repeated daily, the cat habituates and eats without the slightest reaction.

habituation, the learning can be quite long lasting. For example, when placed in a new environment, cats are often skittish when they eat. The slightest sound or movement is likely to send them scurrying under the nearest piece of furniture. With time the animal learns, and the adjustment is typically long lasting (see ▮ Figure 7.1).

We rely on simple learning processes like habituation to help conserve our limited resources. The world is full of events to be noticed, far more than we can ever hope to monitor. Orienting responses guarantee that we will notice the new and unusual, but through habituation we learn to ignore those things that are repeated but are of no significant consequence. Therefore, we're able to solve a very important problem—how to be selective about the events that occur and recur in the world.

Test Yourself | 7.1

Check your knowledge about noticing and ignoring by choosing the best answer for each of the following descriptions. Choose from the following terms: habituation, orienting response, sensitization. *(You will find the answers in the Appendix.)*

1. When Shawn practices his trumpet, he tries repeatedly to hit a high C note. The first time he tries, his roommate says nothing. By the third try, his roommate is banging on the door telling him to be quiet: _____
2. Alonda turns her head and stares intently when a strange howling sound begins in her backyard: _____
3. Kesha loves clocks and has six different varieties in her apartment. Strangely, she never notices any ticking noises: _____
4. Your cat, Comet, used to startle and jump three feet in the air whenever you ground your gourmet coffee beans in the morning. Now he never seems to notice: _____

Learning What Events Signal: Classical Conditioning

LEARNING GOALS

- Describe the basic elements of classical conditioning.
- Discuss why and how conditioned responding develops.
- Differentiate among second-order conditioning, stimulus generalization, and stimulus discrimination.
- Discuss extinction and conditioned inhibition.

EVERYONE KNOWS that a flash of lightning means a clap of thunder is likely to follow; experience has taught us to *associate* lightning with thunder. You also know that a sour smell coming from the milk means it probably won't taste very good. In both these cases, you've learned an association between two events—more specifically, you've learned that one event predicts the other. This knowledge is clearly useful because it allows you to prepare yourself for future events. You know to cover your ears or to avoid drinking the milk.

The scientific study of simple associations, like those just described, began around the turn of the century in the laboratory of a Russian physiologist named Ivan P. Pavlov (1849–1936). Pavlov developed a technique, known as **classical conditioning**, to investigate how these associations are formed. According to most accounts, Pavlov didn't start off with a burning desire to study learning. His main interest was in digestion, which included the study of how dogs salivate, or drool, in the presence of food. We salivate when food is placed in our mouth, as do dogs, because saliva contains certain chemicals that help in the initial stages of digestion. However, to his annoyance, Pavlov found that his dogs often began to drool much too soon—before the food was actually placed in their mouths. Pavlov referred to these premature droolings as "psychic" secretions, and he began to study why they occurred, in part to avoid future contamination of his digestion experiments.

classical conditioning A set of procedures used to investigate how organisms learn about the signaling properties of events. Classical conditioning involves learning relations between events—conditioned and unconditioned stimuli—that occur outside of one's control.

The Terminology of Classical Conditioning

unconditioned stimulus (US) A stimulus that automatically leads to an observable response prior to any training.

unconditioned response (UR) The observable response that is produced automatically, prior to training, on presentation of an unconditioned stimulus.

conditioned response (CR) The acquired response that is produced by the conditioned stimulus in anticipation of the unconditioned stimulus.

conditioned stimulus (CS) The neutral stimulus that is paired with the unconditioned stimulus during classical conditioning.

Pavlov recognized immediately that "psychic" secretions developed as a result of experience. At the same time, he was keenly aware that drooling in response to food is *not* a learned response. He knew that certain stimuli, which he called **unconditioned stimuli (US)**, automatically lead to responses, which he called **unconditioned responses (UR)**. Food is an unconditioned stimulus that automatically produces salivation as an unconditioned response. Neither dogs nor humans need to be taught to drool when food is placed in their mouths; rather, this response is a reflex similar to the jerking of your leg when the doctor taps you just below the knee. The response produced to an unconditioned stimulus is *unconditioned*—that is, no learning, or conditioning, is required.

The problem facing Pavlov was that his dogs began to drool merely at the sight of the food dish or even to the sound of an assistant entering the room. Food dishes and footsteps are not unconditioned stimuli that automatically cause a dog to salivate. Drooling in response to such stimuli is learned; it is *conditioned*, or acquired as a result of experience. For this reason, Pavlov began referring to the "psychic" secretions as **conditioned responses (CR)** and to the stimuli that produced them as **conditioned stimuli (CS)**.

Let's take footsteps as an example. The sound of an approaching feeder leads to drooling because the dog has learned that the sound predicts or *signals* the appearance of the food. Footsteps and food bear a special relation to each other in time: When the footsteps are heard, the food is soon to arrive. To use Pavlov's terminology, the footsteps act as a *conditioned stimulus* that produces salivation, a *conditioned response*, in anticipation of food. This is not unlike what happens to you when your mouth begins to water as you sit down to a delicious-looking meal. Conditioned stimuli typically lead to conditioned responses after the conditioned stimulus and the unconditioned stimulus have been paired together in time—the footsteps (the CS) reliably occur just before presentation of the food (the US).

Forming the CS–US Connection

What are the necessary conditions for forming an association between a conditioned stimulus and an unconditioned stimulus? It helps to remember the following general rule: A conditioned stimulus will become a signal for the unconditioned stim-

Russian physiologist Ivan Pavlov watches one of his experiments on "psychic" secretions in dogs in 1934. Notice the dog's cheek, which is fitted with a device for measuring salivation.

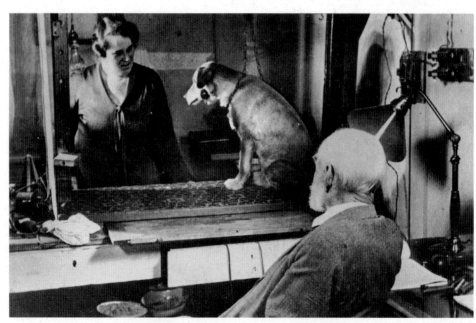

©Sovfoto

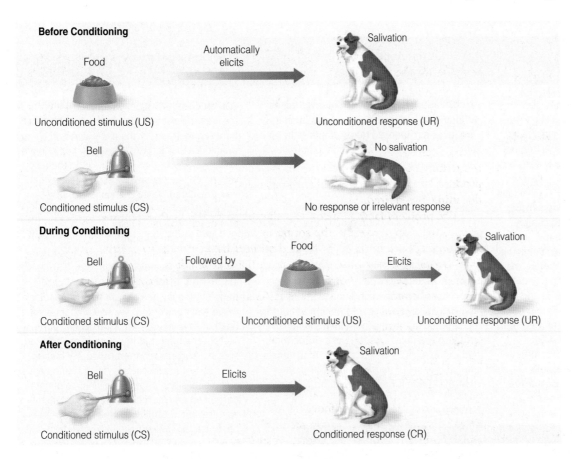

Before Conditioning

Food — Automatically elicits → Salivation

Unconditioned stimulus (US) — Unconditioned response (UR)

Bell → No salivation

Conditioned stimulus (CS) — No response or irrelevant response

During Conditioning

Bell — Followed by → Food — Elicits → Salivation

Conditioned stimulus (CS) — Unconditioned stimulus (US) — Unconditioned response (UR)

After Conditioning

Bell — Elicits → Salivation

Conditioned stimulus (CS) — Conditioned response (CR)

FIGURE 7.2 Classical Conditioning
Through classical conditioning, organisms learn about the signaling properties of events. The presentation of an unconditioned stimulus (US) leads to an automatic unconditioned response (UR) prior to training. A neutral stimulus is paired closely in time with a US. Eventually, the animal learns that this conditioned stimulus (CS) predicts the occurrence of the US and begins to show an appropriate conditioned response (CR) on presentation of the CS.

ulus when it provides *information* about the delivery of the unconditioned stimulus (Rescorla, 1988). If a bell (CS) is struck just before the delivery of food (US), and these pairings are continued over time, the dog will begin to salivate (CR) whenever the bell (CS) is struck (see ▌ Figure 7.2). A connection is formed because the bell provides *information* about the delivery of the food—the dog knows that food will be arriving soon after it hears the bell. This rule helps to explain a number of experimental findings.

First, for an effective association to form, the conditioned stimulus usually needs to be presented *before* the unconditioned stimulus. If the two are presented at the same time (*simultaneous conditioning*), or if the conditioned stimulus is presented *after* the unconditioned stimulus (*backward conditioning*), not much, if any, conditioning will occur. In both cases the conditioned stimulus provides no information about when the unconditioned stimulus will appear, so conditioned responding does not develop. There are some exceptions to this general rule (Cole & Miller, 1999; Rescorla, 1980), but usually the conditioned stimulus needs to be presented first, before the unconditioned stimulus, for effective conditioning.

Second, the unconditioned stimulus needs to follow the conditioned stimulus *closely in time*. Pavlov found that if there was a long delay between when the bell (CS) was struck and the delivery of the food (US), his dogs usually didn't form a connection between the bell and the food. As the gap between presentation of the conditioned stimulus and the unconditioned stimulus increases, one becomes a less efficient signal for the arrival of the other—that is, the conditioned stimulus provides less useful information about the appearance of the unconditioned stimulus. Once again, there are important exceptions to the rule, but they need not concern us here (see Gallistel & Gibbon, 2000). (For one exception, take a look at the Practical Solutions feature on the following page.)

Finally, the conditioned stimulus must provide *new* information about the unconditioned stimulus. If you already know when the unconditioned stimulus will

Taste Aversions

On St. Thomas in the Virgin Islands, researchers Lowell Nicolaus and David Nellis encouraged captured mongooses to eat eggs laced with carbachol, a drug that produces temporary illness. After five days of eating eggs and getting sick, the mongooses reduced their consumption of eggs by about 37% (Nicolaus & Nellis, 1987). In a very different context, in a research program designed to combat the negative effects of chemotherapy, young cancer patients were allowed a taste of some unusually flavored ice cream just before the onset of their normal chemotherapy—a treatment that typically produces nausea and vomiting. Several weeks later, when offered the ice cream, only 21% of the children were willing to taste it again (Bernstein, 1978).

Both of these situations represent naturalistic applications of classical conditioning. Can you identify the critical features of

each? First, let's look for the unconditioned stimulus—the stimulus that unconditionally produces a response prior to training. In both of these cases, the unconditioned stimulus is the illness-producing event, either the drug carbachol or the cancer-fighting chemotherapy. The response that is automatically produced, unfortunately for the participants, is stomach distress. Children don't need to learn to vomit from chemotherapy; a mongoose doesn't need to be taught to be sick after receiving carbachol. These are inevitable consequences that require no prior conditioning.

Now what is the conditioned stimulus—the event that provides information about the occurrence of the unconditioned stimulus? In these examples, it's the taste of the food, either the eggs or the ice cream, that signals the later onset of nausea. It's worth noting that the children were aware that their nausea

was produced by the chemotherapy, not the ice cream, yet an association was still formed between the taste of the ice cream and a procedure that led to sickness. A conditioned response, feelings of queasiness to the food, was produced whenever the opportunity to eat was presented. Taste aversions are easy to acquire. They often occur after a single pairing of a novel food and illness.

It is extremely adaptive for people and mongooses to acquire taste aversions to potentially dangerous foods—it is in their interest to avoid those events that signal something potentially harmful. In the two studies we've just considered, the researchers investigated the aversions for a particular reason. Mongooses often eat the eggs of endangered species (such as marine turtles). By baiting the nests of mongoose prey with tainted eggs and establishing a taste aversion, scientists have been able to reduce the overall rate of egg predation. Similar techniques have also been used to prevent sheep from eating dangerous plants in the pasture (Zahorik, Houpt, & Swartzman-Andert, 1990).

In the case of chemotherapy, Illene Bernstein was interested in developing methods for avoiding the establishment of taste aversions: Cancer patients who are undergoing chemotherapy also need to eat, so it's critical to understand the conditions under which aversions are formed. Taste aversions often develop as a side effect of chemotherapy. Patients tend to avoid foods that they've consumed just before treatment, potentially leading to weight loss that impedes recovery. Researchers have found that associations are particularly likely to form between unusual tastes and nausea. Broberg and Bernstein (1987) found that giving children an unusual flavor of candy just before treatment reduced the likelihood of their forming aversions to their normal diet. These children formed a taste aversion to the candy instead. Another helpful technique is to ask the patient to eat the same, preferably bland, foods before every treatment. Foods that do not have distinctive tastes and that people eat regularly (such as bread) are less likely to become aversive.

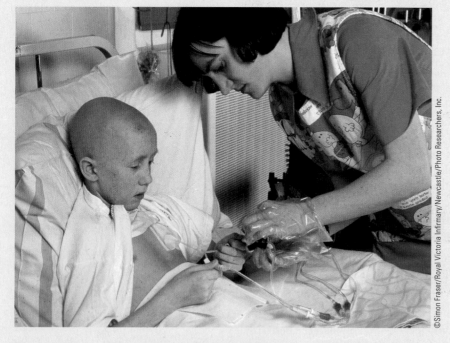

For children undergoing the rigors of chemotherapy, like this boy suffering from leukemia, it's important to prevent taste aversions from developing as a negative side effect. Broberg and Bernstein (1987) found that giving children candy with an unusual flavor just before treatment reduced the chances of a taste aversion forming.

occur, then adding another stimulus that predicts it will lead to little, if any, evidence of conditioning. Suppose you teach some rats that a tone is a reliable signal for an electric shock. Once the rats have begun to freeze when they hear the tone (a typical conditioned response to the expectation of shock), you start turning on a light at the same time as you present the tone. Both the light and the tone are then followed by the shock. Under these conditions, rats typically don't learn that the light is also a reliable signal for the shock (e.g., Kamin, 1968). This result is called *blocking* because the tone appears to prevent, or block, the animal from learning about the light. Blocking occurs because the light provides no new information about the shock—the tone already tells the rat the shock is about to occur—so the animal fails to treat it as a significant signal.

Conditioned Responding: Why Does It Develop?

Forming an association between the conditioned stimulus and the unconditioned stimulus—that is, that one signals the appearance of the other—doesn't really explain conditioned responding. Why should dogs drool to a bell that signals food or rats freeze to a tone that predicts shock? One possibility is that conditioned responses prepare the organism for events that are expected to follow; conditioned responses help the organism interact with the US, which is usually some kind of biologically significant event (Domjan, 2005). Drooling readies the dog to receive food in its mouth, and "freezing" lowers the chances that any predators will see the rat. Because the conditioned stimulus tells the animal that a significant event is about to occur, it responds in a way that's appropriate for the upcoming event.

It was once commonly believed that the pairing of the conditioned stimulus and the unconditioned stimulus simply caused the unconditioned response to "shift" to the conditioned stimulus. Pavlov was convinced, for example, that the conditioned stimulus acts as a kind of substitute for the unconditioned stimulus—you respond to the conditioned stimulus as if it were essentially identical to the unconditioned stimulus. However, this suggests that the conditioned response should always be identical, or at least highly similar, to the unconditioned response. Dogs should always drool to a stimulus that predicts the arrival of food; rats should jump to a stimulus that predicts shock because they usually jump when they're actually shocked. But as you've seen, rats will freeze rather than jump to a signal predicting shock.

The form of the conditioned response depends on many factors. In general, the idea that classical conditioning turns the conditioned stimulus into a substitute for the unconditioned stimulus—or that organisms simply learn to respond to the conditioned stimulus in the same way that they automatically respond to the unconditioned stimulus—is misleading or wrong. Robert Rescorla (1988) put it this way: "Pavlovian conditioning is not the shifting of a response from one stimulus to another. Instead, conditioning involves the learning of relations among events that are complexly represented, a learning that can be exhibited in various ways" (p. 158). This perspective is known as the *cognitive view* of classical conditioning, and it remains widely accepted by current researchers (Holland & Ball, 2003).

Concept Review | Factors Affecting Classical Conditioning

FACTOR	RELATION TO CONDITIONING EFFECTIVENESS
Timing relationship between CS and US	The CS should usually be presented before the US. The US should usually follow the CS closely in time.
Informativeness of CS	The CS should uniquely predict the US. The CS should provide new information about the occurrence of the US (blocking).

Second-Order Conditioning

second-order conditioning A procedure in which an established conditioned stimulus is used to condition a second neutral stimulus.

Pavlov also discovered that conditioned stimuli possess a variety of properties after conditioning. For example, he found that a conditioned stimulus could be used to condition a second signal. In **second-order conditioning**, an established conditioned stimulus, such as a tone that predicts food, is presented immediately after a new event, such as a light; the unconditioned stimulus itself is never actually presented. In such a case, pairing the tone with the light can be sufficient to produce conditioned responding to the light.

An example from Pavlov's laboratory helps to illustrate the procedure. One of Pavlov's associates, Dr. Frolov, first taught a dog that the sound of a ticking metronome signaled meat powder in the mouth. The dog quickly started to drool in the presence of the ticking. A black square was then presented, followed closely by the ticking. After a number of these black square–metronome pairings, even though the ticking was never followed by food powder on these trials, the dog began to drool in the presence of the black square. The dog drooled in response to the square because it signaled the ticking, which the dog had previously learned signaled the food (see ▌Figure 7.3).

The fact that conditioned stimuli can be used to condition other events greatly expands the number of situations in which classical conditioning applies. You don't need an unconditioned stimulus to be physically present to learn something about its occurrence. For example, consider the logic behind using celebrities to endorse products. Advertisers are trying to get you to form a connection between their product and feelings of pleasure or enjoyment. Most people like Tiger Woods because he's linked to something they enjoy—great skill on the golf course. If a product, such as a

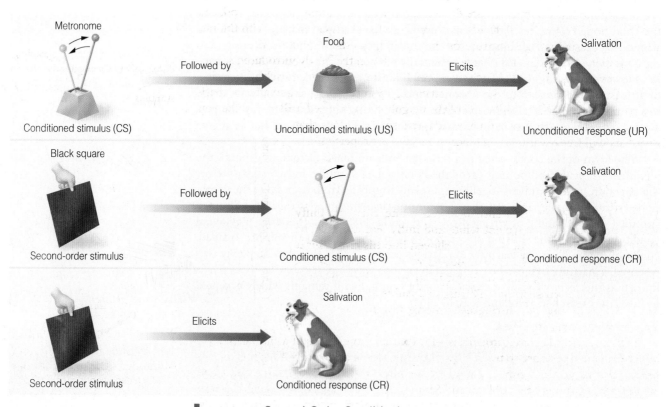

▌**FIGURE 7.3** Second-Order Conditioning

In second-order conditioning, an established CS is used in place of a US to condition a second signal. In Dr. Frolov's experiment, a ticking metronome was first paired with food; after repeated pairings, the ticking elicited salivation as a CR. Next, a black square—which did not produce salivation initially—was paired with the ticking (no US was presented). After repeated pairings, the presentation of the black square began to produce salivation.

new automobile, is repeatedly paired with Tiger, you're likely also to associate it with pleasurable consequences—the product becomes a signal for something that leads to enjoyment. This is a kind of second-order conditioning, and it's been used for decades in the marketplace.

Stimulus Generalization

Pavlov also noticed that conditioned responses tended to generalize to other, related events. If a tone of a particular pitch was established as a signal for food, other similar-sounding tones also produced drooling—even though they had never actually been presented. When a new stimulus produces a response similar to the one produced by the conditioned stimulus, it's called **stimulus generalization**.

Stimulus generalization is aptly demonstrated in a famous study by the behaviorist John Watson and his colleague Rosalie Rayner circa 1920. Watson and Rayner were interested in applying the principles of classical conditioning to a human—in this case to 11-month-old infant known as Little Albert. They presented Albert with a white rat (the conditioned stimulus), which he initially liked, followed quickly by a very loud noise (the unconditioned stimulus), which he did not like. The loud noise, not surprisingly, produced a strong, automatic fear reaction: Albert cried (the unconditioned response). After several pairings of the rat with the noise, Albert began to pucker his face, whimper, and try to withdraw his body (all conditioned responses) immediately at the sight of the rat. (By the way, psychologists now rightly question the ethics of this experiment.) But Albert didn't just cry at the sight of the rat. His crying generalized to other stimuli—a rabbit, a fur coat, a package of cotton, a dog, and even a Santa Claus mask. These stimuli, which all contained white furry elements, had been presented to Albert before the conditioning session, and none had produced crying. Albert cried at the sight of them now because of his experience with the rat; he generalized his crying response from the white rat to the other stimuli.

As a rule, you'll find stimulus generalization when the newly introduced stimulus is similar to the conditioned stimulus (see ▌ Figure 7.4). If you get sick after eating clams, there's a good chance you'll avoid eating oysters; if you've had a bad experience in the dentist's chair, the sound of the neighbor's high-speed drill may make you uncomfortable. Generalization makes adaptive sense: Things that look, sound, or feel the same often share significant properties.

stimulus generalization Responding to a new stimulus in a way similar to the response produced by an established conditioned stimulus.

stimulus discrimination Responding differently to a new stimulus than how one responds to an established conditioned stimulus.

Stimulus Discrimination

Albert did notice the difference between white furry or fluffy things and things that were not white and fluffy. For example, he didn't cry when a block of wood was shoved into his crib. This is called **stimulus discrimination**; it occurs when you respond to a new stimulus in a way that's different from your response to the original conditioned stimulus. Through stimulus discrimination, you reveal that you can distinguish among stimuli, even when those stimuli share properties.

When stimuli do share properties—for example, two tones of a similar pitch— we often need experience to teach us to discriminate. The natural tendency is to generalize, that is, to treat similar things in the same way. Albert could certainly tell the difference among rats, rabbits, and Santa Claus masks; what he needed to learn was which of those white furry things signaled the unfortunate noise. In many cases, the development of stimulus discrimination requires that one directly experience whether or not the unconditioned stimulus will follow a particular event. If event A is followed by the unconditioned stimulus but event B is not, then you learn to discriminate between these two events and respond accordingly.

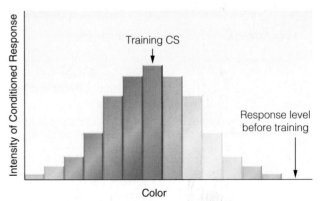

▌ **FIGURE 7.4** Stimulus Generalization After conditioned responding to a CS is established, similar events will often also produce conditioned responding through stimulus generalization. For example, if a red light is trained as a CS, then similar colors that were not explicitly trained will also produce responding if tested. Notice that the less similar the test stimulus is to the training CS, the less generalization occurs.

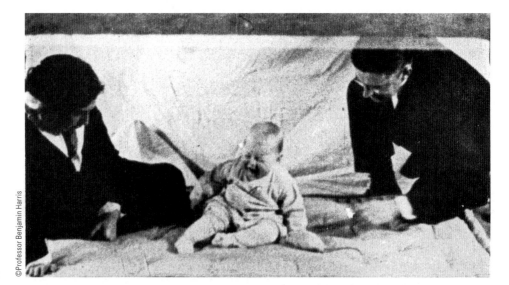

This still from a 1920 film shows Little Albert reacting with dismay to a white rat that had previously been paired with a very unpleasant noise. On the right is behavioral psychologist John Watson; to the left of Albert is Watson's colleague, Rosalie Rayner.

©Professor Benjamin Harris

Extinction: When the CS No Longer Signals the US

extinction Presenting a conditioned stimulus repeatedly, after conditioning, without the unconditioned stimulus, resulting in a loss in responding.

Remember our general rule: A conditioned stimulus becomes a good signal when it provides information about the occurrence of the unconditioned stimulus. But what happens if the conditioned stimulus stops signaling the appearance of an unconditioned stimulus? In the procedure of **extinction**, the conditioned stimulus is presented repeatedly, after conditioning, but it is no longer followed by the unconditioned stimulus. Under these conditions, the conditioned stimulus loses its signaling properties, and conditioned responding gradually diminishes as a result. So if a dog drools to a bell that predicts food, and we suddenly stop delivering the food after striking the bell, the dog will eventually stop drooling.

Concept Review | Major Phenomena of Classical Conditioning

PHENOMENON	DESCRIPTION	PAVLOV'S DOGS
Second-order conditioning	An established CS is presented immediately after a new event; after several pairings, this new event may come to elicit a response.	After a dog has been conditioned to salivate in response to a CS (tone), the CS is presented immediately after a new signal (e.g., a light). After several pairings, the light may come to elicit a response.
Stimulus generalization	A new stimulus produces a response similar to the one produced by the conditioned stimulus.	After a dog has been conditioned to salivate in response to a CS (e.g., a bright light), the same response may be produced by a similar stimulus (e.g., a dimmer light).
Stimulus discrimination	The response to a new stimulus is different from the response to the original CS.	After a dog has been conditioned to salivate in response to a CS (light), the response does not occur to a different stimulus, such as a ringing bell.
Acquisition	Conditioned responding becomes stronger with repeated CS–US pairings.	The more times a dog hears the stimulus (tone) paired with the US (food), the stronger the conditioned response becomes.
Extinction	Conditioned responding diminishes when the CS (after conditioning) is presented repeatedly without the US.	After a dog has been conditioned to salivate in response to a CS (tone), the tone is presented repeatedly without the US (food). The dog's response to the CS lessens.
Spontaneous recovery	Conditioned responding that has disappeared in extinction is recovered spontaneously with the passage of time.	After extinction, a dog no longer responds to the CS (tone). After a rest period, the dog will again respond when presented with the CS (tone).

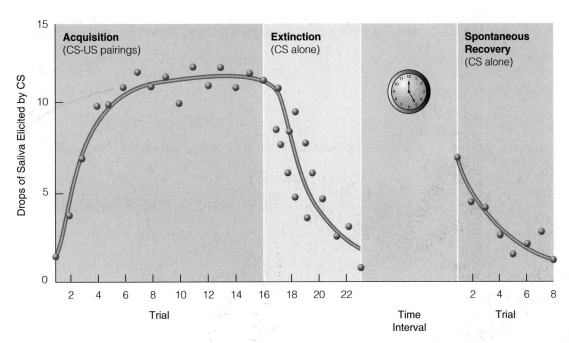

FIGURE 7.5 Training, Extinction, and Spontaneous Recovery During training, Pavlov found that the amount of salivation produced in response to the CS initially increased and then leveled off as a function of the number of CS–US pairings. During extinction, the CS is repeatedly presented without the US, and conditioned responding gradually diminishes. If no testing of the CS occurs for a rest interval following extinction, spontaneous recovery of the CR will often occur if the CS is presented again.

It's sensible for us to change our behavior during extinction because we're learning something new—the conditioned stimulus no longer predicts the unconditioned stimulus. Yet Pavlov discovered an interesting twist: If you wait a while after extinction and present the conditioned stimulus again, sometimes the conditioned response reappears. **Spontaneous recovery** is the recovery of an extinguished response when the conditioned stimulus is presented again, after a delay (see the far right panel in ▌Figure 7.5). In Pavlov's case, his dogs stopped drooling if a bell signaling food was repeatedly presented alone, but when the bell was rung again the day after extinction, the conditioned response reappeared (although often not as strongly). No one is certain exactly why spontaneous recovery occurs, but it tells us that behavior, or performance, isn't always a perfect indicator of what is known or remembered. At the end of extinction, the conditioned stimulus can seem to have lost its signaling properties, but when it is tested after a delay, we see that at least some of the learning remained (Bouton, 2007).

Conditioned Inhibition: Signaling the Absence of the US

During extinction, you learn that a conditioned stimulus no longer predicts the appearance of the unconditioned stimulus. As a result, you stop responding to a stimulus that once elicited a response because you no longer anticipate that the unconditioned stimulus will follow. You've not forgotten about the unconditioned stimulus. Instead you've learned something new: A conditioned stimulus that used to signal the unconditioned stimulus no longer does (Rescorla, 2001).

In **conditioned inhibition**, you learn that an event signals the *absence* of the unconditioned stimulus. There are a variety of ways to create an inhibitory stimulus, but most involve presenting a new stimulus when the unconditioned stimulus is normally expected but is not delivered (Williams, Overmier, & LoLordo, 1992). For example, if dogs are currently drooling to a bell that predicts food, then putting the bell together with a light and then following this compound (bell + light) with no food will establish the light as a conditioned inhibitor for food. The animal learns that when the light is turned on, food does not follow the bell.

What change in behavior is produced by a stimulus that predicts the absence of something? Inhibitory learning can be expressed in various ways, but often you get a reaction that is the *opposite* of that produced by a normal conditioned stimulus.

spontaneous recovery The recovery of an extinguished conditioned response after a period of nonexposure to the conditioned stimulus.

conditioned inhibition Learning that an event signals the absence of the unconditioned stimulus.

Keylight signaling food

Food hopper

a

Keylight signaling no food

b

FIGURE 7.6

Conditioned Inhibition
In conditioned inhibition the CS provides information about the absence of the US. Pigeons will approach and peck at a keylight CS that signals the appearance of food (upper panel), but they will withdraw from a keylight CS signaling no food (lower panel). Notice that the withdrawal response is an indication that the red light has become a conditioned inhibitor—a CS that predicts the absence of food.

For example, if a conditioned stimulus signaling food produces an increase in responding, then an inhibitory conditioned stimulus will lead to a decrease in the normal amount of responding. Several experiments have shown that pigeons and dogs will approach a signal predicting food but will withdraw from a stimulus signaling its absence (see ▌Figure 7.6; Hearst & Franklin, 1977; Jenkins et al., 1978).

The conditions required for establishing the presence of conditioned inhibition are complex and need not concern us here, but it's important to appreciate the value of an inhibitory signal. It's just as adaptive to know that a significant event will not occur as it is to know that the event will occur. For example, every kid knows there are bullies on the playground. The sight of troublemaker Randy might usually make Kelley quake with fear—but not if there's a teacher around. The teacher signals the absence of a negative event—Randy won't be causing any trouble while the teacher is present. Inhibitory stimuli often act as "safety signals," telling people when potentially dangerous events are likely to be absent or when dangerous conditions no longer apply.

Test Yourself 7.2

Check your knowledge about classical conditioning by answering the following questions. (You will find the answers in the Appendix.)

1. Growing up, your little sister Leah had the annoying habit of screaming at the top of her lungs every time she stepped into her bathwater. Her screaming always made you wince and cover your ears. Now, years later, you still wince every time you hear running water. Identify these elements of behavior:
   a. Unconditioned stimulus: _____
   b. Unconditioned response: _____
   c. Conditioned stimulus: _____
   d. Conditioned response: _____

2. Every year when you visit the optometrist, you get a puff of air blown into your eye to test for glaucoma. It always makes you blink. Just before the puff is delivered, the doctor typically asks you if you're "ready." Now, whenever you hear that word, you feel an urge to blink. Identify these elements of behavior:
   a. Unconditioned stimulus: _____
   b. Unconditioned response: _____
   c. Conditioned stimulus: _____
   d. Conditioned response: _____

3. People often wonder whether Little Albert, the subject in the Watson and Rayner experiment, grew up filled with fear and anxiety. Suppose I told you that he suffered no long-term effects from the experiment and, in fact, later grew his own fluffy white beard. Which of the following probably best accounts for his normal development?
   a. Conditioned inhibition
   b. Stimulus generalization
   c. Spontaneous recovery
   d. Extinction

Learning About the Consequences of Behavior: Operant Conditioning

LEARNING GOALS

- Define operant conditioning and discuss the law of effect.
- Explain what we mean by the discriminative stimulus.
- Define reinforcement and punishment and distinguish between their positive and negative forms.
- Discuss and compare the different schedules of reinforcement.
- Explain how complex behaviors can be acquired through shaping.
- Discuss how biological factors might limit the responses that can be learned.

CLASSICAL CONDITIONING ANSWERS an important survival question: How do we learn that certain events signal the presence or the absence of other events? Through classical conditioning, we learn to expect that certain events will or will not occur, at certain times, and we react accordingly. But our actions under these conditions typically don't have any effect on the presentation of the signal and the unconditioned stimulus. Usually, occurrences of the conditioned stimulus and the unconditioned stimulus are outside our control. For example, you can't change the fact that thunder will follow lightning; all you can do is prepare for an event (thunder) when a prior event (lightning) tells you it's coming.

In another type of learning, studied through a procedure called **operant conditioning** (or *instrumental conditioning*), we learn that our own *actions*, rather than conditioned stimuli, lead to outcomes. If you study for hours and hours for an exam and receive an A, you learn that your behavior is *instrumental* in producing a top-notch grade; by *operating* on your environment, you have produced a pleasing consequence. Notice how classical conditioning differs from operant conditioning: In the former you learn that events signal outcomes; in the latter you learn that your own actions produce outcomes (see ▌ Figure 7.7).

operant conditioning A procedure for studying how organisms learn about the consequences of their own voluntary actions (also called instrumental conditioning).

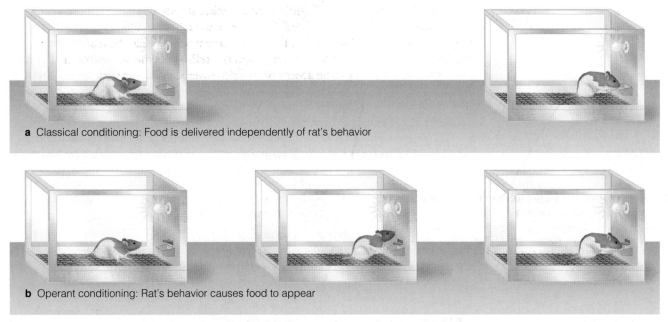

a Classical conditioning: Food is delivered independently of rat's behavior

b Operant conditioning: Rat's behavior causes food to appear

▌ **FIGURE 7.7** Classical Versus Operant Conditioning
In classical conditioning (top row), food is delivered independently of the rat's behavior. The light CS signals the automatic arrival of the food US. In operant conditioning (bottom row), the rat must press the bar in the presence of the light to get the food. The light serves as a discriminative stimulus, indicating that pressing the bar will now produce the food.

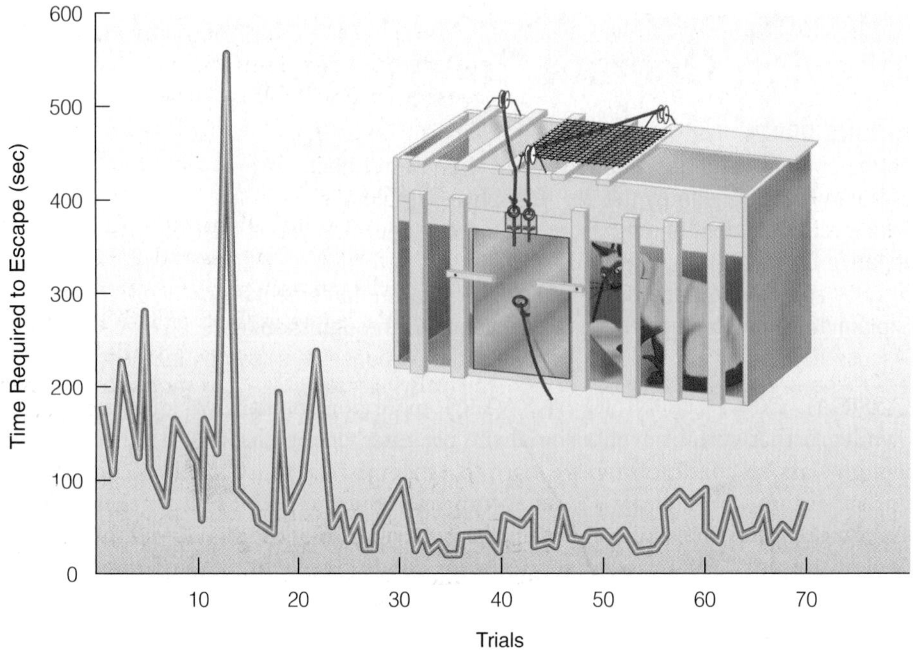

FIGURE 7.8 Operant Conditioning
In Thorndike's famous experiments on animal intelligence, cats learned that some kinds of unusual responses—such as pressing a lever or tilting a pole—allowed them to escape from a puzzle box. The graph shows that the time required to escape gradually diminished over learning trials. Here the cat is learning that its behavior is instrumental in producing escape. (Based on Weiten, 1995)

law of effect If a response in a particular situation is followed by a satisfying consequence, it will be strengthened. If a response in a particular situation is followed by an unsatisfying consequence, it will be weakened.

The Law of Effect

The study of operant conditioning predates Pavlov's historic work by several years. In 1895 Harvard graduate student Edward Lee Thorndike (1874–1949), working in the cellar of his mentor William James, began a series of experiments on "animal intelligence" using cats from around the neighborhood. He built a puzzle box, which resembled a kind of tiny prison, and carefully recorded the time it took for the cats to escape. The boxes were designed so that escape was possible only through an unusual response, such as tilting a pole, pulling a string, or pressing a lever (see ▌Figure 7.8). On release, the cats received a small amount of food as a reward. Thorndike specifically selected escape responses that were unlikely to occur when the animals were first placed in the box. In this way he could observe how the cats learned to escape over time. Through trial and error, the cats eventually learned to make the appropriate response, but the learning process was gradual. Thorndike also found that the time it took for an animal to escape on any particular trial depended on the number of prior successful escapes. The more times the animal had successfully escaped in the past, the faster it could get out of the box on a new trial.

The relationship between escape time and the number of prior successful escapes led Thorndike to formulate the **law of effect**: If a response in a particular situation is followed by a satisfying or pleasant consequence, then the connection between the response and that situation will be strengthened; if a response in a particular situation is followed by an unsatisfying or unpleasant consequence, the connection will be weakened. According to the law of effect, all organisms learn to make certain responses in certain situations; the responses that regularly occur are those that have produced positive consequences in the past. If a response tends to occur initially (e.g., scratching at the walls of the cage) but is not followed by something good (such as freedom from the box), the chances of that same response reoccurring diminish.

The Discriminative Stimulus: Knowing When to Respond

It's important to understand that the law of effect applies only to responses that are rewarded in particular situations. If you are praised for raising your hand in class and asking an intelligent question, you're not likely to begin walking down the street repeatedly raising your hand. You understand that raising your hand is rewarded only in a particular situation, namely, the classroom lecture. What you really learn is the following: If some stimulus situation is present (the classroom), and you act in a certain way (raising your hand), then some consequence will follow (praise).

B. F. Skinner (1938) referred to the stimulus situation as the **discriminative stimulus**. He suggested that a discriminative stimulus "sets the occasion" for a response to be rewarded. Being in class—the discriminative stimulus—sets the occasion for question-asking to be rewarded. In some ways, the discriminative stimulus shares properties with the conditioned stimulus established in classical conditioning. For example, you often find *stimulus generalization* of a discriminative stimulus: If a pigeon is trained to peck a key in the presence of a red light, the bird will later peck the key whenever a light of a similar color is turned on. If you're rewarded for asking questions in psychology, you might naturally generalize your response to another course, such as economics, and raise your hand there. Conversely, *stimulus discrimination* also occurs, usually after experiencing reward in one situation but not in another. You may learn, for instance, that raising your hand in psychology class leads to positive consequences but that a similar behavior in your economics class is frowned on by the professor. In such a case, one setting (psychology) acts as an effective discriminative stimulus for a certain response, but another setting (economics) does not.

discriminative stimulus The stimulus situation that sets the occasion for a response to be followed by reinforcement or punishment.

The Nature of Reinforcement

The law of effect states that responses will be strengthened if they are followed by a pleasant or satisfying consequence. By "strengthened," Thorndike meant that a response was more likely to occur in the future in that particular situation. But what defines a pleasant or satisfying consequence? This is a tricky problem because the concept of a "pleasant" or "satisfying" event is highly personal—what's pleasant for me might not be pleasant for you. Moreover, something that's pleasing at one time might not be pleasing at another. Food, for example, is "positive at the beginning of Thanksgiving dinner, indifferent halfway through, and negative at the end of it" (Kimble, 1993).

For these reasons, psychologists use a technical term—**reinforcement**—to describe consequences that increase the likelihood of responding. As you'll see, it's popular to distinguish between two major types of reinforcement, *positive* and *negative*.

reinforcement Response consequences that increase the likelihood of responding in a similar way again.

Positive Reinforcement When the *presentation* of an event after a response increases the likelihood of that response occurring again, it's called **positive reinforcement**. Usually, the presented event is an *appetitive stimulus*—something the organism likes, needs, or has an "appetite" for. According to Thorndike (1911), an appetitive stimulus is "one which the animal does nothing to avoid, often doing such things as to attain or preserve it" (p. 245). Food and water are obvious examples, but responses can be reinforcing too (such as sexual activity or painting a picture). Remember, though, it's not the subjective qualities of the consequence that matter—what matters in defining positive reinforcement is an increase in a tendency to respond. As long as the consequence makes the response more likely to occur again in that situation, the consequence qualifies as positive reinforcement.

positive reinforcement An event that, when presented after a response, increases the likelihood of that response.

CRITICAL THINKING

Can you think of a case in which presenting an unpleasant event actually increases the likelihood of the response that produces it?

Negative Reinforcement When the *removal* of an event after a response increases the likelihood of the response occurring again, it's called **negative reinforcement**. In most cases negative reinforcement occurs when a response allows you to eliminate, avoid, or escape from an unpleasant situation. For instance, you hang up the phone on someone who is criticizing you unfairly, shut off the blaring alarm clock in the morning, or walk out of a boring movie. These responses are more likely to occur again in the future, given the appropriate circumstance, because they lead to the removal of something negative—criticism, noise, or boredom. But, as you may have guessed, the event that's removed doesn't have to be unpleasant—it simply has to increase the

negative reinforcement An event that, when removed after a response, increases the likelihood of that response occurring again.

Concept Review | Positive and Negative Reinforcement

CONSEQUENCE	DESCRIPTION	EXAMPLE
Positive reinforcement	The presentation of an event after a response increases the likelihood of the response occurring again.	Juan's parents reward him for cleaning his room by giving him $5. This reinforcement increases the likelihood that Juan will clean his room again.
Negative reinforcement	The removal of an event after a response increases the likelihood of the response occurring again.	Hannah's parents nag her continually about cleaning up her room. When she finally cleans her room, her parents stop nagging her. The removal of the nagging increases the probability that Hannah will clean her room again.

CRITICAL THINKING

When you study for an examination or try to do well in school, are you seeking positive reinforcement or negative reinforcement?

conditioned reinforcer A stimulus that has acquired reinforcing properties through prior learning.

punishment Consequences that decrease the likelihood of responding in a similar way again.

positive punishment An event that, when presented after a response, lowers the likelihood of that response occurring again.

likelihood of the "contingent" response (the response that led to the removal). Students are often confused by the term *negative reinforcement* because they think negative reinforcement is a bad thing. Actually, whenever psychologists use the term *reinforcement*, both positive and negative, they're referring to outcomes that increase the probability of responding. Here *positive* and *negative* simply refer to whether the response ends with the presentation of something or the removal of something. In both cases the result is rewarding, and we can expect the response that produced the reinforcement to occur again in that situation.

Conditioned Reinforcers   Sometimes a stimulus can act like a reinforcer even though it seems to have little or no direct value. For example, money serves as a satisfying consequence even though it's only a well-made piece of paper marked with interesting engravings. However, having money predicts something of value—you can buy things—and this is what gives it its reinforcing value. In the same way, if a stimulus or event predicts the absence or removal of something negative, then its presentation is also likely to be reinforcing. Stimuli of this type are called **conditioned reinforcers** because their reinforcing properties are acquired through learning (they are also sometimes called "secondary" reinforcers to distinguish them from more "primary" reinforcers such as food or water). These stimuli are reinforcing because they signal the presence or absence of other events.

Punishment: Lowering the Likelihood of a Response

Now for the dark side: *punishment*. Remember Thorndike claimed that if a response is followed by an unsatisfying or unpleasant consequence, it will be weakened. The term *punishment* is used to refer to consequences that decrease the likelihood of responding. Like reinforcement, **punishment** comes in two forms, *positive* and *negative*.

Positive Punishment   When the *presentation* of an event after a response decreases the likelihood of that response occurring again, it's called **positive punishment**. Notice, as with reinforcement, the concept is defined in terms of its effect on behavior—lowering the likelihood of responding—rather than on its subjective qualities. Often, however, positive punishment occurs when a response leads directly to the presentation of an aversive outcome. As a parent, if your child hassles the cat with her new toy, you could scold the child loudly whenever she engages in the behavior—this qualifies as positive punishment. Provided the aversive event (the scolding) is intense enough, the response that produced the punishment (hassling the cat) will tend to disappear rapidly or become *suppressed*.

Negative Punishment   When the *removal* of an event after responding lowers the likelihood of that response occurring again, it's called **negative punishment**. Instead of scolding your child for hassling the cat, you could simply take her toy away. You're removing something she likes when she engages in an inappropriate behavior—this qualifies as negative punishment. Similarly, if you withhold your child's weekly allowance because his or her room is messy, you are punishing the child by removing something good—money. As with positive punishment, negative punishment is recognized as an effective training procedure for rapidly suppressing an undesirable response.

What accounts for the rapid suppression of the response that's punished? It seems likely that people simply learn the connection between their behavior and the particular outcome. You learn about the consequences of your actions—that a particular kind of behavior will lead to a relatively unpleasant consequence. In this sense, we don't really need two different explanations to account for the behavior changes produced by reinforcement and punishment; the only major difference is that behavior increases in one situation and declines in the other. In both cases you use your knowledge about behavior and its consequences to maximize gain and minimize loss in a particular situation.

Practical Considerations   Punishment works—it's an effective technique for suppressing undesirable behavior. However, punishment isn't always the smartest way to change behavior. Sometimes it can be hard to gauge the appropriate strength of the punishing event. When the punishment is aggressive or violent, such as the forceful spanking of a child, you run the risk of hurting the child either physically or emotionally. At the same time, if a child feels ignored, yelling can actually be reinforcing because of the attention it provides. Children who spend a lot of time in the principal's office may be causing trouble partly because of the attention that the punishment produces. In such cases punishment leads to the exact opposite of the intended result (Martin & Pear, 1999; Wissow, 2002).

Moreover, punishment only suppresses a behavior; it doesn't teach the child how to act appropriately. Spanking your child for lying might reduce the lying, but

negative punishment An event that, when removed after a response, lowers the likelihood of that response occurring again.

Concept Review | Comparing Reinforcement and Punishment

REINFORCEMENT: CONSEQUENCES THAT *INCREASE* THE LIKELIHOOD OF RESPONDING

Outcome	Description	Example
Positive reinforcement	Response leads to the presentation of an event that increases the likelihood of that response occurring again.	Five-year-old Skip helps his mom do the dishes. She takes him to the store and lets him pick out any candy bar he wants. Letting Skip pick out a candy bar increases the likelihood that he'll help with the dishes again.
Negative reinforcement	Response leads to the removal of an event that increases the likelihood of that response occurring again.	Five-year-old Skip has been such a good helper all week that his mom tells him that next week he doesn't have to do any of his scheduled chores. Relieving Skip of his chores increases the likelihood that he'll be a good helper.

PUNISHMENT: CONSEQUENCES THAT *DECREASE* THE LIKELIHOOD OF RESPONDING

Outcome	Description	Example
Positive punishment	Response leads to the presentation of an event that decreases the likelihood of that response occurring again.	Five-year-old Skip runs nearly into the street; his mother pulls him back from the curb and gives him a brief tongue-lashing. This decreases the likelihood that Skip will run into the street.
Negative punishment	Response leads to the removal of an event that decreases the likelihood of that response occurring again.	Five-year-old Skip keeps teasing his 3-year-old sister at the dinner table. His mom sends him to bed without his favorite dessert. Withholding the dessert decreases the likelihood that Skip will tease his sister at the dinner table.

it won't teach the child how to deal more effectively with the social situation that led to the lie. To teach the child about more appropriate forms of behavior, you need to reinforce some kind of alternative response. You must teach the child a positive strategy for dealing with situations that can lead to lying. That's the main advantage of reinforcement over punishment: Reinforcement teaches you what you should be doing—how you should act—whereas punishment only teaches you what you shouldn't be doing.

Schedules of Reinforcement

Actions are more likely to be repeated if they're followed by positive or negative reinforcement. However, just like in classical conditioning, the development of a response in operant conditioning depends importantly on how often, and when, the reinforcements are actually delivered. People must understand that their behavior uniquely predicts the reward—if you deliver the reward in a haphazard way, or when the behavior in question has not occurred, learning can be slow or nonexistent (Miller & Grace, 2003).

A **schedule of reinforcement** is a rule used by the experimenter to determine when particular responses will be reinforced (Ferster & Skinner, 1957). If a response is followed rapidly by reinforcement every time it occurs, the reinforcement schedule is called *continuous*. If reinforcement is delivered only some of the time after the response has occurred, it's called a **partial reinforcement schedule**. There are four major types of partial reinforcement schedules: fixed-ratio, variable-ratio, fixed-interval, and variable-interval. Each produces a distinctive pattern of responding (see ▌Figure 7.9).

schedule of reinforcement A rule that an experimenter uses to determine when particular responses will be reinforced.

partial reinforcement schedule A schedule in which reinforcement is delivered only some of the time after the response has occurred.

Fixed-Ratio Schedules Ratio schedules of reinforcement require a certain number of responses before reinforcement is delivered. In a **fixed-ratio (FR) schedule**, the number of required responses is fixed and doesn't change from one trial to the next. Suppose you're paid a dollar for every 100 envelopes you stuff for a local marketing firm. This schedule of reinforcement is called an "FR 100" (fixed-ratio 100) because it requires 100 responses (envelopes stuffed) before the reinforcement is delivered (a dollar). You can stuff the envelopes as quickly as you like, but you must produce 100 responses before you get the reward.

Fixed-ratio schedules typically produce steady, consistent rates of responding because the relationship between the response and the reinforcement is clear and predictable. For this reason, assembly-line work in factories is often reinforced on a fixed-ratio schedule. The only behavioral quirk occurs when the number of required responses is relatively large. For example, if you have to pick 10 bushels of grapes for each monetary reward, you're likely to pause a bit in your responding immediately after the tenth bushel. This delay in responding after reinforcement is called the *postreinforcement pause*. Pausing after reinforcement is easy to understand in this situation—after all, you have to do a lot of work before you receive the next reward.

fixed-ratio (FR) schedule A schedule in which the number of responses required for reinforcement is fixed and does not change.

Variable-Ratio Schedules A **variable-ratio (VR) schedule** also requires that you make a certain number of responses before reinforcement. (This is the defining feature of a ratio schedule.) However, with a variable-ratio schedule, the required number can change from trial to trial. Reinforcement might be delivered after the first response on trial 1, after the seventh response on trial 2, after the third response on trial 3, and so on. It's called a variable-ratio schedule because the responder doesn't know how many responses are needed to obtain the reward (that is, the number of responses varies, often in a random fashion).

In a variable-ratio schedule, unlike a fixed-ratio schedule, you can never predict which response will get you the reward. As a result, these schedules typically pro-

variable-ratio (VR) schedule A schedule in which a certain number of responses are required for reinforcement, but the number of required responses typically changes.

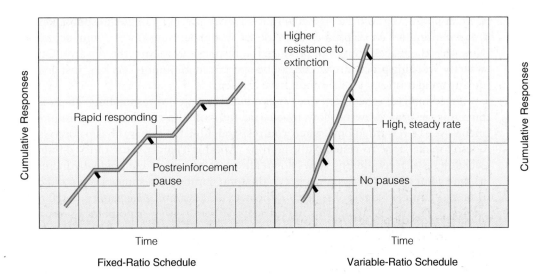

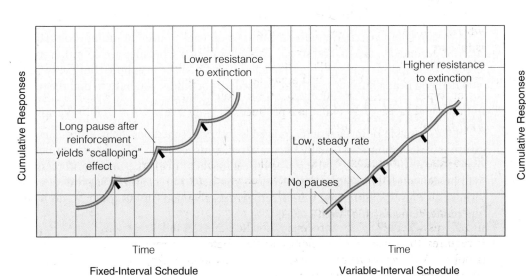

FIGURE 7.9 Schedules of Reinforcement
Schedules of reinforcement are rules that the experimenter uses to determine when responses will be reinforced. Ratio schedules tend to produce rapid rates of responding because reinforcement depends on the number of responses. Interval schedules tend to produce lower rates of responding because reinforcement is delivered only for the first response after a specified time interval. In the cumulative response functions plotted here, the total number of responses is plotted over time.

duce high rates of responding, and the postreinforcement pause, seen in fixed-ratio schedules, is usually absent (after all, the next response might get you the reward again). Gambling is an example of a variable-ratio schedule; because of chance factors, a gambler wins some bets and loses others, but the gambler never knows what to expect on a given bet.

The unpredictability of reward during a variable-ratio schedule makes it difficult to eliminate a response trained on this schedule when the response is no longer reinforced. Consider the typical compulsive slot machine player: Dollar after dollar goes into the machine; sometimes there's a payoff, more often not. Even if the machine breaks and further payments are never delivered (thus placing the responder on *extinction*), many gamblers would continue playing long into the night. On a variable-ratio schedule, it's hard to see that reinforcements are no longer being delivered because you can never predict when reinforcement will occur.

Fixed-Interval Schedules In interval schedules of reinforcement, the reward is delivered for the first response that occurs following a certain interval of time; in a **fixed-interval (FI) schedule**, this time period remains constant from one trial to the

fixed-interval (FI) schedule A schedule in which the reinforcement is delivered for the first response that occurs following a fixed interval of time.

next. Suppose we reward a pigeon with food when it pecks a lighted response key after two minutes have elapsed. In this case we would be using an "FI 2 min" schedule. Note that the pigeon must still produce the response to receive the reward. (Otherwise the learning procedure would not be operant conditioning.) Pecking just doesn't do any good until at least 2 minutes have elapsed.

Fixed-interval schedules typically produce low rates of responding. There is no direct association between how much you respond and the delivery of reinforcement—you're rewarded only when you respond after the interval has passed—so it doesn't make sense to respond all the time. Another characteristic of fixed-interval schedules is that responding slows down after reinforcement and gradually increases as the end of the interval approaches. If the total number of responses is plotted over time in a cumulative response record, the net effect is a *scalloping* pattern of the type shown in Figure 7.9. Again, this makes adaptive sense—there's no point in responding immediately after reinforcement; you should only start responding when you think the interval has passed.

variable-interval (VI) schedule A schedule in which the allotted time before a response will yield reinforcement varies from trial to trial.

Variable-Interval Schedules In a **variable-interval (VI) schedule**, the critical time interval changes from trial to trial. For example, reinforcement might be delivered for a response occurring after 2 minutes on trial 1, after 10 minutes on trial 2, after 30 seconds on trial 3, and so on. Variable-interval schedules are common in everyday life. Suppose you're trying to reach someone on the telephone, but every time you dial you hear a busy signal. To be rewarded, you know you have to dial the number and that a certain amount of time has to elapse, but you're not sure exactly how long you need to wait.

shaping A procedure in which reinforcement is delivered for successive approximations of the desired response.

Like variable-ratio schedules, variable-interval schedules help eliminate the pause in responding that usually occurs after reinforcement. The rate of extinction also tends to be slower because it's never clear when (or if) the next reinforcement will be delivered. For responding to cease, you need to recognize that the relationship between responding and reinforcement has changed—that's tough to do when the reinforcements aren't predictable.

Shaping: Acquiring Complex Behaviors

It is possible to produce unusual behaviors in animals through shaping—reinforcements are delivered for successive approximations of a desired behavior. These rabbits are in the early stages of training for an advertisement that featured them popping out of top hats (circa 1952).

Reinforcement schedules are fine and good, but how do you train a response that never occurs in the first place? For example, suppose you wanted to teach your dog to sit or shake hands—how do you reward your dog for sitting if the dog never sits on command? Most people simply yell "Sit," push the dog's bottom down, and then stuff a food reward in its mouth. Under these conditions, though, you're not really establishing the proper relationship between the dog's own behavior and the delivery of a reward. You've actually set up a kind of classical conditioning procedure—the dog is taught that having his bottom pushed downward is a *signal* for an inviting unconditioned stimulus (food). This might work, but it doesn't teach the animal that its own behavior is instrumental in producing the outcome.

To solve this problem, Skinner (1938) developed a procedure called **shaping**, in which reinforcement is delivered for successive *approximations* to the desired response. Instead of waiting for the complete response—

Concept Review | Schedules of Reinforcement

TYPE OF SCHEDULE	DESCRIPTION	EXAMPLE	EFFECT ON BEHAVIOR
Continuous	Every response is followed rapidly by reinforcement.	Every time Duane cleans his room, his parents give him $1.	Leads to fast acquisition of response, but response is easily extinguished.
Partial	Response is followed by reinforcement only some of the time.	Sometimes Duane gets $1 after he cleans his room.	Acquisition is slower, but learned response is more resistant to extinction.
• fixed-ratio	The number of responses required for reinforcement is fixed.	Duane gets $1 every third time he cleans his room.	Duane cleans his room consistently with a pause in cleaning after each $1; he stops quickly if reward stops.
• variable-ratio	The number of responses required for reinforcement varies.	Duane gets $1 after cleaning his room a certain number of times, but the exact number varies.	Duane cleans his room consistently with few pauses; he continues to clean his room even if the reward isn't delivered for a while.
• fixed-interval	Reinforcement is delivered for the first response after a fixed interval of time.	Every Tuesday, Duane's parents give him $1 if his room is clean.	Duane doesn't do much cleaning until Tuesday is approaching; he stops quickly if reward stops.
• variable-interval	Reinforcement is delivered for the first response after a variable interval of time.	On some random weekday, Duane gets $1 if his room is clean.	Duane cleans his room consistently and doesn't stop even if the reward isn't delivered for a while.

here, sitting to the command "Sit"—you reinforce some part of the response that is likely to occur initially. For instance, you might reward your dog for simply approaching when you say, "Sit." As each part of the response is acquired, you become stricter in your criterion for what constitutes a successful response sequence. Skinner and others have shown that incredibly complex sequences of behavior can be acquired using the successive approximation technique of shaping.

Biological Constraints on Learning

Is it really possible to teach any response, in any situation, provided you have enough time and a reinforcer that works? Probably not. Many psychologists believe there are biological constraints, perhaps based on the genetic code, that limit the responses that can be taught. Thorndike, in his early studies of cats in puzzle boxes, noted that it was basically impossible to increase the probability of yawning or of certain reflexive scratching responses in cats through the application of reinforcement.

Similar observations were reported later by animal trainers Keller and Marion Breland (1961). The Brelands, who were former students of B. F. Skinner, encountered some interesting difficulties while attempting to train a variety of species to make certain responses. In one case, they tried to train a pig to drop large wooden coins into a piggy bank (for a bank commercial). They followed the shaping procedure, where successive approximations of the desired sequence are reinforced, but they could not get the pig to complete the response. The animal would pick up the coin and begin to lumber toward the bank but would stop midway and begin "rooting" the coins along the ground. Despite applying punishment and nonreinforcement of the rooting response, the Brelands could never completely eliminate the response. They encountered similar problems trying to teach a raccoon to put coins in a bank.

In the cases of the pig and the raccoon, biological tendencies connected with feeding and food reinforcement interfered with the learning of certain response sequences. Pigs root in connection with feeding, and raccoons rub and dunk objects related to food (Domjan, 2003). These natural tendencies are adaptive responses for the animals—at least with respect to feeding—but they may limit what the animals can be taught.

In other cases, people and animals may be predisposed to learn relationships between certain stimuli and outcomes. For example, the delay between experiencing a distinctive taste (such as clam pizza) and subsequent illness can be quite long (hours), yet we're still quite likely to form an aversion to the taste (Garcia & Koelling, 1966). We may also be naturally predisposed to learn about and recognize potential predators in our environment, such as snakes. In a classical conditioning procedure, we quickly learn to associate pictures of snakes with aversive events (e.g., shock)—much more quickly, in fact, than we do to nonthreatening events, such as pictures of flowers (Öhman & Mineka, 2001). Some psychologists believe that we have special circuitry in the brain, acquired through evolution, that helps us process and learn about stimuli related to survival threats (Öhman & Mineka, 2003).

Practical Solutions

Superstitious Behavior

Have you ever noticed the odd behavior of a professional baseball player as he approaches the batter's box? He kicks the dirt (a fixed number of times), adjusts his helmet, hitches up his trousers, grimaces, swings toward the pitcher a few times, and adopts a characteristic crouch. Basketball players, as they prepare to make a free throw, endlessly caress the ball with their hands, bounce it a certain number of times, crouch, pause, and release. Such regular patterns are a player's signature—you can identify who's in the batter's box or up at the line by watching these ritualistic preparation patterns.

Let's analyze these behaviors from the perspective of operant conditioning. According to the law of effect, these odd patterns of behavior must have been reinforced—they occurred, perhaps by chance, and were followed by a reward (a hit or a successful free throw). But because the pairing of the behavior with its consequence was really accidental, psychologists refer to this kind of reinforcement as accidental or adventitious reinforcement. In the player's mind, however, a cause-and-effect link has been formed, and he acts in a similar fashion again. Once the player starts to perform the behavior on a regular basis, it's likely that the behavior will continue to be accidentally reinforced, although on a partial schedule of reinforcement. (Can you identify the particular schedule?) The result is called a superstitious act, and because of the partial schedule (a variable-ratio one), it is difficult to eliminate.

Many athletes perform odd rituals on a regular basis. This professional baseball player feels the need to put his gum on a batting helmet every time before going up to the plate. A learning theorist might argue that the player's bizarre behavior was somehow accidentally reinforced in the past, forming a superstitious cause-and-effect link between gum chewing and successful performance.

In 1948 B. F. Skinner developed an experimental procedure to mimic and gain control over the development of superstitious acts. He placed hungry pigeons in a chamber and delivered bits of food every 15 seconds, irrespective of what a bird happened to be doing at the time. In his own words:

In six out of eight cases the resulting responses were so clearly defined that two observers could agree perfectly in counting instances. One bird was conditioned to turn counterclockwise about the cage, making two or three turns between reinforcements. Another repeatedly thrust its head into one of the upper corners of the cage. A third developed a 'tossing' response, as if placing its head beneath an invisible bar and lifting it repeatedly. (Skinner, 1948, p. 168)

Remember, from the experimenter's point of view, no cause-and-effect relationship existed between these quirky behaviors and the delivery of food. Researchers since Skinner have replicated his results, but with some added caveats (Staddon & Simmelhag, 1971). For example, many of the behaviors that Skinner noted are characteristic responses that birds make in preparation for food; therefore, some of the strange behaviors Skinner observed might have been natural pigeon reactions to the expectation of being fed rather than learned responses. Nevertheless, the point Skinner made is important to remember: From the responder's point of view, illusory connections can form between behaviors and outcomes. Once these connections have been made, if the behaviors recur, they might continue to be accidentally reinforced and thus serve as the basis for the familiar forms of superstitious acts.

AP Images/Rick Silva

Test Yourself 7.3

Check your knowledge about operant conditioning by answering the following questions. (You will find the answers in the Appendix.)

1. For each of the following statements, decide which term best applies: *negative punishment, positive punishment, negative reinforcement, positive reinforcement*.
   a. Stephanie is grounded for arriving home well past her curfew: _____
   b. Greg receives a bonus of $500 for exceeding his sales goal for the year: _____
   c. Nikki gets a ticket, at double the normal rate, for exceeding the posted speed limit in a school zone: _____
   d. Little Mowrer cries all the time when her Mom is home because Mom always comforts her with a kiss and a story: _____
   e. With Dad, Mowrer is a perfect angel because crying can be followed by a stern lecture that lasts for an hour or more: _____

2. Identify the schedule of reinforcement that is at work in each of the following situations. Choose from the following: *fixed-interval, fixed-ratio, variable-interval, variable-ratio*.
   a. Rowena feels intense satisfaction after she calls the psychic hotline but only when a psychic named Darlene reads her future: _____
   b. Prana likes to visit the monster truck rally because they always have good corn dogs: _____
   c. Sinead constantly watches music television because her favorite show, *Puck Live*, comes on from time-to-time at odd hours: _____
   d. Mohamed has just joined a coffee club; he gets a free pound of gourmet coffee after the tenth pound that he buys: _____
   e. Charlie hangs around street corners for hours at a time. Occasionally, a pretty woman walks by and gives him a smile: _____

Learning From Others: Observational Learning

LEARNING GOALS

- Describe observational learning and the conditions that lead to effective modeling.
- Explain why observational learning is adaptive and discuss its practical effects.

THE WORLD WOULD BE A VERY UNPLEASANT PLACE if you could learn about the consequences of your behavior only through simple trial and error. You could learn to avoid certain foods through positive punishment, but only after eating them and experiencing an unpleasant consequence. You could learn to avoid illegal drugs, but only if you have a bad experience, such as an arrest or a risky overdose. Clearly, it's sometimes best not to undergo the actual experiences that lead to learning.

In the wild, rhesus monkeys show an adaptive fear response in the presence of snakes. Because snakes are natural predators of monkeys, it makes sense for monkeys to avoid them whenever possible. But how do you suppose that fear is originally acquired? According to a strict interpretation of the law of effect, the animal must learn its fear through some kind of direct reinforcement or punishment—that is, through trial and error. This means that a monkey would probably need to approach a snake and be bitten (or nearly bitten) before it could learn to fear the snake; unfortunately, this single learning experience is likely to be fatal much of the time. This suggests that trial-and-error learning is not always adaptive, especially when you're learning about something dangerous or potentially harmful.

Fortunately, it's possible to learn a great deal without trial and error—by simply observing the experiences of *others*. People and animals can learn from others and this kind of learning, called **observational learning**, has considerable adaptive value (Galef & Laland, 2005; Zentall, 2006). In the wild, newly weaned rats acquire food habits by eating what the older rats eat (Galef, 1985); red-winged blackbirds will

observational learning Learning by observing the experience of others.

refuse to eat a certain food if they've observed another bird getting sick after it has eaten the food (Mason & Reidinger, 1982); chimpanzees in the wild learn how to use stone tools to crack open nuts by observing older chimpanzees eating (Inoue-Nakamura & Matsuzawa, 1997). Rhesus monkeys, it turns out, acquire their fear of snakes partly through observational learning rather than through direct experience (Öhman & Mineka, 2003). They watch other monkeys in their environment showing fear in the presence of a snake and thereby acquire the tendency to show fear themselves.

Is observational learning truly a unique form of learning? This is a difficult question to answer because observational learning can be mediated by many different psychological mechanisms, such as classical conditioning. For example, watching another monkey show fear may itself be fear-inducing, which in turn can lead the monkey to associate the presence of the snake with fear (Zentall, 2006). It is unlikely that nonhuman animals truly "imitate" the behavior of others in the same way that we do, partly because most animals are unable to take the perspective of another—that is, to "see" the world from the perspective of another. However, regardless of the mechanisms involved, avoiding trial-and-error learning has clear advantages for both humans and animals.

CRITICAL THINKING

Do you think monkeys raised in captivity, such as in a zoo, will also show a strong fear of snakes?

Modeling: Learning From Others

We do know something about the conditions that produce effective observational learning in people. One important factor is the presence of a significant role model. We naturally tend to imitate, or **model**, the behavior of significant others. You probably learned a lot of things by watching your parents or your teachers—even though you may never have been aware of doing so. Research has shown that observational learning is particularly effective if the model has positive characteristics, such as attractiveness, honesty, perceived competence, and some kind of social standing (Bandura, 1986; Brewer & Wann, 1998). It's also more likely if you observe the model being rewarded for a particular action or if the model's behavior is particularly successful.

modeling The natural tendency to imitate the behavior of significant others.

In one classic study, Bandura and his colleagues showed nursery-school children a film that portrayed an adult striking, punching, and kicking a large, inflatable, upright "Bobo" doll. Afterward, when placed in a room with Bobo, many of these children imitated the adult and violently attacked the doll (Bandura et al., 1963). In addition, the chances of the children kicking the doll increased if the adult was directly praised in the film for attacking Bobo ("You're the champion!"). Bandura (1986) has claimed that the responses acquired through observational learning are especially strengthened through *vicarious reinforcement*, which occurs when the model is reinforced for an action, or weakened through *vicarious punishment*, in which the model is punished for an action. A clear parallel therefore exists between the law of effect and observational learning; the difference, of course, is that the behavior of others is being reinforced or punished rather than our own.

We naturally tend to imitate, or model, the behavior of significant others. Modeling is adaptive because it allows us to learn things without directly experiencing consequences.

Albert Bandura did much of the early pioneering work on observational learning (you'll find more discussion of his work in Chapter 12). Bandura believes that much of what we learn from an experience depends on our existing beliefs and expectations. You're unlikely to learn from a model, for example, if you believe you're incapable of ever performing the model's behavior. You can watch a great pianist or singer or athlete, but you're not likely to imitate his or her behavior if you feel you're incapable of performing the task. Our beliefs about our own abilities, which Bandura refers to as "self-efficacy," significantly shape and constrain what we gain from observational learning.

Practical Considerations

Psychologists regularly use the techniques of observational learning to improve or change unwanted behaviors. Many studies have shown that observing desirable behavior can lower unwanted or maladaptive behavior. Children have been able to reduce their fear of dental visits (Craig, 1978) or impending surgery (Melamed & Siegel, 1975) by observing films of other children effectively handling their dental or surgical anxieties. Clinical psychologists now use observational learning as a technique to deal with specific fears and as a method for promoting cooperative behavior among preschoolers (Granvold, 1994).

Observational learning has powerful consequences that are not always what we intend. Children imitate significant role models, even when the behavior lacks adaptive value.

At the same time, observational or social learning can have significant negative effects as well. For example, children witness thousands of reinforced acts of violence just by watching Saturday morning cartoons. Although causal connections between TV violence and personal aggression remain somewhat controversial (Freedman, 1988), the consensus among psychologists clearly supports a link (Anderson et al., 2003). In addition, it can be difficult for a society to overcome unproductive stereotypes if they're repeatedly portrayed through the behavior of others. Many gender-related stereotypes, such as submissive or helpless behavior in females, continue to be represented in TV programs and movies. By the age of 6 or 7, children have already begun to shy away from activities that are identified with members of the opposite sex. Although it's unlikely that television is entirely responsible for this trend, it's widely believed that television plays an important role (Ruble, Balaban, & Cooper, 1981).

Even if people don't directly imitate or model a particular violent act, it's still likely that the observation itself influences the way they think. For instance, witnessing repeated examples of fictional violence distorts people's estimates of realistic violence—they're likely to believe, for example, that more people die a violent death than is actually the case. This can lead individuals to show irrational fear and to avoid situations that are in all likelihood safe. People who watch a lot of television tend to view the world in a way that mirrors what they see on the screen. They might think, for example, that a large proportion of the population are professionals (such as doctors or lawyers) and that few people in society are actually old (Gerbner & Gross, 1976). It's not just the imitation of particular acts we need to worry about: Television and other vehicles of observational learning can literally change or determine our everyday view of the world (Bandura, 1986; Bushman & Anderson, 2001).

Finally, suppose the link between witnessed violence and personal aggression is real, but small. Imagine, for example, that only 1% of people who watch a violent television program become more violent after watching the show. Is this a cause for concern? Remember, many millions of people watch television every day. If 10 million people watch a show, and only 1% are affected, that would still mean that 100,000 people might have an increased tendency for violence. Those are scary numbers when you consider that it only takes one or two people to terrorize a building or commit murder in a school (e.g., Columbine). Ironically, recent research suggests that when violence is shown in a television program, it may actually hurt the very industries that are sponsoring the show. Evidence collected from Bushman and Phillips (2001) indicates that television violence actually impairs subsequent memory for the brand names and product information shown in accompanying commercials.

CRITICAL THINKING

Given what you've learned about modeling, do you now favor the passage of laws that will control the amount of violence shown on television? Why or why not?

Test Yourself 7.4

Check your knowledge about observational learning by deciding whether each of the following statements is True or False. *(You will find the answers in the Appendix.)*

1. Observational learning, like classical conditioning, typically involves learning about events that occur outside of your control. *True or False?*
2. People are more likely to imitate the behavior of a role model if the model is observed being rewarded for his or her behavior. Bandura refers to this reward process as vicarious reinforcement. *True or False?*

3. Observational learning is usually a passive process. Our beliefs and expectations about how well we can perform the model's behavior play little or no role. *True or False?*
4. Most psychologists believe that television is a powerful vehicle for observational learning. *True or False?*
5. Clinical psychologists now use observational learning to treat specific fears, such as phobias. *True or False?*

Review *Psychology for a Reason*

As we struggle to survive, our capacity to learn—that is, to change our behavior as a result of experience—represents a great strength. Psychologists have long recognized the importance of understanding how behavior changes with experience; historically, research on learning predates research on virtually all other topics, with the exception of basic sensory and perceptual processes. In this chapter we've concentrated on relatively simple learning processes. To meet the needs of changing environments, each of us must solve certain types of learning problems, and the principles of behavior you've learned about apply generally across animal species.

Learning About Events: Noticing and Ignoring Novel or unusual events lead to an orienting response, which helps ensure that we'll react quickly to sudden changes in our environment. The sound of screeching automobile brakes leads to an immediate reaction; we don't have to stop and think about it. At the same time, no one can attend to all the stimuli that surround us, so we learn to ignore events that are of little adaptive significance. Through the process of habituation, characterized by

the decline in the tendency to respond to an event that has become familiar, we become selective about responding to events that occur repeatedly in our environment.

Learning What Events Signal: Classical Conditioning We also learn about what events signal—it's helpful to know, for example, that a wailing siren means an emergency vehicle is somewhere nearby. Signals, or conditioned stimuli, are established through classical conditioning. Events that provide information about the occurrence or nonoccurrence of other significant events become conditioned stimuli. A conditioned stimulus elicits a conditioned response, which is a response appropriate for anticipating the event that will follow. When we hear the siren, we anticipate the arrival of the ambulance and quickly move out of the way.

Learning About the Consequences of Our Behavior: Operant Conditioning We also learn that our actions produce outcomes that are sometimes pleasing and sometimes not. In operant conditioning, the presentation and removal of events after responding can either increase or decrease the likelihood

of responding in a similar way again. When a response is followed by reinforcement, either positive or negative, the tendency to respond similarly is strengthened. When a response is followed by punishment, either positive or negative, we are less likely to repeat the behavior. It's also important to consider the schedule of reinforcement. Schedules affect not only how rapidly we will learn and respond but also the pattern of responding and how likely we are to change our behavior if the reinforcement stops.

Learning from Others: Observational Learning Through observational or social learning, we imitate and model the actions of others, thereby learning from example rather than from direct experience. We study how other people behave and how their behavior is reinforced or punished, and we change our own behavior accordingly. Whether or not we will imitate the behavior of others depends on several factors, including the social standing of the model. Observational learning can have a number of effects, both positive and negative, on the individual and on society.

Active Summary *(You will find the answers in the Appendix.)*

- Learning is defined by a change in (1) _____ that results from (2) _____.

Learning About Events: Noticing and Ignoring

- The limited resources of the nervous system keep us from attending to every environmental stimulus. Psychological processes help us (3) _____ our mental functioning.

- (4) _____ occurs when we stop responding to an event that has become familiar through repeated presentation. Sensitization occurs when responding to an event (5) _____ with repeated exposure to the event.

Learning What Events Signal: Classical Conditioning

- Stimuli and events in the environment have (6) _____ properties that tell us when one event (7) _____ a second one.

- An (8) _____ stimulus (US) leads to an automatic or unconditioned (9) _____ (UR). Repeated pairing of an event or stimulus with a US results in that event becoming a (10) _____ stimulus (CS), which can then elicit a conditioned response (CR).

- For a CS–US connection to form, the CS must provide new (11) _____ about the delivery of the US.

- Sometimes the CS–US pairing leads to a CR that is (12) _____ from the UR. A CR may be opposite to the UR, but a CR usually prepares the organism for the arrival of the (13) _____.

- In (14) _____ order conditioning, an established CS (e.g., a tone that predicts food) immediately follows a (15) _____ event (e.g., a light). The US itself is never presented again, but the pairing of tone and light can now produce conditioned responding to the light alone. Stimulus (16) _____ occurs when a new stimulus produces a response similar to the one produced by the conditioned stimulus. Stimulus (17) _____ occurs when the response to a new stimulus is (18) _____ from the response to the original stimulus.

- If the CS is presented repeatedly, and is no longer followed by the (19) _____, it loses its signaling properties and the CR gradually becomes weaker. This is called (20) _____. Conditioned (21) _____ occurs when we learn that an event signals the (22) _____ of the US.

Learning About the Consequences of Our Behavior: Operant Conditioning

- Behaviors produce rewards and punishments, so it's clearly adaptive to learn when and how to operate, or act, on your environment.

- (23) _____ conditioning is a procedure for studying how organisms learn about the (24) _____ of their own behavior. Thorndike's law of (25) _____ holds that if a response is followed by a satisfying or pleasant consequence, the connection between the response and that situation will be (26) _____; conversely, if a response leads to an unsatisfying or unpleasant consequence, the connection will be (27) _____.

- The law of effect applies when a response is rewarded in one situation and not the other. The situation is the (28) _____ stimulus.

- (29) _____ reinforcement occurs when the presentation of an event after a response (30) _____ the likelihood of the response occurring again. Negative reinforcement occurs when removing an event after a response (31) _____ the likelihood of the response occurring again. Conditioned, or secondary, (32) _____ are stimuli that acquire reinforcement properties through learning.

- Positive punishment occurs when the presentation of an event (33) _____ the chances of that response occurring again. (34) _____ punishment occurs when the removal of an event (35) _____ the likelihood of responding.

- A schedule of (36) _____ is a rule used to determine when responses will be reinforced. In a (37) _____ schedule, every response is followed by reinforcement; in a (38) _____ schedule, reinforcement is delivered only after some responses. Partial schedules include (39) _____ ratio, variable (40) _____, fixed (41) _____, and (42) _____ interval.

- A subject can be trained to behave in a particular way through (43) _____, which refers to giving reinforcement for successive (44) _____ of the desired behavior.

- Many psychologists believe that (45) _____ constraints, perhaps in the genetic code, limit the responses that can be learned; in addition, we are predisposed to learn relationships between certain stimuli and outcomes, such as taste and illness.

Learning From Others: Observational Learning

• We naturally tend to model the behavior of people who are significant to us. (46) _____ learning is especially likely if the model's characteristics are (47) _____,

or if we see that the person is (48) _____ for certain behaviors.

• It's (49) _____ to model the behavior of others because it reduces the likelihood of coming into contact with something harmful or dangerous. Observing desirable behavior can (50) _____ unwanted or maladaptive behavior. Observational learning can also (51) _____ maladaptive behavior, as when people model the violence they see on TV.

Terms to Remember

classical conditioning, 217
conditioned inhibition, 225
conditioned reinforcer, 230
conditioned response (CR), 218
conditioned stimulus (CS), 218
discriminative stimulus, 229
extinction, 224
fixed-interval (FI) schedule, 233
fixed-ratio (FR) schedule, 232
habituation, 216
law of effect, 228
learning, 213

modeling, 238
negative punishment, 231
negative reinforcement, 229
observational learning, 237
operant conditioning, 227
orienting response, 216
partial reinforcement schedule, 232
positive punishment, 230
positive reinforcement, 229
punishment, 230
reinforcement, 229
schedule of reinforcement, 232

second-order conditioning, 222
sensitization, 216
shaping, 234
spontaneous recovery, 225
stimulus discrimination, 223
stimulus generalization, 223
unconditioned response (UR), 218
unconditioned stimulus (US), 218
variable-interval (VI) schedule, 234
variable-ratio (VR) schedule, 232

Media Resources

 ThomsonNOW

www.thomsonedu.com/ThomsonNOW

Go to this site for the link to ThomsonNow, your one-stop study shop. Take a Pre-Test for this chapter and Thomson-Now will generate a personalized Study Plan based on your test results! The Study Plan will identify the topics you need to review and direct you to online resources to help you master those topics. You can then take a Post-Test to help you determine the concepts you have mastered and what you still need to work on.

 Companion Website

www.thomsonedu.com/psychology/nairne

Go to this site to find online resources directly linked to your book, including a glossary, flashcards, quizzing, weblinks, and more.

 Psyk.trek 3.0

Check out the Psyk.trek CD-ROM for further study of the concepts in this chapter. Psyk.trek's interactive learning modules, simulations, and quizzes offer additional opportunities for you to interact with, reflect on, and retain the material:

Learning: Basic Processes in Classical Conditioning
Learning: Avoidance and Escape Learning

CHAPTER 8

Memory

What if the flow of time suddenly fractured and you were forced to relive the same 10 minutes, over and over again, in an endless pattern? Maybe you'd be driving your car, or reading a book; it wouldn't matter—at the end of the interval you'd begin again, back at the same fork in the road, or the same location on the page. Think about how this might affect you. You wouldn't age, but would you be able to endure?

The answer, I suspect, depends on your capacity to remember and forget. If you've seen the movie *Groundhog Day*, you'll remember that Bill Murray's character was caught in a kind of time warp—he was forced to relive the same day over and over. To make matters worse, he was fully aware of his situation. Like Murray's character, if your memories remained intact from one cycle to the next, if you were aware of the endless repetition, life would quickly become unbearable (even if it was a particularly good day). But if your memories were erased before each new 10-minute interval, you'd lack awareness of your hopeless plight; your life, although existing in an abbreviated form, would continue as usual. It's through **memory**—broadly defined as the capacity to preserve and recover information—that concepts like the past and the present gain meaning in our lives.

Like learning, memory is not something that can be directly observed. It's an *inferred* capacity, one that psychologists assume must be operating when people act on information that's no longer physically present. To understand how memory works, we need to consider how memories are formed, how memories are maintained over time, and how the stored information is recovered and translated into performance. The processes of **encoding** determine and control how memories are initially acquired. **Storage** controls how memories are maintained. **Retrieval** is the term used to describe how stored memories are recovered and translated into performance. Each of these key psychological processes is illustrated in ▌Figure 8.1.

memory The capacity to preserve and recover information.

encoding The processes that determine and control how memories are formed.

storage The processes that determine and control how memories are stored and kept over time.

retrieval The processes that determine and control how memories are recovered and translated into performance.

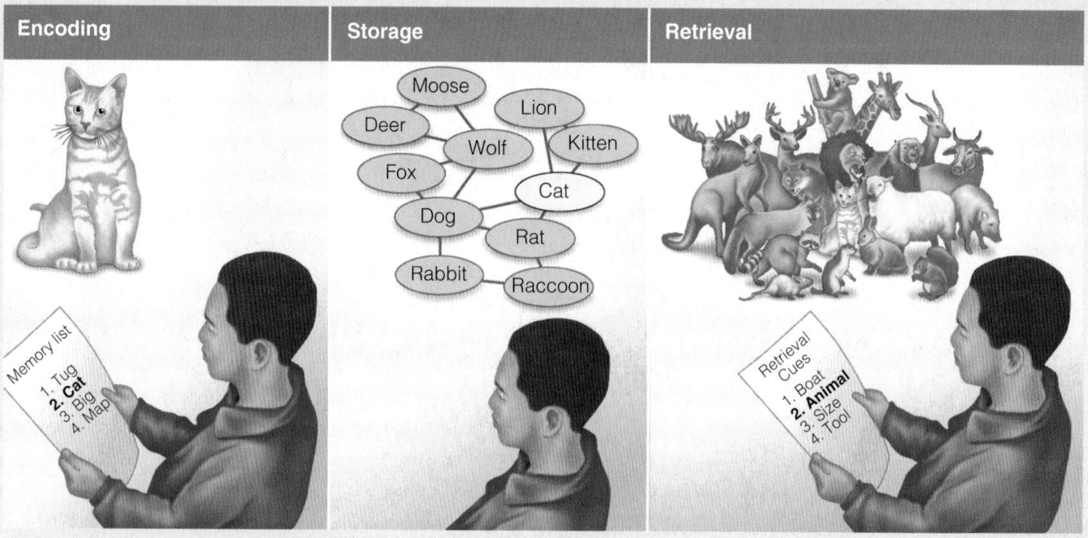

Encoding	Storage	Retrieval

FIGURE 8.1 Basic Memory Processes
How the person thinks about the word CAT will affect how that word is encoded into memory (panel 1). CAT might be stored in long-term memory by activating existing knowledge structures (panel 2). The person uses the cue ANIMAL to help retrieve the memory of CAT (panel 3).

What's It For? *Remembering and Forgetting*

Not surprisingly, memory tends to be highly adaptive. By maintaining and recovering the past, we equip ourselves to better handle the present. We can change our behavior to correct past mistakes, or we can continue to act in ways that led to past success. But memory is far more than simply reexperiencing past events. A world without memory would be devoid of thought and reason. You would never learn; you would never produce spoken language or understand the words of others; your sense of personal history would be lost along with much, if not all, of your personal identity. In this chapter we focus on the key adaptive problems that our memory systems help us solve.

Remembering Over the Short Term
It's natural to link memory to the recovery of events that happened hours, days, or weeks ago, but we need to remember over the very short term as well. Consider the interpretation of spoken language. Because speech unfolds one word at a time, it's necessary to remember the early part of a sentence, after it has receded into the past, before you can hope to understand the meaning of the sentence as a whole.

Likewise, when we perform most mental tasks, such as solving math problems, certain bits of information must be retained during the ongoing solution process. Try adding 28 and 35 in your head without remembering to carry the 1 (or subtract 2 if you round the 28 up to 30). By establishing short-term memories, we're able to prolong the incoming message, giving us more time to interpret it properly.

Storing Information for the Long Term
To remember information for longer periods, it needs to be encoded in a way that promotes lasting storage. Forming a visual image of a to-be-remembered item generally increases its durability in memory. It also helps to think about the meaning of the item, or to relate the item to other material that's already been stored. We'll consider these techniques in some detail, and I'll provide some tips to help you improve your own ability to remember.

Recovering Information From Cues
What initiates an act of remembering? What causes you to remember your appointment with the doctor this afternoon, or what you had for breakfast this morning, or a fleeting encounter with a stranger yesterday? Most researchers believe that the retrieval of stored memories is triggered by other events, or cues, encountered in the environment. When we fail to remember, it's usually because we lack the right retrieval cues. We'll discuss what makes a "good" retrieval cue, and we'll examine how existing knowledge is used to help us reconstruct what happened in the past.

Updating Memory
It's upsetting to forget, but forgetting actually has considerable adaptive properties. Among other things, it prevents us from acting in ways that are no longer appropriate. It's the study assignment you need to complete *today* that's critical, not the one from yesterday or the week before. It's your *current* phone number that you need to remember, not the one from a previous apartment or from the home you lived in as a child. We'll consider the major determinants of forgetting, both the normal kinds and abnormal forgetting of the type that characterizes amnesia.

Remembering Over the Short Term

LEARNING GOALS
- Discuss how visual and auditory sensory memories can be measured.
- Describe how information is represented, maintained, and forgotten over the short term.

WHEN INFORMATION FIRST REACHES the senses, we rely on two memory systems to help us prolong the incoming message over the short term. The first, called **sensory memory**, keeps the message in a relatively pure, unanalyzed form. Sensory memories are like fleeting snapshots of the world. The external message is represented in accurate detail—as a kind of picture or echo—but the memory usually lasts less than a second (Crowder & Surprenant, 2000). The second system, **short-term memory**, is a limited-capacity "working memory" that we use to hold information after it has been analyzed for periods lasting on the order of a minute or two. Short-term memories are also rapidly forgotten, but they can be maintained for extended periods through internal repetition. Let's take a look at each of these systems and consider some of their important properties.

sensory memory An exact replica of an environmental message, which usually lasts for a second or less.

short-term memory A limited-capacity system that we use to hold information after it has been analyzed for periods lasting less than a minute or two.

Sensory Memory: The Icon and the Echo

When you watch a movie or a television program, you experience a continuous flow of movement across the screen. As you probably know, the film does not actually contain moving images; it is composed of still pictures presented rapidly in sequence, each separated by a period of darkness. We perceive a continuous world, some researchers believe, because the nervous system activity left by one picture lingers for a brief period prior to presentation of the next image (Massaro & Loftus, 1996). This extended nervous system activity creates a sensory "memory" that helps to fill the gap, thereby providing a sense of continuous movement.

In vision the lingering sensory memory trace is called an *icon*, and the sensory memory system that produces and stores icons is known as **iconic memory** (Neisser, 1967). It's relatively easy to demonstrate an icon: Simply twirl a flashlight about in a darkened room and you will see a trailing edge. You can obtain a similar effect on a dark night by writing your name in the air with a sparkler or a match. These trails of

iconic memory The system that produces and stores visual sensory memories.

The trails of light created by a whirling sparkler are caused by visual sensory memories, which act like still photographs of the perceptual scene.

©Roger Ressmeyer/CORBIS

echoic memory The system that produces and stores auditory sensory memories.

light are not really present in the night air; they arise from the rapidly fading images of iconic memory, which act as still photographs of the perceptual scene. These images allow the visual sensations to be extended in time so that the brain can more efficiently process the physical message it receives.

In the auditory system, there is a lingering *echo*, or **echoic memory**. Pure sounds can be held for brief intervals to help auditory perception. In Chapter 5 you learned how the brain calculates arrival time differences between the ears to help localize sounds. However, to compare arrival times, the first sound must be retained until the second one arrives; echoic memory may help fill the gap. Echoic memory is also widely believed to play a key role in language processing, perhaps to help retain exact replicas of sounds during sentence and word processing (Crowder, 1976; Nairne, 2003).

Measuring Iconic Memory How can an icon be measured? More than 30 years ago a graduate student in psychology named George Sperling (1960; also see Averbach & Coriell, 1961) developed a clever procedure for studying the properties of iconic memory. Using an apparatus called a *tachistoscope*, which presents visual displays for carefully controlled durations, Sperling showed people arrays of 12 letters arranged in rows. For example:

XLWF

JBOV

KCZR

The person's task was simple: Look at the display and then report the letters. Sounds easy, but the presentation time was extremely brief—the display was shown for only about 50 milliseconds (1/20 of a second). Across several experiments, Sperling found that people could report only 4 or 5 letters correctly in this task (out of 12). But more important, they claimed to see an image—an icon—of the *entire* display for a brief period after it was removed from view. All 12 of the letters could be seen, the people claimed, but the image faded before all could be reported.

To provide evidence for this rapidly decaying image, or icon, Sperling tried asking people to report only the letters shown in a particular row—but, critically, he didn't tell them which row until after the display was turned off. A high, medium, or low tone was presented immediately after the display, which cued participants to recall just the top, middle, or bottom row (see ▌ Figure 8.2). Sperling called this new condition *partial report* because only a part of the display needed to be recalled. Performance was great—people almost always reported the row of letters correctly.

Remember, people heard the tone *after* the display had been turned off. There was no way to predict which row would be cued, so the entire display must have been available in memory for participants to perform so well. Performance improved, Sperling reasoned, because people had enough time to read a single cued row, but not the entire display, before the iconic image had completely faded. In further experiments he was able to measure how quickly the sensory image was lost by delaying presentation of the tone. He discovered that the fleeting image—the iconic memory—was indeed short-lived; it disappeared in about half a second.

Measuring Echoic Memory Sensory memories are produced by each of the five senses, but little work has been done on systems other than vision and audition. An experiment by Efron (1970) demonstrates how it's possible to measure the lingering echoic trace, or echo. People were presented with a series of very brief tones, each lasting less than about 1/10 of a second; the task was to adjust a light so that it appeared exactly when each tone ended. Efron discovered that people always thought the tone ended later than it actually did; that is, people reported hearing the tone for a brief period after it had been turned off. Efron argued that this "phantom tone" was actually caused by a memory—the lingering echo of echoic memory. As in visual sensory memory, auditory sensory memory is believed to last for only a brief period of time—

CRITICAL THINKING

Can you think of a reason it might be adaptive for icons to be lost so quickly?

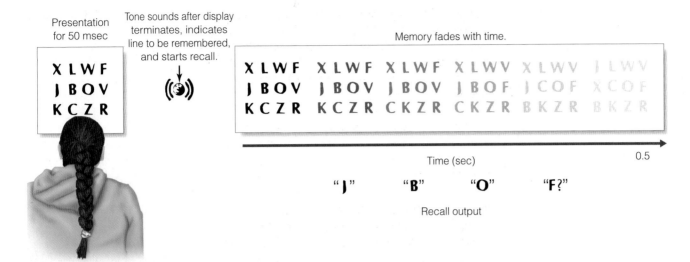

FIGURE 8.2 The Partial Report Technique
After presentation of the display, a tone indicates the row of letters to be recalled. As the participant attempts to recall them, the visual iconic memory fades and becomes less and less accurate. When only part of the display is to be recalled, most of the relevant information can be reported before the image is completely lost.

probably less than a second—although in some circumstances it may last longer, perhaps for as long as 5 or 10 seconds (Cowan, 1995; Cowan, Lichty, & Grove, 1990).

Short-Term Memory: Prolonging the Present

The function of sensory memory is to maintain an exact replica of the environmental message, for a very short period, as an aid to perception. *Short-term memory* is the system we use to temporarily store, think about, and reason with information. The term *working memory* is sometimes used because this temporary storage system often acts as a kind of mental workplace, allowing us to store the components of a problem as we work toward a solution (Baddeley, 2007; Nairne, 2002a).

It's useful to keep recently presented information available over the short term. Consider language: It would be hard to understand spoken language, which occurs sequentially (one word at a time), without remembering the first part of a spoken phrase. It would also be difficult to read any kind of text without keeping themes of the passage, or what was presented in the previous sentence, in mind. Short-term memories help us produce and interpret spoken language, remember telephone numbers, reason and problem solve, and even think. In the following sections we consider some of the properties of short-term memories, including how and why they're forgotten.

The Inner Voice   Unlike sensory memories, short-term memories are not exact copies of the environmental message. When we maintain information over the short term, we tend to use an acoustic code regardless of how the message was originally presented. You can see this for yourself by repeating the word PSYCHOLOGY silently inside your head. Notice that you can repeat the word quickly or slowly, and, if you like, you can even insert internal pauses after each repetition. There's nothing visual about this repetition process; you have *recoded*, or translated, the visual message PSYCHOLOGY into another form—an inner voice.

This notion of an inner voice is supported by the errors that occur during short-term recall. When recalling over the short term, people invariably make errors that are acoustically based. Mistakes tend to *sound* like correct items even when the stimulus materials have never been presented aloud (Conrad, 1964; Hanson, 1990). For example, suppose you're given five letters to remember—B X R C L—but you make a

Short-term memories help us maintain information, such as telephone numbers, over relatively brief time intervals.

©Mauro Panci/CORBIS

mistake and misremember the fourth letter. Your error will probably be a letter that sounds like the correct one; you're likely to incorrectly remember something like T or P. Notice that C and T and P all sound alike, but they *look* nothing alike. It's believed that errors tend to be acoustic because people typically recode the original visual input into an inner voice.

Why do we store things over the short term in an inner voice? It's probably because we're often called on to interpret and produce spoken language. It makes sense to think in a way that's compatible with the way we communicate. In fact, there's some evidence to suggest that deaf or hearing-impaired individuals, particularly those who communicate with American Sign Language, may not rely on an inner voice to the same extent as people with normal hearing; they encode information in a form that's compatible with their normal language format (Flaherty, 2000; Wilson & Emmorey, 1997).

The Inner Eye We usually use our inner voice to store short-term memories, but we can use other codes. For example, sometimes we use visual images (Baddeley, 1992). To illustrate, close your eyes and count the number of windows in your house or apartment. Did you perform this task by visualizing the rooms, one by one, and counting the number of windows you "saw"? Now try forming a visual image of a rabbit standing next to a rat. Does the rabbit in your image have whiskers? If I measure your reaction time, it turns out that you'll answer a question like this more quickly if you imagine the rabbit standing next to a rat instead of next to an elephant (Kosslyn, 1983). This is exactly the kind of result we'd expect if you were looking at an actual picture—the larger the object is in the picture, the easier it is to "see."

Experiments have shown that the imagery produced by the "inner eye" may rely on the same brain mechanisms as normal visual perception. Neuroimaging techniques reveal that imagery and perception activate many of the same regions in the brain (Ganis, Thompson, & Kosslyn, 2004). Other studies have found that people have trouble storing a visual image in their head while they're also performing a visually based tracking task, such as finding locations on a map (Baddeley & Lieberman, 1980).

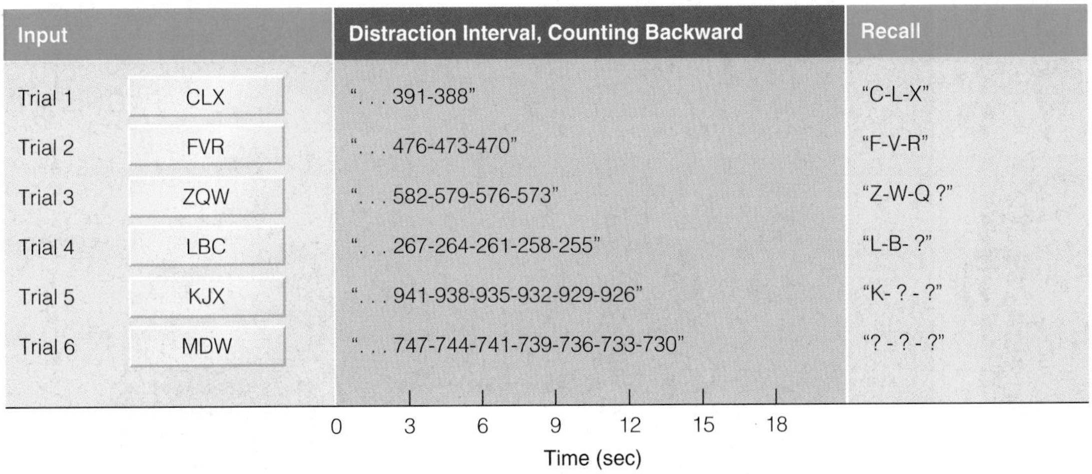

Input	Distraction Interval, Counting Backward	Recall
Trial 1 CLX	"...391-388"	"C-L-X"
Trial 2 FVR	"...476-473-470"	"F-V-R"
Trial 3 ZQW	"...582-579-576-573"	"Z-W-Q ?"
Trial 4 LBC	"...267-264-261-258-255"	"L-B- ?"
Trial 5 KJX	"...941-938-935-932-929-926"	"K- ? - ?"
Trial 6 MDW	"...747-744-741-739-736-733-730"	"? - ? - ?"

Time (sec): 0 3 6 9 12 15 18

FIGURE 8.3 The Petersons' Distractor Task
On each trial, people were asked to recall three letters in correct order, after counting backward aloud for 3 to 18 seconds. The longer the participants counted, the less likely they were to recall the letters correctly.

There are even brain-damaged patients who report corresponding impairments in both imagery and visual perception. For example, some patients whose brain damage has caused them to lose their color vision also have difficulty forming a colorful visual image. Thus there appears to be an important link between the brain systems involved in perception and those involved in mental imagery (Ganis et al., 2003).

Short-Term Forgetting Everyone knows it can be tough to remember telephone numbers or directions long enough to write them down. It's possible to prolong short-term memories indefinitely by engaging in **rehearsal**, which is the process of internal repetition, assuming that you have the time and resources to continue the rehearsal process. (Think about the word *rehearsal* as *re-hear-sal*, as if listening to the inner voice.) Without rehearsal, however, short-term memories are quickly forgotten (Atkinson & Shiffrin, 1968). In an early investigation of short-term forgetting, Lloyd and Margaret Peterson (1959) asked students to recall short lists of three letters (such as CLX) after delays that ranged from 3 to 18 seconds. The task sounds easy—remembering three letters for less than half a minute—but the experiment had an unusual feature: No one was allowed to rehearse the letters during the delay interval; instead, the students were asked to count backward by threes aloud until a recall signal appeared. You can try this experiment for yourself: Ask someone to read you three letters, then try immediately counting backward by threes from the number 832. Finally have your friend signal you to recall after about 10 to 20 seconds. Under these conditions, you'll probably find that you forget the letters relatively quickly (if the first trial seems easy, try a few more with different letters). In the Petersons' experiment, the students were reduced to guessing after about 10 to 15 seconds of counting backward (see Figure 8.3).

Why is information forgotten so rapidly without rehearsal? Some researchers believe that short-term memories are lost spontaneously over time, through a process called *decay*, unless those memories are kept active through rehearsal (Baddeley, 1992; Cowan, Saults, & Nugent, 1997). Decay also explains the rapid forgetting of sensory memories. Other researchers believe that short-term forgetting is caused by *interference* from new information or because people confuse current memories with past memories (Crowder & Neath, 1991; Keppel & Underwood, 1962; Nairne, 1990, 2002a). A third possibility is that both decay and interference operate together to produce information loss. We'll return to the question of what causes forgetting later in the chapter.

Short-Term Memory Capacity Another characteristic of short-term memory is its limited capacity: We can only remember a small amount of information over the short term. Research has shown that short-term **memory span**—which is defined as the number of items a person can recall in the exact order of presentation on half

rehearsal A strategic process that helps to maintain short-term memories indefinitely through the use of internal repetition.

memory span The number of items that can be recalled from short-term memory in their proper presentation order on half of the tested memory trials.

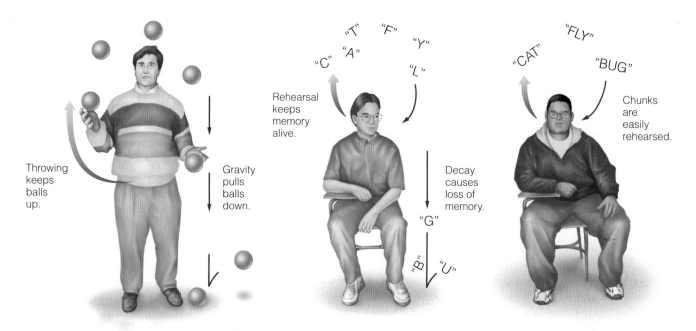

FIGURE 8.4 The Capacity of Short-Term Memory
The amount of information that can be stored in short-term memory depends on rehearsal, which you can think of as roughly analogous to juggling. You return to each rapidly fading short-term memory trace and reactivate it through rehearsal before it is permanently forgotten. "Chunking" the material makes it easier to rehearse and therefore remember the information.

of the tested memory trials—is typically about seven, plus or minus two items. In other words, short-term memory span ranges between five and nine incoming items (Miller, 1956). It's easy to remember a list of four items, but quite difficult to remember a list of eight or nine items (which is one of the reasons telephone numbers are seven digits long).

Most psychologists believe that the capacity of short-term memory is limited because it takes time to execute the process of rehearsal. To illustrate, imagine you're asked to remember a relatively long list of letters arranged this way:

CA TFL YBU G

First, try reading this list aloud, from C to G. You'll find that several seconds elapse from start to finish. Now imagine cycling through the list with your inner voice as you prepare for short-term recall. It turns out that the C to G cycling takes a similar amount of time inside your head (Landauer, 1962).

Remember, however, that items stored in short-term memory are forgotten in a matter of seconds, so the first part of the list tends to be forgotten during execution of the last. By the time you've finished with the last letter and returned to the beginning of the list, the early items have already been lost from memory. You can think about this relationship between forgetting and rehearsal as roughly similar to juggling (see ▌Figure 8.4). To juggle successfully, you need to win the battle against gravity. You throw the dinner plates up, and gravity pulls them down. To prevent one of the plates from crashing, it's necessary to catch and toss it back up before gravity runs it into the ground. Similarly, you need to return to the rapidly fading short-term memory trace and reactivate it through rehearsal before the "forces" of forgetting win out. It's a race between two opposing forces—rehearsal and forgetting.

Chunking   As a general rule, memory span is roughly equal to the amount of material you can internally rehearse in about two seconds (which usually turns out to be about seven plus or minus two items). To improve your ability to remember over the short term, then, it's best to figure out a way to rehearse a lot of information in a short amount of time. One effective strategy is **chunking**, which involves rearranging the incoming information into meaningful or familiar patterns, called *chunks*. Remember that long list of letters presented earlier (CA TFL YBU G)? Perhaps you saw that the same list could be slightly rearranged:

CAT FLY BUG

Forming the letters into words drastically reduces the time it takes to repeat the list internally (try saying CAT FLY BUG over and over internally). In addition, once you remember a chunk, it's easy to recall the letters—in most cases, words are great storage devices for remembering sequences of letters. Of course, the trick lies in finding meaningful chunks in what can appear to be a meaningless jumble of information.

The ability to create meaningful chunks often depends on how much you know about the material that needs to be remembered. Expert chess players can re-create most of the positions on a chessboard after only a brief glance—as long as a meaningful game is in progress (Chase & Simon, 1973). They recognize familiar attack or defense patterns in the game, which allows them to create easy-to-rehearse chunks of position information. Similar results are found when electronics experts are asked to remember complex circuit board diagrams (Egan & Schwartz, 1979). In both cases, if the materials are arranged in a more or less random fashion (for example, the chess pieces are simply scattered about the board), the skilled retention vanishes, and memory reverts to normal levels.

The Working Memory Model

We've focused on the characteristics of short-term memories—how they're stored and forgotten—but we haven't discussed the "system" that controls memory over the short term. Unfortunately, memory researchers still don't completely agree about the mechanisms that enable us to remember over the short term. Some psychologists believe that memory over the short term is controlled by the same machinery that controls memory over the long term (Melton, 1963; Nairne, 2002a), but most psychologists assume we have special equipment for short-term memory because of its importance in language and thought. The most popular current account of the short-term memory system is the *working memory model* developed originally by Baddeley and Hitch (1974) and elaborated more recently by Baddeley (1992, 2000).

In the working memory model, several distinct mechanisms are important for short-term retention. First, the temporary storage of acoustic and verbal information is controlled by the *phonological loop*. The phonological loop is the structure we use to temporarily store verbal information and engage in repetitive rehearsal—it corresponds to the inner voice and is believed to play a critical role in language (Baddeley, Gathercole, & Papagno, 1998). The short-term retention and processing of visual and spatial information is controlled by a different system—the *visuospatial sketchpad*. If you try to count the number of windows in your house by moving through it in your mind's eye, you are probably involving the visuospatial sketchpad. Finally, Baddeley and Hitch (1974) propose that a *central executive* controls and allocates how processing is divided across the loop and the sketchpad. The central executive determines when the loop or sketchpad will be used and coordinates their actions.

One reason the working memory model is popular among memory researchers is that it helps explain the effects of certain types of brain damage. There are patients, for example, who seem to lose very specific verbal skills, such as the ability to learn new words in an unfamiliar language. Other patients retain their language skills but have difficulties with memory for spatial or visual information (Baddeley, 2000, 2007). These results suggest that we have separate systems controlling verbal and visual storage, just as the working memory model proposes. Neuroimaging techniques also show that different areas of the brain are active when we remember spatial and nonspatial information (Jonides, 2000; Wager & Smith, 2003).

chunking A short-term memory strategy that involves rearranging incoming information into meaningful or familiar patterns.

CRITICAL THINKING

Why do you suppose the telephone company encourages you to group the numbers into chunks—for example, 449-5854?

Test Yourself 8.1

Check your knowledge about remembering over the short term by deciding whether each of the following statements best describes sensory memory or short-term memory. (You will find the answers in the Appendix.)

1. Information is forgotten in less than a second: _____
2. Information is stored as a virtually exact copy of the external message: _____
3. Information can be stored indefinitely through the process of rehearsal: _____
4. The system measured through Sperling's partial report procedure: _____

5. Recall errors tend to sound like the correct item even when the item is presented visually: _____
6. May help us calculate message arrival time differences between the two ears: _____
7. Span is roughly equal to the amount of material that you can say to yourself in two seconds: _____
8. Capacity is improved through chunking: _____

Storing Information for the Long Term

LEARNING GOALS

• Define episodic, semantic, and procedural memories.
• Explain why it's important to form an elaborate and distinctive memory record.
• Describe some simple mnemonic techniques.

long-term memory The system used to maintain information for extended periods of time.

Long-term memory is the system we use to maintain information for extended periods. When you remember the name of your fifth grade teacher or the correct route to class, you're using your long-term memory. Most psychologists believe that the capacity of long-term memory is effectively unlimited. There are no limits to what we can potentially remember, but not everything we experience gets stored, nor do we necessarily store information in a way that makes it easy to remember. To promote effective long-term storage, it's necessary to *encode* the experience in a way that makes it easy to *retrieve*. We'll consider the kinds of encoding activities that lead to effective long-term storage momentarily, but first let's briefly consider the general kinds of information that are stored.

What Is Stored in Long-Term Memory?

episodic memory A memory for a particular event, or episode, that happened to you personally, such as remembering what you ate for breakfast this morning or where you went on vacation last year.

Stop for a moment and think about your first kiss. The recollection (assuming you can remember your first kiss) is probably tinged with a measure of warmth, intimacy, and perhaps embarrassment. Do you remember the person's name? The situation? The year? Memories of this type, which tap some moment from our personal past, are called **episodic memories**—they're composed of particular events, or episodes, that happened to us personally. Most experimental research on memory tests episodic memory because people typically are asked to remember information from an earlier point in the experiment. The task is to remember an *event*, such as a word list, that forms a part of the personal history of the participant.

Some psychologists believe that episodic memory is a uniquely human quality (Tulving, 2002). Other animals show memory, in the sense that they can act on the basis of information that's no longer present (such as remembering the location of food), but they lack the ability to mentally travel backward in time and "relive" prior experiences. They live only in the present and show no awareness of the past. Interestingly, some forms of brain damage produce a similar effect in humans. Such patients appear normal in most respects—they can read and write normally, solve problems, and even play chess—but they lack the ability to remember any events or circumstances from their personal past (Wheeler & McMillan, 2001).

Think of a city in Europe that's famous for its fashion and fine wine. The correct response is *Paris*, but did you "remember" or "know" the answer? What about the square root of 9, or the capital city of the United States? These are certainly memories, in the sense that you have preserved and recovered information from the past, but "remembering" these answers feels vastly different from remembering your first kiss. When you reveal what you know about the world, but make no reference whatsoever to a particular episode from your past, you're using **semantic memory** (*semantic* refers to "meaning"). It's through semantic memory that we store facts and remember the rules we need to know to adapt effectively in the world.

Finally, think about how to tie your shoes, drive a car, or ride a bike. The knowledge about how to *do* things is called **procedural memory**. Most skills, including athletic ability, rely on procedural memories. Procedural memories differ from episodic and semantic memories in a fundamental way: They rarely produce any conscious experience of "remembering." Most people have a difficult time consciously reporting how to tie their shoes or ride a bike. They can do these things, but it's extremely difficult to put the knowledge into words. Procedural memories are among the simplest of all memories to recover, but they are among the most difficult for psychologists to study—they seem to be inaccessible to conscious awareness (Tulving, 1983). For a summary of these memory types—episodic, semantic, and procedural—see the concept review table.

It's difficult to teach skills associated with procedural memory because such memories tend to be inaccessible.

Elaboration: Connecting Material to Existing Knowledge

Now let's turn to long-term memory. What's the best way to remember something over the long term? As a general rule, if you want a lasting memory, relate what you want to remember to what you already know. There's a vast storehouse of information in the brain, and memory works best when you make use of it. When you actively relate new information to the already-stored contents of long-term memory, the process is called **elaboration**. Elaboration works for two reasons: First, it helps establish retrieval cues that ease later recovery. Second, it creates a distinctive memory record that stands out and is easy to identify. Elaboration comes in many forms, as the following sections demonstrate.

Think About Meaning   One of the easiest ways to promote elaboration is to think about the *meaning* of the information you want to remember. In an experiment by Craik and Tulving (1975), people were asked questions about single words such as

CRITICAL THINKING

When you take a test in one of your college courses, is the test primarily tapping episodic, semantic, or procedural memory?

semantic memory Knowledge about the world, stored as facts that make little or no reference to one's personal experiences.

procedural memory Knowledge about how to do things, such as riding a bike or swinging a golf club.

Concept Review	**Varieties of Long-Term Memory**	
TYPE OF MEMORY	**DESCRIPTION**	**EXAMPLE**
Episodic	Memories that recall a personal moment from our past	Wanda, the mail carrier, remembers that yesterday 10 inches of snow fell, making her job very difficult.
Semantic	Knowledge about the world, with no specific reference to a particular past episode	Wanda knows that mailing a letter first-class costs 41 cents; she also knows that it costs more to send something by express mail.
Procedural	Knowledge about *how* to do something	Wanda drives the streets of her mail route effortlessly, without really thinking about it.

elaboration An encoding process that involves the formation of connections between to-be-remembered input and other information in memory.

MOUSE. In one condition, the task required everyone to make judgments about the sound of the word (Does the word rhyme with HOUSE?); in another condition, people were required to think about the meaning of the word (Is a MOUSE a type of animal?). Substantially better memory was obtained in this second condition. Thinking about meaning, rather than sound, leads to richer and more elaborate connections between events and other things in memory. The deeper and more elaborative the processing, the more likely that memory will improve (Craik & Lockhart, 1972).

Notice Relationships   Existing knowledge can also be used to look for relationships among the things that need to be remembered. Suppose you're asked to remember the following list of words:

NOTES PENCIL BOOK NEWSPAPER MUSIC COFFEE

If you think about what the words mean and look for properties that they have in common—perhaps things that you would take to a study session or a lecture—you're engaging in a form of elaboration called *relational processing*. Relational processing works because you are embellishing, or adding to, the input. If you're trying to remember the word PENCIL and you relate the word to an involved sequence of events, there are likely to be lots of cues that will remind you of the correct response at a later time. Thinking about music, newspapers, drinking coffee—any of these can lead to the correct recall of PENCIL.

Notice Differences   It also helps to specify how the material you want to remember is *different* from other information in long-term memory. If you simply encode PENCIL as a writing implement, perhaps by thinking about its meaning, you might incorrectly recall things like PEN, CHALK, or even CRAYON when later tested. Instead, you need to specify the particular event in detail—we're talking about a yellow, number 2 pencil, not a crayon—so the memory record becomes *unique*. Unique memory records are remembered better because they stand out—they're easier to distinguish from related, but not appropriate, material in memory.

distinctiveness Refers to how unique or different a memory record is from other things in memory. Distinctive memory records tend to be recalled well.

Elaboration tends to produce **distinctive**—that is, unique—memory records (Neath & Surprenant, 2003; Schmidt, 1991). When you compare to-be-remembered information to other things in memory, noting similarities and differences, you encode how that information both shares properties with other information (relational processing) and is unique or different (distinctive processing). This leads to lots of retrieval cues that will help you remember the encoded material. Generally, if you want to remember something particularly well, you should concentrate on encoding both item similarities and differences (Hunt & McDaniel, 1993).

Form Mental Pictures   Another way to produce an elaborate memory record is to form a visual image of the material when it's first presented. If you're trying to remember COFFEE, try forming a mental picture of a steaming hot, freshly brewed cup. Forming mental pictures is an effective memory strategy because it naturally leads to elaborate, rich encodings. Mental pictures require you to think about the details of the material, and these details create a distinctive memory record. As you'll see later, many memory improvement techniques, called mnemonic devices, rely importantly on the use of **visual imagery**.

visual imagery The processes used to construct an internal visual image.

Visual imagery leads to excellent memory, but the memories themselves are not photographic (as you might assume)—instead, they're surprisingly abstract, and important details are often missing or inaccurate. To demonstrate, try forming a visual image of a penny or a quarter. You use coins every day, so this should be a fairly easy task. Now try to reproduce the image on paper—simply draw the president depicted on the coin, which direction he is facing, and so on. Your performance is apt to be mediocre at best. People are simply unable to reproduce the main features of a coin very accurately, despite the strong belief that they can see an accurate representation in their head. In fact, it's even difficult for people to recognize the correct coin when it is presented along with incorrect versions. For a display like the one shown in ▌ Figure 8.5, fewer than half of the participants pick out the right penny (Nickerson & Adams, 1979). Certainly, if you were looking at a coin, you would be able to trace the features accurately, so the image we form isn't necessarily an accurate representation of physical reality. This in no way detracts from the power of imagery on memory, however. We may not store exact pictures in our head, but the records produced from imagery are among the easiest to retrieve.

Space Your Repetitions   Elaborate memory traces can also be achieved through *repetition*: If information is presented more than once, it will tend to be remembered better. The fact that repetition improves memory is not very surprising, but it might surprise you to learn that repetition alone is not what leads to better memory. It's possible to present an item lots of times without improving memory—what's necessary is that you use each repetition as an opportunity to encode the material in an elaborate and distinctive manner. If you think about the material in exactly the same way every time it's presented, your memory won't improve very much (Greene, 1992; Herrmann, Raybeck, & Gutman, 1993).

How the repetitions are spaced is another important factor. Your memory will be better if you distribute the repetitions—that is, if you insert other events (or time) between each occurrence. This is called **distributed practice**. It means that all-night cram sessions where you read the same chapter over and over again are not very effective study procedures. It's better to study a little psychology, do something else, and then return to your psychology. Why does distributed practice lead to the best memory? Again, what matters to memory is how you process the material when it's presented. If you engage in massed practice—where you simply reread the same material over and over again without a break—you're likely to think about the material in exactly the same way every time it's presented. If you insert a break between presentations, when you see the material again there's a better chance that you'll notice something new or different. Distributed practice leads to memory records that are more elaborate and distinctive.

Consider Sequence Position   Finally, if you're given a long list of items to remember, such as 10 errands to complete, you'll tend to remember the items from the beginning and the end of the sequence best. This pattern is shown in ▌ Figure 8.6, which plots how well items are recalled as a function of their temporal, or serial, position in a list (this graph is often called a *serial position curve*). The improved memory for items at the start of the list is called the **primacy effect**; the end-of-the-list advantage is called the **recency effect**. Memory researchers believe that primacy and recency effects arise because items that occur at the beginning and end of a sequence are more naturally distinctive in memory and are therefore easier to rehearse and/or to recall (Murdock, 1960; Neath, 1993). Practically, then, if you're trying to remember a list of errands, put the most important ones at the beginning and the end of the list.

Mnemonic Devices

Mnemonic devices (*mnemonic* means "pertaining to memory") are special mental tricks developed thousands of years ago as memory aids (Yates, 1966). They're worth discussing because they're relatively easy to use and have lots of practical applications—in fact, virtually all "how to" memory books rely entirely on these techniques.

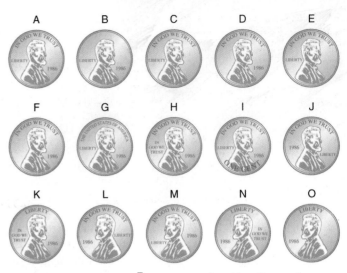

▌ FIGURE 8.5 Can You Recognize a Penny?
We may think we can form an accurate mental image of a penny, but it isn't easy to pick a true penny from a group of fake ones. Can you find the real penny in this display? (From "Long-Term Memory for a Common Object" by R. S. Nickerson and M. J. Adams in *Cognitive Psychology*, Volume 11, 287–307. Copyright 1979, Elsevier Science [USA]. Reproduced by permission of the publisher.)

CRITICAL THINKING

Given what you've learned about repetition and memory, do you think it's a good idea to have children learn arithmetic tables by rote repetition?

distributed practice Spacing the repetitions of to-be-remembered information over time.

primacy effect The better memory of items near the beginning of a memorized list.

recency effect The better memory of items near the end of a memorized list.

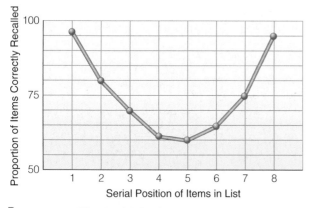

FIGURE 8.6 The Serial Position Curve
When we are asked to recall a list of items, our performance often depends on the temporal, or serial, position of the entries in the list. Items at the beginning of the list are remembered relatively well—the primacy effect—and so are items at the end of the list—the recency effect.

mnemonic devices Special mental tricks that help people think about material in ways that improve later memory. Most mnemonic devices require the use of visual imagery.

method of loci A mnemonic device in which you choose some pathway, such as moving through the rooms in your house, and then form visual images of the to-be-remembered items sitting in locations along the pathway.

peg-word method A mnemonic device in which you form visual images connecting to-be-remembered items with retrieval cues, or pegs.

FIGURE 8.7 The Method of Loci
To-be-remembered items are mentally placed in various locations along a familiar path. They should now be remembered easily because visual imagery promotes an elaborate memory trace and because the stored locations are easy to access.

One of the oldest **mnemonic devices** is the **method of loci** (*loci* is Latin for "places"). According to legend, it traces back to the ancient Greek Simonides, who used it to identify the attendees of a large banquet that ended abruptly in tragedy. Simonides had apparently delivered a lecture at the banquet but was called away just before a portion of the building collapsed, killing many of the diners. To identify the bodies, Simonides formed a visual image of the room and used the seating assignments to reconstruct the guest list.

Like most mnemonic devices, the method of loci relies on visual imagery. You begin by choosing some real-world pathway, or route, that's easy to remember, such as moving through the rooms in your house or along some familiar route to work or school. In your mind, you then place the to-be-remembered material—suppose that you wanted to remember a list of errands—at various locations along the path. It's important to form a visual image of each memory item and to link the image to a specific location. So, if you wanted to remember to pay the gas bill, you could form a mental picture of a large check made out to the gas company and place it in the first location on your path (such as the entry hall in your house).

Depending on the size of your pathway, you can store a relatively large amount of material using this method. At the end of encoding you might have 15 different errands stored. Overdue library books could be linked to the living room sofa, clean shirts encased in plastic could be draped across the kitchen counter, or big bags of dog chow could be associated with a dog on the television screen (see ▮Figure 8.7).

To recover the material later, all you need to do is walk along the pathway in your mind, "looking" in the different locations for the objects you've stored (Higbee, 1988). The method of loci is an effective memory aid because it forces you to use imagery—creating an elaborate and distinctive record—and the stored records are easy to recover because the storage locations are easy to access.

The **peg-word method** resembles the method of loci in that it requires you to link material to specific memory cues, but the cues are usually words rather than mental pathways. One easy technique is to pick "peg words" that rhyme with numbers: For instance, one is a *bun*, two is a *shoe*, three is a *tree*, and so forth. This makes the pegs easy to remember and access. You then form an image linking the to-be-remembered material with each of the pegs. You might picture your overdue library books inside a

hamburger bun, a bag of dog chow sitting inside a shoe, or some clean shirts hanging from a tree. To recover the memory records, you simply start counting, and the peg word should lead you to the image of the to-be-remembered errand. One is a bun—return books; two is a shoe—buy dog chow; three is a tree—pick up shirts.

An alternative version of the peg-word method, called the *linkword system*, has been used successfully to assist in learning foreign language vocabulary (Gruneberg, Sykes, & Gillett, 1994). Suppose you wanted to remember the French word for rabbit (*lapin*). While studying, think of an English word that sounds like the French word; perhaps the word *lap* would do for *lapin*. Next, think about the meaning of the French word and try to form a visual image of the result linked to the English rhyme. For example, you could imagine a white furry rabbit sitting in someone's lap. When the word *lapin* then appears later on a test, the English rhyme should serve as an effective cue for bringing forth a remembered image of the rabbit (*lap* acts as a kind of peg word for rabbit). This method has been shown to produce nearly a doubling of the rate of learning for vocabulary words (Raugh & Atkinson, 1975).

Remembering With a Stone-Age Brain

The fact that forming a visual image is an effective way to remember shouldn't surprise you too much. After all, we rely heavily on our visual system to navigate and understand our world, so it makes sense that memory, too, relies to some extent on visual imagery (Paivio, 2007). Most cognitive processes, including memory, evolved to help us solve particular problems and bear the "footprints" of ancestral selection pressures. For example, if people are asked to think about material in terms of its potential survival value, they remember that material particularly well (Nairne, Thompson, & Pandeirada, 2007).

We also tend to form rich records of the circumstances surrounding emotionally significant and surprising events (Brown & Kulick, 1977). So-called **flashbulb memories** have been reported for lots of events—for example, the assassination of John F. Kennedy, the attempted assassination of Ronald Reagan, the Space Shuttle *Challenger* disaster, and even the verdict in the O. J. Simpson murder trial. People who experience flashbulb memories are convinced they can remember exactly what they were doing when the event occurred. Playing in school, watching television, talking on the phone—whatever the circumstance, people report vivid details about the events surrounding their first exposure to the news. Do you remember what you were doing when you first heard of the September 11, 2001, terrorist attack on the United States?

Surprisingly, flashbulb memories are often not very accurate. Neisser and Harsch (1992) asked college students one day after the Space Shuttle *Challenger* exploded to describe exactly how they first heard the news. The details were recorded, then three years later the same students were asked to recollect their experiences. People were highly confident about their recollections, yet there wasn't much agreement between the original and the delayed memories. The students thought they were remembering things accurately, but the data proved otherwise. The fact that their memories were poor suggests that the psychological experience of flashbulb memories—that is, the strong conviction that one's memories are accurate—may be related more to the emotionality of the original experience than to the presence of a rich and elaborative memory record.

One reason flashbulb memories tend to be inaccurate is that we often incorporate later experiences into our original memories. When something shocking happens, we talk about it a lot, see footage of the event on TV, and hear other people analyze how and why it happened. The events of September 11 are a good example. When President Bush was asked about his memory for the events some months later, he remembered having seen footage of the first plane hitting the tower before he learned about the crash of the second plane. At the time, of course, no footage was available on TV, so his memory of having seen the first plane attack was simply wrong. This led to some conspiracy theories on the Internet—"Bush films his own attack on the World Trade Center"—but a more reasonable explanation is that he simply

flashbulb memories Rich memory records of the circumstances surrounding emotionally significant and surprising events.

You probably have a strong flashbulb memory for the events of September 11— but is the memory accurate?

mistakenly incorporated a later memory (viewing the footage) into his memory for the original event (Greenberg, 2004).

It's important to remember, though, that just because flashbulb memories are sometimes inaccurate doesn't mean they aren't useful and adaptive. We don't necessarily want to remember the past exactly, because the past can never happen again in exactly the same way. Instead, we want to use the past, in combination with the present, to decide on an appropriate action. As you'll see in the next section, remembering often involves reconstructing the past rather than remembering it exactly.

Test Yourself   8.2

Check your knowledge of how information is stored over the long term by answering the following questions. (You will find the answers in the Appendix.)

1. For each of the following, try to decide whether the relevant memory is episodic, semantic, or procedural.
   a. The capital city of Texas is Austin: _____
   b. Breakfast yesterday was ham and eggs: _____
   c. My mother's maiden name is Hudlow: _____
   d. Executing a perfect golf swing: _____
   e. Tying your shoelaces: _____
2. Your little brother Eddie needs to learn a long list of vocabulary words for school tomorrow. Which of the following represents the best advice for improving his memory?
   a. Say the words aloud as many times as possible.
   b. Write down the words as many times as possible.
   c. Form a visual image of each word.
   d. Spend more time studying words at the beginning and end of the list.

3. For each of the following, decide which term best applies. Choose from *distinctiveness, distributed practice, elaboration, method of loci,* and *peg-word technique.*
   a. Visualize each of the items sitting in a location along a pathway: _____
   b. Notice how each of the items is different from other things in memory: _____
   c. Form connections among each of the items to be remembered: _____
   d. Form images linking items to specific cues: _____
   e. Engage in relational processing of the to-be-remembered material: _____

Recovering Information From Cues

LEARNING GOALS
- Discuss the importance of retrieval cues in remembering.
- Discuss the differences between explicit and implicit memory.
- Explain the role of schemas in reconstructive memory.

CAN YOU STILL REMEMBER the memory list from a few pages back? You know, the one based on things you might take to a morning lecture class? If you remembered the items, such as PENCIL, NOTES, and COFFEE, it's probably because you were able to use the common theme—things at a lecture—as a *cue* to help you remember. Psychologists believe that *retrieval*, the process of recovering previously stored memories, is guided primarily by cues, called *retrieval cues*, that are either generated internally (thinking of the lecture scene helps you remember PENCIL) or are present in the environment (a string tied around your finger).

The Importance of Retrieval Cues

free recall A testing condition in which a person is asked to remember information without explicit retrieval cues.

cued recall A testing condition in which people are given an explicit retrieval cue to help them remember.

A classic study conducted by Tulving and Pearlstone (1966) illustrates the important role that retrieval cues play in remembering. People were given lists to remember containing words from several meaningful categories (types of animals, birds, vegetables, and so on). Later, people were asked to remember the words either with or without the aid of retrieval cues. Half were asked to recall the words without cues, a condition called **free recall**; the other half were given the category names to help them remember, known as **cued recall**. People in the cued-recall condition recalled

Can you name all of your fifth-grade classmates? Probably not, but your memory is sure to improve if you're given a class photo to use as a retrieval cue.

nearly twice as many words, presumably because the category names helped them gain access to the previously stored material.

Although these results are not surprising, they have important implications for how we need to think about remembering. Because people performed poorly in the free-recall condition, it's tempting to conclude they never learned the material or simply forgot many of the items from the list. But performance in the cued-recall condition shows that the material wasn't actually lost—it just couldn't be accessed. With the right retrieval cues—in this case the category names—the "lost" material could be remembered with ease. Memory researchers believe that most, if not all, instances of forgetting are caused by a failure to use the right kinds of retrieval cues. Once information is encoded, it is available somewhere in the brain; you simply need appropriate retrieval cues to gain access.

This is the main reason elaboration is an effective strategy for remembering. When you connect material to existing knowledge, creating a rich and elaborate memory record, you're effectively increasing the number of potential retrieval cues. The more retrieval cues, the more likely you'll be able to access the memory record later on. It's also the main reason mnemonic techniques such as the peg-word method work so well—they establish readily available retrieval cues as part of the learning process (counting to 10 provides immediate access to the relevant "pegs").

The Encoding–Retrieval Match Increasing the number of potential retrieval cues helps, but it also helps if the cue *matches* the memory that was encoded. If you think about the sound of a word during its original presentation, rather than its appearance, then a cue that rhymes with the stored word will be more effective than a visual cue. Similarly, if you think about the meaning of a word during study, then an effective cue will get you to think about the encoded word's meaning during retrieval. Retrieval cues are effective to the extent that they match the way information was originally encoded.

In the years to come, this couple may find it easier to remember this blissful reunion if they're happy rather than sad. How does this conclusion reflect the encoding–retrieval match?

Study	Retrieval Match	Retrieval Mismatch
Encoding Input	Retrieval Cue: "Bank"	Retrieval Cue: "Bank"

▌FIGURE 8.8 The Encoding–Retrieval Match

Memory often depends on how well retrieval cues match the way information was originally studied or encoded. Suppose you're asked to remember the word pair BANK–WAGON. You form a visual image of a wagon teetering on the edge of a riverbank. When presented later with the retrieval cue BANK, you're more likely to remember WAGON if you interpret the cue as something bordering a river than as a place to keep money.

Let's consider an example. Suppose you're asked to remember two words: BANK and WAGON. To improve retention, you form a visual image of a WAGON perched on the BANK of a river (see ▌Figure 8.8). Later BANK is provided as a retrieval cue. Will it help you remember WAGON? Probably, but only if you interpret the retrieval cue BANK to mean a slope immediately bordering a river. If for some reason you think about BANK as a place to keep money, you probably won't recover WAGON successfully. A retrieval cue works well only if you interpret it in the proper way. By "proper" psychologists mean that the cue must be interpreted in a way that matches the original encoding. There are some exceptions to this general rule (Nairne, 2002b), but a good encoding–retrieval match is one of the most important factors to consider when seeking a useful retrieval cue.

The encoding–retrieval match helps to explain why remembering is often state or context dependent. It turns out that divers can remember important safety information better if they learn the information while diving rather than on land (Martin & Aggelton, 1993). Presumably, there's a better match between encoding and retrieval when information is learned and tested in the same environment. Another example is childhood, or infantile, amnesia: Most of us have a difficult time remembering things that happened to us before the age of 4 or 5. However, it's likely that we interpreted the world very differently when we were small. Childhood amnesia may result, then, from a poor match between the present and the distant past. We see and interpret events differently now than we did as children, so we have few effective retrieval cues available for remembering childhood events (Courage & Howe, 2004).

Transfer-Appropriate Processing Is there any way to guarantee a good encoding–retrieval match? One way is to pay close attention to the conditions that are likely to be present when you need to remember. You can engage in what psychologists call **transfer-appropriate processing**, which means you should study material using the same kind of mental processes that'll be required during testing. Matching the mental processes used during study and test increases the chances that effective retrieval cues will be available (Lockhart, 2002).

To illustrate, let's assume you're asked to remember the word TUG for a later memory test (see ▌Figure 8.9). If you form a visual image of a tugboat and you're then specifically asked about a tugboat on the memory test, you'll probably perform well.

transfer-appropriate processing The idea that the likelihood of correct retrieval is increased if a person uses the same kind of mental processes during testing that he or she used during encoding.

FIGURE 8.9 Transfer-Appropriate Processing
It's useful to study material with the same type of mental processes that you'll be required to use when tested. Suppose you form a visual image of a to-be-remembered word (panel 1). If the test requires you to recognize an image of the word, you should do well (panel 2). But if the test asks how the word sounds (panel 3) or whether the word was presented originally in upper- or lowercase letters (panel 4), you're likely to perform poorly. You need to study in a way that is appropriate to the test.

But suppose you're asked instead to remember whether the word TUG was printed in upper- or lowercase letters. All of the elaboration in the world isn't going to help you unless you've specifically encoded the way the letters were shaped ("TUG," not "tug"). The lesson of transfer-appropriate processing is that you need to consider the nature of the test before you can decide how to study most effectively. For some hints on how to apply the principle of transfer-appropriate processing when you study for an exam, see the Practical Solutions feature on the following page.

Reconstructive Remembering

Retrieval cues guide remembering in much the same way that an incoming physical message guides the processes of perception. As you may recall from Chapter 5, what you "see" really depends on both the incoming message and the expectations you hold about what's "out there." In a similar way, remembering depends on more than just a retrieval cue—your expectations and beliefs color an act of remembering just as they color what you see and hear. Think about what you had for breakfast two weeks ago. Did you skip breakfast or, perhaps, gulp down a quick bowl of cereal? It turns out that what you "remember" in a case like this often corresponds more to habit than to actual fact. If you regularly eat a bowl of cereal in the morning, then eating cereal is what you're likely to recall, even if you broke the routine on that particular day and had a bagel.

Memory Schemas   To understand why memory acts in this way, we must return to that vast storehouse of information in the brain—the repository of episodic, procedural, and especially semantic memories. As you know, we store more than facts in long-term memory—we also store relationships among facts. You know, for example, that houses contain rooms with walls, require insurance protection, and are susceptible to burning down. You know that college students like to sleep late, wear

Studying for Exams

You're now familiar with some techniques for improving memory. You form an elaborate and distinctive memory record during encoding, possibly through the use of visual imagery, and make certain that relevant retrieval cues are available when you need to remember. It also helps to space your practice—don't cram all of your studying into one marathon session the night before the test. By studying the material at different times, and in different situations, you increase the chances of the information being linked to lots of different, and potentially available, retrieval cues. Perhaps most important is that you pay particular attention to the concept of transfer-appropriate processing: Make certain that how you study resembles the kinds of activities found on the test.

On a practical level, this means that you should think about the characteristics of an exam before you sit down to study. An essay exam, for example, is a kind of *cued-recall* test—you're given a cue in the form of a test question, and you're required to recall the most appropriate answer. To study for such a test, it's best to practice cued recall: Make up questions that are relevant to the material and practice recalling the appropriate answer with only the test question as a cue. For a multiple-choice test, which is a kind of *recognition test*, it's necessary to discriminate a correct answer from a group of incorrect answers (called *distractors*). The best way to study for a multiple-choice test is to practice with multiple-choice questions; either make up your own or use questions from a study guide.

Have you ever thought to yourself, "I'll just read the chapter one more time before I go to bed, and I'll ace the exam tomorrow"? Think about it from the perspective of transfer-appropriate processing—what exactly does the typical exam ask you to do? Exams don't measure the speed or fluency with which the chapter can be *read*. Most exams require you to recall or reproduce material in the presence of cues. Learn the material by reading the chapter, but prepare for the exam by using processes similar to those required by the test. Practice reproducing the material by answering questions from memory or practice discriminating correct from incorrect answers by responding to a variety of multiple-choice questions.

schema An organized knowledge structure in long-term memory.

jeans, and listen to loud music. These large clusters of related facts are organized into knowledge structures called **schemas**. Schemas can be about people, places, or activities—we even have them for routines such as going to a restaurant, visiting the local urgent care center, or following daily eating habits. When you remember, you use these organized knowledge packages to help recover the past. So when someone asks you what you ate for breakfast two weeks ago, you can confidently answer "cereal" because you know cereal is what you usually eat for breakfast. You don't have to remember the specific episode; you can rely on your general knowledge.

The trouble with schema-based remembering is that it can easily lead to false or inaccurate retention. You might remember something that's completely wrong—it didn't really happen—yet still be convinced your memory is accurate. (Remember our earlier discussion of flashbulb memories?) More than 70 years ago an English psychologist named Frederick Bartlett asked undergraduates to read an unfamiliar North American Indian folktale about tribe members who traveled up a river to battle with some warrior "ghosts" (the story's title was "The War of the Ghosts"). In recalling the story sometime later, the students tended to distort facts, omit details, and fill in information that was not included in the original version. For example, familiar things were substituted for unfamiliar things—the word *boat* was substituted for *canoe*; "hunting seals" was replaced with "hunting beavers." Because these things were not actually in the story, Bartlett assumed his participants must have used their prior knowledge to reconstruct what they remembered—even though they were convinced they were remembering the material accurately (Bartlett, 1932).

A similar point was made more recently by Loftus and Palmer (1974). Undergraduates were shown a short film depicting an automobile accident. Later, when questioned about the film, the students were asked to estimate how fast the cars were traveling just prior to the accident. Some students were asked to estimate the speed of the cars just before they *smashed* into each other; others were asked how fast the cars were going before they *contacted* each other. Notice the difference between the words—the schema for *smashed* implies that the cars were traveling at a high rate of speed, whereas *contacted* suggests that the cars were moving slowly. As shown in Figure 8.10, people who heard the word *smashed* in the question estimated that the

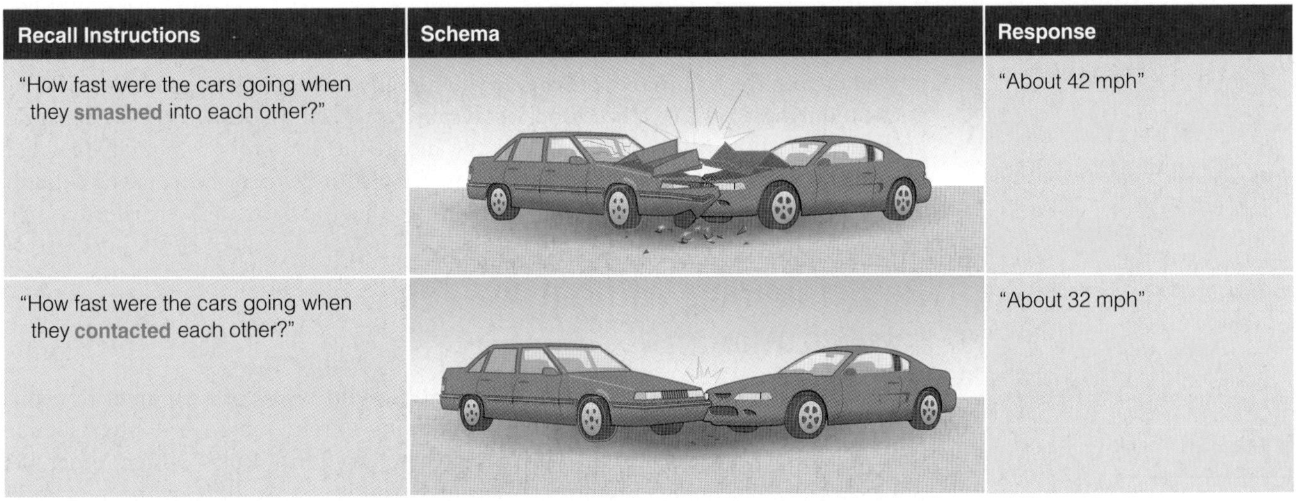

Recall Instructions	Schema	Response
"How fast were the cars going when they **smashed** into each other?"		"About 42 mph"
"How fast were the cars going when they **contacted** each other?"		"About 32 mph"

FIGURE 8.10 Schema-Based Remembering
Loftus and Palmer (1974) found that students remembered cars traveling faster when retrieval instructions used the word *smashed* instead of *contacted*. All people saw the same film, but their different schemas for the words *smashed* and *contacted* presumably caused them to reconstruct their memories differently.

cars were traveling about 42 miles per hour; people in the *contacted* group gave an estimate of about 10 miles per hour slower.

Once again, these results show that memory is importantly influenced by general knowledge, as well as by expectations. Everyone in the Loftus and Palmer experiment saw the same film, but what people remembered depended on how the questions were worded—that is, on whether people were led to believe that the cars were going fast or slow. In addition to giving estimates of speed, some were asked whether any broken glass was present in the accident scene. When *smashed* was used in the speed question, people were much more likely to incorrectly remember seeing broken glass, even though there wasn't any in the original film. By asking the right kinds of questions during testing, it's possible to make people think they experienced things that did not occur. As Loftus (1979, 1991) has emphasized, these findings suggest that caution must be exercised in interpreting the testimony of any eyewitness—reconstructive factors can always be involved.

Here's an easy way to demonstrate schema-based remembering for yourself: Read the following list of words aloud to a group of friends:

BED REST AWAKE TIRED DREAM WAKE SNOOZE
BLANKET DOZE SLUMBER SNORE NAP YAWN DROWSY

Now ask your friends to write down all the words they've just heard. The chances are very good that someone will remember an item that was not on the list, especially the word SLEEP. In experiments using lists of such related items, people have been found to recall nonpresented items (e.g., sleep) nearly 50% of the time (Deese, 1959; Roediger & McDermott, 1995). The chances of false memory increase even more when recognition memory is tested—that is, when you're given the word SLEEP and are asked if it was presented on the list (McDermott & Roediger, 1998). What's behind this effect? Obviously, the word SLEEP is highly related to the words on the list. It seems likely that people recognize the relationships among the words and use this knowledge to help them remember. This is a very effective strategy for remembering, but it can lead to false recollections.

Despite the mistakes, schema-based remembering clearly has adaptive value. By relying on preexisting knowledge to "fill in the gaps" or to help interpret fuzzy recollections, you increase the chances that your responses in new environments will

CRITICAL THINKING

Do you think all remembering is reconstructive? What about sensory memory—isn't that a pure kind of remembering?

be appropriate—after all, the past is usually the best predictor of the future. You can also use your schematic knowledge to "correct" for any minor details you may have missed during the original exposure. If you already have a pretty good idea of what goes on during a visit to a fast-food restaurant, your mind doesn't need to expend a great deal of effort attending to details the next time you enter a McDonald's. You can rely on your prior knowledge to capture the gist of the experience, even though, on the down side, you may recollect a few things that didn't actually happen.

Remembering Without Awareness: Implicit Memory

Up to this point we've concentrated on conscious, willful acts of remembering—that is, situations in which you're consciously intending to remember something (such as what you ate for breakfast or the words from a memory list). But we often remember things without conscious intent or awareness. You speak, walk to work, recognize someone you know—all these things require memory, but you're usually not explicitly trying to remember anything.

Psychologists use the term **implicit memory** to describe this kind of remembering (Graf & Schacter, 1985; Roediger & McDermott, 1993). It turns out that implicit memory—remembering without awareness—acts quite similarly to **explicit memory**, the name researchers use to describe conscious, willful remembering. For example, both implicit and explicit memory are strongly influenced by retrieval cues. If you look at ▌Figure 8.11, you'll see some examples of word and picture fragments. Your ability to complete one of these fragments improves if you've seen the solution word recently during reading (for example, the word fragment E_E_ _AN_ is easier to solve if the word ELEPHANT has been encountered in the prior 24 hours). But importantly, you don't need to remember seeing the word. Your performance improves even if you don't consciously remember the word (which makes the remembering implicit). At the same time, performance depends importantly on whether the earlier encounter matches the fragment. If you need to solve a picture fragment, then you're helped more if the earlier encounter was in the form of a picture—such as seeing a picture of an elephant—rather than a word (McDermott & Roediger, 1994; Weldon & Roediger, 1987). Once again, the conditions during testing need to match the conditions present during the original exposure.

There are situations in which implicit memory appears to act somewhat differently from explicit memory. For example, encoding strategies that typically improve conscious, willful remembering often have little or no effect on implicit memory

implicit memory Remembering that occurs in the absence of conscious awareness or willful intent.

explicit memory Conscious, willful remembering.

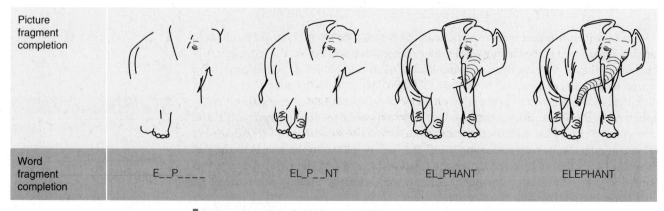

| Picture fragment completion | | | | |
| Word fragment completion | E_ _P_ _ _ _ | EL_P_ _NT | EL_PHANT | ELEPHANT |

▌**FIGURE 8.11** Implicit Memory Tests
The person's task in each test is to complete the picture or word fragment so as to identify the object shown on the far right.

(Roediger et al., 1992). If you think about the meaning of the material, which induces elaboration, you're much more likely to recall it on an explicit test of memory, such as recall or recognition. But the same improvement often isn't found when memory is tested using an implicit test, such as solving word fragment problems (Graf, Mandler, & Haden, 1982). All that seems to matter is that the material be presented in a physically similar way during study and testing.

Test Yourself 8.3

Check your knowledge about how we use cues to help us remember by answering the following questions. Fill in the blanks with one of the following terms: cued recall, explicit memory, free recall, implicit memory, schema, transfer-appropriate processing. (You will find the answers in the Appendix.)

1. An organized knowledge package that's stored in long-term memory: _____
2. Remembering without awareness: _____
3. Studying for a multiple-choice test by writing your own multiple-choice questions: _____
4. Remembering material without the aid of any external retrieval cues: _____

Updating Memory

LEARNING GOALS
- Discuss the contributions of Ebbinghaus and explain why forgetting is often adaptive.
- Describe the mechanisms that cause forgetting, including decay and retroactive and proactive interference.
- Discuss motivated forgetting and the case for repression.
- Describe retrograde and anterograde amnesia and explain where memories might be stored in the brain.

LIKE OTHER STORAGE DEVICES, the mind is susceptible to clutter. Effective remembering often hinges on your ability to successfully discriminate one occurrence from another—you need to remember where you parked your car today not yesterday, or a current phone number (not a previous one). What if you felt the urge to buy two dozen paper cups every time you entered the grocery store because one time last year you needed paper cups for a party? **Forgetting**, the loss of accessibility to previously stored material, is one of the most important and adaptive properties of your memory system (Bjork, 1989; Kraemer & Golding, 1997).

If you need further convincing, consider the strange case of a Russian journalist known as S. who possessed an extraordinary ability to remember. It seems that S., through a fluke of nature, reacted automatically to stimuli in ways that formed unusual and distinctive encodings. When presented with a tone pitched at 500 hertz, S. reported seeing "a dense orange color which made him feel as though a needle had been thrust into his spine" (Luria, 1968, p. 24). For a 3,000-hertz tone, S. claimed that it "looks something like a firework tinged with a pink-red hue. The strip of color feels rough and unpleasant, and it has an ugly taste—rather like that of a briny pickle" (p. 24).

S. had a remarkable memory—he could remember grids of numbers perfectly after 15 years—but he suffered a near fatal flaw: He simply couldn't forget. He had trouble reading

forgetting The loss of accessibility to previously stored material.

Forgetting is often bothersome, but it can have considerable adaptive value.

©David Young-Wolff/PhotoEdit

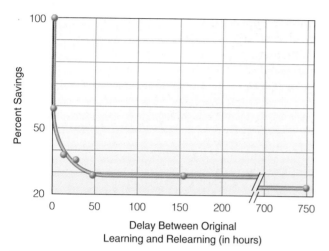

Percent Savings (y-axis: 20, 50, 100)

Delay Between Original Learning and Relearning (in hours) (x-axis: 0, 50, 100, 150, 200, 700, 750)

FIGURE 8.12 The Ebbinghaus Forgetting Curve
The German philosopher Hermann Ebbinghaus memorized lists of nonsense syllables and then measured how long it took to relearn the same material after various delays. Fifty percent savings means it took half as long to relearn the list as it did to learn it originally; 0% savings would mean that it took as long to relearn the list as it did to learn the list originally.

Hermann Ebbinghaus (1859–1909)

books because words or phrases so flooded his mind with previous associations that he had great difficulty concentrating. He would note, for example, small errors in the text: If a character entered the story wearing a cap and in later pages was described without a cap, S. would become greatly disturbed and disappointed in the author. He had trouble holding a job or even a sustained conversation. For S., the failure to forget produced a truly cluttered mind.

How Quickly Do We Forget?

For most people, once an item has left the immediate present, it's forgotten in a regular and systematic way. How quickly an item is forgotten depends on several factors: how the item was initially encoded, whether it was encountered again at some later time, and the kinds of retrieval cues that are present at the point of remembering. But in general the course of forgetting looks like the curve shown in
Figure 8.12. Most of the forgetting occurs early, but you will continue to forget gradually for a long period following the initial exposure (Wixted & Ebbesen, 1991).

The forgetting curve shown in the figure is taken from some classic work by the German philosopher Hermann Ebbinghaus, who was one of the first researchers to investigate memory and forgetting scientifically (Ebbinghaus, 1885/1964). Isolated in his study, he forced himself to learn lists of nonsense syllables (such as ZOK) and then measured how long it took to relearn the same material after various delays (a technique called the *savings method*). As the graph shows, the longer the delay after original learning, the greater effort Ebbinghaus had to spend relearning the list. The Ebbinghaus forgetting function—a rapid loss followed by a more gradual decline—is typical of forgetting. Similar forgetting functions are found for a variety of materials, and even for complex skills such as flying an airplane (Fleishman & Parker, 1962) or performing cardiopulmonary resuscitation (McKenna & Glendon, 1985).

Even memories for everyday things, such as the names of high school classmates or material learned in school, are forgotten in regular and systematic ways. In one study Bahrick (1984) studied memory for a foreign language (Spanish) over intervals that ranged from about 1 to 50 years. In another study Bahrick and Hall (1991) examined the retention of high school mathematics over 50 years. In both cases there was rapid loss of recently learned material, followed by more gradual loss, but a considerable amount of knowledge was retained indefinitely. What's surprising about these studies is that a fair amount of the knowledge remained, even though the participants claimed to have not rehearsed or thought about the material in over half a century. (Maybe there's hope for education yet!)

There's one more characteristic of long-term forgetting that you'll probably find interesting. When older adults are asked to recall and date events from their past, not surprisingly they tend to remember things from the more recent past best. However, there's a "bump" in the forgetting curve for events that happened between late adolescence and about age 30 (Rubin & Schulkind, 1997). For some reason we retain events from this period particularly well—or, at least, these are the events that we're apt to recall in our older years. This is known as the "reminiscence bump," and psychologists aren't exactly certain why it happens. We experience lots of "firsts" during this period (career, possibly marriage and family), so perhaps we simply repeatedly rehearse what happens during the 20-something period throughout our lives (Roediger & Marsh, 2003; Rubin & Bernsten, 2003).

Why Do We Forget?

We can agree that it's adaptive to forget, and we can measure how quickly information becomes unavailable over time, but what causes forgetting? As we discussed earlier, most memory researchers believe that forgetting is cue dependent—you fail to remember a prior event because you don't have the right retrieval cues. But it's also possible that memories simply fade with the passage of time in accordance with a "law of use" (Thorndike, 1914). If you fail to practice a learned habit, such as playing the piano, the habit fades, or *decays*, spontaneously with time.

However, **decay**—the idea that memories fade due to the passage of time—cannot explain most instances of forgetting. For one thing, as you've seen, memories that appear to have been forgotten can be remembered later under the right retrieval conditions. In addition, people often remember trivial things (such as a joke) for years but forget important things that once received a great deal of practice (such as elementary geometry). Even more significant, just because memories are lost with time doesn't mean that *time* alone is the cause. A nail left outside becomes rusty with time, but it is not the passage of time that creates the rust—processes other than time (oxidation, in the case of the rusty nail) actually produce the changes.

Retroactive Interference   In forgetting, the "other processes"—which are correlated with the passage of time but are not created by time—often depend on the establishment of other memories. We constantly learn new things, and these new memories compete, or *interfere*, with the recovery of old memories. When you get a new apartment, you work hard to associate your telephone with a new phone number. But after you succeed, it becomes more difficult to retrieve your old number, even if you actively try to remember. The retrieval cue "telephone number" has now become associated with something new; as a result, it loses its capacity to produce the old number. Psychologists use the term **retroactive interference** to refer to cases where the formation of new memories hurts the retention of old memories.

In a classic study of retroactive interference, Jenkins and Dallenbach (1924) asked two students from Cornell University to live in a laboratory for several weeks and learn lists of nonsense syllables either just before bed or early in the morning. The students were tested 1, 2, 4, or 8 hours after learning. The results, which are shown in ▌Figure 8.13, were clear: When the students slept during the delay interval, they remembered more than when they remained awake. Note that a constant amount of time passed in both conditions, so a decay theory would predict no differences between the conditions. The findings suggest it was the activities that occurred during the students' waking hours that produced the information loss. When awake, the students formed new memories, which interfered with recovery of the old material.

Proactive Interference   It's not just the learning of new information that produces forgetting. Previously learned information can also produce interference. **Proactive interference** occurs when old memories interfere with the establishment and recovery of new memories. Suppose I ask you to recall the word DEATH every time you see the word HAPPY. It's likely that prior associations will interfere with the learning process—the word HAPPY makes you think of things that are inconsistent with DEATH. Alternatively, suppose I ask you to think of PENCIL as a potential weapon to be used in combat. You might be able to think about the word in this way for the experiment, but as time passes you'll certainly revert back to thinking about PENCIL in the usual way. This, in turn, will make it difficult for you to remember later that PENCIL was once encoded as a weapon—you won't be able to generate retrieval cues that match the way the item was encoded. Prior knowledge and habits interfere with the learning and retention of new material.

Most memory researchers believe that forgetting is usually caused by interference, although it's conceivable that decay might operate in certain situations. One possibility is that decay operates when we remember over the very short term—that is, in sensory memory and short-term memory (Cowan, 1995; Cowan et al., 1997). It's also possible that when we learn new material, older memories are "overwritten" and permanently lost (Loftus &

decay The proposal that memories are forgotten or lost spontaneously with the passage of time.

retroactive interference A process in which the formation of new memories hurts the recovery of old memories.

proactive interference A process in which old memories interfere with the establishment and recovery of new memories.

▌**FIGURE 8.13** Interference and Memory
The activities that occur after learning affect how well stored information is remembered. In this study by Jenkins and Dallenbach (1924), the students remembered better if they slept during the retention interval than if they remained awake. Presumably, the waking activities caused interference.

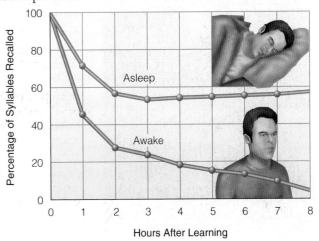

repression A defense mechanism that individuals use, unknowingly, to push threatening thoughts, memories, and feelings out of conscious awareness.

People are more likely to recall pleasant than unpleasant experiences, perhaps because they're reluctant to rehearse unpleasant experiences.

©Robert Cianflone/Getty Images

Loftus, 1980). But generally, we don't *lose* material with time; the material simply becomes harder to remember because other things interfere with the retrieval process. As new memories are encoded, old retrieval cues become less effective because those cues are now associated with new things.

Motivated Forgetting

In our earlier discussion of flashbulb memories, I suggested that highly unusual or emotional events lead to distinctive, and therefore easy to remember, memory records. The adaptive value of a system that "stamps in" significant events is easy to understand—remembering these kinds of events could increase our ability to survive. But what about those cases in which it's adaptive to *forget* something, such as a traumatic instance of child abuse or the witnessing of a violent crime?

The idea that the mind might actively repress, or inhibit, certain memory records is an important ingredient of Sigmund Freud's psychoanalytic theory, as you'll see when we discuss personality theories in Chapter 12. Freud introduced **repression** as a "defense mechanism" unknowingly used by people to push threatening thoughts, memories, and feelings out of conscious awareness. According to Freud, these repressed memories retain the capacity to affect behavior at an unconscious level but cannot be remembered in the conventional sense. The result is a reduction in the experience of anxiety.

The Evidence for Repression   Modern researchers remain undecided about the scientific validity of repression. It's clear that people typically recall more pleasant than unpleasant events (Linton, 1975; Wagenaar, 1986), and painful experiences, such as the pain associated with childbirth, also seem to be recollected less well with the passage of time (Robinson et al., 1980). There are also many cases, reported mainly in clinical settings, of what appear to be the repression of traumatic experiences.

For example, in one study 475 adults who were undergoing psychotherapy were asked about memories of childhood sexual abuse. Each had reported an incident of abuse during childhood, and each was asked the following specific question: "During the period of time between when the first forced sexual encounter happened and your 18th birthday, was there ever a time when you could not remember the forced sexual experience?" (Briere & Conte, 1993). Fifty-nine percent of the people who answered the question responded "Yes," suggesting that the memories had been pushed out of consciousness for at least some period of time. In another study supporting the same conclusion, Williams (1992) asked 100 women who had been medically treated for sexual abuse as children—the abuse was documented by hospital and other records—whether they remembered the incident 17 years later. Thirty-eight percent of those responding reported no memory of the abuse, again providing support for the concept of repression.

But does this really mean that the forgetting was caused by repression? It's possible that people tend to remember positive events because these are the types of events that we rehearse and relate to others. The fact that painful experiences are forgotten with the passage of time can be explained in lots of ways—many things are forgotten with the passage of time, especially those that are unlikely to be rehearsed. Moreover, there's considerable evidence suggesting that people like to cast themselves in a positive light—people often remember donating more to charity than they actually did, or that they raised more intelligent children (Cannell & Kahn, 1968; Myers & Ridl, 1979). Many instances of apparent retrieval failure could be due to the reconstructive "recasting" of prior experiences rather than to the active repression of intact memories (Loftus, 1993; Loftus & Polage, 1999).

There have been attempts to simulate repression in the laboratory. No, people are not exposed to traumatic events; instead they're simply asked to actively prevent previously learned material from coming to mind. For example, if you've been taught to recall TOWN every time you're given CART, I might ask you to actively repress

Concept Review | Mechanisms of Forgetting

MECHANISM	DESCRIPTION	EXAMPLE
Cue dependence	One fails to remember an event due to a lack of appropriate cues.	Although Susan would recognize a definition of semantic memory on a multiple-choice test, she can't think of it for a fill-in-the-blank test.
Decay	Memories fade with the passage of time.	After only a month of lessons, and then six years of not playing the piano, Shao forgets how to play.
Proactive interference	Old memories interfere with the formation and recovery of new memories.	Bruce is so impressed with the first person he met at the party, he can't remember the names of those he met later.
Retroactive interference	New memories interfere with the recovery of old memories.	Filling out a job application, Seth can remember only his most recent address, not the one before it.
Motivated forgetting	Traumatic experiences are forgotten to reduce anxiety.	Jackie can't remember too much about the day her parents were seriously injured in an accident.

thinking about TOWN the next time you see CART. Under these conditions, there's some evidence that TOWN then becomes harder to recall—you've suppressed its representation in memory (Anderson & Green, 2001; but see Bulevich et al., 2006). Researchers even claim to have identified specific areas in the brain that help us keep unwanted memories out of conscious awareness (Anderson et al., 2004).

Whether these laboratory studies really tell us anything about the forgetting of traumatic events remains uncertain. However, as Freud noted, a process of repression might be adaptive in the sense that it can prevent or reduce anxiety. It may also be the case that forgotten events continue to exert indirect influences on behavior in ways that bypass awareness. But the data do suggest that memories, whether "recovered" in therapy or simply in the normal course of everyday activities, should not be taken at face value. It is adaptive for people to use prior knowledge, as well as current expectations, to help them remember—but perhaps at the cost of sometimes remembering things that didn't actually happen.

The Neuroscience of Forgetting

Forgetting can also be caused by physical problems in the brain, such as those induced by injury or illness. Psychologists use the term **amnesia** to refer to forgetting that is caused by some kind of physical problem. (Another type of amnesia that's psychological in origin arises from something called a dissociative disorder, but we'll delay our discussion of this kind of forgetting until Chapter 14.)

amnesia Forgetting that is caused by physical problems in the brain, such as those induced by injury or disease.

Types of Amnesia There are two major kinds of amnesia, retrograde and anterograde. **Retrograde amnesia** is memory loss for events that happened *prior* to the point of injury (you can think of *retro* as meaning backward in time). People who are in automobile accidents, or who receive a sharp blow to the head, often have trouble remembering the events leading directly up to the accident. The memory loss can apply to events that happened only moments before the accident, or the loss can be quite severe; in some cases patients lose their ability to recall personal experiences that occurred years before the accident. In most cases, fortunately, these memory losses are not permanent and recover slowly over time (Cermak, 1982).

retrograde amnesia Memory loss for events that happened prior to the point of brain injury.

Anterograde amnesia is memory loss for events that happen *after* the point of physical damage. People who suffer from anterograde amnesia often seem locked in the past—they're incapable of forming memories for new experiences. The disorder develops as a result of brain damage, which can occur from the persistent use of alcohol (a condition called *Korsakoff syndrome*), from brain infections (such as

anterograde amnesia Memory loss for events that happen after the point of physical injury.

viral encephalitis), or, in some cases, as a by-product of brain surgery. One of the most thoroughly studied amnesic patients, known to researchers as H.M., developed the disorder after surgery was performed to remove large portions of his temporal lobes. The purpose of the operation was to reduce the severity of H.M.'s epileptic seizures; the surgery was successful—his seizures were dramatically reduced—but anterograde amnesia developed as an unexpected side effect.

Over the years patients such as H.M. have been studied in great detail to determine exactly what kinds of memory processing are lost (Milner, 1966). It was originally believed that such patients fail to acquire new memories because some basic encoding mechanisms have been destroyed. It is now clear, however, that these patients can learn a great deal but must be tested in particular ways. If a patient like H.M. is tested implicitly, on a task that does not require *conscious* remembering, performance can approach or even match normal levels.

In one study, Jacoby and Witherspoon (1982) asked Korsakoff patients with anterograde amnesia to learn homophones for a later memory test. Homophones are words that sound alike but have different meanings and spellings, such as READ and REED. To "bias" a particular interpretation for a given homophone, it was presented as part of a word pair, such as BOOK–READ or, in another condition, SAXOPHONE–REED. (Because the words were presented aloud, the only way to distinguish between the homophones READ and REED was through the accompanying context word BOOK or SAXOPHONE.) Later the amnesics were asked to recognize the words, but they were unable to do so—they seemed to have acquired none of the presented information. In a second test, however, the homophones were simply read aloud by the experimenter, and the patients' task was to provide the spelling. Surprisingly, if the amnesics had earlier received the pair BOOK–READ, they spelled the test homophone READ, but if the homophone had been paired with SAXOPHONE, they spelled it REED.

These results suggest that the homophones were learned by the amnesic patients. The way the patients spelled the homophone during the test depended on their prior experience. Other experiments have revealed similar findings. For example, amnesics are more likely to complete a word fragment (such as E_E_ _AN_) correctly if they've seen the word before, but if asked to recall the word, their performance falters (Graf & Schacter, 1985). Patients who suffer from anterograde amnesia fail to retrieve past experiences whenever they must *consciously* recollect the experience; when the past is assessed indirectly, through a task that does not require conscious remembering, these amnesics often perform at normal levels.

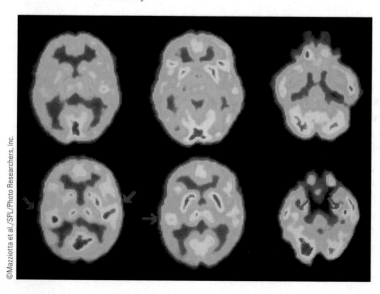

This PET scan shows regions of brain activity during auditory stimulation. The arrows point to areas inside the temporal lobes that become active when words are heard; these same areas are thought to be associated with some kinds of memory.

©Mazziotta et al./SPL/Photo Researchers, Inc.

Where Are Memories Stored? The study of brain-damaged individuals, such as Korsakoff patients, has also encouraged researchers to draw tentative conclusions about how and where memories might be stored in the brain. We touched on this issue in Chapter 3 when we considered biological processes. At that point special attention was paid to a structure called the *hippocampus*, which most brain researchers believe is critically involved in the formation and storage of memories (Squire, 1992). Damage to the hippocampus, as well as to surrounding structures in the brain, leads to memory problems in a wide variety of species, including humans, monkeys, and rats. Areas surrounding the hippocampus also "light up" in neuroimaging studies when people are asked to recall specific material (Cabeza & St Jacques, 2007).

However, no single brain structure, or group of structures, is responsible for all instances of remembering and forgetting. Things are vastly interconnected in the brain, and activities in one part of the brain usually depend on activities in other parts. The regions of the brain involved in the storage of memories also depend on the type of processing involved. For example, episodic memory appears to be controlled by different brain regions from those involved in learning and remembering skills (Gabrieli, 1998). Different hemispheres of the brain may be selectively involved in encoding and retrieval (Habib, Nyberg, & Tulving, 2003) and in whether we're remembering "if" an item occurred versus "where" an item occurred (Mitchell et al., 2004). Emotionally charged memories may involve a structure in the brain called the amygdala (Herz et al., 2004), and different brain regions may even control the remembering of true and false memories (Okada & Stark, 2003; Schacter, 2001).

Certain kinds of memory loss, such as those found in Alzheimer disease, have been linked to inadequate supplies of neurotransmitters in the brain (Albert & Moss, 1992). But damage to a part of the brain tied to the production of a neurotransmitter (such as acetylcholine) probably has consequences for all regions of the brain that depend on that neurotransmitter. This makes it very difficult to pinpoint where a memory is stored or even where the processing relevant to the storage of memories takes place. Modern technological advances are supplying researchers with lots of useful information about activity in the brain, but we still have a long way to go before it will be possible to draw definitive conclusions about the physical basis of learning and remembering.

Test Yourself | 8.4

Check your knowledge about forgetting and the updating of memory by deciding whether each of the following statements is True or False. *(You will find the answers in the Appendix.)*

1. Forgetting is usually slow at first and becomes more rapid as time passes. *True or False?*
2. Most psychologists agree that interference rather than decay is primarily responsible for long-term forgetting. *True or False?*
3. Proactive interference occurs when what you learn at time 2 interferes with what you learned previously at time 1. *True or False?*
4. Anterograde amnesia blocks the learning of new information. *True or False?*
5. People recall more pleasant than unpleasant events over time. *True or False?*
6. Psychologists believe that the hippocampus is involved in some, but not all, instances of remembering. *True or False?*

Review > *Psychology for a Reason*

Time flows continuously, so experiences quickly leave the present and recede backward into the past. To understand the human capacity to preserve and recover this past, we considered some of the problems that our memory systems help us solve.

Remembering Over the Short Term

To improve perception and aid ongoing comprehension, psychologists assume we have internal processes that help us remember over the short term.

In the case of sensory memory, we retain a relatively pure snapshot of the world, or replica of the environmental message. Sensory memories accurately represent the world as recorded by the sensory equipment, but they tend to be short lived, lasting on the order of a second or less. Short-term memory, in contrast, is the system used to store, think about, and reason with the message once it has undergone perceptual analysis. Items are typically maintained in short-term memory in the form of

an "inner voice," and they're forgotten rapidly in the absence of rehearsal. The capacity, or size, of the short-term memory system is determined by a trade-off between the factors that lead to forgetting over the short term (either decay or interference) and the time-limited process of rehearsal.

Storing Information for the Long Term

To store information over the long term, you need to produce elaborate and distinctive memory records.

Focusing on the meaning of the input, relating to-be-remembered information to other things in memory, and forming visual images of the input all lead to distinctive memory records. Forming a visual image is particularly effective, and many memory aids, or mnemonic devices, are based on the use of imagery. Long-term memory also depends on how information is actually presented: Items presented near the beginning and end of a sequence are remembered well, as are items that have been repeated. Spaced or distributed practice turns out to be more effective than massed practice.

Recovering Information From Cues

Successful remembering depends critically on having the right kinds of retrieval cues. Most forms of forgetting are cue dependent, which means that stored information is not really "lost," it simply is inaccessible without the appropriate retrieval cues. Effective retrieval cues are generally those that match the conditions that were present during original learning. It's also the case that when people recover information from cues, they rely on their general knowledge. The past is often reconstructed, and the reconstruction process leads to adaptive, but sometimes inaccurate, recollections of the past.

Updating Memory

Forgetting is an adaptive process. If we didn't constantly change and update our knowledge about the world, our minds would be cluttered with useless facts, such as where the car was parked last Wednesday. Although the psychological mechanisms of forgetting are still being investigated, it seems unlikely that long-term memories fade as a simple by-product of time. Rather, as we learn new things, previously learned material becomes harder to access. New memories compete and interfere with recovery of the old. With the right kinds of cues, however—cues that discriminate one kind of occurrence from another—previously forgotten material becomes refreshed and available for use once again.

Active Summary *(You will find the answers in the Appendix.)*

• Memory is defined as the capacity to (1) _____ and (2) _____ information.

Remembering Over the Short Term

• Both (3) _____ and (4) _____ sensory memory retain relatively (5) _____ replicas of an incoming stimulus. With (6) _____ memory, a visual memory or image is retained for about half a second, long enough to help process the incoming message. With (7) _____ memory, a pure sound is held briefly in auditory memory and may help in language processing.

• We use (8) _____-term memory to store and think about information temporarily, usually as an "inner voice." Information in short-term memory is quickly (9) _____ if not rehearsed, because of (10) _____ (passing time) or (11) _____ (from the environment). Memory (12) _____ is equal to the amount of information that can be (13) _____ in about (14) _____ seconds, usually seven plus or minus two items. Memory span can be increased through a method called (15) _____, which involves rearranging information into meaningful patterns. Some researchers have suggested that we have special systems in a "working" memory that handle spatial (visuospatial sketchpad) and verbal (phonological loop) information.

Storing Information for the Long Term

• We recall personal moments with (16) _____ memory. (17) _____ memories are of facts and knowledge about the world. Our knowledge of how to do things is stored in (18) _____ memory.

• (19) _____ has to do with making (20) _____ among experiences, which allows for easier (21) _____ of stored memories. It helps to think about the (22) _____ of an experience, notice (23) _____, and notice similarities to and (24) _____ from existing knowledge. You can also improve retention by forming mental (25) _____, by spacing your (26) _____, and by considering the (27) _____ position of the material.

• Mnemonic devices, which include the method of (28) _____ and the peg-(29) _____ technique, are mental exercises that use visual imagery to help us remember.

Recovering Information From Cues

• Researchers believe that the amount of information that can be remembered or retrieved is dependent on (30) _____. Good retrieval cues usually (31) _____ the way the information was encoded.

The (32) _____-appropriate processing principle holds that we should study material with the same kinds of (33) _____ processes that will be used during the (34) _____ process.

• (35) _____ are large clusters of related facts about people, activities, and places. Memory schemas are adaptive but can influence what is remembered and may lead to (36) _____ memories.

• When we remember something without conscious awareness, it's called (37) _____ memory. Prior experience and stored memories may influence implicit memory. We use (38) _____ memory when we make a conscious, deliberate effort to recall something.

Updating Memory

• Ebbinghaus found that (39) _____ forgetting occurs soon after initial exposure to an experience, but (40) _____ forgetting can continue for a long time. Forgetting can be extremely (41) _____, as it prevents our minds from becoming cluttered with useless information: We need to remember where we parked our car today, not yesterday.

• The simple passage of time (decay) isn't sufficient to explain most aspects of forgetting. Equally important are (42) _____ interference, in which (43) _____ material interferes with the recovery of old memories, and (44) _____ interference, in which (45) _____ material interferes with the formation and recovery of new memories.

• Freud believed that the mind may deliberately inhibit or (46) _____ certain memories as a form of self-protection. Most researchers are undecided about the scientific (47) _____ of this concept. We do sometimes forget traumatic events, but it's not clear that this forgetting is due to special processes.

• Forgetting caused by a physical problem is called (48) _____. (49) _____ amnesia is loss of memory for events that happened (50) _____ the accident or disease; (51) _____ amnesia causes events that happened (52) _____ the trauma to be forgotten. Although the (53) _____ is important in forming new memories, no single structure is responsible for the complex processes of memory. Amnesia may be regulated by the amount or production of certain (54) _____.

Terms to Remember

amnesia, 271
anterograde amnesia, 271
chunking, 253
cued recall, 260
decay, 269
distinctiveness, 256
distributed practice, 257
echoic memory, 248
elaboration, 256
encoding, 245
episodic memory, 254
explicit memory, 266
flashbulb memories, 259

forgetting, 267
free recall, 260
iconic memory, 247
implicit memory, 266
long-term memory, 254
memory span, 251
memory, 245
method of loci, 258
mnemonic devices, 258
peg-word method, 258
primacy effect, 257
proactive interference, 269
procedural memory, 255

recency effect, 257
rehearsal, 251
repression, 270
retrieval, 245
retroactive interference, 269
retrograde amnesia, 271
schema, 264
semantic memory, 255
sensory memory, 247
short-term memory, 247
storage, 245
transfer-appropriate processing, 262
visual imagery, 256

Media Resources

 **ThomsonNOW**

www.thomsonedu.com/ThomsonNOW

Go to this site for the link to ThomsonNow, your one-stop study shop. Take a Pre-Test for this chapter and Thomson-Now will generate a personalized Study Plan based on your test results! The Study Plan will identify the topics you need to review and direct you to online resources to help you master those topics. You can then take a Post-Test to help you determine the concepts you have mastered and what you still need to work on.

 Companion Website

www.thomsonedu.com/psychology/nairne

Go to this site to find online resources directly linked to your book, including a glossary, flashcards, quizzing, weblinks, and more.

 Psyk.trek 3.0

Check out the Psyk.trek CD-ROM for further study of the concepts in this chapter. Psyk.trek's interactive learning modules, simulations, and quizzes offer additional opportunities for you to interact with, reflect on, and retain the material:

Memory and Thought: Memory Encoding

Language and Thought

Wayne Inges chuckles silently to himself as he completes the deal. "That's right," he says, "center court, floor level—$100 for the pair." Having paid only $50 for the ticket pair himself, Wayne pockets a tidy little profit. But

there are more fools in the world, so he decides to buy the tickets back for $150. With game time approaching, and desperation setting in, this time the pair sells for $200. Can you figure out Wayne's total profit for the evening?

To find the answer, your mind begins an internal, goal-directed activity called **thinking**. In its simplest form, thinking involves the internal manipulation of knowledge and ideas. When we think, we act on our knowledge in a directed and purposeful way to solve problems, to reason and make decisions, and to understand and communicate with others. It's not possible to measure thinking directly, but psychologists learn a lot by watching people think and then listening to their rationales for actions or conclusions.

Let's see, Wayne made $50 on the first transaction but spent $150 to buy the tickets back, so he lost the original $50. He finally sold the pair for $200, so his total profit for the evening must be $50, right? Easy enough. We've used our knowledge about the world, and about mathematics in particular, to work systematically toward a goal. It's easy to see the usefulness of the process. Thinking increases your ability to survive because you can act on your knowledge in precise, systematic, and purposeful ways.

But, as perhaps you guessed, our reasoning in this case is completely wrong. We arrived at the wrong answer, as do many others who try this task. Using a slight variation of the same problem, Maier and Burke (1967) found that people come up with the correct answer less than 40% of the time. The correct answer is $100—Wayne paid out a total of $200 ($50 for the first transaction and $150 for the second) and received $300 back from the buyers. Simple subtraction yields the correct answer of $100.

Why the error? Well, the difficulty comes from thinking about Wayne's sales as one continuous event rather than as two separate transactions. Try framing the problem slightly differently: Wayne bought tickets for Friday night's game for $50 and sold them for $100, then he bought tickets for Saturday's game for $150 and sold them for $200. Under these conditions, people rarely, if ever, make an error. One of the challenges of the modern study of thinking, and problem solving in particular, is to understand why human thought processes sometimes break down and lead to errors.

> **thinking** The processes that underlie the mental manipulation of knowledge, usually in an attempt to reach a goal or solve a problem.

All the topics we'll be considering in this chapter—language, forming categories, problem solving, reasoning—are examples of *cognition*, or reflect the action of *cognitive processes*. The term *cognition* refers simply to the activities that underlie all forms of thought. Psychologists who study cognition are generally known as cognitive psychologists, but there is a more diverse field, called *cognitive science*, that draws on the work of professionals in many disciplines, including linguistics, philosophy, biology, computer science, and engineering. Engineers and computer scientists, for example, often attempt to simulate reasoning and thought in computer programs (i.e., artificial intelligence).

The usefulness, or adaptive value, of cognition is self-evident. As you'll see shortly, our ability to think, reason, and communicate with others is what sets humans apart from other species. As before, we'll tackle the chapter content by focusing on a set of specific tasks, or problems, that our cognitive processes help us solve (see ∎ Figure 9.1).

Communicating With Others
The ability to communicate, especially through written and spoken language, may well be our greatest success story. No other species on the planet can claim our knack for transmitting knowledge through speech and writing. Through language production we transmit thoughts, feelings, and needs to others; through language comprehension we learn and understand. We'll discuss the basics of language, both production and comprehension, and we'll consider whether nonhuman animals, particularly other primates, possess even the simplest form of language.

Classifying and Categorizing
To make sense of our environment, especially the objects in it, we carve the world into meaningful chunks called *categories*. Can you imagine a world in which no two things shared features in common, where each encounter with a cat, or a bird, or a snake was a new and unique experience? The ability to see similarities among things, to classify objects and events into meaningful categories, allows us to simplify our environment and make predictions about how to act. We'll discuss how people define and structure categories, and you'll see there's some "fuzziness" to the process.

Solving Problems
Think about the dozens of practical problems you face and solve each and every day. Did you have trouble finding your keys this morning? Have a difficult time choosing what to wear or what to watch on TV? The adaptive value of problem solving should be relatively obvious—if humans couldn't solve the problem of where to find food and water or how to woo and win the appropriate mate, homo sapiens would quickly follow a path to extinction. We'll discuss the various steps involved in problem solving and some of the pitfalls to avoid.

Making Decisions
Finally, when we make decisions, we're required to choose from among a set of alternatives. Should I buy the tickets for $100, use the money to help pay this month's rent, or gamble the money on the outcome of tonight's game? Note that an important ingredient of decision making is *risk*—choices have consequences, and an incorrect decision can lead to an unpleasant or even fatal outcome. Like problem solving, we use certain strategies to help us make decisions, and these strategies, although generally quite productive, sometimes lead to irrational conclusions.

∎ **FIGURE 9.1** The Adaptive Problems
Thought and language serve a variety of adaptive functions. Summarized here are the four adaptive problems that we'll be considering in this chapter.

Communicating with others

Making decisions

Solving problems

Classifying and categorizing

Communicating With Others

LEARNING GOALS
- Understand the structure of language.
- Isolate the factors that contribute to language comprehension.
- Identify the major milestones of language development.
- Assess language in nonhuman species.
- Evaluate the possibility that language is an adaptation.

WE BEGIN OUR DISCUSSION OF THINKING, curiously enough, with an extended discussion of language. It might seem funny to lump language and thought together, but the two are closely linked: Language importantly influences the way we think about and view our world. Remember from Chapter 8 how use of the word *smashed* led people to infer and recall things about a car accident that they didn't when given the word *contacted*? Think about the words *doctor* and *secretary*—are you likely to picture a man and a woman, respectively? Do you think twice about a sentence such as "The secretary hates his boss"? It's clear that language affects us in ways that extend well beyond simple communication.

According to the *linguistic relativity hypothesis*, language not only shapes how we think but also how we perceive the world (Whorf, 1956). For example, if your language lacks color terms to distinguish between blue and green, which is the case for some African languages, you might have a difficult time telling those colors apart on a color test. Cross-cultural tests have produced some support for this idea: "What you see when you look at a rainbow actually depends on the language that you speak" (Özgen, 2004, p. 94). Additional evidence comes from work on visual discrimination in the laboratory. It turns out that your ability to pick visual targets from distract-

ing stimuli, such as identifying a cat in a lineup of dogs versus other cats, depends on whether the stimuli are presented to the right or left hemisphere. When the stimuli are presented to the left hemisphere, the side of the brain that usually controls language, the composition of the lineup (other cats versus dogs) matters more, presumably because language is influencing your visual ability (Gilbert et al., 2007).

At the same time, few psychologists believe that language completely determines how we think or perceive. We all share certain fundamental cognitive abilities, those rooted in our evolutionary past, and those abilities are likely to remain intact regardless of language particulars or environmental influences (Newcombe & Uttal, 2006). Language influences how we think and perceive the world, no question about it, but it doesn't completely determine thought.

Bees do a characteristic waggle dance that may communicate information about the location of nectar. But would you say bees have really developed language?

The Structure of Language

What is language, and how should it be defined? If you think about it, birds communicate effectively through the production of acoustic sequences (songs). Some believe that bees can convey information about the exact location of food through a tail-wagging dance (von Frisch, 1967, but see also Wenner, 1998). Even your dog barks at outdoor noises in what appears to be an effort to communicate. But to qualify as a true language, the communication system must have rules, known collectively as **grammar**, that enable the communicator to combine arbitrary symbols to convey meaning.

Grammar provides rules about which combinations of sounds and words are permissible and which are not. Grammar has three aspects: (1) **phonology**, the rules for

grammar The rules of language that enable the communicator to combine arbitrary symbols to convey meaning.

phonology Rules governing how sounds should be combined to make words in a language.

syntax Rules governing how words should be combined to form sentences.

semantics The rules used in language to communicate meaning.

phonemes The smallest significant sound units in speech.

morphemes The smallest units in a language that carry meaning.

combining sounds to make words; (2) **syntax**, the rules for combining words to make sentences; and (3) **semantics**, the rules used to communicate meaning. In English we would never say "The cautious the barked nasty at man poodle." This particular combination of words violates a number of rules of syntax, such as the rule that articles (*the*) and adjectives (*nasty*) come before nouns (*man*). We would also never generate a sentence like "Colorless green ideas sleep furiously." Although this is a well-structured sentence, it suffers from a violation of semantics—it has no meaning. We use our knowledge about semantics to pick the appropriate words (perhaps "people" can sleep furiously, but "ideas" cannot) and to infer connections between words and other things in memory (cautious poodles bark at rather than bite nasty people).

Phonemes and Morphemes   All human languages possess a hierarchical structure, which ranges from the fundamental sounds of speech to the more complex levels of spoken conversation. At the bottom of the spoken language hierarchy are **phonemes**, defined as the smallest significant sound units in speech. These speech sounds are produced through a complex coordination of the vocal cords, lungs, lips, tongue, and even the teeth. ▌Table 9.1 lists some examples of phonemes in the English language. Notice there isn't a simple one-to-one mapping between a given letter of the alphabet and a phoneme. The letter *e*, for example, maps onto one kind of speech sound in the word *head* and a different kind in the word *heat*.

Babies greet the world with the ability to produce a large number of fundamental speech sounds, but they quickly restrict the number to a much smaller set (Werker & Tees, 1999). English speakers use only about 40 to 45 phonemes; other languages may use considerably more or fewer. Japanese speakers, for example, do not differentiate between the phonemes *r* and *l* in their native tongue (which makes it difficult for a native Japanese speaker to hear the difference between *race* and *lace*). English speakers do not meaningfully distinguish the *p* sound in *pause* from the *p* sound in *camp*. In Thai or Hindi, these same sound units carry unique and different meanings. Part of the trick to acquiring a foreign language is mastering the basic phonemes of that language.

At the next level in the hierarchy are **morphemes**—the smallest units of language that carry meaning. Morphemes usually consist of single words, such as *cool* or *hip*, but they can also be prefixes and suffixes. For instance, the word *cool* contains a single morpheme, whereas *uncool* contains two—the root word *cool* and the prefix *un*. The grammar of a language dictates the acceptable order of morphemes within a word—*uncool* has definite meaning in our language, *coolun* does not. The morpheme *s*, when placed at the end of a word (*oars*), designates plural. But the phoneme *s*, when placed at the beginning of that same word (*soar*), means something entirely different. All told, the average speaker of English knows and uses somewhere between 50,000 and 80,000 morphemes.

TABLE 9.1	Some Examples of English Phonemes		
Symbol	**Examples**	**Symbol**	**Examples**
b	**b**urger, ru**bb**le	ng	sti**ng**, ri**ng**er
ē	**e**asy, zomb**ie**	oy	c**oi**l, empl**oy**
ĕ	**e**nter, m**e**tric	r	**r**at, c**r**ust
f	**f**ungus, **ph**one	s	**s**todgy, be**s**t
ĭ	**i**cky, w**i**g	t	**t**ramp, miss**ed**
ī	**i**ce, sh**y**	th	**th**at, o**th**er
k	**k**itty, a**ch**e	ŭ	**u**gly, b**u**tter
n	**n**ewt, a**nn**oy		

Words to Sentences   At the higher levels of the language hierarchy are *words, phrases,* and *sentences.* Words combine to form phrases; phrases, in conjunction with other phrases, form sentences. To illustrate, the sentence "Stephanie kissed the crying boy" contains a noun (*Stephanie*) and a verb phrase (*kissed the crying boy*). The verb phrase contains a verb (*kissed*) and a noun phrase (*the crying boy*). Perhaps you can remember diagramming sentences in this way in your high school English class (see ▌Figure 9.2). Breaking sentences into phrases has psychological meaning—we clearly use phrases when we generate spoken sentences. If I accurately time you speaking, for example, I'll find that you pause for a moment at the boundaries between major phrases (Boomer, 1965). When you read a sentence, I'll also find that there are measurable changes in brain activity that correspond to phrase changes (Rösler et al., 1998).

Language researchers have spent decades trying to figure out the rules people use to combine words into phrases and phrases into sentences. It was once thought that a single set of rules might be discovered that would effectively capture all of the nuances of sentence generation—just apply the rules appropriately to words, and you've got language. However, as the linguist Noam Chomsky pointed out, it's unlikely that such a set of rules exists. To bolster his argument, Chomsky came up with sentences such as "Visiting relatives can be a nuisance." It's easy to break this sentence down into its appropriate phrase structure, he argued, but the phrase structure doesn't tell us what the sentence actually means: Are we annoyed that the relatives are visiting, or is it a nuisance to visit relatives? Both meanings apply to the same phrase structure: Visiting relatives—pause—can be a nuisance. Hence, we cannot capture why or how sentences are generated during a meaningful conversation by appealing only to the phrase structure.

Surface and Deep Structure   According to Chomsky (1957), to understand how language really works, you first need to accept that there's a difference between the "surface" structure of a sentence and its accompanying, more abstract, "deep" structure. The **surface structure** of a sentence corresponds to its superficial appearance (the literal ordering of words), whereas **deep structure** refers to the underlying representation of meaning. Thus, two sentences can have the same surface structure but two different deep structures (the "visiting relatives" example). Or two different

surface structure The literal ordering of words in a sentence.

deep structure The underlying representation of meaning in a sentence.

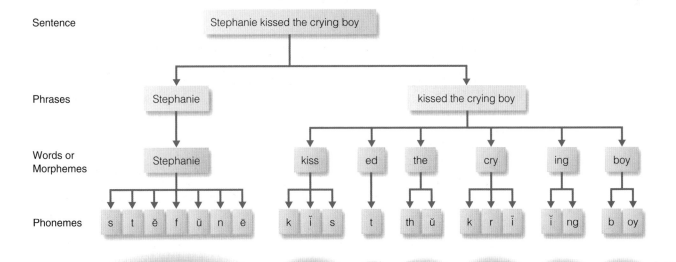

▌FIGURE 9.2 The Units of Language
Languages have a hierarchical structure that includes the fundamental sounds of speech and the more complex levels of spoken conversation. Complex rules determine how words are combined into phrases and sentences, and how fundamental speech sounds (phonemes) combine to create the smallest units of meaning (morphemes) and words.

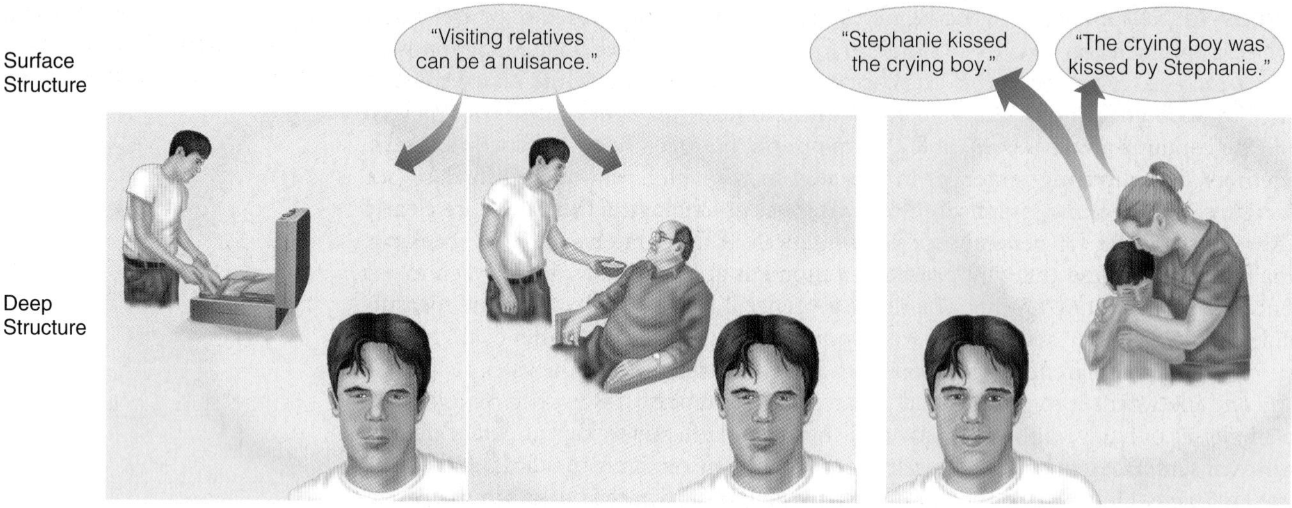

FIGURE 9.3 Surface Structure and Deep Structure
The surface structure of a sentence is its appearance, the literal ordering of words. Deep structure is the meaning of the sentence. This figure shows how the same surface structure—"Visiting relatives can be a nuisance"—can reflect two different deep structures. Similarly, a single deep structure can be transformed into two or more acceptable surface structures.

CRITICAL THINKING

Based on what you've learned about Chomsky's work, why might it be difficult to program a computer to understand speech?

surface structures can arise from the same deep structure ("Stephanie kissed the crying boy"—"The crying boy was kissed by Stephanie").

According to Chomsky, language production requires the transformation of deep structure into an acceptable surface structure (see ▌ Figure 9.3). Most language researchers accept this point, but there are sharp disagreements about how the transformation process actually works (Treiman et al., 2003). Language is clearly more than sets of words or symbols organized in a fixed and rigid way. In the words of psychologist Steven Pinker, there are "hundreds of millions of trillions of thinkable thoughts" (Pinker, 1997), and each can, in principle, be expressed through language and understood. The challenge for language researchers is to discover how this flexibility ultimately arises.

Language Comprehension

The flip side of language production—that is, understanding the structure and rules of grammar—is language comprehension. How do people use their practical knowledge about the world, and the general context of the conversation, to decide what information another person is trying to communicate? This is not a trivial problem because language comprehension presents many difficulties: We don't always hear sounds correctly; words can have many different meanings; the pitch or rhythm in which a phrase is spoken can help or mislead us; and language is full of metaphors that complicate the interpretation process (Lakoff, 1987; Pinker, 1994).

Effective communication seems to rely a great deal on *common knowledge* among speakers (Clark, 1992; Keysar et al., 1998). When you're having a conversation with someone about a mutual friend, you can say "That's typical for him," and there's likely to be no comprehension problem. You both know the statement refers to your friend, and you both have no trouble listing examples of your friend's "typical" behavior. Similarly, when you hear a statement, you don't simply process the sound arriving at your ears into words, phrase structures, and sentences. You make a guess about what the speaker is trying to communicate, perhaps even before he or she makes a sound, and then you use this expectation to interpret the sounds you hear. Thus, in an important sense, language comprehension shares properties with perception: Both rely on a combination of *top-down* and *bottom-up processing* (McClelland & Elman, 1986).

Pragmatic Rules Language researchers use the term **pragmatics** to describe how practical knowledge can be used both to comprehend the intentions of speakers and to produce an effective response. Consider your response to an *indirect* request such as "Could you close the window?" If you process the request directly—that is, if you take its literal interpretation—you might respond, "Yes, I'm capable of putting enough steady pressure on the window to produce closure." You have answered the question, but clearly you have violated some important pragmatic rules. The speaker was making a request, not asking you about your ability to perform the task. In fact, if you had answered the question in this way, the speaker would have probably inferred that you were using irony or sarcasm in your reply (Gibbs, O'Brien, & Doolittle, 1995; Lee & Katz, 1998).

The pragmatics of language make the study of comprehension processes a challenge. How you interpret someone's words—be they babblings or profound commentary on the hypocrisy of our times—will depend on the shared context of the conversation, as well as on your expectations and beliefs. To facilitate effective communication, all good speakers follow certain pragmatic guidelines, or maxims (Grice, 1975):

1. Be informative.
2. Tell the truth.
3. Be relevant.
4. Be clear.

If you choose to answer an indirect request literally ("Yes, I can close the window"), then you're not being relevant—you're violating an accepted guideline for communication. If you don't tell the truth or are purposely vague in answering a request, then you'll soon have trouble finding people who want to talk with you. By following the simple rules presented here and by assuming the same for your conversational partner, you can enhance the ease and flow of conversation.

pragmatics The practical knowledge used to comprehend the intentions of a speaker and to produce an effective response.

Language Development

How does language develop? Are humans born with a genetic plan that directs and shapes their communication skills? Or do we acquire language exclusively as a product of experience? Not all people of the world speak the same language, so experience must certainly play an important role. But many language researchers are convinced that babies arrive in the world prepared to learn language, much as they are born prepared to walk. There is a regularity to language development, as there is to the development of motor skills, that is difficult to explain by appealing only to the environment (Chomsky, 1986; Pinker, 1994).

The universality of language is apparent even at birth. Most babies cry in similar ways, and they move quickly through vocalization milestones that precede formal language development. By 3 to 5 weeks of age, *cooing*—repeating vowel sounds like "ooooh" and "aaaaah"—has been added to the baby's vocalization patterns. *Babbling*—repeating consonant/vowel combinations such as "kaka" or "baba"—begins in virtually all babies between the ages of 4 and 6 months. It doesn't matter where you look in the world, this same sequence—crying then cooing then babbling—is found.

Between the ages of 6 and 18 months, experience begins to play a role, shaping and fine-tuning the baby's babblings into language-specific

Infants and small children develop rather sophisticated ways to communicate meaningfully—cooing, kicking, pointing, and so on—even though their overt language skills are limited.

©Myrleen Ferguson Cate/PhotoEdit

Concept Review | Highlights in Language Development

AGE	LINGUISTIC HIGHLIGHT(S)	INTERPRETATION
3–5 weeks	*Cooing*, or the repetition of vowel sounds such as "oooh" and "aaah."	Both cooing and babbling are vocalization milestones that occur before formal language development, and they are similar across cultures, highlighting the universality of language.
4–6 months	*Babbling*, or the repetition of vowel-consonant combinations such as "kaka" or "baba."	
6–18 months	Vocalizations become specific to the native language; the first word is spoken by the end of the first year.	Experience plays a role in vocalization as a baby's babblings are shaped into language-specific sounds. Language comprehension is rapidly developing.
24 months	Vocabulary of nearly 200 words; child shows *telegraphic speech*, grammatical two-word combinations.	Speech reflects knowledge of syntax, as words are almost always combined in the proper order.
Preschool years	Ability to produce and comprehend sentences.	Child is now showing most of the important features of adult syntax.

sounds. Babies begin to restrict their vocalizations to the phonemes in the language they hear every day from their parents or guardians; they even acquire a kind of language-specific "accent" by around 8 months of age (de Boysson-Bardies, Sagat, & Durand, 1984; Locke, 1994). Simple words—*mama, dada,* and so on—appear by the end of the first year, and by 24 months most babies have developed a vocabulary of nearly 200 words (Nelson, 1973). Language comprehension also develops rapidly during this period—in fact, infants develop the ability to understand the words and commands of language *faster* than they actually learn to produce language.

Child Speak   As every parent knows, infants and young children develop rather sophisticated ways to communicate meaningfully, even though their language production skills may still be limited. An 18-month-old child can point to the bear-shaped jar on the counter and say "ookie" and Mom or Dad immediately knows what the child has in mind. An enormous amount of information can be packed into a single word, even if that word is spoken incorrectly, when its utterance is combined with a gesture or if the utterance occurs in the right context.

As the child approaches the end of his or her second year of life, a phase of *telegraphic speech* begins. Telegraphic speech involves combining two words into simple sentences, such as "Daddy bad" or "Give cookie." It's called telegraphic speech because, as in a telegram, the child characteristically omits articles (*the*) and prepositions (*at, in*) from communications. But a 2-year-old's first sentences reflect a rudimentary knowledge of syntax: Words are almost always spoken in the proper order. For example, a child will reliably say "Want cookie" instead of "Cookie want." During the rest of the child's preschool years, up to around age 5 or 6, sentences become increasingly more complex, to the point where the average child of kindergarten age can produce and comprehend sentences that reveal most of the important features of adult syntax.

It's of enormous interest to psychologists that children develop such sophisticated language skills during their preschool years. After all, few parents sit down with their children and teach them the rules of grammar (such as the differences between present and past tense). Moreover, as we discussed in Chapter 4, children at this age lack the ability to understand most abstract concepts, so they couldn't consciously understand grammatical rules even if parents took the time to try. Children pick up their language skills implicitly; they automatically learn rules for language production.

CRITICAL THINKING

In normal conversation, how much meaning do you think is typically communicated nonverbally—such as through frowning or folding your arms?

The rules children learn during their preschool years are revealed partly by the errors they make. For example, at some point preschoolers acquire the rule "Add *ed* to the ends of verbs to make them past tense." Interestingly, children tend to *overgeneralize* this rule—they say things like "goed" or "falled," which are incorrect in English but represent a correct application of the rule. Notice that *goed* is not something that the child could have learned to use directly from experience. No parent rewards a child for saying *goed*, nor does a child hear the word being used by his or her parents. Rather, the child appears to be naturally "tuned" to pick up communication rules and apply them generally—even if a rule sometimes leads to an incorrect utterance. This natural tendency to learn and apply rules is then shaped by experience as an adult or peer teaches the child that *goed* is incorrect.

Language development continues throughout the school years as children fine-tune their articulation skills and knowledge about grammar. Vocabulary expands, as does the child's ability to communicate abstract concepts. Ultimately, the sophistication of any child's language ability will depend, at least in part, on his or her level of cognitive development. Children think differently as they age, and their increasingly sophisticated cognitive abilities are reflected in their conversations. Keep this fact in mind as we turn our attention to language abilities in nonhuman species.

Language in Nonhuman Species

Psychologists have recognized for decades that nonhuman animals communicate. Anyone who has ever seen a cat indicate that it would rather be inside the house than outside knows this to be true. The question is whether such forms of communication can legitimately be called *language*. We know that animals sometimes express things symbolically, and there's little doubt that an animal's actions can convey meaning. But to qualify as a true language, the animals would need to possess at least a rudimentary form of grammar—that is, a set of rules for deciding how arbitrary symbols can be combined to convey meaning.

Early attempts to foster language development in chimpanzees, in a form resembling human speech, were not very successful. Chimps were raised in homes, like surrogate children, in an effort to provide the ideal environment for language development. In one case, a chimp named Gua was raised along with the researchers' son, Donald (Kellogg & Kellogg, 1933). Donald and Gua were exposed to the same experiences, and careful attention was paid to rewarding the appropriate vocalizations. But in the end, the Kelloggs had merely produced a fine-speaking son and an effectively mute chimp (legend has it that Donald also developed into an excellent tree-climber). Later efforts to teach chimps to speak yielded the same discouraging results (Hayes & Hayes, 1951).

Signs and Symbol Communication   These early attempts were misguided, in a way, because chimps lack the necessary vocal equipment to produce the sounds required for human speech (Hayes, 1952). It's kind of like a bird trying to teach a human to fly by raising a boy in a nest. Without wings, the boy just isn't going to fly. For these reasons, subsequent researchers turned to visual communication mediums. Allen and Beatrice Gardner tried to teach a simplified form of American Sign Language to a chimp named Washoe (Gardner & Gardner, 1969; Gardner, Gardner, & Van Cantfort, 1989). By the age of 4, Washoe was capable of producing about 160 appropriate signs, and apparently she understood a great deal more. Even more impressive was her ability to produce various word combinations, such as "more fruit" or "gimme tickle."

In California, David Premack taught a chimp named Sarah to manipulate plastic shapes that symbolized words (e.g., a plastic triangle stood for the word *banana*). Sarah eventually was able to respond to simple symbol-based sentences that were arranged on a magnetic board (such as "Sarah insert banana into pail"; Premack, 1976). In Georgia, pigmy chimpanzees have been taught to communicate by pressing keys that

Chimpanzees lack the vocal equipment needed to produce the sounds of human speech. But they can be taught to communicate in relatively sophisticated ways with American Sign Language (left) and by pressing keys on a board that represent objects such as food or toys (right).

represent objects such as foods or toys (Rumbaugh, 1977; Savage-Rumbaugh et al., 1986). Again, not only have these chimps learned to associate particular symbols with words or actions, but they've shown the capacity to generate combinations of words by pressing the symbols in sequence (Savage-Rumbaugh et al., 1986).

Work in the Georgia laboratory has also shown that pygmy chimpanzees can understand some spoken English. A chimp named Kanzi can press the appropriate symbol key when a word is spoken (e.g., banana). He can also respond appropriately to a variety of spoken commands. When asked "Can you pour the ice water in the potty?" Kanzi picks up the bowl of ice water, heads to the potty, and carefully pours it in (Savage-Rumbaugh et al., 1993). When asked to "Hide the toy gorilla," Kanzi picks up the toy gorilla and attempts to push it under a fence. Kanzi can even perform these tasks when the command is presented over headphones; this is important because it suggests that Kanzi is not simply responding to subtle cues from his handlers.

Is It Really Language?   These are very impressive demonstrations and are quite convincing when you see them in person or on film. But have chimps like Kanzi really acquired *language*? The jury is still out. Some psychologists believe that the chimps' behaviors simply reflect reinforced learning—like a pigeon who has been taught to peck a key for food—rather than true language ability (Terrace, 1986). At the same time, chimps such as Washoe and Kanzi can apparently generate new combinations of words and respond to requests that have never been given before. Washoe, for example, learned to respond to environmental events by producing novel signs. On seeing a duck for the first time, she reportedly signed "water bird." Moreover, it's been shown that chimps can acquire these language skills through observing other chimps, without being trained directly (Savage-Rumbaugh et al., 1986).

This debate is nowhere near a firm resolution. Much of the critical evidence (such as Washoe's "water bird") has come primarily from trainer anecdotes, so some question its scientific value (Wynne, 2007). It's also possible that some of the novel combinations generated by the chimps are simply imitations of their trainers. We just don't know at this point. Most of the psychologists who work with chimps are firmly convinced that the language abilities are real. Kanzi, for example, doesn't seem to follow rigid scripts—he can follow a request that is worded in various ways, which is far beyond what you would expect from a pigeon trained to peck a key.

As you think about this topic for yourself, it's important to keep in mind that chimpanzees have not evolved to understand or produce human language. Chimps have evolved to solve their own problems—problems that arise from their own unique environments. You should avoid, where possible, adopting too egocentric a view of the world. The human mind has evolved to solve human problems, and those problems may or may not overlap with those of other members of the animal kingdom.

Is Language an Adaptation?

Given that language may be a uniquely human characteristic, it's reasonable to wonder why it developed: Why are humans capable of language but most other species are not? One possibility is that language is an *adaptation*—that is, it evolved specifically as a result of natural selection. It's easy to imagine how language might have conferred an extra advantage to those who possessed it, aiding everything from hunting and gathering to selecting and convincing a mate. Yet, as we've discussed in other chapters, it's notoriously difficult to tell whether a psychological feature is truly an adaptation. It might be that we're capable of language simply because at some point we evolved big and highly flexible brains.

Proponents of the "language as an adaptation" view (e.g., Pinker, 1994) point to several kinds of evidence: (1) Language is associated with particular regions of the brain (e.g., Broca's and Wernicke's areas); (2) children learn language incredibly quickly and, as noted earlier, aren't taught the rules of language in any kind of systematic fashion; (3) the human ear as well as the human vocal tract seem perfectly tailored to meet the needs of speech; (4) some people seem to inherit tendencies to make certain types of grammatical errors. Another consideration is that there doesn't seem to be a simple relationship between the sophistication of a culture and the complexity of the language spoken; one might expect such a relationship if language development depended strongly on cultural or environmental factors (Cartwright, 2000).

Again, though, there are no fossil records to support the evolution of language as there are for certain physical characteristics (such as skull and therefore brain size). Moreover, language is unlikely to have emerged suddenly, in its present form, and some have argued that it's not easy to see the adaptive advantages that would result from simple or intermediate forms of language (Rose & Rose, 2000). Like many issues in modern evolutionary psychology, the question of how and why language emerged remains controversial (Jackendoff & Pinker, 2005).

Test Yourself 9.1

Check your knowledge about language by answering the following questions. (You will find the answers in the Appendix.)

1. Choose the term that best fits the following descriptions. Choose your answers from the following: *deep structure, morphemes, pragmatics, phonemes, phonology, semantics, surface structure, syntax.*
   a. The smallest significant sound units in speech:
      _____
   b. The practical knowledge used to understand the intentions of a speaker and to produce an effective response:
      _____
   c. The rules governing how words should be combined to form sentences: _____
   d. The smallest units in language that carry meaning:
      _____

2. Decide whether each of the following statements about language is *True or False.*
   a. Across the world babies cry, coo, and babble in similar ways. *True or False?*
   b. Children learn the rules of language primarily by copying the words and phrases of their parents. *True or False?*
   c. Telegraphic speech begins toward the end of the child's second year of life. *True or False?*
   d. Chimpanzees lack the vocal equipment needed to produce human speech. *True or False?*
   e. Chimpanzee Kanzi learned to associate symbols with a variety of words but cannot follow spoken instructions from his trainers. *True or False?*

Classifying and Categorizing

LEARNING GOALS
- Understand how categories and category membership are defined.
- Distinguish between prototype and exemplar views of categorization.
- Explain the hierarchical organization of categories.

category A class of objects (people, places, or things) that most people agree belong together.

WE NOW TURN OUR ATTENTION to another useful cognitive process—the ability to classify and categorize objects. A **category** is a class of objects (people, places, or things) that most people agree belong together (Smith, 1989). "Vegetables" is a category that contains such things as peas, carrots, and Brussels sprouts; "psychologists" is a category that includes researchers, clinicians, and applied persons working in the field. Categories allow us to *infer* invisible properties about objects (Murphy, 2002). For example, a kite and a doll share important properties as children's toys even though the two objects bear little physical similarity to each other. Once you've successfully categorized something, you can make *predictions* about the future. You know, for example, that if you bring your child an object from the category "toy," she is likely to be happy and reward you with a hug.

We'll divide our discussion of classifying and categorizing into three main topics. First, what properties of an object make it a member of a particular category? Second, in making decisions about category membership, do we form and store abstract representations called prototypes? Finally, we'll end the section by briefly considering the structure of categories—are they general or highly specific?

defining features The set of features necessary to make objects acceptable members of a category.

Defining Category Membership

Researchers have spent a lot of time trying to discover the criteria people use to define category membership. What is it about a sparrow that allows us to classify it so effortlessly as a bird? How do we know that a trout is a member of the category "fish" and not something to be used in the garden?

People automatically classify objects, even other people, into well-defined categories. How would you categorize this individual, and what invisible properties would you infer about him? Can you predict how he might act in a social situation?

One possibility is that you can easily classify a sparrow as a "bird" because it has certain features that all members of that category share. For example, to be a member of the category "bird," a creature might need to have feathers and be able to do things like sing, fly, and build nests—these are called the necessary or **defining features** of the category "bird." If the object in question has all the defining features, it must be an acceptable member of the category; if the object lacks one or more of these qualities, it must be something else (Medin, 1989). From this standpoint, knowing the right category label for an object is simply a matter of learning the right set of defining features (see ▌ Figure 9.4).

But there are problems with this view. It works well for mathematical categories such as "square" or "triangle," but it breaks down for natural objects. Take the category "vehicle," for example. What are the defining features of a vehicle—something that moves along the ground, has wheels, and can transport people? That applies to cars and trucks, but what about a surfboard or a monorail train? Surfboards move through water; monorail trains don't have wheels. What about an elevator, which doesn't have wheels and doesn't move along the ground? Research on natural categories such as birds, vehicles, furniture, and so on demonstrates that people have a tough time identifying and agreeing on just what constitutes the acceptable defining features of a category (Malt & Smith, 1984; Rosch & Mervis, 1975).

Most natural categories turn out to have *fuzzy boundaries*. In ▌ Figure 9.5 you can see a series of objects that collectively tap the fuzzy boundary of the category "cup." In an experiment by Labov (1973), people were presented with a selected set of these objects, such as those shown in series 1 through 4, and were required to name each object as it was presented. Labov discovered that as the ratio of cup width to cup

CRITICAL THINKING

Although categories are usually adaptive, can you think of any instance in which categorizing an object or a person might not be adaptive? How about when you stereotype someone?

Properties	Generic bird	Robin	Sandpiper	Vulture	Chicken	Penguin
Flies regularly	+	+	+	+	−	−
Sings	+	+	+	−	−	−
Lays eggs	+	+	+	+	+	+
Is small	+	+	+	−	−	−
Nests in trees	+	+	−	+	−	−

▌ FIGURE 9.4 Defining Features of a Category
One way to assign category membership is by defining features. For example, members of the generic category "bird" might be expected to fly regularly, sing, and lay eggs in nests. Unfortunately, people have a tough time identifying and agreeing on the defining features for most natural categories. All of the objects shown here are birds, but they don't necessarily share the same properties. (Based on Smith, 1989)

1   2   3   4   5

▌ FIGURE 9.5 Fuzzy Category Boundaries
Are all of these objects members of the category "cup"? Labov (1973) discovered that as the width of the object increased, the more likely people were to label it as a "bowl." But the cup category boundary was fuzzy rather than firm; a significant number of people remained convinced that the fourth object was indeed a cup. (From Goldstein, 1994)

Does this elevator fit snugly into your category for "vehicle"? If so, what defining features does it share with other members of the category?

depth increased (as the object appeared wider), subjects were increasingly likely to dismiss the "cup" label and characterize the object as a "bowl." But the crossover point was gradual rather than fixed. Even for the object labeled 4, a significant number of people remained convinced that the object was indeed a cup. Results like these suggest that category members have *typical* features that are *characteristic* of the category rather than fixed defining features.

Family Resemblance Another way to think about the idea of typical features is in terms of what Rosch and Mervis (1975) have called **family resemblance**. Members of the same category will share certain core features, but it isn't necessary for each member to have them all. Within an extended family, for instance, there may be a characteristic drooping nose, close-set beady eyes, receding hairlines, and a prominent, cleft chin. Cousin Theodore may lack the cleft or the beady eyes, but he could still possess a family resemblance that enables outsiders to easily fit him into the appropriate family. For the category "vehicle," people know that a monorail train doesn't have wheels, and it's not shaped anything like a car, but it moves people along the ground and in this sense fits the category label for most people.

Family resemblance is determined by the collection of core features that an object possesses. Again, members of the same category will share many family features, but it's unlikely that any single member will have them all. If a given object has most of the family features, it will be seen as a good member of the category; if an object has only a few, it will be seen as a poor member of the category. A car, for example, has most of the basic features that people assign to the category "vehicle"; an

© James L. Amos/CORBIS

elevator does not. A robin has most of the features of "bird"; an ostrich or a flamingo has few. Through the notion of family resemblance, we can begin to see how natural categories achieve their fuzzy status. There is no absolute set of criteria for what constitutes a vehicle or a bird; there are only good and poor examples of a class of objects that share features (Rosch et al., 1976).

Do People Store Category Prototypes?

family resemblance The core features that category members share; a given member of the category may have some but not necessarily all of these features.

prototype The best or most representative member of a category (such as robin for the category "bird").

category exemplars Specific examples of category members that are stored in long-term memory.

Family resemblance, combined with the idea that there are good and poor members of a category, leads us naturally to the concept of a prototype. A **prototype** is the best or most representative member of a category: A robin, for example, is close to the prototype for the category "bird"; an apple resembles the prototype for "fruit." Some psychologists believe that we store category prototypes in long-term memory and use them to help decide category membership. If an object, say a small fuzzy creature with a beak, is similar to the prototype for a certain category, "birds," then we assume that the object must be a member of the prototype's category (Goldstone & Kersten, 2003).

However, it isn't necessary to store prototypes to solve categorization problems. Instead, we could simply store all of the category examples (or **category exemplars**) that we encounter. To decide whether a new object is a member of a specific category, we would then compare the object to all of these stored examples rather than to a single prototype. If the object is similar to many examples in a particular category, then we would categorize the object as a member of that category (see ▌Figure 9.6). You should note the main difference between prototype and exemplar views of categorization: In prototype theory, you compare the object to one thing—the prototype; in the exemplar view, the object is compared to many things—the category exemplars.

Whether prototypes or exemplars are used in categorization is currently unknown, although many cognitive psychologists favor the exemplar view because people seem to know a lot about the individual members of a category (Hintzman, 1986;

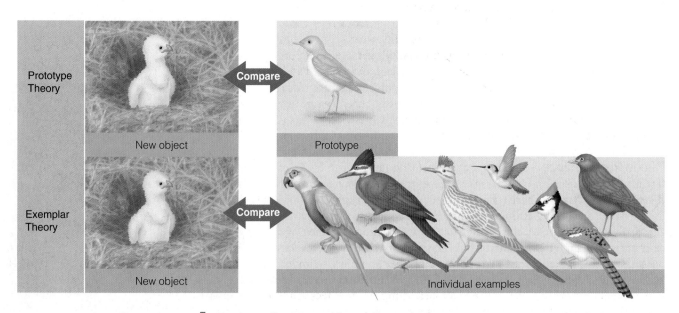

▌**FIGURE 9.6** Prototypes Versus Exemplars
How do we decide whether an object is a member of a particular category? According to prototype theory, we compare the object to the abstract "best" example of the category (a generic bird). If the new object is similar to the prototype, it is assigned to the prototype's category. Exemplar theories of categorization propose instead that we compare the new object to all the individual examples of the category that have been stored in memory. Category membership is based on the summed similarity between the new object and the exemplars.

Concept Review | Defining Category Membership

VIEW OF CATEGORIZATION	BASIS OF CATEGORIZATION	EXAMPLE
Defining features	Certain features are present that define membership in the category.	Inez knows that a robin is a bird, because a robin has all of the features that define a bird, such as feathers, wings, and a beak.
Family resemblance	The degree to which category members share certain core features; a *prototype* is the most representative member of a category.	James knows that a robin is a bird, because it shares common features with other members of the bird family. In fact, "robin" would be considered the *prototype* for the category "bird."
Exemplars	All category examples (*category examplars*) that we encounter are used for categorization.	Semhar knows that a robin is a bird, because it matches so many of the examples of birds stored in her memory.

Medin & Shaffer, 1978; Nosofsky, 1992). For example, people seem to know what features go together—such as the fact that small birds are more likely to sing than large birds—and this kind of result is better handled by theories proposing that we store exemplars. Given the flexibility of the human mind, it seems likely that people can solve categorization problems in many different ways—and, it may depend on the type of category that we're trying to learn (Ashby & Maddox, 2005). Sometimes we may form prototypes; other times we may rely on rules for deciding category membership; and in many situations we may appeal only to category exemplars (e.g., Erickson & Kruschke, 1998; Smith, Patalano, & Jonides, 1998).

The Hierarchical Structure of Categories

Most objects fit nicely into more than one natural category. The reason, in part, is that virtually all categories have a built-in hierarchical structure—that is, there are categories within categories within categories. Consider the class of "living things." Under the umbrella of "living things," we find the category "animals"; under "animals" there are "cats"; under "cats" there are "Siamese cats"; and so on. Most of the time an object, once it's categorized, can easily be recategorized into another, more general level of abstraction. A cat is an animal, a living thing, an object found on the planet Earth, and so on. These levels differ from one another in terms of their degree of inclusion. The more general the level, the more inclusive it becomes—there are more examples of living things than animals and more cats than Siamese cats (Murphy & Lassaline, 1997).

Some levels in the category hierarchy also appear to have special properties—they are in a sense psychologically privileged. When we refer to an object during a normal conversation, we tend to use its basic-level category descriptor. **Basic-level categories** generate the most useful and predictive information (Markman & Wisniewski, 1997). When a furry feline saunters by, you call it a cat, not a living thing or an object found on the planet Earth. The category "cat" provides just the right amount of relevant information. People know you're talking about a four-legged object with fur (rather than the nondescriptive "animal"), but you haven't burdened the conversation with a needless amount of detail ("There's an 18-year-old seal-point Siamese that prefers salmon for dinner").

Basic-level categories tend to be at the intermediate levels of the category hierarchy (see █ Figure 9.7). The top-level categories, or *superordinates*, are simply not very

basic-level categories The level in a category hierarchy that provides the most useful and predictive information; the basic level usually resides at an intermediate level in a category hierarchy.

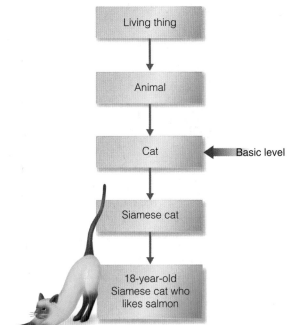

█ FIGURE 9.7 Category Hierarchies
Virtually all categories have a hierarchical structure—there are categories within categories within categories. Most things, like this cat, fit nicely into several natural category levels. But when people refer to something during normal conversation, they tend to use its intermediate, or *basic level*, category label. They call this a "cat" rather than a "living thing," an "animal," or an "18-year-old Siamese cat who likes salmon."

descriptive. When people were asked to list the distinguishing features of top-level categories (such as "living things"), Rosch and her colleagues found that only a few features were actually generated (try it yourself: list the properties that characterize "living things"). At the basic level, more properties were generated, and the generated properties tended to be ones that most members of the category share (Rosch et al., 1976). It is of interest to note that basic-level categories are also the category levels first used by children. It is through basic-level categorization that we cut the world into its most useful and informative slices.

Test Yourself 9.2

Check your knowledge about how people form categories by answering the following questions. (You will find the answers in the Appendix.)

1. For each of the following statements, decide on the category term that seems most appropriate. Choose from the following: *category exemplars, defining features, family resemblance, prototype.*
   a. It must be a bird because all birds have wings, feathers, and a beak. _____
   b. It must be a bird because it looks like all the other birds that I've seen. _____
   c. It must be a bird because it seems to have some features that are typical of birds. _____

   d. It must be a bird because it looks a lot like a robin. _____

2. When people refer to an object, such as your pet, during normal conversation, they tend to use what kind of category descriptor?
   a. Superordinate ("Look, it's an object on the planet Earth.")
   b. Basic level ("Look, it's a cat.")
   c. Subordinate ("Look, it's a seal-point Siamese.")
   d. Functionate ("Look, it's something to cuddle.")

Solving Problems

LEARNING GOALS

- Distinguish between well- and ill-defined problems.
- Describe the pitfalls of problem representation.
- Compare algorithms and heuristics.
- Describe the Aha! moment in problem solving.

NOW LET'S CONSIDER SOME of the thought processes people use when they try to solve problems. Obviously, problem solving is an extremely adaptive skill. When you're faced with a problem, such as how to get your car started in the morning, there's a goal—a running motor—and a certain amount of uncertainty about how to reach that goal. To study the solution process, psychologists typically use problems like the following:

> It's early morning, still dark, and you're trying to get dressed. Your 2-month-old baby, snuggled in her crib at the foot of the bed, sleeps peacefully after a night of sustained wailing. You can't turn on the light—she'll wake up for sure—but the black socks and the blue socks are mixed up in the drawer. Let's see, you recall, I have five pairs of black socks and four pairs of blue socks. How many socks do I need to take out of the drawer to guarantee myself a pair of matching colors?

well-defined problem A problem with a well-stated goal, a clear starting point, and a relatively easy way to tell when a solution has been obtained.

ill-defined problem A problem, such as the search for "happiness," that has no well-stated goal, no clear starting point, and no mechanism for evaluating progress.

Notice there's a goal (selecting a pair of matching socks), and it's not immediately obvious how to get from the problem to the solution. Psychologists call this a **well-defined problem** (even though you may have no idea how to solve it) because there is a well-stated goal, a clear starting point, and a relatively easy way to tell when a solution has been reached. Other kinds of problems do not have well-stated goals, clear starting points, or effective mechanisms for evaluating progress—these are called **ill-defined problems**. An example of an ill-defined problem might be discover-

Certain kinds of problems are well defined, such as finding the correct route on a map. Other problems are ill defined and may not even have a solution. Can you decipher the true meaning of the painting on the right?

ing the secret of happiness. Maybe you can agree on the starting point (I'm not happy enough), but the goal (happiness) is pretty tough to define, and it's not at all clear how to reach that goal or how to measure progress.

Representing Problem Information

To solve a problem quickly and correctly, regardless of whether it's well defined or ill defined, you first need to represent the problem information in the right way. By *problem representation*, psychologists mean you need to understand exactly what information is given and how that information can potentially be used. Take the sock problem. The correct answer is *three*. There are only two colors, so with three samples, you'll get two that match. This is actually an easy problem, but most people fail to "see" it in the right way. Did you start worrying about the four to five ratio of blue to black? Did you briefly consider calculating some sort of probability? If you fail to detect which information is relevant and which is not, if you get hung up with ratios and probabilities and the like, this can be a very tough problem to solve. Let's consider another example.

> Dr. Adams is interrupted from his daily rounds by the arrival of a new patient, a child, who has been injured in a fall. "My god!" Adams cries, "It's my son!" Moments later, Dr. Henderson arrives with the same sense of panic and grief. "My son, my dear son," Henderson moans in despair. Is it a tragic mix-up?

You probably solved this one almost immediately, but it demonstrates the point. The two doctors are the mother and the father, which makes it easy to see why both are panicked about their injured son. But the word *doctor*, with its powerful gender connotations, can create an obstacle to correct problem representation. If you initially identify and define the doctors as men, the solution becomes more involved. Seeing the problem correctly is even more difficult because the doctors have different last names.

Functional Fixedness   The two-doctor problem illustrates a common obstacle to correct problem representation. People allow their preconceptions, even their prejudices, to lock them into an incorrect view of the problem information. Consider another example, illustrated in ▌Figure 9.8, called the Maier two-string problem (after Maier, 1931). Imagine you're standing in a room with two lightweight strings hanging from the ceiling. The strings are hung such a distance apart that, when holding one of the strings, you cannot reach the other. Using only a pair of pliers, which happens to be sitting on a table in the room, can you tie the strings together?

This is a reasonably difficult problem because most people have a certain established, or fixed, way of viewing the function of pliers. The solution is to tie the pliers to one of the strings and swing it, like a pendulum, while you hold onto the other string. The correct solution, however, requires you to *restructure* the way you normally think about pliers. Pliers are good for grabbing and holding, but in this case they can serve as pendulum weights too.

Psychologists use the term **functional fixedness** to refer to this tendency to see objects, and their functions, in certain fixed and typical ways. Doctors are men, pliers are for grabbing, and so on. Functional fixedness is an obstacle to problem solving because it prevents you from recognizing the problem-solving tools that are present in the situation. Here's another one: Try solving the problem illustrated in ▌Figure 9.9. You enter a room in which a candle, a box of tacks, some matches, and a hammer lie on a table. You're told to mount the candle on the wall so that it will still burn properly, using only the objects on the table. Work on the problem for a while before reading on.

Okay: The correct solution is to dump the tacks out of the box, mount the box on the wall with one of the tacks, and then put the candle in the box (Duncker, 1945).

functional fixedness The tendency to see objects, and their functions, in certain fixed and typical ways.

▌FIGURE 9.8 The Maier Two-String Problem
Can you figure out a way to tie these two strings together? Notice there's a pair of pliers on the table.

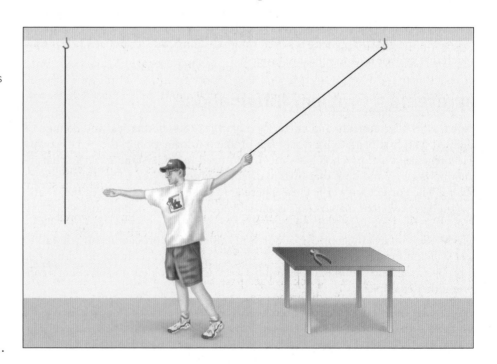

The problem is difficult because most people see the box only as a device for holding the tacks, not as something that can potentially help solve the problem. They become *fixed* in their views about the *functions* of objects and thereby fail to identify and define all of the available problem information correctly. People are more likely to show functional fixedness if they are induced to think about the typical function of the object prior to problem presentation (Chrysikou & Weisberg, 2005). Moreover, the effect seems to occur throughout the world, even in cultures with little exposure to advanced technology (German & Barrett, 2005).

Developing Problem-Solving Strategies

In addition to representing problem information correctly, you also need an arsenal of problem *strategies*—techniques that enable you to move systematically toward a problem solution. Two classes of problem strategies can be used, *algorithms* and *heuristics*.

Algorithms   For some well-defined problems you can use **algorithms**, which are step-by-step rules or procedures that guarantee a solution. You can use algorithms to solve simple math problems, for example, because there are fixed rules for addition, subtraction, and so on. As long as you use the rules properly, you'll always arrive at the correct solution. Solving anagrams, such as MBLOPRE, is another case in point. There are seven letters in the word, which means there are 5,040 possible combinations of the letters. If you systematically work out each of the possible sequences, one will eventually provide a solution to the PROBLEM. But it could take a long time.

Computers are often programmed to use algorithms because computers are capable of examining lots of information very quickly. However, algorithms are not always practical strategies for problem solution, even for computers. Consider chess: In principle, it would be possible to use algorithms to play chess—the computer would simply need to consider all of the possible consequences of a particular move. But practically, computers can't examine all the possible outcomes in a chess game; they can examine only some of them. Overall, there are some 10^{40} possible game sequences, so even if a computer could calculate a game in less than one-millionth of one-thousandth of a second, it would still require 10^{21} centuries to examine all the game possibilities (Best, 1989). It could do so; it would just take a very long time. Another problem with algorithms is that they work for only certain kinds of well-defined problems—there is no algorithm, for example, for deciding how to be happy or for deciding on an appropriate career.

Heuristics   For cases in which it's not feasible to use an algorithm, or for cases in which one is not readily available, people tend to use **heuristics**, which are essentially problem-solving "rules of thumb." To solve an anagram, especially one with seven letters, it's not smart to use an algorithmic approach, examining all 5,040 possible letter sequences. Instead, you turn to heuristics. You know that English words don't usually begin with MB, or end with BL, so you can avoid checking out those possibilities. You can use your knowledge about English words to make guesses about the most likely solution. Heuristics are extremely useful problem-solving tools because they often open the door to a quick and accurate solution. In natural environments, quick solutions can mean the difference between life and death. An organism can't spend its time wrapped in thought, systematically working through a long list of solution possibilities. Instead, it's adaptive for the organism to guess, as long as it's a "reasonable" guess based on prior knowledge.

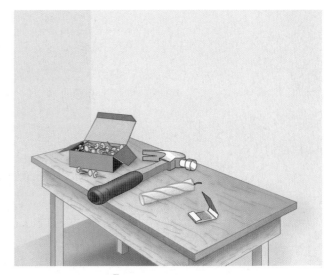

FIGURE 9.9 The Duncker Candle Problem
Using only the materials shown, figure out a way to mount the candle on the wall.

algorithms Step-by-step rules or procedures that, if applied correctly, guarantee a problem solution.

heuristics The rules of thumb we use to solve problems; heuristics can usually be applied quickly, but they do not guarantee that a solution will be found.

People use heuristics—rules of thumb—when they play chess because the human mind simply cannot examine all the possible moves and their consequences during a game.

means–ends analysis A problem-solving heuristic that involves devising actions, or means, that reduce the distance between the current starting point and the desired end (the goal state).

working backward A problem-solving heuristic that involves starting at the goal state and moving backward toward the starting point to see how the goal state can be reached.

searching for analogies A problem-solving heuristic that involves trying to find a connection between the current problem and some previous problem you have solved successfully.

mental set The tendency to rely on well-established strategies when attempting to solve problems.

One common problem-solving heuristic is **means–ends analysis**, which attacks problems by devising *means*, or actions, that reduce the gap between the current starting point and the desired goals, or *ends* (Newell & Simon, 1972). Typically one applies this strategy by breaking down the problem into a series of more manageable subgoals, where the appropriate means to an end are clear. Let's assume that Peter, a normally nonachieving undergraduate, wants to start a relationship with Sonita, the brightest student in his psychology class. Obviously, asking Sonita out immediately is unlikely to succeed, so Peter breaks the problem down into more manageable components.

First, he reasons, he'll impress her in class by making an insightful comment during the lecture. He now has a new goal, acting intelligent in class, for which there is relatively straightforward means—he needs to study hard so he can master the material. Assuming he's successful (everyone now thinks he's an amazingly insightful young man), he devises a new subgoal: making some kind of personal contact with Sonita. Forming a small study group would be a good means to that end, he figures, so he approaches the recently impressed Sonita with the idea. Notice the key ingredients of the problem-solving strategy: Establish where you are, figure out where you want to be, and then devise a means for effectively getting you from here to there. Often, as in Peter's case, means–ends analysis is made more effective by working systematically through subgoals.

Another effective heuristic is **working backward**—starting at the goal state and trying to move back toward the starting point. Suppose someone asked you to generate a set of anagrams. How would you proceed? Would you try to generate sets of randomly arranged letters and then see whether a particular sequence forms a word? Of course not. You would start with the solution, the word, and work backward by mixing up the known sequence.

Here's another example: You're working on a biology project tracking the growth of bacteria in a petri dish. You know this particular strain of bacteria doubles every 2 hours. After starting the experiment, you discover the petri dish is exactly full after 12 hours. After how many hours was the petri dish exactly half full? To solve this one, it's better to work backward. If the dish is full after 12 hours, and it takes 2 hours for the bacteria to double, what did the dish look like after 10 hours? This turns out to be the answer, which is arrived at rather simply if the problem is attacked in reverse.

Another useful heuristic is to **search for analogies**. If you can see a resemblance between the current problem and some task that you solved in the past, you can quickly obtain an acceptable solution. Imagine a man buys a horse for $60 and sells it for $70. Later, he buys the same horse back for $80 and sells it again for $90. How much money did the man make in the horse-trading business? The attentive reader will not miss this one. It's a different version of the ticket scalping problem that opened this chapter. If you see the relationship between the two problems, you're unlikely to suffer the same problem-solving pitfalls you encountered before.

Mental Set   Generally, to solve problems like these, you need to think in creative and novel ways. You may need to look at an everyday object in an unusual way (to break functional fixedness) or even stop using a problem-solving strategy that was successful in the past. Often people adopt **mental sets**, which are tendencies to rely on particular problem-solving strategies that were successful in the past. For example, military commanders lose battles because they rely on tried-and-true attack strategies that simply fail in their current environment. Similarly, your never-fail strategy for getting excellent grades in high school may no longer work in college. You need to formulate a new strategy that's appropriate to the situation you're in now.

At first glance, concepts like functional fixedness and mental sets don't seem very adaptive—so why are they characteristics of how we solve problems? Wouldn't it be better to consider all possible object uses, or all possible strategies? Actually, the answer is "No." Most of the time, if you view objects in fixed ways or use fixed strategies that have worked well in the past, you're likely to be successful. After all, pliers usually do solve problems having to do with holding and grabbing. Many of the problems we've dealt with here are actually quite artificial—they're set up by psychologists in the hope that our "mistakes" will uncover normal problem-solving methods. The fact that we tend to rely on well-established habits of perception and thought is probably an effective overall problem-solving strategy.

Reaching the Aha! Moment: Insight

Anyone who has struggled with problems of the type we've been considering knows there's often a moment—an Aha! moment—when everything falls into place. The solution seems to pop magically into mind, a process that psychologists call **insight**. All the factors we've been considering, especially problem representation, play a role in achieving insight, but the process itself remains poorly understood. There's some suggestion that the Aha! moment is correlated with solution activation in the right cerebral hemisphere (Bowden & Jung-Beeman, 2003), and perhaps the hippocampus in particular (Jing & Kazuhisa, 2003), but the data are merely suggestive at this point.

The phenomenon of insight has been important historically because it suggests that we often don't solve problems through slow and steady trial-and-error learning. Aha! solutions seem to appear spontaneously, in an all-or-none fashion, rather than accumulating slowly over trials. This point was first famously demonstrated in chimpanzees by the Gestalt psychologist Wolfgang Köhler (1925). Köhler was marooned on the Canary Islands during World War I, and he used his free time to experiment with chimpanzees housed in a large outdoor pen. A variety of toys and tools were scattered about in the pen—sticks, boxes, poles, and so forth—which Köhler encouraged the chimps to use in solving problems. For example, he would place food in the pen that was visible, but inaccessible (such as hanging from the ceiling), and record how the chimps managed to reach it. He noticed the chimps would often struggle, failing to get the food, but then suddenly, after seeming to reflect on the situation, they would creatively use a tool (or combination of tools) to secure the food. The solution process wasn't slow, but sudden and reflective—the chimps seemed to display insight.

Psychologists have tried to study insight systematically in the laboratory, but it can be tough to re-create under controlled conditions. One common strategy is to present people with an insight problem, such as the nine-dot problem shown in ▌ Figure 9.10, and then affect solution probability by providing hints or other kinds of information. To solve the nine-dot problem, it's necessary to connect all the dots with exactly four straight lines without lifting the pencil from the paper or retracing. This is an extremely difficult problem to solve, primarily because people are biased perceptually to perceive the nine dots as a square (Maier, 1930). (The solution, shown at the end of the chapter, requires you to break the good figure of the square, drawing outside of the imagined lines.) Researchers have been able to increase performance somewhat through strategy training, such as requiring people to learn visual configurations that resemble the final solution, but performance usually remains low (Kershaw & Ohlsson, 2004). Other researchers have attempted to get inside the problem-solver's head—for example, by tracking eye movements or general brain activity during a solution attempt (Jones, 2003; Lang et al., 2006)—but, unfortunately, the Aha! moment remains largely a mystery to researchers at this point.

insight The moment when a problem solution seems to pop suddenly into one's mind.

▌**FIGURE 9.10** The Nine-Dot Problem
Try connecting all nine dots by drawing exactly four straight lines without lifting your pencil from the paper or retracing.

Having Difficulty? Take a Break!

Have you ever been frustrated with a problem and given up, only to find that the solution suddenly and mysteriously appears at a later time? Psychologists refer to this as an *incubation effect*—sometimes we do better at solving a problem when we stop working on it for a while. What accounts for this effect? Why should putting a problem aside increase the chances of reaching a solution?

One possibility is that our brain continues to work on the problem, even though our conscious awareness is directed elsewhere. The problem is placed in the background where, over time, our unconscious mind churns out a solution. The trouble with this explanation is that we don't really have any solid scientific evidence for this kind of unconscious processing. Psychologists remain undecided about whether the unconscious mind even exists, let alone in a form capable of sophisticated problem solving.

A more likely explanation is that the break stops you from thinking about the problem in the wrong way. When people have trouble solving a problem, they often continue with the same ineffective strategy, coming up with the same wrong answer again and again. You can get locked into a particular way of viewing the problem components and can't break free. As you know, successful problem solving often requires thinking about the problem components in a novel and creative way. When you take a break and stop thinking

© Mary Kate Denny/PhotoEdit

about the problem, you're able to approach it later in a fresh and new way.

Another possibility is that during the break, while you're doing something else, you will come across information that ultimately helps solve the problem. The additional activity may provide clues or hints that lead to a problem breakthrough. Suppose you're having a difficult time solving an anagram, such as THREAGUD. You stop working on it and turn on a television program that shows a happy

Mom with her children, a boy and a girl, playing nearby. That's it, you shout—the solution to the anagram is DAUGHTER! The new activity, watching television, provided the necessary clue to solve the problem. Regardless of the interpretation, it's a good idea to take a break from time to time when you're trying to solve a tough problem. A fresh mind can do wonders for seeing a problem in a new way or simply for renewing your enthusiasm for finding a solution.

Test Yourself 9.3

Check your knowledge about problem solving by answering the following questions. (You will find the answers in the Appendix.)

1. Decide whether each of the following problems is well defined or ill defined. Justify your answer.
   a. Finding your way to a new restaurant in town: _____
   b. Receiving an "A" in your psychology course: _____
   c. Making your lab partner in chemistry fall madly in love with you: _____
   d. Baking a cherry cheesecake that won't taste like plumber's caulk: _____

2. Try to identify the problem-solving strategy at work in each of the following examples. Choose from the following terms: *algorithm, means–ends analysis, working backward, searching for analogies.*

   a. On the final exam Myka looks for connections between the physics problem on the test and the ones he worked on while studying. _____
   b. Rachel needs a three-letter word that begins with *R* to complete the crossword puzzle. She mindlessly considers all possible two-letter combinations, placing them after *R* until she arrives at an acceptable word. _____
   c. Hector really needs an A in his philosophy class, but he has no idea what it takes. He decides to concentrate on writing a really top-notch first paper. _____
   d. Courtney needs to generate a set of anagrams for a school project. To generate each anagram, she starts with a word and then scrambles the letters. _____

Making Decisions

LEARNING GOALS
- Understand how "framing" alternatives influences decision making.
- Identify common decision-making biases.
- Describe the common decision-making heuristics.
- Evaluate the pros and cons of using heuristics.

WE TURN OUR ATTENTION now to **decision making**, which deals with how we evaluate and choose from among alternatives. Obviously, decision making and problem solving are closely related. When you make a decision, you're confronted with a set of alternatives, and you must make a choice. The choice is almost always accompanied by risk, so it's in your interest to evaluate and select among the alternatives with care. Think about the decision of the United States to invade Iraq, or the physician who must choose between risky treatments that may kill or save a patient. Like problem solving, decision making is influenced by how you represent the alternatives in your mind, your personal biases, and by your choice of decision-making strategies. Let's examine how each of these processes affects the choices we make.

> **decision making** The thought processes involved in evaluating and choosing from among a set of alternatives; it usually involves some kind of risk.

Framing Decision Alternatives

The way the alternatives are presented, called **framing**, can have a dramatic influence on what you decide. In a study by McNeil and colleagues (1982), hospital physicians were asked to choose between two forms of treatment for a patient with lung cancer: either a surgical operation on the lungs or a six-week treatment with radiation. Half of the physicians received the following information prior to making the choice:

> **framing** The way in which the alternatives in a decision-making situation are structured.

> Of 100 people having surgery, 10 will die during treatment, 32 will have died by one year, and 66 will have died by five years. Of 100 people having radiation therapy, none will die during treatment, 23 will have died by one year, and 78 will have died by five years.

Put yourself in the doctor's shoes—which would you choose? The other half of the physicians were given the following:

CRITICAL THINKING

Do you think problem solving is a part of decision making, or is decision making a part of problem solving?

> Of 100 people having surgery, 90 will be alive immediately after the treatment, 68 will be alive after one year, and 34 will be alive after five years. Of 100 people having radiation therapy, all will be alive immediately after treatment, 77 will be alive after one year, and 22 will be alive after five years.

Do you want to change your mind? Actually, exactly the same information is given in each of the choice scenarios. The only difference is the treatment outcomes are described, or framed, in terms of who will die or who will survive; the consequences are exactly the same in each case. Believe it or not, the option that physicians choose depends dramatically on the framing: Radiation therapy is chosen 44% of the time when the outcomes are framed in terms of who will die and only 18% of the time when survival rates are given.

This example is unsettling, especially given the medical context, because it suggests that human decision making is not always a rational process. No one wants to think that doctors make life-or-death decisions based on how treatment options happen to be framed. Yet it's not irrational for people to weigh information differently in different situations (Kahneman, Slovic, & Tversky, 1982). When the alternatives were death based, perhaps the doctors simply connected the deaths to the treatment (surgery will kill 10 people and radiation none). In contrast, when the alternatives were framed around who lived, the focus might have been on long-term survival rather than on the hazards of treatment (34 people who receive surgery will be alive after five years, but only 22 radiation patients will survive this long). Thus you can't assume the problem information was perceived in the same way in the two framings—you

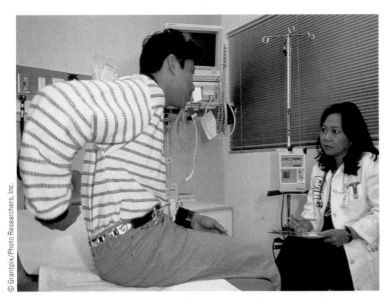

How doctors interpret and frame a patient's treatment options can critically influence the decision-making process.

confirmation bias The tendency to seek out and use information that supports and confirms a prior decision or belief.

belief persistence In decision making, the tendency to cling to initial beliefs when confronted with disconfirming evidence.

representativeness heuristic The tendency to make decisions based on an alternative's similarity, or representativeness, in relation to an ideal. For example, people decide whether a sequence is random based on how irregular the sequence looks.

need to take into account how the problem was actually represented in the mind of the decision maker (Keys & Schwartz, 2007).

Still, experiments on alternative framing have significant implications for everyday decision making. When you're listening to a sales pitch, as you know, the salesperson typically focuses only on the gains: "Eighty-five percent of the people who bought this product report satisfaction after one year." Well, that means that 15% of the customers didn't report satisfaction—if the focus had been on the 15%, would you still be interested in the product? More ominously, think about how politicians or military leaders frame arguments for or against military intervention. Is the focus on saving lives through enhanced security or on the costs of lives lost? The answer is obvious, but tread carefully. How decision alternatives are framed can significantly affect the final judgment you reach.

Decision-Making Biases

Our personal biases also influence our decision making, just as they can when we attempt to solve problems. For example, psychologists have known for some time that people show confirmation biases when they make decisions. In a nutshell, a **confirmation bias** is a tendency to seek out and use information that supports and confirms a prior decision or belief. If a therapist, for instance, believes that all instances of depression are caused by traumatic experiences in childhood (they're not), a confirmation bias might then lead him or her to address and ask only about childhood troubles during the therapy session.

People also tend to remember information that confirms their preconceptions. When asked to read stories about the sexual activities of men and women, for example, people tend to remember more negative things about the women—even if each story contains an equal number of positive and negative statements about the characters. This occurs, presumably, because of the widespread societal belief, or sexual "double standard," that it's okay for men but not women to engage in sexual activity (Marks & Fraley, 2006). To avoid the confirmation bias, you should actively seek out disconfirming evidence; you should ask questions that allow you to reject or rule out one decision alternative over another.

Unfortunately, however, we're also reluctant to believe disconfirming evidence when it occurs. People show **belief persistence** as well, which means that we tend to cling to our initial beliefs even when evidence suggests our belief may be wrong. For example, the strong believer in ESP continues to assume it exists even though countless experiments have failed to support its existence. There is always a reason, or a rationale, to hold onto the belief. In Chapter 13, which covers social psychology, we'll discuss decision-making biases that resemble belief persistence in some detail.

Decision-Making Heuristics

When people are forced to choose from among a set of alternatives, most rely on heuristics, or rules of thumb, just as they do when solving problems. These strategies simplify the decision-making process and often lead to correct judgments, but they sometimes lead you to the wrong decision.

Representativeness Suppose you're asked to judge the likelihood of some event falling into class A or B. In such a case you might rely on a rule of thumb called the **representativeness heuristic**. You arrive at your decision by comparing the similarity of the object or event in question to the average, or prototypical, member of each class. It's easiest to demonstrate with an example. Let's assume your friends, the Renfields, have six children. If B denotes boy and G denotes girl, which of the following two birth order sequences do you think is more likely?

BBBGGG

BGGBGB

If you picked the second alternative, you're like most people. Actually, according to the rules of probability, the two outcomes are equally likely. Whether your next child will be a boy or a girl doesn't depend on the sex of your previous children— each event is independent of the others. Even so, people favor the second alternative because the first sequence clashes with their worldview of randomness. The first sequence just doesn't look like the outcome of a random process—it's not *representative* of randomness.

What if you flipped a coin six times and you got six heads? You'd probably think it was a crooked coin. Again, a sequence of six heads isn't similar to, or representative of, what you think of as a random sequence. You have taken the outcome and compared it to some standard and made your decision accordingly. People often use the representativeness heuristic to make decisions in real-world settings. For example, clerks in stores use the products that a shopper buys as a way of judging age. If someone loads his or her shopping cart with products normally thought to be representative of an older consumer, the clerk's estimate of the shopper's age increases (McCall, 1994).

Using a heuristic such as representativeness is adaptive and beneficial most of the time, but it can lead to irrational decisions. Imagine you're leafing through a stack of questionnaires that have been filled out by some adult men. One of the respondents lists his height as 6 feet 5 inches, but his answers are so sloppily written that you can't make out his circled profession—it's either bank president or basketball player (NBA). You need to make a choice: Which is he? Most people choose NBA player because the applicant is tall and apparently not interested in careful writing (Beyth-Marom & Lichtenstein, 1984). This is actually an illogical choice, however, because the odds of someone in the sample being a professional basketball player is extremely low—bank presidents outnumber NBA players by a wide margin (probably at least 50 to 1). In choosing basketball player, people have ignored the *base rate*, or the proportion of times that an object or event is likely to occur in the population being sampled.

The representativeness heuristic also dupes people into committing what is called the *conjunction error*. Consider the following: Linda is 31 years old, single, outspoken, and very bright. She majored in philosophy. As a student, she was deeply concerned with issues of discrimination and social justice and participated in antinuclear demonstrations. Which of the following alternatives is more likely?

1. Linda is a bank teller.
2. Linda is a bank teller and active in the feminist movement.

In a study conducted by Tversky and Kahneman (1983), 85% of the participants judged alternative 2 to be the more likely. Why? Because Linda's description is more representative of someone active in the feminist movement than it is of a bank teller. But think about it—how can the odds of two things happening together be higher than the likelihood of any one of those events happening alone? Notice the second alternative is actually a subset of the first alternative and therefore cannot be more likely. Those who choose alternative 2 have acted illogically, at least from the standpoint of the rational decision maker.

Availability   At other times, we rely on memory to help us make our decisions. Suppose you're asked to estimate the likelihood that you'll forget to turn off your alarm clock on Friday night. If you can easily remember lots of instances in which your Saturday morning sleep was interrupted by a blasting alarm, your estimate of forgetting

availability heuristic The tendency to base estimates on the ease with which examples come to mind.

is likely to be high. You have relied on your previous experiences—particularly those experiences that easily come to mind—as a basis for judging probability. This kind of judgment relies on an **availability heuristic**. Once again, it's likely to be adaptive much of the time, but as with the representativeness heuristic, researchers can arrange situations that make this decision-making practice ineffective.

Which do you think is more likely, an English word that begins with the letter K or an English word with K in the third position? By now you're probably skeptical about your first choice, but most people think English words that begin with K are more likely (Tversky & Kahneman, 1973). In fact, English words with K in the third position are much more common (the ratio is about 3 to 1). Which do you think is more likely, someone dying from any kind of accident or someone dying from a stroke? Accidents, right? It's not even close. Over twice as many people are likely to die from stroke than from any kind of accident (Slovic, Fischoff, & Lichtenstein, 1982). People make the error because examples of the incorrect alternative are more likely to come to mind. It's easier to think of an English word with K in the first position, and accidental deaths get much more publicity than deaths due to stroke.

Anchoring and Adjustment Judgments are also influenced by starting points—that is, by any initial estimates that you might be given. Tversky and Kahneman (1974) asked people to estimate the proportion of African countries belonging to the United Nations. Prior to answering, subjects were given a number (between 0 and 100) and were asked to pick the correct proportion by moving up or down from this starting point. For example, you might be given the number 10 and asked to estimate the proportion using 10 as a base. For groups that received 10 and 65 as the initial starting points, the estimated proportion of African countries was 25% and 45%, respectively—a whopping difference. The judgments were clearly influenced by the initial estimates, or *anchors*, and people tended to stay relatively close to the starting points as they made their decisions.

In another experiment described by Tversky and Kahneman (1974), one group of people was asked to estimate the product of the following numbers:

$$1 \times 2 \times 3 \times 4 \times 5 \times 6 \times 7 \times 8$$

People are much more likely to worry about terrorism if a recently publicized disaster (such as the September 11, 2001, attack on the Pentagon) is fresh and available in their minds.

© USAF/DoD/Getty Images

Concept Review | Decision-Making Heuristics

HEURISTIC	DESCRIPTION	EXAMPLE
Representativeness	We arrive at a decision by comparing the similarity of the object or event to the average member of each class.	Juan meets his new college roommate, Bryce, who is 6'10" and very athletic looking. Juan assumes that Bryce is a basketball player, probably on scholarship.
Availability	We estimate the odds of some event occurring on the basis of how easily examples come to mind.	Stella reads so much in the newspaper about car accidents that she believes her chances of dying in a car accident are greater than her chances of dying from a stroke.
Anchoring and adjustment	Judgments are influenced by initial estimates.	Stacey holds a garage sale and sells two big items early for a total of $150. Throughout the day, she overestimates how much she is making and in the end is disappointed by her actual profit.

whereas a second group was asked to estimate the product of the same numbers presented in reverse order:

$$8 \times 7 \times 6 \times 5 \times 4 \times 3 \times 2 \times 1$$

The correct answer in both cases is 40,320. But the first group gave an average estimate of 512, whereas the second group's estimate averaged 2,250—quite a difference, given that it's the same problem in both cases. In this example, the early numbers in the sequence serve as the anchors leading to either low or more moderate estimates.

The Value of Heuristics   What are we to make of such an imperfect decision maker? As psychologist Reid Hastie (1991) notes, the heuristic tool user described by Kahneman and Tversky is "an image of a decision maker of 'small brain' attempting to make do with a limited set of useful, imperfect, and not-too-demanding cognitive subroutines" (p. 136).

Imperfect though heuristics may be, there are several points worth making in their favor. First, the use of heuristics may lead to systematic errors under some circumstances, but as Tversky and Kahneman (1974) have argued, they are usually surprisingly effective. Second, heuristics are economical. Optimal, or rational, decision making can be a complex, time-consuming activity. Strategies that lead to quick decisions with little cost are adaptive even if they sometimes lead to error. Third, to act optimally, you must possess all the information needed to calculate a choice; unfortunately, you often don't have all of this information. In these cases, heuristics become useful tools for pointing you in the right direction.

Moreover, as we discussed in the section on framing effects, the fact that people make errors in artificial laboratory situations is somewhat misleading. We can define what the rational decision might be, based on objective information, but people don't always interpret the decision alternatives in the way the researcher intends. We all bring background knowledge to a situation that affects how we think and behave. In the "Linda is a bank teller" example, for instance, people know there are more bank tellers in the world than feminist bank tellers. People understand a great deal about the frequencies of events in the world—the mistake is made because they're thinking about a single case, Linda, rather than about probabilities in general (Fiedler, 1988; Gigerenzer, 1996).

Just because you make decision errors doesn't mean you're using ineffective processes. Think back to Chapter 5 and our discussion of perceptual illusions. It's easy to arrange situations in which you might see or hear things that aren't really there, but your visual system is still highly adaptive. Just because your visual system can be tricked by an illusion doesn't mean it's a bad system. Similarly, when you make decisions, you're relying on adaptive systems that serve you very well in the majority of situations (Gigerenzer, 1997).

Test Yourself 9.4

Check your knowledge about decision making by picking the term that best fits the following statements. Choose your answer from the following: availability heuristic, anchoring and adjustment heuristic, framing, representativeness heuristic. *(You will find the answers in the Appendix.)*

1. Matt used to fly to visit his parents during the Thanksgiving break, but after seeing nonstop coverage of a gory plane accident, he now chooses to drive. _____
2. Larry, a broker, used to tell people that his mutual fund lost money only three times in the last 10 years. Now he tells them that the fund has made money 7 of the last 10 years. He's noticed a very marked improvement in overall sales of the fund. _____
3. Kelley sleeps until noon, she parties at night, and she carries around a big backpack the rest of the time. Her neighbor Eileen assumes that Kelley must be a college student. _____
4. Graham, who made lots of sales early in the morning, estimates that he and Leslie made $700 from their yard sale; Leslie, who had a big afternoon, puts the estimate at $300. _____

Review *Psychology for a Reason*

In this chapter we've discussed how people use their higher mental processes to communicate, categorize, find solutions to problems, and decide among alternatives. Each effectively illustrates how we use our internal processes and existing knowledge to coexist successfully with our environment.

Communicating With Others To communicate effectively, humans have developed rules (grammar) for combining arbitrary symbols in meaningful ways to express thoughts, feelings, and needs to others. A proper grammar consists of rules for combining sounds (phonology), rules for constructing sentences from words (syntax), and rules for meaning (semantics). To understand how language works, language researchers believe it's important to distinguish between the surface structure of a sentence—the literal ordering of words—and its deep structure, which represents the underlying meaning. To

comprehend the communications of others, we rely on mutual knowledge, or pragmatics, to interpret statements or requests that may be riddled with ambiguity.

The sequence of language development turns out to be universal—it doesn't matter where you look in the world, babies show similar milestones in language development. This finding has led many researchers to conclude that people are born ready to learn language in the same way they're born ready to walk. The ability to produce written and spoken language enables people to gather and transmit knowledge in ways that seem to be one of the truly unique characteristics of the human species. Whether or not language is truly an adaptation (a product of natural selection) remains controversial.

Classifying and Categorizing When we categorize, or put objects into meaningful groups, we create a world that's

more sensible and predictable. Categorization skills enable us to infer invisible properties about objects—if X is a member of category Y, then X will have at least some of the properties of category Y members. As a result, we can make accurate predictions about the things we encounter. How is category membership defined? The evidence suggests that people often rely on family resemblance to make the categorization judgment. Members of the same category tend to share certain basic or core features. At the same time, categories are remarkably flexible; their boundaries are fuzzy, which enables us to classify things even when those objects may not share all the typical features of the category members. Categories also have structures that are hierarchical—there are categories within categories within categories. An object that fits the category "Siamese cat" also fits the category "animal" or "living thing." Research indicates that we most commonly assign objects to basic-level categories, which tend to be at intermediate levels of the hierarchy.

Solving Problems When faced with a problem, there is a goal, which may or may not be well defined, and it's not immediately obvious how to get from the problem to the solution. One of the common pitfalls in problem solving occurs when we allow preconceptions to influence how we represent problem information. For example, most people fall prey to functional fixedness, or the tendency to see objects and their functions in certain fixed ways. Algorithms are procedures that guarantee a solution, but they're often time consuming and can't always be applied. Heuristics are problem-solving rules of thumb that can be applied quickly but don't always lead to the correct solution. Examples of problem-solving heuristics include means–ends analysis, working backward, and solving through analogies. Psychologists are also very interested in insight—the Aha! moment that occurs when solutions suddenly become available. Unfortunately, little is known about the psychological processes involved.

Making Decisions The study of decision making looks at how we evaluate and choose from among a set of alternatives. When we make decisions, we're confronted with a set of alternatives and are required to make a choice. Choice in decision making is almost always accompanied by risk, so it's adaptive to evaluate and select among the alternatives with care. As with problem solving, decision making is influenced by how the alternatives are viewed or represented. For example, how alternatives are framed can affect the decision that is made. We commonly use a variety of decision heuristics, including representativeness, availability, and anchoring and adjustment. These strategies may not always cause us to make the right decision, but they allow us to move quickly toward the goal and to use past experience.

Active Summary (You will find the answers in the Appendix.)

Communicating With Others

• To qualify as language, a communication system must have (1) _____, which consists of (a) phonology, the rules for combining (2) _____ to make words; (b) syntax, the rules for combining words to make (3) _____; and (c) semantics, the rules for communicating (4) _____. Languages are hierarchical, ranging from (5) _____, the smallest significant sound units, and (6) _____, the smallest meaningful units, to words and sentences. Sentences have (7) _____ structure, the literal ordering of words, and (8) _____ structure, the underlying meaning; language production turns deep structure into an acceptable surface structure.

• Effective communication relies heavily on the speakers' common (9) _____ and a Combination of bottom-up and (10) _____-_____ processing. (11) _____ refers to how we use (12) _____ knowledge to comprehend what someone says and to respond effectively.

• The universality of language is apparent at birth. Crying, cooing, and babbling are important vocalization milestones. Simple words appear by the end of a child's (13) _____ year. By the age of 2, (14) _____ speech begins: The child communicates without using articles (*the*) or prepositions (*at, in*), showing a rudimentary awareness of (15) _____. Children often (16) _____ grammatical rules.

• Although the vocal (17) _____ of chimps makes actual speech (18) _____, some have been taught to communicate with humans through signs and symbols, including American (19) _____ Language. Researchers disagree about whether such achievements represent true (20) _____.

• Many psychologists assume that language is an (21) _____, which means it evolved as a result of natural selection. Language is associated with particular regions of the (22) _____; children learn language incredibly quickly without specifically being taught the rules; the human (23) _____ and vocal tract seem perfectly tailored to meet the needs of speech; and some people inherit tendencies to make certain types of (24) _____ errors. Even so, the question of how and why language emerged remains controversial.

Classifying and Categorizing

• A (25) _____ is a class of objects—people, places, or things—that belong together. To determine membership in a category, things are classified by their (26) _____ features, which are shared by all (27) _____. (28) _____ categories usually have (29) _____ boundaries, which suggests that members have (30) _____ rather than fixed features. Family (31) _____ is determined by the collection of (32) _____ features that an object possesses. Members of the same category will share many but not all family features.

• Category membership may be determined by comparison to a (33) _____, the one best or most (34) _____ member of a category. Alternatively, we may store category examples, or category (35) _____, of every category and assign category membership based on comparison to many things.

• All categories are (36) _____. (37) _____ level categories generate the most useful and (38) _____ information and are at (39) _____ levels of the category hierarchy. (40) _____ categories are at the top level and aren't especially (41) _____.

Solving Problems

• A (42) _____-_____ problem has a well-stated goal, a clear starting point, and an easy way to tell when a solution has been reached. The goal and starting point of an (43) _____ defined problem aren't (44) _____, and the problem lacks an effective mechanism for evaluating progress.

• To solve a problem quickly and (45) _____, you must represent, or understand, the information you have about the problem and how it can be used. Obstacles to problem representation include functional (46) _____, which is a tendency to see objects and their functions in fixed, typical ways.

• For certain types of well-defined problems we can use (47) _____, step-by-step procedures that guarantee a solution. When algorithms aren't feasible, we can try

problem-solving (48) _____, or "rules of thumb." The three most common heuristics are (49) _____ _____ analysis, working (50) _____, and searching for (51) _____. People often adopt (52) _____ sets, a tendency to rely on particular problem solving strategies that were successful in the past.

• (53) _____ is a process in which a solution seems to "magically" come to mind. The process has been studied in the lab but remains poorly understood.

Making Decisions

• Decisions can be dramatically influenced by (54) _____, the way alternatives are structured or presented, which in turn influences how the problem is (55) _____ in the mind of the decision maker.

• The (56) _____ bias is the tendency to seek out and use information that confirms a previous decision or long-standing (57) _____. We also tend to show belief (58) _____, clinging to our initial beliefs even when confronted with evidence that counters them.

• When asked to judge the likelihood of an event belonging to a class, we often rely on the (59) _____ heuristic, which means that we arrive at a decision by comparing the similarity of the object or event in question to the average or (60) _____ member of each class. If we use the (61) _____ heuristic, we base our estimates on the ease with which examples of the event come to mind. Our judgments are also influenced by starting points, or (62) _____, which are initial estimates we might be given. Though imperfect, heuristics are adaptive because they lead to quick and (63) _____ decisions with little cost. Even when we don't have all the important information about a problem, (64) _____ still help point us in the right direction. However, using heuristics may sometimes lead to (65) _____ in the decision-making process.

Terms to Remember

Media Resources

ThomsonNOW

www.thomsonedu.com/ThomsonNOW

Go to this site for the link to ThomsonNow, your one-stop study shop. Take a Pre-Test for this chapter and Thomson-Now will generate a personalized Study Plan based on your test results! The Study Plan will identify the topics you need to review and direct you to online resources to help you master those topics. You can then take a Post-Test to help you determine the concepts you have mastered and what you still need to work on.

 Companion Website

www.thomsonedu.com/psychology/nairne

Go to this site to find online resources directly linked to your book, including a glossary, flashcards, quizzing, weblinks, and more.

Psyk.trek 3.0

Check out the Psyk.trek CD-ROM for further study of the concepts in this chapter. Psyk.trek's interactive learning modules, simulations, and quizzes offer additional opportunities for you to interact with, reflect on, and retain the material:

Memory and Thought: Problem Solving

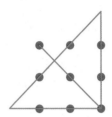

Solution to the nine-dot problem (see Figure 9.10)

CHAPTER 10

Intelligence

On a Saturday morning in October, Jefferson Tarpy drops down his yellow number 2 pencil and glances about the room with a cocky grin. Around him, working feverishly, sit dozens of others, similar in age and general appearance, but with pencils raised and sweat collecting on furrowed brows. Jefferson has finished early, as is his custom, and he's just aced the most important standardized test of his life. Next stop: medical school, a top residency, a lifetime of security.

Meanwhile, outside in a park across the street, Larry Steinway has also dropped his yellow pencil. But he doesn't notice. He'll need to rely on his attendant to recover it. Although physically 22, Larry Steinway's mind drifts in a world occupied by a 4-year-old's thoughts and impulses. He uses language haltingly; his hopes for an elementary school education are limited. Still, he responds quickly when his attendant asks him to calculate the number of seconds elapsing in 65 years, 14 days, and 15 hours. His answer includes the correct number of leap years and arrives in slightly under a minute and a half.

Overhead, unknown to Larry Steinway, flies a single nutcracker in search of a place to deposit his recently harvested supply of pine seeds. On this particular trip, one of many over the past few months, the bird will store its 25,000th seed. Across

© Bettmann/Corbis

Most of us have no trouble accepting that Balamurati Krishna Ambati is "intelligent"—after all, at age 12 he was a third-year premed student at New York University.

© Bettmann/Corbis

Ten-year-old savant Eddie Bonafe was born with severe physical and mental handicaps; but before he learned to walk he could play on the piano every hymn he heard sung in church. Would you call Eddie "intelligent"?

This little bird, Clark's nutcracker, can remember the locations of thousands of seeds scattered across miles of confusing terrain. Wouldn't you call this a form of "intelligent" behavior?

miles of terrain lie thousands of secret caches, all attributable to this one bird, scattered among the storage locations of other nutcrackers. Over the coming winter months, this bird will successfully revisit its own hiding places, ignoring others, and recover some 80% of the hidden seeds.

Each of these sketches demonstrates behavior that *might* be characterized as intelligent. What do you think? Certainly we can agree that Jefferson Tarpy fits the description—ace performer on standardized tests, self-assured; he probably gets all A's and is popular in school. But what about Larry Steinway—someone who is poor at language, who operates at a mental level far below his physical age? Definitely not intelligent, you say; but then how do you explain his extraordinary calculating skills? Isn't "lightning calculation" an odd but nevertheless intelligent form of behavior? Finally, consider the nutcracker. It can't do geometry or calculus, but could you remember where you put 25,000 seeds scattered across miles of confusing terrain? Don't you think this remarkable ability to adapt to the harshness of winter is a prime example of intelligent behavior?

What's It For?   *The Study of Intelligence*

It probably won't surprise you to learn that psychologists can't agree on a definition of intelligence. As you've seen, the term can have a variety of meanings. Practically, when psychologists talk about **intelligence**, they're usually referring to individual differences—specifically, the differences people show in their ability to perform tasks. People clearly differ in ability, and the measurement of these differences is used to infer the capacity called "intelligence."

Think about it: If everyone had the same ability to solve math problems or devise creative ideas, the label "intelligent" would lose its meaning. Psychologists who study intelligence attempt to measure the differences among people and then determine how and why those differences occur. One of the important goals is to use individual differences to predict things like job performance and success in school. In this chapter, we'll focus on three fundamental problems facing the intelligence researcher: conceptualizing, measuring, and discovering the source of individual differences in intellectual ability.

Conceptualizing Intelligence
Many people talk of intelligence as if it's some "thing" that's possessed by a

person, such as blue eyes, long fingers, or a slightly crooked gait. Yet we can neither see intelligence nor measure it directly with a stick. Intelligence may not even be best viewed as a single capacity; it may be better seen as a collection of separate abilities. It's possible that we have multiple intelligences ranging from the more traditional verbal and math skills to musical ability, mechanical ability, or even athletic ability. We'll discuss how psychologists have attempted to conceptualize intelligence over the years and where the brunt of opinion lies today.

Measuring Individual Differences
Regardless of how we may choose to conceptualize intelligence, there's still the practical problem of measuring individual differences. For any particular task, such as performing well in school, there will be a distribution of abilities. Some people will perform extremely well; others will struggle. If these abilities can be measured accurately, through the use of psychological tests, then it should be possible to tailor your activities to fit your skills. You can be advised not to enter cartography school if your spatial abilities are weak, or you can be steered toward a career as

a writer or journalist if your verbal abilities are strong. We'll discuss how intelligence is typically measured and some of the characteristics of effective tests.

Discovering the Sources of Intelligence
Does intelligent behavior come primarily from your genetic background or from life experiences? People do differ in ability, but it's not immediately obvious whether these differences are largely inborn or due simply to peculiarities in one's environmental history. Is poor map reading a permanent condition, resulting from a lack of the right kind of genes, or can a superior ability to read maps be taught? Because of the wiring in my brain, am I doomed to forever have trouble fixing that leaky faucet in my kitchen, or can I be taught mechanical skills? We'll discuss the origins of intelligence from the perspective of nature and nurture and address some of the controversies that still surround the study of individual differences.

intelligence An internal capacity or ability that accounts for individual differences in mental test performance and enables us to adapt to ever-changing environments.

Conceptualizing Intelligence

LEARNING GOALS
- Understand the psychometric approach to intelligence, including Spearman's two-factor theory.
- Distinguish between fluid and crystallized intelligence.
- Explain how the speed of neural transmission might influence intelligence.
- Evaluate the various theories of multiple intelligences.

FROM THE PERSPECTIVE OF THE ADAPTIVE MIND, it certainly makes sense to talk about the adaptive characteristics of intelligence. For example, you might be considered intelligent if you can solve the problems unique to your environment. It turns out this is a fairly common way for psychologists to think about intelligence (Cosmides & Tooby, 2002; Geary, 2005). Adaptive accounts of intelligence present many advantages. For one thing, focusing on adaptation prevents us from thinking that human thoughts and abilities are the only proper measuring sticks for intelligent behavior. The fact that nutcrackers can efficiently hide and relocate thousands of seeds is certainly intelligent from the standpoint of adapting to the harshness of winter (Kamil & Balda, 1990). Recognizing that different species (and people) face different survival problems virtually guarantees that we'll need to establish a wide range of criteria for what it means to be intelligent.

However, conceptualizing intelligence simply in terms of adaptability does not tell us much about what accounts for individual differences. People (and nutcrackers) differ in their ability to fit successfully into their environments, even when they're faced with similar problems. We need to understand the factors that produce individual differences. In this section of the chapter, we'll consider several ways of generally conceptualizing intelligence.

Psychometrics: Measuring the Mind

We begin with the psychometric approach, which proposes that intelligence is a mental capacity that can be understood by analyzing performance on mental tests. The word **psychometric** literally means "to measure the mind." Intelligence is determined by administering a variety of tests that measure specific mental skills, such as verbal comprehension, memory, or spatial ability. The results are then analyzed statistically and conclusions are drawn about underlying mental abilities.

One of the first systematic attempts to treat intelligence in this way was developed in the 19th century by Englishman Sir Francis Galton (1822–1911). Galton was a half-cousin of Charles Darwin, and like his famous relative, he was deeply committed to the idea of "survival of the fittest." Galton (1869) believed individual differences in ability had their basis in heredity and could be measured through a series of tests of sensory discrimination and reaction time. For a small fee, visitors to Galton's laboratory were given a variety of psychological and physical tests, measuring such things as visual acuity, grip strength, and reaction time to sounds. At the end of the test session, they were handed a card with a detailed record of their scores (Hilgard, 1987; Johnson et al., 1985).

Galton believed he was measuring intelligence through performance on his battery of tests. He based his belief partly on the fact that there often appeared to be relationships among the various scores received by a particular individual. If a

psychometrics The use of psychological tests to measure the mind and mental processes.

Sir Francis Galton (1822–1911) and his "anthropometric" laboratory, where he measured intellectual ability.

Archives, History of American Psychology, University of Akron, OH

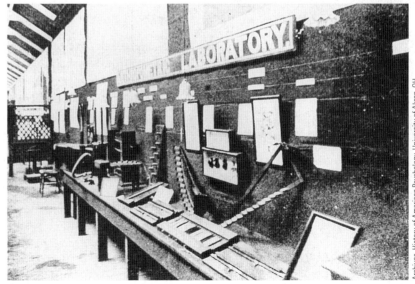

Archives, History of American Psychology, University of Akron, OH

person tended to score high on a certain test, such as sensory acuity, he or she tended to score high on other measures as well. This pattern suggested to Galton that each of the separate tests might be tapping into some general ability—a general intelligence that contributed in some way to each of the different measured skills.

As it turned out, Galton's laboratory investigations into the measurement of intelligence were unsuccessful. His measurements were crude, and his tests were later shown to be poor predictors of actual intellectual performance, such as academic success (Wissler, 1901). For these and other reasons, his contributions are primarily of historical rather than scientific interest. But his methods captured the attention of other researchers, who went on to develop the psychometric approach in a more rigorous way. Among the more influential of those who carried on the Galton tradition was a mathematically inclined psychologist named Charles Spearman (1863–1945).

Spearman and Factor *g* Charles Spearman's principal contribution was the development of a mathematical technique called **factor analysis**, which is a procedure for analyzing the relationships, or correlations, among test scores. Its purpose is to isolate the various factors that can account for test performance. For example, as Galton suggested, it's possible that each of us has a single underlying ability—intelligence—that helps to explain our performance on mental tests. Alternatively, there could be multiple factors involved—we might be intelligent in one way, such as in an ability to remember, and not very intelligent in another, such as in spatial reasoning. Spearman's technique enabled researchers to study these possibilities in a systematic way.

To get an idea of how factor analysis works, think about star athletes who excel in several sports. It's natural to assume that good athletes have general athletic ability that reveals itself in a number of ways. If you were to correlate performance across a variety of skills, you should be able to predict how well they'll perform on one measure of skill, given that you know how well they perform on others. Good athletes, for instance, should run fast, jump high, and have quick reflexes. Correlations exist because presumably an underlying ability—athletic skill—is tapped by each of the individual performance measures. Similar logic applies to intelligence: Someone who is high (or low) in intelligence should perform well (or poorly) on many different kinds of ability tests. If there is general intelligence, you should be able to predict performance on one type of test (such as math) if you know how well the person performs on other tests (such as verbal comprehension or spatial ability).

When Spearman (1904) applied factor analysis to the testing of mental ability, he discovered evidence for general intellectual ability. A single factor in the analysis, which he called *g* for *general intelligence*, helped to explain performance on a wide variety of mental tests. At the same time, it wasn't possible to explain individual test scores entirely by referring to *g*. The correlations among the test scores were high but not perfect. He found, for example, that someone who performed extremely well on a test of verbal comprehension did not necessarily excel on a test of spatial ability. He argued, therefore, that it's necessary to take *specific* abilities into account, reflected in *s*, that are *unique* to each individual test (see ▌Figure 10.1). To predict performance on a test of verbal comprehension, for example, you need a measure of ability that is specific to verbal comprehension in addition to *g*.

Hierarchical Models of Intelligence As you might expect, Spearman's two-factor analysis of intelligence was quite influential in its time, and it remains influential today (Sternberg, 2003). But over the years his conclusions have been challenged, especially the overarching concept of *g*. Psychologist L. L. Thurstone (1938), for example, applied a somewhat different version of factor analysis, as well as a more extensive battery of tests, and dis-

factor analysis A statistical procedure that groups together related items on tests by analyzing the correlations among test scores.

***g* (general intelligence)** According to Spearman, a general factor, derived from factor analysis, that underlies or contributes to performance on a variety of mental tests.

***s* (specific intelligence)** According to Spearman, a specific factor, derived from factor analysis, that is unique to a particular kind of test.

▌**FIGURE 10.1** Spearman's General and Specific Factors
Spearman discovered that to explain performance on a variety of mental tests it was necessary to consider (1) a common factor, called *g* for general intelligence, that contributes to performance on all of the tests, and (2) specific factors—labeled as s_1 through s_7—that are specific to the particular tests.

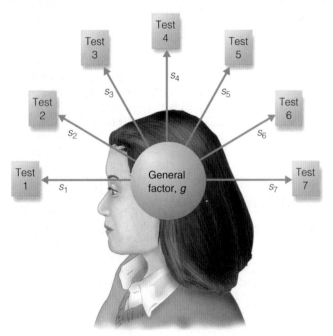

Deion Sanders performed at the highest levels in professional football and professional baseball. Do his skills support the existence of a factor tapping "general athletic ability"?

covered evidence for seven "primary mental abilities": verbal comprehension, verbal fluency, numerical ability, spatial ability, memory, perceptual speed, and reasoning. Thurstone rejected Spearman's notion of a single general intelligence, *g*, because his analysis indicated that these seven primary abilities are largely independent—just because someone is good at verbal reasoning doesn't mean he or she will be good at memory or show perceptual speed. If performance on one type of test tells us little or nothing about performance on a second test, it's unlikely that the two tests are measuring the same general underlying ability.

Psychologists have argued for decades about (a) the proper way to apply factor analysis, (b) the particular kinds of ability tests that should be used, and (c) whether single or multiple factors are needed to explain the data (Jensen & Weng, 1994). But the evidence for a central *g* is hard to dismiss completely, at least when intelligence is defined by performance on tests of mental ability. For this reason, most modern psychometric theories retain the concept of general intelligence but propose more of a hierarchical structure, such as that shown in ▌ Figure 10.2. General intelligence, *g*, occupies a position at the top of the hierarchy, and various subfactors (or abilities) that may or may not operate independently from one another sit at the lower levels. This represents a compromise of sorts between Thurstone's view—that there is more than one primary mental ability—and Spearman's concept of general intelligence or *g*.

CRITICAL THINKING

How well does the notion of general intelligence describe you? If you're good at one subject, does that predict how well you do in others?

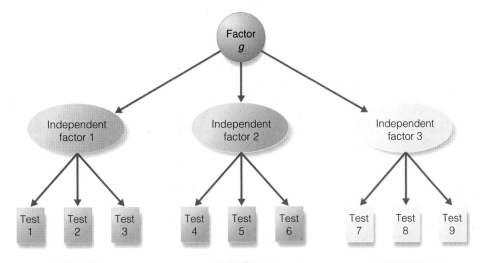

▌ **FIGURE 10.2** Hierarchical Models
Many psychologists now propose hierarchical models of intelligence that include elements found in the theories of both Spearman and Thurstone. Like Thurstone, hierarchical models propose separate factors that contribute independently to certain types of tests (for example, factor 1 contributes to tests 1–3, but not to tests 4–9). Like Spearman, these models also assume that each of the separate factors is influenced by an overall *g*.

Fluid and Crystallized Intelligence

fluid intelligence The natural ability to solve problems, reason, and remember; fluid intelligence is thought to be relatively uninfluenced by experience.

crystallized intelligence The knowledge and abilities acquired as a result of experience (as from schooling and cultural influences).

Most psychologists accept the idea of general intelligence; however, it too may need to be broken down into separate components. Raymond Cattell and John Horn have suggested that *g* contains two distinct components, *fluid* intelligence and *crystallized* intelligence (Cattell, 1963, 1998; Horn & Cattell, 1966). **Fluid intelligence** is a measure of your ability to solve problems, reason, and remember in ways that are relatively uninfluenced by experience. It's the type of intelligence that is probably determined primarily by biological or genetic factors. **Crystallized intelligence**, on the other hand, measures acquired knowledge and ability. You learn things about the world, such as how to solve arithmetic problems, and develop abilities based on level of schooling and other cultural influences.

In most cases, intelligent behavior relies on both fluid and crystallized intelligence. For example, as you know from earlier chapters, people differ in their ability to perform several tasks at the same time. If I ask you to solve math problems while remembering a list of words, your ability to perform this dual task correlates reasonably well with standard measures of intelligence (Engle, 2000). It's likely that you're born with a certain amount of conscious capacity (or mental resources), which is linked to fluid intelligence, but your performance also depends on what you've learned from experience. If you've learned to chunk or rehearse effectively (see Chapter 8), then your performance on the dual task will improve. These acquired strategies reflect crystallized intelligence, which develops with experience.

The distinction between fluid and crystallized intelligence is important because it helps to explain how mental abilities change with age and across different cultures (Horn & Noll, 1997; Parkin & Java, 2001). As you'll see later in the chapter, fluid and crystallized intelligence should change in somewhat different ways as we age. There are also striking differences in performance on psychometric tests of mental ability across different cultures and socioeconomic classes. These differences can't be easily explained from the perspective of general intelligence, unless we assume that an important part of general intelligence is acquired from experience. Distinguishing between fluid and crystallized intelligence can help explain how people who are born with the same amount of natural (fluid) intelligence can end up performing quite differently on tests of mental ability.

CRITICAL THINKING

Which do you think contributes the most to performance on an essay exam: fluid or crystallized intelligence?

Multiple Intelligences: Gardner's Case Study Approach

Before turning to another way of conceptualizing intelligence—the multiple-intelligences approach—let's pause momentarily and return to Larry Steinway, that fictional lightning calculator we met in the opening to the chapter. After reading the previous sections, what do you think psychologists with a psychometric bent would have to say about Larry's intelligence? How does someone with a highly specialized skill—lightning calculation—but with otherwise impaired mental abilities fit into these conceptualizations of intelligence? In some respects Larry has a fast brain, but it's highly doubtful he could read a map very well or solve a complicated analogy problem. We can be sure that Larry will not perform well on a standardized battery of tests, which means that his assigned value of *g* will be far lower than average.

Consider also the gifted athlete, who soars high above the basketball rim but has trouble reading his daughter's nursery rhymes. Or the respected mathematical wizard, full professor at a major university, who has trouble matching her shoes, let alone her socks, in the morning. The point to be made about Larry Steinway, or the athlete or the professor, is that people sometimes show specialized skills or abilities that stand alone and are not representative of a general ability. Spectacular skill can be shown in one area accompanied by profound deficits in another. Perhaps more

think their way out of a paper bag. They lack creativity and seem to have trouble applying what they've learned (Sternberg, 1985).

Practical Intelligence   Finally, people differ in *practical intelligence*, a measure of how well people can take ideas and put them into everyday practice. People with lots of practical intelligence solve the problems that are uniquely posed by their cultural surroundings. They mold themselves well into existing settings, and they can select new environments, if required, that provide a better fit for their talents. In a nutshell, these individuals have "street smarts"—they size up situations well and act accordingly. You probably know someone who seems to lack analytic skills—who fails school or drops out—but still manages to succeed in life.

Sternberg's triarchic theory has helped to broaden the concept of intelligence. Like Howard Gardner's approach, his theory deals with behaviors and skills that aren't normally covered by the standard psychometric approach. Triarchic theory, like Gardner's theory, can also be applied successfully in classroom settings where particular types of intelligence can be nurtured and developed (Sternberg et al., 2006). But breadth is not gained without some cost—concepts such as practical and creative intelligence can be difficult to measure and test. Moreover, even if it is desirable to broaden our conceptualization of intelligence, that doesn't mean that psychometric approaches to intelligence have no value. As you'll see in the next section, psychometric tests are often useful in predicting future performance, even though they may be measuring only narrow dimensions of intelligence.

Test Yourself 10.1

For each of the following statements, pick the term that best describes the approach to conceptualizing intelligence. Choose your answers from the following: psychometric, multiple intelligences, triarchic theory. *(You will find the answers in the Appendix.)*

1. Mitsuko has street smarts—she can mold herself successfully in any situation. _____
2. Jeremy flunks most of his classes, but he's a brilliant pianist, so he considers himself to be highly intelligent. _____
3. Lucy has just finished an exhaustive battery of mental tests; she's waiting to find out if she has a high *g*. _____
4. Natalie wants to understand the concept of intelligence, so she has signed up for a class on factor analysis. _____

5. Verne shows great insight into the feelings of others, which makes him score high on tests of interpersonal intelligence.

6. Shelia scored a perfect 4.0 GPA in high school but has trouble applying what she's learned to new situations. She's beginning to feel that she might not be so intelligent after all. _____

Measuring Individual Differences

LEARNING GOALS
- Understand the components of a good test.
- Understand and evaluate IQ.
- Define mental retardation and giftedness.
- Assess the validity of IQ tests and the effects of labeling.
- Contrast creativity, emotional intelligence, and tacit knowledge.

WE'VE NOW DISCUSSED some of the ways psychologists try to conceptualize intelligence. However, we have yet to discuss how individual differences are actually measured. People differ. Pick just about any attribute—height, weight, friendliness, intelligence—and you're going to find a scattering, or distribution, of individual values. Some people are tall, some are short; some people are friendly, some are not.

As discussed in the previous section, the study of individual differences is important because many psychological concepts, including intelligence and personality, are defined and measured by individual differences.

achievement tests Psychological tests that measure your current level of knowledge or competence in a particular subject.

If we can measure how you compare to others on a psychological dimension, we can then assess your current and future capabilities. For example, **achievement tests** measure your current knowledge or competence in a particular subject (such as math or reading). Researchers or teachers can use the results of an achievement test to gauge the effectiveness of a learning procedure or a curriculum in a school. It's also possible to use individual differences to make predictions about the future, such as how well you can be expected to do in your chosen profession or whether you're likely to succeed in college. **Aptitude tests** measure the ability to learn in a particular area, to acquire the knowledge needed for success in a given domain. Aptitude test results can be used to help choose a career path or even to decide whether to take up something as a hobby, such as car mechanics or the violin.

aptitude tests Psychological tests that measure your ability to learn or acquire knowledge in a particular subject.

The Components of a Good Test

What are the characteristics of a "good" test—that is, a test that can be expected to provide a good measure of individual differences? Given we recognize the need to measure these differences, it's crucial that the measurement device provide information that is scientifically useful. Researchers generally agree on the three characteristics needed for a good test: *reliability*, *validity*, and *standardization*. Please note that these are characteristics of the test, not of the person taking the test.

reliability A measure of the consistency of test results; reliable tests produce similar scores or indices from one administration to the next.

validity An assessment of how well a test measures what it is supposed to measure. *Content validity* assesses the degree to which the test samples broadly across the domain of interest; *predictive validity* assesses how well the test predicts some future criterion; *construct validity* assesses how well the test taps into a particular theoretical construct.

Reliability The first test characteristic, **reliability**, is a measure of the *consistency* of the test results. Reliable tests produce similar scores from one administration to the next. Suppose we want to measure creativity, and we design a test that produces a score from 0 to 100 on a creativity scale. We measure Alan, and he gets a score of 13; we measure Cynthia, and she tops out at 96. Clearly, we conclude, Cynthia is more creative than Alan. But is she really? To be sure about the results, we administer the test again and find that the scores reverse. Sadly, our creativity test lacks reliability—it doesn't produce consistent scores from one administration to the next.

It's important for a test to be reliable so we can draw firm conclusions from the results. Cynthia might be more creative than Alan, but the difference in scores could also be due to an artifact, or failing, of the test. On this particular administration Cynthia scored higher, but that's no guarantee tomorrow's results will produce the same conclusion. One way to measure a test's reliability is to give it to the same group of individuals on two separate occasions. *Test-retest reliability* is then calculated by comparing the scores across the repeated administrations. Often, a correlation coefficient is computed that indicates how well performance on the second test can be predicted from performance on the first. The closer the test-retest correlation comes to a perfect +1.00, the higher the reliability of the test.

Students regularly take standardized tests that measure aptitude or achievement.

Tom McCarthy/PhotoEdit, Inc.

Validity The second test characteristic, **validity**, tells us how well a test measures what it's supposed to measure. A test can yield reliable data—consistent results across repeated administrations—yet not truly measure the psychological characteristic of interest. If a test of creativity actually measures shoe size, then the data are likely to be reliable but not valid. Shoe size isn't going to change much from one measurement to the next, but it has little to do with creativity.

Actually, there are several different forms of validity. *Content validity* measures the degree to which the content of a test samples broadly across the domain of interest. If you're trying to get a general measure of creativity, your test should not be limited to one kind of creativity, such as artistic creativity. For the test to have a high degree of content validity, it should probably measure artistic, verbal, mechanical, mathematical, and other kinds of creativity.

Sometimes psychologists are interested in designing a test that predicts some future outcome, such as job performance or success in school. For a test to have *predictive validity*, it must predict this outcome adequately. The SAT is a well-known case in point. The SAT is designed to predict success in college. So to assess its predictive validity, we need to ask whether the SAT predicts college performance as expressed through a measure such as college grade point average. Various studies have shown that the correlation between SAT scores and the grade point averages of college freshmen is somewhere between +0.40 and +0.50 (Donlon, 1984; Willingham et al., 1990). Statistically, this means that we can predict college performance with the SAT to some degree, but our predictive abilities are not perfect.

Another kind of validity, *construct validity*, measures how well a test applies to a particular theoretical scheme or construct. Suppose we have a theory of creativity that's developed well enough to generate a wide variety of predictions—how creative people act, the kinds of books they read, their susceptibility to mental disorders, and so on. To have high construct validity, our test must predict performance on each of these separate indices of creativity, rather than on just one. If a test has high construct validity, its scores tend to vary in ways that are predicted by the theory. So if the theory predicts that creative people are more likely to suffer from depression, then people who score high on the creativity test should have a greater likelihood of being depressed.

Standardization   The third characteristic of a good test of individual differences is **standardization**. When you take a test such as the SAT, or any national aptitude or achievement test, you quickly learn that the testing procedures are extremely rigid. You can break the test seal only at a certain time, the instructions are spoken in a monotone by a very serious administrator, and your yellow number 2 pencil must be put down at an exact tick of the clock. These tests are *standardized*, which means the testing, scoring, and interpretation procedures remain the same across administrations of the test. Standardization is important because it guarantees that all test takers will be treated the same.

In fact, the proper interpretation of a test score absolutely demands standardization. Remember, we're concerned with individual differences—it doesn't make much sense to compare two or more scores if different instructions or scoring procedures have been used across the test sessions. A person's score on a test of individual differences can be understood only with respect to a reference group, often called a *norm*

CRITICAL THINKING

Pick one of your classes in school. Do you think the tests that you've taken so far have been valid? What specific kind of validity are you using as a basis for your answer?

standardization Keeping the testing, scoring, and interpretation procedures similar across all administrations of a test.

Concept Review | Components of a Good Test

COMPONENT	DESCRIPTION	EXAMPLE
Reliability	Consistency of test results	Taking a test twice should yield similar scores each time.
Validity	Does the test measure what it's supposed to?	
–Content	—The degree to which a test samples broadly across the domain of interest	The items on a test of creativity should cover different types of creativity, such as artistic, mathematical, and verbal.
–Predictive	—The degree to which a test predicts some future outcome	Performance on the American College Test (ACT) should correlate with later performance in college classes.
–Construct	—The degree to which a test taps into a particular theoretical construct	Performance on a creativity test should correlate with other characteristics or indices thought to be associated with creativity.
Standardization	Testing, scoring, and interpretation procedures are the same across all administrations of the test.	Everyone who takes the SAT receives the same instructions, uses a number 2 pencil and standard answer sheet, and has to complete the test within the same specified period of time.

© Bettmann/CORBIS

Alfred Binet was commissioned by the French government to develop a test that would help teachers identify students who might have a difficult time grasping academic concepts.

mental age The chronological age that best fits a child's level of performance on a test of mental ability.

group, and everyone within the group must receive the same test and administration procedures. We'll return to this notion of a norm reference group momentarily when we consider the concept of the IQ.

IQ: The Intelligence Quotient

The most famous index of intelligence is the IQ, or intelligence quotient. The IQ is a single number, derived from performance on a test, and it may well be the most widely applied psychological measure in the world. Yet how can a single number be used to measure intelligence?

This might strike you as odd given our earlier discussion about multiple intelligences and the need to establish a wide variety of criteria for what it means to be intelligent. The key to appreciating the IQ, and to understanding why it is so widely applied, is in the concept of *validity*: What is the IQ designed to measure, and how successfully does it achieve its goal? As you'll see momentarily, it turns out that IQ does a reasonably good job of predicting what it was designed to predict.

The historical roots of the intelligence quotient trace back about a hundred years to the work of the French psychologist Alfred Binet and his associate Théodore Simon. In 1904 Binet and Simon were commissioned by the French government to develop a test that would identify children who were considered "dull"—specifically, children who would have a difficult time grasping concepts in school. It was the French government's intention to help these children, once they were identified, through special schooling. Thus the mission of the test was primarily practical, not theoretical; the charge was to develop a test that would accurately measure individual differences in future academic performance.

Mental Age Not surprisingly, Binet and Simon designed their test to measure the kinds of skills that are needed in school—such as memory, reasoning, and verbal comprehension. The goal was to determine the **mental age**—or what Binet and Simon called the *mental level*—of the child, which was defined as the chronological age that best fit the child's current level of intellectual performance. Mental age is typically calculated by comparing a child's test score with the average scores for different age groups. For example, let's suppose that an average 8-year-old is able to compare two objects from memory, recognize parts of a picture that are missing, count backward from 20 to 0, and give the correct day and time. An average 12-year-old might be able to define abstract words, name 60 words in 3 minutes, and discover the meaning of a scrambled sentence. If Jenny, who is 8, is able to solve the problems of the typical 12-year-old, she would be assigned a mental age of 12.

Notice that mental age and chronological age do not have to be the same, although they will be on average (an average 8-year-old should solve problems at the average 8-year-old level). Because intelligence tests are given to lots of children, it's possible to determine average performance for a given age group and then to determine the appropriate mental age for a particular child. By using mental age, Binet and Simon (1916/1973) were able to identify the slow and quick learners and to recommend appropriate curriculum adjustments.

In the first two decades of the 20th century, Binet and Simon's intelligence test was revised several times and was ultimately translated into English for use in North America. The most popular American version was developed by psychologist Lewis Terman at Stanford University; this test later became known as the *Stanford-Binet* test of intelligence. It was also Terman who popularized the idea of an intelligence quotient (based on an idea originally proposed by German psychologist William Stern), which is defined as follows:

Intelligence quotient (IQ) = Mental age/Chronological age × 100

The IQ is a useful measure because it establishes an easy-to-understand baseline for "average" intelligence—people of average intelligence will have an IQ of 100 because their mental age will always be equal to their chronological age. People with IQs greater than 100 will be above average in intelligence; those below 100 will be below average in intelligence.

Deviation IQ Defining IQ simply in terms of the *ratio* of mental age to chronological age has some problems. For one thing, it's hard to compare the meaning of the ratio across different ages. If a 5-year-old performed like a 7-year-old, she would be given an IQ of 140 (7/5 × 100 = 140). But if a 10-year-old scored at the level of a 12-year-old, his IQ would be only 120 (12/10 × 100 = 120). Both are performing at levels 2 years above their chronological age, but they receive very different IQs. Moreover, how much sense does it make to argue that a 30-year-old who performs comparably to a 60-year-old should be given a vastly higher IQ (60/30 × 100 = 200)?

To overcome this problem, most modern intelligence tests retain the term IQ but define it in terms of a *deviation*, or difference, rather than as a ratio. A **deviation IQ** still uses 100 as a baseline average, but a 100 IQ is redefined as the average score in the distribution of scores for people of a certain age. A particular person's IQ is then calculated by determining where his or her test score "sits," relative to the average score, in the overall distribution of scores. (Note that *age* is the "norm group" used for defining the concept of intelligence.) ❚ Figure 10.3 shows a frequency distribution of scores that might result from administering a test such as the Stanford-Binet to large groups of people. The average of the distribution is 100, and approximately half of the test takers will produce scores above 100 and the other half below 100.

One of the characteristics of modern intelligence tests is their tendency to produce very regular and smooth distributions of scores. With most intelligence tests, for example, not only will the most common score be 100 (by definition), but roughly 68% of the people who take the test will receive an IQ score between 85 and 115. With a distribution like the one shown in Figure 10.3, we can easily calculate the percentage of the population likely to receive a particular IQ score. You will find, for example, that approximately 98% of the people who take the test will receive a score at or below 130. Notice once again that IQ in this case is defined in terms of how a score compares to the scores of other people in the same age group.

intelligence quotient (IQ) Mental age divided by chronological age and then multiplied by 100.

deviation IQ An intelligence score that is derived from determining where your performance sits in an age-based distribution of test scores.

CRITICAL THINKING

Do you see any similarities between the way deviation IQ is interpreted and the way you normally interpret your test scores in a class?

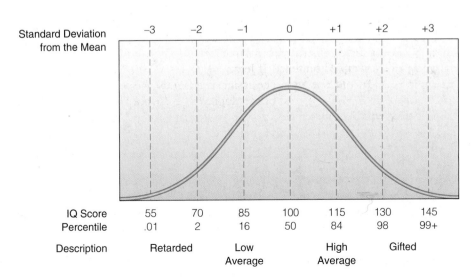

Standard Deviation from the Mean	−3	−2	−1	0	+1	+2	+3
IQ Score	55	70	85	100	115	130	145
Percentile	.01	2	16	50	84	98	99+
Description		Retarded	Low Average		High Average	Gifted	

❚ **FIGURE 10.3** The Distribution of IQ Scores

IQ scores for a given age group are typically distributed in a bell-shaped, or normal, curve. The average and most frequently occurring IQ score is defined as 100. Roughly 68% of the test takers in this age group receive IQ scores between 115 and 85, one *standard deviation* above and below the mean. People labeled "gifted," with an IQ of 130 and above, or "retarded," with an IQ of 70 or below, occur infrequently in the overall population.

Extremes of Intelligence

Tests such as the Stanford-Binet or the related Wechsler Adult Intelligence Scale have been given to thousands and thousands of people. Consequently, we know a great deal about how IQ scores are distributed in the population. Most people fall within a normal or average range, which covers scores from about 70 to about 130. Individuals who fall above or below this range represent *extremes* in intelligence.

Mental Retardation   A score of 70 or below on a standard IQ test often leads to a diagnosis of **mental retardation**, although other factors (such as daily living skills) contribute to the diagnosis (Schalock et al., 2007). The disability must also be diagnosed prior to age 18, which means that limitations in intellectual functioning arising during adulthood—for example, from brain damage—don't lead to the diagnosis (American Association on Intellectual and Developmental Disabilities, 2002). A four-level classification scheme has been developed for mental retardation, which is shown in ▌Table 10.1. This table indicates how each category level for retardation is defined—in terms of IQ—and lists some of the skills that can be expected for individuals who meet the diagnostic criteria.

What causes mental retardation? There are many possible causes, some genetic and some environmental. Down syndrome, for example, is typically associated with low IQ scores and is caused by a genetic abnormality—usually an extra chromosome. Another genetic condition is phenylketonuria (PKU), a metabolic disorder associated with a defective enzyme that can lead to retardation if not corrected early in development. Environmental factors during development, such as inadequate nutrition or illness, can also contribute to mental retardation. In Chapter 4 we talked about the potentially damaging effects of teratogens, such as excessive use of alcohol or other drugs, on the intellectual capacity of the developing fetus. There are probably hundreds of potential causes for extremely low IQ scores and, once again, a low IQ score does not guarantee a diagnosis of mental retardation.

Although mental retardation is assumed to affect somewhere between 1% and 3% of the population, the vast majority of these people (perhaps 85%) are only mildly affected. With the proper support, most are able to lead independent lives and may not even be recognized by the community as having any serious mental deficiencies. By no means does retardation imply an inability to learn or prosper. Even the roughly 15% of cases who are diagnosed as moderate to profoundly retarded can lead satisfying and fulfilling lives. Moreover, numerous agencies such as the American Association on Intellectual and Developmental Disabilities provide useful information and help to support ongoing research (check out their website here: www.aaidd.org).

mental retardation A label generally assigned to someone who scores below 70 on a standard IQ test, although other factors, such as one's ability to adapt to the environment, are also important.

TABLE 10.1	Types of Mental Retardation	
Type	**Approximate IQ Range**	**Adaptation Potential**
Mild	50–70	May develop academic skills comparable to a sixth-grade educational level; with assistance, may develop significant social and vocational skills and be self-supporting.
Moderate	35–50	Unlikely to achieve academic skills over the second-grade level; may become semi-independent.
Severe	20–35	Speech skills will be limited, but communication is possible; may learn to perform simple tasks in highly structured environments.
Profound	Below 20	Little or no speech is possible; requires constant care and supervision.

Giftedness   At the other end of the IQ scale are those considered **gifted**, with IQs at or above approximately 130. Many studies have tracked the intellectual and social accomplishments of gifted children, partly as a means of checking on the validity of the IQ measure. One of the most famous of these studies was begun in the 1920s by Lewis Terman (1925; Terman & Ogden, 1947). Terman was interested in whether children identified early in life as gifted would be likely to achieve success throughout their lives. The answer, on average, was "Yes"—Terman's gifted subjects earned more college degrees than average, made more money, wrote more books, generated more successful patents, and so on. Similar results have been found in other studies, most recently for adolescents with exceptional mathematical or verbal reasoning ability (Lubinski et al., 2001).

gifted A label generally assigned to someone who scores above 130 on a standard IQ test.

Interestingly, the kids studied by Terman (often known collectively as the "Termites") turned out to be emotionally stable and socially skilled as well, which is surprising given the bookworm stereotype that people have of highly intelligent people. Many had successful marriages, and their divorce rate was lower than the general population (Terman, 1954). A more recent study examining gifted children who skipped high school and moved directly to college also found evidence for excellent social adjustment (Nobel, Robinson, & Gunderson, 1993). On the other hand, Ellen Winner (1997) found that profoundly gifted children, those with IQ scores above 180, were more likely to suffer emotional problems, to become socially isolated, and they often ended up as "ordinary" adults (Winner, 2000). In each of these cases, however, the connection between IQ and success is correlational, so it's best to exercise caution in drawing conclusions. In such studies there are apt to be many potentially confounding factors. To list just one example, high-IQ children tend to come from economically privileged households, which might help account for later success and emotional stability (Tomlinson-Keasey & Little, 1990).

Finally, there are *savants*, who may show limited intellectual or social functioning overall but exhibit tremendous "gifts" in a particular domain. Calendrical savants, for example, have the amazing ability to name the weekday corresponding to a particular date, often in a matter of seconds (Cowan, O'Conner, & Samella, 2003). Psychologists have studied savants, and tracked their abilities over time, but remain uncertain about the origins of their remarkable abilities. There's some evidence that the ability is innate, produced by some kind of atypical brain organization or genetic information (Nurmi et al., 2003), but no firm cause has yet been established. Savants are more likely to be male, and savant skills are often associated with disorders such as childhood autism (Heaton & Wallace, 2004). Experience probably plays a role in the development of the special skills, although many appear not to have been explicitly taught (Cowan et al., 2004). Whether most savants truly possess some kind of exceptional cognitive skill, or simply engage in extensive practice of a skill that is rewarded by their peers, remains an open question (Cowan & Carney, 2006).

The Validity of Intelligence Testing

How valid is IQ as a measure of intellectual ability? Does it truly tap some hidden but powerful feature of the mind that accounts for individual differences? Does it adequately measure the ability to adapt and solve the problems of survival? Remember, here we use "validity" in the technical sense: How well does the test measure the thing that it's supposed to measure? To assess the validity of the IQ, then, we must ask: How well do the tests that produce IQ scores predict their criterion of interest?

The most widely applied intelligence tests today are the Stanford-Binet, the Wechsler Adult Intelligence Scale (WAIS), and the Wechsler Intelligence Scale for Children (WISC). These are not the only tests, of course; in fact, if we combine intelligence tests with measures of scholastic aptitude, more than a hundred different tests are currently in use. Often these tests are given for the same reason that originally motivated Binet and Simon—to predict some kind of academic performance, usually grades in high school or college. From this perspective, IQ passes the validity test with flying colors: IQ, as measured by Stanford-Binet or the Wechsler tests, typically correlates about +0.50 or higher with school grades (Ceci, 1991; Murray & Wren, 2003). Notice that the correlation isn't perfect, but it's reasonably high when you consider all of the uncontrolled factors that can affect grades in school (motivation, home environment, participation in extracurricular activities, and so on).

Critics of IQ often point out that it fails to provide a broad index of intelligence. As we discussed earlier, it's proper to define intelligence broadly—there are many ways that people can fit successfully into their environments—and it's certain that not all forms of multiple intelligence are measured by traditional paper-and-pencil IQ tests. This criticism has been recognized for years by the community of intelligence test researchers, and efforts have been made to develop tests that measure a variety of abilities. The influential tests of David Wechsler, for example, were developed in part to measure nonverbal aspects of intellectual ability. The Wechsler tests include not only verbal-mathematical questions of the type traditionally found on the Stanford-Binet test but also nonverbal questions requiring things such as the completion or re-arrangement of pictures (see ▌Figure 10.4). Performance is then broken down into a verbal IQ, a nonverbal (or "performance") IQ, and an overall IQ based on combining the verbal and nonverbal measures.

Again, most intelligence tests are designed to accomplish some specific end, such as predicting future academic performance, not to provide an all-encompassing index of true intellectual ability. So if you develop a test to predict college performance, it probably isn't reasonable to expect it to predict creativity, originality, or the ability for deep thought. As we'll discuss later, this also means that intelligence tests can suffer from cultural limitations—a test designed to measure the abilities of high school students in suburbia may not be valid for students in the barrio or from a different

Wechsler Adult Intelligence Scale (WAIS)		
Test	**Description**	**Example**
Verbal scale		
Information	Taps general range of information.	On what continent is France?
Comprehension	Tests understanding of social conventions and ability to evaluate past experience.	Why are children required to go to school?
Arithmetic	Tests arithmetic reasoning through verbal problems.	How many hours will it take to drive 150 miles at 50 miles per hour?
Performance scale		
Block design	Tests ability to perceive and analyze patterns by presenting designs that must be copied with blocks.	Assemble blocks to match this design:
Picture arrangement	Tests understanding of social situations through a series of pictures that must be arranged in the right sequence to tell a story.	Put the pictures in the right order:
Object assembly	Tests ability to deal with part-to-whole relationships by presenting puzzle pieces that must be assembled to form a complete object.	Assemble the pieces into a complete object:

▌**FIGURE 10.4** Examples from the WAIS
The Wechsler Adult Intelligence Scale measures both verbal and nonverbal aspects of intellectual ability. Included here are samples of the various question types. (From Weiten, 1995)

region of the world. This doesn't mean that intelligence tests aren't useful—you just need to be aware of what the tests were designed to measure.

Labeling Effects   Another potentially serious criticism of IQ concerns the effects of labeling. You take a test as a child, your IQ is calculated by comparing your performance with that of other kids your age, and the score becomes part of your continuing academic record. Once the IQ label is applied—you're smart, you're below average, and so on—expectations are generated in those who have access to your score. A number of studies have shown that intelligence labels influence how teachers interact with their students in the classroom. There is a kind of "rich get richer" and "poor get poorer" effect—the kids with the "smart" label are exposed to more educational opportunities and are treated with more respect. Things are held back from the "slow" kids, so they're less likely to be exposed to factors that might nurture academic growth (Oakes, 1985; Rosenthal & Jacobson, 1968).

Labeling effects were particularly serious in the early decades of the 20th century when intelligence tests were in their formative stages of development. Tests were widely administered—for example, to newly arriving immigrants and to all Army recruits—before the impact of cultural and educational factors on test performance were well understood. As we'll discuss later, people can perform poorly on an intelligence test because the test has certain built-in biases with respect to language and cultural lifestyle. Imagine, for example, that as part of an intelligence test I ask you to identify the vegetable broccoli. Easy, but not if you were raised in a culture that did not include broccoli as part of its diet. In such a case you would probably get the question wrong, but it wouldn't say anything about your intellectual or academic potential.

Researchers were not very sensitive to these concerns when the early intelligence tests were developed. The result was that certain population groups, such as immigrants from Southern and Eastern Europe, generally performed poorly on these tests. Some psychologists even went so far as to label these immigrant groups "feeble-minded" or "defective" based on their test performance. Immigration laws enacted in the 1920s discriminated against poorly performing groups by reducing immigration quotas. In modern times psychologists are more aware of test bias and have worked very hard to reduce its influence on test performance.

Individual Differences Related to Intelligence

To end our discussion of the measurement of individual differences, we'll briefly consider three psychological characteristics that are often aligned with the topic of intelligence: creativity, emotional intelligence, and tacit knowledge. None is necessarily related to *g* (general intelligence), but each is an adaptive characteristic that can potentially increase our ability to succeed or even survive.

Creativity   The term **creativity** refers to the ability to generate ideas that are original and novel. Creative thinkers think in unusual ways, which means they can look at the usual and express it in an unusual way. Creative thinkers tend to see the "big picture" and are able to find connections among things that others might not see. Importantly, however, it's not just the generation of new and different ideas that makes one creative; those ideas must also be useful and relevant—they must potentially have adaptive value.

How is creativity measured? Psychologists have devised a number of ways to measure individual differences in creative ability (Cooper, 1991; Cropley, 1996). One

CRITICAL THINKING

Do you think it makes sense for elementary schools to use "tracking" systems—that is, to divide children early on into different classes based on performance on standardized tests?

© Bettmann/Corbis

Within 24 hours of arriving at Ellis Island, immigrants were subjected to a variety of mental and physical examinations. Unfortunately, these exams were sometimes used to discriminate unfairly among population groups; at the time, administrators were simply not sensitive to the influence of cultural factors on test performance.

creativity The ability to generate ideas that are original, novel, and useful.

popular technique is to supply a group of unrelated words, or unrelated objects in a picture, and ask a person to generate as many connections among the items as possible (Mednick, 1962; Torrance, 1981). Try it yourself: Take these words—*food, catcher, hot*—and try to think of a fourth word (or words) that relates to all three. It turns out that measures such as these reveal individual differences among people—some find this task to be quite easy, others find it extremely hard. Moreover, performance on these creativity tests can then be correlated with other abilities, such as IQ or job success, to see if there is a connection.

What's the relation between creativity and intelligence? When intelligence is conceptualized in a broad way, creativity fits in nicely as a part of general intellectual ability. (You'll remember, for instance, that Sternberg's triarchic theory includes the concept of creative intelligence.) However, there isn't a straightforward relationship between creativity and IQ. Correlations between them are usually low (Horn, 1976; Kee, 2005), although positive correlations have been found between creativity and some measures of verbal intelligence (Harris, 2004). Traditional IQ tests don't really measure creative thinking, so perhaps it's not surprising that the correlations are often low.

Emotional Intelligence   The second psychological characteristic, emotional intelligence, has recently gained some popularity among psychologists and is worthy of brief note. **Emotional intelligence** is essentially the ability to perceive, understand, and express emotion (Mayer & Salovey, 1997; Salovey & Mayer, 1990). The concept applies to perceiving and understanding the emotions of others as well as to understanding and controlling one's own emotions. Emotions, as you'll see in Chapter 11, play a large role in behavior, so it's clearly adaptive to manage and express them appropriately.

People who score high on emotional intelligence can read others' emotions well and tend to be empathetic as a result. They're good at managing conflict, both their own and the conflicts of others. Not surprisingly, emotional intelligence is believed to be an excellent predictor of success in career and social settings; in fact, some have argued that emotional intelligence may be a more important predictor of success in life than more traditional conceptions of intelligence (Goleman, 1995; but see Barchard, 2003). There's clearly overlap between emotional intelligence and the broad conceptions of intelligence proposed by others (e.g., Gardner and Sternberg), but the similarities and differences have yet to be worked out in a systematic way (Matthews, Zedner, & Roberts, 2005). Research on emotional intelligence is in its infancy, but the concept is proving useful to psychologists and is widely applied in the workplace (see Cherniss et al., 2006).

Tacit Knowledge   Finally, most intelligence tests contain questions that are specific and well defined. You must have certain knowledge to perform well; there are right and wrong answers for each question. There's also usually only one method for solving the problem. But to succeed in many areas, such as on a job, you often need knowledge and abilities that are not so cut and dried—unspoken rules and strategies that are rarely, if ever, taught formally. This kind of unspoken practical know-how is called **tacit knowledge**, and some psychologists believe it will turn out to be an even better predictor of job performance than g (Wagner & Sternberg, 1985).

Tacit knowledge is rarely assessed on standardized tests of intelligence. It's a kind of knowledge that isn't written in books, and it's not usually taught. Instead, it comes primarily from experience—from watching and analyzing the behavior of others. Moreover, people clearly differ in their grasp of job-relevant tacit knowledge. Some managers understand the rules for maximizing the performance of their subordinates better than others do. When tacit knowledge is actually measured, by asking people on the job to make ratings about imaginary job scenarios, it seems to do a reasonably good job of predicting job performance. Sternberg and Wagner (1993) found that tacit knowledge correlates significantly with salary, performance ratings, and

emotional intelligence The ability to perceive, understand, and express emotion in ways that are useful and adaptive.

tacit knowledge Unspoken practical knowledge about how to perform well on the job.

Can Mozart's Music Make You Smarter?

People are always looking for ways to boost intelligence, especially new parents, who want to do everything possible to improve their newborn's cognitive functioning. Recently, you may have seen media reports claiming that the music of Mozart can make you smarter, or at least improve your functioning on cognitive tasks. Some years ago, the governor of Georgia actually budgeted money for cassettes of classical music, which could be given to the parents of each new infant born in the state. Other states have considered mandating that classical music be played in all elementary schools. Most agree that Mozart was a genius, but can his music really make you smarter?

The answer is "Yes, and no." In initial work on this topic, undergraduates showed a significant increase in their average spatial-reasoning scores after listening to 10 minutes of Mozart's *Sonata for Two Pianos in D Major*. Control undergraduates, who spent the same amount of time in silence or listening to relaxation tapes, failed to show similar improvements (Rauscher, Shaw, & Ky, 1993, 1995). Some researchers have had trouble repeating this so-called "Mozart Effect" (Steele, Bass, & Cook, 1999), but a number of laboratories have now confirmed the basic finding (see Chabris, 1999, for a review). If you spend time listening to some elegant classical music, rather than sitting in silence, you're likely to perform slightly better on some measures of cognitive ability.

What causes the improvement? One possibility is that Mozart's music, because of its creative and innovative structure, activates the same portions of the brain that handle spatial-reasoning tasks (Rauscher et al., 1995). On the other hand, maybe people simply enjoy listening to music and

Mozart was a musical genius, but can his music really make you smarter?

are therefore in a better mood, or more alert, when they're asked to perform the reasoning tasks. To conclude that Mozart is responsible for the improvement would require experiments to rule out alternative interpretations. In fact, it turns out that listening to a Stephen King short story can also produce a Mozart-like effect, as long as it's enjoyable to the listeners (Nantais & Schellenberg, 1999). Moreover, slow and sad selections of classical music fail to produce improvements in spatial reasoning,

suggesting that it's indeed an enhancement in mood or arousal that is responsible for the effect (Thompson, Schellenberg, & Husain, 2001).

The Mozart Effect is a classic example of how psychological findings can be overblown, or misused, by the popular press (Waterhouse, 2006). Although the original findings probably have some scientific validity, the improvements were always relatively small and lasted only for brief periods. Moreover, the improvements were only shown on particular kinds of spatial-reasoning tasks and not on others. There's certainly no evidence to suggest that listening to 10 minutes of Mozart, or Stephen King, produces lasting improvements in general intelligence. Listening to something you enjoy simply makes you feel better, and you're likely to perform better on certain tasks, but it doesn't really make you smarter in any lasting or significant way.

At the same time, evidence is accumulating that music *lessons* might, in fact, help. In a recent study, children were randomly assigned to groups receiving either music lessons (keyboard or voice), drama lessons, or no lessons for a period of one year. At the end of the year, IQ was measured, and the kids who received the music lessons showed more of an increase than those in the drama or no lesson control groups (Schellenberg, 2004). The IQ boost wasn't large, but it was consistent. Again, it's tough to know what to conclude from this study because researchers have yet to isolate the components of the experience that really matter. Even so, it's intriguing—maybe those hated piano lessons you took as a child really did matter (see also Rauscher & Hinton, 2006).

the prestige of the business or institution where the person is employed. Moreover, tacit knowledge improves with work experience, which is what you would expect. However, tacit knowledge seems to bear little relation to general ability, as measured by *g*. There's almost never a significant correlation with IQ. In fact, in some cultures negative correlations have been reported—the higher the index of tacit knowledge, the lower the measure of *g*—suggesting that practical knowledge is sometimes emphasized at the expense of academic skills (Cianciolo et al., 2006; Sternberg & Hedlund, 2002).

The idea that it's useful to develop and use multiple strategies to perform successfully is almost certain to be true. The adaptive mind soaks up knowledge where it can; and, as we've seen in earlier chapters, modeling others is an important vehicle for guiding behavior. As it stands now, however, the concept of tacit knowledge, while intuitively plausible, remains somewhat slippery scientifically. Critics have questioned whether tacit knowledge is really anything different from job knowledge (Schmidt & Hunter, 1993). It may not tap some human ability, like *g*, that can be scaled by an appropriate test; instead, measurements of tacit knowledge may simply be indices of what's been learned on the job.

Test Yourself 10.2

Check what you know about the measurement of individual differences by answering the following questions. (You will find the answers in the Appendix.)

1. For each of the following statements, pick the test characteristic that is most appropriate. Choose from the following: *reliability, standardization, validity.*
   a. Donna performs poorly on the SAT, so she takes it again and finds herself performing poorly again: _____
   b. Larry has devised a new test of intelligence, but he finds that it predicts nothing about school performance or success on the job: _____
   c. Chei-Wui wants to see how consistent scores are on his new intelligence test, so he correlates answers across repeated administrations of the test: _____
   d. Robert's new job is to administer the Graduate Record Exam. He is very careful to keep the testing and scoring procedures the same for everybody who takes the test: _____

2. Decide whether each of the following statements is *True or False.*
   a. Lucinda has a mental age of 8 and an IQ of 160—this means that she must be 5 years old chronologically. *True or False?*
   b. Average IQ, based on the deviation IQ method, varies with chronological age. *True or False?*
   c. Lewis has just scored below 70 on his IQ test, which means that he will soon be labeled as mentally retarded. *True or False?*
   d. Creativity increases with intellectual ability, as measured by IQ. *True or False?*

Discovering the Sources of Intelligence

LEARNING GOALS

- Understand how IQ changes with age.
- Explain how twin studies are used to evaluate genetic contributions to intelligence.
- Understand environmental influences on intelligence and how they interact with genetic influences.

WE'VE SEEN THAT PEOPLE DIFFER, and we've considered some of the ways to measure those differences. We've also discussed methods for conceptualizing the differences theoretically—there may be differences in *g*; or, perhaps, people may lack one or more of the special "talents" needed for intelligent performance. But what accounts for these differences in the first place? Why is one person's *g* higher or lower than another person's *g*? Can anything be done about these differences, or are they fixed in stone?

There are essentially two ways to explain how differences in intelligence might arise. First, you can appeal to biological processes, particularly the internal *genetic code*—those strands of DNA that determine eye color, thickness of hair, and possibly *g*. According to this view, intellectual potential is established at conception through some particularly fortunate (or unfortunate) combination of genes. Alternatively, you can appeal to an external cause, specifically the *environment*. Variations in *g* might be attributable to one's past history—perhaps Jefferson Tarpy scores high on IQ tests because he was reinforced for intellectual pursuits or went to excellent schools; perhaps Larry Steinway performs poorly because as a child he was exposed to toxins (such as lead paint). In this section, we'll frame this classic nature–nurture debate and consider the evidence relevant to each position. But first we have a practical issue to consider—how stable is the IQ measure itself?

The Stability of IQ

One way to answer questions about the origins of intelligence is to ask whether IQ changes significantly over a lifetime. If intelligence is caused primarily by genetic and/or biological factors we might expect intellectual ability to change very little over time or at least remain stable throughout normal adulthood. On the other hand, if intelligence is determined mainly by the environment, we would probably expect to find changes over time: IQ might rise and fall depending on experience or environmental setting. Neither of these arguments is airtight—for instance, your environment might remain constant over time, or the genetic code might express itself throughout your lifetime; it might also be the case that IQ is determined by early experience and remains fixed after a certain point in development. Even so, examining the stability of IQ seems like a reasonable place to start the search.

When intelligence is measured in the standard way, through performance on a battery of tests, its stability depends on when the measuring process begins. Before the age of about 3 or 4, it's difficult to get an accurate assessment of intellectual ability. Infants can't talk or show lasting attention, so conventional testing procedures can't be used. Investigators resort to indirect measures, such as recording whether babies choose to look at old or new pictures presented on a screen. There's some evidence that babies who quickly habituate, or lose interest, in response to repeated presentations of the same picture, and who prefer to look at novel pictures when they're shown, score higher on intelligence tests later in childhood (Bornstein, 1989; Kavsek, 2004). But in general it's widely believed that you can't get reliable assessments of IQ until somewhere between ages 4 and 7; from that point onward, IQ scores tend to predict performance on later IQ tests reasonably well (Honzik et al., 1948; Sameroff et al., 1993).

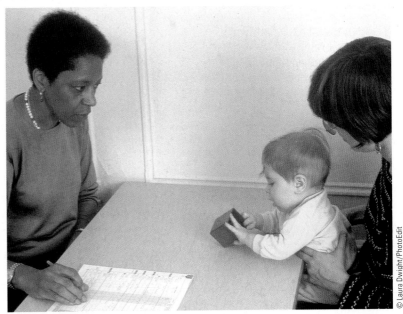

Although tests are available for measuring intelligence in small children, it's difficult to obtain reliable results before age 4.

Longitudinal Studies One of the best ways to measure the stability of IQ is through a longitudinal study, which involves testing the same people repeatedly as they age. The most widely known investigation of the stability of adult intelligence is the Seattle Longitudinal Study, which has examined mental test performance for approximately 5,000 adults ranging in age from 25 through 88 (Schaie, 1983, 1989, 1993, 2005). The participants have been tested in 7-year cycles, dating back to 1956, using a battery of tests to assess such things as verbal fluency, inductive reasoning, and spatial ability. Schaie and his colleagues have found great stability in intellectual ability throughout adulthood. From age 25 to about age 60, there appears to be no uniform decline in general intellectual ability, as measured through the test battery (see ▌Figure 10.5 on page 332). After age 60, abilities begin to decline, although the losses are not great. There are also large individual differences—some people show excellent test performance in their 80s, whereas others do not (Schaie, 1998).

It's difficult to interpret changes in IQ with age because many factors change along with age. Elderly people are more likely to have physical problems, for example, that can affect performance. Declines in intelligence with age also depend on the type of intellectual ability measured. Earlier we discussed the distinction between fluid intelligence, which reflects basic reasoning and processing skills, and crystallized intelligence, which reflects acquired knowledge. The current thinking is that fluid intelligence may decline with age—perhaps because the biology of the brain changes—whereas crystallized intelligence remains constant, or perhaps even increases, until late in adulthood (Beier & Ackerman, 2005; Kaufman & Horn, 1996).

CRITICAL THINKING

Elderly people are often said to possess wisdom. In what ways do you think the label "wise" differs from the label "intelligent"?

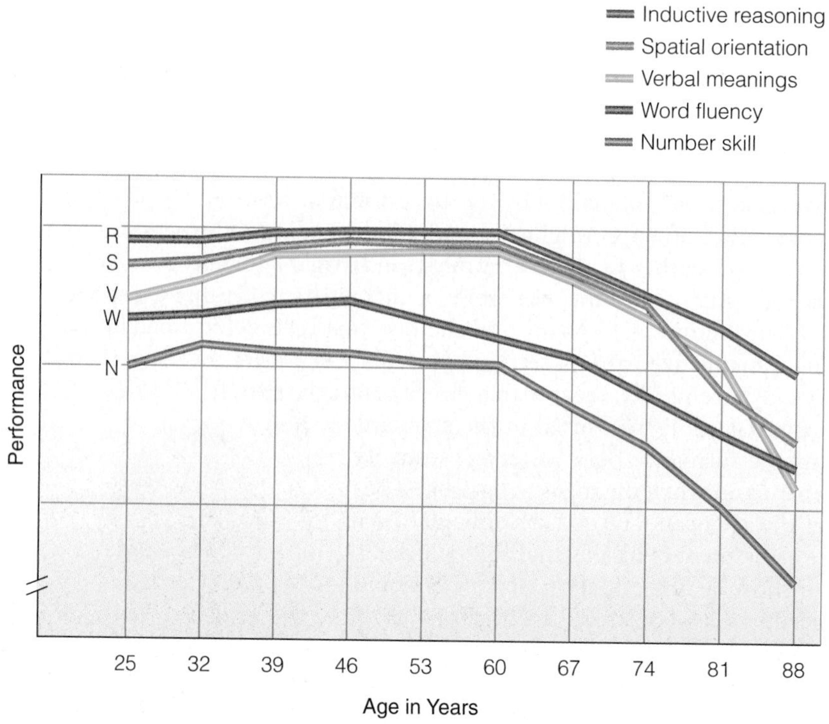

FIGURE 10.5 The Stability of Intellectual Ability
Data from the Seattle Longitudinal Study show how performance changes on a variety of mental tasks between the ages of 25 and 88. Notice that average performance is remarkably stable up to about age 60, when some declines are seen. (Data from Schaie, 1983)

The brain may become a bit slower with age, but people continue to add knowledge and experiences that are invaluable in their efforts to solve the problems of everyday life.

The Flynn Effect Another curious fact about the stability of IQ, although it applies more to populations than to individuals, is that performance on IQ tests seems to be rising steadily and consistently over time. On average, people who take standardized intelligence tests today perform slightly better than people who took similar tests a decade ago, and the same general decade-by-decade increases have been seen since the 1930s (Flynn, 1987, 1999). This trend, known as the *Flynn effect*, has been documented worldwide, but it remains largely unexplained. Most psychologists believe the environment must be responsible because the world's gene pool is unlikely to have changed much in the past 70 years (although see Mingroni, 2007).

Most explanations of the Flynn effect appeal to factors such as increased nutrition or better schooling (Neisser, 1998; Williams, 1998). Better nutrition and health care can certainly lead to better brain functioning, although increases in brain functioning probably can't account for the trend (Nettelbeck & Wilson, 2004). We're also exposed to new technologies, which, in turn, could help develop abstract thinking. (Think about how sophisticated we are about using cell phones and the Internet.) In addition, more and more children are placed in day care or preschool, and these experiences might contribute to better performance on standardized tests as well.

Because of the Flynn effect, IQ tests are periodically "renormed" to adjust for the fact that scores are rising. The average score is reset to 100 (remember our earlier discussion of deviation IQ), which means you now need to do "better" on the test, relative to how the test was scored in the past, to receive a given IQ. Some psychologists believe this rescoring process is having unintended effects. For example, suppose scores are rising less rapidly for people with borderline intellectual functioning (those with IQ scores around 70). Under the new scoring guidelines, significantly more individuals are apt to be diagnosed with mental retardation than in the past. Many other classification decisions are based, in part, on IQ—everything from eligibility for military service to application of the death penalty—so understanding the Flynn effect is likely to remain a priority for psychologists in the future (Kanaya, Scullin, & Ceci, 2003).

Nature: The Genetic Argument

A number of early pioneers in intelligence testing, including Galton, believed strongly that individual differences in mental ability are inherited. After all, Galton argued, it's easy to demonstrate that intellectual skill runs through family lines (remember, his cousin was Charles Darwin, and his grandfather was another famous evolutionist, Erasmus Darwin). But family-tree arguments, used in isolation, aren't very convincing. Environmental factors, such as social and educational opportunities, can explain why members of the same family might show similar skills. Growing up in a family that places value on intellectual pursuits determines to some extent what sort of behaviors will be rewarded in a child, or the particular type of role models that will be available. In fairness to Galton, he realized that both inherited and environmental factors are needed to explain mental ability fully—in fact, it was Galton (1869, 1883) who coined the phrase "nature versus nurture."

To establish a genetic basis for a psychological or physical characteristic, it's necessary to control for the effects of the environment. In principle, if two people are raised in exactly the same environment and have exactly the same experiences, we can attribute any differences in IQ to inherited factors (nature). In this case, you've held any nurturing effects of the environment constant, so any differences must be due to genetics. Alternatively, if two people are born with exactly the same genes but end up with quite different intelligence scores, it must be the environment, not genes, that is responsible (nurture). We can't perform these kinds of experimental manipulations in the laboratory, for obvious reasons, but we can look for relevant natural comparisons.

Some kinds of abilities tend to run in families, such as artistic ability in the Judd family. It's difficult, though, to separate the influences of nature and nurture.

Twin Studies   As discussed in Chapter 3, psychologists often study identical twins, who share nearly complete genetic overlap, to tease apart the nature and nurture components of mind and behavior. In twin studies, researchers search for identical twins who have been raised together in the same household or who have been separated at birth through adoption (Bouchard & McGue, 1981; T. J. Bouchard et al., 1990). The effects of the environment are assumed to be similar for the twins raised together but quite different, at least on average, for twins raised apart. If intelligence comes primarily from genetic factors, we would expect identical twins to have very similar intelligence scores, regardless of the environments in which they've been raised. One way to measure similarity is by correlation. More specifically, you can attempt to predict the IQ of one twin given the IQ of the other.

If genes are largely responsible for intelligence, we would expect to get a strong positive correlation between IQ scores for identical twins. We wouldn't necessarily expect it to be exactly +1.00 because of measurement error or other uncontrolled factors. In reviewing the research literature on this issue, Bouchard and McGue (1981) found strong evidence for the genetic position: The IQ scores of identical twins are indeed quite similar, irrespective of the environment in which the twins have been reared. As shown in ▌Figure 10.6 on page 334, the IQ scores for twins reared together showed an average correlation of .86; when reared apart, the average correlation remained strongly positive at .72 (Bouchard & McGue, 1981).

Researchers who conduct twin studies are actually interested in many different comparisons. For instance, it's useful to compare intelligence scores for fraternal twins (who are genetically no more similar than normal siblings) and among unrelated people who have been reared together or apart. In general, the impressive finding is that the closer the overlap in genes, the more similar the resulting IQs. Notice, for example, that the average correlation for adopted siblings who have been reared together (.30) is much lower than the average correlation for identical twins reared apart (.72). Similarity in environmental history is not as strong a predictor of

CRITICAL THINKING

Do you think it's possible to tease apart the relative contributions of nature and nurture to intelligence by studying animals in the laboratory?

© Russell Einhorn/Getty Images

Type of Relationship

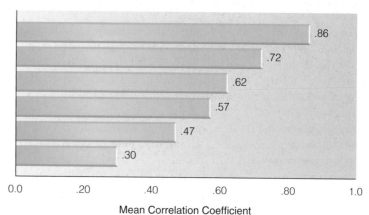

*One or both of the sibling pairs were adopted.

| FIGURE 10.6 Nature Versus Nurture
The horizontal bars show the mean correlation coefficients for pairs of people with differing amounts of genetic overlap who have been reared in similar or different environments. For example, the top bar shows the average correlation for identical twins who have been reared together in the same environment, and the bottom bar shows the correlation coefficient for adopted siblings reared together. Higher correlations mean that the measured IQ scores are more similar. (Data from Bouchard & McGue, 1981)

intelligence as similarity in genetic background. Data such as these suggest that genetic history plays an important role in intelligence, at least when intelligence is measured through conventional IQ testing (see also Plomin et al., 1997).

Heritability Intelligence researchers often use the concept of heritability to describe the influence of genetic factors on intelligence. **Heritability** is a mathematical index that represents the extent to which IQ differences within a population can be accounted for by genetic factors. For any group of people, you will find individual differences in IQ scores; heritability measures the role genetic factors play in producing these differences. It's expressed as a percentage, so if the heritability of intelligence were 100%, all differences in measured IQ could be explained genetically. Most estimates of the heritability of intelligence, derived from twin studies, hover at around 50%, which means that approximately half of the differences in IQ have a genetic basis (Sternberg & Kaufman, 1998). Other researchers propose values that are higher, perhaps closer to 70% (T. J. Bouchard et al., 1990).

It's important to understand that estimates of heritability apply only to groups, not to individuals. A heritability estimate of 70% does not mean that 70% of someone's intelligence is due to his or her genes. To see why, imagine two groups of people with the same genetic histories. Group A is placed in a rigidly controlled environment where everyone is treated exactly the same. For group B, the environment is allowed to vary. If IQ scores are influenced by the environment in any way, we would expect the heritability values to be quite different for these two groups, even though the groups' genetic backgrounds are identical. Because the environment is held constant in group A, all of the differences in measured IQ will be due to genes. In group B, the heritability index will be lower because some of the differences in IQ will be due to environmental effects. Heritability tells us only that for a given group a certain percentage of the differences in intelligence can be explained by genetic factors.

Nurture: The Environmental Argument

Most psychologists agree that intelligence is influenced by genetic factors. But did you notice in Figure 10.6 that identical twins reared together have IQs that are more similar than do twins reared apart? This means that individual differences in intelligence

heritability A mathematical index that represents the extent to which IQ differences in a particular population can be accounted for by genetic factors.

can't be explained completely through genetic background; it's not even close—the environment clearly plays an important role.

In this section, we'll consider some environmental influences on IQ by addressing a controversial topic in the study of intelligence: group differences in IQ. The majority of intelligence researchers agree that there are stable differences in IQ across racial, ethnic, and socioeconomic groups. For example, Asian Americans tend to score 4 or 5 IQ points higher on standardized intelligence tests, on average, than White European Americans. White Americans, on average, score 10 to 15 points higher than African Americans and Hispanic Americans (Brody, 1992; Lynn, 1994).

It's important to understand that group differences in IQ, although stable, reflect average *group* differences. Not every Asian American scores high on an intelligence test, nor does every African American score low. In fact, the differences among IQ scores within a population (African Americans, Asian Americans, and so on) are much larger than the average differences between groups. This means that a large number of African Americans will score higher than the average White score, just as many Asian Americans will have scores below the average for Whites. The average population differences cannot be applied to single individuals, but the group differences are real and should be explained. How can we account for these differences? Although some psychologists have suggested that evolutionary and genetic factors are partly responsible for IQ differences among racial and ethnic groups (Rushton, 2000), most psychologists favor environmental explanations of the type we'll discuss next.

Economic Differences   Significant economic differences continue to exist among racial/ethnic groups that could contribute to performance and that make interpretation of the IQ differences difficult. For example, African Americans and Hispanic Americans are more likely to live at or below the poverty level in the United States. Poverty is often associated with poor nutrition and difficulties in gaining proper health care, and it may hurt one's chances to enter adequate schools. African Americans and Hispanic Americans are also much more likely than Whites to suffer racial discrimination. The impact of these factors on intelligence testing is not completely understood, although they almost certainly play an important role. African Americans, Whites, and Hispanic Americans tend to live in very different and somewhat isolated worlds. As a consequence, it's extremely difficult to disentangle the effects of the environment from any genetic differences that might contribute to intelligence.

Test Bias   It's also possible that test biases contribute to group differences in IQ scores (Bernal, 1984). Racial/ethnic group differences depend, to a certain extent, on the type of intelligence test administered (Brody, 1992). Most traditional IQ tests are written, administered, and scored by White, middle-class psychologists. This raises the very real possibility that cultural biases might be contaminating some of the test questions. For example, if I ask you a question such as "Who wrote *Faust?*" (which once appeared on a Wechsler test), your ability to answer correctly will depend partly on whether your culture places value on exposure to such information. African American psychologist Robert L. Williams has shown that when an intelligence test is used that relies heavily on African American terms and expressions, White students who have had limited experience with African American culture perform poorly.

However, psychologists have worked hard to remove bias from standard intelligence and achievement tests (Raven, Court, & Raven, 1985); in some cases, the development of "culture-fair" tests has reduced racial differences in measured ability. However, significant group differences usually remain even after culture-bound questions have been altered or removed. Consequently, bias can contribute to test performance in some instances, but it's unlikely to be a major determinant of group differences in IQ (Cole, 1981; Kaplan, 1985).

Stereotype Threat   The content of intelligence tests may no longer be biased, but situational factors remain a concern. When people take intelligence tests, they have certain expectations about how they'll perform; these expectations, in turn,

CRITICAL THINKING

Do you think it's possible to eliminate cultural influences completely from a psychological test?

© Paul Chesley/Getty Images/Stone

Most psychologists agree that cultural background plays an important role in the measurement and interpretation of intelligence.

can significantly affect the final score. If you're nervous or expect to bomb the test, you're less likely to do well. Psychologist Claude Steele and his colleagues argue that African Americans, who understand the negative stereotypes people hold about their intelligence, often feel pressured or threatened by stereotypes and perform poorly as a result.

In support of this conclusion, Steele and Aronson (1995) found that African Americans performed more poorly on a verbal test when they thought the test was measuring intelligence rather than general problem solving. Everyone in the experiment took exactly the same test, but they were led to believe, through instructions, that it was either an intelligence or problem-solving test. Presumably the label "intelligence test" activated the negative stereotype, creating pressure and anxiety, and performance suffered as a result. Whether this pressure can account for the differences found between groups on intelligence tests remains uncertain (Sackett, Hardison, & Cullen, 2004; Steele & Aronson, 2004), but stereotype threat is clearly an important factor to consider. We'll return to the effects of stereotypes on expectations and performance in Chapter 13.

Adoption Studies   A more direct test of environmental explanations of racial/ethnic differences comes from IQ studies of African American children who have been reared in White homes. If the average African American childhood experience leads to skills that do not transfer well to standard tests of intelligence (for whatever reason), then we would expect African American children raised in White middle-class homes to produce higher IQ scores. In general, this assumption is supported by the data. Scarr and Weinberg (1976) investigated interracial adoptions in Minnesota and found that the average IQ for African American children reared in economically advantaged White households was significantly higher than the national African American mean score. This finding was confirmed again in later follow-up studies (Waldman, Weinberg, & Scarr, 1994; Weinberg, Scarr, & Waldman, 1992). You shouldn't conclude from this finding that White middle-class households are somehow better than other households. The results simply imply that certain cultural experiences give one an advantage on the kinds of tests currently being used to assess intelligence.

The Interaction of Nature and Nurture

So what are we to conclude about the relative contributions of genetics and the environment to intelligence? Nature–nurture issues are notoriously difficult to resolve, and this is especially true in the politically sensitive area of intelligence (Hunt & Carlson, 2007). It's extremely difficult to control for the effects of either the environment or genetics. Consider the twin studies—how reasonable is it to assume that twins who have been reared apart have had unrelated environmental experiences? Are children who are adopted really representative of the racial or ethnic populations from which they have been drawn (Brody, 2007)? It's difficult to answer these questions because neither the environment nor genetic structure can be manipulated directly in the laboratory (at least for humans).

The most reasonable position to take at the present time is that your intelligence, like many other psychological attributes, is determined by a mixture of genes and environment. The genes you inherit from your parents place upper and lower bounds on intellectual ability. Genes may importantly determine how your brain is wired, and possibly the speed of neural transmission, but the expression of your genetic material is strongly influenced by the environment. Nature always works via nurture and vice versa—one can't happen without the other (Ridley, 2003).

Recall from Chapter 3 that geneticists use the term *genotype* to refer to the genetic message itself and *phenotype* to refer to the observable characteristics that actually result from genetic expression. An analogy of the genotype/phenotype relationship that is sometimes used by intelligence researchers compares the development of intelligence to the nurturing of flowering plants (Lewontin, 1976). Imagine that we have a packet of virtually identical seeds, and we toss half into a pot containing fertile soil and half into a pot of barren soil (see ▌Figure 10.7). The seeds tossed into the poor soil will undoubtedly grow, but their growth will be stunted relative to that of the group planted in the rich soil. Because these are virtually identical groups of seeds, containing similar distributions of genetic information, any differences in growth between the pots are due entirely to the environment (the soil). So, too, with intelligence—two people can be born with similar genetic potential, but the degree to which their intellectual potential will "blossom" will depend critically on the environment.

Consider as well that within each handful of seeds there will be variations in genetic information. Some plants will grow larger than others, regardless of the soil in which they've been thrown. A similar kind of result would be expected for intelligence—variations in the genetic message will produce individual differences in IQ that cannot be adequately explained by environmental variables. In fact, after analyzing the differences within a pot, we might conclude that all of the differences are due to inherited factors. But even if the differences within a group are due to genes, the differences between groups would still be due to the environment (fertile or barren soil). This kind of insight can help account, in part, for the racial/ethnic differences in IQ discussed earlier. Even though genes may exert a strong influence within a population, between-population differences may still be determined primarily by the environment (Eysenck & Kamin, 1981; Lewontin, 1976).

One other feature of the interaction between nature and nurture is worth noting . . . yet again. Environmental experiences do not occur independent of inherited

CRITICAL THINKING

Suppose we broaden the concept of intelligence to include athletic and artistic ability. Would it bother you to think that these abilities are influenced primarily by genetic factors?

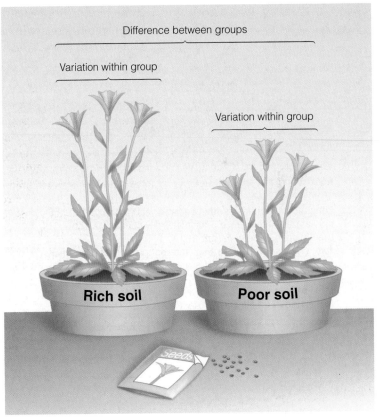

▌ **FIGURE 10.7** Between- and Within-Group Variation
In the plant analogy, all variation in plant height within one pot is due to genetics, but the overall height difference between plants in one pot and plants in the other is attributable to the differing environments (rich soil versus poor soil).

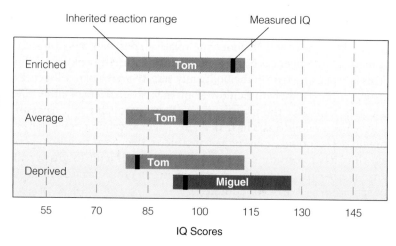

FIGURE 10.8 Reaction Range
Each person may have genes that set limits for intellectual potential (sometimes called a reaction range). In this case, Tom inherited an IQ potential anywhere between 80 and about 112. The IQ that Tom actually obtains (shown as the dark bar) is determined by the kind of environment in which he is reared. Notice that Miguel inherited a greater IQ potential than Tom, but if Tom is raised in an enriched environment, his IQ may actually turn out to be higher than Miguel's.

factors. It's a two-way street. The environment will partly determine how genetic information is expressed, but so too will genetic information determine experience. If you're born with three arms, because of some odd combination of inherited factors, your interactions with the world will be quite different from those of a person with two arms. The fact that you have three arms will color your environment—it will determine how you are treated and the range of opportunities to which you are exposed. If you're born with "smart" genes, then early on you're likely to be exposed to opportunities that will help you realize your full intellectual potential; conversely, if you're born "slow," the environment is likely to shape you away from intellectually nurturing experiences (see ▌Figure 10.8). Such is the way of life and of the world.

Test Yourself 10.3

Check your knowledge about the sources of intelligence by deciding whether each of the following statements is True or False. *(You will find the answers in the Appendix.)*

1. Longitudinal studies of intelligence reveal that fluid, but not crystallized, intelligence remains largely constant across the life span. *True or False?*
2. Twin studies have shown that fraternal twins raised together tend to have more similar IQs than identical twins raised apart. *True or False?*
3. Most psychologists now believe that genetic factors definitely play a role in intelligence. *True or False?*
4. A heritability estimate of 70% means that 70% of someone's intelligence is due to his or her genetic structure. *True or False?*
5. Test bias is recognized as a possible contributor to measured intelligence, but it's unlikely to be a strong determinant of group differences in IQ. *True or False?*

Review *Psychology for a Reason*

What is intelligence? You've seen in this chapter that the concept of intelligence comes primarily from the study of individual differences. People differ, and we can try to develop tests that measure these differences effectively. From an analysis of individual variability, psychologists have tried to develop theories of intellectual functioning: What kinds of mental processes underlie intelligent thought? We've seen that one way to characterize intelligence is by the adaptability of behavior. What makes one species member intelligent, and another not, may be dictated by how well organisms adapt to rapidly changing environments and solve the problems of survival. From this perspective, the nutcracker, in its successful search for a cache of seeds, fits the adaptive view of intelligence just as well as the cocky student who aces the SAT. In this chapter our discussion revolved around three problems that face researchers of intelligence.

Conceptualizing Intelligence

Researchers have attempted to conceptualize intelligence in a number of ways. Proponents of psychometric approaches map out fundamental aspects of the mind by analyzing performance on a battery of mental tests. They traditionally draw distinctions between a general factor of intelligence, *g*, which applies broadly, and specific factors, *s*, which measure separate abilities. The idea that intelligence must be broken down into several, or multiple, kinds of ability remains popular today, although researchers disagree as to how many or what types of intelligence need to be included.

There's some evidence to suggest that performance on traditional tests of mental ability might be related to the speed of processing among neurons in the brain. The multiple-intelligences approach of Howard Gardner and the triarchic theory of Robert Sternberg both suggest that the concept of intelligence must be defined broadly. We cannot rely entirely on academic ability to define intelligence—everyday intelligence and "street smarts" also enhance our ability to adapt.

Measuring Individual Differences

Concepts like intelligence really have little meaning outside of the study of individual differences—it's how the mental ability of Sam differs from the mental ability of Jennifer that makes the concept of intelligence meaningful. A good test of intelligence has three main characteristics: reliability, valid-

ity, and standardization. Understanding the concept of test validity is crucial because it holds the key to appreciating the widespread use of standardized measures such as IQ or tests such as the SAT. Researchers who study individual differences are often primarily interested in using the resulting measurements to make predictions about future success. Will Jennifer perform well in school? Will Sam make it as a graduate student in psychology? As you've seen, the IQ test itself was originally developed to measure academic ability, not as some ultimate measure of mental capacity.

Discovering the Sources of Intelligence

There are two primary ways to explain how measured differences in intelligence might arise, genetics and the environment. Twin studies provide convincing evidence that at least some kinds of mental ability are inherited, although how much remains controversial. However, the role of the environment in determining IQ—cultural background, economic status, stereotype threat, and even built-in test biases—cannot be discounted. Intelligence, like many psychological attributes, grows out of an interaction between nature and nurture.

Active Summary *(You will find the answers in the Appendix.)*

Conceptualizing Intelligence

• The (1) _____ approach proposes that intelligence can be understood by statistically analyzing (2) _____ on tests that measure specific mental skills. Spearman used (3) _____ analysis to study the relationships, or (4) _____, among test scores and to analyze the factors that account for test performance. He proposed that we possess (5) _____ intelligence, or *g*, as well as specific abilities, or *s*.

• (6) _____ intelligence is the ability to reason, (7) _____ problems, and remember; it may be influenced by (8) _____ and biological factors. (9) _____ intelligence reflects the (10) _____ and abilities that we acquire from experience.

• Gardner proposed that traditional views of intelligence be broadened to include special (11) _____ or talents that reflect (12) _____ intelligences. He identified (13) _____ kinds of intelligence: musical, bodily-kinesthetic, logical-mathematical, (14) _____, spatial, interpersonal, (15) _____, and naturalist.

• Sternberg's (16) _____ theory of intelligence proposed that intelligence has three main components. (17) _____ intelligence is the ability to process information; (18) _____ intelligence is used in coping with new kinds of tasks; and (19) _____ intelligence has to do with how well people adapt to the environment.

Measuring Individual Differences

• (20) _____ is a measure of the (21) _____ of test results. (22) _____ is whether a test measures what it is supposed to measure. (23) _____ ensures that the testing, scoring, and interpretation procedures are similar every time the test is administered.

• IQ is an index of (24) _____ that was originally designed to identify children who were likely to have trouble in school. A test was developed that would determine a child's (25) _____ age, which is typically calculated by comparing a child's test score with the (26) _____ score for (27) _____ age groups. Traditionally, IQ was calculated by dividing mental age by (28) _____ age and multiplying the quotient by 100. Now, however, a (29) _____ IQ is calculated by determining where a given test score "sits" in relation to the average score.

• An IQ score of 70 or below is associated with mental (30) _____, although several criteria must be met for a formal diagnosis. An IQ of (31) _____ or above indicates (32) _____.

• Scores on traditional IQ tests (33) _____ well with school test scores or grades, although critics argue that IQ doesn't reflect the whole range of intelligence. (34) _____ effects may occur when teachers' knowledge of IQ scores affect how they interact with students. The effects of the IQ label were particularly serious during the early 20th century when many immigrants who had not mastered (35) _____ were given intelligence tests and were labeled "feebleminded" or "defective" when they failed to perform well.

• (36) _____ is the ability to generate novel and original ideas. (37) _____ intelligence is the ability to perceive, (38) _____, and express emotion. (39) _____ knowledge is an unspoken practical "know-how" that is rarely formally taught and comes primarily from (40) _____.

Discovering the Sources of Intelligence

• One of the best ways to measure the stability of IQ is through a (41) _____ study, which involves testing the same people repeatedly as they age. Current thinking is that (42) _____ intelligence, which reflects basic (43) _____ skills, may (44) _____ with age, whereas (45) _____ intelligence, which reflects acquired (46) _____, remains (47) _____ or increases with age. The (48) _____ effect is a trend that has been documented worldwide and shows that performance on IQ tests seems to be rising steadily and consistently over time.

• (49) _____ studies address the role of (50) _____ and (51) _____ on intelligence. Identical twins have very (52) _____ IQ scores, regardless of whether they were raised in the same (53) _____. (54) _____ is a mathematical index that shows the extent to which IQ differences within a population can be accounted for by (55) _____ factors. Estimates of heritability apply to (56) _____, not to individuals.

• Most researchers agree that there are stable group (57) _____ in IQ across racial, ethnic, and social lines, which may be explained by (58) _____ differences or test (59) _____. Adoption studies support the role of the (60) _____ in explaining group differences. Intelligence is determined by a mixture of (61) _____ and (62) _____ influences. Genes place (63) _____ and lower limits on intellectual ability. However, the environment will partly determine how (64) _____ information is expressed, and genetic information will influence (65) _____.

Terms to Remember

achievement tests, 320
aptitude tests, 320
creativity, 327
crystallized intelligence, 316
deviation IQ, 323
emotional intelligence, 328
factor analysis, 314
fluid intelligence, 316

g (general intelligence), 314
gifted, 325
heritability, 334
intelligence quotient (IQ), 323
intelligence, 312
mental age, 322
mental retardation, 324
multiple intelligences, 317

psychometrics, 313
reliability, 320
s (specific intelligence), 314
standardization, 321
tacit knowledge, 328
triarchic theory, 318
validity, 320

Media Resources

 ThomsonNOW

www.thomsonedu.com/ThomsonNOW

Go to this site for the link to ThomsonNow, your one-stop study shop. Take a Pre-Test for this chapter and Thomson-Now will generate a personalized Study Plan based on your test results! The Study Plan will identify the topics you need to review and direct you to online resources to help you master those topics. You can then take a Post-Test to help you determine the concepts you have mastered and what you still need to work on.

 Companion Website

www.thomsonedu.com/psychology/nairne

Go to this site to find online resources directly linked to your book, including a glossary, flashcards, quizzing, weblinks, and more.

 Psyk.trek 3.0

Check out the Psyk.trek CD-ROM for further study of the concepts in this chapter. Psyk.trek's interactive learning modules, simulations, and quizzes offer additional opportunities for you to interact with, reflect on, and retain the material:

Testing and Intelligence: Understanding IQ Scores
Testing and Intelligence: Key Concepts in Testing
Testing and Intelligence: Heredity, Environment, and Intelligence

Motivation and Emotion

You sense only rapid movement at first—then the cool feel of metal on your cheek. You exhale, gasping, as a bony arm wraps itself around your neck. "Welcome to a nightmare, my friend," a voice growls. "Your wallet or your life." Inside your sympathetic nervous system jumps into action—releasing epinephrine, targeting the critical organs of the body and the neural communication chains. Your mind, flooded with the arousal, struggles to decide on the best response. But you're in a psychological meltdown—you see only jumbled images of the sidewalk and needle tracks dotting the arm grasping your neck. You can't think clearly; in your mind there is only surprise, confusion, and the smothering grip of fear.

Not a very pleasant scenario. Two people, reacting to circumstance, each in a highly activated state. For psychologists, however, the interplay is of special interest. The unfolding action strikes at the core of what psychology is about: understanding the causes and motivations of behavior. What factors initiate and direct behavior? What causes the criminal to attack the victim? Is it the reinforcing value of money? Is it the loss of control driven by an internal need for a "fix"? And what about the emotions that accompany the act—fear, excitement, despair? How do emotions enhance our ability to function? Do the emotions themselves motivate and direct behavior? These are some of the topics we'll be considering in this chapter.

Motivation can be defined as the set of factors that *initiate* and *direct* behavior, usually toward a goal. If you're motivated, your behavior becomes activated and goal directed. Hunger is a classic example; something happens in the body that stimulates us to pursue food. Junkies become motivated to search for the drug of need. As you saw in Chapter 7, rewards can be motivating as well—we're likely to repeat a behavior that led to a reward. **Emotions** are complex psychological events that are often associated with goal-directed behavior. Emotions typically involve (1) a *physiological* reaction, usually arousal; (2) some kind of *expressive* reaction, such as a distinctive facial expression; and (3) some kind of *subjective experience*, such as the conscious feeling of being happy or sad.

Most psychologists are convinced that motivation and emotion should be closely linked. Both terms, in fact, derive from the Latin *movere*, meaning "to move." Many conditions that are motivating also give rise to the experience of emotion. Suppose you're thirsty and put

motivation The set of factors that initiate and direct behavior, usually toward some goal.

emotions Psychological events involving (1) a physiological reaction, usually arousal; (2) some kind of expressive reaction, such as a distinctive facial expression; and (3) some kind of subjective experience, such as the conscious feeling of being happy or sad.

The study of motivation and emotion deals with psychological processes that are critically important. In some sense these are the most basic of all internal processes, the ones that help us survive. Each of the preceding chapters touched in one way or another on the question of *why* behavior occurs, but we'll focus our attention here on goal-directed behaviors—those actions specifically related to the accomplishment of a goal.

Activating Behavior Anyone hoping to survive in a changing environment must react quickly to circumstance. You need to anticipate future outcomes and act accordingly, *now*, with vigor and persistence. Much of the time our actions are controlled by *internal* factors that push us in the direction of a goal. For example, if you're deprived of food or water, a delicate internal balance is disrupted. A specific need is signaled, which you seek to satisfy to restore that balance. At other times we're motivated by *external* events, things in our environment that exert powerful pulling effects. The sight of an attractive person or a recently sliced piece of chocolate cake can be sufficient to initiate and direct behavior. We'll discuss how psychologists think about the "activation" of behavior as well as the general concept of "need."

Meeting Biological Needs: Hunger and Eating We all need to eat—it's a requirement of living. Consequently, there must be internal mechanisms that make us hungry and interested in eating at regular intervals. To understand how our bodies maintain the proper levels of internal energy, we'll consider the relevant internal and external cues that activate and control eating. For example, we'll discuss how the body monitors internal physiological states, using brain mechanisms to check on energy reserves (such as the amount of sugar in the blood). We'll also discuss how external cues in the environment compel us to eat and how these cues can influence food selection. Whether you like broccoli, reject mushrooms, or happily consume squid depends on a variety of factors, including what you've learned about these foods.

Meeting Biological Needs: Sexual Behavior Are you "consumed" by sex? Do you have a reasonably intense sexual "appetite"? Unlike eating, sex isn't necessary for individual survival. You can live a perfectly productive life, at least in principle, without ever once engaging in a sexual act. But adequate sexual performance is needed for survival of the *species*. Consequently, there must be internal systems that help motivate an interest in sex. We'll discuss some of the biological and psychological mechanisms that motivate sexual behavior, as well as some of the physiological characteristics of the human sexual response.

Expressing and Experiencing Emotion Emotions have considerable adaptive significance. Consider anger. Anger occurs in response to an environmental event, usually the perceived misdeed of another, which causes the body to enter a highly aroused state. The arousal activates behavior and leads to reactions that may substantially increase (or decrease) the likelihood of survival. Once the emotion gains hold, overt physical expressions arise, particularly easy-to-identify facial expressions. From an adaptive perspective, the sight of an angry person carries important signaling properties—others know to shy away and avoid interaction. As you'll see, emotions are easy to identify but difficult to define.

change into a Coke machine. If the money gets stuck, blocking your goal, you're likely to get frustrated and angry. The emotional experience, in turn, produces its own "energizing" effect on behavior—maybe you start screaming and kicking the machine (which may or may not help). It's difficult to discuss the topic of motivation without also considering emotion.

Activating Behavior

LEARNING GOALS
- Compare instinct and drive and their roles in activating behavior.
- Understand incentive motivation and its role in activating behavior.
- Compare achievement motivation and intrinsic motivation.
- Describe Maslow's hierarchy of needs.

WHAT FACTORS ACTIVATE AND CONTROL goal-directed behavior? At first, psychologists thought there might be a single source of motivation, based either in the body or in the environment. It's possible, for example, that we're born with biological machinery that compels us to act in fixed ways regardless of what we learn from experience. But as you'll soon see, this idea is largely rejected by modern psychologists, who believe instead that no single explanation of goal-directed behavior is likely to be found. The reason is simple: Virtually all forms of behavior are determined by multiple causes. Factors both inside and outside the body contribute to motivation. In the following sections, we'll consider some examples of these influences.

© Photodisc/Getty Images

Internal Factors: Instincts and Drive

The factors that initiated and are directing this behavior include internal ones, such as depleted energy resources, and external ones, such as the sight of an attractive meal. Hunting behavior may also be controlled to a certain extent by instincts—unlearned, characteristic patterns of responding that are triggered by specific stimuli.

To survive, we all must do certain things. Sleeping, eating, and drinking are activities we need to perform at regular intervals. It makes sense, then, to assume that our motivation to perform these activities comes naturally. But just how rigidly controlled are human goal-directed behaviors? In nature, birds don't need to be taught how to build nests in the springtime or to fly south in the winter; cats don't need to be taught to show interest in small, furry creatures. These are unlearned, characteristic patterns of responding—called **instincts**—that are controlled by events in the environment. Instincts share properties with *reflexes*, which we discussed in Chapter 3, but instincts typically involve more complex patterns of behavior than those covered by simple reflexes.

instincts Unlearned characteristic patterns of responding that are controlled by specific triggering stimuli in the world.

Human Instincts   It's widely accepted that instincts play a role in nonhuman species, but psychologists are more skeptical about human behavior. Early on, psychologists followed the lead of Charles Darwin in suggesting that instincts underlie much of human motivation. Humans don't need to be taught to take care of their young, William James (1890) argued, or to cry as infants, to clean themselves when dirty, or even to play, love, imitate, or be curious. These are ingrained biological "musts" that are as natural to the human as nest building is to the bird.

   Yet just because a behavior occurs on a regular basis doesn't mean it's *instinctive*—that is, unlearned and characteristic in its display. There's no way to measure an instinct directly by looking inside the body, so it's easy to fall into a trap of circular reasoning: Someone shows sympathy for a child in need, and the temptation is to propose a corresponding sympathy instinct (Holt, 1931). Over the years, psychologists argued about which behaviors qualify as instincts. For example, James (1890) identified some 20 physical and 17 mental human instincts; William McDougall (1908) was convinced of only 12 (he later changed his mind and increased the number to 17). Because of the disagreements, instincts eventually fell out of favor as a widely applied explanation for goal-directed human behavior. Today, many evolutionary psychologists are seeking to revive the concept of human instincts, although in a more flexible form.

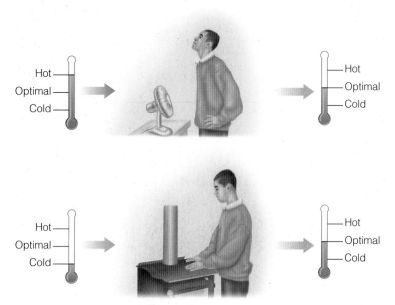

FIGURE 11.1 Homeostasis
It's adaptive for the body to maintain stable and constant internal conditions. If your internal temperature rises above or falls below an optimal level, you are driven to perform actions that will restore the "steady state."

drive A psychological state that arises in response to an internal physiological need, such as hunger or thirst.

homeostasis The process through which the body maintains a steady state, such as a constant internal temperature or an adequate amount of fluids.

incentive motivation External factors in the environment that exert pulling effects on our actions.

Evolutionary psychologists argue that we are born with specific mental "software" that helps control and guide our actions, but those actions need not be as inflexible and characteristic as many of the instincts seen in non-human species (Buss, 2007).

Drive Psychologists next turned to the concept of drive. A **drive** is an internal state that arises in response to a need, such as hunger or thirst. It's clear that the human body is designed to seek fairly stable and constant internal conditions. For example, it's important for the body to maintain an adequate internal supply of fluids and a constant internal temperature. The body maintains its steady state through a process called **homeostasis**, much like the thermostat in a house maintains a constant internal temperature by turning the heat on or off (Cannon, 1929). Once a specific need is detected, drive serves a general activating function—drive energizes the organism, causing it to seek immediate reduction of the need (Berridge, 2004). If your water supply is used up, you're driven to drink and restore the appropriate balance. Similar processes are assumed to operate for hunger and for the maintenance of internal body temperature (see ▌Figure 11.1).

When an organism seeks to reduce drive—to restore homeostatic balance—it doesn't really matter how balance is restored. Drive is a more flexible concept than instinct. People can use what they've learned from experience to help them satisfy the need; they're not stuck with one fixed pattern of behavior that's triggered only by a restricted set of stimuli. You can think about drive as somewhat analogous to the running engine of a car. A properly running engine is necessary for the car to move, just as drive is necessary to start goal-directed behavior, but the engine doesn't determine where the car will travel or how you'll get across town. As you'll see shortly, how hard you'll work toward a goal also depends critically on the value, or *incentive*, of the goal. You're much more likely to eat if you like the food, even though a wide variety of food options may satisfy the internal need. You sometimes even eat in the absence of need—you have that second brownie just because it looks good.

External Factors: Incentive Motivation

As just noted, goal-directed behavior depends on what we learn from experience. External rewards, such as money or a good grade, exert powerful pulling and guiding effects on our actions. Generally, whether you'll be motivated to perform an action depends on the value—positive or negative—of the incentive. For this reason psychologists often use the term **incentive motivation** to help explain goal-directed behavior. For example, Whitney is motivated to jog for an extra five minutes so she can eat that extra brownie; conversely, Charlie is motivated to avoid the kitchen because of the extra calories (and guilt) he knows the brownie will produce. Note this type of motivation differs from drive—drive is an internal push that compels a person to action; incentives are external pulls that tempt people with the prospects of receiving powerful reinforcing or punishing consequences.

Internal factors can interact with external factors in a number of ways. Whether or not you're thirsty, for example, affects the incentive value of water; water tastes better, and is more rewarding, when you've been deprived of it for a while (Blundell & Rogers, 1991; Bolles, 1972). Rewarding you with an end-of-chapter test, thereby motivating you to study, has more of an effect when you're a high procrastinator—that is, someone who finds it difficult to find the motivation to study (Tuckman, 1998). Internal states of deprivation can also act as cues for responding. You might learn to perform a certain type of action when you're thirsty or hungry (Hull, 1943); alternatively, you might learn that hunger or thirst means that food or water will be especially rewarding (Davidson, 1993, 1998). Remember, motivated behavior is virtually always jointly determined by internal and external factors. Neither factor alone is sufficient to explain motivation.

Achievement Motivation

Another example of motivated behavior that clearly depends on both internal and external factors is the push for achievement (Elliot & Thrash, 2001). Many psychologists believe each of us, to varying degrees, has an internally driven need for achievement (Atkinson, 1957; McClelland et al., 1953; Murray, 1938). The **achievement motive** pushes us to seek success and significant accomplishment in our lives. Studies have shown that people who rate high in achievement motivation tend to work harder and more persistently on tasks, and they tend to achieve more than those who rate low in achievement motivation (Atkinson & Raynor, 1974; Cooper, 1983).

External rewards can exert powerful pulling and guiding effects on our actions.

achievement motive An internal drive or need for achievement that is possessed by all individuals to varying degrees.

However, whether you'll work hard on any particular task depends on your expectations of success and on how much you value the task (Atkinson, 1957; Molden & Dweck, 2000). You can have a high internal need for achievement but choose not to persist on a task either because you place no value on it or because you lack confidence in your ability to succeed. For example, young children who experience failure on mathematics problems early in life can develop a helpless attitude that prevents them from persisting and succeeding on mathematical tasks later on. Conversely, children who perform well on such tasks gain confidence in their ability and appear motivated to take on similar tasks in the future (Smiley & Dweck, 1994; Wigfield, 1994).

How can the achievement motive be measured? According to experts, you can't get a very accurate measure by asking. Instead, it's better to examine a person's fantasies, wishes, and dreams. Over time you'll find common themes that clearly illustrate how much the person values and needs achievement. One technique is to present an ambiguous picture and instruct the individual to make up a story about its content. David McClelland and others (1953) have found that people tend to reflect their need for achievement in the repeating themes of their stories. This kind of technique for assessing psychological characteristics—called a *projective test*—is often used to study personality, as you'll discover in Chapter 12.

Concept Review	General Approaches to Motivation

APPROACH	SOURCE OF MOTIVATION	SUMMARY AND EVALUATION
Instinct	Internal	Unlearned, characteristic patterns of responding that are controlled by specific triggering mechanisms in the world. They play a role in nonhuman species but are insufficient to explain goal-directed human behavior.
Drive	Internal	A psychological state that arises in response to a physiological need, such as hunger or thirst. *Homeostasis* is the process through which the body maintains a steady state. A more flexible concept than instinct, but drive does not explain behavior in the absence of need.
Incentive motivation	External	Helps to explain goal-directed behavior. People are driven by external rewards that exert powerful pulling and guiding effects on their actions.

© Bill Binzen/Rainbow

Children who experience failure on mathematical problems early in life can develop a "helpless" attitude that prevents them from persisting and succeeding in mathematics later in life.

Parents and teachers play an important part in determining achievement motivation. If parents value a task, it's likely their child will value it too and be more motivated to succeed. What children are told about their performance on a task is also important. For example, if children are praised for their effort, they tend to work harder, report more enjoyment, and show more interest. On the other hand, if they're told that performance is tied to an ability such as natural intelligence, children show less achievement motivation—especially if they fail or perform poorly on the task (Mueller & Dweck, 1998; Ziegert et al., 2001).

Cultural Factors Every society in the world establishes standards for achievement—the skills and tasks deemed important and unimportant—and these standards influence what the members of the society seek to achieve and perhaps the level of productivity of the society as a whole (McClelland, 1961). For example, whether a society values individual success or collective success seems to affect individual levels of achievement motivation. Middle school athletes in the United States report more self-confidence than comparable students in Korea, and they are more easily motivated, presumably because a greater emphasis is placed on individual success in the United States (Kim, Williams, & Gill, 2003).

Many researchers believe gender differences in achievement—such as the tendency for men to outperform women in mathematics—may be partly tied to such cultural factors. In the United States, for instance, the parents of sons place greater value on success in mathematics than do the parents of daughters (Parsons, Kaczala, & Meece, 1982); at the same time, boys often receive the message that they should study less, which helps explain why girls outperform boys in other subjects (Van Houtte, 2004). Consequently, the expectations and values of the parents help to determine the achievement motivation of the children.

Intrinsic Motivation

So far we've talked about motivation entirely in terms of internal pushes and external pulls, but sometimes we choose to engage in actions for which there's no obvious internal or external motivational source. A child spends hours carefully coloring a picture or playing with a doll; you might become transfixed by a crossword puzzle or by a long walk on the beach. Certainly there's no biological *need* that drives coloring or walking. There's also no clear-cut external incentive: Nobody pays the child for coloring or you for finishing the crossword puzzle. Psychologists use the term **intrinsic motivation** to describe behaviors that appear to be entirely self-motivated. We engage in the action for its own sake, not because someone offers us a reward or because the action restores some internal homeostatic balance (Lepper, Corpus, & Iyengar, 2005; Ryan & Deci, 2000).

intrinsic motivation Goal-directed behavior that seems to be entirely self-motivated.

In fact, it turns out that when we're intrinsically motivated, supplying an external reward can actually lower interest in the task. In a classic study by Lepper, Greene, and Nisbett (1973), preschool children who were naturally interested in drawing were asked to draw either for its own sake or to win a "Good Player" certificate. Psychologically, we would expect the external reward to bolster drawing even more than normal—after all, drawing is now followed by a concrete positive consequence—but it didn't. The children in the reward condition showed less interest in drawing a week later. The reward apparently reduced the value of the behavior, making it less rewarding or interesting than it otherwise would have been.

This study has been repeated with other rewards and with activities other than drawing. The story is much the same: Externally supplied rewards sometimes lower our desire to perform a task. Once a reward is involved, we're less likely to enjoy that task for its own sake in the future. This doesn't always happen, of course, but it can

© Catherine Karnow/Corbis

These food bank volunteers are probably intrinsically motivated; it's unlikely that they're expecting any concrete external reward.

occur in some instances (Henderlong & Lepper, 2002). Think about professional athletes. Many sports fans complain that the external reward of money has ruined professional sports. Even baseball players sometimes complain that the game was more fun back in the sandlot, before millions of dollars entered into the motivational chain.

How can a reward lead to a negative effect? One possibility is people see external rewards, even praise, as an indirect way of controlling behavior. Drawing loses its value because it's now something you're doing to please the person giving you the reward—you're no longer drawing simply because it pleases *you*. Another possibility is the reward degrades the value of the task—for example, the baseball player begins to believe it's the money that makes him play, rather than love for the game. Some researchers have even suggested that traits like creativity should never be rewarded lest the positive internal value of engaging in a creative act be destroyed (Amabile, 1983; Schwartz, 1990).

But not all psychologists are comfortable with these conclusions. External reward enhances creativity under some circumstances, and the negative effects of reward on task motivation only occur in restricted circumstances (Eisenberger & Cameron, 1996). For example, in the study by Lepper and colleagues, children did indeed choose to draw less frequently when they were rewarded for drawing, but this effect occurred only when the children *expected* the reward. When children were given an unexpected reward for drawing, they later spent more time drawing than a group who had received no reward. Therefore, the negative effect of reward on intrinsic motivation may be related to the expectation or promise of reward rather than to the reward itself (Cameron & Pierce, 1994).

CRITICAL THINKING

Suppose you spend every Saturday morning volunteering at a local homeless shelter. How do you think your attitude might change if you started receiving a paycheck for your time?

Maslow's Hierarchy of Needs

Most general theories of motivation appeal primarily to biological factors. The body seeks to maintain a delicate internal balance (homeostasis), and if that balance is disrupted, we're motivated to restore it. However, as you've just seen, not all needs are biological in origin—for example, the need for achievement (Murray, 1938). For this reason, some psychologists have tried to classify need and to determine whether some needs are more important than others.

Among the more influential of these classification systems is the **need hierarchy** introduced by the humanistic theorist Abraham Maslow. The essential component of

need hierarchy The idea popularized by Maslow that human needs are prioritized in a hierarchy.

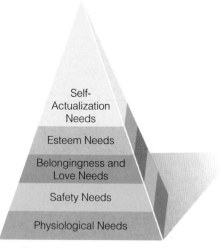

FIGURE 11.2 A Hierarchy of Needs Maslow proposed that human needs are prioritized: Some must be satisfied before others can be addressed, including physiological and safety needs. At the top of the pyramid is the need for self-actualization, our natural desire to reach our true potential.

CRITICAL THINKING

Turn back to the chapter on development and think about the various personal crises people confront as they age. Is there any way you can tie these crises to the needs that Maslow discussed in his hierarchy?

Maslow's theory is the *prioritizing* of needs: Some needs, he argued, have special priority and must be satisfied before others can be addressed. Obviously, if we don't eat or drink water on a regular basis, we'll die. Maslow's theory is usually represented in the form of a pyramid, to emphasize the fact that human motivation rests on a foundation of biological and security "musts" (see ▌Figure 11.2). It's only after satisfying the survival needs—such as hunger and thirst—that we can consider personal security and more social or spiritual needs, such as the need for love or self-esteem. At the top of the structure sits the need for self-actualization, which Maslow believed represented our desire to reach our true potential as human beings.

The pyramid is an appropriate symbol for Maslow's system because it captures the upward thrust of human motivation. As a humanistic psychologist, Maslow (1954) believed all people have a compelling need to grow, to better themselves as functioning individuals. Maslow was strongly influenced by people who he felt had reached their fullest potential, such as Thomas Jefferson and Albert Einstein. He used their personality characteristics as a way of defining what it means to sit at the top of the pyramid—to be self-actualized. These characteristics included spontaneity, openness to experience, and a high degree of ethical sensitivity (Mook, 1995; Ryckman, 2008). In his later years Maslow fine-tuned the hierarchy, adding some additional motivational levels, but they need not concern us here (see Koltko-Rivera, 2006). We'll return to humanistic views on personality in Chapter 12.

Probably the most important feature of the Maslow hierarchy is the laddering of needs. Psychologists might disagree about the specific order that Maslow proposed—does the need to belong and be accepted really have higher priority than the need for self-esteem?—but the idea that humans have a wide variety of needs that must be prioritized has been enormously influential (Rowan, 1998). How we act is often influenced by unfilled needs. If you have to worry about putting food on the table, and consequently steal from others on a regular basis, you might appear to lack moral or ethical values. But this isn't necessarily a permanent fixture of your personality—under different circumstances, with a full stomach, you might act extremely ethically.

Critics of Maslow's theory often point to its lack of scientific rigor. Because the various needs are not defined clearly in a way that each can be individually measured, it's difficult to test the different proposals of the need hierarchy (Wahba & Bridwell, 1976). However, the theory continues to exert considerable influence on how

Abraham Maslow used the personality characteristics of high achievers, such as Thomas Jefferson and Albert Einstein, to define what it means to be self-actualized.

Abraham Maslow

Thomas Jefferson

Albert Einstein

psychologists think. For example, applied psychologists have extended Maslow's ideas to the workplace to help employers better understand the behavior of their employees. Many employers now recognize that an employee's needs change depending on his or her position in the management hierarchy. When people receive low pay or have poor job security, their work behavior is directed toward satisfying basic needs. Promotion may help satisfy the fundamental needs, but new, perhaps more demanding ones will quickly arise. Employers must be sensitive to the particular needs at each level of the management hierarchy (Muchinsky, 2003).

Test Yourself 11.1

Check your knowledge about activating behavior by answering the following questions. (You will find the answers in the Appendix.)

1. Which of the following statements best captures the difference between an instinct and a drive?
   a. A drive is a reflex; an instinct is not.
   b. Instincts are learned; drives are not.
   c. Instincts lead to fixed response patterns; drives do not.
   d. Instincts restore appropriate internal balance; drives do not.

2. Which type of motivation best describes each of the following behaviors: achievement, incentive, or intrinsic?
   a. Whitney never misses her daily jogging session—she loves the brownie she gives herself at the end: _____
   b. Janice spends hours practicing the piano—she just seems to love playing: _____
   c. Candice studies at least six hours a day—she is obsessed with the idea of finishing first in her class: _____
   d. Jerome rarely paints for fun anymore, not since he started teaching art classes at the local college: _____

3. According to Maslow's hierarchy of needs, we can reach our true potential as human beings only after:
   a. restoring a proper level of homeostatic balance.
   b. satisfying basic survival and social needs.
   c. satisfying our need for achievement.
   d. eliminating the need for rewards.

Meeting Biological Needs: Hunger and Eating

LEARNING GOALS
- Understand how internal and external factors influence the desire to eat.
- Explain how body weight is regulated.
- Distinguish between anorexia nervosa and bulimia nervosa.

WHY DO WE EAT? Obviously, from a survival standpoint eating is a no-brainer—we need food and water to survive. But we eat for reasons that are more complex than you might think. If you ask children why they eat, they'll explain they eat "because I'm hungry" or "because my tummy hurts." An adult's response will appear more sophisticated, but it usually amounts to much the same thing: "We eat because our bodies need food, internal energy." This is true; eating is a biologically driven behavior. But eating is a psychologically driven behavior as well. We sometimes feel hungry when there is no physical need; and, as any dieter knows, a strong will can stop consumption even when the physical need is present.

Internal Factors Controlling Hunger

Researchers have spent decades trying to understand the internal mechanisms that influence when and why we eat. We now know that the body monitors itself, particularly its internal supply of resources, in a number of ways. For example, there's a connection between the volume and content of food in the stomach and the frequency of

Such internal factors as the amount of food in the stomach and the amount of glucose in the blood play an important role in making people feel sated after a meal.

glucose A kind of sugar that cells require for energy production.

insulin A hormone released by the pancreas that helps pump nutrients in the blood into the cells, where they can be stored as fat or metabolized into needed energy.

leptin A hormone that may regulate the amount of energy stored in fat cells.

If a particular portion of the hypothalamus is destroyed, a mouse becomes an eating machine and can balloon up to several times its normal weight.

neural activity in certain areas of the brain (Sharma et al., 1961). Psychologically, people report little if any hunger or interest in food when their stomach is full, and hunger increases in a relatively direct way as the stomach empties (Sepple & Read, 1989).

Chemical Signals   It's not only the contents of the stomach that are monitored. The body regularly checks several important suppliers of internal energy. One critical substance is **glucose**, a kind of sugar required for energy production. Receptors in the liver or intestines are thought to react to changes in the amount of glucose in the blood, or perhaps to how this sugar is being used by the cells, and appropriate signals are communicated upward to the brain. When the amount of usable glucose falls below an optimal level, you begin to feel hungry and seek out food (Campfield et al., 1996). If blood glucose levels are high, which occurs after a meal, you lose interest in food. This link between blood sugar levels and hunger is not simply correlational: In the laboratory it is possible to increase or decrease how much an animal will eat by artificially manipulating the amount of glucose in its blood (Smith & Campfield, 1993).

Your body also monitors **insulin**, a hormone released by the pancreas. The body needs insulin to help pump the nutrients present in the blood into the cells, where they can be stored as fat or metabolized into needed energy. At the start of a meal, the brain sends signals to the pancreas to begin the production and release of insulin in preparation for the rise in blood sugar produced by the food. As insulin does its job, the levels of blood sugar go down, and you eventually feel hungry again. Also critical is a hormone called **leptin** that rises and falls with the amount of body fat; high levels of leptin are often found in obese individuals, and leptin levels typically drop when individuals go on a diet (Woods et al., 2000). Leptin plays a critical role in weight loss and if blocked can lead to increased food intake and weight gain. Resistance to leptin probably plays an important role in the development and maintenance of obesity (Morton et al., 2006).

Brain Regions   Ultimately, of course, the experience of hunger originates in the brain. It's the activation of brain structures that kick-starts and directs the search for food. A number of years ago it was discovered that if a particular portion of the hypothalamus is lesioned (destroyed) in laboratory animals, a curious transformation occurs. Lesioned animals appear to be hungry all the time and show a striking tendency to overeat. In fact, each animal becomes an eating machine—if allowed, it balloons up to several times its normal weight (Hetherington & Ranson, 1942). If this same area is stimulated electrically, rather than destroyed, the opposite pattern emerges. Electrical stimulation causes the animal to lose all interest in food, even if there's a real need for nutrients in the body.

Neuroscientists now believe that the hypothalamus contains receptors that are sensitive to the presence of food-related hormones such as insulin and leptin (Schwartz, 2006). Leptin, for example, binds with receptors in the hypothalamus that, in turn, enhance the body's response to satiety signals in the body (stop eating) and lower the reward value of food (e.g., may make food taste less good). Such a process is adaptive because it prevents us from accumulating too many nutrients in the blood—more than our bodies can safely handle. Portions of the hindbrain are also critical in the initiation of eating (Grill & Kaplan, 1990), and the hippocampus may be involved as well. You may remember from Chapter 8 that we discussed an amnesic called H.M. who was doomed to live in a kind of perpetual present—he could remember nothing of what happened to him moments before. It turns out that H.M., who has damage to his temporal lobes and hippocampus, also has trouble monitoring his need for food. He's sometimes convinced he's hungry immediately after finishing a meal. He may have simply forgotten he's eaten; but as Davidson (1993) points out, he's also clearly unable to use internal signals from his body as cues for hunger or satiety. These data suggest an important role for the hippocampus in feeding behavior.

External Factors Controlling Hunger

It's a mistake to think about eating as simply a means to satisfy a variety of internal energy needs. We often eat for reasons unrelated to restoring internal homeostatic balance. Haven't you ever eaten to reduce stress or simply to make yourself feel good? Have you ever eaten to promote social interaction, as in going out to dinner with friends? We all have. People even use food to make ethical statements. For example, some people are vegetarians because they believe it's wrong to eat other animals.

Eating Habits   Most eating habits develop through personal experience and by modeling the behavior of others. These learned habits control much of our decision making about food. I suspect you're probably used to eating at certain times and in certain places. If you're offered a tasty snack, how much you eat is determined partly by the time of day—if the offer comes shortly before dinner, you take less than if the offer comes in the middle of the afternoon (Schachter & Gross, 1968). You also know from past experience how much food you can eat and still feel okay. You know, for instance, that if you eat the whole pizza you will probably feel sick afterward, even though the pizza may taste great at the time.

Cultural and ethnic background is another powerful influence (Rozin et al., 1999). Most people who grow up in the United States will not willingly choose to eat dogs or sheep's eyes, but these are considered delicacies in some parts of the world. Are you hesitant about eating pork or beef? You probably are if you're an Orthodox Jew or a native of India. And it's not just the appearance of food or where it comes from. People around the world often discriminate among eating partners. For example, members of some social classes would never consider eating with those they consider to be social inferiors.

Food Cues   The decision to eat is also strongly influenced by the appearance of food cues. Animals know that certain kinds of food taste good, and the sight of these foods is often enough to make them start eating. If hungry rats are taught that a flashing light predicts food, they'll start eating in the presence of the light even if they've been fully fed moments before (Weingarten, 1983). Waiters at fine restaurants push the dessert tray under your nose because they know the sight of the sugar-filled array will be more likely to break down your reserve than just hearing about what's for dessert. Again, your choice of the New York cheesecake with the strawberry sauce is not driven by internal need. Your blood contains plenty of appropriate nutrients—the sight of the food, and its associations with past pleasures, acts as an external pull, motivating your choice to consume. For more information on potential food cues, take a look at the Practical Solutions feature.

CRITICAL THINKING

Can you think of any factors, besides behavior modeling, that might help to determine eating habits? What about the availability of food—when was the last time you saw sheep's eyes on the menu at the local diner?

One's cultural and ethnic background exerts a powerful effect on food selection. Would you be willing to consume the shrimp shown on the left? How about the delicacies on the right?

© Bill Deering/Getty Images/Taxi

© Anna Mockford Nick Bonetti/AA World Travel/Topfoto/The Image Works

Dietary Variety and Weight Gain

Is variety in your diet a good thing? From a nutritional standpoint, of course, it's essential that you eat foods that deliver needed vitamins and other nutrients. But from a psychological standpoint, variety within a meal can actually make you eat more food. Suppose I let you eat one of your favorite flavors of ice cream, as much as you like, and record how much you eat; in a second case, I give you several different types of ice cream and, again, let you eat to your heart's desire. The evidence indicates you'll eat significantly more in the second instance (Raynor & Epstein, 2001).

Variety, particularly the introduction of a new and different food, has a way of counteracting fullness, or satiety. This is one of the reasons dessert looks good even though you've just pushed away your dinner plate.

The effect of variety on consumption, which occurs for both humans and animals, suggests that satiety is *sensory-specific*—that is, eating makes us lose interest in the particular food we're eating but not necessarily other foods. If people are asked to rate the pleasantness of sweet foods after eating a meal containing sweet food, their ratings drop; but the meal has no effect on their rating of savory foods (Rolls, van Duijvencvoorde, & Rolls, 1984). The effect applies to the taste and color of food as well as to its shape and texture. For instance, your pleasantness ratings for hard foods (such as a baguette or an apple) drop after consumption, but not your ratings for soft foods (Guinard & Brun, 1998).

Some psychologists have suggested that dietary variety may be a factor in the development of obesity. It's possible, for example,

that obese individuals show less sensory-specific satiety, which, in turn, causes them to eat more; alternatively, perhaps they show greater levels of sensory-specific satiety, which leads them to eat a greater variety of foods at a meal. Remember, though, obesity is not caused simply by the amount of food consumed—your weight depends on many factors, including genetics. The variety of foods present in a meal can, however, influence weight gain because variety determines how much you eat. One common reason people give for finishing a meal is that they're "tired" of the food (Hetherington, 1996)—variety, of course, works against this tendency. From a practical standpoint, if you want to eat less, try reducing the amount of variety on your plate. Eat right, but cut down on the variety.

Regulating Body Weight

What determines everyday body weight? Why are some people thin and others obese? Not surprisingly, internal and external factors combine to regulate body weight. Some factors, such as genetic predisposition, play a particularly important role (Kowalski, 2004). For example, when identical twins—those sharing the same genetic material—are fed identical diets, they tend to gain virtually the same amount of weight. But if two unrelated people are given matched diets, the differences in weight gain can be substantial (Bouchard et al., 1990). I'm sure you know people who seem to eat continuously and never gain weight; others balloon considerably after only a small daily increase in caloric intake. In short, the amount of food you eat only partly determines what you normally weigh.

set point A natural body weight, perhaps produced by genetic factors, that the body seeks to maintain.

Set Point Some researchers believe we have a natural body weight, or **set point**, that more or less controls our tendency to gain or lose weight (Keesey & Powley, 1975). Most people show little variation in weight from year to year, presumably because their bodies manipulate the motivation to eat, as needed, to maintain the appropriate set point weight. When people go on a diet and dip below their natural weight, well over 90% of them eventually gain that weight back (Martin, White, & Hulsey, 1991). Here again, the idea is that the body adjusts how much it eats, rebounding after a diet, to produce stability in body weight.

What determines our set point? Genetic factors certainly play an important role: People are born with a certain number of fat cells, and this number may constrain just how much weight they can hope to gain or lose (Faust, 1984). Your metabolic rate—how quickly you burn off calories—is another important internal factor; again, it's determined in part by your genetic makeup but also by experience. Recent research in rats indicates that nicotine may lower metabolic set point; if so, although speculative, this may help explain why people sometimes gain weight after they stop smoking (Frankham & Cabanac, 2003).

Concept Review Factors Involved in Hunger

TYPE OF FACTOR	FACTOR	ITS ROLE IN HUNGER
Internal	Chemical signals	Receptors in the liver respond to changes in the amount of *glucose* in the blood. The body also monitors *insulin*, a hormone released by the pancreas. The glucose–insulin interaction is monitored internally. Insulin lowers blood glucose levels, leading to hunger.
	Brain	Regions of the hypothalamus help to control eating, but the precise role of each is unclear. Portions of the brain stem also seem important in the initiation of eating.
External	Eating habits	Learned habits develop through personal experience and modeling the behavior of others. Cultural and ethnic background also play critical roles in when and what you eat.
	Food cues	Factors such as the attractiveness of food, or its association with past pleasures, can serve as an external pull, motivating eating behavior.

Obesity   What causes **obesity**, the condition characterized by excessive body fat? Obesity rates are on the rise, startlingly so over the last decade or so (Corsica & Perri, 2003). Think about how easy it is to get tasty fast food or prepackaged meals or to stuff yourself at an all-you-can-eat buffet. At one time it was thought that overweight people simply lacked sufficient willpower to resist overeating, especially when appealing food was in view (Schachter, 1971). Overweight people are more likely to order a specific dish in a restaurant after a tasty description; they're also more likely than nonobese people to report that food still tastes good after a filling meal.

Yet to explain obesity by appealing to willpower, or to any one psychological factor, is simplistic and misleading. As noted previously, just because someone eats a lot doesn't mean he or she will gain excessive amounts of weight. Some people can eat a lot and gain little weight; others gain weight on limited diets. It's increasingly apparent that genetic factors predispose people to become overweight (Corsica & Perri, 2003). Even so, the ultimate causes of obesity are certain to lie in a complex combination of biology and psychology: metabolic rate, set point, number of fat cells, learned eating habits, cultural role models, level of stress—all contribute in one way or another to weight control. Given the recent and dramatic increases in obesity rates across the world, it is clear that the environment is extremely important; in turn, excessive and prolonged weight gains may change how the brain and body function—the brain's responsiveness to leptin, for instance, may decrease (Morton et al., 2006). Obviously, proper diet, and gaining some control over how much you eat, is important to maintaining a healthy lifestyle; we'll return to this issue in more detail in Chapter 16.

obesity A weight problem characterized by excessive body fat.

Eating Disorders

The quest for a perfect body shape is a multimillion-dollar industry with worldwide influence. As you know, society sets weight ideals, often through advertising, and our notions about attractiveness have become closely tied to meeting these standards (Jacobi & Cash, 1994). There are adaptive reasons why you might seek to resemble role models in your culture (see Chapter 7), but in the case of weight control you're traveling along a dangerous two-way street. If you're extremely overweight, you're more likely to suffer from health problems, so you need to monitor what you eat carefully. But the pursuit of *unrealistic* weight goals, ones that you can never hope to reach because of your genetic background, can lead to significant psychological and physical problems. Unhappiness and depression are the all-too-often by-products of the failure to reach the proper ideal (Rodin, Schank, & Striegel-Moore, 1989).

Interestingly, people's assessments of their own weight, and its relation to these standards, are typically inaccurate. In addition, most people are simply wrong about

Social standards concerning ideal weight have changed considerably over the years.

what members of the opposite sex consider to be an ideal body weight (Fallon & Rozin, 1985). On average, women tend to think men prefer thinner women than men actually do; when men are asked about their own ideal weight, it tends to be heavier than what the average woman rates as most attractive. Not surprisingly, these mistaken beliefs often help promote a negative body image. A negative body image, in turn, can increase one's susceptibility to eating disorders such as *anorexia nervosa* and *bulimia nervosa* (Polivy & Herman, 2002).

Anorexia Nervosa   In a survey of 8th- and 10th-grade students, it was discovered that more than 60% of the females and 28% of the males were actively dieting (Hunnicutt & Newman, 1993). The concern—some would say obsession—with weight and dieting starts early in Western cultures, and for an unfortunate few the consequences can be life threatening. In the condition called **anorexia nervosa**, otherwise healthy people fail to maintain a normal weight level, typically because they have an irrational fear of being overweight. In such cases, a person can literally be starving to death and still see an overweight person in the mirror. The condition mainly affects young women and usually begins between the ages of 15 and 29 (perhaps as many as 1% of adolescent women are affected). Somewhere between 5% and 8% of those with the disorder will eventually die as a result, either from medical problems or from suicide (Herzog et al., 2000). Not surprisingly, the causes of this disorder are complex and may involve genetic as well as psychological factors (Grice et al., 2002).

One of the many features associated with anorexia nervosa is the slowing or ceasing of menstruation and associated reproductive functions. This has led some evolutionary psychologists to suggest that a predisposition for anorexia may have served an adaptive function at some point in our evolutionary history—perhaps because it lowered the likelihood of a young girl becoming pregnant in a stressful environment (Anderson & Crawford, 1992). Although this may have been true at some point in our ancestral past, anorexia nervosa is certainly not adaptive in modern environments. Besides interfering with reproductive functions, the condition is associated with low blood pressure, loss of bone density, and gastrointestinal problems, and it may lead to death. Anorexia nervosa is a very serious and chronic condition that needs immediate and prolonged treatment.

This young woman suffers from anorexia nervosa, a condition characterized by an intense fear of being overweight.

Bulimia Nervosa   In the eating disorder known as **bulimia nervosa**, the principal symptom is *binge eating*. A binge is an episode in which a person consumes large quantities of food, often junk food, in a limited period of time. You might find a person suffering from bulimia locked in a room, surrounded by his or her favorite snacks, eating literally thousands of calories in a single sitting. The condition is marked by a lack of control—the person feels unable to stop the eating or to control the content of the food being consumed. A bingeing episode is often followed by *purging*, in which the person induces vomiting or uses laxatives in an effort to stop potential weight gain. Like anorexia, bulimia primarily affects women and is characterized by an obsessive desire to be thin.

Bulimia is often associated with serious medical problems, although the condition tends not to be life threatening. One of the defining characteristics of bulimia is that the person can appear normal, without the excessive weight loss found in anorexia. Yet repeated vomiting can damage the intestines, lead to nutritional problems, and even promote tooth decay. Psychologically, bulimia nervosa is associated with a preoccupation or obsession with weight gain and a fear of becoming obese. Bulimia can be harder to diagnose than anorexia because the bingeing and purging usually occur in private (Polivy & Herman, 2002).

Until recently, psychologists assumed that eating disorders such as bulimia and anorexia were caused primarily by cultural factors, specifically, the fixation by many Western cultures on staying thin. Anorexia nervosa, in particular, was believed to be a recent phenomenon, rarely diagnosed prior to the 1970s and confined largely to the West. However, recent work suggests that anorexia nervosa may be neither recent nor culture bound. Cases can be traced back to medieval times, and the disorder occurs today in all parts of the world. Bulimia nervosa, on the other hand, may follow a different pattern. A large and significant increase in bulimia apparently occurred in the latter half of the 20th century, and little evidence for the condition currently exists outside of cultures with Western influences (see Keel & Klump, 2003).

anorexia nervosa An eating disorder diagnosed when an otherwise healthy person refuses to maintain a normal weight level because of an intense fear of being overweight.

bulimia nervosa An eating disorder in which the principal symptom is binge eating (consuming large quantities of food) followed by purging, in which the person voluntarily vomits or uses laxatives to prevent weight gain.

Test Yourself | 11.2

Check your knowledge about hunger and eating by deciding whether each of the following statements is True or False. *(You will find the answers in the Appendix.)*

1. A high level of glucose, or blood sugar, is associated with an increased desire for food. *True or False?*
2. The principal symptoms of anorexia nervosa are bingeing and purging. *True or False?*
3. High levels of a hormone called leptin are often found in obese individuals. *True or False?*

4. Obesity is primarily caused by poor dietary habits. *True or False?*
5. Destruction of portions of the hypothalamus can cause a rat to overeat and gain substantial amounts of weight. *True or False?*

Meeting Biological Needs: Sexual Behavior

LEARNING GOALS
- Describe the human sexual response cycle.
- Consider the role of hormones in sexual behavior.
- List external influences on sexual behavior.
- Understand the factors that influence mate selection.
- Discuss factors that may determine sexual orientation.

DOES YOUR WORLD revolve around sex? Maybe not, but sex is still a powerful motivator of people around the world. Every significant culture has well-established rules and guidelines for the teaching and practice of behavior related to courtship,

Besides reproduction, finding an appropriate mate opens the door for companionship, protection, and love.

© Jeremy Horner/Corbis

mating, and the sexual act. Just think for a moment about advertising, television, and movies. Enough said.

But where exactly is the need? What problem is solved by the pursuit and completion of the sexual act? Is there some kind of internal sex gauge that monitors sexual deprivation and adjusts behavior accordingly? You certainly won't die if your goal-directed sexual pursuits fail, as you might from an unsuccessful search for nutrients. So why sex? Why did we evolve a form of reproduction that requires finding a mate as opposed to some kind of asexual reproduction or cloning process?

Engaging in a sexual act can put you at risk, either from predators or from disease. It also takes a lot of time and effort to find an appropriate mate—time and energy that might be better spent satisfying basic energy needs.

Evolutionary biologists and psychologists have spent a lot of time considering the costs and benefits of sexual reproduction (e.g., Geary, Vigil, & Byrd-Craven, 2004). Some have argued that sex introduces genetic variation within the species, which can help individual genes survive and compete in changing environments. But, of course, sexual motivation has its advantages within a single lifetime too. In addition to the pleasurable and reinforcing aspects of sex, selection of a mate opens the door for companionship, protection, and love. In this section of the chapter, we'll consider some of the specifics of sexual motivation, beginning with a brief discussion of the human sexual response cycle. Then we'll look at the internal and external factors that motivate sexual behavior. We'll conclude with a look at issues involved in mate selection and sexual orientation.

The Sexual Response Cycle

Humans are capable of wide and imaginative varieties of lovemaking, but biologically the sexual response follows a standard four-step sequence (see ▌Figure 11.3). As documented by researchers William Masters and Virginia Johnson (1966), who spent years studying the human sexual response in the laboratory, the response cycle begins with an **excitement phase**. Sexual excitement is characterized by changes in muscle tension, increased heart rate and blood pressure, and a rushing of blood into the genital organs. In men, the increased blood supply causes an erection in the penis; in women, the clitoris swells and the lining of the vaginal walls becomes lubricated.

The excitement phase then shifts into a **plateau phase**, during which sexual arousal continues to increase, at a slower rate, toward a maximum point. The

excitement phase The first component of the human sexual response cycle; it's characterized by changes in muscle tension, increased heart rate and blood pressure, and a rushing of blood into the genital organs.

plateau phase The second stage in the human sexual response cycle. Arousal continues to increase, although at a slower rate, toward a preorgasm maximum point.

penis becomes fully erect, and vaginal lubrication increases. Other changes begin that are appropriate to the reproductive process—the internal shape of the vagina changes in preparation for the receipt of the sperm-laden semen; the testes of men rise up in preparation for ejaculation. Sexual release is next, in the **orgasmic phase**, and occurs in the form of rhythmic contractions in the sex organs; in men, these rhythmic contractions are accompanied by ejaculation. Interestingly, the subjective experience of the orgasm is apparently quite similar for males and females despite the obvious physiological differences (Mah & Binik, 2002). When asked to review written descriptions of the orgasmic experience, outside readers usually can't tell whether a description was written by a man or a woman (Proctor, Wagner, & Butler, 1974).

The sexual response cycle is completed with a **resolution phase**, during which arousal returns to normal levels and, at least for men, there is a *refractory period* where further stimulation fails to produce visible signs of arousal or orgasm. The length of the resolution phase is highly variable—it can last anywhere from a few minutes to several days—and no one is quite sure exactly what determines when it will end. Age and prior frequency of sexual release seem to be important factors, as is the degree of emotional closeness with one's partner (Crooks & Baur, 2008).

Internal Factors

For most of the animal kingdom, including primates, sexual behavior is strongly controlled by chemical messengers (sex hormones) that rise and fall in cycles (Pfaff, 1999). A female rat will assume a characteristic posture—signaling receptivity to mounting and copulation by the male—but only during the time in her hormonal cycle when she is most likely to become impregnated. She'll adjust her posture to prepare for the weight of the male, she'll move her tail aside, and she'll even approach and nuzzle the male to ensure his attention. But these behaviors are tightly locked to the presence of the appropriate hormones—estradiol and progesterone in the case of the female rat. If these hormones are absent, the female will show no interest in sex at all, choosing instead to display indifference or hostility toward the sexually active male. If these hormones are injected artificially, sexual receptivity can be induced under conditions in which it would not normally occur (Lisk, 1978). As with the female,

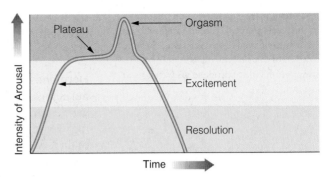

FIGURE 11.3 The Sexual Response Cycle
The human sexual response is believed to follow a four-component biological sequence: (1) During an initial excitement phase, arousal increases rapidly. (2) During the *plateau phase*, arousal increases steadily but more slowly. (3) In the *orgasmic phase*, sexual release occurs. (4) In the *resolution phase*, arousal falls back toward normal levels. For men, the resolution phase is characterized by a refractory period during which further stimulation fails to produce visible signs of arousal or orgasm. (Based on Masters & Johnson, 1966)

orgasmic phase The third stage in the human sexual response cycle. It's characterized by rhythmic contractions in the sex organs; in men, ejaculation occurs. There is also the subjective experience of pleasure, which appears to be similar for men and women.

resolution phase The fourth and final stage in the human sexual response cycle. Arousal returns to normal levels. For men, there is a refractory period during which further stimulation fails to produce visible signs of arousal.

Animals often show rigid courtship and mating rituals that are largely under the control of internal hormones.

resolution phase The fourth and final stage in the human sexual response cycle. Arousal returns to normal levels. For men, there is a refractory period during which further stimulation fails to produce visible signs of arousal.

sexual behavior of the male rat depends on the presence of the appropriate hormone—testosterone. If testosterone is absent, so too is the desire to have sex.

Hormones and Human Sexuality   Humans also show regular variations in the hormones relevant to sex and reproduction. These sets of hormones—*estrogens* in women and *androgens* in men—play a critical role in physical development, affecting everything from the development of the sex organs to the wiring structure of the brain (see Chapter 3). But the initiation and control of adult sexual behavior doesn't appear to be a matter of simply mixing and matching the right internal chemicals. Human sexual behavior remains largely under our control, although learned social and cultural factors exert an influence. Instead of instinctive posturing and fixed courtship rituals, people in most cultures largely choose when, where, and how they engage in sexual activity.

This doesn't mean that hormones aren't important in human sexual behavior. There's some evidence that a woman's peak of sexual desire occurs in the middle of her menstrual cycle, near the time of ovulation, although the nature of the sexual relationship may matter (Pillsworth, Haselton, & Buss, 2004). There's also evidence that testosterone affects both male and female sexual desire. For example, when testosterone levels are reduced sharply—as occurs, for instance, following removal of the testes (medical castration) in men—there's often a loss of interest in sex. In fact, sex offenders are sometimes treated by administering drugs that block the action of testosterone. But neither males nor females are rigidly controlled by these hormones. Some castrated men continue to enjoy and seek out sexual encounters, even without hormone replacement therapy. Similarly, women continue to seek out and enjoy sexual relations after menopause when the levels of female sex hormones decline (Matlin, 2003).

Certain smells can be highly arousing, although in humans it's more learning than biology that makes the perfume industry a success.

© Michael Marzelli/Index Stock Imagery

External Factors

Rather than appealing to hormones to explain sexual desires, many psychologists focus instead on the value, or incentive, of the sexual act. Clearly, there's something about the internal wiring of the brain that makes the sexual act itself immensely rewarding for most people. The sight of an attractive person acts as a signal for something pleasurable, and we are pulled, or motivated, toward an object that may lead to reinforcing sexual release.

Not a very romantic description of sexual desire, to be sure, but it's the sexual "signals" in our environment that often stimulate sexual desire. Both men and women are sexually aroused by explicit visual stimuli, although women, if questioned, are less likely to report the arousal (Murnen & Stockton, 1997). If excitement is measured through physiological recording devices attached to sensitive genital regions, men and women show very similar arousal responses to erotic pictures and movies (Rubinsky et al., 1987). The way people dress and wear their hair, the shapes of their bodies—all contribute to popular conceptions of attractiveness and help to promote sexual interest.

Touch and Smell   Touch is another important external source of sexual arousal. When stimulated, certain regions of the body (known commonly as *erogenous zones*) are highly arousing for most people and may act as one of the few completely natural, or unlearned, arousal sources (although other "erotic zones" may develop or be influenced by experience). We frequently communicate through touch, and touch is an important source of information in all corners of the world (McDaniel & Anderson, 1998).

In contrast, for many animals odor or smell initiates sexual interest. In Chapter 5 we discussed chemicals called *pheromones* that are released by the females of many species during periods of receptivity. Pheromones are odor-producing chemicals, and they drive dogs, pigs, and many other creatures into a sexual frenzy. There's no strong evidence that human pheromones affect sexual desire, but studies have reported increased sexual activity for men wearing synthetic human pheromones (compared to a placebo control; Cutler, Friedman, & McCoy, 1998). How a person smells definitely matters—both men and women report that odor is an important factor in selecting a lover (Herz & Cahill, 1997). Moreover, as you learned in Chapter 5, women seem to prefer the scent of men who show physical traits suggestive of "good genes," such as facial symmetry; moreover, these preferences are strongest when the women are most fertile (Thornhill et al., 2003).

Mate Selection

How do we choose a mate, and what determines who we'll consider attractive and desirable? Not surprisingly, our conceptions of attractiveness are influenced by both biological and sociocultural factors (see Chapter 13). Societies have unique cultural definitions of attractiveness, their own rules for attracting a mate, and different views on what kinds of sexual behavior are considered appropriate.

Sexual Scripts   Many psychologists believe we acquire **sexual scripts** as we develop—these are learned programs that instruct us on how, why, and what to do in our interactions with sexual partners (Gagnon, 1990; Gagnon & Simon, 1973). Sexual scripts may differ from one culture to the next, and they contribute to the differences seen in male and female sexual behavior. Among other things, sexual scripts affect the attitudes we hold toward the sexual act. Boys typically learn, for example, to associate sexual intimacy with genital fondling; girls are more likely to identify intimacy with romantic love. These scripts affect expectations and can result in miscommunication between the sexes. For instance, more than half of teenage girls who engage in premarital sex expect to marry their partners, but this expectation is true for only 18% of their male partners (Coles & Stokes, 1985). Sexual scripts may also account, in part, for why men sometimes employ aggression or strategies based on force to help them achieve their sexual interests (Ryan, 2004).

sexual scripts Learned cognitive programs that instruct us on how, why, and what to do in our interactions with sexual partners.

Evolutionary Influences   Despite the many differences that exist in the formation of sexual scripts, some mating strategies occur worldwide. In nearly every culture men are more likely than women to pursue *short-term* sexual strategies—brief affairs or one-night stands. In interviews with college students, Buss and Schmitt (1993) found that most men weren't bothered very much by the idea of having sexual intercourse with a woman they'd met only an hour before; for most women, the idea of such casual sex was a "virtual impossibility." Across all parts of the world, men seem to value attractiveness in a long-term mating partner, usually prefer to mate with women who are on the average younger than themselves, and report wanting more variety in their sexual partners (D. M. Buss, 1989; Schmitt, 2003). Women, on the other hand, tend to place much greater value on a mating partner's financial prospects than men do—a pattern that again holds across the world (see ▌Figure 11.4).

The fact that these differences are present in every society suggests there may be adaptive reasons for these gender-based behaviors—or that the behaviors themselves may be adaptations. Men might pursue multiple sexual partners to increase the likelihood of successful reproduction (Dawkins, 1986). Women might prefer a man of high economic means because the responsibility of rearing and nurturing a child often falls on the woman's shoulders. According to Buss and Schmitt (1993), the sexual strategies of men and women are best understood from the perspective of evolution. Throughout evolutionary history, men and women have faced gender-specific

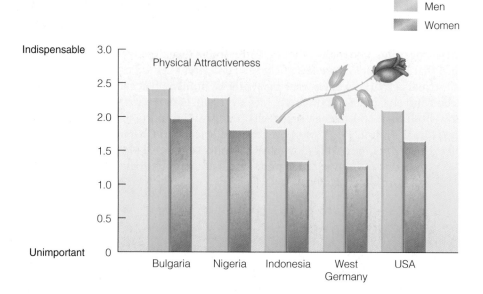

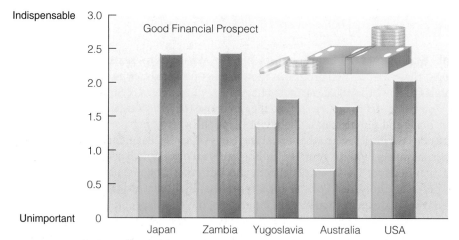

FIGURE 11.4 Cross-Cultural Mating Strategies
Men and women in different parts of the world were asked to rate the importance of physical attractiveness and financial prospects in a long-term partner. On average, men rated physical attractiveness higher than women did, and women were more likely than men to value a partner's financial prospects. (Data from Buss & Schmitt, 1993)

sexual orientation A person's sexual and emotional attraction to members of the same sex or the other sex; homosexuality, heterosexuality, and bisexuality are all sexual orientations.

reproductive problems, and their attitudes and mating rituals have probably developed, in part, to help resolve these problems (Buss, 2000, 2004).

At the same time, it's misleading to focus too much on gender differences—there are many similarities in how men and women view prospective mates. It's also very difficult to disentangle evolutionary influences from what may simply be learned social "roles" (Eagly & Wood, 1999). As noted previously, human sexual behavior shows considerable flexibility—the biological forces of nature influence but need not determine our final behavior. We'll return to the debate about the roles of biology versus the environment, specifically with respect to conceptions of attractiveness, in Chapter 13.

Sexual Orientation

The term **sexual orientation** refers to whether one is sexually and emotionally attracted to members of the same sex or other sex. The term *homosexual* is applied when the attraction is predominantly to members of the same sex; *heterosexual* refers to the more typical other-sex attraction. Estimates of the number of people in the United States who fit the description of homosexual vary, ranging from 1 to 2% to perhaps as high as 10%, depending on how the term is defined (Savin-Williams, 2006). Exact numbers are difficult to determine, partly because people are often reluctant to disclose intimate information about sexual preference. Moreover, in some respects sexual orientation is best seen as a continuum rather than as a category with fixed boundaries. People who are predominantly homosexual sometimes seek out heterosexual relationships, and many heterosexuals have had sexual experiences with members of the same sex.

But what accounts for a sexual and emotional preference for members of the same sex? If the purpose of sexual desire is to procreate—to ensure continuation of the species—in what way can homosexuality be considered adaptive? There's no simple answer to this question, although certainly same-sex relationships have nurturing qualities that go well beyond sexual encounters. For many years psychologists believed that homosexuality developed as the result of experience, particularly the experiences children have with their parents. Homosexuality was considered to be an abnormal condition that arose from dysfunctional home environments, usually as a consequence of having a domineering mother and a passive father. But this view is no longer widely accepted, primarily because a close examination of family histories revealed that the home environments of heterosexuals and homosexuals are actually quite similar (Bell, Weinberg, & Hammersmith, 1981).

Sexual orientation is probably determined, at least in part, by biological factors. When researcher Simon LeVay (1991) compared the autopsied brains of homosexual and heterosexual men, he discovered that a cluster of neurons associated with the hypothalamus was consistently larger in heterosexual men. Exactly how or why this portion of the brain influences sexual orientation is unknown. There have also been reports suggesting a genetic locus for sexual orientation. For example, twin studies have revealed that if one identical twin is homosexual, there is an approximately 50% chance that the other twin will share the same sexual orientation; for fraternal twins or nontwin brothers and sisters, the likelihood that both will be homosexual is considerably lower (Kirk et al., 2000). Systematic analyses of the chromosomes of homosexual brothers have also provided preliminary evidence for what the researchers believe might be a "gay gene" (Hamer et al., 1993), although the data remain controversial (Mustanski, Chivers, & Bailey, 2002).

It's simply too early to tell what all these results mean. The biological findings remain correlational; we simply know that sexual orientation may be *associated* with certain brain structures or genetic markers—but correlational data don't allow us to determine the *cause* of sexual orientation. Moreover, it seems very unlikely that biological factors alone will solve the mysteries of sexual orientation—after all, 50% of identical twins of homosexuals do not share this orientation. The environment is certain to play an important role, but the nature of that role has yet to be determined. Finally, remember that sexual orientation is not really a fixed attribute of a person, like blue eyes or blond hair; we're attracted to others for many reasons, and there may be multiple pathways and reasons for particular sexual preferences.

Test Yourself 11.3

Check your knowledge about the internal and external factors that control sexual behavior by deciding whether each of the following statements is True or False. *(You will find the answers in the Appendix.)*

1. In the human sexual response cycle, the period just prior to orgasm is called the plateau phase. *True or False?*
2. It is possible to affect sexual desire in men by altering the natural levels of the hormone testosterone in the body. *True or False?*
3. Across the world, men value attractiveness in a long-term mating partner and universally prefer to mate with women who are, on average, younger than themselves. *True or False?*
4. Twin studies have revealed that if one identical twin is homosexual, there is an approximately 50% chance that the other twin will share the same sexual orientation. *True or False?*

Expressing and Experiencing Emotion

LEARNING GOALS
- Examine the evidence for and against basic emotions.
- Understand the role of arousal in emotional experience.
- Describe the subjective experiences of anger, happiness, and disgust.
- Differentiate among the James-Lange, Cannon-Bard, and two-factor theories of emotion.

WE TURN NOW to the expression and experience of emotions. As we discussed at the beginning of the chapter, emotions are complex psychological events that involve a mixture of reactions: (1) a *physiological response* (usually arousal), (2) an *expressive reaction* (distinctive facial expression, body posture, or vocalization), and (3) some kind of *subjective experience* (internal thoughts and feelings). Each of these components is shown in ▌Figure 11.5.

Why experience emotions in the first place? Psychologists generally believe emotions help us adapt to rapidly changing environmental conditions. Emotions are powerful motivators of behavior—they help us prioritize our thoughts and force us to focus on finding problem solutions. Physiological arousal, for instance, prepares the body for "fight or flight" and helps us direct and sustain our reactions in the face of danger. Through expressive behaviors, such as the characteristic facial grimace of anger, it's possible to communicate our mental state instantly to others. Emotions can even stimulate social behaviors. People perform better and are more likely to help others when they feel happiness (Hoffman, 1986); people are also more likely to volunteer aid after doing something for which they feel guilt (Carlsmith & Gross, 1969).

Are There Basic Emotions?

Can you name all the important emotions? The English language is full of words, literally hundreds in fact, that relate in one way or another to emotions. But are there hundreds of emotions, or just a basic few? This seems like a simple question, but it's one that's perplexed researchers for decades (Russell, 2003). To get a sense of the difficulty, try compiling your own list of basic emotions. While you're at it, ask your friends and see how much you agree. Let's see: anger, fear, joy . . . how about interest, loathing, jealousy, or distraction? Psychologists have been compiling their own lists for decades without general agreement.

If forced to choose, most people (including emotion researchers) agree on about a half-dozen. Most lists include anger, fear, happiness, and sadness (Ekman, 1999; Ortony & Turner, 1990). Researchers who believe these emotions are basic, or universal, argue convincingly that certain emotions, such as anger, increase the chances of survival. People also have no trouble recognizing expressions of anger, fear, sadness, and happiness in other people. Paul Ekman and his colleagues asked volunteers to match photographs of grimacing, smiling, or otherwise distinctive facial displays to a number of basic emotion labels. There was wide agreement on six fundamental emotions: happiness, surprise, fear, sadness, anger, and disgust combined with contempt (Ekman, 1992; Ekman & Friesen, 1986).

Facial Expressions and Culture   One of the signature characteristics of an emotion is a facial expression. Regardless of where you look in the world, people identify facial expressions with emotional states. For example, a furrowed brow and a square mouth with pursed lips signify anger worldwide (Ekman & Friesen, 1975). Ekman and Friesen even tested members of a rural, isolated culture in New Guinea. These people had no experience with Western culture, yet they correctly identified the emotions expressed in photographs of Caucasian faces. Similarly, when U.S. college students were later shown photos of the New Guinea people acting out various emotions, they too were able to identify the emotions with a high degree of accuracy. Although

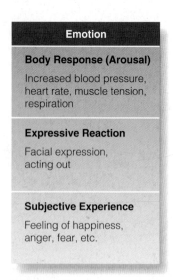

Emotion
Body Response (Arousal)
Increased blood pressure, heart rate, muscle tension, respiration
Expressive Reaction
Facial expression, acting out
Subjective Experience
Feeling of happiness, anger, fear, etc.

▌**FIGURE 11.5** The Composition of Emotion
Emotions are complex experiences that involve (1) a *physiological response*; (2) an *expressive reaction*; and (3) some kind of *subjective experience*.

it's not clear that emotion labels necessarily mean the same thing across cultures (Russell, 1994), most researchers are convinced there's some universal recognition of emotion from facial expressions (Russell, Barchorowski, & Fernandez-Dols, 2003).

The cross-cultural results are important because they suggest the expression of emotion may have a biological or genetic origin. Babies show a wide range of emotional expressions at a very young age (Izard, 1994), and even babies who are born blind, or hearing impaired and blind, show virtually the same facial expressions as sighted babies (Eibl-Eibesfeldt, 1973). It appears people may purse their lips and furrow their brow when they're mad because these tendencies are built directly into the genetic code rather than having been learned. The idea that there are universal facial expressions certainly makes adaptive sense because facial expressions are excellent signals to others about our current internal state (Ekman & Keltner, 1997).

The Facial-Feedback Hypothesis   Some researchers have even suggested that feedback from the muscles in the face helps to determine the internal emotional experience. According to the **facial-feedback hypothesis**, muscles in the face deliver signals to the brain that are then interpreted, depending on the pattern, as subjective

facial-feedback hypothesis The proposal that muscles in the face deliver signals to the brain that are then interpreted, depending on the pattern, as a subjective emotional state.

Different emotions are often associated with particular facial expressions. Can you identify the emotion expressed in each of these photos?

emotional states (Tomkins, 1962). Other researchers suggest there may be direct connections between expressions and physical changes in the brain. For example, smiling can alter the volume of air that is inhaled through the nose; these changes, in turn, can affect the temperature of the brain, which, in turn, might affect mood (McIntosh et al., 1997; Zajonc, Murphy, & McIntosh, 1993).

The facial-feedback hypothesis suggests an interesting possibility: If asked to adopt a particular facial expression artificially, will you experience a corresponding change in emotion? In fact, some kinds of forced smiling, frowning, or grimacing do appear to modulate emotional reports, although the effects may be small (e.g., Soussignan, 2002). You can try this for yourself: Try forcing yourself to smile or grimace in an exaggerated way. Do you feel any different? Some therapists recommend that clients who are depressed literally force themselves to smile when they're feeling depressed.

How Convincing Is the Evidence?   The link among facial expressions, biology, and emotion suggests that certain emotions may be universal (Izard, 2007). But does the fact that people universally have distinct facial expressions for fear, anger, or happiness really allow us to conclude that these emotions are somehow more primary or basic than others? Some psychologists think not. Remember, many psychologists disagree about which emotions belong on the basic list. Does interest, wonder, or guilt belong? How about shame, contempt, or elation? Each of these terms has been identified as basic by at least one prominent emotion researcher. The problem is that humans are capable of an enormous range of emotional experiences. Consider the differences among fear, terror, panic, distress, rage, and anxiety. It is clearly appropriate to use each of these terms in some circumstances and not in others. How can we explain a complex emotion such as terror? If it's not a basic emotion, is it somehow manufactured in the brain by combining or blending more fundamental emotions such as fear, surprise, and possibly anger?

Many psychologists believe it's not possible to explain human emotional experiences by manipulating and combining a set of basic emotions. Rather than basic emotions, they argue, it's better to think of basic response components that are *shared* by a wide variety of emotional experiences (e.g., Barrett, 2006). For example, the furrowed brow commonly seen in anger is not exclusive to anger but also occurs when people are frustrated, puzzled, or even just working hard on a task. The furrowed brow may occur in any situation in which a person is somehow blocked from reaching a goal; its appearance, by itself, is not sufficient to infer that the person is angry.

It may help to think about the analogy of human language. There are hundreds of different languages across the world, and each follows certain universal rules (relating to sound and word combinations). But it doesn't make any sense to argue that some of these languages are more basic than others. Human languages are built up from basic components and share many features in common. Similarly, when people are in the grip of an emotion, they may experience many basic and universal conditions (such as a tendency to smile or frown, approach or avoid), but these are merely the components of emotion, not the emotions themselves (Russell, 2003; Turner & Ortony, 1992).

The Emotional Experience: Arousal

Psychologists may disagree about whether there are basic emotions, but everyone agrees about certain aspects of the emotional *experience*. Virtually all emotions, for instance, lead to *physiological arousal*. Muscles tense, heart rate speeds up, and blood pressure and respiration rates skyrocket. These emotional symptoms come from activity of the autonomic nervous system as it prepares the muscles and organs of the body for a fight-or-flight response. We usually experience emotions in situations that are significant for one reason or another—for instance, the car of a drunken driver swerves sharply into our path, or the sound of breaking glass from the basement

CRITICAL THINKING

Have you ever heard actors talk about how they "become the role" when they're playing emotional parts? What might a psychologist tell an actor to help him or her understand why this happens?

window startles us awake. It's adaptive for the body to react quickly in such cases, and the rapid onset of physiological arousal serves that function well.

But emotional arousal can have a negative side as well. Too much arousal can lead to a breakdown in behavioral, biological, or psychological functioning. ▌Figure 11.6 shows the relationship that exists between level of arousal and task performance. Notice the pattern looks like an arch or an inverted U. For a given task, as arousal levels increase from low to moderate, performance generally rises. Some people perform better under pressure—the track star runs a little faster or jumps a little higher. You may well perform better on a test if the test is particularly important. But too much pressure, which causes too much arousal, causes a sharp drop-off or breakdown in task functioning. Did you have trouble thinking when you took the SAT? Too much emotional pressure can create a level of arousal that hurts rather than helps normal mental functioning.

Understanding the relationship between arousal and performance has helped psychologists interpret behavior in a variety of situations. For example, you may remember from Chapter 8 that people who witness crimes are sometimes inaccurate in their later recollections. One factor that contributes to these inaccuracies is the high level of arousal generated in crime scenes. If someone holds a gun to your head, your level of arousal is likely to block normal cognitive processing. You're simply too aroused to process the details of the crime scene in a manner that will lead to effective remembering. Moreover, as you'll see in Chapter 13, the relationship between arousal and performance also helps us to understand how our behavior changes in the presence of other people—our performance is either facilitated or impaired when other people are around, perhaps because the presence of others changes our overall level of arousal.

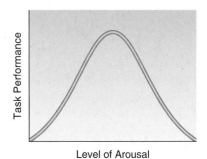

▌**FIGURE 11.6** Arousal and Task Performance
For a given task, performance tends to be best at intermediate levels of arousal. Too little or too much arousal often leads to a decrease in performance.

The Emotional Experience: Subjective Reactions

Experiencing an emotion involves much more than a facial expression or a flood of physiological arousal. Your thoughts, your perceptions, and the things you notice in the environment all change when you experience an emotion. But as we discussed earlier, it's difficult to measure the internal experience accurately and reliably. After all, the emotional experience is by definition personal and subjective. We can ask someone what it feels like to be angry, happy, or scared, but the constraints of language restrict the answers we receive. Some cultures don't even have a word in their language to describe the concept of an emotion. The Ifaluks of Micronesia, for example, have only the word *niferash*, which roughly translates as "our insides" (Lutz, 1982; Matsumoto, 1994).

Anger   It is possible to study the conditions that lead to emotions. For example, in the case of *anger*, people have been asked to keep daily and weekly records, noting the specific situations that made them mad. Most people get angry at least several times a week (but to different degrees); some experience the emotion several times a day (Averill, 1983). Anger clearly serves an adaptive function: It causes us to tackle our problems head on and express our grievances, and it also serves as a signal to others that they should change their ways or avoid interaction.

What causes anger? Not surprisingly, the causes are many (Berkowitz & Harmon-Jones, 2004). If you're restrained in some way, physically or psychologically, you're likely to get mad. More generally, people tend to get angry when their expectations are violated. If you're counting on someone to act a certain way, and these expectations are violated, you'll probably get mad. This is one of the reasons we often get angry at the ones we love. We tend to expect more from the people we love, which, in turn, increases the chances that our expectations will be violated. We also get angry when unpleasant things happen, even if it doesn't involve the violation of an expectation. I bet you get mad when you trip over something on the sidewalk or bang your knee against a wall. Right? Physical pain, physically unpleasant situations, and major social stresses all reliably lead to anger.

Is the expression of anger healthy psychologically? Psychologists remain undecided about the benefits of "venting" anger or blowing off steam. On one hand, expressing your feelings may have a cathartic effect: The expression of anger can lead to an emotional release that is ultimately calming. On the other hand, getting physically angry could well increase the chances that you'll get angry again (Tavris, 1989). When you express anger, and feel the calming effect that follows, you reinforce or reward the anger response. Some psychologists have found that encouraging people to express their feelings of anger or hostility leads to more expressions or feelings of anger in the future (Bushman, 2002). The expression of anger can also lead to increased risk-taking and other kinds of self-defeating behavior. We'll return to the effects of anger, specifically on stress and health, in Chapter 16.

Happiness The idea that anger arises from violations of expectations also helps account for the experience of *happiness*. Overall, there is little, if any, relationship between observable characteristics such as age, sex, race, or income and the experience of happiness (Myers & Diener, 1995). Instead, people seem to gain or lose happiness as a result of the comparisons they make—either with others (a well-known tendency called *social comparison*) or with things or experiences from their past (Cacioppo & Gardner, 1999). People set standards for satisfaction, and they're happy to the extent that these standards are maintained or surpassed. The trouble is that our standards are constantly changing—Eddie and Lucinda may be able to keep up with the Joneses next door, but there's always the Mendenhalls down the street who just bought that new boat. Once people reach a certain level of satisfaction, they form a new level, and then another, and never quite attain complete happiness.

Actually, many psychological judgments, not just emotions, are linked to comparisons with some standard, or *adaptation level*. You may recall from Chapter 5 that whether we hear one tone as louder than another depends on how loud the standard tone is to begin with. Human judgments are relative—there's no sense in which a tone is "loud," a light is "bright," or a person is "happy" or "sad" without answering the question, "Relative to what?" Even negative events can seem positive if they are placed in the right context. For example, arguing with a spouse is rated more positively if it's preceded by the rating of an extremely negative event, such as a death in the family (Schwarz & Strack, 1998). A study of athletes at the 1992 Olympic Games revealed that bronze medal winners (third place) were actually happier than silver medal winners (second place); presumably, the bronze medalists focused on the accomplishment of winning a medal, whereas the silver medalists saw themselves as failing to reach gold (Medvec, Madey, & Gilovich, 1995).

The fact that happiness is relative helps to explain some phenomena that might seem a bit mysterious. Why is the couple who just won the multimillion-dollar lottery still bickering? Why is Ed, who recently succeeded in getting the most popular girl in class to hang out with him, now anxiously seeking the amorous attention of someone else? How can that homeless man, with only scraps to eat and tattered clothes, wake up every morning with a smile on his face? Happiness is not some Holy Grail that can be sought and sometimes found—it's an elusive and fickle condition that depends on constantly changing standards and comparisons.

Disgust Usually included in the group of basic emotions is *disgust*, a marked aversion toward something distasteful (literally meaning "bad taste"). It's easy to appreciate why this emotion is an important tool for the adaptive mind, especially as a mechanism to make certain we select and reject the appropriate foods. The facial expression that typically accompanies disgust is itself an adaptive reaction to a potentially harmful substance. You wrinkle your nose and your mouth drops open in a characteristic gape. Wrinkling the nose closes off the air passages, cutting off any

© John Livzey

Would you use this toothbrush?

offending odor; the gaping expression "causes the contents of the mouth to dribble out" (Rozin & Fallon, 1987, p. 24).

Yet there is a psychology to the emotion of disgust that extends beyond its role in food rejection. To illustrate, suppose you come home one evening and find a cockroach nesting on your toothbrush. Is it conceivable that you would ever use that toothbrush again? Suppose I dropped it into boiling water for a while to ensure sterilization. Would you use it now? Probably not by choice. In a study by Paul Rozin and his colleagues, a dead but sterilized cockroach was dropped into a glass of juice and offered to thirsty subjects. Not surprisingly, few people showed any interest in drinking the juice, even though they knew the roach had been sterilized (Rozin et al., 1986). Most people are also reluctant to consume their favorite soup if they witness the bowl being stirred by a never-used comb or fly swatter (Rozin & Fallon, 1987).

The experience of disgust seems to be universal—appearing cross-culturally—but the emotion takes time to develop. For example, if children under age 4 are presented with what adults consider a disgusting odor (feces or synthetic sweat), they tend not to be bothered, or they may even react positively. Children under age 2, as any parent knows, are happy to put just about anything into their mouths, even "disgusting" objects. In one study, it was found that 62% of tested children under age 2 would put imitation dog feces in their mouth; 31% would mouth a whole, sterilized grasshopper (Rozin et al., 1986). Children simply have no conception that these objects are potentially harmful—they must learn what not to put in their mouths.

Theories of Emotion: Body to Mind

We've seen that emotions are complex events. People subjectively experience happiness or sadness, but they also experience important changes in their body and on their face. Questions about how these various components interact have stumped emotion researchers for decades. For example, what exactly causes the bodily reaction? Is the arousal caused by the internal subjective experience, or are we happy or sad because our bodies have been induced to react in a particular way?

There are a number of possible explanations (for an overview, see ▮ Figure 11.7). The most natural argument is that the subjective experience drives the physiological reaction. We tremble, gasp, and increase our heart rate because some event has caused us to become afraid. We feel fear, and our body reacts with physiological arousal. Surprisingly, this straightforward view of emotion has been rejected by

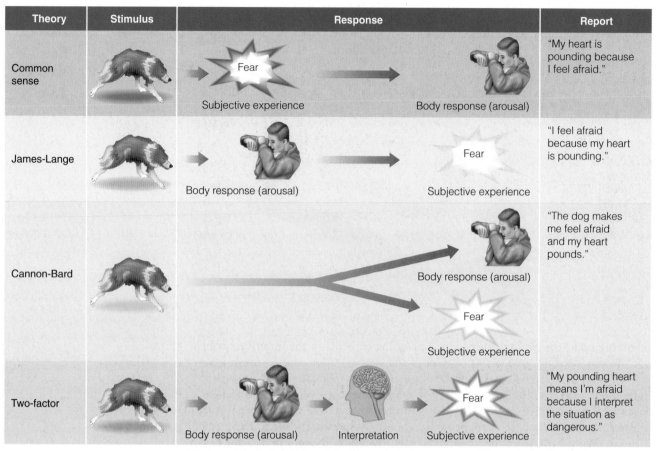

Theory	Stimulus	Response		Report
Common sense		Fear Subjective experience → Body response (arousal)		"My heart is pounding because I feel afraid."
James-Lange		Body response (arousal) → Fear Subjective experience		"I feel afraid because my heart is pounding."
Cannon-Bard		Body response (arousal) Fear Subjective experience		"The dog makes me feel afraid and my heart pounds."
Two-factor		Body response (arousal) → Interpretation → Fear Subjective experience		"My pounding heart means I'm afraid because I interpret the situation as dangerous."

FIGURE 11.7 Four Views of Emotion

The commonsense view, largely rejected by psychologists, assumes that an environmental stimulus creates a subjective experience (fear), which in turn leads to a physiological reaction (arousal). The James-Lange theory proposes instead that the physical reaction drives the subjective experience. In the Cannon-Bard theory, the physical reaction and the subjective experience are assumed to be largely independent processes. In the two-factor theory, it is the cognitive interpretation and labeling of the physical response that drives the subjective experience.

emotion researchers for more than a century. James (1890) saw the commonsense view as backward: "The more rational statement is that we feel sorry because we cry, angry because we strike, afraid because we tremble, and not that we cry, strike, or tremble because we are sorry, angry, or fearful" (p. 1066). Although James believed our interpretation of the situation also plays a role (Ellsworth, 1994; James, 1894), he was convinced that the body reaction occurs before the subjective experience of emotion rather than the other way around.

The James-Lange Theory The idea that the body reaction drives the subjective experience of emotion is known as the **James-Lange theory** of emotion. Lange is coupled with James because Danish physiologist Carl Lange proposed a similar idea at roughly the same time as James. Why reject the commonsense approach in favor of such a counterintuitive view? Actually, neither James nor Lange presented much evidence in support of this account (other than personal impressions). However, some significant predictions can be derived from their view. For instance, imagine we could somehow reduce or eliminate significant body reactions. The James-Lange theory predicts we should lose the corresponding experience of emotion. To test this idea, a number of interviews have been conducted with people suffering from spinal cord injuries. Because of nerve damage, these people have either lost feeling in

James-Lange theory A theory of emotion that argues that body reactions precede and drive the subjective experience of emotions.

Expressing and Experiencing Emotion | 371

major portions of their bodies or at least have reduced sensory feedback. In support of the James-Lange view, some paraplegics have reported a corresponding drop-off in the intensity of their emotional experience (for example, anger lost its "heat"; Hohmann, 1966). Unfortunately, subsequent researchers have failed to confirm this finding (Cobos et al., 2002).

The James-Lange theory also predicts that unique physical changes should accompany each of the different emotional experiences. That is, a particular body response must produce anger, happiness, fear, and so on. But as noted previously, the dominant physiological response during an emotion is *arousal*, and heart rate changes, sweaty palms, and increased breathing rate seem to be characteristic of virtually all emotions rather than just a select few. Think about how your body feels just before an important exam. How about the feelings you have before an important and long-awaited date? Would you describe the emotions as similar?

Recently, sophisticated measuring devices have enabled researchers to record small, previously undetectable changes in body reactions. These new data may eventually help us to distinguish the body reaction for one emotional state from the body reaction of another (Lang, 1994; Levenson, 1992). It turns out that anger, fear, and sadness, for example, may lead to greater heart rate acceleration than an emotion such as disgust; there's also apparently a greater increase in finger temperature during fear than during anger (Levenson, 1992). Neuroimaging studies also reveal differences in patterns of brain activity when people experience different emotions (e.g., Panksepp, 2007), although these data remain somewhat controversial (Barrett & Wager, 2006). Establishing definitive links between emotional states and physiological responses is an important step for emotion researchers, although perhaps not an unexpected one. After all, anger and happiness certainly are experienced differently and therefore must ultimately reflect differences in brain activity.

The Cannon-Bard Theory Historically, it didn't take too long for critics of the James-Lange theory of emotion to emerge. Physiologist Walter Cannon mounted an influential attack in the 1920s. Cannon (1927) recognized that the body reacts in essentially the same way to most emotional experiences. He was also convinced that the conscious experience of emotion has a rapid onset—people feel fear immediately after seeing an attacking dog—but the physiological reactions that come from the autonomic nervous system have a relatively slow onset time (glands need to be activated, hormones need to be released into the bloodstream, and so on). Cannon felt the subjective experience of emotion and the associated body reactions are *independent processes*. Emotions and arousal may occur together, but one doesn't cause the other. Cannon's view was later modified somewhat by Philip Bard, so this approach is now generally known as the **Cannon-Bard theory** of emotion.

The Schachter and Singer Experiment Up to this point, we've discussed three different theories of emotion: (1) people experience emotions subjectively, which then leads to body reactions such as arousal (the commonsense view); (2) the body generates a characteristic internal reaction, which then produces the appropriate emotional experience (James-Lange); and (3) body reactions and subjective experiences occur together, but independently (Cannon-Bard). None of these views remains popular among emotion researchers.

The major problem with this trio of emotion theories is that they fail to take into account the cognitive side of emotion. To understand exactly what this means, we need to consider a rather complex study that was conducted in the early 1960s by psychologists Stanley Schachter and Jerome Singer (see ▌ Figure 11.8). College students were recruited to participate in an experiment they thought was designed to test the effects of vitamin injections on vision. What the students didn't know, however, was that the vitamin cover story was a ploy—rather than vitamins, they were actually injected with either a dose of epinephrine (which produces physiological arousal

Cannon-Bard theory A theory of emotion that argues that body reactions and subjective experiences occur together, but independently.

FIGURE 11.8 The Schacter and Singer Experiment
Volunteer subjects were injected with a drug that produced symptoms of physiological arousal. Half the subjects were informed about the drug's effects; the others were not. When placed in a room with either a euphoric or an angry accomplice, only the uninformed subjects adopted the same mood. Presumably, the informed subjects attributed their arousal symptoms to the drug, whereas the uninformed subjects interpreted the symptoms as an emotional experience.

symptoms) or a dose of saline (which produces no effects). A second manipulated variable was expectation: Half the people in each of the injection groups were told to expect arousal symptoms—as a side effect of the vitamins—and the other half were told to expect no reaction of any kind.

Now let's consider what effect these conditions should have on emotional reactions. Suppose you're sitting in a room, waiting for further instructions from the experimenter, when suddenly your heart begins to race and your palms begin to sweat. According to James-Lange, this arousal should translate into some kind of emotional experience; you might, for example, expect to become scared or irritated. But Schachter and Singer (1962) found that the experience of emotion was determined almost entirely by expectation. Those students who were told to anticipate arousal from the injection showed little emotional reaction to the arousal when it occurred. Only when the arousal was unexpected did people begin to report strong emotions.

Even more interesting, Schachter and Singer were able to influence the quality of the emotion when it occurred. Joining the participant in the waiting room was a disguised member of the experimental team, introduced as another participant in the experiment. Unknown to the real participant, the accomplice was instructed to act in a way that was either playful and euphoric or angry and disagreeable. In later assessments of mood, Schachter and Singer found that aroused but uninformed students tended to adopt the mood of the accomplice. If the accomplice was playful, the students reported feeling happy; if the accomplice was angry, the students reported feeling irritation.

Two-Factor Theory   The results of the Schachter and Singer experiment led to the proposal of the **two-factor theory** of emotion. In two-factor theory, autonomic arousal is still a critical determinant of the emotional experience (factor 1). But equally important is the *cognitive appraisal* or *interpretation* of that arousal when it occurs (factor 2). An intense body reaction may be necessary for the full experience of an emotion, but it's not sufficient. It's how you *interpret* the arousal that ultimately determines your subjective emotion. So, you're scared when you face a venomous snake not only because your body is aroused but also because your mind understands that what's causing the arousal is dangerous. You *label* the arousal and thereby determine the emotion that's experienced.

Like the other theories of emotion we've discussed, two-factor theory has generated its share of criticism. For example, some researchers remain convinced that emotions like anger and fear can arise directly without higher-level interpretation or appraisal (Russell, 2003; Winkielman & Berridge, 2004). However, it's possible to draw several tentative conclusions. First, it's reasonably clear that arousal contributes to the experience of emotion. Second, the situation in which the arousal occurs, and our expectations about the source of the arousal, contribute to the emotional experience. Third, rather than saying the body reaction creates the emotion, or vice versa, it's better to conclude that emotions arise from interactions among several sources: the stimulus event that leads to the reaction, autonomic changes in arousal, and the expectation-based cognitive labels applied to everything involved.

two-factor theory A theory of emotion that argues that the cognitive interpretation, or appraisal, of a body reaction drives the subjective experience of emotion.

CRITICAL THINKING

If expectations play an important role in determining whether an emotion will be experienced, would you expect to find cultural differences in the expression of emotion?

Test Yourself 11.4

Check your knowledge about expressing and experiencing emotion by answering the following questions. (You will find the answers in the Appendix.)

1. For each of the following, pick the component of emotion that best fits the situation: *body response, expressive reaction,* or *subjective experience.*
   a. Sally likes to dance when she's happy: _____
   b. Yolanda grimaces and wrinkles her nose when she sees spaghetti with clam sauce: _____
   c. Mei feels her heart start racing whenever she sees her boyfriend approach: _____
   d. Robert would rather use the words "delighted, glad, pleased, and excited" to describe how he feels, instead of the word "happy": _____
2. Which of the following situations is most likely to produce happiness?
   a. Receiving a B on a test when you were expecting a C
   b. Receiving an A on a test when you were expecting an A
   c. Receiving a C on a test when you were expecting to flunk
   d. Stimulation of the hypothalamus
3. For each of the following, pick the theory of emotion that best fits the situation: *James-Lange, Cannon-Bard,* or *two-factor.*
   a. I love it when my heart starts racing because it makes me feel happy: _____
   b. I must be in love because she just gave me a wink and my heart is racing: _____
   c. I really feel happy right now and, by the way, my heart is also racing: _____
   d. You're not really in love, you just drank too much coffee this morning: _____

Motivation, and its intimate companion, emotion, are highly adaptive processes that help you initiate and direct your behavior, maintain your internal energy needs, and even prolong the species. Each of us simply must do certain things—eat, drink, maintain a constant internal temperature—and psychologists have struggled for decades to discover how the body accomplishes these ends.

Activating Behavior As you've seen, motivation depends on an interplay between internal and external factors. Much of the time behavior is controlled by internal factors that compel us in the direction of a goal. Our bodies are constantly monitoring internal energy levels, and once a disruption in the homeostatic balance is detected, we feel hungry or thirsty and seek to restore the balance. In these cases, it's likely that motivated behavior arises directly as a consequence of biological factors and requires little direct experience with the environment.

But even something as biologically significant as eating or drinking can't be explained by appealing only to innate internal factors. All forms of motivated behavior are influenced by external factors as well. External rewards, or incentives, exert powerful pulling and guiding effects on our actions. Understanding motivation then becomes a matter of specifying how these *external* factors interact with *internal* factors to activate and control behavior. One way in which internal and external factors interact is described by Maslow's notion of a needs hierarchy. The essential component of Maslow's theory is the prioritizing of need: Some needs, especially those critical to survival, must be satis-

fied before others, such as the need for self-actualization, can be pursued.

Meeting Biological Needs: Hunger and Eating Internally, the body monitors everything from the amount and content of food in the stomach to the level of glucose in the blood to determine its energy needs. If the level of glucose falls below a certain level, for example, you start to feel hungry and seek out food. Although researchers are uncertain about its precise function in controlling eating, the hypothalamus is believed to play an important role. But we also eat for reasons that appear unrelated to restoring homeostatic balance. Food, and particularly eating, is clearly reinforcing. As you've seen, people are much more likely to motivate themselves to eat if they like the food—the vigor or intensity with which they respond depends critically on the value, or incentive, of the food. A number of factors, both genetic (such as having a set point) and environmental, play a role in regulating body weight. Eating disorders such as anorexia nervosa and bulimia nervosa tend to have psychological origins related to body image but may be influenced by genetic factors as well.

Meeting Biological Needs: Sexual Behavior Sexual activity is adaptive for a species because it increases the chances that the species will continue. But on an individual level, sex is also reinforcing, and sexual desire compels us to pursue a mate, thereby opening the door for companionship, protection, and love. The sexual response itself consists of four main phases (excitement, plateau, orgasmic, and resolution). Hormones appear to play much less of a role

in controlling sexual desire in humans when compared with other animals. Different cultures have different views of attractiveness and different codes of conduct for sexual activity. Many psychologists believe people acquire sexual scripts that instruct them on how, why, and what to do in their interactions with potential sexual partners. Mate selection and sexual orientation, however, are probably influenced by biological as well as environmental factors.

Expressing and Experiencing Emotion Emotions typically involve a mixture of reactions, including a physiological response (arousal), a characteristic expressive reaction (such as a distinctive facial expression), and some kind of subjective experience (such as the feeling of happiness or sadness). The physical expression of an emotion enables us to communicate our feelings to others. The internal components—arousal, for example—prepare us for action. Thoughts become prioritized, and muscles are ready to respond. Emotions are powerful adaptive tools: They not only increase the likelihood of survival but also make life itself worth living.

The subjective experience of emotion is often relative—whether we feel happy, for example, seems to depend on the comparisons we make with others and with our past experiences. Although a number of theories have tried to explain the relation between arousal and the experience of emotion, most psychologists believe that the experience of emotion depends partly on the presence of a body response—general arousal—and partly on the cognitive appraisals we make about the origin of arousal when it occurs.

Active Summary *(You will find the answers in the Appendix.)*

Activating Behavior

• (1) _____ are unlearned responses controlled by specific external triggering stimuli; they do not adequately explain human behavior. A (2) _____ is an internal state that arises in response to a (3) _____ need. Drives lead to more flexible responses than instincts.

• The term (4) _____ motivation is used to explain (5) _____ directed behavior. The value of the incentive—positive or negative—helps determine whether you'll be motivated to perform a task. An incentive is an external pull with (6) _____ or punishing consequences that helps explain motivated or goal-directed behavior.

• (7) _____ motivation is an internally driven need for success and accomplishment. People who rate high in achievement motivation tend to work (8) _____ and more persistently on tasks. (9) _____ motivation describes behaviors that are entirely self-motivated. (10) _____ rewards sometimes lower intrinsic motivation. (11) _____ factors may explain differences in achievement motivation.

• Usually represented as a pyramid, Maslow's (12) _____ of (13) _____ assumes that needs are prioritized and some must be satisfied before others can be met. Fundamental (14) _____ needs are primary; once they have been met we can work toward fulfilling our needs for personal (15) _____, spiritual meaning, and (16) _____. At the top of the hierarchy is the need to reach our fullest potential, or to (17) _____ - _____.

Meeting Biological Needs: Hunger and Eating

• Both (18) _____ and (19) _____ are involved in the metabolic process, and the levels of each are regulated by the body and (20) _____. Brain areas that signal hunger include the (21) _____, (22) the _____ brain, and the (23) _____. Eating habits are influenced through (24) _____, experience, and modeling. Our eating behavior is partly determined by food (25) _____ and their association with past pleasures and discomforts. Cultural factors can also be important.

• Our natural body weight or (26) _____ point is probably determined partly by (27) _____ and may strongly influence our tendency to gain or lose weight. (28) _____ reflects biological and psychological factors that include set point, (29) _____ rate, number of fat cells, (30) _____ eating habits, cultural role models, and (31) _____ levels.

• People often make inaccurate assessments of their own weight and its relation to (32) _____ ideals, which can result in a (33) _____ body image and increase one's susceptibility to eating disorders. (34) _____ nervosa is a condition in which people fail to maintain a normal body weight. (35) _____ nervosa is a condition in which people purge after binge eating.

Meeting Biological Needs: Sexual Behavior

• The four phases of the human sexual response cycle are (36) _____, (37) _____, (38) _____, and (39) _____. Resolution features a (40) _____ period, during which stimulation fails to produce further (41) _____.

• Hormones control sexual behavior in most species, but human sexual behavior is also influenced largely by (42) _____ cultural factors. Human hormones related to sexual behavior and reproduction differ by sex: the primary sex hormone in females is (43) _____ and (44) _____ are predominant in males.

• Touch is an important source of sexual arousal, especially the stimulation of (45) _____ zones. Odors or smells called (46) _____ may initiate sexual behavior in many species, though not necessarily in humans.

• Attractiveness is strongly influenced by biological and (47) _____ factors. One theory proposes that we acquire sexual (48) _____ that tell us how to interact with sexual partners. Despite individual differences in our scripts, similarities among sexual scripts may be due to (49) _____ influences. In nearly every (50) _____, men are more likely to value physical attractiveness than women, who usually emphasize financial prospects.

• (51) _____ and (52) _____ factors influence sexual (53) _____, or whether a person is attracted to members of the same sex (homosexual) or the other sex (heterosexual).

Expressing and Experiencing Emotion

• The basic (54) _____ expressions of emotions tend to be universal, which suggests that emotions may be (55) _____ in origin. These basic emotions include (56) _____, fear, (57) _____, and sadness. According to the facial-(58) _____ hypothesis, the movement of muscles in the face creates an internal experience that we think of as emotion.

• Emotions are associated with (59) _____ arousal. Very (60) _____ or low levels of arousal tend to disrupt (61) _____.

• Anger is typically associated with having one's (62) _____ violated. Whether or not it's healthful to vent anger is (63) _____. (64) _____ seems to rely on comparing ourselves to others or current experiences with those in the past. (65) _____ is an adaptive emotion that protects us from coming into contact with or ingesting harmful substances and tends to develop with age.

• The most natural way of relating body to mind is to assume that the subjective experience drives the physical reaction (commonsense view). The James-Lange theory assumes the opposite—that the (66) _____ reaction drives the (67) _____ experience of emotion, predicting that unique physical changes should accompany different emotions. The (68) _____-Bard theory proposes that the subjective experience and the physical reaction are (69) _____ processes. Schacter and Singer's (70) _____-factor theory assumes that emotion results from cognitive (71) _____, or interpretation, of autonomic arousal.

Terms to Remember

achievement motive, 347
anorexia nervosa, 357
bulimia nervosa, 357
Cannon-Bard theory, 371
drive, 346
emotions, 343
excitement phase, 358
facial-feedback hypothesis, 365
glucose, 352

homeostasis, 346
incentive motivation, 346
instincts, 345
insulin, 352
intrinsic motivation, 348
James-Lange theory, 370
leptin, 352
motivation, 343
need hierarchy, 349

obesity, 355
orgasmic phase, 359
plateau phase, 359
resolution phase, 359
set point, 354
sexual orientation, 362
sexual scripts, 361
two-factor theory, 373

Media Resources

  ThomsonNOW

www.thomsonedu.com/ThomsonNOW

Go to this site for the link to ThomsonNow, your one-stop study shop. Take a Pre-Test for this chapter and Thomson-Now will generate a personalized Study Plan based on your test results! The Study Plan will identify the topics you need to review and direct you to online resources to help you master those topics. You can then take a Post-Test to help you determine the concepts you have mastered and what you still need to work on.

Companion Website

www.thomsonedu.com/psychology/nairne

Go to this site to find online resources directly linked to your book, including a glossary, flashcards, quizzing, weblinks, and more.

 Psyk.trek 3.0

Check out the Psyk.trek CD-ROM for further study of the concepts in this chapter. Psyk.trek's interactive learning modules, simulations, and quizzes offer additional opportunities for you to interact with, reflect on, and retain the material:

Motivation and Emotion: Elements of Emotion

CHAPTER 12

Personality

In *The Strange Case of Dr. Jekyll and Mr. Hyde*, Robert Louis Stevenson explores the dual nature of human personality through the characters of Jekyll and Hyde. Actually they are one and the same man; Dr. Jekyll transforms himself into the troublesome Mr. Hyde, the personification of evil, by drinking a potion composed of salts and other wholesale chemicals. If you read the novel, you'll see that the results are disastrous for them "both," but the thesis is fascinating for the psychologist to consider.

How reasonable is it to assume that behavior is controlled by fixed psychological characteristics or traits? Are we born with a fundamental "nature," a set of traits that predict our actions throughout our lives? Moreover, assuming these traits exist, is it fair to describe them as "good" or "evil"—are humans, like Luke Skywalker in *Star Wars*, engaged in an unrelenting battle against the dark side of their nature? As you'll see in this chapter, some psychologists believe there are indeed multiple sides to human nature, although few would characterize them as "good" or "evil."

Our topic in this chapter is **personality**, which can be defined as the set of characteristics that distinguishes us from others and leads us to act consistently across situations. At its core the study of personality, like the study of intelligence, is first and foremost the study of individual differences (Cronbach, 1957). People seem to differ in lasting ways: Rowena is outgoing, confident, and friendly; Roger is shy in social settings and has an annoying habit of lying. In a very real sense, personality **traits**, or predispositions to respond in certain ways, define people. Traits make people unique, identifiable, and generally predictable across time. Potentially, we can use them to explain why Rowena's and Roger's actions remain stable and consistent across situations.

personality The distinguishing pattern of psychological characteristics—thinking, feeling, and behaving—that differentiates us from others and leads us to act consistently across situations.

trait A stable predisposition to act or behave in a certain way.

Does every personality have a dark side, waiting to be expressed by the right environmental conditions? Is it possible that mass murderer Henry Lee Lucas, shown here in prison along with photographs of his victims, was simply born with the wrong kind of genes?

© Enrico Ferorelli

From an adaptive perspective, maintaining stability in our thoughts and actions, especially if they lead to successful outcomes, makes sense. Most psychologists believe we possess traits like fearfulness or aggressiveness because those traits increase the likelihood of our survival. But the question of where those traits come from (hint: nature or nurture?) has perplexed researchers for decades. As you read this chapter, think back to the issues we considered in Chapter 10 (intelligence)—you'll find many similarities between the study of intelligence and the study of personality.

Conceptualizing and Measuring Personality

To understand the concept of personality, it's necessary to consider the whole person. This means you can't simply record the actions of someone in a restricted situation or even in several situations. You need to measure the *enduring* aspects of behavior—those things that distinguish you from me consistently across time. To use the analogy of one personality researcher, the focus should be on "not one time at bat in baseball but the season's hitting average, not an evening's flirtation or adventure but marriage or an enduring relationship" (A. H. Buss, 1989, p. 1379). Unfortunately, as you'll see, there's no simple way of addressing this problem; psychologists have relied on a host of techniques to conceptualize and measure personality.

Determining How Personality Develops

What factors in development lead to stable and consistent behaviors? It's one thing to identify and measure a person's lasting traits but quite another to understand their origin. Where do personality traits come from, and what accounts for the individual differences? Why does Roger have that nasty tendency to lie, and why does sweet Rowena always see the sunny side of a rotten situation? It is here, in the study of personality development, that you'll find some of the most ambitious and best-known attempts at psychological theory.

Resolving the Person–Situation Debate

All major theories of personality assume that the environment shapes behavior. However, because personality consists of those traits that remain the same across situations, we're faced with a kind of theoretical puzzle. In essence, personality should be something that's largely independent of the environment. Remember, people are supposed to act the same regardless of the situation. Is behavior really as consistent across situations as many people, including psychologists, assume? In the final section of the chapter, we'll discuss the evidence—and controversy—that bears on this issue.

Conceptualizing and Measuring Personality

LEARNING GOALS
- Discuss how factor analysis helps identify basic personality traits.
- Distinguish among cardinal, central, and secondary traits.
- Describe self-report inventories and projective personality tests.

IT'S NOT NECESSARY to have a complete understanding of personality to identify and measure differences among people. In fact, we probably need some formal way of classifying individual differences before we can know exactly what needs to be explained. **Trait theories** are systems for assessing how people differ, particularly how people differ in their tendencies to act consistently across situations. As a general rule, trait theories use a *psychometric approach*—that is, they seek to identify stable individual differences by analyzing the performances of large groups of people on rating tests or questionnaires.

If you open any dictionary, you'll find thousands of words that fit the everyday definition of a personality trait. In fact, it's been estimated that approximately 1 out of every 22 words in the English language is a trait-related term (Allport & Odbert, 1936). One goal of the trait theorist is to reduce these thousands of descriptive terms to a smaller set of more basic terms—to find a kind of common denominator among groups of terms. For example, when you describe someone with words such as *kind*, *trusting*, and *warm*, you might really be describing a more general characteristic of the person, such as agreeableness or pleasantness. The researcher attempts to identify the basic traits from among the thousands of personality descriptors that are common in the language. How can this be accomplished?

Try coming up with a set of trait words to describe this individual. What are the chances that your words will apply in all situations?

The Factor Analytic Approach

One way to approach the problem is to use the statistical technique of *factor analysis*. As we discussed in Chapter 10, factor analysis is a mathematical procedure that's used to analyze correlations among test responses. The goal is to identify a set of factors that collectively predict test performance. To see how this works in the case of personality, imagine asking a large group of people to rate themselves on a variety of personality characteristics. For example: "On a scale of 1 to 7, how well do you think the term *brooding* is characteristic of you?" When we look at the results, we'll undoubtedly see many individual differences. Some people will see themselves as brooders, others won't; some people will score high on aggressiveness and competitiveness; others will classify themselves as passive and shy.

However, researchers are really interested in how the trait ratings correlate with one another. Do people who rate themselves as, say, "kind" also tend to rate themselves as "warm" and "trusting"? More specifically, can we predict someone's rating on one trait given that we know his or her rating on some other trait? If we can, then it's reasonable to assume that some general personality characteristic, such as pleasantness, is being measured by the more specific personality descriptors. This is the logic behind factor analysis—discover the common denominators for personality by noting which terms cluster statistically in a group.

Source Traits and Superfactors Psychologists frequently apply factor analysis to personality data. For practical reasons, it's common to rely on ratings of personality descriptors, such as "kind" or "warm," which people give about themselves or others. Psychologist Raymond Cattell was able to use rating data of this sort to identify

trait theories Formal systems for assessing how people differ, particularly in their predispositions to respond in certain ways across situations.

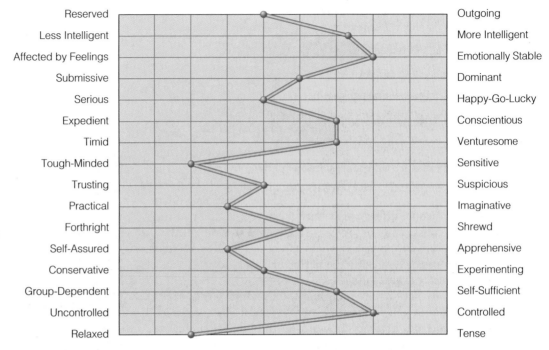

Reserved													Outgoing
Less Intelligent													More Intelligent
Affected by Feelings													Emotionally Stable
Submissive													Dominant
Serious													Happy-Go-Lucky
Expedient													Conscientious
Timid													Venturesome
Tough-Minded													Sensitive
Trusting													Suspicious
Practical													Imaginative
Forthright													Shrewd
Self-Assured													Apprehensive
Conservative													Experimenting
Group-Dependent													Self-Sufficient
Uncontrolled													Controlled
Relaxed													Tense

FIGURE 12.1 A Personality Profile

This is a sample personality profile as measured by Cattell's 16 Personality Factor test. Notice that our personalities are defined by our standing on each of the 16 trait dimensions. (Reprinted with permission from R. B. Cattell, "A 16PF Profile," in *Psychology Today*, pp. 40–46. Copyright © 1973 Sussex Publishers, Inc.)

16 basic personality factors from a set of traits that originally numbered in the thousands (Cattell, Eber, & Tatsuoka, 1970). Cattell's 16 factors, which he called *source traits*, are listed in ▌Figure 12.1. Notice that each factor is shown as a dimension marked by an opposing pole: reserved–outgoing, trusting–suspicious, relaxed–tense, and so on. Any particular individual, such as you, will have a unique personality profile, reflecting your standing on each of the dimensions. So, you might be closer to "reserved" than "outgoing," more "controlled" than "uncontrolled," and have a tendency to be "tough-minded" rather than "sensitive."

However, the factors that are discovered depend partly on how the mathematical technique of factor analysis is applied. Whereas Cattell reported 16 primary factors (along with some additional secondary or second-order factors), Hans Eysenck settled on only three *superfactors*: (1) the dimension of *extroversion*, which refers roughly to how outgoing and sociable you are; (2) the dimension of *neuroticism*, which captures your degree of anxiety, worry, or moodiness; and (3) the dimension of *psychoticism*, which represents your tendencies to be insensitive, uncaring, or cruel toward others (Eysenck, 1970, 1991). Specific personality descriptors, such as "touchy" or "lively," are presumed to reflect some combination of each of the three primary dimensions (see ▌Figure 12.2).

The Big Five Psychologists continue to argue about the number of factors that best characterize personality, which depends partly on the specific types of personality data that are included (Simms, 2007), but increasingly the field is settling on a more intermediate solution: It is now widely believed that the best solution to the factoring problem is to propose *five* basic personality dimensions (McCrae & Costa, 1985, 2003). The so-called **Big Five** personality dimensions include *extroversion, agreeableness, conscientiousness, neuroticism,* and *openness.* Each is listed in ▌Figure 12.3 along with some of the descriptors that identify each trait. So, for example, people who score highly on the extroversion dimension tend to see themselves as talkative, sociable, fun loving, and affectionate.

Notice that *extroversion* and *neuroticism* are two of the three primary dimensions suggested by Eysenck. In fact, Eysenck (1991) believes that psychoticism, his remaining dimension, simply reflects a combination of the Big Five's agreeableness, consci-

Big Five The five dimensions of personality—extroversion, agreeableness, conscientiousness, neuroticism, and openness—that have been isolated through the application of factor analysis.

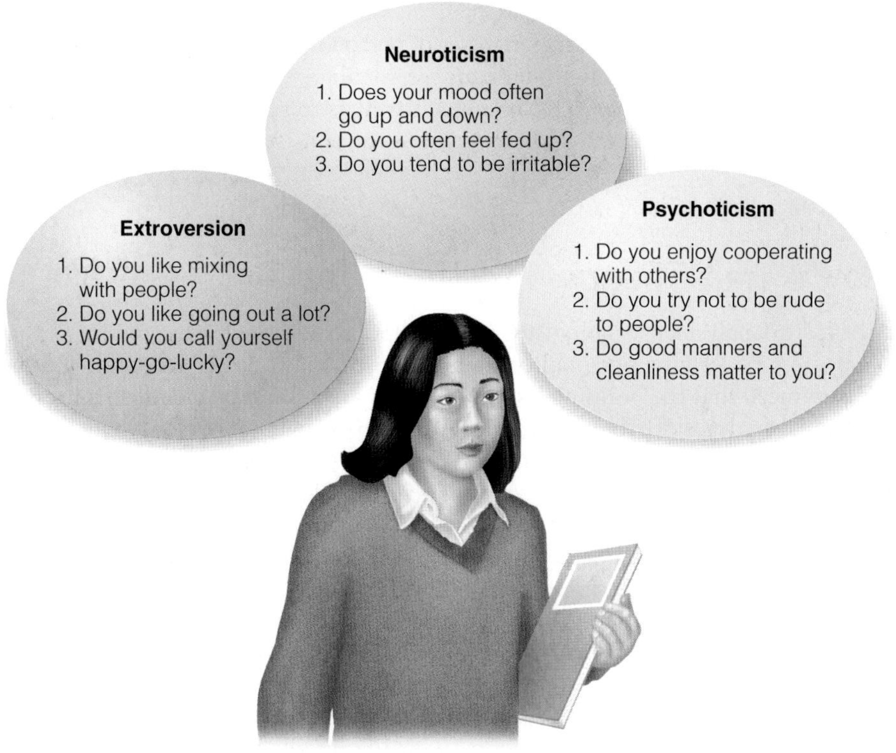

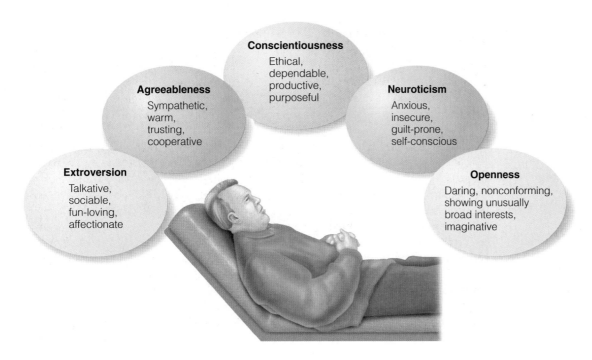

Neuroticism
1. Does your mood often go up and down?
2. Do you often feel fed up?
3. Do you tend to be irritable?

Extroversion
1. Do you like mixing with people?
2. Do you like going out a lot?
3. Would you call yourself happy-go-lucky?

Psychoticism
1. Do you enjoy cooperating with others?
2. Do you try not to be rude to people?
3. Do good manners and cleanliness matter to you?

FIGURE 12.2 Eysenck's Three Primary Dimensions of Personality
Hans Eysenck proposed three primary dimensions of personality: extroversion, neuroticism, and psychoticism. Included in each circle are sample questions of the type used to measure a person's standing on that dimension.
(Questions from Eysenck & Eysenck, 1975)

entiousness, and openness (see also Scholte & De Bruyn, 2004). The debate continues, but the consensus seems to be favoring the Big Five. Studies have analyzed trait ratings collected from around the world, and, regardless of the language used, five basic dimensions seem to best explain the ratings. In addition to supporting the Big Five, the data suggest that the basic structure of personality might be universal rather than dependent on cultural background (Allik & McCrae, 2004).

At the same time, the fact that five (or three) factors can be used to categorize people doesn't tell us anything about the internal processes that determine a

Conscientiousness
Ethical, dependable, productive, purposeful

Agreeableness
Sympathetic, warm, trusting, cooperative

Neuroticism
Anxious, insecure, guilt-prone, self-conscious

Extroversion
Talkative, sociable, fun-loving, affectionate

Openness
Daring, nonconforming, showing unusually broad interests, imaginative

FIGURE 12.3 The Big Five
Many psychologists believe that personality is best analyzed in terms of five fundamental personality dimensions.

personality profile. Some psychologists have also questioned whether all aspects of personality can be captured by any small set of personality dimensions (see Livesley, Jang, & Vernon, 2003). To truly understand personality, the critics argue, you need to understand the ability of people to *change* as well as to stay the same across situations. We'll discuss how the environment affects the consistency of behavior later in the chapter.

Allport's Trait Theory

Like the factor analysts, psychologist Gordon Allport (1897–1967) was convinced that people possess underlying personality traits, or "predispositions to respond." But he wasn't convinced that the building blocks of personality could be gleaned from massive statistical analyses of group responses. Allport believed that personality is a measure of one's *uniqueness* as an individual. So the proper focus should be on individuals, he argued, not on groups. His approach, which he called *idiographic* (which means "relating to the individual"), was to study particular individuals in great detail. An advantage of this kind of case study approach is that consistencies in behavior can be recorded across an entire lifetime rather than just in a limited setting (Barenbaum, 1997).

One of Allport's main contributions was his general classification scheme for identifying personality traits (Allport, 1937). Allport believed some people show what he called *cardinal* personality traits. **Cardinal traits** are the ruling passions that dominate an individual's life. If you spend your life huddled in a mountain monastery, rejecting all worldly possessions, your passion "to serve god" would likely satisfy Allport's description of a cardinal trait. Perhaps you know someone whose every thought or action revolves around the pursuit of wealth, fame, or power. People with cardinal traits do not represent the average—these people are driven and highly focused; every action is motivated by a particular goal. We can't really capture a cardinal trait by applying a technique such as factor analysis, however, because cardinal traits are uniquely defined by the individual rather than by the group.

Allport believed cardinal traits are rare. Most people have personalities that are controlled by several lasting characteristics, which he labeled *central* traits.

cardinal traits Allport's term to describe personality traits that dominate an individual's life, such as a passion to serve others or to accumulate wealth.

Cardinal traits are ruling passions that dominate a person's life, such as a compelling need to help others at the expense of personal comfort.

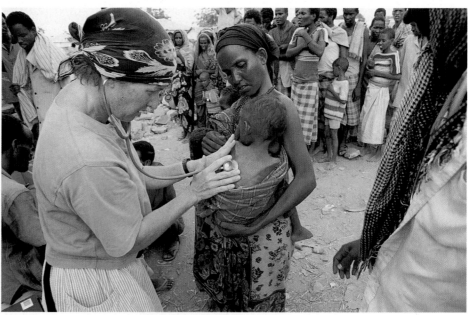

© Betty Press/Woodfin Camp and Associates

Central traits are the five to ten descriptive terms you would use to describe someone you know. Rowena? She's outgoing and friendly, very trustworthy, sentimental, and honest to the core. In addition to central traits, Allport suggested that everyone has **secondary traits**, which are less obvious because they may not always appear in behavior; the particular situation, or context, matters. For example, Rowena might also have a secondary trait of "testiness" that shows up only when she goes on an extended diet. Personality characteristics, therefore, can appropriately be described in terms of *levels* ranging from dominant (cardinal) to representative (central) to occasional (secondary).

Personality Tests

There are practical reasons to measure personality traits. Suppose you're the personnel director at a large nuclear power plant. You need to hire responsible people to run the plant, people who have the right stuff to handle potentially dangerous materials in an emergency. You wouldn't want to hire someone like Roger, with his tendency to lie and act compulsively under pressure. How do you decide for a given individual? You can choose from two main categories of personality tests, *self-report inventories* and *projective tests.*

Self-Report Inventories The most popular personality tests are **self-report inventories**, which use a questionnaire format to identify personality characteristics. People are asked to answer questions about how they typically think, act, and feel. Their responses, or *self-reports*, are scored objectively, and the results are compared to test averages compiled from thousands of other test takers. As a general rule, self-report inventories are easy to administer, and they paint a reliable picture of how someone differs from the average. Roger, for instance, would probably raise red flags on a number of measures; his answers are likely to show some disregard for social customs (compared to the average) and a marked tendency toward impulsiveness. If you were the personnel director, you could easily make your hiring—or more accurately, "no-hire"—decision based partly on the test results.

Professionals use many kinds of self-report inventories. Some tests are based on popular trait theories. For example, to assess normal personality traits you can administer the *16 Personality Factor*, which is a 187-item questionnaire designed to measure the 16 primary personality factors identified by Cattell (Cattell et al., 1970). Alternatively, there is the *NEO-PI-R*, which measures your standing on the Big Five personality traits identified in Figure 12.3 (NEO-PI-R stands for Neuroticism Extroversion Openness–Personality Inventory–Revised). The most widely used self-report inventory is the *Minnesota Multiphasic Personality Inventory (MMPI)*. The MMPI contains hundreds of true-false questions that people answer about themselves (e.g., "I never get angry"); it's now available in several revised forms (see Butcher, 2006). The responses are expressed in a personality profile that describes a person's scores on various subscales (see ▌Figure 12.4 on page 386).

In addition to measuring personality characteristics, the MMPI is often used as a technique for diagnosing psychological disorders. A person's responses are compared to those of average test takers but also to the responses of individuals with known psychological problems. There are records, for example, of how people who suffer from such disorders as paranoia (irrational beliefs of persecution) are likely to answer certain questions. The test responses of someone like Roger can then be compared with the average "paranoia" personality profile to see if he fits the bill. Comparisons of this sort are useful in diagnosing problems and in making judgments about how appropriate an individual might be for a high-risk form of employment.

The main advantage of self-report inventories is that they are objective tests—they're standardized, everyone takes the same test, and they can easily be scored by

CRITICAL THINKING

When comparing Allport's approach to the factor analytic approach, think back to our discussions in Chapter 2. What are the advantages and disadvantages of using case studies, which examine single individuals, versus surveys, which rely on responses from large groups?

central traits Allport's term to describe the five to ten descriptive traits that you would use to describe someone you know—friendly, trustworthy, and so on.

secondary traits The less obvious characteristics of an individual's personality that do not always appear in his or her behavior, such as testiness when on a diet.

self-report inventories Personality tests in which people answer groups of questions about how they typically think, act, and feel; their responses, or self-reports, are then compared to average responses compiled from large groups of prior test takers.

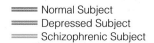

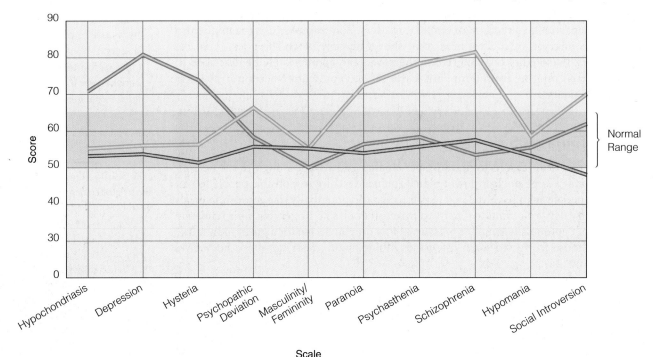

FIGURE 12.4 MMPI Profiles

Psychologists often use the MMPI to help diagnose psychological disorders. A client's scores on the various clinical scales can be compared to average scores from people who are not suffering from psychological problems, as well as from people who have been diagnosed with specific problems, such as depression or schizophrenia. (Adapted from Weiten, 1995)

projective personality test A type of personality test in which individuals are asked to interpret unstructured or ambiguous stimuli.

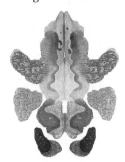

FIGURE 12.5 Projective Tests

In projective personality tests, we are asked to interpret unstructured or ambiguous stimuli. Our answers are presumed to provide insight into our personalities. What do you see hidden in this inkblot—the fundamental decay of human society?

(From Kalat, 1996)

a computer. There have been literally thousands of studies conducted testing the reliability and validity of these measures, especially the MMPI (Ben-Porath, 2003). The fact that the MMPI is one of the most widely applied measures in clinical assessment is one testament to its usefulness. At the same time, self-report inventories depend on the accuracy of the information provided by the test taker. If people choose to be deceptive on the test, or try to make themselves look good in some way, the results can be of little value (Nichols & Greene, 1997).

Projective Personality Tests In a **projective personality test**, you're asked to interpret an unstructured or ambiguous stimulus. The assumption is that you'll "project" your thoughts and true feelings into the stimulus interpretation, thereby revealing elements of your personality. For example, take a look at the inkblot shown in ▌Figure 12.5, which is similar to the kind of unstructured stimulus used on the *Rorschach test*. Clearly, you argue, the inkblot exemplifies the fundamental decay of human society. The image symbolizes the need for aggressive action on the part of all responsible people—we must rise up and defeat the tyranny that, like an out-of-control cancer, is eating away at the virtue and values of common folk. Right? Well . . . Can you see how someone's interpretation of such a stimulus might provide insight into his or her personality? If Roger always sees snakes and decaying dragons in the images, whereas Rowena sees butterflies and flowers, it's not too difficult to infer that they have quite different personality characteristics.

Another popular projective personality test is the *Thematic Apperception Test (TAT)*. Instead of an inkblot, you're shown an ambiguous picture, such as the one shown, and are asked to make up a story. What's happening? What are the characters in the picture thinking and feeling? And so on. Again, the idea is that you'll reveal aspects of yourself in the stories you tell. Both the TAT and the Rorschach test use a standardized set of stimuli, so your responses can be compared to other people who've interpreted the same picture. Many psychologists prefer to use tests like the TAT or the Rorschach, rather than self-report inventories, because projective tests help clients open up and talk about themselves and their problems (Medoff, 2004).

Projective tests allow you to respond freely, in a manner that's less restrictive than the requirements of self-report inventories. But this can create problems of interpretation: How do we know what your responses mean? Psychologists have tried to develop reliable standards for interpreting responses in these kinds of tests. Typically, the researcher or clinician is trained to look for common themes in interpretation (such as a tendency to see death, decay, or aggressiveness) or for qualities such as originality. The clinician might also look for such things as the realistic nature of the interpretation: Does the response really match the perceptual structure of the stimulus? If you claim to see a dragon in an inkblot, your general view of the world may slant toward fantasy rather than reality. The degree to which you seek help in your interpretation may also be instructive. For example, people who constantly seek guidance from the clinician before giving an answer are likely to be classified as dependent.

Again, none of the personality assessment procedures we've discussed is perfect, neither self-report inventories nor projective tests. The scoring procedures for projective tests can be somewhat unreliable; it's not uncommon for administrators to arrive at quite different interpretations of the same subject's responses (see Beutler & Berren, 1995). At the same time, evidence suggests that projective tests, particularly the Rorschach test, are reasonably valid and reliable, "roughly on par with other commonly used tests" (Society for Personality Assessment, 2005, p. 220). Personality tests of this sort remain extremely popular and widely used (Masling, 2002).

Reprinted by permission of the publishers from Henry A. Murray, THEMATIC APPERCEPTION TEST, Plate 12F, Cambridge, Mass.: Harvard University Press, Copyright © 1943 by the President and Fellows of Harvard College. © 1971 by Henry A. Murray

This image from the Thematic Apperception Test can be interpreted in many ways. What do you think the characters in the picture are thinking and feeling? Your answers may tell us something about your personality.

Test Yourself 12.1

Check your knowledge about conceptualizing and measuring personality by answering the following questions. (You will find the answers in the Appendix.)

1. For each of the following, identify the personality dimension of the Big Five that the statement best describes. Choose from the following terms: *extroversion, agreeableness, conscientiousness, neuroticism, openness.*
   a. Joanne is known as a risk-taker; she just loves to bungee jump: _____
   b. It's hard to get Mimi to stop talking: _____
   c. Raphael is very cooperative; he's virtually always sympathetic to my needs: _____
   d. Mark is very insecure; he always seems to feel guilty about something: _____
   e. Maureen is very productive, and she has very high ethical standards: _____

2. For each of the following, pick the personality test that the statement best describes. Choose from the following: *MMPI, NEO-PI-R, 16 Personality Factor, Rorschach, TAT.*
   a. An ambiguous picture is shown and the client is asked to make up a story about its contents: _____
   b. An objective self-report inventory that is often used in clinical settings: _____
   c. A test used primarily to measure someone's standing on the Big Five: _____
   d. A projective personality test using standardized inkblots as stimuli: _____
   e. Designed to create a personality profile representing Cattell's source traits: _____

Sigmund Freud is shown here in 1891, when he was becoming increasingly convinced that certain physical problems may have psychological origins.

Determining How Personality Develops

LEARNING GOALS
• Describe Freud's psychodynamic theory of personality and mind.
• Summarize and evaluate humanistic approaches to personality.
• Describe social–cognitive theories of personality.

AS YOU'VE JUST SEEN, we can describe the personality traits of people like Roger or Rowena—perhaps their standing on the Big Five—and there's a good chance our measurements will be reasonably accurate and reliable. But description is not the same thing as explanation. We may know Rowena has a sunny disposition, but trait theories don't tell us much about the origins of those characteristics. Why do Roger and Rowena differ?

In this section we'll consider three very different approaches to understanding personality development: the psychodynamic theory of Sigmund Freud, humanistic theories, and social–cognitive theories. Each claims that individual uniqueness comes from the operation of general psychological principles. We're not consistent in our behavior by accident or chance; rather, processes inside our head, or in the external environment, shape and mold our actions.

The Psychodynamic Approach of Freud

Consider the following scenario. You're a practicing clinician, and your latest patient, 18-year-old Katharina, complains of persistent physical problems. "I'm often overcome with a frightful choking feeling," she insists. "I have trouble catching my breath and my head begins to spin. I truly think I must be about to die." Extensive examinations reveal no physical cause; the attacks appear suddenly without warning and seem unrelated to activity or general health. Katharina herself provides no insight: "There's nothing in my head when the attacks begin; my mind is a blank." The only additional information you have about Katharina is that she's reluctant to involve herself with members of the opposite sex and she has a persistent dream in which she appears as a young child pursued from room to room by a shadowy figure.

Think about this case study for a moment. Can you draw any general conclusions about Katharina's personality from an analysis of her symptoms? The case itself is typical of the clinical problems Sigmund Freud (1856–1939) studied in the late 19th century. Remember, Freud was a medical doctor by training. He established a private practice in Vienna, where he specialized in a branch of medicine concerned with disorders of the nervous system. Freud routinely encountered patients like Katharina, who seemed to have physical problems without physical causes. He used these cases (known in that time as *hysterics*) as the basis for his highly influential **psychodynamic theory** of personality and mind, as well as for his method of treatment known as *psychoanalysis*.

psychodynamic theory An approach to personality development, based largely on the ideas of Sigmund Freud, that holds that much of behavior is governed by unconscious forces.

conscious mind The contents of awareness—those things that occupy the focus of one's current attention.

preconscious mind The part of the mind that contains all of the inactive but potentially accessible thoughts and memories.

unconscious mind The part of the mind that Freud believed housed all the memories, urges, and conflicts that are truly beyond awareness.

The Structure of the Mind   Freud believed the human mind can be divided into three major parts: the *conscious*, the *preconscious*, and the *unconscious*. The **conscious mind** contains the contents of current awareness—those things that occupy the focus of your attention at the moment. The **preconscious mind** contains inactive but accessible thoughts and memories—those things that you could easily recall, if desired, but are simply not thinking about at the moment. Finally, the **unconscious mind** houses all the memories, urges, and conflicts that are beyond awareness. Freud believed that the contents of the unconscious mind exert powerful and long-lasting influences on behavior, despite the fact that they're hidden and unavailable to consciousness.

From Freud's perspective, Katharina's panicky behavior is likely to be caused by forces originating in her unconscious. Consider her dream of being chased by a shadowy figure. She can remember the details—her appearance as a young child, perhaps the color and shapes of the rooms—but her conscious memory of the dream, according to Freud, is unreliable. The parts of the dream she remembers, its *manifest content*, are merely symbolic of the dream's true unconscious meaning, or *latent content*. As we discussed in Chapter 6, Freud believed that dreams represent wish fulfillment; dreams are simply one way of gratifying desires or dealing with forbidden conflicts that are normally stored in the unconscious. In Katharina's case, the shadowy figure may well have arisen from a traumatic childhood experience—perhaps an unwelcome sexual advance by a relative—or even from her own unconscious desire for a sexual experience. Freud relied heavily on dream interpretation as a technique for mapping out the contents of the unconscious mind. Dreams, Freud argued, represent a "royal road" to the unconscious (Freud, 1900/1990).

The Structure of Personality Freud believed that human personality consists of three parts: the *id*, *ego*, and *superego* (see ▌ Figure 12.6). As a student of biology, Freud was committed to the idea that behavior is influenced by biological forces. He was convinced that each of us is born with powerful instinctual drives, particularly related to sex and aggression, which motivate and control our actions. Freud used the term **id** to represent the portion of personality that is governed by these forces (translated from the Latin, *id* means "it"). As a component of personality, the id seeks immediate satisfaction of natural urges, without concern for the morals and customs of society. It obeys what Freud called the *pleasure principle*—the pursuit of pleasure through the satisfaction of animalistic urges. Ironically, from an adaptive standpoint, it's this dark side of personality—the seeker of pleasure—that guarantees survival of the species by motivating a desire for sexual intercourse.

At the same time, Freud understood that we're more than just irrational sex machines. He suggested that the forces of the id are appropriately balanced by a moral arm of personality called the superego. The **superego** is the part of our personality that encourages us to act in an ideal fashion—to act in accordance with the moral customs defined by parents and culture. The superego is acquired from experience, and it acts, in part, as a conscience; it makes us feel good when we act the way we should and feel guilty when our behavior strays from accepted standards. Like the id, the superego is essentially irrational—it seeks only moral perfection. Left to its own devices, the superego would undercut or block the more basic urges, even though those urges may help us satisfy fundamental survival needs. The superego follows an *idealistic principle*: Always act in a proper and ideal fashion as defined by parents and culture.

Sitting between the forces of the id and superego, and acting as a mediator, is the third component of personality—the ego. The **ego**, which comes from the Latin word for "I," serves an executive role in Freud's conception of personality. The ego encourages you to act with reason and deliberation and helps you conform to the requirements of the external world. Freud suggested that the ego obeys a *reality principle*; it monitors the real world looking for appropriate outlets for the id's needs, but it also listens intently to the moralistic preaching of the superego. The ego's goal is compromise among three demanding masters: the external world, the id, and the superego.

Defense Mechanisms: The Ego's Arsenal As noted previously, Freud believed we're unaware of the conflicts that regularly rage among the id, ego, and superego. We consciously experience only the side effects of these battles. For example, Freud believed the experience of *anxiety* (an unpleasant feeling of dread) is often the result of confrontations between the ego and the id (of course, anxiety can also come from dangers in the real world). But the ego does not enter the battlefield unarmed. Freud proposed that the ego uses a variety of **defense mechanisms**, which are unconscious processes that can ward off the anxiety that comes from confrontation with the id.

CRITICAL THINKING

How do the modern memory concepts of short- and long-term memory relate to Freud's three-part theory of the mind?

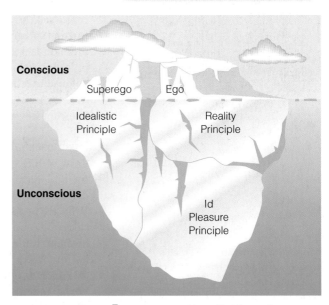

▌ **FIGURE 12.6** Freud's View of Personality
Freud believed that our personalities are influenced by three forces. The *id* is the unconscious and unrepentant seeker of pleasure; the *superego* is the moral seeker of ideal behavior; and the *ego* is the executive that acts in accordance with reality. Just as most of an iceberg lies beneath the water, much of personality operates at an unconscious level.

id In Freud's theory, the portion of personality that is governed by inborn instinctual drives, particularly those related to sex and aggression.

superego In Freud's theory, the portion of personality that motivates people to act in an ideal fashion, in accordance with the moral customs defined by parents and culture.

ego In Freud's theory, the portion of personality that induces people to act with reason and deliberation and helps them conform to the requirements of the external world.

defense mechanisms According to Freud, unconscious processes used by the ego to ward off the anxiety that comes from confrontation, usually with the demands of the id.

CRITICAL THINKING

What are the adaptive qualities of the superego? What would happen to the human species if the superego always controlled behavior?

repression A defense mechanism used to bury anxiety-producing thoughts and feelings in the unconscious.

oral stage The first stage in Freud's conception of psychosexual development, occurring in the first year of life; in this stage, pleasure is derived primarily from sucking and placing things in the mouth.

anal stage Freud's second stage of psychosexual development, occurring in the second year of life; pleasure is derived from the process of defecation.

phallic stage Freud's third stage of psychosexual development, lasting from about age 3 to age 5; pleasure is gained from self-stimulation of the sexual organs.

The most important weapon in the ego's arsenal is **repression**, a process that keeps anxiety-producing thoughts and feelings buried in the unconscious. When a primitive urge from the id rears its ugly head, the ego actively represses the thought or feeling. The urge is blocked, jammed down into the dark recesses of the unconscious. Freud was convinced that we're particularly likely to repress sexual thoughts or experiences. Unrestricted sexual activity is typically discouraged by parents and society—this was particularly true in Freud's time—so sexual thoughts and feelings must be actively blocked by the reality-driven ego. In contrast, we're apt to have few repressed thoughts or memories about eating or normal drinking, although both are instinctual urges, because these behaviors tend to violate few societal norms. Repression is a kind of self-deception—the mind deals with the anxiety-producing impulse by acting as if it isn't there. Similar kinds of self-deception occur with the other defense mechanisms Freud proposed. For a listing of some of these other important defense mechanisms, along with some examples, take a look at the accompanying Concept Review.

Psychosexual Development To Freud, the unconscious mind is a bubbling cauldron of hidden conflicts, repressed memories, and biological urges. In the case of the biological urges, their origin is relatively clear—people are born with instinctual drives for self-preservation and sex. But where do the hidden conflicts come from? Why are people tormented by repressed memories that arise directly from life's experiences? Freud believed that people travel through stages of psychosexual development in their childhood (Freud, 1905/1962). How children deal with their emerging sexuality importantly affects the way they think and feel when they reach adulthood.

Each developmental stage is associated with a sensitive region of pleasure, which Freud called an *erogenous zone*. In roughly the first year of life—during the **oral stage**—pleasure is derived primarily from sucking and from placing things in the mouth (such as the mother's breast). In the second year of life, the focus of pleasure shifts to the anus. During this **anal stage**, pleasure arises from the process of defecation, the passing of feces. From ages 3 through 5, in the **phallic stage**, the genital regions of the body receive the focus of attention. The child obtains intense gratification from self-stimulation of the sexual organs.

Freud believed we move through these stages for primarily biological reasons. All organisms, including humans, need to learn how to gain nourishment, control the elimination of waste, and satisfy the sexual drive. Unfortunately, it's possible to

Concept Review | Defense Mechanisms

MECHANISM	DESCRIPTION	EXAMPLE
Repression	Anxiety-producing thoughts and feelings are kept buried in the unconscious.	Horace doesn't remember the horrible fire that nearly killed him when he was a child.
Denial	You refuse to believe information that leads to anxiety.	Clay continues to deny that his four-martini lunches are a problem.
Rationalization	Explanations are created to deal with threatening thoughts.	Suze explains that she failed the test because the teacher asked the wrong questions.
Projection	Unacceptable wishes or feelings are attributed to others.	Monica deals with her attraction to her married supervisor Bill by accusing fellow employee Kelly of flirting with him.
Reaction formation	You behave in a way that is counter to how you feel.	Although deeply resentful of how his mother treated him as a child, Juan calls her every day and showers her with affection.
Sublimation	Unacceptable impulses are channeled into socially acceptable activity.	Tze is rude and critical and likes to put people down. She decides to become a stand-up comic.

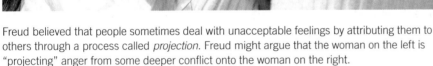

Freud believed that people sometimes deal with unacceptable feelings by attributing them to others through a process called *projection*. Freud might argue that the woman on the left is "projecting" anger from some deeper conflict onto the woman on the right.

Through *sublimation*, unacceptable impulses, such as a desire to hurt others, are channeled into socially acceptable activities.

become stalled, or fixated, at a particular stage, which, in turn, can have long-lasting effects on personality. By *fixation*, Freud meant that a person will continue to act in ways that are appropriate for a particular stage, seeking pleasure in stage-dependent ways, even after he or she has physically matured. There are two primary ways in which the fixation process can occur: First, if the child gains excess gratification from a stage or, second, if the child becomes excessively frustrated. It's the second of these two situations that has received the most attention.

Notice the oral and anal stages are associated with the potentially traumatic experiences of weaning and toilet training. Freud emphasized these experiences because a child can become easily frustrated during either event. People who are fixated in the oral stage, Freud believed, continue to derive pleasure from oral activities into adulthood. They become excessive smokers, or overeaters, or people who bite their nails. Fixation at the anal stage might lead to excessive neatness or messiness. The pleasure-seeking activities in these instances are symbolic, of course; compulsive room cleaning might be a symbolic attempt at the gratification a child sometimes receives from the retention of feces.

Freud's interpretation of the phallic stage of psychosexual development was particularly controversial. He was convinced that small children have intense but unconscious sexual urges that become focused during this stage toward the opposite-sex parent. Boys become erotically attracted to their mother, a condition Freud called the *Oedipus complex* (after the Greek tragedy of Oedipus, who unknowingly killed his father and married his mother); girls can become attracted to their father in what has been called the *Electra complex* (after the mythical Greek Electra, who hated and conspired to murder her mother). Desire for the opposite-sex parent creates enormous unconscious conflicts in the developing child. Freud believed that many adult sexual or relationship problems can be traced back to a failure to resolve these conflicts adequately.

After the age of 5 or 6, boys and girls enter a kind of psychosexual lull—called the **latency period**—during which their sexual feelings are largely suppressed. During

> **CRITICAL THINKING**
>
> Most people deny that they've ever had sexual feelings toward their parents. If you were Freud, how would you explain these denials?

latency period Freud's period of psychosexual development, from age 5 to puberty, during which the child's sexual feelings are largely suppressed.

genital stage Freud's final stage of psychosexual development, during which one develops mature sexual relationships with members of the opposite sex.

this period, children direct their attention to social concerns, such as developing solid friendships. Beginning with the onset of puberty, one enters the **genital stage**. Here, sexuality reawakens, but in what Freud considered to be a more direct and appropriate fashion. Erotic tendencies now tend to be directed toward members of the opposite sex.

Adler, Jung, and Horney Freud's emphasis on the role of sexuality in personality development was received with skepticism by many, even from those who were firmly committed to his general approach. One of the first to split from Freud's inner circle of disciples was Alfred Adler (1870–1937). Adler disagreed strongly with Freud about the role of early psychosexual experience. He felt the important determinant of personality development was not childhood trauma but rather how we come to deal with a basic sense of *inferiority*. To Adler, personality arises from our attempts to overcome or compensate for fundamental feelings of inadequacy. Adler was responsible for coining the popular term *inferiority complex*, a concept, he argued, that motivates a great deal of human behavior. It is our natural drive for superiority that explains motivation, not sexual gratification as envisioned by Freud (Adler, 1927).

Adler was not the only dissenting voice. Others who had been early advocates of Freud's theory began to break away and offer new and revised forms of the theory. One of the biggest personal blows to Freud was the departure of his disciple Carl Jung (1875–1961), whom Freud had picked as his intellectual heir. Jung, like Adler, was dissatisfied with Freud's narrow reliance on sexuality as the dominant source of human motivation. Jung believed instead in the idea of a "general life force," which he adopted from his extensive study of Eastern religions and mythology. This general life force was sexual in part but included other basic sources of motivation as well, such as the need for creativity (Jung, 1923).

collective unconscious The notion proposed by Carl Jung that certain kinds of universal symbols and ideas are present in the unconscious of all people.

Among Jung's more influential ideas was his concept of the **collective unconscious**. Jung believed that each person has a shared unconscious, in addition to the personal unconscious described by Freud, that's filled with mystical symbols and universal images that have accumulated over the lifetime of the human species. These symbols are inherited—passed from one generation to the next—and tend to represent enduring concepts (or *archetypes*), such as god, mother, earth, and water. Actually, the idea that all humans share certain concepts buried deep in a collective unconscious can also be found in the writings of Freud, but Jung expanded on the idea and assigned it a central focus.

Another blow to Freud was the dissenting voice of Karen Horney (1885–1952), one of the first women to learn and practice psychodynamic theory. Horney agreed with Freud's basic approach, but she rebelled against what she felt was Freud's male-dominated views of sexuality. Freud had argued in his writings that women are fundamentally dissatisfied with their sex—they suffer from what he called *penis envy*—a view that Horney found unsatisfactory in many ways. She boldly confronted Freud, both personally and in her writings, and offered revised forms of psychodynamic theory that treated women in a more balanced way (Horney, 1967). One of her more lasting theoretical contributions was her insistence that a link exists between the irrational beliefs people hold about themselves and their psychological problems (Horney, 1945). As you'll see in Chapters 14 and 15, this idea continues to be influential in the conceptualization and treatment of psychological disorders.

Evaluating Psychodynamic Theory Few psychological theories have been as influential as Freud's. Many of the terms and concepts he introduced—particularly his ideas about the unconscious—have become part of modern language and beliefs. You were probably familiar with such Freudian terms as *repression*, *id*, *ego*, and *projection* before you opened this psychology text. Moreover, the suggestion that personality is determined in part by how we learn to satisfy basic biological drives, as well as deal effectively with the demands of society and the outside world, is still a very modern and widely accepted idea (Bornstein, 2003). But psychodynamic theory, as envisioned by Freud, has steadily lost its influence over the years.

© Bettmann/Corbis

Carl Jung believed that everyone shares a collective unconscious filled with mystical symbols and universal images.

Part of the problem is that many of the ideas Freud proposed lack scientific rigor; he never articulated concepts such as the id, superego, and ego with ringing precision. As a result, it's been difficult, if not impossible, to subject them to proper scientific testing. Consider the concept of repression, which Freud believed to be the bedrock of psychodynamic theory. If repressed memories are hidden behind the veil of the unconscious, expressing themselves only in masked and largely symbolic ways, can we ever be certain that we've correctly identified and interpreted these unconscious influences? Most of the evidence for repression has come from clinical case studies, from individuals who are probably not representative of the general population. Psychologists have been unable to study repression in the laboratory, either because of ethical concerns or because it's unclear what conditions need to be met for repression to occur. Moreover, many people have undergone traumatic events in their childhood yet remain psychologically healthy (Loftus, 1993).

In addition to the problems of testability and lack of scientific rigor, Freud's theory is often criticized for its biases against women. As mentioned earlier, he painted women as individuals unsatisfied with their gender, who need to come to grips with the fact that they lack a penis. Freud was also reluctant to believe women's testimonials of rape or childhood sexual abuse—he saw these accounts as symbolic expressions of unconscious conflicts rather than as actual events. Many modern psychologists consider these positions, along with Freud's general male-oriented approach, to be unrealistic and even distasteful (Masson, 1984; Vitz, 1988).

Karen Horney rebelled against what she felt were Freud's male-dominated views on sexuality.

Humanistic Approaches to Personality

There's another reason many psychologists don't like Freud's psychodynamic approach: It paints a very dark picture of human nature. In describing the origins of personality, Freud often compared the mind to a battlefield, where irrational forces are continuously engaged in a struggle for control. According to Freud, our actions are motivated primarily by the need to satisfy animalistic urges related to sex and aggression; our conscious awareness of why we act is misleading and symbolic, representative of conflicts created during toilet training or as a result of being weaned.

Humanistic psychology is largely a reaction against this pessimistic view of the human spirit. Humanistic psychologists don't talk about battlefields and conflict; instead, they speak of growth and potential. It's not animalistic urges that explain personality; it's the *human* with our unparalleled capacity for self-awareness, choice, responsibility, and growth. Humanistic psychologists believe each of us can control our own behavioral destiny—we can consciously rise above whatever animalistic urges might be coded in our genes. We're built and designed for personal growth, to seek our fullest potential, to self-actualize—to become all we are capable of becoming.

humanistic psychology An approach to personality that focuses on people's unique capacity for choice, responsibility, and growth.

To a humanist, there are many ways to explain individual differences in behavior. First, each of us is considered to be naturally *unique*. We're more than the sum of a set of predictable parts—everyone is a unique and individual *whole*. Second, the environment influences the natural growth process. Like plants, people will grow best in fertile and supportive environments; barren environments can't stop the growth process, but they can prevent us from realizing our own true potential (Rogers, 1963). Third, and perhaps most important, how we act is determined by our unique view of the world—our interpretation of reality. How we view ourselves and the environment guides and motivates our actions. Notice the emphasis here is on conscious mental processes. We're assumed to be responsible for our own actions, although sometimes our subjective experience of reality is not an accurate reflection of the real world. We'll consider the views of two prominent humanistic psychologists in this section, Carl Rogers and Abraham Maslow.

Carl Rogers and the Self   To humanist Carl Rogers (1902–1987), the essence of personality is wrapped up in the concept of the self or, more specifically, the *self-concept*. He defined the **self-concept** as an organized set of perceptions about one's

self-concept An organized set of perceptions that we hold about our abilities and characteristics.

abilities and characteristics—it amounts to that keen sense of oneself, what it means to be "I" or "me." Rogers believed that the self-concept comes primarily from social interactions, particularly the interactions we have with our parents, friends, and other significant role models throughout our lifetimes. The people around us mold and shape our self-image through their ongoing evaluations of our actions.

We rely on the judgments of others to tell us who we truly are and what we can hope to become, Rogers argued, because of a basic need for **positive regard**. We value what others think of us and consistently seek others' approval, love, and companionship. Unfortunately, in real life **conditions of worth** tend to be attached to the approval of others. For instance, let's suppose you come from a family that values education and intellectual pursuits. You, however, couldn't care less about such things—your interests are in popular music and athletics. To gain acceptance from your parents, you may deny your true feelings and modify your self-concept to bring it more in line with what your parents believe: "I'm not someone who cares about a trivial activity like sports, I'm someone who cares intensely about the pursuit of knowledge."

But herein lies a major problem, Rogers argued. The self-concept that you work so hard to form inevitably conflicts with what you truly feel from experience. You may decide to spend the evening reading the philosophical musings of Immanuel Kant, but you'll probably find your mind drifting and your feelings of self-worth diminishing. Rogers called this condition **incongruence**, which he defined as a discrepancy between the image you hold of yourself—your self-concept—and the sum of all your experiences. Incongruence leads to the experience of anxiety and ultimately forms the basis for a variety of psychological problems. True psychological health, Rogers suggested, comes when the self-concept is *congruent* (agrees) with your true feelings and experiences—that is, when your opinions and beliefs about yourself accurately reflect your everyday experiences. Chapter 15 outlines what Rogers felt was the appropriate therapeutic solution to conditions of incongruence. To anticipate the discussion just a bit, Rogers was convinced that the therapist's proper role is to be nonjudgmental—to accept the feelings and actions of the client unconditionally. By eliminating the *conditions of worth*, the client is able to develop a self-concept more congruent with reality.

With respect to personality and its development, Rogers believed that regularities in behavior come largely from the structure of the self-concept. Personality is defined by consistent behavior across situations; people tend to act consistently, he

positive regard The idea that we value what others think of us and that we constantly seek others' approval, love, and companionship.

conditions of worth The expectations or standards that we believe others place on us.

incongruence A discrepancy between the image we hold of ourselves—our self-concept—and the sum of all our experiences.

Carl Rogers proposed that we have an inborn need for positive regard—we value what others think of us and consistently seek their approval and companionship.

argued, simply because their actions consistently mirror their established self-concept. We act in ways that support our beliefs about ourselves. More often than not we'll actively seek to protect our self-image. Given a choice, you might consistently choose to read philosophy rather than watch television because it's consistent with your vision of *you*. If you chose television, you would need to reconsider who you really are, which is the sort of confrontation that we tend to avoid.

Abraham Maslow and Self-Actualization   Although Carl Rogers was committed to the role played by the self-concept, he also believed strongly in the potential for personal growth. We may act defensively and seek to protect a rigid self-concept, but at our core we're creative people who have the power to fulfill our personal potential. This idea that everyone has a basic need for **self-actualization**—the need to move forward toward the realization of potential—also plays a pivotal role in Abraham Maslow's view of personality.

We encountered Maslow's views in Chapter 11 when we discussed motivation. Maslow believed that human motivation is grounded in the satisfaction of need. There are certain things that humans must do—such as obtain food and water and protect themselves from danger—before their potential can be fully realized. As you saw in Chapter 11, one of Maslow's main contributions was his proposal of the *need hierarchy*, shown in ▌Figure 12.7, which expresses the order in which needs must be satisfied. Notice that safety and survival needs sit below the need for love and belonging in the need hierarchy. It's unlikely that you'll appear to be spiritual or loving if you're constantly worrying about your next meal. It's only after the basic needs are satisfied—those related to survival—that the more spiritual side of personality can be developed.

Your personality characteristics will reflect where you're positioned in the hierarchy of needs. Maslow had a very positive view of human nature. A person may consistently act unkind, defensive, or aggressive, he argued, but these personality traits come from a failure to satisfy basic needs—they'll never be fundamental to the human spirit. To support this claim, Maslow pointed to the behavior of individuals who he felt had progressed through the entire hierarchy. The characteristics of human personality, he argued, are highly consistent across individuals at the highest levels of the hierarchy. People who are self-actualizing show none of the darker personality traits exhibited by those locked in at lower levels; they tend to be positive, creative, accepting individuals (Leclerc et al., 1998).

Maslow's conclusions were based largely on the study of particular individuals, people whom he knew and admired. He also studied the personality traits of people who were very successful, such as Albert Einstein, Abraham Lincoln, and Eleanor Roosevelt. All self-actualizing people, he argued, share certain personality traits. They tend to be accepting of themselves and others, to be self-motivated and problem oriented, and to have a strong ethical sense and hold democratic values. Self-actualizing people also often undergo what Maslow called *peak experiences*—emotional, often religious, experiences in which one's place in a unified universe becomes clear and meaningful. Notice these are all positive traits; self-actualizing people tend to be at peace with themselves and with the world.

Evaluating Humanistic Theories   The humanistic approach, with its optimistic emphasis on positive growth, has had considerable influence in psychology. Concepts such as the *self* have received a great deal of recent attention and, as you'll see in Chapter 15, humanistic approaches to psychotherapy are popular and widely applied. The humanistic approach provides a nice balance to the pessimism of Freud. Rather than ignoring the conscious influences on behavior, humanists champion personal choice and responsibility. Take a trip to your local bookstore and check the shelves devoted to psychology—you'll find that many of the books emphasize the control *you* can exert over your own behavior. This is one indication of the humanists' widespread impact, especially in tapping the general population's interest in psychology.

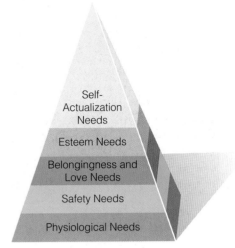

▌ **FIGURE 12.7** Maslow's Hierarchy of Needs
Maslow proposed that our observable personality characteristics will indicate where we are positioned in the hierarchy of needs. Someone who must worry constantly about biological or safety needs will behave differently from someone who is seeking to satisfy needs at the highest levels of the pyramid.

self-actualization The ingrained desire to reach one's true potential as a human being.

Are we all born naturally good, or do we learn to be good because of how we've been rewarded?

But as contributors to scientific psychology, humanistic psychologists are often criticized (see Funder, 2001). Many of the basic concepts we've discussed, such as the potential for growth and self-actualization, are vague and difficult to pin down. It's also not clear where these tendencies come from and under which conditions they'll fully express themselves. Remember, too, that the humanists place important emphasis on personal, subjective experience. This means that researchers must often rely on self-reports to generate data, and some question whether self-reports produce reliable and accurate representations of internal psychological processes (Leclerc et al., 1998). So in addition to problems of conceptual vagueness, humanism lacks adequate testability.

The humanistic approach to personality is also criticized for adopting too optimistic a view of human nature. In part, the arguments of Rogers and Maslow are reactions against the pessimism of Freud. But like Freud, humanistic theorists have adopted a rather extreme view of human nature: People constantly strive for growth, unless constrained in some way by the environment, and are driven to pursue lofty goals. Thus we have the dark view described by Freud (people are driven by unconscious animalistic urges) countered by the extremely optimistic views of the humanists. Many psychologists believe it's better to adopt a balanced approach: People are neither inherently good nor evil; they sometimes act in self-interested ways that may appear animalistic, but these actions are often adaptive and increase one's likelihood of survival. At the same time, placing too much emphasis on unconscious biological motives is itself misleading—we undoubtedly exercise considerable conscious control over our behavior.

Social–Cognitive Approaches to Personality

One particularly important characteristic of both the psychodynamic and humanistic approaches to personality is their emphasis on built-in determinants of behavior. People are born with animalistic urges that must be satisfied, or they greet the world naturally good with a compelling need for personal growth. The environment plays a critical role in determining final personality, but the role is essentially secondary—personal experiences and cultural norms merely constrain or enhance the full expression of natural needs.

social–cognitive theories An approach to personality that suggests it is human experiences, and interpretations of those experiences, that determine personality growth and development.

But what about the possibility that people simply *learn* to act in consistent ways? Isn't it possible that Roger's tendency to lie and Rowena's outgoing and sunny disposition come entirely from experience? Maybe Roger stole candy when he was 4 and was rewarded by not being caught; maybe Rowena learned at an early age that smiles are often met with smiles and that a good deed will be returned in kind. According to **social–cognitive theories** of personality, human experience, not human nature, is the primary cause of personality growth and development. The *social* side of the approach emphasizes the role of experiences delivered by the environment; the *cognitive* side emphasizes how one's interpretation of the experience plays a significant role in determining what's actually learned.

Behaviorist Roots Social–cognitive theories were originally influenced by the behaviorist tradition in psychology. As discussed in Chapter 1, behaviorists believe that psychologists should look to *observable behavior* for answers to psychological questions; the research goal is to understand how behavior changes when rewards and punishments are applied. What we call personality, then, could be nothing more than the collective actions we've learned to produce in various situations. As with all other animals, if our behavior is rewarded in a particular situation, we'll be more likely to repeat it the next time we encounter the same situation.

There are three main ways in which people acquire situation-specific response tendencies (see Chapter 7). First, through *classical conditioning*, we learn that certain kinds of events signal other events. Imagine that as a small child Little Albert is frightened in the presence of a white furry rat; he develops a specific fear, or phobia, of small furry animals that continues on into adulthood. His behavior is consistent over time—he panics at the sight of anything small and furry—due in large part to this early childhood experience. Second, through *operant conditioning*, we learn about the consequences of our behavior. If we're rewarded in some context for acting aggressively, we'll tend to act aggressively in the future. If we are repeatedly put down at parties for being outgoing, we'll learn to be withdrawn and to avoid social situations. Here again it is the environment—one's past history of rewards and punishments—that is shaping behavior.

The third way that regularities in behavior can develop is through observational learning, or *modeling*. We observe the behavior of others around us—especially role models—and imitate the behavior. As we discussed in Chapter 7, it's adaptive for organisms to mimic the behavior of others, because in this way they can learn appropriate behavior without directly experiencing the consequences of an inappropriate action. Rhesus monkeys, for example, learn to show fear in the presence of snakes through modeling their parents' behavior, not from directly experiencing the negative consequences of a bite (Mineka, 1987). Modeling approaches assume that many personality traits come from copying the behavior of others, especially when the behavior of the model regularly leads to positive, reinforcing outcomes (Bandura, 1986; Mischel, 1968).

How we act and feel often depends on how much control we think we have over the environment. Externals, who perceive little connection between their own actions and rewards, tend to see themselves as powerless and to have low levels of self-esteem.

The Role of Internal Beliefs   Very few psychologists actually believe the environment alone determines personality. This is because the psychological effect of most experiences—positive or negative—depends crucially on how you interpret the experience. Suppose we ask two groups of people to perform a relatively difficult task, such as predicting sequences of numbers. We tell one of the groups that performance on the task is based on skill; the other group is told that success or failure is due entirely to chance. (Unknown to the participants, we actually rig the procedure so people in both groups will succeed and fail the same number of times.) What you'll find is that task effort, as well as the amount learned, depends on how much control you think you have over the outcome. People who believe their performance is skill based work harder and learn more from the task (Rotter, Liverant, & Crowne, 1961).

The important point here is that the groups perform differently even though everyone receives exactly the same number of rewards and punishments. So it's not only the literal distribution of rewards and punishments that matters; your belief about the origins of those consequences is also important. Some psychologists believe that enduring personality traits are based partly on one's perceived **locus of control**—how much control you feel you have over your environment (Rotter, 1966). People who are oriented externally, known as *externals*, perceive little connection between their own actions and the occurrence of rewards; they tend to see themselves as powerless and generally have low levels of self-esteem (Lefcourt, 1982). Internally oriented people (*internals*) view the world as responsive to their actions; they feel confident they can control when rewards and punishments occur. Internally oriented people display high levels of self-confidence and tend to score higher than externally oriented individuals on a variety of academic and social indices (Ryckman, 2004).

Interestingly, U.S. college students seem to be trending toward more of an external locus of control. Young Americans increasingly believe they have little direct control over what happens in their lives. One recent analysis found that the average college student in 2002 had more of an external locus of control than 80% of the college students in the early 1960s (Twenge, Zhang, & Im, 2004). Why the trend? No one knows for certain, but greater cynicism, negative social trends (including increased media

locus of control The amount of control that a person feels he or she has over the environment.

How students cope with the problem of performing well in school depends to a certain extent on their degree of self-efficacy.

self-efficacy The beliefs we hold about our own ability to perform a task or accomplish a goal.

coverage of negative events), and the tendency to adopt a "victim mentality" have all been suggested as reasons. It's an unfortunate trend because, again, an external locus of control, and its accompanying feelings of powerlessness, is typically associated with a host of negative consequences.

Locus of control is related to another psychological concept called **self-efficacy** (Bandura, 1986, 2001). Whereas locus of control refers to your beliefs about how much control you can exert over the environment, self-efficacy is defined as the beliefs you hold about your own ability. For example, Raymond might be convinced people can control their environment but feel he personally lacks the skill. In this case, he would be rated as low in self-efficacy, with an internal locus of control. On the other hand, he might be extremely confident in his basic abilities (high self-efficacy) but believe he can do little to control the things around him (external locus of control). Often a person's degree of self-efficacy is related to particular situations or tasks. You might believe strongly in your ability to excel academically but lack any measure of confidence in your social skills.

Locus of control and self-efficacy are important concepts. They tell us that what we learn from the environment depends on more than the delivery of rewards and punishments. What you expect and believe about the world and your abilities influences the types of tasks you'll choose to engage in, as well as the effectiveness of rewards and punishments. If you're convinced you have little or no ability in social settings—your self-efficacy is low—you'll either avoid going to parties or act nervous and uncomfortable when you do go. If you feel you have no chance of succeeding in your psychology course because the teaching assistant doesn't like you—that is, you've adopted an external locus of control—your motivation to work hard is likely to be low. Note in these cases your internal beliefs end up affecting your overt behavior (avoidance of parties or class), which, in turn, affects the likelihood that you'll be rewarded. Psychologist Albert Bandura (1986) has referred to this relationship between beliefs, overt behavior, and the environment as one of **reciprocal determinism**: beliefs, behavior, and the environment interact to shape what's learned from experience (see ▌Figure 12.8).

reciprocal determinism The idea that beliefs, behavior, and the environment interact to shape what is learned from experience.

CRITICAL THINKING

Carla receives an A in her psychology class but attributes it to the fact that her teacher is easy. Does she have an internal or external locus of control? How confident do you think she is of her own abilities?

Evaluating Social–Cognitive Theories   Most psychologists believe learning plays an important role in personality development. Furthermore, the idea that cognitive factors help determine what's learned, rather than just rewards and punishments,

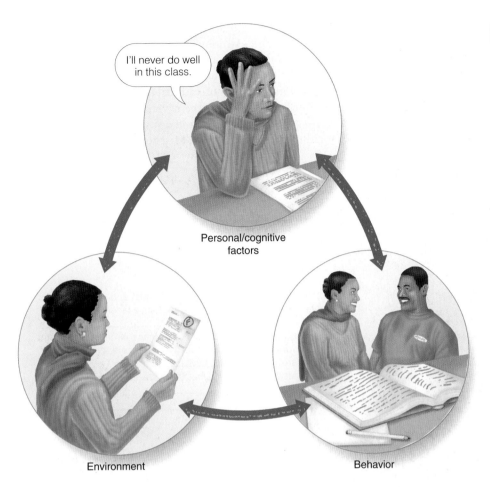

Personal/cognitive factors

Environment

Behavior

I'll never do well in this class.

FIGURE 12.8 Reciprocal Determinism Bandura proposed that personality is shaped by complex interactions among expectations and beliefs, behavior, and the rewards and punishments delivered by the environment. In this case, expecting failure in class (personal/cognitive factors) affects studying (behavior), which in turn affects the likelihood of success on the test (environment). The arrows point both ways, suggesting that these factors can all interact.

is also widely accepted. Critics of the social–cognitive approach simply argue that it is insufficient as a general account of personality development (Feist, 1994; Ryckman, 2008). Social–cognitive theories, for example, tend to neglect the individual as a *whole*, choosing instead to concentrate on how people have learned to respond in particular situations.

Concept Review | View of Personality Development

APPROACH	DESCRIPTION	EXAMPLE
Psychodynamic	Personality can be influenced by forces originating in the unconscious and is made up of three components: *id* (instinctive urges), *ego* (conscious decision making), and *superego* (conscience).	Jane is strongly attracted to men, but her parents are very strict about dating, so her sexual feelings are repressed. As a result she tends to avoid men and is uncomfortable when she is around them.
Humanistic	We ultimately control our own behavioral destiny. Personality reflects our uniqueness, as well as our environment and our personal view of the world.	Because of criticism from her parents during childhood, Jane has developed a poor self-concept. She has not experienced unconditional positive regard and as a result feels uncomfortable with who she is.
Social–cognitive	Personality results from an interaction between the experiences delivered by the environment and our interpretations and expectations about those experiences.	Jane goes to an all-girls high school and doesn't encounter many boys. As a result, she's a bit uncomfortable around them and acts nervous. They then tend to avoid her, and she feels even more uncomfortable.

The approach has been criticized as well for failing to emphasize the role of biological and genetic factors in development. Although biological drives and urges may not be the main determinants of personality, biological ancestry can't be ignored completely. By choosing to focus primarily on the environment, the social–cognitive theorists sometimes ignore potentially important motivational factors that are controlled largely by biological processes. In fairness, more recent versions of social–cognitive theories are seeking to integrate genetic, biological, and environmental factors into a more general theory of personality development (e.g., Mischel & Shoda, 1998).

Test Yourself 12.2

Check your knowledge of how personality develops by deciding whether each of the following statements is most likely to have been made by a psychodynamic, humanistic, or social–cognitive personality theorist. (You will find the answers in the Appendix.)

1. Ethel talks a lot, but that's only because she's trying to cover up her true feelings of inadequacy: _____
2. Teresa is very demanding, but that's because her boyfriend always gets her what she wants: _____
3. Sally can't help herself—her basic needs are preventing her from realizing her true potential: _____
4. Sharma seems to be a tireless volunteer, but in truth she secretly resents people in need: _____
5. Robert isn't really an intellectual—he just acts that way because both of his parents are famous academics and he desperately wants to please them: _____
6. Henry is shy because he lacks confidence in his abilities, and he's convinced that he can't really influence or control the people around him: _____
7. Ralph sleeps around a lot, but that's because he can't control his animalistic nature: _____

Resolving the Person–Situation Debate

LEARNING GOALS
• Define the person–situation debate and discuss its components.
• Discuss how genetic factors influence personality.

ACCORDING TO SOCIAL–COGNITIVE THEORIES, behavior is primarily the product of the environment. As a result, you might be expected to act somewhat inconsistently from one situation to the next. If you're rewarded for acting bold and aggressive when negotiating a deal (such as buying a car), you'll almost certainly act bold and aggressive in such situations in the future. But if similar actions lead to rejection in the classroom or in social situations, you might very well turn meek and mild in class or at a party. If you think about it, you probably know people who seem to change their behavior at the drop of a hat, acting one way in one situation and quite differently in another.

This kind of reasoning really strikes at the core of personality. Remember, personality is defined in terms of lasting qualities—the set of characteristics that distinguishes us from others and leads us to act consistently across situations. Throughout this chapter, we've assumed that such characteristics exist and that they can be measured and interpreted through the application of psychological principles. But the assumption of cross-situational consistency in behavior has been challenged by some prominent psychologists, notably Walter Mischel, and the issue has come to be known as the **person–situation debate**.

person–situation debate A controversial debate centering on whether people really do behave consistently across situations.

The Person–Situation Debate

The argument is really a simple one. If people possess unique and enduring personality traits, we should be able to predict their behavior from one situation to the next. If you believe Roger to be dishonest, perhaps because you witnessed him peering over

Rowena's shoulder during a history test, you expect him to be dishonest in the future. You predict he will pocket a dropped wallet or take the money Rowena left lying on the counter. Put more technically, measurements of behavior should correlate across situations; that is, if you know the chances that someone will perform a trait-related action in situation A, you should be able to predict the chances that he or she will perform a similar action in situation B.

Unfortunately, as Walter Mischel (1968) pointed out four decades ago, there's little evidence for this assumption (see also Peterson, 1968). If you look carefully at studies reporting correlations between measures of behavior that tap a particular kind of personality trait, such as how honest you are at two different points in time, the correlations are almost always low. Whereas a correlation of 1.00 implies perfect behavioral consistency across situations, Mischel found that actual correlations rarely exceeded 0.30 and were usually even lower (see also Kenrick & Funder, 1988; Ross & Nisbett, 1991). To say the least, Mischel's conclusions were quite controversial; in fact, they rocked the foundation of personality theory. Without consistency in behavior, the psychological construct of personality has little meaning.

Situational Consistency   Despite the data, very few psychologists (including Mischel) reject the concept of personality altogether. People may not always act consistently *across* situations, but they do tend to act consistently *within* a situation. For example, in a famous study by Hartshorne and May (1928), the honesty of schoolchildren was tested by placing them in situations in which they could act dishonestly without much likelihood of being caught (money was left on a table, cheating on a test was possible, and so on). Little evidence of cross-situational consistency was found, but the children did tend to act the same way in a similar situation. For instance, kids who cheated on a test were not necessarily more likely to steal money, but they were more likely to cheat on a test again if given the chance. In short, people do act consistently from one situation to the next, as long as the situations are similar (Mischel & Peake, 1982; Mischel & Shoda, 1995).

Results of the type reported by Hartshorne and May and others (see Mischel, 1968) are based primarily on the observation of single individual behaviors (Did the child steal the money on the table?) rather than on collections of behaviors. To get an accurate estimate of a true personality trait, many psychologists believe, you need to collect lots of observations, not just one; single observations tend to be unreliable and not necessarily representative of true behavior (Epstein, 1979). One reason reliable personality traits are often obtained through psychometric tests (see the earlier discussion of trait theorists) might be because the collected ratings are based on a long history of watching oneself or others behave (Ross & Nisbett, 1991).

In fact, if you record how people act across longer periods of time, rather than in single situations, they tend to act quite consistently. For example, Fleeson (2001) asked people to rate themselves on the Big Five trait adjectives (e.g., How "talkative" were you in the last three hours?) five times a day for a period of several weeks. Although people's ratings on the Big Five dimensions varied a lot over the course of a day, their average ratings over a week were quite stable from one week to the next. For any given Big Five dimension, such as extroversion, we're apparently capable of a wide range of expression, but our average rating remains stable and unique over time (Fleeson, 2004).

Self-Monitoring   Some psychologists have argued that the tendency to act consistently or haphazardly across different situations may itself be a kind of personality trait. People differ in the extent to which they engage in chameleon-like **self-monitoring**, which is the tendency to mold or change your behavior to fit the situation at hand (Snyder, 1974, 1987). People who are high self-monitors attend closely to their present situation and change their behavior to best fit their needs. They're likely to alter their behavior, and even their stated opinions and beliefs, simply to please

self-monitoring The degree to which a person monitors a situation closely and changes his or her behavior accordingly; people who are high self-monitors may not behave consistently across situations.

The Value of Self-Monitoring

Not surprisingly, your personality traits can play an important role in determining how well you succeed in life. Consider your ability to self-monitor—that is, your capacity to "act like different persons in different situations and with different people" (Snyder, 1995, p. 39). Clearly, if your goal is politics, self-monitoring would be a plus, but people who rate highly in self-monitoring seem also to have advantages in many other professions and activities. For example, high self-monitors tend to get better performance evaluations on the job—from both peers and supervisors (Miller & Cardy, 2000). High self-monitors even get higher tips when employed as waiters and waitresses at restaurants (Lynn & Simons, 2000).

Why are high self-monitors successful? One factor is their natural tendency to be good actors—they can tell people what they want to hear in a believable way and then act accordingly. High self-monitors also spend time closely observing their environments and, as a result, tend to be perceptive at reading other people. High self-monitors are good at spotting deception, and they're usually quite accurate in judging personality characteristics (Sanz, Sanchez-Bernados, & Avia, 1996). The net result is that high self-monitors tend to occupy central and important positions in social networks, which,

in turn, helps them perform well on the job (Ajay, Kilduff, & Brass, 2001).

Should we all try to become high self-monitors, or at least improve on our self-monitoring skills? As with many other personality traits, there may be a genetic component to self-monitoring (Gangestad & Simpson, 1993), so it's possible that our options are limited. And it's important to note that there are some downsides to the self-monitoring trait. For example, high self-monitors are more concerned with a person's social status than low self-monitors; they also have difficulty committing to romantic relationships, show less marital satisfaction, and are more likely to divorce (Leone & Hall, 2003). In addition, couples that consist of two high self-monitors are less likely to trust one another than couples consisting of two low self-monitors (Norris & Zweigenhaft, 1999). High self-monitors also tend to stick to well-defined social situations that, in turn, allow them to use established social scripts (Ickes et al., 2006).

From a practical standpoint, it might make sense for employers to pay attention to the self-monitoring trait. It seems clear that self-monitoring is related to job performance, especially in jobs that require adapting to social situations. People who adapt well to their

© Bob Daemmrich/The Image Works

Successful politicians are often high self-monitors, which means they attend closely to the situation and behave accordingly.

environment are more likely to see the rewards it can bring, even at the risk of appearing to be a little inconsistent in their behavior across situations.

CRITICAL THINKING

Decide whether each of your friends is a high or a low self-monitor. Whom do you prefer to be around—the high self-monitors or the low self-monitors?

someone with whom they're currently interacting. People who are low self-monitors are less likely to change their actions or beliefs and, consequently, are more likely to show consistency in their behavior across situations (Gangestad & Snyder, 1985).

Scales have been developed to measure self-monitoring tendencies. Typically, you're asked to respond to statements such as the following: "I'm not always the person that I appear to be" or "I might deceive people by acting friendly when I really dislike them." People who score highly on self-monitoring, not surprisingly, are likely to conform to social norms. They also tend to be aware of how their behavior is affecting others. High self-monitors even seem to remember the actions of others better than low self-monitors, especially when those actions are unexpected or unusual (Beers, Lassiter, & Flannery, 1997). Thus, self-monitoring can be quite adaptive: It's usually in our interest to monitor the environment and change our behavior accordingly (Graziano & Bryant, 1998; Mischel & Shoda, 1998). For more on the practical value of self-monitoring, take a look at the Practical Solutions feature.

A Resolution   Most psychologists resolve the person–situation debate by simply assuming that it's necessary to take both the person and the situation into account. It's unlikely that either alone is enough to explain behavior or to allow us to predict consistency (Mischel, 2004). People *interact* with situations, and how they behave will depend partly on what's required by current needs. Personality "traits" will reveal themselves primarily in situations in which they're relevant (Kenrick et al., 1990) and may not otherwise. Similarly, given the right situation, each of us is capable of acting in a way that seems to violate our basic nature. Recognition of the vital role of the person and the situation is so widespread that one prominent personality psychologist recently proclaimed that the person–situation debate "can at least be declared about 98% over" (Funder, 2001, p. 199). (We'll return to this issue, and provide some compelling illustrations of the power of the situation, when we take up the general topic of social psychology in Chapter 13.)

Genetic Factors in Personality

There's other evidence supporting the role of the "person" in personality development. It appears that we may be born with certain genetic predispositions—perhaps our brains are wired in a certain way—that tend to cause us to act in consistent ways throughout our lifetime. It's not unusual for family members to show similar personality traits, although experience could play an important role in producing these similarities. At the same time, brothers and sisters can show strikingly different personality traits, even though they've been raised in what seem to be highly similar environments. Observations like these indicate that more than the environment is at work in determining personality.

Twin Data   Most of the evidence for genetic factors in personality, as in the study of intelligence, comes from twin studies. Identical twins are compared with fraternal twins when the twins have been reared together or apart. Perhaps you've seen reports in the popular media of identical twins who were separated at birth but ended up sharing many of the same personality traits. There's the case of identical twins Oscar and Frank—one raised as a Nazi in Czechoslovakia and the other as a Jew in Trinidad. When they were reunited in 1979, it was discovered that they shared numerous odd but consistent behaviors. For example, they both had a habit of sneezing deliberately in elevators to surprise people, and they both liked to flush toilets before and after use.

However, anecdotes can't be used to make a convincing scientific case (Horgan, 1993). Coincidences are possible, and some of the more famous reunited twins may have had ulterior motives for manufacturing shared traits (for example, Oscar and his brother eventually sold the rights to their story in Hollywood). More compelling evidence comes from group studies, in which the personality characteristics of large numbers of twins are analyzed. In one such study (Tellegen et al., 1988), 217 pairs of identical twins who had been reared together and 44 pairs of twins who had been reared apart were compared with 114 pairs of fraternal twins reared together and 27 pairs reared apart. Each of the participants was administered the MMPI, which, as you remember from our earlier discussion, is a widely used questionnaire for measuring personality traits.

Some of the results of this study are shown in ▌ Figure 12.9, for several of the personality traits measured by the MMPI. Of main interest is the similarity between members of a twin pair, expressed in terms of correlation coefficients. In other words, for a trait such as aggressiveness or positive emotionality, can we predict the score that one twin will receive on the MMPI if we know the score of the other twin? Correlations close to 1.00 suggest that members of a twin pair share many of the same personality traits. As the figure indicates, identical twins tend to show higher

The Williams sisters share tremendous skill on the tennis court, but do they share similar personalities as well?

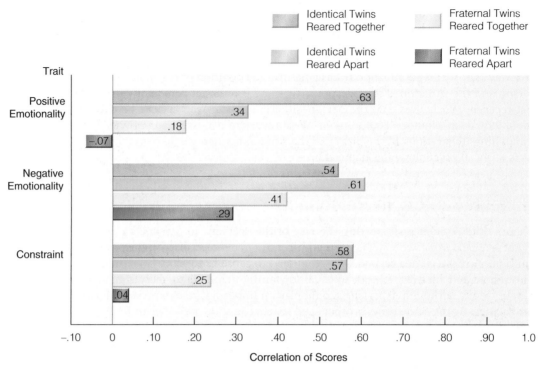

FIGURE 12.9 The Genetics of Personality

Are identical twins more likely than fraternal twins to share basic personality traits? Does the rearing environment matter? These average correlations from Tellegen and colleagues reveal consistent differences between identical and fraternal twins, irrespective of the rearing environment, suggesting that genetics plays a role in determining personality. The environment also had a significant effect in some cases, but overall it appeared to be less important. (Adapted from "Personality Similarity in Twins Reared Apart and Together," by A. Tellegen et al., 1988, *Journal of Personality and Social Psychology*, 54(6), 1031–1039. Copyright (c) 1988 by the American Psychological Association. Adapted by permission of the author.)

correlations than fraternal twins, regardless of whether they've been reared together or apart. Twins who share the same genes but have been reared in different households tend to have more similar personality traits than fraternal twins who have been reared together.

Of course, the twin data are based primarily on self-report inventories such as the MMPI. Psychologists have rarely conducted studies observing actual behaviors among large groups of twins, so some caution must be exercised before drawing firm conclusions (Funder, 2001; Maccoby, 2000). Moreover, as noted in Chapter 10, it's not necessarily the case that twins reared in separate environments have distinctly different experiences. For example, identical twins look similar and so might be treated by the world in similar ways based on their level of attractiveness (see Chapter 13).

Overall, the twin data do indicate that at least some enduring psychological traits may have their origins in genetic predispositions present at birth (Bouchard, 2004). Not surprisingly, psychologists have argued as well that certain traits are likely to be grounded in genetics because of the adaptive role those traits played in the evolutionary history of our species (e.g., Buss, 2006). Of course, the expression of genetic tendencies depends on the nurturing conditions (the environment): Nature interacts with nurture in determining a person's final physical and psychological makeup. Therefore, although genes may play a critical role in determining how personality develops, environmental factors are also extremely important (Beer, Arnold, & Loehlin, 1998; Plomin et al., 1998).

Test Yourself 12.3

Check your knowledge about the person–situation debate by deciding whether each of the following statements is True or False. *(You will find the answers in the Appendix.)*

1. In the Hartshorne and May study, kids who cheated on a test were not more likely to steal money, but they were more likely to cheat on a test again if given the chance. *True or False?*
2. People tend to act consistently from one situation to the next, as long as the situations are similar. *True or False?*
3. People who are low self-monitors tend to change their behaviors to fit the situation at hand. *True or False?*
4. Identical twin studies show little evidence for genetic contributions to personality characteristics, as measured by the MMPI. *True or False?*
5. Most psychologists believe personality traits are revealed in all situations, regardless of the relevance of the trait. *True or False?*

Review *Psychology for a Reason*

There's little question in most people's minds about the status of personality—anyone will tell you that people differ in enduring ways. We all have behavioral quirks that distinguish us from others, and we often give the impression of acting consistently across situations. If asked, people have little trouble making judgments about the personality of others. We quickly and without hesitation identify Rowena as friendly and outgoing and Roger as nasty and generally no good. Moreover, as discussed at the beginning of this chapter, it makes adaptive sense to act consistently, especially when particular actions help us to survive and enjoy productive lives. Thus personality is clearly an important and useful feature of the adaptive mind.

To psychologists, however, the study of personality has proven to be difficult and elusive. Historically, researchers have disagreed about how to best approach the topic. As we've seen, questions have even been raised about the validity of the concept itself—how useful is personality in describing individual differences in behavior? (Remember, similar issues were raised about the study of intelligence.) Still, the vast majority of psychologists agree that personality is a useful construct and that it is needed to describe the full range of human psychological functioning.

Conceptualizing and Measuring Personality Trait theories are formal systems for measuring and identifying personality characteristics, such as emotional stability or extroversion. Currently, the trait theorists seem to agree that there are five basic personality dimensions—the so-called Big Five (extroversion, agreeableness, conscientiousness, neuroticism, and openness)—that accurately and reliably describe a person's unique and consistent attributes. Psychometric techniques such as factor analysis, along with the development of personality tests such as the NEO-PI-R and the MMPI, have proven useful in advancing theory and in applying what we've learned about personality to practical settings. For example, the MMPI and the NEO-PI-R are sometimes used in business settings as part of the decision-making process for hiring new employees.

Determining How Personality Develops Identifying stable personality traits, however, leaves unanswered the general question of how those traits originate. Noted psychologists have developed several grand theories of personality development, including the psychodynamic approach of Freud, the humanistic perspective of Rogers and Maslow, and the social–cognitive

approach of Bandura, Mischel, and others. These theoretical frameworks propose very different mechanisms for personality development and offer quite different conceptions of basic human nature. The pessimism of Freud, with his emphasis on battling unconscious biological urges, is counterbalanced by the optimism of the humanists. From a social–cognitive perspective, the environment and beliefs about controlling that environment produce the consistent actions that define personality. Each of these perspectives has been enormously influential in the past and remains so today.

Resolving the Person–Situation Debate The concept of personality demands at least some consistency in behavior across situations. But evidence suggests that cross-situational consistency in behavior may be low. In light of the person–situation debate, a proper analysis of behavior requires consideration of the interaction between the person and the situation. We must also keep in mind the contribution of genetics to personality—twin studies indicate that there may be a genetic component to enduring behavior.

Active Summary *(You will find the answers in the Appendix.)*

Conceptualizing and Measuring Personality

• (1) _____ analysis studies correlations among test responses, with the goal of identifying a set of factors that together predict test performance on a personality test.

• Raymond Cattell identified (2) _____ factors or source traits. Hans (3) _____ argued that personality can best be described in terms of (4) _____ primary dimensions, or superfactors: extroversion, neuroticism, and (5) _____. The contemporary Big (6) _____ approach holds that extroversion, (7) _____, openness, (8) _____, and (9) _____ best describe personality.

• (10) _____ proposed a classification scheme for identifying personality traits. (11) _____ traits are ruling passions that dominate a person's life. (12) _____ traits are expressed by the (13) _____ to 10 descriptive terms that you'd use to describe someone you know well. (14) _____ traits are less obvious traits that are not always reflected in behavior.

• (15) _____ report inventories are (16) _____, standardized, fill-in-the-answer tests, such as the (17) _____ Personality Factor and the Minnesota (18) _____ Personality Inventory (MMPI). With (19) _____ personality tests, such as the Rorschach and the Thematic (20) _____ Test (TAT), elements of the test taker's personality are revealed in the way he or she interprets an unstructured or (21) _____ stimulus.

Determining How Personality Develops

• Sigmund Freud divided the mind into three parts: (22) _____, (23) _____, and (24) _____, and argued that the (25) _____ mind powerfully affects behavior. Dreams are a window into the unconscious and have an external or (26) _____ content and a (27) _____ or latent content. Personality consists of the (28) _____, which is governed by inborn (29) _____; the (30) _____, which encourages us to act in an ideal fashion; and the (31) _____, which acts to compromise and encourages us to act with reason and deliberation. Conflict among the various aspects of personality results in (32) _____, which we attempt to combat with (33) _____ mechanisms. As children we progress through (34) _____ stages that help determine adult personality.

• (35) _____ psychology developed largely in reaction to Freud's pessimistic view of human nature. The approach emphasizes self-(36) _____, choice, (37) _____, growth, and that we are all unique. According to Carl Rogers, we have a basic need for (38) _____ self-regard. Problems may arise when we mold our self-concept to satisfy others (conditions of worth), which can lead to (39) _____, a discrepancy between the true self and experience. Abraham Maslow stressed the drive toward (40) _____-_____, using a pyramid to prioritize needs—your personality reflects where you fit in the need hierarchy.

• Social-(41) _____ approaches hold that personality growth and development result from interactions between experiences and how we interpret them (cognitions or beliefs). We acquire situation-specific response tendencies through (42) _____ conditioning, operant conditioning, and (43) _____. According to (44) _____ learning theory, we acquire many personality traits by imitating others. How we (45) _____ our experiences is also critical. Perceived (46) _____ of control—how much power we think we have over our environment—and self-(47) _____—our beliefs about our own abilities—determine how we ultimately interpret experience and shape its effects on personality.

Resolving the Person–Situation Debate

• The person–situation debate is about whether people are (48) _____ in their behavior from one situation to another. Most psychologists note that although behavior across situations may not be consistent, behavior is usually consistent (49) _____ a situation. The tendency to act consistently or inconsistently may itself be a personality trait, one known as (50) _____-_____. High self-monitors pay close attention to their own behavior, modifying it as necessary to fit their needs in a situation and are more likely to act (51) _____ across situations. Low self-monitors are less likely to change their beliefs and actions and are more likely to act (52) _____ across situations. Current thinking is that the individual and the situation (53) _____ to produce personality.

• Studies with (54) _____ and fraternal twins that have been raised together or apart indicate that (55) _____ factors contribute to personality. Traits measured by the MMPI reveal that identical twins tend to show more similar traits than (56) _____ twins, whether or not they were raised together. Such data have convinced psychologists that some enduring personality traits are rooted in genetic predispositions present at birth.

Terms to Remember

anal stage, 390
Big Five, 382
cardinal traits, 384
central traits, 385
collective unconscious, 392
conditions of worth, 394
conscious mind, 388
defense mechanisms, 389
ego, 389
genital stage, 392
humanistic psychology, 393
id, 389

incongruence, 394
latency period, 391
locus of control, 397
oral stage, 390
personality, 379
person–situation debate, 400
phallic stage, 390
positive regard, 394
preconscious mind, 388
projective personality test, 386
psychodynamic theory, 388
reciprocal determinism, 398

repression, 390
secondary traits, 385
self-actualization, 395
self-concept, 393
self-efficacy, 398
self-monitoring, 401
self-report inventories, 385
social–cognitive theories, 396
superego, 389
trait theories, 381
trait, 379
unconscious mind, 388

Media Resources

 ThomsonNOW

www.thomsonedu.com/ThomsonNOW

Go to this site for the link to ThomsonNow, your one-stop study shop. Take a Pre-Test for this chapter and Thomson-Now will generate a personalized Study Plan based on your test results! The Study Plan will identify the topics you need to review and direct you to online resources to help you master those topics. You can then take a Post-Test to help you determine the concepts you have mastered and what you still need to work on.

 Companion Website

www.thomsonedu.com/psychology/nairne

Go to this site to find online resources directly linked to your book, including a glossary, flashcards, quizzing, weblinks, and more.

 Psyk.trek 3.0

Check out the Psyk.trek CD-ROM for further study of the concepts in this chapter. Psyk.trek's interactive learning modules, simulations, and quizzes offer additional opportunities for you to interact with, reflect on, and retain the material:

Personality Theory: Freudian Theory
Personality Theory: Behavioral Theory

CHAPTER 13

Social Psychology

It's the annual Christmas party for Everville Industries. Al Hobart has worked at the company for a year and a half now, and he's itching for a promotion to the advertising department. To his left stands the head of advertising,

Mr. Barker, along with several of Hobart's equally ambitious coworkers. The topic of conversation is the company's recent disastrous marketing campaign, spearheaded by Barker, whose shortcomings are recognized by everyone in the group save one—Barker himself.

"It just goes to show you," spouts Barker confidently, "you can never underestimate the ignorance of the people. It was a brilliantly conceived but unappreciated plan."

"Absolutely," says Ms. Adler, "a brilliant plan."

"People are just stupid," employee Jones remarks. "They wouldn't know a good marketing campaign if it came up and bit them on the cheek."

I'm working with jerks, the little voice inside Hobart's head chimes. These people have no values—no sense of personal integrity. Everyone knows that campaign was terrible.

"And what about you, Hobart," Barker says, his eyes meeting Al's. "What do you think?"

"Brilliant plan, sir," Hobart says, hesitating only slightly; "the work of genius. . . ."

Put on your psychological thinking cap for a moment, and let's analyze Hobart's behavior. From this brief exchange, can you draw any conclusions about what kind of person he is? What does your psychological training tell you? He clearly violated his own beliefs and outwardly conformed to the opinions expressed by the people around him. He also drew some rather nasty conclusions about his colleagues, concluding they were jerks for shamelessly agreeing with the misguided boss. Do you think Hobart will now apply those same negative personality traits to himself? Do you suppose he might have acted differently if the head of advertising had been absent, or if the job promotion had already been his? Stop for a moment and think about how *you* might have acted in this situation. Would you have conformed to the opinions of others? Would you, like Hobart, have left the conversation thinking your coworkers suffered from fundamental personality flaws?

By now you've learned that behavior can be importantly influenced by the immediate context. Not only does your behavior change according to circumstance, but you think differently too. Hobart's example is relatively harmless, but other situa-

Social psychology is the discipline that studies how we think about, influence, and relate to other people. As you'll see shortly, how we think and act changes in characteristic ways when we're in the presence of others. In fact, the mere presence of other people, as well as their behaviors, can be among the most powerful and pervasive of environmental influences. We'll tackle the topics of social psychology by focusing on three specific social problems that play a vital role in helping us adjust and adapt successfully to our world (see ▌Figure 13.1).

Interpreting the Behavior of Others

As social animals, living in a social world, we're constantly trying to interpret the behavior of other people. We form impressions of our friends, teachers, and our colleagues in the workplace—we even form impressions of the people we meet on the street. We develop theories about why people behave the way they do; we form attitudes that help us act adaptively in the presence of particular individuals or groups. At the same time, as you'll see, there are systematic biases in the interpretation process as well.

Behaving in the Presence of Others

Everyone's behavior is strongly influenced by the social context. For example, sometimes your ability to perform a task will improve when others are present; sometimes your performance falls apart. Your behavior will also be strongly influenced by the presence of authority figures and by the opinions of fellow members in a group. What are the factors that determine when you'll yield to the demands of others, and what implications do these factors have for the structure of society? We'll expand our psychological analysis of Hobart's behavior and extend it to a broader range of situations.

Establishing Relations With Others

It's certainly adaptive to interpret the behavior of others and to change behavior accordingly in their presence. But among our most important social actions are the relationships we form with others. Without attraction and romantic love, it's unlikely that the human species would survive; but it's not just mating we need—we rely on the relationships within the family as well as the social structures within society to help protect and nurture us and our offspring.

> **social psychology** The discipline that studies how people think about, influence, and relate to other people.

Interpreting the behavior of others.

Behaving in the presence of others.

Establishing relations with others.

▌**FIGURE 13.1** Summarizing the Adaptive Problems
In this chapter we address the three main adaptive problems studied by social psychologists.

tions can have more far-reaching and disturbing consequences. Suppose Mr. Barker wasn't the head of an advertising department but a commanding officer in the military, and the locale was a prison located on the outskirts of Baghdad. The topic of conversation? Not a marketing campaign, but rather Barker's decision to subject Iraqi prisoners to torture and humiliation. How would you react now? Would you still conform to the opinions of your superior?

Interpreting the Behavior of Others: Social Cognition

LEARNING GOALS

- Discuss how physical attractiveness, stereotypes, and social schemas influence our impressions of others.
- Discuss how we attribute causality to the behavior of others, explaining our biases and errors.
- Explain how attitudes are formed and changed.

WE BEGIN OUR TREATMENT of social psychology with a discussion of how people *think about* other people—how impressions of others are formed, how causes are attributed to behavior, and what mechanisms underlie the formation of attitudes about people and things. Social psychologists typically group these topics together under the title of **social cognition**, which is the study of how we use cognitive processes—such as perception, memory, and thought—to help make sense of other people as well as ourselves. First up is the topic of person perception, which deals specifically with how we form impressions of others.

social cognition The study of how people use cognitive processes—such as perception, memory, thought, and emotion—to help make sense of other people as well as themselves.

Person Perception: How Do We Form Impressions of Others?

When we first discussed the topic of perception in Chapter 5, I focused on the processes used to interpret elementary sensations into meaningful wholes. In that chapter you learned that perception is driven by a combination of *bottom-up processing*—the actual physical sensations received by the sensory equipment—and *top-down processing*, which takes into account our expectations and beliefs about the world. We do not simply see what's "out there" in the physical world; our perceptions are also influenced by our *expectations* of what we'll find.

A similar kind of analysis applies to the perception of people. When you encounter a person for the first time, your initial impressions are influenced by physical factors—attractiveness, facial expression, skin color, clothing—and by your meaningful interpretations of those physical attributes. If you see a sloppily dressed, unshaven man weaving down the street, you're likely to form a negative first impression, partly because past experiences have taught you to avoid people who fit this description. You could be wrong, of course, but in the face of limited information, it's usually adaptive to use background knowledge to help predict the possible consequences of an interaction.

Physical Appearance   One of the most powerful determinants of a first impression is a person's *physical appearance*. In fact, evidence suggests that we can form an initial impression, such as how trustworthy a person might be, after looking at a face for as little as 100 ms (Willis & Todorov, 2006)! Studies have shown that when we first look at someone who's physically attractive, we assume that he or she is more intelligent, better adjusted, and more socially aware than someone with average looks (Eagly et al., 1991; Feingold, 1992). In general, physically attractive people are also thought to be healthier (Kalick et al., 1998) and more inclined to succeed academically (Chia et al., 1998), and they're even less likely to get "carded" if they try to buy alcohol (McCall, 1997). These tendencies don't diminish as we age—the elderly also show a strong tendency to attribute positive personality characteristics to attractive people (Larose & Standing, 1998).

Why do we rely on physical appearance to form a first impression? After all, it seems like a rather shallow way to judge a person. The reason is simple: When you form a *first* impression, you use the information that's available. You almost always notice the way a person looks, along with his or her facial expression, and perhaps even the way the person is walking or sitting. These raw materials are combined with your background knowledge to generate an expectation of what an encounter with that person might be like.

Obviously, judging a book by its cover isn't always an effective long-term strategy for impression formation. Not all people rely on physical appearance to the same extent (Livingston, 2001), and cultural background is important too—some cultures don't rely on attractiveness as much as others (Wheeler & Kim, 1997). But it can be reasonable in the short term. If the approaching person appears attractive and well kept, at least you know he or she follows some of the accepted standards and norms of the culture. Think about it. If you were in trouble and needed help, whom would you approach—someone with poor personal hygiene and tattered clothes, or someone neat, clean, and well dressed?

Social Schemas   Psychologists believe much of the knowledge we use in social situations comes from social categories or schemas (Bodenhausen et al., 2003). Schemas are general knowledge structures stored in memory, such as your knowledge about how houses are constructed or about what it's like to go to a restaurant or the doctor's office (see Chapter 8). We use schemas to help us remember but also to help organize and interpret ongoing experience. A schema can be formed about most anything—a person, a place, or a thing. When schemas are about social experiences or people, they're commonly called **social schemas** (Fiske, 1993).

Returning to the unshaven, sloppily dressed man on the street, your initial impression is likely to be negative because his tattered appearance activates a common social schema about people. An unkempt appearance is associated with negative social characteristics—such as laziness or even criminal behavior—and his weaving gait signals possible drunkenness. All these things lead you to categorize the man as "trouble" and make it less likely that you'll either ask him for help or give help to him if he requests it. Both the man's physical appearance and his behavior feed into your existing social schema about seedy characters; and, once he's been categorized, the schema directs you to alter your behavior accordingly.

social schema A general knowledge structure, stored in long-term memory, that relates to social experiences or people.

How other people look is likely to activate social schemas that direct and guide your behavior. Social schemas are generally adaptive, but under some circumstances they can lead to inappropriate conclusions or actions.

Stereotypes   When social schemas revolve around the traits and behaviors of *groups* and their members, they're called **stereotypes**. We form stereotypes about many kinds of social groups, from insurance agents to college professors, but the three most common are based on gender, race, and age (Fiske, 1993). Most people carry around a collection of impressions about men and women. For example, men are typically seen as strong, dominant, and aggressive; women are typically seen as sensitive, warm, and dependent (Deaux & Lewis, 1984).

Stereotypes seem to share many of the properties of categories. Not surprisingly, some of the more popular theories of how stereotypes are formed resemble the theories of categorization discussed in Chapter 9. For example, *prototype theories* of stereotypes assume we store abstract representations of the typical features of a group; we then judge particular individuals based on their similarity to the prototype (Cantor & Mischel, 1978). *Exemplar theories* assume we store memories of particular individuals, or exemplars, and these individual memories form the basis for stereotypes (Smith & Zárate, 1992). So, for example, the stereotypic belief that African Americans are athletic would be based on comparisons with particular individuals (e.g., Serena Williams or Tiger Woods) rather than with some abstract representation (Hilton & von Hippel, 1996).

Stereotypes become "activated" whenever we're exposed to stereotypic beliefs and actions. For example, men are more likely to behave sexually toward a woman if they've recently seen a television commercial in which women were presented as sexual objects (Rudman & Borgida, 1995). In addition, witnessing an African American man engaging in a negative stereotypic behavior influences how a White male evaluates other African American men (Henderson-King & Nisbett, 1996). Recent exposure to behavior consistent with a stereotype apparently activates, or "primes," the stereotype, which in turn affects future behavior (Stewart et al., 1998). At the same time, the effects of stereotypic beliefs and actions depend importantly on the situation. For example, you are more susceptible to the negative effects of an activated stereotype if you're angry and less susceptible if you are being praised (Smith & Semin, 2007).

Self-Fulfilling Prophecies   Once stereotypes are activated, we expect certain kinds of behavior from members of groups. These expectations can produce a **self-fulfilling prophecy effect**, which occurs when your expectations about a person's actions cause that person to behave in the expected way (Merton, 1948). If you expect someone to be unreliable and you act in line with your expectations (such as snubbing or avoiding the person), the chances that he or she will assume that role in the future may actually increase.

Let's consider an experiment demonstrating the effect. In a study by Mark Snyder and colleagues (1977), undergraduate men were asked to talk to undergraduate women, whom they had never met, on the telephone. Prior to the conversation, the men were shown a photograph of their prospective telephone partner. The partner appeared as either physically attractive or unattractive. In reality, the photos were of women from another college; they were not really photos of the women participating in the study. The intention of the experimenters was simply to lead the men to *believe* they were talking to a woman who was attractive or unattractive. As for the women, they were not given a photo of their partner, nor were they told that the man had been biased to think of them in a particular way. All of the telephone calls were taped, and social aspects of the men's and women's conversational styles were then rated by judges who were unaware of the men's assignment group.

Not surprisingly, if the men thought they were talking to an attractive female, their conversational styles were friendly and positive—more so than if their partner had been presented as unattractive. But the important finding of the study focused on the women. It turned out that the women's conversational styles also differed, depending on whether the man they were talking to thought they were attractive. The women who were presumed by their partners to be attractive were rated by the judges as more friendly, open and poised, and generally more pleasant than the

stereotypes The collection of beliefs and impressions held about a group and its members; common stereotypes include those based on gender, race, and age.

self-fulfilling prophecy effect A condition in which our expectations about the actions of another person actually lead that person to behave in the expected way.

CRITICAL THINKING

Do you think the social schemas that were activated in the telephone study were different for the men and the women? If so, in what way?

Perceiver's impression of the other person

Perceiver's behavior based on that impression

Corresponding behavior elicited from the other person

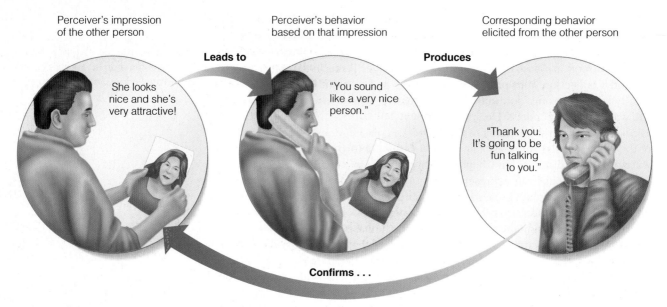

Leads to

Produces

She looks nice and she's very attractive!

"You sound like a very nice person."

"Thank you. It's going to be fun talking to you."

Confirms . . .

▌ FIGURE 13.2 The Self-Fulfilling Prophecy Effect
Our impressions of other people can affect how they behave, leading them to act in the expected ways. In the study by Snyder and colleagues (1977), if a male subject thought he was talking to an attractive female on the phone, his conversational style was rated as more friendly and positive—but so too was the conversational style of the woman on the other end.

women shown as unattractive. Remember, these women had no idea their male partners had preformed opinions about their attractiveness. Apparently, the friendly, positive conversational styles of the men elicited similar qualities from the women. This is the self-fulfilling prophecy effect—the expectations that we have toward others, along with our actions, can actually influence them to act in the expected way (see ▌Figure 13.2).

Self-fulfilling prophecies can have either positive or negative effects on people. As you've just seen, if someone expects you to be unattractive, or intellectually challenged, those expectations can bring out the worst in you. One recent study found that parents' beliefs about whether their adolescent child would engage in illegal drinking predicted the child's subsequent drinking behavior—if both parents expected their child to drink illegally, there was a greater chance their child would, in fact, drink illegally. But if a parent thought illegal drinking was unlikely, then this, too, predicted subsequent drinking behavior (Madon et al., 2004). The fact that expectations can importantly shape behavior has many implications for society, especially when it comes to the expectations generated about groups and cultures.

Prejudice   Stereotypes can lead to rigid interpretations of people. Stereotypes can cause us to overgeneralize and place too much emphasis on the differences that exist *between* groups (for instance, between men and women) and too little emphasis on the differences that exist *within* groups. Not all women are dependent, nor are all men strong. Furthermore, when the beliefs we hold about a group are negative or extreme, stereotypes increase the likelihood of prejudice and discrimination. **Prejudice** occurs when groups and their members are evaluated in a negative way (although you can also prejudge members of a group in a positive way); **discrimination** occurs when those beliefs lead to behaviors that are directed against members of the group. For example, you might be excluded from a job, or even criminally assaulted, just because of negative beliefs activated by your skin color or sexual preference.

Stereotypic beliefs, including those that lead to prejudice, may be automatically activated and not always under our conscious control (Bargh & Williams, 2006). For example, we discussed how simply witnessing a behavior can be enough to activate

prejudice Positive or negative evaluations of a group and its members.

discrimination Behaviors that are directed against members of a group.

prejudicial evaluations. Apparently, we don't even need to be consciously aware of the exposure to act accordingly. In a study by Greenwald and Banaji (1995), words that were consistent with a negative stereotype about African Americans were flashed on a computer screen at speeds too fast to be noticed. The people who were working at the computers were then more likely to evaluate a fictional character as having traits consistent with a negative African American stereotype (e.g., aggressive). This suggests that stereotypes can be activated and influence behavior in ways that are not consciously controlled (Bargh, 1999; Dion, 2003).

The good news is that we can reduce the prejudicial feelings that come from stereotypes through repeated exposure to individuals in the stereotyped group. For instance, as the amount of social contact between heterosexuals and homosexuals increases, negative feelings decrease (Whitely, 1990). However, there are a number of crucial elements at work in the maintenance of stereotypic beliefs. Whether beliefs will change depends on the nature of the social interactions and how representative the contacted individuals are of their stereotyped group. Moreover, the contact must be widespread and repeated; otherwise, people will attempt to defend their stereotypic views by explaining away individual contacts as unrepresentative of the group (Weber & Crocker, 1993).

Being aware of stereotypes can also help. Once you recognize that stereotypical reactions are common, and maybe even automatic, you can take steps to reduce their influence (Wegener & Petty, 1997). One course of action is to consciously adjust your behavior in a way that opposes the presumed influence of the stereotype. For example, if you're a male interviewing a woman for a job, steer away from questions that relate to typical gender stereotypes. It may even be possible to actively suppress stereotypic thoughts under some circumstances—that is, to prevent stereotypic thoughts from ever entering conscious awareness (e.g., Wyer, 2007). For more information on reducing the negative influence of stereotypic beliefs, see the Practical Solutions feature on the following page.

Obviously, prejudging people on the basis of stereotypes can lead to many kinds of discriminatory behavior, including racism, sexism, and ageism. Stereotypes are not necessarily accurate representations of people, nor can they be expected to apply to all individuals within a group. Still, as general rules of thumb, researchers assume that stereotypes do have adaptive value. They help people carve their social worlds into meaningful chunks, thereby providing a sense of direction about how to act when encountering new people. Furthermore, not all components of stereotypes are inaccurate, nor are all instances of prejudice negative. Stereotyping occurs in every culture of the world, and it's simply another way in which our minds organize and categorize the world.

Concept Review | Factors in Person Perception

FACTOR	ROLE IN PERSON PERCEPTION	EXAMPLE
Physical appearance	We tend to assume that physically attractive individuals are more intelligent, well-adjusted, and socially aware.	Tyrone encounters Michelle at a party. He finds her quite attractive. In addition, he perceives her as very personable, good-humored, and intelligent.
Social schemas	We use schemas (e.g., *stereotypes*) to organize and interpret ongoing experiences.	Tyrone believes most women are sensitive, warm, and dependent. He finds that Michelle's behavior fits this pattern.
Self-fulfilling prophecies	The activation of stereotypes leads to expectations of certain types of behavior. These expectations can cause the person to behave in the expected way.	Tyrone is very attentive toward Michelle at the party, bringing her refreshments and introducing her to all of his friends. Michelle relaxes; she begins to open up and make witty comments.

Combating Prejudice

It's generally adaptive for us to form stereotypes—they help us categorize our social world and make quick and efficient decisions about how to act. But when stereotypes lead to prejudice or discrimination, it's obviously in our interest to reduce their influence. There are several ways to combat stereotyping. As our awareness of the group increases, we're less prone to negative beliefs and actions. It's also possible to actively suppress stereotypic beliefs. For example, if undergraduates are asked to write essays about well-defined groups, such as the elderly or African Americans, their essays will show less stereotypic content if they've been instructed to actively avoid thinking about group members in preconceived ways.

Ironically, when people are taught to suppress thoughts and beliefs, there is some evidence for rebound effects. When no lon-

ger attempting to suppress them, those very thoughts seem to become more accessible and influential (Macrae & Bodenhausen, 2000; Wegner, 1994). For example, after suppression of a stereotype, people are more likely to recollect words consistent with the stereotype and are able to identify stereotypic words more quickly. Therefore, thought suppression may not be the best solution to reducing prejudice and discrimination.

Recent research suggests a more promising alternative may be to practice taking the perspective of others. Galinsky and Moskowitz (2000) asked undergraduates to write a narrative essay about a day in the life of an elderly man. One group was told to adopt the perspective of the man: "to imagine a day in the life of this individual as if you were this individual, looking at the world through his eyes and walking through the world in his shoes"

(p. 711). Compared to control conditions, those who adopted the man's perspective produced fewer stereotypic words in their essays and, in fact, tended to write about the subject in a more positive way. Moreover, there were no rebound effects. Similar results were found when White students were asked to take the perspective of an African American. Among other things, perspective taking increased the subjects' awareness of the continued discrimination that is directed against African Americans.

Negative stereotypes, which form the basis for prejudice and discrimination, are widespread and hard to avoid. As our familiarity with group members increases, however, the likelihood of prejudice and discrimination decreases. One reason may be that familiarity enables us to better see the world through another's eyes.

Attribution Theory: Attributing Causes to Behavior

attributions The inference processes people use to assign cause and effect to behavior.

It's natural for us to interpret the behavior of others. A wife tries to understand why her husband sits channel surfing in front of the television during their anniversary dinner; a student tries to understand why the teacher responds to his appeal for a grade change with a gruff "I didn't give you the grade, you earned the grade." When people assign causes to behaviors, psychologists refer to these inferences as **attributions**; attribution theories are concerned primarily with the psychological processes that underlie these inferences of cause and effect (Heider, 1944; Jones & Davis, 1965).

Let's consider an example of the attribution process at work. Suppose you notice that the mood of your friend Ira improves noticeably on Monday, Wednesday, and Friday afternoons, after he returns from lunch. He smiles a lot, exchanges pleasantries, and offers advice freely. These behaviors contrast sharply with his normally gruff manner and generally sour disposition. What accounts for the behavior change? According to the *covariation model of attribution* (Kelley, 1967), the first thing you'll look for is some factor that happens at the same time as, or *covaries* with, the behavior change. You'll try to identify an event or some other factor that's present when the behavior changes and is absent when the behavior change doesn't occur. In this particular example, it turns out Ira goes to his aerobic exercise class between 12:00 P.M. and 1:00 P.M. on those three days.

But covariation by itself is not a sufficient condition for the attribution of causality, for much the same reason that we can't infer causality from a simple correlation (see Chapter 2). Just because Ira's mood improves after his exercise class doesn't mean exercise is the cause of the change—other factors could be involved. According to the covariation model, we rely on three additional pieces of information to help us make the appropriate inference: *consistency*, *distinctiveness*, and *consensus*. When assessing *consistency*, we try to determine whether the change occurs regularly when the causal event is present—does Ira's mood consistently improve after exercise class? *Distinctiveness* provides an indication of whether the change occurs uniquely in the presence of the event—does Ira's mood improve after lunch only if he's been exercising?

Finally, we look for *consensus*, which tells us whether other people show similar reactions when they're exposed to the same causal event—is elevation of mood a common reaction to exercising?

Internal Versus External Attributions These three factors—consistency, distinctiveness, and consensus—work together to help us form an attribution. In the particular example we've been considering, we'll probably assume it's the *external* event—the exercise class—that's the cause of Ira's mood change. People tend to make an **external attribution**, one that appeals to external causes, when the behavior is high in consistency, distinctiveness, and consensus. In the case of Ira's pleasant mood, it's highly consistent (it happens every Monday, Wednesday, and Friday afternoon); its occurrence is distinctive (it occurs only after exercise class); and there is a high level of consensus (exercise tends to make people happy).

But what if no single event can be used to explain someone's behavior? For example, suppose Ira consistently smiles and acts pleasant in the afternoon, but he also smiles during the mornings and on days he's skipped the exercise class. Under these conditions it's doubtful you'll appeal to the environment to explain his behavior; instead, you'll make an **internal attribution**, which means you'll attribute his pleasant behavior to some internal personality trait or disposition: "Ira just has a great personality; he's a friendly, pleasant guy." Internal attributions are common when the consistency of a behavior is high but its distinctiveness and consensus are low. If Ira is pleasant all the time, his behavior after lunch lacks distinctiveness, and you'll be unlikely to appeal to some lunch activity to explain his behavior. Similarly, if the consensus is low—suppose exercise rarely improves mood for most people—you'll again resist attributing his pleasantries to this particular event (see █ Figure 13.3).

The Fundamental Attribution Error The attribution process seems logical enough, but social psychologists have discovered that we often take shortcuts in the attribution process. We're often required to make judgments quickly, and it's effortful and time consuming to consider all possible factors logically, so we cut corners in the attribution process. What happens, however, is that these shortcuts tend to produce consistent biases and errors in the judgment process. One of the most pervasive of these biases is the **fundamental attribution error** (sometimes also known as the *correspondence bias*): When we seek to interpret someone else's behavior, we tend to overestimate the influence of internal personal factors and underestimate the role of external situational factors (Jones, 1990; Ross, 1977).

external attribution Attributing the cause of a person's behavior to an external event or situation in the environment.

internal attribution Attributing the cause of a person's behavior to an internal personality trait or disposition.

CRITICAL THINKING

Suppose you were forced to make an attribution quickly, without much time for thought. Do you think quickly formed attributions are more likely to be internal or external? Explain.

fundamental attribution error When people seek to interpret someone else's behavior, they tend to overestimate the influence of internal personal factors and underestimate the role of situational factors.

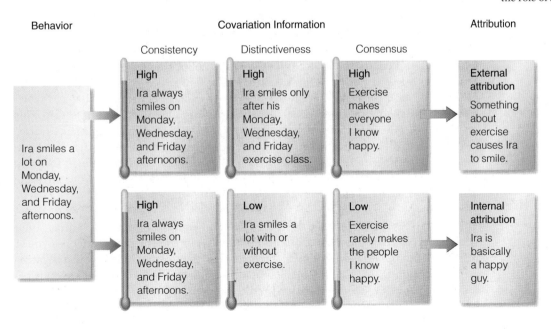

Behavior	Covariation Information			Attribution
	Consistency	Distinctiveness	Consensus	
Ira smiles a lot on Monday, Wednesday, and Friday afternoons.	**High** Ira always smiles on Monday, Wednesday, and Friday afternoons.	**High** Ira smiles only after his Monday, Wednesday, and Friday exercise class.	**High** Exercise makes everyone I know happy.	**External attribution** Something about exercise causes Ira to smile.
	High Ira always smiles on Monday, Wednesday, and Friday afternoons.	**Low** Ira smiles a lot with or without exercise.	**Low** Exercise rarely makes the people I know happy.	**Internal attribution** Ira is basically a happy guy.

█ **FIGURE 13.3** The Covariation Model of Attribution When we make internal attributions, we attribute behavior to internal personality characteristics; external attributions assume behavior reflects factors in the environment. In Kelley's attribution model, whether an internal or external attribution will be made about a particular behavior depends on *consistency, distinctiveness,* and *consensus.*

People often think that game show hosts, such as Alex Trebek, are extremely knowledgeable. What attribution processes might underlie such an inference?

In a classic demonstration of this bias, Jones and Harris (1967) had college students read essays expressing either positive or negative opinions about Fidel Castro's Communist regime in Cuba (at the time Castro's Cuba was a hot topic of discussion). Before reading the essays, one group of students was told that the person writing the essay had been allowed to write freely and choose the position adopted in the text. A second group was told the writer had no choice and had been forced to adopt a particular pro or con position. Afterward, the students in both groups were asked to speculate about the writer's true opinion on the topic. Thinking logically, you might assume if the writer had been given a choice, then the essay position probably reflected his or her true opinion on Castro. Alternatively, if the writer was simply following directions, it would be difficult to tell. To the surprise of the experimenters, however, the students tended to believe the essay always reflected the writer's true opinion, even when the students knew that the essay writer had been forced to adopt a particular position. This represents the fundamental attribution error at work: People tend to attribute an individual's activities to internal personal factors, even when there are strong situational explanations for the behavior (Jones, 1990).

Now consider another example: You're driving down the street, at a perfectly respectable speed, when you glance in your rearview mirror and see a pickup truck bearing down on your bumper. You speed up a bit, only to find the truck mirroring your every move. Being tailgated like this is a relatively common experience. But what kind of attribution do you typically make about the driver? Do you attribute the behavior to the person or to the situation? If you're like most people, your first response is likely to be an internal attribution—you naturally assume that the driver behind you has some severe personality flaw; put simply, the driver is a jerk. You ignore the possibility that situational factors might be compelling the driver to drive fast. Isn't it possible, for instance, that the driver is late for work or has a sick child in the backseat who is in need of a doctor? These kinds of attributions, which focus on the situation, don't usually enter our minds because our first tendency is to attribute behavior to a personal characteristic.

The Actor–Observer Effect Now let's switch gears for a moment. Think about what happens when you make attributions about your own behavior. Suppose you're the one doing the tailgating. Under these conditions, will you blame your tailgating on the fact that you're a jerk? Probably not. Instead, you're likely to explain your behavior by appealing to the situation. You're tailgating, you explain, because you're late for an appointment, or because the driver in front of you is simply driving too slowly. Generally, each of us shows what's called an **actor–observer effect**—we tend to attribute our own behavior to external sources but attribute the behavior of others to internal sources. One exception to this general rule is the **self-serving bias**, which means we take internal credit for our actions when those actions produce positive outcomes—such as attributing a solid A on the psychology test to hard work and intelligence. But we'll blame the situation when our behaviors are questionable or lead to failure. The self-serving bias is adaptive because it allows us to bolster and maintain our self-esteem and project a sense of self-importance and confidence to the world (Snyder, 1989).

These attributional biases have important implications—not just for you but for society as well. The tailgating example is relatively harmless (unless this behavior causes an accident), but think about a situation in which the focus of analysis is on welfare or homelessness. Because of attribution biases, you might naturally attribute, for example, being on welfare or losing a job to laziness, incompetence, or some other negative internal trait. But in many cases an individual is on welfare or out of work because of situational factors, perhaps because of some catastrophic life event. Attribution biases may have considerable adaptive value—because they allow us to make quick decisions about the causes of behavior—and may even be the products of adaptations rooted in our evolutionary past (Andrews, 2001). But they do have a downside; they can lead to misleading or even incorrect conclusions.

Attribution biases are reduced in some situations. For example, you're less likely to show the self-serving bias if you're working on a task with someone you know very well. If you're in a close relationship with your task partner, you're less likely to take credit for success on the task and assign blame for failure; if you don't know your partner very well, he or she gets the blame for failure and you take credit for the success (Sedikides et al., 1998). Your mood also seems to matter. For example, evidence indicates that you're more likely to commit the fundamental attribution error if you're in a positive mood; if you're in a negative mood, you're more willing to blame the situation, rather than the person, for the behavior (Forgas, 1998).

There appear to be cultural differences in these attributional biases as well. For example, people in Eastern cultures may be less susceptible to the fundamental attribution error than people in Western cultures (Norenzayan & Nisbett, 2000). People in Asian cultures, as noted previously, are more likely to focus on situational factors than people raised in the West. When asked to make a causal judgment about someone's behavior, the natural tendency of many Asians is to make a situation-based, external attribution. Although all cultures show the fundamental attribution error under some circumstances, the effect is easier to find among Westerners (Masuda & Kitayama, 2004).

actor–observer effect The overall tendency to attribute our own behavior to external sources but to attribute the behavior of others to internal sources.

self-serving bias The tendency to make internal attributions about one's own behavior when the outcome is positive and to blame the situation when one's behavior leads to something negative.

How we interpret risky behavior on the highway depends on who is doing the driving.

© Martin Mouchy/ Getty Images/Stone

Attitudes and Attitude Change

The final topic we'll consider in our discussion of social cognition is the study of attitudes and attitude change. An **attitude** is simply a positive or negative evaluation or belief held about something, which in turn may affect behavior. Like the other forms of social cognition we've discussed, attitudes are beneficial for a number of reasons. When they guide behavior, attitudes help us remain consistent in our actions and help us use our knowledge about individuals or situations. Attitudes also play an important role in our perception and interpretation of the world. They help us focus our attention on information relevant to our beliefs—particularly information that can help confirm an existing belief. As a result, attitudes may serve a kind of defensive function, protecting people's basic beliefs about themselves and others (Fazio, 1986).

attitude A positive or negative evaluation or belief held about something, which in turn may affect one's behavior; attitudes are typically broken down into cognitive, affective, and behavioral components.

The Components of an Attitude   Typically, social psychologists divide attitudes into three main components: a cognitive component, an affective component, and a behavioral component (Olson & Maio, 2003). The *cognitive component* represents what people know or believe about the object of their attitude; the *affective component* is made up of the feelings that the object produces; and the *behavioral component* is a predisposition to act toward the object in a particular way.

To see how these three components work together, let's suppose you've formed an unfavorable attitude toward your landlord. Your attitude rests on a foundation of facts and beliefs about behavior. You know, for instance, that the landlord has raised your rent three times in the last year, that he enters your apartment without first asking permission, and that he won't let you keep your pet cat Kepler without a huge pet deposit. These facts and beliefs form the cognitive component of your attitude. Accompanying these facts are your emotional reactions, which make up the affective component—when you see or think about your landlord, you get angry and slightly sick to your stomach. Finally, the behavioral component of your attitude predisposes you to act in certain ways. You may spend every Sunday reading the classified ads looking for a new apartment, and you may constantly complain about your landlord to anyone who'll listen. It's these three factors in combination—cognitive, affective, and behavioral—that compose what psychologists mean by an attitude (see ▌Figure 13.4).

Notice the behavioral component of the attitude is described as a *predisposition* to act. This is an important point to remember because attitudes don't always directly affect behavior. As you know, people sometimes act in ways that are inconsistent with their attitudes (Ajzen, 2001; Ajzen & Fishbein, 1977). When directly confronting your landlord, for instance, you may be all smiles even though underneath you're steaming. Attitudes do not always connect with behavior because behavior is usually determined by multiple factors—especially external factors. In some situations it's simply unwise to express your true feelings, such as when dealing with the landlord. In other situations, people act quickly and mindlessly without considering the true meaning or ramifications of their behavior (Langer, 1989). For example, people often sign petitions for activities they may not completely believe in or buy products that they don't really want, simply because they're in a hurry and don't want to be bothered further.

Attitude
Cognitive
Knowledge about the object
Affective
Emotional feelings
Behavioral
Predisposition to act

▌**FIGURE 13.4** The Three Components of Attitudes

Social psychologists typically divide attitudes into *cognitive*, *affective*, and *behavioral* components.

How Are Attitudes Formed?   Where do attitudes come from, and how are they acquired? There are many routes to attitude formation. We use our everyday experiences as the basis for many of our ideas and beliefs. How we interpret those experiences also depends partly on our inborn intellectual and personality traits (Tesser, 1993). Even something as simple as *mere exposure* can be sufficient to change your feelings about an object (Greenwald & Banaji, 1995). In classic work by Robert Zajonc

(1968), subjects were shown photographs of undergraduate men taken from a school yearbook. Some of the photos were shown only once or twice; others were shown up to 25 times. Following exposure, everyone was asked to give an estimate of how much they liked each of the men shown. The results revealed that the more often a photo had been presented, the more the subjects claimed to "like" the person shown. It's not clear exactly how to interpret this finding, in part because people's ratings change on a whole host of dimensions following exposure (Mandler, Nakamura, & Van Zandt, 1987). But it demonstrates how easily attitudes can be affected (Zajonc, 2001).

Experience is generally agreed to be the single most important factor affecting attitude formation. For instance, attitudes can be conditioned through experiences of the type discussed in Chapter 7. Events that occur outside of our control can acquire signaling properties, through *classical conditioning*, and then serve as an initial foundation for an attitude (Petty, DeSteno, & Rucker, 2001). Advertisers commonly try to manipulate how we feel toward consumer products by pairing the product with something pleasurable, such as an attractive model or a successful athlete. Through *operant conditioning*, attitudes are influenced by the rewards and punishments we receive for our actions. Certainly if you express a tentative opinion on a subject—"We've got too much big government in this country"—and this opinion is reinforced by people whom you respect, you're likely to express this same attitude again. Operant conditioning teaches us about the consequences of our behavior, and direct experience of this sort plays a significant role in attitude formation.

Finally, much of what we acquire from experience is the result of *observational learning*. We model significant others—our parents, peers, teachers, and so on—when it comes to both attitudes and behavior. The political convictions of most people, for example, mirror quite closely the political attitudes of their parents (McGuire, 1985). People use their peers, too, as a kind of reference group for judging the acceptability of their behaviors and beliefs. All you need to do is take a random sample of the behavior of teenagers in the local mall to see how important modeling behavior can be. Everything from language to musical taste to hairstyle to shoe type is replicated from one teen to the next.

Central and Peripheral Routes to Persuasion

For decades, social psychologists have been interested not only in how attitudes are formed initially but also in how attitudes can be changed (Petty, Wheeler, & Tormala, 2003). We're bombarded daily by dozens of persuasive messages from sources in business, politics, religion, and the arts. For obvious reasons, psychologists have tried to determine the important ingredients of persuasion: What are the factors that determine whether you'll be convinced to buy a particular product or support a particular political campaign? According to one popular theory of attitude change, known as the **elaboration likelihood model**, there are two primary routes to persuasion, one that is central and one that is peripheral (Petty & Cacioppo, 1986; Wegener & Carlston, 2005).

The *central route* to persuasion is the most obvious and familiar one. It operates when we're motivated and inclined to process an incoming persuasive communication with care and attention; we'll listen carefully to the arguments of the message, then judge those arguments according to their merits. Suppose you've recently changed your views on the topic of abortion after listening to a persuasive speaker at your school. If you carefully weighed the quality and strength of the arguments and then changed your attitude accordingly, you've been convinced via the central route. Not surprisingly, attitude changes that result from this kind of central processing tend to be stable and long lasting (Olson & Zanna, 1993).

The *peripheral route* to persuasion operates when we're either unable to process the message carefully or are unmotivated to do so. When we process a message peripherally, our attitudes are much more susceptible to change from superficial cues or from mere exposure (Petty & Wegener, 1997). Think about the typical beer

How closely do your attitudes mirror the positions and beliefs of your peer group?

© John Giustina/Photodisc/Getty Images

Do you think it's likely that all people have an innate attitude, or preference, for pleasurable things over painful things? What other kinds of attitudes might be influenced by genetic factors?

elaboration likelihood model A model proposing two primary routes to persuasion and attitude change: a *central* route, which operates when we are motivated and focusing our attention on the message, and a *peripheral* route, which operates when we are either unmotivated to process the message or are unable to do so.

source characteristics Features of the person who is presenting a persuasive message, such as his or her attractiveness, amount of power, or fame.

Why do you suppose this company chose to use Tiger Woods in its ad?

cognitive dissonance The tension produced when people act in a way that is inconsistent with their attitudes.

commercial on television. You don't see logical arguments about the quality of the product—you see talking frogs or partying dogs. The same is true for fast-food commercials. There's no discussion of nutrition—again, it's talking animals or anecdotes about families and minivans. When our motivation to process the message is low, we're much more likely to be persuaded by **source characteristics**—things such as celebrity, attractiveness, or power.

Advertisers typically capitalize on the peripheral route to persuasion because most of the time we don't process advertisements on television or in magazines with a high level of involvement. We're also more likely to rely on processing shortcuts (*heuristics*) to form opinions when we process a message peripherally (Chaiken, Liberman, & Eagly, 1989). For instance, you might adopt a favorable attitude toward an expensive product because you believe that "better products are more expensive," or you might buy the product endorsed by Tiger Woods because "Tiger wouldn't endorse something that isn't quality."

The Festinger and Carlsmith Study   We can also be persuaded to change our attitudes because of our own actions. In a highly influential study of attitude change conducted by Festinger and Carlsmith (1959), male college students were asked to perform some incredibly boring tasks, such as placing sewing spools onto a tray, during an hour session. At the end of the hour, some of the participants (the experimental group) were given a bogus cover story. They were told that one purpose of the study was to examine the effects of motivation on task performance. The next student, the researcher explained, needed to be told that the experiment was actually filled with interesting and enjoyable tasks. Would they mind going into the adjacent waiting room and telling him that the experiment was interesting and enjoyable? To provide an incentive, the experimenter offered some of the participants a monetary reward of $1 and others a reward of $20.

The point of the offer was to get the members of the experimental group to act in a way that contradicted their true feelings, or attitudes, about the experiment. The task was clearly boring, so they were essentially asked to lie for either a small or a large reward. Festinger and Carlsmith were interested in what effect this behavior would have on people's attitudes about the experiment. After accepting the offer, and trying to convince the next participant, the students' attitudes about the experimental tasks were assessed through an interview. The researchers found that attitudes about the experimental tasks did indeed change—they became more positive relative to the attitudes of a control group, who had not been asked to lie. Moreover, the positive shift was larger for people receiving $1 than for those receiving $20. The more money people were paid to act inconsistently with their true feelings, the less likely their attitudes were to change (see ▌Figure 13.5).

Cognitive Dissonance   These results may seem perplexing. You would probably have predicted that the students receiving $20 would show the greatest attitude change—after all, wouldn't a large reward have a greater reinforcing effect? The answer, according to Festinger's (1957) theory of **cognitive dissonance**, is that the inconsistent behavior produces tension—or what he called *dissonance*. Think about it. Which action is going to lead to greater internal turmoil, lying to receive $1 or lying to receive $20? Most people can easily justify a simple white lie when offered a reasonable amount of money, especially when asked by an authority figure (remember that $20 was worth a lot more in the 1950s than it is now). But to lie for a measly $1 is tough to justify—unless, of course, you can justify the action by changing your initial attitude about the task. According to cognitive dissonance theory, if the discrepancy between what you believe and how you act is great, you will either (1) change your behavior or (2) change your beliefs.

Since cognitive dissonance theory was first introduced in the 1950s, hundreds of follow-up studies have been conducted (Aronson, 1992). Most have confirmed Festinger and Carlsmith's basic finding: When people are induced to act in ways that are inconsistent with their attitudes, their attitudes often change as a consequence. But not all psychologists are convinced that internal tension, or dissonance, results from acting inconsistent with your beliefs. You might, for example, simply feel uncomfortable about your actions (Elliot & Devine, 1994), or you might feel personally responsible for creating an unwanted or negative situation (Blanton et al., 1997; Cooper, 1992). The concept of cognitive dissonance remains both vague and difficult to measure. It's tough to predict when dissonance will occur and, if it's present, how people will choose to reduce it (Joule, 1986). However, the idea continues to be influential among social psychologists (Crano & Prislin, 2006).

Self-Perception Theory   One of the best-known alternatives to dissonance theory is psychologist Daryl Bem's (1967, 1972) **self-perception theory**. The idea behind it is that we are active observers of our own behavior. We learn from our behavior and use our actions as a basis for inferring internal beliefs. For example, if I sit down and practice the piano for two hours a day, it must be the case that I like music and think I have at least a bit of musical talent. If I regularly stop for hamburgers and fries for lunch, it must be the case that I like fast food. The basis for the attitude is self-perception—behavior is observed, and attitudes follow from the behavior (see ▌Figure 13.6).

Many experimental findings support these basic ideas. For example, the Festinger and Carlsmith study can be interpreted from this perspective. You observe yourself telling someone that a boring task is interesting, for a measly $1, and conclude that because you engaged in this behavior your attitude toward the task must not have been that negative. In another classic example, known as the *foot-in-the-door technique,*

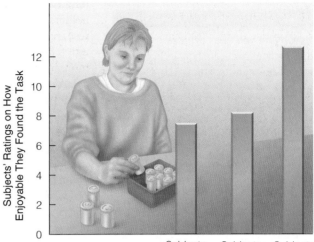

Subjects' Ratings on How Enjoyable They Found the Task

Subjects Not Asked to Lie | Subjects Receiving $20 to Lie | Subjects Receiving $1 to Lie

▌**FIGURE 13.5** Cognitive Dissonance
Festinger proposed that attitudes change when there is a discrepancy between what we believe and how we act. Presumably, it was tough to justify lying for a small amount of money, which created a lot of cognitive dissonance, so the subjects in the $1 condition simply changed their original attitude about the task. (Data from Festinger & Carlsmith, 1959)

self-perception theory The idea that people use observations of their own behavior as a basis for inferring their internal beliefs.

"Do you like hamburgers?"

"I guess so."

▌**FIGURE 13.6** Self-Perception Theory
Some psychologists believe we form attitudes at least in part by observing our own behavior. If I regularly eat hamburgers, then my attitude about hamburgers must be positive.

CRITICAL THINKING

How might you use cognitive dissonance theory to explain the foot-in-the-door technique?

Jonathan Freedman and Scott Fraser (1966) convinced a group of California house-holders to sign a petition expressing support for safe driving. Several weeks later, the researchers returned with a request that the householders now place a large and quite ugly "Drive Safely" billboard in their yards. The petition signers were three times more likely to comply with this new request than a control group of people who were not asked to sign a petition. What's the interpretation? The signing of the original petition triggered *self-perception*, which then helped shape the attitude: If I signed the petition, then I must be a strong advocate for safe driving (see also Burger & Caldwell, 2003).

A related phenomenon is the *lowball technique*. You wander into the local electronics store to look around. You're not really ready to buy, but the salesperson offers you a tremendous price on a piece of high-quality equipment. You agree, convinced you've received a great deal. The salesperson leaves to finish the paperwork with the manager of the store. He returns a few minutes later with some bad news: The offered price was a mistake—the manager rejected the deal—but he will be able to sell you the equipment at a price that is still lower than what most people pay. Reluctantly you agree to buy, even though you probably would have rejected this deal if it had been offered first. In this case, by getting you to agree verbally to the initial purchase, the salesperson has lowered your resistance to buying the product (Burger & Cornelius, 2003).

Of course, there are boundary conditions for these effects—we do not always match our attitudes to our behaviors—but monitoring behavior is clearly an important ingredient of attitude formation and change. It may be that we're particularly likely to use our own actions as a guide when we're unsure or undecided about our attitude. Or we may use our own behavior to see if our attitudes or opinions have recently changed: "Do I still like playing video games? Well, let's see. I haven't played a game for a while, so I must not be crazy about them anymore." It's adaptive for us to use multiple sources of information for establishing our beliefs, including our own actions.

Concept Review | Roots of Attitudes and Attitude Change

MECHANISM	DESCRIPTION	EXAMPLE ("WHO SHOULD I VOTE FOR?")
Central route	When motivated to process an incoming message, we listen carefully to the arguments given and judge them on their merits.	Jaraan is not sure who to vote for in the governor's race. He obtains detailed information on the candidates' views on the major issues and, after considering each, decides on the Democratic candidate.
Peripheral route	When we are unable or unwilling to process a message carefully, our attitudes are affected more by superficial cues or mere exposure.	Yvette hasn't really kept up with the governor's race but has seen commercials on TV. She gets a kick out of the Republican candidate's humorous ad, so she decides to vote for him.
Cognitive dissonance	Behavior that is inconsistent with attitudes produces tension (i.e., *dissonance*). If this discrepancy is large enough, attitudes or behavior will change.	Jeremy has always considered himself a Republican, and he backs his party's candidate for governor. Lately he's been dating a woman who is very involved in the Democratic candidate's campaign. Jeremy finds that his attitudes toward this candidate are becoming more and more favorable.
Self-perception	We learn from our behavior, using our actions as a basis for inferring beliefs: Attitudes follow behavior.	Felicia gets a phone call from the third-party campaign headquarters pleading for help. The third party can't compete with the other two campaigns unless it raises more money for its candidate. Felicia agrees to donate $20 to the cause. Looking back, she decides she must really favor the third-party candidate.

Test Yourself 13.1

Check your knowledge about how we form impressions of others by answering the following questions. (You will find the answers in the Appendix.)

1. Decide whether each of the following statements about person perception is *True or False*.
   a. On average, attractive people are assumed to be more intelligent, better adjusted, and more socially aware than people with average looks. *True or False*?
   b. Prototype theories assume that we represent stereotypes with particular individuals, or exemplars. *True or False*?
   c. Stereotypes can be activated automatically and can influence our later behavior in ways that seem to bypass awareness. *True or False*?
   d. Studies suggest that it might be possible to reduce the prejudicial feelings that arise from stereotypes through repeated exposure to individuals in the stereotyped group. *True or False*?
2. For each of the following, decide whether you are most likely to make an internal or an external attribution for the behavior described.
   a. A perfect score on your psychology exam: _____
   b. Josie always smiles after her psychology lecture, but everyone else in the class leaves mad: _____

   c. A failing score on your psychology exam: _____
   d. Eagerly anticipating your food, you notice your waiter seems to spend a lot of time talking to the hostess: _____
3. Decide whether each of the following statements about attitudes and attitude change is *True or False*.
   a. For an attitude to guide behavior, it should be appropriate or relevant to the situation. *True or False*?
   b. The peripheral route to persuasion operates when our level of involvement in or commitment to a message is high. *True or False*?
   c. According to cognitive dissonance theory, it is inconsistencies between internal beliefs and our actions that lead to attitude change. *True or False*?
   d. Mere exposure can lead to attitude change, but only if we're processing an incoming communication with care and attention. *True or False*?

Behaving in the Presence of Others: Social Influence

LEARNING GOALS
- Define and discuss social facilitation and interference.
- Describe the bystander effect and diffusion of responsibility.
- Describe how behavior changes in a group setting.
- Discuss some aspects of group decision making.
- Describe the Milgram experiment and discuss what it implies about the power of authority.
- Discuss how culture affects social influence.

WE NOW TURN OUR ATTENTION to the topic of **social influence**: How is our behavior affected by the presence of others? Obviously, by the word *others*, social psychologists mean the general social context, but it can have a variety of meanings in practice. Our behavior might change as a consequence of interacting with a single individual, perhaps an authority figure such as our boss or an intimate friend, or by the collective behavior of people in a group. Moreover, the presence of others can cause us to act in a new or different way or change our attitudes and beliefs. Think back to Al Hobart, the ambitious underling we met in the chapter opening. His behavior certainly changed in the presence of others; he violated his beliefs and conformed to the opinions of his colleagues and his self-serving boss.

social influence The study of how the behaviors and thoughts of individuals are affected by the presence of others.

Social Facilitation and Interference

One of the simplest and most widely documented examples of social influence is the phenomenon of social facilitation. **Social facilitation** is the *enhancement* in performance that is sometimes found when we perform in the presence of others. To

social facilitation The enhancement in performance that is sometimes found when an individual performs in the presence of others.

© Gary Houlder/Corbis

Demonstrating the phenomenon of social facilitation, people tend to eat more in the presence of others.

social interference The impairment in performance that is sometimes found when an individual performs in the presence of others.

demonstrate social facilitation, you need to compare someone's task performance in two conditions, when performing alone and when performing in the presence of other people. If performance improves when other people are around, you've demonstrated social facilitation. In an early investigation of this effect, Norman Triplett (1898) discovered that adolescents would wind in a fishing line faster when working in pairs than when working alone. Task performance *improved* in the presence of others, which is the defining characteristic of social facilitation.

Social facilitation is a widespread effect, occurring in many kinds of social environments and for many kinds of tasks (Aiello & Douthitt, 2001). Motorists drive through intersections faster when another car is traveling in the lane beside them (Towler, 1986); people run faster when others are present (Worringham & Messick, 1983); people even eat more when dining out with friends than when eating alone (Clendenen, Herman, & Polivy, 1994). In fact, the effect is not restricted to humans—ants will excavate dirt more quickly to build their nests when other ants are present (Chen, 1937); hungry chickens will eat more when other chickens observe passively though a clear plastic wall (Tolman, 1968); cockroaches will even run faster down an alleyway when a "spectator" roach watches from a small plastic enclosure (Zajonc, Heingartner, & Herman, 1969).

But there's another side to the coin. It's easy to think of examples of how we've "risen to the occasion" and excelled when an audience was present, but the opposite can occur as well. Sometimes performing in a crowd impairs performance—we "choke," a tendency referred to as **social interference**. Talented Angela, who finally performs Bach's Invention No. 1 perfectly in her last practice session, finds her fingers fumbling helplessly during the piano recital. Confident Eddie, who thought he had learned his lines to perfection, stands embarrassingly silent on center stage on opening night. Social interference is the opposite of social facilitation, but both represent cases in which our ability to perform a task is influenced by the presence of others.

© Berthold Litjes/Corbis

When a task is difficult, performing in the presence of others can lead to social interference: What seemed easy in private becomes a nightmare in public.

Social Influences on Altruism:
The Bystander Effect

In addition to task performance, the presence of other people influences whether we show **altruism**—that is, whether we'll act in a way that shows unselfish concern for the welfare of others. Both people and animals engage in altruistic behaviors—we help others in need, and these behaviors may arise, in part, from adaptations rooted in our evolutionary past (Buss, 2007; Stevens & Hauser, 2004). We're more likely to engage in kin-directed altruism, which means there's a greater chance we'll help relatives, but we'll help strangers under some circumstances—even if it means putting ourselves at risk. Some have suggested that we act altruistically because we anticipate that the favor will be returned in kind—a concept called *reciprocal altruism* (Trivers, 1985). Putting yourself at risk can be considered adaptive, therefore, because it increases the likelihood that you will be helped in other situations.

Altruistic behavior is strongly controlled by the social environment. Think about the last time you were driving on the highway and noticed some poor person standing alongside his or her disabled car. Did you stop and help? Did you at least pull out your cell phone and inform the police or highway patrol? If you're like most people, you probably did nothing. In all likelihood, you failed to accept responsibility for helping—you left that job for someone else.

The problem is more serious than you might think. In March of 1964, while walking home from work at 3:30 in the morning, Catherine "Kitty" Genovese was stalked and then brutally attacked by a knife-wielding assailant outside her apartment building in Queens, New York. "Oh my god, he stabbed me!" Kitty screamed. "I'm dying! I'm dying!" Inside the apartment building, awakened by the screams, many of her neighbors sat silently listening as the attacker finished the job. Kitty was stabbed repeatedly before she eventually died; in fact, the attacker actually left and came back before finally ending her life. Few, if any, in the apartment building came to her aid or called the police. Did they simply not want to get involved in such a situation, or was some other, more general psychological process at work?

The reluctance to come to someone's aid when other people are present is known generally as the **bystander effect** (Darley & Latané, 1968). Although it's relatively easy to document in natural environments, it's also possible to study the bystander effect in the laboratory. Consider the following scenario. You've volunteered to participate in a psychology experiment that involves groups of students discussing the problems of college life. To minimize embarrassment, you're allowed to sit in a small cubicle where you can communicate with the others via an intercom system. Before the experiment begins, you're told that one, two, or five other people will be participating. The session begins, and suddenly one of the group members, who had previously mentioned being subject to epileptic seizures, begins to have a seizure. Over the intercom, his voice begins to garble—"Somebody-er-er-help-er-uh-uh-uh"—followed by silence. What do you do? Do you get up and help, or sit where you are?

In the actual version of this experiment, of course, no one had a seizure; the incident was manufactured by the experimenters to observe the bystander effect. There was also only one real participant in the experiment—the "others" were simply voices recorded on tape. The researchers found that whether the real participant would offer some kind of help to the imaginary seizure victim depended on how many other people he or she believed to be present. When the participant was convinced that only one other person was participating in the group, he or she almost immediately rose to intervene. But when it was presumed that four others (in addition to the seizure victim) were present, only 62% of the subjects offered aid (Darley & Latané, 1968).

Diffusion of Responsibility   Most social psychologists are convinced that the behavior of the people in these experiments, including the actions of the Queens apartment dwellers, is neither atypical nor representative of general apathy. Instead, the

altruism Acting in a way that shows unselfish concern for the welfare of others.

bystander effect The reluctance to come to the aid of a person in need when other people are present.

diffusion of responsibility The idea that when people know (or think) that others are present in a situation, they allow their sense of responsibility for action to diffuse, or spread out widely, among those who are present.

reluctance to get involved—to help others—can be explained by appealing once again to the powerful role of social context. We tend not to lend a hand, or get involved, because the presence of others leads to **diffusion of responsibility**—we believe others have already done something to help or will soon get involved. If we know that others are present in the situation, and certainly many occupants of the apartment building heard the terrible screams, we allow our sense of responsibility to *diffuse*, or spread out widely, among the other people presumed to be present.

The bystander effect is a disturbing but powerful example of social influence. Again, it has been replicated many times in numerous social settings that extend beyond the laboratory (Latané & Nida, 1981). As a general rule, the more witnesses there are, the less likely it is that any one will step forward to offer aid. In fact, this relationship holds even if you simply imagine yourself in a group. One recent study found that people who imagined themselves eating dinner with 30 of their friends were less likely to pledge money to a charity than people who imagined themselves eating with only 10 people or just one other person (Garcia et al., 2002).

There are exceptions to the rule. For instance, people are more likely to help if they've recently observed others being helpful, if they don't think the people around them have the ability to help, or if they truly perceive the situation as an emergency with high potential danger (Fischer et al., 2006). Still, diffusion of responsibility remains the rule rather than the exception. The tendency to diffuse responsibility doesn't mean that people are bad or selfish; it simply provides yet another indication of how behavior can be strongly influenced by social factors. Our behavior changes when we are in the presence of others, and although the forces that produce the bystander effect may not make us feel good about ourselves, this behavior may be adaptive. Stopping to help someone in need could place one in danger—there may be a definite cost to helping behavior—and diffusion of responsibility is one way of reducing the risk.

The Power of the Group

The power of social context over human behavior is especially noticeable when we act as members of a well-defined group. Our behavior is shaped not only by the characteristics of the group—its size and the unanimity of its members—but even by the mere fact that we're *in* a group. Social psychologists have identified a number of psychological phenomena that illustrate the power of group membership. We'll consider three in the following sections: social loafing, deindividuation, and conformity.

social loafing The tendency to put out less effort when working in a group compared to when working alone.

Social Loafing During our discussion of social facilitation, you learned that a person's performance often changes when others are present. Whether performance improves or declines depends on factors such as the difficulty of the task or one's general level of arousal. But when participating as a member of a group, most people show a strong tendency to engage in **social loafing**, which means they put out less effort than when they are alone (Latané, Williams, & Harkens, 1979). Social loafing is easy to demonstrate in the laboratory. In one study, volunteer subjects were instructed to clap and cheer as loudly as possible while blindfolded and listening to noise over headphones. Just before they began the task, the participants were told they would be clapping either with a group of other subjects or by themselves. When the volunteers believed they were part of a clapping group, their individual output dropped considerably.

Like many of the phenomena we've discussed in this chapter, social loafing is a complex phenomenon. Whether it occurs in a particular situation will depend on many factors, including the importance of the task, the cohesiveness of the group, and the personalities of the group members (Karau & Hart, 1998; Smith et al., 2001). The effect also occurs widely across cultures, although it may be especially common in cultures that stress individuality (Karau & Williams, 1993). Some social psychologists believe there may be a connection between social loafing and the bystander effect.

Bibb Latané (1981) has argued that both effects result from diffusion of responsibility. In the bystander effect, people suspect that others either will or have become involved; in social loafing, we assume that others will carry the load. In both cases, the fact that we are simply one of many makes us feel less accountable for our behavior. We fail to step up and take full responsibility, or to work to our fullest capabilities, because the responsibility can be diffused or spread to the other members of the group.

Deindividuation   The idea that we feel less accountable for our behavior when we're in a group setting can lead to a phenomenon called **deindividuation**. Imagine yourself at a particularly lively party: The people around you are acting crazy—they're drinking too much, damaging the furniture, and some are even beginning to shed their clothes. Are you likely to start doing the same? Some psychologists believe that people in large groups lose their sense of individuality. We can enter a depersonalized state of mind called deindividuation, which increases the chances of engaging in destructive, aggressive, or deviant behavior. Under most circumstances, it's highly unlikely that you would trash the furniture in a friend's home. But when you're part of a large rowdy group, deindividuation can lead you to do things that you might not otherwise do.

> **deindividuation** The loss of individuality, or depersonalization, that comes from being in a group.

Once again, diffusion of responsibility is likely to play a role in such situations. When you're in a large group, you're less likely to feel accountable for your actions. You feel anonymous, which lowers your normal restraints on destructive actions. You also feel less self-conscious—you go along with the group, as a whim, because you're not thinking about your normal standards, values, and morals. Whether you truly enter a depersonalized state of mind is debatable, but your actions do differ from your normal tendencies. Some psychologists have argued that deindividuation is simply an example of situation-specific behavior; your behavior is being controlled by an unusual situation, and your actions probably don't provide much information about how you typically behave (Postmes & Spears, 1998).

At the same time, deindividuation often plays a central role in prejudice, discrimination, and racism (Zimbardo, 2007). Group membership can lead individuals to perform actions, particularly toward members of an "out-group," that they would be less likely to perform otherwise. History is full of egregious examples of group-based behavior—e.g., lynching, looting—that are fueled, in part, by deindividuation.

People can feel less accountable for their behavior in a group setting, a phenomenon known as deindividuation.

Conformity   Another disturbing property of group membership is **conformity**, which occurs when a person's opinions, feelings, and behaviors start to move toward the group norm. When you're in a group setting, you feel social pressure, which, in turn, causes you generally to comply, or go along, with the wishes of the group—even though you may not always be aware that you're doing so. Studies investigating issues of conformity and compliance to group norms are among the oldest and best known of all social psychology experiments.

> **conformity** The tendency to comply with the wishes of the group; when people conform, their opinions, feelings, and behaviors generally start to move toward the group norm.

In one classic study of conformity, psychologist Solomon Asch (1951, 1955) rigged the following experimental setup. People were asked to participate in a simple perception experiment that required them to make judgments about line length. Two cards were shown, one displaying a standard line of a particular length and the other showing three comparison lines of differing lengths. The participant was required to state aloud which of the three comparison lines was the same length as the standard line (see ▌Figure 13.7). The task was really quite simple—there was no question as to

| FIGURE 13.7 The Asch Study of Conformity
Do you think you would have any trouble choosing the correct comparison line in this task? Asch found that people often conformed to the group opinion. The photo shown here is taken from one of his actual experiments.

the correct answer. The catch was that this was a group experiment, and the other members of the group were really confederates of the experimenter—they were not volunteers but rather were there to put social pressure on the true participant.

The confederates were instructed to lie on a certain number of the trials. They were told to give a response, aloud, that was clearly wrong (such as picking comparison line 1 as the correct answer). Asch was mainly concerned with how often these incorrect answers would affect the answers of the real participant. Imagine yourself in this situation—you know the answer is line 2, but four of your fellow participants have already given 1 as a response. Do you conform to the opinions of your peers, even though doing so conflicts with what you know to be true? The results were not particularly encouraging for those who champion individualism. Asch found that in approximately 75% of the sessions people complied on at least one of the trials, and the overall rate of conformity was around 37%. Although peer pressure wasn't always effective in altering the behavior of the subjects—in fact, only 5% of the participants conformed on every trial—it was a powerful influence. In describing his results, Asch (1955) put it this way: "That reasonably intelligent and well-meaning young people are willing to call white black is a matter of concern" (p. 34).

As you might imagine, the Asch experiments had quite an impact on the psychological community. Similar experiments have been conducted on dozens of occasions, not only in the United States but in many other countries around the world. Generally, Asch's results have held up well, although a number of variables affect the likelihood that conformity will occur. Asch himself found, for example, that the rate of compliance dropped dramatically when one of the confederates dissented from the majority and gave the correct answer. It was also discovered that the size of the group is not as important as you might think. Conformity increases as the size of the pressure group gets larger, but it levels off relatively quickly. The pressure to conform does not increase directly with group size; after a certain point, usually when the majority group contains three to five members, adding even more pressure has less of an effect (Tanford & Penrod, 1984). Your feelings about the status of the group as a whole also matter; if you have little or no respect for the other members of the group, you're less likely to conform. Conformity is particularly likely when pressure comes from an **in-group**—that is, a group of individuals with whom you share features in common or with whom you identify (see Cialdini & Goldstein, 2004).

Why do we conform to the majority opinion? One possibility is that we generally seek approval in social settings and try to avoid rejection, so we act to please by complying with social customs and norms. Clearly, voicing a dissenting opinion increases the risk of rejection by the group, so we choose to conform. But it may also be the case that we use the majority group opinion as a source of information. If four

CRITICAL THINKING

When people conform, they act in ways that are inconsistent with their attitudes. What implications should this have for attitude change?

in-group A group of individuals with whom one shares features in common or with whom one identifies.

or five people around you are convinced that comparison line 1 is the correct answer, perhaps your perception of the stimulus is flawed in some way. Perhaps your angle of sight is misleading, or your memory for the comparison line is wrong. Consequently, you use the opinions of the others in the group as information or evidence about what has really been presented.

Group Decision Making

As you've just seen, members of an in-group can exert considerable pressure on one another to conform to the standards or norms of the group. One of the consequences of these internal pressures is that groups tend to take on behavioral characteristics of their own, especially when group decisions need to be made. Obviously, the psychology of group decision making is critically important—it affects everything from how verdicts are reached by juries, to how families decide where to go on vacation, to decisions made by Congress. Psychologists have identified two important characteristics of group decision making, group polarization and groupthink.

Group Polarization   When members of an in-group arrive at a consensus of opinion, there is a tendency for the group's opinion to polarize. **Group polarization** means that the group's dominant point of view—which is usually determined by the initial views of the majority—becomes stronger and even more extreme with time. If you join a local action group dedicated to exposing corporate corruption and the group tends to believe initially that corporate corruption is a significant and rising problem, it's likely that over time you and the rest of the members of the group will become even more convinced of that position (see Nowak et al., 2003).

group polarization The tendency for a group's dominant point of view to become stronger and more extreme with time.

What accounts for group polarization? Not surprisingly, some of the same factors that promote conformity promote polarization. For example, group discussions tend to provide information that consolidates initial opinions. Those who enter the group with strong opinions make strong cases for their viewpoint and dissenting viewpoints are less likely to be heard (Stewart & Stasser, 1995). At the same time, the social aspects of the discussion play an important role. People want to be liked by the other members of the group, so they shift their attitude toward the group consensus. You're more likely to be accepted by the group if you forcefully argue in favor of the group's dominant viewpoint.

Groupthink   The trend toward consensus and polarization of opinion may also be influenced by what psychologist Irving Janis has labeled **groupthink**: Members of a group become so interested in seeking a consensus of opinion that they start to ignore and even suppress dissenting views. Janis (1982, 1989) found evidence for groupthink when he looked at how well-established in-groups arrived at decisions, particularly policy decisions by members of the government. He and others analyzed a number of watershed events in U.S. policymaking, including the decision to escalate the war in Vietnam, the decision by President John F. Kennedy to invade Cuba in 1961, and even the decision by NASA to launch the ill-fated *Challenger* Space Shuttle. Not all psychologists are satisfied with the interpretations that Janis provided for groupthink (e.g., Kramer, 1998), but there is still wide agreement that the phenomenon exists (Esser, 1998).

groupthink The tendency for members of a group to become so interested in seeking a consensus of opinion that they start to ignore and even suppress dissenting views.

In an alarming number of cases, Janis discovered that group members systematically sought consensus at the expense of critical analysis. Group members often acted as if they were trying to convince themselves of the correctness of their position. When alternative views were expressed, those views were either suppressed or dismissed. The management at NASA had clear evidence that freezing launch temperatures might pose a problem for *Challenger*, but the managers chose to ignore that evidence in the interest of going forward with the mission. The result of groupthink is general closed-mindedness and an overestimation of the uniformity of opinion.

Can groupthink be avoided? According to Janis (1982), it's possible to counteract groupthink by following certain prescriptions. For instance, it helps to have a leader

Concept Review | Influences of the Group

PHENOMENON	DESCRIPTION
Social facilitation	An enhancement in performance sometimes found when we perform in the presence of others. This is especially likely with easy or well-practiced tasks.
Social interference	A decline in performance when one is in the presence of others. This is especially likely with tasks that are unique or not well learned.
Bystander effect	The reluctance to come to someone's aid when other people are present. This is characterized by diffusion of responsibility, the tendency to believe that others will help.
Social loafing	Most people show a strong tendency to put in less effort when they are working in a group compared to when they work alone.
Deindividuation	When in large groups, we can lose our sense of individuality and be more likely to engage in destructive, aggressive, or deviant behavior.
Conformity	A person's opinions, feelings, and behaviors start to move toward the group norm.

Influences on Decision Making

PHENOMENON	DESCRIPTION
Group polarization	A group's dominant point of view becomes stronger and even more extreme with time.
Groupthink	Members of a group become so interested in seeking a consensus of opinion that they ignore and suppress dissenting views.

who acts impartial, one who does not quickly endorse a particular position. One or more members of the group can also be assigned a kind of devil's advocate role in which they are expected and encouraged to represent a dissenting position. Perhaps most important, however, is the simple recognition by the group that social influences such as groupthink are real phenomena that affect behavior, irrespective of group members' intelligence or commitment to the truth. Groupthink can be avoided, but it requires reconsidering how group decision making is normally conducted.

Polarization occurs when a group's majority opinion becomes stronger and more extreme with time. What's the likelihood that people in this group will adopt more tolerant views in the future?

AP Images/Jim Mone

The Power of Authority: Obedience

Up to this point in our discussion of social influence, we've concentrated on how behavior is affected by the presence of others, where the others have simply been any individuals who happen to be present in the social context. But in many cases it does matter *who* these others happen to be—and what roles these people play in your life. Think back once again to Al Hobart. Do you think he would have agreed so readily with his coworkers if the head of advertising had not been standing there, drink in hand, listening intently to his opinions? To what degree was Hobart's behavior changed because it was someone in a position of authority who had asked him his opinion?

Psychologists use the term **obedience** to describe the form of compliance that occurs when people respond to the orders of an authority figure. You're of course aware that during World War II millions of Jewish men, women, and children were systematically executed by scores of German soldiers working under orders from Nazi officials. In 1978 in a rural area of Guyana, South America, hundreds of converts to the religious teachings of Reverend Jim Jones chose, under his direct orders, to commit mass suicide. Most people find it extremely difficult to understand such events and consider them to be social aberrations committed by people far different from themselves. Admittedly, you might toe the line in front of your boss, and do and say things that you don't really believe, but murder innocent people? Drink Kool-Aid laced with cyanide? Never.

The Milgram Experiment   In what is perhaps the most controversial social psychology experiment ever conducted, psychologist Stanley Milgram (1963) set out to determine just how resistant the average person is to the demands of authority. He placed an advertisement in a local newspaper recruiting men for what was billed as a study looking at the effects of punishment on learning. The participants were told that for a small fee they would be asked to play one of two roles in the experiment: either a *learner*, which required memorizing and then recalling lists of word pairs, or a *teacher*, whose task it would be to administer an electric shock to the learner whenever he made any

recall errors. Each session required two participants, one teacher and one learner, and the assignment of condition was decided by drawing slips of paper out of a hat.

But things were not exactly what they appeared to be. In fact, in every case the true volunteer, the one who had actually responded to the ad, was picked to be the teacher. The learner was a confederate of the experimenter, someone who was fully informed about the true nature of the study. Although it was rigged to look as though he was receiving shocks throughout the session, he was never actually shocked. The idea was to get the confederate to make learning errors and then to assess how willing the teacher would be to administer the shock under the authority of a hovering and demanding experimenter.

To begin the setup, the unwitting teacher watched as the learner was led away to an adjacent room and hooked up to a shock-administering apparatus. Back in the original room, the teacher was then placed in front of an imposing-looking electrical shock generator, which contained some 30 different switches. It was explained that each switch was able to generate a particular level of shock intensity,

obedience The form of compliance that occurs when people respond to the orders of an authority figure.

Obedience to authority reached shocking levels in 1978 when more than 900 followers of Reverend Jim Jones obeyed his direct orders to commit suicide by drinking a fruit drink laced with cyanide.

These photos were taken during one of Milgram's early experiments on obedience to authority. The first shows the shock generator used during the experiment; the second shows the "learner"— actually a confederate of the experimenter—being hooked up to the shock-delivery apparatus; and in the third, the "teacher" sits in front of the shock generator, in the presence of the demanding experimenter.

ranging from 15 volts (Slight Shock), through 150 volts (Strong Shock), and finally up to 450 volts (labeled simply XXX). With the experimenter standing by his side, the teacher was instructed to begin reading and then testing the learner's memory for the words, via intercom, and to administer a shock whenever the learner failed to call out the correct answer. Moreover, to see how the degree of punishment influenced learning, the teacher was instructed to increase the voltage level of the shock, by moving to a new switch, with each new mistake.

Remember, no one was actually shocked in this experiment; the learner was *in on* the experiment, and he was told to make mistakes consistently throughout the session. To add to the cover, he was also instructed to respond vocally and actively to the shocks, via the intercom, whenever they were delivered (the learner's responses were actually prerecorded). At first, when the shock levels were low, there wasn't much response. But as the prearranged mistakes continued—which, of course, necessitated the teacher to continue increasing the voltage of the shock—loud protests began to come over the intercom. By the time the mistake-prone learner was receiving 150-volt shocks, he was demanding to be released from the experiment. By around 300 volts, he was screaming in agony in response to each delivered shock and pounding on the wall; after the 330-volt level, the shocks yielded no response at all—simply silence.

Listening to these disturbing pleas for help did not make the average teacher very comfortable. In fact, most quickly expressed concern over the consequences of the shocking and wanted to discontinue the experiment. But the teacher's concerns were met with resistance from the authoritative experimenter, who demanded that the shocks go on. "Please continue," the experimenter responded. "You have no other choice, you must go on." What would you do in this situation? You're participating in an experiment, which is being conducted in the name of science, but the task requires you to inflict quite a bit of pain and suffering on someone else. Do you blindly go forward, delivering shocks in compliance with the requests of the authority figure, or do you quit and give the experimenter a piece of your mind? Of course, this was exactly the question of interest to Milgram—how obedient would people be to the unreasonable requests of an authority figure?

Interestingly, before the experiment actually began Milgram asked a number of people, including professionals, to predict how much voltage participants would be willing to deliver in his task. Most predicted that obedience would be low; the estimates were that only a few people in a thousand would deliver shocks up to 450 volts and that most would defy the experimenter after discomfort was expressed by the learner. In reality, the results were far different. Milgram found that 65% of the 40 people who participated were willing to deliver shocks up to 450 volts, and no one quit before the pounding on the wall started. This means that 26 of the 40 participants went all the way to the final switch—the one with the ominous XXX label—despite the agonized

CRITICAL THINKING

Why might it be adaptive for us to respond so readily to the demands of an authority figure?

pleas from the learner. This remarkable finding rocked the psychological community and initiated a great deal of subsequent research, as well as a firestorm of controversy.

Controversies and Ethical Concerns Milgram's (1963) experiment was controversial for two main reasons. First, the manner in which it was conducted raised serious ethical questions. The people in his study were misled from the beginning and became severely distressed during their participation. Milgram observed a number of indications of distress during the experiment—the "teachers" sometimes groaned, bit their lips, trembled, stuttered, and even broke into a sweat. Many critics feel that this kind of psychological manipulation—even though done to advance knowledge—cannot be justified (Baumrind, 1964; Schlenker & Forsyth, 1977). In response, Milgram (1974) argued that his participants were thoroughly debriefed at the end of the experiment—they were told in detail about the true nature of the experiment—and were generally glad they had participated. Follow-up questionnaires sent to the participants months later revealed that only a handful felt negatively about the experiment.

The other major question raised about the experiment concerned the procedure itself. Some critics argued that perhaps the participants had seen through the cover and were simply trying to please the experimenter; others argued that the results, although interesting, had no general applicability beyond the laboratory. People must have assumed that things were okay, these critics reasoned; otherwise no one would have believed that an experiment of this type could be conducted. In response, Milgram again pointed out that his participants tended to get extremely distressed in the setting, which suggests that they couldn't have figured out the hoax and were expressing their true feelings.

In the four-plus decades since Milgram's original experiment was conducted, his general procedure has been repeated a number of times, in many countries around the world (see Blass, 2000; Meeus & Raaijmakers, 1987). Few psychologists today question the validity of his basic findings, although it's clear that the degree of compliance that people will show to authority depends on many factors. For example, the Milgram experiment was conducted at a prestigious university (Yale); when the same study was conducted in a less prestigious setting—a rundown office building—compliance dropped (although it remained alarmingly high). People were also less likely to comply if the authority figure left the room after explaining the experiment or if the person giving the orders looked ordinary rather than official or scientific (Milgram, 1974). Thus, obedience to authority is not absolute—it depends on the characteristics of the situation as well as on the characteristics of the person giving the orders.

Finally, a cautionary note: Although behavior can certainly change in the presence of an authority figure, even dramatically in some cases, obedience shouldn't be used to explain away the actions of people who commit egregious crimes. In the case of Nazi Germany, for example, "I was just following orders" became the standard rallying cry for those accused of some truly horrendous actions. Social psychologists are careful to draw distinctions between obedience to authority, as witnessed in Milgram's settings, and the cruelties practiced by many executioners in concentration camps (Cialdini & Goldstein, 2004). There's no question that we can all be pushed to extremes in the presence of an authority figure, but obedience (or deindividuation) can't be used as an overriding excuse, or even explanation, for genocide or other horrendous acts.

The Role of Culture

You've now seen how our thoughts and actions change when we're in the presence of others, particularly groups. The group can exert a powerful influence on members' judgments, leading to conformity, groupthink, and obedience to authority. In some cases, you may find yourself giving in to the group's demands at the expense of your own personal convictions. Remember Al Hobart and the questions we posed at the opening to this chapter? Have the preceding discussions changed your mind about how you might act in such a situation?

Is the tendency to conform, or to sacrifice one's individual desires for the collective, necessarily bad? Is conformity or obedience a sign of weakness, or is it a sign of strength? The answer depends partly on the culture in which you are raised. In most Western cultures, such as the United States, people are taught from a very young age to adopt an *independent* view of the self; that is, people are rewarded for viewing themselves as unique individuals, with special and distinctive qualities. American children, for example, are likely to be told things like "the squeaky wheel gets the grease." Be someone different, be an individual with unique qualities—these are the things that count. Although Western cultures certainly value acts of charity or unselfish devotion to others, such acts are typically viewed as reflecting distinctive personal qualities—qualities that make someone stand out as an admirable individual.

In many non-Western cultures, particularly Asian cultures, people adopt a very different, *interdependent* view of the self (Markus & Kitayama, 1991, 1994). In Japan, for example, children are taught to think of themselves from the perspective of the collective—as members of a group with common goals—rather than as individuals striving to be different. In Japan, children are told, "The nail that stands out gets pounded down." Such cultural differences are reflected in people's inner thoughts and feelings. When asked to write self-descriptions, Asians are likely to list personal qualities that they share with others ("I come from Kyoto") and to think they are more similar to others than others are to them. Westerners, in contrast, tend to describe themselves as dissimilar to others, and they use individualistic characteristics ("I'm very talented on the flute") to describe themselves (Trafimow, Triandis, & Goto, 1991). The majority of Westerners also tend to think of themselves as above average in intelligence and leadership ability, which is a trend rarely seen among Asians (Markus & Kitayama, 1991).

What do such findings mean? They should reinforce the idea that cultural factors can't be ignored in the interpretation and study of behavior and mind. Our thoughts and actions often arise from our efforts to adapt successfully to our individual environments. As cultural demands on the individual vary, so too will his or her actions.

In some Asian cultures children are encouraged to adopt an "interdependent" view of self; that is, they view themselves primarily as members of a group with common goals rather than as individuals striving to be unique.

Test Yourself | 13.2

Check your knowledge about social influence by answering the following questions. (You will find the answers in the Appendix.)

1. Pick the psychological term that best fits each of these statements. Choose from the following: *social facilitation, social loafing, deindividuation, bystander effect, conformity, group polarization, groupthink, obedience.*

   a. Casey is normally shy and polite, but at the rock concert last night he was loud and shouted obscenities at the police: _____

   b. Megan writes extremely well, but she contributes little to group discussions during class: _____

   c. Sergio is convinced that his study group is dead wrong about their interpretation of the Milgram experiment, but he chooses to nod in agreement with the others in the group: _____

   d. Landlord Sang-Woo notices that the grievances coming from his tenant group have become increasingly more rigid and demanding over time: _____

   e. Gabriella never calls 911 when she sees a broken-down car by the side of the road—she assumes everyone has a cell phone: _____

   f. Teresa notices that she always talks more when she's at a large party: _____

2. Which of the following situations should lead to the greatest reduction in obedience to authority?

   a. The authority figure wears a uniform in front of the teacher.

   b. The authority figure stands close to the teacher.

   c. The experiment is conducted in a federal building.

   d. The experiment is conducted in the teacher's home.

Establishing Relations With Others

LEARNING GOALS

- Describe the factors that influence our perception of facial attractiveness.
- Explain the factors that influence us to like or love others.
- Define the components of romantic love and explain the triangular theory.

WE'VE DEFINED SOCIAL PSYCHOLOGY as the discipline that studies how we think about, influence, and relate to other people. So far we've dealt with social thought and social influence. We now turn our attention to a third and final component: How do we establish and maintain *relations* with others? People are not merely objects to be interpreted or forces that exert influences on behavior. For most of us, it is the personal relationships we establish that are paramount in our lives. Most people depend on their interactions with friends, lovers, and family not only for protection and sustenance but also to help give meaning to their lives.

We've encountered the topic of social relations several times in earlier chapters. In Chapter 4, when we discussed social development, we dealt in detail with the topic of *attachment*. But in that case we were concerned with how people use social bonds to help solve the problems that arise during development. Infants are born with limited motor skills and somewhat immature perceptual systems; consequently, they need to establish strong bonds with their caregivers to survive. In Chapter 11, when we discussed motivation and emotion, we saw how people use facial expressions to communicate their emotions to others and how people are motivated to secure sexual partners. Again, the emphasis was placed on the adaptive value of the relationship rather than on understanding the role the social context plays in the process. In this section we'll consider some of the factors that influence interpersonal attraction, which often forms the basis for relationship development, and then we'll discuss how psychologists have attempted to tackle the mysterious subject of love.

Our relationships with others protect us, nurture us, and give meaning to our lives.

© Clarissa Leahy/Getty Images/Stone

What Makes a Face Attractive?

Few things are as alluring as the sight of an attractive face. Beauty is a powerful motivator of behavior, a fact confirmed by the many millions of dollars spent annually on cosmetics and other beauty aids. The concept of attractiveness is important to the psychologist because people's physical appearance often helps shape how their behavior will be interpreted and therefore how they will be treated by others. As you learned earlier in the chapter, people commonly rely on social schemas to form impressions, and there is considerable evidence to suggest that physical attractiveness is used as a basis for generating expectations about others (Eagly et al., 1991). Just think about the words of the 19th-century German poet Johann Schiller: "Physical beauty is the sign of an interior beauty, a spiritual and moral beauty." Schiller's insight is certainly not lost on modern advertisers who, as you know, rely heavily on the power of an attractive face to help sell their clients' products.

An Evolutionary Perspective   What exactly is it that makes a face physically beautiful? What are the qualities that determine whether someone's looks are considered desirable? One way to think about this problem is from the perspective of evolutionary theory. If the purpose of attraction is to snare an ideal mate, then preferably it should be someone with a high reproductive capacity or someone who is able to provide protection for his or her children and compete successfully for needed resources. This kind of reasoning predicts that people should be attracted to opposite-sex members who are youthful, vigorous, and healthy looking because these qualities increase the likelihood of successful reproduction and child rearing (Alley & Cunningham, 1991; Buss, 2007; Johnston, 2000).

Another prediction of evolutionary theory is that features of attractiveness should cut across cultural boundaries. If attractiveness is grounded somewhere deep in our genetic ancestry, then it shouldn't matter much where you are reared and what experiences you have; in general, there should be worldwide agreement about what constitutes attractiveness. Notice this conclusion contrasts sharply with the generally accepted idea that "beauty is in the eye of the beholder," but it's supported, at least in part, by empirical research. A number of studies have found that when ratings of attractiveness are compared cross-culturally, attractive faces share a number of basic structural features (Bernstein, Lin, & McClelland, 1982; McArthur & Berry, 1987). It's also been discovered that babies, within hours of birth, prefer to look at pictures of faces that adults have rated as attractive over faces that have been rated as unattractive (Langlois et al., 1987; Slater et al., 1998). It's unlikely that we can appeal to experience—that is, sustained exposure to some culturally based definition of beauty—to account for this preference.

Attractive Faces May Be Average   Some research suggests that the universality of attractiveness may be partly due to the fact that people are programmed to prefer faces that are *average* representations of faces in the population (Langlois & Roggman, 1990; Langlois, Roggman, & Musselman, 1994). Average in this case does not necessarily mean common, typical, or frequently occurring faces. Instead, it means prototypical faces—that is, faces that are good representations of the category "faces." In Chapter 9 we defined category prototypes as the best or most representative members of a category—a robin, for example, is probably close to the prototype for the category "bird." Accordingly, attractive faces are those that are particularly *facelike*, or representative of the category of faces.

Langlois and Roggman (1990) supported this view by asking people to rate the attractiveness of average faces that were generated electronically on a computer. To create these faces, hundreds of individual black-and-white photographs, composed of either male or female Caucasians, Asians, and Hispanics, were first scanned by a computer and then digitized into matrices of individual gray values. Each of these gray values corresponded to a shade of gray sitting at a particular small location on the

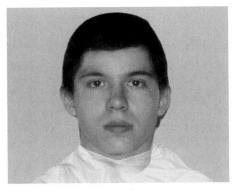
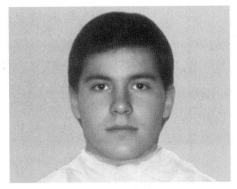

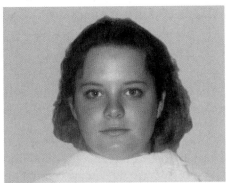
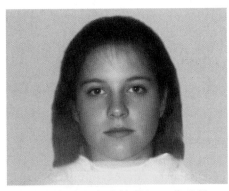
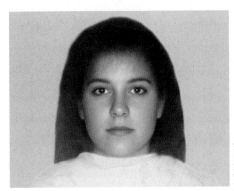

Judith Langlois

The faces in each row are composites created by averaging either two individual faces (far left), eight faces (middle photos in each row), or 32 faces (far right). The stimuli were created using the averaging process employed by Langlois and Roggman (1977).

scanned face. A whole face was represented by many thousands of these gray values, as they are in a typical newspaper photo or video display. As you probably know, any image you see in a newspaper or on a video monitor is actually a configuration of many rows and columns of individual intensity dots or pixels. When viewed as a whole, the dots blend together to form a familiar image on the page or screen.

The unique feature of the Langlois and Roggman research was that people were sometimes shown faces that were generated by averaging the gray values across a large collection of individual faces. An individual dot in one of these composite faces was set by averaging the values of all the dots at the same relative location in the face pool. The result was a "blended face" that did not look exactly like any one of the individual faces but rather represented a kind of prototype face in the population. Volunteer participants were asked to rate these faces for attractiveness, along with the individual faces that had been used to form the composite. The surprising result was that people generally rated the composite faces as more attractive than the individual faces (see also Rhodes & Tremewan, 1996).

Why would people prefer faces that are prototypical? Langlois and Roggman offer several speculative reasons. One possibility is that prototypical faces are easy to identify and classify as human faces. Classifying something as a face may not seem like much of task for adults, but it could well be difficult for the newborn infant. It is critical for infants to be able to recognize a looming visual configuration as a face because they are dependent on their social interactions with people for survival. Yet the visual acuity of the newborn is limited, so faces that are particularly facelike may make this critical classification process easier. Another possibility is that people are programmed biologically to prefer prototypical faces because individuals with average features may be less likely to harbor potentially harmful genetic mutations—that is, they may be "signals" for genetic health. Likewise, faces that are symmetrical in appearance tend to be preferred as well—perhaps, again, because they provide clues about the genetic health of a potential mating partner (Rhodes, 2006).

The perception of beauty has subjective components that are culturally dependent.

The Subjective Components   Despite the evidence for universality in how people conceive of attractiveness, most psychologists recognize that there is a strong subjective component to the perception of beauty. As discussed in Chapter 11, standards of beauty have changed over time in most cultures of the world. In Western societies, for instance, our icon of beauty, the fashion model, has ranged from a "curvaceous bustiness" at one point to slender tomboyishness at the next (Silverstein et al., 1986).

It's also the case that features considered attractive in one culture—pierced noses, liposuctioned thighs, elongated ear lobes—may be considered unattractive in another. Perceptions of attractiveness and beauty also clearly change with experience. We generally rate people we like as more attractive than people we don't like; moreover, if you've just been shown a picture of a strikingly attractive person, your ratings of average-looking people go down (Kenrick, Gutierres, & Goldberg, 1989). Beauty is not entirely in the eye of the beholder, as the research of Langlois and Roggman (1990) indicates, but there is indeed a measurable subjective component that cannot be ignored.

Determinants of Liking and Loving

If you had to list all the things you look for in a friend, what would they be? Understanding? A sense of humor? Intelligence? What if the word *husband*, *wife*, or *lover* was substituted for *friend*—would the characteristics on your list change? Might you add wealth, security, or attractiveness? If you ask people to create such a list—and psychologists have done so numerous times—most people have no trouble coming up with a wish list of characteristics for "friend" or "marriage partner of my dreams." But how important do these well-thought-out and carefully chosen factors turn out to be? Do we really form friendships, or choose marriage partners, based on some relationship equation that sums desirable and undesirable attributes in a logical and rational way?

One of the most important lessons of this textbook, and certainly of this chapter, is that our behavior is strongly influenced by external forces in the environment. People act the way they do partly because of conscious, internally driven processes but also because the environment shapes and constrains the possible behaviors. In the case of interpersonal attraction, it turns out that the environment often plays a major role in determining both whom you choose to spend time with and whom you consider to be an appropriate mate. As you learned earlier in the chapter, even mere exposure to something can be sufficient to increase its likeability (Zajonc, 1968). People like things that are familiar, even when that familiarity has been created by simple repetition in the environment.

Proximity   In a classic study conducted almost 60 years ago, psychologist Leon Festinger and his colleagues (1950) analyzed the friendships that formed among students living in an apartment complex near the Massachusetts Institute of Technology. Festinger and his colleagues found that they could predict the likelihood of a friendship forming by simply noting the *proximity*—defined in terms of the closeness of living quarters—between two people in the building. When the students were asked to list their three closest friends, two-thirds of the time they named students who lived in their same apartment complex. Moreover, when a fellow apartment dweller was listed as a friend, two-thirds of the time he or she lived on the same floor as the respondent. Clearly, the choice of friends is strongly influenced by where one lives. People tend to end up with friends who live nearby.

Of course, it isn't proximity by itself that leads to liking and loving. When somebody lives close by, you see him or her a lot, and it may be the increased exposure that promotes the attraction. We've already seen that increased exposure leads to an increase in rated likeability, but it also provides the opportunity for interaction. When you consistently interact with someone, mutual feelings of connectedness and belonging tend to follow (Cantor & Malley, 1991). You see each other as members of the

Birds of a feather do tend to flock together—our lasting relationships are usually with people who are similar to us.

same *in-group*—that is, as people who share features in common. In fact, you don't even have to interact physically with someone for increased liking to occur. Psychologists John Darley and Ellen Berscheid (1967) found that even the anticipation of an interaction with someone you don't already know can cause you to rate that person as more attractive.

Similarity   We also tend to like and form relationships with people who are *similar* to us. Friends and intimate partners typically resemble each other in age, social status, education level, race, religious beliefs, political attitudes, intelligence, and even physical attractiveness; we even pick dogs that, at least on some dimensions, seem to resemble us physically (Roy & Christenfeld, 2004). People may report preferring physically attractive mates, but most end up marrying someone who is approximately equal to them in degree of physical attractiveness (Feingold, 1988, 1990). So, if you believe in the idea that "opposites attract," think again—in reality, it is the birds of a feather that tend consistently to flock together.

Although few psychologists question the finding that similarities attract, there are disagreements about how best to interpret this finding. The fact that similarities are found between the physical and attitudinal dimensions of friends and lovers doesn't provide any insight into why these similarities exist. As we discussed in Chapter 2, correlations do not imply causality. One possibility is that we like others who share our beliefs and attitudes because they *validate* those beliefs, which further helps convince us that our beliefs are the right ones (Byrne, 1971; Laprelle et al., 1990). Another possibility is that we spend time with others like ourselves because we dislike people who hold different views (Rosenbaum, 1986). It's not so much that we want to spend time with those who resemble us; it's that we don't want to spend time with those we despise.

A third possibility is that environmental factors are responsible. Partners in romantic relationships might be similarly attractive because attractiveness dictates to some extent who you can find as a mate. Physically unattractive people, for example, might be unable to attract mates who are more attractive; or it could be that society dictates that attractive people reject those who are less attractive. Socioeconomic class also tends to limit our options. If we are poor and live in a run-down section of town, our interactions are likely to be with people who are members of the same socioeconomic class. Generally, people who live in the same neighborhood, attend the

CRITICAL THINKING

Think about your own relationship experiences. Have you ever felt peer pressure to find a partner who meets a well-defined set of standards? How important were these factors in your decisions?

same church, or go off to the same university already share many features in common, and it is from this pool that people typically find their companions.

Reciprocity   There's also a role in the dynamics of interpersonal attraction for **reciprocity**, or our tendency to return in kind the feelings that are shown toward us. If someone doesn't like you and displays hostility at every turn, you usually have similarly negative feelings toward him or her. If someone likes you, or even if you simply think the person likes you, then you tend to like that person back (Curtis & Miller, 1986; Kelley, 1983). In a study by Curtis and Miller (1986), participants were asked to have a conversation with someone who they believed had been told either positive or negative information about them (actually, the conversation partner hadn't been told anything). If the people believed they were talking to someone who perceived them in a positive light, they tended to be friendlier and more open in their conversation—they acted as if they liked their partner more.

Reciprocity helps lead to interpersonal attraction because it is self-fulfilling and because people who like you tend to be reinforcing and accepting of your actions. But it doesn't always work. If you feel that the positive actions of another are motivated for some selfish reason—as part of a con job or to get something such as a promotion—then your reaction will typically be negative (Jones, 1964). Ingratiation, in which a person consciously tries to win the affections of another for some ulterior motive, is likely to backfire as a strategy if it is discovered.

The Psychology of Romantic Love

When psychologists study *interpersonal attraction*, it's likely to be seen as interesting and important research by most casual observers. But when psychologists turn to the study of "love," the reactions are often far different. How, you ask, can someone understand, define, or attempt to measure such a thing as love? Love is a topic to be tackled by the poet or the artist, not the questionnaire-laden social psychologist. Perhaps. But as you'll soon see, that hasn't stopped psychologists from trying.

Defining Love   Psychologists recognize that love is a complex emotion that can be expressed in a variety of forms. There is the love that exists between parent and child, between lovers, between husband and wife, even between friends. In each case, when it's measured through a questionnaire, the relationship is typically characterized by the giving and receiving of support, a kind of mutual understanding, and intense personal satisfaction (Fehr & Russell, 1991; Sternberg & Grajek, 1984). Although there may be fundamental similarities in how love is experienced, the amount of love that is reported depends on the type of relationship studied. Women, for example, might report *loving* their lover more than a best friend but *liking* their best friend more; men, on the other hand, report liking *and* loving their lover more than they report these feelings for their friends (Sternberg, 1986).

When the relationship between two individuals is romantic, it is popular to distinguish further between passionate love and companionate love. **Passionate love** is an intense emotional state in which the individual is enveloped by a powerful longing to be with the other person (Hatfield, 1988). For many people, passionate love resembles a ride on a kind of emotional roller coaster—they experience intense joy if the feelings are shared, and intense pain and despair if their feelings are unrequited. **Companionate love** tends to be less emotional and intense, but its feelings of trust and warmth can be more enduring. Whereas passionate love leads to intense arousal, companionate love leads to self-disclosure—we are willing to reveal our innermost secrets because the relationship sits on a bedrock of trust. It is, of course, possible for both passionate love and companionate love to be present in the same relationship, but this is not always the case.

reciprocity The tendency for people to return in kind the feelings that are shown toward them.

passionate love An intense emotional state characterized by a powerful longing to be with a specific person; passionate love is marked by a combination of intimacy and passion, but commitment may be lacking.

companionate love A kind of emotional attachment characterized by feelings of trust and companionship; companionate love is marked by a combination of intimacy and commitment, but passion may be lacking.

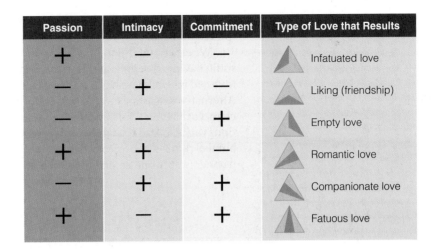

Passion	Intimacy	Commitment	Type of Love that Results
+	−	−	Infatuated love
−	+	−	Liking (friendship)
−	−	+	Empty love
+	+	−	Romantic love
−	+	+	Companionate love
+	−	+	Fatuous love

FIGURE 13.8 The Triangular View of Love
Robert Sternberg proposed that there are many kinds of love, each defined by the degree of *passion*, *intimacy*, and *commitment* present in the relationship. (Based on Sternberg, 1986)

The Triangular View of Love Psychologist Robert Sternberg (1986, 1999) has argued for what he calls a triangular view of love. He sees love as being composed of three major dimensions—intimacy, passion, and commitment—that vary in relation to one another (see ▌Figure 13.8). *Intimacy* is the emotional component that brings closeness, connectedness, and warmth to a relationship. *Passion* is the motivational component that underlies arousal, physical attraction, and sexual behavior. *Commitment* is the decision-making arm of love—how willing are the partners to stick with the relationship in times of trouble? All forms of love can be seen as some combination of these three components. For example, according to Sternberg (1986), *romantic love* is marked by a combination of intimacy and passion (but it may lack commitment), companionate love is high in intimacy and commitment (but without passion), and *empty love* occurs when there is commitment but little or no passion or intimacy.

In addition to using his triangle as a vehicle for defining love, Sternberg has followed other researchers in attempting to determine how the components of love change over time (see Berscheid, 1985; Hatfield & Rapson, 1993). What patterns have been found? Do couples gain intimacy? Lose passion? Become increasingly willing to commit? It is impossible to predict for any particular relationship, but the theory proposes some general trends. On average, the passion component of love builds early and rapidly in a relationship—it can even be experienced almost immediately on meeting another—but it's difficult to sustain for long periods. Commitment, on the other hand, is slow to develop but can be quite long lasting. Intimacy, too, is unlikely to be found early in a relationship (there is too much uncertainty), but it grows and maintains itself in most successful relationships. The components of love are fluid, changing over time in ways that reflect the successes and failures of the interactions between the partners.

Can we predict how long a specific love relationship will last? A number of studies have been conducted on this topic with some surprising results. For instance, it turns out that for college students your roommate is a better predictor, on average, of how long your romantic relationship will last than you and your romantic partner (MacDonald & Ross, 1999). It's also the case that your original ratings of the quality of the relationship correlate more highly with the eventual outcome than your predictions about how long the relationship will last. Often our "hopes" for what a relationship will become are inaccurate; what matters is our ongoing assessment of the quality of the relationship (and, of course, you might consider paying some attention

CRITICAL THINKING

If you had to write a prescription for a successful marriage, how would you rate the dimensions of the triangle?

to what your roommate thinks because he or she tends to be more "objective" about the relationship).

Whether you'll end up staying in a close relationship depends on many factors, some having little or nothing to do with "love." For example, people who are highly invested in a relationship—if they share property, friends, or kids—tend to stick it out. Alternatives matter as well: How easily can you survive on your own, and what are the chances that you'll find another relationship partner? Strong personal or moral convictions can also lead to stability in a relationship. You may dislike your partner intensely but feel that it's wrong to break up a relationship. Satisfaction, or happiness, with your partner is only one determinant of a relationship that lasts (Clark & Grote, 2003).

Test Yourself 13.3

Check your knowledge about how we establish relationships with other people by deciding whether each of the following statements is True or False. (You will find the answers in the Appendix.)

1. Babies, within hours of birth, show a preference for attractive over unattractive faces. *True or False*?
2. Blending studies of facial attractiveness indicate that faces that are unusual or distinct tend to receive higher ratings of attractiveness than averaged faces. *True or False*?
3. Studies have found that if you've just been shown a picture of a strikingly attractive person, your ratings of an average-looking person go up. *True or False*?
4. Friends and intimate partners typically resemble each other in age, social status, education level, race, religious beliefs, political attitudes, intelligence, and even physical attractiveness. *True or False*?
5. According to the triangular theory of love, infatuated love represents passion without intimacy or commitment. *True or False*?
6. Passionate love typically leads to more feelings of warmth and trust than does companionate love. *True or False*?

Review *Psychology for a Reason*

Our actions, thoughts, and feelings arise out of the interactions we have with ever-changing environments. Among the most powerful components of these environments are *social* ones—our thoughts and actions are strongly influenced by the people around us. Social psychology is the discipline that studies how people think about, influence, and relate to others. In this chapter we tackled the topic areas of social psychology from the perspective of three major social problems.

Interpreting the Behavior of Others

As we move through the social world, it's extremely adaptive for us to try and make sense of the people around us. We form initial impressions of others by using the information we have available—such as the physical appearance of the person—and by relying on preexisting knowledge categories, called social schemas, which help us interpret that information. Schemas are useful features of the adaptive mind because they help us to direct our actions in uncertain situations. But schemas can also lead to stereotypes—beliefs about people belonging to groups—which, although useful in many ways, can produce prejudice.

Attributions—how we infer the causes of another's behavior—form another important part of the overall interpretation process. When attempting to explain the actions of others, we look for factors that covary with the behavior, and we assess the consistency of the behavior, its distinctiveness, and whether there is consensus among people. Whether you place the locus of causality in the external environment or within the person depends on how these three factors work together. Some basic attribution biases—such as the fundamental attribution error—also help shape our inferences.

Attitudes, which are positive or negative evaluations, are typically separated into three components: a cognitive component, an affective component, and a behavioral component. Attitude formation is influenced by a number of factors, but direct experience plays a major role. One popular theory of attitude change is the elaboration likelihood model, which proposes that there are central and peripheral routes to persuasion. It's clear from a number of research studies that when people are induced to act in ways that are inconsistent with their existing attitudes, their attitudes often change as a result.

Behaving in the Presence of Others Psychologists use the term *social influence* to describe how behavior is affected by other people in one's environment. Sometimes social influence can produce positive effects, as in social facilitation, and sometimes the presence of others hinders performance, as in social interference. The presence of others can also affect our willingness to deliver aid to people in need. The bystander effect reveals that we're generally reluctant to come to someone's aid when other people are present. One interpretation of this effect appeals to diffusion of responsibility: We believe that others have already done something to help or will soon get involved.

Behavior is also strongly influenced by the social pressures of groups and of authority. Participation as a member of a well-defined group can make us conform, which means that our opinions and behaviors will tend to move toward the group norm. Conformity operates on the group level also. It is common for groups to polarize, which means that the group's dominant point of view tends to become stronger and more extreme with the passage of time. If the phenomenon of groupthink is present, members have become so interested in seeking a consensus of opinion that dissenting views start to be ignored or suppressed. Milgram's famous experiment on obedience to authority demonstrated that people can be induced by an authority figure to engage in behavior that they would not engage in otherwise. The degree of compliance depends on the characteristics of the situation and on the characteristics of the person giving the orders.

Establishing Relations With Others Often the most meaningful things in our lives are the social relations that we've established with others. How are relationships formed? We examined facial attractiveness and discovered that attractiveness may be determined, in part, by innate biological factors. People tend to prefer average, or prototypical, faces—perhaps because they're easier to identify or signal genetic health. Among the factors that influence liking and loving are familiarity, proximity, similarity, and reciprocity. We're more likely to be attracted to someone we know, who lives nearby, who is similar to ourselves, and who likes us back. Psychologists have also attempted to understand love, which is typically defined in terms of multiple components—such as intimacy, passion, and commitment. Whether a person ends up in a relationship based on passionate love or companionate love depends on how these components work together in the relationship.

Active Summary (You will find the answers in the Appendix.)

Interpreting the Behavior of Others: Social Cognition

• Our perceptions of others are guided by bottom-up processing—actual physical sensations—and (1) _____-down processing—our beliefs and (2) _____. For example, physical attractiveness significantly shapes our interpretations, and so do existing social schemas and (3) _____. In the self-fulfilling prophecy effect, social (4) _____ lead us to expect certain kinds of behavior from members of certain groups, and these expectations can cause the expected behavior. Stereotypes also lead to (5) _____ and discrimination. Prejudice can be reduced through repeated exposure to individual members of the stereotyped group or by adopting the perspective of group members.

• Attributions are the causes we assign to behaviors. According to the covariation model, we rely on consistency, (6) _____, and consensus to make the appropriate inference. When a behavior is high on all three dimensions, we tend to make (7) _____ attributions—to credit an outside source; when a behavior is high in consistency but low in consensus and distinctiveness, we tend to make (8) _____ attributions—to credit inherent personality traits. When we consider the behavior of others and overestimate the role of (9) _____ factors and underestimate outside influences, we are making the (10) _____ _____ _____. The general rule in which we tend to attribute our own behavior to external sources and the behavior of others to internal sources is known as the (11) _____-_____ _____. An exception to this rule is a (12) _____-_____ bias, our tendency to take credit for actions that produce positive outcomes and to blame other people when our actions are questionable or lead to failure.

• Attitudes have (13) _____, (14) _____, and (15) _____ components. (The behavioral component is a predisposition to behave in a certain way; our attitudes don't always directly affect our behavior.) Attitudes form primarily from (16) _____, through classical and (17) _____ conditioning and (18) _____ learning. According to the elaboration (19) _____ model, our attitudes can be changed through a (20) _____ route, when we listen carefully to a message and judge it on its merits, or through a (21) _____ route, when superficial cues or mere exposure to a message affect us more. According to cognitive (22) _____ theory, inconsistencies between behavior and (23) _____ lead to internal (24) _____, or dissonance, that is relieved by changing one's attitude. According to self-(25) _____ theory, we may also use our own behavior as the basis for our attitudes about ourselves.

Behaving in the Presence of Others: Social Influence

• When we're in the presence of others, social (26) _____ may improve our (27) _____. Social (28) _____ occurs when being around others (29) _____ our performance.

• The sense of (30) _____ causes us to act out of (31) _____ concern for others. But the (32) _____ effect makes us reluctant to step forward and help when other people are present. A diffusion of (33) _____ comes from believing that someone else has already taken action or will soon get involved.

• People have a tendency toward social (34) _____, putting out (35) _____ effort when working with a (36) _____ than when working alone. (37) _____ occurs when we feel less accountable in the presence of others than when we're on our own. When someone's opinions, feelings, and behaviors reflect a group norm rather than individual preference, (38) _____ has occurred; this is especially likely if pressure to fit in arises from an in-group with which you share common features or identify with.

• When the (39) _____ point of view within a group becomes stronger and more extreme with time, group (40) _____ has occurred. (41) _____ has occurred when group members become so interested in achieving a (42) _____ of opinion that they (43) _____ and even suppress dissenting views.

• When we respond to the orders of an authority figure or institution, we are showing (44) _____. In the Milgram experiment, (45) _____% of the research participants

willingly followed orders to deliver electric shocks up to 450 volts to another person, despite the subject's pleas. The study has been criticized on ethical grounds, as well as for its procedures. However, in the 30 years since the experiment, the general procedure has been repeated and has (46) _____ Milgram's findings, although the degree of compliance that people will show depends on many factors.

• In most Western cultures, including the United States, people are taught from a very young age to adopt an (47)_____ view of the self; that is, they are rewarded for viewing themselves as unique individuals. In many non-Western cultures, especially in Asia, people adopt a very different, (48) _____ view of the self. They are taught to consider themselves as members of a group with common goals rather than as individuals striving to be different.

Establishing Relations With Others

• Physical attractiveness powerfully influences our behavior. An (49) _____ perspective predicts that we will be attracted to people who look youthful, vigorous, and (50) _____, or who may be able to provide protection and sustenance, because these qualities increase the likelihood of successful reproduction and child rearing. The universality of attractiveness may reflect the fact that we seem programmed to prefer faces that represent the average, or represent the category of (51) _____. The perception of beauty does, however, have a strong (52) _____ component.

• Attraction to others depends on their proximity and (53) _____ to us, and on (54) _____, the tendency to return feelings that are shown toward us.

• (55) _____ love is an intense emotional state in which one individual is possessed by the powerful longing to be with another. (56) _____ love tends to be less emotional and intense and is characterized by feelings of trust and warmth. According to the (57) _____ theory, the experience of love has three major aspects: (58) _____, (59) _____, and (60) _____, components that change with time.

Terms to Remember

actor–observer effect, 419
altruism, 427
attitude, 420
attributions, 416
bystander effect, 427
cognitive dissonance, 422
companionate love, 442
conformity, 429

deindividuation, 429
diffusion of responsibility, 428
discrimination, 414
elaboration likelihood model, 421
external attribution, 417
fundamental attribution error, 417
group polarization, 431
groupthink, 431

in-group, 430
internal attribution, 417
obedience, 433
passionate love, 442
prejudice, 414
reciprocity, 442
self-fulfilling prophecy effect, 413
self-perception theory, 423

Media Resources

 ThomsonNOW

www.thomsonedu.com/ThomsonNOW
Go to this site for the link to ThomsonNow, your one-stop study shop. Take a Pre-Test for this chapter and Thomson-Now will generate a personalized Study Plan based on your test results! The Study Plan will identify the topics you need to review and direct you to online resources to help you master those topics. You can then take a Post-Test to help you determine the concepts you have mastered and what you still need to work on.

 Companion Website

www.thomsonedu.com/psychology/nairne
Go to this site to find online resources directly linked to your book, including a glossary, flashcards, quizzing, weblinks, and more.

 Psyk.trek 3.0

Check out the Psyk.trek CD-ROM for further study of the concepts in this chapter. Psyk.trek's interactive learning modules, simulations, and quizzes offer additional opportunities for you to interact with, reflect on, and retain the material:

Social Psychology: Attribution Processes
Social Psychology: Attitude Change
Social Psychology: Theories of Love

Psychological Disorders

"You shouldn't really be reading this book, you know. In fact, put it down—now. The author's intentions are not pure . . . he doesn't have your best interest in mind. He wants to convince you that you have no true control over your life.

To him, you're nothing more than a machine shaped by the whims of changing environments; you're the product of forces outside of your control—biological drives, toilet-training habits, unbalanced mixtures of neurotransmitters in your brain.

"But you and I are more than that—we're more than the product of brain biochemistry or dirty little habits. We have inner control over our lives. You and I are in touch with the essence of the inner one, although perhaps it is only I who recognizes this fact at the moment. I've stopped you because it's time to prepare ourselves now . . . the first of the tribe arrived weeks ago . . . he's here, inside my head, and he's telling me the real truth. There's nothing to fear . . . we're still in control . . . it will be our choice, not theirs, to submit. And when we do, the truth about the conspiracy will be revealed to all. . . ."

Imagine being on the receiving end of such a conversation. What would be your reaction? At best, I suspect you'd categorize this person as odd; more likely, you'd label him as disturbed. His thinking is certainly distorted, and he is more than a bit paranoid. But does he suffer from a *true psychological disorder* needing treatment, or is he simply eccentric? How can we tell? What are the criteria used to define and describe psychological disorders and abnormal behavior? Is distorted thinking merely a personal choice, a way to be different or unique, or is it something more like strep throat or a bladder infection—something that we should try to treat and cure?

In this chapter and the next one, we turn our attention to the classification and treatment of psychological disorders. Obviously, before treating a psychological problem, you must

© Ex-Rouchon/Photo Researchers, Inc.

To help you understand how psychologists view psychological disorders, our discussion will revolve around the following three-part question: How do we conceptualize, classify, and understand abnormal behavior? Once you see how psychologists think about abnormality, the stage will be set for treatment, which is covered in depth in Chapter 15.

Conceptualizing Abnormality A person who suffers from one or more psychological problems is typically classified as abnormal. Indeed, the terms *abnormal* and *abnormal behavior* are often used as roughly equivalent to the term *psychological disorder*. But over the years, psychologists have struggled with how best to define abnormality. When people act abnormally, their behavior tends to be unusual or dysfunctional, and they often appear to be suffering from considerable personal distress. But for reasons we'll discuss in the first section of the chapter, none of these criteria alone is

sufficient to capture the concept. Most conceptualizations of abnormality rely on multiple criteria.

Classifying Psychological Disorders Even if we reach agreement about the proper way to define abnormality, we still need a means for naming and classifying the underlying disorders that lead to abnormal behavior. Psychologists and psychiatrists have worked hard to develop a rigorous system for the diagnosis and classification of psychological disorders. We'll consider the current system, which is detailed in the *Diagnostic and Statistical Manual of Mental Disorders*, and you'll see how it's used to diagnose a variety of mental problems. There are many kinds of known psychological disorders— ranging from anxiety disorders to depression to schizophrenia—and each is classified on the basis of a relatively fixed set of criteria. Although it's a common belief among the general

public that psychological disorders are idiosyncratic—which means they arise in different ways for different individuals—you'll see that most disorders actually produce symptoms that are consistent and reliable.

Understanding Psychological Disorders In the final section of the chapter, we'll discuss how researchers attempt to understand the causes of psychological disorders. What causes an anxiety disorder, depression, or schizophrenia? Do psychological disorders result from some kind of mental breakdown, or are they simply adaptive reactions to stress? If it's a breakdown, is the cause of the breakdown biological or environmental? We'll consider the major theoretical tools used by mental health professionals to explain abnormal behavior. Not surprisingly, the answer to many psychological problems lies partly in biology and partly in the environment.

determine whether there is indeed a problem that requires treatment. Making this determination is more difficult than you might think. Let's imagine you arrive home tonight and find your roommate awake but slumped in a corner with his cap pulled down over his eyes. You ask him to explain, but he tells you to mind your own business. Later that night, you hear sobbing and crying coming from behind his locked bedroom door. His bizarre behavior continues for the next two days. He refuses to respond to questions, he stops going to class, and he refuses to eat or clean himself. He's suffering from a psychological disorder, right? Perhaps. But suppose you learn that his father and mother were just killed in an automobile accident. What would your reaction be now? Would you conclude that he's psychologically disturbed or that he's simply showing an intense but normal grief reaction?

Conceptualizing Abnormality: What Is Abnormal Behavior?

LEARNING GOALS
• Evaluate the various criteria that have been used to define abnormality.
• Discuss the legal definition of insanity.
• Explain how the medical model classifies and categorizes abnormality.
• Discuss the effects of diagnostic labeling.

WHEN YOU ENCOUNTER SOMEONE who babbles on about how voices in his or her head are busy plotting a conspiracy, it's not difficult to categorize this behavior as abnormal; clearly, this person is in trouble and in need of some professional help. But as you've seen, sharp dividing lines don't always exist between normal and abnormal behavior. Sometimes behavior that appears abnormal can turn out to be a reasonable reaction to a stressful event, such as the roommate's reaction to the death of his parents. It's also the case that a behavior that seems abnormal in one culture can appear to be perfectly normal in another (Marsella & Yamada, 2000). Entering a trance state and experiencing visual hallucinations is considered abnormal in Western cultures, but in other cultures it may not be (Bentall, 1990).

Even within a culture, conceptions of abnormality can change over time. For many years homosexuality was considered abnormal by the psychological community—in fact, it was considered a psychological disorder. But this view of homosexuality is rejected by psychologists today. Fifty years ago, a strong dependence on tobacco wouldn't have raised an eyebrow, but today if you're hooked on tobacco, you could easily be classified as having a substance-related disorder. Given these changing conceptions, psychologists are justifiably cautious when applying the label of abnormality. Behavior usually must meet a set of criteria before it's considered abnormal (Widiger & Sankis, 2000).

Characteristics of Abnormal Behavior

Over the years, researchers have proposed a number of defining criteria for abnormality. In each case, as you'll see, the proposed criteria capture some but not all of the important features of what is agreed to be abnormal behavior.

Statistical Deviance   One way to define abnormal behavior is in terms of **statistical deviance**, or infrequency. For any given behavior, such as arguing with your neighbors or hearing voices, there is a certain probability that the behavior will occur in society at large. Most people have argued with their neighbors at one time or another, but few actually converse with disembodied voices. According to the concept of statistical deviance, a behavior is abnormal if it occurs infrequently among the members of a population. As you've learned elsewhere in this text, it's not unusual for psychologists to classify behavior on the basis of statistical frequency. For example, terms such as *gifted* and *mentally retarded* are defined with respect to statistical frequencies. So it should come as no surprise that statistical frequencies have been used to define abnormality.

But statistical deviance—that is, something that is extreme or different from the average—can't be used as the sole criterion for labeling a behavior as abnormal. It's easy to come up with a list of behaviors that are statistically infrequent but are not abnormal in a psychological sense. For example, Kobe Bryant and Shaquille O'Neal have skills on the basketball court that are extreme, and thereby statistically deviant, but to be a great athlete does not make one abnormal. Similarly, only a handful of individuals have reached the intellectual heights of Albert Einstein or Isaac Newton, but superior intelligence is not abnormal in the usual psychological sense of the word. An additional problem is the establishment of a criterion point: Just how infrequent or unusual must a behavior be to be characterized as abnormal? So far, psychologists have failed to produce a satisfactory answer to this question.

Cultural Deviance   Another criterion is **cultural deviance**, which compares behavior to existing cultural norms. In this case, a behavior would be considered abnormal if it violates the accepted standards of society. In most cultures, for example, it's not considered normal or acceptable to walk to class in the nude or to engage in sexual relations with children. These behaviors break the established rules of our culture, and if you engage in either, it's likely that people will think you have a serious problem.

statistical deviance A criterion of abnormality stating that a behavior is abnormal if it occurs infrequently among the members of a population.

> **CRITICAL THINKING**
>
> Suppose a 70-year-old entered college and started acting exactly the same way as a 20-year-old sophomore. Would you consider his or her behavior to be abnormal?

cultural deviance A criterion of abnormality stating that a behavior is abnormal if it violates the rules or accepted standards of society.

Although Bill Gates and Yo-Yo Ma are statistically deviant in some respects, would you classify them as psychologically abnormal?

emotional distress A criterion of abnormality stating that abnormal behaviors are those that lead to personal distress or emotional upset.

dysfunction A breakdown in normal functioning; abnormal behaviors are those that prevent one from pursuing adaptive strategies.

A trance state is likely to be classified as abnormal in Western cultures, but not necessarily in other cultures.

But once again, cultural deviance by itself fails as a sufficient criterion. Many criminals violate the established norms of society—stealing cars or embezzling money, for example. Such behavior might be abnormal by both statistical and cultural standards, but that doesn't mean all criminals suffer from psychological disorders. There are also many individuals who suffer from legitimate psychological problems, such as anxiety or depression, who never violate a law or established standard of society. Finally, as we just discussed, behaviors that are abnormal in one culture may be considered normal in another. There are cultures in the world, for instance, where nakedness in public breaks no established cultural rules. People who suffer from psychological disorders may indeed violate cultural norms in some instances, but often they do not.

Emotional Distress A third characteristic of many kinds of abnormal behavior is the presence of personal or **emotional distress**. People who suffer from psychological disorders often experience great despair and unhappiness. They feel hopeless, lost, and alienated from others. In fact, it's the emotional distress that usually leads them to seek professional help for their problems. But not all disorders make people unhappy; there are lots of people who have little contact with reality but seem perfectly content in their fantasy world. Likewise, there are many distressed people in the world—for example, those who have recently lost a loved one or a job—who would not be classified as abnormal by the psychological community.

Dysfunction A final criterion for abnormality is general adaptiveness: Is there a breakdown in normal functioning—a **dysfunction**—that prevents the person from successfully following adaptive strategies? People who suffer from psychological disorders are often unable to function well in typical daily activities—they may not eat properly, clean themselves, or be able to hold a job. Their ability to think clearly may be impaired, which affects their ability to adapt successfully in their environment. As you'll see later, the assessment of global functioning—defined as the ability to adapt in social, personal, and occupational environments—plays a large role in the diagnosis and treatment of psychological disorders.

Summarizing the Criteria You've seen that abnormal behavior can be statistically or culturally deviant, it can involve personal or emotional distress, and it can signal impairment or dysfunction. Normal behavior, then, could be any behavior that's relatively common, does not cause personal distress, or generally leads to adaptive consequences. However, psychologists will usually refuse to label any behavior as normal or abnormal unless it satisfies several of these criteria. Crying hysterically for hours at a time may be a normal grief reaction, or it may signal a serious disorder. Even a behavior that seems to be clearly abnormal—such as a paranoid delusion that people are out to get you—might be adaptive in some environments. To paraphrase comedian Woody Allen, paranoids can have enemies too.

You should also recognize that "abnormal" and "normal" are not rigid categories. Each of us can relate in one way or another to the criteria of abnormality we've just discussed. We all know people who have occasionally acted unusually, suffered from emotional distress, or failed to follow an adaptive strategy. Many psychological disorders are characterized by behaviors or feelings that are merely exaggerations of normal ones, such as anxiety, feelings of sadness, or concerns about one's health. Consequently, it's better to think about normal and abnormal behavior as endpoints on a continuum rather than as nonoverlapping categories (see ▌ Figure 14.1).

Normal	Criterion	Abnormal
Common	Statistical deviance	Rare
Acceptable	Cultural deviance	Unacceptable
Low	Emotional distress	High
Adaptive	Dysfunction	Maladaptive

▌**FIGURE 14.1** The Normal-to-Abnormal Continuum
"Abnormal" and "normal" are not fixed categories but endpoints on a continuum. To a certain degree, everyone has acted unusually, suffered from emotional distress, or failed to follow an adaptive strategy.

The Concept of Insanity

Behavior can mean different things depending on the context in which it occurs—something that's abnormal in one situation may be quite normal in another. Yet regardless of where you travel in the world, some behaviors will always be recognized as abnormal: Consider serial killer Jeffrey Dahmer, who admitted butchering, cannibalizing, and having sex with the dead bodies of more than a dozen young men and boys. Everyone, including the mental health professionals who examined Dahmer, was in agreement—this was a man suffering from some serious psychological problems.

But from a legal standpoint Jeffrey Dahmer was judged by a jury to be perfectly sane. Despite the best efforts of his legal team to have him declared mentally unfit, and thus not responsible for his crimes, Dahmer was found legally sane. He stood trial and

Concept Review | **Criteria for Defining Abnormality**

CRITERION	DESCRIPTION	EXAMPLE
Statistical deviance	Behavior that occurs infrequently among the members of a population	Jon goes back to make sure his front door is locked exactly 12 times each morning. As he walks to the door, he mutters over and over, "lock the door . . ." No one else in the neighborhood does this.
Cultural deviance	Behavior that violates the accepted standards of society	Jon notices that each time he comes back to his front door, talking to himself, his neighbors look at him rather nervously, and they tend to avoid him at other times.
Emotional distress	Great despair and unhappiness	Jon is very distressed by his compulsive behavior.
Dysfunction	A breakdown in normal functioning	Jon's routine of checking his front door 12 times every morning has made him late for work a number of times, and his job is in jeopardy.

insanity A legal term usually defined as the inability to understand that certain actions are wrong, in a legal or moral sense, at the time of a crime.

Everyone agrees that Andrea Yates, who drowned her five young children, suffers from severe psychological problems, yet a jury failed to accept that she was legally insane.

medical model The view that abnormal behavior is symptomatic of an underlying "disease," which can be "cured" with the appropriate therapy.

CRITICAL THINKING

How might acceptance of the medical model influence the availability of treatment options? Might it cause an overemphasis on biological treatments for psychological problems?

diagnostic labeling effects The fact that labels for psychological problems can become self-fulfilling prophecies; the label may make it difficult to recognize normal behavior when it occurs, and it may actually increase the likelihood that a person will act in an abnormal way.

was convicted of his crimes (later, while serving his life sentence, he was brutally murdered by a fellow inmate). Sounds perplexing, but *insanity* is a *legal* concept rather than a psychological one. Its definition varies somewhat from state to state, but **insanity** is usually defined in terms of the defendant's thought processes *at the time of the crime*: A criminal is insane, and therefore not guilty by reason of insanity, if, because of a "mental disease," he or she fails to appreciate or understand that certain actions are wrong in a legal or moral sense (Ogloff, Roberts, & Roesch, 1993). Dahmer was judged capable of understanding the wrongfulness of his actions; as a result, he failed the insanity test, even though he was clearly suffering from serious psychological problems.

Most mental health professionals accept that people with serious psychological disorders are sometimes incapable of judging the appropriateness of their actions. As you'll soon see, psychological disorders can lead to distorted views of the world—affected individuals not only act in ways that are abnormal, but their very thoughts, beliefs, and perceptions of the world can be wildly distorted as well. But exercise caution: It's important not to confuse the concept of insanity with the concept of a psychological disorder.

The Medical Model: Conceptualizing Abnormality as a Disease

To understand how disorders are classified by the psychological community, we need to discuss the *medical model* of diagnosis. According to the **medical model**, abnormal behavior is caused by an underlying *disease*—a kind of mental *illness*—that can be *cured* with the appropriate therapy. This conception of abnormality has been quite influential. As you already know, there are good reasons to believe that behavior is strongly influenced by biological factors, such as the actions of neurotransmitters in the brain. In addition, biomedical therapies, such as the administration of psychoactive drugs, are often effective in treating psychological problems. It's also the case that most psychological disorders can be classified in terms of *symptoms*. Depression, for example, typically leads to one or more of the following: sad mood, diminished interest in pleasure, difficulty in sleeping, feelings of worthlessness, and so on. The medical influence is deeply ingrained in the very language used by psychologists—they speak of mental health, mental illness, or psychopathology in much the same way a physician describes a medical condition.

But is the medical model an appropriate way to view abnormality? Some researchers believe it's wrong to draw direct comparisons between physical illness and psychological problems (Szasz, 1961, 2000). Both strep throat and depression lead to a set of reliable symptoms. But we know that strep throat is caused by a physical problem—bacteria; at this point the cause of depression is still being debated. In addition, people often seek treatment for psychological problems that are perhaps more accurately described as problems in living. How these adjustment problems are interpreted also seems to depend on the particular social or cultural context, which is not the case for most medical conditions. Some kinds of bizarre behavior thought to be abnormal in one culture can be considered normal in another, but strep throat produces fever and pain regardless of the cultural environment.

Problems Associated With Labeling

Critics of the medical model also express concern about **diagnostic labeling effects**. Labeling a psychological problem as an illness or a disorder tends to attach a stigma that can be difficult to overcome (Link & Phelan, 1999). A number of studies have found that applying the label "mental patient" leads one to interpret an individual's behavior in a far different light than you would otherwise. In one study, professional therapists watched a videotape of a man describing his personal adjustment problems (Langer & Abelson, 1974). If, prior to viewing the tape, the therapists were told that the man was a mental patient, they rated his adjustment problems more negatively than did other therapists who were simply told he was a job applicant (see ▌Figure 14.2). People's expectations, as I've stressed in previous chapters, importantly influence how they interpret new information.

The Rosenhan Study In one particularly influential study of labeling effects, David Rosenhan, along with seven other coinvestigators, arrived separately at several psychiatric hospitals in the early 1970s with the complaint that they were hearing voices (Rosenhan, 1973). Actually, each of the participants was perfectly normal. They simply adopted the role of a pseudopatient—they feigned, or faked, a disorder to see how labeling would affect their subsequent treatment. On arrival they reported to the psychiatric staff that they were hearing a disembodied voice in their head, a voice that repeated things like "empty," "hollow," and "thud." They were all admitted to hospitals, and virtually all received the diagnosis of schizophrenia (schizophrenia, as you'll see later, is a condition characterized by serious disturbances in thought and emotion).

Again, the purpose of the study was to see how an initial diagnosis of schizophrenia would affect subsequent treatment. From the point of admission, none of the participants continued to act strangely. In all interactions with the hospital staff, they acted normally and gave no indications that they were suffering from a disorder. However, despite their normal behavior, none of the staff ever recognized them as pseudopatients; indeed, written hospital reports later revealed that the staff members tended to interpret normal behaviors as symptomatic of a disorder. It was the real patients, in fact, who felt the researchers somehow did not belong; several actually voiced their suspicions, claiming, "You're not crazy. You're a journalist or a professor" (these comments were partly made in reaction to the fact that the pseudopatients spent time taking notes). Once the pseudopatients had been admitted and labeled as "abnormal," their behaviors were seen by the staff through the lens of expectation, and normal, sane behavior was never recognized as such. On average, the pseudopatients remained in the hospital for 19 days—the stays ranged from under a week to almost two months—and on release all were given the diagnosis of schizophrenia "in remission" (which means not currently active).

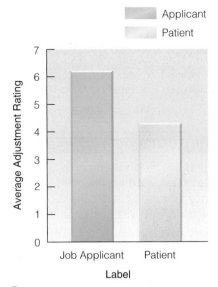

▌**FIGURE 14.2** Labeling Effects
In one study therapists were asked to provide adjustment ratings for people labeled as "patient" or "job applicant." The people were judged to be better adjusted when the therapists thought they were job applicants, not patients. (Data from Langer & Abelson, 1974)

Most mental health professionals are careful not to apply rigid labels to clients because diagnostic labels can become self-fulfilling prophecies.

The Rosenhan study is important because it suggests that diagnostic labels can become self-fulfilling prophecies. Once you're diagnosed, you're likely to be treated as if you're suffering from a disorder, and this treatment (1) may make it difficult to recognize normal behavior when it occurs and (2) may actually increase the likelihood that you'll act in an abnormal way. If the people in your environment expect you to act abnormally, you may very well start to act in a way that's consistent with those expectations (see Chapter 13).

Since its publication in 1973, the Rosenhan study has been widely analyzed in psychological circles. Its lessons about the hazards of labeling are clear. But at the same time, two points about the study are worth noting. First, you should appreciate that the admission of the pseudopatients by the hospital staff, as well as the subsequent diagnoses, were reasonable given the patients' reported symptoms. The diagnosis of a psychological disorder is often dependent on what the patient reports, and the trained professionals in this case had no reason to assume that the patients were lying or manufacturing symptoms. Second, it's possible and even reasonable to dispute the claim that the attending staff failed to recognize that the pseudopatients were acting normally. After all, they were released with the label "in remission," so the staff must have recognized that they were no longer acting in an abnormal way (Spitzer, 1975).

Test Yourself 14.1

Check your knowledge of how abnormality is conceptualized by deciding whether each of the following statements is True or False. (You will find the answers in the Appendix.)

1. When a behavior occurs infrequently among members of a population, it meets the criterion of cultural deviance. *True or False?*
2. To receive the diagnosis of a psychological disorder, a person must be suffering from a certain amount of emotional distress. *True or False?*
3. In many cases, abnormal behaviors are simply exaggerated versions of normal behaviors. *True or False?*
4. According to the medical model, psychological disorders can and should be classified in terms of symptoms. *True or False?*
5. In the Rosenhan study, hospital staff members quickly picked up on the fact that the pseudopatients were no longer acting abnormally. *True or False?*

Classifying Psychological Disorders: The DSM-IV-TR

LEARNING GOALS
- Describe the DSM-IV-TR.
- Describe the common anxiety disorders.
- Describe the somatoform disorders.
- Describe the common dissociative disorders.
- Describe the common mood disorders.
- Describe the characteristics of schizophrenia.
- Describe the common personality disorders.

DSM-IV-TR The *Diagnostic and Statistical Manual of Mental Disorders* (4th ed.), which is used for the diagnosis and classification of psychological disorders. The DSM-IV-TR is composed of five major rating dimensions, or *axes*.

NOW, FINALLY, WE TURN TO the actual classification process. As mentioned in the previous section, specific psychological disorders are often diagnosed in terms of defining criteria or symptoms. This is the approach used by the *Diagnostic and Statistical Manual of Mental Disorders*, published by the American Psychiatric Association (2000). From this point forward, I'll refer to this manual by its more commonly used acronym: **DSM-IV-TR**. The "IV" designates that the classification system is currently in its fourth edition; the "TR" refers to some revisions in the descriptive text that have occurred in recent years. The purpose of the DSM-IV-TR is to provide clinicians with a well-defined classification system, based on objective and measurable criteria, so that reliable diagnoses of psychological disorders can be produced worldwide; it is also designed to coordinate with the tenth edition of the World Health Organization's International Classification of Diseases (ICD-10), which covers medical as well as psychological problems. The DSM-IV-TR is intended only for the purposes of diagnosis and classification; it does not suggest therapies or methods of treatment.

How does the classification system work? The DSM-IV-TR is composed of five major rating dimensions, or *axes* (see ▌Figure 14.3). We'll focus our attention mainly

Axis I	Axis II	Axis III	Axis IV
Clinical Disorders and Other Conditions That May Be a Focus of Clinical Attention	Personality Disorders and Mental Retardation	General Medical Conditions	Psychosocial and Environmental Problems
Examples:	**Examples:**	**Examples:**	**Examples:**
Substance-related disorders Schizophrenia and other psychotic disorders Mood disorders Anxiety disorders Somatoform disorders Dissociative disorders Sexual and gender identity disorders Eating disorders Sleep disorders	Paranoid personality disorder Schizotypal personality disorder Antisocial personality disorder Borderline personality disorder Narcissistic personality disorder Dependent personality disorder	Infectious and parasitic diseases Endocrine, nutritional, and metabolic diseases and immunity disorders Diseases of the nervous system and sense organs Diseases of the circulatory system Diseases of the respiratory system Diseases of the digestive system Diseases of the genitourinary system Congenital anomalies	Problems with primary support group Problems related to the social environment Educational problems Occupational problems Housing problems Economic problems

Axis V

Global Assessment of Functioning (GAF) Scale

Code	Examples of symptoms:
100	Superior functioning in a wide range of activities
90	Absent or minimal symptoms, good functioning in all areas
80	Symptoms transient and expectable reactions to psychosocial stressors
70	Mild symptoms or impairment in social, occupational, or school functioning, but general functioning is pretty good
60	Moderate symptoms or impairment in social, occupational, or school functioning
50	Serious symptoms or impairment in social, occupational, or school functioning
40	Major impairment in work or school, family relations, judgment, thinking, mood; some communication impairment
30	Influenced by delusions or hallucinations, serious impairment in communication or judgment
20	Some danger of severely hurting self or others, gross impairment in communication, sporadic personal hygiene
10	Persistent danger of severely hurting self or others

▌**FIGURE 14.3** The Five Axes of the DSM-IV-TR Diagnostic System
The DSM-IV-TR is composed of five major rating dimensions, or axes. Information collected from each axis is integrated into final diagnosis and treatment decisions. (Reprinted with permission from *Diagnostic and Statistical Manual of Mental Disorders*, Fourth Edition, Text Revision. Copyright 2000, American Psychiatric Association.)

on the first axis, which lists the major clinical syndromes (such as depression and schizophrenia), although all five are important to the complete diagnostic process. The clinician uses the criteria outlined in Axis I (Clinical Syndromes) and Axis II (Personality Disorders) to classify and label any abnormal behavior that may be present. Axis III allows the clinician to record any medical conditions that the individual may be experiencing. It's important for the clinician to know a person's medical history because some medical conditions (such as Alzheimer disease) can contribute to abnormal behavior. Axis IV rates any environmental or psychosocial problems that may be present. For example, is the client going through a difficult divorce, or has he or she recently been fired? Finally, on Axis V the clinician codes the individual's current level of adaptive or global functioning. Is the client able to function adequately in social, personal, and occupational settings?

The clinician uses this multiaxial classification system to get the widest possible assessment of one's current psychological status. It matters to the clinician how someone is functioning in daily life, for example, because it often determines the most effective kind of treatment program. If the person is so severely impaired that he or she cannot hold a job, go to school, or even keep clean, it may be necessary to initiate a period of hospitalization. Our discussion focuses primarily on the diagnostic criteria used to classify the most common psychological disorders, as depicted on Axis I. We'll consider the major clinical syndromes and end the section with a brief discussion of Axis II–based personality disorders. But remember, labeling or categorizing the disorder is only part of the diagnostic process—the remaining axes also play an important role in the diagnosis. ▌Figure 14.4 summarizes some of the syndromes we'll be discussing and presents data showing how likely each disorder is to occur in the population at large.

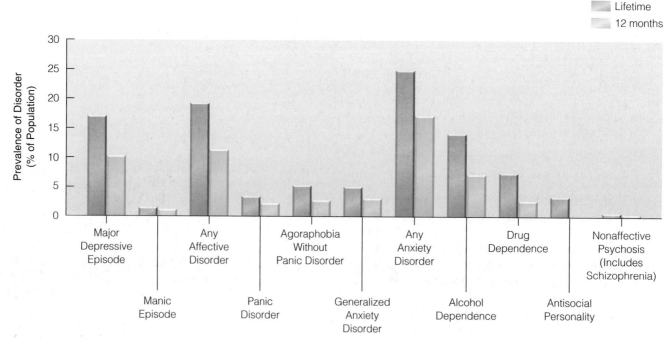

▌**FIGURE 14.4** Prevalence Rates for Various Psychological Disorders
Each bar shows the percentage of individuals in a sample of more than 8,000 participants who reported suffering from the listed psychological disorder during the previous 12 months or earlier. *Note:* A given individual might have reported suffering from more than one of these disorders concurrently. (Data from Kessler et al., 1994)

Anxiety Disorders: Fear and Apprehension

We begin with the anxiety disorders. Although it may be difficult to understand the paranoid delusions of the severely disordered, it's not difficult to understand the apprehension, worry, and fear that characterize anxiety. Most people understand anxiety because it's often an important part of our everyday experience. We become anxious when we meet someone new, when awaiting the beginning of an exam, or when an out-of-control car swerves dangerously close to our path. Moreover, even though the physical and psychological changes that accompany anxiety can seem unpleasant, anxiety is basically an adaptive human response. The physical changes prepare the body to take action—to fight or flee—and thereby increase the chances of survival. The psychological changes cause us to become attentive—we monitor our environment more closely so we're more apt to notice a potentially dangerous event when it occurs.

But there is a dark side to anxiety. When anxiety becomes too persistent and intense, it interferes with the ability to function. **Anxiety disorders** are diagnosed when the levels of apprehension and worry become so extreme that overall behavior is impaired in some way. For example, if you consistently fail exams because you can't collect your thoughts, or if you refuse to leave the house because you're convinced you'll experience a frightening panic attack, you're likely to be suffering from an anxiety disorder. There are several kinds of anxiety disorders, and each is defined by its own set of DSM-IV-TR diagnostic criteria. We'll concentrate on some common ones in this section: generalized anxiety disorder, panic disorder, obsessive–compulsive disorder, and phobias.

anxiety disorders A class of disorders marked by excessive apprehension and worry that in turn impairs normal functioning.

Generalized Anxiety Disorder The defining characteristic of **generalized anxiety disorder** is excessive and chronic worrying that lasts for a period of at least six months. The anxiety is "free-floating," as Freud described it, and can't be attributed to any single identifiable source. People who suffer from this problem worry in *general* (which is captured in the name *generalized* anxiety disorder), and they fret constantly about any number of minor things (Brown, O'Leary, & Barlow, 2001). More important, the worrying is unrealistic—there's usually little, if any, chance that the feared event will actually occur.

generalized anxiety disorder Excessive worrying, or free-floating anxiety, that lasts for at least six months and that cannot be attributed to any single identifiable source.

People afflicted with generalized anxiety disorder are chronically tense. Not surprisingly, they often report a range of physical symptoms, especially muscle tension and fatigue, and they're likely to have trouble sleeping and become easily irritated as well. They're also likely to spend a lot of time worrying about the future—more so than someone suffering from the other anxiety disorders we'll consider (Dugas et al., 1998). These kinds of symptoms are relatively easy to understand—after all, these people are living in a world of perpetual worry; the worst, they assume, is always about to happen.

panic disorder A condition marked by recurrent discrete episodes or attacks of extremely intense fear or dread.

A person with agoraphobia may be reluctant to leave home, fearing that once outside a panic attack will result in helplessness.

Panic Disorder Generalized anxiety is marked by chronic, unfocused worrying. In **panic disorder**, people suffer from recurrent episodes, or attacks, of extremely intense fear or dread (Craske & Barlow, 1993). A *panic attack* is a sudden and alarming event, and it can make you feel as if you're about to die (or, sometimes, go crazy). Panic attacks are brief, but they produce high levels of anxiety and, as a result, are accompanied by a collection of physical symptoms: a pounding heart, shortness of breath, sweating, nausea, chest pains, and so on. These symptoms can be devastating experiences, and they often lead to persistent concern about the possibility of having additional attacks (Barlow, 2002). It's worth noting

agoraphobia An anxiety disorder that causes an individual to restrict his or her normal activities; someone suffering from agoraphobia tends to avoid public places out of fear that a panic attack will occur.

that a single isolated panic attack is not sufficient for diagnosis of a panic disorder; the attacks need to occur repeatedly.

Panic disorder is sometimes associated with an additional complication, called *agoraphobia*, that comes from the worry that further panic attacks might occur. **Agoraphobia**—which translates from the Greek as "fear of the marketplace"—can cause people to restrict their normal activities in an extreme way (Mennin, Heimberg, & Holt, 2000). People with agoraphobia typically avoid crowded or public places, such as shopping malls or restaurants, because they're afraid they'll experience a panic attack and be unable to cope effectively with the situation (especially the accompanying physical symptoms). In severe cases, people with agoraphobia might simply refuse to leave their house; home, they reason, is the only really safe place in the world. For obvious reasons, panic disorder with accompanying agoraphobia can significantly reduce one's ability to function successfully.

obsessive–compulsive disorder An anxiety disorder that manifests itself through persistent and uncontrollable thoughts, called *obsessions*, or by the compelling need to perform repetitive acts, called *compulsions*.

Obsessive–Compulsive Disorder In **obsessive–compulsive disorder**, anxiety manifests itself through persistent, uncontrollable thoughts, called *obsessions*, or by the presence of a compelling need to perform one or more actions repeatedly, which is called a *compulsion*. Have you ever had part of a song or jingle ramble endlessly through your head—one that keeps repeating despite your best efforts to stop it? This is somewhat like an obsession, although in obsessive–compulsive disorder the obsessions tend to focus on fears (such as being contaminated by germs), doubts (such as forgetting to turn off the stove), and impulses (such as hurting oneself or another).

Compulsions consist of cleaning or checking or other actions that prevent some inappropriate impulse from occurring. For example, you might repeat the alphabet aloud over and over in an effort to divert your thinking away from a frightening or inappropriate aggressive or sexual impulse. Generally, the compulsive behaviors are designed to reduce the anxiety or distress caused by the obsessions. In extreme cases, the compulsions are so repetitive and ritualistic that they essentially prevent the sufferer from leading anything resembling a normal life. Some people become housebound, relentlessly cleaning rooms; others feel irresistibly compelled to leave work 10 to 15 times a day to check and make sure the stove wasn't left on. Interestingly, in the majority of such cases the suffering individuals understand that their actions are irrational and of little adaptive value. The disorder simply compels the action.

How do you feel about spiders and lightning? Both are common sources of phobias.

Phobic Disorders   The defining feature of a **phobic disorder** is a highly focused fear of a specific object or situation—such as a bug, a snake, flying, heights, an animal, a closed place, or a storm. Like the other anxiety disorders we've discussed, phobias are irrational, which means that the level of anxiety the object or situation produces is in no way justified by reality. Elevators do fall, snakes can bite, planes do crash—but these events are rare and do not justify daily worry. Many people show mild forms of phobic reactions—and, again, in some cases the object of the anxiety might indeed be dangerous (some snakes do kill)—but in specific phobic disorder the fear and distress can be severely disabling. To avoid the anxiety-producing object or situation, people with a phobic disorder might significantly disrupt their normal routines; they may avoid work or school or travel in the slight chance that they will encounter the object of their fear.

Phobias typically revolve around one of four classes of fear-inducing objects or situations: (1) animals (insects, snakes, dogs, and the like), (2) natural environments (storms, heights, water, and the like), (3) blood-injection-injury (the sight of blood or even the thought of an injection), and (4) specific situations (fears associated with public transportation or closed-in places). There are other phobias as well—such as fear of choking or fear of costumed characters—that don't fit easily into these established categories. Most people who suffer from phobias tend to have more than one, and often more than one type (Stinson et al., 2007). For a look at how likely the various phobias are to occur among the general population see ▌ Figure 14.5.

Social Anxiety Disorder   Also known as social phobia, **social anxiety disorder** occurs when people become extremely anxious and self-conscious in everyday social situations. People with this disorder often have an excessive fear of being watched and judged by others and of performing actions that might embarrass them. Like the other anxiety disorders, social anxiety disorder is often accompanied by physical symptoms (blushing, sweating, trembling, nausea), which only magnify the level of worry. The disorder might manifest itself only in very specific situations, such talking to other people, or it can occur broadly across a variety of social situations. Social anxiety disorder is recognized currently as one of the most common psychological disorders affecting individuals (Swinson, 2005).

Gender and Culture   In general, women are more likely to suffer from anxiety disorders than men, although this trend differs somewhat across cultures (Barlow & Durand, 2005). About two-thirds of those with generalized anxiety disorder are

phobic disorder A highly focused fear of a specific object or situation.

CRITICAL THINKING

Can you think of reasons it might be adaptive for people to show specific reactions for each of the four classes of phobic stimuli described in the text?

social anxiety disorder Intense fear of being watched, judged, and embarrassed in social situations.

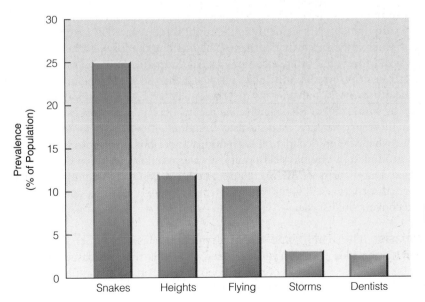

▌FIGURE 14.5 Prevalence Rates for Various Phobias
Each bar shows the percentage of people in a large sample who reported suffering from a particular kind of phobia. (Data from Agras, Sylvester, & Oliveau, 1969)

women, three-fourths with agoraphobia, and the ratio of women to men for specific phobic disorder is about 4 to 1. Why is there a sex difference? Researchers are not certain, although most current accounts focus on cultural explanations (Arrindell et al., 2003). Men are typically raised to "tough things out," which means they're less likely to report the symptoms of anxiety or seek treatment. Men are also more likely to "treat" the symptoms of anxiety by turning to alcohol or drugs (with sometimes devastating consequences).

Anxiety disorders occur in all cultures of the world, but the focus of the anxiety can differ, as well as the chances that the disorder will be reported. For example, for unknown reasons, Hispanics and Asians in the United States have a somewhat lower risk of developing a specific phobic disorder than White Americans (Stinson et al., 2007). In developing countries, people are more likely to focus on the physical symptoms of anxiety and tend not to report the subjective feelings associated with panic, dread, or worry. In Arab countries the obsessions of obsessive–compulsive disorder are apt to be religious-based, often focusing on the Muslim emphasis on cleanliness. Culture undoubtedly plays a significant role in the onset of these disorders as well, but we'll delay our discussion of this possibility until later in the chapter.

Concept Review | Anxiety Disorders

DISORDER	DESCRIPTION
Generalized anxiety disorder	Excessive and chronic worrying that lasts for a period of at least 6 months. Accompanied by excessive autonomic activity (e.g., increased respiration, heart rate).
Panic disorder	Recurrent episodes or "attacks" of extremely intense fear or dread. Sometimes accompanied by agoraphobia, the fear of being in public due to anticipation of another panic attack.
Obsessive–compulsive disorder	Anxiety that is manifested through *obsessions* (persistent uncontrollable thoughts) and/or *compulsions* (a compelling need to perform one or more actions repeatedly).
Phobic disorder	A highly focused fear of a specific object or situation. Most focus on animals, natural environments, blood–injection–injury, or specific situations.

Somatoform Disorders: Body and Mind

A common phenomenon, called the *medical student syndrome*, often plagues medical students as they first learn about the various diseases of the body. The students find that the symptoms described in class, or in the text, are increasingly familiar and personal. A deep pain that appears suddenly in the night is interpreted as a signal for the final stages of pancreatic cancer; that darkening blemish on the forehead becomes the rare form of skin cancer that often accompanies AIDS. In almost every case the student is perfectly healthy, but the mind plays its tricks, and the student fears the worst.

somatoform disorders Psychological disorders that focus on the physical body.

Mental health professionals classify psychological problems that focus on the physical body as **somatoform disorders** (*soma* means "body"). Obviously, like medical students, most people have experienced imagined illnesses at some point in their lives. But when the preoccupation with bodily functions or symptoms is excessive and not grounded in any physical reality, a true psychological disorder may be indicated (Iezzi, Duckworth, & Adams, 2001). The DSM-IV-TR lists a number of basic somatoform disorders; we'll focus briefly on three: hypochondriasis, somatization disorder, and conversion disorder.

hypochondriasis A long-lasting preoccupation with the idea that one has developed a serious disease, based on what turns out to be a misinterpretation of normal body reactions.

Hypochondriasis The main symptom of **hypochondriasis** is a persistent preoccupation with the idea that you've developed a serious disease, based on what turns out to be a misinterpretation of normal bodily reactions. The pain in the side, the slight case of indigestion, or the occasional irregular heartbeat is interpreted as symptomatic of a serious medical condition. Moreover, unlike the situation for the normal medical student, these preoccupations persist for months and often cause significant distress and impaired functioning. Hypochondriasis is typically associated with excessive anxiety and may be strongly related to the types of anxiety disorders discussed earlier (Otto et al., 1998).

Somatization Disorder **Somatization disorder** is related to hypochondriasis; in fact, mental health professionals sometimes have a difficult time distinguishing between the two. Both involve the persistent complaint of symptoms with no identifiable physical cause, but in somatization disorder it's the *symptoms* that receive the focus of attention rather than an underlying disease. In both cases, the person searches endlessly for doctors who will confirm his or her symptoms, usually with little or no success (because there is no real physical problem). The major difference between hypochondriasis and somatization disorder seems to be that in hypochondriasis the anxiety arises because of a presumed underlying disease, whereas in somatization disorder the presence of the symptoms themselves causes the anxiety. People with somatization disorder are not typically afraid of dying from a serious disease; rather, they are looking for someone to understand and sympathize with their countless physical problems.

> **somatization disorder** A long-lasting preoccupation with body symptoms that have no identifiable physical cause.

Conversion Disorder In **conversion disorder**, unlike the other two somatoform disorders we've considered, there appears to be real physical or neurological impairment. Someone suffering from a conversion disorder might report being blind, or paralyzed, or unable to speak. The affected person might even experience seizures resembling those found in epilepsy or other neurological disorders (Bowman, 1998). These are not feigned symptoms; that is, these problems are not intentionally produced by the individual to gain sympathy or attention. These are real problems, although no physical cause can be discovered. Neuroscientists are currently using imaging techniques in an effort to understand how and why the brain produces the physical effects (e.g., de Lange, Roelofs, & Toni, 2007).

> **conversion disorder** The presence of real physical problems, such as blindness or paralysis, that seem to have no identifiable physical cause.

Obviously, in such cases there's always the possibility that a true neurological or other physical problem does exist; physical problems are indeed sometimes misdiagnosed as conversion disorders. But when the reported problems disappear after effective therapy, a psychological origin is usually indicated. You may remember from our discussion of personality in Chapter 12 that Sigmund Freud often used his psychoanalytic techniques to treat patients with conversion disorders (although the problem was known as *hysteria* in his day). In fact, the term *conversion*, as used here, originates from psychodynamic theory and the proposal that unconscious conflicts have been converted into a physical form.

Gender and Culture Although somatization and conversion disorders occur somewhat more frequently in women, hypochondriasis occurs at roughly the same rate in men and women (Kirmayer, Looper, & Taillefer, 2003). Each of the disorders occurs cross-culturally as well, but there are some unique expressions in specific cultures. A condition called *koro*, for example, occurs mainly in Asian men—it's characterized by a persistent fear that the genitals will retract into the abdomen. A related condition, known as *dhat*, occurs mainly in India and is characterized by anxiety associated with the loss of semen from sexual activity (Ranjith, Moran, & Ismail, 2004).

Dissociative Disorders: Disruptions of Identity or Awareness

Some of the more colorful types of psychological disorders, at least as seen by Hollywood or the popular press, come from a class of problems called **dissociative disorders**. Dissociative disorders are defined by the separation, or *dissociation*, of

> **dissociative disorders** A class of disorders characterized by the separation, or dissociation, of conscious awareness from previous thoughts or memories.

conscious awareness from previous thoughts or memories. If you're affected by one of these disorders, you lose memory for some specific aspect of your life, or even your entire sense of identity. The theme of the confused amnesiac, searching for his or her lost identity, has been explored repeatedly in films throughout the years. We'll focus our attention on three types of dissociative disorder: dissociative amnesia, dissociative fugue, and dissociative identity disorder.

Dissociative Amnesia   In Chapter 8, when we tackled remembering and forgetting, we discussed various kinds of *amnesia*, or the inability to remember or retain personal experiences. It was noted that amnesia could result from either physical factors (such as brain damage) or psychological factors (such as traumatic stress). In **dissociative amnesia**, which is assumed to be psychological in origin, the person is unable to remember important personal information. The amnesia can be general, as in the failure to remember one's identity or family history, or it can be localized, such as the failure to remember a specific traumatic life experience. In dissociative amnesia, the forgetting can last for hours or years. It often disappears as mysteriously as it arises.

dissociative amnesia A psychological disorder characterized by an inability to remember important personal information.

Dissociative Fugue   In **dissociative fugue**, there is also a loss of personal identity—people forget who they are—but it's accompanied by an escape or flight from the home environment (*fugue* literally means "flight"). Imagine leaving for work or school as usual only to "awaken" some time later in a different city or state. Sometimes the fugue state can last months or even years; some individuals experiencing this disorder have even adopted different identities in their new locale. Recovery can be sudden and often complete, but affected individuals will typically claim that they have no knowledge of their activities during the blackout period.

dissociative fugue A loss of personal identity that is often accompanied by a flight from home.

Dissociative Identity Disorder   In what is perhaps the most baffling of all dissociative disorders, **dissociative identity disorder**, a person alternates among what appear to be two or more distinct identities or personality states (hence the alternative name, *multiple personality disorder*). Some cases of this disorder have been widely publicized. For example, you may be familiar with Sybil Dorsett, who was diagnosed with 16 personalities (Schreiber, 1973); she was portrayed by Sally Field in the television movie *Sybil*. Another well-known case is "Eve," who alternated among three personality types (Thigpen & Cleckley, 1957); she was portrayed by Joanne Woodward in the film *The Three Faces of Eve*.

dissociative identity disorder A condition in which an individual alternates between what appear to be two or more distinct identities or personalities (also known as *multiple personality disorder*).

© Bettman/Corbis

Kenneth Bianchi, known as the Hillside Strangler, claimed that he could not be held responsible for the rape and murder of several California women because he suffered from dissociative identity disorder. The evidence presented at trial suggested that Bianchi was faking the disorder; he was later convicted and sentenced to life imprisonment.

In dissociative identity disorder, the unique personalities or identities appear to take control of one's thoughts and actions, one personality at a time. More important, the personality in control will profess to have only limited awareness of the other personality inhabitants. Commonly, there is interpersonality amnesia, which means that events experienced while the person is inhabited by personality A cannot be remembered when he or she is occupied by personality B (Eich et al., 1997). It's for this reason that the disorder is classified as *dissociative*—there is a separation of current conscious awareness from prior thoughts and memories. Dozens of different identities may be involved, including both males and females, and a given identity will tend to have unique physical attributes, such as a distinct tone of voice, facial expression, handwriting style, or behavioral habit.

Dissociative identity disorder is recognized as a legitimate disorder in the DSM-IV-TR, but not all mental health professionals are comfortable with this designation. Controversy often surrounds the diagnosis, for a number of reasons. First, this disorder often co-occurs with other psychological problems (such as depression and somatization disorder), so it's difficult to pinpoint the ultimate cause of any particular symptom (Ross et al., 1990). Second, although each of the observed personalities may be distinguished on the basis of personality tests or physiological measures, we still cannot be completely sure about the origins of these differences—other factors, such as mood or arousal differences, may partly account for the distinct performance patterns (Fahy, 1988; Lilienfeld, 1994). Third, recent studies have found that the interpersonality "amnesia" that helps to characterize the disorder is found only with certain kinds of memory tests (e.g., Huntjens et al., 2007).

Finally, several studies have shown that it's relatively easy to fake or simulate multiple personalities (Spanos, Weeks, & Bertrand, 1985). This raises the possibility that people with dissociative identity disorder may actually be role playing in some fashion, perhaps in a way comparable to those who have been hypnotized. As you might recall from Chapter 6, many psychologists question whether hypnosis truly represents some kind of dissociated state; instead, hypnotized people often seem eager to please the hypnotist by acting in accordance with a hypnotized role. This is not necessarily a conscious choice made by those who have been hypnotized; instead, it may represent a kind of unconscious or involuntary compliance (Lynn et al., 1990). Some researchers are convinced that dissociative identity disorder is best interpreted as a kind of self-hypnosis that arises partly to please the therapist. There has been an unusually rapid rise in the number of cases of dissociative identity disorder as the disorder has been publicized in the media, which lends support to the role-playing hypothesis.

Despite the controversy, dissociative identity disorder was retained as a diagnostic disorder in the DSM-IV-TR. It does seem clear that not all aspects of the disorder can be consciously faked (Kluft, 1991). Highly specific physiological differences have been reported across personalities—such as differences in visual acuity or eye muscle balance (Miller, 1989)—and it seems unlikely that such things could be easily faked (see ▌Figure 14.6). There also appear to be certain similarities in the past histories of affected individuals that have convinced many of the validity of the diagnosis. For example, the occurrence of abuse, usually sexual or physical, tends to be a significant predictor of the disorder (Sar et al., 2007). The diagnosis of dissociative identity disorder remains controversial, but it is considered to be a legitimate disorder by the psychological community at large (Gleaves, May, & Cardena, 2001).

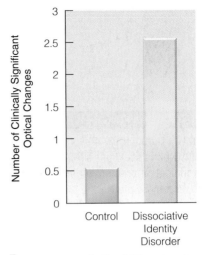

▌FIGURE 14.6 Optical Changes Across Personalities

Individuals diagnosed with dissociative identity disorder were asked to undergo ophthalmological (eye) exams while "inhabited" by three different personalities in turn. Significant differences were found in optical functioning across personalities, more so than occurred for normal control subjects who were asked to fake different personalities during each exam. (Data from Miller, 1989)

Disorders of Mood: Depression and Mania

From time to time everyone experiences depression, that overwhelming feeling that things are completely hopeless and sad. For most, thankfully, the experience is brief; moreover, most of us can usually account for our depressed mood by pointing to a particular experience or event in our lives: We failed the test; our beloved pet died; our once-trusted romantic partner now prefers the affections of another. But when an extreme mood swing is not short lived and is accompanied by other symptoms, such as a prolonged loss of appetite and a negative self-concept, a mood disorder may be present. **Mood disorders**—which are defined as prolonged and disabling disruptions in emotional state—are of two types: (1) *depressive disorders*, in which one suffers primarily from depression, and (2) *bipolar disorders*, which are characterized by mood swings between extreme highs, called manic states, and the lows of depression. We'll consider each of these types of disorders separately.

mood disorders Prolonged and disabling disruptions in emotional state.

Depressive Disorders The DSM-IV-TR lists specific criteria for the diagnosis of depressive disorders, which are among the most common of all psychological disorders. For something to qualify as a **major depressive episode**, for instance, you must show five or more of the following types of symptoms for a period of at least two weeks: (1) depressed mood for most of the day; (2) loss of interest in normal daily activities; (3) a significant change in weight (either a loss or a gain); (4) difficulty sleeping or a desire to sleep all the time; (5) a change in activity level (either extreme restlessness or lethargy); (6) daily fatigue or loss of energy; (7) a negative self-concept, including feelings of worthlessness or excessive guilt; (8) trouble concentrating or in making decisions; and (9) suicidal thoughts.

major depressive episode A type of mood disorder characterized by depressed mood and other symptoms.

When you enter a major depressive episode, the world is seen through a kind of dark filter. You feel extremely sad and full of self-doubt, and the environment seems overwhelming, imposing, and full of obstacles that can't be overcome. This worldview

bipolar disorder A type of mood disorder in which the person experiences disordered mood shifts in two directions—from depression to a manic state.

manic state A disordered state in which the person becomes hyperactive, talkative, and has a decreased need for sleep; a person in a manic state may engage in activities that are self-destructive or dangerous.

of a depressed person is a particularly grim aspect of the disorder—if you're depressed, the future seems hopeless with little or no possibility of a reprieve. Moreover, the accompanying negative self-image appears to be solidly grounded in reality; depressed people are absolutely convinced about the truth of their hopelessness, which tragically leads some to consider suicide as their only outlet.

Major depression is more than just feeling sad. You literally view and interpret the world differently when you're depressed, which tends to feed back and confirm your negative self-concept. Normal activities are interpreted as indicating some dire consequence (for example, if a friend fails to call, it must mean the friend no longer cares). As you'll see in the next chapter, one of the goals of therapy in treating depression is to change depressed individuals' thought patterns—to make them see the world in a more realistic way.

Mental health professionals distinguish among several types of depressive disorders, based partly on the length and severity of the depressive episode. For example, a major depressive episode can be classified as *recurrent*, which means that it has occurred more than once in an individual's lifetime (but separated by a period of at least two months). There is also a condition called *dysthymic disorder*, in which the depressive symptoms tend to be milder and less disruptive but more chronic. Most major depressive episodes end after a period of weeks or months and the person returns to normal, but people affected by dysthymic disorder show a relatively continuous depressed mood for a period of at least two years. A major depressive episode can even occur at the same time as dysthymic disorder, in which case the condition is referred to as *double depression*.

Bipolar Disorder   When depression is *unipolar*, the depressive episode typically runs its course, and the individual returns to a normal state. The depression may occur again, but the disorder is defined by a mood shift in only one direction—toward the negative. In a **bipolar disorder**, one experiences mood shifts in two directions, traveling from the depths of depression (a major depressive episode) to a hyperactive, euphoric condition called a **manic state**. When in a manic state, people act as if they're on top of the world—they are hyperactive, talkative, and seem to have little need for sleep. These symptoms may seem positive and desirable, but they're balanced by tendencies toward grandiosity, distractibility, and risk taking. In a manic state, a person might attempt a remarkable feat—such as scaling the Statue of Liberty—or perhaps will go on a sudden spending spree, cashing in all his or her savings. People who are in a manic state report feeling great, but their thinking is far from normal or rational. Their speech can appear disrupted because they shift rapidly from one fleeting thought to another.

To be classified as a manic episode in the DSM-IV-TR, this abnormally elevated mood state must last for at least a week, although it can last for months. Like a depressive episode, the manic state typically goes away, even without treatment, and the person either returns to normal or roller-coasters into another depressive episode. People who suffer from bipolar disorders live lives of extreme highs and lows; not surprisingly, their ability to function normally in society is often severely impaired. Moreover, tragically, it's been estimated that as many as 19% of individuals who are affected with bipolar disorder eventually end up committing suicide (Ostacher & Eidelman, 2006).

Suicide   As just noted, suicide can be one fatal consequence of suffering from a mood disorder such as bipolar disorder. It's worth pausing for a moment and considering suicide because it's a significant problem worldwide; suicide rates have been on the rise for decades, especially among adolescents, although the overall rates have leveled off somewhat since 1994 (Gould & Kramer, 2001). Suicide is the third leading cause of death among adolescents. Suicide is highest for White males, at least in the United States. Men are 4 to 5 times more likely to commit suicide than women (although women are more likely to *attempt* suicide), and the average suicide rates for

minorities are often reported to be lower than those for Whites (Colucci & Martin, 2007). The vast majority of people who kill themselves suffer from some kind of psychological disorder (Garland & Zigler, 1993).

What are the risk factors associated with suicide? In addition to a psychological disorder, many different factors can be involved. Alcohol use and abuse are particularly likely in adolescent suicides, present in perhaps the majority of suicides. Another important factor is the sudden occurrence of a very stressful event—something like the death of a loved one, failure or rejection in a personal relationship, or even a natural disaster. Evidence suggests that suicide rates increase after natural disasters, such as floods, hurricanes, or earthquakes (Krug et al., 1998). Suicide may also be contagious: There are increased suicide rates following widely publicized suicides, especially among adolescents, suggesting that imitation or modeling is an important factor (Gould & Kramer, 2001).

Among the most significant predictors of suicide, however, are prior suicide attempts and suicidal thoughts. Among adolescents there is somewhere between a 3:1 and 6:1 ratio of serious suicidal thoughts to actual suicide attempts. Not everyone who thinks about suicide makes an attempt—and the ratio of attempted suicides to successful suicides is perhaps 25:1 (Moscicki, 2001). But suicidal thinking is a serious warning sign. Treatment options for the psychological conditions associated with suicide are discussed in Chapter 15, but a variety of intervention programs are currently being used to tackle the suicide problem nationally. For example, the Centers for Disease Control recommends that teams of mental health professionals be sent to schools, for counseling and screening, whenever a student or visible member of the community commits suicide. Moreover, most cities and towns now have 24-hour suicide hotline services that enable people in need to voice their concerns and learn alternative ways of dealing with their crises. Most psychologists are optimistic that as the risk factors associated with suicide are identified, and treatment options become more accessible, suicide rates can be slowed or reversed (Kosky et al., 1998). For more on the prevention of suicide, take a look at the Practical Solutions feature on page 468.

Gender and Culture   As noted previously, women are significantly more likely to attempt suicide than men (although men are more often successful); overall, women are more likely to report, and be treated for, major depression (by a factor of about

Suicide Prevention

Suicide is relatively rare in childhood and early adolescence but increases significantly in the late teens and early 20s. Suicide is now the third leading cause of death among young adults. Although the causes of suicide are many, and may differ from early to late adulthood, psychologists are attempting to isolate the factors that can lead to prevention (at any age). Let's consider some recommendations being offered to reduce suicide among young adults (see Gould & Kramer, 2001):

1. *Gatekeeper Training.* Most professionals are convinced that suicidal youths are underidentified. There is a compelling need to train members of the community to recognize the warning signs of suicide and to offer educated assistance. We need programs to train people who come in contact with potential suicides—both in schools and in the community. Interestingly, current research indicates that it may be better to train school officials (teachers, coaches, counselors) to screen for potential victims because student-centered educational programs have met with limited success.

2. *Skills Training.* Rather than focusing on student programs that deal specifically with suicide and its prevention, it may be more effective to develop programs that teach students basic problem-solving, decision-making, and communication skills. Life-skills training and teaching general coping strategies can reduce the risk factors typically associated with suicide (Eggert et al., 1995). By teaching students skills to handle the problems that arise in day-to-day living, we increase their self-esteem and their ability to handle stressors in the environment.

3. *Increase Media Awareness.* Social learning and modeling can significantly increase the risk of suicide among the young. Considerable evidence supports contagion effects (copycat suicides). When suicidal behavior is given wide exposure in the media, even fictional suicides in movies, it can be followed by a significant increase in the number of suicides and suicide attempts (Gould, 2001). Members of the media should be educated about the risks associated with modeling suicide and encouraged to reduce the amount or emphasis of such coverage.

4. *Crisis Centers.* Crisis centers, or suicide hotlines, are an important and widely available method for reducing suicide risk. Suicides are often associated with significant traumatic or stressful events, so providing a social network for someone in need is clearly a useful strategy. Unfortunately, significant risk groups tend not to take advantage of these centers. For example, young White females are the most frequent users of telephone hotlines—males tend to stay away. Accordingly, although effective for the groups that use them, crisis centers are not a compete solution to suicide prevention.

---

2 to 1), which may help explain the trend (Hammen, 2003). Cross-cultural studies have found that the rates of major depression are higher for women across the world, ranging from developing countries to major industrialized nations. Interestingly, though, there doesn't appear to be a similar sex difference for bipolar disorder.

The symptoms reported for major depression are also quite similar across the world, particularly loss of energy, insomnia, and thoughts of death or suicide. People's internal thoughts about depression, however, do seem to depend partly on their cultural worldview. For example, in cultures stressing individuality, such as Western nations, people talk about their symptoms in terms of their personal identity ("I feel blue"); in cultures stressing an interdependent (collective) view of the self, symptoms might be described in terms of the group ("Our life has lost its meaning") (cf. Barlow & Durand, 2005).

Schizophrenia: Faulty Thought Processes

schizophrenia A class of disorders characterized by fundamental disturbances in thought processes, emotion, or behavior.

For most of the psychological disorders considered so far, you probably experienced at least a glimmer of recognition. Everyone can identify with anxiety, the occasional obsessive thought, or even a slight case of depression. It's only when these tendencies become *excessive* and interfere with normal functioning that someone is likely to be diagnosed with an actual psychological disorder. But in the case of **schizophrenia**, which translates literally as "split mind," the psychological changes can be so profound that one is thrust into a world that bears little resemblance to everyday experience. A person with schizophrenia lives in an internal world marked by thought processes that have gone awry; delusions, hallucinations, and generally disordered thinking become the norm.

Schizophrenia is actually a group or class of disorders. There are different subtypes of schizophrenia, defined by different DSM-IV-TR criteria, but each case is identified with some kind of fundamental disturbance in thought processes, emotion, or behavior. Schizophrenia is a bit unusual compared to the other disorders we've considered because it doesn't always reveal itself in the same way; whereas everyone who suffers from an anxiety disorder feels apprehensive, or in depression feels sad, the symptoms of schizophrenia are not necessarily shared by all affected individuals. Schizophrenia is a complex disorder that is expressed in a variety of complex ways—no single symptom must be present for the diagnosis to be applied (Walker et al., 2004).

Despite the translation of schizophrenia as "split mind," it's not the same thing as a dissociative identity disorder. Schizophrenia leads to faulty thought processes and inappropriate emotions—not to dissociations among distinct personality types. In fact, when the Swiss psychiatrist Eugen Bleuler (1908) originally introduced the term *schizophrenia*, he was referring primarily to the fact that affected individuals have trouble holding onto a consistent line of thought. Their thinking is disorganized; their thought lines and associations seem to split apart and move forward in inconsistent ways. Both schizophrenia and dissociative identity disorder are serious psychological problems, but they fall into completely different categories in the DSM-IV-TR.

Diagnostic Symptoms There are three main types of symptoms in schizophrenia: positive, negative, and cognitive. *Positive symptoms* usually include observable expressions of abnormal behavior, such as delusions or hallucinations; *negative symptoms* consist of deficits in behavior, such as an inability to express emotion; *cognitive symptoms* include difficulties in memory and decision making and in the ability to sustain attention. The DSM-IV-TR requires that two or more characteristic symptoms be present for the diagnosis of schizophrenia, but a particular person may have many or only a few. As with the other disorders we've considered, these symptoms must last for a significant period of time, they must cause social or job distress, and they cannot be due to the effects of a general medical condition or to the use of a drug or medication.

Let's consider some of the major positive symptoms of schizophrenia in more detail. As noted earlier, one of the main problems in schizophrenia is distorted or disorganized thinking. People with schizophrenia often suffer from *delusions*, which are thoughts with inappropriate content. If someone sitting next to you in class leaned over and claimed to be Elvis in disguise, or Jesus Christ, or Adolf Hitler, the content of his or her thoughts would clearly be inappropriate or deviant—this individual would be suffering from a delusion. People suffering from schizophrenia sometimes hold a *delusion of grandeur*, which is a belief that they are more famous or important than they actually are, or a *delusion of persecution*, which is a belief that others are conspiring or plotting against them. These latter symptoms are especially characteristic of one subtype of schizophrenia called *paranoid schizophrenia*.

It's also not unusual for people with schizophrenia to report distorted perceptions of the world. For them, objects can seem to change their shape or size; distances can be perceived in ways that are different from reality. Frequently, these *hallucinations*—which are perceptions that have no basis in external stimulation—are auditory. People with schizophrenia claim to hear disembodied voices in their heads, giving them commands or commenting on the quality of their activities ("You're an idiot," "You should stay away from that person," and so on). Some researchers believe

Highlighted in this PET scan are areas of the brain that appear to be selectively activated during auditory and visual hallucinations. A young man suffering from schizophrenia was asked to press a button, initiating the scan, every time he experienced a hallucination.

© Wellcome/Cognitive Neurology/SPL/Photo Researchers, Inc.

these voices may originate from the same areas of the brain that control language production. It may be the case that people with schizophrenia are actually "listening" to their inner voice (see Chapter 8) but fail to recognize the voice as their own. Instead, they falsely attribute the source of the voice to something external (Allen et al., 2007; Evans, McGuire, & David, 2000).

Other positive symptoms of schizophrenia include *disorganized speech* and *catatonia*. Sometimes the speech patterns of a person with schizophrenia appear jumbled and incoherent; the affected individual jumps repeatedly from one disconnected topic to another ("I went to the beach today where the moon pulls the rabbit out of the hat. I'm the world's greatest cook, but that's because volcanic magma heats the glaciers and makes the water and the sand.") It's as if the mind has lost its internal editor—ideas or thoughts no longer flow in a connected way. In addition to displaying speech problems, someone with schizophrenia can behave in ways that are quite disorganized and bizarre. The person might engage in repetitive activities, such as swirling his or her arms repeatedly, or will appear to laugh or cry at inappropriate times. When *catatonia* is present, people may adopt a peculiar stance or position and remain immobile for hours, or they may wildly and suddenly change position for no apparent reason. Catatonia is a defining feature of a subtype called *catatonic schizophrenia*. Fortunately, because of modern medications, severe forms of catatonia have declined in recent years (Stompe, Ritter, & Schanda, 2007).

Negative symptoms of schizophrenia are expressed by the elimination or reduction of normal behavior. For example, it's common for people with schizophrenia to display *flat affect*, which means they show little or no emotional reaction to events. Show someone with flat affect an extremely funny movie or a tragic, heartrending photo, and the person is unlikely to crack a smile or shed a tear. People with schizophrenia may also refuse to engage in the most basic and important of everyday activities. They may refuse to speak, or interact socially, and they may even refuse to wash themselves, to eat, or to get dressed. Activities that are pleasurable to most people become unpleasurable or uninteresting to some individuals with schizophrenia.

Finally, the cognitive symptoms of schizophrenia can be more subtle and difficult to detect, often appearing only after neuropsychological testing. Schizophrenia can produce marked deficits in the ability to absorb information and process it effectively. People with schizophrenia sometimes have difficulties associated with "working memory," that portion of our memory system that enables us to maintain information in consciousness and use it in ongoing tasks. People with schizophrenia often have difficulty concentrating and integrating thoughts and feelings. There is evidence suggesting that cognitive difficulties may be apparent even before the onset of the more severe symptoms discussed above (Reichenberg & Harvey, 2007).

For obvious reasons, people with schizophrenia are often unable to cope successfully at school or at work. In many cases, their behavior becomes so maladaptive that hospitalization is required. As you'll see later in the chapter, there are reasons to believe that people with schizophrenia may be suffering from problems in the brain itself—fundamental neurological problems may cause the bizarre thinking and behaviors that plague people affected with the disorder.

Gender and Culture   Researchers remain uncertain about how gender affects the likelihood of developing schizophrenia. Historically, it's been assumed that men and women are equally likely to develop the disorder, but recent research suggests that men may be at slightly greater risk (Aleman, Kahn, & Selten, 2003). Moreover, men tend to develop the disorder earlier in life, about four years earlier on average, whereas women show an increased risk of developing schizophrenia in later years. For unknown reasons, women are also more likely than men to benefit favorably from treatment (Walker et al., 2004).

Schizophrenia is a worldwide phenomenon, occurring in every studied racial and cultural group. However, there are differences in the rates of diagnosis—for example,

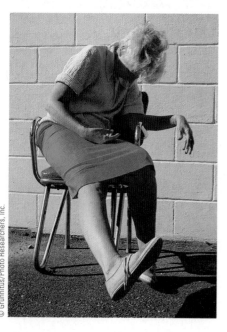

In catatonia, a symptom of schizophrenia, the affected person adopts a peculiar stance or position and remains immobile for hours.

© Grunnitus/Photo Researchers, Inc.

more African Americans are diagnosed with schizophrenia than Whites—and people seem to recover better in some cultures than in others (Kulhara & Chakrabarti, 2001). These patterns are puzzling to researchers and poorly understood. Some researchers have suggested that the racial differences in diagnosis may be related to bias or discrimination (Goater et al., 1999), but other possibilities remain, including differences in genetic susceptibility (Barlow & Durand, 2005) or socioeconomic status (Bresnahan et al., 2007).

Personality Disorders

All of the psychological disorders we've considered up to now are described on Axis I of the DSM-IV-TR (Clinical Syndromes). Axis II describes **personality disorders**, which are essentially chronic or enduring patterns of behavior that lead to significant impairments in social functioning. People with personality disorders have a tendency to act repeatedly in an inflexible and maladaptive way. They may show an exaggerated distrust of others, as in **paranoid personality disorder**, or they may show an excessive and persistent need to be taken care of by others, as in **dependent personality disorder**. One of the best-known examples of a personality disorder, occurring mainly in males, is the **antisocial personality disorder**. People with this type of disorder show little respect for social customs or norms. They act as if they have no conscience—they lie, cheat, or steal at the drop of a hat and show no remorse for their actions if caught. Someone with antisocial personality disorder is likely to have no qualms about committing criminal acts, even murder. Many end up with long criminal records and spend significant periods of time in jail (Cunningham & Reidy, 1998). Another common personality disorder is **borderline personality disorder**, which affects mainly young women. This disorder is associated with an inability to regulate emotions and can be associated with aggression, self-injury, and substance abuse. People with borderline personality disorder often have unstable patterns of social relationships and a poor sense of self.

What is it about personality disorders that requires them to be placed on their own classification axis? Do personality disorders have characteristics that fundamentally distinguish them from the major clinical syndromes described on Axis I? Most mental health professionals believe personality disorders are unique primarily because they tend to be more *ingrained* and *inflexible* than the major clinical syndromes outlined on Axis I. These are not problems that typically appear and disappear over time, which is the case with many psychological disorders. These problems reflect basic personality and, as a result, tend to continue throughout adulthood and are resistant to therapy. Personality disorders are placed on a separate axis in the DSM-IV-TR in part to force the clinician to consider the possibility that it's a personality characteristic, rather than a major clinical syndrome, that's contributing to the appearance of abnormal behavior.

Because personality disorders are linked to personality, some mental health professionals have argued that it's wrong to think of them as *disorders* in the same sense as a phobia or depression (Gunderson, 1992; Trull & McCrae, 1994). In Chapter 12 we discussed the idea that personality can be defined by the Big Five personality dimensions (McCrae & Costa, 1985). Some researchers have argued it's better to think about people with personality disorders as simply extreme or deviant on one or more of these five dimensions—extroversion, agreeableness, conscientiousness, neuroticism, and openness (Clark & Livesley, 1994). For example, the dimension of *agreeableness* measures how kind, warm, and trusting an individual is. It's possible that people classified with a paranoid personality disorder may simply lie near an extreme pole on the agreeableness scale—they trust almost no one. At present, debate continues about the proper way to think about personality disorders, and it remains uncertain whether the Big Five will be sufficient to account for the complexities of the disorders (Trull & Widiger, 2003).

personality disorders Chronic or enduring patterns of behavior that lead to significant impairments in social functioning.

paranoid personality disorder A personality disorder characterized by pervasive distrust of others.

dependent personality disorder A personality disorder characterized by an excessive and persistent need to be taken care of by others.

antisocial personality disorder A personality disorder characterized by little, if any, respect for social laws, customs, or norms.

borderline personality disorder A personality disorder characterized by problems with emotional regulation, social relationships, and sense of self.

CRITICAL THINKING

Think back to our earlier discussion of how to conceptualize abnormality. Do you think personality disorders should be labeled as "abnormal" behaviors?

Test Yourself 14.2

Check your knowledge about how psychological disorders are classified by picking the diagnostic category that best describes each of the following behavior patterns. Pick from among the following terms: anxiety disorder, somatoform disorder, dissociative disorder, mood disorder, schizophrenia, personality disorder. *(You will find the answers in the Appendix.)*

1. Sharma is convinced that the ringing in her ears means she has a brain tumor, even though a variety of doctors can find nothing wrong: _____

2. Gabriella is a checker—she often drives home five or six times a day to make sure she hasn't left the oven on: _____

3. Kunal hasn't left his house for 6 years—it's the only place he really feels safe: _____

4. Otto hates himself. He's convinced that he's worthless, stupid, and unlovable. No one can convince him otherwise: _____

5. Sergio is found wandering aimlessly in the park. When questioned, he can't remember who he is or how he got to the park: _____

6. Roger is a habitual con artist with little regard for the truth. He steals regularly and feels no guilt or remorse about his actions: _____

7. Melissa is convinced that her psychology professor is beaming his thoughts directly into her brain; she feels empowered and ready to complete her takeover of the world: _____

8. Billy shows little or no emotional reaction to events in his world; in fact, he usually stands in the corner for hours at a time with his right arm resting on his head: _____

Understanding Psychological Disorders: Biological, Cognitive, or Environmental?

LEARNING GOALS
- Explain how biological and genetic factors can contribute to psychological disorders.
- Discuss how maladaptive thoughts can contribute to psychological disorders.
- Explain how environmental factors can contribute to psychological disorders.

THE DSM-IV-TR CLASSIFICATION SYSTEM is designed to provide a reliable way for mental health professionals to diagnose psychological problems. The word *reliable* in this case refers to whether professional clinicians will tend to arrive at the same or similar diagnoses for people with a given set of symptoms. In general, the DSM system is considered to be very reliable, although agreement is higher for some diagnostic categories than for others (Nathan & Langenbucher, 2003). Still, it's important to remember that the DSM-IV-TR is only a classification system—it does not indicate anything about the root cause, or etiology, of the underlying disorder. What factors, alone or in combination, conspire to produce a major clinical syndrome like depression, anxiety, or schizophrenia? The answer—in a nutshell—is that we don't know for sure. But most current explanations, as well as most approaches to therapy, appeal to *biological, cognitive,* or *environmental* factors.

The recognition that psychological disorders are influenced by these three factors is sometimes called the **bio-psycho-social perspective**. Biological factors (*bio*) include physiological problems with the body, particularly the brain, and genetic influences that are present at birth. Cognitive factors (*psycho*) include our beliefs, styles of thought, and any other psychological mechanisms that potentially influence behavior. Finally, environmental factors (*social*) include what we learn from the environment, cultural influences, and how other people treat us in our daily lives. We'll consider each of these three major factors in greater detail in the following sections.

bio-psycho-social perspective The idea that psychological disorders are influenced, or caused, by a combination of biological, psychological (cognitive), and social (environmental) factors.

Biological Factors: Is It in the Brain or Genes?

Over the past several decades, there have been significant advances in our understanding of the brain and its functions. Most researchers are now convinced that at least some kinds of abnormal behavior result directly from brain dysfunction. The

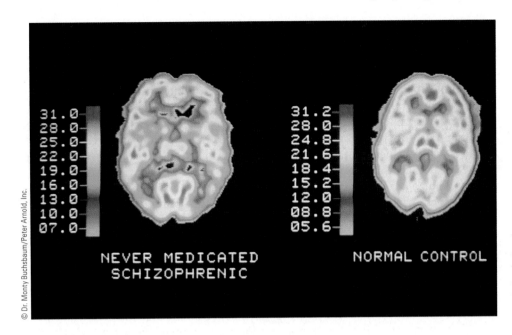

NEVER MEDICATED SCHIZOPHRENIC

NORMAL CONTROL

These PET scans, taken from a person diagnosed with schizophrenia (left) and from one without the disorder (right), show dramatic differences in brain activity levels. The blue and purple areas show relatively low activity.

disordered thoughts of schizophrenia, for example, may be partly due to a malfunctioning brain. What's the evidence? Biological accounts are typically supported by two kinds of findings. First, it's been discovered that abnormal brain chemistry or abnormal brain structures accompany some kinds of mental disorders. Second, it turns out that a number of psychological disorders may have a powerful genetic component—psychological disorders tend to run in families in ways that can't be easily explained by environmental histories. We discussed some of these findings in Chapter 3; we'll review and expand on that discussion here.

Neurotransmitter Imbalances   As you may recall from Chapter 3, schizophrenia has been linked to the neurotransmitter *dopamine* (Snyder, 1976), or possibly to an interaction between dopamine and other neurotransmitters (Iverson & Iverson, 2007). Support for the link has come primarily from studying how different drugs affect the disorder. Among the most effective treatments for schizophrenia are medications that act as dopamine *antagonists*, which means they reduce or block dopamine use in the brain. Medications that increase the level of dopamine in the brain can also produce side effects that resemble the symptoms found in schizophrenia. Abnormal dopamine levels are probably not the only cause of schizophrenia—for example, not all people with schizophrenia are helped by dopamine-reducing medications—but problems in brain neurochemistry are widely believed to be involved in the disorder. Currently, the neurotransmitters glutamate, GABA, and serotonin are also being considered as factors in the development and maintenance of schizophrenia (e.g., Javitt, 2006).

Neurotransmitter imbalances may also contribute to mood disorders, such as manic states and depression. Once again, most of the effective medications for these problems act by altering the actions of neurotransmitters in the brain. Fluoxetine (more commonly known by its brand name, *Prozac*) is one of the most commonly prescribed treatments for depression; it acts by slowing the reuptake of *serotonin*, thereby prolonging the neurotransmitter's effectiveness. More generally, depression and mania have been linked to neurotransmitters called *monoamines*, which include serotonin, norepinephrine, and dopamine. Researchers currently believe these neurotransmitters are involved in the regulation of mood, although the specifics have yet to be worked out (Hammen, 2003). It's unlikely that mood disorders are caused by an inadequate supply of any one of these neurotransmitters. Instead, a decrease in one may have multiple effects on the others. A decrease in serotonin, for instance, may permit the levels of other neurotransmitters in the brain to vary more widely; these

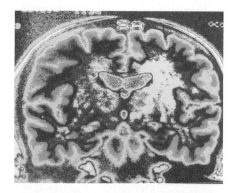

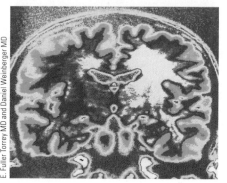

Schizophrenia is sometimes associated with structural abnormalities. The top scan is taken from someone with schizophrenia. Notice that the central, wing-shaped ventricles are larger than in the normal control brain shown on the bottom.

CRITICAL THINKING

Based on our earlier discussion of schizophrenia, can you think of any reason people diagnosed with schizophrenia might not all show the same neurological problems?

more complex interactions probably work together in some way to alter mood abnormally. Recent research suggests that stress hormones, such as cortisol, may play an important role as well in mood disorders like depression (Sher, 2004).

Structural Problems   In addition to neurochemical problems, such as imbalances in neurotransmitters, there may also be structural problems in the brains of people suffering from serious psychological problems. In the case of schizophrenia, anatomical and brain-imaging studies have revealed that people with schizophrenia tend to have larger *ventricles*, which are the liquid-filled cavities in the brain. (For reasons that are not yet clear, increased ventricle size tends to be more likely in men who suffer from schizophrenia.) Larger ventricles are associated with the loss, or shrinkage, of brain tissue, which may help explain some instances of schizophrenia (Osuji et al., 2007). There's also evidence that activity in the frontal areas of the brain may be abnormally low in schizophrenia patients (Berman & Weinberger, 1990). Although it's not clear why these activity levels are low, decreased brain activity in certain prefrontal regions may directly or indirectly alter the neural pathways associated with the neurotransmitter dopamine (Davis et al., 1991). Postmortem studies have also found abnormalities in how neurons are interconnected in certain regions of the brain, suggesting that schizophrenia may involve faulty wiring in the neural circuits (Walker et al., 2004).

These data are convincing, but it's important to remember that not all people with schizophrenia show these kinds of neurological problems; not all people with schizophrenia have larger ventricles or show lower frontal lobe activity. Moreover, not all people who have been diagnosed with depression respond to drug therapies that alter the levels or actions of monoamines. So we're left with a somewhat cloudy picture. There's little doubt that psychological disorders are sometimes associated with observable abnormalities in brain chemistry or function. But whether these factors are the true cause of disorders such as schizophrenia or depression, or simply one cause, or occur somehow as a consequence of having the disorder, is not currently known. For example, larger ventricle size is observed more often in people who have suffered from schizophrenia for a long time, so it's conceivable that the structural abnormality is partly a consequence of the disorder or even of its treatment (DeLisi et al., 1997).

Genetic Contributions   Increasingly, researchers are concluding that people may inherit predispositions toward abnormality. For example, the odds that any particular individual in the population will develop schizophrenia are roughly 1 in 100. But if you have a brother, sister, or parent with the disorder, the odds increase dramatically, perhaps to 1 in 10. If you have an identical twin—someone who has essentially the same genetic information as you do—and your twin has been diagnosed with schizophrenia, the odds that you will develop the disorder during your lifetime jump to about 1 in 2 (Gottesman, 1991) (see ▌Figure 14.7). Notice that the disorder can't be explained entirely by appealing to genetic factors—otherwise, identical twins would always share the disorder—but these data suggest that genetic background plays a significant role.

As you know from our many discussions of the nature–nurture issue throughout this book, it's not easy to separate inherited characteristics from those acquired through experience. Just because there's a family history of a disorder doesn't mean the cause is genetic; family members are typically raised in similar environments, so experience could account for the shared psychological problems. In the case of schizophrenia, however, even when children are adopted and raised apart from their biological parents, there still appears to be a familial link. Adopted children who have biological parents with schizophrenia are more likely to be diagnosed with schizophrenia themselves, even if they've had little or no contact with the parents (Tienari, Wahlberg, & Wynne, 2006).

A similar pattern emerges with mood disorders. Depression and bipolar disorder tend to run in families, and the concordance rate, which measures the likelihood of

Type of Relationship

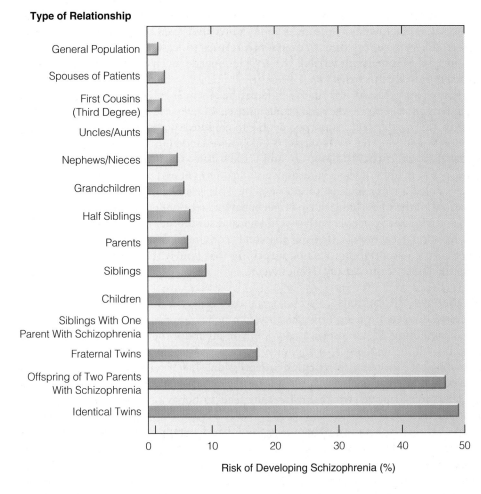

Risk of Developing Schizophrenia (%)

FIGURE 14.7 The Genetics of Schizophrenia
Each bar shows the risk of developing schizophrenia when one or more relatives have been diagnosed with the disorder. In general, the closer an individual is genetically to the person with schizophrenia, the more likely he or she is to develop the disorder. (Based on Gottesman, 1991)

sharing a disorder, is quite high between identical twins. A number of studies have shown that if one twin is diagnosed with depression, there is a 50% or greater chance that the other twin will also be diagnosed with depression; the concordance rate may be even higher for bipolar disorders (Gershon, 1990). It is also the case that adoptees with biological parents who suffer from a mood disorder are themselves more likely to suffer from a mood disorder. It's the biological history rather than the environmental history that, on average, predicts the chances of becoming affected.

Genetic factors help predict the likelihood that someone will suffer from certain psychological disorders, but genetic factors are not sufficient to explain abnormal behavior. Once again, having an identical twin with schizophrenia or bipolar disorder does not guarantee that you'll have a similar problem. Your genetic code may predispose you to a disorder—it may set the stage—but other environmental factors must be present for the disorder to actually develop (Schneider & Deldin, 2001). For example, problems during childbirth may help to explain why one twin eventually develops schizophrenia whereas the other does not (McNeil, Cantor-Graae, & Weinberger, 2000). Anxiety disorders may be likely to occur in people who are born with sensitive temperaments, but experience will determine whether a full-blown disorder actually develops. To repeat a common theme, it is the interaction between nature and nurture that is important.

Cognitive Factors: Thinking Maladaptive Thoughts

If you look closely into the mind of someone with a psychological disorder, you'll often find disordered styles of thinking. People with anxiety disorders, somatoform disorders, or the other disorders we've discussed typically believe things about themselves or about the world that have little or no basis in reality. Robert, who is depressed, is convinced that he lacks ability and drive, even though he is a successful banker. Jill, who suffers from agoraphobia, refuses to leave her house because she's convinced that something terrible will happen outside, even though she can think of no real reason for this belief.

Many psychologists feel that such faulty beliefs may be more than symptoms of an underlying disorder—they may contribute to, or even cause, the disorder itself. To see how this might work, suppose I'm able to convince you, by feeding you false but convincing reports, that evil extraterrestrials have landed in a nearby city. Your anxiety level would certainly shoot up, and there's little question your behavior would change. You might not leave your house, and you might end up spending a lot of your time huddled under a table in your basement. This is abnormal behavior, but it would be rational if the underlying cause of the behavior—the belief that the world may end soon—is true. Many people with psychological disorders act the way they do because they have incorrect beliefs. If you're absolutely convinced that you're no good and can never succeed at anything, it's not surprising that you withdraw from social situations and fail to secure steady employment.

Maladaptive Attributions   Psychologists use the term *attribution* to refer to the processes involved in assigning causality to a behavior (see Chapter 13). When you fail at something, like a test or a new job, you attribute the failure to a cause, such as your own incompetence or the lousy teacher. It turns out that people who have psychological disorders, particularly depression, have relatively distinctive and predictable attributional or explanatory styles. Unfortunately, the attributions are often maladaptive, which means they lead to behaviors that are abnormal or unproductive.

As ▮Figure 14.8 shows, when something bad happens to a person prone to depression, he or she is likely to explain it in terms of *internal* ("I'm to blame rather than the situation"), *stable* (long lasting), and *global* (widespread) attributions (Abramson, Metalsky, & Alloy, 1989; Barlow, 2002). Let's suppose you fail a test at school. If you're depressed, you'll probably attribute that failure to some personal inadequacy (internal) that is likely to be long lasting (stable) and that will apply in lots of situations other than school (global). People who are not prone to depression tend to have more flexible explanatory styles. They might attribute the failure to some *external* source ("I've got a rotten teacher") and consider the failure to be *unstable* ("I had a bad day"), and they'll probably make a *specific* rather than global attribution. Nondepressed people have less of a tendency to overgeneralize from a situation at school to other areas of life.

learned helplessness A general sense of helplessness that is acquired when people repeatedly fail in their attempts to control their environment; learned helplessness may play a role in depression.

▮**FIGURE 14.8** Maladaptive Thoughts in Depression
Depressed individuals tend to attribute failure to internal, stable, and global conditions.

Stable
"I was born stupid."

Internal
"It's totally my fault."

Global
"I'll probably fail all my courses."

Learned Helplessness   What produces these different explanatory styles? It's difficult to know whether people who make maladaptive attributions do so because they're depressed or whether it's the unfortunate explanatory style that creates the depression. Some researchers have argued that prolonged experience with failure may be one contributing factor. According to the **learned helplessness** theory of depression (Seligman, 1975), if individuals repeatedly fail while attempting to control their environment, they acquire a general sense of helplessness. They give up and become passive, which, the theory proposes, leads to depression. Still, it's unlikely that we can account for all forms of depression by appealing only to repeated failure. Experience with failure may be a necessary condition for acquiring depression, but it is not a sufficient condition. Many people fail repeatedly yet show no tendencies toward depression.

Moreover, it isn't really the failure that leads to depression but rather one's attributions about the failure. Instead of learning to be helpless, it may be the sense of *hopelessness*—the belief that things cannot become better because of internal, stable, and global factors—that is more likely to produce depression, at least in some people (Joiner et al., 2001). Whether this sense of hopelessness can be explained by appealing to experience alone or to some interaction between experience and biological or genetic predispositions remains to be seen (Alloy et al., 2001).

CRITICAL THINKING

Try to identify your own attributional style. Do you tend to attribute outcomes to global, stable, and internal causes?

Environmental Factors: Do People Learn to Act Abnormally?

All theories of psychological disorders ultimately appeal either directly or indirectly to environmental factors. Even if a researcher believes a disorder such as schizophrenia is primarily caused by a genetically induced problem in the brain, it's still necessary to explain why identical twins don't always share the disorder. Experience clearly plays a pivotal role. Similarly, the irrational beliefs and explanatory styles that characterize depression must be learned somewhere, although two people with the same experiences may not always share the same set of beliefs. Once again, experience is the bedrock on which the psychological interpretation is built.

The Role of Culture   As we've discussed throughout this chapter, cultural factors also play an obvious and important role (Harper, 2001). Although the symptoms of most serious psychological disorders—such as schizophrenia and depression—are generally similar across the world, culture-based differences do exist. For example, the types of delusions found in schizophrenia depend to a certain extent on cultural background (Tateyama et al., 1998). Different cultural groups may also be more or less likely to show symptoms of disorders because of cultural "rules" for expressing emotion and action (Manson, 1995). If an individual lives in a culture that discourages the expression of emotion, then depression will be somewhat harder to detect and treat.

People's cultural background may also determine the chances that they'll be exposed to environmental events that could trigger the onset of psychological disorders. Obviously, those who live somewhere in the world where war or extreme poverty is a way of life are likely to encounter more stressful events, which, in combination with a genetic predisposition, could lead to psychological problems. Cultural goals or ideals can also influence psychological health. For example, living in a society that places enormous emphasis on weight ideals can increase the chances that individuals will suffer from an eating disorder such as bulimia or anorexia nervosa (see Chapter 11). (You'll learn more about how cultural ideals and stressors in everyday life can affect your physical and psychological health in Chapter 16.)

Conditioning Disorders   A number of mental health professionals feel that at least some psychological disorders may be essentially *learned*. People can learn to act and think abnormally in the same way they might learn how to bake a cake, make friends, or avoid talking in class. Experts with this view of abnormality propose that learning principles of the type discussed in Chapter 7 help explain why psychological disorders develop and how they can be best treated. A phobia, for example, could be acquired through *classical conditioning*; an individual might learn to associate a particular stimulus or event with another event that makes him or her afraid. Alternatively, people might learn to act abnormally through *operant conditioning* because they've been reinforced for those actions. Acting in a strange way thus becomes more likely than it was before.

Learning theorists believe that *modeling*, or observational learning, might play a particularly important role in the development of some psychological disorders. As we discussed in Chapter 7, there are reasons to believe that phobias are sometimes acquired through modeling (Mineka & Zinbarg, 2006). Some of the best evidence has come from animal studies, where it's possible to control how the fear reaction is initially acquired. Rhesus monkeys who are raised in the wild show an extremely strong fear response to snakes; monkeys who have been reared in the laboratory will show a similar reaction, but only if they've witnessed other monkeys reacting fearfully when snakes are introduced into the cage. This research has made it clear that it's not necessary for the animal to experience something negative directly, such as getting attacked and bitten by the snake; the animal can acquire its fear simply by watching other monkeys act afraid (Cook & Mineka, 1989). Modeling in this case makes adaptive sense because appropriate actions can be learned without directly experiencing negative consequences.

The monkey data are important because they show how modeling can lead to the acquisition of a strong fear response. Obviously, for monkeys in the wild it's quite adaptive to be afraid of snakes. For humans, we know that modeling is also a powerful way to learn, but the evidence that modeling underlies phobias—which, after all, are essentially irrational fears—is still largely indirect at this point. We know that many people with phobias can't remember having a traumatic experience with the object of their fear (Rachman, 1990). It's also the case that phobias tend to run in families—if your father is afraid of heights, there's an increased chance that you'll share that same fear (Fyer et al., 1990). This kind of evidence is consistent with a modeling account of phobias, but it doesn't preclude alternative accounts. It seems likely, for instance, that some kind of biological predisposition might also be needed (Bouton et al., 2001).

As with the biological, genetic, and cognitive factors we've considered, it's unlikely that learning principles alone will be able to account for why people develop psychological disorders. People probably can't learn to be schizophrenic, for example, although stressful events in the environment undoubtedly play an important role in this disorder (Walker et al., 2004). Even with phobias, which may be largely learning based, it's probably necessary to be predisposed to anxiety for a full-blown phobia to develop (Barlow, 2002). Experience plays a significant role in the development of most psychological disorders, but it doesn't act alone. Behavior, both normal and abnormal, is virtually always produced by multiple causes.

CRITICAL THINKING

Do you suffer from any kind of phobia? Can you trace the fear to any particular experience in your life? Does anyone else in your family share the same fear?

Concept Review | Causes of Psychological Disorders

FACTOR	DESCRIPTION	EXAMPLE
Biological	Physiological problems, particularly in the brain. Could include neurotransmitter imbalances, structural problems, and genetic influences.	Danae feels extremely depressed. She goes to a psychologist who asks her whether anyone else in her family has suffered from depression. Danae reports that her mother and grandmother did have bouts of severe depression.
Cognitive	Our beliefs and styles of thought, such as maladaptive attributions and a sense of hopelessness.	Danae is struggling with her studies. She receives a D on a big exam. She is disgusted with herself and keeps thinking, "How could I be so stupid? I am such a loser!"
Environmental	The influence of experience and culture. Cultural background, events, and learning all have an impact on psychological disorders.	Danae's family has always struggled financially, and now her parents are going through a nasty divorce. Danae acts disruptively because it's one of the few ways she can get any attention from them.

Test Yourself 14.3

Check your knowledge about how psychologists have attempted to understand psychological disorders by answering the following questions. (You will find the answers in the Appendix.)

1. Which of the following biological conditions is most likely to be a contributing factor in schizophrenia?
   a. Slowed reuptake of the neurotransmitter serotonin
   b. Excessive amounts of the neurotransmitter dopamine
   c. Smaller-than-normal ventricles in the brain
   d. Increased random activity in the frontal lobes
2. Studies examining the genetics of schizophrenia have discovered that:
   a. Schizophrenia is a learned rather than an inherited disorder.
   b. Living with two parents with schizophrenia increases your risk of developing schizophrenia by about 65%.
   c. Identical twins are more likely to develop schizophrenia than fraternal twins.
   d. If your identical twin has schizophrenia, you have about a 50% chance of developing the disorder yourself.
3. Psychologists studying depression have found that depressed people tend to make the following kinds of personal attributions:
   a. External, stable, and global
   b. Internal, unstable, and global
   c. Internal, stable, and specific
   d. Internal, stable, and global
4. Studies examining how monkeys develop a strong fear response to snakes have been used to support which of the following accounts of phobias?
   a. Operant conditioning
   b. Observational learning
   c. Learned helplessness
   d. Classical conditioning

Review *Psychology for a Reason*

In this chapter we've considered what happens when a person's thoughts and actions become disordered. Most mental health professionals believe it's possible and useful to distinguish between normal and abnormal behavior. In addition, as you've seen, a relatively precise and rigorous classification system exists for the diagnosis and labeling of psychological disorders when they occur. But what are the implications for our general theme of the adaptive mind? It hardly seems adaptive to suffer from a psychological disorder—in fact, lack of adaptiveness is often used as a criterion for labeling a behavior as abnormal.

It's important to keep in mind that abnormal behaviors are often simply extreme versions of behaviors that otherwise have adaptive qualities. Anxiety, for instance, is an adaptive body response that prepares us for action and helps keep us vigilant in our surroundings. It becomes a problem only in its extreme form, when it is prolonged and chronic enough to impair normal functioning.

Sigmund Freud believed certain kinds of psychologically based amnesias are adaptive because they prevent traumatic memories from intruding into conscious awareness. To paraphrase William Shakespeare, there may indeed be a bit of method in madness. On the other hand, it's also reasonable to propose that psychological disorders may represent a kind of breakdown in the system. In particular, schizophrenia may arise from faulty brain functioning—the system ceases to be adaptive because it no longer has the capacity to function properly.

Conceptualizing Abnormality

Conceptualizing *abnormal* behavior turns out to be a rather difficult thing to do. A number of criteria have been proposed, including the notions of statistical and cultural deviance. By *deviance*, psychologists typically mean behavior that is essentially unusual in some way, either with respect to its statistical likelihood or with respect to the accepted norms of the culture. Abnormality can also be defined

in terms of emotional distress or dysfunction. None of these criteria alone is sufficient to capture the concept. The concept of abnormality is usually defined by a combination of these factors.

Currently, many mental health professionals conceive of abnormal behavior from a medical model. According to this view, psychological disorders are best described as "illnesses" that can be "cured" through appropriate treatment. There are advantages and disadvantages to this approach, and it should not be taken too literally. Physical illnesses often have clearly identifiable causes, but this is seldom true for psychological disorders. Also of concern are the effects of diagnostic labeling of disorders: Diagnostic labels can sometimes become self-fulfilling prophecies, which can make it harder for a suffering person to recover.

Classifying Psychological Disorders

Most mental health professionals rely on the DSM-IV-TR, which lists objective criteria for the diagnosis of psychological disorders. The DSM-IV-TR is composed of five major rating dimensions, or axes, which are used to record the presence of clinical or personality disorders, existing medical conditions, environmental problems, and the ability of the individual to function globally. In this chapter we focused our attention primarily on Axis I, which lists the major clinical syndromes.

Anxiety disorders are diagnosed when a person's apprehension and worry become so extreme that behavior is impaired. Generalized anxiety disorder is characterized by chronic worrying that can't be attributed to any obvious source. Obsessive–compulsive disorders are characterized by the presence of persistent, uncontrollable thoughts (obsessions) or by compelling needs to perform actions repetitively (compulsions). Phobias are highly focused fears of specific objects or events.

In somatoform disorders, the focus of the disorder revolves around the body: You might have a persistent preoccupation with the possibility that you've contracted a serious disease (hypochondriasis), or you might appear to suffer from an actual physical problem that has no identifiable physical cause (conversion disorder).

In dissociative disorders, the person appears to separate, or dissociate, previous thoughts and memories from current conscious awareness. These disorders include dissociative amnesia, dissociative fugue states, and the more controversial dissociative identity disorder, in which the person appears to have two or more distinct personalities.

Mood disorders typically come in two forms: depressive disorder, in which the affected individual is mired in depression; and bipolar disorder, in which the individual alternates between the highs of mania and the lows of depression. Schizophrenia, the final clinical syndrome we discussed, is characterized by distorted thoughts and perceptions. The symptoms of schizophrenia include delusions, hallucinations, and disorganized speech and behavior. Negative symptoms include flat affect, which means that the person shows little or no emotional reaction to events. Personality disorders are listed in Axis II because they tend to be more ingrained and inflexible than the major clinical syndromes described on Axis I.

Understanding Psychological Disorders

Mental health professionals currently believe that the root cause, or etiology, of most disorders lies in a combination of biological, cognitive, and environmental factors. Some disorders may result from disordered or malfunctioning brains. There's evidence to support the idea that some psychological problems result from neurotransmitter problems in the brain or perhaps from structural problems in brain anatomy. Many psychological disorders also appear to have a genetic basis—individuals may inherit a predisposition for a particular kind of problem.

Psychological disorders are also typically characterized by maladaptive thinking, and it has been suggested that maladaptive beliefs and attributions contribute to the appearance of abnormal behavior. Depressed individuals, for example, tend to attribute negative events to internal, stable, and global causes; these attributions are often associated with a sense of hopelessness, or the faulty belief that things cannot get better.

Finally, all theories of psychological disorders rely in one form or another on the environment. For example, your cultural background may play a role in the expression of biological or genetic predispositions and may even determine the kinds of personal attributions you make. It's possible that some psychological problems may arise almost entirely from environmental influences. It's possible that people learn to act abnormally, either through conditioning or through modeling the behavior of significant people around them.

Active Summary *(You will find the answers in the Appendix.)*

Conceptualizing Abnormality: What Is Abnormal Behavior?

• "Abnormal" and "normal" are best understood as ends of a (1) _____ rather than as distinct categories. Statistical (2) _____ refers to behavior that occurs infrequently among members of a population. (3) _____ deviance is a criterion used to compare behaviors to current cultural (4) _____. The extent of (5) _____ distress is also relevant in evaluating whether a condition is abnormal. A final criterion is the extent of (6) _____, a breakdown in the ability to perform typical daily activities.

• "Insanity" is a (7) _____ concept, not a (8) _____ one. A criminal is insane, and therefore not guilty by reason of insanity, if, because of a mental condition, he or she fails to (9) _____ that certain actions are (10) _____ or (11) _____ wrong at the time of a crime.

• According to the (12) _____ model, abnormal behavior is caused by an underlying (13) _____. This model is influential, and (14) _____ have been developed that are effective in treating a variety of psychological disorders. Some researchers feel that it is difficult to make direct comparisons between (15) _____ and psychological illnesses.

• Critics of the medical model are concerned that (16) _____ a psychological disorder as an illness attaches a (17) _____ to the person that is hard to overcome. Research has shown that labeling someone as "abnormal" can lead people to interpret (18) _____ behaviors as signs of a (19) _____ disorder.

Classifying Psychological Disorders: The DSM-IV-TR

• The *Diagnostic and Statistical Manual (DSM) of Mental Disorders*, now in its fourth edition (IV-TR), is a well-defined (20) _____ system for psychological disorders. Based on (21) _____ and (22) _____ criteria, it consists of (23) _____ major ratings dimensions, or *axes*, that assess clinical syndromes (Axis 1), (24) _____ disorders (Axis 2), medical conditions (Axis 3), environmental or psychosocial problems (Axis 4), and the client's current level of adaptive or (25) _____ functioning (Axis 5). The DSM-IV-TR does not suggest therapies or methods of treatment.

• A person may be diagnosed with an (26) _____ disorder if the level of (27) _____ and worry is so extreme that behavior is impaired. (28) _____ anxiety disorder is characterized by excessive, chronic, and unfocused worry-

ing that lasts for a period of at least (29) _____ months. (30) _____ disorder is characterized by (31) _____ attacks of intense (32) _____ or dread and is sometimes complicated by (33) _____, the fear of being in public. In (34) _____–_____ disorder, anxiety is apparent in persistent thoughts (obsessions) or the compelling need to perform actions (compulsions). The defining feature of specific (35) _____ disorder is a highly focused fear of a particular object or situation.

• (36) _____ disorders are associated with the (37) _____ body. In (38) _____, a healthy person misinterprets normal bodily signs as evidence of (39) _____. In the related (40) _____ disorder, people focus on physical symptoms rather than a possible disease state. In (41) _____ disorder, there is real physical impairment with no apparent physical cause.

• People with a (42) _____ disorder have a loss of memory. In (43) _____ amnesia, a person is unable to remember important personal information. Dissociative (44) _____ involves a loss of personal (45) _____ followed by a flight from home. A person with dissociative (46) _____ disorder alternates among distinct (47) _____ or identity states; controversy surrounds such a diagnosis.

• The prolonged emotional disruptions known as (48) _____ disorders come in two varieties, (49) _____ disorders and (50) _____ disorders. A major (51) _____ episode is characterized by numerous symptoms, which may include loss of interest in daily activities, chronic fatigue, trouble concentrating, and suicidal thoughts. In (52) _____ disorder, the depression is milder but chronic. A person with (53) _____ disorder alternates between (54) _____ and the hyperactive euphoria associated with (55) _____. A mood disorder may result in (56) _____; risk factors include substance abuse, a sudden very stressful event, the recent occurrence of other suicides, and prior suicide attempts and suicidal thoughts.

• Schizophrenia is a class of disorders that is characterized by fundamental disturbances in thought processes, (57) _____, or behavior. Both (58) _____ and negative symptoms are associated with schizophrenia. Positive symptoms include (59) _____, thoughts with bizarre content and (60) _____, perceptions that aren't triggered by external stimuli. Negative symptoms involve the elimination or reduction of normal behavior such as (61) _____ affect, showing little emotional reaction. Other symptoms can include (62) _____, a general physical immobility or sudden wild adjustment of position, and disorganized (63) _____.

• In (64) _____ disorders, chronic behavior patterns lead to significant impairment in (65) _____ functioning. (66) _____ personality disorder features an exaggerated distrust of others; (67) _____ personality disorder features an excessive need to be taken care of by others; and a person with (68) _____ personality disorder shows little or no respect for social norms. Some psychologists believe that people with these disorders are simply at an extreme on one or more of the Big (69) _____ personality dimensions.

Understanding Psychological Disorders: Biological, Cognitive, or Environmental?

• Some psychological disorders coincide with abnormal brain (70) _____ or structure. Many psychological disorders have a strong (71) _____ basis; people may inherit a predisposition toward certain disorders. Schizophrenia has been linked to an oversupply of (72) _____, and to the interaction of dopamine and other neurotransmitters such as glutamate, GABA, and (73) _____. Mood disorders may also reflect (74) _____ imbalances.

• People with psychological disorders (especially depression) have distinctive and predictable (75) _____ styles. Someone with a tendency toward depression is likely to respond to a negative event with (76) _____, stable, and (77) _____ attributions. According to the (78) _____ _____ theory of depression, people who repeatedly fail to (79) _____ their environment give up and may have a sense of hopelessness, which leads to depression.

• (80) _____ plays a pivotal role in psychological disorders. For example, (81) _____ can affect whether you will be exposed to an event that triggers the onset of a disorder and how the disorder will be (82) _____. Some psychologists believe that certain disorders can be (83) _____ through (84) _____ conditioning or modeling, such as a phobia, or through operant conditioning.

Terms to Remember

agoraphobia, 460
antisocial personality disorder, 471
anxiety disorders, 459
bio-psycho-social perspective, 472
bipolar disorder, 466
borderline personality disorder, 471
conversion disorder, 463
cultural deviance, 451
dependent personality disorder, 471
diagnostic labeling effects, 454
dissociative amnesia, 464
dissociative disorders, 463

dissociative fugue, 464
dissociative identity disorder, 464
DSM-IV-TR, 456
dysfunction, 452
emotional distress, 452
generalized anxiety disorder, 459
hypochondriasis, 462
insanity, 454
learned helplessness, 476
major depressive episode, 465
manic state, 466
medical model, 454

mood disorders, 465
obsessive–compulsive disorder, 460
panic disorder, 459
paranoid personality disorder, 471
personality disorders, 471
phobic disorder, 461
schizophrenia, 468
social anxiety disorder, 461
somatization disorder, 463
somatoform disorders, 462
statistical deviance, 451

Media Resources

 **ThomsonNOW**

www.thomsonedu.com/ThomsonNOW
Go to this site for the link to ThomsonNow, your one-stop study shop. Take a Pre-Test for this chapter and Thomson-Now will generate a personalized Study Plan based on your test results! The Study Plan will identify the topics you need to review and direct you to online resources to help you master those topics. You can then take a Post-Test to help you determine the concepts you have mastered and what you still need to work on.

 Companion Website

www.thomsonedu.com/psychology/nairne
Go to this site to find online resources directly linked to your book, including a glossary, flashcards, quizzing, weblinks, and more.

 Psyk.trek 3.0

Check out the Psyk.trek CD-ROM for further study of the concepts in this chapter. Psyk.trek's interactive learning modules, simulations, and quizzes offer additional opportunities for you to interact with, reflect on, and retain the material:

Abnormal Behavior and Therapy: Anxiety Disorders
Abnormal Behavior and Therapy: Mood Disorders
Abnormal Behavior and Therapy: Schizophrenia Disorders

CHAPTER 15

Therapy

If you're hearing voices in your head, and you're convinced that the alien takeover is on schedule for next Tuesday, it's likely you're having trouble leading a normal life. You probably can't hold a job or make lasting friends, and you may even have difficulty carrying on a meaningful conversation. Clearly, you need some kind of treatment—**psychotherapy**—to deal with your mental, emotional, and behavioral problems. But as you'll discover in this chapter, even those with less severe disturbances can benefit from the right kind of therapy. Suppose Carlos turns down the job of national sales manager simply because he's afraid of flying; what if Julie spends most of her time alone in her apartment because she's convinced she'll embarrass herself in social settings?

Treatment options are available to tackle these kinds of problems in everyday living as well—psychotherapy isn't just for the severely impaired. Mental health professionals have a variety of tools at their disposal to help people regain their ability to function well in their surroundings. The particular tool used by the therapist depends on a number of factors, including the specific type of disorder being treated and the personality of the person seeking treatment. Treatment can be administered in a variety of ways. Some people respond well to one-on-one encounters with a therapist; others thrive best in group settings. As we discussed in Chapter 1, good therapists tailor the treatment to meet the needs of the particular client. This doesn't mean that therapists must abandon all theoretical orientations, but it does require flexibility. Good therapists recognize that a method that proves effective for one person can be ineffective for another.

> **psychotherapy** Treatment designed to help people deal with mental, emotional, or behavioral problems.

As you saw in Chapter 14, when psychologists study the cause of a psychological disorder, they usually look for contributions from biological, cognitive, or environmental factors. Abnormal behavior can be caused by problems in the brain, irrational beliefs, environmental experiences, or some combination of these factors. As a result, most kinds of psychotherapy are specifically designed to treat either the body, the mind, or the environment (see ▌Figure 15.1).

Treating the Body Abnormal functioning in the brain is thought to contribute to a number of disorders. Schizophrenia, for example, might be due in part to imbalances in neurotransmitters; depression and mania have also been linked to the activities of neurotransmitters. To address these kinds of problems, it makes sense to consider treating the body itself through *biomedical therapies*. One option might be to administer a drug that restores the proper balance of neurotransmitters; other options might include surgery to fix the damage that exists in a particular region of the brain or even the use of electric shock treatment.

Treating the Mind Psychological disorders are often associated with abnormal thoughts and beliefs. Many psychologists are convinced that the key to improvement is insight—you must gain awareness of your own thought processes. When you think of psychotherapy, do you imagine someone lying on a couch talking about dreams and early childhood experiences? Although this stereotypical image is accurate in some respects, you'll see in the discussion of *insight therapies* that many therapists have abandoned the couch, as well as the emphasis on dreams and early experiences. What remains is the idea that exploring one's thought processes can be an effective tool for solving psychological problems.

Treating the Environment Psychologists also accept that certain kinds of disorders might be learned. We might learn to think and act in abnormal ways in much the same way that we acquire other thoughts and actions—through operant conditioning, classical conditioning, or by modeling the actions of others. The idea behind *behavioral therapies* is to use basic learning principles to change dysfunctional behavior patterns into adaptive behavior patterns. For example, if experience has taught you to associate high places with disabling fear, it might be possible to alter the association either through extinction or by counterconditioning relaxation to replace the fear.

Evaluating and Choosing Psychotherapy Do all forms of therapy work, or are some more effective than others? Therapy can be a costly and time-consuming process, so it's important to evaluate the advantages and disadvantages of the intervention. A number of studies have been conducted comparing people who have undergone therapy with those left untreated. Although many studies demonstrate the effectiveness of psychotherapy, some of the findings may surprise you.

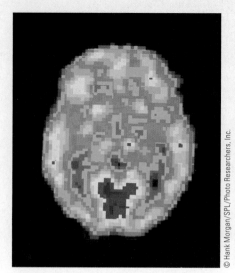
Treating the body.

Treating the mind.

Treating the environment.

▌**FIGURE 15.1** Treatment Options
Psychologists consider three main treatment options in the administration and evaluation of therapy.

Treating the Body: Biomedical Therapies

LEARNING GOALS
- Explain how drug therapies are used to treat psychological disorders.
- Discuss and evaluate electroconvulsive therapy.
- Explain why psychosurgery is sometimes used to treat psychological disorders.

PSYCHOLOGICAL DISORDERS HAVE BEEN AROUND since the beginning of recorded history. And for just as long, people have speculated about what causes abnormal behavior and have offered remedies for its treatment. At one time it was popular to appeal to supernatural forces: People who exhibited bizarre or deviant behavior were believed to be possessed by evil spirits or demons. The cure, if we can call it that, was to torture the sufferer in an effort to drive out the evil inhabitants.

But not all serious thinkers adopted such views. In fact, more than 2000 years ago Hippocrates (469–377 B.C.E.) and his followers suggested that psychological disorders should be treated as products of the body. Hippocrates believed people get depressed or exhibit manic states for much the same reason we fall victim to the common cold—the body and brain, and hence the mind, are affected by some kind of "disease." Hippocrates even went so far as to recommend changes in diet and exercise as a way of treating depression, a course of action that many modern therapists consider appropriate today.

The medical approach to understanding disorders gained scientific respectability in the 19th and early 20th centuries as researchers began to establish links between known physical problems and the symptoms of psychological disorders. For example, by the end of the 19th century it was recognized that the venereal disease *syphilis* is responsible not only for a steady deterioration in physical health (and eventually death) but also for the appearance of paranoia and hallucinations. Establishing a link between syphilis and mental problems was an important step in the eventual development of biologically based therapies. Early "cures" for the disease included injecting sufferers with the blood of malaria patients in an effort to induce a high fever that would "burn out" the syphilis bacteria; today, of course, doctors use antibiotics to treat syphilis.

In this section of the chapter we'll consider several modern biological approaches to the treatment of psychological disorders. **Biomedical therapies** use physiological interventions to reduce or eliminate the symptoms of psychological disorders. By far the most popular approach is treatment with medication, and we'll consider this approach first, but other biomedical therapies are available, including electroconvulsive therapy and psychosurgery.

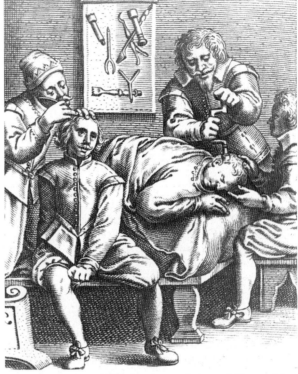

This engraving from 1598 shows an early form of "therapy" for psychological disorders—drilling holes in the head to promote the release of evil spirits.

biomedical therapies Biologically based treatments for reducing or eliminating the symptoms of psychological disorders.

Drug Therapies

The psychological community began to recognize the remarkable potential of drug therapy in the early 1950s when two French psychiatrists, Jean Delay and Pierre Deniker, reported success in treating the positive symptoms of schizophrenia with a drug called *chlorpromazine* (often sold under the brand name Thorazine). Patients suffering from delusions and hallucinations showed considerable improvement after prolonged use of the drug. Since that time, dozens of other drugs have proved successful in treating a wide variety of psychological disorders. In fact, specific medications are now available to treat most of the disorders we considered in Chapter 14—everything from obsessive–compulsive disorder to depression. Unfortunately, these drugs do not work for all people, and as you'll see, some drugs have disturbing side effects. But they've helped thousands, and in many ways they've revolutionized the mental health profession.

antipsychotic drugs Medications that reduce the positive symptoms of schizophrenia.

Antipsychotic Drugs Medications that treat the positive symptoms of schizophrenia—for example, delusions or hallucinations—are commonly called **antipsychotic drugs**. Chlorpromazine is an example of such a drug, but a number of others are also available. The majority of these antipsychotic drugs are believed to act on the neurotransmitter *dopamine* in the brain. As we discussed in Chapter 14, many researchers believe schizophrenia is caused partly by abnormalities in the regulation of dopamine. Chlorpromazine acts as a dopamine *antagonist*, meaning that it blocks or slows down the use of dopamine in the brain (e.g., Weiden, 2007; see Figure 15.2). The fact that dopamine antagonists work so well in treating positive symptoms is considered strong support for the dopamine hypothesis of schizophrenia (Walker et al., 2004).

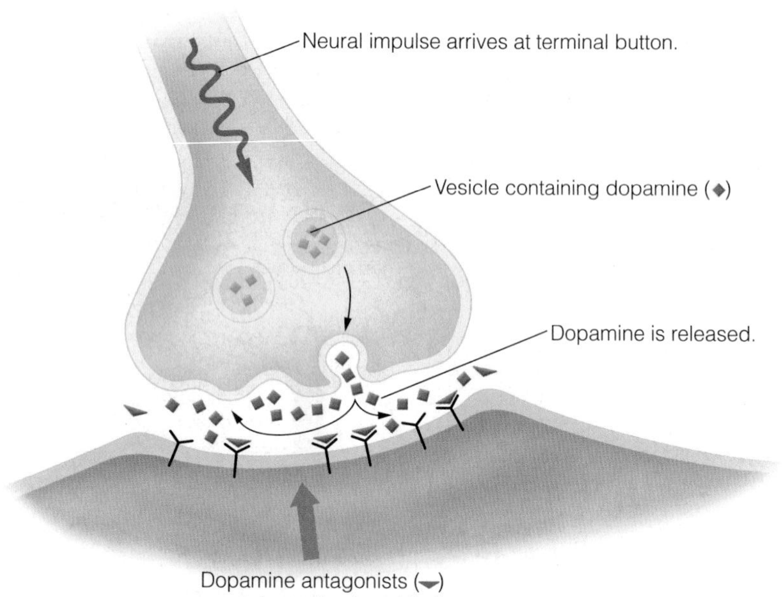
Neural impulse arrives at terminal button.
Vesicle containing dopamine (◆)
Dopamine is released.
Dopamine antagonists (⌣) prevent dopamine from binding to membrane receptors (Y).

FIGURE 15.2 Dopamine Antagonists
Some antipsychotic medications act as antagonists, which means they block or slow down the action of neurotransmitters in the brain. Here, a dopamine antagonist binds with the receptor membrane, blocking the neurotransmitter.

But dopamine antagonists don't work for all sufferers of schizophrenia. Moreover, these drugs tend to work almost exclusively on positive symptoms. The negative symptoms of schizophrenia, such as the sharp decline in the normal expression of emotions, are rarely affected by the administration of traditional antipsychotic medications. Antipsychotic drugs can also produce unwanted and persistent side effects in some patients, including drowsiness, difficulties in concentrating, blurry vision, and movement disorders. One particularly serious side effect is a condition called *tardive dyskinesia*, which produces involuntary movements of the tongue, jaw, mouth, and face. These side effects can be permanent, and they act as a two-edged sword: Not only are they extremely uncomfortable, but they increase the chances that the patient will stop taking the medication. Without the medication, of course, the positive symptoms of the disorder are likely to reemerge.

In recent years new medications, including *clozapine* and *risperidone*, have been introduced that work well for patients who don't respond to the more traditional dopamine antagonists (Chakos et al., 2001). These medications do not produce movement side effects such as tardive dyskinesia, although medical complications can still be a concern in some cases. From a research standpoint, the effectiveness of the newer "second-generation" medications is noteworthy because they don't work by simply regulating the amount of dopamine in the brain. It's believed they affect a number of neurotransmitters, including dopamine and serotonin (Richtand et al., 2007). This suggests that dopamine alone, as we noted in Chapter 14, can't account entirely for schizophrenic disorders.

CRITICAL THINKING

Just because dopamine antagonists reduce the positive symptoms of schizophrenia does not necessarily mean that dopamine causes schizophrenia. Why not?

Antidepressant Drugs The 1950s also witnessed the introduction of medications for treating manic states and depression. Mood disorders have been linked to several neurotransmitters, including norepinephrine and serotonin. **Antidepressant drugs** act by modulating the availability or effectiveness of these neurotransmitters. The group of antidepressants called *tricyclics*, for example, alter mood by acting primarily on norepinephrine; tricyclics apparently allow norepinephrine to linger in synapses longer than normal, which eventually modulates its effectiveness. The most commonly prescribed antidepressants act on serotonin. So-called *selective serotonin reuptake inhibitors* (SSRIs) block the reabsorption (or "reuptake")

antidepressant drugs Medications that modulate the availability or effectiveness of the neurotransmitters implicated in mood disorders.

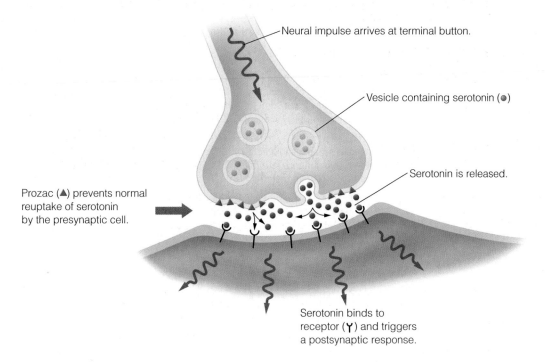

Neural impulse arrives at terminal button.

Vesicle containing serotonin (●)

Serotonin is released.

Prozac (▲) prevents normal reuptake of serotonin by the presynaptic cell.

Serotonin binds to receptor (Υ) and triggers a postsynaptic response.

FIGURE 15.3 Reuptake Blockers
Some kinds of antidepressant medications block the reabsorption of neurotransmitters, which then linger longer in the synapse and continue to activate receptor neurons. Prozac is in the class of antidepressants that block the reabsorption of serotonin.

of serotonin into the neuron, thereby allowing it to linger longer in the synapse and continue to activate receptor neurons (see ▌Figure 15.3). Commonly prescribed examples of SSRIs include Prozac, Paxil, and Zoloft.

Researchers don't know exactly how or why these medications affect mood, outside of the belief that they alter the effectiveness of neurotransmitters. Fortunately, they do work well for many individuals affected with depression. It's been estimated that sustained use of antidepressants successfully controls depression in well over 50% of all depressed patients (Hammen, 2003). On the downside, it typically takes several weeks for these medications to begin working (the time period may differ across the different types of antidepressants), and potential side effects must be monitored. SSRIs, for example, can produce agitation or restlessness, difficulty sleeping, weight gain, and even diminished sexual desire.

Effective medications are also available for treating bipolar disorders, which produce mood swings between depression and hyperactive manic states. Bipolar disorders are usually treated by administering a common salt called *lithium carbonate*. Lithium is more effective for bipolar disorder than the antidepressants because it works well on the manic state; it puts people on a more "even keel" and helps to prevent the reoccurrence of future manic episodes. But it, too, needs to be monitored closely because lithium use can lead to a variety of medical complications (Holtzheimer & Neumaier, 2003).

Antianxiety Drugs   For the treatment of psychological problems associated with anxiety, mental health professionals typically use **antianxiety drugs**, known more generally as *tranquilizers*. Tranquilizers come from a class of chemicals called *benzodiazepines*—Valium and Xanax are popular trade names—and they are quite effective for reducing tension and anxiety. In the mid-1970s it was estimated that 10 to 20% of adults in the Western world were "popping" tranquilizers (Greenblatt & Shader, 1978), which gives you some idea of their widespread use. In recent years tranquilizer use has been on the decline, primarily because mental health professionals recognize a downside to their continued use.

Most benzodiazepines appear to work on the neurotransmitter GABA, which produces primarily inhibitory effects. The effectiveness of GABA increases after

antianxiety drugs Medications that reduce tension and anxiety.

Concept Review | Drug Therapies

TYPE OF DRUG	TREATMENT USED IN:	EXAMPLES AND EFFECTS
Antipsychotic	Positive symptoms of schizophrenia, including delusions, hallucinations, and disorganized speech	*Chlorpromazine*, one example, is a *dopamine antagonist*. It blocks or impedes the flow of dopamine in the brain. *Clozapine* has also proven effective in alleviating some symptoms of schizophrenia.
Antidepressants	Mood disorders	*Tricyclics* alter mood by acting primarily on norepinephrine, allowing it to linger in synapses longer. *Fluoxetine* (e.g., Prozac) works primarily on serotonin, blocking its reuptake into the neuron. *Lithium carbonate* is used to treat bipolar disorder.
Antianxiety	Psychological problems associated with anxiety	*Tranquilizers* come from a class of chemicals called *benzodiazepines*. They appear to work on the neurotransmitter GABA, which produces primarily inhibitory effects. The result is a lowering of excitation in affected neurons, reducing tension and anxiety.

taking the drug, which leads to a lowering of excitation in affected neurons (Lickey & Gordon, 1991). Potential side effects include drowsiness, impaired motor coordination, and possible psychological dependence (Wells & Carter, 2006). Tranquilizers can act as a psychological crutch after lengthy use, so the majority of clinicians now recommend that they be used primarily as a short-term remedy for anxiety rather than as a long-term cure. Newer antianxiety drugs, such as *buspirone*, may not produce the same degree of dependency. However, increasingly, therapists are finding that antidepressants, particularly SSRIs, are effective in treating anxiety disorders, and they're now being widely prescribed (Golden, 2004).

Electroconvulsive Therapy

electroconvulsive therapy (ECT) A treatment used primarily for depression in which a brief electric current is delivered to the brain.

When traditional medications fail, particularly for depression, clinicians sometimes turn to a more controversial form of biomedical therapy: "shock" treatment. As you know, the language of the nervous system is partly electrical in nature. If electric shock is administered to the brain, a brief brain seizure will occur that produces, among other things, convulsions and loss of consciousness. When **electroconvulsive therapy (ECT)** was first introduced in the 1930s, it was a terrifying and hazardous procedure; patients suffered serious side effects that included the occasional broken bone from the convulsions. Fortunately, modern applications of ECT are much less physically traumatic; the patient is given a light anesthetic and medications that relax the muscles so injuries won't occur.

Many mental health professionals believe ECT is a reasonably safe and effective form of treatment for patients who suffer from severe depression. It's used almost exclusively for depression, although some clinicians believe it benefits other psychological problems as well (Fink, 2001). It's considered to be a treatment of last resort, to be used only when people have shown little or no response to antidepressant drugs or other conventional forms of psychotherapy. Controlled research studies have found that ECT is successful some 50 to 70% of the time in lessening the symptoms of depression in patients who have not otherwise responded to treatment (Carney et al., 2003). Typically, these studies involve direct comparisons between depressed patients who receive ECT and patients who undergo the same procedural preparations but don't actually receive the shock.

Controversies　Despite the demonstrated effectiveness of ECT as a treatment for severe depression, the procedure remains controversial for several reasons. First, no one is certain exactly why the treatment works. It's possible that shocking the brain affects the release of neurotransmitters or changes some structural feature of the

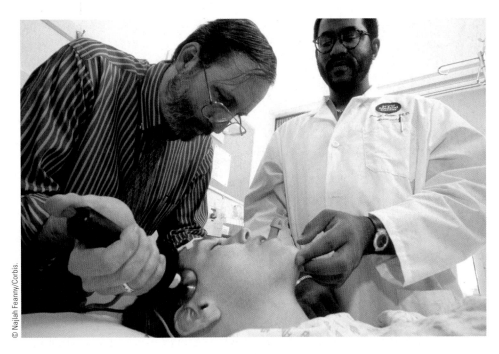

ECT is a reasonably safe and effective form of treatment for patients suffering from severe depression, but it is still considered controversial by mental health professionals.

brain, but at present there's no definitive answer as to why the procedure changes mood. Second, ECT produces side effects, particularly confusion and a loss of memory for events surrounding the treatment (e.g., McCall, 2007). These side effects are usually temporary, and they're not serious for most patients, but they remain a concern. Third, patients who receive ECT for depression have a relatively high relapse rate, which means they're likely to tailspin into another depressive episode at some point (McCall, 2001). Finally, some researchers are concerned that ECT might cause permanent brain damage. Effective ECT usually requires repeated administrations of the shock over several weeks, and it's not known what long-term effects these treatments have on the brain.

Is ECT worth the risks? The answer depends mainly on the needs of the particular patient. If you're deeply depressed and no other treatment options have provided relief, or if the side effects of traditional medications cannot be tolerated, ECT can literally be a lifesaver. Many clinicians believe that if it comes down to a desperate choice between ending your life and suffering some confusion and memory loss, trying ECT is certainly worth the risk. Newer treatment options on the horizon may eventually prove more effective and have fewer side effects. For example, transcranial magnetic stimulation (TMS) works by placing a magnetic coil around the head, which, in turn, sets up a magnetic field that alters electrical activity in the brain. Early results have been promising in treating major depressive disorders (Sampson et al., 2007).

Psychosurgery

A direct connection exists between biological problems in the brain and the occurrence of some psychological disorders. People suffering from schizophrenia, for example, sometimes show structural abnormalities in the brain. It makes sense, then, to consider the possibility of direct intervention, through brain surgery, to fix these problems permanently. Certainly if your appendix or gall bladder was infected and the diseased organ was creating a whole host of physical symptoms, you wouldn't think twice about calling the local surgeon. Wouldn't it be nice if we could adopt a similar approach for psychological problems?

Actually, the use of **psychosurgery**—surgery that destroys or alters tissue in the brain in an effort to affect behavior—has been around for decades. In the 1930s a surgical

CRITICAL THINKING

Imagine you're treating a severely depressed person who is clearly suicidal. Remember, drug therapies can take weeks to work. Would you consider ECT for such a person? How about an elderly patient who refuses to eat, just wants to die, and cannot be given medications because of side effects?

psychosurgery Surgery that destroys or alters tissues in the brain in an effort to affect behavior.

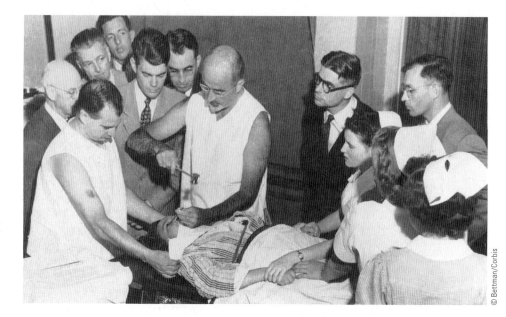

© Bettman/Corbis

Dr. Walter Freeman is shown here in 1949, demonstrating psychosurgery. He is inserting an instrument under the patient's upper eyelid to sever certain neural connections in the brain and thereby relieve symptoms of a psychological disorder. Operations of this type are no longer performed.

procedure called the *prefrontal lobotomy* was pioneered by a Portuguese physician, Egas Moniz (and later in the United States by Walter Freeman and James Watts). The operation involved a crude separation of the frontal lobes from the rest of the brain. The surgery was designed to sever various connections in the brain's circuitry in the hope that it might produce calming tendencies in disturbed patients. The procedure was widely used for several decades, and, in fact, Moniz was awarded the Nobel Prize for his work in 1949. But prefrontal lobotomies eventually fell into disrepute. Many patients were killed by the procedure, and it produced serious cognitive deficits in many others. They lost their ability to plan and coordinate actions, capabilities associated with activity in the frontal lobes.

Psychosurgery is still used as a way of treating problems that have failed to respond to conventional forms of therapy, but its use is exceedingly rare. One modern form of psychosurgery, called a *cingulotomy*, is sometimes used to treat obsessive–compulsive disorder and severe forms of depression (Jenike, 1998; Matthews & Eljamel, 2003). The surgery destroys a small portion of tissue in the limbic system of the brain. As with ECT, however, physicians really have no idea why this procedure works, nor can they explain why it works in some patients but not in others. It's another treatment of last resort that has proven effective for some but has not gained wide acceptance among the general psychological community. As our understanding of the brain increases, however, it seems likely that surgical approaches to treatment may rise in popularity (Hurley et al., 2000).

Test Yourself 15.1

Check your knowledge about biomedical therapies by answering the following questions. (You will find the answers in the Appendix.)

1. Pick the psychological disorder that is best treated by each of the following therapies or medications. Choose your answers from among the following: *depression, manic state, generalized anxiety disorder, schizophrenia, hypochondriasis.*
    a. Clozapine: _____
    b. Prozac: _____
    c. Cingulotomy: _____
    d. ECT: _____
    e. Benzodiazepine: _____

2. Which of the following statements about ECT (electroconvulsive therapy) is false?
    a. ECT is an effective treatment for depression.
    b. Researchers are uncertain how ECT works.
    c. ECT can produce confusion and some memory loss.
    d. ECT is used regularly to treat schizophrenia.

Treating the Mind: Insight Therapies

LEARNING GOALS
- Evaluate psychoanalysis as a form of insight therapy.
- Evaluate cognitive therapies.
- Evaluate humanistic therapies.
- Discuss group and family therapy.

PEOPLE WHO SUFFER from psychological disorders often carry around faulty or irrational beliefs about the world and about themselves. Many clinicians are convinced that the proper role for the therapist is to confront these irrational thoughts and beliefs directly through what are called insight therapies. **Insight therapies** are designed to give clients self-knowledge, or *insight*, into the content of their thought processes, usually through extensive one-on-one verbal interactions. The hope is that with insight people will adopt a more realistic, adaptive view of the world and change their behavior accordingly.

There are many types of insight therapy. We'll consider three in this section: *psychoanalysis, cognitive therapies*, and *humanistic approaches*. Most other insight therapies are related in one form or another to these three main approaches. The common thread that ties them together is the belief that cognitive or mental insight can produce significant changes in one's psychological condition. The therapies differ in the kinds of beliefs or memories that are considered to be important and in how the client's insight can best be obtained. Finally, we'll end this section by briefly discussing the value of group and family therapy.

insight therapies Treatments designed to give clients self-knowledge, or insight, into the contents of their thought processes.

Psychoanalysis: Resolving Unconscious Conflicts

Probably the best-known insight therapy is **psychoanalysis**, which comes originally from the work of Sigmund Freud. As you may remember from Chapter 12, Freud placed enormous emphasis on the concept of the *unconscious mind*. He believed that each of us houses a kind of hidden reservoir that is filled with memories, primitive urges, and conflicts. We can't directly think about the urges and memories stored in the unconscious mind, but they affect our behavior nonetheless. Freud believed that through psychoanalysis these hidden impulses and memories can be brought to the surface of awareness, thereby freeing us from unwanted thoughts and behaviors.

Freud based his theory primarily on case studies. He routinely treated patients with troubling psychological problems, and he discovered he could often help these people by getting them to recall and relive traumatic experiences they had apparently forgotten, or repressed. Freud was particularly interested in the emotionally significant experiences of childhood because he believed that during childhood we progress through a number of psychologically "fragile" stages of psychosexual development (see Chapter 12). Traumatic experiences are, by definition, anxiety provoking and therefore difficult for the young mind to deal with, so they're buried in the unconscious. Although no longer consciously available, these experiences continue to dominate and color behavior.

psychoanalysis Freud's method of treatment that attempts to bring hidden impulses and memories, which are locked in the unconscious, to the surface of awareness, thereby freeing the patient from disordered thoughts and behaviors.

The Tools of Psychoanalysis   The goal of psychoanalysis is to help the patient uncover, and thereby relive, unconscious conflicts. Obviously, because the patient is unaware of the conflicts, the therapist needs certain tools to access the contents of the unconscious mind. Freud liked to compare psychoanalysis to excavating a buried city, but instead of picks and shovels his tools were the uncensored expressions and feelings of his patients. Freud relied heavily on a technique called **free association**, in which patients were asked to relax and freely express whatever thoughts and feelings happened to come into their minds. To the untrained eye, the result was a series of meaningless and unrelated streams of thought, but to Freud these free associations represented symbolic clues to the contents of the unconscious.

free association A technique used in psychoanalysis to explore the contents of the unconscious; patients are asked to freely express whatever thoughts and feelings happen to come into their minds.

dream analysis A technique used in psychoanalysis; Freud believed that dreams are symbolic and contain important information about the unconscious.

© Bettman/Corbis

CRITICAL THINKING

What do you think Freud would have thought about the value of biomedical therapies? Would he have supported or rejected the idea of treating psychological disorders through medications, ECT, or psychosurgery?

resistance In psychoanalysis, a patient's unconsciously motivated attempts to subvert or hinder the process of therapy.

transference In psychoanalysis, the patient's expression of thoughts or feelings toward the therapist that are actually representative of the way the patient feels about other significant people in his or her life

Freud's other important therapeutic tool was patient dreams. Through **dream analysis**, he felt the therapist was handed a royal road to the unconscious. As we discussed in Chapter 6, Freud was convinced that dreams are partly a psychological mechanism for wish fulfillment, a way to satisfy hidden desires that are too anxiety provoking to come to consciousness directly. The storyline of dreams, he believed, is largely symbolic—there is a hidden meaning to dreams, a *latent content*, that reveals the unconscious. This latent content can be contrasted with the actual events and symbols of the dream, which Freud called its *manifest content*. Freud encouraged his patients to describe their dreams so he could acquire further clues in his search for hidden psychological truth.

Resistance and Transference   In classic psychoanalysis, the therapist seeks to understand the contents of the unconscious, but it's really the patient who needs the insight. The therapist can't simply relay the hidden meanings that he or she uncovers—explanation is not enough. Instead, the patient needs to face the emotional conflicts directly and relive them, and the therapist acts only as a kind of learned guide. But the journey toward insight is not an easy one, and the therapist must usually maneuver around a number of roadblocks. For example, patients typically go through periods in which they are uncooperative. They show **resistance**, which is an unconsciously motivated attempt to subvert or hinder the therapy.

Why would people try to block their own therapy? Hidden conflicts are anxiety provoking, so the patient uses defense mechanisms to reduce the anxiety. As Freud (1912/1964) put it, "Resistance accompanies the treatment at every step; every single association, every act of the patient's . . . represents a compromise between the forces aiming at cure and those opposing it" (p. 140). The resistance can express itself in a variety of ways; the patient might become inattentive, claim to forget dreams, skip therapy sessions, or argue with the directions suggested by the therapist.

Overcoming patient resistance is a major challenge for the therapist. Freud believed that a turning point comes when the patient begins to show a type of resistance called transference. **Transference** occurs when the patient starts to express thoughts or feelings toward the therapist that are actually representative of the way the patient feels about other significant people in his or her life. The patient "transfers" feelings of love, hate, or dependence onto a substitute figure, the therapist. Depending on the repressed feelings being tapped, the patient might turn the therapist into an object of passionate love or into a hated and despised individual (see ■ Figure 15.4).

Transference is a significant event in analysis because it means that the patient's hidden memories and conflicts are bubbling up close to the surface of consciousness. The patient is fully aware of the strong feelings he or she is experiencing—although the object of those feelings is inappropriate—and this gives the therapist an opportunity to help the patient work through what those feelings might mean. The patient is no longer in denial of powerful emotional urges—they're right there on the surface, ready to be dealt with. At the same time, it's important for the therapist to recognize that the patient's feelings at this point are symbolic. It's not uncommon for the patient to express feelings of strong sexual desire for the therapist, for example, and it would be inappropriate and unethical for the therapist to take them as literal truth (American Psychological Association, 2002a).

Current Applications   Classical psychoanalysis, as practiced by Freud and his contemporaries, is a very time-consuming process. It can take years for the analyst to excavate the secrets of the unconscious, and the patient needs to be properly prepared to accept the insights when they're delivered. Remember, the patient is setting up roadblocks throughout the process. So this kind of therapy is certainly far from a quick fix. It's not only time consuming but also expensive.

For these reasons, modern practitioners of psychoanalysis often streamline the therapeutic process (Coren, 2001). So-called brief forms of psychoanalysis encourage the therapist to take a more active role. Rather than waiting for patients to find insight themselves, the analyst is much more willing to offer interpretations in the early stages of therapy. Instead of waiting for transference to occur on its own, the analyst might actually encourage role playing in an attempt to get the patient to deal with deep-seated feelings. Using these techniques, progress can occur in weeks or months rather than requiring years of analysis (see Charman, 2004).

In addition to increasing the speed of treatment, modern versions of psychoanalysis are often tailored to meet the needs of the particular patient. No attempt is made to excavate and reconstruct the patient's entire personality; instead, the analyst focuses on selective defense mechanisms or conflicts that are more pertinent to the individual's particular symptoms. Often a greater emphasis is placed on improving the patient's interpersonal and social skills, and less attention is given to sexual and aggressive drives. Because these forms of treatment differ from classical psychoanalysis, they usually go by the more general name *psychodynamic therapy*.

Cognitive Therapies: Changing Maladaptive Beliefs

According to Freud's theory, a person's conscious thoughts, beliefs, and feelings are important primarily because they provide clues to the inner workings of the unconscious mind. **Cognitive therapies**, in contrast, place a much greater emphasis on the conscious beliefs themselves, rather than on what those beliefs may mean symbolically. Cognitive therapists assume that irrational beliefs and negative thoughts are primarily responsible for psychological disorders. If you can change the negative thoughts and beliefs, the psychological disorder will be changed as well.

Let's take depression as an example. People who are depressed usually don't think productively. They view themselves as essentially worthless and unlovable, and they see little chance that things will change for the better in the future. Thinking in such a way clouds the interpretation of normal events; everyday experiences are passed through a kind of negative filter, which means that depressed people often jump to irrational conclusions. For instance, a depressed woman whose husband arrives home slightly late from work might be immediately convinced that her husband is having an affair. The depressed student who fails the test might see the F as confirmation of a dull and stupid mind.

Cognitive therapists believe it's not direct experience, such as failure on a test, that actually produces depression. Think about it. It's not particularly difficult to fail a test—just stop going to class or refrain from studying. The F by itself doesn't logically mean much. You can fail a test for many reasons, and most of these reasons have nothing to do with your intrinsic worth as a human being. But in the mind of a depressed person, the event (failing the test) is accompanied by an irrational belief ("I'm incredibly stupid"), and it's this belief that leads to negative emotional consequences (feeling sad and depressed). Thus, it's the *interpretation* of the event, not the event itself, that leads to problems (Beck, 1991; Ellis, 1962, 1993; see ▌Figure 15.5).

Rational-Emotive Therapy The goal of cognitive therapy, then, is to remove these irrational beliefs. But how can irrational beliefs be changed? One technique is to challenge the beliefs directly, through active and aggressive confrontation. In **rational-emotive therapy**, developed by Albert Ellis, the therapist acts as a kind of

Resistance

"I know I'm late. I ... uh... couldn't find my dream notes."

Transference

"You really understand me. I cherish our time together."

▌FIGURE 15.4 Resistance and Transference
Freud believed that uncooperative actions by the client, which he called *resistance*, were unconsciously motivated attempts to subvert the therapeutic process. Through *transference*, Freud believed, clients transfer unconscious feelings for significant others onto the therapist.

cognitive therapies Treatments designed to remove irrational beliefs and negative thoughts that are presumed to be responsible for psychological disorders.

rational-emotive therapy A form of cognitive therapy in which the therapist acts as a kind of cross-examiner, verbally assaulting the client's irrational thought processes.

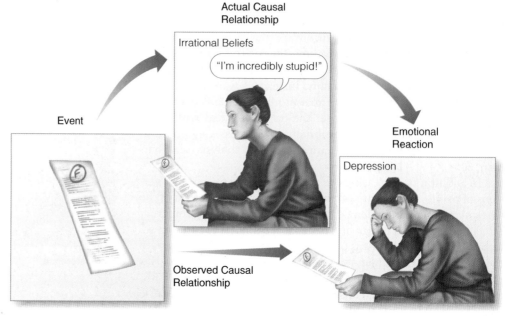

FIGURE 15.5 The Cognitive View of Depression
Cognitive therapists believe that internal thoughts and beliefs, not direct experience, lead to depression.

cross-examiner, verbally questioning the client's irrational thought processes. Here's an excerpt from an exchange between a therapist practicing rational-emotive therapy and a client showing signs of depressed thinking (from Walen, DiGuiseppe, & Dryden, 1992, pp. 204–205):

Therapist: You really believe that you're an utterly worthless person. By definition, that means that you're doing things poorly. Can you prove to me that that's correct?

Client: But I've failed at so many things.

Therapist: Just how many?

Client: I've lost my job, my wife is threatening to leave me, I don't get along with my kids—my whole life's a mess!

Therapist: Well, let me make two points. First of all, that's not every aspect of your life. Second, you seem to take total responsibility for all of those events, rather than only partial responsibility.

Client: But even if I'm not totally responsible, I'm still a failure.

Therapist: No. You've failed at those things. There are other things you haven't failed at.

Client: Like what?

Therapist: You still manage to get up every morning, you keep up appearances, you manage your finances well considering your economic plight—there's lots of things you do well.

Client: But they don't count!

Therapist: They don't count to you right now because you're overly concerned with negative issues, but they certainly *do* count. There are lots of people who don't do those things well. Are *they* failures?

Client: No, but . . .

Therapist: You know, Jack, you're one of the most conceited people I've ever met!

Client: What do you mean? I've just been telling you how lousy I am!

Therapist: The fact that you hold two different standards tells me how conceited you are. You hold much higher standards for yourself than for anyone else, which implies that you think you're much better than others. It's okay for those lowly slobs to have problems, but not a terrific person like you. Isn't that contradictory to your notion that you're worthless?

Client: Hmmmmm.

Therapist: How about instead of rating yourself as worthless, you just accept the failings that you do have and try your best to improve them?

Client: That sounds sensible.

Therapist: Let's take one of those problem areas now and see how we can improve things . . .

The important part of rational-emotive therapy is the therapist's attack on the rationality of the client's beliefs. The therapist points out the irrationality of the client's thought processes, sometimes in a confrontational manner, in the hope that his or her beliefs will ultimately be rejected, lessening their emotional consequences. The creator of rational-emotive therapy, Albert Ellis (1962), identified what he believed to be the irrational beliefs that affect most people who seek treatment for psychological disorders. The therapist tries initially to pinpoint which of these beliefs the client holds, so they can be changed accordingly. Here are a few examples from Ellis' list:

1. I must be loved and approved of by every significant person in my life, and if I'm not, it's awful.
2. It's awful when things are not the way I'd like them to be.
3. I should be very anxious about events that are uncertain or potentially dangerous.
4. I am not worthwhile unless I am thoroughly competent, adequate, and achieving at all times, or at least most of the time in at least one major area.
5. I need someone stronger than myself on whom to depend or rely.

What makes these beliefs irrational is their inflexibility and absoluteness. I *must* be loved and approved; I *must* be thoroughly competent; I *need* someone stronger than myself. The client firmly believes things must be a particular way or something awful or catastrophic will happen. Ellis has used the term *musterbation* to refer to this

> **CRITICAL THINKING**
>
> Where do you think these irrational beliefs come from? Is it possible that people are taught to think in absolute and inflexible ways by their parents, role models, or by the general culture?

Albert Ellis developed rational-emotive therapy to help free people from irrational thoughts and beliefs.

kind of irrational thinking. Any time you find yourself thinking that something *must* be a particular way, you're guilty of musterbation.

Beck's Cognitive Therapy   Although all forms of cognitive therapy focus on changing irrational thought processes, not all treatments are as direct and harsh as rational-emotive therapy. The rational-emotive therapist will essentially lecture—and in some instances even belittle—the client in an effort to attack faulty beliefs. Other cognitive therapies, such as the treatment procedures pioneered by Aaron Beck, take a more subtle tack. Rather than directly confronting clients with their irrational beliefs, Beck suggests it's more therapeutic for clients to identify negative forms of thinking themselves. The therapist acts as an adviser, or coinvestigator, helping clients discover their own unique kinds of faulty beliefs (Young, Weinberger, & Beck, 2001).

In a sense, clients who undergo Beck's cognitive therapy are asked to become psychological detectives. Part of the therapy involves extensive record keeping or "homework." Between therapeutic sessions, Beck asks his clients to record their automatic (or knee-jerk) thoughts and emotions in a notebook as they experience various situations during the day. Clients are then asked to write rational responses to those thoughts and emotions, as if they were scientists evaluating data. Is the thought justified by the actual event? What's the evidence for and against the conclusions that I reached? The therapist hopes clients will eventually discover the contradictions and irrationality in their thinking and realign their beliefs accordingly (see ❚ Figure 15.6).

Situation	Emotion(s)	Automatic Thought(s)	Rational Response	Outcome
1. Actual event leading to unpleasant emotion, or 2. Stream of thoughts, daydreams or recollections, leading to unpleasant emotion.	1. Specify sad/ anxious/ angry, etc. 2. Rate degree of emotion, 1–100.	1. Record automatic thought(s) that preceded emotion(s). 2. Rate belief in automatic thought(s), 0–100%.	1. Write rational response to automatic thought(s). 2. Rate belief in rational response, 0–100%.	1. Rerate belief in automatic thought(s), 0–100%. 2. Specify and rate subsequent emotions, 0–100.
7/15 Audre didn't return my phone call.	Anxious – 75 Sad – 55 Angry – 40	People don't like talking to me – 75% I'm incompetent. 65 %	She's out walking the dog so she hasn't had the time to call back. 70%	1. 35 % 15% 2. Relieved – 35

Explanation: When you experience an unpleasant emotion, note the situation that seemed to stimulate the emotion. (If the emotion occurred while you were thinking, daydreaming, etc., please note this.) Then note the automatic thought associated with the emotion. Record the degree to which you believe this thought: 0% = not at all, 100% = completely. In rating degree of emotion: 1 = a trace, 100 = the most intense possible.

❚ **FIGURE 15.6** Homework From a Cognitive Therapist
During cognitive therapy, people are often asked to record their automatic thoughts and emotions in a daily log, which requires the person to construct a rational response to the situation and then rerate the emotional reaction. (Adapted from "Depression," by A. T. Beck and J. E. Young. In D. H. Barlow (Ed.), *Clinical Handbook of Psychological Disorders: A Step by Step Treatment Manual*, pp. 667–668. Copyright ©1985 Guilford Press. Reprinted by permission.)

Humanistic Therapies: Treating the Human Spirit

In cognitive therapy, the goal is for clients to gain insight into their faulty and irrational ways of thinking. In classical psychoanalysis, the focus is on hidden conflicts and desires. In the final type of insight-based treatment that we'll consider—**humanistic therapy**—the purpose of therapy is to help the client gain insight into his or her own fundamental *self-worth* and *value* as a human. Therapy is a process of discovering one's own unique potential, one's ingrained capacity to grow and better oneself as a human being.

Humanistic therapists believe that all people are capable of controlling their own behavior—we can "fix" our own problems—because each of us ultimately has free will. The problem is that we sometimes lose sight of our potential because we're concerned about what others think of us and of our actions. We let others control how we think and feel. It is the therapist's job to help clients rediscover their natural self-worth—to help them get back in touch with their own true feelings, desires, and needs—by acting as a confidant and friend.

Client-Centered Therapy Humanistic therapies resemble cognitive therapies in their emphasis on conscious thought processes. But the intention of humanistic therapy is not to criticize or correct irrational thinking; quite the contrary, it's to be totally supportive in all respects. The therapist's proper role is to be nonjudgmental, which means the client should be accepted unconditionally. According to humanistic therapists such as Carl Rogers, the most effective form of therapy is **client centered**—it is the client, not the therapist, who ultimately holds the key to psychological health and happiness.

We discussed the theoretical ideas of humanistic psychologists, especially Carl Rogers, in some detail in Chapter 12. Rogers was convinced that most psychological problems originate from *incongruence*, which he defined as the discrepancy between our self-concept and the reality of our everyday experiences. People often hold an inaccurate view of themselves and their abilities, Rogers argued, because of an ingrained need for *positive regard*—they seek the approval, love, and companionship of

humanistic therapy Treatments designed to help clients gain insight into their fundamental self-worth and value as human beings.

client-centered therapy A form of humanistic therapy proposing that it is the client, not the therapist, who holds the key to psychological health and happiness; the therapist's role is to provide genuineness, unconditional positive regard, and empathy.

In humanistic therapies, the therapist tries to provide a completely supportive environment, which allows clients to rediscover their natural self-worth.

significant others (such as their parents). But these significant others tend to attach *conditions of worth* to their approval: They demand that we think and act in ways that may not be consistent with our true inner feelings. Improvement comes from providing a warm and supportive environment—without conditions of worth—that will encourage clients to accept themselves as they truly are.

In client-centered therapy, the therapist seeks to provide three essential core qualities to the client: *genuineness, unconditional positive regard,* and *empathy.* As the client's confidant, the therapist must be completely genuine—he or she must act without phoniness and express true feelings in an open and honest way. The second quality, unconditional positive regard, means that the therapist cannot place conditions of worth on the client. The therapist must be totally accepting and respectful of the client at all times, even if the client thinks and acts in a way that seems irrational or inappropriate. Remember, humanists believe all people are essentially good—they simply need to be placed in an environment that will nurture their natural tendencies toward positive growth.

CRITICAL THINKING

Think about the interactions you've had with a really close friend. Do you see any similarities to the client-centered approach advocated by Carl Rogers?

The third quality, empathy, is achieved when the therapist is able to truly understand and accept what the client is feeling—to see things from the client's perspective. Through empathy, the therapist acquires the capacity to reflect those feelings back in a way that helps the client gain insight into him- or herself. Consider the following interaction between Carl Rogers and one of his clients, a woman coming to grips with deep feelings of betrayal and hurt that she's tried to cover up (from Rogers, 1961, p. 94):

> *Client:* I never did really know. But it's—you know, it's almost a physical thing. It's—it's sort of as though I were looking within myself at all kinds of—nerve endings and bits of things that have been sort of mashed.
> *Rogers:* As though some of the most delicate aspects of you physically almost have been crushed or hurt.
> *Client:* Yes. And you know, I do get the feeling, "Oh, you poor thing." (Pause)
> *Rogers:* Just can't help but feel very deeply sorry for the person that is you.
> *Client:* I don't think I feel sorry for the whole person; it's a certain aspect of the thing.
> *Rogers:* Sorry to see the hurt.
> *Client:* Yeah.

Notice that Rogers reflects back the feelings of the client in a completely nonjudgmental fashion. He is seeking to understand and empathize with her feelings, thereby validating their existence and helping her to work through them. Notice also that it's the client, not the therapist, who is doing the analyzing. Client-centered therapy is founded on the idea that it's the clients who understand what truly hurts them psychologically, and it's the clients who have the best sense of how to proceed with therapy. All the therapist can do is provide the right kind of supportive environment and help clients recognize their own self-worth and trust their own instincts.

Other Humanistic Approaches   Client-centered therapy is the most popular form of humanistic therapy, but it's not the only one. *Gestalt therapy*, developed by Fritz Perls (1969; Perls, Hefferline, & Goodman, 1951), also places the burden of treatment in the hands of a "naturally good" client, but the approach is far less gentle and nondirective than client-centered therapy. In Gestalt therapy, clients are actively encouraged—even forced—to express their feelings openly. The emphasis is on the "here and now," and the therapist uses a variety of techniques to get the client to open up. For example, in the "empty chair" technique, clients are asked to project their feelings onto an empty chair in the room and then, literally, "talk" to those feelings (or to the person who is the source of those feelings). The idea is that only through fully understanding and overtly expressing oneself as a whole person (the word *Gestalt* roughly translates from the German as "whole"), can a person hope to take responsibility for those feelings and change them for the better.

Concept Review | Insight Approaches to Psychotherapy

APPROACH	PSYCHOPATHOLOGY ATTRIBUTED TO:	APPROACH TO TREATMENT FOR DEPRESSION
Psychoanalysis	Unconscious conflict, often rooted in childhood trauma	Debbie is depressed because of repressed fears that her parents don't really love her. They were not very affectionate while she was growing up. Her therapist tries to get Debbie to talk about her childhood relationship with her parents.
Cognitive	Conscious processes, including irrational beliefs and negative thoughts	Troy is having a tough time with his parents. They want him to major in business, which he hates. He feels like a terrible person for not following his parents' wishes; after all, they're paying his tuition. His therapist attempts to show him that disagreeing with his parents over his college major does not reflect badly on him as a person.
Humanistic	Problems with self-concept, or *incongruence* between self-concept and reality	Azra feels guilty. She plans on having only one child, but her parents would like lots of grandchildren, and Azra is an only child. Azra feels bad about herself and her failure to gain acceptance from her parents. Her therapist listens as Azra describes her feelings and tries to be warm, supportive, and open to what she is saying.

Another group of humanistic treatments is known collectively as *existential therapies*. Existential therapists believe psychological problems originate from the anxieties created by personal choices, such as whether to stay in school, get married, or quit a job. These fundamental choices—choices that relate to one's daily existence as a human being—are often difficult to face, and individuals may choose not to deal with them directly. Existential therapists encourage their clients to accept responsibility for these decisions, but in a supportive environment that encourages positive growth (Trull, 2005).

Group Therapy

Therapy is most commonly perceived as a one-on-one experience—you and the therapist sit alone in a room discussing your problems. But there is no principled reason why the therapies we've been discussing can't be conducted in group rather than individual sessions. In **group therapy**, you join other people who are undergoing treatment for a similar problem. Typically, group sessions include the therapist and somewhere between 4 and 15 clients, although there are few hard-and-fast rules for conducting group sessions; for example, in some cases there may be more than one therapist involved in the session (Yalom, 1995).

At first glance, the idea of group therapy seems troubling to most people. After all, who wants to talk about their personal problems in front of others? It's hard enough to open up to one person—the therapist—but at least he or she is a trained professional. Yet groups offer a number of advantages over individual sessions (MacKenzie, 2000). First, group therapy can be much more cost effective because the therapist can meet with multiple clients at the same time. Second, hearing other people talk about problems that match your own can be educational. You can learn about their strategies for coping with problems, and you can see firsthand how their symptoms compare to your own. Third, and perhaps most important, when you hear testimonies from other people, it's easier to realize that you're not alone—you're not the only person who is suffering from psychological problems. As you'll discover later in this chapter, empathy is a very important predictor of success in therapy; group settings can improve the trusting relationship you have with your therapist as well as with other people who share your problem.

group therapy A form of therapy in which several people are treated simultaneously in the same setting.

family therapy A form of group therapy in which the therapist treats the family as whole, as a kind of social *system*. The goals of the treatment are often to improve interpersonal communication and collaboration.

Family Therapy   One place where group therapy can be particularly appropriate is with the family. Rather than just treating an individual, in **family therapy** the therapist treats the family as whole, as a kind of social *system*. Clearly, if one member of a family suffers from a psychological problem, such as depression, all family members tend to be affected, and all can benefit from treatment. Moreover, the family environment can play either a positive or a negative role in helping a particular family member recover from a psychological problem. If the family understands the disorder and what's necessary for treatment, the odds of successful treatment go up considerably. Family therapists work on ways to improve interpersonal communication and collaboration among family members.

Test Yourself 15.2

Check your knowledge of insight therapies by matching each of the following statements to a type of therapy. Choose from among the following: psychoanalysis, Gestalt therapy, rational-emotive therapy, Beck's cognitive therapy, client-centered therapy, family therapy. *(You will find the answers in the Appendix.)*

1. "You think you're worthless? Well, I'm sitting here spending time with you so how can you be completely worthless? It's a ridiculous idea." _____

2. "I want you to keep a record of your thoughts, and the situations that produce them, so that you can judge whether those thoughts are really appropriate given the situation." _____

3. "Don't leave. Sit down and tell me again about the dream you had last night." _____

4. "You feel pain, deep pain, and you just can't get beyond the hurt that you feel inside." _____

5. "Talk to the chair . . . be the chair. Open up and let your true feelings come out." _____

6. "It's not just your problem. Each of you needs to communicate better and learn to work together to solve problems and avoid conflicts." _____

Treating the Environment: Behavioral Therapies

LEARNING GOALS
- Explain how conditioning techniques can be used in therapy.
- Explain how rewards and punishments can be used in therapy.

TRADITIONAL INSIGHT THERAPISTS address psychological problems by searching the minds of their clients for hidden conflicts, faulty beliefs, or damaged self-worth. But there are alternative approaches to therapy that essentially leave the mind alone. Behavioral therapies treat *behavior* rather than thoughts or memories. **Behavioral therapies** are designed to change unwanted or maladaptive behavior through the application of basic learning principles.

As we discussed in Chapter 14, many psychologists are convinced that psychological problems can be learned, or acquired, as a result of experience. Afraid of snakes? Perhaps you had a frightening experience at some point in your life—you may have been bitten by a snake—and this experience caused you to associate snakes with a negative emotional consequence. The snake isn't symbolic of some hidden sexual conflict—you just learned that when snakes are around you can be bitten; as a result, snakes have become "signals" for something bad.

If you believe that a psychological problem has been learned, it doesn't make a lot of sense to spend months or years searching for a hidden reason for the problem. It's better to treat the surface symptoms by learning something new. More productive actions need to be rewarded, or the negative associations you've formed need to be extinguished or counteracted. We'll consider several behavioral approaches in this section of the chapter, beginning with an effective technique for treating phobias that is based on the principles of *classical conditioning*.

behavioral therapies Treatments designed to change behavior through the use of established learning techniques.

CRITICAL THINKING
Can you think of a role that reinforcement might play in maintaining a phobia? Isn't it true that every time you stay away from a snake you avoid being bitten?

Conditioning Techniques

In Chapter 7 we discussed how dogs and people learn about the signaling properties of events. In Pavlov's classic experiments, dogs learned that one event, called the *conditioned stimulus*, signaled the occurrence of a second event, called the *unconditioned stimulus*. After pairing the conditioned stimulus and the unconditioned stimulus together in time, Pavlov found that his dogs responded to the conditioned stimulus in a way that anticipated the arrival of the unconditioned stimulus. For example, if a bell (the conditioned stimulus) was repeatedly presented just prior to food (the unconditioned stimulus), the dogs would begin to drool (the conditioned response) to the bell in anticipation of the food. Pavlov also showed that this conditioned response, the drooling, was sensitive to how well the conditioned stimulus predicted the occurrence of the unconditioned stimulus: If the bell was rung repeatedly after conditioning but the food was no longer presented, the dog eventually stopped drooling to the bell (a procedure Pavlov called *extinction*).

Now let's consider the case of a specific phobia, such as fear of snakes. Specific phobias are highly focused fears of objects or situations. When the feared object is present, it produces an intense anxiety reaction. In the 1920s, psychologist Mary Cover Jones proposed that such intense fear reactions can be treated as if they're classically conditioned responses. A snake produces fear because some kind of earlier experience has taught you to associate snakes with something fearful. Perhaps while standing near one as a child, your brother or sister screamed in terror, thereby scaring you. Jones' analysis suggested a treatment: It might be possible to eliminate phobias by teaching a new association between the feared object and something pleasurable. As she reported in 1924, she was able to use this logic to treat a little boy's fear of rabbits. She fed the boy some tasty food in the presence of the rabbit, which extinguished the association between the rabbit and an earlier negative experience and replaced it with a more pleasurable association (Jones, 1924).

Systematic Desensitization   The treatment pioneered by Mary Cover Jones was later refined by psychiatrist Joseph Wolpe into a technique known as **systematic desensitization** (Wolpe, 1958, 1982). As with Jones' approach, systematic desensitization uses *counterconditioning* as a way of reducing the fear and anxiety that have become associated with a specific object or event. The therapist attempts to replace the negative association with something relaxing and pleasurable. It's a gradual process that involves three major steps:

1. The therapist helps the client construct an *anxiety hierarchy*, which is an ordered list of situations that lead to fearful reactions. The client is asked to imagine a series of anxiety-provoking situations, beginning with the least fear-arousing and ending with the feared situation itself.
2. The therapist spends time teaching the client ways to achieve deep muscle relaxation. A state of deep relaxation is inconsistent with the experience of anxiety—you can't be afraid and relaxed at the same time.
3. With the help of the therapist the client then attempts to work through the anxiety hierarchy, forming an image of each of the scenes while maintaining the state of relaxation. The idea is to pair the images of fearful situations with the pleasurable state of relaxation so as to extinguish the old negative association and replace it with something relaxing.

Let's imagine you have a deep, irrational fear of flying in an airplane. Treatment starts by having you create a list of flying-related situations that are increasingly frightful. Next, you would receive lessons in how to relax yourself fully. Finally, you would begin working through your hierarchy. Perhaps you might start by simply imagining a picture of an airplane. If you can remain relaxed under these conditions, the therapist will direct you to move up the hierarchy to the next most stressful situation—perhaps imagining the airplane actually taking off. Gradually, over time, you

Psychologist Mary Cover Jones proposed that intense fear reactions could be treated as if they were classically conditioned responses.

systematic desensitization A technique that uses counterconditioning and extinction to reduce the fear and anxiety that have become associated with a specific object or event.

CRITICAL THINKING

In what ways is shaping, which we discussed in Chapter 7, similar to and different from the procedures of systematic desensitization?

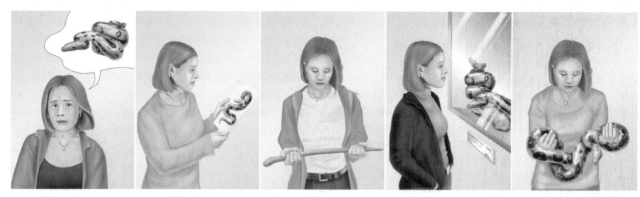

FIGURE 15.7 Systematic Desensitization
After learning relaxation techniques, the client works slowly through an anxiety hierarchy. At first she simply imagines the feared object. Eventually, the relaxation response can be maintained while she experiences the actual feared situation.

will learn to relax in increasingly more stressful situations, even to the point where you can imagine yourself strapped in the seat as the plane rolls down the runway. If you can stay relaxed—which is incompatible with fear and anxiety—the fearful association with planes should extinguish and be replaced by an association that is neutral or positive. Eventually, when you move to a real situation, the learning will generalize and you will no longer be afraid to fly in a plane. This type of therapy is summarized in ▌Figure 15.7 using another specific phobia—the fear of snakes.

The idea that we can reduce our fear by confronting the very thing that we fear the most has proven to be extremely effective in the treatment of phobic disorders. Interestingly, though, it turns out that repeated exposure to the feared object or event may be what matters most. Many clinicians today find that neither progressive muscle relaxation nor construction of the hierarchy is necessary for substantial improvements to occur. Simple exposure to the feared object is often sufficient for improvement (see McNally, 2007).

Aversion Therapy Systematic desensitization attempts to eliminate unpleasant associations by replacing them with pleasant ones. In **aversion therapy**, the therapist tries to replace a pleasant reaction to a harmful stimulus with something unpleasant, such as making the client feel bad rather than good after smoking a cigarette or having a drink of alcohol. Once again, the idea is to use a kind of counterconditioning, but the goal is to make the target situation something to be avoided rather than approached.

In the case of alcohol dependency, it's possible to give people a drug (Antabuse) that causes them to be become nauseated and vomit if they take a drink of alcohol. The drug interacts with alcohol, causing extreme discomfort. Under these conditions, the person who is drinking learns a new association that helps combat the alcohol dependency—drinking leads to an unpleasant feeling. A similar technique can be used for smoking, wherein drugs containing certain chemicals leave an extremely bad taste in one's mouth after smoking. The old association connecting pleasure with smoking is replaced by a new association that connects smoking with a terrible taste.

Aversion therapy can be quite effective if the client takes the aversive drug for a sufficient period of time. However, people who undergo aversion therapy are often reluctant to continue the treatment unless they're closely supervised. If the client stops the treatment and returns to normal drinking or smoking, the newly learned negative association will extinguish and be replaced by the old, positive association. Ethical concerns have also been raised about this form of treatment. Although those who participate do so voluntarily, they are often people who are desperately seeking a solution to their problems. Because the treatment directly induces extremely unpleasant experiences, many therapists are convinced that it should be used only as a treatment of last resort.

aversion therapy A treatment for replacing a positive reaction to a harmful stimulus, such as alcohol, with something negative, such as feeling nauseated. Aversion therapy replaces positive associations with negative ones, such as making a smoker feel bad rather than good after having a cigarette.

© John Chiasson/Getty Images

Aversion therapy replaces positive associations with negative ones, such as making a smoker feel bad rather than good after having a cigarette.

Applying Rewards and Punishments

As we discussed in Chapter 7, it's possible to change behavior by teaching people about the direct consequences of their behavior. You can be shaped, through the application of rewards and punishments, away from abnormal actions and toward more normal behaviors. Although aversion therapy involves elements of punishment—the act of drinking is followed by an extremely unpleasant consequence—its goal is mainly to replace prior pleasant emotional associations with unpleasant ones. Behavioral therapies that use rewards and punishments are designed to modify specific unwanted behaviors by teaching people about the consequences of their actions.

Token Economies   Shaping behavior through the delivery of rewards has proven to be particularly effective in institutional settings. When people are confined to mental hospitals or other kinds of institutions, it's usually because they can't cope successfully without constant supervision. If people can't care for themselves—if they don't wash, eat proper foods, or protect themselves from harm—they need a structured environment around them. In institutional settings, therapists have found that setting up token economies—in which patients are rewarded for behaving appropriately—can be quite effective in teaching patients how to cope with the realities of everyday life (e.g., Seegert, 2003).

In a **token economy**, institutionalized patients are rewarded with small tokens (such as poker chips) whenever they engage in an appropriate activity. Certain rules are established and explained to the patient, which determine when tokens are handed out (or taken away). For example, if Forrest, who is suffering from schizophrenia, takes his medication without complaint, he is given a plastic token. Candita might receive tokens for getting out of bed in the morning, washing her hair, and brushing her teeth. The tokens can later be exchanged for certain privileges, such as being able to watch a DVD or stay in a private room. Similarly, if a patient acts in an inappropriate manner, the therapist might choose to take tokens away as a form of punishment. This technique is called a token *economy* because it represents a voluntary exchange of goods and services—the patient exchanges appropriate behavior for the privileges that tokens provide.

token economy A type of behavioral therapy in which patients are rewarded with small tokens when they act in an appropriate way; the tokens can then be exchanged for certain privileges.

Token economies are highly successful in helping patients develop the skills they'll need to function well inside and outside of the institution. Not only do the everyday maintenance activities of the patients improve, but social behavior and even vocational skills can be shaped using token rewards. Token economies have also been used in classroom settings to reward children for showing appropriate individual and group behavior and even to increase participation in large college courses (Boniecki & Moore, 2003).

Punishment Token economies tend to be based primarily on the application of reward as a way of changing unwanted behaviors. But as we've seen, punishment can also be an effective way to teach people about the consequences of their behavior. And, indeed, there are instances in which therapists feel that following a behavior with an aversive stimulus (sometimes even a shock) or removing something pleasant is justified. Consider someone who is extremely self-destructive—perhaps a disturbed child who continually bangs his or her head against the wall. Under these conditions, the safe delivery of an aversive event has been shown to reduce these self-destructive behaviors, thereby preventing serious injury (Lovaas, 1987; Lovaas et al., 1973).

But punishment is rarely used as the sole kind of behavioral intervention, for several reasons. First, punishment has side effects—for example, it can damage the working relationship between the therapist and the client. Second, punishment by itself only teaches someone what not to do; it doesn't teach someone the appropriate way to act. Third, punishing someone who is in the grips of a psychological disorder raises ethical concerns. We can't be sure the person on the receiving end of the aversive event approves of the treatment, even though the therapist may be convinced it's in the client's best interest.

Social Skills Training

Serious psychological disorders can have a devastating effect on a person's ability to function successfully in virtually all environments, especially social ones. In schizophrenia, for example, social or occupational dysfunction is one of the defining characteristics of the disorder. Patients with schizophrenia tend to isolate themselves from others, and when they do interact socially, they typically act in odd or peculiar ways.

In such cases, therapists face a practical problem: How can they improve the social skills of the person with the disorder? This is a particularly important concern

Concept Review | Behavioral Therapies

CONDITIONING TECHNIQUES

APPROACH	BASED ON THE IDEA THAT:	THERAPEUTIC APPROACH
Systematic desensitization	Intense anxiety is the result of classically conditioned associations.	Uses counterconditioning to reduce the fear and anxiety that are associated with a particular object or event. The therapist attempts to replace a negative association with something relaxing and pleasurable.
Aversion therapy	Problem behaviors are based partly in classically conditioned associations.	The therapist tries to replace a pleasant reaction to a harmful stimulus with an unpleasant reaction. For example, the pleasurable reaction associated with smoking is replaced by a new association between smoking and a terrible taste.

REWARDS AND PUNISHMENTS

Token economies	Behavior can be changed by teaching people about the direct consequences of their behavior.	Therapist and patient have a voluntary exchange of goods and services—the patient exchanges appropriate behavior for privileges provided by tokens.
Punishment	Behavior can be changed by teaching people about the direct consequences of their behavior.	An inappropriate (e.g., self-injurious) behavior is followed by an aversive stimulus or by the removal of a pleasant stimulus.

in schizophrenia, which is often difficult to treat. Even with effective medications, many patients suffer relapses of symptoms, and some symptoms of the disorder, including social withdrawal and flat affect, are not always affected by conventional psychoactive drugs. For these reasons, therapists sometimes turn to *social skills training*, which is a form of behavioral therapy that uses modeling and reinforcement to shape appropriate adjustment skills.

Social skills training is usually a multistep process. To teach conversational skills, for example, the therapist might begin with a discussion of appropriate verbal responses in a conversation, followed by a videotaped demonstration. The patient is then asked to "role play" an actual conversation, and the therapist provides either corrective feedback or positive reinforcement. "Homework" might then be assigned, in which the patient is encouraged to practice his or her skills outside of the training session, preferably in new situations. If the training is conducted in an institutional setting, such as a mental hospital, the therapist must monitor the patient's subsequent interactions carefully so that appropriate reinforcement can be delivered.

Social skills training usually takes place over many sessions, and it's often combined with other forms of treatment (such as psychoactive drugs or some form of insight therapy). Reviews of the research literature indicate that the application of these simple learning principles—positive reinforcement and modeling—can lead to significant improvements in social functioning, and in the quality of life for individuals affected with psychological disorders (Bustillo et al., 2001). You should understand that one of the most important goals of any therapy is to improve global functioning; at times focusing on specific symptoms—even something as simple as knowing how to answer a casual question in an appropriate way—can make an enormous difference in the life of a troubled individual.

Test Yourself 15.3

Check your knowledge about behavioral therapies by answering the following questions. (You will find the answers in the Appendix.)

1. According to the classical conditioning account of phobias, the feared stimulus, such as a snake, acts as a(n):
   a. Unconditioned stimulus.
   b. Conditioned stimulus.
   c. Conditioned response.
   d. Conditioned reinforcer.
2. In systematic desensitization, the fear that has become associated with a specific object or event is reduced through:
   a. Counterconditioning and extinction.
   b. Second-order conditioning.
   c. Delivery of an aversive consequence.
   d. Token rewards.
3. Which of the following is not a major concern in aversion therapy?
   a. Clients cannot truly give informed and voluntary consent.
   b. Effective punishments can't be delivered because pain thresholds are high.
   c. Clients are often reluctant to continue treatment.
   d. Newly learned negative associations can extinguish.
4. In a token economy, the token acts as which of the following?
   a. Conditioned stimulus
   b. Punishment
   c. Conditioned inhibitor
   d. Reinforcement

Evaluating and Choosing Psychotherapy

LEARNING GOALS
- Discuss the major findings of clinical evaluation research.
- Describe the factors that are common across psychotherapies.

WHEN PEOPLE MAKE THE DECISION to enter therapy, they do so because they're in need of help. Carlos is unable to advance his career in sales because of his extreme fear of flying; Julie lives a life of quiet desperation, mostly alone in her room, because she suffers from a social phobia. We've now examined the major types of therapy, but we've said little about their relative effectiveness. How well does psychotherapy actually work? Are all forms of therapy equally effective, or do some forms of therapy work better than others?

To assess the effectiveness of any therapy requires carefully controlled research. As discussed in Chapter 2, just because someone's behavior changes after a manipulation doesn't mean it was the manipulation that caused the change. Someone might enter therapy and leave improved some time later, but the change could have occurred for reasons unrelated to the actual treatment. Perhaps the person simply improved spontaneously over time. Most people who get the flu improve over time—even if they never see a doctor—and it could be that the same kind of thing happens with psychological disorders. A control group—in which no treatment is given—is needed to confirm that the therapy was indeed responsible for the improvement. Fortunately, a number of such controlled research studies have been conducted.

Clinical Evaluation Research

Let's begin by considering a famous example of a clinical evaluation study (Sloane et al., 1975). In this study, conducted at a Philadelphia psychiatric clinic in the mid-1970s, men and women who were seeking treatment primarily for anxiety disorders were assigned at random to one of three treatment conditions. One group of patients was assigned to therapists experienced in the practice of *psychodynamic* techniques (the analysis of unconscious conflicts and memories); a second group was assigned to experienced *behavioral* therapists (using systematic desensitization and other learning-based techniques); a third group—the *control* group—was placed on a "waiting list" and received no immediate treatment. After four months, an independent team of therapists, who were unaware of the treatment assignments, was called in to evaluate the progress of the patients in each of the three groups.

The results were somewhat surprising. The good news is that the therapies clearly worked. As shown in ▌Figure 15.8, the people who were given either psychodynamic or behavioral therapy showed significantly more improvement after four months than the people who were left on the waiting list (although it's interesting to note that the waiting list people improved also). But there were no significant differences between the two treatment conditions—the behavioral approach worked just as well as the psychodynamic approach. Even more surprising was the finding that eight months later, at a year-end follow-up assessment, the patients in the control group had essentially caught up with the treatment patients—they had improved enough to be comparable to the patients in the other two groups. Thus, the treatments worked, but it seems that their primary effect was simply to speed up natural improvement.

Meta-Analysis The Philadelphia study is important because it's an example of how evaluation research should be conducted—random assignment to groups, the use of a no-treatment control, and an independent assessment procedure (Wolpe, 1975). Since that study was first reported, hundreds of other studies have been conducted (although not all have included the same rigorous control procedures). Rather than picking and choosing from among these studies, mental health professionals often rely on a technique called meta-analysis to help them draw conclusions about this research. In a **meta-analysis**, many different studies are compared statistically on some common evaluation measure. The comparison standard is usually something called an *effect size*, which is essentially a standardized measure of the difference between treatment and control conditions.

In one of the first extensive meta-analytic studies, Smith and colleagues analyzed the results of 475 research studies designed to evaluate one or more forms of psychotherapy (Smith & Glass, 1977; Smith, Glass, & Miller, 1980). Although the individual

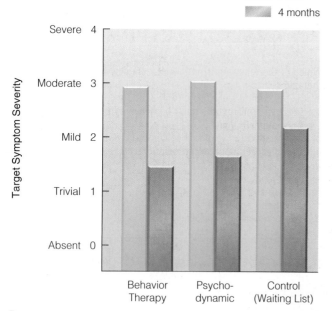

▌FIGURE 15.8 Evaluating Forms of Treatment
After four months, people receiving therapy showed significantly less severe symptoms than people in the control group, but there were no significant differences in the results of behavioral and psychodynamic therapy.
(Data from Sloane et al., 1975)

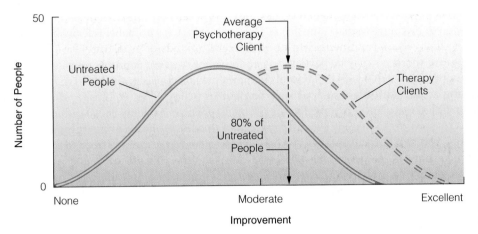

studies covered a wide range of psychological problems and therapeutic techniques, in each case it was possible to compare a treatment condition to some kind of control condition (usually an untreated group). Smith and colleagues reached two major conclusions from their meta-analysis of the data. First, there was a consistent and large treatment advantage (see ▌Figure 15.9). People who experienced some kind of active psychotherapy were better off, on average, than roughly 80% of the people who were left untreated. Second, when the various kinds of psychotherapy were compared, few, if any, differences were found. It really didn't matter whether the patient was receiving an insight therapy or a behavioral therapy—all produced the same amount of improvement (see also Wampold et al., 1997).

There have been hundreds of other attempts to meta-analyze evaluation studies. Some have sought to exercise more control over the research quality of the studies included (Lipsey & Wilson, 1993); others have attempted to extend the areas of examination to include client characteristics, experience of the therapist, or length of the treatment (Lambert & Bergin, 1994). In general, the findings support two main conclusions: Therapy works, and the effects of therapy are long-lasting. For example, one review of meta-analysis studies, which examined some 302 published meta-analyses, found that only six produced negative effect sizes (which means that patients undergoing therapy actually got worse than untreated controls), and that the vast majority were overwhelmingly positive (Lipsey & Wilson, 1993).

Controversies There is widespread agreement among professionals that psychotherapy works, but clinical evaluation studies remain the subject of debate. For example, what should constitute the proper evaluation "control"? Let's return to the Philadelphia experiment in which two treatment groups (psychodynamic and behavioral) were compared with a group containing people who were left on a waiting list. Remember, the control patients actually got considerably better over time, to a point at which, after a year, they had improved to the same levels as the treatment groups. Psychologists call this kind of improvement in the absence of treatment **spontaneous remission**, and it's been estimated that psychological disorders may improve on their own as much as 30% or more of the time (Eysenck, 1952; Lambert & Bergin, 1994).

But did the people who were left on the waiting list in the Philadelphia experiment really receive no treatment? This is a difficult question to answer—it depends on how you define "treatment." Although these people received no formal psychotherapy, they were given initial psychological tests and were called frequently and given support. Their simple involvement in the study, along with the expectation that they would be receiving some help, may itself have acted as a kind of therapy. Similar effects are commonly found with many placebo controls, in which clients are given attention and support but not formal therapy. Many critics have argued that these no-treatment conditions actually involve factors—such as social support—that are common to most forms of therapy (see Lambert, 2005). We'll return to this issue in the next section.

meta-analysis A statistical technique used to compare findings across many different research studies; comparisons are based on some common evaluation measure, such as the difference between treatment and control conditions.

spontaneous remission Improvement in a psychological disorder without treatment—that is, simply as a function of the passage of time.

The reported finding that all types of psychotherapy are equally effective has also proven to be controversial (Hunsley & Di Giulio, 2002). It's probably reasonable to assume that certain treatments work best for certain kinds of problems. For example, cognitive therapies may be particularly effective for treating depression or its relapse (Vittengl et al., 2007), and behavioral therapies may be consistently effective for combating anxiety disorders such as specific phobias (Choy, Fyer, & Lipsitz, 2007). But even if the treatment is matched to the problem, client variables can also influence the effectiveness of the therapy. Not all people have the desire or capacity to respond to rational, verbal arguments of the type used by some cognitive therapists, or to the probing questions of the psychoanalyst. As a result, it's very difficult to conduct an evaluation study that properly takes all of these factors into account. Moreover, often one finds a correlation between a particular form of therapy and an effective outcome, but the causal mechanisms behind the improvement remain mysterious (Kazdin, 2007).

Common Factors Across Psychotherapies

Clinical researchers have also considered the possibility that there may be common, nonspecific factors shared by all therapies, regardless of surface differences. Although the various therapies we've considered seem to be very different, and they're clearly driven by very different assumptions about human psychology, they do share features in common (Grencavage & Norcross, 1990; Rosenzweig, 1936). Michael Lambert and Allen Bergin (1994) have suggested that these common factors can be grouped into three main categories: *support factors*, *learning factors*, and *action factors*.

Support Factors   Virtually all therapies that produce positive outcomes provide tangible support for the client. People who enter therapy find themselves face to face with a person who is willing to accept and understand their problems. Both the therapist and the client have a common goal, which is to help the client get better. Regardless of their theoretical orientation—psychodynamic, cognitive, behavioral, or humanistic—effective therapists are clearly interested in listening to and reassuring their clients and in developing a positive, trusting relationship. A number of studies have found a strong correlation between the amount of empathy that the therapist establishes with the client and the effectiveness of the treatment (Lafferty, Beutler, & Crago, 1991).

It's also important that the client and the therapist form a *therapeutic alliance*, which means that the client and the therapist must work together to deal with the problems at hand. If the client perceives the therapeutic alliance to be strong, and works hard to maintain a strong alliance, there is a greater chance that the therapy will be successful (Zuroff & Blatt, 2006).

Learning Factors   When people go through therapy, they learn things about themselves. They learn about their thought processes, or about their behavior, or about important factors in their past that might be contributing to current discomforts. Effective therapists often act as mirrors, reflecting a client's beliefs and actions in ways that provide critical insight. Regardless of the method of treatment, effective therapists also give feedback about how various experiences relate to one another. They point out connections among experiences—how we might behave and think similarly across different situations. People are often helped because they're given a reason or a rationale for their problems.

To take a case in point, consider the homework assignments common in cognitive therapy. Here, the client is simply asked to list the specific situations that led to unpleasant thoughts (emotions) and to provide alternative responses. Even without the development of rational response alternatives, it's useful simply to know the particular situations that make you upset or unhappy. If you learn, for instance, that you tend to get emotionally upset regularly after talking to an old boyfriend or girlfriend, then you can work to avoid encounters in the future. Knowledge is useful, and therapy is an excellent vehicle for learning things about yourself.

Action Factors Finally, all forms of therapy ultimately provide people with a set of specific suggestions for action. Troubled clients might be asked to face their fears, take risks, or directly test irrational beliefs. They might be given specific strategies for coping with anxiety or training in how to relax. Irrespective of the specific suggestions, providing clients with a tangible course of action may be sufficient to give them hope and allow them to feel in control of their problem.

Practical Solutions

Choosing a Therapist

At some point in your life, you might find yourself in need of a psychotherapist. Perhaps you'll experience a simple problem in living, or maybe something more serious. What should you do? Given our discussion about the relative effectiveness of the various treatment options, it might seem natural to conclude that it doesn't make much difference whom you choose. But remember, one of the best predictors of treatment success is the amount of empathy between the client and the therapist. Therefore, it's critical that you find someone you trust and with whom you feel comfortable interacting. The level of trust you feel with the therapist is very important;

don't be afraid to shop around a bit to find the right person.

Currently, most psychotherapists describe themselves as *eclectic* in their orientation. This means they're willing to pick and choose from among treatment options to find the techniques that work best for the individual client. It used to be the case that therapists would align themselves with a particular approach or "school"—such as psychoanalysis or behavior therapy—but in one survey of 800 therapists, 68% of those responding described their orientation as eclectic (Jensen, Bergin, & Greaves, 1990). You can expect most therapists to be flexible in their

approach, and if one form of treatment is not yielding results—or if you feel uncomfortable with the approach—you can expect the therapist to be open to trying something different. Effective therapy requires open communication, and the therapist is dependent on your feedback as a client throughout the treatment process.

Mental health professionals also recognize that cultural factors are important in both the diagnosis and the treatment of psychological disorders (Gaw, 2001). For many years, cultural barriers made it difficult for members of ethnic minorities to use and benefit from mental health resources. Language differences between the client and the therapist clearly undermine effective communication, as do differences between the therapist's and the client's worldview. To take a case in point, many Asians feel uncomfortable with open self-disclosure and the expression of emotions. As a result, it's unlikely that many Asians will benefit from Western therapists who encourage "letting it all hang out" (Sue, Zane, & Young, 1994).

Does this mean you should always seek a therapist with a cultural background identical to your own? Not necessarily. For one thing, there is still a shortage of therapists from ethnic minorities in the United States (Mays & Albee, 1992). This means that finding a cultural match may be difficult. Moreover, with the increased exposure to cultural influences, many therapists are now making concerted efforts to become culturally sensitive. In fact, special training programs are now available to help therapists break down some of the barriers that exist for clients from diverse cultural backgrounds. By gaining knowledge about a variety of customs and lifestyles and working directly with culturally diverse clients, therapists hope to remove barriers to effective empathy.

© Michael Newman/PhotoEdit

Cultural barriers sometimes prevent members of ethnic minorities from benefiting from mental health resources. It's essential for a therapist to be sensitive to a client's cultural background and general worldview.

Test Yourself 15.4

Check your knowledge about evaluating and choosing psychotherapy by deciding whether each of the following statements is True or False. *(You will find the answers in the Appendix.)*

1. Psychological disorders may improve on their own as much as 30% or more of the time. *True or False?*
2. According to most meta-analytic studies, people who experience active psychotherapy are better off, on average, than roughly 80% of the people who are left untreated. *True or False?*
3. Most evaluation studies show that specific disorders, such as depression, require specific forms of therapy, such as psychoanalysis. *True or False?*
4. One factor common to all forms of psychotherapy is the need to investigate the traumatic events of childhood. *True or False?*
5. In choosing a therapist, perhaps the most important factor is empathy—finding someone you trust and with whom you feel comfortable. *True or False?*

Review *Psychology for a Reason*

In this chapter, we've discussed the various tools therapists use to treat psychological disorders. In each case, the goal of the therapist is to find a way to improve the client's ability to function successfully in the world. As you've seen, most forms of therapy address one or more of the three basic factors thought to contribute to psychological disorders: biological factors, cognitive factors, and environmental factors.

Treating the Body Therapies that use medical interventions to treat the symptoms of psychological problems are called *biomedical therapies*. The idea that psychological disorders might be treated as "illnesses," in the same way that physicians might treat the common cold, has a long history in human thought. The most popular form of biomedical therapy is drug therapy, in which certain medications are given to affect thought and mood by altering the actions of neurotransmitters in the brain. Antipsychotic drugs, for example, reduce the symptoms of schizophrenia by acting as antagonists to the neurotransmitter dopamine in the brain. The antidepressant drug Prozac acts on the neurotransmitter serotonin, and antianxiety drugs—tranquilizers—are believed to act on neurotransmitters in

the brain that have primarily inhibitory effects.

In the event that drug therapies fail, mental health professionals sometimes turn to other forms of biomedical intervention, particularly electroconvulsive therapy (ECT) and psychosurgery. Shock therapy is used to treat severe forms of depression, but usually only if more conventional forms of treatment have failed. No one is completely sure how or why the administration of electric shock affects mood, but there's wide agreement that ECT works for many patients. Even more controversial than ECT is the use of psychosurgery, in which some portion of the brain is destroyed or altered in an attempt to eliminate the symptoms of a mental disorder. The infamous prefrontal lobotomies of yesteryear are no longer conducted (partly because they produced unacceptable side effects), but some kinds of surgical intervention in the brain are still used.

Treating the Mind In *insight therapy*, the psychotherapist attempts to treat psychological problems by helping clients gain insight, or self-knowledge, into the contents of their thought processes. Usually, this insight is obtained through prolonged verbal, one-on-one

interactions between the therapist and the client. Perhaps the best-known form of insight therapy is Freudian psychoanalysis. The goal of psychoanalysis is to help the client uncover and relive conflicts that have been hidden in the unconscious mind. The psychoanalyst uses such techniques as free association and dream analysis to help probe the contents of the unconscious. As hidden conflicts begin to surface during the course of therapy, the client will typically show what Freud called resistance—an attempt to hinder the progress of therapy—and transference, in which the client transfers feelings about others onto the therapist.

Cognitive therapists believe that psychological problems arise primarily from irrational beliefs and thought processes. The therapist attempts to change the client's negative beliefs and thoughts by actively attacking them in verbal exchanges. The therapist points out the irrationality of negative thoughts, using evidence where possible, in the hope that the client will reject the beliefs, thereby lessening their emotional consequences. *Humanistic therapies* have a quite different goal. Here, the idea is to help clients gain insight into their own self-worth and value as humans. It is the client, not the therapist, who holds the key to self-improvement. Humanistic therapists view therapy as a process of discovering one's natural tendencies toward growth and free will. In client-centered therapy, the therapist tries to provide an approving and nonjudgmental environment, thereby allowing the client to better recognize and trust his or her own true instincts.

Treating the Environment *Behavioral therapies* are designed to treat actual behavior rather than inner thought processes. Behavioral therapists assume that many kinds of psychological problems have been learned and can be treated through the application of learning principles. With many counterconditioning techniques, for example, the therapist attempts to replace learned associations that are negative with new, pleasurable associations. Thus, in systematic desensitization, specific phobias are treated by having the subject (1) construct an anxiety hierarchy of

fear-inducing situations, (2) learn relaxation techniques, and (3) work through the anxiety hierarchy, imagining each of the scenes while maintaining a feeling of relaxation. Pairing the feared object with relaxation is intended to extinguish the old, negative association and replace it with something pleasurable. Other behavioral therapies make use of rewards and punishments to change behavior. In token economies, patients are rewarded with small tokens whenever they engage in normal or appropriate behaviors. The tokens can then be exchanged later for more tangible rewards or privileges.

Evaluating and Choosing Psychotherapy Evaluating any form of psychotherapy requires controlled research in which treatment groups are compared with appropriate control conditions. Hundreds of such studies have been conducted, and meta-analyses of their results typically reach two main conclusions. First, people who receive

psychotherapy do significantly better than those left untreated. Second, there are few, if any, advantages for one type of psychotherapy over another.

One reason most forms of treatment are equally effective may be that common factors are shared by all psychotherapies. These common factors can be grouped into three main categories: support, learning, and action. All therapists provide some kind of support for their clients, and therapist empathy has been shown to be important to outcome success. All forms of therapy also help clients learn about themselves and their behavior, and clients are provided with specific prescriptions for action or behavior change. In choosing a therapist, it's critical that you find someone you trust and with whom you feel comfortable interacting. Cultural factors are also important, because for therapy to work the therapist must be sensitive to the client's cultural worldview.

Active Summary *(You will find the answers in the Appendix.)*

Treating the Body: Biomedical Therapies

• Most typical antipsychotic drugs work primarily on the neurotransmitter (1) _____ and are used to treat schizophrenia. These medications, which include chlorpromazine (Thorazine), are limited in their effectiveness, and side effects may include (2) _____ dyskinesia, which produces disabling involuntary movements. Clozapine and risperidone are newer antipsychotics that act on several neurotransmitters and help people who don't respond to typical antipsychotic medication. (3) _____ drugs also modulate the effectiveness of neurotransmitters, particularly norepinephrine and (4) _____. (5) _____ disorders have traditionally been treated with the common salt (6) _____ carbonate. (7) _____ medications, or tranquilizers, are in a class of drugs called benzodiazepines, which work primarily on the neurotransmitter (8) _____.

• Many professionals believe that (9) _____ therapy (ECT) is a reasonably (10) _____ and effective treatment 50 to 70% of the time for (11) _____ depression, though it is usually used as a last resort. The treatment is controversial for a number of reasons. No one completely understands why it is effective, and it can produce temporary side effects such as (12) _____ and memory loss.

• (13) _____ affects behavior by destroying or altering (14) _____ tissue. (15) _____ lobotomy (now in disrepute) produces "calming" effects in disturbed patients. Although cingulotomy is sometimes used to treat obsessive–(16) _____ disorder and severe forms of depression, psychosurgery is performed very (17) _____.

Treating the Mind: Insight Therapies

• Sigmund Freud believed that (18) _____ brings hidden memories and impulses to awareness, freeing the client from unwanted thoughts and behaviors. The tools used to uncover unconscious conflicts include (19) _____ association and (20) _____ analysis. (21) _____, seen in unconsciously motivated attempts to hinder therapy, and (22) _____, where a client begins to express thoughts and feelings toward the therapist that are really how he or she feels about other people, also provide clues about (23) _____ conflicts. Modern psychoanalysts (24) _____ the therapeutic process, which is often tailored to meet specific individual needs.

• (25) _____ therapists emphasize the contents of the (26) _____ mind, believing that irrational beliefs and negative thoughts influence our interpretations of events. In (27)_____-emotive therapy the therapist cross-examines the client, challenging (28) _____ thought processes. Aaron Beck's (29) _____ therapy helps clients more subtly to identify their own faulty beliefs through record-keeping and other types of homework.

• In (30) _____ therapy, clients gain insight into their own fundamental self-worth and (31) _____. Client-(32) _____ therapy supports the client in all respects. The key to improvement is a warm supportive environment that helps the client overcome (33) _____, a discrepancy between the (34) _____-_____ and the reality of our everyday experiences. The therapist provides genuineness, unconditional (35) _____ regard, and empathy. (36) _____ therapy is a version of humanistic therapy that encourages and even forces clients to express their feelings openly.

• (37) _____ therapy brings together clients who are experiencing (38) _____ problems. (39) _____ therapy treats the family as a social system; the therapist helps members improve their (40) _____ communication styles and learn to collaborate with each other.

Treating the Environment: Behavioral Therapies

• A person with a phobia associates a certain object or situation with (41) _____. (42) _____ techniques may be used to change the association to something plea-

surable. In (43) _____ _____ the therapist uses (44) _____ to systematically associate relaxation with feared objects, as rated in an anxiety (45) _____. In (46) _____ therapy a pleasant reaction to a harmful stimulus, such as alcohol, is replaced with an unpleasant reaction and results in a new association.

• People can be shaped by (47) _____ and (48) _____ to give up abnormal behaviors in exchange for functional ones. In a (49) _____ economy, whenever institutionalized patients engage in an appropriate activity they are rewarded with tokens that they can exchange for (50) _____. (51) _____ may also be effective in teaching people to understand the (52) _____ of their actions and is sometimes used to discourage self-injurious behavior. (53) _____ skills training is a form of behavioral therapy that uses modeling and reinforcement to shape appropriate adjustment skills.

Evaluating and Choosing Psychotherapy

• A study that compared psychodynamic and (54) _____ therapies with a control condition demonstrated that therapy clearly worked, but that there were no reliable (55) _____ in the effectiveness of the two approaches. A (56) _____-analysis of psychotherapy evaluation studies also showed that therapy works and that the effects are long-lasting. In addition, some problems may improve on their own through spontaneous (57) _____. Although all kinds of therapy show similar effectiveness, certain kinds of treatment may work best with certain kinds of problems.

• All forms of therapy involve (58) _____, (59) _____, and (60) _____ factors. The therapist provides support for the client by expressing understanding and empathy. People in therapy usually learn something about themselves, and all therapies offer suggestions for action. Such common factors may account for the finding that various approaches are equally (61) _____.

Terms to Remember

antianxiety drugs, 489
antidepressant drugs, 488
antipsychotic drugs, 488
aversion therapy, 504
behavioral therapies, 502
biomedical therapies, 487
client-centered therapy, 499
cognitive therapies, 495
dream analysis, 494

electroconvulsive therapy (ECT), 490
family therapy, 502
free association, 493
group therapy, 501
humanistic therapy, 499
insight therapies, 493
meta-analysis, 509
psychoanalysis, 493

psychosurgery, 492
psychotherapy, 485
rational-emotive therapy, 495
resistance, 494
spontaneous remission, 509
systematic desensitization, 503
token economy, 505
transference, 494

Media Resources

 ThomsonNOW

www.thomsonedu.com/ThomsonNOW
Go to this site for the link to ThomsonNow, your one-stop study shop. Take a Pre-Test for this chapter and Thomson-Now will generate a personalized Study Plan based on your test results! The Study Plan will identify the topics you need to review and direct you to online resources to help you master those topics. You can then take a Post-Test to help you determine the concepts you have mastered and what you still need to work on.

 Companion Website

www.thomsonedu.com/psychology/nairne
Go to this site to find online resources directly linked to your book, including a glossary, flashcards, quizzing, weblinks, and more.

 Psyk.trek 3.0

Check out the Psyk.trek CD-ROM for further study of the concepts in this chapter. Psyk.trek's interactive learning modules, simulations, and quizzes offer additional opportunities for you to interact with, reflect on, and retain the material:

Abnormal Behavior and Therapy: Behavioral and Biomedical Therapies
Abnormal Behavior and Therapy: Insight Therapies

CHAPTER 16

Stress and Health

Push, push, push. It hits you from all sides—school, work, relationships, family. Although we can't claim exclusive rights to the "age of stress," we certainly live in a demanding time. Everybody expects something from us, and they seem to want it now. Your teachers expect the subject matter to be learned, the paper written; your boss expects overtime in addition to your regular hours; your parents expect that weekly phone call, delivered in a pleasant and friendly tone. Add in the constant threat of a terrorist attack or a further breakdown in the international scene, and . . . well, enough said. Is it any wonder you can't seem to shake that cold, or that you feel the need to leave the antacid tablets by your bedside at night?

The idea that there's a close relationship between your psychological state and the physical reactions of your body should, by now, be firmly implanted in your mind. The mind and the body interact, and the interaction works in two directions. As we've discussed, disruptions in the delicate balance of neurotransmitters in the brain probably contribute significantly to psychological problems such as schizophrenia and depression. At the same time, beliefs, expectations, and reactions to the environment affect how those neurotransmitters are manufactured and used in the brain. In this chapter you'll see that the mind-to-body connection affects not only the way you think, feel, and react but your overall state of health as well.

Our focus is the general topic of health psychology. **Health psychology** is part of a broad movement, known as *behavioral medicine*, that seeks to understand the role of biological, psychological, environmental, and cultural factors in the promotion of physical health and the prevention of illness. Not surprisingly, health psychologists are particularly interested in psychological and environmental contributions to health (see Stanton, Revenson, & Tennen, 2007). They tend to focus on questions such as these: Are there particular personality characteristics that determine who becomes sick or who will recover from illness? Can the same theories that have been used successfully to diagnose and treat psychological disorders be applied to the promotion of physical health? Is it possible to identify the kinds of working environments that lead to illness or promote recovery? Are there specific strategies, or lifestyle choices, that reduce the likelihood of getting sick?

> **health psychology** The study of how biological, psychological, environmental, and cultural factors are involved in physical health and the prevention of illness.

Much of our discussion in this chapter deals with the topic of psychological stress and its effects on health. Stress is essentially an adaptive reaction to events in the world, but prolonged exposure to stressful environments can have a negative impact on health. Our discussion in this chapter revolves around four key issues related to stress and to health psychology in general.

Experiencing Stress Everyone has an intuitive sense of what *stress* is, but the term can be defined in a variety of ways. We'll discuss some of the meanings of the term as well as various components of the stress response. It's popular to conceive of stress not as a single reaction, such as a sudden release of activating hormones, but rather as an extended response that occurs over time.

Reacting to Prolonged Stress The human body is usually ably equipped to deal with unexpected trauma by activating those systems that are needed to respond to the emergency. But if the threat continues for an extended period of time, the body's defenses begin to break down. We'll consider some of the physical consequences of prolonged exposure to stress, including the role stress plays in the immune system.

Reducing and Coping With Stress Given that prolonged exposure to stress can have negative long-term consequences, psychologists have developed specific treatment methods for reducing and controlling stress. A number of techniques are available for managing stress, and we'll consider some of them later in the chapter.

Living a Healthy Lifestyle Whether you'll remain healthy throughout your life depends importantly on the lifestyle habits you choose. Obviously, if you choose to engage in risky behaviors—such as smoking, failing to get adequate nutrition, or practicing unsafe sex—you increase your chances of illness or death. Health psychologists have joined with other professionals, including physicians, to offer prescriptions for a healthful lifestyle. We'll discuss some of these recommendations along with their foundations in psychological theory.

Experiencing Stress

LEARNING GOALS
- Describe the stress response.
- Explain the function of cognitive appraisal as part of the stress response.
- Discuss external sources of stress.
- Discuss internal sources of stress.

"STRESS" IS ONE OF THOSE CONCEPTS that's easy to identify but difficult to define precisely. Part of the problem is that the term can be used in a variety of ways. For example, we frequently describe stress as if it was an actual *stimulus* (such as an event or a person) that places a demand on us or threatens our well-being ("That final next week is going to kill me"). On the other hand, we're just as likely to describe stress as a physical *response* or reaction that we feel ("I'm really stressed out"). To complicate matters even further, whether we feel stress depends on how we interpret the situation we're in (Lazarus, 1966, 2007). Consequently, some researchers describe stress as an internal psychological *process* through which external events are interpreted as threatening or demanding.

stress People's physical and psychological reactions to demanding situations.

stressors The demanding or threatening situations that produce stress.

For our purposes, we'll define **stress** as the physical and psychological reaction people have to demanding situations, and we'll refer to the demanding or threatening situations that produce stress as **stressors**. For example, the jackknifed tractor trailer blocking your speedy route home from school is a stressor, whereas your fuming physical and emotional reaction to it is stress. First, we'll consider some of the physical and psychological characteristics of stress; then we'll examine the external and internal factors that contribute to stress.

The Stress Response

If you're like most people, you probably think stress is a bad thing. Certainly when you're "stressed out," you tend to feel lousy, and there's no question that extended exposure to stressful situations can have long-term negative consequences. But it's important to understand that stress is in many ways an adaptive reaction. When you're in a threatening situation, or when someone is placing demands on you, it's important that your body become activated so you can respond to the threat in the most appropriate way. The experience of stress does exactly that, at least initially—it activates you (Korte et al., 2005).

Prolonged exposure to stress can lead to physical and psychological problems.

Physiological Reactions In the 1930s a physician named Hans Selye (1936, 1952, 1974) introduced an influential model of the stress reaction that he called the **general adaptation syndrome (GAS)**. Selye was convinced that our reaction to stressful situations is general and nonspecific, by which he meant that people are biologically programmed to respond to most threats in the same way. He was initially led to this idea as a medical student when he was struck by the similarities he saw among his patients. Across wildly different illnesses and injuries, his patients seemed to share a "syndrome of just being sick" that suggested to Selye that the body was reacting to each threatening situation in a very general way (no matter what the illness or the injury). Later, working in the laboratory with rats, he was able to confirm his hypothesis under controlled experimental conditions. Rats subjected to a variety of different kinds of threat—cold, heat, shock, restraint—produced a similar pattern of responses.

Selye's concept of the GAS proposes that the body reacts to threat in three stages, or phases (see ▌Figure 16.1). The first phase, the *alarm reaction*, corresponds to the adaptive fight-or-flight response we've discussed in previous chapters (Cannon, 1932). The body becomes energized, through activation of the sympathetic division of the autonomic nervous system, and hormones are released by the glands of the endocrine system. Heart rate and respiration rate increase, as does blood flow to the muscles; each of these actions helps prepare the body for immediate defensive or evasive action. The alarm reaction enables us to get out of life-threatening jams, but it's extremely intense and can't be sustained for long periods without serious negative consequences (even death).

If the threat continues but is not serious enough to demand a continued alarm reaction, the body enters a *resistance* phase. During this phase, the body adjusts its physiological reaction to reduce, or cope with, the still-present threat. Arousal levels remain higher than normal, but the body is capable of replenishing at least some of its resources. During the resistance phase, people are able to function reasonably well, but they're particularly susceptible to other stressors in the environment and may begin to suffer from health problems, or what Selye called "diseases of adaptation."

Finally, if the person is unable to find a way to neutralize the threat, the body eventually enters the *exhaustion phase* of the GAS. The body simply can't continue to maintain a high state of readiness for extended periods of time. Eventually, energy reserves become so taxed and depleted that the body starts to give up. During this period, resistance declines to the point at which the stress reaction becomes more and more maladaptive. Death, or some kind of irreversible damage, becomes a real possibility.

Selye's notion of the GAS has remained influential over the years. But researchers no longer believe the body's reaction to threat is as general and nonspecific as Selye suggested. Different stressors may well produce

general adaptation syndrome (GAS) Hans Selye's model of stress as a general, nonspecific reaction that occurs in three phases: alarm, resistance, and exhaustion.

▌**FIGURE 16.1** The General Adaptation Syndrome
Hans Selye proposed that the body reacts to threat or demand in three stages or phases: **(1)** an *alarm reaction* that corresponds to the fight-or-flight response; **(2)** *resistance*, during which the body adjusts its reaction in an effort to cope with a threat that is still present; and **(3)** *exhaustion*, which occurs when the body's energy reserves become so depleted that it starts to give up.

General Adaptation Syndrome

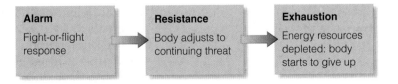

Alarm	Resistance	Exhaustion
Fight-or-flight response	Body adjusts to continuing threat	Energy resources depleted: body starts to give up

The early stages of the stress response are clearly adaptive because they help initiate a "fight-or-flight" response.

CRITICAL THINKING

Just because two things occur together, such as illness and empathy, doesn't mean that one causes the other. How would you determine whether physical illness truly causes increased empathy?

somewhat different patterns of response in the body (Goldstein & Kopin, 2007). Moreover, as you'll see a little later, the stress reaction depends on the cognitive interpretation, or appraisal, of the threatening situation.

Psychological Reactions   Stress is not just a physiological reaction to threat; there are also emotional and behavioral components to the reaction. We'll consider the psychological consequences of prolonged exposure to stressful situations later in the chapter, but emotional reactions are an important part of the stress response regardless of when or how long it occurs. *Fear* is a common reaction to threat, as is *anger*. Stressful situations can also lead to feelings of *sadness, dejection,* or even *grief* (Lazarus, 1991). These emotional reactions further suggest that stress is not completely general and nonspecific—people are capable of responding emotionally to different stressors in very different ways.

The psychological experience of stress is not even necessarily negative. Stress can have significant short- and long-term psychological benefits. For example, one study that examined the psychological characteristics of people who suffered from frequent physical illness found them to be more understanding (empathetic) of others and more tolerant of uncertainty (Haan, 1977). Stressful situations require people to use their skills and to interact with the environment. As individuals deal with stress, they often learn useful things about themselves and their abilities (Haan, 1993). Moreover, people who can successfully resolve a stressful situation gain confidence in their abilities. Laboratory work has even found that rats allowed to escape from shock, thereby reducing stress, have better-functioning immune systems than rats who receive no shock (Laudenslager et al., 1983). A similar reaction may happen to people: Stress may, at times, lead to the release of hormones that are health enhancing (de Kloet, Joëls, & Holsboer, 2005).

Gender Differences   Although the basic physiological stress reaction (e.g., activation of the sympathetic nervous system) doesn't differ much between males and females, some psychologists believe there are important behavioral differences. For example, rather than showing the typical fight-or-flight response, which is characteristic of males, females seem predisposed to react to stressors with "tending and befriending" behavior (Taylor, 2002, 2006). Because of evolutionary pressures, females may have evolved to respond by tending and protecting offspring (in addition to themselves) rather than fighting or fleeing the scene.

According to Taylor and her colleagues, it's more adaptive for males to react to potential harm by being aggressive or fleeing; females are faced with different pressures, especially the care of the young, and often lack the necessary physical equipment to ward off threats through aggression. Although women can certainly become physically aggressive in some settings, aggression and flight are secondary reactions to threat. Instead, the first line of defense is to protect and calm offspring, which increases the chances of offspring survival. In addition, compared to males, females appear more likely to create and maintain social networks that potentially can aid in protecting themselves and their offspring.

The proposal that males and females differ fundamentally in their behavioral reactions to stressors is new and likely to be controversial—especially the idea that gender-specific stress reactions may be adaptations arising from evolutionary pressures (Geary & Flinn, 2002). However, gender differences appear across the animal kingdom and may have some basis in the biology of male and female brains. As Taylor and her colleagues note, the vast majority of research on the behavioral components of the stress response has been conducted on males, so much remains to be learned about the role of gender in the basic stress response.

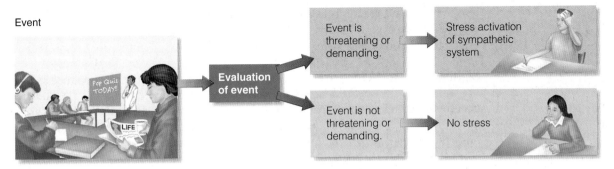

FIGURE 16.2 Cognitive Appraisal
Whether an event will create stress depends on how that event is interpreted. A stress reaction is more likely if you feel your resources are inadequate to deal with the potential threat.

Cognitive Appraisal

Most psychologists are convinced that stress is closely related to the concept of emotion because the experience of stress is critically influenced by the way we perceive or *appraise* the situation (Lazarus, 1993, 2007). To feel stress, it's necessary (1) to perceive there's some kind of demand or threat present and (2) to conclude that you may not have adequate resources available to deal with that threat. If you have a black belt in the martial arts, then the sudden appearance of an unarmed thug is not likely to cause much stress—the threat is there, but you have adequate defensive resources should you need to use them.

This idea that our stress reaction depends on the **cognitive appraisal** of the situation is reminiscent of what we know about the experience of emotions. As you may remember from Chapter 11, the same physiological reaction can lead to different emotional experiences, depending on how we interpret the arousal experienced. The same is true for stress. Identical environmental events can lead to two very different stress reactions, depending on how the event is interpreted. Consider an upcoming exam: Everyone in the class receives the same test, but not everyone will feel the same amount of stress. Those people who are prepared for the exam—the people like you who read the chapter—are likely to feel less stress. Again, you perceive the threat, but you have adequate resources to deal with it (see ▌Figure 16.2). The converse is also true—dangerous situations must be perceived as dangerous for a stress response to be produced. A small child doesn't necessarily understand that a loaded gun is dangerous and may feel no stress while handling it.

There's a great deal of support for cognitive appraisal in the experience of stress (Folkman & Moskowitz, 2004). In one study of elementary school children, urine samples were taken from the children on both normal school days and on days when they were about to take standardized achievement tests. The urine sample measured the amount of cortisol, an important stress hormone, that each child produced (notice that the researchers provided an operational definition of stress in terms of the amount of hormone measured). Not surprisingly, more cortisol was found on test days, suggesting a higher level of stress, but the increase in stress depended on the child's previously recorded overall intelligence score. The children with higher intelligence scores showed less of a stress reaction on test days, presumably because they considered the test to be less of a threat (Tennes & Kreye, 1985).

cognitive appraisal The idea that to feel stress you need to perceive a threat and come to the conclusion that you may not have adequate resources to deal with the threat.

External Sources of Stress

Because the stress reaction depends on one's appraisal of the given situation, it's impossible to compile an exhaustive list of life's stressors. We can never predict how everyone will react to an environmental event, even though it may seem clearly stressful to the majority. All we can do is catalogue external situations, or life events, that induce stress reactions in *most* individuals. We'll consider three major classes of external stressors in this section: significant life events, daily hassles, and other factors in the environment.

Significant Life Events   Certain events are virtually guaranteed to produce stress. We can all agree that the death of a loved one or getting fired from a job is likely to lead to an extended stress reaction in most people. On a larger scale, natural disasters or catastrophes—such as the terrorist attacks that occurred in the United States on September 11, 2001—unquestionably produce stress that is prolonged and widespread. In the case of September 11, a national phone survey conducted three to five days after the attack found that more than 44% of the people surveyed reported one or more substantial symptoms of stress, and more than 90% reported feeling symptoms of stress to at least some degree (Schuster et al., 2001).

Many studies have found clear links between these kinds of events and subsequent physical and psychological problems, particularly for the September 11 attack (e.g., Heim et al., 2004). In the seven months following the 1980 volcanic eruption of Mount Saint Helens in Washington state, one nearby town reported more than a 30% increase in the number of hospital emergency room visits compared to a similar period in the year prior to the eruption (Adams & Adams, 1984; see ▌Figure 16.3). These visits were *not* for injuries directly caused by the eruption but rather for general health problems that may have been created or enhanced by the experience of stress.

Over the years researchers have tried to compile lists of external life stressors. The best-known example is the Social Readjustment Rating Scale, which was put together by researchers Thomas Holmes and Richard Rahe (1967). Holmes and Rahe interviewed thousands of people who were suffering from health problems and then tried to determine whether certain kinds of events preceded the onset of the health problems. The results are shown in ▌Table 16.1, which lists the various significant life events mentioned by the people interviewed, ranked in terms of "life change units" (roughly representing the amount of adjustment the event caused in the person's life).

There are two interesting things to notice about the results shown in the table. First, most of these life events are connected with some kind of *change* in day-to-day activities. This suggests that the disruption caused by the event is just as important as the event itself in causing the stress reaction. People feel stress, in part, because something happens that requires them to alter their ways or lifestyle. Second, notice that many of the events listed in the table are actually quite *positive*. For example, marriage and retirement make the top 10. Even vacations and Christmas make the list. This is not really too surprising if you think about it, because each is associated with some kind of temporary or long-lasting disruption of normal routines.

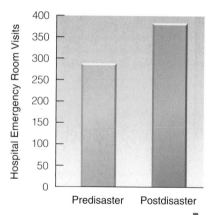
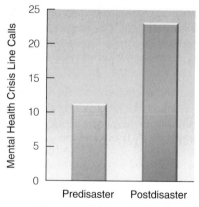
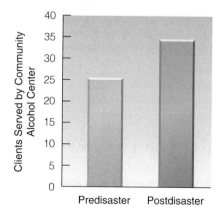

▌**FIGURE 16.3** Reacting to a Natural Disaster
The data shown here present the mean monthly hospital emergency room visits, mental health crisis line calls, and number of clients served by a community alcohol center for comparable time periods before and after the eruption of Mount Saint Helens in 1980. (Data from Adams & Adams, 1984)

TABLE 16.1 Social Readjustment Rating Scale		
Rank	**Life Event**	**Point Value**
1	Death of spouse	100
2	Divorce	73
3	Marital separation	65
4	Jail term	63
5	Death of close family member	63
6	Personal injury or illness	53
7	Marriage	50
8	Fired at work	47
9	Marital reconciliation	45
10	Retirement	45
11	Change in health of family member	44
12	Pregnancy	40
13	Sex difficulties	39
14	Gain of new family member	39
15	Business readjustment	39
16	Change in financial state	38
17	Death of close friend	37
18	Change to different line of work	36
19	Change in number of arguments with spouse	35
20	Mortgage over $10,000	31
21	Foreclosure of mortgage or loan	30
22	Change in responsibilities at work	29
23	Son or daughter leaving home	29
24	Trouble with in-laws	29
25	Outstanding personal achievement	28
26	Wife begins or stops work	26
27	Begin or end school	26
28	Change in living conditions	25
29	Revision of personal habits	24
30	Trouble with boss	23
31	Change in work hours or conditions	20
32	Change in residence	20
33	Change in schools	20
34	Change in recreation	19
35	Change in church activities	19
36	Change in social activities	18
37	Mortgage or loan less than $10,000	17
38	Change in sleeping habits	16
39	Change in number of family get-togethers	15
40	Change in eating habits	15
41	Vacation	13
42	Christmas	12
43	Minor violations of the law	11

Source: Reprinted from *Journal of Psychosomatic Research, 11,* T. H. Holmes and R. H. Rahe, "The Social Readjustment Rating Scale," pp. 213–218. Copyright © 1967, with permission of Elsevier Science.

CRITICAL THINKING

Try listing and ranking the life events that cause, or have caused, you the most stress. How do your rank orderings differ from those listed in Table 16.1?

The results listed in Table 16.1 are roughly 40 years old, but they continue to be used by researchers as a vehicle for predicting the likelihood of stress. Dozens of studies have found significant correlations between these rankings and various measures of stress, including physical and psychological problems (see Cooper & Dewe, 2007). However, not all experts are satisfied with the methods that were used to devise the scale, and it's been revised to take into account such factors as gender, age, and amount of education (Hobson & Delunas, 2001; Miller & Rahe, 1997). You should also remember that change by itself does not necessarily lead to stress reactions in all individuals. So you can't automatically assume that if one of these events happens to you, you'll feel stress. Remember, it's how you appraise the event that's really important, along with your assessment of whether you have adequate resources to deal with the life change when it occurs.

Daily Hassles Psychologists also recognize that it's not just the big events that cause problems. The little things, the daily irritations and hassles of life, also contribute significantly to the experience of stress. Think about how you feel when you're stuck in a long checkout line at the market, when someone's tailgating you on the freeway, or when you're hungry and you've waited a half hour or more for your order at a restaurant. Some psychologists believe the cumulative effect of these "daily hassles" may actually be more important in creating lasting stress than are significant life events (Lazarus & Folkman, 1984; Miller, 1993). Kanner and colleagues (1981) have developed a Hassles Scale, and it seems to predict the likelihood of physical and mental health problems. The more hassles you experience in your daily life, the more likely you'll experience health problems. Included on the scale are such things as concern about one's weight and physical appearance, home maintenance, and worries about misplacing or losing something. There is even a version of the Hassles Scale that is specifically designed to measure hassles among university students (Pett & Johnson, 2005)!

Environmental Factors We're also subjected to stress by our environment. *Noise* is a good example. Think about how difficult it is to study when someone is talking loudly nearby or how irritated you get when you're roused from sleep by the whirring, clanging sounds of the morning garbage truck. Chronic exposure to noise interferes with everyday activities, and it's been linked with the appearance of such stress-related disorders as ulcers and high blood pressure (Evans, 1997; Nagar & Panady, 1987) and with a general decline in the perceived quality of life (Evans, Hygge, & Bullinger, 1995). Schoolchildren experience more stress when they're exposed to chronic noise, and cognitive measures (such as reading comprehension) appear to suffer (Haines et al., 2001).

CRITICAL THINKING

Suppose you discover a group of people living in a crowded and noisy environment who show little or no stress reaction. How would you interpret your findings?

Another environmental factor that has been linked to stress is *crowding*. The more people who live or work around you, the more likely you'll experience a stress reaction (Regoeczi, 2003). Living in a crowded environment makes us generally more susceptible to health problems and increases the likelihood of aggression. People who live in high-rise apartment buildings, filled with tenants, are more likely to behave aggressively than those who live in apartment buildings with fewer floors (Bell et al., 1990). The effects of crowding on health and aggression have also been studied extensively in prison settings—inmates who live in crowded environments suffer more health problems and are more likely to act aggressively than inmates housed in less crowded environments (Haney, 2006; Paulus, 1988).

Crowding and noise are two examples of environmental stressors, but there are many others. For example, stress and health have been closely linked to the family social environment, peer interactions, conditions in the workplace, socioeconomic class, and the general characteristics of the neighborhood in which you live (Cutrona, Wallace, & Wesner, 2006). There is, in fact, an entire specialty in psychology—called **environmental psychology**—devoted to the study of environmental effects on behavior and health. Environmental psychologists have shown particular interest in the psychology of urban living because living in a large city is likely to expose one to a

environmental psychology A specialty area in psychology devoted to the study of environmental effects on behavior and health, such as the effects of crowding or noise.

A crowded urban environment is a source of stress for many people.

variety of environmental stressors (particularly noise and crowding). In general, people succumb to stress when they're forced to live in situations in which there is excessive stimulation, movement is constrained, or resources are limited.

Internal Sources of Stress

As you're now aware, no single event or set of living conditions will automatically lead to stress in everyone. Stressors are very much in the eye of the beholder, which means we need to know something about the internal characteristics of the individual before we can predict whether he or she will experience stress. Stress arises out of an interaction between individuals and events in the world—neither alone is sufficient to predict the reaction. But what exactly are these internal characteristics? We'll consider three in this section: perceived control, explanatory style, and personality characteristics.

Perceived Control To experience stress, you need to perceive a threat or some kind of demand, and you need to feel you lack the resources to deal effectively with that threat. This second part of the appraisal process, the assessment of resources, is influenced by a psychological construct called **perceived control**, which is the amount of influence you feel you have over the situation and your reaction to it. It turns out that perceived control significantly affects the amount of stress you'll experience. If you perceive a demand or threat and you think you have no control over the situation, your body is likely to react with arousal, the release of stress hormones, and there will be changes in the activities of your immune system (Brosschot et al., 1998). If the situation continues for a prolonged period, negative physical and psychological consequences are likely to result.

Many examples, both scientific and anecdotal, support the link between perceived control and stress (Kemeny, 2003). Early in the manned space program, for instance, the Mercury astronauts insisted that manual controls and windows be placed in the orbiting space capsule. Although not necessary from an engineering standpoint, doing so gave the astronauts a "sense of control" over their environment, which reduced their stress. In laboratory studies, animals that are exposed to shocks that they can turn off by turning a wheel are less likely to develop ulcers than animals who

perceived control The amount of influence you feel you have over a situation and your reaction to it.

receive the same amount of shock but cannot control it (Weiss, 1977). Moreover, people with an internal locus of control, those who feel they generally have control over the events in their environment, show less of a stress response when allowed to control a stressor in the laboratory than people with an external locus of control (Bollini et al., 2004). Finally, anxious individuals who feel they lack control after a heart attack are more likely to suffer complications than those with high perceived control (Moser et al., 2007).

Explanatory Style   The results of the cognitive appraisal process, and therefore susceptibility to stress, are also influenced by one's general style of thinking. At several points in the text we've discussed the importance of *attributions*, or our conclusions about cause and effect. People offer different kinds of explanations for the positive and negative events that occur in their world. For example, someone with an *internal*, *stable*, and *global* explanatory style is likely to attribute a negative event to some long-lasting personal inadequacy that applies in lots of situations: "My spouse left me because I'm witless; I've always been witless, and I can never hope to convince anyone otherwise."

We've seen elsewhere that a person's explanatory style contributes to psychological disorders such as depression (see Chapter 14). Perhaps not surprisingly, explanatory style has also been linked to physical health and susceptibility to stress. People who consistently make internal, stable, and global attributions for negative events have been found to suffer from increased stress-related health problems in midlife as well as later in life (Kamen-Siegel et al., 1991; Peterson, Seligman, & Vaillant 1988). In one particularly intriguing study, Peterson and Seligman (1987) analyzed the explanatory styles of 94 members of the Baseball Hall of Fame who had played at some point between 1900 and 1950. Many of these players were dead at the time of the study, so the researchers had to glean the players' explanatory styles from stories and quotations in old newspapers. The players with negative explanatory styles were found, on average, to have lived shorter lives.

Personality Characteristics   Both perceived control and explanatory style are related more generally to personality. Previously, we defined *personality* as the set of psychological characteristics that distinguishes us from others and leads us to act consistently across situations. Explanatory style may be linked to a personality characteristic such as *optimism*—the belief that good things will happen—which some psychologists have argued is a relatively enduring trait that changes little over a lifetime (Scheier & Carver, 1993). "Optimism scales" have been developed and used to look for a connection between personality and health. In one study, optimism was assessed on the day before a group of men underwent coronary bypass surgery. The optimists reacted physiologically to the surgery in ways that lowered the risk of heart attack; they also recovered more quickly after the surgery (Scheier et al., 1989). More recent studies have demonstrated links between psychosocial factors like optimism and improved functioning of the immune system (see Antoni & Lutgendorf, 2007).

An optimistic view of life can clearly reduce stress. In one recent study, rescue and recovery workers at the crash site of an airline accident (USAir Flight 427) were studied two, six, nine, and twelve months after the crash. Those individuals who maintained an optimistic outlook reported less stress and generally better coping strategies. They also tended to have better social support networks and thereby improved resources for dealing with the stress associated with the accident (Dougall et al., 2001). Consequently, an optimistic outlook not only can help you establish and maintain friends but it may help you live longer too (Smith, 2006).

The most widely recognized personality characteristics that have been linked to stress-related health disorders, particularly coronary heart disease, are the famous **Type A** and **Type B** behavior patterns. You're familiar with the Type A personality: hard driving, ambitious, easily annoyed, and impatient. Those with a Type A personality seem to be immersed in a sea of perpetual self-imposed stress; they're too busy to notice or enjoy the things around them because they're engaged in a relentless pur-

Type A An enduring pattern of behavior linked to stress-related health disorders; it is characterized by being hard driving, ambitious, easily annoyed, and impatient.

Type B People who lack the Type A traits—they put themselves under less pressure and appear more relaxed.

Concept Review | Sources of Stress

EXTERNAL

Source	Description
Significant life events	Major life events associated with a change in day-to-day activities; they can be positive (e.g., getting married) or negative (e.g., death of a loved one)
Daily hassles	Daily irritations and hassles, such as getting stuck in traffic
Environmental factors	Stressors present in the environment, such as noise and crowding

INTERNAL

Source	Description
Perceived control	The amount of influence you feel you have over a situation. A sense of control often lessens the stress.
Explanatory style	One's general style of thinking about and explaining events. People who make internal, stable, and global attributions for negative events are more likely to suffer from stress-related health problems.
Personality characteristics	*Optimism* (the belief that good things will happen) generally reduces stress. A *Type A* behavior pattern (hard driving, ambitious, easily annoyed, impatient) is associated with elevated stress and heart problems.

suit of success. Type B personality types are essentially people who lack the Type A attributes—they put themselves under less pressure and appear more relaxed.

The connection between Type A behavior patterns and heart disease was first noted by cardiologists Meyer Friedman and Ray Rosenman (1974). Friedman and Rosenman were interested in explaining why only some people with known risk factors for heart disease—such as smoking, obesity, inactivity, and so on—actually develop heart problems. People can appear to have identical risk profiles but end up healthy in one instance and disease prone in another. Friedman and Rosenman proposed that the solution lies in the connection between personality and stress. People who are psychologically prone to stress—Type A personalities—will prove more susceptible to diseases of the heart.

Over the past several decades, a number of very ambitious studies have been conducted to explore the health consequences of Type A behavior patterns. Thousands of individuals have participated, and they've been studied over long periods of time. Generally, the results have supported the proposals of Friedman and Rosenman: People who are classified as Type A personality types are at least twice as likely to develop coronary heart problems as Type B personality types (Lyness, 1993). Not all studies have found this result, and there have even been studies showing the opposite pattern (Ragland & Brand, 1988).

Recent work suggests that a more complete answer lies in further analyzing the Type A behavior pattern or personality, which turns out to be quite complex. To be classified as a Type A personality requires that a person be rated on a number of dimensions—competitiveness, ambition, hostility, and so on—and not all of these attributes are equally important. Some researchers believe it's hostility, anger, or the expression of anger that is most responsible for producing subsequent coronary artery disease, although not all studies have found this relationship (Krantz & McCeney, 2002). Others have stressed the need to consider cultural factors—some societies encourage competition, and others do not (Thoresen & Powell, 1992). There's probably also an interaction between personality and explanatory style—that is, whether you attribute consequences to internal or external factors (Kirkcaldy, Cooper, & Furnham, 1999). At this point, it's widely believed that personality characteristics do affect susceptibility to stress and disease (Friedman, Hawley, & Tucker, 1994), but we can't just draw a sharp line between Type A and Type B personality types and hope to explain all the data (Smith, 2006).

Type A personalities seem to be immersed in a sea of perpetual stress, and they're significantly more likely to develop coronary heart problems than Type B personalities.

© Arlene Collins

Test Yourself 16.1

Check your knowledge about the stress response by answering each of the following questions. (You will find the answers in the Appendix.)

1. Hans Selye's concept of the general adaptation syndrome (GAS) proposes that the body reacts to stress in three phases. Which of the following shows the correct sequence of these phases?
   a. Resistance, alarm, exhaustion
   b. Exhaustion, resistance, alarm
   c. Alarm, resistance, exhaustion
   d. Exhaustion, alarm, resistance
2. The experience of stress is related to the experience of emotion in which of the following ways?
   a. The experience of stress, like emotion, is an inevitable reaction to threat.
   b. The experience of stress, like emotion, is accompanied by very distinctive facial expressions.
   c. The experience of stress, like emotion, depends on the appraisal of the event rather than on the event itself.

   d. The experience of different kinds of stress, like emotion, leads to highly specific kinds of body reactions.
3. According to the Social Readjustment Rating Scale, which of the following events is most likely to cause stress-related health problems?
   a. Marriage
   b. Death of a close friend
   c. Sex difficulties
   d. Trouble with your boss
4. Which of the following internal characteristics is least likely to be associated with stress-related health problems?
   a. Low levels of perceived control
   b. Type A behavior pattern
   c. An optimistic outlook
   d. Internal, stable, and global attributions

Reacting to Prolonged Stress

LEARNING GOALS
- Describe the physical consequences of prolonged stress.
- Describe the psychological consequences of prolonged stress.

THERE'S A DEFINITE CONNECTION between prolonged stress and physical and psychological health. Stress is an adaptive reaction to threat—it helps us to fight or flee. But when it's prolonged, when we're not able to reduce or eliminate the perceived threat, the mind and body start to break down. If the stress reaction is extreme enough, the breakdown can be sudden and may even result in death; in most cases, however, the effects are gradual and reveal themselves slowly through a growing list of physical and psychological problems. In this section of the chapter, we'll consider the nature of these breakdowns and how and why they occur.

Physical Consequences of Stress

Stress has been implicated in a wide variety of health problems. In addition to ulcers and heart disease, stress has been linked to everything from the common cold to chronic back pain, multiple sclerosis, and even cancer (Schneiderman et al., 2001). Most of the scientific evidence is correlational, which means a statistical relationship has been found between the incidence of a health problem such as heart disease and some measurement of stress. Large numbers of people are interviewed, and health histories as well as stress levels are measured. The net result is that we can predict whether someone, on average, will have an increased chance of developing a particular kind of health problem by knowing the amount of stress that person experiences on a regular basis. But this doesn't tell us whether a causal relationship exists between stress and illness. To determine that, we must turn to experimental research.

It's difficult to conduct experimental research on the relationship between stress and health for obvious ethical reasons. Ethically, we can't randomly divide people into groups, subject some of them to high levels of stress, and then monitor the later consequences of that manipulation on health. But experimental studies have been conducted on groups of people who have been previously identified as having either a high or low level of stress in their lives. In one study (Cohen, Tyrell, & Smith, 1993), high- and low-stress people were given nasal drops that either contained or did not contain a common cold virus. It was a double-blind study, so neither the participants nor the researchers were aware during the course of the study who was getting the actual virus and who was not. Afterward, when the assignments were "decoded," it was found that the high-stress people who received the virus were the ones most likely to show cold symptoms. Living a stressful life apparently lowers one's ability to fight off disease.

The Immune Response   To understand why stress increases susceptibility to illness, we need to consider the human *immune system*, a complex defense system that's constantly on the lookout for foreign substances, such as viruses or bacteria. The primary weapons of the immune system are **lymphocytes**, which are specialized white blood cells that attack and destroy most of these foreign invaders. Stress can lower the immune response by either decreasing the number of lymphocytes in the bloodstream or by suppressing the response of the lymphocytes to foreign substances that have invaded the body (see Gonzalez-Quijano et al., 1998). The underlying mechanisms that produce these changes have not been completely determined, although the prolonged release of stress hormones into the bloodstream probably plays a significant role (Kiecolt-Glaser et al., 2002).

lymphocytes Specialized white blood cells that have the job of attacking foreign substances, such as viruses and bacteria.

Several investigations have shown that stressful life events directly affect the immune response. Medical students, on average, have fewer lymphocytes in their blood during a period of final exams compared to levels found before exams (Kiecolt-Glaser et al., 1984); they're also more likely to get sick during exams. People who have recently had a spouse or loved one die also show a suppressed immune response. One investigative team tracked the immune response in men married to women with advanced breast cancer. Samples of the men's blood were taken during a period of months preceding and following their wives' deaths. On average, the existing lymphocytes in blood samples drawn *after* the wives had died showed a weaker response to foreign substances (Schleifer et al., 1983).

The fact that stress weakens the immune system has led researchers to wonder about the effects of stress on more chronic illnesses, such as cancer. In the laboratory

People who are subjected to chronic stress by environmental conditions can have weakened immune systems.

© Scott Nelson/Getty Images

it's been shown that stress can increase the growth rate of cancerous tumors in animals (Antoni & Lutgendorf, 2007). There have also been reports that cancer patients who are optimistic, or who are given therapy to help reduce anxiety and depression, survive longer than patients who are hopeless or depressed (Andersen, 1992; Spiegel et al., 1989). Stress may affect not only the body's ability to fight cancer but also the likelihood that cancer cells will form in the first place (Antoni & Lutgendorf, 2007).

At present, however, most researchers remain cautious about the link between psychology, the immune system, and cancer. Not all studies have found associations between psychological factors and cancer, and the fact that data linking cancer to stress have come primarily from correlational studies means that it's difficult to draw conclusions about cause and effect. It's possible that "stressful" people, on average, have a greater risk of acquiring cancer because they tend to engage in unhealthful behaviors—such as smoking—as a way of dealing with the stress. It may also be the case that people who are optimistic about their survival from cancer tend to comply more with the recommendations of their doctors. Although there may be a statistical association between stress and cancer, that does not necessarily mean that stress is causing cancer by compromising the functioning of the immune system. In addition, questions have been raised about whether psychotherapy actually increases the likelihood of survival among cancer patients (Coyne, Stefanek, & Palmer, 2007).

Cardiovascular Disease Health psychologists have also intensively studied the well-documented relationship between stress and cardiovascular disease (problems connected with the heart and blood vessels). We discussed the connection between Type A behavior and heart problems earlier, but we left the mechanisms through which stress undermines cardiovascular health unspecified. The two most important risk factors in heart disease are (1) high cholesterol levels in the blood and (2) high blood pressure. Prolonged exposure to stress increases exposure to both of these risk factors (O'Callahan, Andrews, & Krantz, 2003).

Increased blood pressure, a natural by-product of the stress response, is generally helpful over the short term in preparing us to react to a threat. But if the elevated pressure continues, it causes wear and tear on the blood vessels in the body, which can lead to both cardiovascular disease and kidney problems. Stress can also directly affect the level of cholesterol in the blood. For example, when college students are anticipating an upcoming exam, samples of their blood show higher levels of cholesterol (Van Doornen & Van Blokland, 1987). People who display Type A behavior patterns have also been found, on average, to have higher levels of blood cholesterol. It's possible that when people sense threat, the body directs the blood flow to the muscles and away from internal organs, such as the liver, that remove fat and cholesterol from the blood.

Psychological Consequences of Stress

CRITICAL THINKING

How might the onset of a psychological disorder, such as depression, be an adaptive reaction to prolonged stress?

Think about how you feel when you're "stressed out." That recurring cold or sour stomach seems like it'll never go away. But the mental and emotional changes can be just as profound. You feel anxious, out of control, emotionally drained, and, after a while, possibly even sad and depressed. Stress is not a pleasant experience, and if the stress reaction is intense enough, or if it continues long enough, serious psychological problems can result.

Psychologists are convinced that stressful life events play a significant role in the onset of many psychological disorders. If you interview people who have suffered from major depression or a bipolar disorder, you'll find that most have experienced some kind of major stressor just before or early into the depressive episode—they got fired from their job, they moved to a new town, they're mired in a nasty divorce, and so on (Barlow & Durand, 2005). Stress has been implicated in the onset of schizophrenia as well. Several studies have shown that stressful life events tend to immediately precede schizophrenic episodes (Harvey, 2001).

But, importantly, not all people who experience intense stress go on to develop serious psychological problems. In fact, the majority of people who experience a traumatic life stressor do not subsequently develop psychological disorders. Psychologists assume there must be some kind of vulnerability, perhaps rooted in the genetic recipe, before stress leads to an extreme disorder such as major depression or schizophrenia. Similar arguments apply to anxiety disorders such as posttraumatic stress disorder.

Posttraumatic Stress Disorder   You're familiar with this scenario: Soldier returns home from war, shell shocked, suffering from sleepless nights and flashbacks of traumatic episodes in battle. Hollywood has exploited this image to the point where the "unstable Vietnam vet" has become an unfortunate part of our collective sense of the Vietnam experience. In reality, the vast majority of soldiers who returned from Vietnam or both Gulf Wars have experienced no long-term psychological problems. At the same time, even though the percentages are small, psychologists do recognize that exposure to extreme stress can produce a serious psychological condition known as **posttraumatic stress disorder**. This disorder is not limited to battle veterans; it can occur in any individual who has undergone a traumatic episode, such as a physical attack, rape, or a natural disaster. In fact, the disorder is somewhat more likely to occur in women than in men (Olff et al., 2007).

In the DSM-IV-TR, posttraumatic stress disorder is classified as an anxiety disorder, and the diagnosis is made if the following three types of symptoms occur for a period lasting longer than one month:

1. *Flashbacks.* When a flashback occurs, the person relives the traumatic event in some way. These flashbacks can take the form of persistent thoughts or images of the traumatic scene, and they can even involve vivid hallucinations; the affected person seems at times to be reexperiencing the event—fighting the battle anew or fending off the attacker.
2. *Avoidance of stimuli associated with the trauma.* People with posttraumatic stress disorder actively try to avoid anything that reminds them of the event. This avoidance behavior can lead to significant disruptions in normal social functioning as the affected person turns away from friends and loved ones who in some way remind him or her of the trauma.

posttraumatic stress disorder A trauma-based anxiety disorder characterized by flashbacks, avoidance of stimuli associated with the traumatic event, and chronic arousal symptoms.

Traumatic events, such as the bombing of the World Trade Center on September 11, 2001, can lead to disabling psychological conditions.

© Jose Jimenez/Getty Images/Primera Hora

3. *Chronic arousal symptoms.* These symptoms can include sleep problems, irritability or outbursts of anger, and difficulties in concentrating.

Obviously, posttraumatic stress disorder is a disabling condition, not only for the individuals who are directly affected but also for family and friends. The cause of the disorder is clear—traumatic stress—but the reason only some people who experience trauma develop posttraumatic stress disorder remains a mystery. There's evidence that the intensity of the trauma may be important. For example, Vietnam veterans who were in heavy combat were significantly more likely to develop posttraumatic stress disorder than those serving in noncombat roles (Goldberg et al., 1990). But, once again, this doesn't explain why the disorder remains relatively rare even among people who have experienced extreme trauma. As with most psychological disorders, the chances that posttraumatic stress disorder will develop undoubtedly depend on a complex mix of biological and environmental factors (Craske, 1999; O'Shea, 2001).

Burnout Stress does not need to be extreme to produce unpleasant psychological consequences. In the 1970s the term *burnout* was introduced by psychologists to describe a syndrome that develops in certain people who are exposed to stressful situations that are demanding but not necessarily traumatic (Freudenberger, 1974; Maslach, 1976). Although the term **burnout** has become a household word, to psychologists it refers to "a state of physical, emotional, and mental exhaustion caused by long-term involvement in emotionally demanding situations" (Pines & Aronson, 1988, p. 9). When burnout occurs, affected individuals essentially lose their spirit—they become emotionally drained, they feel used up, and they lose their sense of personal accomplishment.

As with posttraumatic stress disorder, stress is a necessary component but is not a sufficient condition for producing burnout. Not everyone who has a demanding and stressful job becomes burned out. Burnout seems to occur only in idealistic individuals—people who have entered their careers with a high sense of motivation and commitment. In the words of psychologist Ayala Pines (1993), "You cannot burn out unless you were 'on fire' initially" (p. 386). Because burnout tends to occur only in highly motivated individuals, it can have a high cost for organizations as well as for the individual. People who suffer from burnout lose their edge on the job—they become disillusioned with their work, are frequently absent from the job, and usually are at increased risk for a host of physical problems (Maslach, Schaufeli, & Leiter, 2001).

burnout A state of physical, emotional, and mental exhaustion created by long-term involvement in an emotionally demanding situation.

Concept Review | Consequences of Stress

PHYSICAL

Stress Affects	Nature of the Effect
Immune response	Stressful events directly affect the immune response, lowering the number of disease-fighting *lymphocytes*. Some believe that stress also influences chronic illnesses, such as cancer.
Cardiovascular disease	Increased blood pressure from prolonged stress causes wear and tear on blood vessels, which can lead to cardiovascular disease.

PSYCHOLOGICAL

Stress Leads To	Nature of the Effect
Posttraumatic stress disorder	A serious psychological condition that can result from exposure to extreme stress. Classified as an anxiety disorder, it's characterized by flashbacks, avoidance of trauma-associated stimuli, and chronic arousal symptoms.
Burnout	A state of physical, emotional, and mental exhaustion caused by long-term involvement in emotionally demanding situations. It seems to occur in idealistic individuals who are highly motivated, perhaps due to a loss of control or a loss of meaning in life.

Why does burnout occur? The underlying cause may well be related to a loss of meaning in life (Pines, 1993) or to a loss of control in the workplace (McKnight & Glass, 1995). People who are subject to burnout are usually those who think of their work as a kind of "calling." They use success on the job as a way of validating their existence. They identify so closely with their work that when failure happens, their entire life loses meaning. Failure is much more likely when the job is demanding and taxes the individual's resources, which is probably the reason stress is typically associated with the syndrome. If the overall stress levels can be reduced, perhaps by providing a better support system within the work environment, burnout is less likely to occur (see Leiter & Maslach, 2005).

Test Yourself | **16.2**

Check your knowledge about reacting to stress by deciding whether each of the following statements is True or False. *(You will find the answers in the Appendix.)*

1. Lymphocytes are the primary weapons of the human immune system. *True or False?*
2. Much of the data linking cancer and stress have come from correlational studies; researchers are unable, therefore, to draw firm conclusions about cause and effect. *True or False?*
3. Stress is known to affect blood pressure, but no links have been established between stress and cholesterol levels. *True or False?*

4. Posttraumatic stress disorder is a common reaction to experiencing a traumatic event. *True or False?*
5. Burnout is more likely to occur in people who use success on the job as a way of giving life meaning. *True or False?*

Reducing and Coping With Stress

LEARNING GOALS
- Explain how relaxation techniques can be used to reduce stress.
- Explain how stress can be managed through cognitive reappraisal of the stressful situation.

BECAUSE STRESS IS ASSOCIATED with so many physical and psychological problems, it's obviously important to develop techniques for reducing stress. Unfortunately, stressors are often outside of our direct control—you can't prevent the tornado that skirts the neighborhood trailer park or the death of a valued friend from accident or illness. But techniques are available for coping with stressors when they're present. **Coping** is a term psychologists use to describe efforts to manage conditions of threat or demand that tax one's resources (Lazarus, 1993). In this section, we'll consider three coping strategies for controlling or reducing stress: (1) learning relaxation techniques, (2) forming effective social support systems, and (3) learning to reappraise the environment in a less threatening way.

coping Efforts to manage or master conditions of threat or demand that tax one's resources.

Relaxation Techniques

By definition, the stress response is incompatible with relaxation. You cannot be prepared to fight or flee if your body is calm, relaxed, and free from arousal-inducing stress hormones. Studies have shown that high-stress individuals can reduce the physically threatening components of the stress reaction—such as high blood pressure—by simply practicing a regimen of relaxation techniques. You may remember that we discussed how relaxation can be used effectively in the treatment of anxiety disorders (Chapter 15); similar relaxation techniques have proven effective in reducing long-term stress reactions.

Exercise, meditation, and even social support can be excellent vehicles for coping with stress.

A number of relaxation procedures are available to help manage stress. In *progressive muscle relaxation*, you're taught to concentrate on specific muscle groups in the body, to note whether there is any tension, and then to try to relax those specific groups. Often in progressive relaxation you learn to address muscle groups in sequence. For example, you might begin with the muscle groups in the neck, move to the shoulders, and so on, first tensing and then relaxing each group. In this way you learn to pay attention to how muscles in your body feel when tense or relaxed. Progressive relaxation has been used successfully to treat a variety of stress-related health problems, everything from tension headaches (Myers, Wittrock, & Foreman, 1998) to posttraumatic stress syndrome (Frueh, de Arellano, & Turner, 1997). In a somewhat different technique, called *autogenic relaxation*, you're taught to focus on directing blood flow toward tense muscle groups, "warming" and relaxing each group; once again, autogenic relaxation has proven beneficial in treating stress-related conditions (Friedlander et al., 1997).

Relaxation techniques such as these are sometimes accompanied by *meditation* training. We discussed some of the benefits of meditation in Chapter 6. Meditation essentially involves learning how to relax, using techniques similar to progressive muscle relaxation. But you're also taught some time-tested mental exercises, such as repeating a string of words or sounds over and over in your head. The mental repetition focuses awareness and helps prevent potentially distracting or stress-producing thoughts from interfering with the relaxation response. (For instance, if you're concentrating on repeating the phrase "I'm at one with the universe," you can't simultaneously be worrying about whether the relaxation technique is working.) Daily meditation sessions clearly help people deal with stress-related arousal and are likely to prevent the later development of health problems such as high blood pressure (Barnes, Treiber, & Davis, 2001).

Biofeedback The goal of relaxation training is to lower components of the stress response, such as blood pressure, heart rate, and muscle tension. For example, if stress-related headaches are caused by tension in the muscles of the head and scalp, then people should be able to reduce or eliminate the pain by relaxing these specific muscle groups. Some researchers have suggested that it helps to give people feedback—*biofeedback*—about the effectiveness of their relaxation efforts. With biofeedback, monitoring equipment provides a continuous reading of your physiological state. In the case of tension headaches, the feedback would indicate the tension levels in the muscles of the head; for blood pressure or heart rate, you would be able to read your blood pressure and heart rate directly from appropriate monitoring equipment.

biofeedback Specific physiological feedback people are given about the effectiveness of their relaxation efforts.

Not surprisingly, biofeedback works. When people are given information about how well their relaxation efforts are succeeding, compared with control subjects who are given no feedback, it's clearly easier to control the relevant physiological response (Nestoriuc & Martin, 2007). But interestingly, it's also likely to be the subsequent feeling of *control* that leads to reductions in the stress response. For instance, in one study on tension headaches, three groups of people were given a feedback signal that they were led to believe indicated a successful lowering of muscle tension in their foreheads. Actually, unknown to them, the signal had three different meanings: In one group, it appeared only when participants successfully increased the amount of tension in their foreheads; in a second group, the signal appeared whenever the amount of tension decreased; in a third group, it appeared when tension levels remained the same. Remarkably, despite the misleading feedback in two of the groups, everyone reported headache improvement (see ▌Figure 16.4, page 536). Apparently, feeling that you have some control over your body can be sufficient to lower stress-induced pain (Andrasik & Holroyd, 1980). Remember, whether you'll experience a stress response depends on a cognitive appraisal of your resources. If you feel you have the ability to control the threat or demand, even if that control is illusory, you're less likely to experience stress.

Social Support

Although it may seem like a cliché, having a good friend to lean on during a time of stress really does matter. Psychologists use the term **social support** to refer to the resources we receive from other people or groups, often in the form of comfort, caring, or help. There is a great deal of evidence to suggest that social support can improve one's psychological and physical health (Taylor, 2007). People with well-established social support systems are less likely to suffer a second heart attack (Case et al., 1992), are more likely to survive life-threatening cancer (Speigel, 2004), and are less likely to consider suicide if they're infected with HIV (Schneider et al., 1991). Other studies have established that social support plays a role in lowering the likelihood of depression and in speeding recovery (McLeod, Kessler, & Landis, 1992).

social support The resources we receive from other people or groups, often in the form of comfort, caring, or help.

Social support probably helps reduce stress for many reasons. Once again, the evidence tends to be correlational (researchers can't manipulate the amount of support someone receives, for ethical reasons), so firm cause-and-effect relationships have been difficult to establish. One possibility is that social contacts help people maintain a healthful lifestyle. Friends and family push you out the door for your morning jog, force you to take your medications, or encourage you to visit the doctor

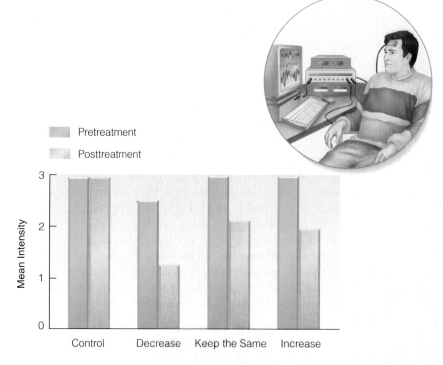

FIGURE 16.4 Biofeedback, Perceived Control, and Stress
Subjects in three groups were led to believe that they could lower the amount of muscle tension in their foreheads through biofeedback. Actually, they learned to increase, decrease, or keep the tension levels the same. Yet all three groups showed significant improvement in headache symptoms, irrespective of condition. Apparently, the mere fact that the subjects believed they were lowering the tension levels was sufficient to produce improvement. Also shown are the data for control subjects who received no biofeedback. (Data from Andrasik & Holroyd, 1980)

CRITICAL THINKING

Do you think it's possible that people who are healthier tend to get more social support than those who are sick? Might this fact account for the correlation?

regularly. Family and friends also bolster your confidence in times of stress, so you're more likely to feel that you have the necessary resources to cope with the demand. In a time of loss, such as immediately after the death of a spouse, social support lowers the chances that a grieving person will engage in unhealthful behaviors, such as drinking. (For a discussion of how pets can act as a form of positive social support, see the Practical Solutions feature.)

It's also the case that simply having someone to talk things over with can help you cope with stress. James Pennebaker (1990) has conducted a number of studies in which college students were encouraged to talk or write about upsetting events in their lives (everything from a divorce in the family to fears about the future). When compared to "control" students, who were asked to talk or write about trivial things, the students who opened up showed improved immune functioning and were less likely to visit the college health center over the next several months. Pennebaker has found similar benefits for people who lived through natural disasters (such as earthquakes) or were part of the Holocaust. Opening up, talking about things, and confiding in others really seems to help people cope (Pennebaker & Chung, 2007).

At the same time, psychologists recognize that social support can have a negative side as well. For example, if you've come to depend on another for support and that support is no longer delivered, your ability to cope can be compromised. Social support can also reduce self-reliance in some people, which may produce psychological distress and impair their ability to cope. Whether people respond favorably to social support and the receipt of aid, or consider it to be a meddling nuisance, depends to some extent on how much control they feel they have over their own actions and the outcomes of their actions.

Reappraising the Situation

When thinking about how to cope with stress, it's important to remember that the origin of the stress reaction is essentially psychological. In most instances, it's not the sudden life event or the daily hassle that leads us to experience stress—it's our *interpretation* of the event that really matters. Even the death of a spouse or the occurrence of a natural disaster, cruel as it may seem, will create significant stress only if the

Pet Support

Having a loved one or a good friend to talk to about your problems makes a difference, and that friend doesn't even need to be human. The companionship of pets—dogs, cats, even birds—has repeatedly been found to be an effective form of social support. Heart attack victims who own pets, for example, are more likely to survive the first year after the attack than are non–pet owners. Correlational studies among the elderly have found that pet ownership is inversely related to the severity of psychological problems: People who are attached to their pets are less likely to show the symptoms of depression (Garrity et al., 1989). Ownership of a dog, in particular, is an excellent predictor of whether or not an elderly person will feel the need to visit a doctor (Siegel, 1990).

There's some evidence to suggest that having a pet may even be a more effective buffer against stress than having a human companion. In an experiment conducted by Karen Allen and her colleagues (1991), female dog owners agreed to have several physiological reactions monitored while they tried to solve relatively difficult math problems. Prior to starting the task, the women were randomly divided into three groups. In one group, the women were allowed to have their dog with them in the room while completing the math task. In a second group, no dogs were allowed, but each woman was allowed the presence of a close human friend. In the third group, no social support was present during the testing.

A variety of physiological reactions were measured, including heart rate and blood pressure. Not surprisingly, solving difficult math problems led directly to stress-related arousal—heart rate increased, as did blood pressure. But the amount of reactivity depended on the group: The women who were allowed to have their dog with them showed the lowest arousal effects compared to the women in the other two groups (see ▌Figure 16.5). The presence of the pet apparently acted as an effective buffer against stress. The surprise finding of the study was that having a close human friend sit nearby while solving the math problems actually led to the highest relative stress reaction.

Does this mean that pets are more therapeutic than friends or loved ones? For some people in some situations, the answer may

Pets are effective buffers against stress for many people.

well be "Yes." Allen and her colleagues argued that pets are often effective buffers against stress because they're essentially nonevaluative. Pets don't make value judgments about their caretakers. Your dog or cat doesn't care one bit about how well you're doing on some math task, but your close human friend might. A friend's expectations can place added pressure on you as you perform an already stressful task. A woman who participated in the study by Allen and colleagues put it this way: "Pets never withhold their love, they never get angry and leave, and they never go out looking for new owners" (p. 588). Another woman offered the following: "Whereas husbands may come and go, and children may grow up and leave home, a 'dog is forever' " (p. 588). The opinions of these women may not be shared by everyone, nor do you need to hold these strong views to appreciate the value of pet companionship. The data simply indicate that pets can be an important part of your social network and that they can clearly help you cope with stress.

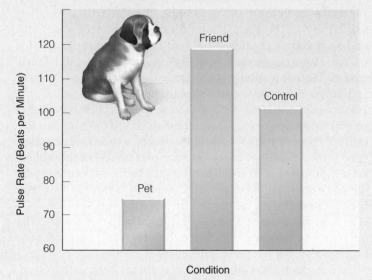

▌FIGURE 16.5 Pets as Stress Moderators
In one study, a pet's presence during a stressful task significantly lowered the stress reaction (measured here in terms of pulse rate) compared to when a friend was present or to a control condition in which neither a friend nor a pet was present. (Data from Allen et al., 1991)

The support of family and friends can be especially helpful when the environment itself acts as a stressor.

event is appraised in a negative way. Imagine if your spouse were suffering from an incurable disease, one that produced extreme and persistent pain. Under these conditions, death could be seen as a kind of blessing.

Remember, too, that many instances of stress are caused by the little things, the daily hassles of life. Getting stuck in traffic, or in the wrong line at the supermarket, makes us feel stressed only because we have a tendency to "catastrophize" the situation: "This is absolutely awful . . . I can't stand waiting here any longer . . . I'm going to get home late, and my family will be mad." It's not the delay that creates the stress, it's the things we tell ourselves about the delay that cause the problems. As a result, many psychologists feel that stress can be managed effectively through logical reanalysis and positive reappraisal. If you can interpret the hassle in a more logical and positive manner, you can reduce or eliminate the stress reaction.

Stress management techniques that rely on cognitive reappraisal take a variety of forms. For instance, you can be taught to focus on certain aspects of the situation that distract you from catastrophizing. If you're stuck in the wrong checkout line, rather than concentrating on how you "must" get home on time, pick up one of the tabloids and read about the latest sighting of Elvis. Alternatively, try using your past experiences to reappraise the consequences: "Let's see, this certainly is not the first time I've been stuck in a checkout line, and my family and friends still think I'm okay." Another approach would be to analyze the situation logically and derive alternatives for the future: "Every time I come to the market at 5:30, right after work, I get stuck in a line—maybe if I wait and go after dinner, there will be less of a wait."

Some stress management programs recommend that clients keep daily records of the specific situations that have led to stress, as well as the specific symptoms and thoughts that arose (an example is shown in ▌Figure 16.6). The value of a stress record is that it allows the client to recognize any unrealistic thoughts or conclusions on the spot because they need to be written down. With time, clients get a pretty good idea of the situations that lead to the highest stress, and they gain insight into the thought processes that underlie their reactions. As each unrealistic thought is recognized, the client can work at reappraising the situation and confronting any negative attitudes or beliefs (Barlow, Rapee, & Reisner, 2001).

CRITICAL THINKING

What's the link between these stress management programs and the techniques used in cognitive therapies, such as rational-emotive therapy?

Sample Daily Stress Record

Week of _____

Stress thermometer:
8 — Extreme stress
7
6 — Great stress
5
4 — Moderate stress
3
2 — Mild stress
1
0 — No stress

Date	(1) Starting time	(2) Ending time	(3) Highest stress (0-8)	(4) Triggers	(5) Symptoms	(6) Thoughts
1–5	10:00 am	11:00 am	7	Sales meeting	Sweating, headache	My figures are bad.
1–7	5:15 pm	5:35 pm	6	Traffic jam	Tension, impatience	I'll never get home.
1–8	12:30 pm	12:32 pm	3	Lost keys	Tension	I can't find my keys.
1–9	3:30 pm	4:30 pm	4	Waiting for guests	Sweating, nausea	Are they lost?

FIGURE 16.6 A Daily Stress Record
Stress management programs often recommend that clients keep daily records of situations that lead to stress, along with the specific symptoms and thoughts that arise. (From D. H. Barlow, R. M. Rapee, & L. C. Reisner, "Daily Stress Record," *Mastering Stress 2001—A LifeStyle Approach*, p. 12. Copyright © 2001. Reproduced with permission of American Health Publishing Company, Dallas, Texas. All rights reserved.)

Test Yourself 16.3

Check on your knowledge about stress management techniques by answering the following questions. (You will find the answers in the Appendix.)

1. Relaxation techniques, such as meditation or progressive muscle relaxation, appear to work because:
   a. They promote a sense of "connectedness" with the therapist.
   b. They lead to positive cognitive reappraisals.
   c. The stress response is incompatible with relaxation.
   d. They cause you to open up and express feelings.
2. Biofeedback may be effective for managing stress because it:
   a. Gives you a feeling of control.
   b. Leads to muscle relaxation.
   c. Trains neurons to fire in sequence.
   d. Works well with meditation.
3. Which of the following statements about the influence of social support on stress is false?
   a. Social contacts help you maintain a healthy lifestyle.
   b. Social support increases the chances that you'll open up and express feelings.
   c. Social support can reduce the chances of a second heart attack.
   d. Social support makes it easier to cope if the support is no longer delivered.
4. Elroy no longer fumes when he gets stuck in traffic because he's stopped catastrophizing about the consequences. Which of the following stress management techniques is Elroy probably using?
   a. Cognitive reappraisal
   b. Autogenic relaxation
   c. Progressive muscle relaxation
   d. Cathartic exploration

Living a Healthy Lifestyle

LEARNING GOALS

- Discuss the physical and psychological benefits of aerobic exercise.
- Discuss the consequences of tobacco use and explain why quitting smoking is so difficult.
- Discuss the value of proper nutrition.
- Describe the different types of prevention programs and explain how they're used to target AIDS.

ONE OF THE CHALLENGES of the health psychology movement is to devise a comprehensive and workable framework for health promotion (Marks, Sykes, & McKinley, 2003). In offering prescriptions for healthful lifestyles, psychologists recognize that not all risk factors can be controlled. Men, for example, have a much greater risk of developing heart disease than women, and the elderly are at a greater risk of developing a whole host of health-related problems. Obviously, people have no control over heredity, and they can't help the fact that they grow old. But there are lifestyle choices that can make a difference.

Get Fit: The Value of Aerobic Exercise

Exercise is an excellent example of an activity that can have a substantial positive impact on physical and psychological health, especially if the exercise is sustained and aerobic. **Aerobic exercise** consists of high-intensity activities that increase both heart rate and oxygen consumption, such as fast walking, running, dancing, rowing, swimming, and so on. As you probably know, regular aerobic exercise improves cardiovascular fitness over the long term and, on average, increases the chances that you'll live longer.

Psychologically, regular exercise improves mood and makes people more resistant to the effects of stressors. Much of the evidence is correlational (studies have shown statistical relationships between the regularity of exercise and reported mental health), but controlled experimental studies have reached the same conclusion.

aerobic exercise High-intensity activities, such as running and swimming, that increase both heart rate and oxygen consumption.

Regular exercise is an important ingredient in a healthful lifestyle.

© George Shelley/Corbis

For example, in a study by McCann and Holmes (1984), volunteer female college students who were suffering from mild depression were asked to (1) engage in a regular program of aerobic exercise, (2) learn relaxation techniques, or (3) do nothing. After ten weeks the aerobic exercise group showed the largest improvement in mood. More recent work indicates that 30 minutes of moderate exercise daily may be sufficient to increase mood (Hansen, Stevens, & Coast, 2001). In another study of stress resistance, men were randomly assigned to exercise conditions that involved either aerobic activity or nonaerobic strength-and-flexibility training. After 12 weeks of training, the men in the aerobic group showed lower blood pressure and heart rate when they were exposed to situations involving mental stress (Blumenthal et al., 1988).

Researchers have yet to understand fully how or why exercise improves psychological health and functioning. Over the short term, vigorous exercise increases the amount of oxygen that reaches the brain, which undoubtedly improves cognitive functioning, and sustained exercise may alter mood-inducing neurotransmitters in the brain. It is also clearly the case that aerobic exercise, as it improves cardiovascular health, will lessen the physiological effects of the stress reaction. But there may also be placebo-like effects involved: People who choose to exercise regularly are convinced they're going to improve their health, and they subsequently rate themselves as more psychologically healthy than they may in fact be (Pierce et al., 1993).

Don't Smoke: Tobacco and Health

Virtually everyone knows that smoking or the oral ingestion (chewing) of tobacco is bad for your health. There is no shortage of correlational and experimental studies available to document this fact. Few researchers question, for example, that smoking contributes annually to hundreds of thousands of deaths in the United States alone, from associated heart disease, cancer, stroke, and emphysema. And it's not just the smokers who are affected—the babies of women who smoke during pregnancy tend to have lower birth weights and are at increased risk for birth defects; even people who are simply exposed to smoke secondhand may suffer from subsequent health problems. So why, given that it is so damaging to their health, do people smoke?

First, despite what you might have heard on television (especially from tobacco company executives), smoking is recognized to be *addictive* by the vast majority of mainstream researchers in the health-related sciences (Swan, Hudmon, & Khroyan, 2003). Many people who smoke regularly become dependent on their daily dosage, and when they try to quit, they suffer physical and psychological withdrawal symptoms. The DSM-IV-TR lists criteria for a diagnosis of "nicotine withdrawal" that include insomnia, irritability, difficulty concentrating, and increased appetite or weight gain. The symptoms of withdrawal can be severe enough to cause a significant disruption in normal everyday functioning (Piasecki, Fiore, & Baker, 1998). This conclusion, of course, comes as no surprise to anyone who has ever tried to quit smoking after prolonged use.

The reinforcing effects of cigarette smoking can be explained by appealing to chemical reactions in the brain and to factors in the culture at large. Within the brain, it takes only seconds for nicotine—the active agent in cigarette smoke—to stimulate the central nervous system, elevating heart rate, blood pressure, and mood. Many smokers report that cigarettes not only improve mood but help alleviate anxiety and stress. At the same time, tobacco companies launch advertising campaigns designed to make smoking appear desirable. Tobacco use is identified with role models—often thin, vigorous, and healthy people on horseback or frolicking on the beach—or is associated with independence and nonconformity. Unfortunately, these types of advertising campaigns are often particularly effective for those in adolescence, which is the time when most smokers begin their habit.

You've probably heard the saying that the best way to stop smoking is never to start. It's undoubtedly true because, once started, tobacco use is a difficult habit to

Tobacco companies often associate their products with healthy, vigorous lifestyles.

break. The psychological and physical withdrawal symptoms associated with tobacco use make quitting extraordinarily difficult. Furthermore, cues in the environment (such as seeing someone else smoking) regularly trigger the habit (Tiffany, Cox, & Elash, 2000). A variety of smoking cessation techniques have been developed that rely on psychological principles, but they tend to be effective only over the short term. For example, some programs use learning principles to "punish" tobacco use and encourage users to replace positive associations with negative ones. These programs often prove effective initially, but in the long run the vast majority of smokers return to the habit. In the words of Mark Twain: "To cease smoking is the easiest thing I ever did; I ought to know because I've done it a thousand times."

But the news is not all bad. There has been a significant drop in the percentage of people who smoke in the United States and Canada, especially over the past two or three decades. In the mid-1960s, for example, a little over 40% of people in the United States smoked; today the number has dropped below 25%, and approximately 70% of those who currently smoke want to quit (Swan et al., 2003). More and more people are quitting—although often only after many relapses. Perhaps more significantly, large numbers of people are choosing never to start.

Eat Right: The Value of Proper Nutrition

In Chapter 11 we dealt with the adaptive problem of how to motivate eating behavior. Obviously, to maintain proper functioning of body and mind, people need to consume the necessary amounts of food. In our earlier discussion of eating, we didn't pay too much attention to the quality of the food that people consume; instead, our concern was mainly with the internal and external factors that underlie the motivation to eat. But proper nutrition is vitally important in maintaining a healthful body and mind, and health psychologists are engaged in a vigorous campaign to improve people's dietary habits.

The dietary habits of most North Americans leave much to be desired. After a long period of relative stability, overweight and obesity rates in the United States

CRITICAL THINKING

Do you think there's a connection between age and the chances of living a healthy lifestyle? If so, why do you think this is?

began to increase in the 1980s and have continued to increase to the present day. Adjusting for age and height, there has been nearly a 10% increase in average body weight during this period, and the rate of obesity has virtually doubled (Jeffery & Utter, 2003). Our diet tends to be too high in calories, fat, cholesterol, sugar, protein, and salt. High-fat diets have been linked to heart disease, stroke, and several kinds of cancer, as well as to obesity. Diets that are high in cholesterol contribute to heart disease because the cholesterol can lodge in the walls of arteries, leading to a hardening and narrowing that restricts blood flow. Of course, not everyone who maintains a diet high in fat or cholesterol will develop these problems (because genetic predispositions are also a factor), but there's no question that many people eat themselves into an early grave.

Given the overwhelming amount of evidence linking diet to health, why don't people eat better? For many people, it's not the amount of food they eat but their choice of food that creates the problems. Consider the following: A baked potato has 0.5% of its calories as fat; when that same potato is french fried, it has 42% of its calories as fat (Winikoff, 1983). Everyone has a handy list of reasons for choosing to stop for fast food, including the fact that it tastes good. But from a nutritional standpoint, fast foods tend to come up short because they're packed with fat and sodium. The best advice is to avoid foods with too much fat, cholesterol, sugar, and sodium. This is not a new message for you, I'm sure, but remember: You're now much more sophisticated about the psychological factors that influence your choice of foods (see Chapter 11). So think before you eat—it might make a difference.

Avoid Risky Behavior: Protect Yourself From Disease

Choosing a healthful lifestyle requires having the right kind of information about how to prevent health-impairing habits. Health psychologists often distinguish among three main types of prevention programs (Winett, 1995):

1. *Primary prevention* is designed to educate the public as a whole in ways to reduce or eliminate a problem before it starts. Teaching children about the potential hazards of smoking or drug use is an example of primary prevention.
2. *Secondary prevention* involves the early identification of risk factors in specific population groups, such as checking for HIV infection in intravenous drug users or looking for early signs of disease through screening.
3. *Tertiary prevention* seeks to handle and contain an illness or habit once it has been acquired.

All three types of prevention programs are needed, but stopping an illness or habit before it starts—primary prevention—obviously has greater long-term significance.

AIDS   Living in the age of AIDS (acquired immune deficiency syndrome) dramatically underscores the need for primary prevention programs. As you probably know, **AIDS** is an infectious disease that involves a gradual weakening and disabling of the immune system. AIDS is "acquired," meaning that it's not a by-product of the genetic code, and it's thought to develop as a result of infection with the *human immunodeficiency virus* (HIV). HIV does its damage by attacking cells in the immune system, which leaves the body unable to fight off opportunistic infections that would otherwise be controlled. The disease AIDS is diagnosed in the latter stages of HIV infection when the immune system has been sufficiently compromised.

Because infection with HIV can lead to AIDS and death, it's crucial that all three types of prevention programs be initiated, with special emphasis on primary prevention (Kalichman et al., 1997; Strombeck & Levy, 1998). Infection with HIV is preventable when the proper steps are taken to control its transmission. HIV is transmitted through contact with bodily fluids, particularly blood and semen. The virus is found

AIDS Acquired immune deficiency syndrome, a disease that gradually weakens and disables the immune system.

he's real cute and he's got a great job
but when
**he didn't
put on a condom**
I said, **Hello!**
DO I LOOK *STUPID?*

AIDS
IT AIN'T OVER YET
1 800 235 2331

© Better World Advertising/www.socialmarketing.com

Primary prevention is crucial in battling the AIDS epidemic.

in saliva, urine, and tears, but the amount is so small that infection through casual contact—even kissing—is extremely unlikely. The most likely means of transmission is through sexual contact or sharing intravenous needles with someone infected with the virus. The use of latex condoms during sexual activity dramatically reduces the chances of infection.

Although AIDS and HIV infection are medical conditions, psychologists have two important roles to play. First, the only effective way to control widespread HIV transmission is to prevent risk-taking behavior. The public needs to be educated about how HIV spreads, and the many misconceptions that currently exist need to be countered. For example, there are still people who are convinced that AIDS is a homosexual problem only, despite the fact that the disease can be—and is being—readily transmitted through heterosexual contact. Indeed, in most parts of the world unprotected heterosexual contact is primarily responsible for spreading the virus. The other key role being played by psychologists in the AIDS epidemic is a therapeutic one. Once infected, people with HIV are subjected to an overwhelming amount of stress. Not only are these individuals faced with the prospects of an early death, but they must face the stigma that often accompanies the disease. Psychologists are actively involved in establishing treatment programs that can help AIDS patients cope with their disease (Carey & Vanable, 2003).

Test Yourself 16.4

Check your knowledge of living a healthy lifestyle by deciding whether each of the following statements is True or False. *(You will find the answers in the Appendix.)*

1. Aerobic exercise improves cardiovascular health and general mood but produces few changes in the physiological effects of the stress reaction. *True or False?*
2. Smoking is recognized to be addictive by the vast majority of mainstream researchers in the health-related sciences. *True or False?*
3. For many people, it's not the amount of food they eat but their choice of food that creates health problems. *True or False?*
4. Teaching children about the hazards of smoking or drugs would be classified as an example of secondary prevention. *True or False?*

The close relationship between thoughts and emotions and the physical reactions of the body means that understanding and promoting physical health requires some attention to psychological factors. Health psychology is part of a broader movement, called behavioral medicine, that is seeking to understand the medical consequences of the interaction between body and mind. Health psychologists in particular are interested in the psychological and environmental factors—everything from personality characteristics to the work environment—that both produce illness and affect the likelihood of recovery.

Experiencing Stress Stress has historically been a somewhat difficult concept to define. It can be conceived of as a stimulus, as a response, or as a process through which external events are interpreted as threatening or demanding. We chose to treat stress as the physical and psychological reaction to demanding situations. The stress response is often treated as an extended reaction that occurs in phases. According to the general adaptation syndrome proposed by Hans Selye, the body initially reacts to threat with a highly adaptive fight-or-flight response (although there may be gender differences in the behavioral response); if the threat continues, the body goes through resistance and exhaustion phases that make it vulnerable to disease.

Our reactions are critically influenced by the way we perceive or appraise a situation. To experience stress, it's necessary to both perceive a threat and feel that you lack the necessary resources to deal with it effectively. This means that identical environmental events can lead to very different stress reactions, depending on how the situation is interpreted. Overall, however, it is possible to identify some common sources of stress. External sources of stress include significant life events, daily hassles, and environmental factors such as noise and crowding. Internal sources of stress include perceived control—how much influence you feel you have over the situation—and explanatory style.

Certain personality characteristics have been linked to stress. Type A individuals—those who are hard driving, ambitious, and impatient—appear to be at increased risk for subsequent heart disease. The Type A behavior pattern is complex, however, and researchers are in the process of trying to determine which of the many components of this personality type contribute most to the onset of disease.

Reacting to Prolonged Stress Stress is an adaptive reaction to threat, but if the threat is extended over time, both body and mind can start to break down. Stress has been implicated in a wide variety of health problems, ranging from heart disease to the common cold. A number of studies have shown that prolonged stress can affect immune functioning, which is the body's method for fighting off disease. Stress can compromise the immune response by either lowering the number of specialized white blood cells (lymphocytes) or by somehow suppressing the response of those lymphocytes to foreign substances that have invaded the body.

Two chronic psychological consequences of prolonged stress are posttraumatic stress disorder and burnout. Posttraumatic stress disorder results from exposure to extreme trauma, such as that experienced during battle or as a result of a physical assault such as rape. The symptoms of the disorder include flashbacks in which the traumatic event is reexperienced, avoidance of stimuli associated with the trauma, and chronic arousal problems. Burnout is a term that psychologists use to describe a state of physical, emotional, and mental exhaustion that sometimes develops after prolonged stress.

Reducing and Coping With Stress We use coping strategies to manage conditions of threat that tax our resources. Effective coping techniques include relaxation training, the use of social support, and reappraisal. The stress response is incompatible with relaxation, and relaxation training can help lower components of the stress response (such as blood pressure and heart rate). In progressive relaxation training, the client is taught to concentrate on specific muscle groups in the body, note whether they seem tense, and then relax those specific groups. Sometimes it's useful to provide biofeedback as well.

Additional evidence indicates that social support—the resources received from other people—can also help you cope effectively with stress. Friends and family help us maintain a healthful lifestyle, boost confidence, or simply provide an avenue for us to open up and express our feelings. Talking about things and confiding in others really seem to help people deal with stress. Finally, because stress depends on how you interpret the threatening or demanding situation, it can often be managed effectively through cognitive reappraisal. You can be taught to reinterpret significant life events or daily hassles in a less stressful way. Some stress management programs encourage clients to keep daily stress records. By identifying the kinds of situations that create stress, as well as the negative thoughts those situations induce, you become better prepared to reinterpret those situations and thoughts in a more adaptive manner.

Living a Healthy Lifestyle Aerobic exercise is one example of an activity that can have a substantial effect on physical and psychological health. Regular exercise improves mood and makes people more resistant to the effects of stressors. Another lifestyle choice that directly affects physical health is the decision not to smoke. Smoking and other tobacco use contribute to hundreds of thousands of deaths annually in the United States alone, from associated heart disease, cancer, stroke, and emphysema. Tobacco use stimulates activity in the central nervous system, which is immediately reinforcing, but prolonged use leads to addiction or dependence that can be difficult to overcome.

Proper nutrition is another important ingredient in maintaining a healthy body and mind. The North American diet tends to be too high in calories, fat, cholesterol, sugar, protein, and salt. Poor dietary habits can lead to significant long-term health problems. Finally, maintaining a healthful lifestyle includes avoiding risky behaviors and preventing disease. For example, psychologists are playing an important role in the AIDS epidemic by educating the public about risky behavior, and through the establishment of treatment programs they're helping AIDS patients cope with the psychological effects of the disease.

Active Summary *(You will find the answers in the Appendix.)*

Experiencing Stress

• According to the general (1) _____ syndrome (GAS), we respond to threats or demands in (2) _____ phases. The (3) _____ reaction corresponds to the fight-or-flight response; during the (4) _____ stage the body adjusts its reaction to cope with the continuing threat; finally, if we can't neutralize the effect, the (5) _____ phase sets in. Common psychological reactions to stress include (6) _____, anger, (7) _____, dejection, and grief.

• Most psychologists believe stress is closely related to the experience of (8) _____. How stress is experienced is affected by how people (9) _____ the situation they're in. A greater stress response will be produced if people perceive a threat directly and believe that their resources are inadequate to deal with it.

• (10) _____ life events can create a great deal of stress. According to the (11) _____ Readjustment Rating Scale, both positive and (12) _____ life events that are associated with (13) _____ may produce stress. Psychologists recognize that (14) _____ hassles and environmental factors such as (15) _____ and crowding are important determinants of chronic stress. (16) _____ psychology is devoted to the study of environmental effects on behavior and health.

• (17) _____ control is how much influence we believe we have over a situation. Generally, the less perceived control, the (18) _____ the resulting stress. (19) _____ style can also contribute to stress and influence health. People with Type A personalities are hard-driving, ambitious, easily annoyed, and impatient, all stress-producing characteristics linked with (20) _____ disease.

Reacting to Prolonged Stress

• Stress lowers the (21) _____ response, and therefore decreases either the number of (22) _____ or their ability to respond to the presence of foreign substances.

The link between stress and the immune system has led to speculation about a possible relationship between stress and illnesses such as cancer, although researchers offer such conclusions cautiously. Prolonged exposure to stress is also associated with (23) _____ blood pressure and high (24) _____, which are major risk factors in cardiovascular disease.

• Psychologists are convinced that (25) _____ life events may produce (26) _____ disorders, possibly through an interaction with (27) _____ vulnerability. Extreme stress produced by traumatic experiences is sometimes associated with (28) _____ stress disorder, which is characterized by (29) _____, avoidance of trauma-associated stimuli, and chronic arousal symptoms. (30) _____, another effect of prolonged stress, is a state of emotional and mental (31) _____ caused by lasting involvement in situations that are emotionally demanding. Burnout may be caused by loss of (32) _____ in the workplace or of (33) _____ in life.

Reducing and Coping With Stress

• Stress is incompatible with (34) _____, which is therefore an effective stress reducer. Progressive (35) _____ relaxation involves concentrating on specific muscle groups, noting tension and deliberately relaxing the affected areas. In (36) _____ relaxation, the focus is on directing blood flow toward specific muscle groups, warming and relaxing them. (37) _____ is also an effective relaxation technique. (38) _____ has been shown to facilitate relaxation by providing information about the effectiveness of the techniques the person is using. (39) _____ support helps to reduce stress but may have a negative effect as well in certain situations.

• How we (40) _____ events partly determines how stressful they are, so many stress management techniques involve cognitive (41) _____. This may include focusing on aspects of the situation that aren't upsetting, which prevents the reaction that a catastrophe has occurred, or analyzing the situation in a logical fashion.

Living a Healthy Lifestyle

• (42) _____ exercise increases heart rate and oxygen consumption and can have a highly positive impact on both (43) _____ and (44) _____ health. It can improve (45) _____ and increase (46) _____ to stressors. Why exercise improves functioning hasn't been exactly determined, but it may involve improved cardiovascular and cognitive function and alterations in mood-enhancing chemicals.

• Correlational and experimental evidence have demonstrated the link between (47) _____ use and serious (48) _____ problems. Smoking seems to produce (49) _____ reactions in the brain that reinforce the habit. Although many smokers fail to quit because tobacco is highly (50) _____ and is associated with

(51) _____ effects, smoking rates have been on the decline over the past two to three decades.

• Proper (52) _____ is vital to a healthy (53) _____ and (54) _____, yet in the United States many people maintain a diet that is high in calories, cholesterol, fat, and other substances that are damaging when consumed in excess. Nutritional problems usually have to do with the (55) _____ of food that is eaten, not necessarily the amount.

• (56) _____ prevention is aimed at reducing health problems or eliminating them (57) _____ they start. (58) _____ prevention involves early identification of risk factors in specific (59) _____. (60) _____ prevention seeks to handle and contain an illness that has already developed. The prevalence of AIDS underscores the important need for a special emphasis on (61) _____ prevention programs.

Terms to Remember

aerobic exercise, 540
AIDS, 543
biofeedback, 535
burnout, 532
cognitive appraisal, 521
coping, 533
environmental psychology, 524

general adaptation syndrome (GAS), 519
health psychology, 517
lymphocytes, 529
perceived control, 525
posttraumatic stress disorder, 531

social support, 535
stress, 518
stressors, 518
Type A, 526
Type B, 526

Media Resources

 ThomsonNOW

www.thomsonedu.com/ThomsonNOW

Go to this site for the link to ThomsonNOW, your one-stop study shop. Take a Pre-Test for this chapter, and ThomsonNOW will generate a Personalized Study Plan based on your results. The Study Plan will identify the topics you need to review and direct you to online resources to help you master those topics. You can then take a Post-Test to help you determine the concepts you have mastered and what you still need to work on.

 Companion Website

www.thomsonedu.com/psychology/nairne

Go to this site to find online resources directly linked to your book, including a glossary, flashcards, quizzing, weblinks, and more.

 Psyk.trek 3.0

Check out the Psyk.trek CD-ROM for further study of the concepts in this chapter. Psyk.trek's interactive learning modules, simulations, and quizzes offer additional opportunities for you to interact with, reflect on, and retain the material:

Stress and Health: Types of Stress
Stress and Health: Elements of Emotion
Stress and Health: Responding to Stress

Appendix

Chapter 1

Test Yourself 1.1

1. False. Internal thoughts and feelings are often studied by psychologists; a thought or a feeling can be considered as a type of behavior when it is revealed through written or spoken expression.
2. True.
3. True.
4. False. Psychiatrists are medical doctors who receive specialized training in psychology, but their interests do not differ in any fundamental way from those of psychologists. Both psychologists and psychiatrists work on severe psychological problems such as a schizophrenia.

Test Yourself 1.2

1. b. Most psychologists believe that mental events arise entirely from activity in the brain.
2. Functionalists and structuralists used the technique of introspection to understand immediate conscious experience. The structuralists believed that it was best to break the mind down into basic parts, much as a chemist would seek to understand a chemical compound. The functionalists were influenced by Darwin's views on natural selection and focused primarily on the purpose and adaptive value of mental events. Behaviorism, founded by John Watson, steered psychology away from the study of immediate conscious experience to an emphasis on behavior.
3. d. Psychoanalysis often places a strong emphasis on hidden urges and memories related to sex and aggression.

Test Yourself 1.3

1. c. Clinical psychologists who adopt an eclectic approach often consider the preferences of the client, as well as the type of problem presented, in deciding on the most appropriate therapy.
2. Over the past several decades, psychologists have returned to the study of internal mental phenomena such as consciousness. This shift away from strict behaviorism has been labeled the cognitive revolution. An important factor that helped fuel this revolution was the development of the computer, which became a model of sorts for the human mind. Developments in biology are also playing an important role in shaping modern psychology and in creating effective treatments for psychological problems.
3. True.
4. b. Our cultural background can influence how we think, reason, and remember.

Active Summary

1. behavior
2. mind
3. observation
4. behavior
5. Clinical
6. Applied
7. Research
8. philosophy
9. physiology
10. Descartes
11. mind
12. Empiricism
13. Nativism
14. Darwin
15. genes or nature
16. experience or nurture
17. Structuralism
18. Functionalism
19. Behaviorism
20. psychoanalysis
21. unconscious
22. Humanistic
23. Calkins
24. Washburn
25. Wooley
26. Ladd-Franklin
27. Martin
28. Howard
29. Bernal
30. Eclectic
31. memory
32. chemical
33. Evolutionary
34. values

Chapter 2

Test Yourself 2.1

1. The middle point in an ordered set of scores is the median.
2. The case study technique, which focuses on the study of a single instance of behavior of condition, is open to criticism because its results may lack external validity.
3. When behavior changes as a result of the observation process, the recorded data are said to suffer from a problem of reactivity.

4. The descriptive research technique used to gather limited amounts of information from many people is called a survey.

Test Yourself 2.2

1. negative
2. positive
3. positive
4. zero

Test Yourself 2.3

1. In experimental research, the researcher actively manipulates the environment to observe its effect on behavior. The aspect of the environment that is manipulated is called the independent variable; the behavior of interest is measured by the dependent variable. To draw conclusions about cause and effect, the experimenter must make certain that the independent variable is the only thing changing systematically in the environment.
2. b. The independent variable—Tom Cruise versus Barney—is not the only thing changing across the groups.
3. c. increases the chances that subject differences will be equally represented in each group.

Test Yourself 2.4

1. Psychologists have a responsibility to respect the rights and dignity of other people. To ensure that research participants are treated ethically, psychologists use (a) informed consent, which means that everyone is fully informed about the potential risks of the project, (b) confidentiality, which assures the subject's rights to privacy will be maintained, and (c) debriefing, which is designed to provide more information about the purpose and procedures of the research.
2. c. is justified, but only under some circumstances.
3. c. animals can give no informed consent.

Active Summary

1. Descriptive
2. observe
3. Behavior
4. noninterfering
5. Case
6. hypotheses
7. responses
8. representative
9. individual
10. regularities
11. hypotheses
12. Descriptive
13. Inferential
14. correlation
15. variables
16. predict
17. causality
18. experimental control
19. experimental
20. environment
21. hypothesis
22. independent
23. manipulated
24. dependent
25. observed
26. control
27. independent
28. two
29. control group
30. experimental
31. single-blind
32. double-blind
33. experimenter
34. controls
35. participate
36. Debriefing
37. Confidentiality
38. control
39. humane

Chapter 3

Test Yourself 3.1

1. The soma is the main body of the cell, where excitatory and inhibitory messages combine.
2. The axon is the long tail-like part of a neuron that serves as the cell's main transmitter device.
3. The action potential is the all-or-none electrical signal that leads to the release of chemical messengers.
4. The dendrites are the branchlike fibers that extend outward and receive messages from other neurons.
5. Each is an example of a neurotransmitter.

Test Yourself 3.2

1. The hindbrain is the primitive part of the brain that controls basic life support functions such as heart rate and respiration.
2. The hypothalamus is a structure thought to be involved in a variety of motivated activities, including eating, drinking, and sexual behavior.
3. The frontal lobes are believed to be involved in higher-order thought processes (such as planning) as well as the initiation of motor movements.
4. The cerebellum is a structure near the base of the brain that is involved in coordination of complex activities such as walking.
5. An EEG is a device used to monitor gross electrical activity in the brain.

Test Yourself 3.3

1. nervous system
2. endocrine system
3. endocrine system

4. endocrine system
5. nervous system

Test Yourself 3.4

1. False. Reading and writing skills developed too recently in the history of the species to be adaptations.
2. *Genotype* refers to the actual genetic information inherited from your biological parents.
3. Dominant genes play a stronger role.
4. Psychologists study genetic effects in identical twins because they have essentially the same genetic material.

Active Summary

1. neuroscience
2. integrate
3. electrochemically
4. dendrites
5. axons
6. Interneurons
7. Motor
8. behavioral
9. chemically
10. activation
11. spinal cord
12. axons
13. autonomic
14. somatic
15. organ
16. lesions
17. electrodes
18. electroencephalograph (EEG)
19. positron emission tomography (PET)
20. hindbrain
21. pons
22. midbrain
23. forebrain
24. limbic
25. lateralized
26. hormones
27. pituitary
28. endocrine
29. survival
30. Adaptations
31. chromosomes
32. Genes
33. recessive
34. Family
35. twin
36. fraternal
37. environmental

Chapter 4

Test Yourself 4.1

1. False. The period from implantation to the end of the eighth week is called the embryonic period.

2. True.
3. False. The cells increase in size and complexity, not in number. The number of glial cells in the brain, however, may increase with age.
4. False. The timing of motor development is determined primarily by nature—the genetic code—although the environment may play some role.
5. False. We all lose brain cells with age, but the vast majority of people over 70 will not develop dementia.

Test Yourself 4.2

1. a. Reward. In the reward technique, the baby is given reinforcement when he or she performs a movement, such as kicking a leg, in response to a presented event.
   b. Habituation. The decline in responsiveness to repeated presentations, called habituation, can be used to infer that the baby recognizes that elements of the event have been repeated.
   c. Cross-sectional. In a cross-sectional design, different age groups are studied at the same time.
   d. Longitudinal. In a longitudinal design, the same individual is tested repeatedly across the life span.
2. a. Conservation. Conservation refers to the ability to recognize that certain physical properties of an object, such as mass, remain the same despite changes in the object's appearance.
3. a. Conventional. According to Kohlberg, individuals at the conventional level of moral reasoning decide the correctness of actions on the basis of whether or not the action disrupts the social order.
   b. Postconventional. At the postconventional level, moral reasoning is based on abstract principles that may or may not conflict with accepted standards.
   c. Preconventional. At the preconventional level, moral decisions are made on the basis of the action's immediate consequences.

Test Yourself 4.3

1. a. secure
   b. avoidant
   c. resistant
   d. resistant
2. d. Not all teenagers suffer anxiety during this period.
3. False. Gender identity is already being formed by age 2 or 3.
4. a. False. Most elderly people are not sick and disabled, although certainly physical problems do increase with age.
   b. False. Some stereotypes about the elderly are positive, such as the belief that all elderly are wise and kind.
   c. False. Research suggests the opposite.
   d. False. Research suggests that most elderly prefer to strive to keep on living in such circumstances.

Active Summary

1. Zygote
2. germinal

3. implantation
4. embryonic
5. fetal
6. 7
7. plasticity
8. predictable
9. Adolescence
10. psychological
11. puberty
12. physically
13. dementia
14. preference
15. habituation
16. rewarding
17. sensory
18. shapes
19. memory
20. schemata
21. assimilation
22. accommodation
23. sensorimotor
24. preoperational
25. operational
26. formal
27. preconventional
28. conventional
29. postconventional
20. attachment
31. contact
32. Temperament
33. Strange
34. secure
35. avoidant
36. psychosocial
37. autonomy
38. inferiority
39. role
40. gender roles
41. schema
42. Ageism
43. myths
44. stages
45. bargaining

Chapter 5

Test Yourself 5.1

1. a. Fovea. The "central pit" is where the cone receptors tend to be located.
   b. Cones. These receptors are responsible for visual acuity, or our ability to see fine detail.
   c. Accommodation. Through this process, the lens changes its shape temporarily to help focus light.
   d. Retina. This "film" at the back of the eye contains the light-sensitive receptor cells.

e. Cornea. This is the protective outer covering of the eye.
2. a. False. The majority of visual messages are analyzed in the lateral geniculate and primary visual cortex, although some messages are relayed to the superior colliculus.
   b. True.
   c. True.
   d. True.
3. a. Top-down processing. This is the part of perception that is controlled by our beliefs and expectations about how the world is organized.
   b. Perceptual constancy. This can be defined as perceiving an object, or its properties, to remain the same even though the physical message delivered to the eyes is changing.
   c. Phi phenomenon. This is an illusion of motion.
   d. Convergence. This depth cue is based on calculating the degree to which the two eyes have turned inward.
   e. Recognition by components. This is the view that object perception is based on the analysis of simple building blocks, called geons.

Test Yourself 5.2

1. True.
2. False. Place, not frequency, theory proposes that the location of activation on the basilar membrane is a critical cue for pitch.
3. False. Hair cells are located in the cochlea, not the pinna, and they are "bent" by movement of the basilar membrane.
4. False. Figure-ground organization occurs in hearing as well as in vision.
5. True.

Test Yourself 5.3

1. b. Our perception of temperature is influenced by the changes that occur from one environment to the next.
2. c. Psychological factors are thought to somehow block pain messages from reaching higher neural centers.
3. d. The vestibular sacs are part of the structures of the inner ear.

Test Yourself 5.4

1. Chemoreceptors. The general term for receptor cells that are activated by invisible molecules scattered about the air or dissolved in liquids.
2. Olfactory bulb. One of the main brain destinations for odor messages.
3. Flavor. A psychological term used to describe the entire gustatory experience.
4. Olfaction. The technical name for the sense of smell.
5. Gustation. The technical name for the sense of taste.

Test Yourself 5.5

1. False. There is no single point in an intensity curve at which detection reliably begins.
2. True.

3. False. Detection of a jnd in magnitude depends on the intensity of the standard.
4. True.

Active Summary

1. eye
2. pupil
3. lens
4. retina
5. rods
6. cones
7. optic chiasm
8. thalamus
9. Feature detectors
10. three
11. opponent-process theory
12. top-down
13. proximity
14. closure
15. binocular
16. depth
17. constancy
18. frequency
19. amplitude
20. eardrum
21. cochlea
22. basilar membrane
23. brain
24. place theory
25. hair cells
26. frequency
27. auditory cortex
28. expectations
29. organize
30. localization
31. time
32. intensity
33. pressure-sensitive
34. somatosensory
35. parietal
36. increasing
37. changes
38. gate-control
39. spinal cord
40. brain
41. endorphins
42. Kinesthesia
43. position
44. somatosensory
45. vestibular
46. acceleration
47. Semicircular
48. olfaction
49. chemoreceptors
50. nasal
51. bulb
52. thalamus
53. absolute threshold
54. 50
55. signal detection
56. false
57. difference threshold
58. magnitude
59. detected
60. just noticeable difference
61. adaptation
62. stimulus
63. sensitivity
64. constant

Chapter 6

Test Yourself 6.1

1. False. The cocktail party effect suggests that we do at least some monitoring of unattended messages. We hear our name when it's spoken from across the room.
2. True.
3. True.
4. False. In visual neglect, damage to the right side of the brain means that people will fail to recognize things on the left side of the body.
5. False. Although some aspects of attention deficit/hyperactivity disorder may be learned, most researchers believe that some kind of neurological problem also contributes to the disorder.

Test Yourself 6.2

1. a. Theta waves. The characteristic pattern found in stage 1 sleep.
   b. K complex. Often triggered by loud noises during stage 2 sleep.
   c. Delta activity. Another name for the slow-wave patterns that are found during stage 3 and stage 4 sleep.
   d. REM. The characteristic pattern of paradoxical sleep.
2. c. Cats sleep more than cows.
3. a. Insomnia. Difficulty initiating and maintaining sleep.
   b. Night terror. Sleeper awakens suddenly, screaming, but the EEG pattern indicates a period of non-REM sleep.
   c. Sleep apnea. Sleeper repeatedly stops breathing during the night, usually for short periods lasting more than 1 minute.
   d. Nightmare. An anxiety-producing dream that usually occurs during the REM stage of sleep.

Test Yourself 6.3

1. Stimulant. Increases central nervous system activity.
2. Opiate. Reduces pain by mimicking the brain's own natural pain-reducing chemicals.
3. Depressant. Tends to produce inhibitory effects by increasing the effectiveness of the neurotransmitter GABA.
4. Hallucinongen. Distorts perception and may lead to flashbacks.

5. Stimulant. The type of active ingredient in your morning coffee.

Test Yourself 6.4

1. False. The EEG patterns of a hypnotized person more closely resemble the patterns found when you're awake, not asleep.
2. False. Hypnosis increases the chances of fabrication and does not generally lead to better memory.
3. True.
4. False. Hilgard's experiments support the idea of hypnotic dissociations.
5. True.

Active Summary

1. Attention
2. priorities
3. limits
4. neurons
5. dichotic listening
6. monitor
7. awareness
8. cocktail party effect
9. Automaticity
10. fast
11. attention
12. conscious
13. divided
14. neglect
15. parietal
16. left
17. distractibility
18. clocks
19. rhythms
20. waking
21. hormone
22. circadian
23. 90
24. height
25. four
26. slow
27. 90
28. repair
29. survival
30. mental
31. memories
32. wish fulfillment
33. synthesis
34. random
35. threats
36. hypersomnia
37. narcolepsy
38. dyssomnias
39. terrors
40. parasomnias
41. neurotransmitters
42. mental
43. tolerance
44. psychological
45. dependency
46. Depressants
47. alcohol
48. increase
49. pain
50. Halucinogens
51. perception
52. environmental
53. familiarity
54. set
55. suggestibility
56. relaxed
57. pain
58. enhance
59. relaxation
60. dissociations
61. consciousness
62. social
63. awareness
64. anxiety

Chapter 7

Test Yourself 7.1

1. sensitization
2. orienting response
3. habituation
4. habituation

Test Yourself 7.2

1. a. The unconditioned stimulus is the screaming.
   b. The unconditioned response is wincing and covering your ears.
   c. The conditioned stimulus is the sound of running water.
   d. The conditioned response is wincing.
2. a. The unconditioned stimulus is the puff of air.
   b. The unconditioned response is blinking.
   c. The conditioned stimulus is the word *ready*.
   d. The conditioned response is the urge to blink.
3. d. Extinction. It's likely that the stimuli presented in the experiment (soft furry things) occurred again many times in Albert's life without the accompanying loud noise. So, the association was extinguished.

Test Yourself 7.3

1. a. Negative punishment. Arriving home late is punished by the removal of freedom.
   b. Positive reinforcement. The bonus is presented to increase the chances of similar sales behavior again.
   c. Positive punishment. The ticket is delivered to lower the likelihood of speeding in a school zone (although

one might argue that the ticket also removes something positive—money).

    d. Positive reinforcement. Crying increases because Mom delivers a kiss and a story.

    e. Positive punishment. Dad delivers a stern lecture for crying, which lowers the likelihood of crying in his presence.

2. a. Variable-ratio. Reinforcement depends on the number of calls, but the number of calls is not constant or predictable.

    b. Fixed-ratio. Reinforcement always occurs when she goes to a rally.

    c. Variable-interval. Reinforcement cannot be predicted and depends on the passage of time rather than the number of responses.

    d. Fixed-ratio. Reinforcement is delivered after a fixed number of purchases.

    e. Variable-interval. Reinforcement is not predictable and depends on the passage of time.

Test Yourself 7.4

1. False. Observational learning often applies to our own behavior—we learn to act in a certain way by observing a role model.
2. True.
3. False. Our beliefs about how well we can perform a task (self-efficacy) plays an important role in observational learning.
4. True.
5. True.

Active Summary

1. behavior
2. experience
3. prioritize
4. Habituation
5. increases
6. signaling
7. predicts
8. unconditioned
9. response
10. conditioned
11. information
12. different
13. US
14. second
15. new
16. generalization
17. discrimination
18. different
19. US
20. extinction
21. inhibition
22. absence
23. Operant
24. consequences
25. effect
26. strengthened
27. weakened
28. discriminative
29. Positive
30. increases
31. increases
32. reinforcers
33. decreases
34. Negative
35. decreases
36. reinforcement
37. continuous
38. partial
39. fixed
40. ratio
41. interval
42. variable
43. shaping
44. approximations
45. biological
46. Observational
47. positive
48. rewarded
49. adaptive
50. reduce
51. increase

Chapter 8

Test Yourself 8.1

1. sensory memory
2. sensory memory
3. short-term memory
4. sensory memory
5. short-term memory
6. sensory memory
7. short-term memory
8. short-term memory

Test Yourself 8.2

1. a. semantic
    b. episodic
    c. semantic
    d. procedural
    e. procedural
2. c. Form a visual image of each word.
3. a. Method of loci. A mnemonic device in which you visualize items sitting in different locations.
    b. Distinctiveness. The appropriate term to use when you notice how an item is different from other things in memory.
    c. Elaboration. The formation of connections between an item and other things in memory.

   d. Peg-word technique. The formation of an image linking the to-be-remembered item to a specific cue.

   e. Elaboration. The process of engaging in relational processing.

Test Yourself 8.3

1. Schema. An organized knowledge package in long-term memory.
2. Implicit memory. Remembering without awareness.
3. Transfer-appropriate processing. Studying for a multiple choice test by writing your own multiple-choice questions.
4. Free recall. Remembering without using external cues.

Test Yourself 8.4

1. False. Most forgetting occurs early and is followed by more gradual loss.
2. True.
3. False. Proactive interference occurs when prior learning interferes with later remembering.
4. False. People with anterorgrade amnesia can learn new things, but they lose the ability to access those memories consciously.
5. True.
6. True.

Active Summary

1. preserve
2. recover
3. visual
4. auditory
5. exact
6. iconic
7. echoic
8. short
9. forgotten
10. decay
11. interference
12. span
13. rehearsed
14. two
15. chunking
16. episodic
17. Semantic
18. procedural
19. Elaboration
20. connections
21. retrieval
22. meaning
23. relationships
24. differences
25. images
26. repetitions
27. sequence
28. loci
29. word
30. cues
31. match
32. transfer
33. mental
34. retrieval
35. Schemas
36. false
37. implicit
38. explicit
39. most
40. gradual
41. adaptive
42. retroactive
43. new
44. proactive
45. old
46. repress
47. validity
48. amnesia
49. Retrograde
50. before
51. anterograde
52. after
53. hippocampus
54. neurotransmitters

Chapter 9

Test Yourself 9.1

1. a. Phonemes. The smallest significant sound units in speech.
   b. Pragmatics. The practical knowledge used to understand the intentions of a speaker and produce an effective response.
   c. Syntax. The rules governing how words should be combined into sentences.
   d. Morphemes. The smallest units in a language that carry meaning.
2. a. True.
   b. False. Babies appear to learn language rules implicitly and often produce phrases, and commit errors, that they never hear from their parents.
   c. True.
   d. True.
   e. False. Kanzi appears able to understand and follow spoken requests from his trainers.

Test Yourself 9.2

1. a. defining features
   b. category exemplars
   c. family resemblance
   d. prototype
2. b. basic level ("Look, it's a cat.")

Test Yourself 9.3

1. a. well-defined problem
   b. well-defined problem

  c. ill-defined problem
  d. ill-defined problem
 2. a. searching for analogies
  b. algorithm
  c. means-ends analysis
  d. working backward

Test Yourself 9.4

 1. availability heuristic
 2. framing
 3. representativeness
 4. anchoring and adjustment

Active Summary

 1. grammar
 2. sounds
 3. sentences
 4. meaning
 5. phonemes
 6. morphemes
 7. surface
 8. deep
 9. knowledge
 10. top-down
 11. Pragmatics
 12. practical
 13. first
 14. telegraphic
 15. syntax
 16. overgeneralize
 17. anatomy or tract
 18. impossible
 19. Sign
 20. language
 21. adaptation
 22. brain
 23. ear
 24. grammatical
 25. category
 26. defining
 27. members
 28. Natural
 29. fuzzy
 30. typical
 31. resemblance
 32. core
 33. prototype
 34. representative
 35. exemplars
 36. hierarchical
 37. Basic
 38. predictive
 39. intermediate
 40. Superordinate
 41. descriptive
 42. well-defined
 43. ill
 44. clear
 45. correctly
 46. fixedness
 47. algorithms
 48. heuristics
 49. means-ends
 50. backward
 51. analogies
 52. mental
 53. Insight
 54. framing
 55. represented
 56. confirmation
 57. belief
 58. persistence
 59. representativeness
 60. prototypical
 61. availability
 62. anchors
 63. effective
 64. heuristics
 65. errors

Chapter 10

Test Yourself 10.1

 1. Triarchic theory. "Street smarts" is an example of practical intelligence.
 2. Multiple intelligences. Musical ability is considered to be a type of intelligence in Gardner's theory.
 3. Psychometric. Intelligence is measured by analyzing performance on mental tests.
 4. Psychometric. Factor analysis is a statistical technique used to analyze test performance.
 5. Multiple intelligence. Insight into the feelings of others is a type of intelligence in Gardner's theory.
 6. Triarchic theory. Applying what's been learned to new situations is a kind of creative intelligence.

Test Yourself 10.2

 1. a. Reliability. Donna's performance is consistent across testing.
  b. Validity. Larry's new test doesn't measure what it's supposed to measure.
  c. Reliability. Chei-Wui is checking on the consistency of test scores.
  d. Standardization. Robert makes certain that the testing and scoring procedures are the same for everybody who takes the test.
 2. a. True.
  b. False. Average IQ, based on the deviation IQ method, is always 100 regardless of age.
  c. False. The diagnosis of mental retardation depends on many factors, such as one's ability to adapt.
  d. False. Creativity doesn't correlate very highly with IQ.

Test Yourself 10.3

1. False. Fluid intelligence shows some decline over the life span.
2. False. Identical twins reared apart tend to have more similar IQs than fraternal twins raised together.
3. True.
4. False. Heritability tells us only that, for a given group, a certain percentage of the differences in intelligence can be explained by genetic factors.
5. True.

Active Summary

1. psychometric
2. performance
3. factor
4. correlations
5. general
6. Fluid
7. solve
8. genetic
9. Crystallized
10. knowledge
11. abilities
12. multiple
13. eight
14. linguistic
15. intrapersonal
16. triarchic
17. Analytic
18. creative
19. practical
20. Reliability
21. consistency
22. Validity
23. Standardization
24. intelligence
25. mental
26. average
27. different
28. chronological
29. deviation
30. retardation
31. 130
32. giftedness
33. correlate
34. Labeling
35. English
36. Creativity
37. Emotional
38. understand
39. Tacit
40. experience
41. longitudinal
42. fluid
43. reasoning
44. decline
45. crystallized
46. knowledge
47. constant
48. Flynn
49. Twin
50. genetics
51. environment
52. similar
53. environment
54. Heritability
55. genetic
56. groups
57. differences
58. economic
59. bias
60. environment
61. genetic
62. environmental
63. upper
64. genetic
65. experience

Chapter 11

Test Yourself 11.1

1. c. Instincts lead to fixed response patterns; drives do not.
2. Choose the appropriate term:
   a. Incentive motivation. Whitney jogs because of the reward.
   b. Intrinsic motivation. Janice's playing is self-motivated.
   c. Achievement motivation. Candice studies to satisfy a need for achievement.
   d. Intrinsic motivation. Jerome has become less motivated because of the reward.
3. b. Satisfying basic survival and social needs.

Test Yourself 11.2

1. False. A high level of glucose, or blood sugar, is associated with a decreased desire for food.
2. False. Bingeing and purging are the principal symptoms of bulimia nervosa.
3. True. High levels of leptin are often found in obese individuals.
4. False. Obesity is caused by many factors, not necessarily poor dietary habits.
5. True. Destruction of the hypothalamus can lead to overeating in the rat.

Test Yourself 11.3

1. True
2. True.
3. True.
4. True.

Test Yourself 11.4

1. a. Dancing is an expressive reaction.

b. Grimacing and wrinkling her nose is an expressive reaction.

c. A racing heart is a body response.

d. Robert is telling us about his subjective experience.

2. c. Receiving a C when you expected to flunk is the largest change in expectation (i.e., adaptation level).

3. a. James-Lange

b. two-factor

c. Cannon-Bard

d. two-factor

Active Summary

1. Instincts
2. drive
3. physiological
4. incentive
5. goal
6. reinforcing
7. Achievement
8. harder
9. Intrinsic
10. External
11. Cultural
12. hierarchy
13. needs
14. biological
15. security
16. relationships
17. self-actualize
18. glucose
19. insulin
20. brain
21. hypothalamus
22. hind
23. hippocampus
24. learning
25. cues
26. set
27. genetics
28. Obesity
29. metabolic
30. learned
31. stress
32. cultural
33. negative
34. Anorexia
35. Bulimia
36. excitement
37. plateau
38. orgasm
39. resolution
40. refractory
41. arousal
42. learned
43. estrogen
44. androgens
45. erogenous
46. pheromones
47. cultural
48. scripts
49. evolutionary
50. culture
51. Biological
52. environmental
53. orientation
54. facial
55. biological
56. anger
57. happiness
58. feedback
59. physiological
60. high
61. performance
62. expectations
63. controversial
64. Happiness
65. Disgust
66. physical
67. subjective
68. Cannon
69. independent
70. two
71. appraisal

Chapter 12.1

Test Yourself 12.1

1. a. openness

b. extroversion

c. agreeableness

d. neuroticism

e. conscientiousness

2. a. TAT

b. MMPI

c. NEO-PI-R

d. Rorschach

e. 16 personality factor

Test Yourself 12.2

1. psychodynamic
2. social-cognitive
3. humanistic
4. psychodynamic
5. humanistic
6. social-cognitive
7. psychodynamic

Test Yourself 12.3

1. True.
2. True.
3. False. High self-monitors tend to adapt their behavior to the situation.

4. False. Genetics appears to play a significant role in personality as measured by the MMPI.
5. False. Personality traits may only reveal themselves if they are relevant, or needed, in the situation.

Active Summary

1. Factor
2. 16
3. Eysenck
4. three
5. psychoticism
6. Five
7. agreeableness
8. neurocitism
9. conscientiousness
10. Allport
11. Cardinal
12. Central
13. 5
14. Secondary
15. Self
16. objective
17. 16
18. Multiphasic
19. projective
20. Apperception
21. ambiguous
22. conscious
23. preconscious
24. unconscious
25. unconscious
26. manifest
27. hidden
28. id
29. drives
30. superego
31. ego
32. anxiety
33. defense
34. psychosexual
35. Humanistic
36. awareness
37. responsibility
38. positive
39. incongruence
40. self-actualization
41. cognitive
42. classical
43. modeling
44. social
45. interpret
46. locus
47. efficacy
48. consistent
49. within
50. self-monitoring
51. inconsistent
52. consistent
53. interact
54. identical
55. genetic
56. fraternal

Chapter 13

Test Yourself 13.1

1. a. True.
   b. False. Exemplar, not prototype, theories assume that we represent stereotypes with particular individuals, or exemplars.
   c. True.
   d. True.
2. a. internal
   b. internal
   c. external
   d. internal
3. a. True.
   b. False. The central, not peripheral, route to persuasion operates when our level of involvement in or commitment to a message is high.
   c. True.
   d. False. Mere exposure is most likely to lead to attitude change when we're processing a message peripherally.

Test Yourself 13.2

1. a. deindividuation
   b. social loafing, although conformity is also a possibility
   c. conformity
   d. group polarization
   e. bystander effect
   f. social facilitation
2. d. The experiment is conducted in the teacher's home.

Test Yourself 13.3

1. True.
2. False. Averaged faces tend to be rated as most attractive.
3. False. Your ratings would go down.
4. True.
5. True.
6. False. Companionate love typically leads to more feelings of warmth and trust.

Active Summary

1. top
2. expectations
3. stereotypes
4. schemas
5. prejudice
6. distinctiveness
7. external
8. internal
9. internal
10. fundamental attribution error
11. actor-observer effect

12. self-serving
13. cognitive
14. affective
15. behavioral
16. experience
17. operant
18. observational
19. likelihood
20. central
21. peripheral
22. dissonance
23. attitudes
24. tension
25. perception
26. facilitation
27. performance
28. interference
29. impairs
30. altruism
31. unselfish
32. bystander
33. responsibility
34. loafing
35. less
36. group
37. Deindividuation
38. conformity
39. dominant
40. polarization
41. Groupthink
42. consensus
43. ignore
44. obedience
45. 65
46. validated
47. independent
48. interdependent
49. evolutionary
50. healthy
51. faces
52. subjective
53. similarity
54. reciprocity
55. Passionate
56. Companionate
57. triangular
58. intimacy
59. passion
60. commitment

Chapter 14

Test Yourself 14.1

1. False. When a behavior occurs infrequently among members of a population, it meets the criterion of statistical deviance.

2. False. Not all people with psychological disorders are emotionally distressed.
3. True.
4. True.
5. False. In many cases, hospital staff members appeared not to notice or classify the pseudopatients' behavior as normal—at least not quickly.

Test Yourself 14.2

1. somatoform disorder (hypochondriasis or conversion disorder)
2. anxiety disorder (obsessive-compulsive disorder)
3. anxiety disorder (panic disorder, agoraphobia)
4. mood disorder (depressive disorder)
5. dissociative disorder (dissociative fugue)
6. personality disorder (antisocial personality disorder)
7. schizophrenia (paranoia)
8. schizophrenia (catatonia)

Test Yourself 14.3

1. b. Excessive amounts of the neurotransmitter dopamine.
2. d. If your identical twin has schizophrenia, you have about a 50% chance of developing the disorder yourself.
3. d. Internal, stable, and global
4. b. Observational learning

Active Summary

1. continuum
2. deviance
3. Cultural
4. norms
5. emotional
6. dysfunction
7. legal
8. psychological
9. understand
10. legally
11. morally
12. medical
13. disease
14. medications
15. physical
16. labeling
17. stigma
18. normal
19. mental
20. classification
21. objective
22. measurable
23. five
24. personality
25. global
26. anxiety
27. apprehension
28. Generalized

29. six
30. Panic
31. sudden
32. fear
33. agoraphobia
34. obsessive-compulsive
35. phobia
36. Somatoform
37. physical
38. hypochondriasis
39. disease
40. somatization
41. conversion
42. dissociative
43. dissociative
44. fugue
45. identity
46. identity
47. personalities
48. mood
49. depressive
50. bipolar
51. depressive
52. dysthymic
53. bipolar
54. depression
55. mania
56. suicide
57. emotion
58. positive
59. delusions
60. hallucinations
61. flat
62. catatonia
63. speech
64. personality
65. social
66. Paranoid
67. dependent
68. antisocial
69. Five
70. chemistry
71. genetic
72. dopamine
73. serotonin
74. neurotransmitter
75. explanatory
76. internal
77. global
78. learned helplessness
79. control
80. Experience
81. culture
82. expressed
83. learned
84. classical

Chapter 15

Test Yourself 15.1

1. a. schizophrenia
   b. depression
   c. depression
   d. depression
   e. generalized anxiety disorder
2. d. ECT is used regularly to treat schizophrenia.

Test Yourself 15.2

1. rational-emotive therapy
2. Beck's cognitive therapy
3. psychoanalysis
4. client-centered therapy
5. Gestalt therapy
6. family therapy

Test Yourself 15.3

1. b. conditioned stimulus.
2. a. counterconditioning and extinction.
3. b. Effective punishments can't be delivered because pain thresholds are high.
4. d. reinforcement

Test Yourself 15.4

1. True.
2. True.
3. False. Many evaluation studies show that the particular form of treatment doesn't matter.
4. False. Some types of treatment, such as most behavioral therapies, show concern only for the present symptoms.
5. True.

Active Summary

1. dopamine
2. tardive
3. Antidepressant
4. serotonin
5. Bipolar
6. lithium
7. Antianxiety
8. GABA
9. electroconvulsive
10. safe
11. severe
12. confusion
13. Psychosurgery
14. brain
15. Prefrontal
16. compulsive
17. rarely
18. psychoanalysis
19. free
20. dream
21. Resistance

22. transference
23. unconscious
24. streamline
25. Cognitive
26. conscious
27. rational
28. faulty or irrational
29. cognitive
30. humanistic
31. value
32. centered
33. incongruence
34. self-concept
35. positive
36. Gestalt
37. Group
38. similar
39. Family
40. interpersonal
41. anxiety
42. Conditioning
43. systematic desensitization
44. counterconditioning
45. hierarchy
46. aversion
47. rewards
48. punishments
49. token
50. privileges
51. Punishments
52. consequences
53. Social
54. behavioral
55. differences
56. meta
57. remission
58. support
59. learning
60. action
61. effective

Chapter 16

Test Yourself 16.1

1. c. alarm, resistance, exhaustion
2. c. The experience of stress, like emotion, depends on the appraisal of the event rather than on the event itself.
3. a. marriage
4. c. an optimistic outlook

Test Yourself 16.2

1. True.
2. True.
3. False. Stress has been shown to affect cholesterol levels.

4. False. Most people who suffer trauma do not develop posttraumatic stress disorder.
5. True.

Test Yourself 16.3

1. c. The stress response is incompatible with relaxation.
2. a. gives you a feeling of control.
3. d. Social support makes it easier to cope if the support is no longer delivered.
4. a. cognitive reappraisal

Test Yourself 16.4

1. False. Aerobic exercise can lessen the physiological effects of the stress reaction.
2. True.
3. True.
4. False. Teaching children about the hazards of smoking or drugs would be classified as an example of primary prevention.

Active Summary

1. adaptation
2. three
3. alarm
4. resistance
5. exhaustion
6. fear
7. sadness
8. emotion
9. appraise
10. Significant
11. Social
12. negative
13. change
14. daily
15. noise
16. Environmental
17. Perceived
18. greater
19. Explanatory
20. heart
21. immune
22. lymphocytes
23. high
24. cholesterol
25. stressful
26. psychological
27. genetic
28. posttraumatic
29. flashbacks
30. Burnout
31. exhaustion
32. control
33. meaning
34. relaxation
35. muscle

36. autogenic
37. Meditation
38. Biofeedback
39. Social
40. interpret
41. reappraisal
42. Aerobic
43. physical
44. mental or psychological
45. mood
46. resistance
47. tobacco
48. health
49. chemical
50. addictive
51. withdrawal
52. nutrition
53. body
54. mind
55. type
56. Primary
57. before
58. Secondary
59. populations
60. Tertiary
61. primary

Glossary

absolute threshold The level of intensity that lifts a stimulus over the threshold of conscious awareness; it's usually defined as the intensity level at which people can detect the presence of the stimulus 50% of the time.

accommodation The process through which we change or modify existing schemata to accommodate new experiences. In vision, the process through which the lens changes its shape temporarily to help focus light on the retina.

acetylcholine A neurotransmitter that plays multiple roles in the central and peripheral nervous systems, including the excitation of muscle contractions.

achievement motive An internal drive or need for achievement that is possessed by all individuals to varying degrees.

achievement tests Psychological tests that measure your current level of knowledge or competence in a particular subject.

action potential The all-or-none electrical signal that travels down a neuron's axon.

activation-synthesis hypothesis The idea that dreams represent the brain's attempt to make sense of the random patterns of neural activity generated during sleep.

actor–observer effect The overall tendency to attribute our own behavior to external sources but to attribute the behavior of others to internal sources.

adaptation A trait that has been selected for by nature because it increases the reproductive "fitness" of the organism.

aerobic exercise High-intensity activities, such as running and swimming, that increase both heart rate and oxygen consumption.

ageism Discrimination or prejudice against an individual based on physical age.

agoraphobia An anxiety disorder that causes an individual to restrict his or her normal activities; someone suffering from agoraphobia tends to avoid public places out of fear that a panic attack will occur.

AIDS Acquired immune deficiency syndrome, a disease that gradually weakens and disables the immune system.

algorithms Step-by-step rules or procedures that, if applied correctly, guarantee a problem solution.

alpha waves The pattern of brain activity observed in someone who is in a relaxed state.

altruism Acting in a way that shows unselfish concern for the welfare of others.

amnesia Forgetting that is caused by physical problems in the brain, such as those induced by injury or disease.

anal stage Freud's second stage of psychosexual development, occurring in the second year of life; pleasure is derived from the process of defecation.

anorexia nervosa An eating disorder diagnosed when an otherwise healthy person refuses to maintain a normal weight level because of an intense fear of being overweight.

anterograde amnesia Memory loss for events that happen after the point of physical injury.

antianxiety drugs Medications that reduce tension and anxiety.

antidepressant drugs Medications that modulate the availability or effectiveness of the neurotransmitters implicated in mood disorders.

antipsychotic drugs Medications that reduce the positive symptoms of schizophrenia.

antisocial personality disorder A personality disorder characterized by little, if any, respect for social laws, customs, or norms.

anxiety disorders A class of disorders marked by excessive apprehension and worry that in turn impair normal functioning.

applied psychologists Psychologists who extend the principles of scientific psychology to practical problems in the world.

aptitude tests Psychological tests that measure your ability to learn or acquire knowledge in a particular subject.

assimilation The process through which we fit—or assimilate—new experiences into existing schemata.

attachments Strong emotional ties formed to one or more intimate companions.

attention The internal processes used to set priorities for mental functioning.

attention deficit/hyperactivity disorder (ADHD) A psychological disorder marked by difficulties in concentrating or in sustaining attention for extended periods; can be associated with hyperactivity.

attitude A positive or negative evaluation or belief held about something, which in turn may affect one's behavior; attitudes are typically broken down into cognitive, affective, and behavioral components.

attributions The inference processes people use to assign cause and effect to behavior.

automaticity Fast and effortless processing that requires little or no focused attention.

autonomic system The collection of nerves that control the more automatic needs of the body (such as heart rate, digestion, blood pressure); part of the peripheral nervous system.

availability heuristic The tendency to base estimates on the ease with which examples come to mind.

aversion therapy A treatment for replacing a positive reaction to a harmful stimulus, such as alcohol, with something negative, such as feeling nauseated. Aversion therapy replaces positive associations with negative ones, such as making a smoker feel bad rather than good after having a cigarette.

axon The long tail-like part of a neuron that serves as the cell's transmitter.

basic-level categories The level in a category hierarchy that provides the most useful and predictive information; the basic level usually resides at an intermediate level in a category hierarchy.

basilar membrane A flexible membrane running through the cochlea that, through its movement, displaces the auditory receptor cells, or hair cells.

behavior Observable actions such as moving about, talking, gesturing, and so on; behaviors can also refer to the activities of cells and to thoughts and feelings.

behavioral therapies Treatments designed to change behavior through the use of established learning techniques.

behaviorism A school of psychology proposing that the only proper subject matter of psychology is observable behavior rather than immediate conscious experience.

belief persistence In decision making, the tendency to cling to initial beliefs when confronted with disconfirming evidence.

Big Five The five dimensions of personality—extroversion, agreeableness, conscientiousness, neuroticism, and openness—that have been isolated through the application of factor analysis.

binocular depth cues Cues for depth that depend on comparisons between the two eyes.

biofeedback Specific physiological feedback people are given about the effectiveness of their relaxation efforts.

biological clocks Brain structures that schedule rhythmic variations in bodily functions by triggering them at the appropriate times.

biomedical therapies Biologically based treatments for reducing or eliminating the symptoms of psychological disorders.

bio-psycho-social perspective The idea that psychological disorders are influenced, or caused, by a combination of biological, psychological (cognitive), and social (environmental) factors.

bipolar disorder A type of mood disorder in which the person experiences disordered mood shifts in two directions—from depression to a manic state.

blind spot The point where the optic nerve leaves the back of the eye.

borderline personality disorder A personality disorder characterized by problems with emotional regulation, social relationships, and sense of self.

bottom-up processing Processing that is controlled by the physical message delivered to the senses.

brightness The aspect of the visual experience that changes with light intensity; in general, as the intensity of light increases, so does its perceived brightness.

bulimia nervosa An eating disorder in which the principal symptom is binge eating (consuming large quantities of food) followed by purging, in which the person voluntarily vomits or uses laxatives to prevent weight gain.

burnout A state of physical, emotional, and mental exhaustion created by long-term involvement in an emotionally demanding situation.

bystander effect The reluctance to come to the aid of a person in need when other people are present.

Cannon-Bard theory A theory of emotion that argues that body reactions and subjective experiences occur together, but independently.

cardinal traits Allport's term to describe personality traits that dominate an individual's life, such as a passion to serve others or to accumulate wealth.

case study A descriptive research technique in which the effort is focused on a single case, usually an individual.

category A class of objects (people, places, or things) that most people agree belong together.

category exemplars Specific examples of category members that are stored in long-term memory.

central nervous system The brain and the spinal cord.

central traits Allport's term to describe the five to ten descriptive traits that you would use to describe someone you know—friendly, trustworthy, and so on.

cerebellum A hindbrain structure at the base of the brain that is involved in the coordination of complex motor skills.

cerebral cortex The outer layer of the brain, considered to be the seat of higher mental processes.

chemoreceptors Receptor cells that react to invisible molecules scattered about in the air or dissolved in liquids, leading to the senses of smell and taste.

chunking A short-term memory strategy that involves rearranging incoming information into meaningful or familiar patterns.

circadian rhythms Biological activities that rise and fall in accordance with a 24-hour cycle.

classical conditioning A set of procedures used to investigate how organisms learn about the signaling properties of events. Classical conditioning involves learning relations between events—conditioned and unconditioned stimuli—that occur outside of one's control.

client-centered therapy A form of humanistic therapy proposing that it is the client, not the therapist, who holds the key to psychological health and happiness; the therapist's role is to provide genuineness, unconditional positive regard, and empathy.

clinical psychologists Psychologists who specialize in the diagnosis and treatment of psychological problems.

cochlea The bony, snail-shaped sound processor in the inner ear where sound is translated into nerve impulses.

cocktail party effect The ability to focus on one auditory message and ignore others; also refers to the tendency to notice when your name suddenly appears in a message that you've been actively ignoring.

cognitive appraisal The idea that to feel stress you need to perceive a threat and come to the conclusion that you may not have adequate resources to deal with the threat.

cognitive dissonance The tension produced when people act in a way that is inconsistent with their attitudes.

cognitive revolution The shift away from strict behaviorism, begun in the 1950s, characterized by renewed interest in fundamental problems of consciousness and internal mental processes.

cognitive therapies Treatments designed to remove irrational beliefs and negative thoughts that are presumed to be responsible for psychological disorders.

cold fibers Neurons that respond to a cooling of the skin by increasing the production of neural impulses.

collective unconscious The notion proposed by Carl Jung that certain kinds of universal symbols and ideas are present in the unconscious of all people.

companionate love A kind of emotional attachment characterized by feelings of trust and companionship; companionate love is marked by a combination of intimacy and commitment, but passion may be lacking.

computerized tomography scan (CT scan) The use of highly focused beams of X-rays to construct detailed anatomical maps of the living brain.

concrete operational period Piaget's third stage of cognitive development, lasting from ages 7 to 11. Children acquire the capacity to perform a number of mental operations but still lack the ability for abstract reasoning.

conditioned inhibition Learning that an event signals the absence of the unconditioned stimulus.

conditioned reinforcer A stimulus that has acquired reinforcing properties through prior learning.

conditioned response (CR) The acquired response that is produced by the conditioned stimulus in anticipation of the unconditioned stimulus.

conditioned stimulus (CS) The neutral stimulus that is paired with the unconditioned stimulus during classical conditioning.

conditions of worth The expectations or standards that we believe others place on us.

cones Receptor cells in the central portion of the retina that transduce light energy into neural messages; they operate best when light levels are high, and they are primarily responsible for the ability to sense color.

confidentiality The principle that personal information obtained from a participant in research or therapy should not be revealed without the individual's permission.

confirmation bias The tendency to seek out and use information that supports and confirms a prior decision or belief.

conformity The tendency to comply with the wishes of the group; when people conform, their opinions, feelings, and behaviors generally start to move toward the group norm.

confounding variable An uncontrolled variable that changes along with the independent variable.

conscious mind The contents of awareness—those things that occupy the focus of one's current attention.

consciousness The subjective awareness of internal and external events.

conventional level In Kohlberg's theory of moral development, the stage in which actions are judged to be right or wrong based on whether they maintain or disrupt the social order.

convergence A binocular cue for depth that is based on the extent to which the two eyes move inward, or converge, when looking at an object.

conversion disorder The presence of real physical problems, such as blindness or paralysis, that seem to have no identifiable physical cause.

coping Efforts to manage or master conditions of threat or demand that tax one's resources.

cornea The transparent and protective outer covering of the eye.

corpus callosum The collection of nerve fibers that connects the two cerebral hemispheres and allows information to pass from one side to the other.

correlation A statistic that indicates whether two variables vary together in a systematic way; correlation coefficients vary from $+1.00$ to -1.00.

creativity The ability to generate ideas that are original, novel, and useful.

cross-sectional design A research design in which people of different ages are compared at the same time.

crystallized intelligence The knowledge and abilities acquired as a result of experience (as from schooling and cultural influences).

cued recall A testing condition in which people are given an explicit retrieval cue to help them remember.

cultural deviance A criterion of abnormality stating that a behavior is abnormal if it violates the rules or accepted standards of society.

culture The shared values, customs, and beliefs of a group or community.

dark adaptation The process through which the eyes adjust to dim light.

debriefing At the conclusion of an experimental session, informing the participants about the general purpose of the experiment, including any deception that was involved.

decay The proposal that memories are forgotten or lost spontaneously with the passage of time.

decision making The thought processes involved in evaluating and choosing from among a set of alternatives; it usually involves some kind of risk.

deep structure The underlying representation of meaning in a sentence.

defense mechanisms According to Freud, unconscious processes used by the ego to ward off the anxiety that comes from confrontation, usually with the demands of the id.

defining features The set of features necessary to make objects acceptable members of a category.

deindividuation The loss of individuality, or depersonalization, that comes from being in a group.

delta activity The pattern of brain activity observed in stage 3 and stage 4 sleep; it's characterized by synchronized slow waves. Also called slow-wave sleep.

dementia Physically based losses in mental functioning.

dendrites The fibers that extend outward from a neuron and receive information from other neurons.

dependent personality disorder A personality disorder characterized by an excessive and persistent need to be taken care of by others.

dependent variable The behavior that is measured or observed in an experiment.

depressants A class of drugs that slow or depress the ongoing activity of the central nervous system.

descriptive research Methods designed to observe and describe behavior.

descriptive statistics Mathematical techniques that help researchers describe their data.

development The age-related physical, intellectual, social, and personal changes that occur throughout an individual's lifetime.

deviation IQ An intelligence score that is derived from determining where your performance sits in an age-based distribution of test scores.

diagnostic labeling effects The fact that labels for psychological problems can become self-fulfilling prophecies; the label may make it difficult to recognize normal behavior when it occurs, and it may actually increase the likelihood that a person will act in an abnormal way.

dichotic listening Different auditory messages are presented separately and simultaneously to each ear. The subject's task is to repeat aloud one message while ignoring the other.

difference threshold The smallest detectable difference in the magnitude of two stimuli.

diffusion of responsibility The idea that when people know (or think) that others are present in a situation, they allow their sense of responsibility for action to diffuse, or spread out widely, among those who are present.

discrimination Behaviors that are directed against members of a group.

discriminative stimulus The stimulus situation that sets the occasion for a response to be followed by reinforcement or punishment.

dissociative amnesia A psychological disorder characterized by an inability to remember important personal information.

dissociative disorders A class of disorders characterized by the separation, or dissociation, of conscious awareness from previous thoughts or memories.

dissociative fugue A loss of personal identity that is often accompanied by a flight from home.

dissociative identity disorder A condition in which an individual alternates between what appear to be two or more distinct identities or personalities (also known as *multiple personality disorder*).

distinctiveness Refers to how unique or different a memory record is from other things in memory. Distinctive memory records tend to be recalled well.

distributed practice Spacing the repetitions of to-be-remembered information over time.

dopamine A neurotransmitter that often leads to inhibitory effects; decreased levels have been linked to Parkinson disease, and increased levels have been linked to schizophrenia.

double-blind study Neither participants nor research observers are aware of who has been assigned to the experimental and control groups; it's used to control for both subject and experimenter expectancies.

dream analysis A technique used in psychoanalysis; Freud believed that dreams are symbolic and contain important information about the unconscious.

drive A psychological state that arises in response to an internal physiological need, such as hunger or thirst.

drug dependency A condition in which one experiences a physical or a psychological need for continued use of a drug.

DSM-IV-TR The *Diagnostic and Statistical Manual of Mental Disorders* (4th ed.), which is used for the diagnosis and classification of psychological disorders. The DSM-IV-TR is composed of five major rating dimensions, or *axes*.

dysfunction A breakdown in normal functioning; abnormal behaviors are those that prevent one from pursuing adaptive strategies.

echoic memory The system that produces and stores auditory sensory memories.

eclectic approach The idea that it's useful to select information from several sources rather than to rely entirely on a single perspective or school of thought.

ego In Freud's theory, the portion of personality that induces people to act with reason and deliberation and helps them conform to the requirements of the external world.

egocentrism The tendency to see the world from one's own unique perspective only; a characteristic of thinking in the preoperational period of development.

elaboration An encoding process that involves the formation of connections between to-be-remembered input and other information in memory.

elaboration likelihood model A model proposing two primary routes to persuasion and attitude change: a *central* route, which operates when we are motivated and focusing our attention on the message, and a *peripheral* route, which operates when we are either unmotivated to process the message or are unable to do so.

electroconvulsive therapy (ECT) A treatment used primarily for depression in which a brief electric current is delivered to the brain.

electroencephalograph (EEG) A device used to monitor the gross electrical activity of the brain.

embryonic period The period of prenatal development lasting from implantation to the end of the eighth week.

emotional distress A criterion of abnormality stating that abnormal behaviors are those that lead to personal distress or emotional upset.

emotional intelligence The ability to perceive, understand, and express emotion in ways that are useful and adaptive.

emotions Psychological events involving (1) a physiological reaction, usually arousal; (2) some kind of expressive reaction, such as a distinctive facial expression; and (3) some kind of subjective experience, such as the conscious feeling of being happy or sad.

empiricism The idea that knowledge comes directly from experience.

encoding The processes that determine and control how memories are formed.

endocrine system A network of glands that uses the bloodstream, rather than neurons, to send chemical messages that regulate growth and other internal functions.

endorphins Morphinelike chemicals that act as the brain's natural painkillers.

environmental psychology A specialty area in psychology devoted to the study of environmental effects on behavior and health, such as the effects of crowding or noise.

episodic memory A memory for a particular event, or episode, that happened to you personally, such as remembering what you ate for breakfast this morning or where you went on vacation last year.

evolutionary psychology A movement proposing that we're born with mental processes and "software" that guide our thinking and behavior. These innate mechanisms were acquired through natural selection in our ancestral past and help us to solve specific adaptive problems.

excitement phase The first component of the human sexual response cycle; it's characterized by changes in muscle tension, increased heart rate and blood pressure, and a rushing of blood into the genital organs.

experimental research A technique in which the investigator actively manipulates the environment to observe its effect on behavior.

explicit memory Conscious, willful remembering.

external attribution Attributing the cause of a person's behavior to an external event or situation in the environment.

external validity The extent to which results generalize to other situations or are representative of real life.

extinction Presenting a conditioned stimulus repeatedly, after conditioning, without the unconditioned stimulus, resulting in a loss in responding.

facial-feedback hypothesis The proposal that muscles in the face deliver signals to the brain that are then interpreted, depending on the pattern, as a subjective emotional state.

factor analysis A statistical procedure that groups together related items on tests by analyzing the correlations among test scores.

family resemblance The core features that category members share; a given member of the category may have some but not necessarily all of these features.

family studies The similarities and differences among biological (blood) relatives are studied to help discover the role heredity plays in physical or psychological traits.

family therapy A form of group therapy in which the therapist treats the family as whole, as a kind of social *system*. The goals of the treatment are often to improve interpersonal communication and collaboration.

feature detectors Cells in the visual cortex that respond to very specific visual events, such as bars of light at particular orientations.

fetal period The period of prenatal development lasting from the ninth week until birth.

fixed-interval (FI) schedule A schedule in which the reinforcement is delivered for the first response that occurs following a fixed interval of time.

fixed-ratio (FR) schedule A schedule in which the number of responses required for reinforcement is fixed and does not change.

flashbulb memories Rich memory records of the circumstances surrounding emotionally significant and surprising events.

flavor A psychological term used to describe the gustatory experience. Flavor is influenced by taste, smell, and the visual appearance of food, as well as by expectations about the food's quality.

fluid intelligence The natural ability to solve problems, reason, and remember; fluid intelligence is thought to be relatively uninfluenced by experience.

forebrain The outer portion of the brain, including the cerebral cortex and the structures of the limbic system.

forgetting The loss of accessibility to previously stored material.

formal operational period Piaget's last stage of cognitive development; thought processes become adultlike, and people gain mastery over abstract thinking.

fovea The "central pit" area in the retina where the cone receptors are located.

framing The way in which the alternatives in a decision-making situation are structured.

free association A technique used in psychoanalysis to explore the contents of the unconscious; patients are asked to freely express whatever thoughts and feelings happen to come into their minds.

free recall A testing condition in which a person is asked to remember information without explicit retrieval cues.

frequency theory The idea that pitch perception is determined partly by the frequency of neural impulses traveling up the auditory pathway.

frontal lobe One of four anatomical regions of each hemisphere of the cerebral cortex, located on the top front of the brain; it contains the motor cortex and may be involved in higher-level thought processes.

functional fixedness The tendency to see objects, and their functions, in certain fixed and typical ways.

functionalism An early school of psychology; functionalists believed that the proper way to understand mind and behavior is to first analyze their function and purpose.

fundamental attribution error When people seek to interpret someone else's behavior, they tend to overestimate the influence of internal personal factors and underestimate the role of situational factors.

g (general intelligence) According to Spearman, a general factor, derived from factor analysis, that underlies or contributes to performance on a variety of mental tests.

gamma-amino-butyric acid (GABA) A neurotransmitter that may play a role in the regulation of anxiety; it generally produces inhibitory effects.

gate-control theory The idea that neural impulses generated by pain receptors can be blocked, or gated, in the spinal cord by signals produced in the brain.

gender roles Specific patterns of behavior that are consistent with how society dictates males and females should act.

general adaptation syndrome (GAS) Hans Selye's model of stress as a general, nonspecific reaction that occurs in three phases: alarm, resistance, and exhaustion.

generalized anxiety disorder Excessive worrying, or free-floating anxiety, that lasts for at least six months and that cannot be attributed to any single identifiable source.

genes Segments of chromosomes that contain instructions for influencing and creating particular hereditary characteristics.

genital stage Freud's final stage of psychosexual development, during which one develops mature sexual relationships with members of the opposite sex.

genotype The actual genetic information inherited from one's parents.

germinal period The period in prenatal development from conception to implantation of the fertilized egg in the wall of the uterus.

Gestalt principles of organization The organizing principles of perception proposed by the Gestalt psychologists. These principles include the laws of proximity, similarity, closure, continuation, and common fate.

Gestalt psychology A movement proposing that certain organizing principles of perception are innate and cannot be altered by experience.

gifted A label generally assigned to someone who scores above 130 on a standard IQ test.

glial cells Cells that fill in space between neurons, remove waste, or help neurons to communicate efficiently.

glucose A kind of sugar that cells require for energy production.

grammar The rules of language that enable the communicator to combine arbitrary symbols to convey meaning.

group polarization The tendency for a group's dominant point of view to become stronger and more extreme with time.

group therapy A form of therapy in which several people are treated simultaneously in the same setting.

groupthink The tendency for members of a group to become so interested in seeking a consensus of opinion that they start to ignore and even suppress dissenting views.

gustation The sense of taste.

habituation The decline in the tendency to respond to an event that has become familiar through repeated exposure, or a stimulus that is repeatedly presented.

hallucinogens A class of drugs that tend to disrupt normal mental and emotional functioning, including distorting perception and altering reality.

health psychology The study of how biological, psychological, environmental, and cultural factors are involved in physical health and the prevention of illness.

heritability A mathematical index that represents the extent to which IQ differences in a particular population can be accounted for by genetic factors.

heuristics The rules of thumb we use to solve problems; heuristics can usually be applied quickly, but they do not guarantee that a solution will be found.

hindbrain A primitive part of the brain that sits at the juncture point where the brain and spinal cord merge. Structures in the hindbrain, including the medulla, pons, and reticular formation, act as the basic life-support system for the body.

homeostasis The process through which the body maintains a steady state, such as a constant internal temperature or an adequate amount of fluids.

hormones Chemicals released into the blood by the various endocrine glands to help control a variety of internal regulatory functions.

hue The dimension of light that produces color; hue is typically determined by the wavelength of light reflecting from an object.

humanistic psychology A movement in psychology and approach to personality that focuses on people's unique capacities for choice, responsibility, and growth.

humanistic therapy Treatments designed to help clients gain insight into their fundamental self-worth and value as human beings.

hypersomnia A chronic condition marked by excessive sleepiness.

hypnosis A form of social interaction that produces a heightened state of suggestibility in a willing participant.

hypnotic dissociation A hypnotically induced splitting of consciousness during which multiple forms of awareness already exist.

hypnotic hypermnesia The supposed enhancement in memory that occurs under hypnosis; there is little if any evidence to support the existence of this effect.

hypochondriasis A long-lasting preoccupation with the idea that one has developed a serious disease, based on what turns out to be a misinterpretation of normal body reactions.

hypothalamus A forebrain structure thought to play a role in the regulation of various motivational activities, including eating, drinking, and sexual behavior.

iconic memory The system that produces and stores visual sensory memories.

id In Freud's theory, the portion of personality that is governed by inborn instinctual drives, particularly those related to sex and aggression.

ill-defined problem A problem, such as the search for "happiness," that has no well-stated goal, no clear starting point, and no mechanism for evaluating progress.

implicit memory Remembering that occurs in the absence of conscious awareness or willful intent.

incentive motivation External factors in the environment that exert pulling effects on our actions.

incongruence A discrepancy between the image we hold of ourselves—our self-concept—and the sum of all our experiences.

independent variable The aspect of the environment that is manipulated in an experiment. It must consist of at least two conditions.

inferential statistics Mathematical techniques that help researchers decide whether data are representative of a population or whether differences among observations can be attributed to chance.

informed consent The principle that before consenting to participate in research, people should be fully informed about any significant factors that could affect their willingness to participate.

in-group A group of individuals with whom one shares features in common or with whom one identifies.

insanity A legal term usually defined as the inability to understand that certain actions are wrong, in a legal or moral sense, at the time of a crime.

insight The moment when a problem solution seems to pop suddenly into one's mind.

insight therapies Treatments designed to give clients self-knowledge, or insight, into the contents of their thought processes.

insomnia A chronic condition marked by difficulties in initiating or maintaining sleep, lasting for a period of at least one month.

instincts Unlearned characteristic patterns of responding that are controlled by specific triggering stimuli in the world.

insulin A hormone released by the pancreas that helps pump nutrients in the blood into the cells, where they can be stored as fat or metabolized into needed energy.

intelligence An internal capacity or ability that accounts for individual differences in mental test performance and enables us to adapt to ever-changing environments.

intelligence quotient (IQ) Mental age divided by chronological age and then multiplied by 100.

internal attribution Attributing the cause of a person's behavior to an internal personality trait or disposition.

internal validity The extent to which an experiment has effectively controlled for confounding variables; internally valid experiments allow for the determination of causality.

interneurons Cells that transfer information from one neuron to another; interneurons make no direct contact with the outside world.

intrinsic motivation Goal-directed behavior that seems to be entirely self-motivated.

iris The ring of colored tissue surrounding the pupil.

James-Lange theory A theory of emotion that argues that body reactions precede and drive the subjective experience of emotions.

kinesthesia In perception, the ability to sense the position and movement of one's body parts.

latency period Freud's period of psychosexual development, from age 5 to puberty, during which the child's sexual feelings are largely suppressed.

latent content According to Freud, the true psychological meaning of dream symbols.

law of effect If a response in a particular situation is followed by a satisfying consequence, it will be strengthened. If a response in a particular situation is followed by an unsatisfying consequence, it will be weakened.

learned helplessness A general sense of helplessness that is acquired when people repeatedly fail in their attempts to control their environment; learned helplessness may play a role in depression.

learning A relatively permanent change in behavior, or potential behavior, that results from experience.

lens The flexible piece of tissue that helps focus light toward the back of the eye.

leptin A hormone that may regulate the amount of energy stored in fat cells.

light The small part of the electromagnetic spectrum that is processed by the visual system.

limbic system A system of structures thought to be involved in motivational and emotional behaviors (the amygdala) and memory (the hippocampus).

locus of control The amount of control that a person feels he or she has over the environment.

longitudinal design A research design in which the same people are studied or tested repeatedly over time.

long-term memory The system used to maintain information for extended periods of time.

lymphocytes Specialized white blood cells that have the job of attacking foreign substances, such as viruses and bacteria.

magnetic resonance imaging (MRI) A device that uses magnetic fields and radio-wave pulses to construct detailed, three-dimensional images of the brain; "functional" MRIs can be used to map changes in blood oxygen use as a function of task activity.

major depressive episode A type of mood disorder characterized by depressed mood and other symptoms.

manic state A disordered state in which the person becomes hyperactive, talkative, and has a decreased need for sleep; a person in a manic state may engage in activities that are self-destructive or dangerous.

manifest content According to Freud, the actual symbols and events experienced in a dream.

mean The arithmetic average of a set of scores.

means–ends analysis A problem-solving heuristic that involves devising actions, or means, that reduce the distance between the current starting point and the desired end (the goal state).

median The middle point in an ordered set of scores; half of the scores fall at or below the median score, and half fall at or above the median score.

medical model The view that abnormal behavior is symptomatic of an underlying "disease," which can be "cured" with the appropriate therapy.

meditation A technique for self-induced manipulation of awareness, often used for the purpose of relaxation and self-reflection.

memory The capacity to preserve and recover information.

memory span The number of items that can be recalled from short-term memory in their proper presentation order on half of the tested memory trials.

menopause The period during which a woman's menstrual cycle slows down and finally stops.

mental age The chronological age that best fits a child's level of performance on a test of mental ability.

mental retardation A label generally assigned to someone who scores below 70 on a standard IQ test, although other factors, such as one's ability to adapt to the environment, are also important.

mental set The tendency to rely on well-established strategies when attempting to solve problems.

meta-analysis A statistical technique used to compare findings across many different research studies; comparisons are based on some common evaluation measure, such as the difference between treatment and control conditions.

method of loci A mnemonic device in which you choose some pathway, such as moving through the rooms in your house, and then form visual images of the to-be-remembered items sitting in locations along the pathway.

midbrain The middle portion of the brain, containing such structures as the tectum, superior colliculus, and inferior colliculus; midbrain structures serve as neural relay stations and may help coordinate reactions to sensory events.

middle ear The portion between the eardrum and the cochlea containing three small bones (the malleus, incus, and stapes) that help to intensify and prepare the sound vibrations for passage into the inner ear.

mind The contents and processes of subjective experience: sensations, thoughts, and emotions.

mnemonic devices Special mental tricks that help people think about material in ways that improve later memory. Most mnemonic devices require the use of visual imagery.

mode The most frequently occurring score in a set of scores.

modeling The natural tendency to imitate the behavior of significant others.

monocular depth cues Cues for depth that require input from only one eye.

mood disorders Prolonged and disabling disruptions in emotional state.

morality The ability to distinguish between appropriate and inappropriate actions.

morphemes The smallest units in a language that carry meaning.

motivation The set of factors that initiate and direct behavior, usually toward some goal.

motor neurons Cells that carry information away from the central nervous system to the muscles and glands that directly produce behavior.

multiple intelligences The notion proposed by Howard Gardner that people possess a set of separate and independent "intelligences" ranging from musical to linguistic to interpersonal ability.

mutation A spontaneous change in the genetic material that occurs during the gene replication process.

myelin sheath An insulating material that protects the axon and helps to speed up neural transmission.

narcolepsy A rare sleep disorder characterized by sudden extreme sleepiness.

nativism The idea that some knowledge is innate, or present at birth.

naturalistic observation A descriptive research technique that records naturally occurring behavior as opposed to behavior produced in the laboratory.

need hierarchy The idea popularized by Maslow that human needs are prioritized in a hierarchy.

negative punishment An event that, when removed after a response, lowers the likelihood of that response occurring again.

negative reinforcement An event that, when removed after a response, increases the likelihood of that response occurring again.

nerves Bundles of axons that make up neural "transmission cables."

neurons The cells in the nervous system that receive and transmit information.

neuroscience An interdisciplinary field of study directed at understanding the brain and its relation to behavior.

neurotransmitters Chemical messengers that relay information from one neuron to the next.

night terrors Terrifying experiences, which occur mainly in children, in which the sleeper awakens suddenly in an extreme state of panic.

nightmares Frightening and anxiety-arousing dreams that occur primarily during the REM stage of sleep.

obedience The form of compliance that occurs when people respond to the orders of an authority figure.

obesity A weight problem characterized by excessive body fat.

object permanence The ability to recognize that objects still exist when they're no longer in sight.

observational learning Learning by observing the experience of others.

obsessive–compulsive disorder An anxiety disorder that manifests itself through persistent and uncontrollable thoughts, called *obsessions*, or by the compelling need to perform repetitive acts, called *compulsions*.

occipital lobe One of four anatomical regions of each hemisphere of the cerebral cortex, located at the back of the brain; visual processing is controlled here.

olfaction The sense of smell.

operant conditioning A procedure for studying how organisms learn about the consequences of their own voluntary actions (also called instrumental conditioning).

operational definitions Definitions that specify how concepts can be observed and measured.

opiates A class of drugs that reduce anxiety, lower sensitivity to pain, and elevate mood; opiates often act to depress nervous system activity.

opponent-process theory A theory of color vision proposing that cells in the visual pathway increase their activation levels to one color and decrease their activation levels to another color—for example, increasing to red and decreasing to green.

oral stage The first stage in Freud's conception of psychosexual development, occurring in the first year of life; in this stage, pleasure is derived primarily from sucking and placing things in the mouth.

orgasmic phase The third stage in the human sexual response cycle. It's characterized by rhythmic contractions in the sex organs; in men, ejaculation occurs. There is also the subjective experience of pleasure, which appears to be similar for men and women.

orienting response An inborn tendency to notice and respond to novel or surprising events.

pain An adaptive response by the body to any stimulus that is intense enough to cause tissue damage.

panic disorder A condition marked by recurrent discrete episodes or attacks of extremely intense fear or dread.

paranoid personality disorder A personality disorder characterized by pervasive distrust of others.

parietal lobe One of four anatomical regions of each hemisphere of the cerebral cortex, located roughly on the top middle portion of the brain; it contains the somatosensory cortex, which controls the sense of touch.

partial reinforcement schedule A schedule in which reinforcement is delivered only some of the time after the response has occurred.

passionate love An intense emotional state characterized by a powerful longing to be with a specific person; passionate love is marked by a combination of intimacy and passion, but commitment may be lacking.

peg-word method A mnemonic device in which you form visual images connecting to-be-remembered items with retrieval cues, or pegs.

perceived control The amount of influence you feel you have over a situation and your reaction to it.

perception The collection of processes used to arrive at a meaningful interpretation of sensations.

perceptual constancy Perceiving the properties of an object to remain the same even though the physical properties of the sensory message are changing.

perceptual illusions Inappropriate interpretations of physical reality. Perceptual illusions often occur as a result of the brain's using otherwise adaptive organizing principles.

peripheral nervous system The network of nerves that links the central nervous system with the rest of the body.

personal identity A sense of who one is as an individual and how well one measures up against peers.

personality The distinguishing pattern of psychological characteristics—thinking, feeling, and behaving—that differentiates us from others and leads us to act consistently across situations.

personality disorders Chronic or enduring patterns of behavior that lead to significant impairments in social functioning.

person–situation debate A controversial debate centering on whether people really do behave consistently across situations.

phallic stage Freud's third stage of psychosexual development, lasting from about age 3 to age 5; pleasure is gained from self-stimulation of the sexual organs.

phenotype A person's observable characteristics, such as red hair. The phenotype is controlled mainly by the genotype, but it can also be influenced by the environment.

phi phenomenon An illusion of movement that occurs when stationary lights are flashed in succession.

phobic disorder A highly focused fear of a specific object or situation.

phonemes The smallest significant sound units in speech.

phonology Rules governing how sounds should be combined to make words in a language.

pinna The external flap of tissue normally referred to as the "ear"; it helps capture sounds.

pitch The psychological experience that results from the auditory processing of a particular frequency of sound.

pituitary gland A kind of master gland in the body that controls the release of hormones in response to signals from the hypothalamus.

place theory The idea that the location of auditory receptor cells activated by movement of the basilar membrane underlies the perception of pitch.

placebo An inactive, or inert, substance that resembles an experimental substance.

plateau phase The second stage in the human sexual response cycle. Arousal continues to increase, although at a slower rate, toward a preorgasm maximum point.

positive punishment An event that, when presented after a response, lowers the likelihood of that response occurring again.

positive regard The idea that we value what others think of us and that we constantly seek others' approval, love, and companionship.

positive reinforcement An event that, when presented after a response, increases the likelihood of that response.

positron emission tomography (PET) A method for measuring how radioactive substances are absorbed in the brain; it can be used to detect how specific tasks activate different areas of the living brain.

postconventional level Kohlberg's highest level of moral development, in which moral actions are judged on the basis of a personal code of ethics that is general and abstract and that may not agree with societal norms.

posttraumatic stress disorder A trauma-based anxiety disorder characterized by flashbacks, avoidance of stimuli associated with the traumatic event, and chronic arousal symptoms.

pragmatics The practical knowledge used to comprehend the intentions of a speaker and to produce an effective response.

preconscious mind The part of the mind that contains all of the inactive but potentially accessible thoughts and memories.

preconventional level In Kohlberg's theory, the lowest level of moral development, in which decisions about right and wrong are made primarily in terms of external consequences.

prejudice Positive or negative evaluations of a group and its members.

preoperational period Piaget's second stage of cognitive development, lasting from ages 2 to about 7; children begin to think symbolically but often lack the ability to perform mental operations such as conservation.

primacy effect The better memory of items near the beginning of a memorized list.

principle of conservation The ability to recognize that the physical properties of an object remain the same despite superficial changes in the object's appearance.

proactive interference A process in which old memories interfere with the establishment and recovery of new memories.

procedural memory Knowledge about how to do things, such as riding a bike or swinging a golf club.

projective personality test A type of personality test in which individuals are asked to interpret unstructured or ambiguous stimuli.

prototype The best or most representative member of a category (such as robin for the category "bird").

psychiatrists Medical doctors who specialize in the diagnosis and treatment of psychological problems.

psychoactive drugs Drugs that affect behavior and mental processes through alterations of conscious awareness.

psychoanalysis A term used by Freud to describe his theory of mind and system of therapy; a method of treatment that attempts to bring hidden impulses and memories, which are locked in the unconscious, to the surface of awareness, thereby freeing the patient from disordered thoughts and behaviors.

psychodynamic theory An approach to personality development, based largely on the ideas of Sigmund Freud, that holds that much of behavior is governed by unconscious forces.

psychology The scientific study of behavior and mind.

psychometrics The use of psychological tests to measure the mind and mental processes.

psychophysics A field of psychology in which researchers search for ways to describe the transition from the physical stimulus to the psychological experience of that stimulus.

psychosurgery Surgery that destroys or alters tissues in the brain in an effort to affect behavior.

psychotherapy Treatment designed to help people deal with mental, emotional, or behavioral problems.

puberty The period during which a person reaches sexual maturity and is potentially capable of producing offspring.

punishment Consequences that decrease the likelihood of responding in a similar way again.

pupil The hole in the center of the eye that allows light to enter.

random assignment A technique ensuring that each participant in an experiment has an equal chance of being assigned to any of the conditions in the experiment.

random sampling A procedure guaranteeing that everyone in the population has an equal likelihood of being selected for the sample.

range The difference between the largest and smallest scores in a distribution.

rational-emotive therapy A form of cognitive therapy in which the therapist acts as a kind of cross-examiner, verbally assaulting the client's irrational thought processes.

reactivity When behavior changes as a result of the observation process.

recency effect The better memory of items near the end of a memorized list.

receptive field In vision, the portion of the retina that, when stimulated, causes the activity of higher order neurons to change.

reciprocal determinism The idea that beliefs, behavior, and the environment interact to shape what is learned from experience.

reciprocity The tendency for people to return in kind the feelings that are shown toward them.

recognition by components The idea proposed by Biederman that people recognize objects perceptually via smaller components called geons.

reflexes Largely automatic body reactions—such as the knee jerk—that are controlled primarily by spinal cord pathways.

refractory period The period of time following an action potential when more action potentials cannot be generated.

rehearsal A strategic process that helps to maintain short-term memories indefinitely through the use of internal repetition.

reinforcement Response consequences that increase the likelihood of responding in a similar way again.

reliability A measure of the consistency of test results; reliable tests produce similar scores or indices from one administration to the next.

REM A stage of sleep characterized by rapid eye movements and low-amplitude, irregular EEG patterns resembling those found in the waking brain. REM is typically associated with dreaming.

REM rebound The tendency to increase time spent in REM sleep after REM deprivation.

representativeness heuristic The tendency to make decisions based on an alternative's similarity, or representativeness, in relation to an ideal. For example, people decide whether a sequence is random based on how irregular the sequence looks.

repression A defense mechanism that individuals use, unknowingly, to push threatening thoughts, memories, and feelings out of conscious awareness.

research psychologists Psychologists who try to discover the basic principles of behavior and mind.

resistance In psychoanalysis, a patient's unconsciously motivated attempts to subvert or hinder the process of therapy.

resolution phase The fourth and final stage in the human sexual response cycle. Arousal returns to normal levels. For men, there is a refractory period during which further stimulation fails to produce visible signs of arousal.

resting potential The tiny electrical charge in place between the inside and the outside of the resting neuron.

retina The thin layer of tissue that covers the back of the eye and contains the light-sensitive receptor cells for vision.

retinal disparity A binocular cue for depth that is based on location differences between the images in each eye.

retrieval The processes that determine and control how memories are recovered and translated into performance.

retroactive interference A process in which the formation of new memories hurts the recovery of old memories.

retrograde amnesia Memory loss for events that happened prior to the point of brain injury.

rods Receptor cells in the retina, located mainly around the sides, that transduce light energy into neural messages; these visual receptors are highly sensitive and are active in dim light.

s (specific intelligence) According to Spearman, a specific factor, derived from factor analysis, that is unique to a particular kind of test.

schedule of reinforcement A rule that an experimenter uses to determine when particular responses will be reinforced.

schema An organized knowledge structure in long-term memory.

schemata Mental models of the world that we use to guide and interpret our experiences.

schizophrenia A class of disorders characterized by fundamental disturbances in thought processes, emotion, or behavior.

scientific method A multistep technique that generates empirical knowledge—that is, knowledge derived from systematic observations of the world.

searching for analogies A problem-solving heuristic that involves trying to find a connection between the current problem and some previous problem you have solved successfully.

secondary traits The less obvious characteristics of an individual's personality that do not always appear in his or her behavior, such as testiness when on a diet.

second-order conditioning A procedure in which an established conditioned stimulus is used to condition a second neutral stimulus.

self-actualization The ingrained desire to reach one's true potential as a human being.

self-concept An organized set of perceptions that we hold about our abilities and characteristics.

self-efficacy The beliefs we hold about our own ability to perform a task or accomplish a goal.

self-fulfilling prophecy effect A condition in which our expectations about the actions of another person actually lead that person to behave in the expected way.

self-monitoring The degree to which a person monitors a situation closely and changes his or her behavior accordingly; people who are high self-monitors may not behave consistently across situations.

self-perception theory The idea that people use observations of their own behavior as a basis for inferring their internal beliefs.

self-report inventories Personality tests in which people answer groups of questions about how they typically think, act, and feel; their responses, or self-reports, are then compared to average responses compiled from large groups of prior test takers.

self-serving bias The tendency to make internal attributions about one's own behavior when the outcome is positive and to blame the situation when one's behavior leads to something negative.

semantic memory Knowledge about the world, stored as facts that make little or no reference to one's personal experiences.

semantics The rules used in language to communicate meaning.

semicircular canals A receptor system attached to the inner ear that responds to movement and acceleration and to changes in upright posture.

sensations The elementary components, or building blocks, of an experience (such as a pattern of light and dark, a bitter taste, or a change in temperature).

sensitization Increased responsiveness, or sensitivity, to an event that has been repeated.

sensorimotor period Piaget's first stage of cognitive development, lasting from birth to about 2 years of age; schemata revolve around sensory and motor abilities.

sensory adaptation The tendency of sensory systems to reduce sensitivity to a stimulus source that remains constant.

sensory memory An exact replica of an environmental message, which usually lasts for a second or less.

sensory neurons Cells that carry environmental messages toward the spinal cord and brain.

serotonin A neurotransmitter that has been linked to sleep, dreaming, and general arousal and may also be involved in some psychological disorders such as depression and schizophrenia.

set point A natural body weight, perhaps produced by genetic factors, that the body seeks to maintain.

sexual orientation A person's sexual and emotional attraction to members of the same sex or the other sex; homosexuality, heterosexuality, and bisexuality are all sexual orientations.

sexual scripts Learned cognitive programs that instruct us on how, why, and what to do in our interactions with sexual partners.

shaping A procedure in which reinforcement is delivered for successive approximations of the desired response.

short-term memory A limited-capacity system that we use to hold information after it has been analyzed for periods lasting less than a minute or two.

signal detection A technique used to determine the ability of someone to detect the presence of a stimulus.

single-blind study Experimental participants do not know to which condition they have been assigned (e.g., experimental versus control); it's used to control for subject expectancies.

sleepwalking The sleeper arises during sleep and wanders about.

social anxiety disorder Intense fear of being watched, judged, and embarrassed in social situations.

social cognition The study of how people use cognitive processes—such as perception, memory, thought, and emotion—to help make sense of other people as well as themselves.

social–cognitive theories An approach to personality that suggests it is human experiences, and interpretations of those experiences, that determine personality growth and development.

social facilitation The enhancement in performance that is sometimes found when an individual performs in the presence of others.

social influence The study of how the behaviors and thoughts of individuals are affected by the presence of others.

social interference The impairment in performance that is sometimes found when an individual performs in the presence of others.

social loafing The tendency to put out less effort when working in a group compared to when working alone.

social psychology The discipline that studies how people think about, influence, and relate to other people.

social schema A general knowledge structure, stored in long-term memory, that relates to social experiences or people.

social support The resources we receive from other people or groups, often in the form of comfort, caring, or help.

soma The cell body of a neuron.

somatic system The collection of nerves that transmits information toward the brain and connects to the skeletal muscles to initiate movement; part of the peripheral nervous system.

somatization disorder A long-lasting preoccupation with body symptoms that have no identifiable physical cause.

somatoform disorders Psychological disorders that focus on the physical body.

sound The physical message delivered to the auditory system; a mechanical energy that requires a medium such as air or water in order to move.

source characteristics Features of the person who is presenting a persuasive message, such as his or her attractiveness, amount of power, or fame.

spontaneous recovery The recovery of an extinguished conditioned response after a period of nonexposure to the conditioned stimulus.

spontaneous remission Improvement in a psychological disorder without treatment—that is, simply as a function of the passage of time.

standard deviation An indication of how much individual scores differ or vary from the mean.

standardization Keeping the testing, scoring, and interpretation procedures similar across all administrations of a test.

statistical deviance A criterion of abnormality stating that a behavior is abnormal if it occurs infrequently among the members of a population.

stereotypes The collection of beliefs and impressions held about a group and its members; common stereotypes include those based on gender, race, and age.

stimulants A class of drugs that increase central nervous system activity, enhancing neural transmission.

stimulus discrimination Responding differently to a new stimulus than how one responds to an established conditioned stimulus.

stimulus generalization Responding to a new stimulus in a way similar to the response produced by an established conditioned stimulus.

storage The processes that determine and control how memories are stored and kept over time.

strange situation test Gradually subjecting a child to a stressful situation and observing his or her behavior toward the parent or caregiver. This test is used to classify children according to type of attachment—secure, resistant, avoidant, or disorganized/disoriented.

stress People's physical and psychological reactions to demanding situations.

stressors The demanding or threatening situations that produce stress.

structuralism An early school of psychology; structuralists tried to understand the mind by breaking it down into basic parts, much as a chemist might try to understand a chemical compound.

superego In Freud's theory, the portion of personality that motivates people to act in an ideal fashion, in accordance with the moral customs defined by parents and culture.

surface structure The literal ordering of words in a sentence.

survey A descriptive research technique designed to gather limited amounts of information from many people, usually by administering some kind of questionnaire.

synapse The small gap between the terminal buttons of a neuron and the dendrite or cell body of another neuron.

syntax Rules governing how words should be combined to form sentences.

systematic desensitization A technique that uses counterconditioning and extinction to reduce the fear and anxiety that have become associated with a specific object or event.

systematic introspection An early technique used to study the mind; systematic introspection required people to look inward and describe their own experiences.

tacit knowledge Unspoken practical knowledge about how to perform well on the job.

taste buds The receptor cells on the tongue.

temperament A child's general level of emotional reactivity.

temporal lobe One of four anatomical regions of each hemisphere of the cerebral cortex, located roughly on the sides of the brain; it's involved in certain aspects of speech and language perception.

teratogens Environmental agents—such as disease organisms or drugs—that can potentially damage the developing embryo or fetus.

terminal buttons The tiny swellings at the end of the axon that contain chemicals important to neural transmission.

thalamus A relay station in the forebrain thought to be an important gathering point for input from the senses.

theta waves The pattern of brain activity observed in stage 1 sleep.

thinking The processes that underlie the mental manipulation of knowledge, usually in an attempt to reach a goal or solve a problem.

token economy A type of behavioral therapy in which patients are rewarded with small tokens when they act in an appropriate way; the tokens can then be exchanged for certain privileges.

tolerance An adaptation made by the body to compensate for the continued use of a drug, such that increasing amounts of the drug are needed to produce the same physical and behavioral effects.

top-down processing Processing that is controlled by one's beliefs and expectations about how the world is organized.

trait A stable predisposition to act or behave in a certain way.

trait theories Formal systems for assessing how people differ, particularly in their predispositions to respond in certain ways across situations.

transduction The process by which external messages are translated into the internal language of the brain.

transfer-appropriate processing The idea that the likelihood of correct retrieval is increased if a person uses the same kind of mental processes during testing that he or she used during encoding.

transference In psychoanalysis, the patient's expression of thoughts or feelings toward the therapist that are actually representative of the way the patient feels about other significant people in his or her life.

triarchic theory Robert Sternberg's theory of intelligence; it proposes three types of intelligence: analytic, creative, and practical.

trichromatic theory A theory of color vision proposing that color information is extracted by comparing the relative activations of three different types of cone receptors.

twin studies Identical twins, who share genetic material, are compared to fraternal twins in an effort to determine the roles heredity and environment play in psychological traits.

two-factor theory A theory of emotion that argues that the cognitive interpretation, or appraisal, of a body reaction drives the subjective experience of emotion.

tympanic membrane The eardrum, which responds to incoming sound waves by vibrating.

Type A An enduring pattern of behavior linked to stress-related health disorders; it is characterized by being hard driving, ambitious, easily annoyed, and impatient.

Type B People who lack the Type A traits—they put themselves under less pressure and appear more relaxed.

unconditioned response (UR) The observable response that is produced automatically, prior to training, on presentation of an unconditioned stimulus.

unconditioned stimulus (US) A stimulus that automatically leads to an observable response prior to any training.

unconscious mind The part of the mind that Freud believed housed all the memories, urges, and conflicts that are truly beyond awareness.

validity An assessment of how well a test measures what it is supposed to measure. *Content validity* assesses the degree to which the test samples broadly across the domain of interest; *predictive validity* assesses how well the test predicts some future criterion; *construct validity* assesses how well the test taps into a particular theoretical construct.

variability A measure of how much the scores in a distribution of scores differ from one another.

variable-interval (VI) schedule A schedule in which the allotted time before a response will yield reinforcement varies from trial to trial.

variable-ratio (VR) schedule A schedule in which a certain number of responses are required for reinforcement, but the number of required responses typically changes.

vestibular sacs Organs of the inner ear that contain receptors thought to be primarily responsible for balance.

visual acuity The ability to process fine detail in vision.

visual imagery The processes used to construct an internal visual image.

visual neglect A complex disorder of attention characterized by a tendency to ignore things that appear on one side of the body (usually the left side).

warm fibers Neurons that respond vigorously when the temperature of the skin increases.

Weber's law The principle stating that the ability to notice a difference in the magnitude of two stimuli is a constant proportion of the size of the standard stimulus. Psychologically, the more intense a stimulus is to begin with, the more intense it will need to become for one to notice a change.

well-defined problem A problem with a well-stated goal, a clear starting point, and a relatively easy way to tell when a solution has been obtained.

withdrawal Physical reactions, such as sweating, vomiting, changes in heart rate, or tremors, that occur when a person stops taking certain drugs after continued use.

working backward A problem-solving heuristic that involves starting at the goal state and moving backward toward the starting point to see how the goal state can be reached.

zygote The fertilized human egg, containing 23 chromosomes from the father and 23 chromosomes from the mother.

References

Abdullaev, Y. G., & Posner, M. I. (1997). Time course of activating brain areas in generating verbal associations. *Psychological Science, 8*, 56–59.

Abel, E. L. (1981). Behavioral teratology of alcohol. *Psychological Bulletin, 90*, 564–581.

Abramson, L. Y., Metalsky, G. I., & Alloy, L. B. (1989). Hopelessness depression: A theory-based subtype of depression. *Psychological Review, 96*, 358–372.

Achenbach, T. M. (1992). Developmental psychopathology. In M. H. Bornstein & M. E. Lamb (Eds.), *Developmental psychology: An advanced textbook*. Hillsdale, NJ: Erlbaum.

Adair, R., Bauchner, H., Phillip, B., Levenson, S., & Zuckerman, B. (1991). Night waking during infancy: Role of parent presence at bedtime. *Pediatrics, 87*, 500–504.

Adams, P. R., & Adams, G. R. (1984). Mount Saint Helens's ash-fall: Evidence for a disaster stress reaction. *American Psychologist, 39*, 252–260.

Adeyemo, S. A. (2002). Can the action of amphetamine on dopamine cause schizophrenia? *Psychology & Education, 39*, 29–39.

Adler, A. (1927). *Understanding human nature*. New York: Greenberg.

Adolphs, R., & Tranel, D. (2004). Impaired judgments of sadness but not happiness following bilateral amygdala damage. *Journal of Cognitive Neuroscience, 16*, 453–462.

Agras, W. S., Sylvester, D., & Oliveau, D. (1969). The epidemiology of common fears and phobia. *Comprehensive Psychiatry, 10*, 151–156.

Ahern, J., Galea, S., Resnick, H., & Vlahov, D. (2004). Television images and probable posttraumatic stress disorder after September 11. *Journal of Nervous and Mental Disease, 192*, 217–226.

Aiello, J. R., & Douthitt, E. A. (2001). Social facilitation from Triplett to electronic performance monitoring. *Group Dynamics, 5*, 163–180.

Ainsworth, M. D. S. (1979). Attachment as related to mother-infant interactions. In J. S. Rosenblatt, R. A. Hinde, C. Beer, & M. Busnel (Eds.), *Advances in the study of behavior* (Vol. 9). New York: Academic Press.

Ainsworth, M. D. S., Blehar, M., Waters, E., & Wall, S. (1978). *Patterns of attachment*. Hillsdale, NJ: Erlbaum.

Ainsworth, M. D. S., & Wittig, B. A. (1969). Attachment and exploratory behavior of one-year-olds in a strange situation. In B. M. Foss (Ed.), *Determinants of infant behaviour* (Vol. 4). London: Methuen.

Ajay, M., Kilduff, M., & Brass, D. J. (2001). The social networks of high and low self-monitors: Implications for workplace performance. *Administrative Science Quarterly, 46*, 121–146.

Ajzen, I. (2001). Nature and operation of attitudes. *Annual Review of Psychology, 52*, 27–58.

Ajzen, I., & Fishbein, M. (1977). Attitude-behavior relations: A theoretical analysis and review of empirical research. *Psychological Bulletin, 84*, 888–918.

Albert, M. S., & Moss, M. B. (1992). The assessment of memory disorders in patients with Alzheimer's disease. In L. R. Squire & N. Butters (Eds.), *Neuropsychology of memory* (2nd ed.). New York: Guilford.

Aleman, A., Kahn, R. S., & Selten, J. (2003). Sex differences in the risk of schizophrenia: Evidence from meta-analysis. *Archives of General Psychiatry, 60*, 565–571.

Allen, K. M., Blascovich, J., Tomaka, J., & Kelsey, R. M. (1991). Presence of human friends and pet dogs as moderators of autonomic responses to stress in women. *Journal of Personality and Social Psychology, 61*, 582–589.

Allen, P., Amaro, E., Fu, C.H.Y., Williams, S. C., Brammer, M. J., Johns, L. C., & McGuire, P. K. (2007). Neural correlates of the misattribution of speech in schizophrenia. *British Journal of Psychiatry, 190*, 162–169.

Alley, T. R., & Cunningham, M. R. (1991). Average faces are attractive, but very attractive faces are not average. *Psychological Science, 2*, 123–125.

Allik, J., & McCrae, R. R. (2004). Escapable conclusions: Toomela (2003) and the universality of trait structure. *Journal of Personality and Social Psychology, 87*, 261–265.

Allison, T., & Cicchetti, D. V. (1976). Sleep in mammals: Ecological and constitutional correlates. *Science, 194*, 732–734.

Alloy, L. B., Abramson, L. Y., Tashman, N. A., Berrebbi, D. S., Hogan, M. E., Whitehouse, W. G., Crossfield, A. G., & Moroco, A. (2001). Developmental origins of cognitive vulnerability to depression: Parenting, cognitive, and inferential feedback styles of the parents of individuals at high and low cognitive risk for depression. *Cognitive Therapy & Research, 25*, 397–423.

Allport, A. (1989). Visual attention. In M. I. Posner (Ed.), *Foundation of cognitive science*. Cambridge, MA: MIT Press.

Allport, G. W. (1937). *Personality: A psychological interpretation*. New York: Holt.

Allport, G. W., & Odbert, H. H. (1936). Trait-names: A psycho-lexical study. *Psychological Monographs, 47*(1, Whole No. 211).

Amabile, T. M. (1983). *The social psychology of creativity*. New York: Springer-Verlag.

American Association on Intellectual and Developmental Disabilities. (2002). *Mental retardation: Definition, classification, and systems of supports* (10th ed.). Annapolis, MD: Author.

American Psychiatric Association. (2000). *Diagnostic and statistical manual of mental disorders*, 4th ed., text revision (DSM-IV-TR). Washington, DC: Author.

American Psychological Association. (2002a). Ethical principles of psychologists and code of conduct. *American Psychologist, 57,* 1060–1073.

American Psychological Association. (2002b). *Profile of all APA members: 2000.* Washington, DC: Author.

Andersen, B. L. (1992). Psychological interventions for cancer patients to enhance quality of life. *Journal of Consulting and Clinical Psychology, 60,* 552–568.

Anderson, C. A., Berkowitz, L., Donnerstein, E., Huesmann, L. R., Johnson, J. D., Linz, D., Malamuth, N. M., & Wartella, E. (2003). The influence of media violence on youth. *Psychological Science in the Public Interest, 4,* 81–110.

Anderson, J. L., & Crawford, C. B. (1992). Modeling the costs and benefits of reproductive suppression. *Human Nature, 3,* 299–334.

Anderson, M. C., Bulevich, J. B., Roediger, H. L., Balota, D. A., & Butler, A. C. (2004). Neural systems underlying the suppression of unwanted memories. *Science, 303,* 232–235.

Anderson, M. C., & Green, C. (2001). Suppressing unwanted memories through executive control. *Nature, 410,* 366–369.

Anderson, N. D., & Craik, F. I. M. (2000). Memory in the aging brain. In E. Tulving and F. I. M. Craik (Eds.), *The Oxford handbook of memory.* Oxford, U.K.: Oxford University Press.

Andrasik, F., & Holroyd, K. A. (1980). A test of specific and nonspecific effects in the biofeedback treatment of tension headache. *Journal of Consulting and Clinical Psychology, 48,* 575–586.

Andrews, P. W. (2001). The psychology of social chess and the evolution of attribution mechanisms: Explaining the fundamental attribution error. *Evolution and Human Behavior, 22,* 11–29.

Andrews, P. W., Gangestad, S. W., & Matthews, D. (2002). Adaptationism—How to carry out an exadaptationist program. *Behavioral and Brain Sciences, 25,* 489–553.

Angell, J. R. (1903). The relations of structural and functional psychology to philosophy. *Philosophical Review, 12,* 203.

Antoni, M. H., & Lutgendorf, S. (2007). Psychosocial factors and disease progression in cancer. *Current Directions in Psychological Science, 16,* 42–46.

Antonio, A. L., Chang, M. J., Hakuta, K., Kenny, D. A., Levin, S., & Milem, J. F. (2004). Effects of racial diversity on complex thinking in college students. *Psychological Science, 15,* 507–510.

Apgar, V., & Beck, J. (1974). *Is my baby all right?* New York: Pocket Books.

Araoz, D. L. (1982). *Hypnosis and sex therapy.* New York: Brunner/Mazel.

Arnold, L. E., et al. (2004). Nine months of multicomponent behavioral treatment for ADHD and effectiveness of MTA fading procedures. *Journal of Abnormal Child Psychology, 32,* 39–51.

Arnold, M. L. (2000). Stage, sequence, and sequels: Changing conceptions of morality, post-Kohlberg. *Educational Psychology Review, 12,* 365–383.

Aronson, E. (1992). The return of the repressed: Dissonance theory makes a comeback. *Psychological Inquiry, 3,* 303–311.

Arrindell, W. A., Eisemann, M., Richter, J., Oei, T. P. S., Caballo, V. E., van der Ende, J., Sanavio, E., Nuri Bagés, Feldman, L., Torres, B., Sica, C., Iwawaki, S., Edelmann, R. J., Crozier, W. R., Furnham, A., & Hudson, B. L. (2003). Phobic anxiety in 11 nations Part 1: Dimensional constancy of the five-factor model. *Behaviour Research and Therapy, 41,* 461–479.

Asch, S. E. (1951). Effects of group pressure on the modification and distortion of judgments. In H. Guetzkow (Ed.), *Groups, leadership, and men.* Pittsburgh, PA: Carnegie Press.

Asch, S. E. (1955, May). Opinions and social pressures. *Scientific American, 193,* 31–35.

Aschoff, J., & Wever, R. (1981). The circadian system of man. In J. Aschoff (Ed.), *Handbook of behavioral neurobiology: Vol. 4. Biological rhythms.* New York: Plenum.

Aserinsky, E., & Kleitman, N. (1955). Two types of ocular motility occurring in sleep. *Journal of Applied Physiology, 8,* 1–10.

Ashby, F. G., & Maddox, W. T. (2005). Human category learning. *Annual Review of Psychology, 56,* 149–178.

Atkinson, J. W. (1957). Motivational determinants of risk-taking behavior. *Psychological Review, 64,* 359–372.

Atkinson, J. W., & Raynor, J. O. (Eds.). (1974). *Motivation and achievement.* Washington, DC: Winston.

Atkinson, R. C., & Shiffrin, R. M. (1971, August). The control of short-term memory. *Scientific American, 225,* 82–90.

Averbach, E., & Coriell, A. S. (1961). Short-term memory in vision. *Bell System Technical Journal, 40,* 309–328.

Averill, J. R. (1983). Studies on anger and aggression: Implications for theories of emotion. *American Psychologist, 38,* 1145–1160.

Baddeley, A. D. (1992). Working memory. *Science, 255,* 556–559.

Baddeley, A. D. (2000). The episodic buffer: A new component of working memory? *Trends in Cognitive Sciences, 4,* 417–423.

Baddeley, A. D. (2007). *Working memory, thought, and action.* Oxford, U.K.: Oxford University Press.

Baddeley, A. D., Gathercole, S. E., & Papagno, C. (1998). The phonological loop as a language learning device. *Psychological Review, 105,* 158–173.

Baddeley, A. D., & Hitch, G. (1974). Working memory. In G. H. Bower (Ed.), *The psychology of learning and motivation* (Vol. 8, pp. 47–89). New York: Academic Press.

Baddeley, A. D., & Lieberman, K. (1980). Spatial working memory. In R. Nickerson (Ed.), *Attention and performance VIII.* Hillsdale, NJ: Erlbaum.

Bahrick, H. P. (1984). Semantic memory content in permastore: 50 years of memory for Spanish learned in school. *Journal of Experimental Psychology: General, 113,* 1–29.

Bahrick, H. P., & Hall, L. K. (1991). Lifetime maintenance of high school mathematics content. *Journal of Experimental Psychology: General, 120,* 20–33.

Baillargeon, R. (1994). How do infants learn about the physical world? *Psychological Science, 5,* 133–140.

Baillargeon, R. (2004). Infants' physical world. *Current Directions in Psychological Science, 13,* 89–94.

Baldo, J. V., & Shimamura, A. P. (1998). Letter and category fluency in patients with frontal lobe lesions. *Neuropsychology, 12,* 259–267.

Balota, D. A., Dolan, P. O., & Duchek, J. M. (2000). Memory changes in healthy older adults. In E. Tulving and F. I. M. Craik (Eds.), *The Oxford handbook of memory.* Oxford, U.K.: Oxford University Press.

Bandura, A. (1986). *Social foundations of thought and action.* Englewood Cliffs, NJ: Prentice-Hall.

Bandura, A. (2001). Social cognitive theory: An agentic perspective. *Annual Review of Psychology, 52,* 1–26.

Bandura, A., Ross, D., & Ross, S. A. (1963). Imitation of film-mediated aggressive models. *Journal of Abnormal and Social Psychology, 66,* 3–11.

Banks, M. S., & Shannon, E. (1993). Spatial and chromatic visual efficiency in human neonates. In C. E. Granrud (Ed.), *Visual perception and cognition in infancy.* Hillsdale, NJ: Erlbaum.

Barber, T. X. (1976). *Pitfalls in human research: Ten pivotal points.* New York: Pergamon.

Barber, T. X., Spanos, N. P., & Chaves, J. (1974). *Hypnosis, imagination, and human potentialities.* New York: Pergamon.

Barchard, K. A. (2003). Does emotional intelligence assist in the prediction of academic success? *Education & Psychological Measurement, 63,* 840–858.

Barenbaum, N. B. (1997). The case(s) of Gordon Allport. *Journal of Personality, 65,* 743–755.

Bargh, J. A. (1999). The cognitive monster: The case against the controllability of automatic stereotype effects. In S. Chaiken & Y. Trope (Eds.), *Dual process theories in social psychology.* New York: Guilford.

Bargh, J. A., & Williams, E. L. (2006). The automaticity of social life. *Current Directions in Psychological Science, 15,* 1–4.

Bargones, J. Y., & Werner, L. A. (1994). Adults listen selectively; infants do not. *Psychological Science, 5,* 170–174.

Barkley, R. A. (1997). Behavioral inhibition, sustained attention, and executive functions: Constructing a unified theory of ADHD. *Psychological Bulletin, 121,* 65–94.

Barlow, D. H. (2002). *Anxiety and its disorders: The nature and treatment of anxiety and panic* (2nd ed.). New York: Guilford.

Barlow, D. H., & Durand, V. M. (2005). *Abnormal psychology: An integrative approach* (4th ed.). Belmont, CA: Wadsworth.

Barlow, D. H., Rapee, R. M., & Reisner, L. C. (2001). *Mastering stress 2001—A lifestyle approach.* Dallas, TX: American Health.

Barnes, V. A., Treiber, F., & Davis, H. (2001). Impact of Transcendental Meditation (R) on cardiovascular function at rest and during acute stress in adolescents with high normal blood pressure. *Journal of Psychosomatic Research, 51,* 597–605.

Barrett, L. F. (2006). Are emotions natural kinds? *Perspectives on Psychological Science, 1,* 28–58.

Barrett, L. F., & Wager, T. D. (2006). The structure of emotion: Evidence from neuroimaging studies. *Current Directions in Psychological Science, 15,* 79–83.

Bartlett, F. C. (1932). *Remembering.* Cambridge, U.K.: Cambridge University Press.

Bastien, C., & Campbell, K. (1992). The evoked K-complex: All or none phenomenon? *Sleep, 15,* 236–245.

Battelli, L., Alvaro, P-L., & Cavanagh, P. (2007). The 'when' pathway of the right parietal lobe. *Trends in Cognitive Sciences, 11,* 204–210.

Baumrind, D. (1964). Some thoughts on the ethics of research: After reading Milgram's "Behavioral study of obedience." *American Psychologist, 19,* 421–423.

Baumrind, D. (1985). Research using intentional deception: Ethical issues revisited. *American Psychologist, 40,* 165–174.

Beck, A. T. (1991). Cognitive therapy: A 30-year retrospective. *American Psychologist, 46,* 368–375.

Beck, A. T., & Young, J. E. (1985). Depression. In D. H. Barlow (Ed.), *Clinical handbook of psychological disorders.* New York: Guilford.

Beer, J. M., Arnold, R. D., & Loehlin, J. C. (1998). Genetic and environmental influences on MMPI factor scales: Joint model fitting to twin and adoption data. *Journal of Personality & Social Psychology, 74,* 818–827.

Beers, M. J., Lassiter, G. D., & Flannery, B. C. (1997). Individual differences in person memory: Self-monitoring and the recall of consistent and inconsistent behavior. *Journal of Social Behavior & Personality, 12,* 811–820.

Beier, M. E., & Ackerman, P. L. (2005). Age, ability, and the role of prior knowledge on the acquisition of new domain knowledge: Promising results in a real-world learning environment. *Psychology and Aging, 20,* 341–355.

Békésy, G. von (1960). *Experiments in hearing.* New York: McGraw-Hill.

Bell, A. P., Weinberg, M. S., & Hammersmith, S. K. (1981). *Sexual preference: Its development in men and women.* Bloomington: Indiana University Press.

Bell, P. A., Fisher, J. D., Baum, A., & Greene, T. E. (1990). *Environmental psychology* (3rd ed.). Fort Worth, TX: Holt, Rinehart and Winston.

Belsky, J., Burchinal, M., McCartney, K., Vandell, D. L., Clarke-Stewart, K. A., & Owen, M. T. (2007). Are there long-term effects of early child-care? *Child Development, 78,* 681–701.

Bem, D. J. (1967). Self-perception: An alternative interpretation of cognitive dissonance phenomena. *Psychological Review, 74,* 183–200.

Bem, D. J. (1972). Self-perception theory. In L. Berkowitz (Ed.), *Advances in experimental social psychology* (Vol. 6). New York: Academic Press.

Bem, S. L. (1981). Gender schema theory: A cognitive account of sex-typing. *Psychological Review, 88,* 354–364.

Benes, F. M. (1989). Myelination of cortical-hippocampal relays during late adolescence. *Schizophrenia Bulletin, 15,* 585–593.

Benes, F. M., Turtle, M., Khan, Y., & Farol, P. (1994). Myelination of a key relay zone in the hippocampal formation occurs in the human brain during childhood, adolescence, and adulthood. *Archives of General Psychiatry, 51,* 477–484.

Ben-Porath, Y. S. (2003). Assessing personality and psychopathology with self-report inventories. In J. R. Graham & J. A.

Naglieri (Eds.), *Handbook of psychology: Assessment psychology* (Vol. 10, pp. 553–577). New York: Wiley.

Benson, H. (1975). *The relaxation response.* New York: Morrow.

Bentall, R. P. (1990). The illusion of reality: A review and integration of psychological research on hallucinations. *Psychological Bulletin, 107,* 82–95.

Bergvall, A., Fahlke, C., & Hansen, S. (1996). An animal model for Type 2 alcoholism? Alcohol consumption and aggressive behavior following lesions in the raphe nuclei, medial hypthothalamus, or ventral striatum-septal area. *Physiology & Behavior, 60,* 1125–1135.

Berkowitz, L., & Harmon-Jones, E. (2004). Toward an understanding of the determinants of anger. *Emotion, 4,* 107–130.

Berman, K. F., & Weinberger, D. R. (1990). Lateralization of cortical function during cognitive tasks: Regional cerebral blood flow studies of normal individuals and patients with schizophrenia. *Journal of Neurology, Neurosurgery, and Psychiatry, 53,* 150–160.

Bernal, E. M. (1984). Bias in mental testing: Evidence for an alternative to the heredity-environment controversy. In C. R. Reynolds & R. T. Brown (Eds.), *Perspectives on bias in mental testing.* New York: Plenum.

Berndt, T. J. (2004). Children's friendships: Shifts over a half-century in perspectives on their development and their effects. *Merrill-Palmer Quarterly, 50,* 206–223.

Berndt, T. J., & Keefe, K. (1995). Friends' influence on adolescents' adjustments to school. *Child Development, 66,* 1312–1329.

Bernstein, I. H., Lin, T., & McClelland, P. (1982). Cross- vs. within-racial judgments of attractiveness. *Perception & Psychophysics, 32,* 495–503.

Bernstein, I. L. (1978). Learned taste aversions in children receiving chemotherapy. *Science, 200,* 1302–1303.

Berridge, K. C. (2004). Motivation concepts in behavioral neuroscience. *Physiology & Behavior, 81,* 179–209.

Berridge, K. C., & Robinson, T. E. (2003). Parsing reward. *Trends in Neurosciences, 26,* 507–513.

Berscheid, E. (1985). Interpersonal attraction. In G. Lindzey & E. Aronson (Eds.), *Handbook of social psychology* (Vol. 2). New York: Random House.

Bertenthal, B. I., Campos, J. J., & Kermoian, R. (1994). An epigenetic perspective on the development of self-produced locomotion and its consequences. *Current Directions in Psychological Science, 3,* 140–145.

Best, J. B. (1989). *Cognitive psychology* (2nd ed.). St. Paul, MN: West.

Beutler, L. E., & Berren, M. R. (Eds.). (1995). *Integrative assessment of adult personality.* New York: Guilford.

Beyth-Marom, R., & Lichtenstein, S. (1984). *An elementary approach to thinking under uncertainty.* Hillsdale, NJ: Erlbaum.

Bhardwaj, R. D., Curtis, M. A., Spalding, K. L., Buchholz, B. A., Fink, D., Bjork-Eriksson, T., Nordborg, C., Gage, F. H., Druid, H., Eriksson, P. S., & Frisen, J. (2006). Neocortical neurogenesis in humans is restricted to development. *Proceedings of the National Academy of Sciences, 103,* 12564–12568.

Biederman, I. (1987). Recognition-by-components: A theory of human image understanding. *Psychological Review, 94,* 115–147.

Biederman, I. (1990). Higher-level vision. In D. H. Osherson, S. M. Kosslyn, & J. M. Hollerbach (Eds.), *An invitation to cognitive science: Visual cognition and action* (Vol. 2). Cambridge, MA: MIT Press.

Bigelow, H. J. (1850). Dr. Harlow's case of recovery from the passage of an iron bar through the head. *American Journal of Medical Science, 20,* 13–22.

Binet, A., & Simon, T. (1973). *The development of intelligence in children.* New York: Arno Press. (Original work published 1916)

Bisiach, E. (1992). Understanding consciousness: Clues from unilateral neglect and related disorders. In A. D. Milner & M. D. Rugg (Eds.), *The neuropsychology of consciousness.* London: Academic Press.

Bisiach, E., & Rusconi, M. L. (1990). Break-down of perceptual awareness in unilateral neglect. *Cortex, 26,* 643–649.

Bjork, R. A. (1989). Retrieval inhibition as an adaptive mechanism in human memory. In H. L. Roediger & F. I. M. Craik (Eds.), *Varieties of memory and consciousness: Essays in honor of Endel Tulving.* Hillsdale, NJ: Erlbaum.

Bjorklund, D. F. (1997). The role of immaturity in human development. *Psychological Bulletin, 122,* 153–169.

Blagrove, M. (1996). Problems with the cognitive psychological modeling of dreaming. *Journal of Mind and Behavior, 17,* 99–134.

Blakemore, S., & Choudhury, S. (2006). Development of the adolescent brain: Implications for executive function and social cognition. *Journal of Child Psychology and Psychiatry, 47,* 296–312.

Blanton, H., Cooper, J., Skurnik, I., & Aronson, J. (1997). When bad things happen to good feedback: Exacerbating the need for self-justification with self-affirmations. *Personality & Social Psychology Bulletin, 23,* 684–692.

Blass, Thomas (Ed). (2000). *Obedience to authority: Current perspectives on the Milgram paradigm.* Mahwah, NJ: Erlbaum.

Bleuler, E. (1908). Die prognose der Dementia praecox (Schizophreniegruppe). *Allgemeine Zeitschrift fur Psychiatrie, 65,* 436–464.

Blumenthal, J. A., Emery, C. F., Walsh, M. A., Cox, D. R., Kuhn, C. M., Williams, R. B., & Williams, R. S. (1988). Exercise training in healthy Type A middle-aged men: Effects on behavioral and cardiovascular responses. *Psychosomatic Medicine, 50,* 418–433.

Blundell, J. E., & Rogers, P. J. (1991). Hunger, hedonics, and the control of satiation and satiety. In M. I. Friedman, M. G. Tordoff, & M. R. Kare (Eds.), *Chemical senses* (Vol. 4). New York: Marcel Dekker.

Bodenhausen, G. V., Macrae, C. N., & Hugenberg, K. (2003). Social Cognition. In T. Millon & M. J. Lerner (Eds.), *Handbook of psychology: Personality and social psychology,* Vol. 5 (pp. 257–282). Hoboken, NJ: John Wiley & Sons.

Bolanowski, S. J., Jr. (1989). Four channels mediate vibrotaction: Facts, models, and implications. *Journal of the Acoustical Society of America, 85,* S62.

Bolanowski, S. J., Gescheider, G. A., & Verrillo, R. T. (1994). Hairy skin: Psychophysical channels and their physiological substrates. *Somatosensory and Motor Research, 11,* 279–290.

Bolla, K. I., Brown, K., Eldreth, D., & Cadet, J. L. (2002). Dose-related neurocognitive effects of marijuana use. *Neurology, 59,* 1337–1343.

Bolles, R. C. (1972). Reinforcement, expectancy, and learning. *Psychological Review, 79,* 394–409.

Bolles, R. C. (1993). *The story of psychology: A thematic history.* Pacific Grove, CA: Brooks/Cole.

Bollini, A. M., Walker, E. F., Hamann, S., & Kestler, L. (2004). The influence of perceived control and locus of control on the cortisol and subjective response to stress. *Biological Psychology, 67,* 245–260.

Boniecki, K. A., & Moore, S. (2003). Breaking the silence: Using a token economy to reinforce classroom participation. *Teaching of Psychology, 30,* 224–227.

Boomer, D. S. (1965). Hesitation and grammatical encoding. *Language and Speech, 8,* 145–158.

Bootzin, R. R., Manber, R., Perlis, M. L., Salvio, M., & Wyatt, J. K. (1993). Sleep disorders and the elderly. In P. B. Sutker & H. F. Adams (Eds.), *Comprehensive handbook of psychopathology* (2nd ed.). New York: Plenum.

Boring, E. G. (1950). *A history of experimental psychology* (2nd ed.). New York: Appleton-Century-Crofts.

Bornstein, M. H. (1989). Stability in early mental development: From attention and information processing in infancy to language and cognition in childhood. In M. H. Bornstein & N. A. Krasnegor (Eds.), *Stability and continuity in mental development: Behavioral and biological perspectives.* Hillsdale, NJ: Erlbaum.

Bornstein, M. H. (1992). Perception across the life span. In M. H. Bornstein & M. E. Lamb (Eds.), *Developmental psychology: An advanced textbook* (3rd ed.). Hillsdale, NJ: Erlbaum.

Bornstein, M. H., Kessen, W., & Weiskopf, S. (1976). Color vision and hue categorization in young human infants. *Journal of Experimental Psychology: Human Perception and Performance, 2,* 115–129.

Bornstein, R. F. (2003). Psychodynamic models of personality. In T. Millon & M. J. Lerner (Eds.), *Handbook of psychology: Personality and social psychology* (Vol. 5, pp. 117–134). New York: Wiley.

Bortz, W. M. (1990). The trajectory of dying: Functional status in the last year of life. *Journal of the American Geriatrics Society, 38,* 146–150.

Bouchard, C., Tremblay, A., Despres, J., Nadeau, A., Lupien, P. J., Theriault, G., Dussault, J., Moorjani, S., Pinault, S., & Fournier, G. (1990). The response to long-term overfeeding in identical twins. *New England Journal of Medicine, 322,* 1477–1487.

Bouchard, T. J., Jr. (1997). IQ similarity in twins reared apart: Findings and responses to critics. In R. J. Sternberg & E. L. Grigorenko (Eds.), *Intelligence, heredity, and environment.* New York: Cambridge University Press.

Bouchard, T. J., Jr. (2004). Genetic influence on human psychological traits. *Current Directions in Psychological Science, 13,* 148–151.

Bouchard, T. J., Jr., Lykken, D. T., McGue, M., Segal, N. L., & Tellegean, A. (1990). Sources of human psychological differences: The Minnesota study of twins reared apart. *Science, 250,* 223–228.

Bouchard, T. J., Jr., & McGue, M. (1981). Familial studies of intelligence: A review. *Science, 212,* 1055–1059.

Bouton, M. E. (2007). *Learning and behavior: A contemporary synthesis.* Sunderland, MA: Sinauer Associates.

Bouton, M. E., Mineka, S., & Barlow, D. H. (2001). A modern learning theory perspective on the etiology of panic disorder. *Psychological Review, 108,* 4–32.

Bouvier, S. E., & Engel, S. A. (2006). Behavioral deficits and cortical damage loci in cerebral achromatopsia. *Cerebral Cortex, 16,* 183–191.

Bowden, E. M., & Jung-Beeman, M. (2003). Aha! Insight experience correlates with solution activation in the right hemisphere. *Psychonomic Bulletin & Review, 10,* 730–737.

Bower, T. G. R. (1982). *Development in infancy* (2nd ed.). San Francisco: Freeman.

Bowlby, J. (1969). *Attachment and loss: Vol. 1. Attachment.* New York: Basic Books.

Bowman, E. S. (1998). Pseudoseizures. *Psychiatric Clinics of North America, 21,* 649–657.

Boynton, R. M. (1979). *Human color vision.* New York: Holt, Rinehart & Winston.

Braungart, J. M., Plomin, R., DeFries, J. C., & Fulker, D. W. (1992). Genetic influence on tester-rated infant temperament as assessed by Bayley's Infant Behavior Record: Non-adoptive and adoptive siblings and twins. *Developmental Psychology, 28,* 40–47.

Bregman, A. S. (1990). *Auditory scene analysis.* Cambridge, MA: Bradford/MIT Press.

Breland, K., & Breland, M. (1961). The misbehavior of organisms. *American Psychologist, 16,* 681–684.

Brennan, P. A., & Zufall, F. (2006). Pheromonal communication in vertebrates. *Nature, 444,* 308–315.

Bresnahan, M., Begg, M. D., Brown, A., Schaefer, C., Sohler, N., Insel, B., Vella, L., & Susser, E. (2007). Race and risk of schizophrenia in a US birth cohort: another example of health disparity? *International Journal of Epidemiology, 36,* in press.

Brewer, K. R., & Wann, D. L. (1998). Observational learning effectiveness as a function of model characteristics: Investigating the importance of social power. *Social Behavior & Personality, 26,* 1–10.

Briere, J., & Conte, J. (1993). Self-reported amnesia for abuse in adults molested as children. *Journal of Traumatic Stress, 6,* 21–31.

Broad, W., & Wade, N. (1982). *Betrayers of the truth.* New York: Simon & Schuster.

Broadbent, D. E. (1952). Failures of attention in selective listening. *Journal of Experimental Psychology, 44,* 428–433.

Broadbent, D. E. (1958). *Perception and communication.* London: Pergamon Press.

Broberg, D. J., & Bernstein, I. L. (1987). Candy as a scapegoat in the prevention of food aversions in children receiving chemotherapy. *Cancer, 60,* 2344–2347.

Broca, P. (1861). Remarques sur le siege de la faculte du langage articule, suivies d'une observation d'aphemie (perte de la parole). *Bulletin de la Societé Anatomique (Paris), 36,* 330–357.

Brody, N. (1992). *Intelligence* (2nd ed.). San Diego, CA: Academic Press.

Brody, N. (2007). Barriers to understanding racial differences in intelligence. *Perspectives on Psychological Science, 2,* 214–215.

Bromley, D. B. (1986). *The case-study method in psychology and related disciplines.* Chichester, U.K.: Wiley.

Brosschot, J. F., Godaert, G. L. R., Benschop, R. J., Olff, M., Ballieux, R. E., & Heijnen, C. J. (1998). Experimental stress and immunological reactivity: A closer look at perceived uncontrollability. *Psychosomatic Medicine, 60,* 359–361.

Brown, R., & Kulick, J. (1977). Flashbulb memories. *Cognition, 5,* 73–99.

Brown, T. A., O'Leary, T. A., & Barlow, D. H. (2001). Generalized anxiety disorder. In D. H. Barlow (Ed.), *Clinical handbook of psychological disorders: A step-by-step treatment manual* (3rd ed.). New York: Guilford Press.

Bruce, D. (1985). The how and why of ecological memory. *Journal of Experimental Psychology: General, 114,* 78–90.

Buccino, G., Binkofski, F., & Riggio, L. (2003). The mirror neuron system and action recognition. *Brain and Language, 89,* 370–376.

Buccino, G., Canessa, L. F., Patteri, I., Lagravinesi, G., Benuzzi, F., Porro, C. A., & Rizzolatti, G. (2004). Neural circuits involved in the recognition of actions performed by non-conspecifics: An fMRI study. *Journal of Cognitive Neuroscience, 16,* 114–126.

Buck, L. (1996). Information coding in the vertebrate olfactory system. *Annual Review of Neuroscience, 19,* 517–544.

Buck, L., & Axel, A. (1991). A novel multigene family may encode odorant receptors: A molecular basis for odor recognition. *Cell, 65,* 175–187.

Buell, S. J., & Coleman, P. D. (1979). Dendritic growth in the aged human brain and failure of growth in senile dementia. *Science, 206,* 854–856.

Bulevich, J. B., et al. (2006). Failure to find suppression of episodic memories in the think/nothink paradigm. *Memory & Cognition, 34,* 1569–1577.

Buller, D. (2005). Evolutionary psychology: The emperor's new paradigm. *Trends in Cognitive Sciences, 9,* 277–283.

Burger, J. M., & Caldwell, D. F. (2003). The effects of monetary incentives and labeling on the Foot-in-the-Door Effect: Evidence for a self-perception process. *Basic & Applied Social Psychology, 25,* 235–241.

Burger, J. M., & Cornelius, T. (2003). Raising the price of agreement: Public commitment and the low-ball compli-

ance procedure. *Journal of Applied Social Psychology, 33,* 923–934.

Burgess, A. (2007) On the contribution of neurophysiology to hypnosis research: Current state and future directions. In G. A. Jamieson (Ed.), *Hypnosis and conscious states: The cognitive neuroscience perspective.* New York: Oxford University Press.

Burns, N. R., Bryan, J., & Nettelbeck, T. Ginkgo biloba: No robust effect on cognitive abilities or mood in healthy young or older adults. *Human Psychopharmacology: Clinical and Experimental, 21,* 27–37.

Bushman, B. J. (2002). Does venting anger feed or extinguish the flame? Catharsis, rumination, distraction, anger and aggressive responding. *Personality & Social Psychology Bulletin, 28,* 724–731.

Bushman, B. J., & Anderson, C. A. (2001). Media violence and the American public. *American Psychologist, 56,* 477–489.

Bushman, B. J., & Phillips, C. M. (2001). If the television program bleeds, memory for the advertisement recedes. *Current Directions in Psychological Science, 10,* 43–47.

Buss, A. H. (1989). Personality as traits. *American Psychologist, 44,* 1378–1388.

Buss, D. M. (1989). Sex differences in human preferences: Evolutionary hypotheses tested in 37 cultures. *Behavioral and Brain Sciences, 12,* 1–49.

Buss, D. M. (2000). *The dangerous passion: Why jealousy is as necessary as love and sex.* New York: Free Press.

Buss, D. M. (2004). *Evolutionary psychology: The ultimate origins of human behavior* (2nd ed.). Boston: Allyn & Bacon.

Buss, D. M. (2006). The evolutionary genetics of personality: Does mutation load signal relationship load? *Behavioral and Brain Sciences, 29,* 409.

Buss, D. M. (2007). *Evolutionary psychology: The new science of the mind* (3rd ed.). Boston: Allyn & Bacon.

Buss, D. M., & Schmitt, D. P. (1993). Sexual strategies theory: An evolutionary perspective on human mating. *Psychological Review, 100,* 204–232.

Bustillo, J. R., Lauriello, J., Horan, W. P., & Keith, S. J. (2001). The psychosocial treatment of schizophrenia: An update. *American Journal of Psychiatry, 158,* 163–175.

Butcher, J. N. (Ed.) (2006). *MMPI-2: A practitioner's guide.* Washington, DC: APA.

Butterworth, G. (1992). Origins of self-perception in infancy. *Psychological Inquiry, 3,* 103–111.

Byrne, D. (1971). *The attraction paradigm.* New York: Academic Press.

Cabeza, R., & St Jacques, P. (2007). Functional neuroimaging of autobiographical memory. *Trends in Cognitive Sciences, 11,* 219–227.

Cacioppo, J. T., & Gardner, W. L. (1999). Emotion. *Annual Review of Psychology, 50,* 191–214.

Cameron, J., & Pierce, W. D. (1994). Reinforcement, reward, and intrinsic motivation: A meta-analysis. *Review of Educational Research, 64,* 363–423.

Campbell, D. T., & Stanley, J. C. (1966). *Experimental and quasi-experimental designs for research.* Chicago: Rand McNally.

Campfield, L. A., Smith, F. J., Rosenbaum, M., & Hirsch, J. (1996). Human eating: Evidence for a physiological basis using a modified paradigm. *Neuroscience & Biobehavioral Reviews, 20*, 1133–1137.

Campos, J. J., Langer, A., & Krowitz, A. (1970). Cardiac responses on the visual cliff in prelocomotor human infants. *Science, 170*, 196–197.

Cannell, C. G., & Kahn, R. L. (1968). Interviewing. In G. Lindzey and E. Aronson (Eds.), *Handbook of social psychology: Research methods* (Vol. 2). Reading, MA: Addison-Wesley.

Cannon, W. B. (1927). The James-Lange theory of emotions: A critical examination and an alternative theory. *American Journal of Psychology, 39*, 106–124.

Cannon, W. B. (1929). *Bodily changes in pain, hunger, fear, and rage.* New York: Appleton.

Cannon, W. B. (1932). *The wisdom of the body.* New York: Norton.

Cantor, N., & Malley, J. (1991). Life tasks, personal needs, and close relationships. In G. Fletcher & F. Fincham (Eds.), *Cognition in close relationships.* Hillsdale, NJ: Erlbaum.

Cantor, N., & Mischel, W. (1978). Prototypes in person perception. *Advances in Experimental Social Psychology, 12*, 3–52.

Cantwell, D. P. (1996). Attention deficit disorder: A review of the past 10 years. *Journal of the American Academy of Child and Adolescent Psychiatry, 35*, 978–987.

Carey, M. P., & Vanable, P. A. (2003). AIDS/HIV. In A. M. Nezu, C. M. Nezu, & P. A. Gellar (Eds.), *Handbook of psychology: Health psychology* (Vol. 9, pp. 219–244). New York: Wiley.

Carlsmith, J. M., & Gross, A. E. (1969). Some effects of guilt on compliance. *Journal of Personality and Social Psychology, 11*, 240–244.

Carney, S., et al. (2003). Efficacy and safety of electroconvulsive therapy in depressive disorders: A review and meta-analysis. *Lancet, 36*, 799–808.

Carstensen, L. L. (1995). Evidence for a life-span theory of socioemotional selectivity. *Current Directions in Psychological Science, 4*, 151–156.

Cartwright, J. (2000). *Evolution and human behavior.* Cambridge, MA: MIT Press.

Cartwright, R. (1991). Dreams that work: The relation of dream incorporation to adaptation to stressful events. *Dreaming, 1*, 2–9.

Cartwright, R. (1996). Dreams and adaptation to divorce. In D. Barrett (Ed.), *Trauma and dreams.* Cambridge, MA: Harvard University Press.

Case, R. B., Moss, A. J., Case, N., McDermott, M., & Eberly, S. (1992). Living alone after myocardial infarction: Impact on prognosis. *Journal of American Medical Association, 267*, 515–519.

Caspi, A., & Silva, P.A. (1995). Temperamental qualities at age three predict personality traits in young adulthood: Longitudinal evidence from a birth cohort. *Child Development, 66*, 486–498.

Castle, L., Aubert, R. E., Verbrugge, R. R., Khalid, M., &

Epstein, R. S. (2007). Trends in medication treatment for ADHD. *Journal of Attention Disorder, 10*, 335-342.

Cattell, R. B. (1963). Theory of fluid and crystallized intelligence: A critical experiment. *Journal of Educational Psychology, 54*, 1–22.

Cattell, R. B. (1973, July). A 16PF profile. *Psychology Today,* 40–46.

Cattell, R. B. (1998). Where is intelligence? Some answers from the triadic theory. In J. J. McArdle & R. W. Woodcock (Eds.), *Human cognitive abilities in theory and practice.* Mahwah, NJ: Erlbaum.

Cattell, R. B., Eber, H. W., & Tatsuoka, M. M. (1970). *Handbook of the 16 personality factor questionnaire (16PF).* Champaign, IL: Institute for Personality and Ability Testing.

Cavanaugh, J. C., & Blanchard-Fields, F. (2002). *Adult development and aging* (4th ed.). Belmont, CA: Wadsworth.

Ceci, S. J. (1991). How much does schooling influence intellectual development and its cognitive components? A reassessment of the evidence. *Developmental Psychology, 27*, 703–722.

Cermak, L. S. (1982). The long and the short of it in amnesia. In L. S. Cermak (Ed.), *Human memory and amnesia.* Hillsdale, NJ: Erlbaum.

Chabris, C. F. (1999). Prelude or requiem for the "Mozart effect"? *Nature, 400*, 826.

Chaiken, S., Liberman, A., & Eagly, A. H. (1989). Heuristic and systematic information processing: Within and beyond the persuasion context. In J. S. Uleman & J. A. Bargh (Eds.), *Unintended thought.* New York: Guilford.

Chakos, M., Lieberman, J., Hoffman, E., Bradford, D., & Sheitman, B. (2001). Effectiveness of second-generation antipsychotics in patients with treatment-resistant schizophrenia: A review and meta-analysis of randomized trials. *American Journal of Psychiatry, 158*, 518–526.

Chandrashekar, J., Hoon, M. A., Ryba, N. J., & Zuker, C. S. (2006). The receptors and cells for mammalian taste. *Nature, 444*, 288–294.

Charman, D. P. (Ed.) (2004). *Core processes in brief psychodynamic psychotherapy.* Mahwah, NJ: Erlbaum.

Chase, W. G., & Simon, H. A. (1973). The mind's eye in chess. In W. G. Chase (Ed.), *Visual information processing.* New York: Academic Press.

Chen, S. C. (1937). Social modification of the activity of ants in nest-building. *Physiological Zoology, 10*, 420–436.

Chernis, C., Extein, M., Goleman, D., & Weissberg, R. P. (2006). Emotional intelligence: What does the research really indicate? *Educational Psychologist, 41*, 239–245.

Cherrier, M. M., Matsumoto, A. M., Amory, J. K., Asthana, S., Bremner, W., Peskind, E. R., Raskind, M. A., & Craft, S. (2005). Testosterone improves spatial memory in men with Alzheimer disease and mild cognitive impairment. *Neurolog, 64*, 2063–2068.

Cherry, E. C. (1953). Some experiments on the recognition of speech with one and with two ears. *Journal of the Acoustical Society of America, 25*, 975–979.

Chia, R. C., Allred, L. J., Grossnickle, W. F., & Lee, G. W. (1998). Effects of attractivness and gender on the perception of achievement-related variables. *Journal of Social Psychology, 138,* 471–477.

Child Care Action Campaign. (1996). *A child care primer for parents.* New York: Child Care Action Campaign.

Chomsky, N. (1957). *Syntactic structures.* The Hague: Mouton.

Chomsky, N. (1986). *Knowledge of language: Its nature, origins, and use.* New York: Praeger.

Choy, Y., Fyer, A. J., & Lipsitz, J. D. (2007). Treatment of specific phobia in adults. *Clinical Psychology Review, 27,* 266–286.

Chrysikou, E. G., & Weisberg, R. W. (2005). Following the wrong footsteps: Fixation effects of pictorial examples in a design problem-solving task. *Journal of Experimental Psychology: Learning, Memory, and Cognition, 31,* 1134–1148.

Chumlea, W. C. (1982). Physical growth in adolescence. In B. J. Wolman (Ed.), *Handbook of developmental psychology.* Englewood Cliffs, NJ: Prentice-Hall.

Cialdini, R. B., & Goldstein, N. J. (2004). Social influence: Compliance and comformity. *Annual Review of Psychology, 55,* 591–621.

Cianciolo, A. T., Grigorenko, E. L., Jarvin, L., Gil, G., Drebot, M. E., & Sternberg, R. J. (2006). Practical intelligence and tacit knowledge: Advancements in the measurement of developing expertise. *Learning and Individual Differences, 16,* 235–253.

Cicirelli, V. G. (1997). Relationship of psychosocial and background variables to older adults' end-of-life decisions. *Psychology and Aging, 12,* 72–83.

Cicirelli, V. G. (2002). *Older adults' views on death.* New York: Springer.

Clark, H. H. (1992). *Arenas of language use.* Chicago: University of Chicago Press.

Clark, L. A., & Livesley, W. J. (1994). Two approaches to identifying the dimensions of personality disorder: Convergence on the five-factor model. In P. T. Costa Jr. & T. A. Widiger (Eds.), *Personality disorders and the five-factor model of personality.* Washington, DC: American Psychological Association.

Clark, M. S., & Grote, N. K. (2003). Close relationships. In T. Millon & M. J. Lerner (Eds.), *Handbook of psychology: Personality and social psychology* (Vol. 5, pp. 447–461). New York: Wiley.

Clarke, S., & Thiran, A. B. (2004). Auditory neglect: What and where in auditory space. *Cortex, 40,* 291–300.

Clementz, B. A., Keil, A., & Kissler, J. (2004). Aberrant brain dynamics in schizophrenia: Delayed build-up and prolonged decay of the visual steady-state response. *Cognitive Brain Research, 18,* 121–129.

Clendenen, V. I., Herman, C. P., & Polivy, J. (1994). Social facilitation of eating among friends and strangers. *Appetite, 23,* 1–13.

Cobos, P., Sanchez, M., Garcia, C., Vera, M., & Vila, J. (2002). Revisiting the James versus Cannon debate on emotion: Startle and autonomic modulation in patients with spinal cord injuries. *Biological Psychology, 61,* 251–269.

Cohen, S., Tyrrell, D. A., & Smith, D. A. (1993). Negative life events, perceived stress, negative affect, and susceptibility to the common cold. *Journal of Personality and Social Psychology, 64,* 131–140.

Coile, D. C., & Miller, N. E. (1984). How radical animal activists try to mislead humane people. *American Psychologist, 39,* 700–701.

Cole, M. (1992). Culture in development. In M. H. Bornstein & M. E. Lamb (Eds.), *Developmental psychology: An advanced textbook.* Hillsdale, NJ: Erlbaum.

Cole, N. S. (1981). Bias in testing. *American Psychologist, 36,* 1067–1077.

Cole, R. P., & Miller, R. R. (1999). Conditioned excitation and conditioned inhibition acquired through backward conditioning. *Learning & Motivation, 30,* 129–156.

Coleman, P. (1993). Overview of substance abuse. *Primary Care, 20,* 1–18.

Coles, R., & Stokes, G. (1985). *Sex and the American teenager.* New York: Harper & Row.

Colombo, J., Frick, J. E., & Gorman, S. A. (1997). Sensitization during visual habituation sequences: Procedural effects and individual differences. *Journal of Experimental Child Psychology, 67,* 223–235.

Colucci, E., & Martin, G. (2007). Ethnocultural aspects of suicide in young people: A systematic literature review. Part 2: Risk factors, precipitating agents, and attitudes toward suicide. *Suicide and Life-Threatening Behavior, 37,* 222–237.

Compas, B. E., Hinden, B. R., & Gerhardt, C. A. (1995). Adolescent development: Pathways and processes of risk and resilience. *Annual Review of Psychology, 46,* 265–293.

Conrad, R. (1964). Acoustic confusion in immediate memory. *British Journal of Psychology, 55,* 75–84.

Conway, M. A., Anderson, S. J., Larsen, S. F., Donnelly, C. M., McDaniel, M. A., McClelland, A. G. R., Rawles, R. E., & Logie, R. H. (1994). The formation of flashbulb memories. *Memory & Cognition, 22,* 326–343.

Cook, M., & Mineka, S. (1989). Observational conditioning of fear to fear-relevant versus fear-irrelevant stimuli in rhesus monkeys. *Journal of Abnormal Psychology, 98,* 448–459.

Cook, T. D., & Campbell, D. T. (1979). *Quasi-experimentation: Design and analysis for field settings.* Chicago: Rand McNally.

Cooper, C. L., & Dewe, P. (2007). Stress: A brief history from the 1950s to Lazarus. In A. Monat, R. S. Lazarus, & G. Reevy (Eds.), *The Praeger handbook on stress and coping.* Westport, CT: Praeger.

Cooper, E. (1991). A critique of six measures for assessing creativity. *Journal of Creative Behavior, 25,* 194–204.

Cooper, J. (1992). Dissonance and the return of the self-concept. *Psychological Inquiry, 3,* 320–323.

Cooper, J., & Cooper, G. (2002). Subliminal motivation: A story revisited. *Journal of Applied Social Psychology, 32,* 2213–2227.

Cooper, W. H. (1983). An achievement motivation nomological network. *Journal of Personality and Social Psychology, 44,* 841–861.

Corballis, M. C. (1991). *The lopsided ape: Evolution of the generative mind.* New York: Oxford University Press.

Coren, A. (2001). *Short-term psychotherapy: A psychodynamic approach*. New York: Palgrave.

Coren, S. (1996). *Sleep thieves*. New York: Free Press.

Coren, S., Porac, C., & Theodor, L. H. (1987). Set and subjective contour. In S. Petry & G. E. Meyer (Eds.), *The perception of illusory contours*. New York: Springer-Verlag.

Coren, S., Ward, L. M., & Enns, J. T. (1994). *Sensation and perception* (4th ed.). Fort Worth, TX: Harcourt Brace.

Corsica, J. A., & Perri, M. G. (2003). Obesity. In A. M. Nezu, C. M. Nezu, & P. A. Geller (Eds.), *Handbook of psychology, Vol. 9, Health psychology*, pp. 121–146. New York: Wiley.

Cosmides, L., & Tooby, J. (1992). Cognitive adaptations for social exchange. In J. H. Barkow, L. Cosmides, & J. Tooby (Eds.), *The adapted mind*. New York: Oxford University Press.

Cosmides, L., & Tooby, J. (2002). Unraveling the enigma of human intelligence: Evolutionary psychology and the multimodular mind. In R. J. Sternberg & J. C. Kaufman (Eds.), *The evolution of intelligence*. Mahwah, NJ: Erlbaum.

Courage, M. L., & Howe, M. L. (2004). Advances in early memory development research: Insights about the dark side of the moon. *Developmental Review, 24*, 6–32.

Cowan, G., & Hoffman, C. D. (1986). Gender stereotyping in young children: Evidence to support a concept-learning approach. *Sex Roles, 14*, 211–224.

Cowan, N. (1995). *Attention and memory: An integrated framework*. New York: Oxford University Press.

Cowan, N., Lichty, W., & Grove, T. R. (1990). Properties of memory for unattended spoken syllables. *Journal of Experimental Psychology: Learning, Memory, & Cognition, 16*, 258–269.

Cowan, N., Saults, J. S., & Nugent, L. D. (1997). The role of absolute and relative amounts of time in forgetting within immediate memory: The case of tone-pitch comparisons. *Psychonomic Bulletin & Review, 4*, 393–397.

Cowan, R., & Carney, D. P. J. (2006). Calendrical savants: Exceptionality and practice. *Cognition, 100*, B1–B9.

Cowan, R., O'Conner, N., & Samella, K. (2003). The skills and methods of calendrical savants. *Intelligence, 31*, 51–65.

Cowan, R., Stainthorp, R., Kapnogianni, S., & Anastasiou, M. (2004). The development of calendrical skills. *Cognitive Development, 19*, 169–178.

Coyne, J. C., Stefanek, M., & Palmer, S. C. (2007). Psychotherapy and survival in cancer: The conflict between hope and evidence. *Psychological Bulletin, 133*, 367–394.

Craig, J. C. (1985). Attending to two fingers: Two hands are better than one. *Perception & Psychophysics, 38*, 496–511.

Craig, K. D. (1978). Social disclosure, coactive peer companions, and social modeling determinants of pain communications. *Canadian Journal of Behavioural Science, 10*, 91–104.

Craik, F. I. M. (1994). Memory changes in normal aging. *Current Directions in Psychological Science, 5*, 155–158.

Craik, F. I. M., & Lockhart, R. S. (1972). Levels of processing: A framework for memory research. *Journal of Verbal Learning and Verbal Behavior, 11*, 671–684.

Craik, F. I. M., & McDowd, J. M. (1987). Age differences in recall and recognition. *Journal of Experimental Psychology: Learning, Memory, & Cognition, 13*, 474–479.

Craik, F. I. M., & Tulving, E. (1975). Depth of processing and the retention of words in episodic memory. *Journal of Experimental Psychology: General, 104*, 268–294.

Crano, W. D., & Prislin, R. (2006). Attitudes and persuasion. *Annual Review of Psychology, 57*, 345374.

Craske, M. G. (1999). *Anxiety disorders: Psychological approaches to theory and treatment*. Boulder, CO: Westview Press.

Craske, M. G., & Barlow, D. H. (1993). Panic disorder and agoraphobia. In D. H. Barlow (Ed.), *Clinical handbook of psychological disorders* (2nd ed.). New York: Guilford.

Crawford, C. B. (2007). Reproductive success: Then and now. In S. W. Gangestad & J. A. Simpson (Eds.), *The evolution of mind: Fundamental questions and controversies*. New York: The Guilford Press.

Cronbach, L. J. (1957). The two disciplines of scientific psychology. *American Psychologist, 12*, 671–684.

Crooks, R., & Baur, K. (2008). *Our sexuality* (10th ed.). Belmont, CA: Wadsworth.

Cropley, A. J. (1996). Recognizing creative potential: An evaluation of the usefulness of creativity tests. *High Ability Studies, 7*, 203–219.

Crosby, F. J., Iyer, A., & Sincharoen, S. (2006). Understanding affirmative action. *Annual Review of Psychology, 57*, 585–611.

Crowder, R. G. (1976). *Principles of learning and memory*. Hillsdale, NJ: Erlbaum.

Crowder, R. G., & Neath, I. (1991). The microscope metaphor in human memory. In W. E. Hockley & S. Lewandowsky (Eds.), *Relating theory and data: Essays on human memory in honor of Bennet B. Murdock*. Hillsdale, NJ: Erlbaum.

Crowder, R. G., & Surprenant, A. M. (2000). Sensory memory. In A. E. Kazdin (Ed.), *Encyclopedia of psychology* (pp. 227–229). New York: Oxford University Press and American Psychological Association.

Cummings, E. M., Braungart-Rieker, J. M., & Du Rocher-Schudlich, T. (2003). Emotion and personality development in childhood. In R. M. Lerner, M. A. Easterbrooks, & J. Mistry (Eds.), *Handbook of psychology. Vol. 6: Developmental psychology* (pp. 211–239). New York: Wiley.

Cunningham, M. D., & Reidy, T. J. (1998). Antisocial personality disorder and psychopathy: Diagnostic dilemmas in classifying patterns of antisocial behavior in sentencing evaluations. *Behavioral Sciences & the Law, 16, 333–351.*

Curtis, R. C., & Miller, K. (1986). Believing another likes or dislikes you: Behaviors making the beliefs come true. *Journal of Personality and Social Psychology, 51*, 284–290.

Cutler, W. B., Friedmann, E., & McCoy, N. L. (1998). Pheromonal influences on sociosexual behavior in men. *Archives of Sexual Behavior, 27*, 1–13.

Cutrona, C. E., Wallace, G., & Wesner, K. A. (2006). Neighborhood characteristis and depression: An examination of stress processes. *Current Directions in Psychological Science, 15*, 188–192.

Dackis, C. A., & Miller, N. S. (2003). Neurobiological effects determine treatment options for alcohol, cocaine, and heroin addiction. *Psychiatric Annals, 33,* 585–592.

Damon, W., & Hart, D. (1992). Self-understanding and its role in social and moral development. In M. H. Bornstein & M. E. Lamb (Eds.), *Developmental psychology: An advanced textbook.* Hillsdale, NJ: Erlbaum.

Daniels, H., Cole, M., & Wertsch, J. V. (Eds.). (2007). *The Cambridge companion to Vygotsky.* New York: Cambridge University Press.

Daprati, E., & Sirigu, A. (2006). How we interact with objects: Learning from brain lesions. *Trends in cognitive sciences, 10,* 265–270.

Darley, J. M., & Berscheid, E. (1967). Increased liking as a result of the anticipation of personal contact. *Human Relations, 20,* 29–39.

Darley, J. M., & Latané, B. (1968). Bystander intervention in emergencies: Diffusion of responsibilities. *Journal of Personality and Social Psychology, 8,* 377–383.

Darwin, C. (1859). *On the origin of species.* London: Murray.

Darwin, C. (1871). *Descent of man.* London: Murray.

Davidson, T. L. (1993). The nature and function of interoceptive signals to feed: Toward integration of physiological and learning perspectives. *Psychological Review, 100,* 640–657.

Davidson, T. L. (1998). Hunger cues as modulatory stimuli. In N. A. Schmajuk & P. C. Holland (Eds.), *Occasion setting: Associative learning and cognition in animals.* Washington, DC: American Psychological Association.

Davis, K. L., Kahn, R. S., Ko, G., & Davidson, M. (1991). Dopamine in schizophrenia: A review and reconceptualization. *American Journal of Psychiatry, 148,* 1474–1486.

Dawkins, R. (1976). *The selfish gene.* New York: Oxford University Press.

Dawkins, R. (1986). Wealth, polygyny, and reproductive success. *Behavioral and Brain Sciences, 9,* 190–191.

Dawson, G., Ashman, S., & Carver, L. J. (2000). The role of early experience in shaping behavioral and brain development and its implications for social policy. *Development and Psychopathology, 12,* 695–712.

Dawson, G., & Fischer, K. W. (Eds.). (1994). *Human behavior and the developing brain.* New York: Guilford.

Day, N. L., & Richardson, G. A. (1994). Comparative teratogenicity of alcohol and other drugs. *Alcohol Health and Research World, 18,* 42–48.

de Boysson-Bardies, B., Sagat, L., & Durand, C. (1984). Discernable differences in the babbling of infants according to target language. *Journal of Child Language, 11,* 1–16.

De Kloet, E. R., Joëls, M., & Holsboer, F. (2005). Stress and the brain: From adaptation to disease. *Nature Reviews Neuroscience, 6,* 463–475.

de Lange, F. P., Roelofs, K., & Toni, I. (2007). Increased self-monitoring during imagined movements in conversion paralysis. *Neuropsychologia, 45,* 2051–2058.

De Vries, G. J., & Boyle, P. A. (1998). Double duty for sex differences in the brain. *Behavioural Brain Research, 92,* 205–213.

Deaux, K., & Lewis, L. L. (1984). The structure of gender stereotypes: Interrelationships among components and gender label. *Journal of Personality and Social Psychology, 46,* 991–1004.

DeCasper, A. J., & Fifer, W. P. (1980). Of human bonding: Newborns prefer their mothers' voices. *Science, 208,* 1174–1176.

DeCasper, A. J., & Spence, M. J. (1986). Prenatal maternal speech influences newborns' perception of speech sounds. *Infant Behavior and Development, 9,* 133–150.

Deese, J. (1959). On the prediction of occurrence of particular verbal intrusions in immediate recall. *Journal of Experimental Psychology, 58,* 17–22.

DeGrandpre, R. (2000). *Ritalin nation: Rapid-fire culture and the transformation of human consciousness.* New York: Norton.

DeLisi, L. E., Sakuma, M., Tew, W., Kushner, M., Hoff, A. L., & Grimson, R. (1997). Schizophrenia as a chronic active brain process: A study of progressive brain structural change subsequent to the onset of schizophrenia. *Psychiatry Research: Neuroimaging, 74,* 129–140.

Dement, W. C. (1978). *Some must watch while some must sleep.* New York: Norton.

Dennett, D. C. (1995). *Darwin's dangerous idea: Evolution and the meanings of life.* New York: Simon & Schuster.

Dennis, W., & Dennis, M. G. (1940). The effect of cradling practices upon the onset of walking in Hopi children. *Journal of Genetic Psychology, 56,* 77–86.

DeSaint, V., Smith, C., Hull, P., & Loboschefski, T. (1997). Ten-month-old infants' retrieval of familiar information from short-term memory. *Infant Behavior & Development, 20,* 111–122.

DeValois, R. L., & DeValois, K. K. (1980). Spatial vision. *Annual Review of Psychology, 31,* 309–341.

Dewey, J. (1896). The reflex arc concept in psychology. *Psychological Review, 3,* 357–370.

Dinges, D. F., Whitehouse, W. G., Orne, E. C., & Powell, J. W. (1992). Evaluating hypnotic memory enhancement (hypermnesia and reminiscence) using multitrial forced recall. *Journal of Experimental Psychology: Learning, Memory, and Cognition, 18,* 1139–1147.

Dion, K. L. (2003). Prejudice, racism, and discrimination. In T. Millon & M. J. Lerner (Eds.), *Handbook of psychology: Personality and social psychology* (Vol. 5, pp. 507–536). New York: Wiley.

DiPietro, J. A. (2004). The role of prenatal maternal stress in child development. *Current Directions in Psychological Science, 13,* 71–78.

Dittmar, H., Long, K., & Meek, R. (2004). Buying on the Internet: Gender differences in on-line and conventional buying motivations. *Sex Roles, 50,* 423–444.

Dixon, W. E., Jr., & Smith, P. H. (2000). Links between early temperament and language acquisition. *Merrill-Palmer Quarterly, 46,* 417–440.

Domhoff, G. (1996). *Finding meaning in dreams: A quantitative analysis.* New York: Plenum.

Domhoff, G. (2003). *The scientific study of dreams: Neural networks, cognitive development, and content analysis.* Washington, DC: American Psychological Association.

Domhoff, G. (2005). Refocusing the neurocognitive approach to dreams: A critique of the Hobson versus Solms debate. *Dreaming, 15,* 3–20.

Domjan, M. (2003). *The principles of learning and behavior* (5th ed.). Belmont, CA: Wadsworth.

Domjan, M. (2005). Pavlovian conditioning: A functional perspective. *Annual Review of Psychology. 56,* 179–206.

Domjan, M., & Purdy, J. E. (1995). Animal research in psychology: More than meets the eye of the general psychology student. *American Psychologist, 50,* 496–503.

Dong, W. K., Chudler, E. H., Sugiyama, K., Roberts, V. J., & Hayashi, T. (1994). Somatosensory, multisensory, and task-related neurons in cortical area 7b (PF) of unanesthetized monkeys. *Journal of Neurophysiology, 72,* 542–564.

Donlon, T. F. (Ed.). (1984). *The College Board technical handbook for the Scholastic Aptitude Test and achievment tests.* New York: College Entrance Examination Board.

Dorward, F. M. C., & Day, R. H. (1997). Loss of 3-D shape constancy in interior spaces: The basis of the Ames-room illusion. *Perception, 26,* 707–718.

Dougall, A. L., Hyman, K. B., Hayward, M. C., McFeeley, S., & Baum, A. (2001). Optimism and traumatic stress: The importance of social support and coping. *Journal of Applied Social Psychology, 31,* 223–245.

Douvan, E. (1997). Erik Erikson: Critical times, critical theory. *Child Psychiatry and Human Development, 28,* 15–21.

Drevets, W. C., Burton, H., Videen, T. O., & Snyder, A. Z. (1995). Blood flow changes in human somatosensory cortex during anticipated stimulation. *Nature, 373,* 249–252.

Drosopoulos, S., Schulze, C., Fishcer, S., & Born, J. (2007). Sleep's function in the spontaneous recovery and consolidation of memories. *Journal of Experimental Psychology: General, 136,* 169–183.

Druckman, D., & Bjork, R. A. (1991). *In the mind's eye: Enhancing human performance.* Washington, DC: National Academy Press.

Dugas, M. J., Freeston, M. H, Ladouceur, R., Rheaume, J., Provencher, M., & Boisvert, J. (1998). Worry themes in primary GAD, secondary GAD, and other anxiety disorders. *Journal of Anxiety Disorders, 12,* 253–261.

Duncker, K. (1945). On problem solving. *Psychological Monographs, 58*(5, Whole No. 270).

Durie, D. J. (1981). Sleep in animals. In D. Wheatley (Ed.), *Psychopharmacology of sleep.* New York: Raven Press.

Eagle, M. (1997). Contributions of Erik Erikson. *Psychoanalytic Review, 84,* 337–347.

Eagly, A. H., Ashmore, R. D., Makhijani, M. G., & Longo, L. C. (1991). What is beautiful is good, but . . . : A meta-analytic review of research on the physical attractiveness stereotype. *Psychological Bulletin, 110,* 109–128.

Eagly, A. H., & Wood, W. (1999). The origins of sex differences in human behavior: Evolved dispositions versus social roles. *American Psychologist, 54,* 408–423.

Ebbinghaus, H. (1964). *Memory: A contribution to experimental psychology.* New York: Dover. (Original work published 1885)

Eccles, J. S., Wigfield, A., & Byrnes, J. (2003). Cognitive development in adolescence. In R. M. Lerner, M. A. Easterbrooks, & J. Mistry (Eds.), *Handbook of psychology. Vol. 6: Developmental psychology* (pp. 325–350). New York: Wiley.

Edelman, G. M. (1987). *Neural Darwinism.* New York: Basic Books.

Efron, R. (1970). The relationship between the duration of a stimulus and the duration of a perception. *Neuropsychologia, 8,* 37–55.

Egan, D., & Schwartz, B. (1979). Chunking in recall of symbolic drawings. *Memory & Cognition, 7,* 149–158.

Eggert, L. L., Thompson, E. A., Herting, J. R., Randell, B., & Mazza, J. (1995). Reducing suicide potential among high-risk youth: Tests of a school-based prevention program. *Suicide and Life-Threatening Behavior, 25,* 276–296.

Eibl-Eibesfeldt, I. (1973). The expressive behavior of the deaf-and-born-blind. In M. von Cranach & I. Vine (Eds.), *Social communication and movement.* San Diego: Academic Press.

Eich, E., Macaulay, D., Loewenstein, R. J., & Dihle, P. H. (1997). Memory, amnesia, and dissociative identity disorder. *Psychological Science, 8,* 417–422.

Eichenbaum, H. (2003). How does the hippocampus contribute to memory? *Trends in Cognitive Sciences, 7,* 427–429.

Eisenberger, R., & Cameron, J. (1996). Detrimental effects of reward: Reality or myth? *American Psychologist, 51,* 1153–1166.

Ekman, P. & Keltner, D. (1997). Universal facial expressions of emotion: An old controversy and new findings. In U. C. Segerstrale & P. Molnar (Eds.), *Nonverbal communication: Where nature meets culture.* Mahwah, NJ: Erlbaum.

Ekman, P. (1992). Are there basic emotions? *Psychological Review, 99,* 350–353.

Ekman, P. (1999). Basic emotions. In T. Dalgleish and M. Power (Eds.), *Handbook of cognition and emotion.* Chichester, UK: Wiley.

Ekman, P., & Friesen, W. V. (1975). *Unmasking the face.* Englewood Cliffs, NJ: Prentice-Hall.

Ekman, P., & Friesen, W. V. (1986). A new pan-cultural facial expression of emotion. *Motivation and Emotion, 10,* 159–168.

Elicker, J., Englund, M., & Sroufe, L. A. (1992). Predicting peer competence and peer relationships in childhood from early parent-child relationships. In R. D. Parke & G. W. Ladd (Eds.), *Family-peer relationships: Modes of linkage.* Hillsdale, NJ: Erlbaum.

Elliot, A. J., & Devine, P. G. (1994). On the motivational nature of cognitive dissonance: Dissonance as psychological discomfort. *Journal of Personality and Social Psychology, 67,* 382–294.

Elliot, A. J., & Thrash, T. M. (2001). Achievement goals and the hierarchical model of achievement motivation. *Educational Psychology Review, 13,* 139–156.

Ellis, A. (1962). *Reason and emotion in psychotherapy.* Secaucus, NJ: Prentice-Hall.

Ellis, A. (1993). Fundamentals of rational-emotive therapy for the 1990s. In W. Dryden & L. K. Hill (Eds.), *Innovations in rational-emotive therapy*. Newbury Park, CA: Sage.

Ellis, W. D. (1938). *A source book of Gestalt psychology*. London: Routledge & Kegan Paul.

Ellman, S. J., Spielman, A. J., Luck, D., Steiner, S. S., & Halperin, R. (1991). REM deprivation: A review. In S. J. Ellman & J. S. Antrobus (Eds.), *The mind in sleep* (2nd ed.). New York: Wiley.

Ellsworth, P. C. (1994). William James and emotion: Is a century of fame worth a century of misunderstanding? *Psychological Review, 101*, 222–229.

Elmes, D. G., Kantowitz, B. H., & Roediger, H. L. (2006). *Experimental psychology: Understanding psychology research* (8th ed.). Belmont, CA: Wadsworth.

Engle, R. W. (2000). What is working memory capacity? In H. L. Roediger et al. (Eds.), *The nature of remembering*. Washington, DC: American Psychological Association.

Epstein, S. (1979). The stability of behavior: On predicting most of the people much of the time. *Journal of Personality and Social Psychology, 37*, 1097–1126.

Erickson, M. A., & Kruschke, J. K. (1998). Rules and exemplars in category learning. *Journal of Experimental Psychology: General, 127*, 107–140.

Erickson, M. H. (1964). A hypnotic technique for resistant patients. *American Journal of Clinical Hypnosis, 7*, 8–32.

Erikson, E. (1963). *Childhood and society*. New York: Norton.

Erikson, E. (1968). *Identity: Youth and crisis*. New York: Norton.

Erikson, E. (1982). *The life cycle completed: Review*. New York: Norton.

Esser, J. K. (1998). Alive and well after 25 years: A review of groupthink research. *Organizational Behavior & Human Decision Processes, 73*, 116–141.

Evans, C. L., McGuire, P. K., & David, A. S. (2000). Is auditory imagery defective in patients with auditory hallucinations? *Psychological Medicine, 30*, 137–148.

Evans, E. F. (1982). Functions of the auditory system. In H. B. Barlow & J. D. Mollon (Eds.), *The senses*. Cambridge, U.K.: Cambridge University Press.

Evans, G. W. (1997). Environmental stress and health. In A. Baum, T. Revenson, & J. E. Singer (Eds.), *Handbook of health psychology*. Hillsdale, NJ: Erlbaum.

Evans, G. W., Hygge, S., & Bullinger, M. (1995). Chronic noise and psychological stress. *Psychological Science, 6*, 333–338.

Eysenck, H. J. (1952). The effects of psychotherapy: An evaluation. *Journal of Consulting Psychology, 16*, 319–324.

Eysenck, H. J. (1970). *The structure of human personality* (3rd ed.). London: Methuen.

Eysenck, H. J. (1991). Dimensions of personality: 16, 5, or 3?: Criteria for a taxonomic paradigm. *Personality and Individual Differences, 12*, 773–790.

Eysenck, H. J., & Eysenck, S. B. G. (1975). *Manual of the Eysenck Personality Questionnaire*. San Diego: EdITS.

Eysenck, H. J., & Kamin, L. (1981). *The intelligence controversy: H. J. Eysenck vs. Leon Kamin*. New York: Wiley.

Fagan, T. J., Ax, R. K., Liss, M., Resnick, R. J., & Moody, S. (2007). Prescriptive authority and preferences for training. *Professional Psychology: Research and Practice, 38*, 104–111.

Fahy, T. A. (1988). The diagnosis of multiple personality: A critical review. *British Journal of Psychiatry, 153*, 597–606.

Fallon, A. E., & Rozin, P. (1985). Sex differences in perceptions of desirable body shape. *Journal of Abnormal Psychology, 94*, 102–105.

Fantz, R. L. (1961, May). The origin of form perception. *Scientific American, 204*, 66–72.

Faust, I. M. (1984). Role of the fat cell in energy balance physiology. In A. J. Stunkard & E. Stellar (Eds.), *Eating and its disorders*. New York: Raven.

Fazio, R. H. (1986). How do attitudes guide behavior? In R. M. Sorrentino & E. T. Higgins (Eds.), *Handbook of motivation and cognition: Foundations of social behavior* (Vol. 1). New York: Guilford.

Fehr, B., & Russell, J. A. (1991). The concept of love: Viewed from a prototype perspective. *Journal of Personality and Social Psychology, 60*, 425–438.

Feingold, A. (1988). Matching for attractiveness in romantic partners and same-sex friends: A meta-analysis and theoretical critique. *Psychological Bulletin, 104*, 226–235.

Feingold, A. (1990). Gender differences in effects of physical attractiveness on romantic attraction: A comparison across five research paradigms. *Journal of Personality and Social Psychology, 59*, 981–993.

Feingold, A. (1992). Good-looking people are not what we think. *Psychological Bulletin, 111*, 304–341.

Feist, J. (1994). *Theories of personality* (3rd ed.). Fort Worth, TX: Harcourt Brace.

Feldman, D. H. (2003). Cognitive development in childhood. In R. M. Lerner, M. A. Easterbrooks, & J. Mistry (Eds.), *Handbook of psychology. Vol. 6: Developmental psychology* (pp. 195–210). New York: Wiley.

Ferris, C. F., Snowdon, C. T., King, J. A., Duong, T. Q., Ziegler, T. E., Ugurbil, K., Ludwig, R., et al. (2001). Functional imaging of brain activity in conscious monkeys responding to sexually arousing cues. *Neuroreport: For Rapid Communication of Neuroscience Research, 12*, 2231–2236.

Ferster, C. B., & Skinner, B. F. (1957). *Schedules of reinforcement*. New York: Appleton-Century-Crofts.

Festinger, L. (1957). *A theory of cognitive dissonance*. Stanford, CA: Stanford University Press.

Festinger, L., & Carlsmith, J. M. (1959). Cognitive consequences of forced compliance. *Journal of Abnormal and Social Psychology, 58*, 203–210.

Festinger, L., Riecken, H. W., & Schacter, S. (1956). *When prophecy fails*. Minneapolis: University of Minnesota Press.

Festinger, L., Schachter, S., & Black, K. (1950). *Social pressures in informal groups: A study of human factors in housing*. New York: Harper.

Fiedler, K. (1988). The dependence of the conjunction fallacy on subtle linguistic factors. *Psychological Research, 50*, 123–129.

Fink, M. (2001). Convulsive therapy: A review of the first 55 years. *Journal of Affective Disorders, 63,* 1–15.

Fischer, P., Greitemeyer, T., Pollozek, F., & Frey, D. (2006). The unresponsive bystander: Are bystanders more responsive in dangerous emergencies? *European Journal of Social Psychology, 36,* 267–278.

Fiske, S. T. (1993). Social cognition and social perception. *Annual Review of Psychology, 44,* 155–194.

Fiss, H. (1991). Experimental strategies for the study of the function of dreaming. In S. J. Ellman & J. S. Antrobus (Eds.), *The mind in sleep* (2nd ed.). New York: Wiley.

Flaherty, M. (2000). Acoustic and visual confusion in immediate memory in people who are deaf hard of hearing. *Volta Review, 101,* 213–221.

Flanagan, O. (2000). Dreaming is not an adaptation. *Behavioral and Brain Sciences, 23,* 936–937.

Flavell, J. H. (1971). Stage-related properties of cognitive development. *Cognitive Psychology, 2,* 421–453.

Flavell, J. H. (1999). Cognitive development: Children's knowledge about the world. *Annual Review of Psychology, 50,* 21–45.

Flavell, J. H., Miller, P. A., & Miller, S. A. (1993). *Cognitive Development* (3rd ed.). Englewood Cliffs, NJ: Prentice-Hall.

Flaxman, S. M., & Sherman, P. W. (2000). Morning sickness: A mechanism for protecting mother and embryo. *Quarterly Review of Biology, 75,* 113–148.

Fleeson, W. (2001). Towards a structure- and process-integrated view of personality: Traits as density distributions of states. *Journal of Personality and Social Psychology, 80,* 1011–1027.

Fleeson, W. (2004). Moving personality beyond the person-situation debate. *Current Directions in Psychological Science, 13,* 83–87.

Fleishman, E. A., & Parker, J. F., Jr. (1962). Factors in the retention and relearning of perceptual motor skill. *Journal of Experimental Psychology, 64,* 215–226.

Flynn, J. R. (1987). Massive IQ gains in 14 nations: What IQ tests really measure. *Psychological Bulletin, 101,* 171–191.

Flynn, J. R. (1999). Searching for justice: The discovery of IQ gains over time. *American Psychologist, 54,* 5–20.

Folkman, S., & Moskowitz, J. T. (2004). Coping: Pitfalls and promise. *Annual Review of Psychology, 55,* 745–774.

Forgas, J. P. (1998). On being happy and mistaken: Mood effects on the fundamental attribution error. *Journal of Personality & Social Psychology, 75,* 318–331.

Foulkes, D. (1985). *Dreaming: A cognitive-psychological analysis.* Hillsdale, NJ: Erlbaum.

Frankham, C., & Cabanac, M. (2003). Nicotine lowers the body-weight set-point in male rats. *Appetite, 41,* 1–5.

Freedman, J. L. (1988). Television violence and aggression: What the evidence shows. In S. Oskamp (Ed.), *Television as a social issue* (Vol. 8). Beverly Hills, CA: Sage.

Freedman, J. L., & Fraser, S. C. (1966). Compliance without pressure: The foot-in-the-door technique. *Journal of Personality and Social Psychology, 4,* 195–202.

Freud, S. (1900). *The interpretation of dreams.* (Translated by A. A. Brill, 1913). New York: Macmillan.

Freud, S. (1910). The origin and development of psychoanalysis. *American Journal of Psychology, 21,* 181–218.

Freud, S. (1940). *An outline of psychoanalysis.* New York: Norton.

Freud, S. (1962). *Three contributions to the theory of sexuality.* New York: Dutton. (Original work published 1905)

Freud, S. (1964). The dynamics of transference. In J. Strachey (Trans. & Ed.), *The standard edition of the complete works of Sigmund Freud* (Vol. 12). London: Hogarth Press. (Original work published 1912)

Freudenberger, H. J. (1974). Staff burnout. *Journal of Social Issues, 30,* 159–165.

Friedlander, L., Lumley, M. A., Farchione, T., & Doyal, G. (1997). Testing the alexithymia hypothesis: Physiological and subjective responses during relaxation and stress. *Journal of Nervous & Mental Disease, 185,* 233–239.

Friedman, H. S., Hawley, P. H., & Tucker, J. S. (1994). Personality, health, and longevity. *Current Directions in Psychological Science, 3,* 37–41.

Friedman, M., & Rosenman, R. F. (1974). *Type A behavior and your heart.* New York: Knopf.

Frueh, B. C., de Arellano, M. A., & Turner, S. M. (1997). Systematic desensitization as an alternative exposure strategy for PTSD. *American Journal of Psychiatry, 154,* 287–288.

Fuchs, A. H., & Milar, K. S. (2003). Psychology as a science. In D. K. Freedheim (Ed.), *Handbook of psychology* (Vol. 1: History of psychology; pp. 1–26). New York: Wiley.

Funder, D. C. (2001). Personality. *Annual Review of Psychology, 52,* 197–221.

Fyer, A. J., Mannuzza, S., Gallops, M. S., Martin, L. Y., Aaronson, C., Gorman, J. M., Liebowitz, M. R., & Klein, D. F. (1990). Familial transmission of simple phobias and fears: A preliminary report. *Archives of General Psychiatry, 47,* 252–256.

Gabrieli, J. D. E. (1998). Cognitive neuroscience of human memory. *Annual Reviews of Psychology, 49,* 87–115.

Gagnon, J. H. (1990). The explicit and implicit use of the scripting perspective in sex research. *Annual Review of Sex Research, 1,* 1–43.

Gagnon, J., & Simon, W. (1973). *Sexual conduct: The social sources of human sexuality.* Chicago: Aldine.

Galef, B. G., Jr. (1985). Social learning in wild Norway rats. In T. D. Johnston & A. T. Pietrewicz (Eds.), *Issues in the ecological study of learning.* Hillsdale, NJ: Erlbaum.

Galef, B. G., & Laland, K. N. (2005). Social learning in animals: Empirical studies and theoretical models. *BioScience, 55,* 489–499.

Galinsky, A. D., & Moskowitz, G. B. (2000). Perspective-taking: Decreasing stereotype expression, stereotype accessibility, and In-Group favoritism. *Journal of Personality and Social Psychology, 78,* 708–724.

Gallistel, C. R., & Gibbon, J. (2000). Time, rate, and conditioning. *Psychological Review, 107,* 289–344.

Galton, F. (1869). *Hereditary genius: An inquiry into its laws and consequences*. New York: Appleton.

Galton, F. (1883). *Inquiries into human faculty and development*. London: Macmillan.

Gandelman, R. (1992). *Psychobiology of behavior development*. New York: Oxford University Press.

Gandevia, S. C., McCloskey, D. I., & Burke, D. (1992). Kinaesthetic signals and muscle contraction. *Trends in Neurosciences, 15*, 62–65.

Gangestad, S. W., & Simpson, J. A. (1993). Development of a scale measuring genetic variation related to expressive control. *Journal of Personality, 61*, 133–158.

Gangestad, S. W., & Snyder, M. (1985). On the nature of self-monitoring: An examination of latent causal structure. In P. Shaver (Ed.), *Review of personality and social psychology* (Vol. 6). Beverly Hills, CA: Sage.

Ganis, G., Thompson, W. L., & Kosslyn, S. M. (2004). Brain areas underlying visual mental imagery and visual perception: An fMRI study. *Cognitive Brain Research, 20*, 226–241.

Ganis, G., Thompson, W. L., Mast, F. W., & Kosslyn, S. M. (2003). Visual imagery in cerebral visual dysfunction. *Neurologic Clinics, 21*, 631–646.

Garcia, J., & Koelling, R. A. (1966). Relation of cue to consequence in avoidance learning. *Psychonomic Science, 4*, 123–124.

Garcia, S. M., Weaver, K., Moskowitz, G. B., & Darley, J. M. (2002). Crowded minds: The implicit bystander effect. *Journal of Personality and Social Psychology, 83*, 843–853.

Gardner, E. B., & Costanzo, R. H. (1981). Properties of kinesthetic neurons in somatosensory cortex of awake monkeys. *Brain Research, 214*, 301–319.

Gardner, E. L. (1997). Brain reward mechanisms. In J. H. Lowinson, P. Ruiz, R. B. Millman, & J. G. Langrod (Eds.), *Substance abuse: A comprehensive textbook*. Baltimore: Williams & Wilkins.

Gardner, H. (1983). *Frames of mind: The theory of multiple intelligences*. New York: Basic Books.

Gardner, H. (1993). *Multiple intelligences: The theory in practice*. New York: Basic Books.

Gardner, H. (1999). *Intelligence reframed: Multiple intelligences for the 21st century*. New York: Basic Books.

Gardner, H., & Moran, S. (2006). The science of multiple intelligences theory: A response to Lynn Waterhouse. *Educational Psychologist, 41*, 227–232.

Gardner, R. A., & Gardner, B. T. (1969). Teaching sign language to a chimpanzee. *Science, 165*, 664–672.

Gardner, R. A., Gardner, B. T., & Van Cantfort, T. E. (Eds.). (1989). *Teaching sign language to chimpanzees*. Albany, NY: SUNY Press.

Garland, A. F., & Zigler, E. (1993). Adolescent suicide prevention: Current research and social policy implications. *American Psychologist, 48*, 169–182.

Garrity, T. F., Stallones, L., Marx, M. B., & Johnson, T. P. (1989). Pet ownership and attachment as supportive factors in the health of the elderly. *Anthrozoos, 3*, 35–44.

Gaw, A. C. (2001). *Concise guide to cross-cultural psychiatry*. Washington, DC: American Psychiatric Association.

Gazzaniga, M. S., Bogen, J. E., & Sperry, R. W. (1965). Observations on visual perception after disconnection of the cerebral hemispheres in man. *Brain, 88*, 221–236.

Gazzaniga, M. S., Eliassen, J. C., Nisenson, L., Wessinger, C. M., Fendrich, R., & Baynes, K. (1996). Collaboration between the hemispheres of a callosotomy patient: Emerging right hemisphere speech and the left hemisphere interpreter. *Brain, 119*, 1255–1263.

Gazzaniga, M. S., & LeDoux, J. E. (1978). *The integrated mind*. New York: Plenum.

Geary, D. C. (2005). *The origin of mind: Evolution of brain, cognition, and general intelligence*. Washington, DC: APA.

Geary, D. C., & Flinn, M. V. (2002). Sex differences in behavioral and hormonal response to social threat: Commentary on Taylor et al. (2000). *Psychological Review, 109*, 745–750.

Geary, D. C., Vigil, J., & Byrd-Craven, J. (2004). Evolution of human mate choice. *Journal of Sex Research, 41*, 101–112.

Gegenfurtner, K. R., & Kiper, D. C. (2003). Color vision. *Annual Review of Neuroscience, 26*, 181–206.

Geiselman, R. E., Fisher, R. P., MacKinnon, D. P., & Holland, H. L. (1985). Eyewitness memory enhancement in the police interview: Cognitive retrieval mnemonics versus hypnosis. *Journal of Applied Psychology, 70*, 401–412.

Gerbner, G., & Gross, L. (1976). Living with television: The violence profile. *Journal of Communications, 26*, 172–199.

German, T. P., & Barrett, H. C. (2005). Functional fixedness in a technologically sparse culture. *Psychological Science, 16*, 1–5.

Gershon, E. S. (1990). Genetics. In F. K. Goodwin & K. R. Jamison (Eds.), *Manic-depressive illness*. New York: Oxford University Press.

Gibbs, R. W., O'Brien, J. E., & Doolittle, S. (1995). Inferring meanings that are not intended: Speakers' intentions and irony comprehension. *Discourse Processes, 20*, 187–203.

Gibson, E. J., & Walk, R. D. (1960, April). The "visual cliff." *Scientific American, 202*, 64–71.

Gigerenzer, G. (1996). On narrow norms and vague heuristics: A reply to Kahneman & Tversky. *Psychological Review, 103*, 592–596.

Gigerenzer, G. (1997). Ecological intelligence: An adaptation for frequencies. In D. Cummins & C. Allen (Eds.), *The evolution of mind*. New York: Oxford University Press.

Gilbert, A. L., Regier, T., Kay, P., & Ivry, R. B. (2007). Support for lateralization of the Whorf effect beyond the realm of color discrimination. *Brain and Language*, in press.

Gilligan, C. (1982). *In a different voice: Psychological theory and women's development*. Cambridge, MA: Harvard University Press.

Gillin, J. C. (1993). Clinical sleep-wake disorders in psychiatric practice: Dyssomnias. In D. L. Dunner (Ed.), *Current psychiatric therapy*. Philadelphia: Saunders.

Glaser, B. G., & Strauss, A. L. (1968). *Time for dying*. Chicago: Aldine.

Gleaves, D. H., May, M. C., & Cardena, E. (2001). An examination of the diagnostic validity of dissociative identity disorder. *Clinical Psychology Review, 21,* 577–608.

Gluck, J. P., & Bell, J. (2003). Ethical issues in the use of animals in biomedical and psychopharmacological research. *Psychopharmacology, 171,* 6–12.

Goater, N., King, M., Cole, E., Leavey, G., Johnson-Sabine, E., Blizard, R., & Hoar, A. (1999). Ethnicity and outcomes of psychosis. *British Journal of Psychiatry, 175,* 34–42.

Gold, P. E., Cahill, L., & Wenk, G. L. (2002). Ginkgo biloba: A cognitive enhancer? *Psychological Science in the Public Interest, 3,* 2–11.

Goldberg, J., True, W. R., Eisen, S. A., & Henderson, W. G. (1990). A twin study of the effects of the Vietnam War on posttraumatic stress disorder. *Journal of the American Medical Association, 263,* 1227–1232.

Golden, R. N. (2004). Making advances where it matters: Improving outcomes in mood and anxiety disorders. *CNS Spectrums, 9,* 14–22.

Goldstein, B. (1994). *Psychology.* Pacific Grove, CA: Brooks/Cole.

Goldstein, D. S., & Kopin, I. J. (2007). Evolution of concepts of stress. *Stress: The International Journal on the Biology of Stress, 10,* 109–120.

Goldstone, R. L., & Kersten, A. (2003). Concepts and categorization. In A. Healy & R. Proctor (Eds.), *Handbook of psychology. Vol. 4: Experimental psychology,* pp. 599–621. New York: Wiley.

Goleman, D. (1995). *Emotional intelligence.* New York: Bantam.

Golub, S. (1992). *Periods: From menarche to menopause.* Newbury Park, CA: Sage.

Gonzalez-Quijano, M. I., Martin, M., Millan, S., & Lopez-Calderon, A. (1998). Lymphocyte response to mitogens: Influence of life events and personality. *Neuropsychobiology, 38,* 90–96.

Goodall, J. (1990). *Through a window: My thirty years with the chimpanzees of Gombe.* Boston: Houghton Mifflin.

Goodenough, D. R. (1991). Dream recall: History and current status of the field. In S. J. Ellman & J. S. Antrobus (Eds.), *The mind in sleep* (2nd ed.). New York: Wiley.

Goodman, M. J., Tijerina, L., Bents, F. D., & Wierwille, W. W. (1999). Using cellular telephones in vehicles: Safe or unsafe? *Transportation Human Factors, 1,* 3–42.

Gore-Felton, C., Koopman, C., Thoresen, C., Arnow, B., Bridges, E., & Spiegel, D. (2000). Psychologists' beliefs and clinical characteristics: Judging the veracity of childhood sexual abuse memories. *Professional Psychology: Research and Practice, 31,* 372–377.

Gottesman, I. I. (1991). *Schizophrenia genesis: The origins of madness.* New York: Freeman.

Gould, E., Tanapat, P., Hastings, N. B., & Shors, T. J. (1999). Neurogenesis in adulthood: A possible role in learning. *Trends in Cognitive Sciences, 3,* 186–192.

Gould, M. S. (2001). Suicide and the media. In H. Hendin & J. J. Mann (Eds.), *Suicide prevention: Clinical and scientific aspects.* New York: New York Academy of Sciences.

Gould, M. S., & Kramer, R. A. (2001). Youth suicide prevention. *Suicide and Life-Threatening Behavior, 31*(Supplement), 6–31.

Gould, R. L. (1978). *Transformations: Growth and change in adult life.* New York: Simon & Schuster.

Gould, S. J. (2000). More things in heaven and earth. In H. Rose & S. Rose (Eds.). *Alas, poor Darwin: Arguments against evolutionary psychology.* New York: Harmony Books.

Gould, S. J., & Lewontin, R. C. (1979). The spandrels of San Marco and the Panglossian paradigm: A critique of the adaptionist program. *Proceedings of Royal Society of London, 205,* 581–598.

Graf, P., Mandler, G., & Haden, P. E. (1982). Simulating amnesic symptoms in normal subjects. *Science, 218,* 1243–1244.

Graf, P., & Schacter, D. L. (1985). Implicit and explicit memory for new associations in normal and amnesic subjects. *Journal of Experimental Psychology: Learning, Memory, & Cognition, 11,* 501–518.

Graffen, N. F., Ray, W. J., & Lundy, R. (1995). EEG concomitants of hypnosis and hypnotic susceptibility. *Journal of Abnormal Psychology, 104,* 123–131.

Granrud, C. E. (Ed.). (1993). *Visual perception and cognition in infancy.* Hillsdale, NJ: Erlbaum.

Granvold, D. K. (Ed.). (1994). *Cognitive and behavioral treatment: Methods and applications.* Pacific Grove, CA: Brooks/Cole.

Graziano, W. G., & Bryant, W. H. M. (1998). Self-monitoring and the self-attribution of positive emotions. *Journal of Personality & Social Psychology, 74,* 250–261.

Greenberg, D. L. (2004). President Bush's false "flashbulb" memory of 9/11/01. *Applied Cognitive Psychology, 18,* 363–370.

Greenblatt, D. J., & Shader, R. I. (1978). Pharmacotherapy of anxiety with benzodiazepines and beta-adrenergic blockers. In M. Lipton, A. DiMascio, & F. Killiam (Eds.), *Psychopharmacology: A generation of progress.* New York: Raven.

Greene, R. L. (1992). *Human memory: Paradigms and paradoxes.* Hillsdale, NJ: Erlbaum.

Greenough, W. T., Black, J. E., & Wallace, C. S. (1987). Experience and brain development. *Child Development, 58,* 539–559.

Greenwald, A. G., & Banaji, M. R. (1995). Implicit social cognition: Attitides, self-esteem, and stereotypes. *Psychological Review, 102,* 4–27.

Greenwald, A. G., Spangenberg, E. R., Pratkanis, A. R., & Eskenazi, J. (1991). Double-blind tests of subliminal self-help audiotapes. *Psychological Science, 2,* 119–122.

Grencavage, L. M., & Norcross, J. C. (1990). Where are the common factors? *Professional Psychology: Research and Practice, 21,* 372–378.

Grice, D. E., Halmi, K. A., Fitcher, M. M., Strober, M., Woodside, D. B., & Treasure, J. T. (2002). Evidence for a susceptibility gene for anorexia nervosa on Chromosome 1. *American Journal of Human Genetics, 70,* 787–792.

Grice, H. P. (1975). Logic and conversation. In P. Cole & J. L. Morgan (Eds.), *Syntax and semantics. Vol. 3. Speech acts.* New York: Seminar Press.

Grill, H. J., & Kaplan, J. M. (1990). Caudal brainstem participates in the distributed neural control of feeding. In E. M. Stricker (Ed.), *Handbook of behavioral neurobiology* (Vol. 10). New York: Plenum.

Grossberg, S. (2003). Filling-in the forms: Surface and boundary interactions in visual cortex. In L. Pessoa & P. De Weerd (Eds.), *Filling-in: From perceptual completion to cortical reorganization.* London: Oxford University Press.

Groves, P. M., & Thompson, R. F. (1970). *Habituation: A dual-process theory. Psychological Review, 77,* 419–450.

Gruneberg, M. M., Sykes, R. N., & Gillett, E. (1994). The facilitating effects of mnemonic strategies on two learning tasks in learning disabled adults. *Neuropsychological Rehabilitation, 4,* 241–254.

Guinard, J. X., & Brun, P. (1998). Sensory-specific satiety: Comparison of taste and texture effects. *Appetite, 31,* 141–157.

Gunderson, J. G. (1992). Diagnostic controversies. In A. Tasman & M. B. Riba (Eds.), *Review of psychiatry* (Vol. 11). Washington, DC: American Psychiatric Press.

Gurman, E. B. (1994). Debriefing for all concerned: Ethical treatment of human subjects. *Psychological Science, 5,* 139.

Haan, N. (Ed.). (1977). *Coping and defending: Processes of self-environment organization.* New York: Academic Press.

Haan, N. (1993). The assessment of coping, defense, and stress. In L. Goldberger & S. Brezitz (Eds.), *Handbook of stress: Theoretical and clinical aspects* (2nd ed.). New York: Free Press.

Habib, R., Nyberg, L., & Tulving, E. (2003). Hemispheric asymmetries of memory: the HERA model revisited. *Trends in Cognitive Sciences, 7,* 241–245.

Hadjikhani, N., & de Gelder, B. (2002). Neural basis of prosopagnosia: An fMRI study. *Human Brain Mapping, 16,* 176–182.

Haines, M. M., Stansfeld, S. A., Job, R. F. S., Berglund, B., & Head, J. (2001). Chronic aircraft noise exposure, stress responses, mental health and cognitive performance in school children. *Psychological Medicine, 31,* 265–277.

Halpern, D. F. (2000). *Sex differences in cognitive abilities* (3rd ed.). Mahwah, NJ: Erlbaum.

Hamer, D. H., Hu, S., Magnuson, V. L., Hu, N., & Pattatucci, A. M. L. (1993). A linkage between DNA markers on the X chromosome and male sexual orientation. *Science, 261,* 321–327.

Hamilton, W. D. (1964). The genetical evolution of social behavior, I and II. *Journal of Theoretical Biology, 7,* 1–52.

Hammen, C. (2003). Mood disorders. In G. Stricker & T. A. Widiger (Eds.), *Handbook of psychology: Clinical psychology* (Vol. 8, pp. 93–118). New York: Wiley.

Haney, C. (2006). Overcrowding and the situational pathologies of prison. In C. Haney (Ed.), *Reforming punishment: Psychological limits to the pains of imprisonment.* Washington, DC: American Psychological Association.

Hansen, C. H. (1989). Priming sex-role stereotypic event schemas with rock music videos: Effects on impression favorability, trait inferences, and recall of a subsequent male-female interaction. *Basic and Applied Social Psychology, 10,* 371–391.

Hansen, C. J., Stevens, L. C., & Coast, J. R. (2001). Exercise duration and mood state: How much is enough to feel better? *Health Psychology, 20,* 267–275.

Hanson, V. L. (1990). Recall of order information by deaf signers: Phonetic coding in temporal order recall. *Memory & Cognition, 18,* 604–610.

Harlow, H. F., Harlow, M. K., & Meyer, D. R. (1971). From thought to therapy: Lessons from a primate laboratory. *American Scientist, 59,* 538–549.

Harlow, H. F., & Zimmerman, R. R. (1959). Affectional responses in the infant monkey. *Science, 130,* 421–432.

Harmon, T. M., Hynan, M. T., & Tyre, T. E. (1990). Improved obstetric outcomes using hypnotic analgesia and skill mastery combined with childbirth education. *Journal of Consulting and Clinical Psychology, 58,* 525–530.

Harper, G. (2001). Cultural influences on diagnosis. *Child & Adolescent Psychiatric Clinics of North America, 10,* 711–728.

Harris, J. A. (2004). Measured intelligence, achievement, openness to experience, and creativity. *Personality and Individual Differences, 36,* 913–929.

Harris, J. R. (1998). *The nurture assumption: Why children turn out the way they do.* New York: Free Press.

Harris, J. R. (2000). Socialization, personality development, and the child's environments: Comment on Vandell (2000). *Developmental Psychology, 36,* 711–723.

Hart, D., & Fegley, S. (1995). Prosocial behavior and caring in adolescence: Relations to self-understanding and social judgment. *Child Development, 66,* 1346–1359.

Hartshorne, H., & May, A. (1928). *Studies in the nature of character: Vol. 1. Studies in deceit.* New York: Macmillan.

Hartup, W. W., & Stevens, N. (1997). Friendships and adaptation in the life course. *Psychological Bulletin, 121,* 355–370.

Harvey, P. D. (2001). Vulnerability to schizophrenia in adulthood. In R. E. Ingram & J. M. Price (Eds.), *Vulnerability to psychopathology: Risk across the lifespan.* New York: Guilford.

Hasher, L., Stolzfus, E. R., Zacks, R. T., & Rypma, B. (1991). Age and inhibition. *Journal of Experimental Psychology: Learning, Memory, & Cognition, 17,* 163–169.

Hasher, L., & Zacks, R. R. (1979). Automatic and effortful processes in memory. *Journal of Experimental Psychology: General, 108,* 356–388.

Hasselmo, M. E., Rolls, E. T., & Baylis, G. C. (1989). The role of expression and identity in the face-selective responses of neurons in the temporal visual cortex of the monkey. *Behavioral Brain Research, 32,* 203–218.

Hastie, R. (1991). A review from a high place: The field of judgment and decision making as revealed in its current textbooks. *Psychological Science, 2,* 135–138.

Hatfield, E. (1988). Passionate and companionate love. In R. J. Sternberg & M. L. Barnes (Eds.), *The psychology of love.* New Haven, CT: Yale University Press.

Hatfield, E., & Rapson, R. L. (1993). *Love, sex, and intimacy.* New York: HarperCollins.

Hauri, P. (1982). *The sleep disorders.* Kalamazoo, MI: Upjohn.

Hayes, C. (1952). *The ape in our house.* London: Gollacz.

Hayes, K. J., & Hayes, C. (1951). The intellectual development of a home-raised chimpanzee. *Proceedings of the American Philosophical Society, 95,* 105–109.

Hays, W. S. T. (2003). Human pheromones: Have they been demonstrated? *Behavioral Ecology and Sociobiology, 54,* 89–97.

Hearst, E., & Franklin, S. R. (1977). Positive and negative relations between a signal and food: Approach-withdrawal behavior to the signal. *Journal of Experimental Psychology: Animal Behavior Processes, 3,* 37–52.

Heaton, P., & Wallace, G. L. (2004). Annotation: The savant syndrome. *Journal of Child Psychology & Psychiatry, 45,* 899–911.

Heider, F. (1944). Social perception and phenomenal causality. *Psychological Review, 51,* 358–374.

Heim, C., Bierl, C., Nisenbaum, R., Wagner, D., & Reeves, W. C. (2004). Regional and prevalence of fatiguing illnesses in the United States before and after the terrorist attacks of September 11, 2001. *Psychosomatic Medicine, 66,* 672–678.

Heiman, G. A. (1995). *Research methods in psychology.* Boston: Houghton Mifflin.

Heimann, M. (1989). Neonatal imitation gaze aversion and mother-infant interaction. *Infant Behavior and Development, 12,* 495–505.

Hellige, J. B. (1990). Hemispheric asymmetry. *Annual Review of Psychology, 41,* 55–80.

Hellige, J. B. (1993). Unity of thought and action: Varieties of interaction between the left and right cerebral hemispheres. *Current Directions in Psychological Science, 2,* 21–25.

Henderlong, J., & Lepper, M. R. (2002). The effects of praise on children's intrinsic motivation: A review and synthesis. *Psychological Bulletin, 128,* 774–795.

Henderson-King, E. I., & Nisbett, R. E. (1996). Anti-Black prejudice as a function of exposure to the negative behavior of a single Black person. *Journal of Personality and Social Psychology, 71,* 654–664.

Herrmann, D., Raybeck, D., & Gutman, D. (1993). *Improving student memory.* Seattle, WA: Hogrefe & Huber.

Herz, R. S., & Cahill, E. D. (1997). Differential use of sensory information in sexual behavior as a function of gender. *Human Nature, 8, 1997,* 275–286.

Herz, R. S., Eliassen, J., Beland, S., & Souza, T. (2004). Neuroimaging evidence for the emotional potency of odor-evoked memory. *Neuropsychologia, 42,* 371–378.

Herzog, D. B., Greenwood, D. N., Dorer, D. J., Flores, A. T., & Ekeblad, E. R. (2000). Mortality in eating disorders: A descriptive study. *Journal of Eating Disorders, 28,* 20–26.

Hetherington, A. W., & Ranson, S. W. (1942). The relation of various hypothalamic lesions to adiposity in the rat. *Journal of Comparative Neurology, 76,* 475–499.

Hetherington, M. M. (1996). Sensory-specific satiety and its importance in meal termination. *Neuroscience and Biobehavioral Reviews, 20,* 113–117.

Hickok, G., & Poeppel, D. (2007). The cortical organization of speech processing. *Nature Reviews Neuroscience, 8,* 393–402.

Higbee, K. L. (1988). *Your memory* (2nd ed.). Englewood Cliffs, NJ: Prentice-Hall.

Hilgard, E. R. (1965). *Hypnotic susceptibility.* New York: Harcourt, Brace, & World.

Hilgard, E. R. (1986). *Divided consciousness: Multiple controls in human thought and action* (Rev. ed.). New York: Wiley.

Hilgard, E. R. (1987). *Psychology in America: An historical survey.* New York: Harcourt Brace Jovanovich.

Hilgard, E. R. (1992). Dissociation and theories of hypnosis. In E. Fromm & M. Nash (Eds.), *Contemporary hypnosis research.* New York: Guilford.

Hilton, J. L., & von Hippel, W. (1996). Stereotypes. *Annual Review of Psychology, 47,* 237–271.

Hines, M. (1982). Prenatal gonadal hormones and sex differences in human behavior. *Psychological Bulletin, 92,* 56–80.

Hintzman, D. L. (1986). "Schema abstraction" in a multiple-trace memory model. *Psychological Review, 93,* 411–428.

Hirsh, I. J., & Watson, C. S. (1996). Auditory psychophysics and perception. *Annual Review of Psychology, 47,* 461–484.

Hobson, C. J., & Delunas, L. (2001). National norms and life-event frequencies for the revised Social Readjustment Rating Scale. *International Journal of Stress Management, 8,* 299–314.

Hobson, J. A., & McCarley, R. W. (1977). The brain as a dream state generator: An activation-synthesis hypothesis of the dream process. *American Journal of Psychiatry, 134,* 1335–1348.

Hobson, J. A., Pace-Schott, E. F., & Stickgold, R. (2000). Dreaming and the brain: Toward a cognitive neuroscience of conscious states. *Behavioral and Brain Sciences, 23,* 793–842.

Hodges, J., & Tizard, B. (1989). IQ and behavioral adjustment of ex-institutional adolescents. *Journal of Child Psychology and Psychiatry, 30,* 53–75.

Hofferth, S. (1996). Child care in the United States today. *The Future of Children, 6,* 41–61.

Hoffman, M. L. (1986). Affect, cognition, motivation. In R. M. Sorrentino & E. T. Higgins (Eds.), *Handbook of motivation and cognition: Foundations of social behavior.* New York: Guilford.

Hofstadter, M. C., & Reznick, J. S. (1996). Response modality affects human infant delayed-response performance. *Child Development, 67,* 646–658.

Hohmann, G. W. (1966). Some effects of spinal cord lesions on experienced emotional feelings. *Psychophysiology, 3,* 143–156.

Holland, P. C., & Ball, G. F. (2003). The psychology and ethology of learning. In M. Gallagher & R. J. Nelson (Eds.), *Handbook of Psychology* (Vol. 3: Biological psychology; pp. 457–497). New York: Wiley.

Holmes, D. S. (1976). Debriefing after psychological experiments: I. Effectiveness of postdeception dehoaxing. *American Psychologist, 31,* 858–867.

Holmes, D. S. (1987). The influence of meditation versus rest on physiological arousal: A second examination. In M. A.

West (Ed.), *The psychology of meditation.* Oxford, U.K.: Clarendon Press.

Holmes, T. H., & Rahe, R. H. (1967). The Social Readjustment Rating Scale. *Journal of Psychosomatic Research, 11,* 213–218.

Holt, E. B. (1931). *Animal drive and the learning process: An essay toward radical empiricism.* New York: Holt.

Holtzheimer, P. E., & Neumaier, J. F. (2003). Treatment of acute mania. *CNS Spectrums, 8,* 917–928.

Honzik, M. P., Macfarlane, J. W., & Allen, L. (1948). The stability of mental test performance between two and eighteen years. *Journal of Experimental Education, 17,* 309–324.

Hopkins, B. (1991). Facilitating early motor development: An intracultural study of West Indian mothers and their infants living in Britain. In J. K. Nugent, B. M. Lester, & T. B. Brazelton (Eds.), *The cultural context of infancy: Vol. 2. Multicultural and interdisciplinary approaches to parent-infant relations.* Norwood, NJ: Ablex.

Horgan, J. (1993, June). Eugenics revisited. *Scientific American, 268,* 123–131.

Horn, J. L. (1976). Human abilities: A review of research and theory in the early 1970s. *Annual Review of Psychology, 27,* 437–485.

Horn, J. L., & Cattell, R. B. (1966). Refinement and test of the theory of fluid and crystallized ability intelligences. *Journal of Educational Psychology, 57,* 253–270.

Horn, J. L., & Noll, J. (1997). Human cognitive capabilities: Gf-Gc theory. In D. P. Flanagan & J. L. Genshaft (Eds.), *Contemporary intellectual assessment: Theories, tests, and issues.* New York: Guilford.

Horne, J. A. (1988). *Why we sleep: The functions of sleep in humans and other mammals.* Oxford, U.K.: Oxford University Press.

Horne, J. A., & Minard, A. (1985). Sleep and sleepiness following a behaviourally "active" day. *Ergonomics, 28,* 567–575.

Horney, K. (1945). *Our inner conflicts: A constructive theory of neurosis.* New York: Norton.

Horney, K. (1967). *Feminine psychology.* New York: Norton.

Houle, M., McGrath, P. A., Moran, G., & Garrett, O. J. (1988). The efficacy of hypnosis- and relaxation-induced analgesia on two dimensions of pain for cold pressor and electrical tooth pulp stimulation. *Pain, 33,* 241–251.

Hser, Y., Anglin, M. D., & Powers, K. (1993). A 24-year follow-up of California narcotics addicts. *Archives of General Psychiatry, 50,* 577–584.

Hubbel, J. C. (1990, January). Animal rights war on medicine. *Reader's Digest,* 70–76.

Hubel, D. H., & Wiesel, T. N. (1962). Receptive fields, binocular interaction, and functional architecture in the cat's visual cortex. *Journal of Physiology, 160,* 106–154.

Hubel, D. H., & Wiesel, T. N. (1979, September). Brain mechanisms and vision. *Scientific American, 241,* 150–162.

Hull, C. L. (1943). *Principles of behavior.* New York: Appleton-Century.

Hull, J. G., & Bond, C. F., Jr. (1986). Social and behavioral consequences of alcohol consumption and expectancy: A meta-analysis. *Psychological Bulletin, 99,* 347–360.

Hunnicutt, C. P., & Newman, I. A. (1993). Adolescent dieting practices and nutrition knowledge. *Health Values, 17,* 35–40.

Hunsley, J., & Di Giulio, G. (2002). Dodo bird, phoenix, or urban legend? The question of psychotherapy effectiveness. *The Scientific Review of Mental Health Practice, 1,* 11–22.

Hunt, E., & Carlson, J. (2007). Considerations relating to the study of group differences in intelligence. *Perspectives on Psychological Science, 2,* 194–213.

Hunt, R. R., & McDaniel, M. A. (1993). The enigma of organization and distinctiveness. *Journal of Memory and Language, 32,* 421–445.

Huntjens, R. J. C., Peters, M. L., Woertman, L., van der Hart, O., & Postma, A. (2007). Memory transfer for emotionally valenced words between identities in dissociative identity disorder. *Behavior Research and Therapy, 45,* 775–789.

Hurley, R. A., Black, D. N., Stip, E., & Taber, K. H. (2000). Surgical treatment of mental illness: Impact of imaging. *Journal of Neuropsychiatry & Clinical Neurosciences, 12,* 421–424.

Hurvich, L. M., & Jameson, D. (1951). The binocular fusion of yellow in relation to color theories. *Science, 114,* 199–202.

Iacoboni, M., & Dapretto, M. (2006). The mirror neuron system and the consequences of its dysfunction. *Nature Reviews Neuroscience, 7,* 942–951.

Ickes, W., Holloway, R., Stinson, L. L., & Hoodenpyle, T. G. (2006). Self-monitoring in social interaction: The centrality of self-affect. *Journal of Personality, 74,* 659–684.

Iezzi, T., Duckworth, M. P., & Adams, H. E. (2001). Somatoform and factitious disorders. In P. B. Sutker & H. E. Adams (Eds). *Comprehensive handbook of psychopathology* (3rd ed.). New York: Kluwer Academic/Plenum.

Inoue-Nakamura, N., & Matsuzawa, T. (1997). Development of stone tool use by wild chimpanzees (Pan troglodytes). *Journal of Comparative Psychology, 111,* 159–713.

Iverson, S. D., & Iverson, L. L. (2007). Dopamine: 50 years in perspective. *Trends in Neurosciences, 30,* 188–193.

Izard, C. E. (1994). Innate and universal facial expressions: Evidence from developmental and cross-cultural research. *Psychological Bulletin, 115,* 288–299.

Izard, C. E. (2007). A few basic emotions and countless emotion schemas. *Perspectives on Psychological Science, 2,* in press.

Jackendoff, R., & Pinker, S. (2005). The nature of the language faculty and its implications for evolution of language (Reply to Fitch, Hauser, and Chomsky). *Cognition, 97,* 211–225.

Jacobi, L., & Cash, T. F. (1994). In pursuit of the perfect appearance: Discrepancies among self-ideal percepts of multiple physical attributes. *Journal of Applied Social Psychology, 24,* 379–396.

Jacobs, B. L. (2004). Depression: The brain finally gets into the act. *Current Directions in Psychological Sciences, 13,* 103–106.

Jacobson, J. L., & Jacobson, S. W. (1994). Prenatal alcohol exposure and neurobehavioral development: Where is the threshold? *Alcohol Health and Research World, 18,* 30–36.

Jacoby, L. L., & Witherspoon, D. (1982). Remembering without awareness. *Canadian Journal of Psychology, 36,* 300–324.

James, W. (1884). Some omissions of introspective psychology. *Mind, 9,* 1–26.

James, W. (1890). *The principles of psychology.* New York: Holt. (Reprinted Cambridge, MA: Harvard University Press, 1983).

James, W. (1894). The physical basis of emotion. *Psychological Review, 1,* 516–529.

Jameson, K. A. (2005). Culture and cognition: What is universal about the representation of color experience? *The Journal of Cognition & Culture, 5* (3–4), 293–347.

Janis, I. L. (1982). *Victims of groupthink* (2nd ed.). Boston: Houghton Mifflin.

Janis, I. L. (1989). *Crucial decisions: Leadership in policymaking and crisis management.* New York: Free Press.

Janowsky, J. S. (2006). Thinking with your gonads: testosterone and cognition. *Trends in Cognitive Sciences, 10,* 77–81.

Jarrad, L. E. (1993). On the role of the hippocampus in learning and memory in the rat. *Behavioral and Neural Biology, 60,* 9–26.

Jaskiw, G. E., & Popli, A. P. (2004). A meta-analysis of the response to chronic L-Dopa in patients with schizophrenia: Therapeutic and heuristic implications. *Psychopharmacology, 171,* 365–374.

Javitt, D. C. (2006). Glutamate involvement in schizophrenia: Focus on N-methyl-D-aspartate receptors. *Primary Psychiatry, 13,* 38–46.

Jeffery, R. W., & Utter J. (2003). The changing environment and population obesity in the United States. *Obesity Research, 11,* 12S–22S.

Jenike, M. A. (1998). Neurosurgical treatment of obsessive-compulsive disorder. *British Journal of Psychiatry, 173,* 79–90.

Jenkins, H. M., Barrera, F. J., Ireland, C., & Woodside, B. (1978). Signal-centered action patterns of dogs in appetitive classical conditioning. *Learning and Motivation, 9,* 272–296.

Jenkins, J. G., & Dallenbach, K. M. (1924). Obliviscence during sleep and waking. *American Journal of Psychology, 35,* 605–612.

Jensen, A. R., & Weng, L. (1994). What is a good *g*? *Intelligence, 18,* 231–258.

Jensen, J. P., Bergin, A. E., & Greaves, D. W. (1990). The meaning of eclecticism: New survey and analysis of components. *Professional Psychology: Research and Practice, 21,* 124–130.

Jing, L., & Kazuhisa, N. (2003). Function of hippocampus in "Insight" of problem solving. *Hippocampus, 13,* 316–323.

Johnson, A. (2003). Procedural memory and skill acquisition. In A. F. Healy & R. W. Proctor (Eds.), *Handbook of psychology* (Vol. 4: Experimental psychology; pp. 499–523). New York: Wiley.

Johnson, A., & Proctor, R. W. (2004). *Attention: Theory and practice.* Thousand Oaks, CA: Sage.

Johnson, J. D., Noel, N. E., & Sutter-Hernandez, J. (2000). Alcohol and male acceptance of sexual aggression: The role of perceptual ambiguity. *Journal of Applied Social Psychology, 30,* 1186–1200.

Johnson, L. M., & Morris, E. K. (1987). Public information on research with nonhumans. *American Psychologist, 42,* 103–104.

Johnson, M. H., Dziurawiec, S., Ellis, H., & Morton, J. (1991). Newborns' preferential tracking of face-like stimuli and its subsequent decline. *Cognition, 40,* 1–19.

Johnson, R. C., McClearn, C. G., Yuen, S., Nagoshi, C. T., Ahern, F. M., & Cole, R. E. (1985). Galton's data a century later. *American Psychologist, 40,* 875–892.

Johnson, S. P. (1997). Young infants' perception of object unity: Implications for the development of attentional and cognitive skills. *Current Directions in Psychological Science, 6,* 5–11.

Johnston, V. S. (2000). Female facial beauty: The fertility hypothesis. *Pragmatics & Cognition, 8,* 107–122.

Joiner, T. E., Jr., Steer, R. A., Abramson, L. Y., Alloy, L. B., Metalsky, G. I., & Schmidt, N. B. (2001). Hopelessness depression as a distinct dimension of depressive symptoms among clinical and non-clinical samples. *Behaviour Research & Therapy, 39,* 523–536.

Jones, E. E. (1964). *Ingratiation.* New York: Appleton-Century-Crofts.

Jones, E. E. (1990). *Interpersonal perception.* New York: Freeman.

Jones, E. E., & Davis, K. E. (1965). A theory of correspondent inferences: From acts to dispositions. In L. Berkowitz (Ed.), *Advances in experimental social psychology* (Vol. 2). New York: Academic Press.

Jones, E. E., & Harris, V. A. (1967). The attribution of attitudes. *Journal of Experimental Social Psychology, 3,* 1–24.

Jones, G. (2003). Testing two cognitive theories of insight. *Journal of Experimental Psychology: Learning, Memory, and Cognition, 29,* 1017–1027.

Jones, M. C. (1924). A laboratory study of fear: The case of Peter. *Pedagogical Seminary, 31,* 308–315.

Jones, R. T. (1971). Tetrahydrocannabinol and the marijuana-induced social "high" or the effects on the mind of marijuana. In A. J. Singer (Ed.), Marijuana: Chemistry, pharmacology, and patterns of social use. *Annals of the New York Academy of Sciences, 191,* 155–165.

Jonides, J. (2000). Mechanisms of verbal working memory revealed by neuroimaging studies. In B. Landau & J. Sabini (Eds.), *Perception, cognition, and language: Essays in honor of Henry and Lila Gleitman.* Cambridge, MA: MIT Press.

Joule, R. V. (1986). Twenty-five on: Yet another version of cognitive dissonance theory? *European Journal of Social Psychology, 16,* 65–78.

Jung, C. G. (1923). *Psychological types.* New York: Pantheon Books.

Kagan, J. (1997). Temperament and the reactions to unfamiliarity. *Child Development, 68,* 139–143.

Kahneman, D. (1973). *Attention and effort.* Englewood Cliffs, NJ: Prentice-Hall.

Kahneman, D., Slovic, P., & Tversky, A. (Eds.). (1982). *Judgment under uncertainty: Heuristics and biases.* Cambridge, U.K.: Cambridge University Press.

Kail, R. (1991). Developmental change in speed of processing during childhood and adolescence. *Psychological Bulletin, 109,* 490–501.

Kail, R., & Salthouse, T. A. (1994). Processing speed as a mental capacity. *Acta Psychologica, 86,* 199–225.

Kalat, J. W. (1996). *Introduction to psychology* (4th ed.). Pacific Grove, CA: Brooks/Cole.

Kalichman, S. C., Belcher, L., Cherry, C., & Williams, E. A. (1997). Primary prevention of sexually transmitted HIV infections: Transferring behavioral research technology to community programs. *Journal of Primary Prevention, 18,* 149–172.

Kalick, S. M., Zebrowitz, L. A., Langlois, J. H., & Johnson, R. M. (1998). Does human facial attractiveness honestly advertise health? Longitudinal data on an evolutionary question. *Psychological Science, 9,* 8–13.

Kamen-Siegel, L., Rodin, J., Seligman, M. E. P., & Dwyer, J. (1991). Explanatory style and cell-mediated immunity in elderly men and women. *Health Psychology, 10,* 229–235.

Kamil, A. C., & Balda, R. P. (1990). Differential memory for different cache sites by Clark's nutcrackers (Nucifraga columbiana). *Journal of Experimental Psychology: Animal Behavior Processes, 16,* 162–168.

Kamin, L. J. (1968). "Attention-like" processes in classical conditioning. In M. R. Jones (Ed.), *Miami symposium on the prediction of behavior: Aversive stimulation.* Miami, FL: University of Miami Press.

Kanaya, T., Scullin, M. H., & Ceci, S. J. (2003). The Flynn effect and U.S. policies. *American Psychologist, 58,* 778–790.

Kanner, A. D., Coyne, J. C., Schaefer, C., & Lazarus, R. S. (1981). Comparison of two modes of stress measurement: Daily hassles and uplifts versus major life events. *Journal of Behavioral Medicine, 4,* 1–39.

Kaplan, R. M. (1985). The controversy related to the use of psychological tests. In B. B. Wolman (Ed.), *Handbook of intelligence: Theories, measurements, and applications.* New York: Wiley.

Kaplan, R. M., & Saccuzzo, D. P. (2005). *Psychological testing: Principles, applications, and issues* (6th ed.). Belmont, CA: Wadsworth.

Karau, S. J., & Hart, J. W. (1998). Group cohesiveness and social loafing: Effects of a social interaction manipulation on individual motivation within groups. *Group Dynamics, 2,* 185–191.

Karau, S. J., & Williams, K. D. (1993). Social loafing: A meta-analytic review and theoretical integration. *Journal of Personality and Social Psychology, 65,* 681–706.

Karni, A., Tanne, D., Rubenstein, B. S., Askenasy, J., & Sagi, D. (1994). Dependence on REM sleep of overnight improvement of a perceptual skill. *Science, 265,* 679–682.

Karremans, J. C., Stroebe, W., & Claus, J. (2006). Beyond Vicary's fantasies: The impact of subliminal priming and brand choice. *Journal of Experimental Social Psychology, 42,* 792–798.

Kaufman, A. S., & Horn, J. L. (1996). Age changes on tests of fluid and crystallized ability for women and men on the Kaufman Adolescent and Adult Intelligence Test (KAIT) at ages 17–94 years. *Archives of Clinical Neuropsychology, 11,* 97–121.

Kavanau, J. L. (2002). REM and NREM sleep as natual accompaniments of the evolution of warm-bloodedness. *Neuroscience and Biobehavioral Reviews, 26,* 889–906.

Kavsek, M. (2004). Predicting later IQ from infant visual habituation and dishabituation: A meta-analysis. *Journal of Applied Developmental Psychology, 25,* 369–393.

Kazdin, A. E. (2007). Mediators and mechanisms of change in psychotherapy research. *Annual Review of Clinical Psychology, 3,* 1–27.

Kee, K. H. (2005). Can only intelligent people be creative? A meta-analysis. *Journal of Secondary Gifted Education, 16,* 57–66.

Keel, P. K., & Klump, K. L. (2003). Are eating disorder culture-bound syndromes? Implications for conceptualizing their etiology. *Psychological Bulletin, 129,* 747–769.

Keesey, R. E., & Powley, T. L. (1975). Hypothalamic regulation of body weight. *American Scientist, 63,* 558–565.

Kelley, H. H. (1967). Attribution theory in social interaction. In E. E. Jones, D. E. Kanouse, H. H. Kelley, R. E. Nisbett, S. Valins, & B. Weiner (Eds.), *Attribution: Perceiving the causes of behavior.* Morristown, NJ: General Learning Press.

Kelley, H. H. (1983). Love and commitment. In H. H. Kelley, E. Berscheid, A. Christensen, J. H. Harvey, T. L. Huston, G. Levinger, E. McClintock, L. A. Peplau, & D. R. Peterson (Eds.), *Close relationships.* New York: Freeman.

Kellogg, W. N., & Kellogg, L. A. (1933). *The ape and the child.* New York: McGraw-Hill.

Kelly, D. D. (1991). Sleep and dreaming. In E. R. Kandel, J. H. Schwartz, & T. M. Jessell (Eds.), *Principles of neural science* (3rd ed.). New York: Elsevier.

Kemeny, M. E. (2003). The psychobiology of stress. *Current Directions in Psychological Science, 12,* 124–129.

Kenrick, D. T., & Funder, D. C. (1988). Profiting from controversy: Lessons of the person-situation debate. *American Psychologist, 43,* 23–34.

Kenrick, D. T., Gutierres, S. E., & Goldberg, L. (1989). Influence of erotica on judgments of strangers and mates. *Journal of Experimental Social Psychology, 25,* 159–167.

Kenrick, D. T., McCreath, H. E., Govern, J., King, R., & Bordin, J. (1990). Person-environment intersections: Everyday settings and common trait dimensions. *Journal of Personality and Social Psychology, 58,* 685–698.

Keppel, G., & Underwood, B. J. (1962). Proactive inhibition in short-term retention of single items. *Journal of Verbal Learning and Verbal Behavior, 1,* 153–161.

Kershaw, T. C., & Ohlsson, S. (2004). Multiple causes of difficulty in insight: The case of the nine-dot problem. *Journal of Experimental Psychology: Learning, Memory, and Cognition, 30,* 3–13.

Kessler, R. C., McGonagle, K. A., Shanyang, Z., Nelson, C. B., Hughes, M., Eshleman, S., Wittchen, H., & Kendler, K. S. (1994). Lifetime and 12–month prevalence of DSM-III-R psychiatric disorders in the United States. *Archives of General Psychiatry, 51,* 8–19.

Key, W. B. (1973). *Subliminal seduction.* Englewood Cliffs, NJ: Prentice-Hall.

Keys, D. J., & Schwartz, B. (2007). "Leaky" Rationality. *Perspectives on Psychological Science, 2*, 162–180.

Keysar, B., Barr, D. J., Balin, A., & Paekm T. S. (1998). Definite reference and mutual knowledge: Process models of common ground in comprehension. *Journal of Memory and Language, 39*, 1–20.

Kiecolt-Glaser, J. K., McGuire, L., Robles, T. F., & Glaser, R. (2002). Emotions, morbidity, and mortality: New perspectives from psychoneuroimmunology. *Annual Review of Psychology, 53*, 83–107.

Kihlstrom, J. (1985). Hypnosis. *Annual Review of Psychology, 36*, 385–418.

Kihlstrom, J., & McConkey, K. M. (1990). William James and hypnosis: A centennial reflection. *Psychological Science, 1*, 174–178.

Kim, B. J., Williams, L., & Gill, D. L. (2003). A cross-cultural study of achievement orientation and intrinsic motivation in young USA and Korean athletes. *International Journal of Sport Psychology, 34*, 168–184.

Kimble, G. A. (1993). A modest proposal for a minor revolution in the language of psychology. *Psychological Science, 4*, 253–255.

Kimura, D. (1992, September). Sex differences in the brain. *Scientific American, 267*, 118–125.

Kimura, D. (1999). *Sex and cognition.* Cambridge, MA: Bradford/MIT Press.

Kimura, D., & Hampson, E. (1994). Cognitive pattern in men and women is influenced by fluctuations in sex hormones. *Current Directions in Psychological Science, 3*, 57–61.

Kirk, K. M., Bailey, J. M., Dunne, M. P., & Martin, N. G. (2000). Measurement models for sexual orientation in a community twin sample. *Behavior Genetics, 30*, 345–356.

Kirkcaldy, B. D., Cooper, C. L., & Furnham, A. F. (1999). The relationship between Type A, internality-externality, emotional distress and perceived health. *Personality & Individual Differences, 26*, 223–235.

Kirmayer, L. J., Looper, K. J., & Taillefer, S. (2003). Somatoform disorders. In M. Hersen & S. M. Turner (Eds.), *Adult psychopathology and diagnosis* (4th ed.). New York: Wiley.

Kirsch, I. (2003). Hidden administration as ethical alternatives to the balanced placebo design. *Prevention and Treatment, 6*, 1–5.

Kite, M. E. (1996). Age, gender, and occupational label. *Psychology of Women Quarterly, 20*, 361–374.

Kite, M. E., & Johnson, B. J. (1988). Attitudes toward older and younger adults: A meta-analysis. *Psychology and Aging, 3*, 233–244.

Klatzky, R. L. (1984). *Memory and awareness: An information-processing perspective.* New York: Freeman.

Klatzky, R. L., Lederman, S. J., & Metzger, V. A. (1985). Identifying objects by touch: An "expert system." *Perception & Psychophysics, 37*, 299–302.

Klinger, E. (1977). *Meaning and void: Inner experience and the incentive in people's lives.* Minneapolis: University of Minnesota Press.

Kluft, R. P. (1991). Multiple personality disorder. In A. Tasman & S. M. Goldfinger (Eds.), *Review of psychiatry* (Vol. 10). Washington, DC: American Psychiatric Press.

Koch, C., & Tsuchiya, N. (2007) Attention and consciousness: two distinct brain processes. *Trends in Cognitive Science, 11*(1):16–22.

Kohlberg, L. (1963). The development of children's orientations toward a moral order: I. Sequence in the development of moral thought. *Vita Humana, 6*, 11–33.

Kohlberg, L. (1969). Stage and sequence: The cognitive-developmental approach to socialization. In D. A. Goslin (Ed.), *Handbook of socialization theory and research.* Chicago: Rand McNally.

Kohlberg, L. (1986). *The psychology of moral development.* New York: Harper & Row.

Köhler, W. (1925). *The mentality of apes.* London: Pelican.

Kolb, B. (1999). Synaptic plasticity and the organization of behavior after early and late brain injury. *Canadian Journal of Experimental Psychology, 53*, 62–75.

Kolb, B., Gibb, R., & Robinson, T. E. (2003). Brain plasticity and behavior. *Current Directions in Psychological Science, 12*, 1–5.

Kolb, B., & Whishaw, I. Q. (1990). *Fundamentals of human neuropsychology* (3rd ed.). New York: Freeman.

Koltko-Rivera, M. E. (2006). Rediscovering the later version of Maslow's hierarchy of needs: Self-transcendence and opportunities for theory, research, and unification. *Review of General Psychology, 10*, 302–317.

Korte, S. M., Koolhaas, J. M., Wingfield, J. C., & McEwen, B. S. (2005). The Darwinian concept of stress: Benefits of allostatsis and costs of allostatic load and the trade-offs in health and disease. *Neuroscience and Biobehavioral Reviews, 29*, 3–38.

Kosky, R. J., Eshkevari, H. S., Goldney, R. D., & Hassan, R. (1998). *Suicide prevention: The global context.* New York: Plenum Press.

Kosslyn, S. M. (1983). *Ghosts in the mind's machine: Creating and using images in the brain.* New York: Horizon.

Kowalski, T. J. (2004). The future of genetic research on appetitive behavior. *Appetite, 42*, 11–14.

Kraemer, D. J., Macrae, C. N., Green, A. E., & Kelley, W. M. (2005). Sounds of silence activates auditory cortex. *Nature, 434*, 158.

Kraemer, P. J., & Golding, J. M. (1997). Adaptive forgetting in animals. *Psychonomic Bulletin & Review, 4*, 480–490.

Kramer, P. D. (1993). *Listening to Prozac.* New York: Viking.

Kramer, R. M. (1998). Revisiting the Bay of Pigs and Vietnam decisions 25 years later: How well has the groupthink hypothesis stood the test of time? *Organizational Behavior & Human Decision Processes, 73*, 236–271.

Krantz, D. S., & McCeney, M. K. (2002). Effects of psychological and social factors on organic disease: A critical assessment of research on coronary heart disease. *Annual Review of Psychology, 53*, 341–369.

Krug, E. G., Kresnow, M., Peddicord, J., Dahlberg, L., Powell, K., Crosby, A., & Annest, J. (1998). Suicide after natural disasters. *New England Journal of Medicine, 338*, 373–378.

Kübler-Ross, E. (1969). *On death and dying.* New York: Macmillan.

Kübler-Ross, E. (1974). *Questions and answers on death and dying.* New York: Macmillan.

Kulhara, P., & Chakrabarti, S. (2001). Culture and schizophrenia and other psychotic disorders. *Psychiatric Clinics of North America, 24,* 449–464.

Kuncel, N. R., Hezlett, S. A., & Ones, D. S. (2004). Academic performance, career potential, creativity, and job performance: Can one construct predict them all? *Journal of Personality and Social Psychology, 86,* 148–161.

Labov, W. (1973). The boundaries of words and their meanings. In C. J. N. Bailey & R. W. Shiny (Eds.), *New ways of analyzing variation in English* (Vol. 1). Washington, DC: Georgetown University Press.

Lachman, M. E. (2004). Development in midlife. *Annual Review of Psychology, 55,* 305–331.

Lackner, J. R., & DiZio, P. (1991). Decreased susceptibility to motion sickness during exposure to visual inversion in microgravity. *Aviation, Space, and Environmental Medicine, 62,* 206–211.

Lafferty, P., Beutler, L. E., & Crago, M. (1991). Differences between more or less effective psychotherapists: A study of select therapist variables. *Journal of Consulting and Clinical Psychology, 57,* 76–80.

Laiacona, M., Barbarotto, R., & Capitani, E. (2006). Human evolution and the brain representation of semantic knowledge: Is there a role for sex differences? *Evolution and Human Behavior, 27,* 158–168.

Lakoff, G. (1987). *Women, fire, and dangerous things: What categories reveal about the human mind.* Chicago: University of Chicago Press.

Lamb, M. E., Ketterlinus, R. D., & Fracasso, M. P. (1992). Parent-child relationships. In M. H. Bornstein & M. E. Lamb (Eds.), *Developmental psychology: An advanced textbook.* Hillsdale, NJ: Erlbaum.

Lamb, M. E., & Sternberg, K. L. (1990). Do we really know how day care affects children? *Journal of Applied Developmental Psychology, 11,* 351–379.

Lambert, M. J. (2005). Early response in psychotherapy: Further evidence for the importance of common factors rather than "placebo effects." *Journal of Clinical Psychology, 61,* 855–869.

Lambert, M. J., & Bergin, A. E. (1994). The effectiveness of psychotherapy. In A. E. Bergin & S. L. Garfield (Eds.), *Handbook of psychotherapy and behavior change* (4th ed.). New York: Wiley.

Lancet, D., Gross-Isseroff, R., Margalit, T., & Seidemann, E. (1993). Olfaction: From signal transduction and termination to human genome mapping. *Chemical Senses, 18,* 217–225.

Landauer, T. K. (1962). Rate of implicit speech. *Perceptual and Motor Skills, 15,* 646.

Lang, P. J. (1994). The varieties of emotional experience: A meditation on James-Lange theory. *Psychological Review, 101,* 211–221.

Lang, S., Kanngieser, N., Jaskowski, P., Haider, H., Rose, M., & Verleger, R. (2006). Precursors of insight in event-related brain potentials. *Journal of Cognitive Neuroscience, 18,* 2152–2166.

Langer, E. J. (1989). *Mindfulness.* Reading, MA: Addison-Wesley.

Langer, E. J., & Abelson, R. P. (1974). A patient by any other name: Clinician group differences in labeling bias. *Journal of Consulting and Clinical Psychology, 42,* 4–9.

Langlois, J. H., & Roggman, L. A. (1990). Attractive faces are only average. *Psychological Science, 1,* 115–121.

Langlois, J. H., Roggman, L. A., Casey, R. J., Ritter, J. M., Rieser-Danner, L. A., & Jenkins, V. Y. (1987). Infant preferences for attractive faces: Rudiments of a stereotype? *Developmental Psychology, 23,* 363–369.

Langlois, J. H., Roggman, L. A., & Musselman, L. (1994). What is average and what is not average about attractive faces? *Psychological Science, 5,* 214–220.

Laprelle, J., Hoyle, R. H., Insko, C. A., & Bernthal, P. (1990). Interpersonal attraction and descriptions of the traits of others: Ideal similarity, self similarity, and liking. *Journal of Research in Personality, 24,* 216–240.

Larose, H., & Standing, L. (1998). Does the halo effect occur in the elderly? *Social Behavior & Personality, 26,* 147–150.

Latané, B. (1981). The psychology of social impact. *American Psychologist, 36,* 343–356.

Latané, B., & Nida, S. A. (1981). Ten years of research on group size and helping. *Psychological Bulletin, 89,* 308–324.

Latané, B., Williams, K., & Harkins, S. (1979). Many hands make light the work: The causes and consequences of social loafing. *Journal of Personality and Social Psychology, 37,* 822–832.

Latta, F., & Van Cauter, E. (2003). Sleep and biological clocks. In M. Gallagher & R. J. Nelson (Eds.), *Handbook of Psychology* (Vol. 3: Biological psychology; pp. 355–377). New York: Wiley.

Laudenslager, M. L., Ryan, S. M., Drugen, R. L., Hyson, R. L., & Maier, S. F. (1983). Coping and immunosuppression: Inescapable but not escapable shock suppresses lymphocyte proliferation. *Science, 221,* 568–570.

Lavie, P. (2001). Sleep-wake as a biological rhythm. *Annual Review of Psychology, 52,* 277–303.

Lawton, M. P., Kleban, M. H., & Rajagopal, D., & Dean, J. (1992). Dimensions of affective experience in three age groups. *Psychology and Aging, 7,* 171–184.

Lazarus, R. S. (1966). *Psychological stress and the coping process.* New York: McGraw-Hill.

Lazarus, R. S. (1991). *Emotion and adaptation.* New York: Oxford University Press.

Lazarus, R. S. (1993). Why we should think of stress as a subset of emotion. In L. Goldberger & S. Breznitz (Eds.), *Handbook of stress: Theoretical and clinical aspects* (2nd ed.). New York: Free Press.

Lazarus, R. S. (2007). Stress and emotion: A new synthesis. In A. Monat, R. S. Lazarus, & G. Reevy (Eds.), *The Praeger handbook on stress and coping.* Westport CT: Praeger.

Lazarus, R. S., & Folkman, S. (1984). *Stress, appraisal and coping*. New York: Springer.

Leach, M. M., & Harbin, J. J. (1997). Psychological ethics codes: A comparison of 24 countries. *International Journal of Psychology, 32,* 181–192.

Lecendreux, M., Bassetti, C., Dauvilliers, Y., Mayer, G., Neidhart, E., & Tafti, M. (2003). HLA and genetic susceptibility to sleepwalking. *Molecular Psychiatry, 8,* 114–117.

Leclerc, G., Lefrancois, R., Dube, M., Hebert, R., & Gaulin, P. (1998). The self-actualization concept: A content validation. *Journal of Social Behavior & Personality, 11,* 69–84.

Lee, C. J., & Katz, A. N. (1998). The differential role of ridicule in sarcasm and irony. *Metaphor & Symbol, 13,* 1–15.

Lefcourt, H. M. (1982). *Locus of control: Current trends in theory and research.* Waterloo, Ontario: University of Waterloo.

Lehman, D. R., Chiu, C., & Schaller, M. (2004). Psychology and culture. *Annual Review of Psychology, 55,* 689–714.

Leibowitz, H. W. (1971). Sensory, learned, and cognitive mechanisms of size perception. *Annals of the New York Academy of Sciences, 188,* 47–62.

Leiter, M. P., & Maslach, C. (2005). A mediation model of job burnout. In A. Antoniou & C. Cooper (Eds.), *Research companion to organizational health psychology.* Northampton, MA: Elgar Publishing.

Lenneberg, E. H. (1967). *Biological foundations of language.* New York: Wiley.

Leon, M. I., & Gallistel, C. R. (1998). Self-stimulating rats combine subjective reward magnitude and subjective reward rate multiplicatively. *Journal of Experimental Behavior: Animal Behavior Processes, 24,* 165–277.

Leone, C., & Hall, I. (2003). Self-monitoring, marital dissatisfaction, and relationship dissolution: Individual differences in orientations to marriage and divorce. *Self & Identity, 2,* 189–202.

Lepper, M. R., Corpus, J. H., & Iyengar, S. S. (2005). Intrinsic and extrinsic motivational orientations in the classroom: Age differences and academic correlates. *Journal of Educational Psychology, 97,* 184–196.

Lepper, M. R., Greene, D., & Nisbett, R. E. (1973). Undermining children's intrinsic interest with external reward: A test of the "overjustification" hypothesis. *Journal of Personality and Social Psychology, 28,* 129–137.

LeVay, S. (1991). A difference in hypothalamic structure between heterosexual and homosexual men. *Science, 253,* 1034–1037.

Levenson, R. W. (1992). Autonomic nervous system differences among emotions. *Psychological Science, 3,* 23–27.

Levine, G., & Parkinson, S. (1994). *Experimental methods in psychology.* Hillsdale, NJ: Erlbaum.

Levinson, D. J., Darow, C. N., Klein, E. B., Levinson, M. H., & McKee, B. (1978). *The seasons of a man's life.* New York: Knopf.

Levy, B., & Langer, E. (1994). Aging free from negative stereotypes: Successful memory in China and among American deaf. *Journal of Personality and Social Psychology, 66,* 989–997.

Lewis, J. W. (2006). Cortical networks related to human use of tools. *The Neuroscientist, 12,* 211–231.

Lewis, M., & Brooks-Gunn, J. (1979). *Social cognition and the acquisition of self.* New York: Plenum.

Lewontin, R. (1976). Race and intelligence. In N. J. Block & G. Dworkin (Eds.), *The IQ controversy: Critical readings.* New York: Pantheon.

Lickey, M. E., & Gordon, B. (1991). *Medicine and mental illness: The use of drugs in psychiatry.* New York: Freeman.

Lilienfeld, S. O. (1994). Conceptual problems in the assessment of psychopathy. *Clinical Psychology Review, 14,* 17–38.

Linde, L., & Bergstrom, M. (1992). The effect of one night without sleep on problem solving and immediate recall. *Psychological Research, 54,* 127–136.

Lindsay, D. S., & Poole, D. A. (1998). The Poole et al. (1995) survey of therapists: Misinterpretations by both sides of the recovered memories controversy. *Journal of Psychiatry and Law, 26,* 383–399.

Link, B. G., & Phelan, J. C. (1999). The labeling theory of mental disorder (II): The consequences of labeling. In A. Horwitz & T. Scheid (Eds.), *A handbook for the study of mental health: Social contexts, theories, and systems.* New York: Cambridge University Press.

Linton, M. (1975). Memory for real-world events. In D. A. Norman & D. E. Rumelhart (Eds.), *Explorations in cognition.* San Francisco: Freeman.

Lipsey, M. W., & Wilson, D. B. (1993). The efficacy of psychological, educational, and behavioral treatment: Confirmation from meta-analysis. *American Psychologist, 48,* 1181–1209.

Lisk, R. D. (1978). The regulation of sexual "heat." In J. B. Hutchinson (Ed.), *Biological determinants of sexual behaviour.* New York: Wiley.

Liu, Z. (1996). Viewpoint dependency in object representation and recognition. *Spatial Vision, 9,* 491–521.

Livesley, W. J., Jang, K. L., & Vernon, P. A. (2003). Genetic basis of personality structure. In T. Millon & M. J. Lerner (Eds.), *Handbook of Psychology: Personality and Social Psychology* (Vol. 5, pp. 59–84). New York: Wiley.

Livingston, R. W. (2001). What you see is what you get: Systematic variability in perceptual-based social judgment. *Personality & Social Psychology Bulletin, 27,* 1086–1096.

Locke, J. L. (1994). Phases in the child's development of language. *American Scientist, 82,* 436–445.

Lockhart, R. S. (2002). Levels of processing, transfer-appropriate processing, and the concept of robust encoding. *Memory, 10,* 397–403.

Loftus, E. L. (1979). *Eyewitness testimony.* Cambridge, MA: Harvard University Press.

Loftus, E. L. (1991). *Witness for the defense.* New York: St. Martin's.

Loftus, E. L. (1993). The reality of repressed memories. *American Psychologist, 48,* 518–537.

Loftus, E. L., & Loftus, G. R. (1980). On the permanence of stored information in the brain. *American Psychologist, 35,* 409–420.

Loftus, E. L., & Palmer, J. C. (1974). Reconstruction of automobile destruction: An example of the interaction between language and memory. *Journal of Verbal Learning and Verbal Behavior, 13,* 585–589.

Loftus, E. L., & Polage, D. C. (1999). Repressed memories: When are they real? How are they false? *Psychiatric Clinics of North America, 22,* 61–70.

Logan, G. D. (1991). Automaticity and memory. In W. E. Hockley & S. Lewandowsky (Eds.), *Relating theory and data: Essays on human memory in honor of Bennet B. Murdock.* Hillsdale, NJ: Erlbaum.

Lorenz, K. Z. (1958, December). The evolution of behavior. *Scientific American, 199,* 67–78.

Lovaas, O. I. (1987). Behavioral treatment and normal educational and intellectual functioning in young autistic children. *Journal of Consulting and Clinical Psychology, 55,* 3–9.

Lovaas, O. I., Koegel, R., Simmons, J. Q., & Long, J. S. (1973). Some generalization and follow-up measures on autistic children in behavior therapy. *Journal of Applied Behavior Analysis, 6,* 131–166.

Lovdal, L. T. (1989). Sex role messages in television commercials: An update. *Sex Roles, 21,* 715–724.

Lubinski, D., Webb, R. M., Morelock, M. J., & Benbow, C. P. (2001). Top 1 in 10,000: A 10-year follow-up of the profoundly gifted. *Journal of Appled Psychology, 86,* 718–729.

Luders, E., Narr, K. L., Thompson, P. M., Rex, D. E., Woods, R. P., DeLuca, H., Jancke, L., & Toga, A. W. (2006). Gender effects on cortical thickness and the influence of scaling. *Human Brain Mapping, 27,* 314–324.

Luria, A. R. (1968). New York: Basic Books.

Lutz, C. (1982). The domain of emotion words in Ifaluk. *American Ethnologist, 9,* 113–128.

Lyness, S. A. (1993). Predictors of differences between Type A and Type B individuals in heart rate and blood pressure reactivity. *Psychological Bulletin, 114,* 266–295.

Lynn, M., & Simons, T. (2000). Predictors of male and female servers' average tip earnings. *Journal of Applied Social Psychology, 30,* 241–252.

Lynn, R. (1994). Some reinterpretations of the Minnesota transracial adoption study. *Intelligence, 19,* 21–27.

Lynn, S. J., Rhue, J. W., & Weekes, J. R. (1990). Hypnotic involuntariness: A social cognitive analysis. *Psychological Review, 97,* 169–184.

Maccoby, E. (2000). Parenting and its effects on children: On reading and misreading behavioral genetics. *Annual Review of Psychology, 51,* 1–27.

MacDonald, T. K., & Ross, M. (1999). Assessing the accuracy of predictions about dating relationships: How and why do lovers' predictions differ from those made by observers? *Personality and Social Psychology Bulletin, 25,* 1417–1429.

MacKenzie, K. R. (2000). Current approaches to time-limited group psychotherapy services. In F. Flach (Ed.), *The Hatherleigh guide to psychiatric disorders, Part II. The Hatherleigh guides series.* Long Island City, NY: Hatherleigh.

Macrae, C. N., & Bodenhausen, G. V. (2000). Social cognition: Thinking categorically about others. *Annual Review of Psychology, 51,* 93–120.

Madon, S., Guyll, M., Spoth, R., & Willard, J. (2004). Self-fulfilling prophecies: The synergistic accumaltive effect of parents' beliefs on children's drinking behavior. *Psychological Science, 15,* 837–845.

Mah, K., & Binik, Y. M. (2002). Do all orgasms feel alike? Evaluating a two-dimensional model of the orgasm experience across gender and sexual context. *Journal of Sex Research, 39,* 104–113.

Maier, N. R. F. (1930). Reasoning in humans I: On direction. *Journal of Comparative Psychology, 10,* 115–143.

Maier, N. R. F. (1931). Reasoning in humans II: The solution to a problem and its appearance in consciousness. *Journal of Comparative Psychology, 12,* 181–194.

Maier, N. R. F., & Burke, R. J. (1967). Response availability as a factor in the problem-solving performance of males and females. *Journal of Personality and Social Psychology, 5,* 304–310.

Main, M., & Soloman, J. (1990). Procedures for identifying infants as disorganized/disoriented during the Ainsworth Strange Situation. In M. Greenburg, D. Cicchetti, & M. Cummings (Eds.), *Attachment in the preschool years.* Chicago: Chicago University Press.

Malt, B. C., & Smith, E. E. (1984). Correlated properties in natural categories. *Journal of Verbal Learning and Verbal Behavior, 23,* 250–269.

Mandler, G., Nakamura, Y., & Van Zandt, B. J. S. (1987). Nonspecific effects of stimuli that cannot be recognized. *Journal of Experimental Psychology: Learning, Memory, & Cognition, 13,* 646–648.

Mandler, J. M. (1992). How to build a baby: II. Conceptual primitives. *Psychological Review, 99,* 587–604.

Manning, M. A., & Hoyme, H. E. (2007). Fetal alcohol spectrum disorders: A practical clinical approach to diagnosis. *Neuroscience & Biobehavioral Reviews, 31,* 230–238.

Manson, S. M. (1995). Culture and major depression: Current challenges in the diagnosis of mood disorders. *Psychiatric Clinics of North America, 18,* 487–501.

Maracek, J., Kimmel, E. B., Crawford, M., & Hare-Mustin, R. T. (2003). Psychology of women and gender. In D. K. Freedheim (Ed.), *Handbook of psychology* (Vol. 1: History of psychology; pp. 249–268). New York: Wiley.

Maratos, O. (1998). Neonatal, early and later imitation: Same order of phenomena? In F. Simion & G. Butterworth (Eds.), *The development of sensory, motor and cognitive capacities in early infancy: From perception to cognition.* Hove, U.K.: Psychology Press/Erlbaum (UK) Taylor & Francis.

Marcia, J. E. (1966). Development and validation of ego identity status. *Journal of Personality and Social Psychology, 3,* 551–558.

Marcus, D. E., & Overton, W. F. (1978). The development of cognitive gender constancy and sex-role preferences. *Child Development, 49,* 434–444.

Markman, A. B., & Wisniewski, E. J. (1997). Similar and different: The differentiation of basic-level categories. *Journal of

Experimental Psychology: Learning, Memory, & Cognition, 23, 54–70.

Marks, D. F., Sykes, C. M., & McKinley, J. M. (2003). Health psychology: Overview and professional issues. In A. M. Nezu, C. M. Nezu, & P. A. Gellar (Eds.), *Handbook of psychology: Health psychology* (Vol. 9, pp. 5–23). New York: Wiley.

Marks, M. J., & Fraley, R. C. (2006). Confirmation bias and the sexual double standard. *Sex Roles, 54*, 19–26.

Markus, H., & Kitayama, S. (1991). Culture and the self: Implications for cognition, emotion, and motivation. *Psychological Review, 98*, 224–253.

Markus, H., & Kitayama, S. (1994). A collective fear of the collective: Implications for selves and theories of selves. *Personality and Social Psychology Bulletin, 20*, 568–579.

Marsella, A. J., & Yamada, A. M. (2000). Culture and mental health: An introduction and overview of foundations, concepts, and issues. In I. Cuellar & F. A. Paniagua (Eds.), *Handbook of multicultural mental health.* San Diego, CA: Academic Press.

Marshall, J. C., & Halligan, P. W. (1988). Blindsight and insight in visuo-spatial neglect. *Nature, 336*, 766–767.

Marson, L., & McKenna, K. E. (1994). Stimulation of the hypothalamus initiates the urethrogenital reflex in male rats. *Brain Research, 638*, 103–108.

Martens, A., Goldenberg, J. L., & Greenberg, J. (2005). A terror management perspective on ageism. *Journal of Social Issues, 61*, 223–239.

Martens, A., Greenberg, J., Schimel, J., & Landau, M. J. (2004). Ageism and death: Effects of mortality and perceived similarity to elders on reactions to elderly people. *Personality and Social Psychology Bulletin, 30*, 1524–1536.

Martin, A. (2007). The representation of object concepts in the brain. *Annual Review of Psychology, 58*, 25–45.

Martin, C. L., & Ruble, D. (2004). Children's search for gender cues: Cognitive perspectives on gender development. *Current Directions in Psychological Science, 13*, 67–70.

Martin, G., & Pear, J. (1999). *Behavior modification: What it is and how to do it* (6th ed.). Upper Saddle River, NJ: Prentice-Hall.

Martin, K. M., & Aggleton, J. P. (1993). Contextual effects on the ability of divers to use decompression tables. *Applied Cognitive Psychology, 7*, 311–316.

Martin, P., & Bateson, P. (1993). *Measuring behavior: An introductory guide* (2nd ed.). Cambridge, U.K.: Cambridge University Press.

Martin, R. J., White, B. D., & Hulsey, M. G. (1991). The regulation of body weight. *American Scientist, 79*, 528–541.

Marx, M. H., & Cronan-Hillix, W. A. (1987). *Systems and theories in psychology.* New York: McGraw-Hill.

Maslach, C. (1976). Burned out. *Human Behavior, 5*, 16–22.

Maslach, C., Schaufeli, W. B., & Leiter, M. P. (2001). Job burnout. *Annual Review of Psychology, 52*, 397–422.

Masling, J. (2002). How do I score thee? Let me count the ways. On some different methods of categorizing Rorschach responses. *Journal of Personality Assessment, 79*, 399–421.

Maslow, A. H. (1954). *Motivation and personality.* New York: Harper.

Mason, J. R., & Reidinger, R. F. (1982). Observational learning of aversions in red-winged blackbirds (Agelaius phoeniceus). *Auk, 99*, 548–554.

Massaro, D. W., & Loftus, G. R. (1996). Sensory and perceptual storage: Data and theory. In E. L. Bjork & R. A. Bjork (Eds.), *Handbook of perception and cognition* (Vol. 10: Memory). New York: Academic Press.

Masson, J. (1984). *The assault on truth: Freud's suppression of the seduction theory.* New York: Farrar, Straus, & Giroux.

Masters, W. H., & Johnson, V. E. (1966). *Human sexual response.* Boston: Little, Brown.

Masuda, T., & Kitayama, S. (2004). Perceiver-induced constraint and attitude attribution in Japan and the US: A case for the cultural dependence of the correspondence bias. *Journal of Experimental Social Psychology, 40*, 409–416.

Matlin, M. W. (2003). From menarche to menopause: Misconceptions about women's reproductive lives. *Psychology Science, 45*, 106–122.

Matsumoto, D. (1994). *People: Psychology from a cultural perspective.* Pacific Grove, CA: Brooks/Cole.

Mattay, V. S., Berman, K. F., Ostrem, J. L., Esposito, G., Van-Horn, J. D., Bigelow, L. B., & Weinberger, D. R. (1996). Dextroamphetamine enhances "neural network-specific" physiological signals: A positron-emission tomography rCBF study. *Journal of Neuroscience, 16*, 4816–4822.

Matthews, G., Zeidner, M., & Roberts, R. D. (2005). Emotional intelligence: An elusive ability. In O. Wilheim & R. Engle (Eds.), *Understanding and measuring intelligence.* Thousand Oaks, CA: Sage.

Matthews, K., & Eljamel, M. S. (2003). Status of neurosurgery for mental disorder in Scotland: Selective literature review and overview of current clinical activity. *British Journal of Psychiatry, 182*, 404–411.

Matthews, K. A. (1992). Myths and realities of the menopause. *Psychosomatic Medicine, 54*, 1–9.

Mauk, M. D., Medina, J., Nores, W., & Ohyama, T. (2000). Cerebellar function: Coordination, learning or timing? *Current Biology, 10*, 522–525.

Mayer, J. D., & Salovey, P. (1997). What is emotional intelligence? In P. Salovey & D. Sluyter (Eds.), *Emotional development, emotional literacy, and emotional intelligence.* New York: Basic Books.

Mays, V. M., & Albee, G. W. (1992). Psychotherapy and ethnic minorities. In D. K. Freedheim (Ed.), *History of psychotherapy: A century of change.* Washington, DC: American Psychological Association.

McArthur, L. Z., & Berry, D. S. (1987). Cross-cultural agreement in perceptions of babyfaced adults. *Journal of Cross-Cultural Psychology, 18*, 165–192.

McCall, M. (1994). Decision theory and the sale of alcohol. *Journal of Applied Social Psychology, 24*, 1593–1611.

McCall, M. (1997). The effects of physical attractiveness on gaining access to alcohol: When social policy meets social decision making. *Addiction, 92*, 597–600.

McCall, W. V. (2001). Electroconvulsive therapy in the era of modern psychopharmacology. *International Journal of Neuropsychopharmacology, 4,* 315–324.

McCall, W. V. (2007). The persistence or the disintegration of memory: Cognitive side effects of electroconvulsive therapy. *Journal of ECT, 23,* 59–60.

McCann, I. L., & Holmes, D. S. (1984). Influence of aerobic exercise on depression. *Journal of Personality and Social Psychology, 46,* 1142–1147.

McClelland, D. C. (1961). *The achieving society.* Princeton, NJ: Von Nostrand.

McClelland, D. C., Atkinson, J. W., Clark, R. A., & Lowell, E. W. (1953). *The achievement motive.* New York: Appleton-Century-Crofts.

McClelland, J. L., & Elman, J. L. (1986). The TRACE model of speech perception. *Cognitive Psychology, 18,* 1–86.

McCrae, R. R., & Costa, P. T., Jr. (1985). Updating Norman's "adequate taxonomy": Intelligence and personality dimensions in natural language and in questionnaires. *Journal of Personality and Social Psychology, 49,* 710–721.

McCrae, R. R., & Costa, P. T., Jr. (2003). *Personality in adulthood* (2nd ed.). New York: Guilford.

McDaniel, E., & Andersen, P. A. (1998). International patterns of interpersonal tactile communication: A field study. *Journal of Nonverbal Behavior, 22,* 59–75.

McDaniel, M. A., Maier, S. F., & Einstein, G. O. (2002). "Brain-specific" nutrients: A memory cure? *Psychological Science in the Public Interest, 3,* 12–38.

McDermott, K. B., & Roediger, H. L. III. (1994). Effects of imagery on perceptual implicit memory tests. *Journal of Experimental Psychology: Learning, Memory, & Cognition, 20,* 1379–1390.

McDermott, K. B., & Roediger, H. L. III. (1998). Attempting to avoid illusory memories: Robust false recognition of associates persists under conditions of explicit warnings and immediate testing. *Journal of Memory and Language, 39,* 508–520.

McDougall, W. (1908). *An introduction to social psychology.* London: Methuen.

McGhee, P. E., & Frueh, T. (1980). Television viewing and the learning of sex-role stereotypes. *Sex Roles, 6,* 179–188.

McGuire, W. J. (1985). Attitudes and attitude change. In G. Lindzey & E. Aronson (Eds.), *Handbook of social psychology* (Vol. 2). New York: Random House.

McIntosh, D. N., Zajonc, R. B., Vig, P. S., & Emerick, S. W. (1997). Facial movement, breathing, temperature, and affect: Implications of the vascular theory of emotional efference. *Cognition & Emotion, 11,* 171–195.

McKenna, S. P., & Glendon, A. I. (1985). Occupational first aid training: Decay in cardiopulmonary resuscitation (CPR) skills. *Journal of Occupational Psychology, 58,* 109–117.

McKinlay, S. M., Brambilla, D. J., & Posner, J. G. (1992). The normal menopause transition. *Maturitas, 14,* 103–115.

McKnight, J. D., & Glass, D. C. (1995). Perceptions of control, burnout, and depressive symptomatology: A replication and extension. *Journal of Consulting & Clinical Psychology, 63,* 490–494.

McLeod, J. D., Kessler, R. C., & Landis, K. R. (1992). Speed of recovery from major depressive episodes in a community sample of married men and women. *Journal of Abnormal Psychology, 101,* 277–286.

McNally, R. J. (2007). Mechanisms of exposure therapy: How neuroscience can improve psychological treatments for anxiety disorders. *Clinical Psychology Review, 27,* 750–759.

McNeil, B. J., Pauker, S. G., Cox, H. C., Jr., & Tversky, A. (1982). On the elicitation of preferences for alternative therapies. *New England Journal of Medicine, 306,* 1259–1262.

McNeil, T. F., Cantor-Graae, E., & Weinberger, D. R. (2000). Relationship of obstetric complications and differences in size of brain structures in monozygotic twin pairs discordant for schizophrenia. *American Journal of Psychiatry, 157,* 203–212.

Medin, D. L. (1989). Concepts and conceptual structure. *American Psychologist, 44,* 1469–1481.

Medin, D. L., & Shaffer, M. M. (1978). A context theory of classification learning. *Psychological Review, 85,* 207–238.

Mednick, S. A. (1962). The associative basis of the creative process. *Psychological Review, 69,* 220–232.

Medoff, D. (2004). Assessing clinical personality assessment. *Journal of Personality Assessment, 82,* 241–243.

Medveck, V. H., Madey, S. F., & Gilovich, T. (1995). When less is more: Counterfactual thinking and satisfaction among Olympic medalists. *Journal of Personality and Social Psychology, 69,* 603–610.

Meeus, W. H. J., & Raaijmakers, Q. A. W. (1987). Administrative obedience as a social phenomenon. In W. Doise & S. Moscovici (Eds.), *Current issues in European social psychology* (Vol. 2). Cambridge, U.K.: Cambridge University Press.

Melamed, B. G., & Siegel, L. J. (1975). Reduction of anxiety in children facing hospitalization and surgery by use of filmed modeling. *Journal of Consulting and Clinical Psychology, 43,* 511–521.

Melton, A. W. (1963). Implications of short-term memory for a general theory of memory. *Journal of Verbal Learning and Verbal Behavior, 2,* 1–21.

Melzack, R. (1973). *The puzzle of pain.* New York: Basic Books.

Melzack, R., & Wall, P. D. (1965). Pain mechanisms: A new theory. *Science, 150,* 971–979.

Melzack, R., & Wall, P. D. (1982). *The challenge of pain.* Harmondsworth, U.K.: Penguin.

Mennin, D. S., Heimberg, R. G., & Holt, C. S. (2000). Panic, agoraphobia, phobias, and generalized anxiety disorder. In M. Hersen & A. S. Bellack (Eds.), *Psychopathology in adulthood* (2nd ed.). Needham Heights, MA: Allyn & Bacon.

Merikle, P. M. (1988). Subliminal auditory messages: An evaluation. *Psychology & Marketing, 5,* 355–372.

Merikle, P. M., & Skanes, H. E. (1992). Subliminal self-help audiotapes: A search for placebo effects. *Journal of Applied Psychology, 77,* 772–776.

Merton, R. (1948). The self-fulfilling prophecy. *Antioch Review, 8,* 193–210.

Milgram, S. (1963). Behavioral study of obedience. *Journal of Abnormal and Social Psychology, 67,* 371–378.

Milgram, S. (1974). *Obedience to authority.* New York: Harper & Row.

Miller, D. B. (1977). Roles of naturalistic observation in comparative psychology. *American Psychologist, 32,* 211–219.

Miller, G. A. (1956). The magical number seven plus or minus two: Some limits on our capacity for processing information. *Psychological Review, 63,* 81–97.

Miller, G. A., Galanter, E., & Pribram, K. H. (1960). *Plans and the structure of behavior.* New York: Holt.

Miller, J. G. (1994). Cultural diversity in the morality of caring: Individually oriented versus duty-based interpersonal moral codes. *Cross-Cultural Research: The Journal of Comparative Social Science, 28,* 3–39.

Miller, J. S., & Cardy, R. L. (2000). Self-monitoring and performance appraisal: Rating outcomes in project teams. *Journal of Organizational Behavior, 21,* 609–626.

Miller, M. A., & Rahe, R. H. (1997). Life changes scaling for the 1990s. *Journal of Psychosomatic Research, 43,* 279–292.

Miller, N. E. (1991). Commentary on Ulrich: Need to check truthfulness of statements by opponents of animal research. *Psychological Science, 2,* 422–424.

Miller, R. R., & Grace, R. C. (2003). Conditioning and learning. In A. Healy & R. Proctor (Eds.), *Handbook of psychology. Vol. 4: Experimental psychology,* pp. 357–397. New York: Wiley.

Miller, S. D. (1989). Optical differences in cases of multiple personality disorder. *Journal of Nervous and Mental Disease, 177,* 480–486.

Miller, T. W. (1993). The assessment of stressful life events. In L. Goldberger & S. Breznitz (Eds.), *Handbook of stress: Theoretical and clinical aspects* (2nd ed.). New York: Free Press.

Milner, B. (1966). Amnesia following operation on the temporal lobes. In C. W. M. Whitty & O. L. Zangwill (Eds.), *Amnesia.* London: Butterworths.

Mineka, S. (1987). A primate model of phobic fears. In H. Eysenck & I. Martin (Eds.), *Theoretical foundations of behavior therapy.* New York: Plenum.

Mineka, S., & Zinbarg, R. (2006). A contemporary learning theory perspective on the etiology of anxiety disorders. *American Psychologist, 61,* 10–26.

Mingroni, M. A. (2007). Resolving the IQ paradox: Heterosis as a cause of the Flynn effect and other trends. *Psychological Review, 114,* 806–829.

Mischel, W. (1968). *Personality and assessment.* New York: Wiley.

Mischel, W. (2004). Toward an integrative science of the person. *Annual Review of Psychology, 55,* 1–22.

Mischel, W., & Peake, P. K. (1982). Beyond déja vu in the search for cross-situational consistency. *Psychological Review, 89,* 730–755.

Mischel, W., & Shoda, Y. (1995). A cognitive-affective system theory of personality: Reconceptualizing situations, dispositions, dynamics, and invariance in personality structure. *Psychological Review, 102,* 246–268.

Mischel, W., & Shoda, Y. (1998). Reconciling processing dynamics and personality dispositions. *Annual Review of Psychology, 49,* 229–258.

Mitchell, K. J., Johnson, M. K., Raye, C. L., & Greene, E. J. (2004). Prefrontal cortex activity associated with source monitoring in a working memory task. *Journal of Cognitive Neuroscience, 16,* 921–934.

Molden, D. C., & Dweck, C. S. (2000). Meaning and motivation. In C. Sansone & J. M. Harackiewicz (Eds.), *Intrinsic and extrinsic motivation: The search for optimal motivation and performance* (pp. 131–159). San Diego, CA: Academic Press.

Moldin, S. Q., & Gottesman, I. I. (1997). Genes, experience, and chance in schizophrenia—Positioning for the 21st century. *Schizophrenia Bulletin, 23,* 547–561.

Montoya, A. G., Sorrentino, R., Lukas, S., & Price, B. H. (2002). Long-term neuropsychiatric consequences of "Ecstasy" (MDMA): A review. *Harvard Review of Psychiatry, 10,* 212–220.

Mook, D. G. (1995). *Motivation: The organization of action* (2nd ed.). New York: Norton.

Moray, N. (1959). Attention in dichotic listening: Affective cues and the influence of instructions. *Quarterly Journal of Experimental Psychology, 11,* 56–60.

Moret, V., Forster, A., Laverriere, M. C., & Lambert, H. (1991). Mechanism of analgesia induced by hypnosis and acupuncture: Is there a difference? *Pain, 45,* 135–140.

Morgan, R. (1990). Analyses of the predictive validity of the SAT and high school grades from 1976–1985. In W. W. Willingham, C. Lewis, R. Morgan, & L. Ramist (Eds.), *Predicting college grades: An analysis of institutional trends over two decades* (pp. 195–212). Princeton, NJ: Educational Testing Service.

Morton, G. J., Cummings, D. E., Baskin, D. G., Barsh, G. S., & Schwartz, M. W. (2006). Central nervous system control of food intake and body weight. *Nature, 443,* 289–295.

Moscicki, E. K. (2001). Epidemiology of completed and attempted suicide: toward a framework for prevention. *Clinical Neuroscience Research, 1,* 310–323.

Moser, D. K., Riegel, B., McKinley, S., Doering, L. V., An, K., & Sheahan, S. (2007). Impact of anxiety and perceived control on in-hospital complications after myocardial infarction. *Psychosomatic Medicine, 69,* 10–16.

Mozell, M. M., Smith, B., Smith, P., Sullivan, R., & Swender, P. (1969). Nasal chemoreception in flavor identification. *Archives of Otolaryngology, 90,* 367–373.

Muchinsky, P. M. (2003). *Psychology applied to work* (7th ed.). Belmont, CA: Wadsworth.

Mueller, C. M., & Dweck, C. S. (1998). Praise for intelligence can undermine children's motivation and performance. *Journal of Personality & Social Psychology, 75,* 33–52.

Munakata, Y., McClelland, J.L., Johnson, M.H., & Siegler, R.S. (1997). Rethinking infant knowledge: Toward an adaptive process account of successes and failures in object permanence tasks. *Psychological Review, 104,* 686–713.

Murdock, B. B., Jr. (1960). The distinctiveness of stimuli. *Psychological Review, 67,* 16–31.

Murnen, S. K., & Stockton, M. (1997). Gender and self-reported sexual arousal in response to sexual stimuli: A meta-analytic review. *Sex Roles, 37,* 135–153.

Murphy, G. L. (2002). *The big book of concepts.* Cambridge, MA: MIT Press.

Murphy, G. L., & Lassaline, M. E. (1997). Hierarchical structure in concepts and the basic level of categorization. In K. Lamberts & D. R. Shanks (Eds.), *Knowledge, concepts and categories: Studies in cognition.* Cambridge, MA: MIT Press.

Murray, C., & Wren, C. T. (2003). Cognitive, academic, and attitudinal predictors of the grade point averages of college students with learning disabilities. *Journal of Learning Disabilities, 36,* 407–415.

Murray, H. A. (1938). *Explorations in personality.* New York: Oxford University Press.

Mustanski, B. S., Chivers, M. L., & Bailey, J. M. (2002). A critical review of recent biological research on human sexual orientation. *Annual Review of Sex Research, 13,* 89–140.

Myers, D. G., & Diener, E. (1995). Who is happy? *Psychological Science, 6,* 10–19.

Myers, D. G., & Ridl, J. (1979, August). Can we all be better than average? *Psychology Today,* pp. 89–98.

Myers, T. C., Wittrock, D. A., & Foreman, G. W. (1998) Appraisal of subjective stress in individuals with tension-type headache: The influence of baseline measures. *Journal of Behavioral Medicine, 21,* 469–484.

Nadon, R., Hoyt, I. P., Register, P. A., & Kihlstrom, J. F. (1991). Absorption and hypnotizability: Context effects reexamined. *Journal of Personality and Social Psychology, 60,* 144–153.

Nagar, D., & Panady, J. (1987). Affect and performance on cognitive tasks as a function of crowding and noise. *Journal of Applied Social Psychology, 17,* 147–157.

Nairne, J. S. (1990). A feature model of immediate memory. *Memory & Cognition, 18,* 251–269.

Nairne, J. S. (2002a). Remembering over the short-term: The case against the standard model. *Annual Review of Psychology, 53,* 53–81.

Nairne, J. S. (2002b). The myth of the encoding-retrieval match. *Memory, 10,* 389–395.

Nairne, J. S. (2003). Sensory and working memory. In A. Healy & R. Proctor (Eds.), *Handbook of psychology. Vol. 4: Experimental Psychology,* pp. 423–444. New York: Wiley.

Nairne, J. S. (2005). The functionalist agenda in memory research. In A. F. Healy (Ed.), *Experimental cognitive psychology and its applications* (pp. 115–126). Washington, DC: American Psychological Association.

Nairne, J. S., Thompson, S. R., & Pandeirada, J. N. S. (2007). Adaptive memory: Survival processing enhances retention. *Journal of Experimental Psychology: Learning, Memory, and Cognition, 33,* 263–273.

Nantais, K. M., & Schellenberg, E. G. (1999). The Mozart effect: An artifact of preference. *Psychological Science, 10,* 370–373.

Nathan, P. E., & Langenbucher, J. (2003). Diagnosis and classification. In G. Stricker & T. A. Widiger (Eds.) *Handbook of psychology: Clinical psychology* (Vol. 8, pp. 3–26). New York: Wiley.

Nawrot, M. (2003). Disorders of motion and depth. *Neurologic Clinics, 21,* 609–621.

Neath, I. (1993). Distinctiveness and serial position effects in recognition. *Memory & Cognition, 21,* 689–698.

Neath, I., & Surprenant, A. (2003). *Human memory: An introduction to research, data, and theory* (2nd ed.). Belmont, CA: Wadsworth.

Neisser, U. (1967). *Cognitive psychology.* New York: Appleton-Century-Crofts.

Neisser, U. (Ed.). (1998). *The rising curve: Long-term gains in IQ and related measures.* Washington, DC: American Psychological Association.

Neisser, U., & Harsch, N. (1992). Phantom flashbulbs: False recollections of hearing the news about *Challenger.* In E. Winograd & U. Neisser (Eds.), *Affect and accuracy in recall: Studies of "flashbulb memories."* Cambridge, U.K.: Cambridge University Press.

Neisser, U., & Hyman, I. (Eds.). (1999). *Memory observed: Remembering in natural contexts* (2nd ed.). New York: Worth.

Nelson, K. (1973). Structure and strategy in learning to talk. *Monographs of the Society for Research in Child Development, 38*(Serial No. 149).

Nestoriuc, Y., & Martin, A. (2007). Efficacy of biofeedback for migraine: A meta-analysis. *Pain, 128,* 111–127.

Nettelbeck, T., & Wilson, C. (2004). The Flynn effect: Smarter not faster. *Intelligence, 32,* 85–93.

Newcomb, A. F., & Bagwell, C. L. (1995). Children's friendship relations: A meta-analytic review. *Psychological Bulletin, 117,* 306–347.

Newcombe, N. S., & Uttal, D. H. (2006). Whorf versus Socrates, round 10. *Trends in Cognitive Sciences, 10,* 394–396.

Newell, A., & Simon, H. A. (1972). *Human problem solving.* Englewood Cliffs, NJ: Prentice-Hall.

Nichols, D. S., & Greene, R. L. (1997). Dimensions of deception in personality assessment: The example of the MMPI-2. *Journal of Personality Assessment, 68,* 251–266.

Nickerson, R. S., & Adams, M. J. (1979). Long-term memory for a common object. *Cognitive Psychology, 11,* 287–307.

Nicolaus, L. K., & Nellis, D. W. (1987). The first evaluation of the use of conditioned taste aversion to control predation by mongooses upon eggs. *Applied Animal Behaviour Science, 17,* 329–346.

Nilsson, L., & Ohta, N. (Eds.). (2006). *Memory and society: Psychological perspectives.* New York: Psychology Press.

Nisbett, R. E., Peng, K., Choi, I., & Norenzayan, A. (2001). Culture and systems of thought: Holistic versus analytic cognition. *Psychological Review, 108,* 291–310.

Nithianantharajah, J., & Hannan, A. J. (2006). Enriched environments, experience-dependent plasticity and disorders of the nervous system. *Nature Reviews Neuroscience, 7,* 697–709.

Nobel, K. D., Robinson, N. M., & Gunderson, S. A. (1993). All rivers lead to the sea: A follow-up study of gifted young adults. *Roeper Review, 15,* 124–130.

Norenzayan, A., & Nisbett, R. E. (2000). Culture and causal cognition. *Current Directions in Psychological Science, 9,* 132–135.

Norris, S. L., & Zweigenhaft, R. L. (1999). Self-monitoring, trust, and commitment in romantic relationships. *The Journal of Social Psychology, 139,* 215–220.

Nosofsky, R. M. (1992). Exemplars, prototypes, and similarity rules. In A. F. Healy & S. M. Kosslyn (Eds.), *Essays in honor of William K. Estes. Vol. 2: From learning processes to cognitive processes* (pp. 149–167) Hillsdale, NJ: Erlbaum.

Nowak, A., Vallacher, R. R., & Miller, M. E. (2003). Social influence and group dynamics. In T. Millon & M. J. Lerner (Eds.), *Handbook of psychology: Personality and social psychology* (Vol. 5, pp 383–417). New York: Wiley.

Nowakowski, R. S. (1987). Basic concepts of CNS development. *Child Development, 58,* 568–595.

Nurmi, E. L., Dowd, M., Tadevosyan-Leyfer, O., Haynes, J. L., Folstein, S. E., & Sutcliffe, J. S. (2003). Exploratory subsetting of autism families based on savant skills improves evidence of genetic linkage to 15q11-q13. *Journal of the American Academy of Child & Adolescent Psychiatry, 42,* 856–863.

Oakes, J. (1985). *Keeping track: How schools structure inequality.* New Haven, CT: Yale University Press.

O'Callahan, M., Andrews, A. M., & Krantz, D. S. (2003). Coronary heart disease and hypertension. In A. M. Nezu, C. M. Nezu, & P. A. Gellar (Eds.), *Handbook of psychology: Health psychology* (Vol. 9, pp. 339–364). New York: Wiley.

Offer, D., & Schonert-Reichl, K. A. (1992). Debunking the myths of adolescence. *Journal of the American Academy of Child and Adolescent Psychiatry, 31,* 1003–1013.

Ogilvie, C. M., Crouch, N. S., Rumsby, G., Creighton, S. M., Liao, L., & Conway, G. S. (2006). Congenital adrenal hyperplasia in adults: A review of medical, surgical and psychological issues. *Clinical Endocrinology, 64,* 2–11.

Ogloff, J. R. P., Roberts, C. F., & Roesch, R. (1993). The insanity defense: Legal standards and clinical assessment. *Applied & Preventive Psychology, 2,* 163–178.

Öhman, A., & Mineka, S. (2001). Fear, phobias, and preparedness: Toward an evolved module of fear and fear learning. *Psychological Review, 108,* 483–522.

Öhman, A., & Mineka, S. (2003). The malicious serpent: Snakes as a prototype stimulus for an evolved module for fear. *Current Directions in Psychological Science, 12,* 5–9.

Okada, Y., & Stark, C. (2003). Neural processing associated with true and false memory retrieval. *Cognitive, Affective, & Behavioral Neuroscience, 3,* 323–334.

Olds, J. (1958). Satiation effects in self-stimulation of the brain. *Journal of Comparative and Physiological Psychology, 51,* 675-678.

Olff, M., Langeland, W., Draijer, N., & Gersons, B. P. (2007). Gender differences in posttraumatic stress disorder. *Psychological Bulletin, 133,* 183–204.

Olson, J. M., & Maio, G. R. (2003). Attitudes in social behavior. In T. Millon & M. J. Lerner (Eds.), *Handbook of psychology: Personality and social psychology* (Vol. 5, pp. 299–325). New York: Wiley.

Olson, J. M., & Zanna, M. P. (1993). Attitudes and attitude change. *Annual Review of Psychology, 44,* 117–154.

O'Mahony, M. (1978). Smell illusions and suggestion: Reports of smells contingent on tones played on television and radio. *Chemical Senses and Flavor, 3,* 183–187.

Orne, M. T. (1959). The nature of hypnosis: Artifact and essence. *Journal of Abnormal and Social Psychology, 58,* 277–299.

Orne, M. T. (1969). Demand characteristics and the concept of quasi-controls. In R. Rosenthal & R. L. Rosnow (Eds.), *Artifact in behavioral research.* New York: Academic Press.

Ortmann, A., & Hertwig, R. (1997). Is deception acceptable? *American Psychologist, 52,* 746–747.

Ortony, A., & Turner, T. J. (1990). What's basic about basic emotions? *Psychological Review, 97,* 315–331.

O'Shea, B. (2001). Post-traumatic stress disorder: A review for the general psychiatrist. *International Journal of Psychiatry in Clinical Practice, 5,* 11–18.

Ostacher, M. J., & Eidelman, P. (2006). Suicide in bipolar depression. In R. El-Mallakh & N. Ghaemi (Eds.), *Bipolar depression: A comprehensive guide.* Washington, DC: American Psychiatric Publishing.

Otto, M. W., Demopulos, C. M., McLean, N. E., Pollack, M. H., & Fava, M. (1998). Additional findings on the association between anxiety sensitivity and hypochondriacal concerns: Examination of patients with major depression. *Journal of Anxiety Disorders, 12,* 225–232.

Ousji, I. J., McGarrahan, A., Mihalakos, P., Garver, D., Kingsbury, S., & Cullum, C. M. (2007). Neuropsychological functioning in MRI-derived subgroups of schizophrenia. *Schizophrenia Research, 92,* 189–196.

Özgen, E. (2004). Language, leaning, and color perception. *Current Directions in Psychological Science, 13,* 95–98.

Paivio, A. (2007). *Mind and its evolution.* Mahwah, NJ: Erlbaum.

Palmore, E. B. (1990). *Ageism: Negative and positive.* New York: Springer.

Panksepp, J. (2007). Neurologizing the psychology of affects. *Perspectives on Psychological Science, 2,* in press.

Parkes, J. D., & Block, C. (1989). Genetic factors in sleep disorders. *Journal of Neurology, Neurosurgery, and Psychiatry, 52,* 101–108.

Parkin, A. J., & Java, R. (2001). Determinents of age-related memory loss. In T. J. Perfect & E. L. Maylor (Eds.), *Models of cognitive aging.* New York: Oxford University Press.

Parmelee, A. H., & Sigman, M. D. (1983). Perinatal brain development and behavior. In M. M. Haith & J. J. Campos (Eds.), *Handbook of child psychology: Vol. 2. Infancy and developmental psychobiology.* New York: Wiley.

Parsons, J. E., Kaczala, C., & Meece, J. L. (1982). Socialization of achievement attitudes and beliefs: Classroom influences. *Child Development, 53,* 322–339.

Parvizi, J., & Damasio, A. (2001). Consciousness and the brainstem. In S. Dehaene (Ed.), *The cognitive neuroscience of consciousness.* Cambridge, MA: MIT Press.

Paulus, P. B. (1988). *Prison crowding: A psychological perspective.* New York: Springer.

Pedersen, D. M., & Wheeler, J. (1983). The Müller-Lyer illusion among Navajos. *Journal of Social Psychology, 121,* 3–6.

Peissig, J. J., & Tarr, M. J. (2007). Visual object recognition: Do we know more now than we did 20 years ago? *Annual Review of Psychology, 58,* 75–96.

Pelphrey, K. A., Mack, P. B., Song, A., Guzeldere, G., & McCarthy, G. (2003). Faces evoke spatially differentiated patterns of BOLD activation and deactivation. *Neuroreport, 14,* 955–959.

Penfield, W., & Perot, P. (1963). The brain's record of auditory and visual experience. *Brain, 86,* 595–696.

Pennebaker, J. W. (1990). *Opening up: The healing power of confiding in others.* New York: Morrow.

Pennebaker, J. W., & Chung, C. K. (2007). Expressive writings, emotional upheavals, and health. In H. S. Friedman & R. C. Silver (Eds.), *Foundations of health psychology.* New York: Oxford University Press.

Pepeu, G., & Giovannini, M. G. (2004). Changes in acetylcholine extracellular levels during cognitive processes. *Learning & Memory, 11,* 21–27.

Perls, F. S. (1969). *Gestalt therapy verbatim.* Moab, UT: Real People Press.

Perls, F. S., Hefferline, R. F., & Goodman, P. (1951). *Gestalt therapy.* New York: Julian.

Perrett, D. I., & Mistlin, A. M. (1987). Visual neurones responsive to faces. *Trends in Neuroscience, 10,* 358–364.

Persson, J., Bringlov, E., Nilsson, L., & Nyberg, L. (2004). The memory-enhancing effects of Ginseng and Ginkgo biloba in healthy volunteers. *Psychopharmacology, 172,* 430–434.

Pert, C. B. (2002). The wisdom of the receptors: Neuropeptides, the emotions, and bodymind. *Advances in Mind-Body Medicine, 18,* 30–35.

Pert, C. B., & Snyder, S. H. (1973). The opiate receptor: Demonstration in nervous tissue. *Science, 179,* 1011–1014.

Peterson, A. C. (1988). Adolescent development. *Annual Review of Psychology, 39,* 583–607.

Peterson, C., & Seligman, M. E. P. (1987). Explanatory style and illness. *Journal of Personality, 55,* 237–265.

Peterson, C., Seligman, M. E. P., & Vaillant, G. E. (1988). Pessimistic explanatory style is a risk factor for physical illness: A thirty-five-year longitudinal study. *Journal of Personality and Social Psychology, 55,* 23–27.

Peterson, D. R. (1968). *The clinical study of social behavior.* New York: Appleton-Century-Crofts.

Peterson, L. R., & Peterson, M. J. (1959). Short-term retention of individual items. *Journal of Experimental Psychology, 58,* 193–198.

Pett, M. A., & Johnson, M. M. (2005). Development and psychometric evaluation of the revised University Student Hassles Scale. *Educational and Psychological Measurement, 65,* 984–1010.

Petty, R. E., & Cacioppo, J. T. (1986). *Communication and persuasion: Central and peripheral routes to attitude change.* New York: Springer-Verlag.

Petty, R. E., DeSteno, D., & Rucker, D. D. (2001). The role of affect in attitude change. In J. P. Forgas (Ed.), *Handbook of affect and social cognition.* Mahwah, NJ: Erlbaum.

Petty, R. E., & Wegener, D. T. (1997). Attitude change: Multiple roles for persuasion variables. In D. Gilbert, S. Fiske, & G. Lindzey (Eds.), *Handbook of social psychology* (4th ed.). New York: McGraw-Hill.

Petty, R. E., Wheeler, C., & Tormala, Z. L. (2003). Persuasion and attitude change. In T. Millon & M. J. Lerner (Eds.), *Handbook of psychology: Personality and social psychology* (Vol. 5, pp. 353–382). New York: Wiley.

Pfaff, D. W. (1999). *Drive: Neurobiological and molecular mechanisms of sexual motivation.* Cambridge, MA: MIT Press.

Piaget, J. (1929). *The child's conception of the world.* New York: Harcourt Brace.

Piaget, J. (1970). Piaget's theory. In P. H. Mussen (Ed.), *Carmichael's manual of child psychology* (Vol. 1). New York: Wiley.

Piasecki, T. M., Fiore, M. C., & Baker, T. B. (1998). Profiles in discouragement: Two studies of variability in the time course of smoking withdrawal symptoms. *Journal of Abnormal Psychology, 107,* 238–251.

Pickles, J. O. (1988). *An introduction to the physiology of hearing* (2nd ed.). London: Academic Press.

Pierce, T. W., Madden, D. J., Siegel, W. C., & Blumenthal, J. A. (1993). Effects of aerobic exercise on cognitive and psychosocial functioning in patients with mild hypertension. *Health Psychology, 12,* 286–291.

Pillsworth, E. G., Haselton, M. G., & Buss, D. M. (2004). Ovulatory shifts in female sexual desire. *Journal of Sex Research, 41,* 55–65.

Pinel, J. (1999). Rhinal cortex, but not medial thalamic, lesions cause retrograde amnesia for objects in rats. *Neuroreport, 10,* 2853–2858.

Pines, A. (1993). Burnout. In L. Goldberger & S. Breznitz (Eds.), *Handbook of stress: Theoretical and clinical aspects* (2nd ed.). New York: Free Press.

Pines, A., & Aronson, E. (1988). *Career burnout: Causes and cures* (2nd ed.). New York: Free Press.

Pinker, S. (1994). *The language instinct.* New York: HarperCollins.

Pinker, S. (1997). *How the mind works.* New York: Norton.

Pinker, S. (2002). *The blank slate: The modern denial of human nature.* New York: Viking.

Pizlo, Z., & Stevenson, A. K. (1999). Shape constancy from novel views. *Perception & Psychophysics, 61,* 1299–1307.

Plomin, R., Corley, R., Caspi, A., Fulker, D. W., & DeFries, J. (1998). Adoption results for self-reported personality: Evidence for nonadditive genetic effects? *Journal of Personality & Social Psychology, 75,* 211–218.

Plomin, R., Fulker, D. W., Corley, R., & DeFries, J. C. (1997). Nature, nurture, and cognitive development from 1 to 16 years: A parent-offspring adoption study. *Psychological Science, 8,* 442–447.

Plous, S. (1991). An attitude survey of animal rights activists. *Psychological Science, 2,* 194–196.

Poldrack, R. A., & Wagner, A. D. (2004). What can nueroimaging tell us about the mind? *Current Directions in Psychological Science, 13,* 177–181.

Polivy, J., & Herman, C. P. (2002). Causes of eating disorders. *Annual Review of Psychology, 53*, 187–213.

Porter, R. H., Makin, J. W., Davis, L. B., & Christensen, K. M. (1992). Breast-fed infants respond to olfactory clues from their own mother and unfamiliar lactating females. *Infant Behavior and Devlopment, 15*, 85–93.

Posner, M. I. (1993). Interaction of arousal and selection in the posterior attention network. In A. Baddeley & L. Weiskrantz (Eds.), *Attention: Selection, awareness, and control. A tribute to Donald Broadbent.* Oxford, U.K.: Clarendon Press.

Posner, M. I., & Rothbart, M. K. (2007) Research on attention networks as a model for the integration of psychological science. *Annual Review of Psychology, 58*, 1–23.

Postmes, T., & Spears, R. (1998). Deindividuation and antinormative behavior: A meta-analysis. *Psychological Bulletin, 123*, 238–259.

Pratt, G. J., Wood, D., & Alman, B. M. (1988). *A clinical hypnosis primer.* New York: Wiley.

Premack, D. (1976). *Intelligence in ape and man.* Hillsdale, NJ: Erlbaum.

Proctor, F., Wagner, N., & Butler, J. (1974). The differentiation of male and female orgasm: An experimental study. In N. Wagner (Ed.), *Perspectives on human sexuality.* New York: Behavioral Publications.

Proctor, R. W., & Capaldi, E. J. (2001). Empirical evaluation and justification of methodologies in psychological science. *Psychological Bulletin, 127*, 759–772.

Profet, M. (1992). Pregnancy sickness as adaptation: A deterrent to maternal ingestion of teratogens. In J. H. Barkow, L. Cosmides, & J. Tooby (Eds.), *The adapted mind.* New York: Oxford University Press.

Provence, S. A., & Lipton, R. C. (1962). *Infants in institutions.* New York: International Universities Press.

Prud'homme, M. J. L., Cohen, D., & Kalaska, J. F. (1994). Tactile activity in primate somatosensory cortex during active arm movements: Cytoarchitectonic distribution. *Journal of Neurophysiology, 71*, 173–181.

Przedborski, S. (2005). Pathogenesis of nigral cell death in Parkinson's disease. *Parkinsonism and Related Disorders, 11(Suppl 1)*, S3–S7.

Rachman, S. J. (1990). *Fear and courage.* New York: Freeman.

Ragland, D. R., & Brand, R. J. (1988). Type A behavior and mortality from coronary heart disease. *New England Journal of Medicine, 318*, 65–69.

Rakic, P. (1991). Plasticity of cortical development. In S. E. Brauth, W. S. Hall, & R. J. Dooling (Eds.), *Plasticity of development.* Cambridge, MA: Bradford/MIT Press.

Ranjith, G., Mohan, R., & Ismail, K. (2004). Dhat syndrome: A functional somatic syndrome? *British Journal of Psychiatry, 185*, 77.

Rao, H., Zhou, T., Zhou, Y., Fan, S., & Chen, L. (2003). Spatiotemporal activation of the two visual pathways in form discrimination and spatial location: A brain mapping study. *Human Brain Mapping, 18*, 78–89.

Raugh, M. R., & Atkinson, R. C. (1975). A mnemonic method for learning a second-language vocabulary. *Journal of Educational Psychology, 67*, 1–16.

Rauscher, F. H., & Hinton, S. C. (2006). The Mozart effect: Music listening is not music instruction. *Educational Psychologist, 41*, 233–238.

Rauscher, F. H., Shaw, G. L., & Ky, K. N. (1993). Music and spatial task performance. *Nature, 365*, 611.

Rauscher, F. H., Shaw, G. L., & Ky, K. N. (1995). Listening to Mozart enhances spatial-temporal reasoning: Toward a neurophysiological basis. *Neuroscience Letters, 185*, 44–47.

Raven, J. C., Court, J. H., & Raven, J. (1985). *A manual for Raven's progressive matrices and vocabulary scales.* London: H. K. Lewis.

Raynor, H. A., & Epstein, L. H. (2001). Dietary variety, energy regulation, and obesity. *Psychological Bulletin, 127*, 325–341.

Rechtschaffen, A., & Bergmann, B. M. (1995). Sleep deprivation in the rat by the disk-over-water method. *Behavioural Brain Research, 69*, 55–63.

Redelmeier, D. A., & Tibshriani, R. J. (1997). Association between cellular-telephone calls and motor vehicle collisions. *New England Journal of Medicine, 336*, 543–458.

Ree, M. J., & Earles, J. A. (1992). Intelligence is the best predictor of job performance. *Current Directions in Psychological Science, 1*, 86–89.

Regoeczi, W. C. (2003). When context matters: A multilevel analysis of household and neighborhood crowding on aggression and withdrawl. *Journal of Environmental Psychology, 23*, 457–470.

Reichenberg, A., & Harvey, P. D. (2007). Neuropsychological impairments in schizophrenia: Integration of performance-based and brain imaging studies. *Pyschological Bulletin, 133*, 833–858.

Rescorla, R. A. (1980). Simultaneous and successive associations in sensory preconditioning. *Journal of Experimental Psychology: Animal Behavior Processes, 6*, 207–216.

Rescorla, R. A. (1988). Pavlovian conditioning: It's not what you think it is. *American Psychologist, 43*, 151–160.

Rescorla, R. A. (2001). Retraining of extinguished Pavlovian stimuli. *Journal of Experimental Psychology: Animal Behavior Processes, 27*, 115–124.

Resnick, S. M., Berenbaum, S. A., Gottesman, I. I., & Bouchard, T. J. (1986). Early hormonal influences on cognitive functioning in congenital adrenal hyperplasia. *Developmental Psychology, 22*, 191–198.

Revonsuo, A. (2000). The reinterpretation of dreams: An evolutionary hypothesis of the function of dreaming. *Behavioral and Brain Sciences, 23*, 877–901.

Rhodes, G. (2006). The evolutionary psychology of facial beauty. *Annual Review of Psychology, 57*, 199–226.

Rhodes, G., & Tremewan, T. (1996). Averageness, exaggeration, and facial attractiveness. *Psychological Science, 7*, 105–110.

Ribaupierre, F. de. (1997). Acoustical information processing in the auditory thalamus and cerebral cortex. In G. Ehret

& R. Romand (Eds.), *The central auditory system*. New York: Oxford University Press.

Richtand, N. M., Welge, J. A., Logue, A. D., Keck, P. E., Strakowsi, S. M., & McNamara, R. K. (2007). Dopamine and serotonin receptor binding and antipsychotic efficacy. *Neuropsychopharmacology, 32,* 1715–1726.

Ridley, M. (2003). *Nature via nurture: Genes, experience, & what makes us human*. New York: HarperCollins.

Rieber, R. W. (1999). Hypnosis, false memory, and multiple personality: A trinity of affinity. *History of Psychology, 10,* 3–11.

Roberts, C. J., & Lowe, C. R. (1975). Where have all the conceptions gone? *Lancet, 1,* 498–499.

Robinson, J. O., Rosen, M., Revill, S. I., David, H., & Rus, G. A. D. (1980). Self-administered intravenous and intramuscular pethidine. *Anaesthesia, 35,* 763–770.

Rodin, J., Schank, D., & Striegal-Moore, R. H. (1989). Psychological features of obesity. *Medical Clinics of North America, 73,* 47–66.

Roediger, H. L. III, & Marsh, E. J. (2003). Episodic and autobiographical memory. In A. Healy & R. Proctor (Eds.) *Handbook of psychology. Vol. 4: Experimental psychology*, pp. 475–497. New York: Wiley.

Roediger, H. L. III, & McDermott, K. B. (1993). Implicit memory in normal human subjects. In F. Boller & J. Grafman (Eds.), *Handbook of neuropsychology* (Vol. 8). Amsterdam: Elsevier.

Roediger, H. L. III, & McDermott, K. B. (1995). Creating false memories: Remembering words not presented in lists. *Journal of Experimental Psychology: Learning, Memory, & Cognition, 21,* 803–814.

Roediger, H. L. III, Weldon, M. S., Stadler, M. L., & Riegler, G. L. (1992). Direct comparison of two implicit memory tests: Word fragment and word stem completion. *Journal of Experimental Psychology: Learning, Memory, & Cognition, 18,* 1251–1269.

Rogers, C. R. (1951). *Client-centered therapy*. Boston: Houghton Mifflin.

Rogers, C. R. (1963). The actualizing tendency in relation to "motives" and to consciousness. In M. R. Jones (Ed.), *Nebraska symposium on motivation*. Lincoln: University of Nebraska.

Rolls, B. J., van Duijvencvoorde, P. M., & Rolls, E. T. (1984). Pleasantness changes and food intake in a varied four course meal. *Appetite, 5,* 337–348.

Rolls, E. T. (1995). Central taste anatomy and neurophysiology. In R. L. Doty (Ed.), *Handbook of olfaction and gustation*. New York: Dekker.

Romans, S. E., Martin, M., & Herbison, G. P. (2003). Age of menarche: The role of some psychosocial factors. *Psychological Medicine, 33,* 933–939.

Rosch, E., & Mervis, C. B. (1975). Family resemblances: Studies in the internal structure of categories. *Cognitive Psychology, 7,* 573–605.

Rosch, E., Mervis, C. B., Gray, W. D., Johnson, D. M., & Bayes-Braem, P. (1976). Basic objects in natural categories. *Cognitive Psychology, 8,* 382–439.

Rose, H., & Rose, S. (2000). *Alas, poor Darwin: Arguments against evolutionary psychology*. New York: Harmony Books.

Rosen, D. L., & Singh, S. (1992). An investigation of subliminal embed effect on multiple measures of advertising effectiveness. *Psychology & Marketing, 9,* 157–173.

Rosenbaum, M. E. (1986). The repulsion hypothesis: On the nondevelopment of relationships. *Journal of Personality and Social Psychology, 51,* 1156–1166.

Rosenhan, D. L. (1973). On being sane in insane places. *Science, 179,* 250–258.

Rosenthal, R. (1966). *Experimenter effects in behavioral research*. New York: Appleton-Century-Crofts.

Rosenthal, R. (1994). Science and ethics in conducting, analyzing, and reporting psychological research. *Psychological Science, 5,* 127–134.

Rosenthal, R., & Jacobson, L. (1968). *Pygmalion in the classroom: Teachers' expectations and pupils' intellectual development*. New York: Holt, Rinehart & Winston.

Rosenthal, R., & Rosnow, R. L. (Eds.). (1969). *Artifact in behavioral research*. New York: Academic Press.

Rosenthal, R., & Rosnow, R. L. (1975). *The volunteer subject*. New York: Wiley.

Rosenzweig, M. R. (1984). Experience, memory, and the brain. *American Psychologist, 39,* 365–376.

Rosenzweig, S. (1936). Some implicit common factors in diverse methods of psychotherapy. *American Journal of Orthopsychiatry, 6,* 422–425.

Roser, M., & Gazzaniga, M. S. (2004). Automatic brains—Interpretive minds. *Current Directions in Psychological Science, 13,* 56–59.

Rösler, F., Pechmann, T., Streb, J., Röder, B., & Hennighausen, E. (1998). Parsing of sentences in a language with varying word order: Word-by-word variations of processing demands are revealed by event-related potentials. *Journal of Memory and Language, 38,* 150–176.

Rosnow, R. L., & Rosenthal, R. (1996). *Beginning behavioral research: A conceptual primer* (2nd ed.). New York: Macmillan.

Ross, C. A., Miller, S. D., Reagor, P., Bjornson, L., Fraser, G. A., & Anderson, G. (1990). Structured interview data on 102 cases of multiple personality disorder from four centers. *American Journal of Psychiatry, 147,* 596–601.

Ross, L. (1977). The intuitive psychologist and his shortcomings: Distortions in the attribution process. In L. Berkowitz (Ed.), *Advances in experimental social psychology* (Vol. 10). New York: Academic Press.

Ross, L., & Nisbett, R. E. (1991). *The person and the situation: Perspectives of social psychology*. New York: McGraw-Hill.

Rothbaum, F., & Morelli, G. (2005). Attachment and culture: Bridging relativism and universalism. In W. Friedlemeier, P. Chakkarath, & B. Schwarz (Eds.). *Culture and human development: The importance of cross-cultural research in the social sciences*. Hove, U.K.: Psychology Press.

Rothbaum, F., Weisz, J., Pott, M., Kazuo, M., & Morelli, G. (2000). Attachment and culture: Security in the United States and Japan. *American Psychologist, 55,* 1093–1104.

Rotter, J. B. (1966). Generalized expectancies for internal versus external locus of control of reinforcement. *Psychological Monographs, 80* (Whole No. 609).

Rotter, J. B., Liverant, S., & Crowne, D. P. (1961). The growth and extinction of expectancies in change controlled and skilled tasks. *Journal of Psychology, 52,* 161–177.

Rovee-Collier, C. (1993). The capacity for long-term memory in infancy. *Current Directions in Psychological Science, 2,* 130–135.

Rowan, J. (1998). Maslow amended. *Journal of Humanistic Psychology, 38,* 81–92.

Roy, M. M., & Christenfeld, N. (2004). Do dogs resemble their owners? *Psychological Science, 15,* 361–363.

Rozin, P., & Fallon, A. E. (1987). A perspective on disgust. *Psychological Review, 94,* 23–41.

Rozin, P., Fischler, C., Imada, S., Sarubin, A., & Wrzesniewski, A. (1999). Attitudes to food and the role of food in life in the U.S.A., Japan, Flemish Belgium and France: Possible implications for the diet–health debate. *Appetite, 33,* 163–180.

Rozin, P., Hammer, L., Oster, H., Horowitz, T., & Marmara, V. (1986). The child's conception of food: Development of categories of accepted and rejected substances. *Journal of Nutrition Education, 18,* 75–81.

Rubin, D. C., & Bernsten, D. (2003). Life scripts help to maintain autobiographical memories of highly positive, but not highly negative, events. *Memory & Cognition, 31,* 1–14.

Rubin, D. C., & Schulkind, M. D. (1997). The distribution of autobiographical memory across the lifespan. *Memory & Cognition, 25,* 859–866.

Rubinsky, H., Eckerman, D., Rubinsky, E., & Hoover, C. (1987). Early-phase physiological response patterns to psychosexual stimuli: Comparisons of male and female patterns. *Archives of Sexual Behavior, 16,* 45–55.

Ruble, D. N., Balaban, T., & Cooper, J. (1981). Gender constancy and the effects of sex-typed televised toy commercials. *Child Development, 52,* 667–673.

Rudman, L. A., & Borgida, E. (1995). The afterglow of construct accessibility: The behavioral consequences of priming men to view women as sexual objects. *Journal of Experimental Social Psychology, 31,* 493–517.

Rumbaugh, D. M. (Ed.). (1977). *Language learning by a chimpanzee: The Lana project.* New York: Academic Press.

Rushton, J. P. (2000). *Race, evolution, and behavior: A life-history perspective* (3rd ed.). Port Huron, MI: Charles Darwin Research Institute.

Russell, J. A. (1994). Is there universal recognition of emotion from facial expression? A review of the cross-cultural studies. *Psychological Bulletin, 115,* 102–141.

Russell, J. A. (2003). Core affect and the psychological construction of emotion. *Psychological Review, 110,* 145–172.

Russell, J. A., Bachorowski, J., & Fernandez-Dols, J. (2003). Facial and vocal expressions of emotion. *Annual Review of Psychology, 54,* 329–349.

Ryan, K. M. (2004). Further evidence for a cognitive component of rape. *Aggression & Violent Behavior, 9,* 579–604.

Ryan, R. M., & Deci, E. L. (2000). Intrinsic and extrinsic motivations: Classic definitions and new directions. *Contemporary Educational Psychology, 25,* 54–67.

Ryckman, R. M. (2004). *Theories of personality* (8th ed.). Belmont, CA: Wadsworth.

Ryckman, R. M. (2008). *Theories of personality* (9th ed.). Belmont, CA: Wadsworth.

Saab, C. Y., & Willis, W. D. (2003). The cerebellum: Organization, functions, and its role in nociception. *Brain Research-Brain Research Reviews, 42,* 85–95.

Sable, P. (2004). Attachment, ethology, and psychotherapy. *Attachment & Human Development, 6,* 3–19.

Sackett, P. R., Hardison, C. M., & Cullen, M. J. (2004). On interpreting stereotype threat as accounting for African American-White differences on cognitive tests. *American Psychologist, 59,* 7–13.

Sacks, O. (1985). *The man who mistook his wife for a hat and other clinical tales.* New York: Summit Books.

Sagvolden, T., & Sergeant, J. A. (1998). Attention deficit/hyperactivity disorder: From brain dysfunctions to behaviour. *Behavioural Brain Research, 94,* 1–10.

Sakai, F., Stirling Meyer, J., Karacan, I., Yamaguchi, F., & Yamamoto, M. (1979). Narcolepsy: Regional cerebral blood flow during sleep and wakefulness. *Neurology, 29,* 61–67.

Sala, S. D., & Young, A. W. (2003). Quaglino's 1867 case of prosopagnosia. *Cortex, 39,* 533–540.

Salovey, P., & Mayer, J. D. (1990). Emotional intelligence. *Imagination, cognition, and personality, 9,* 185–211.

Salthouse, T. A. (1994). The nature of the influence of speed on adult age differences in cognition. *Developmental Psychology, 30,* 240–259.

Saltzstein, H. D. (Ed.). (1997). *Culture as a context for moral development: New perspectives on the particular and the universal.* San Francisco: Jossey-Bass.

Sameroff, A. J., Seifer, R., Baldwin, A., & Baldwin, C. (1993). Stability of intelligence from preschool to adolescence: The influence of social and family risk factors. *Child Development, 64,* 80–97.

Sampson, S. M., Solvason, H. B., & Husain, M. M. (2007). Envisioning transcranial magnetic stimulation (TMS) as a clinical treatment option for depression. *Psychiatric Annals, 37,* 189–196.

Sanders, R. J. (1989). Sentence comprehension following agenesis of the corpus callosum. *Brain and Language, 37,* 59–72.

Sanson, A., & Di Muccio, C. (1993). The influence of aggressive and neutral cartoons and toys on the behaviour of preschool children. *Australian Psychologist, 28,* 93–99.

Santarcangelo, E. L., & Sebastiani, L. (2004). Hypnotizability as an adaptive trait. *Contemporary Hypnosis, 21,* 3–13.

Sanz, J., Sanchez-Bernados, M. L., & Avia, M. D. (1996). Self-monitoring and the prediction of one's own and others' personality test scores. *European Journal of Personality, 10,* 173–184.

Sar, V., Akyuz, G., & Dogan, O. (2007). Prevalence of dissociative identity disorder among women in the general population. *Psychiatry Research, 149,* 169–176.

Sarbin, T. R., & Coe, W. C. (1972). *Hypnosis: A social psychological analysis of influence communication.* New York: Holt, Rinehart & Winston.

Saron, C. D., & Davidson, R. J. (1989). Visual evoked potential measures of interhemispheric transfer times in humans. *Behavioral Neuroscience, 103,* 1115–1138.

Saucier, D. A., & Cain, M. E. (2006). The foundations of attitudes about animal research. *Ethics & Behavior, 16,* 117–133.

Savage-Rumbaugh, S., McDonald, D., Sevcik, R., Hopkins, W., & Rupert, E. (1986). Spontaneous symbol acquisition and communicative use by pygmie chimpanzees. *Journal of Experimental Psychology: General, 115,* 211–235.

Savage-Rumbaugh, S., Murphy, J., Sevcik, R., Brakke, K., Williams, S., & Rumbaugh, D. M. (1993). Language comrephension in ape and child. *Monographs of the Society for Research in Child Development, 58* (3–4, Serial No. 233).

Savin-Williams, R. C. (2006). Who's gay? Does it matter? *Current Directions in Psychological Science, 15,* 40–44.

Scarborough, E., & Furumoto, L. (1987). *Untold lives: The first generation of American women psychologists.* New York: Columbia University Press.

Scarr, S., & Weinberg, R. A. (1976). IQ test performance of Black children adopted by White families. *American Psychologist, 31,* 726–739.

Schachter, S., & Gross, L. (1968). Manipulated time and eating behavior. *Journal of Personality and Social Psychology, 10,* 98–106.

Schachter, S., & Singer, J. E. (1962). Cognitive, social, and physiological determinants of emotional state. *Psychological Review, 69,* 379–399.

Schacter, D. L. (2001). *The seven sins of memory.* Boston, MA: Houghton Mifflin.

Schacter, D. L., Gallo, D. A., & Kensinger, E. A. (2007). The cognitive neuroscience of implicit and false memories: Perspectives on processing specificity. In J. S. Nairne (Ed.), *The foundations of remembering: Essays in honor of Henry L. Roediger, III.* New York: Psychology Press.

Schachter, S. (1971). *Emotion, obesity, and crime.* New York: Academic Press.

Schaie, K. W. (1983). The Seattle Longitudinal Study: A twenty-one-year exploration of psychometric intelligence in adulthood. In K. W. Schaie (Ed.), *Longitudinal studies of adult psychological development.* New York: Guilford.

Schaie, K. W. (1989). The hazards of cognitive aging. *Gerontologist, 29,* 484–493.

Schaie, K. W. (1993). The Seattle Longitudinal Studies of adult intelligence. *Current Directions in Psychological Science, 2,* 171–175.

Schaie, K. W. (1998). The Seattle Longitudinal Studies of adult intelligence. In M. P. Lawton, & T. A. Salthouse (Eds.), *Essential papers on the psychology of aging. Essential papers in psychoanalysis.* New York: New York University Press.

Schaie, K. W. (2005). *Developmental influences on adult intelligence: The Seattle longitudinal study.* New York, NY: Oxford University Press.

Schall, J. D. (2004). On building a bridge between brain and behavior. *Annual Review of Psychology, 55,* 23–50.

Schalock, R. L., Buntinz, W., Borthwick-Duffy, S., Luckasson, R., Snell, M., Tassé, M. J., & Wehmeyer, M. (2007). *User's guide: Mental retardation* (10th ed.). Washington, DC: American Association on Intellectual and Developmental Disabilities.

Scheich, H., & Zuschratter, W. (1995). Mapping of stimulus features and meaning in gerbil auditory cortex with 2–deoxyglucose and c-fos antibodies. *Behavioural Brain Research, 66,* 195–205.

Scheier, M. F., & Carver, C. S. (1993). On the power of positive thinking: The benefits of being optimistic. *Current Directions in Psychological Science, 2,* 26–30.

Scheier, M. F., Matthews, K. A., Owens, J. F., Magovern, G. J., Sr., Lefebvre, R. C., Abbott, R. A., & Carver, C. S. (1989). Dispositional optimism and recovery from coronary artery bypass surgery: The beneficial effects on physical and psychological well-being. *Journal of Personality and Social Psychology, 57,* 1024–1040.

Schellenberg, E. G. (2004). Music lessons enhance IQ. *Psychological Science, 15,* 511–514.

Schirmer, A., & Kotz, S. A. (2006). Beyond the right hemisphere: Brain mechanisms mediating vocal emotional processing. *Trends in Cognitive Sciences, 10,* 24–30.

Schleifer, S. J., Keller, S. E., Meyerson, A. T., Raskin, M. J., Davis, K. L., & Stein, M. (1983). Suppression of lymphocyte stimulation following bereavement. *Journal of the American Medical Association, 250,* 374.

Schlenker, B. R., & Forsyth, D. R. (1977). On the ethics of psychological research. *Journal of Experimental Social Psychology, 13,* 369–396.

Schmidt, F. L., & Hunter, J. E. (1993). Tacit knowledge, practical intelligence, general mental ability, and job knowledge. *Current Directions in Psychological Science, 2,* 8–9.

Schmidt, S. R. (1991). Can we have a distinctive theory of memory? *Memory & Cognition, 19,* 523–542.

Schmitt, D. P. (2003). Universal sex differences in the desire for sexual variety: Tests from 52 nations, 6 continents, and 13 islands. *Journal of Personality and Social Psychology, 85,* 85–104.

Schmuckler, M. A. (1996). Development of visually-guided locomotion: Barrier crossing by toddlers. *Ecological Psychology, 8,* 209–236.

Schneider, F., & Deldin, P. J. (2001). Genetics and schizophrenia. In P. B. Sutker & H. E. Adams (Eds.), *Comprehensive handbook of psychopathology* (3rd ed.). New York: Kluwer Academic/Plenum.

Schneider, S. G., Taylor, S. E., Hammen, C., Kemeny, M. E., & Dudley, J. (1991). Factors influencing suicide intent in gay and bisexual suicide ideators: Differing models for men with and without human immunodeficiency virus. *Journal of Personality and Social Psychology, 61,* 776–788.

Schneiderman, N., Antoni, M. H., Saab, P. G., & Ironson, G. (2001). Health psychology: Psychosocial and biobehavioral aspects of chronic disease management. *Annual Review of Psychology, 52,* 555–580.

Scholte, R., & De Bruyn, E. (2004). Comparison of the giant three and the big five in early adolescents. *Personality and Individual Differences, 36,* 1353–1371.

Schreiber, F. (1973). *Sybil.* New York: Warner Books.

Schuster, M. A., Stein, B. D., Jaycox, L. H., Collins, R. L., Marshall, G. N., Elliott, M. N., Zhou, A. J., Kanouse, D. E., Morrison, J. L., & Berry, S. H. (2001). A national survey of stress reactions after the September 11, 2001, terrorist attacks. *New England Journal of Medicine, 345,* 1507–1512.

Schwartz, B. (1990). The creation and destruction of value. *American Psychologist, 45,* 7–15.

Schwartz, M. W. (2006). Central nervous system regulation of food intake. *Obesity, 14,* 1S–8S.

Schwarz, N., & Strack, F. (1998). Reports of subjective well-being: Judgmental processes and their methodological implications. In D. Kahneman et al. (Eds.), *Hedonic psychology: Scientific perspectives on enjoyment, suffering, and well-being.* New York: Cambridge University Press.

Sclafani, A. (1994). Eating rates in normal and hypothalamic hyperphagic rats. *Physiology and Behavior, 55,* 489–494.

Scott, T. R., Plata-Salamn, C. R., & Smith-Swintosky, V. L. (1994). Gustatory neural coding in the monkey cortex: The quality of saltiness. *Journal of Neurophysiology, 71,* 1692–1701.

Sedikides, C., Campbell, W. K., Reeder, G. D., & Elliot, A. J. (1998). The self-serving bias in relational context. *Journal of Personality & Social Psychology, 74,* 378–386.

Seegert, C. R. (2003). Token economies and incentive programs: Behavioral improvement in mental health inmates housed in state prisons. *Behavior Therapist, 208,* 210–211.

Seeman, T. E., Dublin, L. F., & Seeman, M. (2003). Religiosity/spirituality and health: A critical review of the evidence for biological pathways. *American Psychologist, 58,* 53–63.

Segall, M. H., Dasen, P. R., Berry, J. W., & Poortinga, Y. (1990). *Human behavior in global perspective.* New York: Pergamon.

Sekular, R., & Blake, R. (1990). *Perception* (2nd ed.). New York: McGraw-Hill.

Seligman, M. E. P. (1975). *Helplessness: On depression, development, and death.* San Francisco: Freeman.

Selye, H. (1936). A syndrome produced by diverse nocuous agents. *Nature, 138,* 32.

Selye, H. (1952). *The story of the adaptation syndrome.* Montreal: Acta.

Selye, H. (1974). *Stress without distress.* Philadelphia: Lippincott.

Sepple, C. P., & Read, N. W. (1989). Gastrointestinal correlates of the development of hunger in man. *Appetite, 13,* 183–191.

Shaffer, D. R. (2007). *Developmental psychology: Childhood and adolescence* (7th ed.). Belmont, CA: Wadsworth.

Shapiro, A. K. (1960). A contribution to a history of the placebo effect. *Behavioral Science, 5,* 109–135.

Sharma, K. N., Anand, B. K., Due, S., & Singh, B. (1961). Role of stomach in regulation of activities of hypothalamic feeding centers. *American Journal of Physiology, 201,* 593–598.

Shaywitz, S. E., Fletcher, J. M., & Shaywitz, B. A. (1994). Issues in the definition and classification of attention deficit disorder. *Topics in Language Disorders, 14,* 1–25.

Shearer, B. (2004). Multiple intelligences theory after 20 years. *Teachers College Record, 106,* 2–16.

Shepard, G. M. (2006). Smell images and the flavour system in the human brain. *Nature, 444,* 316–321.

Sher, L. (2004). Hypothalamic-pituitary-adrenal function and preventing major depressive episodes. *Canadian Journal of Psychiatry, 49,* 574–575.

Shields, S. A. (1975). Functionalism, Darwinism, and the psychology of women: A study in social myth. *American Psychologist, 30,* 739–754.

Shiffrin, R. M., & Schneider, W. (1977). Controlled and automatic human information processing II: Perceptual learning, automatic attending, and a general theory. *Psychological Review, 84,* 127–190.

Shirley, M. M. (1933). *The first two years: A study of 25 babies. Vol. 1: Postural and locomotor development.* Minneapolis: University of Minnesota Press.

Shirley, S. G., & Persaud, K. C. (1990). The biochemistry of vertebrate olfaction and taste. *Seminars in the Neurosciences, 2,* 59–68.

Shweder, R. A., Mahapatra, M., & Miller, J. G. (1990). Culture and moral development. In J. W. Stigler, R. A. Shweder, & G. Herdt (Eds.), *Cultural psychology.* New York: Cambridge University Press.

Siegel, J. M. (1990). Stressful life events and use of physician services among the elderly: The moderating role of pet ownership. *Journal of Personality and Social Psychology, 58,* 1081–1086.

Siegler, R. S. (1994). Cognitive variability: A key to understanding cognitive development. *Psychological Science, 3,* 1–5.

Siegler, R. S. (1996). *Children's thinking: Beyond the immaculate transition.* New York: Oxford University Press.

Sigelman, C. K., & Rider, E. A. (2006). *Lifespan human development* (5th ed.). Belmont, CA: Wadsworth.

Sigmundson, H. K. (1994). Pharmacotherapy of schizophrenia: A review. *Canadian Journal of Psychiatry, 39,* 570–575.

Silverstein, B., Perdue, L., Peterson, B., & Kelly, E. (1986). The role of the mass media in promoting a thin standard of bodily attractiveness for women. *Sex Roles, 14,* 519–532.

Simms, L. J. (2007). The big seven model of personality and its relevance to personality pathology. *Journal of Personality, 75,* 65–94.

Sim-Selley, L. J. (2003). Regulation of cannabinoid CB1 receptors in the central nervous system by chronic cannabinoids. *Critical Reviews in Neurobiology, 15,* 91–119.

Sincich, L. C., & Horton, J. C. (2005). The circuitry of V1 and V2: Integration of color, form, and motion. *Annual Review of Neuroscience, 28,* 303–326.

Siqueland, E. R., & DeLucia, C. A. (1969). Visual reinforcement of nonnutritive sucking in human infants. *Science, 165,* 1144–1146.

Skinner, B. F. (1938). *The behavior of organisms: An experimental analysis.* New York: Appleton-Century.

Skinner, B. F. (1948). "Superstition" in the pigeon. *Journal of Experimental Psychology, 38,* 168–172.

Skinner, B. F. (1969). *Contingencies of reinforcement: A theoretical analysis.* New York: Appleton-Century-Crofts.

Slater, A., Von der Schulenburg, C., Brown, E., Badenoch, M., Butterworth, G., Parsons, S., & Samuels, C. (1998). Newborn infants prefer attractive faces. *Infant Behavior & Development, 21,* 345–354.

Slick, D. J., Hopp, G., Strauss, G., & Spellacy, F. J. (1996). Victoria Symptom Validity Test: Efficiency for detecting feigned memory impairment and relationship to neuropsychological tests and MMPI 2 validity scales. *Journal of Experimental and Clinical Neuropsychology, 18,* 911–922.

Sloane, R. B., Staples, F. R., Cristol, A. H., Yorkston, N. J., & Whipple, K. (1975). *Psychotherapy versus behavior therapy.* Cambridge, MA: Harvard University Press.

Slovic, P., Fischoff, B., & Lichtenstein, S. (1982). Facts versus fears: Understanding perceived risk. In D. Kahneman, P. Slovic, & A. Tversky (Eds.), *Judgment under uncertainty: Heuristics and biases.* Cambridge, U.K.: Cambridge University Press.

Smiley, P. A., & Dweck, C. S. (1994). Individual differences in achievement goals among young children. *Child Development, 65,* 1723–1743.

Smith, B. N., Kerr, N. A., Markus, M. J., & Stasson, M. F. (2001). Individual differences in social loafing: Need for cognition as a motivator in collective performance. *Group Dynamics: Theory, Research, & Practice, 5,* 150–158.

Smith, D. (2003). Five principles for research ethics. *Monitor on Psychology, 34,* 56–60.

Smith, D. V., & Margolskee, R. F. (2001, March). Making sense of taste. *Scientific American,* 32–39.

Smith, E. E. (1989). Concepts and induction. In M. Posner (Ed.), *Foundations of cognitive science.* Cambridge, MA: MIT Press.

Smith, E. E., Patalano, A. L., & Jonides, J. (1998). Alternative strategies of categorization. *Cognition, 65,* 167–196.

Smith, E. R., & Semin, G. R. (2007). Situated social cognition. *Current Directions in Psychological Science, 16,* 132–135.

Smith, E. R., & Zárate, M. A. (1992). Exemplar-based model of social judgment. *Psychological Review, 99,* 3–21.

Smith, F. J., & Campfield, L. A. (1993). Meal initiation occurs after experimental induction of transient declines in blood glucose. *American Journal of Physiology, 265,* R1423–R1429.

Smith, M. L., & Glass, G. V. (1977). Meta-analysis of psychotherapy outcome studies. *American Psychologist, 32,* 752–760.

Smith, M. L., Glass, G. V., & Miller, T. I. (1980). *The benefits of psychotherapy.* Baltimore, MD: Johns Hopkins University Press.

Smith, T. W. (2006). Personality as risk and resilience in physical health. *Current Directions in Psychological Science, 15,* 227–231.

Snarey, J. R. (1995). In a communitarian voice: The sociological expansion of Kohlbergian theory, research, and practice. In W. M. Kurtines & J. L. Gewirtz (Eds.), *Moral development: An introduction.* Boston: Allyn & Bacon.

Snowden, P. T., & Schyns, P. G. (2006). Channel surfing in the visual brain. *Trends in Cognitive Sciences, 10,* 538–545.

Snyder, C. R. (1989). Reality negotiation: From excuses to hope and beyond. Self-illusions: When are they adaptive? [Special issue] *Journal of Social and Clinical Psychology, 8,* 130–157.

Snyder, F. (1967). In quest of dreaming. In H. A. Witkin & H. B. Lewis (Eds.), *Experimental studies of dreaming.* New York: Random House.

Snyder, M. (1974). The self-monitoring of expressive behavior. *Journal of Personality and Social Psychology, 30,* 526–537.

Snyder, M. (1987). *Public appearances/private realities: The psychology of self-monitoring.* New York: Freeman.

Snyder, M. (1995). Self-monitoring: Public appearances versus private reality. In G. G. Brannigan & M. R. Merrens (Eds.), *The social psychologists: Research adventures.* New York: McGraw Hill.

Snyder, M., Tanke, E. D., & Berscheid, E. (1977). Social perception and interpersonal behavior: On the self-fulfilling nature of social stereotypes. *Journal of Personality and Social Psychology, 35,* 656–666.

Snyder, S. H. (1976). The dopamine hypothesis of schizophrenia: Focus on the dopamine receptor. *American Journal of Psychiatry, 133,* 197–202.

Society for Personality Assessment (2005). The status of the Rorschach in clinical and forensic practice: An official statement by the Board of Trustees of the Society for Personality Assessment. *Journal of Personality Assessment, 85,* 219–237.

Sommers, S. R. (2006). On racial diversity and group decision-making: Identifying multiple effects of racial composition on jury deliberations. *Journal of Personality and Social Psychology, 90,* 597–612.

Soussignan, R. (2002). Duchenne smile, emotional experience, and autonomic reactivity: A test of the facial feedback hypothesis. *Emotion, 2,* 52–74.

Spanos, N. P. (1982). Hypnotic behavior: A cognitive, social psychological perspective. *Research Communications in Psychology, Psychiatry, and Behavior, 7,* 199–213.

Spanos, N. P. (1986). Hypnotic behavior: A social psychological interpretation of amnesia, analgesia, and "trance logic." *The Behavioral and Brain Sciences, 9,* 449–502.

Spanos, N. P. (1996). *Multiple identities and false memories: A sociocognitive perspective.* Washington, DC: American Psychological Association.

Spanos, N. P., Weeks, J. R., & Bertrand, L. D. (1985). Multiple personality: A social psychological perspective. *Journal of Abnormal Psychology, 92,* 362–376.

Spearman, C. (1904). "General intelligence," objectively determined and measured. *American Journal of Psychology, 15,* 201–293.

Speigel, D. (1995). Hypnosis and suggestion. In D. L. Schacter (Ed.), *Memory distortion.* Cambridge, MA: Harvard University Press.

Spelke, E. S., Breinlinger, K., Macomber, J., & Jacobson, K. (1992). Origins of knowledge. *Psychological Review, 99,* 605–632.

Sperling, G. (1960). The information available in brief visual presentations. *Psychological Monographs, 74*(Whole No. 48).

Spiegel, D. (1998). Social psychological theories cannot completely account for hypnosis: The record was never crooked. *American Journal of Clinical Hypnosis, 41*, 158–161.

Spiegel, D. (2004). Commentary. *Journal of Psychosomatic Research, 57*, 133–135.

Spiegel, D., Bloom, J. R., Kramer, H. C., & Gotheil, E. (1989). Effect of psychosocial treatment on survival of patients with metastatic breast cancer. *Lancet, 14*, 888–891.

Spitz, R. A. (1945). Hospitalism: An inquiry into the genesis of psychiatric conditions in early childhood. *Psychoanalytic Study of the Child, 1*, 53–74.

Spitzer, R. L. (1975). On pseudoscience in science, logic in remission, and psychiatric diagnosis: A critique of Rosenhan's "On being sane in insane places." *Journal of Abnormal Psychology, 84*, 442–452.

Springer, S. P., & Deutsch, G. (1989). *Left brain, right brain.* (3rd ed.). New York: Freeman.

Squire, L. R. (1992). Memory and the hippocampus: A synthesis of findings with rats, monkeys, and humans. *Psychological Review, 99*, 195–231.

Staddon, J. E. R., & Simmelhag, V. L. (1971). The "superstition" experiment: A reexamination of its implications for the principles of adaptive behavior. *Psychological Review, 78*, 3–43.

Stanton, A. L., Revenson, T. A., & Tennen, H. (2007). Health psychology: Psychological adjustment to chronic disease. *Annual Review of Psychology, 58*, 565–592.

Steblay, N. M., & Bothwell, R. K. (1994). Evidence for hypnotically refreshed testimony: The view from the laboratory. *Law and Human Behavior, 18*, 635–651.

Steele, C. M., & Aronson, J. A. (1995). Stereotype threat and the intellectual test performance of African Americans. *Journal of Personality and Social Psychology, 69*, 797–811.

Steele, C. M., & Aronson, J. A. (2004). Stereotype threat does not live by Steele and Aronson (1995) alone. *American Psychologist, 59*, 47–48.

Steele, K. M., Bass, K. E., & Cook, M. D. (1999). The mystery of the Mozart effect: Failure to replicate. *Psychological Science, 10*, 366–369.

Steinberg, L., & Morris, A. S. (2001). Adolescent development. *Annual Review of Psychology, 52*, 83–100.

Steiner, J. E. (1977). Facial expressions of the neonate infant indicating the hedonics of food-related chemical stimuli. In J. M. Weiffenbach (Ed.), *Taste and development.* Bethesda, MD: Department of Health, Education, and Welfare.

Sternberg, R. J. (1985). *Beyond IQ: A triarchic theory of human intelligence.* New York: Cambridge University Press.

Sternberg, R. J. (1986). A triangular theory of love. *Psychological Review, 93*, 119–135.

Sternberg, R. J. (1988). *The triarchic theory of mind: A new theory of human intelligence.* New York: Viking Press.

Sternberg, R. J. (1999). *Cupid's arrow: The course of love through time.* New York: Cambridge University Press.

Sternberg, R. J. (2003). Intelligence. In D. K. Freedheim (Ed.) *Handbook of psychology. Vol. 1: History of psychology,* pp. 135–156. New York: Wiley.

Sternberg, R. J., & Grajek, S. (1984). The nature of love. *Journal of Personality and Social Psychology, 47*, 312–329.

Sternberg, R. J., & Hedlund, J. (2002). Practical intelligence, g, and work psychology. *Human Performance, 15*, 143–160.

Sternberg, R. J., & Kaufman, J. C. (1998). Human abilities. *Annual Review of Psychology, 49*, 479–502.

Sternberg, R. J., and the Rainbow Project Collaborators. (2006). The Rainbow Project: Enhancing the SAT through assessments of analytical, practical, and creative skills. *Intelligence, 34*, 321–350.

Sternberg, R. J., & Wagner, R. K. (1993). The g-ocentric view of intelligence and job performance is wrong. *Current Directions in Psychological Science, 2*, 1–5.

Stevens, J. R., & Hauser, M. D. (2004). Why be nice? Psychological constraints on the evolution of cooperation. *Trends in Cognitive Sciences, 8*, 60–65.

Stevens, S. S. (1939). Psychology and the science of science. *Psychological Bulletin, 36*, 221–263.

Stewart, A. J., & McDermott, C. (2004). Gender in psychology. *Annual Review of Psychology, 55*, 519–544.

Stewart, D. D., & Stasser, G. (1995). Expert role assignment and information sampling during collective recall and decision making. *Journal of Personality & Social Psychology, 69*, 619–628.

Stewart, S.T. (2004). Do out-of-pocket health expenditures rise with age among older Americans? *Gerontologist, 44*, 48–57.

Stewart, T. L., Doan, K. A., Gingrich, B. E., & Smith, E. R. (1998). The actor as context for social judgments: Effects of prior impressions and stereotypes. *Journal of Personality and Social Psychology, 75*, 1132–1154.

Stinson, F. S., Dawson, D. A., Chou, S. P., Smith, S., Goldstein, R. B., Ruan, W. J., & Grant, B. F. (2007). The epidemiology of DSM-IV specific phobia in the USA: results from the National Epidemiologic Survey on Alcohol and Related Conditions. *Psychological Medicine, 37*, 1047–1059.

Stompe, T., Ritter, R., & Schanda, H. (2007). Catatonia as a subtype of schizophrenia. *Psychiatric Annals, 37*, 31–37.

Strassman, R. J. (1992). Human hallucinogen interactions with drugs affecting serotonergic neurotransmission. *Neuropsychopharmacology, 7*, 241–243.

Strayer, D. L., & Drews, F. A. (2007). Cell-phone-induced driver distraction. *Psychological Science, 16*, 128–131.

Strayer, D. L., & Johnston, W. A. (2001). Driven to distraction: Dual-task studies of simulated driving and conversing on a cellular telephone. *Psychological Science, 6*, 462–466.

Stricker, L. J., Rock, D. A., & Burton, N. W. (1996). Using the SAT and high school record in academic guidance. *Educational and Psychological Measurement, 56*, 626–641.

Strombeck, R., & Levy, J. A. (1998). Educational strategies and interventions targeting adults age 50 and older for HIV/AIDS prevention. *Research on Aging, 20*, 912–936.

Sue, S., Zane, N., & Young, K. (1994). Research on psychotherapy with culturally diverse populations. In A. E. Bergin &

S. L. Garfield (Eds.), *Handbook of psychotherapy and behavior change* (4th ed.). New York: Wiley.

Sufta, K. J., & Price, D. D. (2002). Gate control theory reconsidered. *Brain & Mind, 3,* 277–290.

Susman, E. J., Dorn, L. D., & Schiefelbein, V. L. (2003). Puberty, sexuality, and health. In R. M. Lerner, M. A. Easterbrooks, & J. Mistry (Eds.), *Handbook of psychology. Vol. 6: Developmental psychology* (pp. 395–424). New York: Wiley.

Sussman, J. R., & Levitt, B. (1989). *Before you conceive: The complete pregnancy guide.* New York: Bantam Books.

Swan, G. E., Hudmon, K. S., & Khroyan, T. V. (2003). Tobacco dependence. In A. M. Nezu, C. M. Nezu, & P. A. Gellar (Eds.), *Handbook of psychology: Health psychology* (Vol. 9, pp. 147–168). New York: Wiley.

Swinson, R. P. (2005). Social anxiety disorder. *The Canadian Journal of Psychiatry, 50,* 305–307.

Symons, D. (1992). On the use and misuse of Darwinism in the study of human behavior. In J. H. Barkow, L. Cosmides, & J. Tooby (Eds.), *The adapted mind.* New York: Oxford University Press.

Szasz, T. (1961). *The myth of mental illness: Foundations of a theory of personal conduct.* New York: Hoeber-Harper.

Szasz, T. (2000). Second commentary on "Aristotle's function argument." *Philosophy, Psychiatry, & Psychology, 7,* 3–16.

Tamm, L., Menon, V., & Reiss, A. (2006). Parietal attentional system abberations during target detection in adolescents with attention deficit hyperactivity disorder: Event-related fMRI evidence. *Amercian Journal of Psychiatry, 163,* 1033–1043.

Tanford, S., & Penrod, S. (1984). Social influence model: A formal integration of research on majority and minority influence processes. *Psychological Bulletin, 95,* 189–225.

Tanner, J. M. (1990). *Foetus into man: Physical growth from conception to maturity* (Rev. ed.). Cambridge, MA: Harvard University Press.

Tarlowski, A. (2006). If it's an animal it has axons: Experience and culture in preschool children's reasoning about animates. *Cognitive development, 21,* 249–265.

Tateyama, M., Asai, M., Hashimoto, M., Bartels, M., & Kasper, S. (1998). Transcultural study of schizophrenic delusions: Tokyo versus Vienna versus Tuebingen (Germany). *Psychopathology, 31,* 59–68.

Tavris, C. (1989). *Anger: The misunderstood emotion* (Rev. ed.). New York: Touchstone Books/Simon & Schuster.

Taylor, F. W. (1911). *Principles of scientific management.* New York: Harper.

Taylor, H. (1997). The very different methods used to conduct telephone surveys of the public. *Journal of the Marketing Research Society, 39,* 421–432.

Taylor, S .E. (2007). Social support. In H. S. Friedman & R. C. Silver (Eds.), *Foundations of health psychology.* New York: Oxford University Press.

Taylor, S. E. (2002). *The tending instinct: Women, men, and the biology of relationships.* New York: Henry Holt.

Taylor, S. E. (2006). Tend and befriend: Biobehavioral bases of affiliation under stress. *Current Directions in Psychological Science, 15,* 273–276.

Teeter, J. H., & Brand, J. G. (1987). Peripheral mechanisms of gustation: Physiology and biochemistry. In T. E. Finger & W. L. Silver (Eds.), *Neurobiology of taste and smell.* New York: Wiley.

Tellegen, A., Lykken, D. T., Bouchard, T. J., Jr., Wilcox, K. J., Segal, N. L., & Rich, S. (1988). Personality similarity in twins reared apart and together. *Journal of Personality and Social Psychology, 54,* 1031–1039.

Tennes, K., & Kreye, M. (1985). Children's adrenocortical responses to classroom activities and tests in elementary school. *Psychosomatic Medicine, 47,* 451–460.

Terman, L. M. (1925). *Mental and physical traits of a thousand gifted children.* Stanford, CA: Stanford University Press.

Terman, L. M. (1954). The discovery and encouragement of exceptional talent. *American Psychologist, 9,* 221–238.

Terman, L. M., & Ogden, M. (1947). *Genetic studies of genius. Vol. 5. The gifted child grows up.* Stanford, CA: Stanford University Press.

Terrace, H. S. (1986). *Nim: A chimpanzee who learned sign language.* New York: Columbia University Press.

Tesser, A. (1993). The importance of heritability in psychological research: The case of attitudes. *Psychological Review, 100,* 129–142.

Thigpen, C. H., & Cleckley, H. A. (1957). *Three faces of Eve.* New York: McGraw-Hill.

Thomas, A., & Chess, S. (1977). *Temperament and development.* New York: Bruner/Mazel.

Thompson, S. K. (1975). Gender labels and early sex-role development. *Child Development, 46,* 339–347.

Thompson, W. F., Schellenberg, E. G., & Husain, G. (2001). Arousal, mood, and the Mozart effect. *Psychological Science, 12,* 248–251.

Thoresen, C. E., & Powell, L. H. (1992). Type A behavior pattern: New perspectives on theory, assessment and intervention. *Journal of Consulting and Clinical Psychology, 60,* 595–604.

Thorndike, E. L. (1898). Animal intelligence: An experimental study of the associative processes in animals. *Psychological Review, Monograph Supplements, 2* (Serial No. 8).

Thorndike, E. L. (1911). *Animal intelligence: Experimental studies.* New York: Macmillan.

Thorndike, E. L. (1914). *The psychology of learning.* New York: Teacher's College.

Thornhill, R., Gangestad, S. W., Miller, R., Scheyd, G., McCollough, J. K., & Frankin, M. (2003). Major histocompatibility complex genes, symmetry, and body scent attractiveness in men and women. *Behavioral Ecology, 14,* 668–678.

Thurstone, L. L. (1938). *Primary mental abilities.* Chicago: University of Chicago Press.

Tienari, P., Wahlberg, K., & Wynne, L. (2006). Finnish adoption study of schizophrenia: Implications for family interventions. *Family, Systems, & Health, 24,* 442–451.

Tiffany, S. T., Cox, L. S., & Elash, C. A. (2000). Effects of transdermal nicotine patches on abstinence-induced and cue-elicited craving in cigarette smokers. *Journal of Consulting & Clinical Psychology, 68,* 233–240.

Timberlake, W., & Silva, F. J. (1994). Observation of behavior, inference of function, and the study of learning. *Psychonomic Bulletin and Review, 1,* 73–88.

Tinbergen, N. (1951). *The study of instinct.* London: Oxford University Press.

Titchener, E. B. (1899). Structural and functional psychology. *Philosophical Review, 8,* 290–299.

Tolman, C. W. (1968). The role of the companion in social facilitation of animal behavior. In E. C. Simmel, R. A. Hoppe, & G. A. Milton (Eds.), *Social facilitation and imitative behavior.* Boston: Allyn & Bacon.

Tomkins, S. S. (1962). *Affect, imagery, and conciousness* (Vol. 1). New York: Springer.

Tomlinson-Keasey, C., & Little, T. D. (1990). Predicting educational attainment, occupational achievement, intellectual skill, and personal adjustment among gifted men and women. *Journal of Educational Psychology, 82,* 442–455.

Torrance, E. P. (1981). Empirical validation of criterion-referenced indicators of creative ability through a longitudinal study. *Creative Child and Adult Quarterly, 6,* 136–140.

Tourangeau, R. (2004). Survey research and societal change. *Annual Review of Psychology, 55,* 775–801.

Towler, G. (1986). From zero to one hundred: Coaction in a natural setting. *Perceptual and Motor Skills, 62,* 377–378.

Trafimow, D., Triandis, H. C., & Goto, S. G. (1991). Some tests of the distinction between the private self and the collective self. *Journal of Personality and Social Psychology, 60,* 649–655.

Travis, F., & Wallace, R. K. (1999). Autonomic and EEG patterns during eyes-closed rest and transcental mediation (TM) practice: The basis for a neural model of TM practice. *Consciousness and Cognition, 8,* 302–318.

Treiman, R. A., Clifton, C., Meyer, A. S., & Wurm, L. H. (2003). Language comprehension and production. In A. Healy & R. Proctor (Eds.) *Handbook of psychology. Vol. 4: Experimental psychology,* pp. 527–547. New York: Wiley.

Treisman, A. (1960). Contextual cues in selective listening. *Quarterly Journal of Experimental Psychology, 12,* 242–248.

Triplett, N. (1898). The dynamogenic factors in pacemaking and competition. *American Journal of Psychology, 9,* 507–533.

Trivers, R. (1985). *Social evolution.* Menlo Park, CA: Benjamin/ Cummings.

Trull, T. J. (2005). *Clinical psychology* (7th ed.). Belmont, CA: Wadsworth.

Trull, T. J., & McCrae, R. R. (1994). A five-factor perspective on personality disorder research. In P. T. Costa Jr. & T. A. Widiger (Eds.), *Personality disorders and the five-factor model of personality.* Washington, DC: American Psychological Association.

Trull, T. J., & Widiger, T. A. (2003). Personality disorders. In G. Stricker & T. A. Widiger (Eds.) *Handbook of psychology: Clinical psychology* (Vol. 8, pp. 149–172). New York: Wiley.

Tuckman, B. W. (1998). Using tests as an incentive to motivate procrastinators to study. *Journal of Experimental Education, 66,* 141–147.

Tulving, E. (1983). *Elements of episodic memory.* Oxford, U.K.: Oxford University Press.

Tulving, E. (2002). Episodic memory: From mind to brain. *Annual Review of Psychology, 53,* 1–25.

Tulving, E., & Pearlstone, Z. (1966). Availability versus accessibility of information in memory for words. *Journal of Verbal Learning and Verbal Behavior, 5,* 381–391.

Turati, C. (2004). Why faces are not special to newborns: An alternative account of the face preference. *Current Directions in Psychological Science, 13,* 5–8.

Turnbull, C. (1961). Some observations regarding the experiences and behavior of Manbuti pygmies. *American Journal of Psychology, 74,* 304–308.

Turner, T. J., & Ortony, A. (1992). Basic emotions: Can conflicting criteria converge? *Psychological Review, 99,* 566–571.

Tversky, A., & Kahneman, D. (1973). On the psychology of prediction. *Psychological Review, 80,* 237–251.

Tversky, A., & Kahneman, D. (1974). Decision making under uncertainty: Heuristics and biases. *Science, 185,* 1124–1131.

Tversky, A., & Kahneman, D. (1983). Extensional versus intuitive reasoning: The conjunction fallacy in probability judgment. *Psychological Review, 90,* 293–315.

Twenge, J. M., Zhang, L., & Im, C. (2004). It's beyond my control: A cross-temporal meta-analysis of increasing externality in locus of control, 1960–2002. *Personality and Social Psychology Review, 8,* 308–319.

Ulrich, R. E. (1991). Commentary: Animal rights, animal wrongs and the question of balance. *Psychological Science, 2,* 197–201.

U.S. Department of Transportation. (1998). *Transportation statistics annual report, 1998: Long-distance travel and freight, Chapter 3.* Retrieved from: www.bts.gov/publications/ transportation_statistics_annual_report/1998/.

Van Doornen, L. J., & Van Blokland, R. (1987). Serum-cholesterol: Sex-specific psychological correlates during rest and stress. *Journal of Psychosomatic Research, 31,* 239–249.

Van Houtte, M. (2004). Why boys achieve less at school than girls: The difference between boys' and girls' academic culture. *Educational Studies, 30,* 159–173.

Vandell, D. L. (2000). Parents, peer groups, and other socializing influences. *Developmental Psychology, 36,* 699–710.

Verschueven, S., Cordo, P. J., & Swinnen, S. P. (1998). Representation of wrist joint kinematics by the ensemble of muscle spindles from synergistic muscles. *Journal of Neurophysiology, 79,* 2265–2276.

Vertes, R. P., & Eastman, K. E., (2000). The case against memory consolidation in REM sleep. *Behavioral and Brain Sciences, 23,* 867–876.

Vittengl, J. R., Clark, L. A., Dunn, T. W., & Jarrett, R. B. (2007). Reducing relapse and recurrence in unipolar depression: A comparative meta-analysis of cognitive-behavioral therapy's effects. *Journal of Consulting and Clinical Psychology, 75,* 475–488.

Vitz, P. C. (1988). *Sigmund Freud's Christian unconscious.* New York: Guilford.

Vogel, G. W., Buffenstein, A., Minter, K., & Hennessey, A. (1990). Drug effects on REM sleep and on endogenous depression. *Neuroscience and Biobehavioral Reviews, 14,* 49–63.

Vokey, J. R., & Read, J. D. (1985). Subliminal messages: Between the media and the devil. *American Psychologist, 40,* 1231–1239.

von Frisch, K. (1967). *The dance language and orientation of bees.* Cambridge, MA: Belknap Press.

Vygotsky, L. S. (1978). *Mind in society: The development of higher psychological processes.* Cambridge MA: Harvard University Press.

Wagenaar, W. A. (1986). My memory: A study of autobiographical memory over six years. *Cognitive Psychology, 18,* 225–252.

Wager, T. D., & Smith, E. E. (2003). Neuroimaging studies of working memory: A meta-analysis. *Cognitive, Affective, & Behavioral Neuroscience, 3,* 255–274.

Wagner, R. K., & Sternberg, R. J. (1985). Practical intelligence in real-world pursuits: The role of tacit knowledge. *Journal of Personality and Social Psychology, 49,* 436–458.

Wahba, M. A., & Bridwell, L. G. (1976). Maslow reconsidered: A review of research on the need hierarchy theory. *Organizational Behavior and Human Performance, 15,* 212–240.

Waldman, I. D., Weinberg, R. A., & Scarr, S. (1994). Racial-group differences in IQ in the Minnesota Transracial Adoption Study: A reply to Levin and Lynn. *Intelligence, 19,* 29–44.

Walen, S. T., DiGuiseppe, R., & Dryden, W. (1992). *A practitioner's guide to rational-emotive therapy.* New York: Oxford University Press.

Walker, E., Kestler, L., Bollini, A., & Hochman, K. M. (2004). Schizophrenia: Etiology and course. *Annual Review of Psychology, 55,* 401–430.

Walker, L. J. (1989). A longitudinal study of moral reasoning. *Child Development, 60,* 157–166.

Wallhagen, M. I., Strawbridge, W., & Shema, S. (1997). *Perceived control: Mental health correlates in a population-based aging cohort.* Paper presented at the 50th Annual Scientific Meeting of the Gerontological Society of America.

Walters, J. M., & Gardner, H. (1986). The theory of multiple intelligences: Some issues and answers. In R. J. Sternberg & R. K. Wagner (Eds.), *Practical intelligence: Nature and origins of competence in the everyday world.* New York: Cambridge University Press.

Walton, G. E., & Bower, T. G. R. (1993). Newborns form "prototypes" in less than 1 minute. *Psychological Science, 4,* 203–205.

Wampold, B. E., Mondin, G. W., Moody, M., Stich, F., Benson, K., & Ahn, H. (1997). A meta-analysis of outcome studies comparing bona fide psychotherapies: Empiricially, "all must have prizes." *Psychological Bulletin, 122,* 203–215.

Washburn, M. F. (1908). *The animal mind.* New York: Macmillan.

Waterhouse, L. (2006). Multiple intelligences, the Mozart effect, and emotional intelligence: A critical review. *Educational Psychologist, 41,* 207–225.

Waters, E., Wippman, J., & Sroufe, L. A. (1979). Attachment, positive affect, and competence in the peer group: Two studies in construct validation. *Child Development, 50,* 821–829.

Watson, J. B. (1913). Psychology as a behaviorist views it. *Psychological Review, 20,* 158–177.

Watson, J. B. (1919). *Psychology from the standpoint of a behaviorist.* Philadelphia: Lippincott.

Watson, J. B. (1930). *Behaviorism.* New York: Norton.

Watson, J. B., & Rayner, R. (1920). Conditioned emotional reactions. *Journal of Experimental Psychology, 3,* 1–14.

Webb, E. J., Campbell, D. T., Schwartz, R. D., Sechrist, L., & Grove, J. B. (1981). *Nonreactive research in the social sciences.* Boston: Houghton Mifflin.

Webb, W. B. (1981). The return of consciousness. *G. Stanley Hall Lecture Series, 1,* 129–152.

Webb, W. B. (1992). *Sleep: The gentle tyrant.* Bolton, MA: Anker.

Weber, R., & Crocker, J. (1993). Cognitive processes in the revision of stereotypic beliefs. *Journal of Personality and Social Psychology, 45,* 961–977.

Wegener, D. T., & Carlston, D. E. (2005). Cognitive processes in attitude formation and change. In D. Albarracín, B. Johnson, & M. Zanna (Eds.), *The handbook of attitudes.* Hillsdale, NJ: Erlbaum.

Wegener, D. T., & Petty, R. E. (1997). The flexible correction model: The role of naive theories of bias in bais correction. *Advances in Experimental Social Psychology, 29,* 141–208.

Wegner, D. M. (1994). Ironic processes of mental control. *Psychological Review, 101,* 34–52.

Weiden, P. J. (2007). EPS profiles: The atypical antipsychotics are not all the same. *Journal of Psychiatric Practice, 13,* 13–24.

Weinberg, R. A., Scarr, S., & Waldman, I. D. (1992). The Minnesota Transracial Adoption Study: A follow-up of IQ test performance at adolescence. *Intelligence, 16,* 117–135.

Weingarten, H. P. (1983). Conditioned cues elicit feeding in sated rats: A role for learning in meal initiation. *Science, 220,* 431–433.

Weinstein, L. N., Schwartz, D. G., & Arkin, A. M. (1991). Qualitative aspects of sleep mentation. In S. J. Ellman & J. S. Antrobus (Eds.), *The mind in sleep* (2nd ed.). New York: Wiley.

Weiskrantz, L. (1992). Introduction: Dissociated issues. In A. D. Milner & M. D. Rugg (Eds.), *The neuropsychology of consciousness.* London: Academic Press.

Weiss, J. M. (1977). Psychological and behavioral influences on gastrointestinal lesions in animal models. In J. D. Maser & M. E. P. Seligman (Eds.), *Psychopathology: Experimental models.* San Francisco: Freeman.

Weiten, W. (1995). *Psychology: Themes and variations* (3rd ed.). Pacific Grove, CA: Brooks/Cole.

Weldon, M. S., & Roediger, H. L., III. (1987). Altering retrieval demands reverses the picture superiority effect. *Memory & Cognition, 15,* 269–280.

Wells, A., & Carter, K. (2006). Generalized anxiety disorder. In

A. Carr & M. McNulty (Eds.), *The handbook of adult clinical psychology: An evidence-based practice approach.* New York: Routledge/Taylor & Francis Group.

Wenner, A. (1998). Honey bee "dance language" controversy. In G. Greenberg & M. M. Haraway (Eds.), *Comparative psychology: A handbook.* New York: Garland.

Werker, J. F., & Tees, R. C. (1999). Influences on infant speech processsing: Toward a new synthesis. *Annual Review of Psychology, 50,* 509–535.

Wernicke, C. (1874). *Der Aphasische Symptomenkomplex.* Breslau, Poland: Cohn & Weigert.

Wertheimer, M. (1987). *A brief history of psychology* (3rd ed.). New York: Holt, Rinehart & Winston.

Wesnes, K. A., Ward, T., McGinty, A., & Petrini, O. (2000). The memory enhancing effects of a Ginkgo biloba/Panax ginseng combination in healthy middle-aged volunteers. *Psychopharmacology, 152,* 353–361.

Wever, E. G. (1949). *Theory of hearing.* New York: Wiley.

Wexler, M., & van Boxtel, J. (2005). Depth perception by the active observer. *Trends in Cognitive Sciences, 9,* 431–438.

Wheeler, L., & Kim, Y. (1997). What is beautiful is culturally good: The physical attractiveness stereotype has different content in collectivistic cultures. *Personality & Social Psychology Bulletin, 23,* 795–800.

Wheeler, M. A., & McMillan, C. T. (2001). Focal retrograde amnesia and the episodic-semantic distinction. *Cognitive, Affective, & Behavioral Neuroscience, 1,* 22–37.

Whitbourne, S. K. (1985). *The aging body.* New York: Springer.

Whitbourne, S. K., Zuschlag, M. K., Elliot, L. B., & Waterman, A. S. (1992). Psychosocial development in adulthood: A 22–year sequential study. *Journal of Personality and Social Psychology, 63,* 260–271.

White, L., Tursky, B., & Schwartz, G. E. (1985). *Placebo: Theory, research, and mechanisms.* New York: Guilford.

Whitely, B. E., Jr. (1990). The relationship of heterosexuals' attributions for the causes of homosexuality to attitudes toward lesbians and gay men. *Personality and Social Psychology Bulletin, 16,* 367–377.

Whorf, B. L. (1956). *Language, thought, and reality: Selected writings of Benjamin Lee Whorf.* New York: Wiley.

Widiger, T. A., & Sankis, L. M. (2000). Adult psychopathology: Issues and controversies. *Annual Review of Psychology, 51,* 377–404.

Wigfield, A. (1994). Expectancy-value theory of achievement motivation: A developmental perspective. *Educational Psychology Review, 6,* 49–78.

Williams, D. A., Overmier, J. B., & LoLordo, V. M. (1992). A reevaluation of Rescorla's early dictums about Pavlovian conditioned inhibition. *Psychological Bulletin, 111,* 275–290.

Williams, G. C. (1966). *Adaptation and natural selection.* Princeton, NJ: Princeton University Press.

Williams, L. M. (1992). Adult memories of childhood abuse: Preliminary findings from a longitudinal study. *The Advisor, 5,* 19–20.

Williams, W. M. (1998). Are we raising smarter children today? School- and home-related influences on IQ. In U. Neisser (Ed.), *The rising curve: Long-term gains in IQ and related measures.* Washington, DC: American Psychological Association.

Willingham, W. W., Lewis, C., Morgan, R., & Ramsit, L. (1990). *Predicting college grades: An analysis of institutional trends over two decades.* Princeton, NJ: Educational Testing Service.

Willis, J., & Todorov, A. (2006). First impressions: Making up your mind after a 100-ms exposure to a face. *Psychological Science, 17,* 592–598.

Wilson, E. O. (1963, May). Pheromones. *Scientific American, 208,* 100–114.

Wilson, M., & Emmorey, K. (1997). Working memory for sign language: A window into the architecture of the working memory system. *Journal of Deaf Studies and Deaf Education, 2,* 121–130.

Wilson, R. S., Mendes C., Barnes, L. L., Schneider, J. A., Bienias, J. L., Evans, D. A., & Bennett, D. A. (2002). Participation in cognitively stimulating activities and risk of incident Alzheimer disease. *JAMA: Journal of the American Medical Association, 287,* 742–748.

Winett, R. A. (1995). A framework for health promotion and disease prevention programs. *American Psychologist, 50,* 341–350.

Winikoff, B. (1983). Nutritional patterns, social choices, and health. In D. Mechanic (Ed.), *Handbook of health, health care, and the health professions.* New York: Free Press.

Winkielman, P., & Berridge, K. C. (2004). Unconscious emotion. *Current Directions in Psychological Science, 13,* 120–123.

Winner, E. (1997). Exceptionally high intelligence and schooling. *American Psychologist, 52,* 1070–1081.

Winner, E. (2000). The origins and ends of giftedness. *American Psychologist, 55,* 159–169.

Wise, R. A., & Bozarth, M. A. (1987). A psychomotor theory of addiction. *Psychological Review, 94,* 469–492.

Wissler, C. (1901). The correlation of mental and physical tests. *Psychological Review, Monograph Supplement 3* (No. 6).

Wissow, L. S. (2002). Child discipline in the first three years of life. In N. Haflon & McLearn, K. F. (Eds.), *Child rearing in America: Challenges facing parents with young children.* New York: Cambridge University Press.

Witherington, D. C., Campos, J. J., Anderson, D. I., Lejeune, L., & Seah, E. (2005). Avoidance of heights on the visual cliff in newly walking infants. *Infancy, 7,* 285–298.

Wixted, J. T., & Ebbesen, E. B. (1991). On the form of forgetting. *Psychological Science, 2,* 409–415.

Wollberg, Z., & Newman, J. D. (1972). Auditory cortex of squirrel monkey: Response patterns of single cells to species-specific vocalizations. *Science, 175,* 212–214.

Wolpe, J. (1958). *Psychotherapy by reciprocal inhibition.* Stanford, CA: Stanford University Press.

Wolpe, J. (1975). Forward. In B. Sloane, F. Staples, A. Cristol, N. Yorkston, & K. Whipple (Eds.), *Psychotherapy versus behavior therapy.* Cambridge, MA: Harvard University Press.

Wolpe, J. (1982). *The practice of behavior therapy.* New York: Pergamon.

Woods, S. C., Schwartz, M. W., Baskin, D. G., & Seeley, R. J. (2000). Food intake and the regulation of body weight. *Annual Review of Psychology, 51,* 255–277.

Woody, G. E., & Cacciola, J. (1997). Diagnosis and classification: DSM-IV and ICD-10. In J. H. Lowinson, P. Ruiz, R. B. Millman, & J. G. Langrod (Eds.), *Substance abuse: A comprehensive textbook.* Baltimore: Williams & Wilkins.

Wooley, H. T. (1910). Psychological literature: A review of the recent literature on the psychology of sex. *Psychological Bulletin, 7,* 335–342.

Worringham, C. J., & Messick, D. M. (1983). Social facilitation of running: An unobtrusive study. *Journal of Social Psychology, 121,* 23–29.

Wundt, W. (1896). *Outlines of psychology.* C. M. Judd (Trans.). New York: Stechart.

Wyer, N. A. (2007). Motivational influences on compliance with and consequences of instructions to suppress stereotypes. *Journal of Experimental Social Psychology, 43,* 417–424.

Wynne, C. D. L. (2007). What the ape said. *Ethology, 113,* 411–413.

Yalom, I. D. (1995). *The theory and practice of group psychotherapy* (4th ed.). New York: Basic Books.

Yang, T. T., Menon, V., Eliez, S., Blasey, C., White, C. D., Reid, A. J., Gotlib, I. H., & Reiss, A. L. (2002). Amygdalar activation associated with positive and negative facial expressions. *NeuroReport, 13,* 1737–1741.

Yapko, M. D. (1994). Suggestibility and repressed memories of abuse: A survey of psychotherapists' beliefs. *American Journal of Clinical Hypnosis, 36,* 163–179.

Yates, F. A. (1966). *The art of memory.* Chicago: University of Chicago Press.

Yin, R. K. (1998). The abridged version of case study research: Design and method. In Leonard Bickman & Debra J. Rog (Eds.), *Handbook of applied social research methods.* Thousand Oaks, CA: Sage.

Young, J. E., Weinberger, A. D., & Beck, A. T. (2001). Cognitive therapy for depression. In D. H. Barlow (Ed.), *Clinical handbook of psychological disorders* (3rd ed.). New York: Guilford.

Zacks, J. M., Vettel, J. M., & Michelon, P. (2003). Imagined viewer and object rotations dissociated with event-related fMRI. *Journal of Cognitive Neuroscience, 15,* 1002–1018.

Zacks, R. T., & Hasher, L. (1994). Directed ignoring: Inhibitory regulation of working memory. In D. Dagenbach & T. H. Carr (Eds.), *Inhibitory processes in attention, memory, and language.* San Diego, CA: Academic Press.

Zadra, A., Desjardines, S., & Marcotte, E. (2006). Evolutionary function of dreams: A test of the threat simulation theory in recurrent dreams. *Consciousness and Cognition, 15,* 450–463.

Zahorik, D. M., Houpt, K. A., & Swartzman-Andert, J. (1990). Taste-aversion learning in three species of ruminants. *Applied Animal Behaviour Science, 26,* 27–39.

Zajonc, R. B. (1968). Attitudinal effects of mere exposure. *Journal of Personality and Social Psychology, 9,* Monograph Supplement (No. 2, part 2).

Zajonc, R. B. (2001). Mere exposure: A gateway to the subliminal. *Current Directions in Psychological Science, 10,* 224–228.

Zajonc, R. B., Heingartner, A., & Herman, E. M. (1969). Social enhancement and impairment of performance in the cockroach. *Journal of Personality and Social Psychology, 13,* 83–92.

Zajonc, R. B., Murphy, S. T. & McIntosh, D. N. (1993). Brain temperature and subjective emotional experience. In M. Lewis & J. M. Haviland (Eds.), *Handbook of emotions.* New York: Guilford.

Zatorre, R. J. (2005). Finding the missing fundamental. *Nature, 436,* 1093–1094.

Zeki, S. (1992, September). The visual image in mind and brain. *Scientific American, 267,* 68–76.

Zelazo, P. R., Zelazo, N. A., & Kolb, S. (1972). "Walking" in the newborn. *Science, 176,* 314–315.

Zentall, T. R. (2006). Imitation: definitions, evidence, and mechanisms. *Animal Cognition, 9,* 335–353.

Ziegert, D. I., Kistner, J. A., Castro, R., & Robertson, B. (2001). Longitudinal study of young children's responses to challenging achievement situations. *Child Development, 72,* 609–624.

Zimbardo, P. (2007). *The Lucifer effect: Understanding how good people turn evil.* New York: Random House.

Zotterman, Y. (1959). Thermal sensations. In J. Fields, H. W. Magoun, & V. E. Hall (Eds.), *Handbook of physiology: Section I. Neurophysiology* (pp. 431–458). Washington, DC: Physiological Society.

Zur, D., & Ullman, S. (2003). Filling-in of retinal scotomas. *Vision Research, 43,* 971–982.

Zuroff, D. C., & Blatt, S. J. (2006). The therapeutic relationship in the brief treatment of depression: Contributions to clinical improvement and enhanced adaptive capacities. *Journal of Consulting and Clinical Psychology, 74,* 130–140.

Name Index

Subject Index

Theme Index